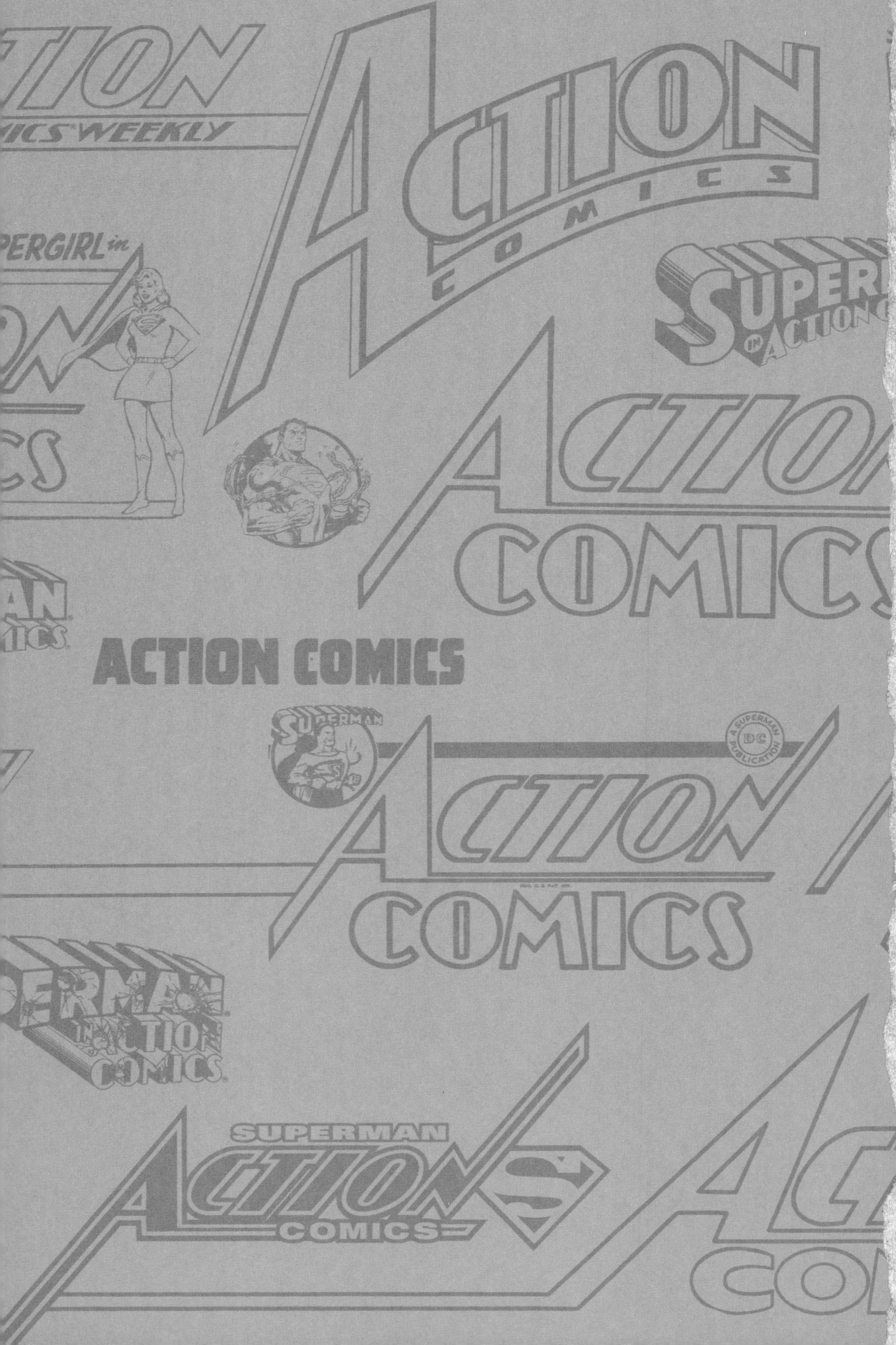
ACTION COMICS
ACTION COMICS
SUPERGIRL in
SUPERMAN IN ACTION COMICS
ACTION COMICS
ACTION COMICS
SUPERMAN
ACTION COMICS
A SUPERMAN DC PUBLICATION
SUPERMAN
ACTION COMICS

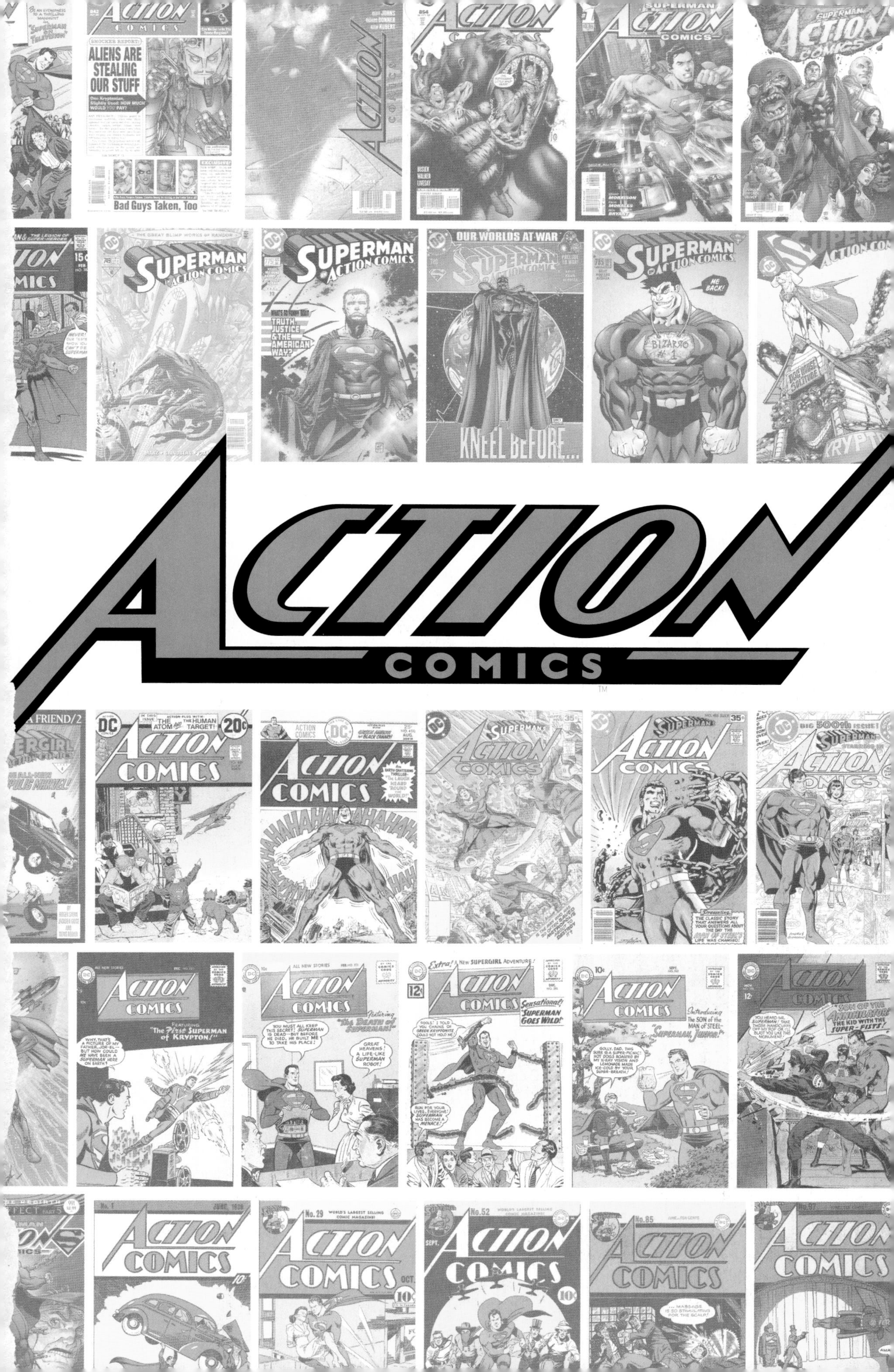
ACTION COMICS
™
ALIENS ARE STEALING OUR STUFF
Bad Guys Taken, Too
OUR WORLDS AT WAR
KNEEL BEFORE...
ME BACK!
BIZARRO #1
TRUTH, JUSTICE & THE AMERICAN WAY?
SUPERMAN IN ACTION COMICS
The First SUPERMAN of KRYPTON!
SUPERMAN GOES WILD!
The SON of the MAN of STEEL
SON OF THE ANNIHILATOR

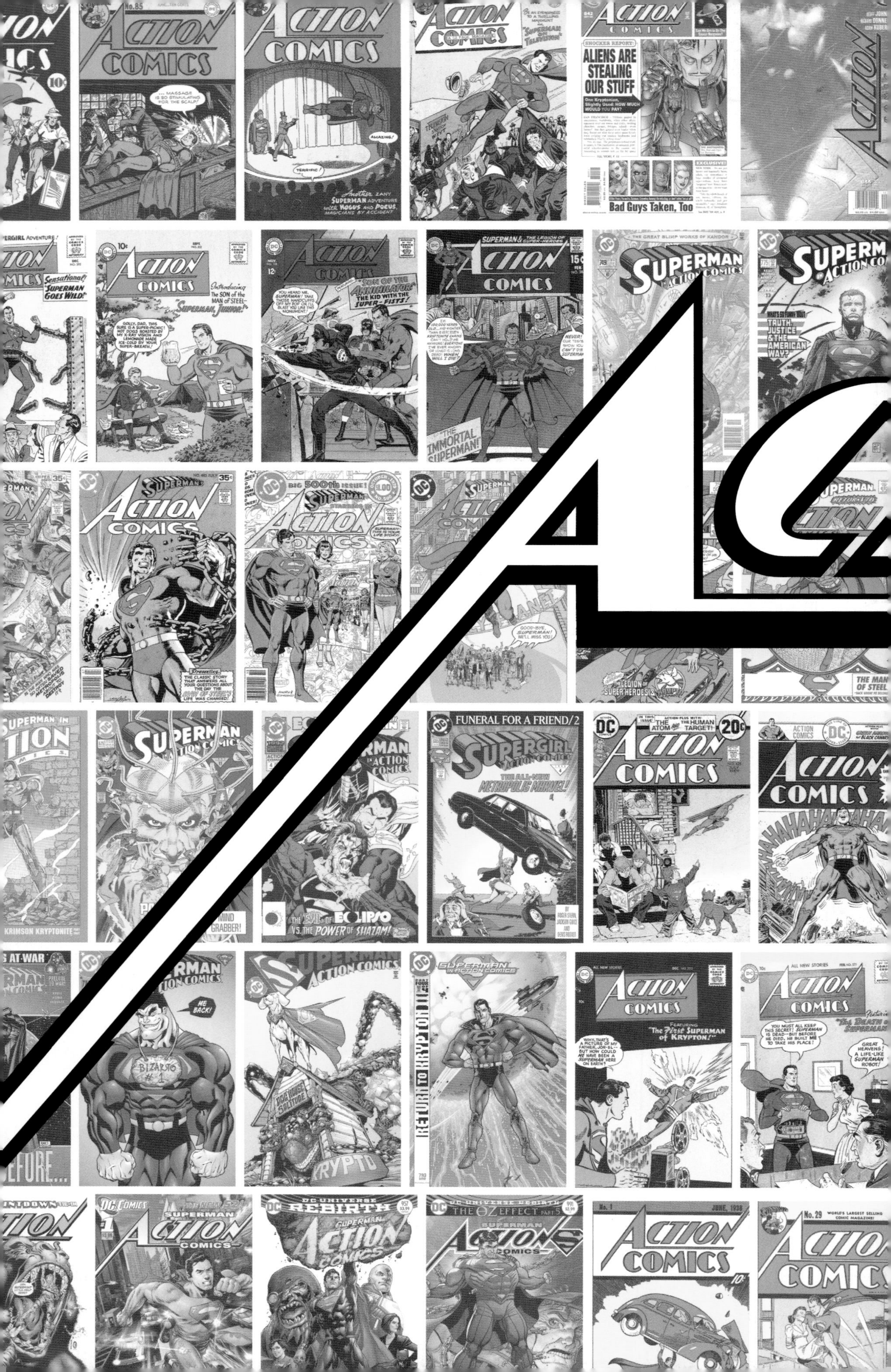

ACTION COMICS
10¢
No. 85
... MASSAGE IS SO STIMULATING FOR THE SCALP!
ACTION COMICS
AMAZING!
TERRIFIC!
Another ZANY SUPERMAN ADVENTURE with HOGUS and POCUS, MAGICIANS BY ACCIDENT
ACTION COMICS
SUPERMAN ON TELEVISION
ACTION COMICS
SHOCKER REPORT!
ALIENS ARE STEALING OUR STUFF
One Kryptonian, Slightly Used: HOW MUCH WOULD YOU PAY?
EXCLUSIVE!
Bad Guys Taken, Too
SUPERGIRL ADVENTURE!
ACTION COMICS
Sensational! SUPERMAN GOES WILD!
10¢
ACTION COMICS
Introducing The SON of the MAN of STEEL- "SUPERMAN, JUNIOR!"
GOLLY, DAD, THIS SURE IS A SUPER-PICNIC! HOT DOGS ROASTED BY MY X-RAY VISION AND LEMONADE MADE ICE-COLD BY YOUR SUPER-BREATH!
ACTION COMICS
12¢
"SON OF THE ANNIHILATOR" THE KID WITH THE SUPER-FISTS!
YOU HEARD ME, SUPERMAN! TAKE THOSE HANDCUFFS OFF MY POP OR I'LL BLAST YOU LIKE THIS MONUMENT!
SUPERMAN & THE LEGION OF SUPER-HEROES
ACTION COMICS
15¢
NEVER!
"THE IMMORTAL SUPERMAN!"
THE GREAT BLIMP WORKS OF KANDOR
SUPERMAN IN ACTION COMICS
SUPERMAN IN ACTION COMICS
WHAT'S SO FUNNY 'BOUT TRUTH, JUSTICE & THE AMERICAN WAY?
SUPERMAN'S
ACTION COMICS
35¢
Presenting: THE CLASSIC STORY THAT ANSWERS ALL YOUR QUESTIONS ABOUT THE DAY THE MAN OF STEEL'S LIFE WAS CHANGED!
BIG 500th ISSUE!
SUPERMAN
ACTION COMICS
GOOD-BYE, SUPERMAN! WE'LL MISS YOU!
THE LEGION OF SUPER-HEROES
THE MAN OF STEEL
SUPERMAN IN ACTION COMICS
KRIMSON KRYPTONITE
SUPERMAN IN ACTION COMICS
MIND GRABBER!
SUPERMAN IN ACTION COMICS
THE EVIL OF ECLIPSO VS. THE POWER OF SHAZAM!
FUNERAL FOR A FRIEND/2
SUPERGIRL ACTION COMICS
THE ALL-NEW METROPOLIS MARVEL!
IN THIS ISSUE ACTION-PLUS WITH THE ATOM AND THE HUMAN TARGET!
20¢
ACTION COMICS
ACTION COMICS
ACTION COMICS
BLACK CANARY
HAHAHAHAHA
SUPERMAN IN ACTION COMICS
ME BACK!
BIZARRO #1
SUPERMAN ACTION COMICS
KRYPTO
RETURN TO KRYPTON II
SUPERMAN IN ACTION COMICS
ALL NEW STORIES
ACTION COMICS
Featuring "The First SUPERMAN of Krypton!"
WHY, THAT'S A PICTURE OF MY FATHER, JOR-EL-- BUT HOW COULD HE HAVE BEEN A SUPERMAN HERE ON EARTH?
ALL NEW STORIES
ACTION COMICS
YOU MUST ALL KEEP THIS SECRET! SUPERMAN IS DEAD--BUT BEFORE HE DIED, HE BUILT ME TO TAKE HIS PLACE!
GREAT HEAVENS! A LIFE-LIKE SUPERMAN ROBOT!
DC COMICS
THE NEW 52!
SUPERMAN ACTION COMICS
DC UNIVERSE REBIRTH
SUPERMAN ACTION COMICS
DC UNIVERSE REBIRTH
THE OZ EFFECT PART 5
ACTION COMICS
No. 1
JUNE, 1938
ACTION COMICS
10¢
No. 29
WORLD'S LARGEST SELLING COMIC MAGAZINE!
ACTION COMICS

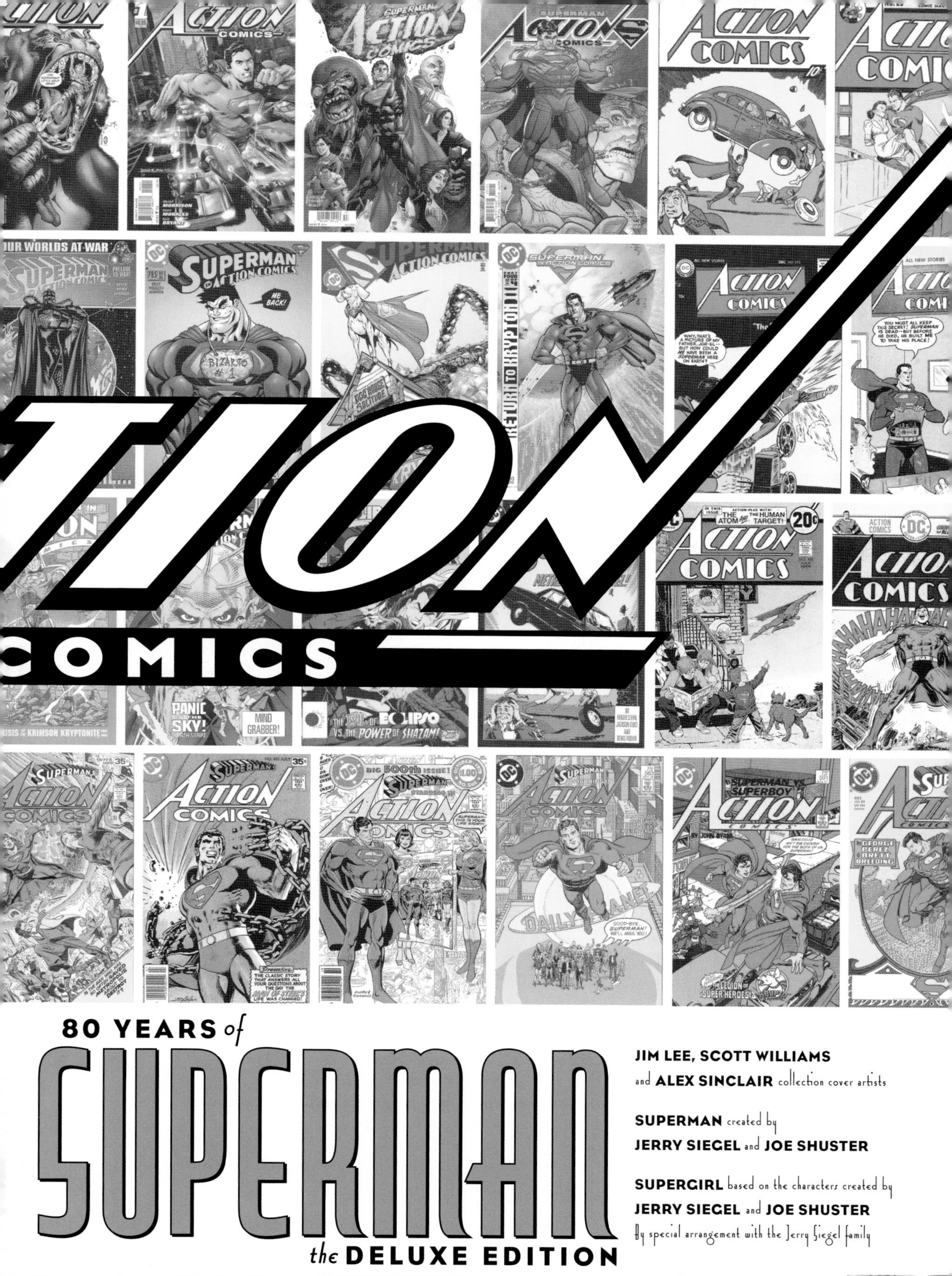

ACTION COMICS
ACTION COMICS
SUPERMAN ACTION COMICS
SUPERMAN ACTION COMICS
ACTION COMICS
ACTION COMICS
OUR WORLDS AT WAR
SUPERMAN IN ACTION COMICS
SUPERMAN IN ACTION COMICS
ME BACK!
BIZARRO #1
SUPERMAN ACTION COMICS
SUPERMAN IN ACTION COMICS
RETURN TO KRYPTON II
ACTION COMICS
WHY, THAT'S A PICTURE OF MY FATHER, JOR-EL -- BUT HOW COULD HE HAVE BEEN A SUPERMAN HERE ON EARTH?
YOU MUST ALL KEEP THIS SECRET! SUPERMAN IS DEAD--BUT BEFORE HE DIED, HE BUILT ME TO TAKE HIS PLACE!
COMICS
PANIC IN THE SKY!
MIND GRABBER!
THE EVIL OF ECLIPSO VS. THE POWER OF SHAZAM!
IN THIS ISSUE: THE ATOM AND THE HUMAN TARGET!
20¢
ACTION COMICS
ACTION COMICS
SUPERMAN ACTION COMICS
SUPERMAN'S ACTION COMICS
BIG 500th ISSUE!
SUPERMAN ACTION COMICS
SUPERMAN ACTION COMICS
DAILY PLANET
GOOD-BYE, SUPERMAN! WE'LL MISS YOU!
SUPERMAN VS. SUPERBOY
ACTION COMICS
BY JOHN BYRNE
THE LEGION OF SUPER HEROES
GEORGE PEREZ BRETT BREEDING

80 YEARS of

SUPERMAN

the DELUXE EDITION

JIM LEE, SCOTT WILLIAMS and **ALEX SINCLAIR** collection cover artists

SUPERMAN created by **JERRY SIEGEL** and **JOE SHUSTER**

SUPERGIRL based on the characters created by **JERRY SIEGEL** and **JOE SHUSTER**
By special arrangement with the Jerry Siegel family

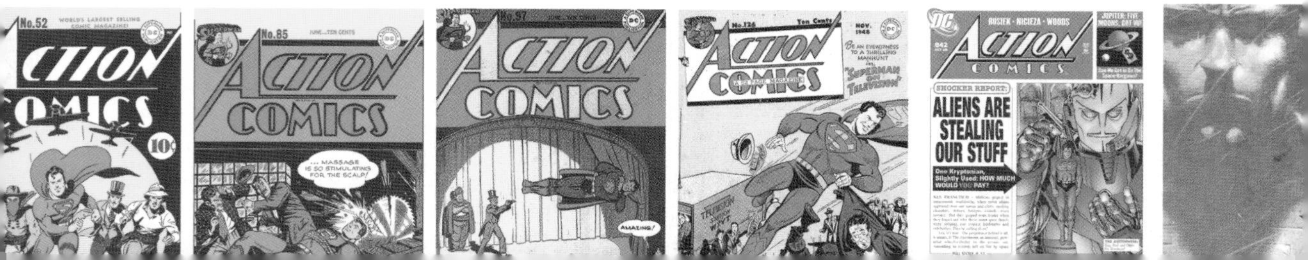

No. 52
WORLD'S LARGEST SELLING COMIC MAGAZINE!
ACTION COMICS
10¢
No. 85
ACTION COMICS
... MASSAGE IS SO STIMULATING FOR THE SCALP!
No. 97
ACTION COMICS
AMAZING!
No. 126
ACTION COMICS
BUSIEK • NICIEZA • WOODS
ACTION COMICS
JUPITER: FIVE MOONS, GUT UP!
SHOCKER REPORT:
ALIENS ARE STEALING OUR STUFF
One Kryptonian, Slightly Used: HOW MUCH WOULD YOU PAY?

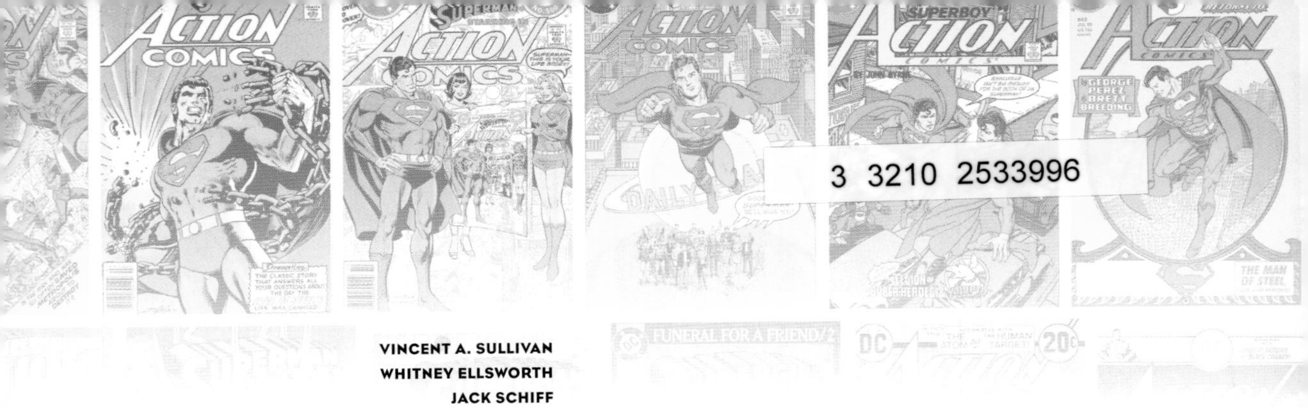

VINCENT A. SULLIVAN	
WHITNEY ELLSWORTH	
JACK SCHIFF	
MORT WEISINGER	
JULIUS SCHWARTZ	
ANDREW HELFER	
MIKE CARLIN	
EDDIE BERGANZA	
PAUL KAMINSKI	EDITORS – ORIGINAL SERIES
JON PETERSON	
TOM PALMER JR.	
WIL MOSS	ASSOCIATE EDITORS – ORIGINAL SERIES
GEORGE KASHDEN	
DAN THORSLAND	
ANDREA SHEA	ASSISTANT EDITORS – ORIGINAL SERIES
PAUL LEVITZ	EDITOR – COLLECTED EDITION
LIZ ERICKSON	ASSISTANT EDITOR – COLLECTED EDITION
STEVE COOK	DESIGN DIRECTOR – BOOKS
AMIE BROCKWAY-METCALF	PUBLICATION DESIGN
BOB HARRAS	SENIOR VP – EDITOR-IN-CHIEF, DC COMICS
PAT McCALLUM	EXECUTIVE EDITOR, DC COMICS
DIANE NELSON	PRESIDENT
DAN DiDIO	PUBLISHER
JIM LEE	PUBLISHER
GEOFF JOHNS	PRESIDENT & CHIEF CREATIVE OFFICER
AMIT DESAI	EXECUTIVE VP – BUSINESS & MARKETING STRATEGY, DIRECT TO CONSUMER & GLOBAL FRANCHISE MANAGEMENT
SAM ADES	SENIOR VP & GENERAL MANAGER, DIGITAL SERVICES
BOBBIE CHASE	VP & EXECUTIVE EDITOR, YOUNG READER & TALENT DEVELOPMENT
MARK CHIARELLO	SENIOR VP – ART, DESIGN & COLLECTED EDITIONS
JOHN CUNNINGHAM	SENIOR VP – SALES & TRADE MARKETING
ANNE DePIES	SENIOR VP – BUSINESS STRATEGY, FINANCE & ADMINISTRATION
DON FALLETTI	VP – MANUFACTURING OPERATIONS
LAWRENCE GANEM	VP – EDITORIAL ADMINISTRATION & TALENT RELATIONS
ALISON GILL	SENIOR VP – MANUFACTURING & OPERATIONS
HANK KANALZ	SENIOR VP – EDITORIAL STRATEGY & ADMINISTRATION
JAY KOGAN	VP – LEGAL AFFAIRS
JACK MAHAN	VP – BUSINESS AFFAIRS
NICK J. NAPOLITANO	VP – MANUFACTURING ADMINISTRATION
EDDIE SCANNELL	VP – CONSUMER MARKETING
COURTNEY SIMMONS	SENIOR VP – PUBLICITY & COMMUNICATIONS
JIM (SKI) SOKOLOWSKI	VP – COMIC BOOK SPECIALTY SALES & TRADE MARKETING
NANCY SPEARS	VP – MASS, BOOK, DIGITAL SALES & TRADE MARKETING
MICHELE R. WELLS	VP – CONTENT STRATEGY
	DIGITAL COVER ARCHIVING BY JOSEPH DALEY

ACTION COMICS 80 YEARS OF SUPERMAN: THE DELUXE EDITION

Published by DC Comics. Compilation, cover and all new material Copyright © 2018 DC Comics. All Rights Reserved.
Originally published in single magazine form in ACTION COMICS 1, 2, 42, 64, 241, 242, 252, 285, 309, 419, 484, 554, 584, 655, 662, 800, 0.
Copyright © 1938, 1941, 1943, 1958, 1959, 1961, 1963, 1972, 1978, 1984, 1986, 1990, 1991, 2003, 2012 DC Comics. All Rights Reserved.
All characters, their distinctive likenesses and related elements featured in this publication are trademarks of DC Comics.
The stories, characters and incidents featured in this publication are entirely fictional.
DC Comics does not read or accept unsolicited submissions of ideas, stories or artwork.

DC Comics, 2900 West Alameda Ave., Burbank, CA 91505
Printed by Transcontinental Interglobe, Beauceville, QC, Canada. 5/4/18. Second Printing.
ISBN: 978-1-4012-7887-8

Library of Congress Cataloging-in-Publication Data is available.

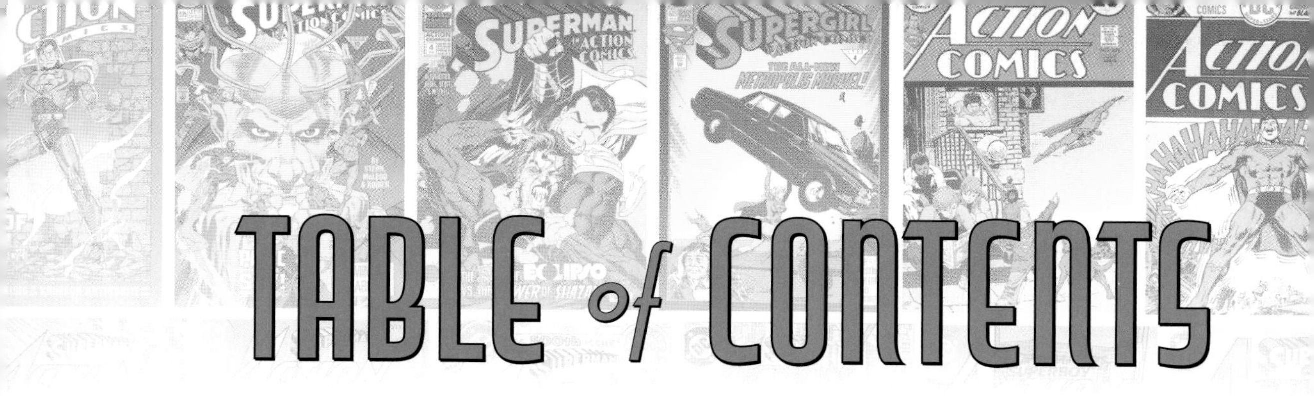
SUPERMAN
SUPERGIRL
ACTION COMICS
ACTION COMICS

TABLE of CONTENTS

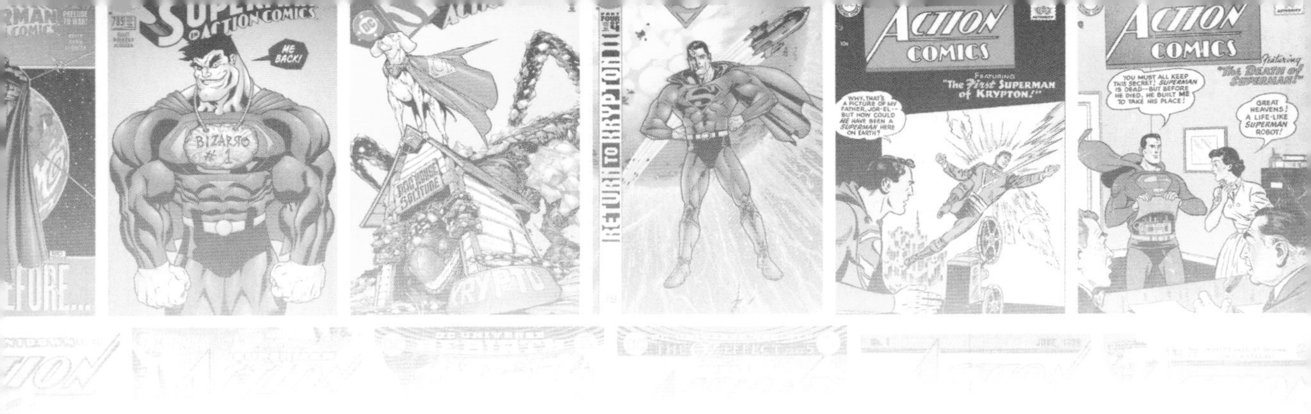
ACTION COMICS
ME BACK!
BIZARRO #1
RETURN TO KRYPTON
ACTION COMICS
The First Superman of Krypton!
ACTION COMICS
The Death of Superman!
GREAT HEAVENS! A LIFE-LIKE SUPERMAN ROBOT!

*Stories in parentheses were originally untitled

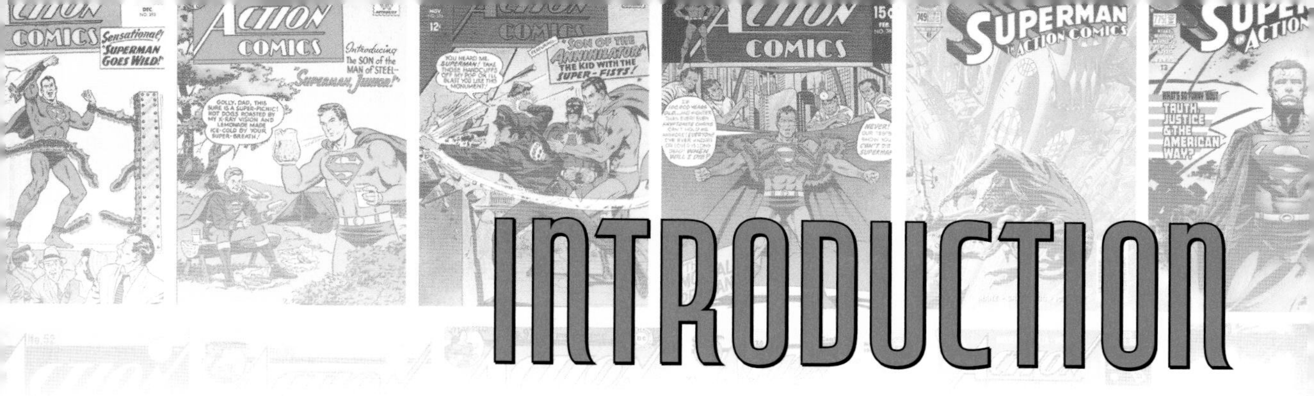

INTRODUCTION

by **PAUL LEVITZ**

There's never been a comic quite like ACTION COMICS. Born only a handful of years after comics were first assembled in the format we recognize as the "comic book" as FUNNIES ON PARADE (1933) or sold to the public that way (FAMOUS FUNNIES, also 1933); only three years after the first regularly published original comic (NEW FUN, 1935), ACTION COMICS #1 showed up on newsstands in 1938 when there was only a tiny section for comics. Only a dozen or so titles were published in any given month, so they didn't need very much space. ACTION changed all that.

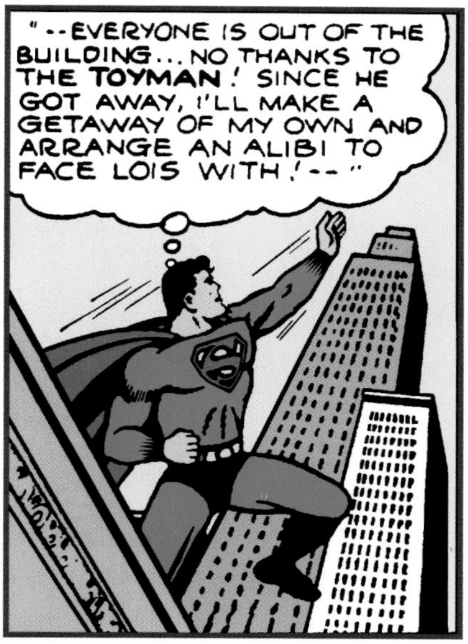
" --EVERYONE IS OUT OF THE BUILDING... NO THANKS TO THE TOYMAN ! SINCE HE GOT AWAY, I'LL MAKE A GETAWAY OF MY OWN AND ARRANGE AN ALIBI TO FACE LOIS WITH ! -- "

Superman changed all that—his first super-powered feat. He took a mild-mannered infant industry and art form and revealed that it had the power to make imaginations leap tall buildings, to make hearts pound faster than a locomotive and to make the business bullets that would fell his competitors bounce off his chest.

Superman was born in the imagination of two Cleveland teenagers, Jerry Siegel and Joe Shuster, and had a long and rough journey to life. Rejected by all the newspaper syndicates of the time (newspaper comics being then the most successful form of cartooning, with by far the largest audience and economic rewards), he was considered too different to succeed. Jerry's daughter, Laura Larson, contributes her reminiscences next in this volume. There are many tales of how the strip came to headline that first issue of ACTION, and little definitive history. Malcolm Wheeler-Nicholson (the entrepreneur who launched NEW FUN) was developing ACTION with his new partners, Harry Donenfeld and Jack Liebowitz, until a Christmas-season bankruptcy took Wheeler-Nicholson out of the picture. Editor Vince Sullivan certainly played a role in assembling the issue. And there's a joyous irony in the likely version that Max Gaines (who helped create the comic book as a printing salesman), spurred on by his boy-genius editor, Shelly Mayer, sent Superman over to Donenfeld to fill a gap in ACTION.

In any case, it was the roar of the crowd that signaled Superman's success. The first issue of ACTION sold an impressive two-thirds of its print run of 200,000 copies, according to Michael Uslan's memory of early DC records he once saw, and within a year the phenomenon had taken hold nationally. ACTION was selling a half-million copies, a solo comic was spun off, and SUPERMAN became the first comic to sell a million copies. Siegel and Shuster achieved their dream of a Superman newspaper comic strip, and a radio show would soon follow. The extraordinarily acclaimed creator and historian Jules Feiffer offers his perspective on that moment in a few pages.

Tally up those cultural precedents: the concept of the superhero is crystallized here, combining elements from science fiction, the pulps and even prose historical novels *(The Scarlet Pimpernel,* anyone?) into a form that would invade and conquer virtually all modern forms of popular media for the next 80 years.

And the business landmarks are vital, too: ACTION inspired dozens of publishers to come into the comics business, in search of their own Superman. Many would follow the path, but few would survive or triumph. It is not exaggeration to say that without ACTION, there would

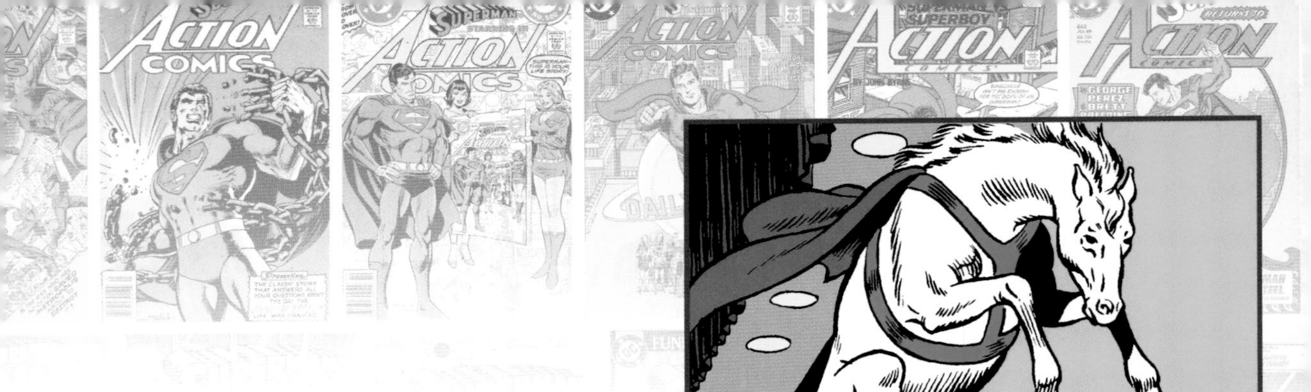

ACTION COMICS

have been no comics industry.

The importance of ACTION didn't end with that first issue, of course, or with the revolutionary effects just discussed. Superman affected our language and inspired several generations of young people. The iconic power of the Man of Steel filled songs' imagery, and words from his mythology infiltrated everyday language (how often have you read about something being a person's "Kryptonite" or heard someone derided as being a "brainiac"?). Perhaps more subtly, our hero's nobility influenced the career choices of many, especially people who looked at the lives Clark Kent and Lois Lane were leading and followed them into journalism. *The Ten-Cent Plague* author and Columbia University journalism professor David Hajdu will examine that aspect a bit deeper in this volume.

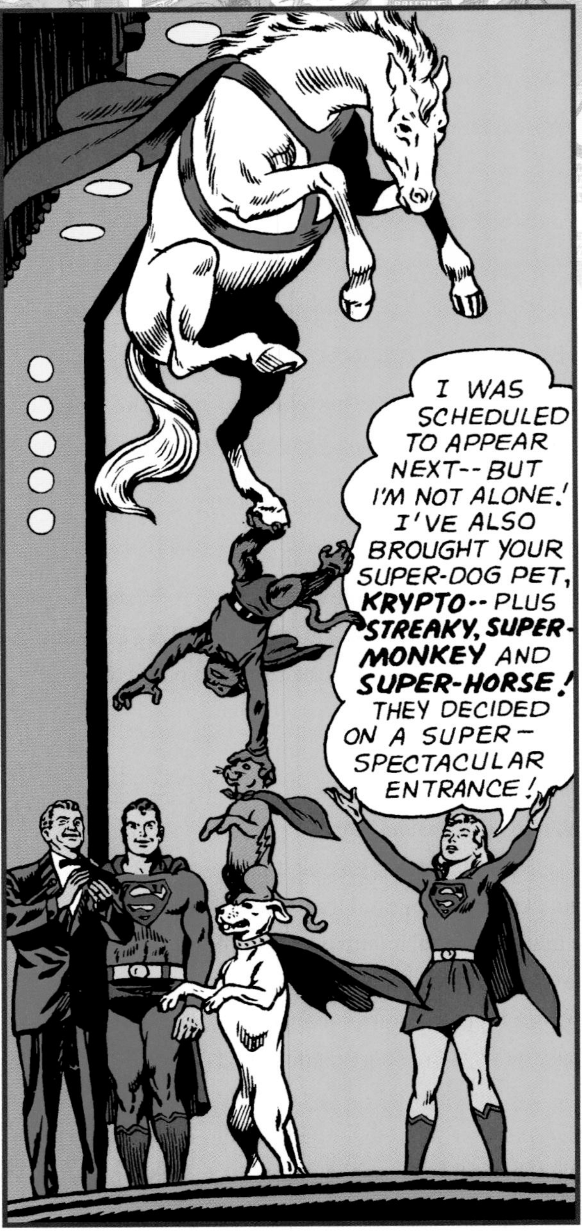

I WAS SCHEDULED TO APPEAR NEXT-- BUT I'M NOT ALONE! I'VE ALSO BROUGHT YOUR SUPER-DOG PET, **KRYPTO**-- PLUS **STREAKY, SUPER-MONKEY** AND **SUPER-HORSE!** THEY DECIDED ON A SUPER-SPECTACULAR ENTRANCE!

Some of it was the times in which Superman was born, tides from the Great Depression and the upcoming World War. Tom DeHaven, who has eloquently written of those days, will contribute his thoughts as well. But some of the effect was purely the genius of Jerry and Joe, and the ability their work had to shape their many collaborators' efforts. Included in this volume, thanks to a long-ago act of salvage by then-young fan Marv Wolfman, is the sole surviving *unpublished* Superman story to come out of their studio in the Golden Age of Comics they did so much to create.

The impact of ACTION was not limited to Superman. Unlike any other comic, ACTION spawned not just one, but four multimedia stars. The Vigilante debuted three years later (#42, 1941) and went on to his own movie serial in 1947. A little over a decade later (#252, 1959), Supergirl began as a companion piece in the back of ACTION, and she's had her turn as a movie star (1984) and now a television series. And in 1971 the Human Target premiered, and he would go on to not one but two different television incarnations in 1992 and 2010. And even though he never got the big spotlight, Zatara gave birth to a daughter magician, Zatanna, who became an important part of the DC Universe and got her own moments at center stage.

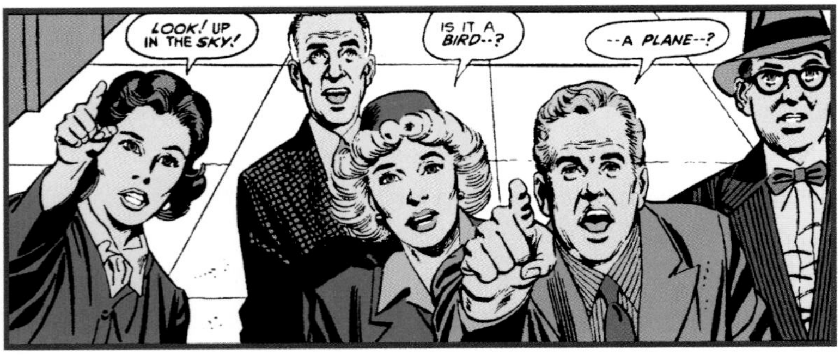

LOOK! UP IN THE SKY!
IS IT A BIRD--?
--A PLANE--?

Back in its own medium, ACTION made a significant contribution in keeping alive the continuous publication of two "second-string" heroes, who otherwise might

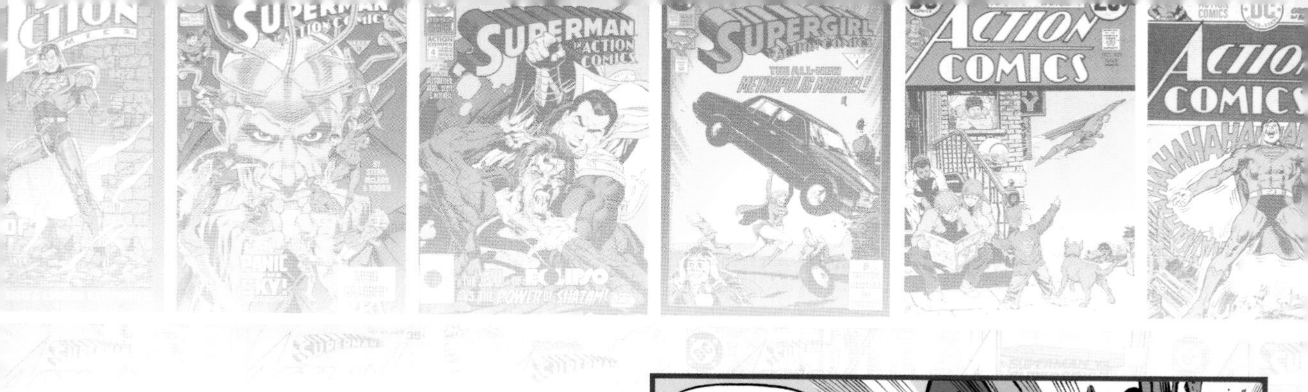

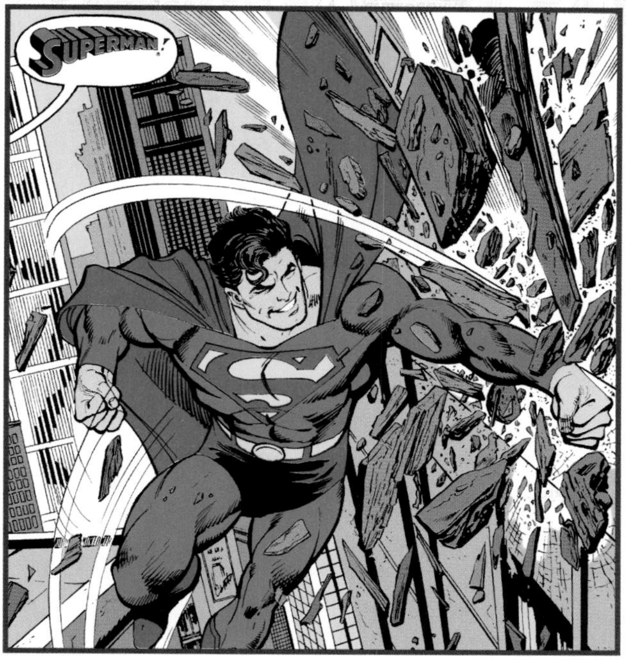
SUPERMAN!

have become history with the rest of the costumed adventurers of the Golden Age when only Superman, Batman and Wonder Woman survived in their own comics. It's likely that editor Mort Weisinger's own role in the creation of Aquaman and Green Arrow motivated him to keep them in ACTION for so long, but regardless, it's clearly that survival that contributed to their becoming important in the DC pantheon. No tales of the duo are included here because they didn't debut in ACTION, but they're part of its mark on history nonetheless.

Superman's mark on history looms far larger, of course, as his near-constant presence on movie screens and television sets extends greater in its reach than the comics themselves. But it is the comics that gave birth to the possibilities, the ideas and the themes that made the legend of Superman enduring. Author Larry Tye, whose biography, *Superman*, explored the subject deeply, offers a few thoughts on that topic within this volume.

ACTION has changed and evolved over the years, becoming thinner as comics shrank after World War Two, becoming a Superman "team-up" title during the era of John Byrne's relaunch of the Last Kryptonian, even becoming ACTION COMICS WEEKLY for a year (allowing it to pass its slightly older sibling, DETECTIVE COMICS, to the one-thousand-issues mark). Wonderful creative writers, artists, editors and craftspeople have come and gone, moving with shifting tastes and the changes in the American public itself (would our last creative commentator, Gene Luen Yang, have been imaginable in the culture of 1938 as a contributor to ACTION? And yet today he has served as the Library of Congress' ambassador for children's literature, as well as an amazing cartoonist and contributor to the Superman legend). But ACTION has remained a constant presence in readers' lives, an almost unique benchmark (name anything else from the culture of 1938 that has been uninterrupted for any material time) and an outsize influence. There never has been a comic like ACTION COMICS, and there probably never will be again.

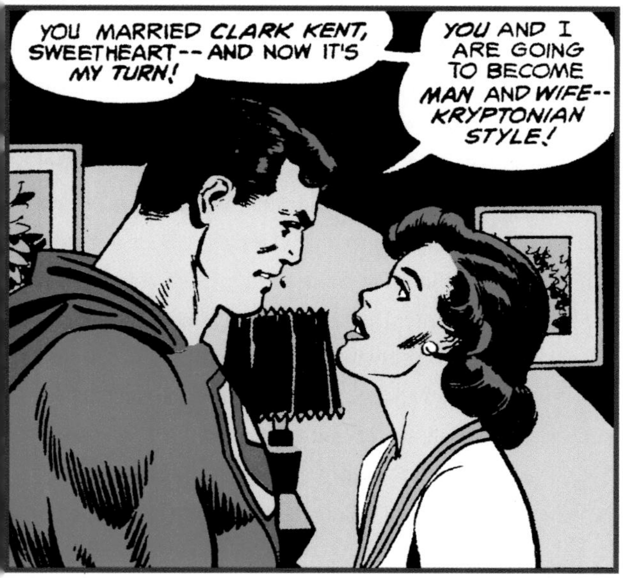
YOU MARRIED CLARK KENT, SWEETHEART--AND NOW IT'S MY TURN!
YOU AND I ARE GOING TO BECOME MAN AND WIFE--KRYPTONIAN STYLE!

PAUL LEVITZ has edited reprint collections for DC since 1974's CHRISTMAS WITH THE SUPER-HEROES, and has also written, edited and served as an executive for the company. His Eisner Award-winning 75 YEARS OF DC COMICS *(Taschen, 2010) was reissued in a new edition last year.*

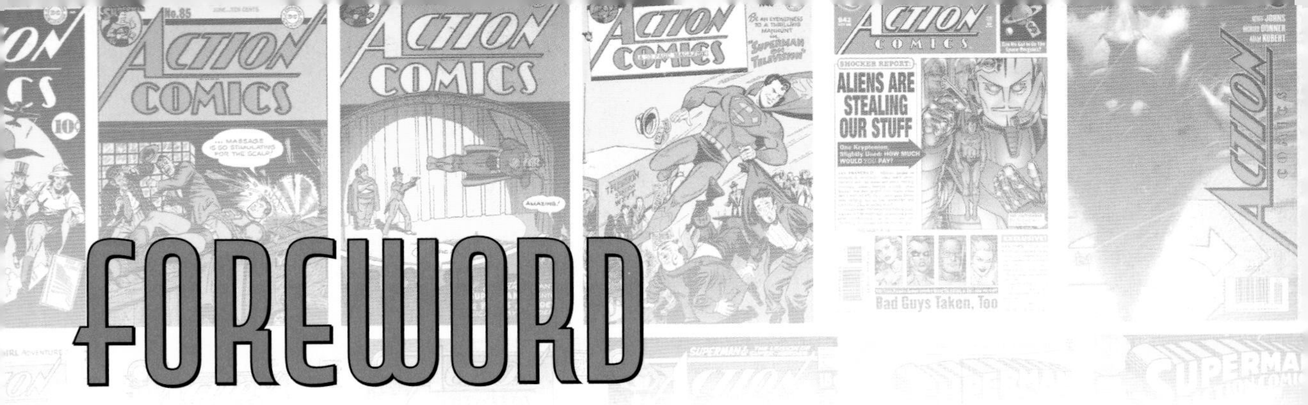
ACTION COMICS
ACTION COMICS
ACTION COMICS
ACTION COMICS
ALIENS ARE STEALING OUR STUFF
Bad Guys Taken, Too

FOREWORD

by LAURA SIEGEL LARSON

Let me tell you about the man who created Superman. My father Jerry Siegel was a bundle of creative energy and determination. Long before superheroes existed, he dreamed of flying. One day his oldest brother Harry brought home a copy of the premiere science fiction pulp magazine of its day, *Amazing Stories,* and placed it in his eager hands. The gorgeous cover art and breathtaking stories exploded from the pages and flew into his imagination, filling him with wonder unlike any he'd felt before. He wanted more!

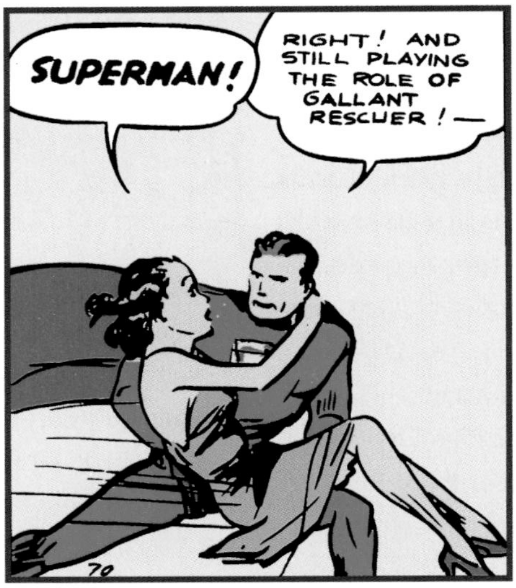
SUPERMAN!
RIGHT! AND STILL PLAYING THE ROLE OF GALLANT RESCUER! —

Dad was the youngest of six children, a shy, lonely daydreamer who felt invisible to the world around him. His parents, immigrants who'd escaped from anti-Semitism in their Lithuanian village, moved to Cleveland, Ohio where his father worked as a tailor and had little time for anything but work. Like other children of Jewish immigrants my dad struggled to fit in but always felt like an outsider. He longed to be accepted by his peers but they couldn't care less about him. Girls ignored him. Classmates teased him because he read books instead of playing sports. But those books were astonishing--filled with action, adventure, brave heroes, and brilliant plot twists! His favorites were science fiction tales that took him to unknown parts of the universe or to societies inhabited by robots. As he got older, Edgar Rice Burroughs' works depicting worlds facing conflicts between compassion and cruelty changed his desire from reading stories to writing them. He knew it was his destiny.

Dad wrote to the Letters Section of *Amazing Stories* and networked with other fans. He wrote every waking minute and got his work read any way he could--in his school newspaper--the *Glenville Torch*--or by creating, writing and self-publishing his own science fiction fanzines--*Cosmic Stories* (1931) and *Science Fiction: The Advance Guard of Future Civilization* (1932).

While he was self-publishing, Dad met another child of immigrants who had transferred to Glenville High. Joe Shuster was even quieter than my dad, wore thick glasses, and was a terrific artist. Best of all, he loved science fiction, the pulps, and swashbuckling movies just like Dad. They became best friends and created projects written by Dad and illustrated by Joe such as "The Reign of the Superman" in *Science Fiction #3* (January 1933). Fueled by Dad's ambition to be a professional author as soon as possible, Siegel and Shuster set out to conquer the world of newspaper comic strips. My dad wanted these strips to be dynamic and fresh.

They put so much time into creating comics that they fell behind with their schoolwork and didn't graduate until the following year.

During that final year of high school it occurred to Dad that the key to real success was to put more of himself and his view of the world into his work. His mind was filled with snippets--what he was and what he wanted to be. My dad believed in fighting for what's right no matter how difficult it might be. His mother taught him compassion for the less fortunate. He had a burning desire for people, especially girls, to see what was inside him and not dismiss him as a goofy geek. He put this in a science fiction context and created a consummate hero, a Super-hero, SUPERMAN--the ideal immigrant who comes from another planet, uses his magnificent powers to help those who

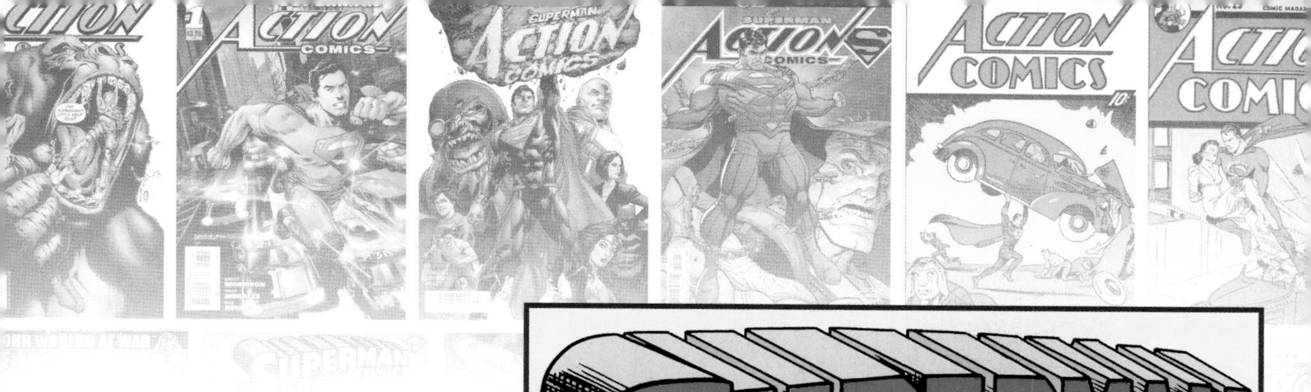
ACTION COMICS

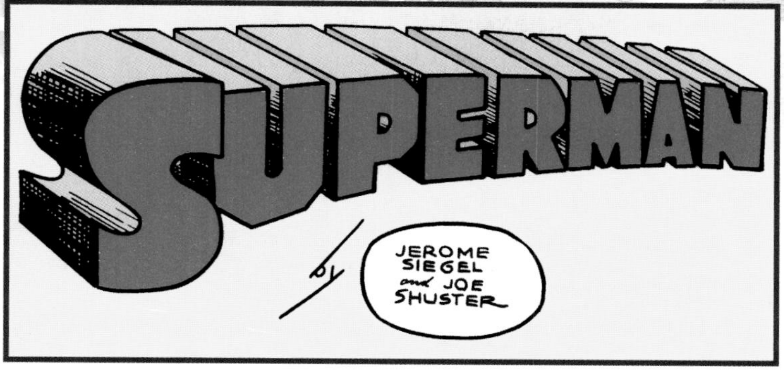
SUPERMAN
by
JEROME SIEGEL and JOE SHUSTER

can't help themselves, and is always right, always good, and always loved by the woman he loves. He added the newspaper setting he was familiar with, the secret identity of Clark Kent, and the love triangle between Clark, Lois Lane and Superman for comic irony.

He and Joe worked to make Superman burst from the page with powerful action sequences that pioneered how to show the movement and incredible strength of a superhero. The iconic looks for Superman and Clark were created. For Lois Lane, Joe wanted a model and in a stroke of luck he saw an ad in the *Cleveland Plain Dealer* placed by an attractive teenager, Jolan Kovacs. She had the perfect look that Joe and my dad wanted for the smart, resourceful reporter Superman loves. She made such an impression on my dad that 13 years later when they met again, he married her.

Dad knew in his gut that Superman was a winner. He submitted it to every newspaper syndicate in America. While he and Joe waited for responses, they came up with enthusiastic advertising slogans —

SUPERMAN! THE SMASH HIT! THE GREATEST SINGLE EVENT SINCE THE BIRTH OF COMIC STRIPS! SUPERMAN!

They were prophetic words. It took years of rejections and offers that fell through but finally, in 1938 Superman lifted a car on the cover of Action Comics #1 and the effect was magical. Newsstands were flooded with requests for "that book with Superman in it." Lois Lane became a role model for career women. Superman's high values and adventures as "champion of the oppressed" inspired readers, young and old.

Dad wasn't surprised. He believed in Superman and in himself from the start.

After *Action #1* Dad wrote Superman in *Action Comics #2* and the issues after that for many years. He gave Superman additional powers, added new characters, villains, and made the stories entertaining and action-packed.

Years passed. In 1976 Dad and Joe received a pension and were assured of a "created by" credit for all time. Dad spent his final years meeting fans at comic conventions, getting well-deserved credit for launching the superhero industry and praise for making that first Action Comics issue the most collected and valuable comic book of all time.

When I look at *Action #1*, I see my father's drive and my mother's face. Now, nearly 80 years after that, the book and Superman are still going strong. Just think of it—*Action Comics #1000!* That's a massive amount of material that started with a thought in my dad's brain!

From the time they were teenagers my parents and Joe never doubted that Superman would be loved all over the world long after they were gone. I'm sure they are smiling down on all of us right now, knowing they were right.

LAURA SIEGEL LARSON is the daughter of Superman co-creator Jerry Siegel and original Lois Lane model Joanne Carter Siegel, and is currently producing a documentary on her father's life and work.

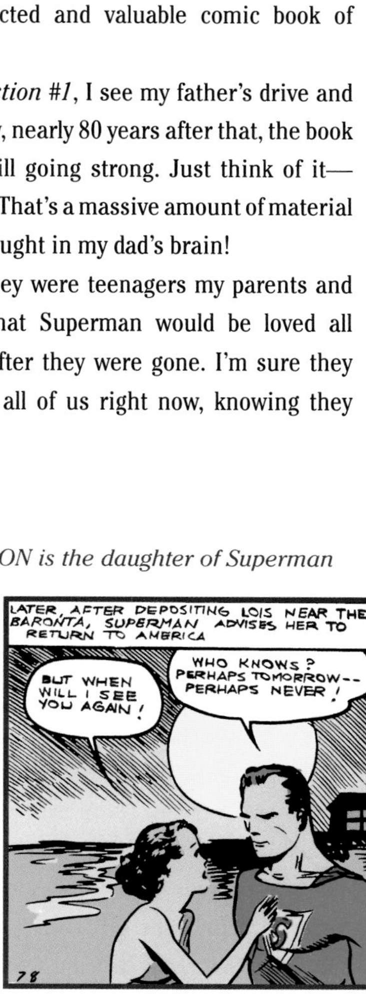
LATER, AFTER DEPOSITING LOIS NEAR THE BARONTA, SUPERMAN ADVISES HER TO RETURN TO AMERICA
BUT WHEN WILL I SEE YOU AGAIN!
WHO KNOWS? PERHAPS TOMORROW-- PERHAPS NEVER!

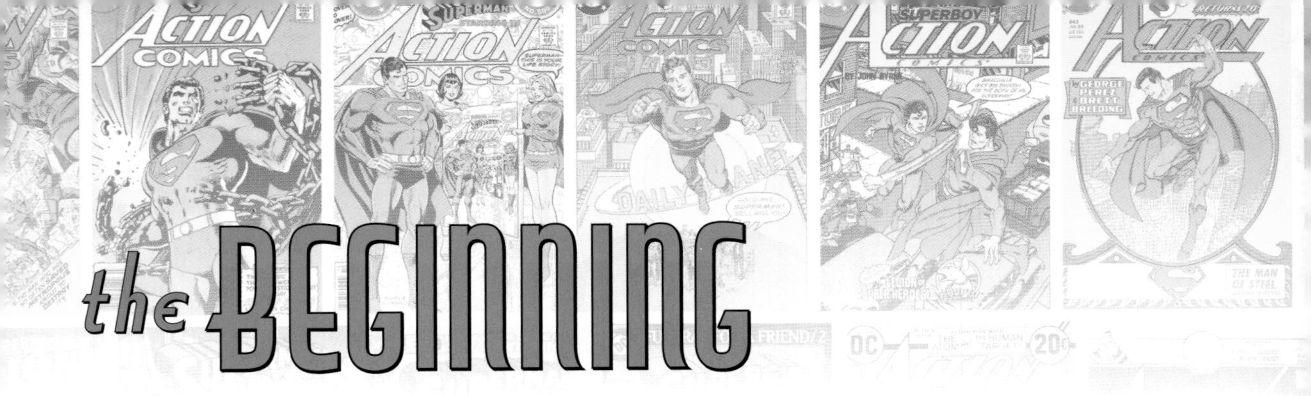

the BEGINNING

by **JULES FEIFFER**

Thumb through ACTION COMICS #1.

Who, 80 years later, doesn't know the lead feature? It changed the game. It carved out a niche in popular culture that expanded, until it, like its arch-villain, Lex Luthor, came close to conquering the universe.

Compared to the other comics in ACTION #1, Siegel and Shuster's story and art could have come from another planet. I'll get back to them a little later.

Original comic book material in 1938 (works that were not reprints of newspaper strips), were derivative and stumbling wannabes that borrowed style and characters from their syndicated betters. They were works in progress, and for young readers, their crudity made them more accessible than the static, wordy strips their parents read in the family paper.

Homer Fleming, who wrote and drew the second feature in ACTION #1 "Chuck" Dawson (a Western), was in his forties, an old man in this new business and a skilled draftsman, far better than his colleagues herein. His serious drawback was that he was not so much a comics artist as a magazine illustrator with a style better fitted for pulps. And like pulps, his story is printed in black and white with tints of blue for color.

Fleming knew zilch about dramatizing a story in words and pictures. The skill of his art was undone by his unwieldy prose. His well-drawn panels just sat there, motionless: galloping horses, fistfights, and shoot-outs, stillborn in their frames. He was the best draftsman in the issue, but there was no action in his "ACTION."

"Zatara, Master Magician," our next feature, is—how can I put this delicately?—a case of pure and slavish thievery. Writer Lee Falk created "Mandrake The Magician," a popular strip in newspaper syndication for decades, whose slicked-back hair, pencil-thin mustache, tux and top hat became an international pop symbol. Federico Fellini, the great Italian director, liked to slip him into cameos in his movies. Guardineer's "Zatara" was a double for Mandrake; his identical twin. Even down to assistants. Mandrake had a giant, half-naked black African. Zatara had a giant, half-naked East Indian.

Guardineer had a diagrammatic drawing style. He drew beefed-up stick figures. Somehow, it worked. His pages were fast-moving and easy to follow, one panel leading smoothly into the next. What he lacked as an artist, he overcame in cinematic storytelling. Odd, after 80 years, but "Zatara" is the only feature, after "Superman," that one still remembers.

Next in line, pages and pages of dopey filler, with which publishers, back then, seemed obligated to impose on perfectly good comic books, perhaps for arcane legal reasons that I'm unaware of. Awful, page-wasting stuff: a typeset pulp-like adventure story, an out-of-place "big foot" (unfunny) funny feature and a four-page

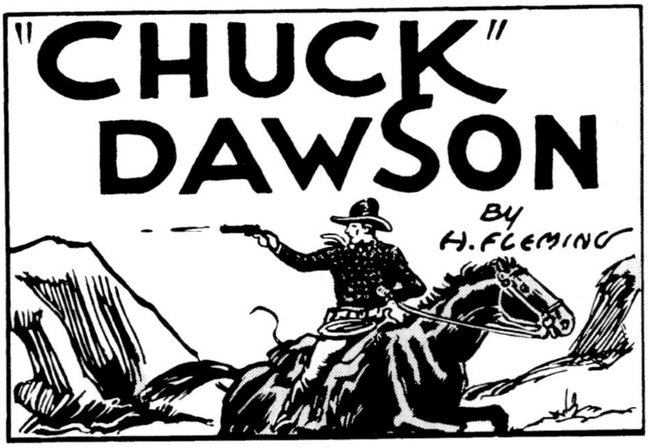
"CHUCK" DAWSON
BY H. FLEMING

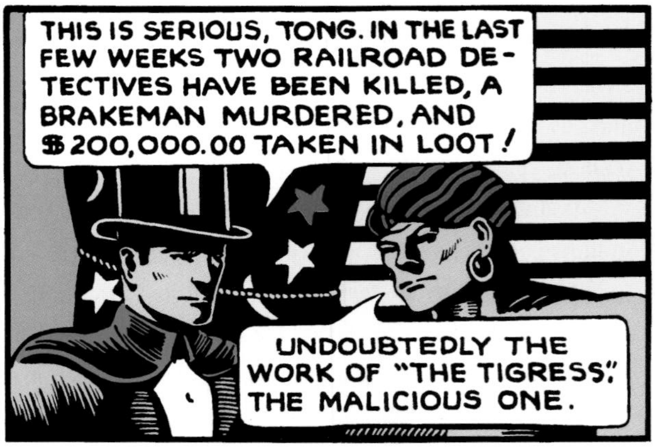
THIS IS SERIOUS, TONG. IN THE LAST FEW WEEKS TWO RAILROAD DETECTIVES HAVE BEEN KILLED, A BRAKEMAN MURDERED, AND $200,000.00 TAKEN IN LOOT!
UNDOUBTEDLY THE WORK OF "THE TIGRESS," THE MALICIOUS ONE.

ACTION COMICS

"educational" history lesson on Marco Polo, dressed up in high-toned book-illustration panels, crafted for young readers to skip by.

And then—lo and behold—another Fred Guardineer feature; two in one book! And drawn in an unwoodeny style. "'Pep' Morgan". A boxer. The art here is swiped from gritty, Ashcan School fine artists such as George Bellow, or *Saturday Evening Post* magazine illustrators, or stills from Hollywood fight films. And it's casually racist. But racism was an accepted staple of mass entertainment media in the 1930s.

Two more comics close down the book. Another black-and-white strip by Will Ely, "Scoop Scanlon, Five Star Reporter," styled to look like (and swiped from) Milton Caniff's "Terry and The Pirates." And "Tex Thomson," entirely swiped from Big Little Book illustrator Henry E. Vallely, and notable only because its young artist Bernard Baily matured, a few years later, into creating one of the more memorable characters in comic book history, the Spectre.

But not as memorable as Superman.

All the other comics in ACTION #1 are consistent with the sort of stuff readers expected from the DC line. But Jerry Siegel and Joe Shuster's lead feature is eye-poppingly different. Every other story in this book is influenced by other comics or movies or radio shows that came before. But "Superman" has only distant and vague antecedents in popular culture. Rather, "Superman" is the closeted fantasy of two nerdy, Jewish high school boys from Cleveland, who mythologize their inadequacies into legend. And because their time frame is the 1930s, and the ascendance of Hitler in Germany, and galloping home-grown anti-Semitism in the Midwest, their dreams of grandeur soon take on a social-democratic construct. Superman may start out by catching robbers and assorted bad guys, but it doesn't take long before he is revealed as an FDR New Dealer.

WHEN MATURITY WAS REACHED, HE DISCOVERED HE COULD EASILY:
LEAP ⅛TH OF A MILE; HURDLE A TWENTY-STORY BUILDING . . .
RAISE TREMENDOUS WEIGHTS . . .
. . . RUN FASTER THAN AN EXPRESS TRAIN . . .
. . AND THAT NOTHING LESS THAN A BURSTING SHELL COULD PENETRATE HIS SKIN!

And the directness of Shuster's art, its sense of immediacy—it bounces off the page as if inked just minutes ago—separates him from the more cautious and studied artists who follow.

Shuster's influences, Roy Crane's "Wash Tubbs and Captain Easy" and Alex Raymond's "Flash Gordon," are effortlessly lifted and blended into his free-wheeling, impressionist style. One quick look at "Superman," Siegel's brisk and rich-in-character storytelling set free by Shuster's leaps-over-tall-buildings-in-a-single-bound artistry, and we fans knew we were in for a game change.

But such a game change? Eighty years later, and who can count the radio shows, movies, TV series and games?

Who can count the imitators and the influenced? Or the rascals out to get you, who finally got you?

Jerry and Joe, you self-mythologized!

Your mothers would be proud.

JULES FEIFFER is a groundbreaking comics historian (The Great Comic Book Heroes), *as well as an extraordinary talent in too many fields to mention, whose major awards include an Oscar, a Pulitzer, an Obie and the Eisner Hall of Fame. His next graphic novel is* The Ghost Ship, *due out in June.*

WHY, YOU—!
GOOD FOR YOU, LOIS!
LOIS--DON'T!

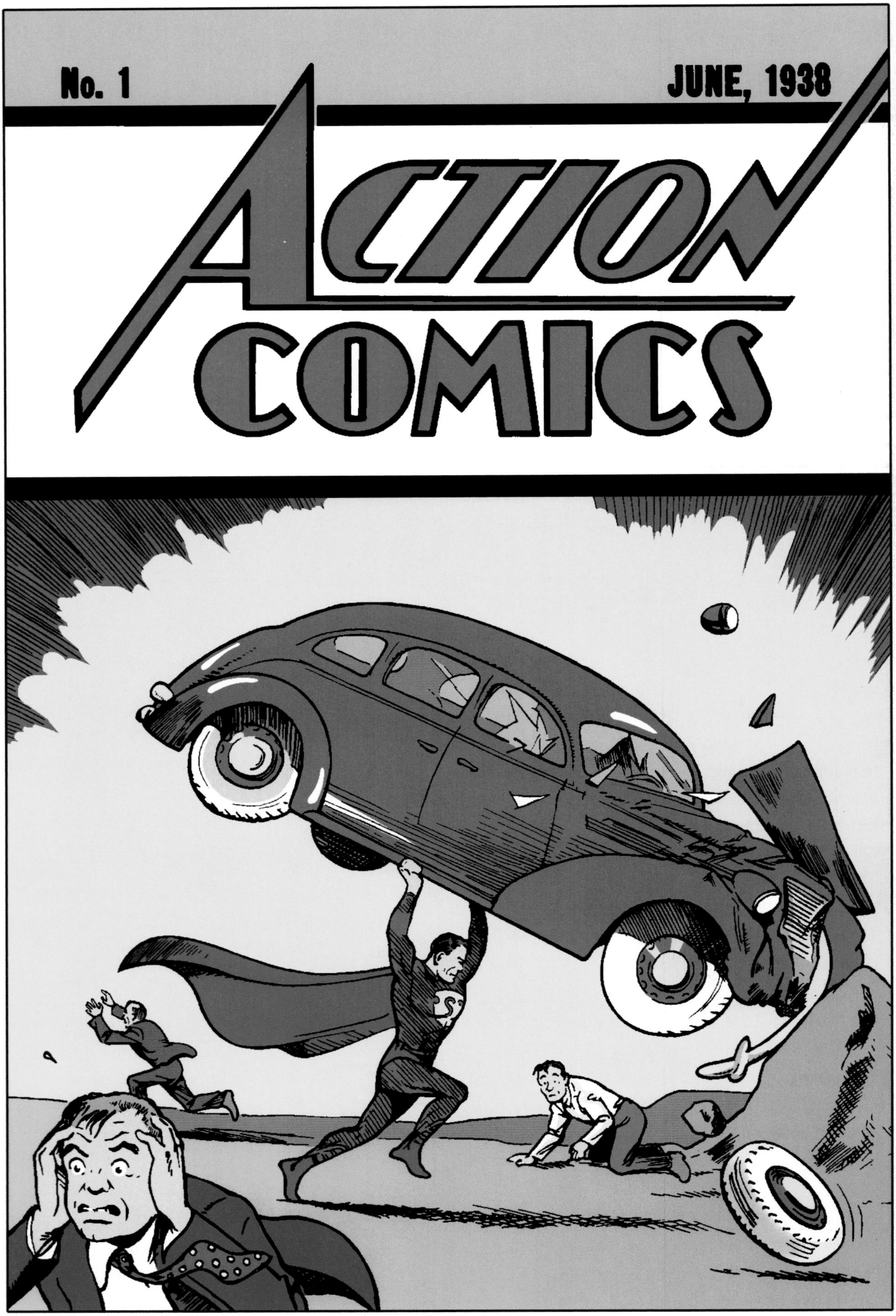
No. 1
JUNE, 1938
ACTION
COMICS

SUPERMAN
JEROME SIEGEL & JOE SHUSTER
AS A DISTANT PLANET WAS DESTROYED BY OLD AGE, A SCIENTIST PLACED HIS INFANT SON WITHIN A HASTILY DEVISED SPACE-SHIP, LAUNCHING IT TOWARD EARTH! 1.
WHEN THE VEHICLE LANDED ON EARTH, A PASSING MOTORIST, DISCOVERING THE SLEEPING BABE WITHIN, TURNED THE CHILD OVER TO AN ORPHANAGE 2.
ATTENDANTS, UNAWARE THE CHILD'S PHYSICAL STRUCTURE WAS MILLIONS OF YEARS ADVANCED OF THEIR OWN, WERE ASTOUNDED AT HIS FEATS OF STRENGTH 3.
WHEN MATURITY WAS REACHED, HE DISCOVERED HE COULD EASILY:
LEAP 1/8TH OF A MILE; HURDLE A TWENTY-STORY BUILDING . . . 4.
RAISE TREMENDOUS WEIGHTS . . . 5.
. . . RUN FASTER THAN AN EXPRESS TRAIN . . .
. . AND THAT NOTHING LESS THAN A BURSTING SHELL COULD PENETRATE HIS SKIN! 6
EARLY, CLARK DECIDED HE MUST TURN HIS TITANIC STRENGTH INTO CHANNELS THAT WOULD BENEFIT MANKIND
AND SO WAS CREATED . . .
SUPERMAN!
CHAMPION OF THE OPPRESSED, THE PHYSICAL MARVEL WHO HAD SWORN TO DEVOTE HIS EXISTENCE TO HELPING THOSE IN NEED! 7
A SCIENTIFIC EXPLANATION OF CLARK KENT'S AMAZING STRENGTH
KENT HAD COME FROM A PLANET WHOSE INHABITANTS' PHYSICAL STRUCTURE WAS MILLIONS OF YEARS ADVANCED OF OUR OWN. UPON REACHING MATURITY, THE PEOPLE OF HIS RACE BECAME GIFTED WITH TITANIC STRENGTH!
--INCREDIBLE? NO! FOR EVEN TODAY ON OUR WORLD EXIST CREATURES WITH SUPER-STRENGTH!
THE LOWLY ANT CAN SUPPORT WEIGHTS HUNDREDS OF TIMES ITS OWN 8
THE GRASSHOPPER LEAPS WHAT TO MAN WOULD BE THE SPACE OF SEVERAL CITY BLOCKS 9

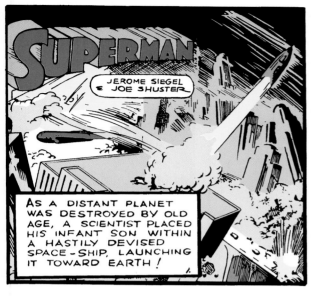

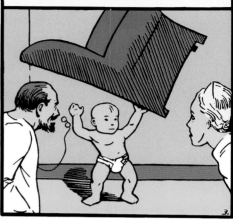

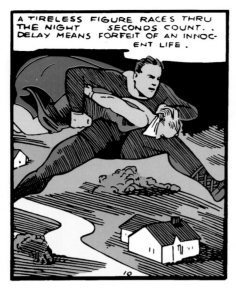

A TIRELESS FIGURE RACES THRU THE NIGHT... SECONDS COUNT.. DELAY MEANS FORFEIT OF AN INNOCENT LIFE.

THE GOVERNOR'S ESTATE FINALLY IS REACHED.

MAKE YOURSELF COMFORTABLE! I HAVEN'T TIME TO ATTEND TO IT

WHAT DO YOU MEAN BY KNOCKING THIS HOUR OF THE NIGHT?

I MUST SEE THE GOVERNOR. IT'S A MATTER OF LIFE AND DEATH!

SEE HIM IN THE MORNING!

CLICK

I'LL SEE HIM NOW!

THIS IS ILLEGAL ENTRY! I'LL HAVE YOU ARRESTED!

ANSWER MY QUESTION! ARE YOU GOING TO TAKE ME TO THE GOVERNOR?

NO! I WON'T!

THEN I'LL TAKE YOU TO HIM!

HELP! HELP!

YES, THIS IS THE GOVERNOR'S SLEEPING ROOM. — DON'T THINK YOU'RE GOING TO GET AWAY WITH THIS OUTRAGE!

18

IT'S LOCKED!

YES! AND MADE OF *STEEL*! TRY AND KNOCK *THIS* DOOR DOWN!

19

20

IT WAS *YOUR* IDEA!

21

WHAT'S THE MEANING OF THIS?

EVELYN CURRY IS TO BE ELECTROCUTED IN 15 MINUTES FOR MURDER. I HAVE PROOF HERE OF HER INNOCENCE — A SIGNED CONFESSION!

22

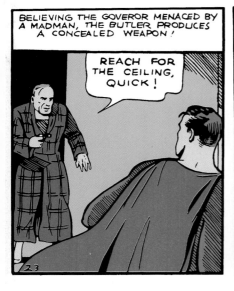

BELIEVING THE GOVEROR MENACED BY A MADMAN, THE BUTLER PRODUCES A CONCEALED WEAPON!

REACH FOR THE CEILING, QUICK!

23

PUT THAT TOY AWAY!

I WARN YOU! TAKE ANOTHER STEP AND *I SHOOT*!

24

25

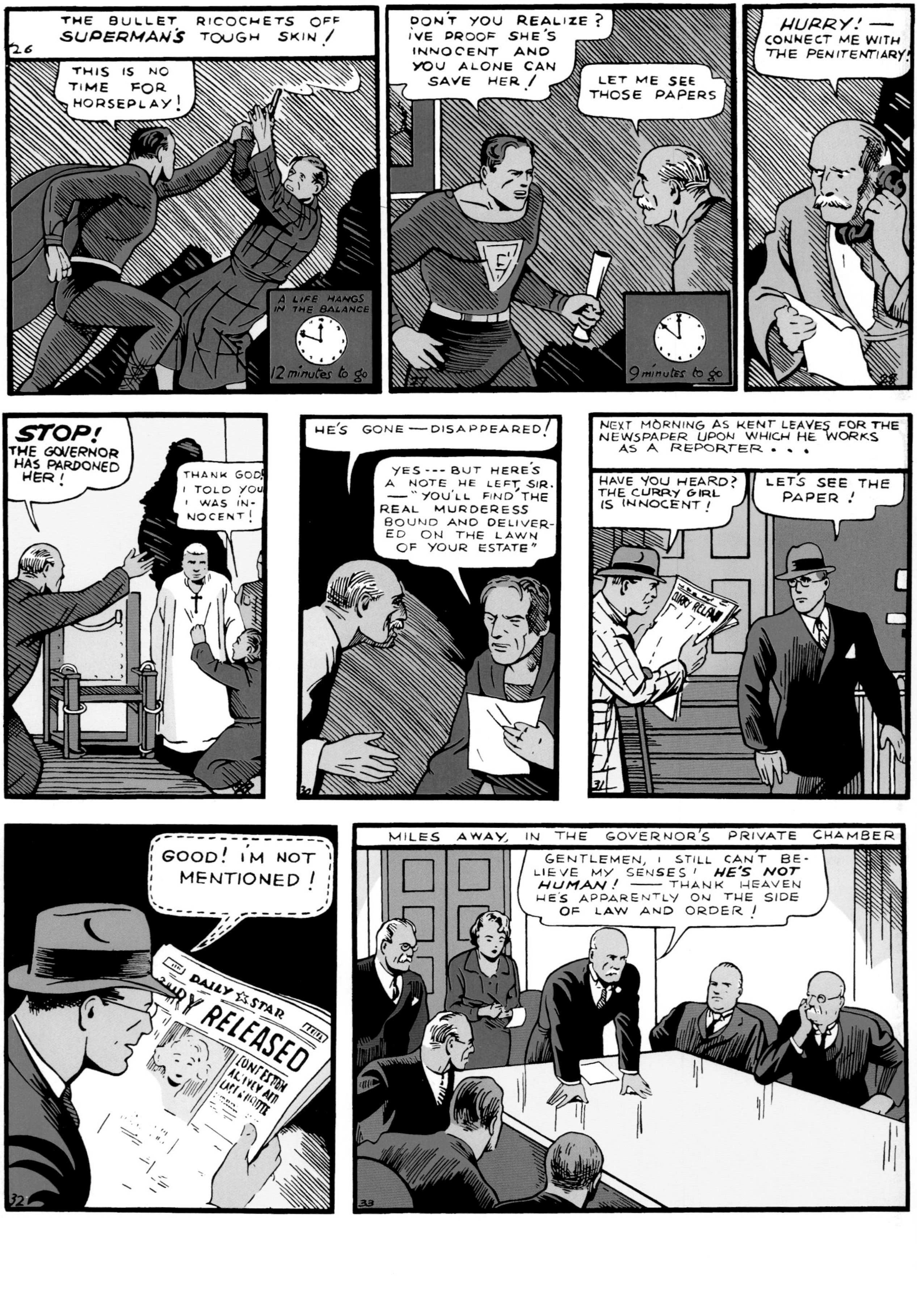
THE BULLET RICOCHETS OFF SUPERMAN'S TOUGH SKIN!
THIS IS NO TIME FOR HORSEPLAY!
A LIFE HANGS IN THE BALANCE
12 minutes to go
DON'T YOU REALIZE? I'VE PROOF SHE'S INNOCENT AND YOU ALONE CAN SAVE HER!
LET ME SEE THOSE PAPERS
9 minutes to go
HURRY! — CONNECT ME WITH THE PENITENTIARY!
STOP! THE GOVERNOR HAS PARDONED HER!
THANK GOD! I TOLD YOU I WAS INNOCENT!
HE'S GONE — DISAPPEARED!
YES --- BUT HERE'S A NOTE HE LEFT, SIR. — "YOU'LL FIND THE REAL MURDERESS BOUND AND DELIVERED ON THE LAWN OF YOUR ESTATE"
NEXT MORNING AS KENT LEAVES FOR THE NEWSPAPER UPON WHICH HE WORKS AS A REPORTER . . .
HAVE YOU HEARD? THE CURRY GIRL IS INNOCENT!
LET'S SEE THE PAPER!
GOOD! I'M NOT MENTIONED!
DAILY STAR
RELEASED
MILES AWAY, IN THE GOVERNOR'S PRIVATE CHAMBER
GENTLEMEN, I STILL CAN'T BELIEVE MY SENSES! HE'S NOT HUMAN! — THANK HEAVEN HE'S APPARENTLY ON THE SIDE OF LAW AND ORDER!

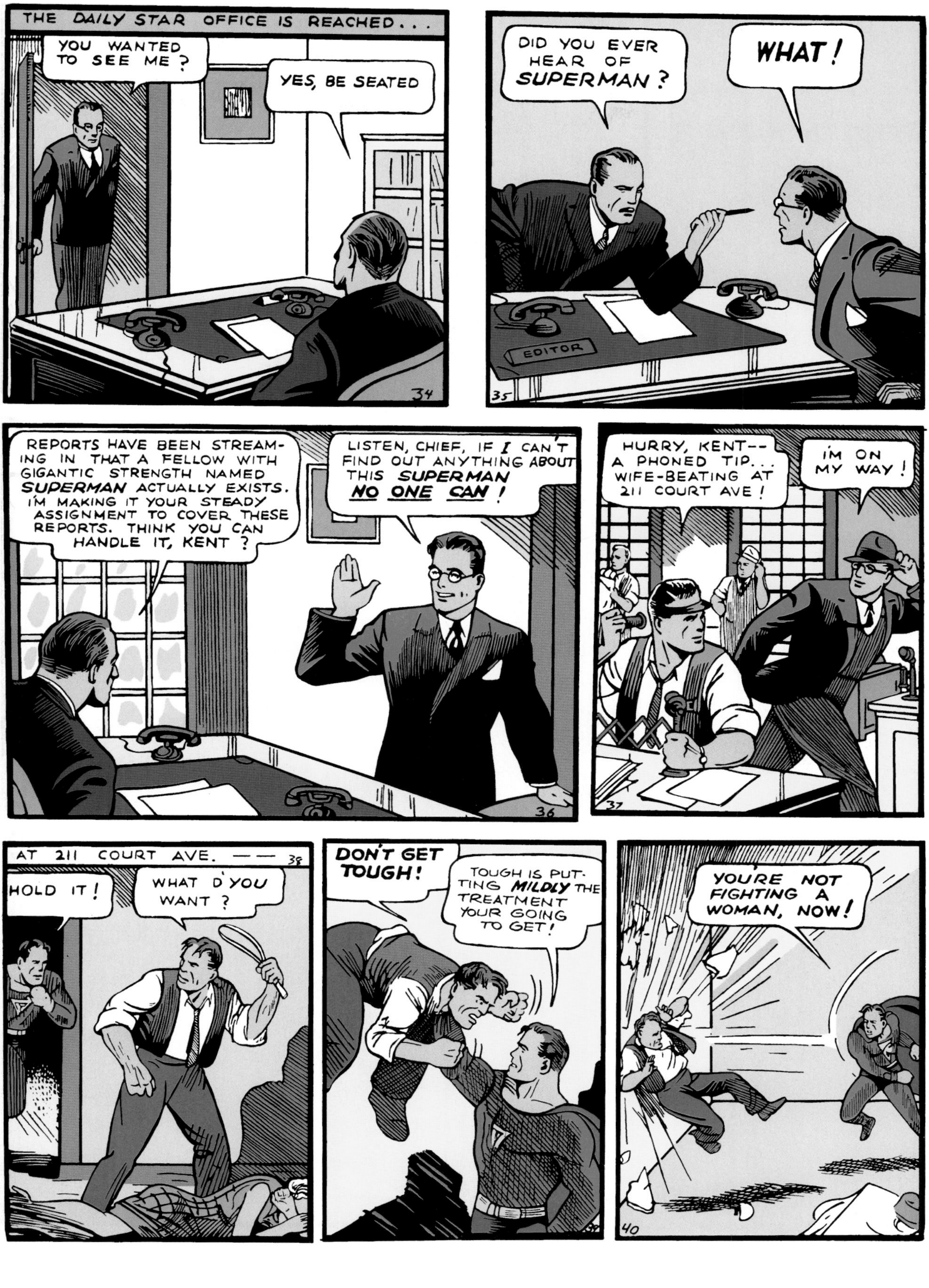
THE DAILY STAR OFFICE IS REACHED...
YOU WANTED TO SEE ME?
YES, BE SEATED
34
DID YOU EVER HEAR OF SUPERMAN?
WHAT!
EDITOR
35
REPORTS HAVE BEEN STREAMING IN THAT A FELLOW WITH GIGANTIC STRENGTH NAMED SUPERMAN ACTUALLY EXISTS. I'M MAKING IT YOUR STEADY ASSIGNMENT TO COVER THESE REPORTS. THINK YOU CAN HANDLE IT, KENT?
LISTEN, CHIEF, IF I CAN'T FIND OUT ANYTHING ABOUT THIS SUPERMAN NO ONE CAN!
36
HURRY, KENT-- A PHONED TIP... WIFE-BEATING AT 211 COURT AVE!
I'M ON MY WAY!
37
AT 211 COURT AVE. ——
38
HOLD IT!
WHAT D'YOU WANT?
DON'T GET TOUGH!
TOUGH IS PUTTING MILDLY THE TREATMENT YOUR GOING TO GET!
39
YOU'RE NOT FIGHTING A WOMAN, NOW!
40

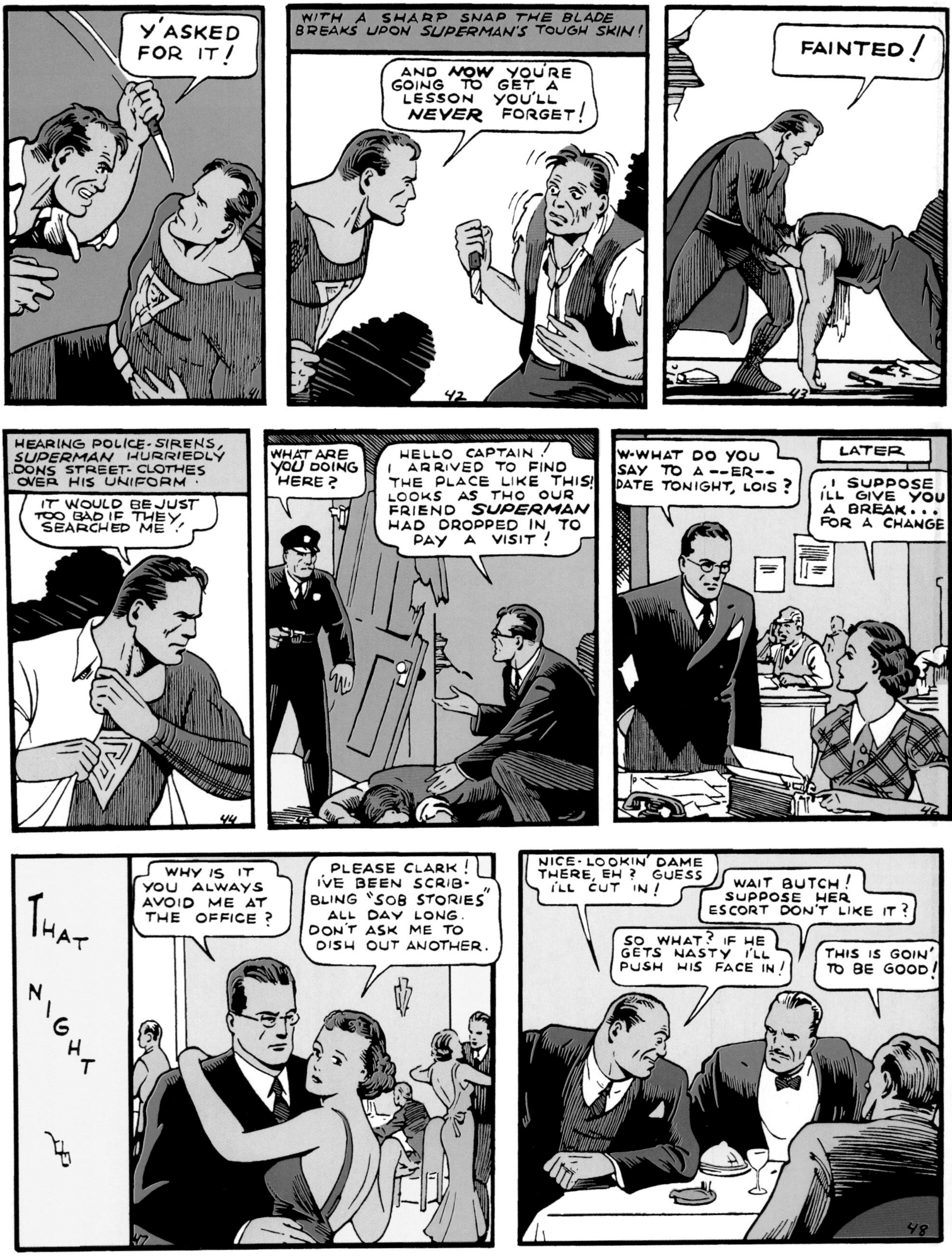
Y'ASKED FOR IT!
WITH A SHARP SNAP THE BLADE BREAKS UPON SUPERMAN'S TOUGH SKIN!
AND NOW YOU'RE GOING TO GET A LESSON YOU'LL NEVER FORGET!
FAINTED!
HEARING POLICE-SIRENS, SUPERMAN HURRIEDLY DONS STREET-CLOTHES OVER HIS UNIFORM.
IT WOULD BE JUST TOO BAD IF THEY SEARCHED ME!
WHAT ARE YOU DOING HERE?
HELLO CAPTAIN! I ARRIVED TO FIND THE PLACE LIKE THIS! LOOKS AS THO OUR FRIEND SUPERMAN HAD DROPPED IN TO PAY A VISIT!
LATER
W-WHAT DO YOU SAY TO A--ER--DATE TONIGHT, LOIS?
I SUPPOSE I'LL GIVE YOU A BREAK... FOR A CHANGE
THAT NIGHT
WHY IS IT YOU ALWAYS AVOID ME AT THE OFFICE?
PLEASE CLARK! I'VE BEEN SCRIBBLING "SOB STORIES" ALL DAY LONG. DON'T ASK ME TO DISH OUT ANOTHER.
NICE-LOOKIN' DAME THERE, EH? GUESS I'LL CUT IN!
WAIT BUTCH! SUPPOSE HER ESCORT DON'T LIKE IT?
SO WHAT? IF HE GETS NASTY I'LL PUSH HIS FACE IN!
THIS IS GOIN' TO BE GOOD!

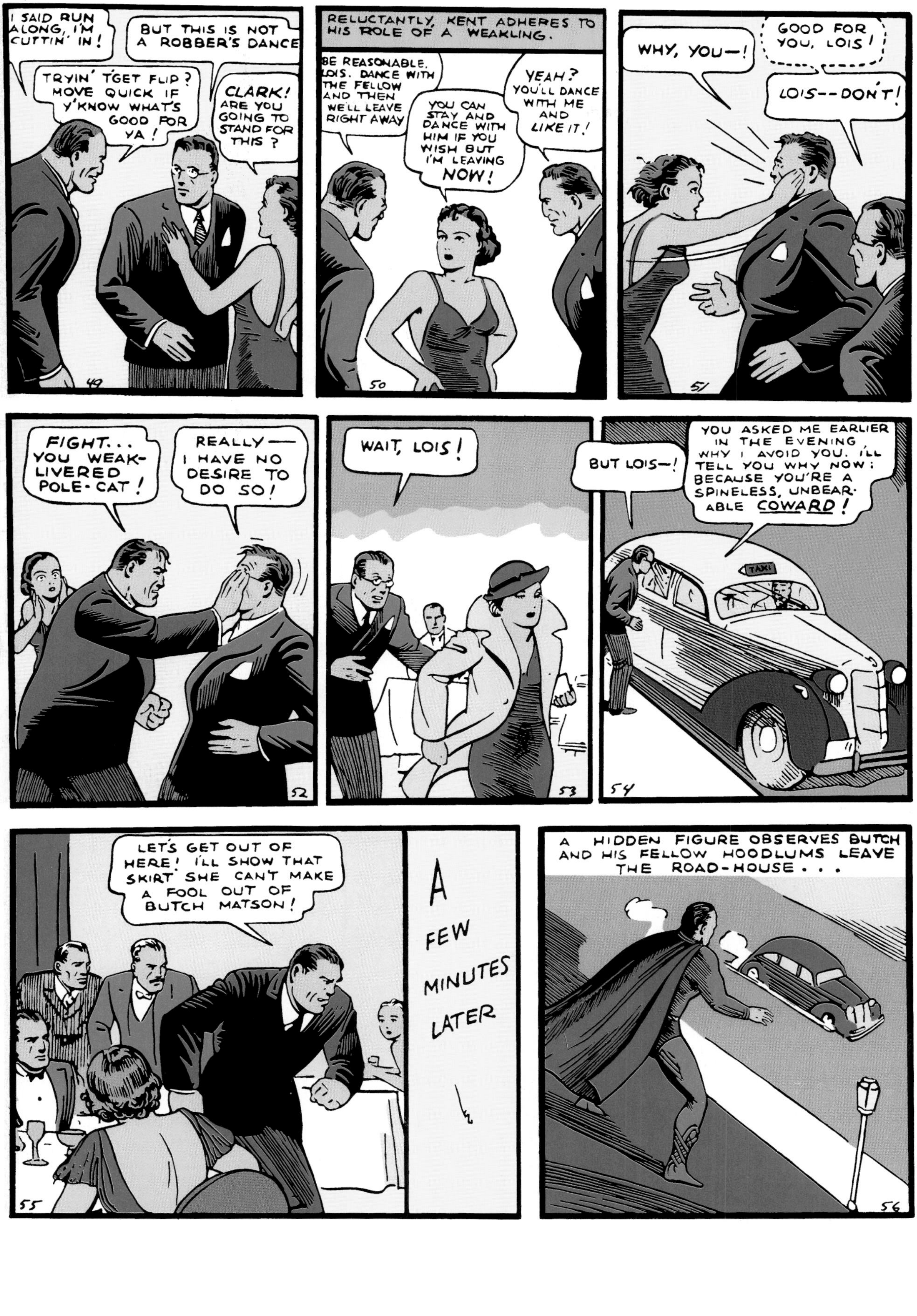
I SAID RUN ALONG, I'M CUTTIN' IN!
BUT THIS IS NOT A ROBBER'S DANCE
TRYIN' T'GET FLIP? MOVE QUICK IF Y'KNOW WHAT'S GOOD FOR YA!
CLARK! ARE YOU GOING TO STAND FOR THIS?
RELUCTANTLY, KENT ADHERES TO HIS ROLE OF A WEAKLING.
BE REASONABLE, LOIS. DANCE WITH THE FELLOW AND THEN WE'LL LEAVE RIGHT AWAY
YOU CAN STAY AND DANCE WITH HIM IF YOU WISH BUT I'M LEAVING NOW!
YEAH? YOU'LL DANCE WITH ME AND LIKE IT!
WHY, YOU—!
GOOD FOR YOU, LOIS!
LOIS--DON'T!
FIGHT... YOU WEAK-LIVERED POLE-CAT!
REALLY— I HAVE NO DESIRE TO DO SO!
WAIT, LOIS!
BUT LOIS—!
YOU ASKED ME EARLIER IN THE EVENING WHY I AVOID YOU. I'LL TELL YOU WHY NOW: BECAUSE YOU'RE A SPINELESS, UNBEARABLE COWARD!
TAXI
LET'S GET OUT OF HERE! I'LL SHOW THAT SKIRT SHE CAN'T MAKE A FOOL OUT OF BUTCH MATSON!
A FEW MINUTES LATER
A HIDDEN FIGURE OBSERVES BUTCH AND HIS FELLOW HOODLUMS LEAVE THE ROAD-HOUSE . . .

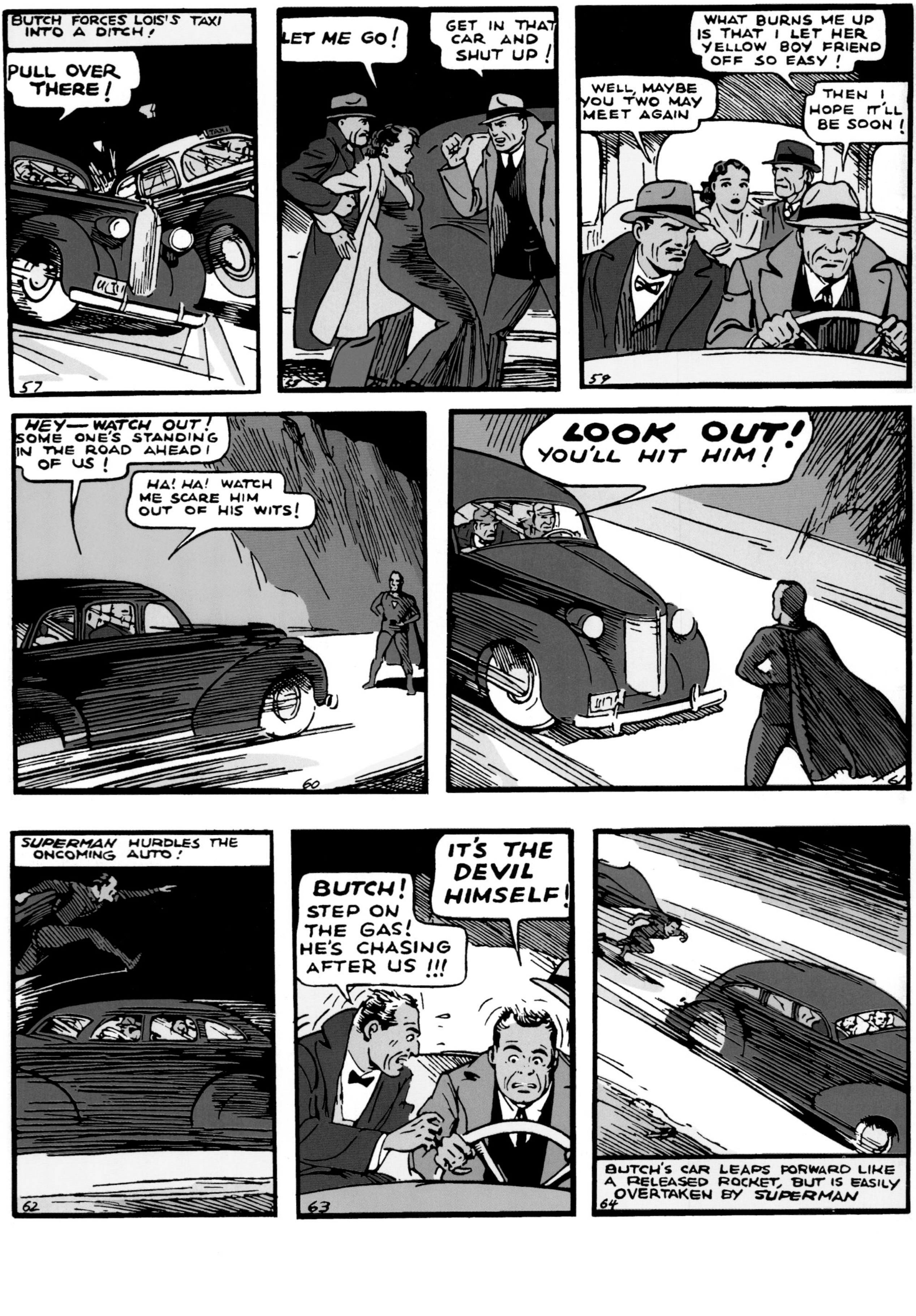
BUTCH FORCES LOIS'S TAXI INTO A DITCH!
PULL OVER THERE!
TAXI
57
LET ME GO!
GET IN THAT CAR AND SHUT UP!
WHAT BURNS ME UP IS THAT I LET HER YELLOW BOY FRIEND OFF SO EASY!
WELL, MAYBE YOU TWO MAY MEET AGAIN
THEN I HOPE IT'LL BE SOON!
59
HEY—WATCH OUT! SOME ONE'S STANDING IN THE ROAD AHEAD OF US!
HA! HA! WATCH ME SCARE HIM OUT OF HIS WITS!
60
LOOK OUT! YOU'LL HIT HIM!
61
SUPERMAN HURDLES THE ONCOMING AUTO!
62
BUTCH! STEP ON THE GAS! HE'S CHASING AFTER US !!!
IT'S THE DEVIL HIMSELF!
63
BUTCH'S CAR LEAPS FORWARD LIKE A RELEASED ROCKET, BUT IS EASILY OVERTAKEN BY SUPERMAN
64

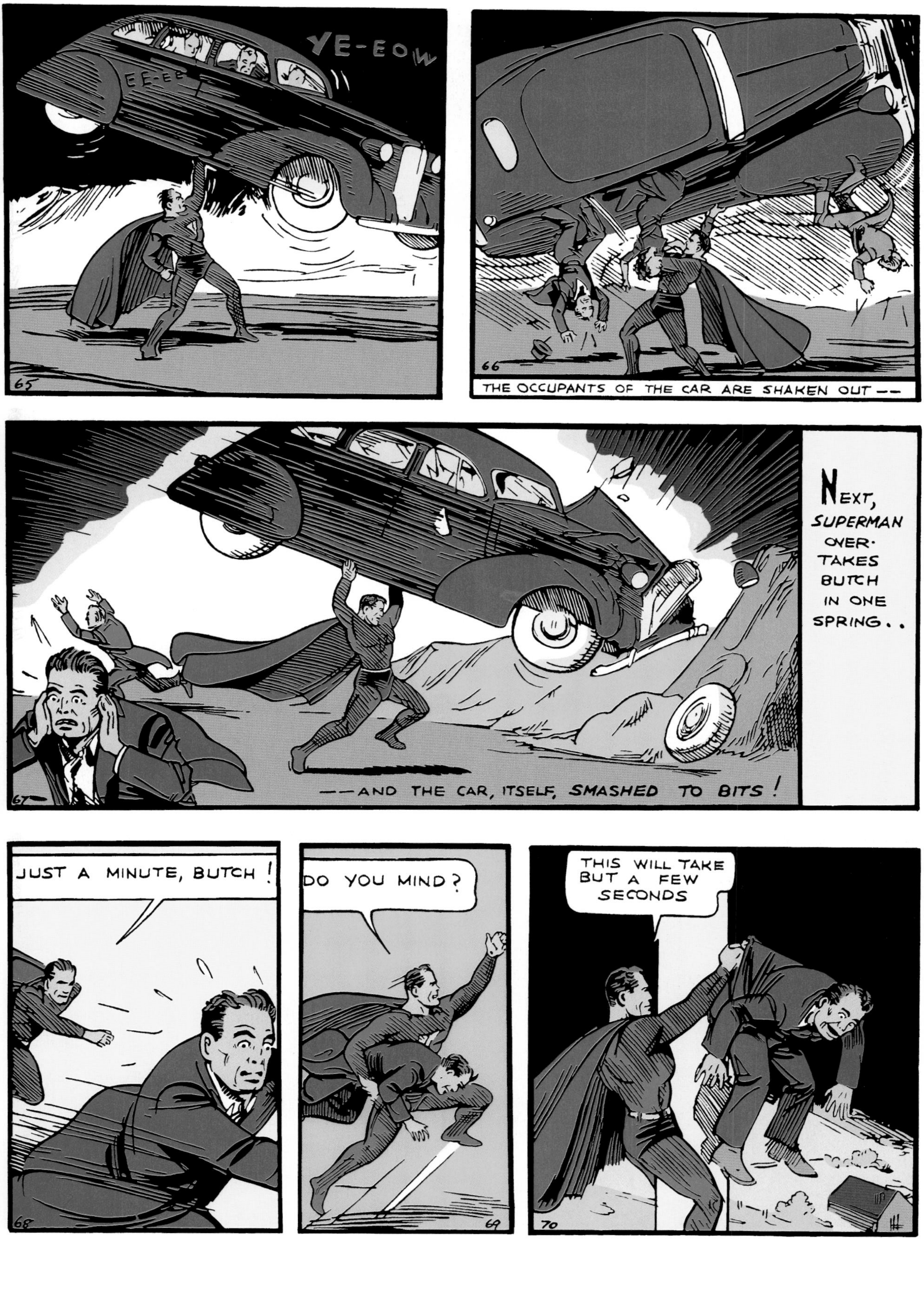
YE-EOW
EE-EE
THE OCCUPANTS OF THE CAR ARE SHAKEN OUT --
NEXT, SUPERMAN OVER-TAKES BUTCH IN ONE SPRING..
--AND THE CAR, ITSELF, SMASHED TO BITS!
JUST A MINUTE, BUTCH!
DO YOU MIND?
THIS WILL TAKE BUT A FEW SECONDS

GET ME OFFA HERE!

OKAY! I'LL CUT YOU LOOSE!

DON'T!

YOU NEEDN'T BE AFRAID OF ME. I WON'T HARM YOU

BEARING LOIS IN HIS ARMS *SUPERMAN* HEADS TOWARD THE CITY — —

— — DEPOSITING HER UPON ITS OUTSKIRTS

I'D ADVISE YOU NOT TO PRINT THIS LITTLE EPISODE

NEXT MORNING

BUT I TELL YOU I SAW *SUPERMAN* LAST NIGHT!

ARE YOU SURE IT WASN'T PINK ELEPHANTS YOU SAW?

EDITOR

LOIS TREATS CLARK COLDER THAN EVER

I'M SORRY ABOUT LAST NIGHT — PLEASE DON'T BE ANGRY WITH ME

CLARK RECIEVES AN ASSIGNMENT

KENT, THE FRONT PAGE IS GETTING SO DULL I'VE EVEN GOT TO HEADLINE CARD-GAMES. — — THERES A WAR GOING ON IN A SMALL SOUTH AMERICAN RE-PUBLIC, SAN MONTE; AND TO STIR UP NEWS I'M SENDING YOU DOWN THERE AS CORRESPONDENT. TAKE ALONG A CAMERA AND TRY TO SEND BACK SOME GOOD SHOTS WITH YOUR ARTICLES

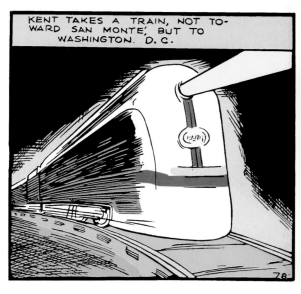

KENT TAKES A TRAIN, NOT TO-WARD SAN MONTE, BUT TO WASHINGTON. D.C.

24

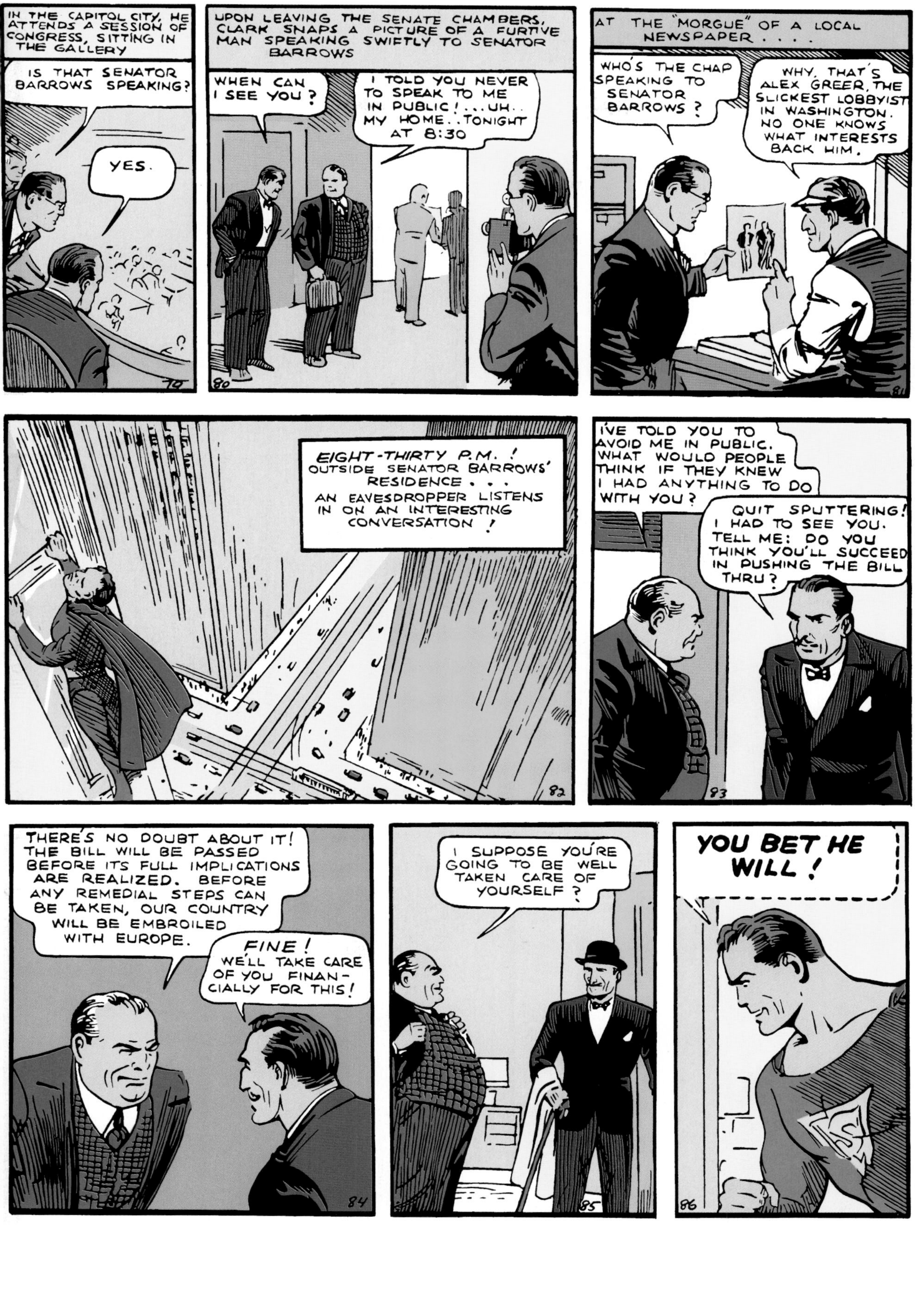
IN THE CAPITOL CITY, HE ATTENDS A SESSION OF CONGRESS, SITTING IN THE GALLERY
IS THAT SENATOR BARROWS SPEAKING?
YES.
UPON LEAVING THE SENATE CHAMBERS, CLARK SNAPS A PICTURE OF A FURTIVE MAN SPEAKING SWIFTLY TO SENATOR BARROWS
WHEN CAN I SEE YOU?
I TOLD YOU NEVER TO SPEAK TO ME IN PUBLIC!...UH.. MY HOME..TONIGHT AT 8:30
AT THE "MORGUE" OF A LOCAL NEWSPAPER . . . .
WHO'S THE CHAP SPEAKING TO SENATOR BARROWS?
WHY, THAT'S ALEX GREER, THE SLICKEST LOBBYIST IN WASHINGTON. NO ONE KNOWS WHAT INTERESTS BACK HIM.
EIGHT-THIRTY P.M.! OUTSIDE SENATOR BARROWS' RESIDENCE . . . AN EAVESDROPPER LISTENS IN ON AN INTERESTING CONVERSATION!
I'VE TOLD YOU TO AVOID ME IN PUBLIC. WHAT WOULD PEOPLE THINK IF THEY KNEW I HAD ANYTHING TO DO WITH YOU?
QUIT SPUTTERING! I HAD TO SEE YOU. TELL ME: DO YOU THINK YOU'LL SUCCEED IN PUSHING THE BILL THRU?
THERE'S NO DOUBT ABOUT IT! THE BILL WILL BE PASSED BEFORE ITS FULL IMPLICATIONS ARE REALIZED. BEFORE ANY REMEDIAL STEPS CAN BE TAKEN, OUR COUNTRY WILL BE EMBROILED WITH EUROPE.
FINE! WE'LL TAKE CARE OF YOU FINANCIALLY FOR THIS!
I SUPPOSE YOU'RE GOING TO BE WELL TAKEN CARE OF YOURSELF?
YOU BET HE WILL!

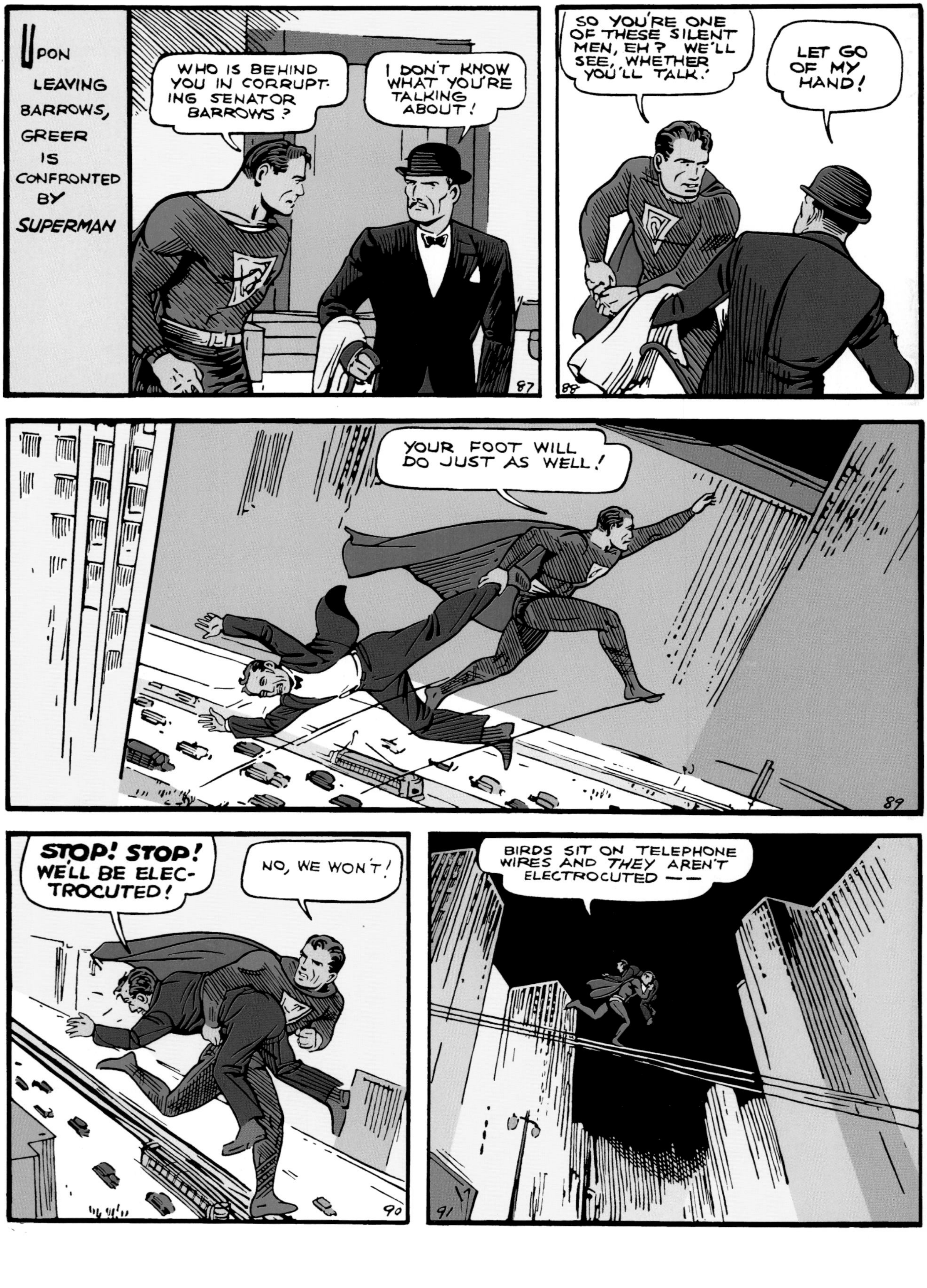
UPON LEAVING BARROWS, GREER IS CONFRONTED BY SUPERMAN
WHO IS BEHIND YOU IN CORRUPTING SENATOR BARROWS?
I DON'T KNOW WHAT YOU'RE TALKING ABOUT!
87
SO YOU'RE ONE OF THESE SILENT MEN, EH? WE'LL SEE, WHETHER YOU'LL TALK!
LET GO OF MY HAND!
88
YOUR FOOT WILL DO JUST AS WELL!
89
STOP! STOP! WE'LL BE ELECTROCUTED!
NO, WE WON'T!
90
BIRDS SIT ON TELEPHONE WIRES AND THEY AREN'T ELECTROCUTED ——
91

—— NOT UNLESS THEY TOUCH A TELEPHONE-POLE AND ARE *GROUNDED!*

OOPS! —— ALMOST TOUCHED THAT POLE!

YE-OW!

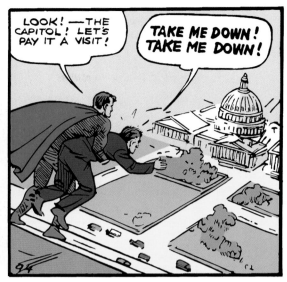

LOOK! —THE CAPITOL! LET'S PAY IT A VISIT!

TAKE ME DOWN! TAKE ME DOWN!

WHAT A MAGNIFICENT VIEW!

HELP! HELP!

I WONDER IF WE COULD JUMP ALL THE WAY TO THAT BUILDING?

NO! DON'T!

DESPITE GREER'S FRENZIED PROTESTS, SUPERMAN LEAPS OUT INTO THE NIGHT!

MISSED —— DOGGONE IT!

TO BE CONTINUED

AND SO BEGINS THE STARTLING ADVENTURES OF *THE MOST SENSATIONAL STRIP CHARACTER OF ALL TIME:* SUPERMAN!

A PHYSICAL MARVEL, A MENTAL WONDER, SUPERMAN IS DESTINED TO RESHAPE THE DESTINY OF A WORLD!

Only in ACTION COMICS CAN YOU THRILL AT THE DARING DEEDS OF THIS SUPERB CREATION! DON'T MISS AN ISSUE!

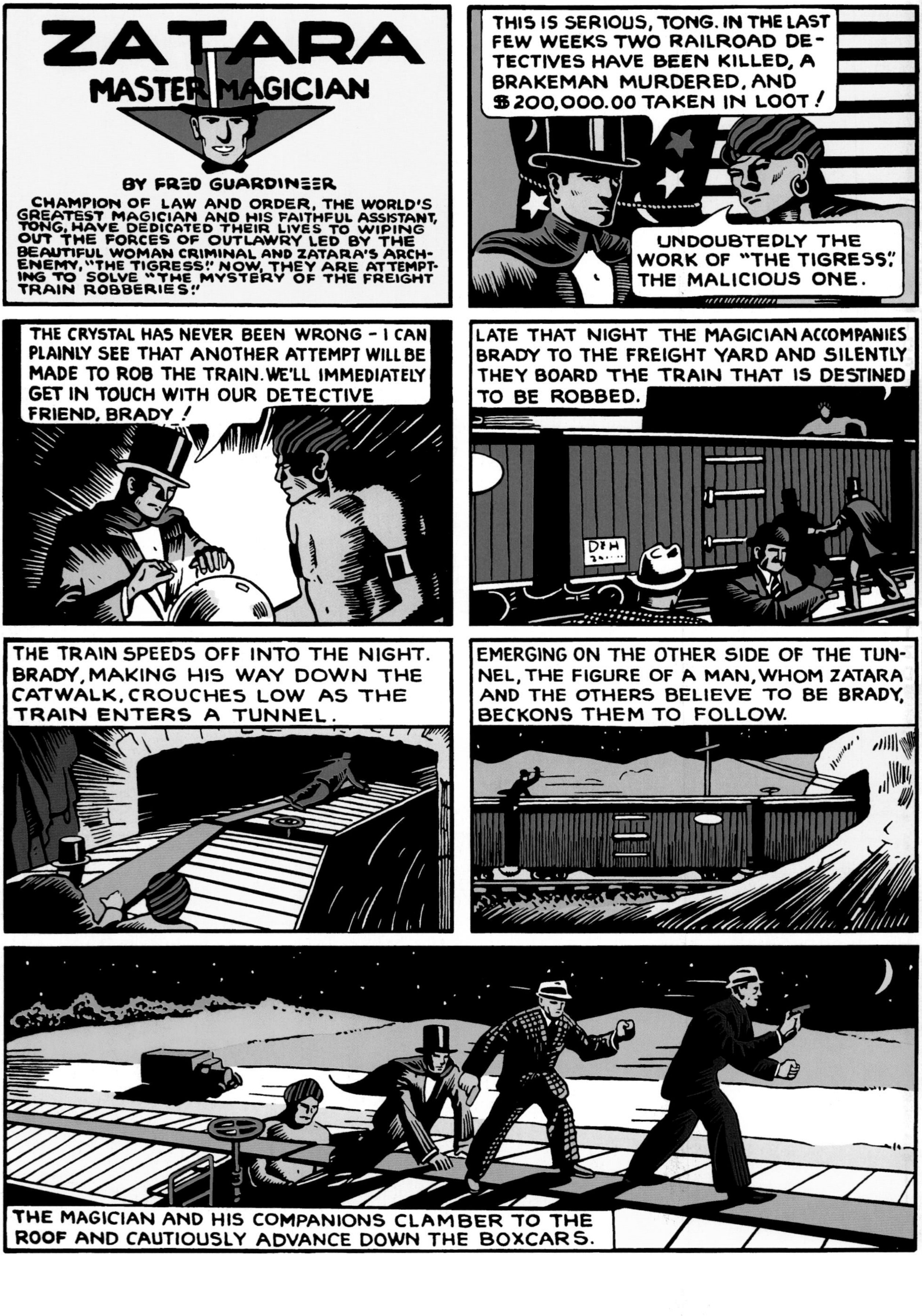
ZATARA
MASTER MAGICIAN
BY FRED GUARDINEER
CHAMPION OF LAW AND ORDER, THE WORLD'S GREATEST MAGICIAN AND HIS FAITHFUL ASSISTANT, TONG, HAVE DEDICATED THEIR LIVES TO WIPING OUT THE FORCES OF OUTLAWRY LED BY THE BEAUTIFUL WOMAN CRIMINAL AND ZATARA'S ARCH-ENEMY, "THE TIGRESS!" NOW, THEY ARE ATTEMPTING TO SOLVE "THE MYSTERY OF THE FREIGHT TRAIN ROBBERIES!"
THIS IS SERIOUS, TONG. IN THE LAST FEW WEEKS TWO RAILROAD DETECTIVES HAVE BEEN KILLED, A BRAKEMAN MURDERED, AND $200,000.00 TAKEN IN LOOT!
UNDOUBTEDLY THE WORK OF "THE TIGRESS," THE MALICIOUS ONE.
THE CRYSTAL HAS NEVER BEEN WRONG - I CAN PLAINLY SEE THAT ANOTHER ATTEMPT WILL BE MADE TO ROB THE TRAIN. WE'LL IMMEDIATELY GET IN TOUCH WITH OUR DETECTIVE FRIEND, BRADY!
LATE THAT NIGHT THE MAGICIAN ACCOMPANIES BRADY TO THE FREIGHT YARD AND SILENTLY THEY BOARD THE TRAIN THAT IS DESTINED TO BE ROBBED.
D&H
THE TRAIN SPEEDS OFF INTO THE NIGHT. BRADY, MAKING HIS WAY DOWN THE CATWALK, CROUCHES LOW AS THE TRAIN ENTERS A TUNNEL.
EMERGING ON THE OTHER SIDE OF THE TUNNEL, THE FIGURE OF A MAN, WHOM ZATARA AND THE OTHERS BELIEVE TO BE BRADY, BECKONS THEM TO FOLLOW.
THE MAGICIAN AND HIS COMPANIONS CLAMBER TO THE ROOF AND CAUTIOUSLY ADVANCE DOWN THE BOXCARS.

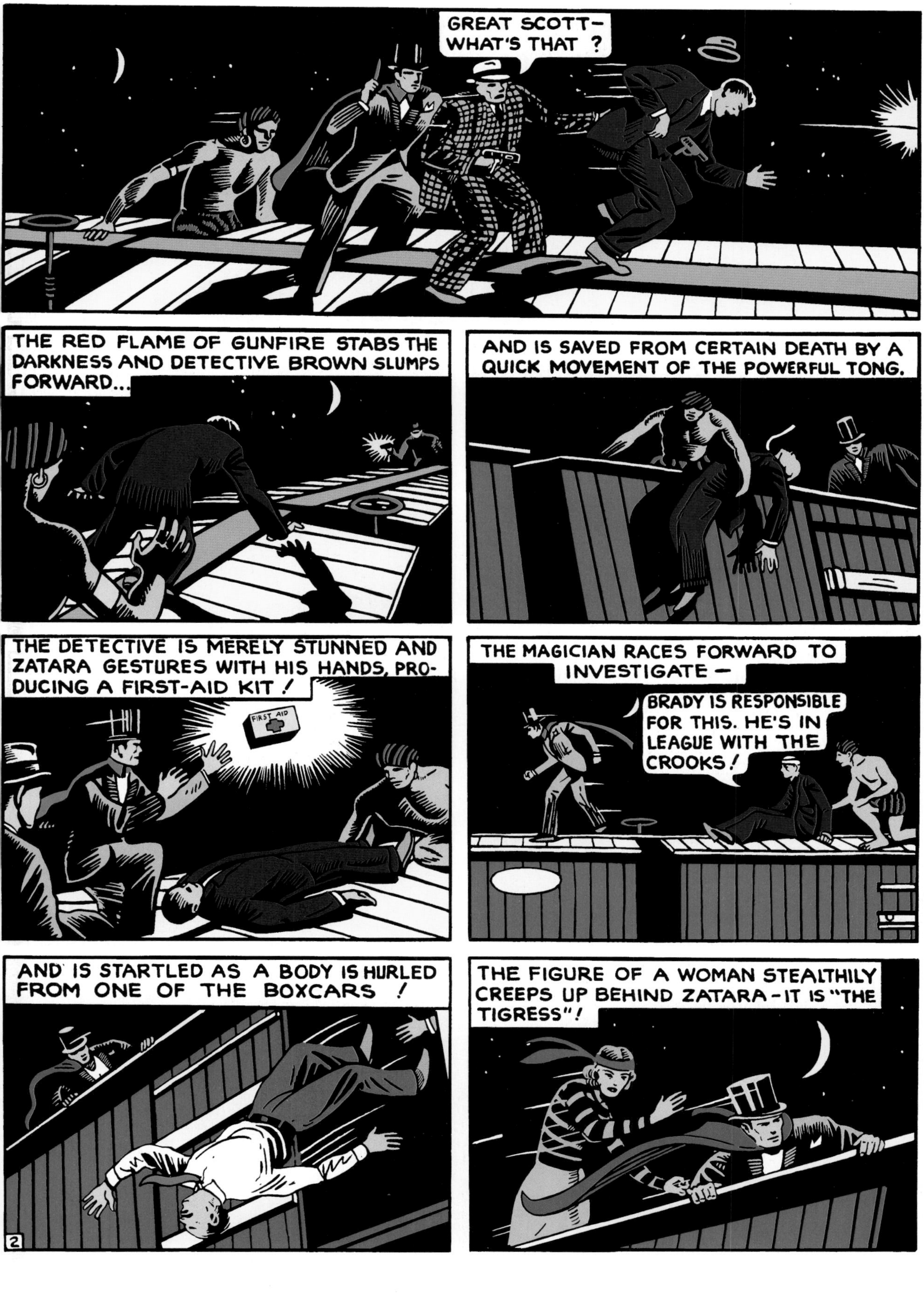

GREAT SCOTT- WHAT'S THAT ?
THE RED FLAME OF GUNFIRE STABS THE DARKNESS AND DETECTIVE BROWN SLUMPS FORWARD...
AND IS SAVED FROM CERTAIN DEATH BY A QUICK MOVEMENT OF THE POWERFUL TONG.
THE DETECTIVE IS MERELY STUNNED AND ZATARA GESTURES WITH HIS HANDS, PRODUCING A FIRST-AID KIT !
FIRST AID
THE MAGICIAN RACES FORWARD TO INVESTIGATE —
BRADY IS RESPONSIBLE FOR THIS. HE'S IN LEAGUE WITH THE CROOKS !
AND IS STARTLED AS A BODY IS HURLED FROM ONE OF THE BOXCARS !
2
THE FIGURE OF A WOMAN STEALTHILY CREEPS UP BEHIND ZATARA - IT IS "THE TIGRESS"!

"THE TIGRESS" ATTACKS!

THIS TIME YOU DIE, ZATARA!

AND WITH A POWERFUL LUNGE SHE SHOVES THE MAGICIAN FROM THE SPEEDING TRAIN!

BUT ZATARA'S MAGICAL POWERS SAVE HIM AND HE FLOATS GENTLY DOWN TO EARTH!

— AND LANDS SOFTLY IN THE UNDERBRUSH ALONG THE TRACKS!

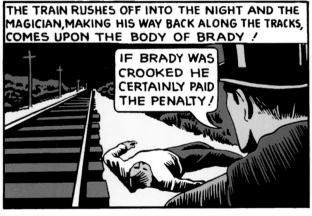
THE TRAIN RUSHES OFF INTO THE NIGHT AND THE MAGICIAN, MAKING HIS WAY BACK ALONG THE TRACKS, COMES UPON THE BODY OF BRADY!

IF BRADY WAS CROOKED HE CERTAINLY PAID THE PENALTY!

MEANWHILE TONG SUCCEEDS IN WARNING THE ENGINEER AND THE TRAIN GRINDS TO A HALT.

THE STATE POLICE HURRY TO INVESTIGATE THIS LATEST OUTRAGE —

3

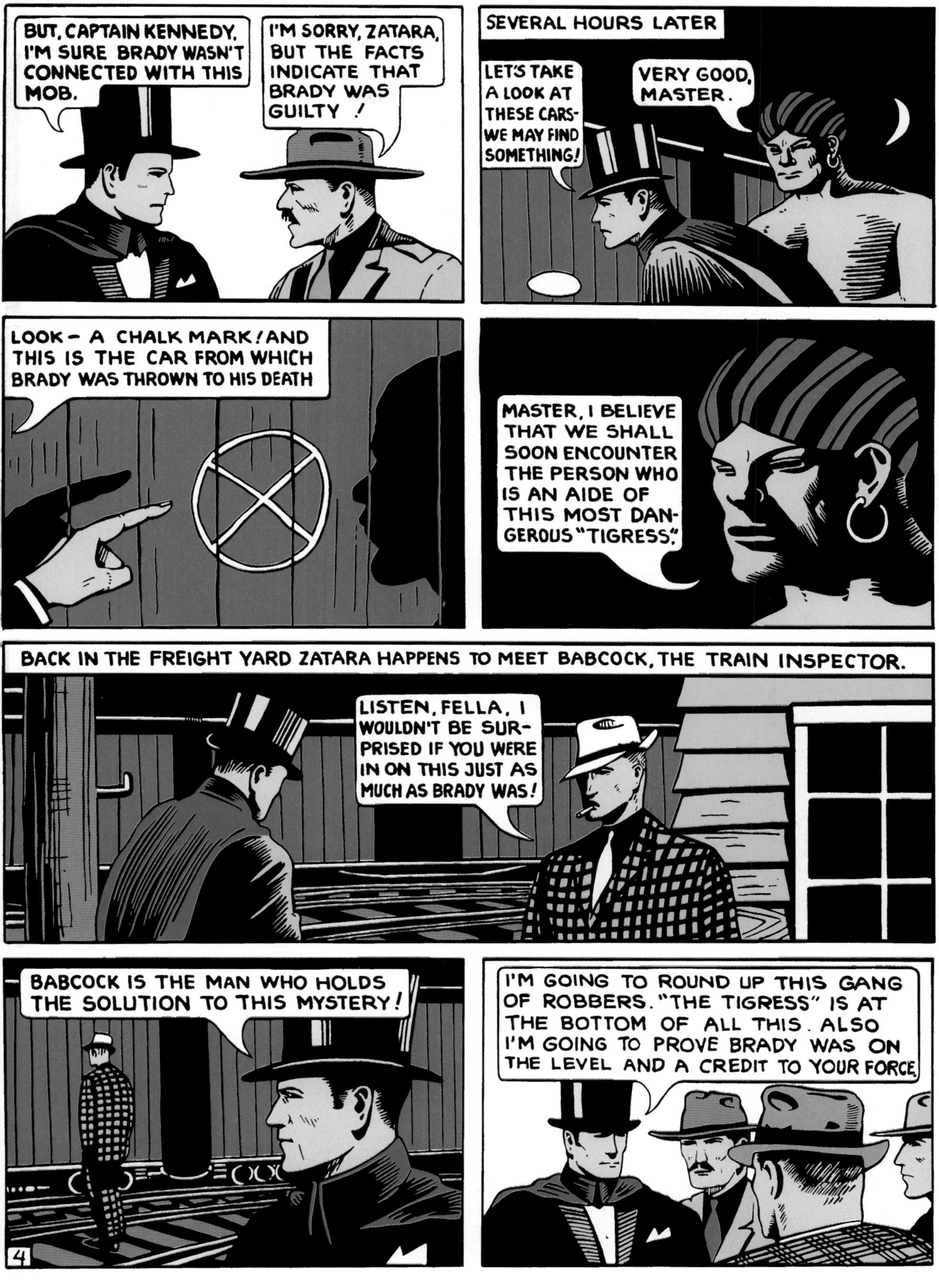

BUT, CAPTAIN KENNEDY, I'M SURE BRADY WASN'T CONNECTED WITH THIS MOB.
I'M SORRY, ZATARA, BUT THE FACTS INDICATE THAT BRADY WAS GUILTY !
SEVERAL HOURS LATER
LET'S TAKE A LOOK AT THESE CARS- WE MAY FIND SOMETHING!
VERY GOOD, MASTER.
LOOK - A CHALK MARK! AND THIS IS THE CAR FROM WHICH BRADY WAS THROWN TO HIS DEATH
MASTER, I BELIEVE THAT WE SHALL SOON ENCOUNTER THE PERSON WHO IS AN AIDE OF THIS MOST DANGEROUS "TIGRESS."
BACK IN THE FREIGHT YARD ZATARA HAPPENS TO MEET BABCOCK, THE TRAIN INSPECTOR.
LISTEN, FELLA, I WOULDN'T BE SURPRISED IF YOU WERE IN ON THIS JUST AS MUCH AS BRADY WAS!
BABCOCK IS THE MAN WHO HOLDS THE SOLUTION TO THIS MYSTERY!
4
I'M GOING TO ROUND UP THIS GANG OF ROBBERS. "THE TIGRESS" IS AT THE BOTTOM OF ALL THIS. ALSO I'M GOING TO PROVE BRADY WAS ON THE LEVEL AND A CREDIT TO YOUR FORCE.

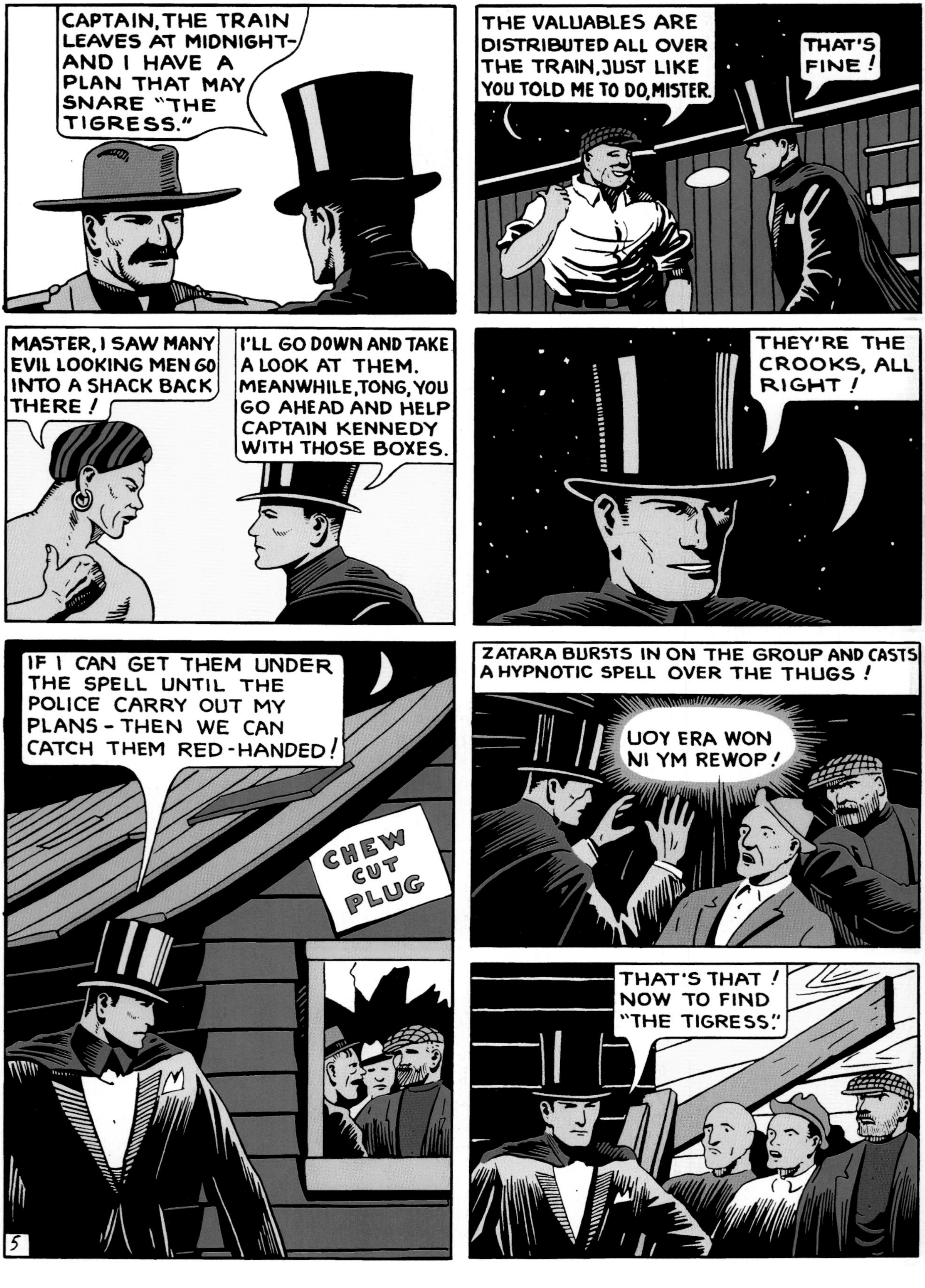
CAPTAIN, THE TRAIN LEAVES AT MIDNIGHT- AND I HAVE A PLAN THAT MAY SNARE "THE TIGRESS."
THE VALUABLES ARE DISTRIBUTED ALL OVER THE TRAIN, JUST LIKE YOU TOLD ME TO DO, MISTER.
THAT'S FINE!
MASTER, I SAW MANY EVIL LOOKING MEN GO INTO A SHACK BACK THERE!
I'LL GO DOWN AND TAKE A LOOK AT THEM. MEANWHILE, TONG, YOU GO AHEAD AND HELP CAPTAIN KENNEDY WITH THOSE BOXES.
THEY'RE THE CROOKS, ALL RIGHT!
IF I CAN GET THEM UNDER THE SPELL UNTIL THE POLICE CARRY OUT MY PLANS - THEN WE CAN CATCH THEM RED-HANDED!
CHEW CUT PLUG
5
ZATARA BURSTS IN ON THE GROUP AND CASTS A HYPNOTIC SPELL OVER THE THUGS!
UOY ERA WON NI YM REWOP!
THAT'S THAT! NOW TO FIND "THE TIGRESS."

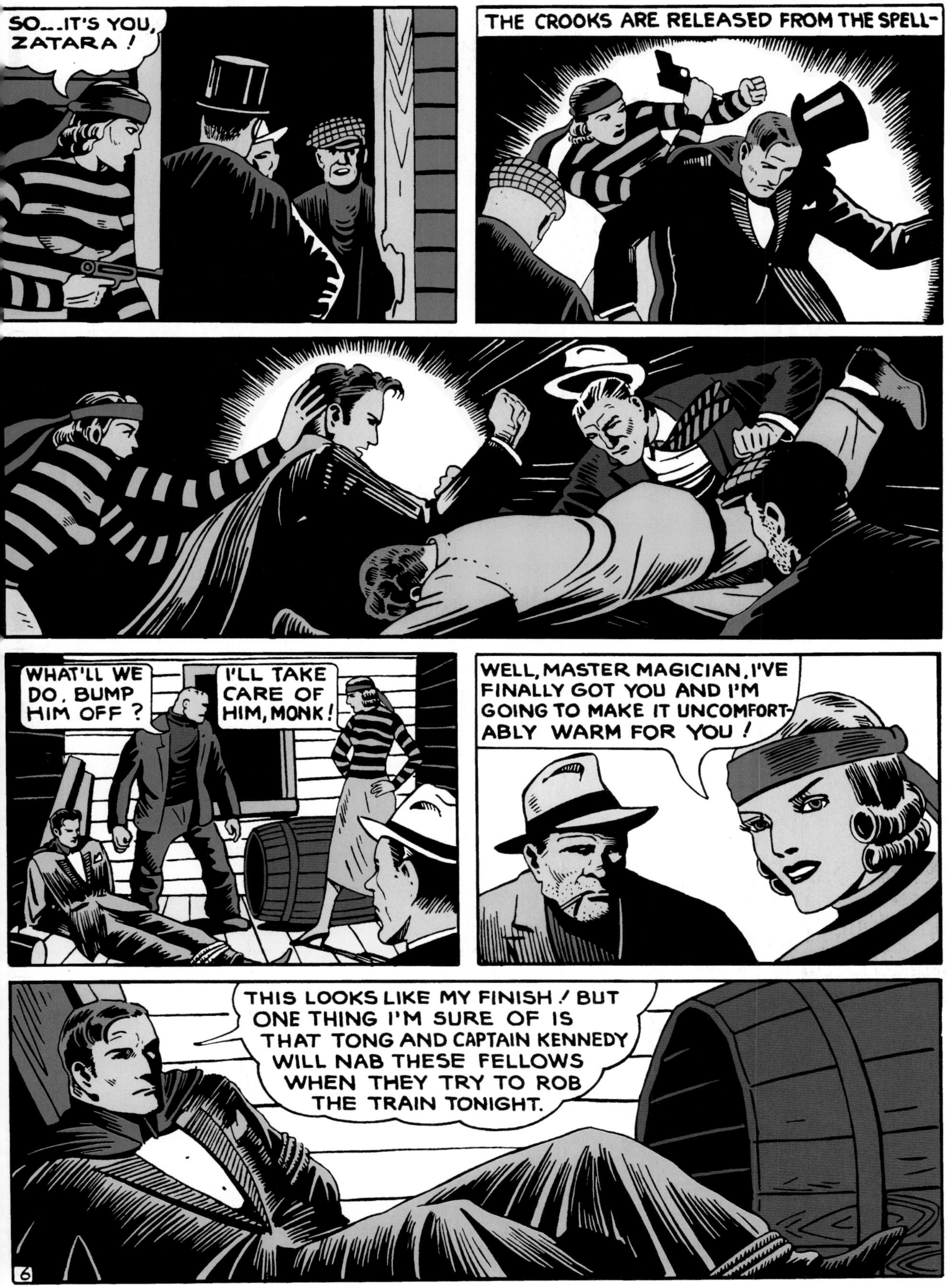
SO...IT'S YOU, ZATARA!
THE CROOKS ARE RELEASED FROM THE SPELL-
WHAT'LL WE DO, BUMP HIM OFF?
I'LL TAKE CARE OF HIM, MONK!
WELL, MASTER MAGICIAN, I'VE FINALLY GOT YOU AND I'M GOING TO MAKE IT UNCOMFORTABLY WARM FOR YOU!
THIS LOOKS LIKE MY FINISH! BUT ONE THING I'M SURE OF IS THAT TONG AND CAPTAIN KENNEDY WILL NAB THESE FELLOWS WHEN THEY TRY TO ROB THE TRAIN TONIGHT.
6

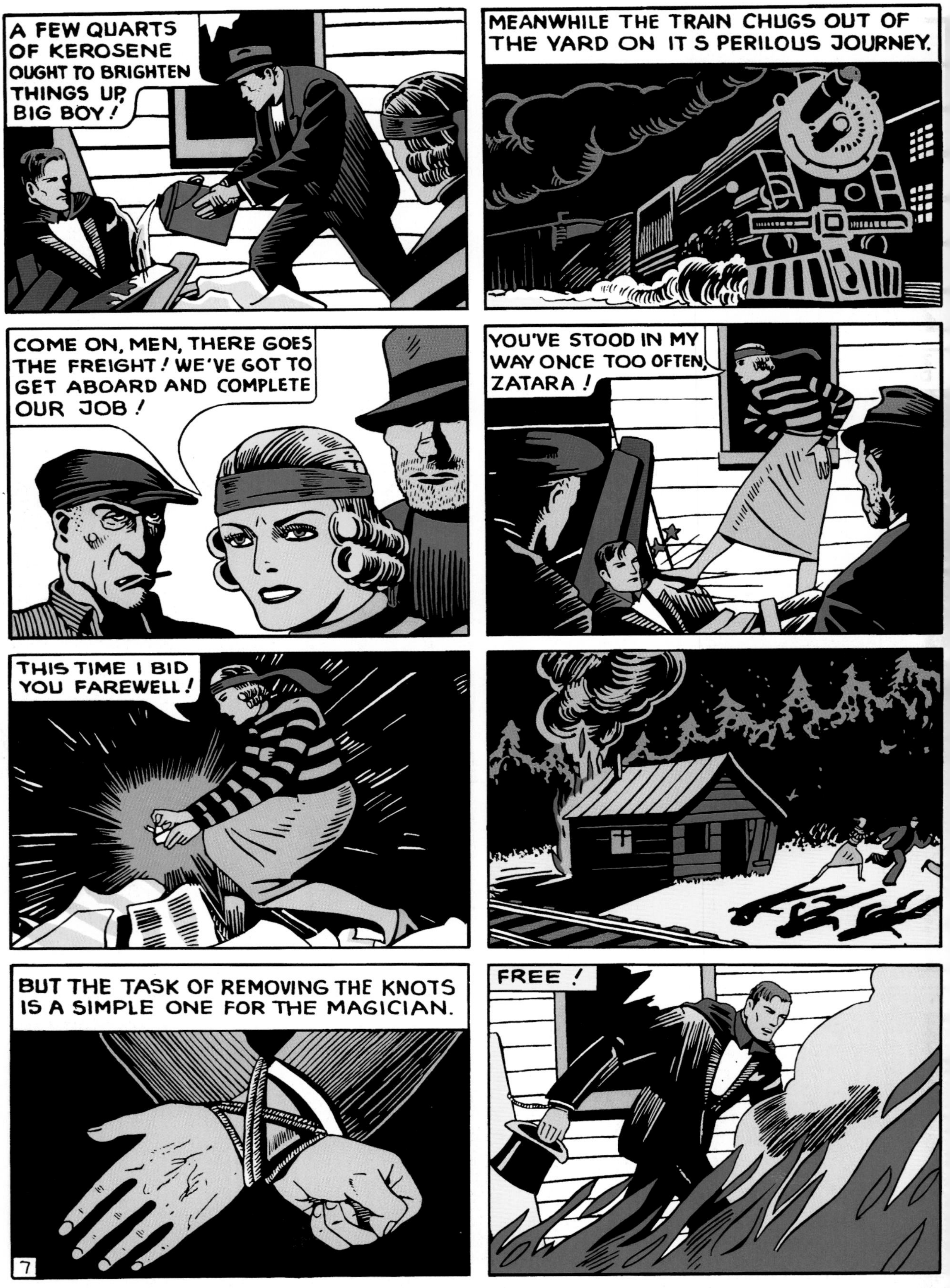
A FEW QUARTS OF KEROSENE OUGHT TO BRIGHTEN THINGS UP, BIG BOY!
MEANWHILE THE TRAIN CHUGS OUT OF THE YARD ON IT S PERILOUS JOURNEY.
COME ON, MEN, THERE GOES THE FREIGHT! WE'VE GOT TO GET ABOARD AND COMPLETE OUR JOB!
YOU'VE STOOD IN MY WAY ONCE TOO OFTEN, ZATARA!
THIS TIME I BID YOU FAREWELL!
BUT THE TASK OF REMOVING THE KNOTS IS A SIMPLE ONE FOR THE MAGICIAN.
7
FREE!

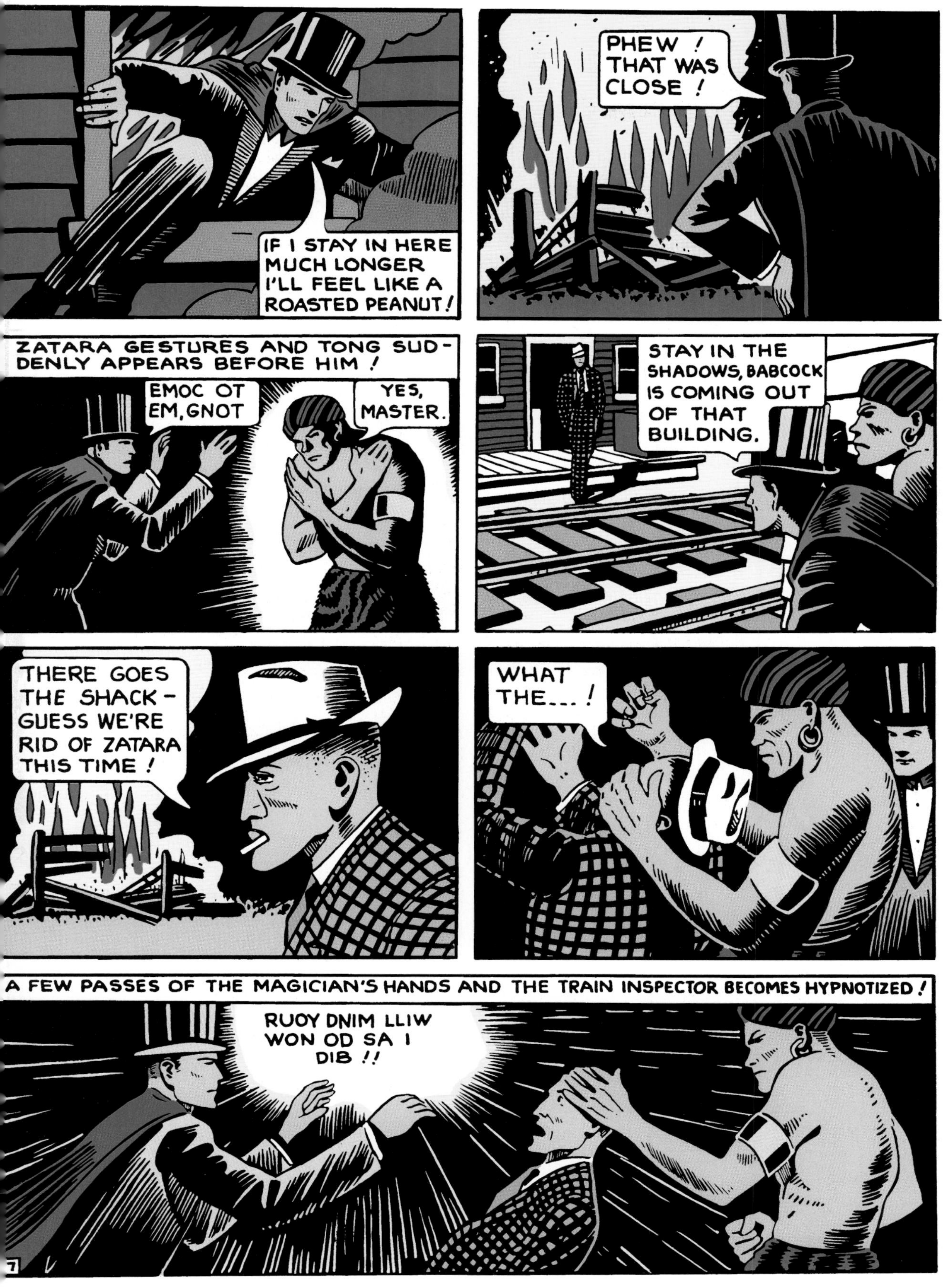
IF I STAY IN HERE MUCH LONGER I'LL FEEL LIKE A ROASTED PEANUT!
PHEW ! THAT WAS CLOSE !
ZATARA GESTURES AND TONG SUDDENLY APPEARS BEFORE HIM !
EMOC OT EM, GNOT
YES, MASTER.
STAY IN THE SHADOWS, BABCOCK IS COMING OUT OF THAT BUILDING.
THERE GOES THE SHACK - GUESS WE'RE RID OF ZATARA THIS TIME !
WHAT THE... !
A FEW PASSES OF THE MAGICIAN'S HANDS AND THE TRAIN INSPECTOR BECOMES HYPNOTIZED !
RUOY DNIM LLIW WON OD SA I DIB !!
7

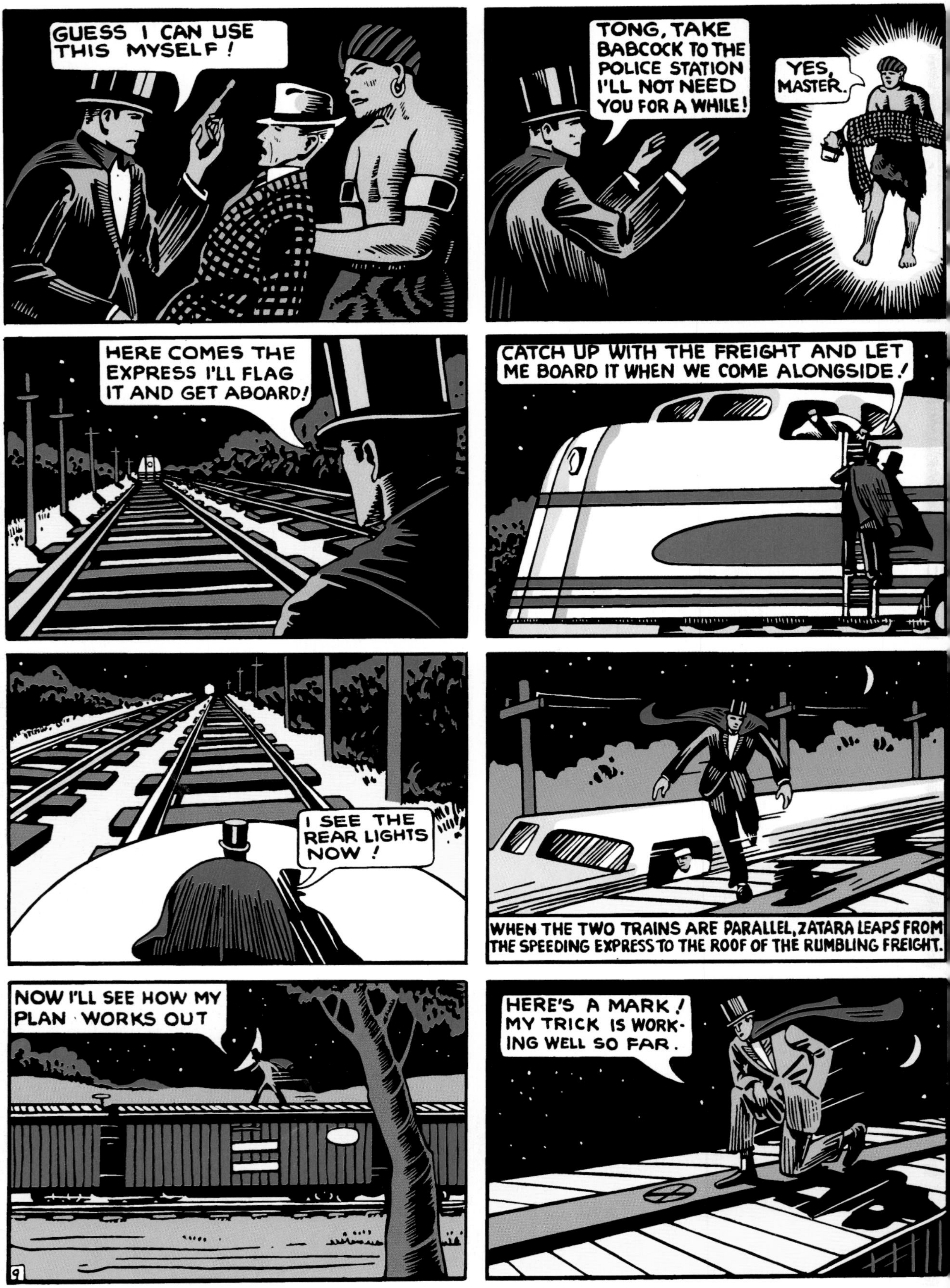
GUESS I CAN USE THIS MYSELF!
TONG, TAKE BABCOCK TO THE POLICE STATION I'LL NOT NEED YOU FOR A WHILE!
YES, MASTER.
HERE COMES THE EXPRESS I'LL FLAG IT AND GET ABOARD!
CATCH UP WITH THE FREIGHT AND LET ME BOARD IT WHEN WE COME ALONGSIDE!
I SEE THE REAR LIGHTS NOW!
WHEN THE TWO TRAINS ARE PARALLEL, ZATARA LEAPS FROM THE SPEEDING EXPRESS TO THE ROOF OF THE RUMBLING FREIGHT.
NOW I'LL SEE HOW MY PLAN WORKS OUT
9
HERE'S A MARK! MY TRICK IS WORKING WELL SO FAR.

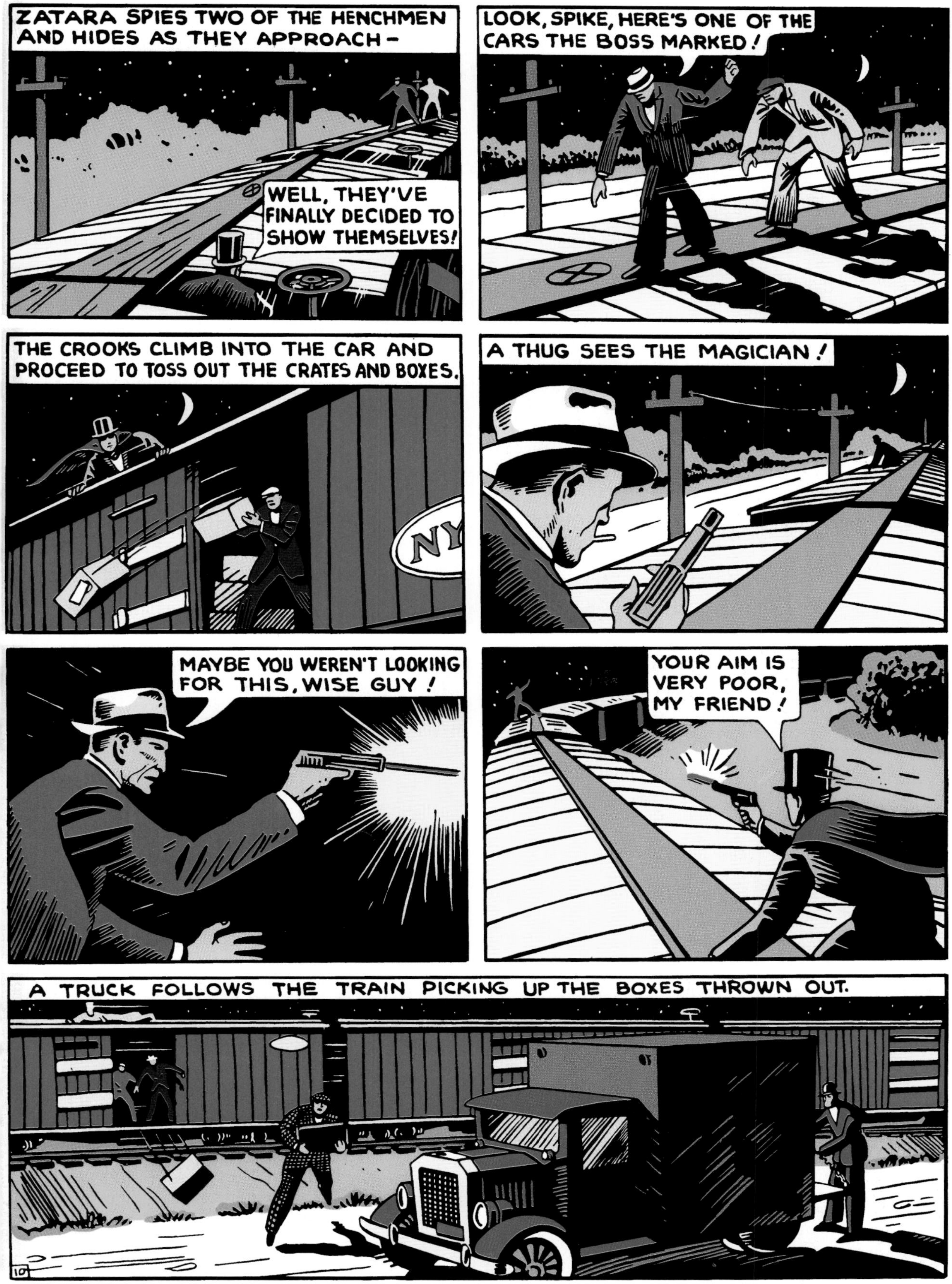
ZATARA SPIES TWO OF THE HENCHMEN AND HIDES AS THEY APPROACH -
WELL, THEY'VE FINALLY DECIDED TO SHOW THEMSELVES!
LOOK, SPIKE, HERE'S ONE OF THE CARS THE BOSS MARKED!
THE CROOKS CLIMB INTO THE CAR AND PROCEED TO TOSS OUT THE CRATES AND BOXES.
NY
A THUG SEES THE MAGICIAN!
MAYBE YOU WEREN'T LOOKING FOR THIS, WISE GUY!
YOUR AIM IS VERY POOR, MY FRIEND!
A TRUCK FOLLOWS THE TRAIN PICKING UP THE BOXES THROWN OUT.
10

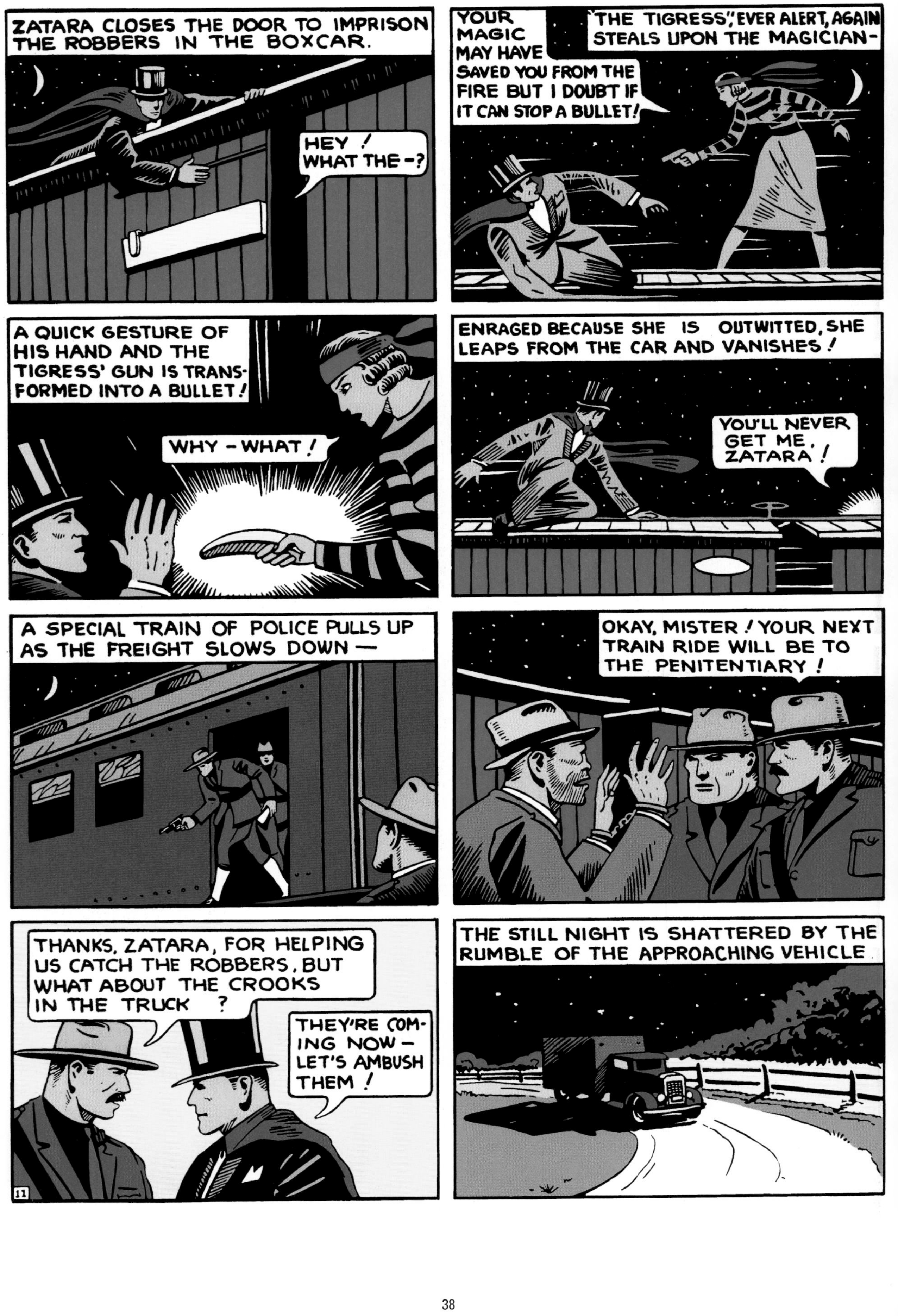
ZATARA CLOSES THE DOOR TO IMPRISON THE ROBBERS IN THE BOXCAR.
HEY ! WHAT THE -?
"THE TIGRESS," EVER ALERT, AGAIN STEALS UPON THE MAGICIAN-
YOUR MAGIC MAY HAVE SAVED YOU FROM THE FIRE BUT I DOUBT IF IT CAN STOP A BULLET!
A QUICK GESTURE OF HIS HAND AND THE TIGRESS' GUN IS TRANSFORMED INTO A BULLET!
WHY - WHAT !
ENRAGED BECAUSE SHE IS OUTWITTED, SHE LEAPS FROM THE CAR AND VANISHES !
YOU'LL NEVER GET ME, ZATARA !
A SPECIAL TRAIN OF POLICE PULLS UP AS THE FREIGHT SLOWS DOWN —
OKAY, MISTER ! YOUR NEXT TRAIN RIDE WILL BE TO THE PENITENTIARY !
THANKS, ZATARA, FOR HELPING US CATCH THE ROBBERS, BUT WHAT ABOUT THE CROOKS IN THE TRUCK ?
THEY'RE COMING NOW - LET'S AMBUSH THEM !
11
THE STILL NIGHT IS SHATTERED BY THE RUMBLE OF THE APPROACHING VEHICLE

THE POLICE SPRING FROM THE SIDES OF THE ROAD AND FORCE THE REMAINING ROBBERS INTO SUBMISSION

RAISE THEM HIGH, FELLOW.

YOU SEE, CAPTAIN KENNEDY; BABCOCK, THE CROOKED TRAIN INSPECTOR, USED TO LEAVE A CAR OPEN FOR THE THIEVES AND THEN LATER THEY ENTERED THE CAR MARKED WITH ⊗. THEY THREW OUT THE FREIGHT AND IT WAS PICKED UP BY THE MEN IN THE TRUCK!

WHILE THEY WERE HOLDING ME IN THE SHACK I HAD TONG SUBSTITUTE THOSE BOXES FOR THE VALUABLE CARGO WHICH IS STILL SAFE AND SOUND ON THE FREIGHT TRAIN —

SO BABCOCK TIPPED THEM OFF?

CORRECT! AND TONG HAS HIM NOW AT THE POLICE STATION BACK IN TOWN!

BACK IN THE STATION HOUSE BABCOCK CONFESSES BRADY'S INNOCENCE –

NO, BRADY WASN'T IN WITH US-THEY BUMPED HIM OFF THAT NIGHT WE WENT THROUGH THE TUNNEL! ONE OF THE BOYS PUT ON HIS HAT AND COAT AND MOTIONED YOU TO COME AHEAD.

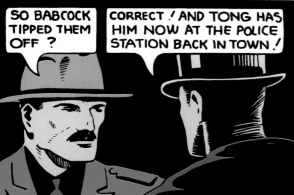

CONGRATULATIONS, ZATARA, YOU CERTAINLY AIDED THE CAUSE OF JUSTICE. TOO BAD "THE TIGRESS" IS STILL AT LARGE.

THANK YOU, CAPTAIN.

WELL, THAT CLOSES THIS CASE. NOW TO WATCH WHERE "THE TIGRESS" STRIKES NEXT!

THIS HUMBLE PERSON SEEKS A BIT OF SLEEP BEFORE THE NEXT "TIGRESS" HUNT!

FRED GUARDINEER

12

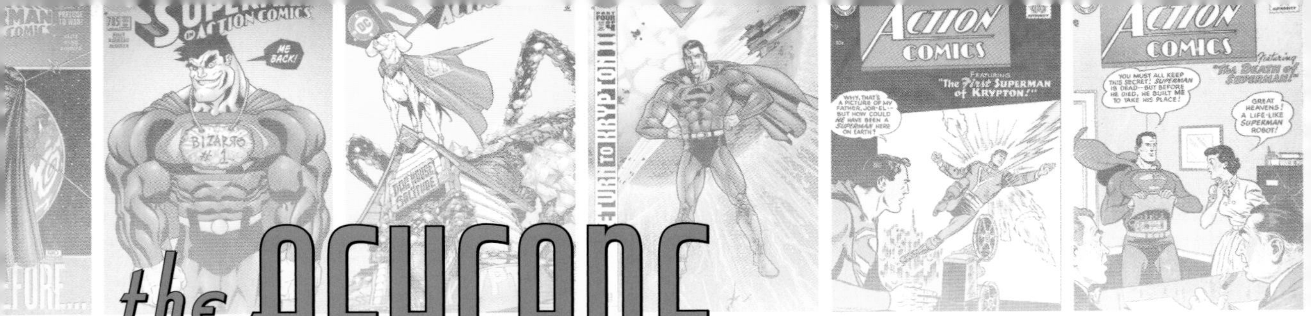
ME BACK!
BIZARRO #1
ACTION COMICS
The First SUPERMAN of KRYPTON!
ACTION COMICS
The Death of SUPERMAN!
GREAT HEAVENS! A LIFE-LIKE SUPERMAN ROBOT!

the ASHCANS

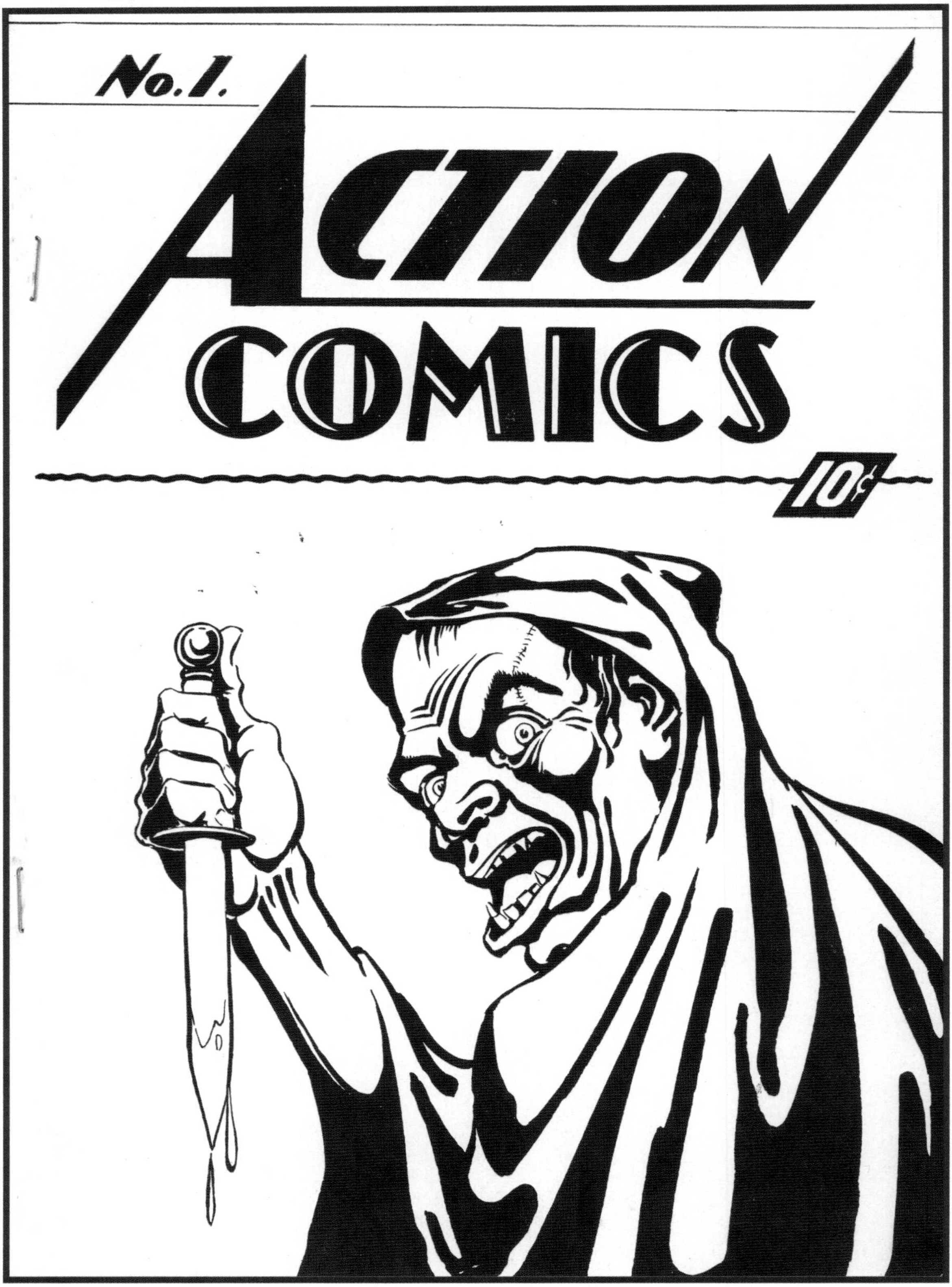
No. 1.
ACTION COMICS
10¢

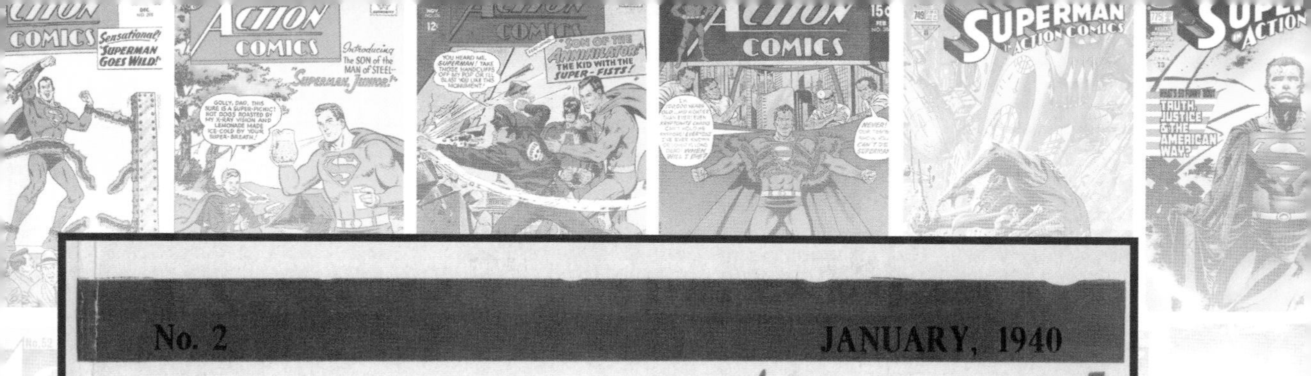
ACTION COMICS
Sensational! "SUPERMAN GOES WILD!"
ACTION COMICS
Introducing The SON of the MAN of STEEL— "Superman, Junior!"
ACTION COMICS
ACTION COMICS
SUPERMAN ACTION COMICS
TRUTH, JUSTICE & THE AMERICAN WAY?

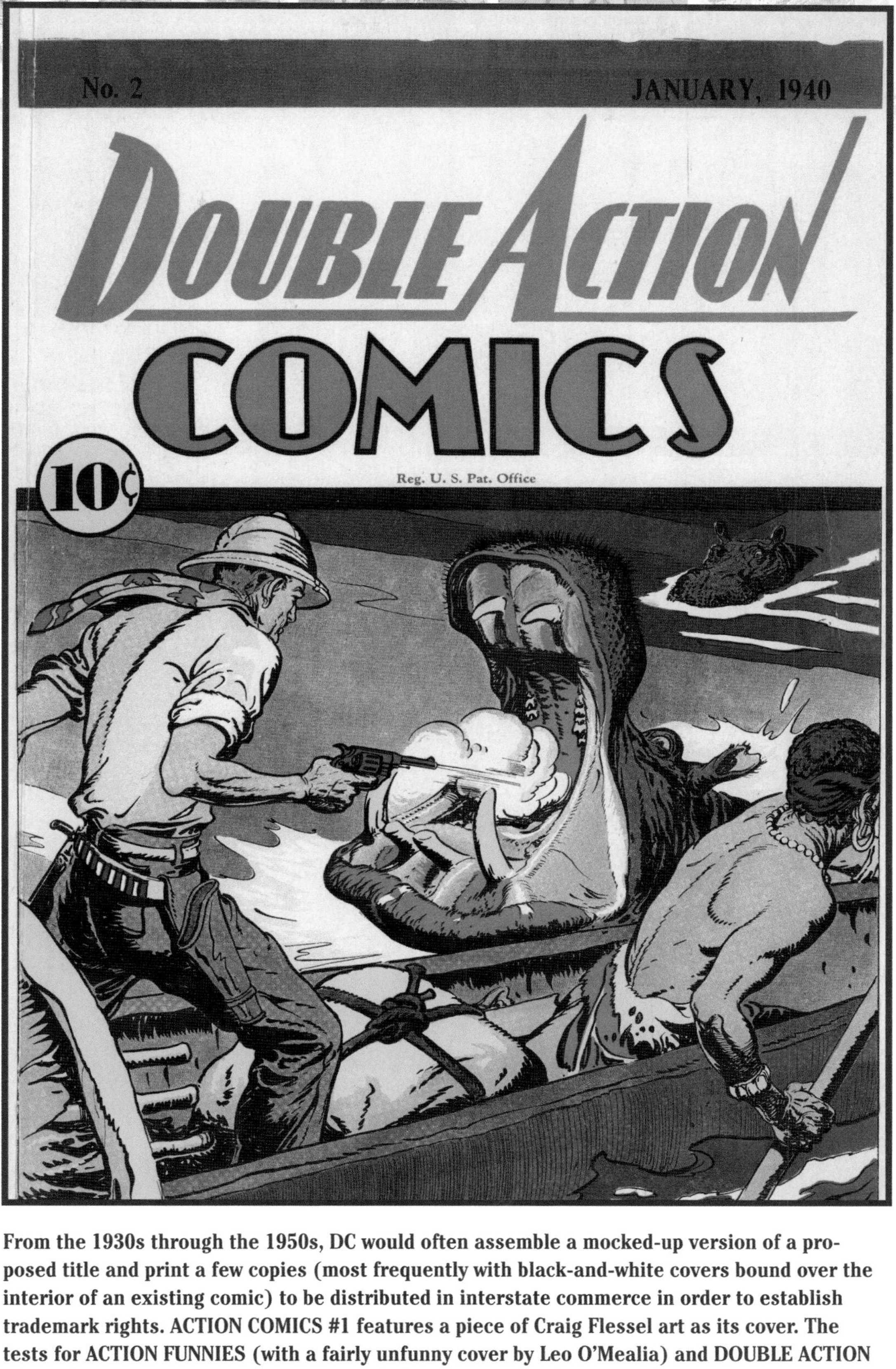
No. 2
JANUARY, 1940
DOUBLE ACTION
COMICS
10¢
Reg. U. S. Pat. Office

From the 1930s through the 1950s, DC would often assemble a mocked-up version of a proposed title and print a few copies (most frequently with black-and-white covers bound over the interior of an existing comic) to be distributed in interstate commerce in order to establish trademark rights. ACTION COMICS #1 features a piece of Craig Flessel art as its cover. The tests for ACTION FUNNIES (with a fairly unfunny cover by Leo O'Mealia) and DOUBLE ACTION COMICS (using covers from ADVENTURE COMICS by Flessel) were for spin-off titles that never happened, but SUPERMAN COMICS (with Joe Shuster's ACTION COMICS #7 cover) certainly did.

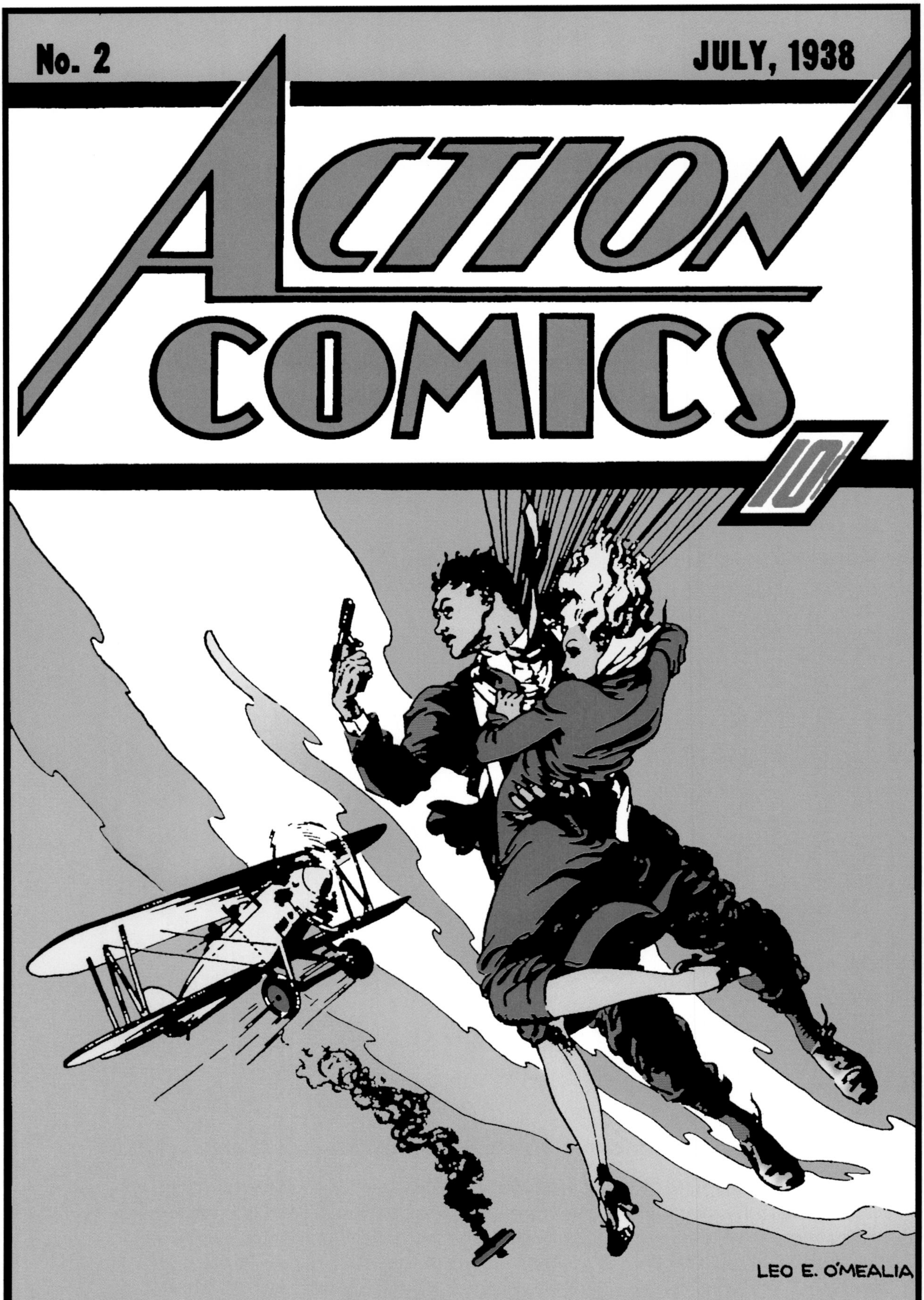
No. 2
JULY, 1938
ACTION COMICS
10¢
LEO E. O'MEALIA

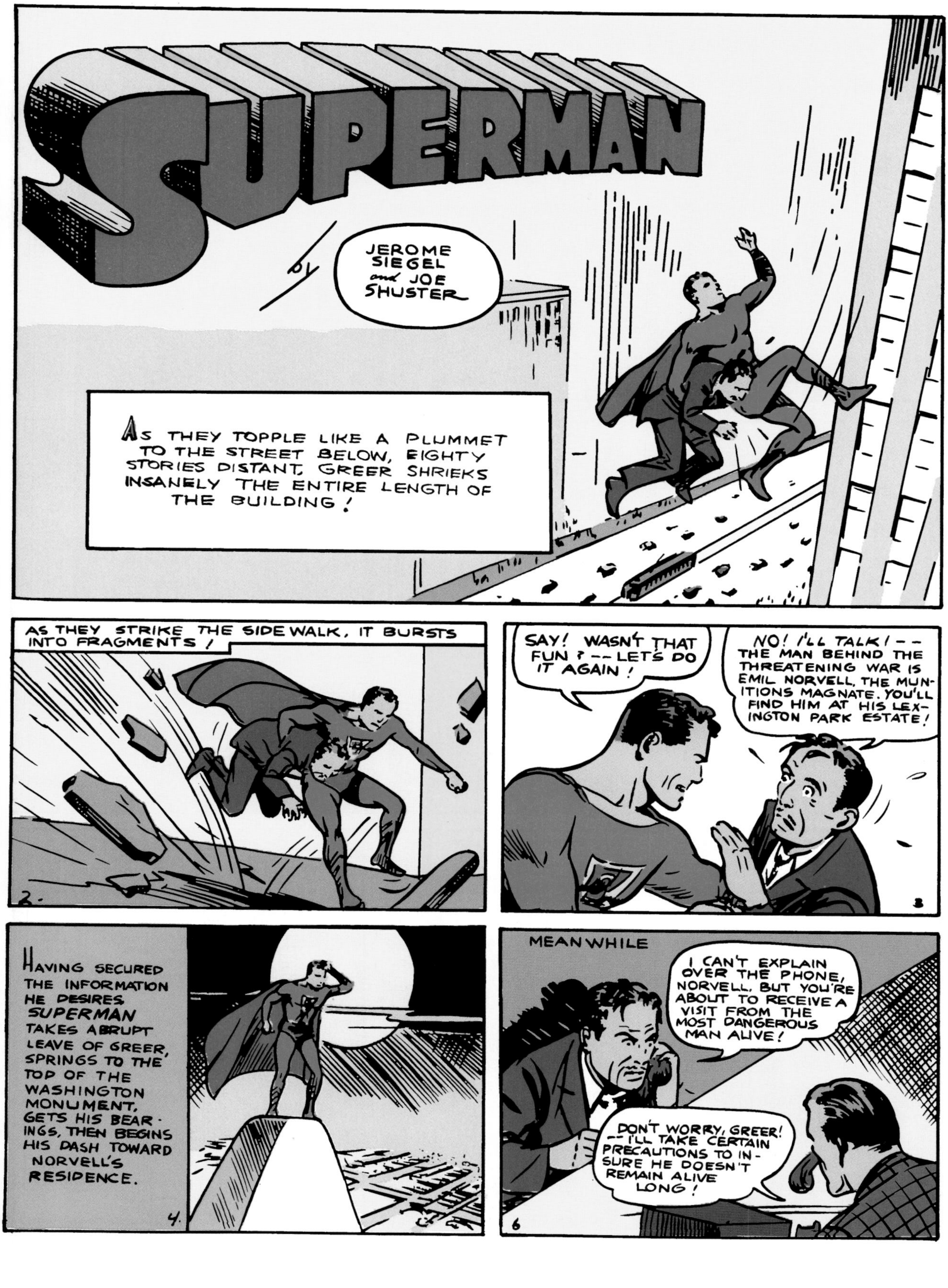
SUPERMAN
by
JEROME SIEGEL and JOE SHUSTER
AS THEY TOPPLE LIKE A PLUMMET TO THE STREET BELOW, EIGHTY STORIES DISTANT, GREER SHRIEKS INSANELY THE ENTIRE LENGTH OF THE BUILDING!
AS THEY STRIKE THE SIDEWALK, IT BURSTS INTO FRAGMENTS!
SAY! WASN'T THAT FUN? -- LET'S DO IT AGAIN!
NO! I'LL TALK! -- THE MAN BEHIND THE THREATENING WAR IS EMIL NORVELL, THE MUNITIONS MAGNATE. YOU'LL FIND HIM AT HIS LEXINGTON PARK ESTATE!
HAVING SECURED THE INFORMATION HE DESIRES SUPERMAN TAKES ABRUPT LEAVE OF GREER, SPRINGS TO THE TOP OF THE WASHINGTON MONUMENT, GETS HIS BEARINGS, THEN BEGINS HIS DASH TOWARD NORVELL'S RESIDENCE.
MEANWHILE
I CAN'T EXPLAIN OVER THE PHONE, NORVELL, BUT YOU'RE ABOUT TO RECEIVE A VISIT FROM THE MOST DANGEROUS MAN ALIVE!
DON'T WORRY, GREER! -- I'LL TAKE CERTAIN PRECAUTIONS TO INSURE HE DOESN'T REMAIN ALIVE LONG!

FIVE MINUTES ELAPSE -- THEN...
...SUPERMAN STEPS THRU THE WINDOW OF EMIL NORVELL'S STUDY AND CALMLY CONFRONTS HIM...

WHETHER YOU LIKE IT OR NOT, NORVELL, YOU'RE COMING WITH ME!

SORRY, BUT I HAVE OTHER PLANS!

7

AS HE SPEAKS, THE MUNITIONS MANUFACTURER SURREPTITIOUSLY REACHES BEHIND HIM TO PRESS A BUTTON ON HIS DESK.

8

WHAT ARE YOU HOLDING BEHIND YOU? --GIVE IT TO ME!

ALL RIGHT BOYS! -- HE ASKED FOR IT! LET HIM HAVE IT!!

9

INSTANTLY SEVERAL PANELS ABOUT THE ROOM SLIDE ASIDE AND OUT STEP A NUMBER OF ARMED GUARDS!

NEXT MOMENT SUPERMAN IS THE CENTER OF A DEAFENING MACHINE-GUN BARRAGE!

10

UNHARMED BY THE RAIN OF MACHINE-GUN BULLETS, SUPERMAN STREAKS TOWARD HIS WOULD-BE MURDERERS!

GOOD HEAVENS! HE WON'T DIE!

GLAD I CAN'T SAY THE SAME FOR YOU!

11

A MOMENT LATER A DOZEN BODIES FLY HEADLONG OUT THE WINDOW INTO THE NIGHT, THE MACHINE-GUNS WRAPPED FIRMLY ABOUT THEIR NECKS!

12

YOU SEE HOW EFFORTLESSLY I CRUSH THIS BAR OF IRON IN MY HAND? -- THAT BAR COULD JUST AS EASILY BE YOUR NECK!... NOW, FOR THE LAST TIME: ARE YOU COMING WITH ME?

YES! YES! IMMEDIATELY!

13

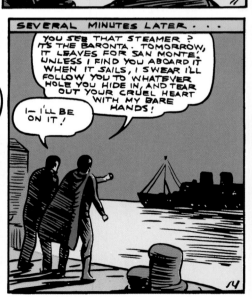

SEVERAL MINUTES LATER...

YOU SEE THAT STEAMER? IT'S THE BARONTA. TOMORROW, IT LEAVES FOR SAN MONTE. UNLESS I FIND YOU ABOARD IT WHEN IT SAILS, I SWEAR I'LL FOLLOW YOU TO WHATEVER HOLE YOU HIDE IN, AND TEAR OUT YOUR CRUEL HEART WITH MY BARE HANDS!

I-- I'LL BE ON IT!

14

44

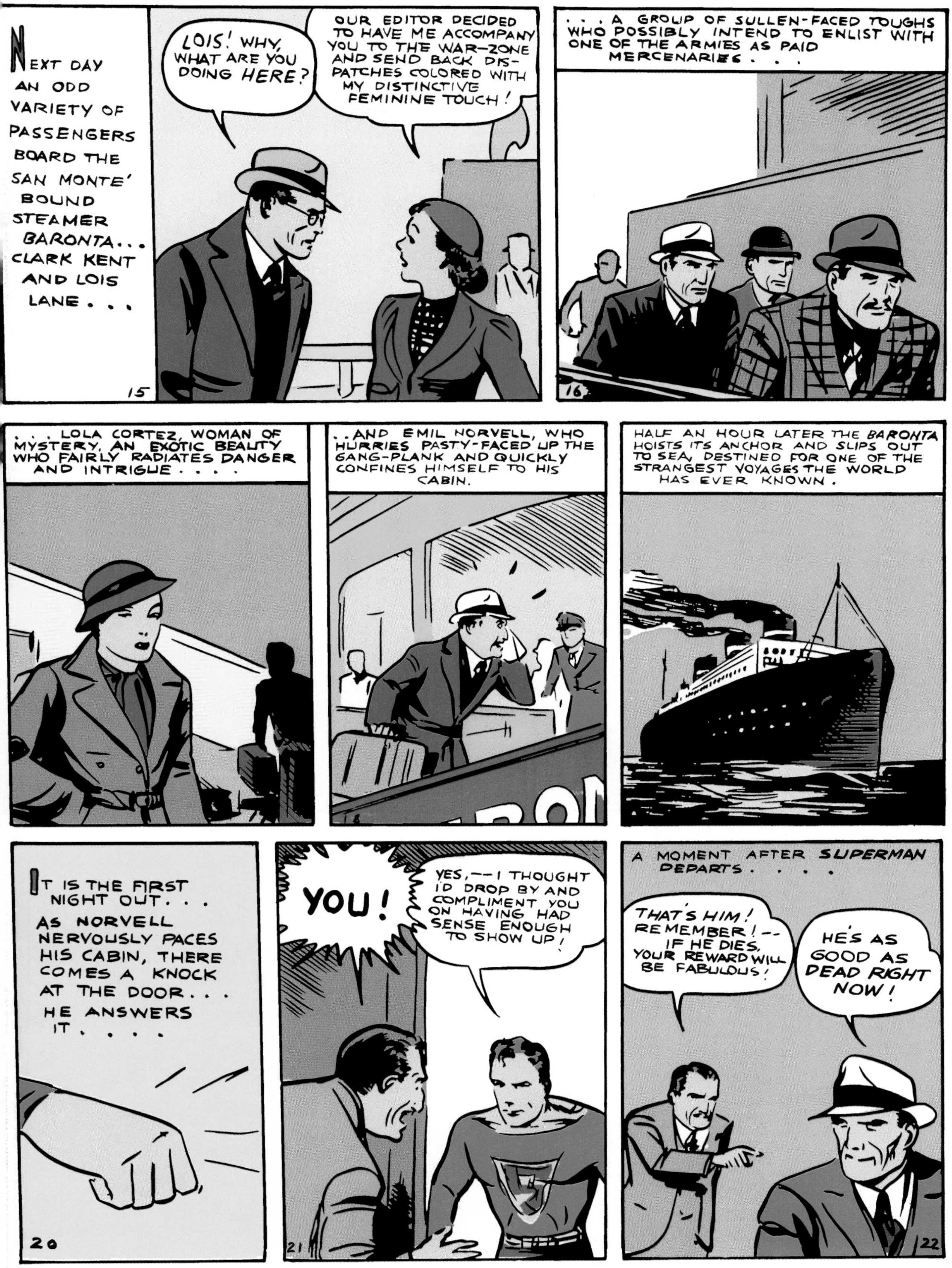
NEXT DAY AN ODD VARIETY OF PASSENGERS BOARD THE SAN MONTE' BOUND STEAMER BARONTA... CLARK KENT AND LOIS LANE . . .
LOIS! WHY, WHAT ARE YOU DOING HERE?
OUR EDITOR DECIDED TO HAVE ME ACCOMPANY YOU TO THE WAR-ZONE AND SEND BACK DIS-PATCHES COLORED WITH MY DISTINCTIVE FEMININE TOUCH!
. . . A GROUP OF SULLEN-FACED TOUGHS WHO POSSIBLY INTEND TO ENLIST WITH ONE OF THE ARMIES AS PAID MERCENARIES . . .
. . . LOLA CORTEZ, WOMAN OF MYSTERY, AN EXOTIC BEAUTY WHO FAIRLY RADIATES DANGER AND INTRIGUE . . . .
..AND EMIL NORVELL, WHO HURRIES PASTY-FACED UP THE GANG-PLANK AND QUICKLY CONFINES HIMSELF TO HIS CABIN.
HALF AN HOUR LATER THE BARONTA HOISTS ITS ANCHOR AND SLIPS OUT TO SEA, DESTINED FOR ONE OF THE STRANGEST VOYAGES THE WORLD HAS EVER KNOWN.
IT IS THE FIRST NIGHT OUT. . . AS NORVELL NERVOUSLY PACES HIS CABIN, THERE COMES A KNOCK AT THE DOOR. . . HE ANSWERS IT . . .
YOU!
YES,--I THOUGHT I'D DROP BY AND COMPLIMENT YOU ON HAVING HAD SENSE ENOUGH TO SHOW UP!
A MOMENT AFTER SUPERMAN DEPARTS . . .
THAT'S HIM! REMEMBER!--IF HE DIES, YOUR REWARD WILL BE FABULOUS!
HE'S AS GOOD AS DEAD RIGHT NOW!

AS SUPERMAN STANDS SILENTLY AT THE SHIP'S RAIL, ADMIRING THE MOONLIGHT, HE WHIRLS SUDDENLY AT THE SOUND OF FOOTSTEPS!

ALL TOGETHER, NOW: — GET HIM!

FOR AN INSTANT SUPERMAN BRACES HIMSELF AGAINST THE RAIL -- AND IN THAT SECOND IT GIVES WAY!

HE IS FLUNG, TWISTING AND TURNING, INTO THE OCEAN!

THE THUGS REPORT BACK TO NORVELL...

IT WAS SIMPLE! A LITTLE SHOVE AND HE TOPPLED OVERBOARD! -- NOW HOW ABOUT THAT DOUGH YOU PROMISED US!

YOU'LL GET NOTHING! GET OUT OF HERE, YOU TRUSTING FOOLS, AND BE GLAD I DON'T TURN YOU OVER TO THE POLICE!

MEANWHILE -- AT THAT VERY INSTANT SUPERMAN, SWIMMING VIGOROUSLY, HAS CAUGHT UP WITH THE STEAMER . . .

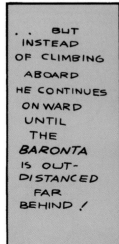

. . BUT INSTEAD OF CLIMBING ABOARD HE CONTINUES ONWARD UNTIL THE BARONTA IS OUT- DISTANCED FAR BEHIND!

SEE YOU LATER!

NEXT EVENING, A FEW MINUTES AFTER THE STEAMER LANDS . . NORVELL IS ATTACKED BY HIS DOUBLE-CROSSED HENCHMEN.

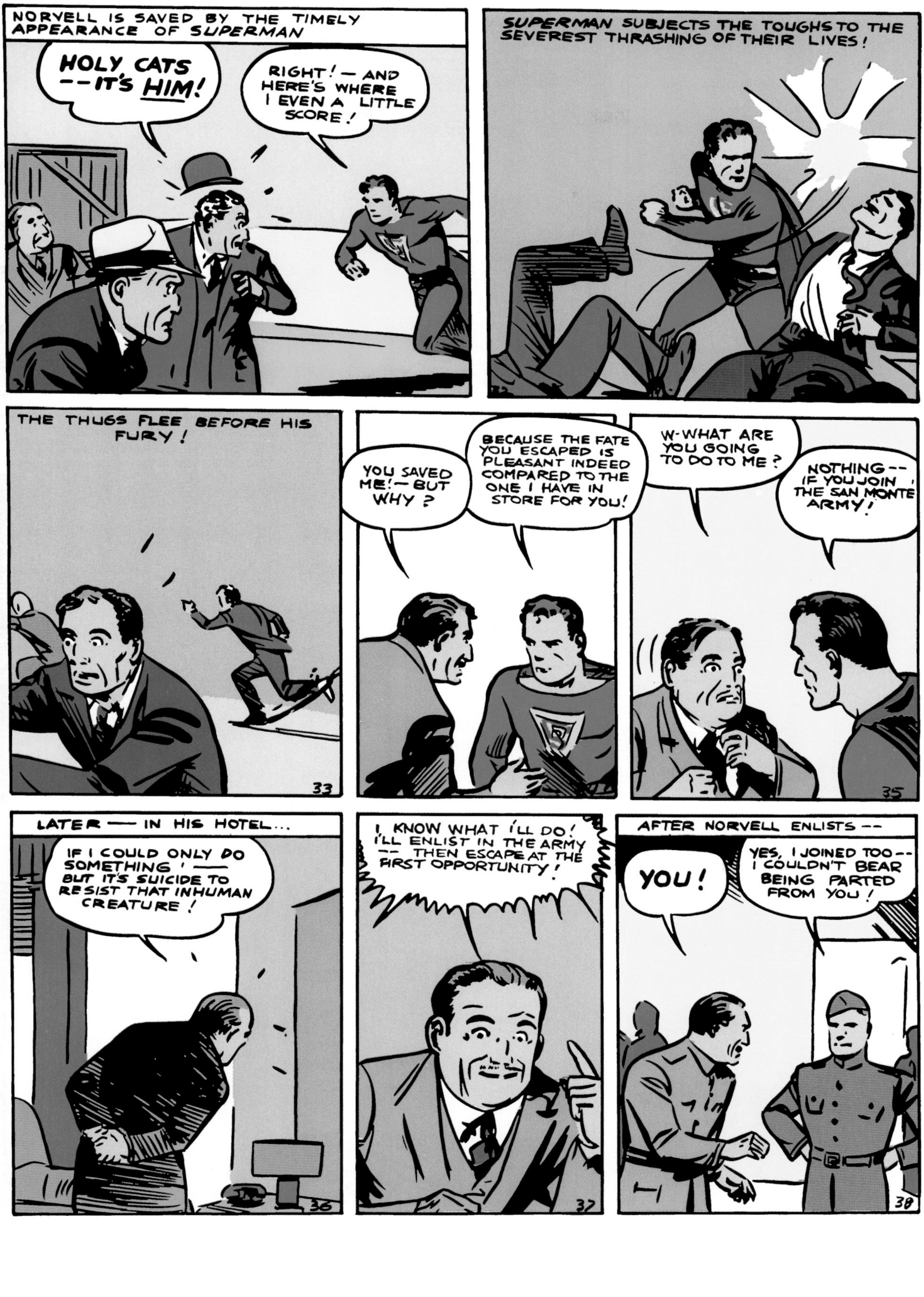
NORVELL IS SAVED BY THE TIMELY APPEARANCE OF SUPERMAN
HOLY CATS --IT'S HIM!
RIGHT! — AND HERE'S WHERE I EVEN A LITTLE SCORE!
SUPERMAN SUBJECTS THE TOUGHS TO THE SEVEREST THRASHING OF THEIR LIVES!
THE THUGS FLEE BEFORE HIS FURY!
33
YOU SAVED ME!— BUT WHY?
BECAUSE THE FATE YOU ESCAPED IS PLEASANT INDEED COMPARED TO THE ONE I HAVE IN STORE FOR YOU!
W-WHAT ARE YOU GOING TO DO TO ME?
NOTHING -- IF YOU JOIN THE SAN MONTE ARMY!
35
LATER — IN HIS HOTEL...
IF I COULD ONLY DO SOMETHING! — BUT IT'S SUICIDE TO RESIST THAT INHUMAN CREATURE!
36
I KNOW WHAT I'LL DO! I'LL ENLIST IN THE ARMY -- THEN ESCAPE AT THE FIRST OPPORTUNITY!
37
AFTER NORVELL ENLISTS --
YOU!
YES, I JOINED TOO -- I COULDN'T BEAR BEING PARTED FROM YOU!
38

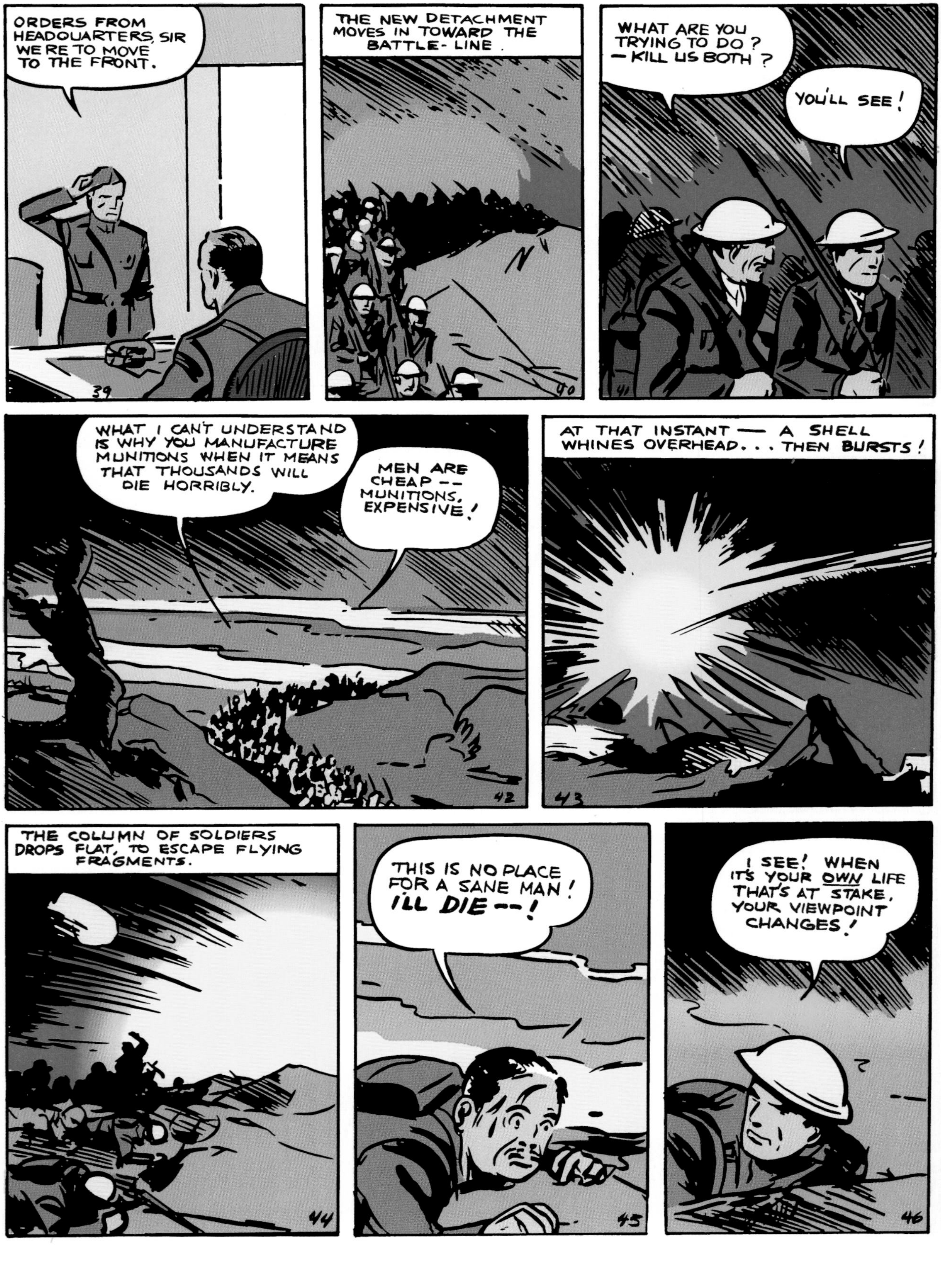
ORDERS FROM HEADQUARTERS, SIR WE'RE TO MOVE TO THE FRONT.
THE NEW DETACHMENT MOVES IN TOWARD THE BATTLE-LINE.
WHAT ARE YOU TRYING TO DO? —KILL US BOTH?
YOU'LL SEE!
WHAT I CAN'T UNDERSTAND IS WHY YOU MANUFACTURE MUNITIONS WHEN IT MEANS THAT THOUSANDS WILL DIE HORRIBLY.
MEN ARE CHEAP -- MUNITIONS, EXPENSIVE!
AT THAT INSTANT — A SHELL WHINES OVERHEAD... THEN BURSTS!
THE COLUMN OF SOLDIERS DROPS FLAT, TO ESCAPE FLYING FRAGMENTS.
THIS IS NO PLACE FOR A SANE MAN! I'LL DIE --!
I SEE! WHEN IT'S YOUR OWN LIFE THAT'S AT STAKE, YOUR VIEWPOINT CHANGES!

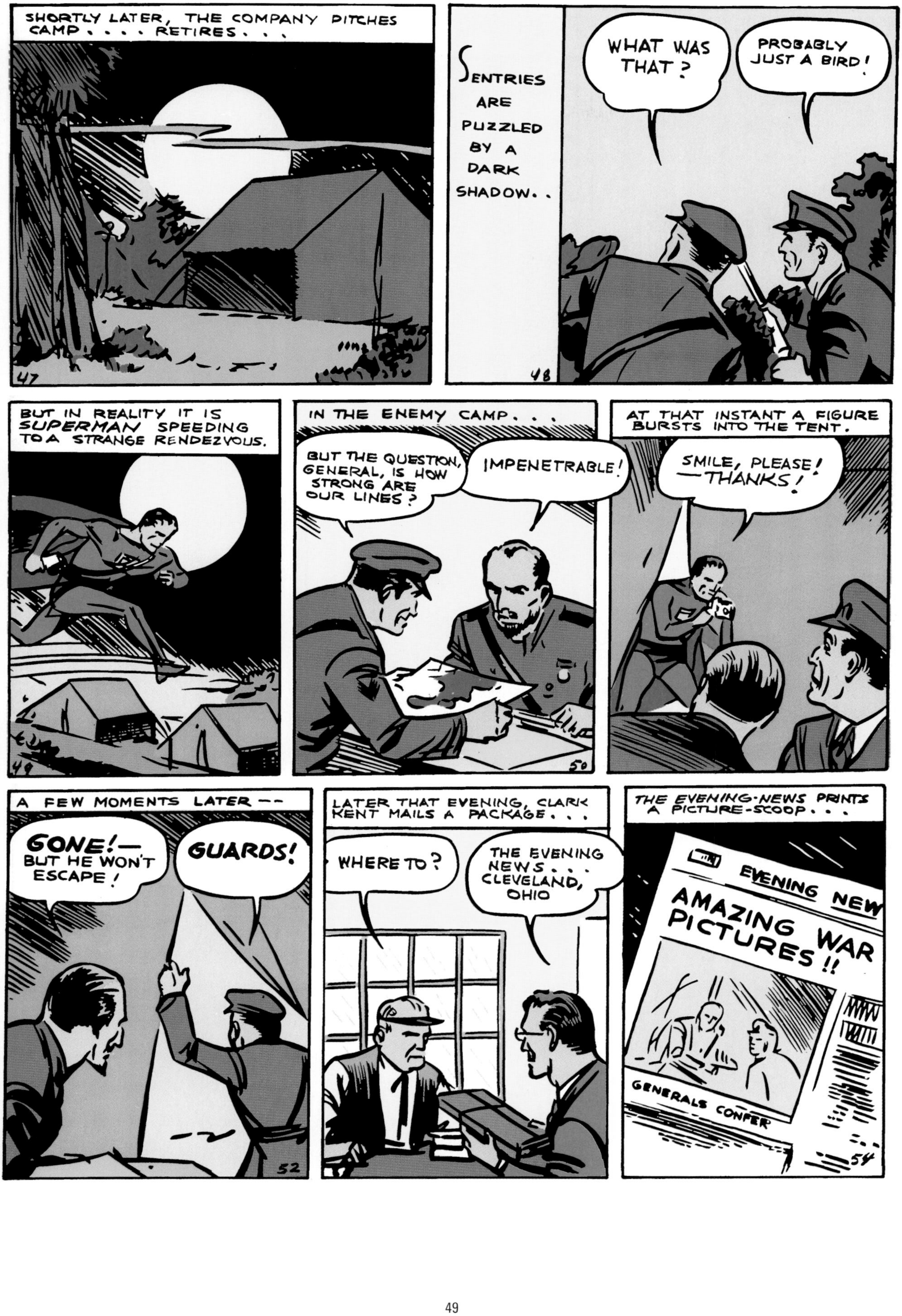
SHORTLY LATER, THE COMPANY PITCHES CAMP . . . . RETIRES . . .
SENTRIES ARE PUZZLED BY A DARK SHADOW . .
WHAT WAS THAT ?
PROBABLY JUST A BIRD !
BUT IN REALITY IT IS SUPERMAN SPEEDING TO A STRANGE RENDEZVOUS.
IN THE ENEMY CAMP . . .
BUT THE QUESTION, GENERAL, IS HOW STRONG ARE OUR LINES ?
IMPENETRABLE !
AT THAT INSTANT A FIGURE BURSTS INTO THE TENT .
SMILE, PLEASE ! —THANKS !
A FEW MOMENTS LATER --
GONE! — BUT HE WON'T ESCAPE !
GUARDS!
LATER THAT EVENING, CLARK KENT MAILS A PACKAGE . . .
WHERE TO ?
THE EVENING NEWS . . . CLEVELAND, OHIO
THE EVENING-NEWS PRINTS A PICTURE-SCOOP . . .
EVENING NEW
AMAZING WAR PICTURES !!
GENERALS CONFER

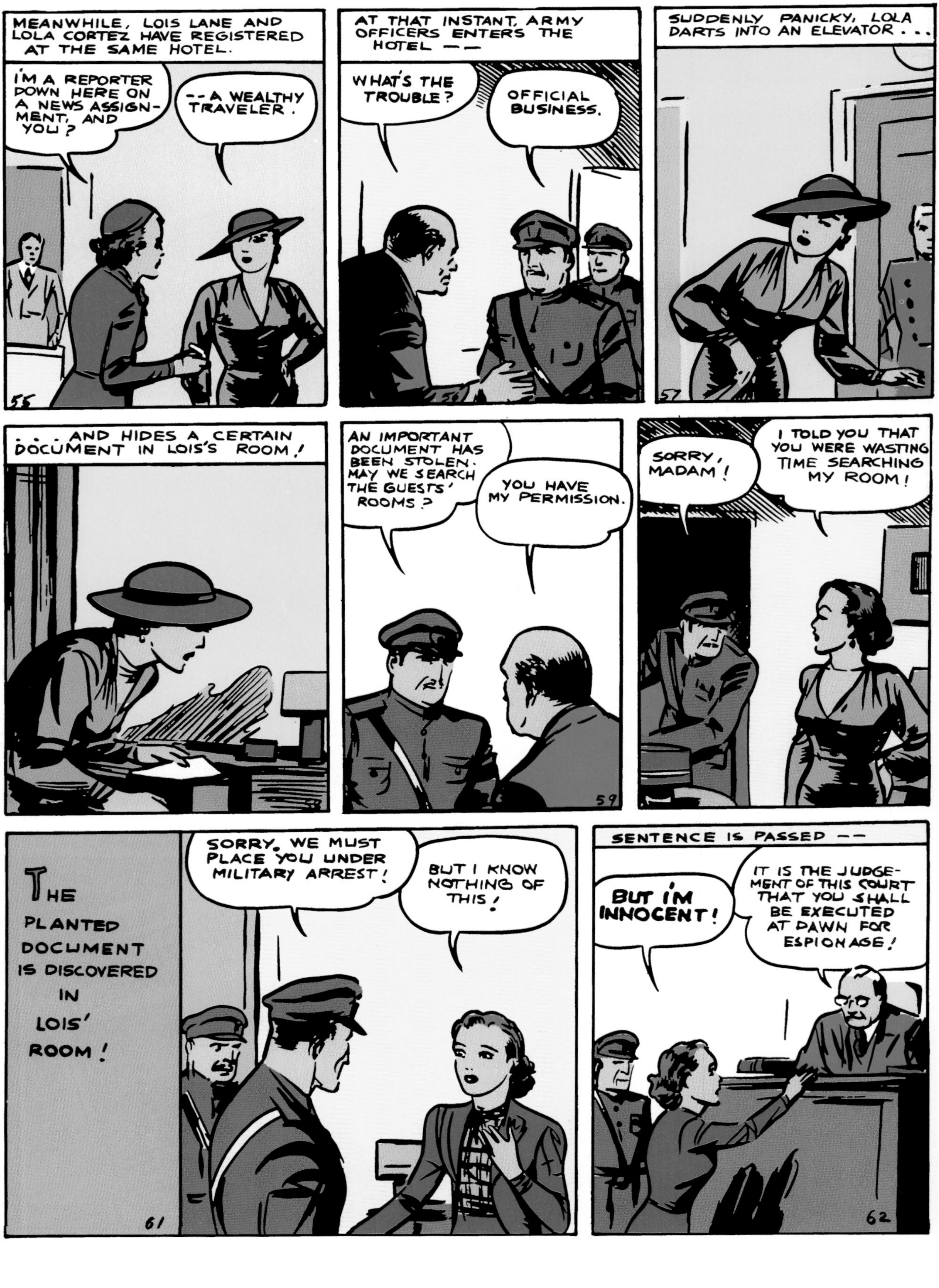
MEANWHILE, LOIS LANE AND LOLA CORTEZ HAVE REGISTERED AT THE SAME HOTEL.
I'M A REPORTER DOWN HERE ON A NEWS ASSIGNMENT, AND YOU?
--A WEALTHY TRAVELER.
AT THAT INSTANT, ARMY OFFICERS ENTERS THE HOTEL --
WHAT'S THE TROUBLE?
OFFICIAL BUSINESS.
SUDDENLY PANICKY, LOLA DARTS INTO AN ELEVATOR . . .
. . . AND HIDES A CERTAIN DOCUMENT IN LOIS'S ROOM!
AN IMPORTANT DOCUMENT HAS BEEN STOLEN. MAY WE SEARCH THE GUESTS' ROOMS?
YOU HAVE MY PERMISSION.
SORRY, MADAM!
I TOLD YOU THAT YOU WERE WASTING TIME SEARCHING MY ROOM!
THE PLANTED DOCUMENT IS DISCOVERED IN LOIS' ROOM!
SORRY. WE MUST PLACE YOU UNDER MILITARY ARREST!
BUT I KNOW NOTHING OF THIS!
SENTENCE IS PASSED --
BUT I'M INNOCENT!
IT IS THE JUDGEMENT OF THIS COURT THAT YOU SHALL BE EXECUTED AT DAWN FOR ESPIONAGE!

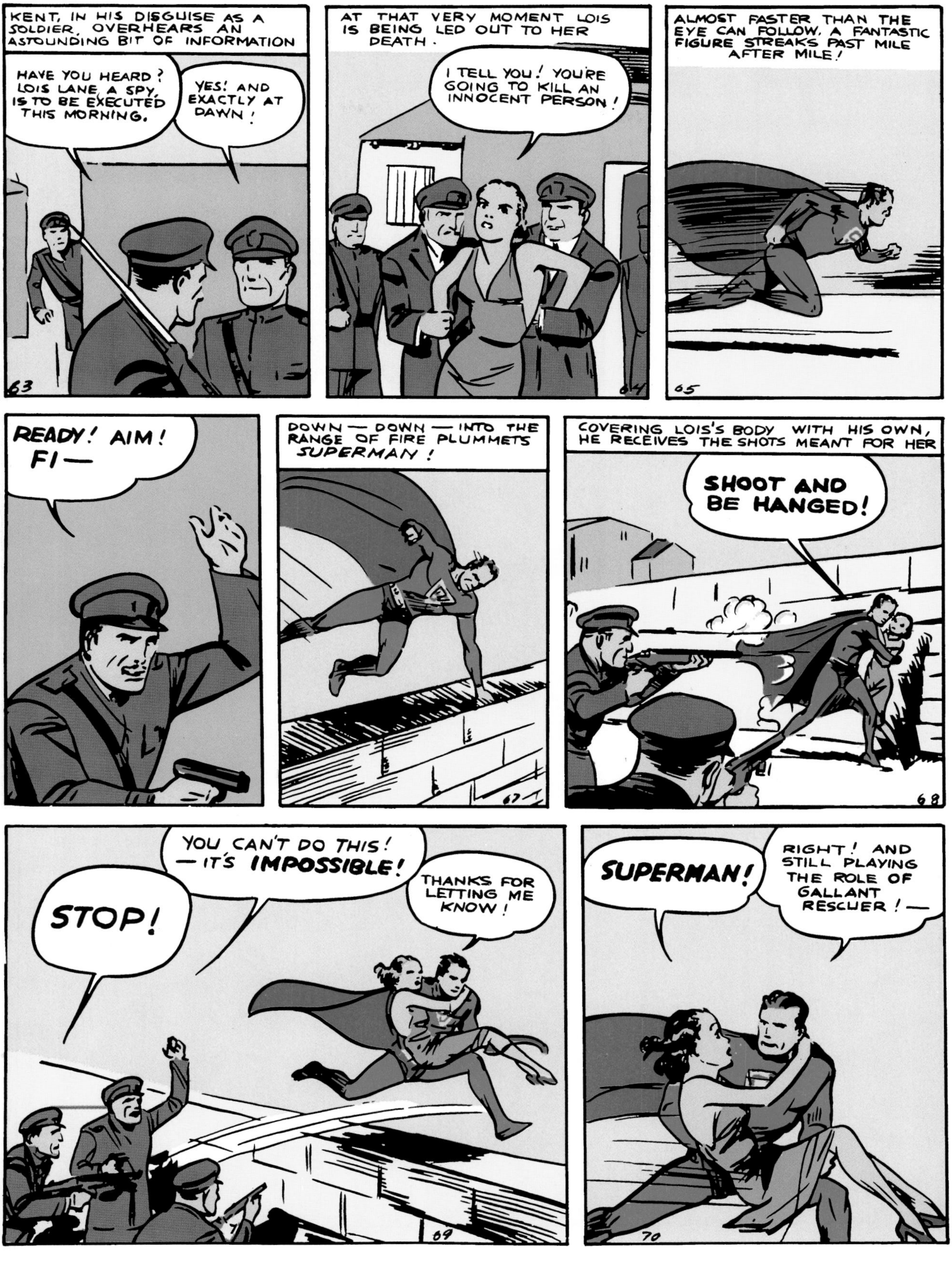
KENT, IN HIS DISGUISE AS A SOLDIER, OVERHEARS AN ASTOUNDING BIT OF INFORMATION
HAVE YOU HEARD? LOIS LANE, A SPY, IS TO BE EXECUTED THIS MORNING.
YES! AND EXACTLY AT DAWN!
AT THAT VERY MOMENT LOIS IS BEING LED OUT TO HER DEATH.
I TELL YOU! YOU'RE GOING TO KILL AN INNOCENT PERSON!
ALMOST FASTER THAN THE EYE CAN FOLLOW, A FANTASTIC FIGURE STREAKS PAST MILE AFTER MILE!
READY! AIM! FI—
DOWN — DOWN — INTO THE RANGE OF FIRE PLUMMETS SUPERMAN!
COVERING LOIS'S BODY WITH HIS OWN, HE RECEIVES THE SHOTS MEANT FOR HER
SHOOT AND BE HANGED!
STOP!
YOU CAN'T DO THIS! — IT'S IMPOSSIBLE!
THANKS FOR LETTING ME KNOW!
SUPERMAN!
RIGHT! AND STILL PLAYING THE ROLE OF GALLANT RESCUER! —

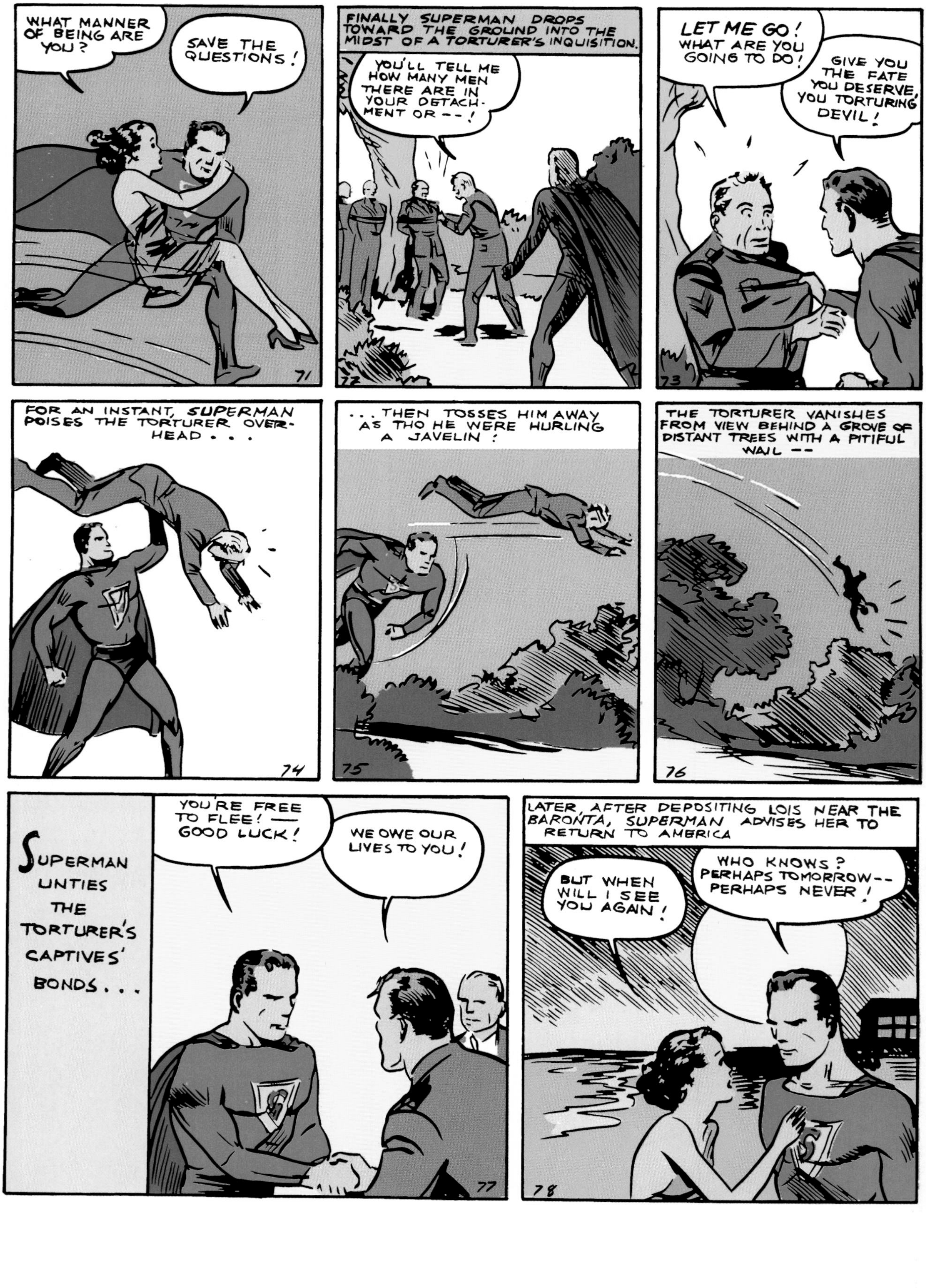
WHAT MANNER OF BEING ARE YOU?
SAVE THE QUESTIONS!
71
FINALLY SUPERMAN DROPS TOWARD THE GROUND INTO THE MIDST OF A TORTURER'S INQUISITION.
YOU'LL TELL ME HOW MANY MEN THERE ARE IN YOUR DETACHMENT OR --!
72
LET ME GO! WHAT ARE YOU GOING TO DO!
GIVE YOU THE FATE YOU DESERVE, YOU TORTURING DEVIL!
73
FOR AN INSTANT, SUPERMAN POISES THE TORTURER OVERHEAD . . .
74
. . . THEN TOSSES HIM AWAY AS THO HE WERE HURLING A JAVELIN!
75
THE TORTURER VANISHES FROM VIEW BEHIND A GROVE OF DISTANT TREES WITH A PITIFUL WAIL --
76
SUPERMAN UNTIES THE TORTURER'S CAPTIVES' BONDS . . .
YOU'RE FREE TO FLEE! — GOOD LUCK!
WE OWE OUR LIVES TO YOU!
77
LATER, AFTER DEPOSITING LOIS NEAR THE BARONTA, SUPERMAN ADVISES HER TO RETURN TO AMERICA
BUT WHEN WILL I SEE YOU AGAIN!
WHO KNOWS? PERHAPS TOMORROW-- PERHAPS NEVER!
78

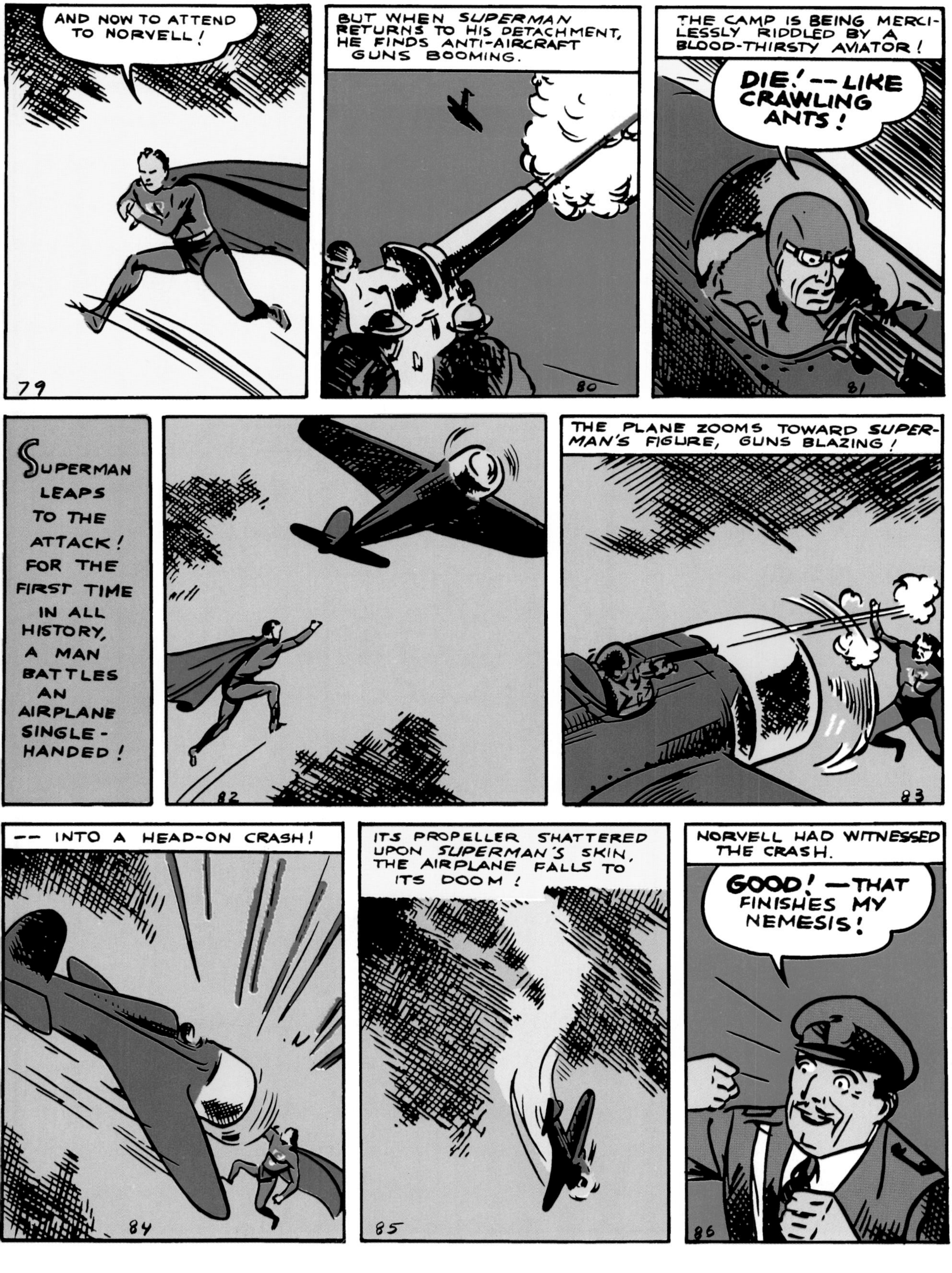
AND NOW TO ATTEND TO NORVELL!
79
BUT WHEN SUPERMAN RETURNS TO HIS DETACHMENT, HE FINDS ANTI-AIRCRAFT GUNS BOOMING.
80
THE CAMP IS BEING MERCILESSLY RIDDLED BY A BLOOD-THIRSTY AVIATOR!
DIE! -- LIKE CRAWLING ANTS!
81
SUPERMAN LEAPS TO THE ATTACK! FOR THE FIRST TIME IN ALL HISTORY, A MAN BATTLES AN AIRPLANE SINGLE-HANDED!
82
THE PLANE ZOOMS TOWARD SUPERMAN'S FIGURE, GUNS BLAZING!
83
-- INTO A HEAD-ON CRASH!
84
ITS PROPELLER SHATTERED UPON SUPERMAN'S SKIN, THE AIRPLANE FALLS TO ITS DOOM!
85
NORVELL HAD WITNESSED THE CRASH.
GOOD! —THAT FINISHES MY NEMESIS!
86

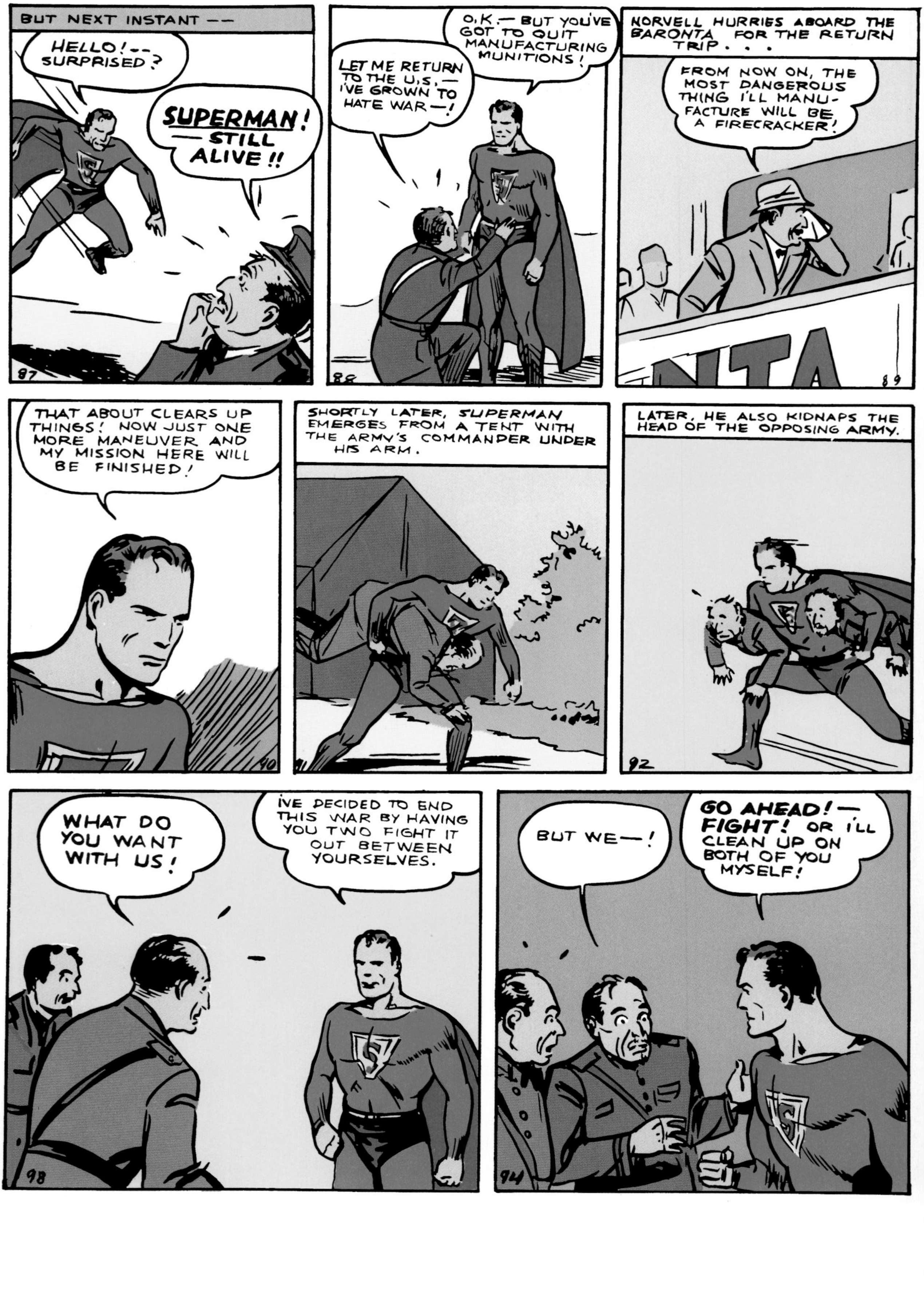

BUT NEXT INSTANT --
HELLO! -- SURPRISED?
SUPERMAN! — STILL ALIVE!!
87
LET ME RETURN TO THE U.S.— I'VE GROWN TO HATE WAR—!
O.K.— BUT YOU'VE GOT TO QUIT MANUFACTURING MUNITIONS!
88
NORVELL HURRIES ABOARD THE BARONTA FOR THE RETURN TRIP . . .
FROM NOW ON, THE MOST DANGEROUS THING I'LL MANUFACTURE WILL BE A FIRECRACKER!
NTA
89
THAT ABOUT CLEARS UP THINGS! NOW JUST ONE MORE MANEUVER AND MY MISSION HERE WILL BE FINISHED!
90
SHORTLY LATER, SUPERMAN EMERGES FROM A TENT WITH THE ARMY'S COMMANDER UNDER HIS ARM.
91
LATER, HE ALSO KIDNAPS THE HEAD OF THE OPPOSING ARMY.
92
WHAT DO YOU WANT WITH US!
I'VE DECIDED TO END THIS WAR BY HAVING YOU TWO FIGHT IT OUT BETWEEN YOURSELVES.
93
BUT WE—!
GO AHEAD!— FIGHT! OR I'LL CLEAN UP ON BOTH OF YOU MYSELF!
94

BUT WHY SHOULD WE FIGHT ?
WE'RE NOT ANGRY AT EACH OTHER!
THEN WHY ARE YOUR ARMIES BATTLING ?
I DON'T KNOW! CAN YOU TELL ME ?
NO. CAN YOU ?
GENTLEMEN, IT'S OBVIOUS YOU'VE BEEN FIGHTING ONLY TO PROMOTE THE SALE OF MUNITIONS! — WHY NOT SHAKE HANDS AND MAKE UP ?
AND SO, DUE TO THE CONCILIATORY EFFORTS OF SUPERMAN, THE WAR IS HALTED.
WHEN KENT REPORTS BACK TO HIS EDITOR . .
SINCE YOU'VE BEEN GONE, THERE'S BEEN NO SUPERMAN NEWS. MAYBE HE'S RETIRED FOR GOOD!
SOMEHOW, CHIEF, I'VE A HUNCH HE'LL MAKE HIS APPEARANCE AGAIN--SOON!
THE END

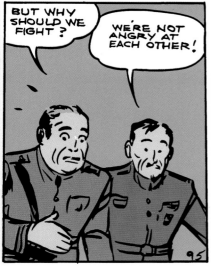

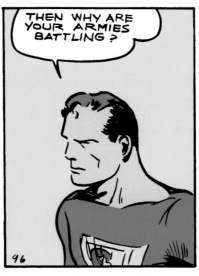

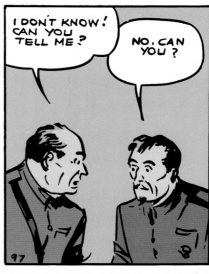

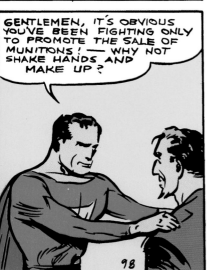

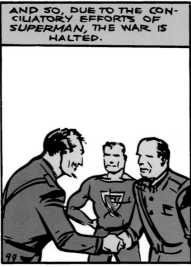

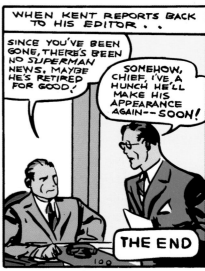

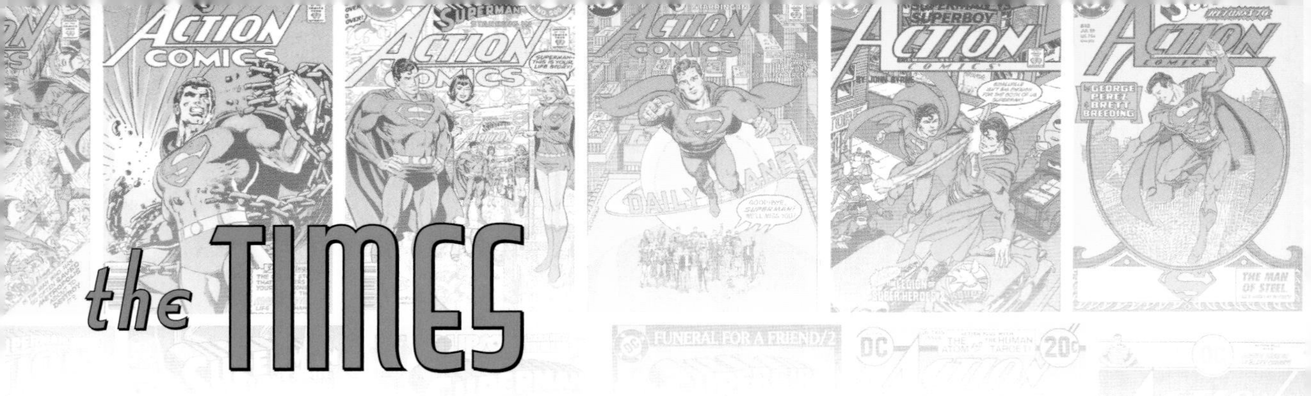
ACTION COMICS
SUPERBOY
GEORGE PEREZ BRETT BREEDING
THE MAN OF STEEL
FUNERAL FOR A FRIEND/2

the TIMES

by TOM DeHAVEN

Whenever I've taught a class on comics, or given a talk about them somewhere, I've illustrated my lectures with magazine cartoons and newspaper comic strips, comic books, underground comics and so on—at first relying on bad slides I took myself and projected using a Kodak Carousel, and more recently, as recently as fall 2017, using classroom media consoles. Over the years, I've shown thousands of different comics images. Different ones for different courses and lectures. But there is one image, and just one, that I've shown every time I've talked publicly about comics: ACTION COMICS #1.

Whether my topic or focus is the history or the sociology or the business of comics, or whether it's pure comics iconography, the cover of ACTION COMICS #1, drawn by Joe Shuster, is essential. But so is the magazine. And so is Superman, of course. The character, the commodity, the concept, the brand. The impact of that cover, that cover image, that magazine and that character on the fantasy component of American mass culture, at home and worldwide, across the past 80 years is incalculable. ACTION COMICS #1. The smallish figure in the middle distance in a blue bodysuit has hoisted up a green Hupmobile and is now, his red *Prisoner of Zenda* cape flared out behind him, canting it down, smashing the hood against a boulder; a wheel has flown off, a headlamp. Nearby, an ordinary-looking little guy in a white shirt and dark pants is on his knees looking dazed. Two men are fleeing, one deep in the picture plane, the other looming in the lower left-hand corner, wide-eyed, traumatized. This feels like somewhere in the desert. There's no glimpse of a road. Your eye is bouncing every which way; the draftsmanship is crude, but the graphic is strong and active.

Above the yellow burst that surrounds the scene, stately but insistent, hangs a steeply slanted, aggressively thrusting, bright red logo. One of the world's most recognizable logos, especially that classy giant *A*. Apparently, the designer is unknown. I tried looking it up, and that's what it says. Designer unknown. But whoever it was, that logo is a hall of famer, and with only occasional graphic updating, it stands in use today.

Some years back, Abbeville Press put out two chunky books that collected the covers of ACTION COMICS, in color and in chronological order, from the first, originally published in 1938, through #600, from 1988. They're fun to look through, to flip through, but for me the covers from the 1940s and '50s are the most fun to revisit. All of Superman's action poses—and hence virtually all of the "costumed superhero's action poses"—are worked up and finessed across the first few dozen issues. There were a lot of *save* covers in the early years, Superman saves this or that—a train from plunging off the rails, a foundering submarine full of desperate sailors from the ocean floor—along with some odd, I-guess-you-might-call-them preparedness-themed covers, Superman lugging artillery shells or featured along with gigantic warheads. The dependable save-style covers predominated for a while, interspersed with the occasional thwarted crime or getaway cover, and then suddenly it was world-at-war covers—Superman delivering ammunition, disabling a U-boat or a Nazi tank, assisting wounded soldiers. But long before the World War was over, beginning in 1944, ACTION covers gradually veered back toward civilian premises; the tone lightened, could even become slapstick, and with only the rare exception they remained in that sphere for more than 10 years. The Prankster turned up, the Toyman, Mr. Mxyztplk. Superman was depicted as an Indian chief, a Super-Cowboy, a Super-Caveman, was shown about to marry a veiled mystery bride. And then, gradually, Mort Weisinger, in full editorial charge of ACTION as well as the other Superman books by the mid-1950s, begins to burnish the franchise with more and more science fiction. Bizarro Superman. The Phantom Zone. Red Kryptonite. More and more Kryptonian survivors, all with the -El suffix on their names.

SUPERGIRL
ACTION COMICS
ACTION COMICS

YOU'RE DUE FOR A SUPER-SHOCK, SUPERMAN!
DON'T WORRY, SUPERMAN! I'M ALIVE WITHOUT A SCRATCH!
GREAT SCOTT, A YOUNG GIRL, UNHARMED! BUT... BUT THAT MEANS YOU'RE INVULNER-ABLE LIKE ME!

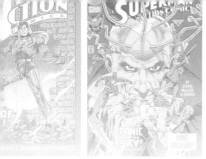

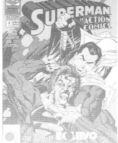

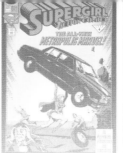

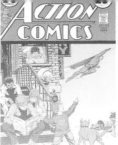

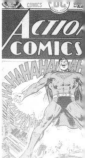

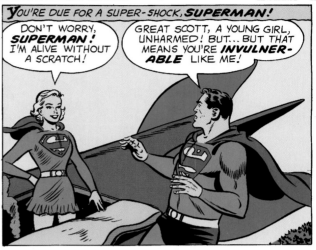

Supergirl.

As far as I can remember, my first issue of ACTION COMICS (but whether I was just a reader or a full-blown purchaser-reader already, I couldn't say) was issue #242, cover dated July 1958, "The Super-Duel in Space," the story that introduced Brainiac and the miniaturized Kryptonian city of Kandor in a bottle. It's a nice Curt Swan/Stan Kaye cover. Brainiac (unnamed there, just referred to by Superman in a thought balloon as a "super outlaw") is planted confidently on a small asteroid while Superman hovers nearby in purple-colored space, poised for a fight; he seems daunted, though, fretting silently in the face of his adversary's mocking threats, "This may be my greatest challenge!" Hardly, but not bad. Certainly good enough to hook me.

That particular issue of ACTION came out just around the time I turned nine. After that, I was not only a regular purchaser, I was a collector, a careful keep-them-in-grocery-store-cartons collector of all the titles in the Superman line, but ACTION was the flagship; it seemed that all of the major changes or additions to the Superman universe happened first on a cover of a new issue of ACTION COMICS, and then in the story, usually drawn by Curt Swan, behind the cover. ACTION was Superman headquarters; it all happened there first. But I also liked it as a title; I liked the short backup stories featuring Tommy Tomorrow or Congorilla, the latter especially. The art on those was retro, from the school of Milton Caniff, and the stories were punchy, often clever. When Supergirl showed up—naturally, in ACTION COMICS for the first time, #252—and took over the backup slot, I just wasn't interested. Were those stories any good? I didn't know, I still don't, I never read them. Jim Mooney's art struck me as a cross between nurse comics and love comics; there were too many close-ups, and everyone looked like they could be a robot. The plots seemed to revolve around teen chores done super-fast. There was a super-kitten. Not for me.

But I still read the Superman story in ACTION every month, all through high school, college and graduate school. After I got married and had kids. Thinking about it now, I guess I bought every issue from the late 1950s through the mid-1970s, and since then not monthly but consistently—picking up a copy now and then or following it again, getting every issue for a couple of years at a time. I still like seeing how Superman is drawn, portrayed, I like to see what his dialogue reads like. The tenor of it. I like knowing his concerns. I like to see what's the same about Superman, and what's different. (His uniform looks better with trunks, though. I think. Just saying.)

Anyhow, this milestone is worth celebrating: ACTION COMICS #1000. Definitely worth celebrating. So here's to all the casts of characters that have lived and raved and fought to fight again on all the many thousands of pages of those thousand issues; and here's to the many, many artists and writers and colorists and letterers and editors and assistant editors and editorial assistants and publishers who produced the stories that filled the pages; here's to the winners and the losers and the in-betweeners; here's to something for the history books.

TOM DeHAVEN teaches creative writing at Virginia Commonwealth University, and has authored several novels centering on the world of comics, including It's Superman!.

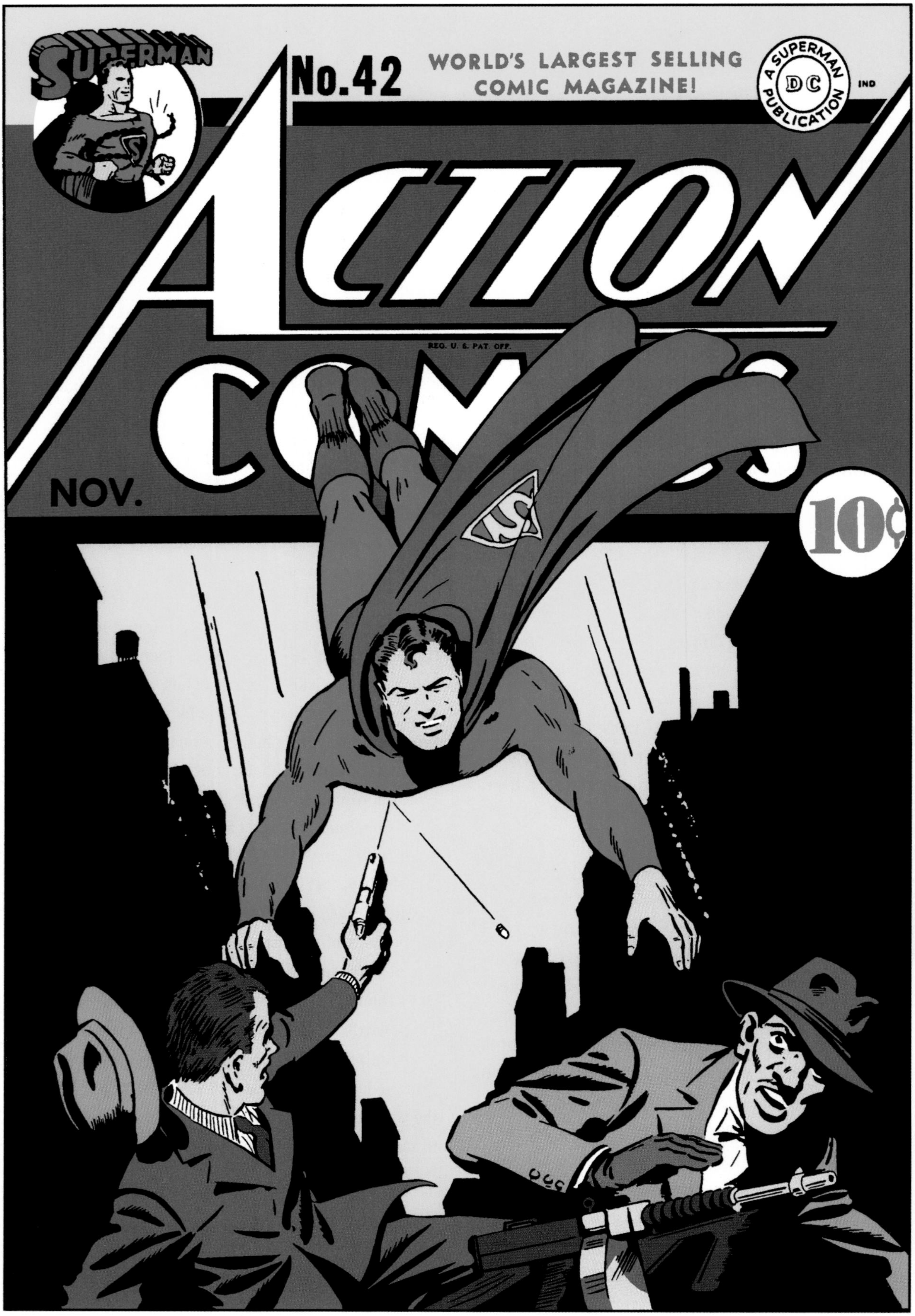
SUPERMAN
No. 42
WORLD'S LARGEST SELLING COMIC MAGAZINE!
A SUPERMAN DC PUBLICATION
IND
ACTION COMICS
REG. U. S. PAT. OFF.
NOV.
10¢

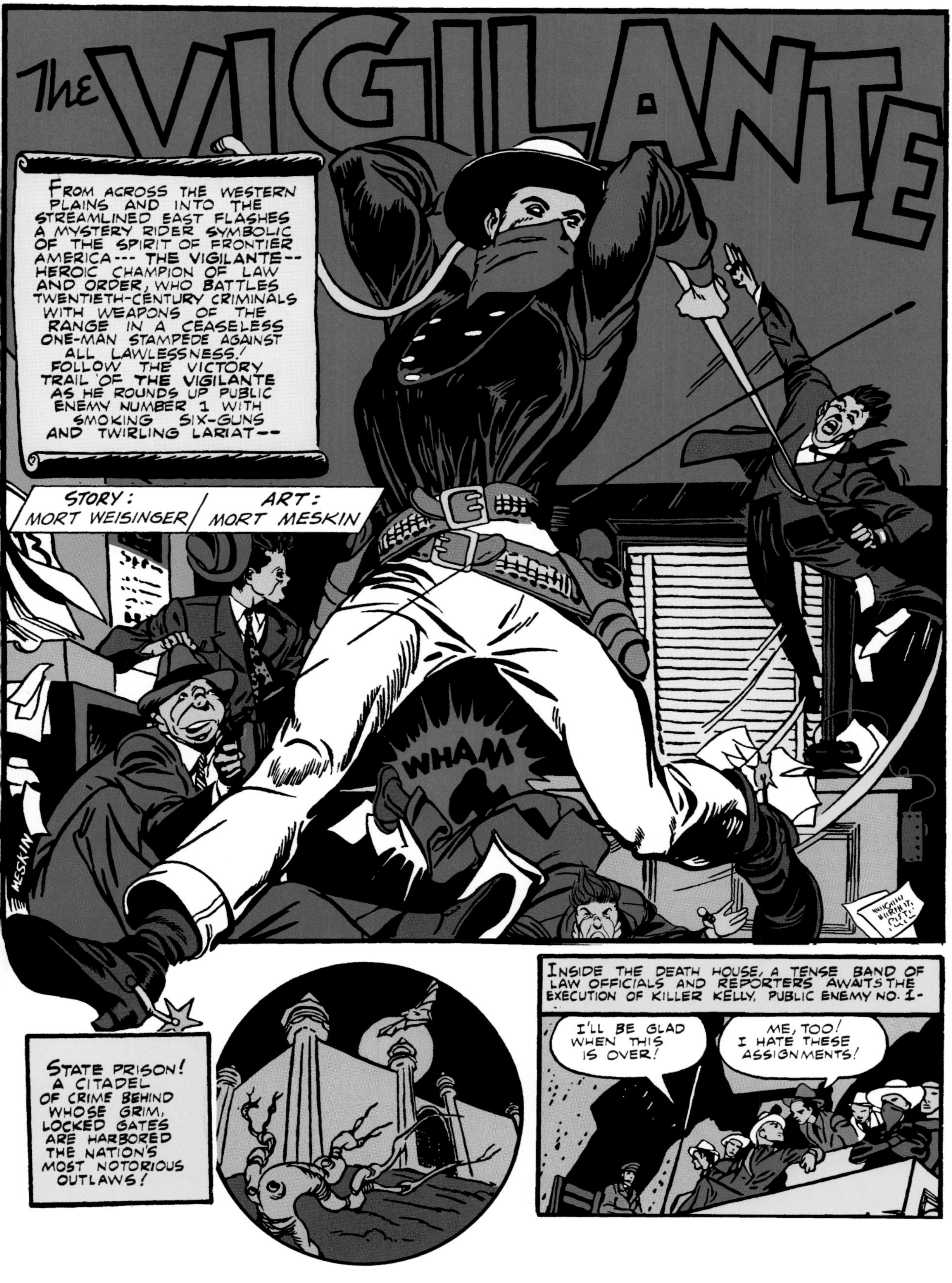

The VIGILANTE
FROM ACROSS THE WESTERN PLAINS AND INTO THE STREAMLINED EAST FLASHES A MYSTERY RIDER SYMBOLIC OF THE SPIRIT OF FRONTIER AMERICA--- THE VIGILANTE-- HEROIC CHAMPION OF LAW AND ORDER, WHO BATTLES TWENTIETH-CENTURY CRIMINALS WITH WEAPONS OF THE RANGE IN A CEASELESS ONE-MAN STAMPEDE AGAINST ALL LAWLESSNESS! FOLLOW THE VICTORY TRAIL OF THE VIGILANTE AS HE ROUNDS UP PUBLIC ENEMY NUMBER 1 WITH SMOKING SIX-GUNS AND TWIRLING LARIAT--
STORY: MORT WEISINGER
ART: MORT MESKIN
WHAM
MESKIN
STATE PRISON! A CITADEL OF CRIME BEHIND WHOSE GRIM, LOCKED GATES ARE HARBORED THE NATION'S MOST NOTORIOUS OUTLAWS!
INSIDE THE DEATH HOUSE, A TENSE BAND OF LAW OFFICIALS AND REPORTERS AWAITS THE EXECUTION OF KILLER KELLY, PUBLIC ENEMY NO. 1-
I'LL BE GLAD WHEN THIS IS OVER!
ME, TOO! I HATE THESE ASSIGNMENTS!

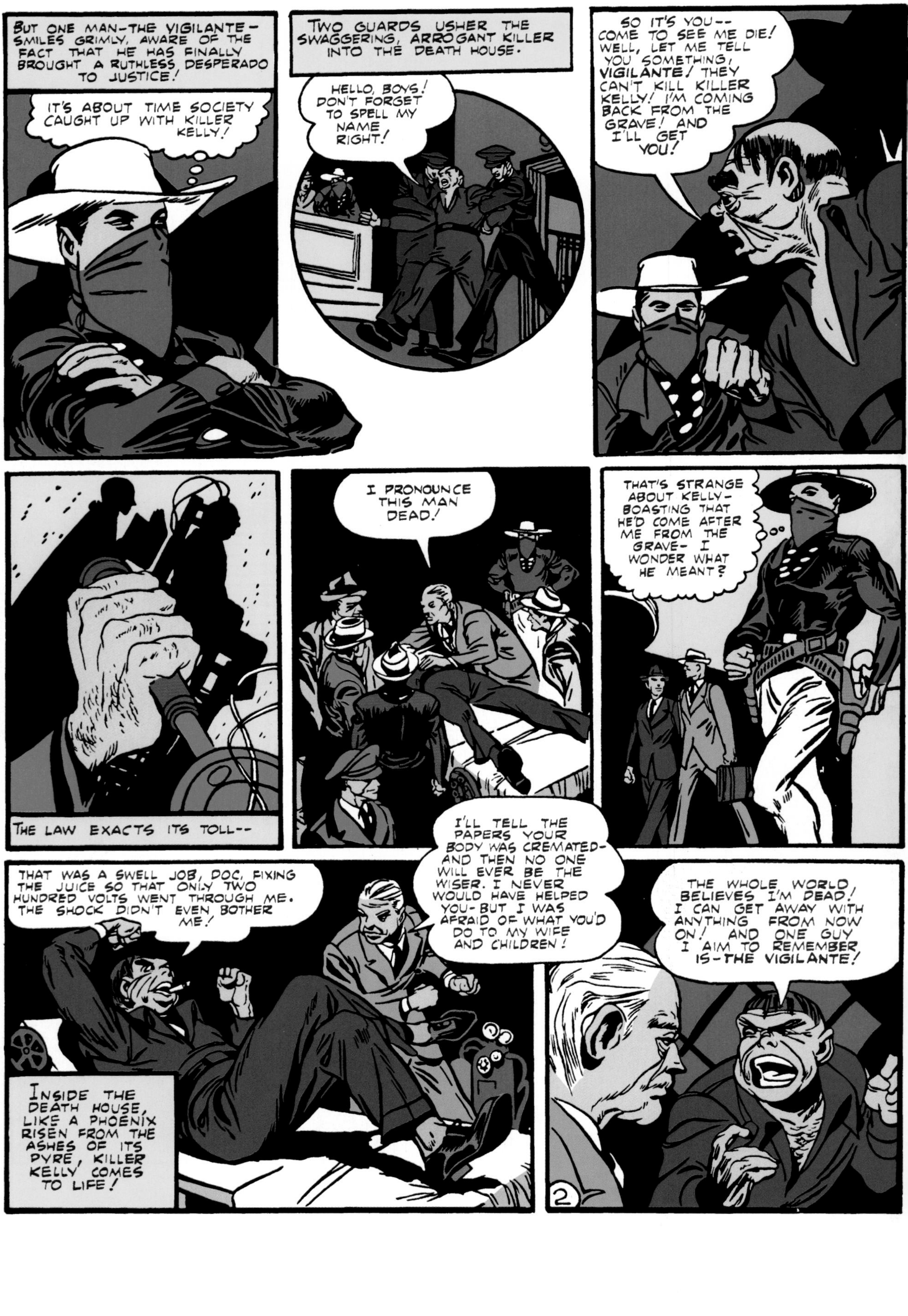
BUT ONE MAN-THE VIGILANTE-SMILES GRIMLY, AWARE OF THE FACT THAT HE HAS FINALLY BROUGHT A RUTHLESS DESPERADO TO JUSTICE!
IT'S ABOUT TIME SOCIETY CAUGHT UP WITH KILLER KELLY!
TWO GUARDS USHER THE SWAGGERING, ARROGANT KILLER INTO THE DEATH HOUSE.
HELLO, BOYS! DON'T FORGET TO SPELL MY NAME RIGHT!
SO IT'S YOU-- COME TO SEE ME DIE! WELL, LET ME TELL YOU SOMETHING, VIGILANTE! THEY CAN'T KILL KILLER KELLY! I'M COMING BACK FROM THE GRAVE! AND I'LL GET YOU!
THE LAW EXACTS ITS TOLL--
I PRONOUNCE THIS MAN DEAD!
THAT'S STRANGE ABOUT KELLY-BOASTING THAT HE'D COME AFTER ME FROM THE GRAVE- I WONDER WHAT HE MEANT?
INSIDE THE DEATH HOUSE, LIKE A PHOENIX RISEN FROM THE ASHES OF ITS PYRE, KILLER KELLY COMES TO LIFE!
THAT WAS A SWELL JOB, DOC, FIXING THE JUICE SO THAT ONLY TWO HUNDRED VOLTS WENT THROUGH ME. THE SHOCK DIDN'T EVEN BOTHER ME!
I'LL TELL THE PAPERS YOUR BODY WAS CREMATED-AND THEN NO ONE WILL EVER BE THE WISER. I NEVER WOULD HAVE HELPED YOU-BUT I WAS AFRAID OF WHAT YOU'D DO TO MY WIFE AND CHILDREN!
THE WHOLE WORLD BELIEVES I'M DEAD! I CAN GET AWAY WITH ANYTHING FROM NOW ON! AND ONE GUY I AIM TO REMEMBER IS-THE VIGILANTE!
2

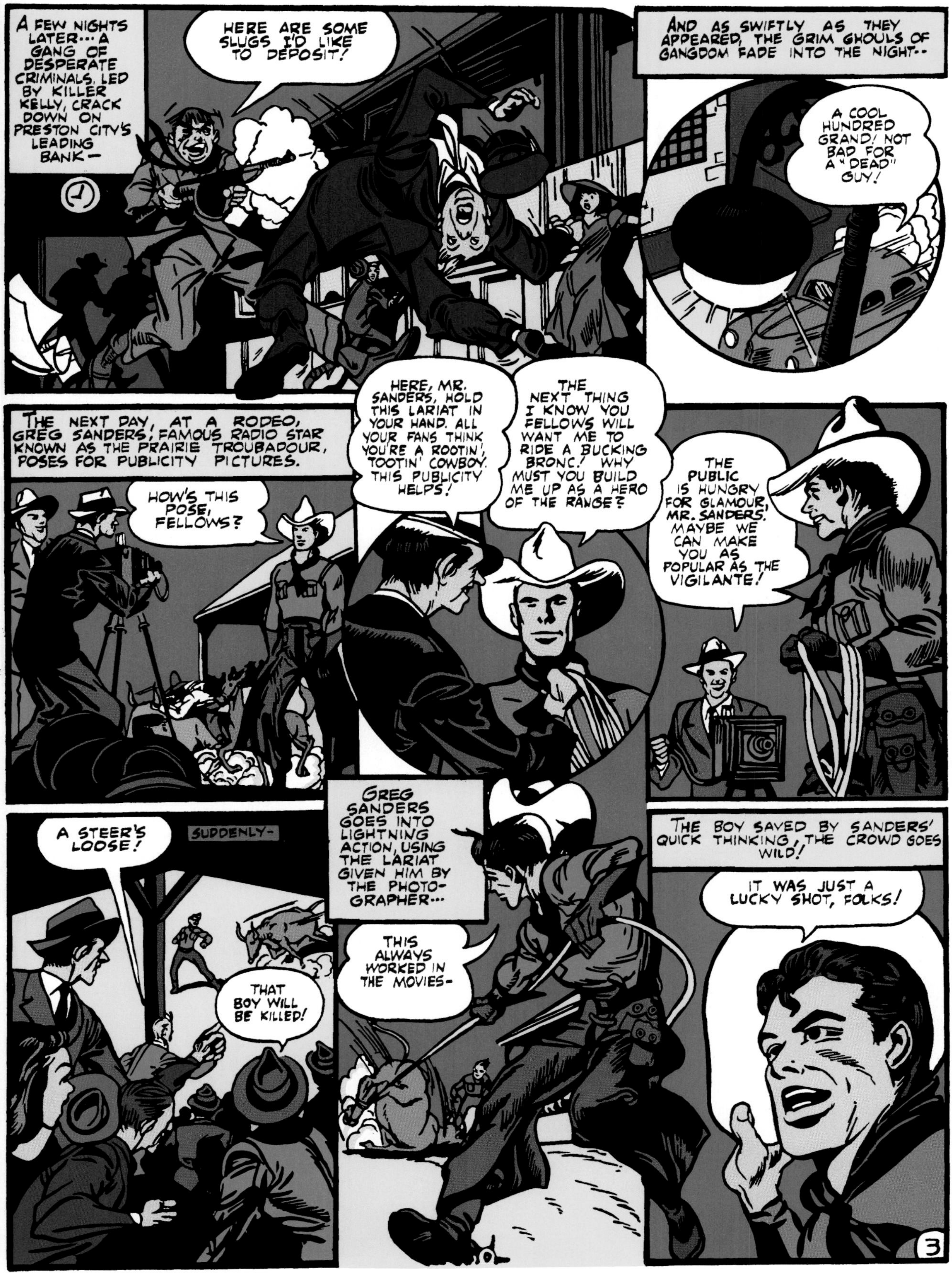
A FEW NIGHTS LATER... A GANG OF DESPERATE CRIMINALS, LED BY KILLER KELLY, CRACK DOWN ON PRESTON CITY'S LEADING BANK—
HERE ARE SOME SLUGS I'D LIKE TO DEPOSIT!
AND AS SWIFTLY AS THEY APPEARED, THE GRIM GHOULS OF GANGDOM FADE INTO THE NIGHT--
A COOL HUNDRED GRAND! NOT BAD FOR A "DEAD" GUY!
THE NEXT DAY, AT A RODEO, GREG SANDERS, FAMOUS RADIO STAR KNOWN AS THE PRAIRIE TROUBADOUR, POSES FOR PUBLICITY PICTURES.
HOW'S THIS POSE, FELLOWS?
HERE, MR. SANDERS, HOLD THIS LARIAT IN YOUR HAND. ALL YOUR FANS THINK YOU'RE A ROOTIN', TOOTIN' COWBOY. THIS PUBLICITY HELPS!
THE NEXT THING I KNOW YOU FELLOWS WILL WANT ME TO RIDE A BUCKING BRONC! WHY MUST YOU BUILD ME UP AS A HERO OF THE RANGE?
THE PUBLIC IS HUNGRY FOR GLAMOUR, MR. SANDERS! MAYBE WE CAN MAKE YOU AS POPULAR AS THE VIGILANTE!
A STEER'S LOOSE!
SUDDENLY—
THAT BOY WILL BE KILLED!
GREG SANDERS GOES INTO LIGHTNING ACTION, USING THE LARIAT GIVEN HIM BY THE PHOTOGRAPHER...
THIS ALWAYS WORKED IN THE MOVIES—
THE BOY SAVED BY SANDERS' QUICK THINKING, THE CROWD GOES WILD!
IT WAS JUST A LUCKY SHOT, FOLKS!
3

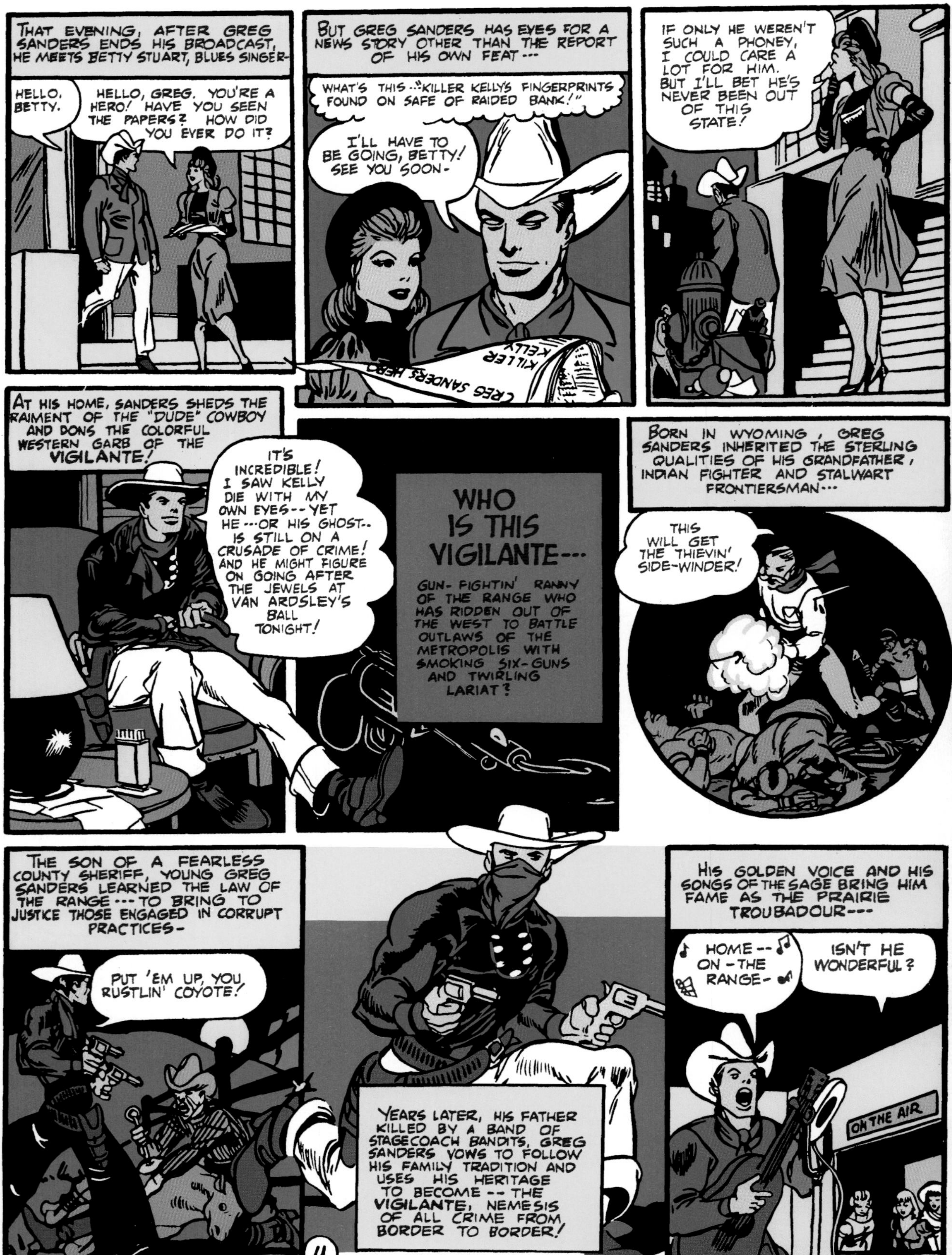
THAT EVENING, AFTER GREG SANDERS ENDS HIS BROADCAST, HE MEETS BETTY STUART, BLUES SINGER-
HELLO, BETTY.
HELLO, GREG. YOU'RE A HERO! HAVE YOU SEEN THE PAPERS? HOW DID YOU EVER DO IT?
BUT GREG SANDERS HAS EYES FOR A NEWS STORY OTHER THAN THE REPORT OF HIS OWN FEAT ---
WHAT'S THIS --"KILLER KELLY'S FINGERPRINTS FOUND ON SAFE OF RAIDED BANK!"
I'LL HAVE TO BE GOING, BETTY! SEE YOU SOON-
GREG SANDERS HERO
KILLER KELLY
IF ONLY HE WEREN'T SUCH A PHONEY, I COULD CARE A LOT FOR HIM. BUT I'LL BET HE'S NEVER BEEN OUT OF THIS STATE!
AT HIS HOME, SANDERS SHEDS THE RAIMENT OF THE "DUDE" COWBOY AND DONS THE COLORFUL WESTERN GARB OF THE VIGILANTE!
IT'S INCREDIBLE! I SAW KELLY DIE WITH MY OWN EYES-- YET HE ---OR HIS GHOST-- IS STILL ON A CRUSADE OF CRIME! AND HE MIGHT FIGURE ON GOING AFTER THE JEWELS AT VAN ARDSLEY'S BALL TONIGHT!
WHO IS THIS VIGILANTE---
GUN- FIGHTIN' RANNY OF THE RANGE WHO HAS RIDDEN OUT OF THE WEST TO BATTLE OUTLAWS OF THE METROPOLIS WITH SMOKING SIX-GUNS AND TWIRLING LARIAT?
BORN IN WYOMING, GREG SANDERS INHERITED THE STERLING QUALITIES OF HIS GRANDFATHER, INDIAN FIGHTER AND STALWART FRONTIERSMAN---
THIS WILL GET THE THIEVIN' SIDE-WINDER!
THE SON OF A FEARLESS COUNTY SHERIFF, YOUNG GREG SANDERS LEARNED THE LAW OF THE RANGE --- TO BRING TO JUSTICE THOSE ENGAGED IN CORRUPT PRACTICES-
PUT 'EM UP, YOU RUSTLIN' COYOTE!
YEARS LATER, HIS FATHER KILLED BY A BAND OF STAGECOACH BANDITS, GREG SANDERS VOWS TO FOLLOW HIS FAMILY TRADITION AND USES HIS HERITAGE TO BECOME -- THE VIGILANTE, NEMESIS OF ALL CRIME FROM BORDER TO BORDER!
4
HIS GOLDEN VOICE AND HIS SONGS OF THE SAGE BRING HIM FAME AS THE PRAIRIE TROUBADOUR---
HOME -- ON - THE RANGE-
ISN'T HE WONDERFUL?
ON THE AIR

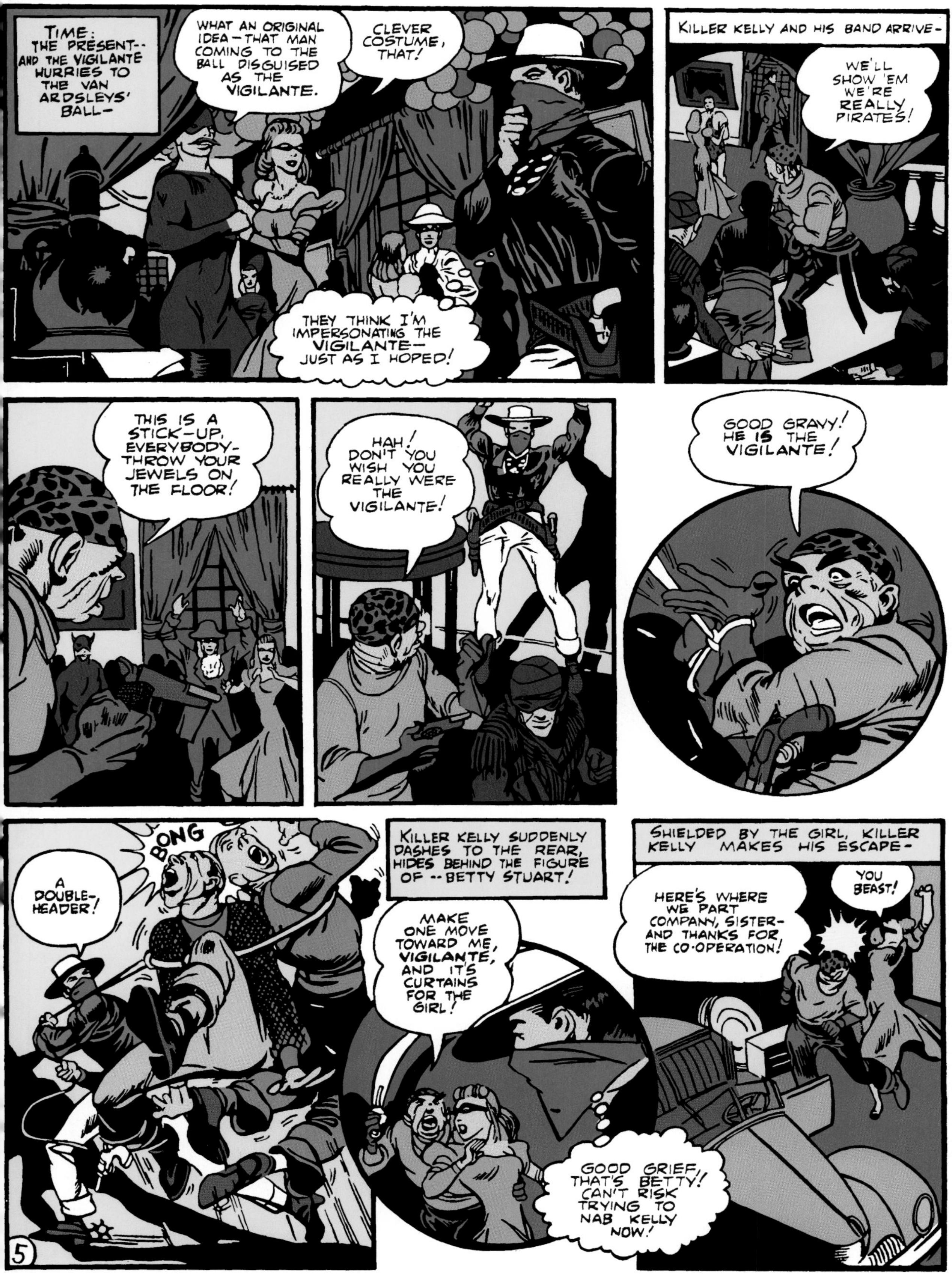

TIME: THE PRESENT-- AND THE VIGILANTE HURRIES TO THE VAN ARDSLEYS' BALL-
WHAT AN ORIGINAL IDEA-THAT MAN COMING TO THE BALL DISGUISED AS THE VIGILANTE.
CLEVER COSTUME, THAT!
THEY THINK I'M IMPERSONATING THE VIGILANTE-JUST AS I HOPED!
KILLER KELLY AND HIS BAND ARRIVE-
WE'LL SHOW 'EM WE'RE REALLY PIRATES!
THIS IS A STICK-UP, EVERYBODY-THROW YOUR JEWELS ON THE FLOOR!
HAH! DON'T YOU WISH YOU REALLY WERE THE VIGILANTE!
GOOD GRAVY! HE IS THE VIGILANTE!
BONG
A DOUBLE-HEADER!
KILLER KELLY SUDDENLY DASHES TO THE REAR, HIDES BEHIND THE FIGURE OF --BETTY STUART!
MAKE ONE MOVE TOWARD ME, VIGILANTE, AND IT'S CURTAINS FOR THE GIRL!
GOOD GRIEF! THAT'S BETTY! CAN'T RISK TRYING TO NAB KELLY NOW!
SHIELDED BY THE GIRL, KILLER KELLY MAKES HIS ESCAPE-
HERE'S WHERE WE PART COMPANY, SISTER-AND THANKS FOR THE CO-OPERATION!
YOU BEAST!
5

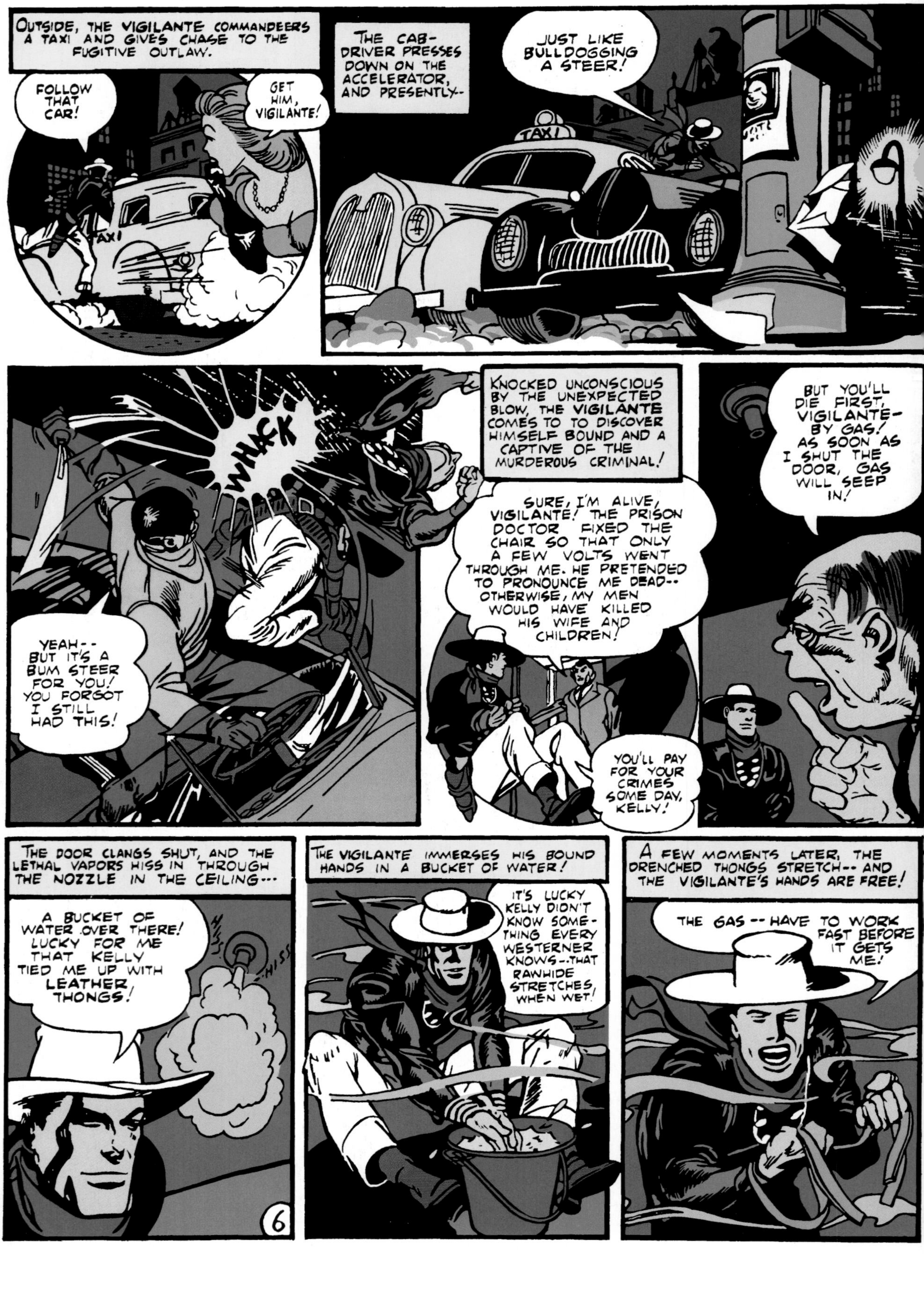

OUTSIDE, THE VIGILANTE COMMANDEERS A TAXI AND GIVES CHASE TO THE FUGITIVE OUTLAW.
FOLLOW THAT CAR!
GET HIM, VIGILANTE!
TAXI
THE CAB-DRIVER PRESSES DOWN ON THE ACCELERATOR, AND PRESENTLY--
JUST LIKE BULLDOGGING A STEER!
TAXI
WHACK
YEAH-- BUT IT'S A BUM STEER FOR YOU! YOU FORGOT I STILL HAD THIS!
KNOCKED UNCONSCIOUS BY THE UNEXPECTED BLOW, THE VIGILANTE COMES TO TO DISCOVER HIMSELF BOUND AND A CAPTIVE OF THE MURDEROUS CRIMINAL!
SURE, I'M ALIVE, VIGILANTE! THE PRISON DOCTOR FIXED THE CHAIR SO THAT ONLY A FEW VOLTS WENT THROUGH ME. HE PRETENDED TO PRONOUNCE ME DEAD-- OTHERWISE, MY MEN WOULD HAVE KILLED HIS WIFE AND CHILDREN!
YOU'LL PAY FOR YOUR CRIMES SOME DAY, KELLY!
BUT YOU'LL DIE FIRST, VIGILANTE-BY GAS! AS SOON AS I SHUT THE DOOR, GAS WILL SEEP IN!
THE DOOR CLANGS SHUT, AND THE LETHAL VAPORS HISS IN THROUGH THE NOZZLE IN THE CEILING---
A BUCKET OF WATER OVER THERE! LUCKY FOR ME THAT KELLY TIED ME UP WITH LEATHER THONGS!
HISS
6
THE VIGILANTE IMMERSES HIS BOUND HANDS IN A BUCKET OF WATER!
IT'S LUCKY KELLY DIDN'T KNOW SOME-THING EVERY WESTERNER KNOWS--THAT RAWHIDE STRETCHES WHEN WET!
A FEW MOMENTS LATER, THE DRENCHED THONGS STRETCH-- AND THE VIGILANTE'S HANDS ARE FREE!
THE GAS -- HAVE TO WORK FAST BEFORE IT GETS ME!

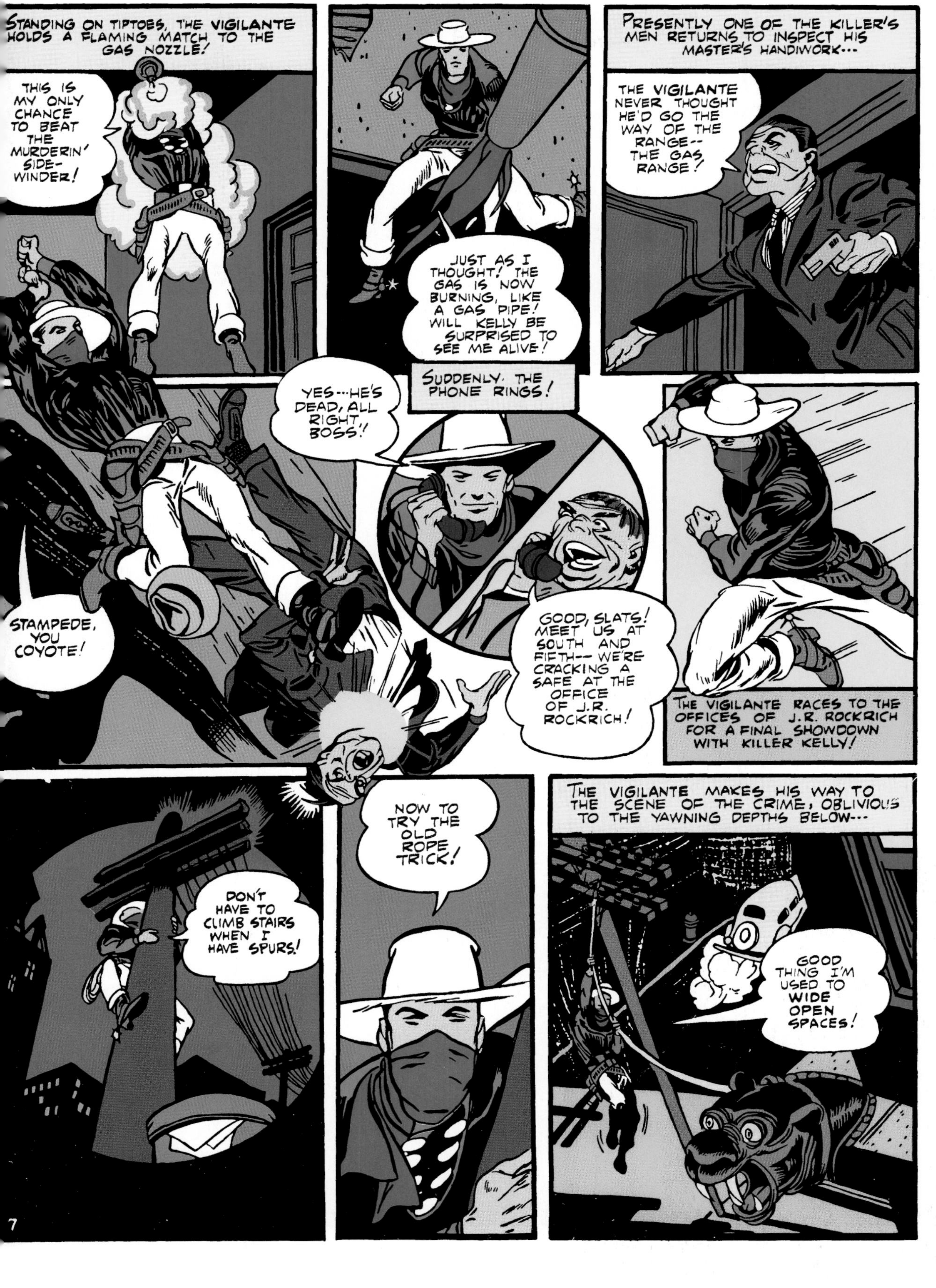
STANDING ON TIPTOES, THE VIGILANTE HOLDS A FLAMING MATCH TO THE GAS NOZZLE!
THIS IS MY ONLY CHANCE TO BEAT THE MURDERIN' SIDE-WINDER!
JUST AS I THOUGHT! THE GAS IS NOW BURNING, LIKE A GAS PIPE! WILL KELLY BE SURPRISED TO SEE ME ALIVE!
PRESENTLY ONE OF THE KILLER'S MEN RETURNS TO INSPECT HIS MASTER'S HANDIWORK...
THE VIGILANTE NEVER THOUGHT HE'D GO THE WAY OF THE RANGE-- THE GAS RANGE!
STAMPEDE, YOU COYOTE!
SUDDENLY, THE PHONE RINGS!
YES...HE'S DEAD, ALL RIGHT, BOSS!!
GOOD, SLATS! MEET US AT SOUTH AND FIFTH-- WE'RE CRACKING A SAFE AT THE OFFICE OF J.R. ROCKRICH!
THE VIGILANTE RACES TO THE OFFICES OF J.R. ROCKRICH FOR A FINAL SHOWDOWN WITH KILLER KELLY!
DON'T HAVE TO CLIMB STAIRS WHEN I HAVE SPURS!
7
NOW TO TRY THE OLD ROPE TRICK!
THE VIGILANTE MAKES HIS WAY TO THE SCENE OF THE CRIME, OBLIVIOUS TO THE YAWNING DEPTHS BELOW---
GOOD THING I'M USED TO WIDE OPEN SPACES!

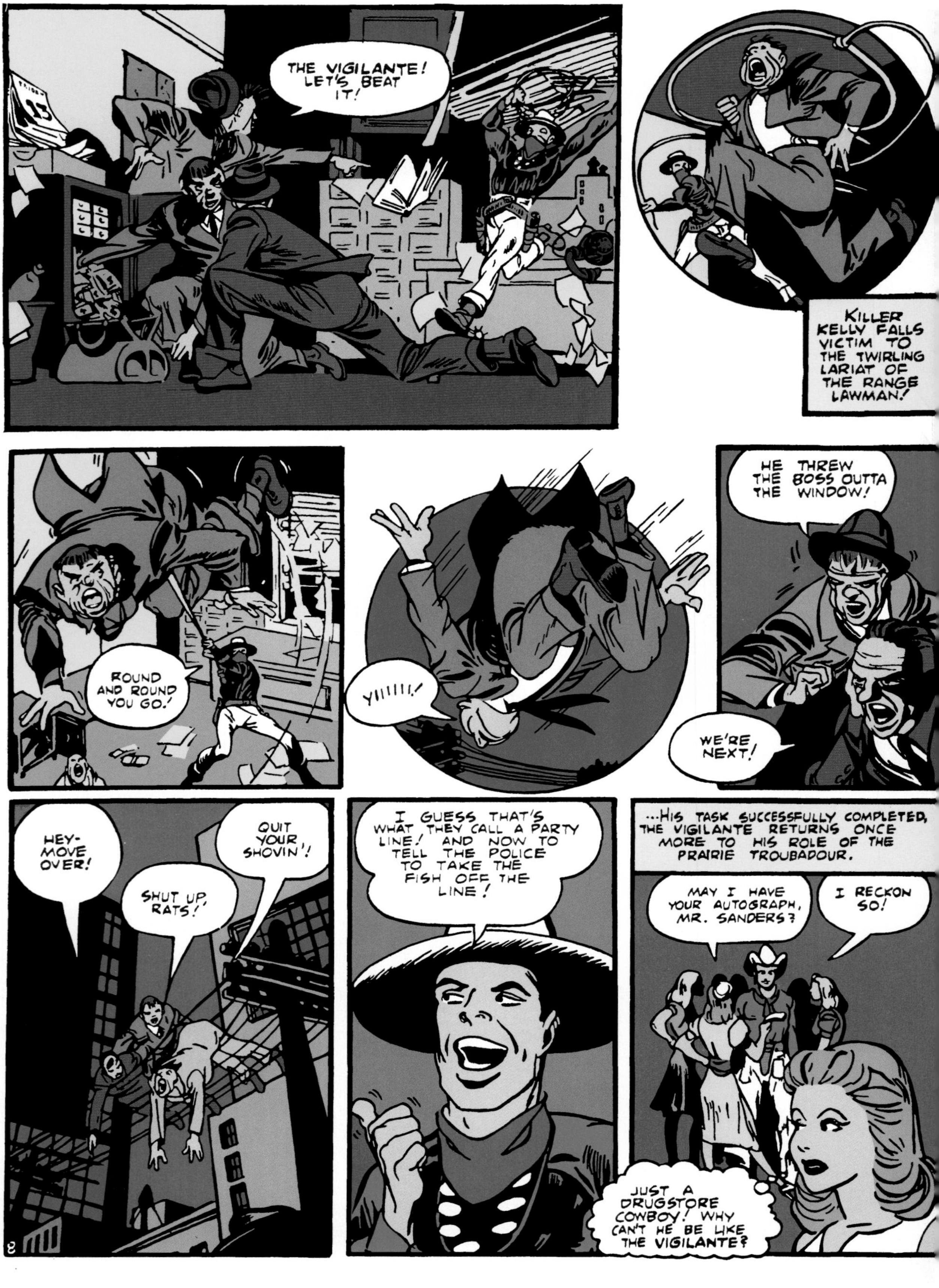
THE VIGILANTE! LET'S BEAT IT!
KILLER KELLY FALLS VICTIM TO THE TWIRLING LARIAT OF THE RANGE LAWMAN!
ROUND AND ROUND YOU GO!
YIIIIII!
HE THREW THE BOSS OUTTA THE WINDOW!
WE'RE NEXT!
HEY- MOVE OVER!
QUIT YOUR SHOVIN'!
SHUT UP, RATS!
I GUESS THAT'S WHAT THEY CALL A PARTY LINE! AND NOW TO TELL THE POLICE TO TAKE THE FISH OFF THE LINE!
...HIS TASK SUCCESSFULLY COMPLETED, THE VIGILANTE RETURNS ONCE MORE TO HIS ROLE OF THE PRAIRIE TROUBADOUR.
MAY I HAVE YOUR AUTOGRAPH, MR. SANDERS?
I RECKON SO!
JUST A DRUGSTORE COWBOY! WHY CAN'T HE BE LIKE THE VIGILANTE?
8

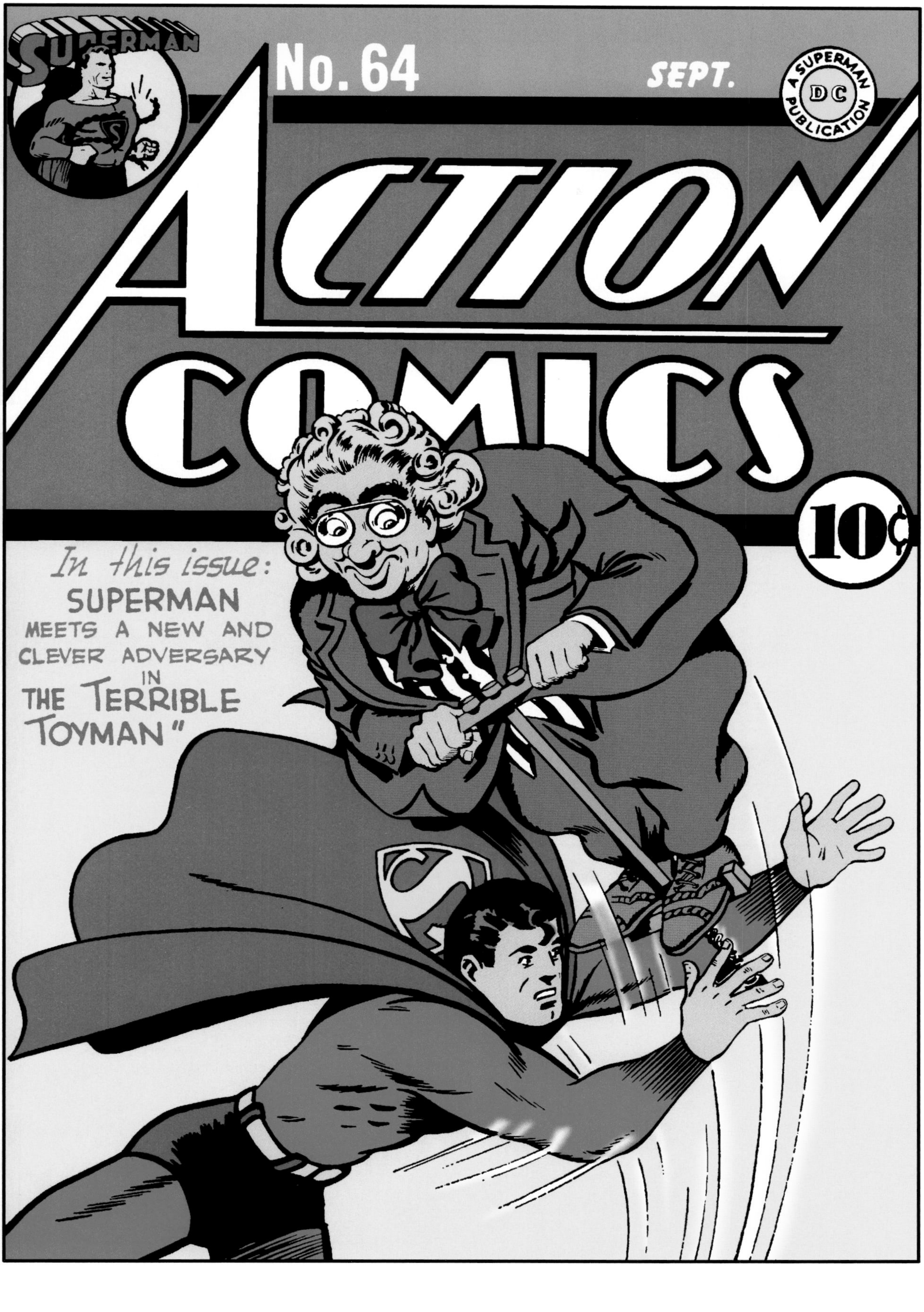
SUPERMAN
No. 64
SEPT.
A SUPERMAN DC PUBLICATION
ACTION COMICS
10¢
In this issue:
SUPERMAN
MEETS A NEW AND
CLEVER ADVERSARY
IN
THE TERRIBLE
TOYMAN"

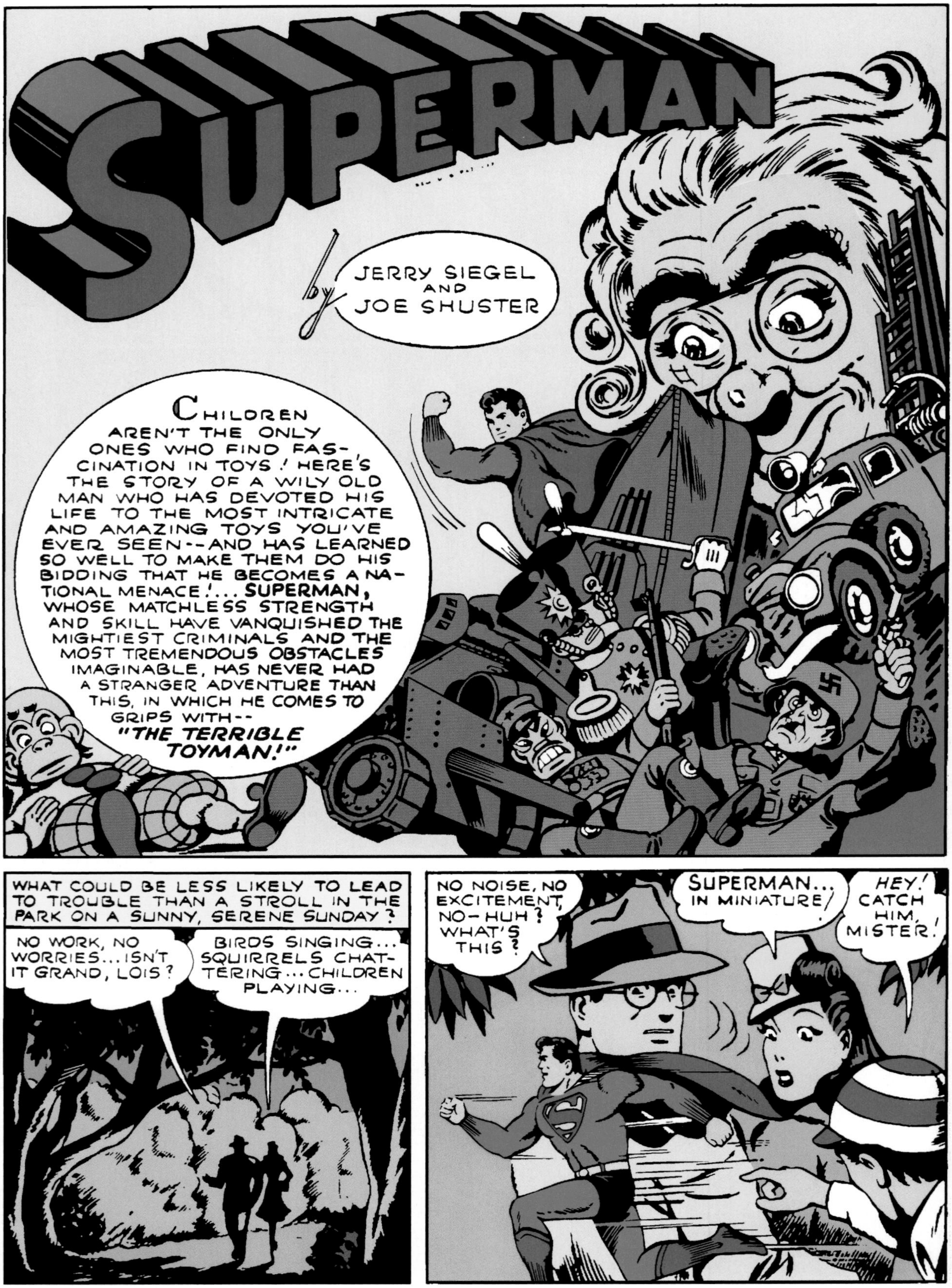
SUPERMAN
by JERRY SIEGEL AND JOE SHUSTER
CHILDREN AREN'T THE ONLY ONES WHO FIND FAS-CINATION IN TOYS! HERE'S THE STORY OF A WILY OLD MAN WHO HAS DEVOTED HIS LIFE TO THE MOST INTRICATE AND AMAZING TOYS YOU'VE EVER SEEN--AND HAS LEARNED SO WELL TO MAKE THEM DO HIS BIDDING THAT HE BECOMES A NA-TIONAL MENACE!... SUPERMAN, WHOSE MATCHLESS STRENGTH AND SKILL HAVE VANQUISHED THE MIGHTIEST CRIMINALS AND THE MOST TREMENDOUS OBSTACLES IMAGINABLE, HAS NEVER HAD A STRANGER ADVENTURE THAN THIS, IN WHICH HE COMES TO GRIPS WITH--"THE TERRIBLE TOYMAN!"
WHAT COULD BE LESS LIKELY TO LEAD TO TROUBLE THAN A STROLL IN THE PARK ON A SUNNY, SERENE SUNDAY?
NO WORK, NO WORRIES...ISN'T IT GRAND, LOIS?
BIRDS SINGING... SQUIRRELS CHAT-TERING...CHILDREN PLAYING...
NO NOISE, NO EXCITEMENT, NO-HUH? WHAT'S THIS?
SUPERMAN... IN MINIATURE!
HEY! CATCH HIM, MISTER!

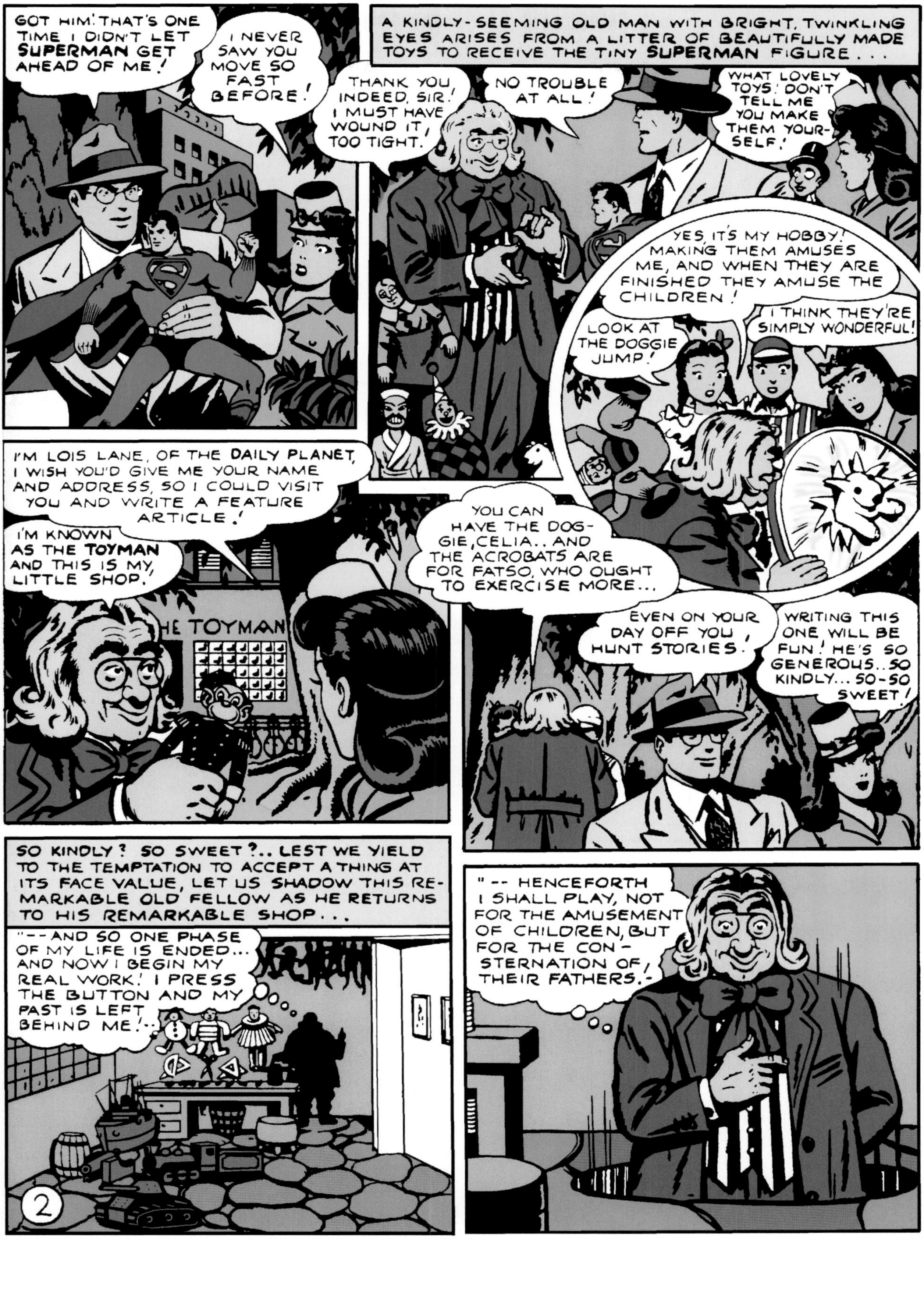
GOT HIM! THAT'S ONE TIME I DIDN'T LET SUPERMAN GET AHEAD OF ME!
I NEVER SAW YOU MOVE SO FAST BEFORE!
A KINDLY-SEEMING OLD MAN WITH BRIGHT, TWINKLING EYES ARISES FROM A LITTER OF BEAUTIFULLY MADE TOYS TO RECEIVE THE TINY SUPERMAN FIGURE . . .
THANK YOU INDEED, SIR! I MUST HAVE WOUND IT TOO TIGHT.
NO TROUBLE AT ALL!
WHAT LOVELY TOYS! DON'T TELL ME YOU MAKE THEM YOURSELF!
YES, IT'S MY HOBBY! MAKING THEM AMUSES ME, AND WHEN THEY ARE FINISHED THEY AMUSE THE CHILDREN!
LOOK AT THE DOGGIE JUMP!
I THINK THEY'RE SIMPLY WONDERFUL!
I'M LOIS LANE, OF THE DAILY PLANET, I WISH YOU'D GIVE ME YOUR NAME AND ADDRESS, SO I COULD VISIT YOU AND WRITE A FEATURE ARTICLE!
I'M KNOWN AS THE TOYMAN AND THIS IS MY LITTLE SHOP.
HE TOYMAN
YOU CAN HAVE THE DOGGIE, CELIA.. AND THE ACROBATS ARE FOR FATSO, WHO OUGHT TO EXERCISE MORE...
EVEN ON YOUR DAY OFF YOU HUNT STORIES.
WRITING THIS ONE WILL BE FUN! HE'S SO GENEROUS.. SO KINDLY... SO-SO SWEET!
SO KINDLY? SO SWEET?.. LEST WE YIELD TO THE TEMPTATION TO ACCEPT A THING AT ITS FACE VALUE, LET US SHADOW THIS REMARKABLE OLD FELLOW AS HE RETURNS TO HIS REMARKABLE SHOP . . .
"--AND SO ONE PHASE OF MY LIFE IS ENDED... AND NOW I BEGIN MY REAL WORK! I PRESS THE BUTTON AND MY PAST IS LEFT BEHIND ME!--
"-- HENCEFORTH I SHALL PLAY, NOT FOR THE AMUSEMENT OF CHILDREN, BUT FOR THE CONSTERNATION OF THEIR FATHERS!-
2

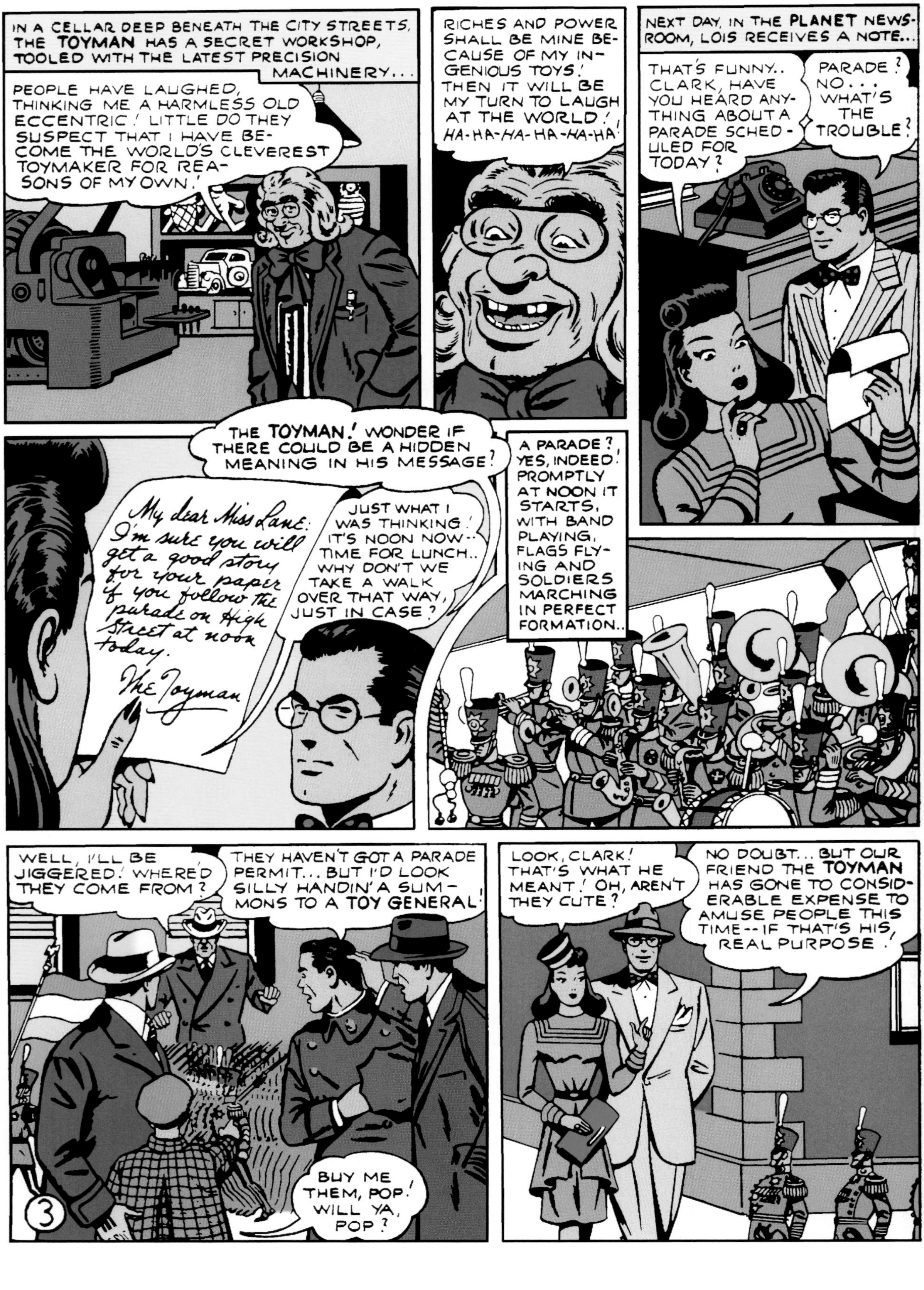

IN A CELLAR DEEP BENEATH THE CITY STREETS, THE TOYMAN HAS A SECRET WORKSHOP, TOOLED WITH THE LATEST PRECISION MACHINERY...
PEOPLE HAVE LAUGHED, THINKING ME A HARMLESS OLD ECCENTRIC! LITTLE DO THEY SUSPECT THAT I HAVE BECOME THE WORLD'S CLEVEREST TOYMAKER FOR REASONS OF MY OWN!
RICHES AND POWER SHALL BE MINE BECAUSE OF MY INGENIOUS TOYS! THEN IT WILL BE MY TURN TO LAUGH AT THE WORLD! HA-HA-HA-HA-HA-HA!
NEXT DAY, IN THE PLANET NEWSROOM, LOIS RECEIVES A NOTE...
THAT'S FUNNY.. CLARK, HAVE YOU HEARD ANYTHING ABOUT A PARADE SCHEDULED FOR TODAY?
PARADE? NO... WHAT'S THE TROUBLE?
THE TOYMAN! WONDER IF THERE COULD BE A HIDDEN MEANING IN HIS MESSAGE?
My dear Miss Lane: I'm sure you will get a good story for your paper if you follow the parade on High Street at noon today. The Toyman
JUST WHAT I WAS THINKING! IT'S NOON NOW-- TIME FOR LUNCH.. WHY DON'T WE TAKE A WALK OVER THAT WAY, JUST IN CASE?
A PARADE? YES, INDEED! PROMPTLY AT NOON IT STARTS, WITH BAND PLAYING, FLAGS FLYING AND SOLDIERS MARCHING IN PERFECT FORMATION..
WELL, I'LL BE JIGGERED! WHERE'D THEY COME FROM?
THEY HAVEN'T GOT A PARADE PERMIT... BUT I'D LOOK SILLY HANDIN' A SUMMONS TO A TOY GENERAL!
BUY ME THEM, POP! WILL YA, POP?
3
LOOK, CLARK! THAT'S WHAT HE MEANT! OH, AREN'T THEY CUTE?
NO DOUBT... BUT OUR FRIEND THE TOYMAN HAS GONE TO CONSIDERABLE EXPENSE TO AMUSE PEOPLE THIS TIME--IF THAT'S HIS REAL PURPOSE!

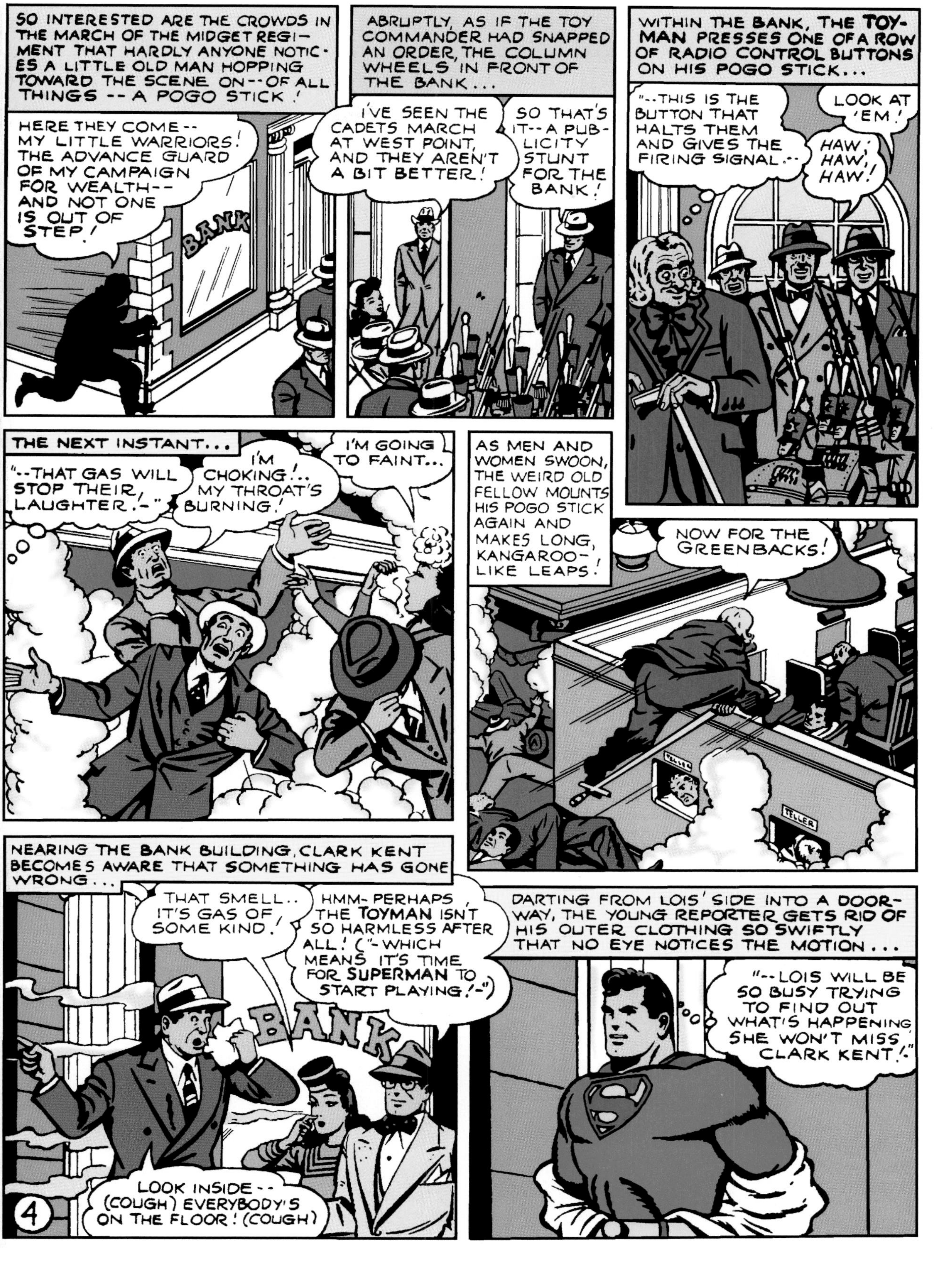
SO INTERESTED ARE THE CROWDS IN THE MARCH OF THE MIDGET REGIMENT THAT HARDLY ANYONE NOTICES A LITTLE OLD MAN HOPPING TOWARD THE SCENE ON--OF ALL THINGS --A POGO STICK!
HERE THEY COME-- MY LITTLE WARRIORS! THE ADVANCE GUARD OF MY CAMPAIGN FOR WEALTH-- AND NOT ONE IS OUT OF STEP!
BANK
ABRUPTLY, AS IF THE TOY COMMANDER HAD SNAPPED AN ORDER, THE COLUMN WHEELS IN FRONT OF THE BANK...
I'VE SEEN THE CADETS MARCH AT WEST POINT, AND THEY AREN'T A BIT BETTER!
SO THAT'S IT--A PUBLICITY STUNT FOR THE BANK!
WITHIN THE BANK, THE TOYMAN PRESSES ONE OF A ROW OF RADIO CONTROL BUTTONS ON HIS POGO STICK...
"--THIS IS THE BUTTON THAT HALTS THEM AND GIVES THE FIRING SIGNAL.--"
LOOK AT 'EM!
HAW! HAW! HAW!
THE NEXT INSTANT...
"--THAT GAS WILL STOP THEIR LAUGHTER.-"
I'M CHOKING!.. MY THROAT'S BURNING!
I'M GOING TO FAINT...
AS MEN AND WOMEN SWOON, THE WEIRD OLD FELLOW MOUNTS HIS POGO STICK AGAIN AND MAKES LONG, KANGAROO-LIKE LEAPS!
NOW FOR THE GREENBACKS!
TELLER
TELLER
NEARING THE BANK BUILDING, CLARK KENT BECOMES AWARE THAT SOMETHING HAS GONE WRONG...
THAT SMELL.. IT'S GAS OF SOME KIND!
HMM- PERHAPS, THE TOYMAN ISN'T SO HARMLESS AFTER ALL! ("-WHICH MEANS IT'S TIME FOR SUPERMAN TO START PLAYING!-")
BANK
LOOK INSIDE-- (COUGH) EVERYBODY'S ON THE FLOOR! (COUGH)
4
DARTING FROM LOIS' SIDE INTO A DOORWAY, THE YOUNG REPORTER GETS RID OF HIS OUTER CLOTHING SO SWIFTLY THAT NO EYE NOTICES THE MOTION...
"--LOIS WILL BE SO BUSY TRYING TO FIND OUT WHAT'S HAPPENING SHE WON'T MISS CLARK KENT!"

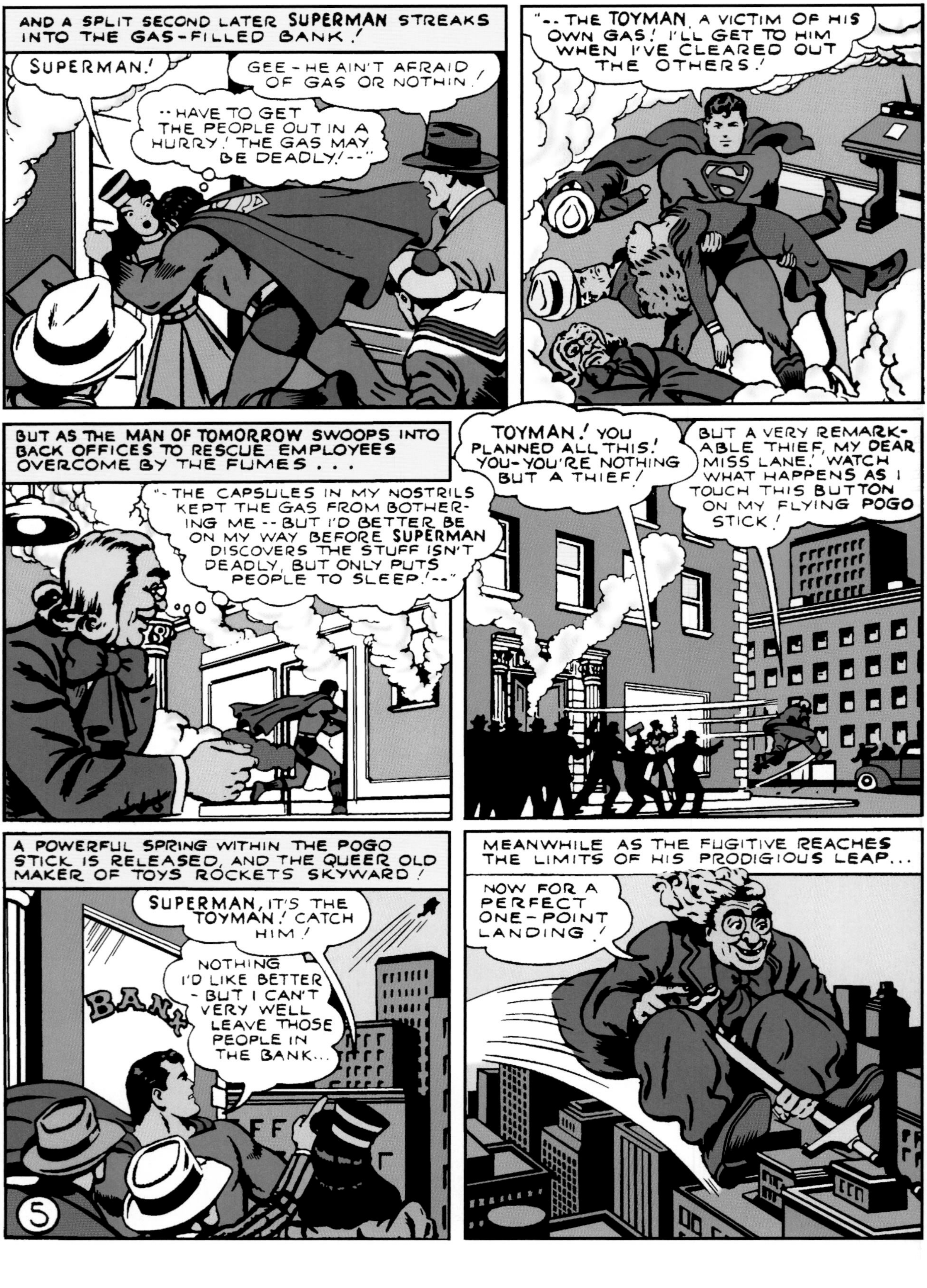
AND A SPLIT SECOND LATER SUPERMAN STREAKS INTO THE GAS-FILLED BANK!
SUPERMAN!
GEE-HE AIN'T AFRAID OF GAS OR NOTHIN'!
"--HAVE TO GET THE PEOPLE OUT IN A HURRY! THE GAS MAY BE DEADLY!--"
"--THE TOYMAN, A VICTIM OF HIS OWN GAS! I'LL GET TO HIM WHEN I'VE CLEARED OUT THE OTHERS!
BUT AS THE MAN OF TOMORROW SWOOPS INTO BACK OFFICES TO RESCUE EMPLOYEES OVERCOME BY THE FUMES . . .
"--THE CAPSULES IN MY NOSTRILS KEPT THE GAS FROM BOTHERING ME--BUT I'D BETTER BE ON MY WAY BEFORE SUPERMAN DISCOVERS THE STUFF ISN'T DEADLY, BUT ONLY PUTS PEOPLE TO SLEEP!--"
TOYMAN! YOU PLANNED ALL THIS! YOU-YOU'RE NOTHING BUT A THIEF!
BUT A VERY REMARKABLE THIEF, MY DEAR MISS LANE! WATCH WHAT HAPPENS AS I TOUCH THIS BUTTON ON MY FLYING POGO STICK!
A POWERFUL SPRING WITHIN THE POGO STICK IS RELEASED, AND THE QUEER OLD MAKER OF TOYS ROCKETS SKYWARD!
SUPERMAN, IT'S THE TOYMAN! CATCH HIM!
NOTHING I'D LIKE BETTER - BUT I CAN'T VERY WELL LEAVE THOSE PEOPLE IN THE BANK...
BANK
5
MEANWHILE AS THE FUGITIVE REACHES THE LIMITS OF HIS PRODIGIOUS LEAP...
NOW FOR A PERFECT ONE-POINT LANDING!

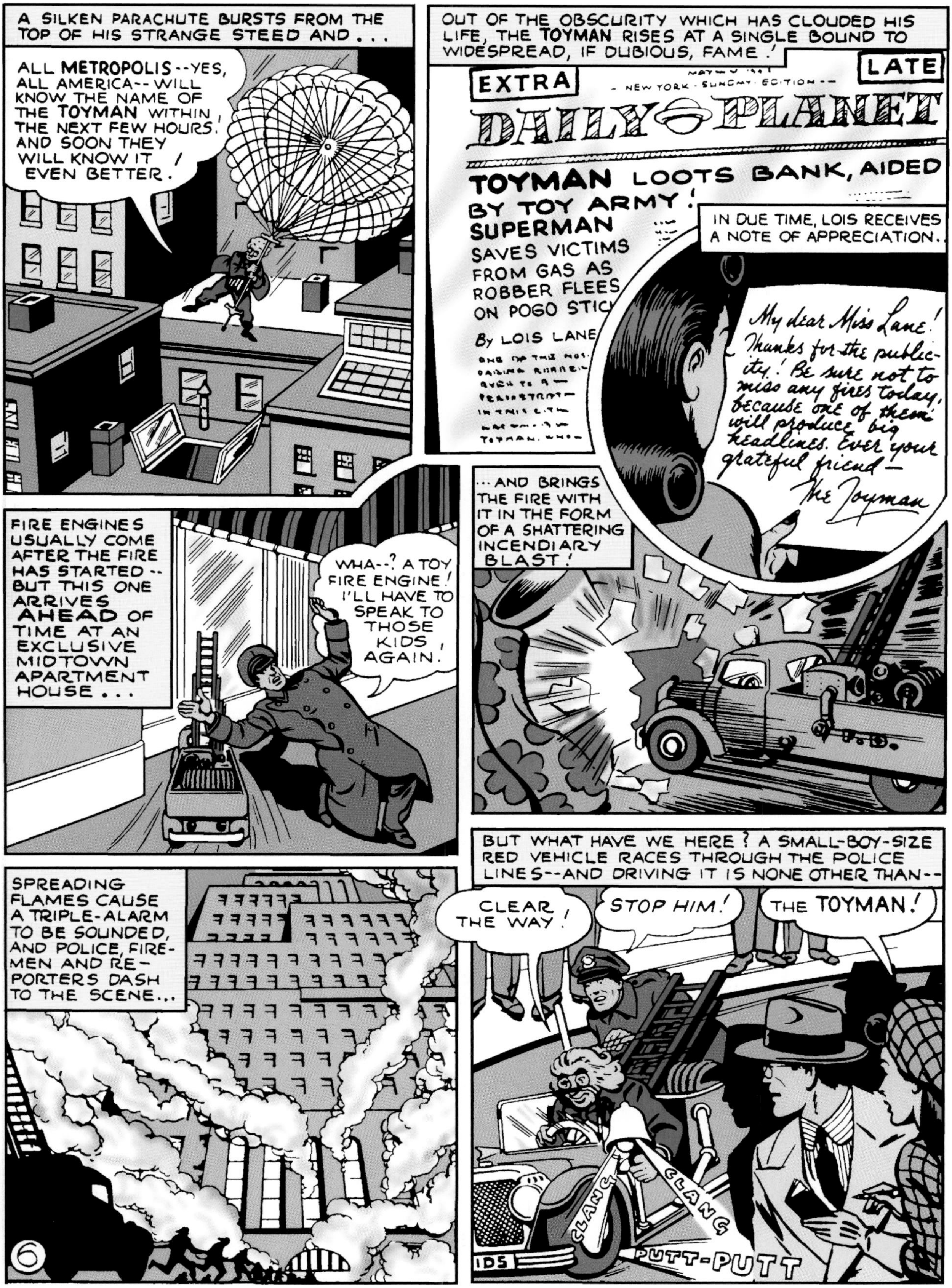
A SILKEN PARACHUTE BURSTS FROM THE TOP OF HIS STRANGE STEED AND . . .
ALL METROPOLIS--YES, ALL AMERICA--WILL KNOW THE NAME OF THE TOYMAN WITHIN THE NEXT FEW HOURS! AND SOON THEY WILL KNOW IT EVEN BETTER!
OUT OF THE OBSCURITY WHICH HAS CLOUDED HIS LIFE, THE TOYMAN RISES AT A SINGLE BOUND TO WIDESPREAD, IF DUBIOUS, FAME!
EXTRA
LATE
NEW YORK - SUNDAY - EDITION
DAILY PLANET
TOYMAN LOOTS BANK, AIDED BY TOY ARMY!
SUPERMAN SAVES VICTIMS FROM GAS AS ROBBER FLEES ON POGO STIC
By LOIS LANE
IN DUE TIME, LOIS RECEIVES A NOTE OF APPRECIATION.
My dear Miss Lane! Thanks for the publicity! Be sure not to miss any fires today, because one of them will produce big headlines. Ever your grateful friend— The Toyman
FIRE ENGINES USUALLY COME AFTER THE FIRE HAS STARTED -- BUT THIS ONE ARRIVES AHEAD OF TIME AT AN EXCLUSIVE MIDTOWN APARTMENT HOUSE . . .
WHA--? A TOY FIRE ENGINE! I'LL HAVE TO SPEAK TO THOSE KIDS AGAIN!
...AND BRINGS THE FIRE WITH IT IN THE FORM OF A SHATTERING INCENDIARY BLAST!
F.D.
SPREADING FLAMES CAUSE A TRIPLE-ALARM TO BE SOUNDED, AND POLICE, FIREMEN AND REPORTERS DASH TO THE SCENE...
6
BUT WHAT HAVE WE HERE? A SMALL-BOY-SIZE RED VEHICLE RACES THROUGH THE POLICE LINES--AND DRIVING IT IS NONE OTHER THAN--
CLEAR THE WAY!
STOP HIM!
THE TOYMAN!
CLANG
CLANG
PUTT-PUTT

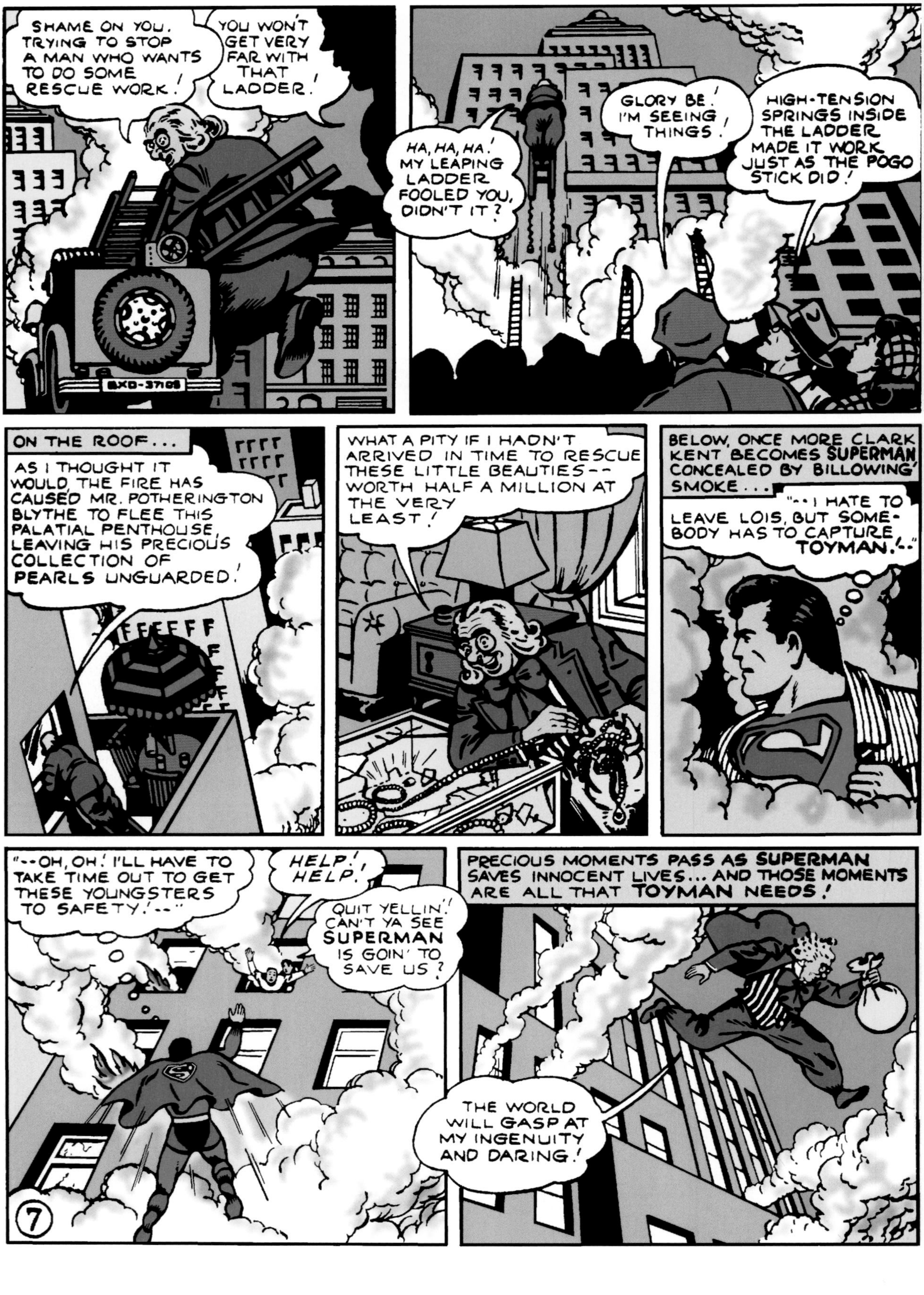
SHAME ON YOU. TRYING TO STOP A MAN WHO WANTS TO DO SOME RESCUE WORK!
YOU WON'T GET VERY FAR WITH THAT LADDER!
BXD-37108
HA, HA, HA! MY LEAPING LADDER FOOLED YOU, DIDN'T IT?
GLORY BE! I'M SEEING THINGS!
HIGH-TENSION SPRINGS INSIDE THE LADDER MADE IT WORK JUST AS THE POGO STICK DID!
ON THE ROOF...
AS I THOUGHT IT WOULD, THE FIRE HAS CAUSED MR. POTHERINGTON BLYTHE TO FLEE THIS PALATIAL PENTHOUSE, LEAVING HIS PRECIOUS COLLECTION OF PEARLS UNGUARDED!
WHAT A PITY IF I HADN'T ARRIVED IN TIME TO RESCUE THESE LITTLE BEAUTIES-- WORTH HALF A MILLION AT THE VERY LEAST!
BELOW, ONCE MORE CLARK KENT BECOMES SUPERMAN CONCEALED BY BILLOWING SMOKE...
"--I HATE TO LEAVE LOIS, BUT SOMEBODY HAS TO CAPTURE TOYMAN!--"
"--OH, OH! I'LL HAVE TO TAKE TIME OUT TO GET THESE YOUNGSTERS TO SAFETY!--"
HELP! HELP!
QUIT YELLIN'! CAN'T YA SEE SUPERMAN IS GOIN' TO SAVE US?
7
PRECIOUS MOMENTS PASS AS SUPERMAN SAVES INNOCENT LIVES... AND THOSE MOMENTS ARE ALL THAT TOYMAN NEEDS!
THE WORLD WILL GASP AT MY INGENUITY AND DARING!

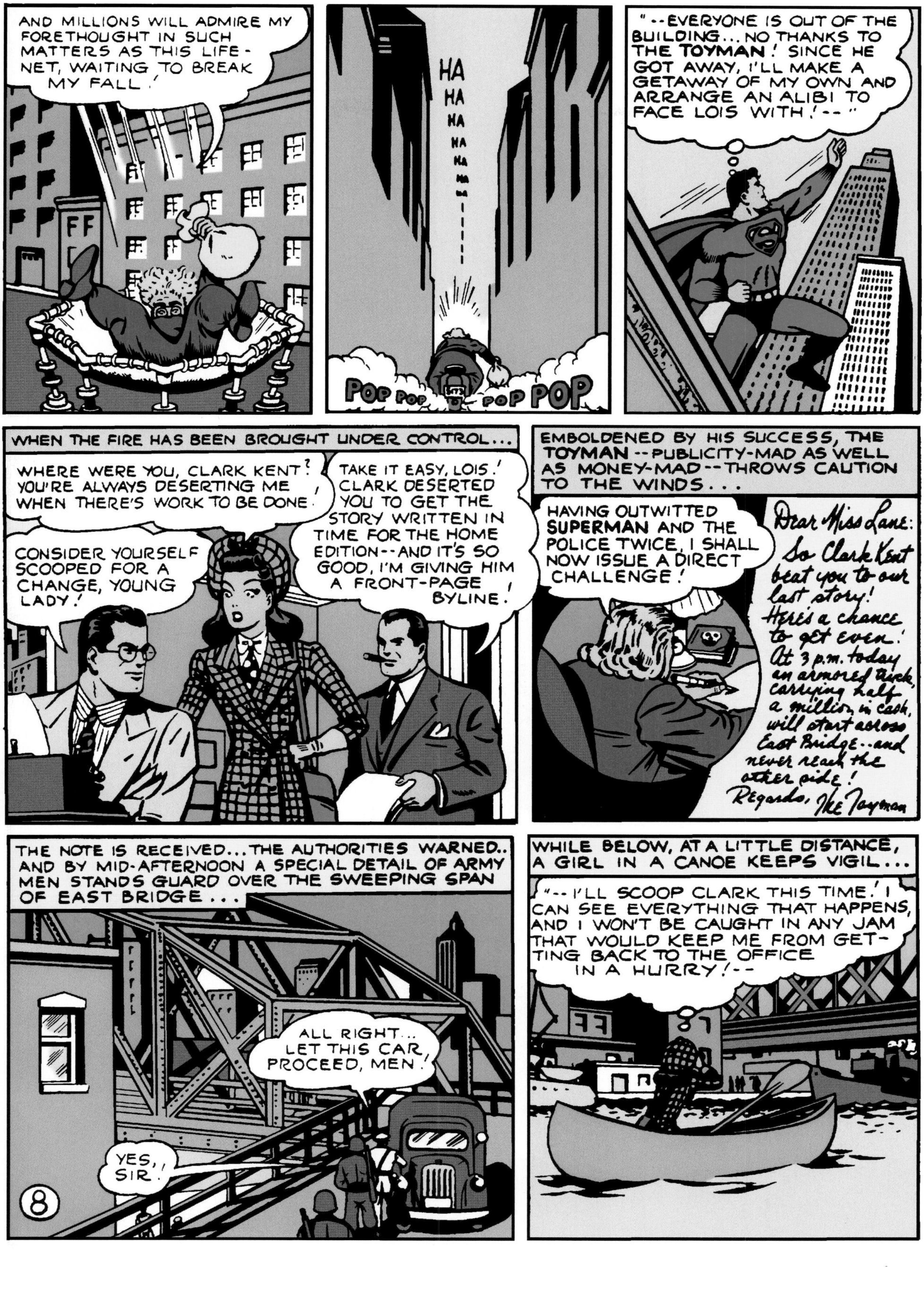
AND MILLIONS WILL ADMIRE MY FORETHOUGHT IN SUCH MATTERS AS THIS LIFE-NET, WAITING TO BREAK MY FALL!
HA HA HA HA HA
POP POP POP POP
"--EVERYONE IS OUT OF THE BUILDING... NO THANKS TO THE TOYMAN! SINCE HE GOT AWAY, I'LL MAKE A GETAWAY OF MY OWN AND ARRANGE AN ALIBI TO FACE LOIS WITH!--"
WHEN THE FIRE HAS BEEN BROUGHT UNDER CONTROL...
WHERE WERE YOU, CLARK KENT? YOU'RE ALWAYS DESERTING ME WHEN THERE'S WORK TO BE DONE!
TAKE IT EASY, LOIS! CLARK DESERTED YOU TO GET THE STORY WRITTEN IN TIME FOR THE HOME EDITION--AND IT'S SO GOOD, I'M GIVING HIM A FRONT-PAGE BYLINE!
CONSIDER YOURSELF SCOOPED FOR A CHANGE, YOUNG LADY!
EMBOLDENED BY HIS SUCCESS, THE TOYMAN --PUBLICITY-MAD AS WELL AS MONEY-MAD--THROWS CAUTION TO THE WINDS...
HAVING OUTWITTED SUPERMAN AND THE POLICE TWICE, I SHALL NOW ISSUE A DIRECT CHALLENGE!
Dear Miss Lane: So Clark Kent beat you to our last story! Here's a chance to get even! At 3 p.m. today an armored truck, carrying half a million in cash, will start across East Bridge..and never reach the other side! Regards, The Toyman
THE NOTE IS RECEIVED... THE AUTHORITIES WARNED.. AND BY MID-AFTERNOON A SPECIAL DETAIL OF ARMY MEN STANDS GUARD OVER THE SWEEPING SPAN OF EAST BRIDGE...
ALL RIGHT... LET THIS CAR PROCEED, MEN!
YES, SIR!
8
WHILE BELOW, AT A LITTLE DISTANCE, A GIRL IN A CANOE KEEPS VIGIL...
"--I'LL SCOOP CLARK THIS TIME! I CAN SEE EVERYTHING THAT HAPPENS, AND I WON'T BE CAUGHT IN ANY JAM THAT WOULD KEEP ME FROM GETTING BACK TO THE OFFICE IN A HURRY!--

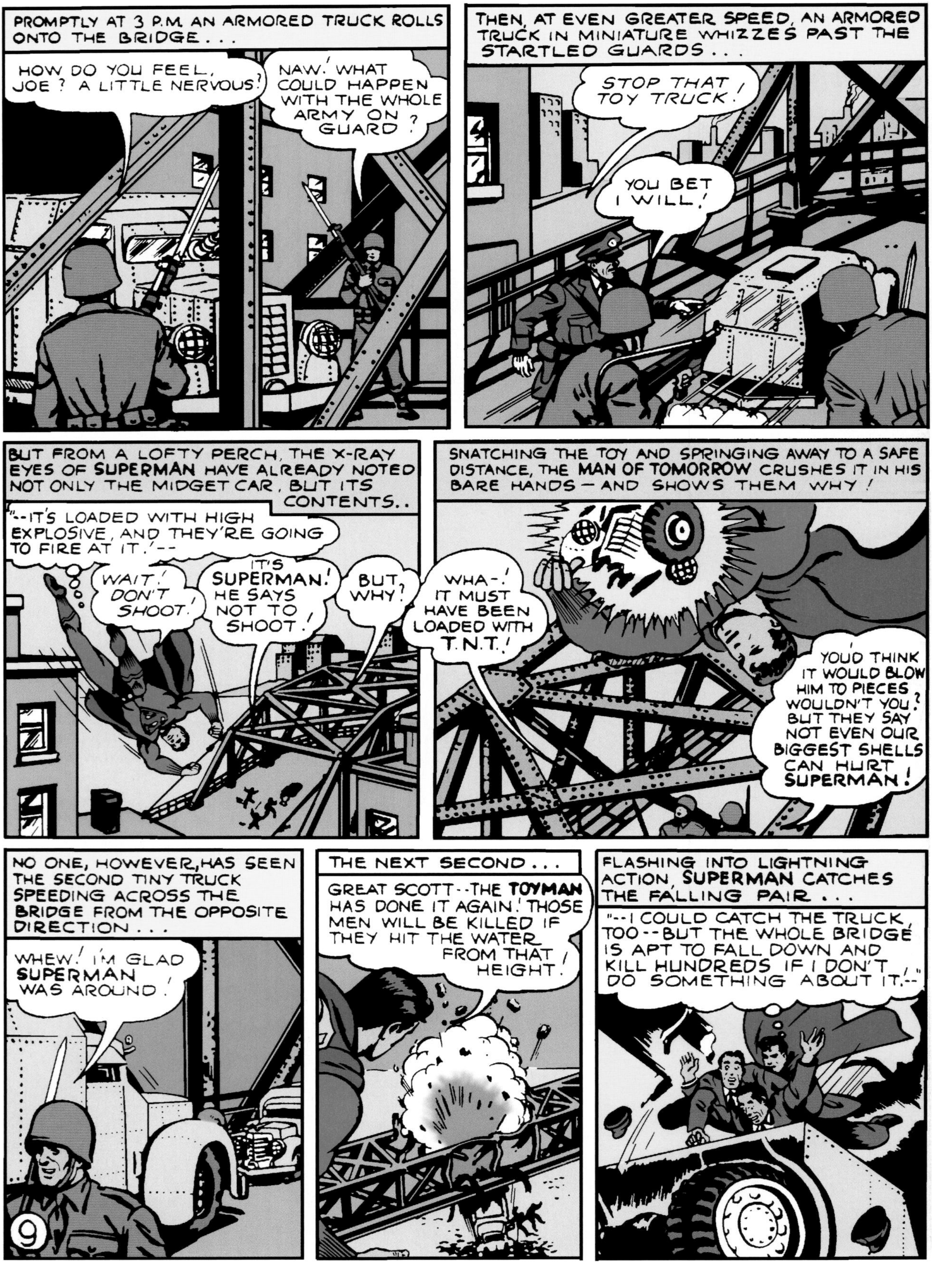
PROMPTLY AT 3 P.M. AN ARMORED TRUCK ROLLS ONTO THE BRIDGE . . .
HOW DO YOU FEEL, JOE ? A LITTLE NERVOUS?
NAW! WHAT COULD HAPPEN WITH THE WHOLE ARMY ON GUARD ?
THEN, AT EVEN GREATER SPEED, AN ARMORED TRUCK IN MINIATURE WHIZZES PAST THE STARTLED GUARDS . . .
STOP THAT TOY TRUCK!
YOU BET I WILL!
BUT FROM A LOFTY PERCH, THE X-RAY EYES OF SUPERMAN HAVE ALREADY NOTED NOT ONLY THE MIDGET CAR, BUT ITS CONTENTS..
"--IT'S LOADED WITH HIGH EXPLOSIVE, AND THEY'RE GOING TO FIRE AT IT.'--
WAIT! DON'T SHOOT!
IT'S SUPERMAN! HE SAYS NOT TO SHOOT!
BUT, WHY?
SNATCHING THE TOY AND SPRINGING AWAY TO A SAFE DISTANCE, THE MAN OF TOMORROW CRUSHES IT IN HIS BARE HANDS — AND SHOWS THEM WHY!
WHA-! IT MUST HAVE BEEN LOADED WITH T.N.T.!
YOU'D THINK IT WOULD BLOW HIM TO PIECES, WOULDN'T YOU? BUT THEY SAY NOT EVEN OUR BIGGEST SHELLS CAN HURT SUPERMAN!
NO ONE, HOWEVER, HAS SEEN THE SECOND TINY TRUCK SPEEDING ACROSS THE BRIDGE FROM THE OPPOSITE DIRECTION . . .
WHEW! I'M GLAD SUPERMAN WAS AROUND!
9
THE NEXT SECOND . . .
GREAT SCOTT--THE TOYMAN HAS DONE IT AGAIN! THOSE MEN WILL BE KILLED IF THEY HIT THE WATER FROM THAT HEIGHT!
FLASHING INTO LIGHTNING ACTION, SUPERMAN CATCHES THE FALLING PAIR . . .
"--I COULD CATCH THE TRUCK, TOO--BUT THE WHOLE BRIDGE IS APT TO FALL DOWN AND KILL HUNDREDS IF I DON'T DO SOMETHING ABOUT IT!--"

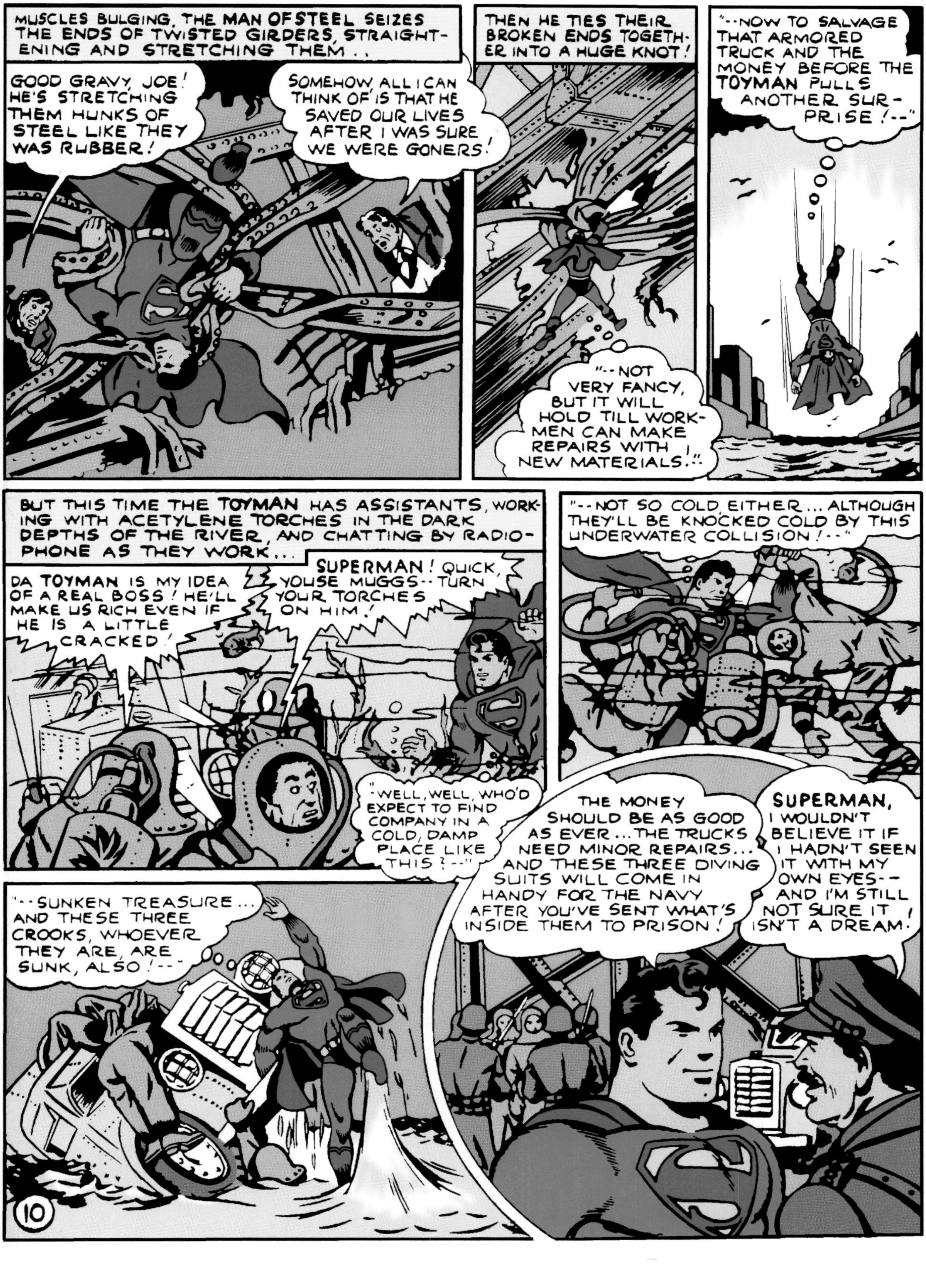
MUSCLES BULGING, THE MAN OF STEEL SEIZES THE ENDS OF TWISTED GIRDERS, STRAIGHTENING AND STRETCHING THEM . .
GOOD GRAVY, JOE! HE'S STRETCHING THEM HUNKS OF STEEL LIKE THEY WAS RUBBER!
SOMEHOW, ALL I CAN THINK OF IS THAT HE SAVED OUR LIVES AFTER I WAS SURE WE WERE GONERS!
THEN HE TIES THEIR BROKEN ENDS TOGETHER INTO A HUGE KNOT!
"--NOT VERY FANCY, BUT IT WILL HOLD TILL WORKMEN CAN MAKE REPAIRS WITH NEW MATERIALS!--"
"--NOW TO SALVAGE THAT ARMORED TRUCK AND THE MONEY BEFORE THE TOYMAN PULLS ANOTHER SURPRISE!--"
BUT THIS TIME THE TOYMAN HAS ASSISTANTS, WORKING WITH ACETYLENE TORCHES IN THE DARK DEPTHS OF THE RIVER, AND CHATTING BY RADIO-PHONE AS THEY WORK...
DA TOYMAN IS MY IDEA OF A REAL BOSS! HE'LL MAKE US RICH EVEN IF HE IS A LITTLE CRACKED!
SUPERMAN! QUICK, YOUSE MUGGS--TURN YOUR TORCHES ON HIM!
"-WELL, WELL, WHO'D EXPECT TO FIND COMPANY IN A COLD, DAMP PLACE LIKE THIS?--"
"--NOT SO COLD, EITHER... ALTHOUGH THEY'LL BE KNOCKED COLD BY THIS UNDERWATER COLLISION!--"
"--SUNKEN TREASURE... AND THESE THREE CROOKS, WHOEVER THEY ARE, ARE SUNK, ALSO!--"
SUPERMAN, I WOULDN'T BELIEVE IT IF I HADN'T SEEN IT WITH MY OWN EYES--AND I'M STILL NOT SURE IT ISN'T A DREAM!
THE MONEY SHOULD BE AS GOOD AS EVER... THE TRUCKS NEED MINOR REPAIRS... AND THESE THREE DIVING SUITS WILL COME IN HANDY FOR THE NAVY AFTER YOU'VE SENT WHAT'S INSIDE THEM TO PRISON!
10

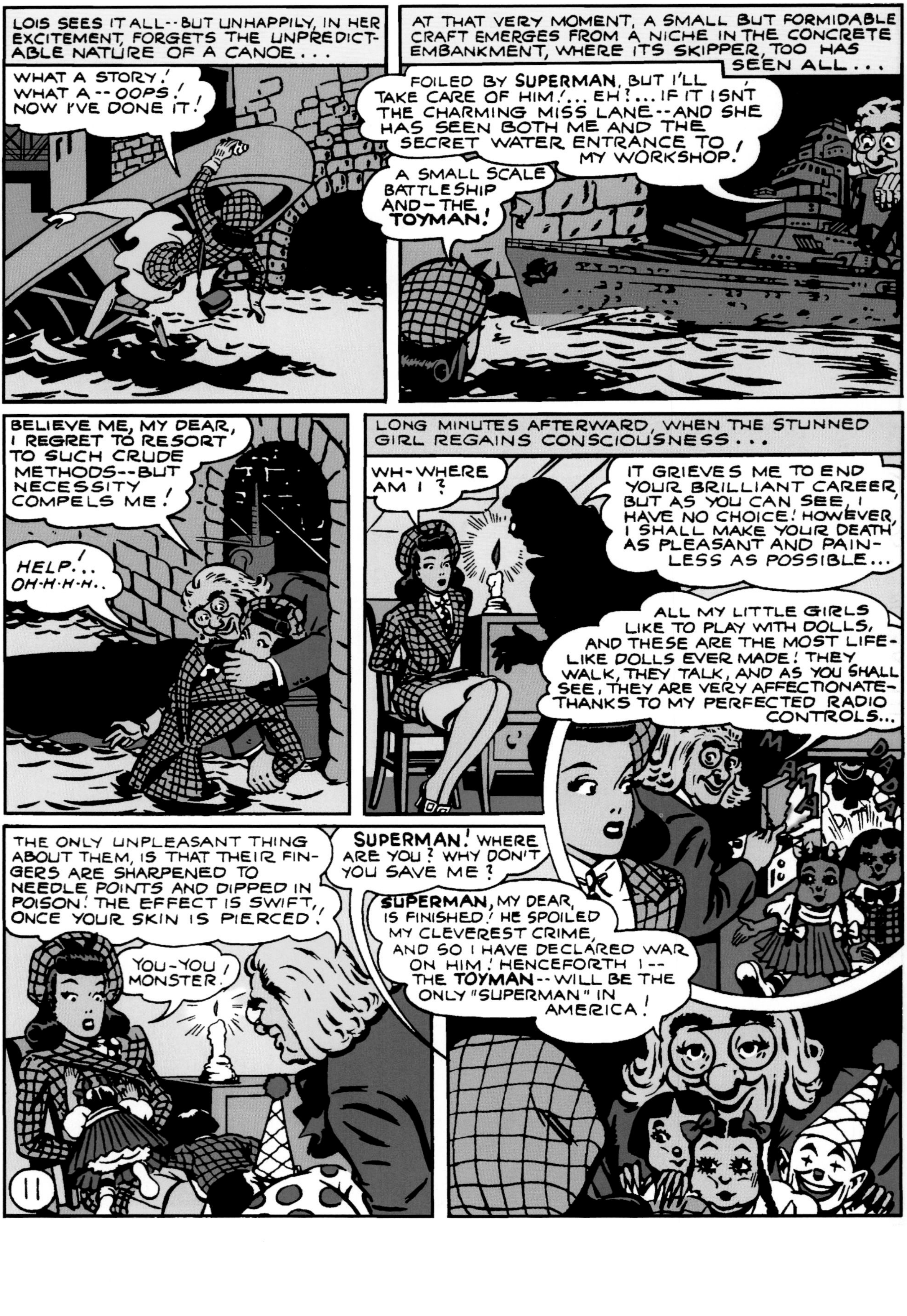
LOIS SEES IT ALL--BUT UNHAPPILY, IN HER EXCITEMENT, FORGETS THE UNPREDICTABLE NATURE OF A CANOE...
WHAT A STORY! WHAT A--OOPS! NOW I'VE DONE IT!
AT THAT VERY MOMENT, A SMALL BUT FORMIDABLE CRAFT EMERGES FROM A NICHE IN THE CONCRETE EMBANKMENT, WHERE ITS SKIPPER, TOO HAS SEEN ALL...
FOILED BY SUPERMAN, BUT I'LL TAKE CARE OF HIM!... EH?... IF IT ISN'T THE CHARMING MISS LANE--AND SHE HAS SEEN BOTH ME AND THE SECRET WATER ENTRANCE TO MY WORKSHOP!
A SMALL SCALE BATTLESHIP AND--THE TOYMAN!
BELIEVE ME, MY DEAR, I REGRET TO RESORT TO SUCH CRUDE METHODS--BUT NECESSITY COMPELS ME!
HELP!... OH-H-H-H..
LONG MINUTES AFTERWARD, WHEN THE STUNNED GIRL REGAINS CONSCIOUSNESS...
WH-WHERE AM I?
IT GRIEVES ME TO END YOUR BRILLIANT CAREER, BUT AS YOU CAN SEE, I HAVE NO CHOICE! HOWEVER, I SHALL MAKE YOUR DEATH AS PLEASANT AND PAINLESS AS POSSIBLE...
ALL MY LITTLE GIRLS LIKE TO PLAY WITH DOLLS, AND THESE ARE THE MOST LIFE-LIKE DOLLS EVER MADE! THEY WALK, THEY TALK, AND AS YOU SHALL SEE, THEY ARE VERY AFFECTIONATE--THANKS TO MY PERFECTED RADIO CONTROLS...
MAMA
DADA
THE ONLY UNPLEASANT THING ABOUT THEM, IS THAT THEIR FINGERS ARE SHARPENED TO NEEDLE POINTS AND DIPPED IN POISON! THE EFFECT IS SWIFT, ONCE YOUR SKIN IS PIERCED!
YOU-YOU MONSTER!
SUPERMAN! WHERE ARE YOU? WHY DON'T YOU SAVE ME?
SUPERMAN, MY DEAR, IS FINISHED! HE SPOILED MY CLEVEREST CRIME, AND SO I HAVE DECLARED WAR ON HIM! HENCEFORTH I--THE TOYMAN--WILL BE THE ONLY "SUPERMAN" IN AMERICA!
11

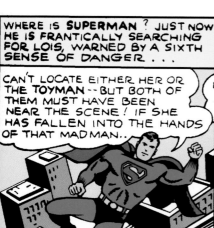

WHERE IS **SUPERMAN**? JUST NOW HE IS FRANTICALLY SEARCHING FOR LOIS, WARNED BY A SIXTH SENSE OF DANGER...

CAN'T LOCATE EITHER HER OR THE TOYMAN--BUT BOTH OF THEM MUST HAVE BEEN NEAR THE SCENE! IF SHE HAS FALLEN INTO THE HANDS OF THAT MADMAN...

ABRUPTLY, HIS SUPER-SENSITIVE EARS PICK UP THE PECULIAR WHINE OF RADIO CONTROL EQUIPMENT...

ULTRA-SHORT WAVES, COMING FROM THE DIRECTION OF THE **TOYMAN'S** SHOP! HMM... AND HE'S LEFT THAT PLACE!

ONCE AGAIN, IN THE SUPPOSEDLY EMPTY TOY SHOP, THE PHENOMENAL X-RAY VISION OF THE **MAN OF TOMORROW** REVEALS SECRETS HIDDEN FROM ORDINARY EYES...

"--EMPTY--BUT THE RADIO IMPULSES ARE COMING FROM BELOW! ...AND THERE SHE IS.--"

FFFFFFF

SOLID STONE CRUMBLES BEFORE A BLASTING SHOWER OF BLOWS!

NOBODY INVITED ME--BUT THEN, THE HOST RARELY DOES IN CASES LIKE THIS!

SUPERMAN! THANK GOODNESS YOU'RE IN TIME

BE CAREFUL! YOU'RE BREAKING MY BEAUTIFUL DOLLS!

YOU HAVE YOUR IDEA OF FUN--AND THIS IS MINE!

OH, WHAT WILL I DO NOW? YOU'VE RUINED EVERYTHING! ALL MY DREAMS--MY SENSATIONAL PLANS--

I'M SURE THE WARDEN AT STATE PRISON WILL APPRECIATE YOUR PECULIAR TALENTS, **TOYMAN**!

I'LL STAY THERE JUST LONG ENOUGH TO THINK OF A PLAN TO DESTROY YOU, AND THEN I'LL BE BACK. HOW THE WORLD WILL LAUGH WHEN **SUPERMAN** IS DEFEATED BY A TOY! HA-HA-HA-HA-HA-HA-HA!

⑫

MINUTES LATER...

CLARK GET ME OUT OF THESE ROPES! SUPERMAN LEFT ME THIS WAY, AND EVERYBODY SEEMS TO THINK IT'S FUNNY! IT MAKES ME SO MAD...

I DON'T BLAME YOU FOR BEING MAD! I'LL UNTIE YOU IN A JIFFY...

JUST AS SOON AS I FINISH WRITING THE BIG STORY **SUPERMAN** GAVE ME ABOUT THE END OF THE **TOYMAN**!

WHY, YOU--YOU--YOU--I'LL FIX YOU! WAIT AND SEE IF I DON'T!

The END

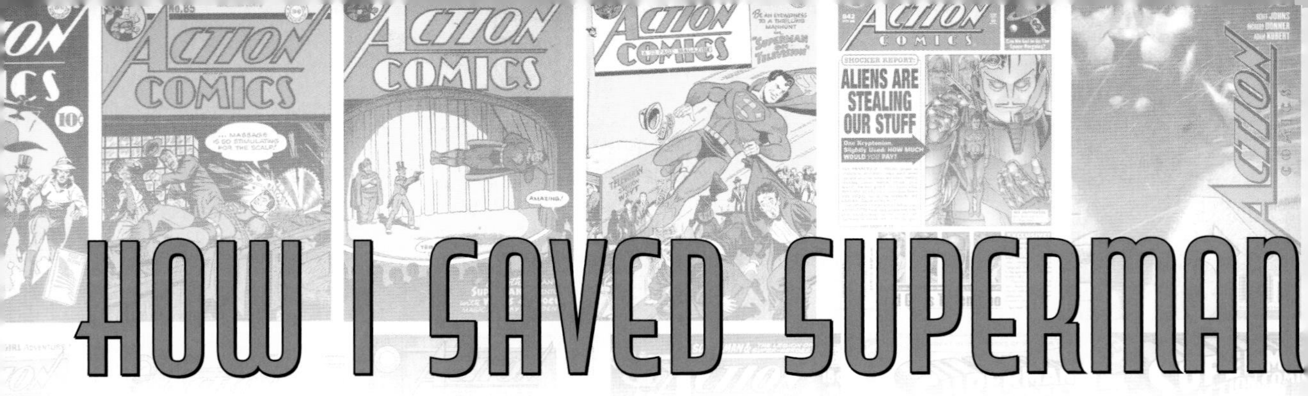
ACTION COMICS
ACTION COMICS
ACTION COMICS
ACTION COMICS
ALIENS ARE STEALING OUR STUFF

HOW I SAVED SUPERMAN

by **MARV WOLFMAN**

In a time of the Internet, where comic book news spreads throughout the galaxy the very moment someone thinks of it, and often before then, it's impossible to understand that there was a long-lost era when comics fans had no idea what was going to happen to their favorite characters until their comics magically appeared at the corner candy store.

Ravenously hungry for our four-color heroes, once a week on magazine delivery day we would pounce on the racks, grabbing every comic we could afford at 10¢ each. Or if you were like me, you made a deal with the store owner to open the bundled comics and put them on the shelves for him (saving him time). Of course, first we would sort through the books and keep the best-condition comics for ourselves. We were young, not stupid.

Buying the books off the racks was how most fans got their weekly dose of real-time comic book news and enjoyment.

Of course, if you were one of the select few comic book fans growing up in New York City in the 1960s, well, you could get news, and it turns out more, by taking DC Comics' weekly office tour. For comic book fans, touring those offices was the ultimate. No way it could get any better than that.

Until it did. But I'm getting ahead of myself.

Although I lived in the borough of Queens, I went to the High School of Art & Design in Manhattan. That required a bus ride to the train station, then another hour's ride to the heart of the city. A long daily trip made worthwhile because: a) I wanted to be a comic book artist, and many of my favorite artists had also gone to A&D; and b) even more important than my future as an artist, the school was only a very few blocks away from DC's office at 51st Street and Lexington Avenue.

Their proximity meant that after classes I could high-tail it down to DC just in time to take the tour.

And the tour was great. Several of us fans would wait in the reception area. To pass the time until the tour began, they let us read bound volumes of DC's comics. You read that right. We might be given a bound volume from the 1940s to read. Or the '50s. Nobody was worried that the kids would steal the volumes; that just didn't happen. Everyone read the books, then handed them back as the tour began.

Ahhh. Innocence.

We were brought into a long corridor. To our right were the editors' offices, followed by the business offices. To our left were file cabinets filled with original comics art for upcoming books (seeing them is how we got our news!). We then made a left turn into the production office, where everything was put together. Almost all of DC's writers and artists worked out of their homes, but every time I took the tour I'd see two of my absolute favorite artists, Carmine Infantino and Murphy Anderson, working away on a new issue of THE FLASH or ADAM STRANGE or some other upcoming project (more news!).

On rare occasions, when the stars aligned, the person giving the tour, or Sol Harrison, DC's production manager, would ask if we would like a page of original art. Yes. They asked us.

Let's pause for a moment. Back in those days, before Atlantis sunk into legend, and before artists started drawing digitally on their computers or tablets, artists put pencil to paper and hand-drew each page. Then another artist would ink over the pencils and make them ready for printing. Oddly, back then, in the days before those artists (and the writers) got credit for their work, very few of the artists actually wanted any of their original art back. There was no value to the pages, and for many artists, when they did get the pages, it was just an ever-growing stack of paper cluttering up their studio.

As comic book fandom came into being, the fans desperately wanted these one-of-a-kind hand-drawn pages. The fans knew these pages had value. Maybe not monetary—yet—but we loved comics. It took several years before the professional artists realized that fans were selling the pages for real money, and decided, finally, they should be able to benefit from their art. Sadly, comic book artists were not among the rich and famous, and original art sales definitely helped pay the bills.

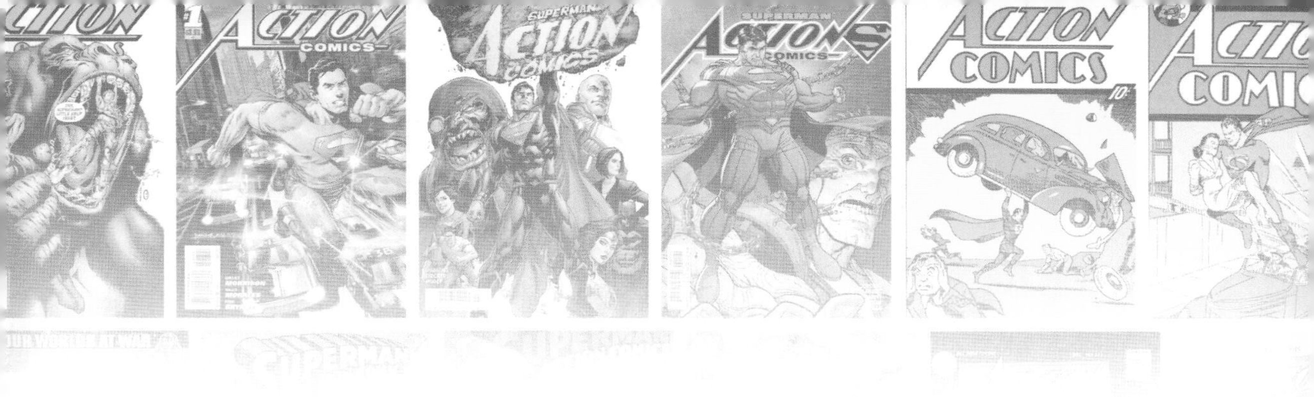
ACTION COMICS
ACTION COMICS
ACTION COMICS
ACTION COMICS

But this was before that dawning of reality. At the moment we're talking about here, except for the fans, nobody thought comic book art had any value. Most of the time, the art was simply destroyed so nobody could use it to illegally reprint stories (I don't know if anyone had ever done that, but it was the excuse we were told).

So it was only a minor surprise when a bunch of us went on the DC tour one afternoon, only to see Sol Harrison pushing a giant mail/utility cart filled nearly to the top with 1940s artwork that was heading to the building's incinerator.

To reiterate: the cart, I'm guessing from memory, was about four feet wide, maybe six feet long and four feet deep. And it was almost filled to the top.

The art was from the 1940s, when the size of original art was 12" x 18" as opposed to today's 10" x 15" size.

Oh, and before I forget, there was something else that made this art unique. None of these hundreds of pages had ever been printed. All the pages I saw were stamped, "Written off."

Hundreds and hundreds of pages of never-printed original art from the Golden Age of Comics were being wheeled to the incinerator, soon to be little more than Golden Age ash.

Before you curse the companies, remember, there was no recognized value to them. The artists almost never asked for or wanted the pages back, and it was just filling up storeroom after storeroom, seemingly for no apparent purpose.

No value to the company, but lots of value to us fans on the tour.

So when Sol Harrison casually asked if we kids wanted any of the art before it was forever destroyed, we dove into that mail cart and swam through the pages like Uncle Scrooge in his money bin.

My memory says we didn't even bother to take the tour. We grabbed as much art as our muscleless arms could carry (reminder, we were comic book fans, not sports fans) and hightailed it to the building's lobby, where the trading began. I flipped through my pages and saw I had almost all the pages of a written-off Superman story. Superman was, and remains, my favorite comic book character, and here was a Superman story nobody had ever seen before. I traded two of some other pages for one of the Superman pages I needed. With apologies to a local car commercial, I wheeled and dealed like I never whelt and dealt before.

And I came out of the trading session with a complete Superman story and tons of other original art pages that, for reasons that escape me now in our money-driven culture, I gave to all my friends.

Over the years I traded and sold pages, but because I've always been a Superman fan, I kept the entire Superman story.

Once I became a professional writer, I started to do research on the story's origin. The story was drawn in 1945 and was 12 pages long. I'm not sure who the artist was (payment was made to Joe Shuster for his studio) or why the story was written off, but in 1947 the story was shortened to 10 pages and redrawn by artist Wayne Boring. I'm not sure that Jerry Siegel actually wrote it, but he received the payment and I don't think he was using ghostwriters. So this 12-page original is the first time it's ever seen print.

As far as I know, there might only be one other unpublished Superman story out there, but I have no idea if those pages are still intact or together. This story has been preserved exactly the way it was when I pulled it from that doomed stack of art and traded pages for those that were missing.

And that's the story of how I saved Superman, or at least how I saved 12 pages' worth of him.

Next time I'll tell the story of being hired by DC's production department to cut up original art before throwing it out, and how I instead carefully cut between the panel borders to save as much of that art as possible. True story!

MARV WOLFMAN remade the DC Universe in CRISIS ON INFINITE EARTHS and has written, edited or created most of the major superheroes in comics.

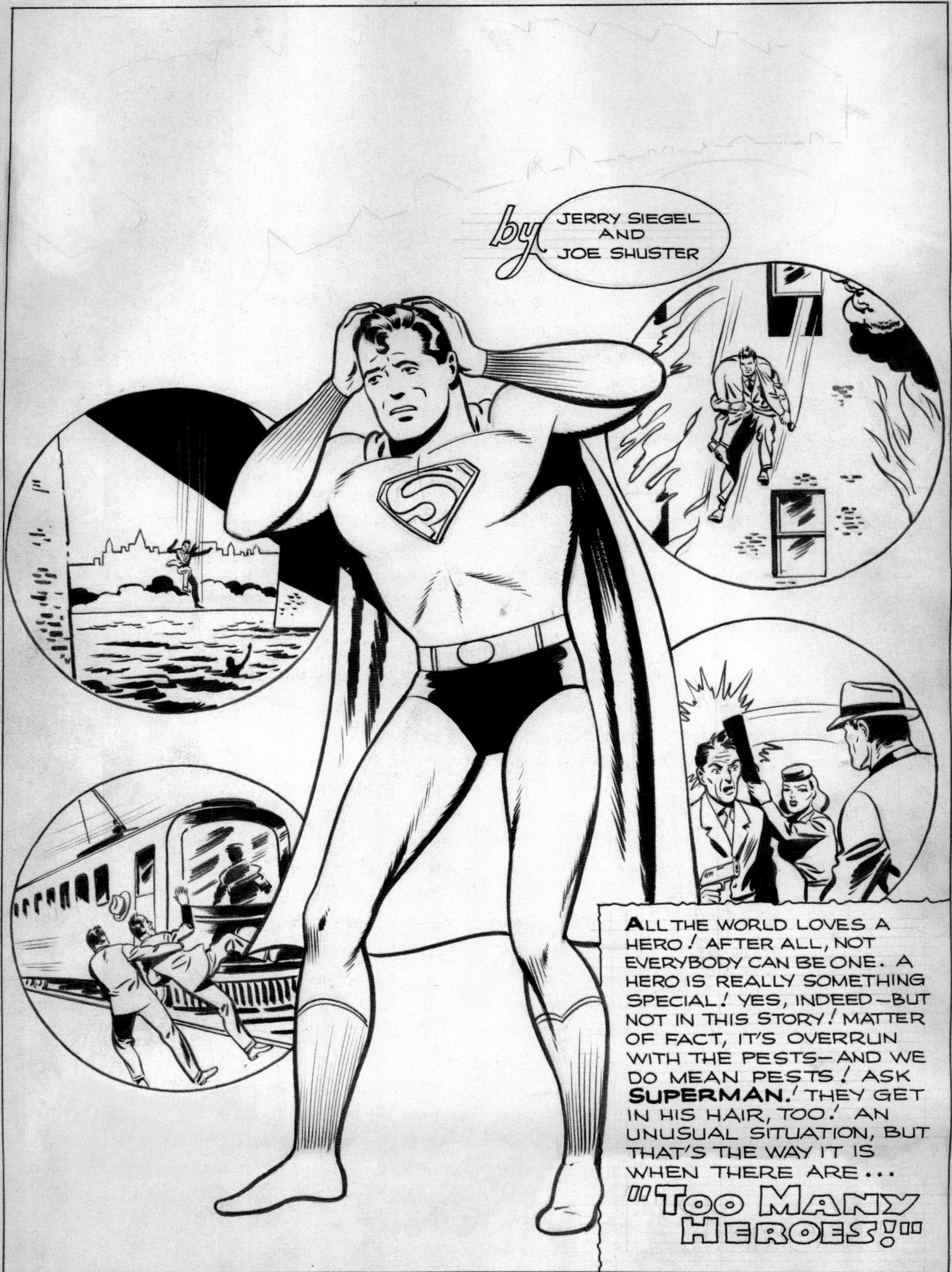

by JERRY SIEGEL AND JOE SHUSTER
ALL THE WORLD LOVES A HERO! AFTER ALL, NOT EVERYBODY CAN BE ONE. A HERO IS REALLY SOMETHING SPECIAL! YES, INDEED—BUT NOT IN THIS STORY! MATTER OF FACT, IT'S OVERRUN WITH THE PESTS—AND WE DO MEAN PESTS! ASK SUPERMAN! THEY GET IN HIS HAIR, TOO! AN UNUSUAL SITUATION, BUT THAT'S THE WAY IT IS WHEN THERE ARE...
"TOO MANY HEROES!"

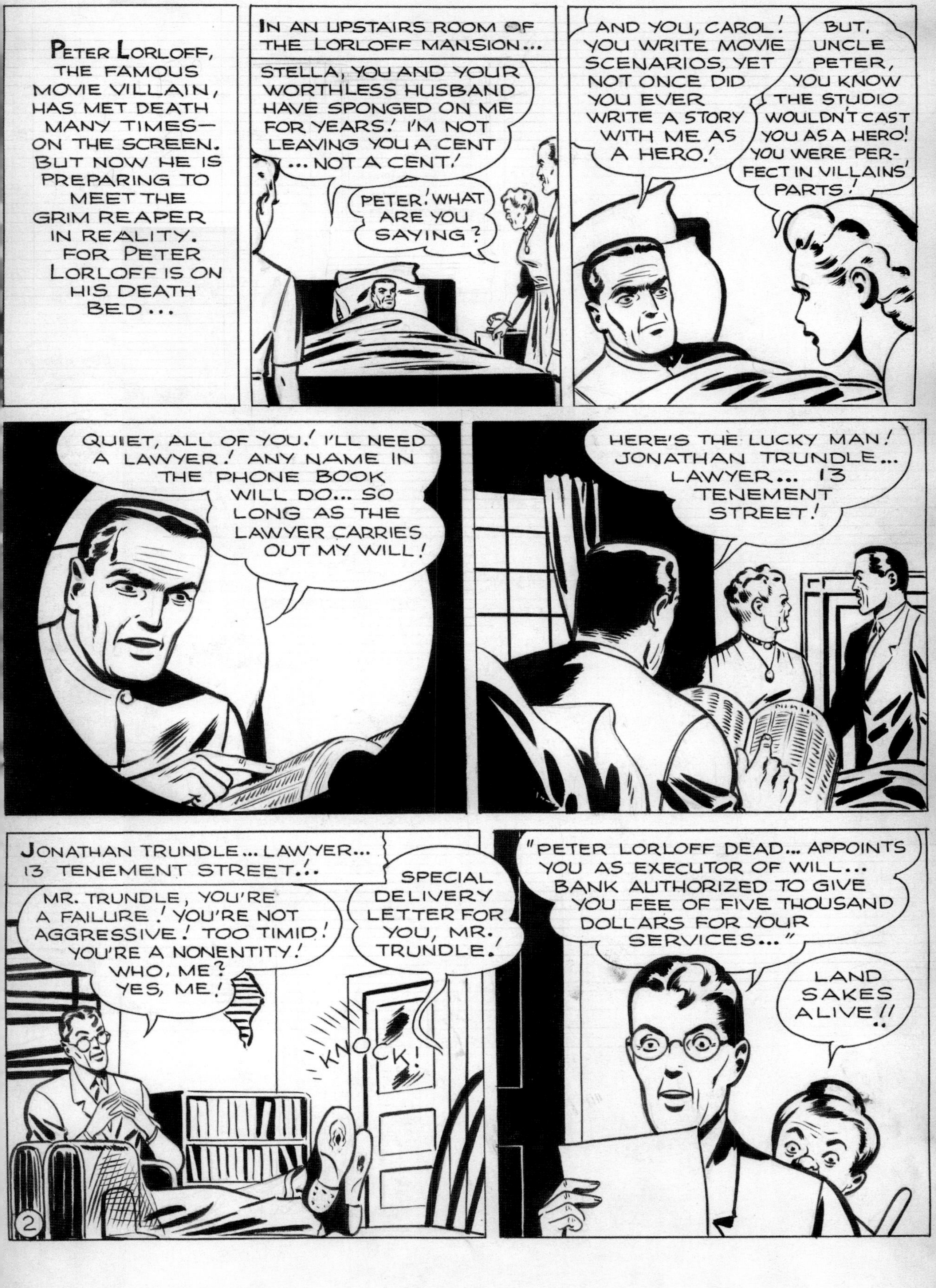

PETER LORLOFF, THE FAMOUS MOVIE VILLAIN, HAS MET DEATH MANY TIMES— ON THE SCREEN. BUT NOW HE IS PREPARING TO MEET THE GRIM REAPER IN REALITY. FOR PETER LORLOFF IS ON HIS DEATH BED...
IN AN UPSTAIRS ROOM OF THE LORLOFF MANSION...
STELLA, YOU AND YOUR WORTHLESS HUSBAND HAVE SPONGED ON ME FOR YEARS! I'M NOT LEAVING YOU A CENT ... NOT A CENT!
PETER! WHAT ARE YOU SAYING?
AND YOU, CAROL! YOU WRITE MOVIE SCENARIOS, YET NOT ONCE DID YOU EVER WRITE A STORY WITH ME AS A HERO!
BUT, UNCLE PETER, YOU KNOW THE STUDIO WOULDN'T CAST YOU AS A HERO! YOU WERE PERFECT IN VILLAINS' PARTS!
QUIET, ALL OF YOU! I'LL NEED A LAWYER! ANY NAME IN THE PHONE BOOK WILL DO... SO LONG AS THE LAWYER CARRIES OUT MY WILL!
HERE'S THE LUCKY MAN! JONATHAN TRUNDLE... LAWYER... 13 TENEMENT STREET!
JONATHAN TRUNDLE... LAWYER... 13 TENEMENT STREET!..
MR. TRUNDLE, YOU'RE A FAILURE! YOU'RE NOT AGGRESSIVE! TOO TIMID! YOU'RE A NONENTITY! WHO, ME? YES, ME!
SPECIAL DELIVERY LETTER FOR YOU, MR. TRUNDLE!
KNOCK!
"PETER LORLOFF DEAD... APPOINTS YOU AS EXECUTOR OF WILL... BANK AUTHORIZED TO GIVE YOU FEE OF FIVE THOUSAND DOLLARS FOR YOUR SERVICES..."
LAND SAKES ALIVE!!
2

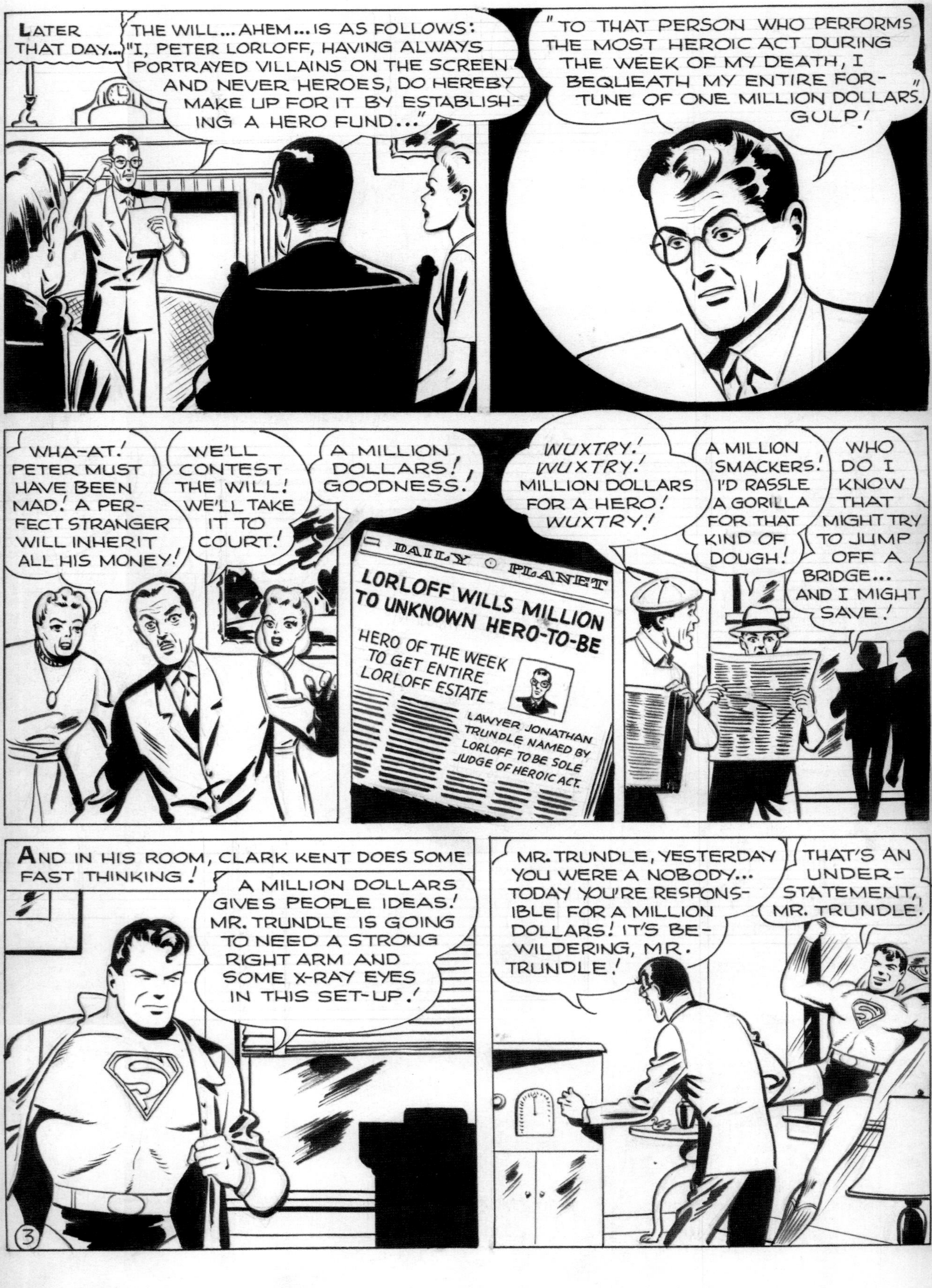
LATER THAT DAY...
THE WILL... AHEM... IS AS FOLLOWS: "I, PETER LORLOFF, HAVING ALWAYS PORTRAYED VILLAINS ON THE SCREEN AND NEVER HEROES, DO HEREBY MAKE UP FOR IT BY ESTABLISHING A HERO FUND..."
"TO THAT PERSON WHO PERFORMS THE MOST HEROIC ACT DURING THE WEEK OF MY DEATH, I BEQUEATH MY ENTIRE FORTUNE OF ONE MILLION DOLLARS." GULP!
WHA-AT! PETER MUST HAVE BEEN MAD! A PERFECT STRANGER WILL INHERIT ALL HIS MONEY!
WE'LL CONTEST THE WILL! WE'LL TAKE IT TO COURT!
A MILLION DOLLARS! GOODNESS!
DAILY PLANET
LORLOFF WILLS MILLION TO UNKNOWN HERO-TO-BE
HERO OF THE WEEK TO GET ENTIRE LORLOFF ESTATE
LAWYER JONATHAN TRUNDLE NAMED BY LORLOFF TO BE SOLE JUDGE OF HEROIC ACT.
WUXTRY! WUXTRY! MILLION DOLLARS FOR A HERO! WUXTRY!
A MILLION SMACKERS! I'D RASSLE A GORILLA FOR THAT KIND OF DOUGH!
WHO DO I KNOW THAT MIGHT TRY TO JUMP OFF A BRIDGE... AND I MIGHT SAVE!
AND IN HIS ROOM, CLARK KENT DOES SOME FAST THINKING!
A MILLION DOLLARS GIVES PEOPLE IDEAS! MR. TRUNDLE IS GOING TO NEED A STRONG RIGHT ARM AND SOME X-RAY EYES IN THIS SET-UP!
3
MR. TRUNDLE, YESTERDAY YOU WERE A NOBODY... TODAY YOU'RE RESPONSIBLE FOR A MILLION DOLLARS! IT'S BEWILDERING, MR. TRUNDLE!
THAT'S AN UNDERSTATEMENT, MR. TRUNDLE!

Panel 1: I KNOW YOU! YOU'RE MR. SUPERMAN WHO FLIES IN THE SKY!

A SPECIAL NEWS-FLASH! ON THE HEELS OF THE MILLION DOLLAR HERO FUND, COMES WORD THAT AN ATTEND-ANT IN THE CITY ZOO HAS JUST AVERTED A...

Panel 2: ...NEAR PANIC WHEN SATAN, A BENGAL TIGER, ESCAPED FROM HIS CAGE.

IT'S BEGINNING! WE'RE OFF, TRUNDLE!

Panel 3: THE CITY ZOO...

AW, IT WAS NOTHIN'!

NOTHING? YOU CALL IT NOTHING TO FORCE BACK A FEROCIOUS TIGER WITH A BIT OF TIMBER! YOU'RE A HERO, SIR!

("HOW DID THAT LOCK EVER COME OFF THAT CAGE-DOOR IN THE FIRST PLACE?")

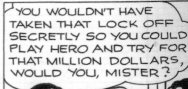

Panel 4: AND **SUPERMAN'S** X-RAY EYES SUPPLY THE ANSWER!

Panel 5: YOU WOULDN'T HAVE TAKEN THAT LOCK OFF SECRETLY SO YOU COULD PLAY HERO AND TRY FOR THAT MILLION DOLLARS, WOULD YOU, MISTER?

Panel 6: STAY AWAY FROM ME! DON'T... OOPS!

THE TIGER! THE TIGER!

Panel 7: YOU MEAN OL' TABBY CAT?

④

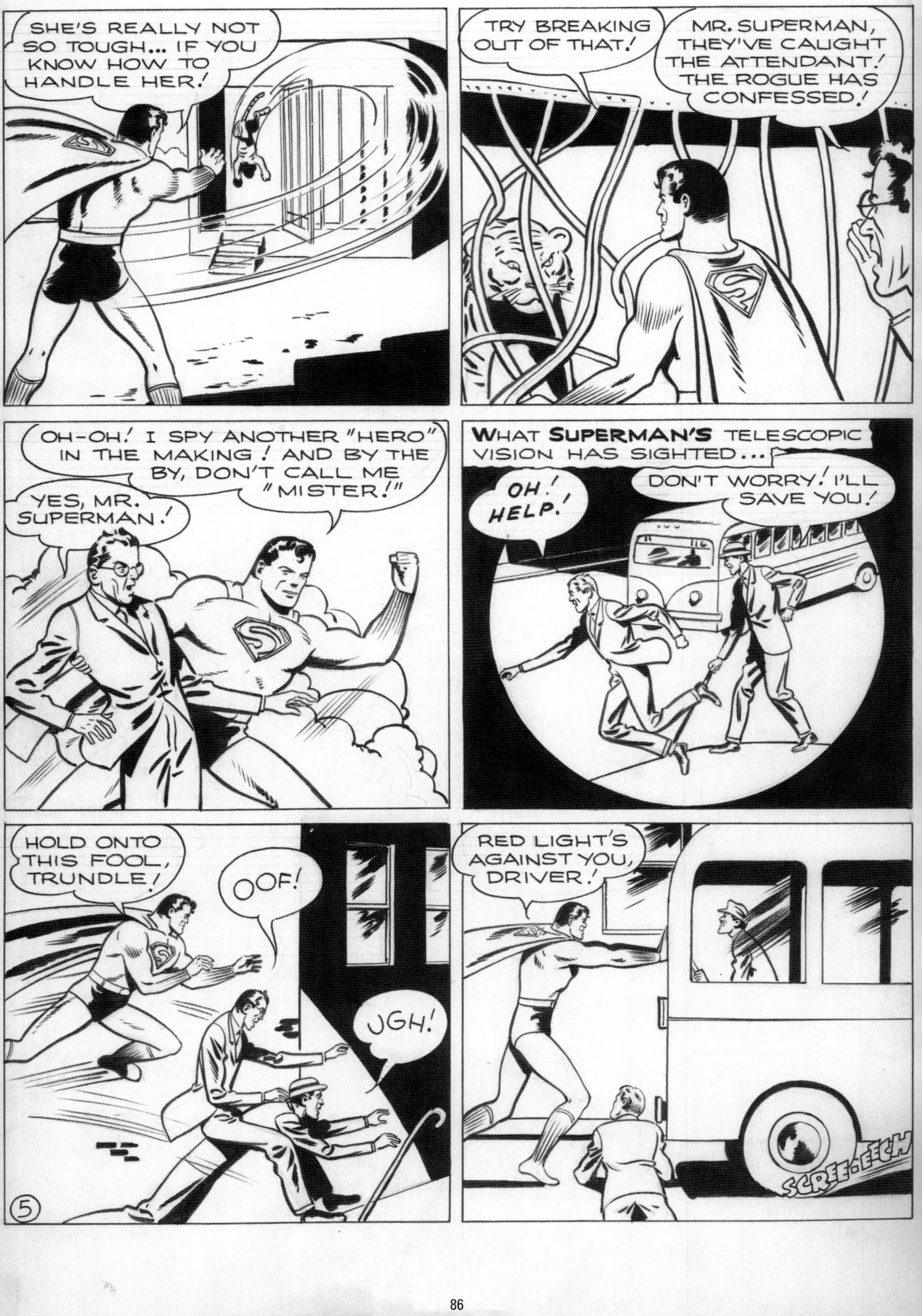
SHE'S REALLY NOT SO TOUGH... IF YOU KNOW HOW TO HANDLE HER!
TRY BREAKING OUT OF THAT!
MR. SUPERMAN, THEY'VE CAUGHT THE ATTENDANT! THE ROGUE HAS CONFESSED!
OH-OH! I SPY ANOTHER "HERO" IN THE MAKING! AND BY THE BY, DON'T CALL ME "MISTER!"
YES, MR. SUPERMAN!
WHAT SUPERMAN'S TELESCOPIC VISION HAS SIGHTED...
OH! HELP!
DON'T WORRY! I'LL SAVE YOU!
HOLD ONTO THIS FOOL, TRUNDLE!
OOF!
UGH!
5
RED LIGHT'S AGAINST YOU, DRIVER!
SCREE-EECH

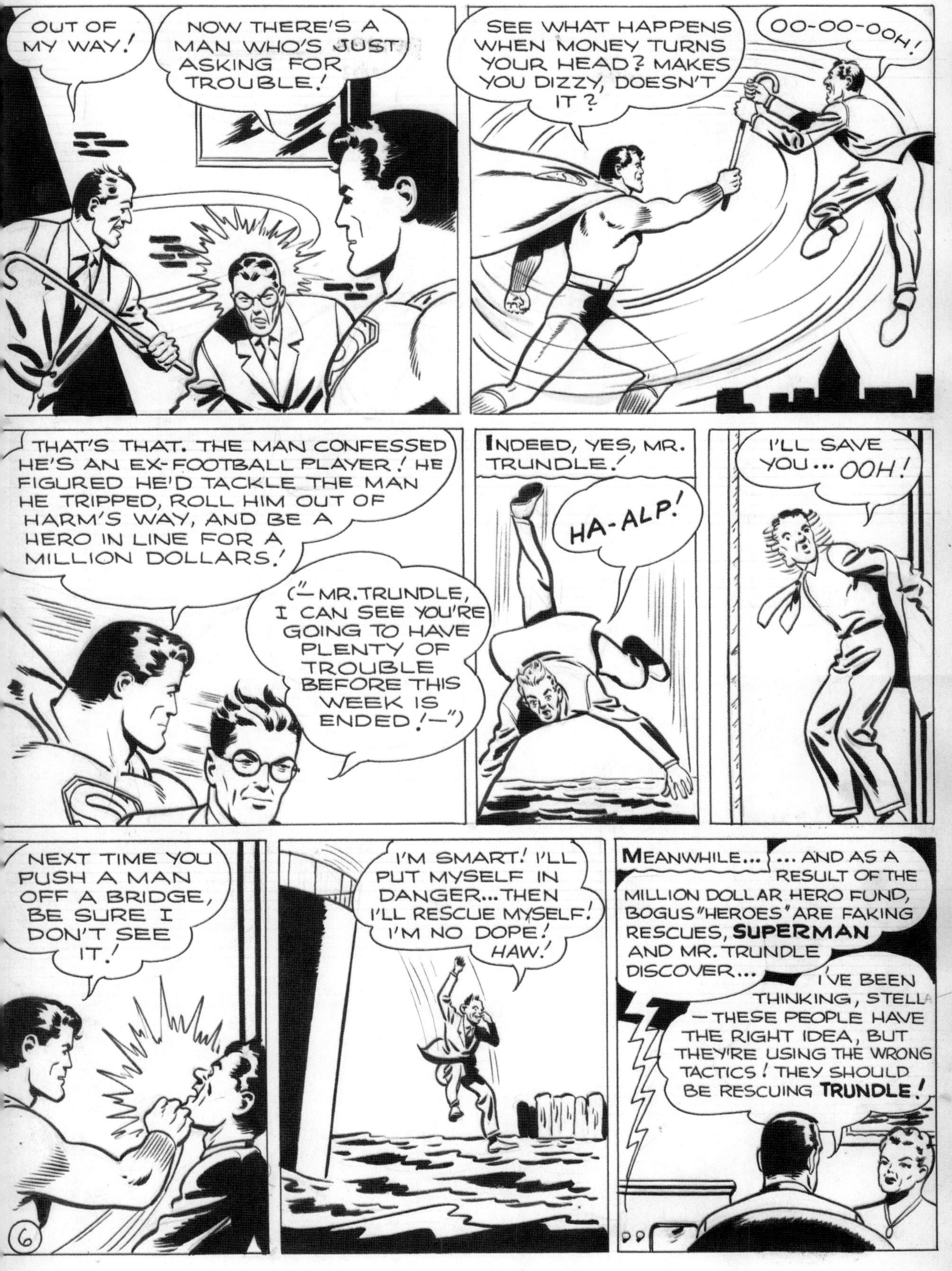

OUT OF MY WAY!
NOW THERE'S A MAN WHO'S JUST ASKING FOR TROUBLE!
SEE WHAT HAPPENS WHEN MONEY TURNS YOUR HEAD? MAKES YOU DIZZY, DOESN'T IT?
OO-OO-OOH!
THAT'S THAT. THE MAN CONFESSED HE'S AN EX-FOOTBALL PLAYER! HE FIGURED HE'D TACKLE THE MAN HE TRIPPED, ROLL HIM OUT OF HARM'S WAY, AND BE A HERO IN LINE FOR A MILLION DOLLARS!
("—MR. TRUNDLE, I CAN SEE YOU'RE GOING TO HAVE PLENTY OF TROUBLE BEFORE THIS WEEK IS ENDED!—")
INDEED, YES, MR. TRUNDLE!
HA-ALP!
I'LL SAVE YOU... OOH!
NEXT TIME YOU PUSH A MAN OFF A BRIDGE, BE SURE I DON'T SEE IT!
6
I'M SMART! I'LL PUT MYSELF IN DANGER... THEN I'LL RESCUE MYSELF! I'M NO DOPE! HAW!
MEANWHILE...
... AND AS A RESULT OF THE MILLION DOLLAR HERO FUND, BOGUS "HEROES" ARE FAKING RESCUES, SUPERMAN AND MR. TRUNDLE DISCOVER...
I'VE BEEN THINKING, STELLA — THESE PEOPLE HAVE THE RIGHT IDEA, BUT THEY'RE USING THE WRONG TACTICS! THEY SHOULD BE RESCUING TRUNDLE!

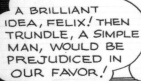

A BRILLIANT IDEA, FELIX! THEN TRUNDLE, A SIMPLE MAN, WOULD BE PREJUDICED IN OUR FAVOR!

AND THE COURT WOULD FAVOR OUR **UNSELFISH ACT!** WE'D BE RESCUING THE ONE THAT COULD DEPRIVE US OF A MILLION DOLLARS!

("—WHAT SHALL I DO? WARN TRUNDLE? OR TELL FELIX AND STELLA I OVERHEARD THEM? THEY'D HAVE TO CUT ME IN ON THE MILLION, THEN! WHAT SHALL I DO?—")

THAT NIGHT, IN THE OLD TENEMENT WHERE TRUNDLE ROOMS, FIRE LEAPS UP ITS WOODEN BEAMS!

FIRE! FIRE!

MR. TRUNDLE! ARE YOU IN THERE?

HE COULDN'T POSSIBLY BE SLEEPING THROUGH ALL THIS RACKET! HE'S NOT HOME! LET'S GET OUT! THIS HALL WILL GO UP IN A MINUTE!

BAM BAM!

MEANWHILE, AT THE DAILY PLANET, CLARK LISTENS TO A PANICKY GIRL...

FELIX MIGHT NOT BE ABLE TO RESCUE TRUNDLE FROM WHATEVER DANGER HE PUT HIM IN! I COULDN'T GO TO THE POLICE! AFTER ALL, STELLA IS MY AUNT! I'VE HEARD YOU CAN GET **SUPERMAN!** YOU MUST CALL HIM NOW!

OKAY! YOU GO OVER TO TRUNDLE'S FLAT! I'LL GET **SUPERMAN!**

A LIGHTNING SWITCH, AND **SUPERMAN** IS AWAY!

TAXI!

⑦

88

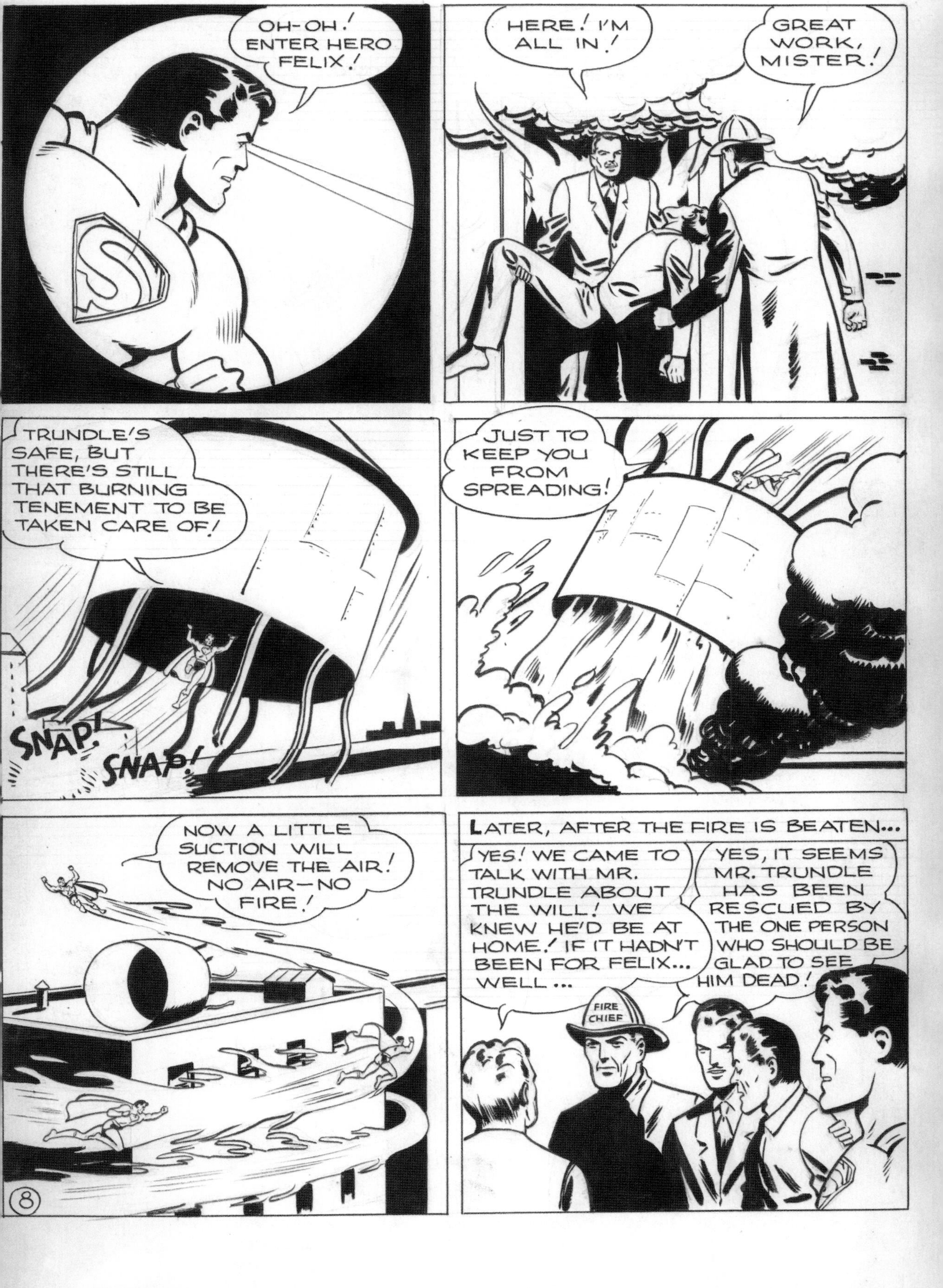
OH-OH! ENTER HERO FELIX!
HERE! I'M ALL IN!
GREAT WORK, MISTER!
TRUNDLE'S SAFE, BUT THERE'S STILL THAT BURNING TENEMENT TO BE TAKEN CARE OF!
SNAP! SNAP!
JUST TO KEEP YOU FROM SPREADING!
NOW A LITTLE SUCTION WILL REMOVE THE AIR! NO AIR—NO FIRE!
8
LATER, AFTER THE FIRE IS BEATEN...
YES! WE CAME TO TALK WITH MR. TRUNDLE ABOUT THE WILL! WE KNEW HE'D BE AT HOME! IF IT HADN'T BEEN FOR FELIX... WELL...
YES, IT SEEMS MR. TRUNDLE HAS BEEN RESCUED BY THE ONE PERSON WHO SHOULD BE GLAD TO SEE HIM DEAD!
FIRE CHIEF

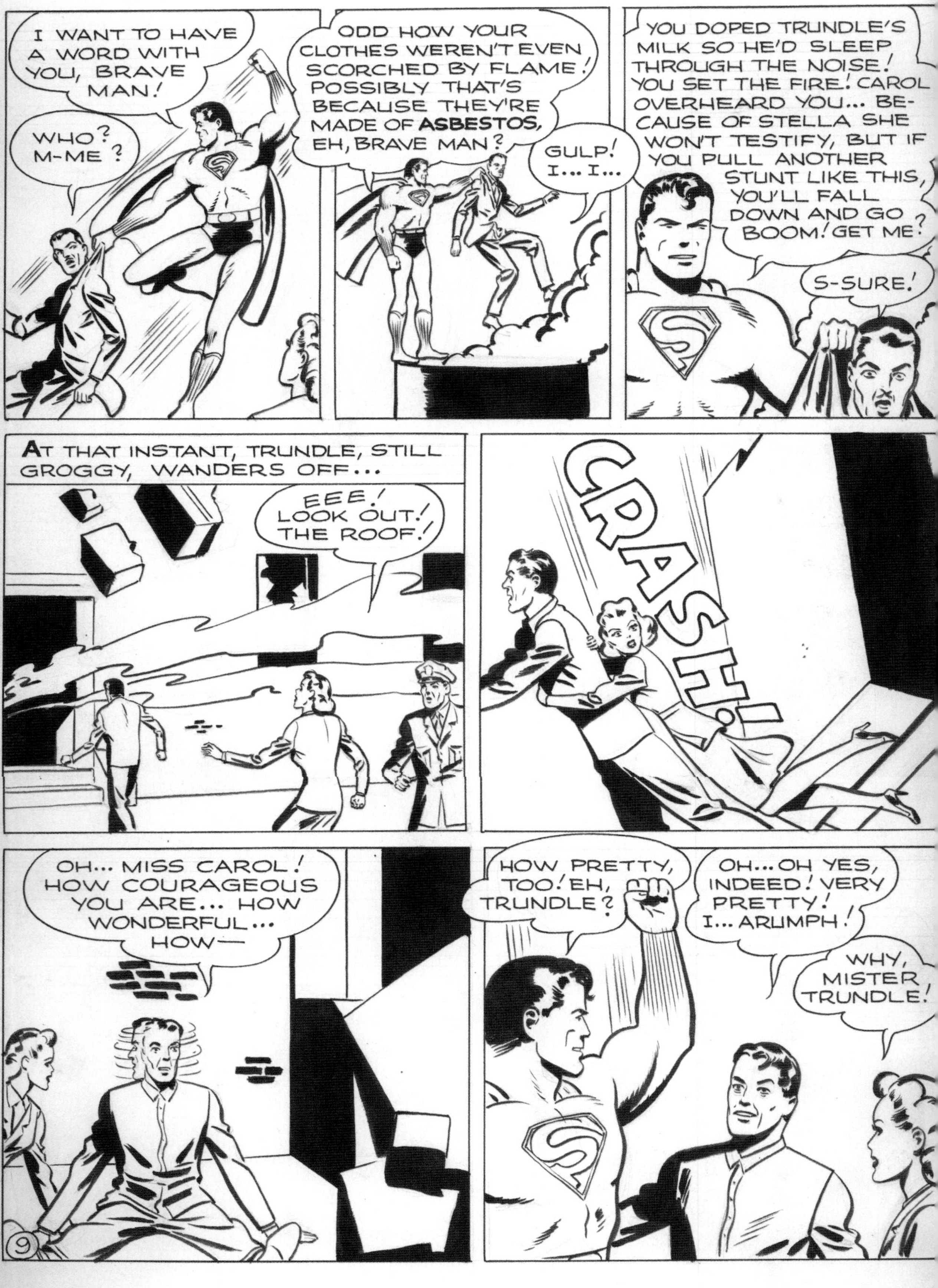

I WANT TO HAVE A WORD WITH YOU, BRAVE MAN!
WHO? M-ME?
ODD HOW YOUR CLOTHES WEREN'T EVEN SCORCHED BY FLAME! POSSIBLY THAT'S BECAUSE THEY'RE MADE OF ASBESTOS, EH, BRAVE MAN?
GULP! I... I...
YOU DOPED TRUNDLE'S MILK SO HE'D SLEEP THROUGH THE NOISE! YOU SET THE FIRE! CAROL OVERHEARD YOU... BECAUSE OF STELLA SHE WON'T TESTIFY, BUT IF YOU PULL ANOTHER STUNT LIKE THIS, YOU'LL FALL DOWN AND GO BOOM! GET ME?
S-SURE!
AT THAT INSTANT, TRUNDLE, STILL GROGGY, WANDERS OFF...
EEE! LOOK OUT! THE ROOF!
CRASH!
OH... MISS CAROL! HOW COURAGEOUS YOU ARE... HOW WONDERFUL... HOW—
HOW PRETTY, TOO! EH, TRUNDLE?
OH... OH YES, INDEED! VERY PRETTY! I... ARUMPH!
WHY, MISTER TRUNDLE!

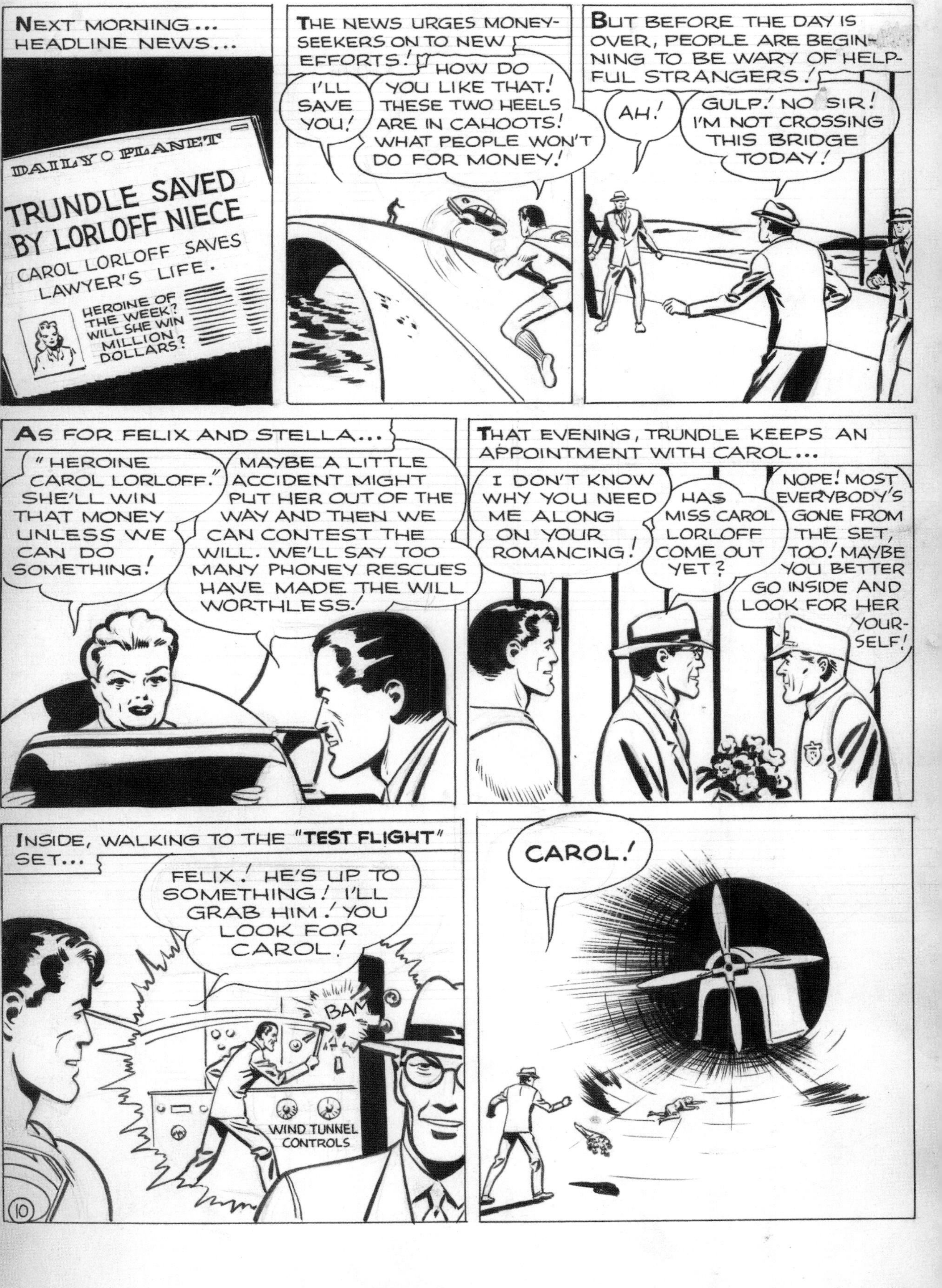
NEXT MORNING... HEADLINE NEWS...
DAILY PLANET
TRUNDLE SAVED BY LORLOFF NIECE
CAROL LORLOFF SAVES LAWYER'S LIFE.
HEROINE OF THE WEEK? WILL SHE WIN MILLION DOLLARS?
THE NEWS URGES MONEY-SEEKERS ON TO NEW EFFORTS!
I'LL SAVE YOU!
HOW DO YOU LIKE THAT! THESE TWO HEELS ARE IN CAHOOTS! WHAT PEOPLE WON'T DO FOR MONEY!
BUT BEFORE THE DAY IS OVER, PEOPLE ARE BEGINNING TO BE WARY OF HELPFUL STRANGERS!
AH!
GULP! NO SIR! I'M NOT CROSSING THIS BRIDGE TODAY!
AS FOR FELIX AND STELLA...
"HEROINE CAROL LORLOFF." SHE'LL WIN THAT MONEY UNLESS WE CAN DO SOMETHING!
MAYBE A LITTLE ACCIDENT MIGHT PUT HER OUT OF THE WAY AND THEN WE CAN CONTEST THE WILL. WE'LL SAY TOO MANY PHONEY RESCUES HAVE MADE THE WILL WORTHLESS!
THAT EVENING, TRUNDLE KEEPS AN APPOINTMENT WITH CAROL...
I DON'T KNOW WHY YOU NEED ME ALONG ON YOUR ROMANCING!
HAS MISS CAROL LORLOFF COME OUT YET?
NOPE! MOST EVERYBODY'S GONE FROM THE SET, TOO! MAYBE YOU BETTER GO INSIDE AND LOOK FOR HER YOURSELF!
INSIDE, WALKING TO THE "TEST FLIGHT" SET...
FELIX! HE'S UP TO SOMETHING! I'LL GRAB HIM! YOU LOOK FOR CAROL!
BAM
WIND TUNNEL CONTROLS
10
CAROL!

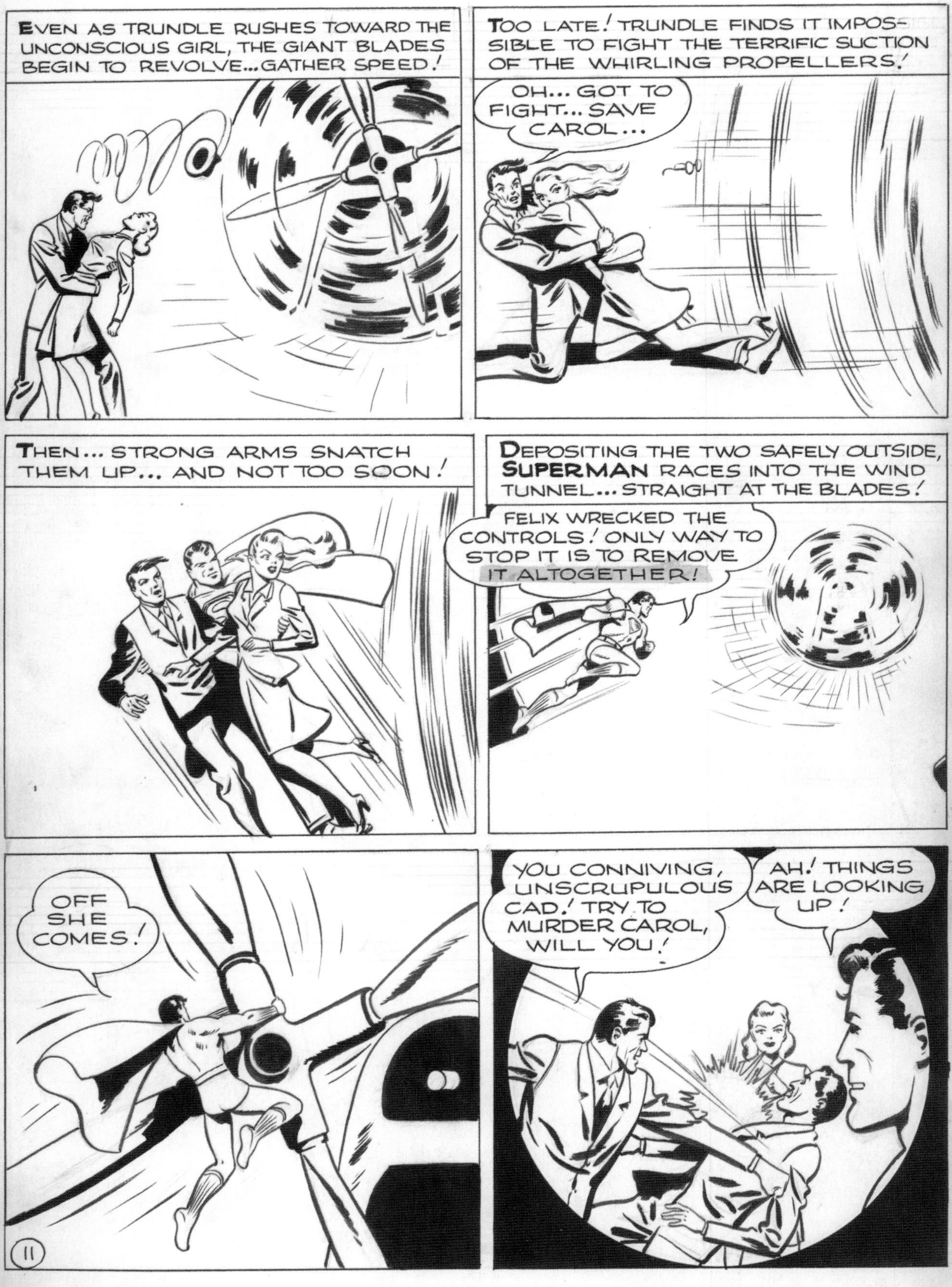
EVEN AS TRUNDLE RUSHES TOWARD THE UNCONSCIOUS GIRL, THE GIANT BLADES BEGIN TO REVOLVE...GATHER SPEED!
TOO LATE! TRUNDLE FINDS IT IMPOSSIBLE TO FIGHT THE TERRIFIC SUCTION OF THE WHIRLING PROPELLERS!
OH... GOT TO FIGHT... SAVE CAROL...
THEN... STRONG ARMS SNATCH THEM UP... AND NOT TOO SOON!
DEPOSITING THE TWO SAFELY OUTSIDE, SUPERMAN RACES INTO THE WIND TUNNEL... STRAIGHT AT THE BLADES!
FELIX WRECKED THE CONTROLS! ONLY WAY TO STOP IT IS TO REMOVE IT ALTOGETHER!
OFF SHE COMES!
11
YOU CONNIVING, UNSCRUPULOUS CAD! TRY TO MURDER CAROL, WILL YOU!
AH! THINGS ARE LOOKING UP!

OH, JONATHAN, YOU'RE WONDERFUL!

SAY, WHAT'S HAPPENING AROUND HERE!

CAN'T YOU SEE?

BUT STELLA IS NOT BEATEN YET! AS THE WEEK ENDS, SHE CONTESTS THE WILL IN COURT...

ALL THESE NEWSPAPERS TELL OF FAKE RESCUES BY EAGER, MONEY-SEEKING STRANGERS! HOW CAN TRUNDLE GIVE THAT MONEY TO A HERO WHEN THERE ARE TOO MANY "HEROES" BEING CREATED?

I'M AFRAID MRS. SAVAT IS RIGHT, MR. TRUNDLE! THIS WILL HAS ALREADY INSTIGATED MASS COLLUSION IN METROPOLIS! UNLESS YOU CAN FIND ONE REAL HERO, I MUST DECLARE THE WILL NULL AND VOID.

I KNOW OF ONE HERO, JUDGE!

WHOM HAVE YOU IN MIND, SUPERMAN?

TRUNDLE, HIMSELF!

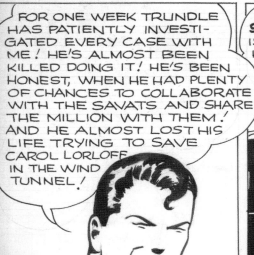

FOR ONE WEEK TRUNDLE HAS PATIENTLY INVESTIGATED EVERY CASE WITH ME! HE'S ALMOST BEEN KILLED DOING IT! HE'S BEEN HONEST, WHEN HE HAD PLENTY OF CHANCES TO COLLABORATE WITH THE SAVATS AND SHARE THE MILLION WITH THEM! AND HE ALMOST LOST HIS LIFE TRYING TO SAVE CAROL LORLOFF IN THE WIND TUNNEL!

YOU'RE RIGHT, SUPERMAN! MR. TRUNDLE IS REALLY THE WEEK'S HERO! I HEREBY APPOINT MR. TRUNDLE TO AWARD THE MILLION DOLLARS, TO MR. TRUNDLE!

GOODNESS ME!

CAROL, NOW I'VE ENOUGH MONEY! NOW I CAN ASK YOU! WILL YOU MARRY ME?

OF COURSE I WILL!

THANK YOU, JUDGE!

THANK YOU!

12

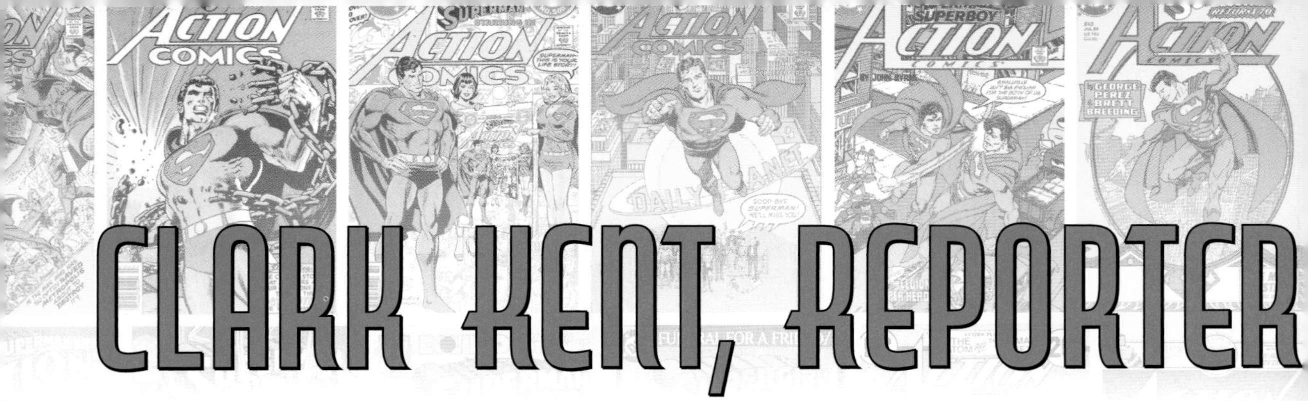
ACTION COMICS
ACTION COMICS
ACTION COMICS
SUPERBOY
ACTION COMICS
ACTION COMICS
GEORGE PEREZ
BRETT BREEDING

CLARK KENT, REPORTER

by **DAVID HAJDU**

Who fights for truth?

It is the first principle, followed by justice, in the manifesto of the "never-ending battle" that Superman has fought for eight decades now. Truth and justice would always be the guiding ideals of the displaced Kal-El's life on Earth. In fact, they were the only values mentioned explicitly when the credo of his mission was adapted from the pages of Golden Age comics and crystallized in the narration for the *Adventures of Superman* radio series (broadcast from 1940 to 1951). "The American way" would be added, strategically, when Superman came to television in 1952, during the heat of the Red Scare. To this day, truth and justice—and, hell, sure, the American way, too—are the words we tend to tend to think of when we try to articulate what Superman represents.

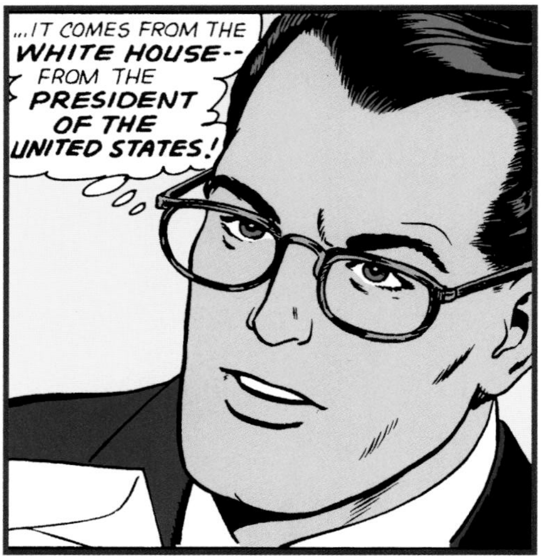
...IT COMES FROM THE WHITE HOUSE-- FROM THE PRESIDENT OF THE UNITED STATES!

Yet in his role as a godly endowed hero among humans, Superman has always been much more concerned with the dispensing of justice than the revealing of truth. He hunts and catches villains, crooks and evildoers of all kinds—earthly, alien, extradimensional or inexplicable—and enforces a resolutely held super-code of right and wrong. If he sometimes skips over the niceties of due process, it's in the name of bringing redress to wrongdoing. He's serving justice, in or out of the judicial system.

It's not Superman, but Kal-El's other terrestrial persona, Clark Kent, whose public mission is to serve the truth. He's a reporter, working full time, five days a week—with hours that are apparently very, very flexible, and time off for holidays and intergalactic crises—at a profession dedicated to the pursuit of the facts.

In the early issues of ACTION COMICS and SUPERMAN, co-creators Jerry Siegel and Joe Shuster made clear that they saw both sides of their cleverly dualistic character as companionably heroic. Clark's work as a journalist often drove the narratives, much as it would in the radio shows, movie serials, George Reeves TV series and, later, in many episodes of *Lois and Clark.* As various early versions of Superman's origin explained, Clark took up journalism in the first place because he saw it as helpful to his second job as a superhero.

"I've got it!" he realizes in a thought balloon. "I could become a reporter on the leading paper in Metropolis! As a reporter, I could investigate criminals without their suspecting I'm really Superman!"

In another account of this decision, he tells himself, "As a reporter, I'd be among the first to learn of crimes and disasters." It is a sign of the awe in which journalistic methods were held at the time that a super-powered alien (and his creators) would think that the skills of good interview technique and careful note-taking would be more useful than X-ray vision, telescopic vision, microscopic vision, super-hearing, super-speed and the power of flight.

Actually, Clark Kent never showed much talent as a reporter in the comics pages, his typing speed notwithstanding—at least not until the John Byrne reboot in the mid-1980s. (Byrne's Kent was not only a Pulitzer Prize-winning journalist but the author of two best-selling novels, *The Janus Contract* and *Under a Yellow Sun.*) Until then, Clark's defining traits were not the perseverance, the resourcefulness, the wile and the intellectual dexterity that distinguish great journalists, but cowardice, social awkwardness, klutziness and physical weakness. When an effective reporter would need to stand firm in the face of danger or stand up to the forces of oppression or abuse,

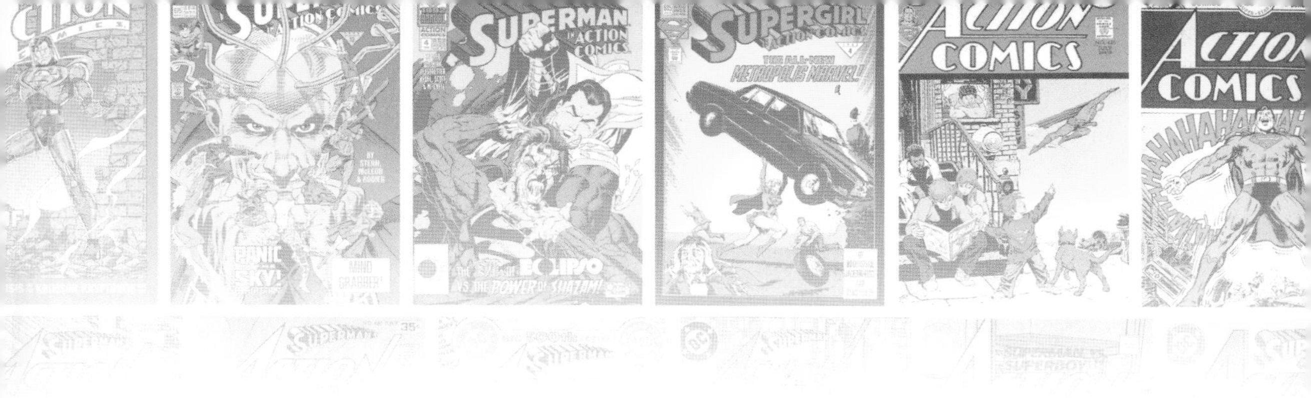
SUPERMAN IN ACTION COMICS
ACTION COMICS
ACTION COMICS

Clark would generally hide or run away or faint. One comic tracing the story of his career shows him as a student at Metropolis University on Graduation Day, about to receive his Bachelor's degree in Journalism when he trips and falls in front of the entire student body.

Readers all knew that his goofus act was just part of his "disguise as Clark Kent," of course—a ruse to protect his secret identity. It worked, with considerable suspension of disbelief by both comics readers and the citizens of Metropolis, because it was a characterization not far removed from the image of journalists in the popular imagination. Movies and magazine fiction had already implanted a conception of reporters as sloths and drunkards, bottom-feeders of dubious integrity, more than likely on the take. Clark Kent, stumbling and cowering, would fit right in with the groggy, spineless hack reporters in movies such as Frank Capra's *Meet John Doe* (1936) and *Mr. Smith Goes to Washington* (1939).

Even after DC editors transferred him to TV news in an attempt to update the character in the 1970s, Clark's "mild-mannered" shtick made him ill-suited to his job. The comics made a contorted attempt to deal with this quandary in a story called "The Man in the Public Eye." Morgan Edge, the head of the company producing the news broadcasts, Galaxy Communications, summons Clark to his office to bawl him out. "There's no *zing* in your broadcasts, Kent!" Edge barks. "You've had the charisma of a grape!" (As part of the upgrade of his status, Clark has relocated from a *Planet* to a Galaxy.)

The one incontestably, consistently excellent journalist in Metropolis was already established as a star reporter when Clark Kent was hired at the *Daily Planet*: Lois Lane. Fearless and determined to get her story at all costs, she upstaged Clark with countless banner headlines, usually having to do with the exploits of Superman. While Lois gloats over yet another front-page scoop in a typical early story, Clark pleads, "Please don't rub it in! The boss has already warned me to wake up—or hunt for another job!"

Lois turns to him and says, "I'm sorry! I hate to make you look like a fool all the time—but if you are one, can I help it?"

Lois, unlike Clark himself, has no reason to want him to seem too flawed to do his job well. But she's a journalist, and she has a duty to the truth.

DAVID HAJDU is a professor at Columbia University's Graduate School of Journalism and author of several books on American cultural history, including The Ten-Cent Plague: The Great Comic Book Scare and How It Changed America.

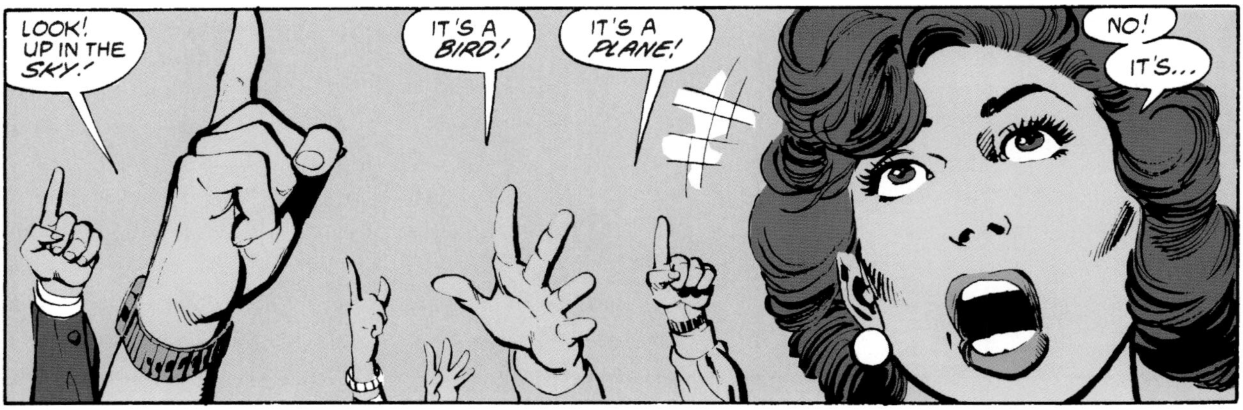
LOOK! UP IN THE SKY!
IT'S A BIRD!
IT'S A PLANE!
NO! IT'S...

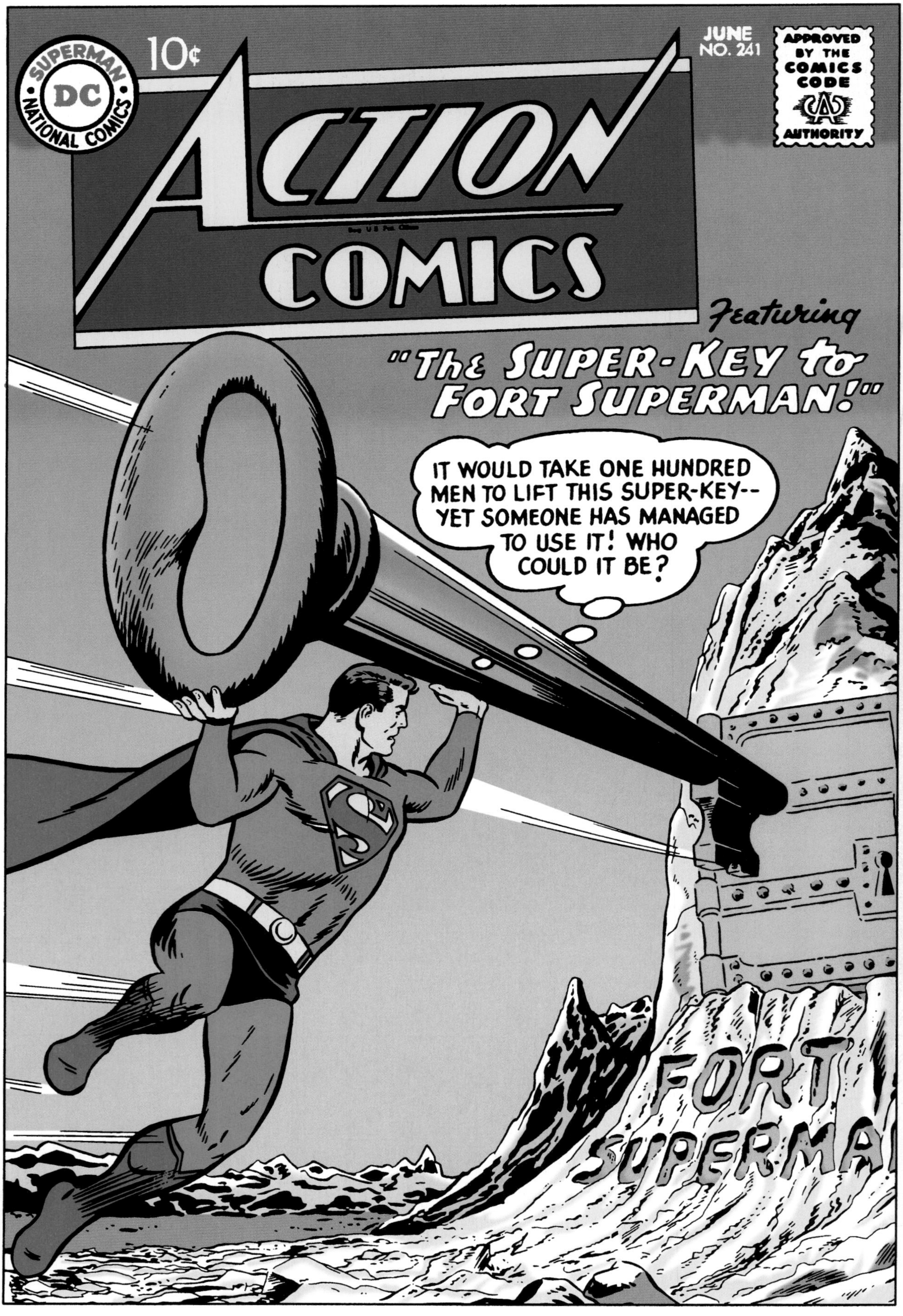
SUPERMAN DC NATIONAL COMICS
10¢
ACTION COMICS
JUNE NO. 241
APPROVED BY THE COMICS CODE AUTHORITY
Featuring "The SUPER-KEY to FORT SUPERMAN!"
IT WOULD TAKE ONE HUNDRED MEN TO LIFT THIS SUPER-KEY-- YET SOMEONE HAS MANAGED TO USE IT! WHO COULD IT BE?
FORT SUPERMA

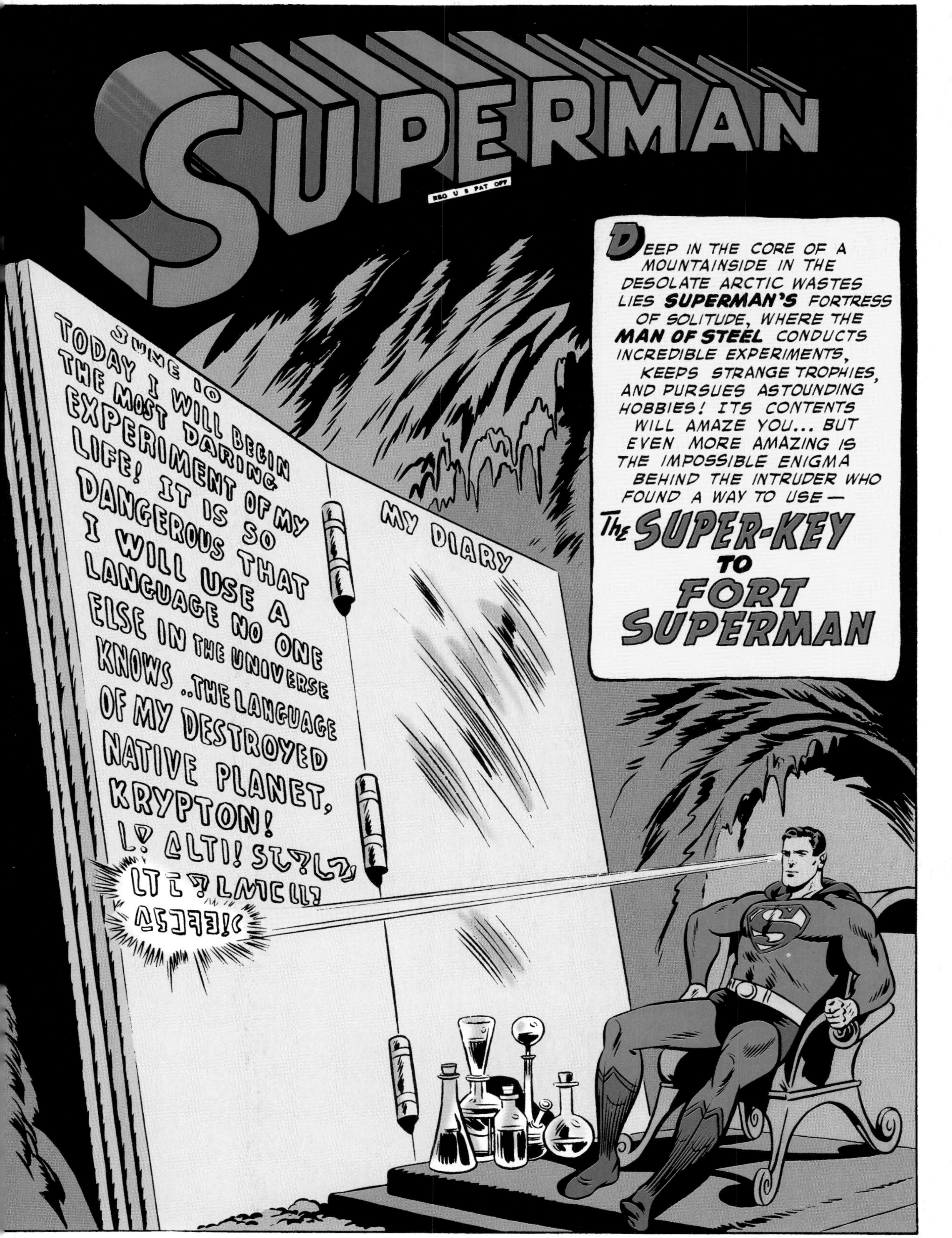
SUPERMAN
REG U S PAT OFF
DEEP IN THE CORE OF A MOUNTAINSIDE IN THE DESOLATE ARCTIC WASTES LIES SUPERMAN'S FORTRESS OF SOLITUDE, WHERE THE MAN OF STEEL CONDUCTS INCREDIBLE EXPERIMENTS, KEEPS STRANGE TROPHIES, AND PURSUES ASTOUNDING HOBBIES! ITS CONTENTS WILL AMAZE YOU... BUT EVEN MORE AMAZING IS THE IMPOSSIBLE ENIGMA BEHIND THE INTRUDER WHO FOUND A WAY TO USE—
The SUPER-KEY TO FORT SUPERMAN
JUNE 10
TODAY I WILL BEGIN THE MOST DARING EXPERIMENT OF MY LIFE! IT IS SO DANGEROUS THAT I WILL USE A LANGUAGE NO ONE ELSE IN THE UNIVERSE KNOWS ..THE LANGUAGE OF MY DESTROYED NATIVE PLANET, KRYPTON!
MY DIARY

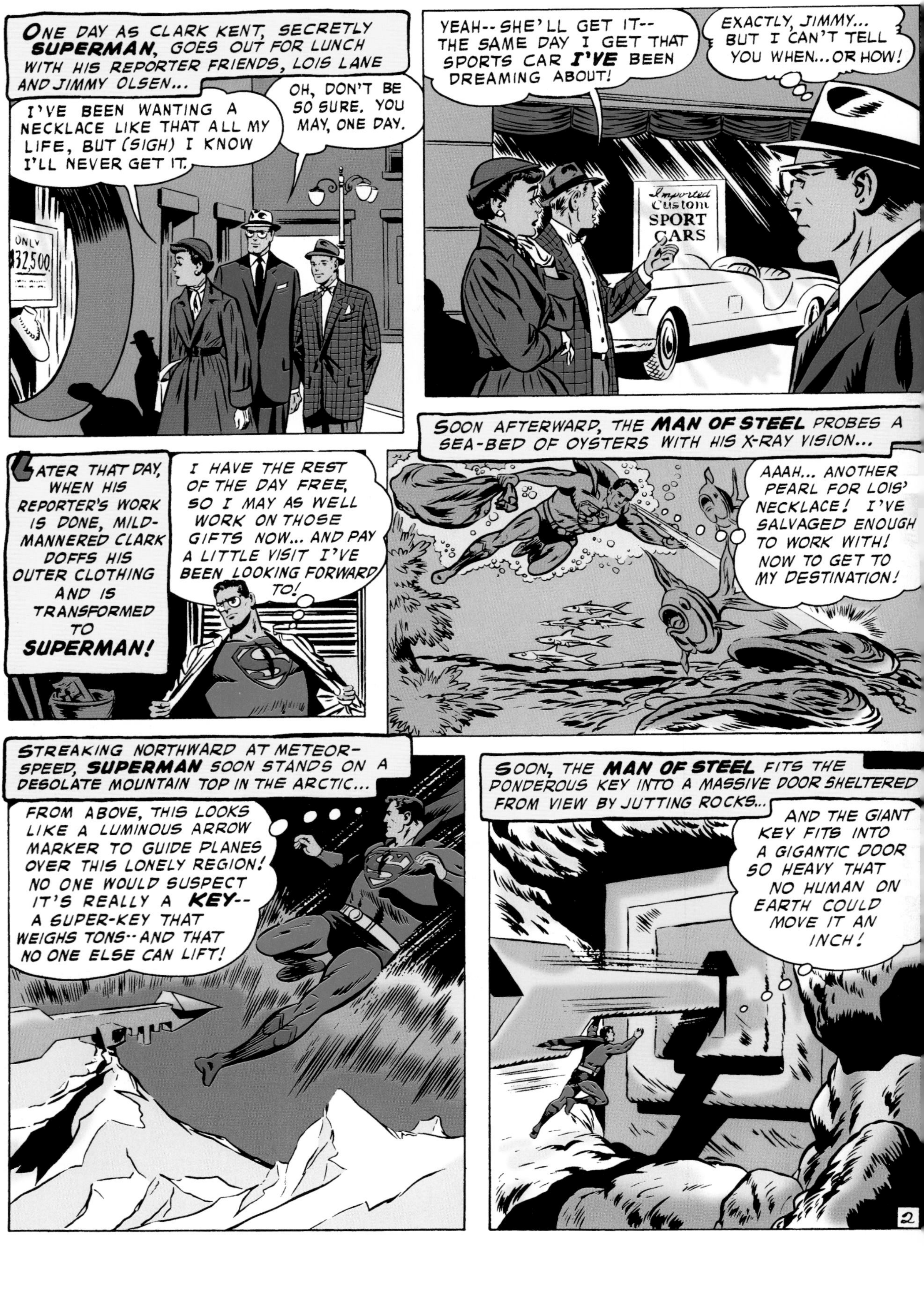
ONE DAY AS CLARK KENT, SECRETLY SUPERMAN, GOES OUT FOR LUNCH WITH HIS REPORTER FRIENDS, LOIS LANE AND JIMMY OLSEN...
I'VE BEEN WANTING A NECKLACE LIKE THAT ALL MY LIFE, BUT (SIGH) I KNOW I'LL NEVER GET IT.
OH, DON'T BE SO SURE. YOU MAY, ONE DAY.
ONLY
$32,500
YEAH--SHE'LL GET IT--THE SAME DAY I GET THAT SPORTS CAR I'VE BEEN DREAMING ABOUT!
EXACTLY, JIMMY... BUT I CAN'T TELL YOU WHEN...OR HOW!
Imported Custom SPORT CARS
LATER THAT DAY, WHEN HIS REPORTER'S WORK IS DONE, MILD-MANNERED CLARK DOFFS HIS OUTER CLOTHING AND IS TRANSFORMED TO SUPERMAN!
I HAVE THE REST OF THE DAY FREE, SO I MAY AS WELL WORK ON THOSE GIFTS NOW... AND PAY A LITTLE VISIT I'VE BEEN LOOKING FORWARD TO!
SOON AFTERWARD, THE MAN OF STEEL PROBES A SEA-BED OF OYSTERS WITH HIS X-RAY VISION...
AAAH... ANOTHER PEARL FOR LOIS' NECKLACE! I'VE SALVAGED ENOUGH TO WORK WITH! NOW TO GET TO MY DESTINATION!
STREAKING NORTHWARD AT METEOR-SPEED, SUPERMAN SOON STANDS ON A DESOLATE MOUNTAIN TOP IN THE ARCTIC...
FROM ABOVE, THIS LOOKS LIKE A LUMINOUS ARROW MARKER TO GUIDE PLANES OVER THIS LONELY REGION! NO ONE WOULD SUSPECT IT'S REALLY A KEY-- A SUPER-KEY THAT WEIGHS TONS--AND THAT NO ONE ELSE CAN LIFT!
SOON, THE MAN OF STEEL FITS THE PONDEROUS KEY INTO A MASSIVE DOOR SHELTERED FROM VIEW BY JUTTING ROCKS...
AND THE GIANT KEY FITS INTO A GIGANTIC DOOR SO HEAVY THAT NO HUMAN ON EARTH COULD MOVE IT AN INCH!
2

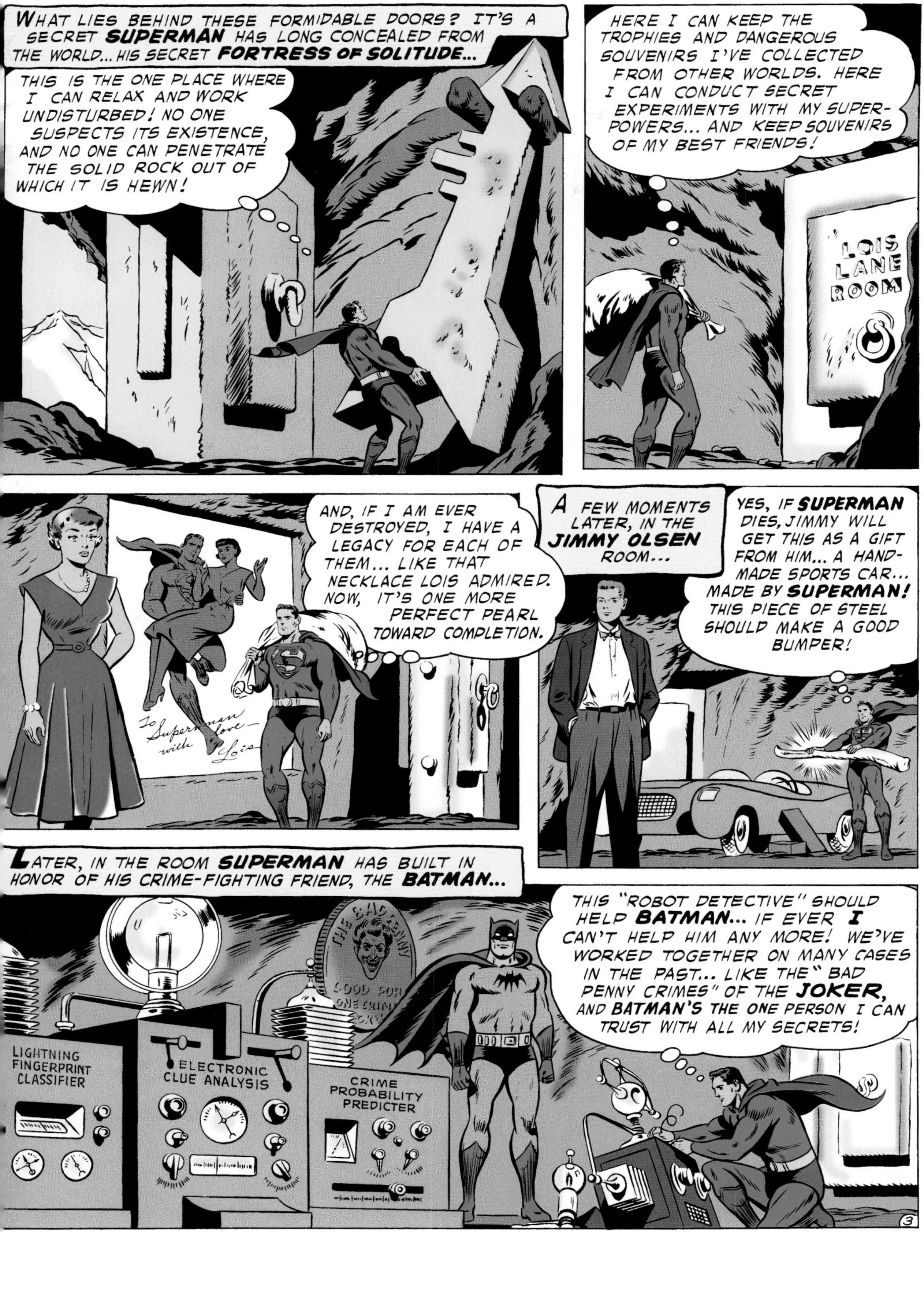

WHAT LIES BEHIND THESE FORMIDABLE DOORS? IT'S A SECRET SUPERMAN HAS LONG CONCEALED FROM THE WORLD... HIS SECRET FORTRESS OF SOLITUDE...
THIS IS THE ONE PLACE WHERE I CAN RELAX AND WORK UNDISTURBED! NO ONE SUSPECTS ITS EXISTENCE, AND NO ONE CAN PENETRATE THE SOLID ROCK OUT OF WHICH IT IS HEWN!
HERE I CAN KEEP THE TROPHIES AND DANGEROUS SOUVENIRS I'VE COLLECTED FROM OTHER WORLDS. HERE I CAN CONDUCT SECRET EXPERIMENTS WITH MY SUPER-POWERS... AND KEEP SOUVENIRS OF MY BEST FRIENDS!
LOIS LANE ROOM
AND, IF I AM EVER DESTROYED, I HAVE A LEGACY FOR EACH OF THEM... LIKE THAT NECKLACE LOIS ADMIRED. NOW, IT'S ONE MORE PERFECT PEARL TOWARD COMPLETION.
To Superman with love — Lois
A FEW MOMENTS LATER, IN THE JIMMY OLSEN ROOM...
YES, IF SUPERMAN DIES, JIMMY WILL GET THIS AS A GIFT FROM HIM... A HAND-MADE SPORTS CAR... MADE BY SUPERMAN! THIS PIECE OF STEEL SHOULD MAKE A GOOD BUMPER!
LATER, IN THE ROOM SUPERMAN HAS BUILT IN HONOR OF HIS CRIME-FIGHTING FRIEND, THE BATMAN...
THE BAD PENNY
GOOD FOR ONE CRIME JOKER
THIS "ROBOT DETECTIVE" SHOULD HELP BATMAN... IF EVER I CAN'T HELP HIM ANY MORE! WE'VE WORKED TOGETHER ON MANY CASES IN THE PAST... LIKE THE "BAD PENNY CRIMES" OF THE JOKER, AND BATMAN'S THE ONE PERSON I CAN TRUST WITH ALL MY SECRETS!
LIGHTNING FINGERPRINT CLASSIFIER
ELECTRONIC CLUE ANALYSIS
CRIME PROBABILITY PREDICTER
3

PRESENTLY, IN STILL ANOTHER CHAMBER OF THIS UNDERGROUND LABYRINTH OF WONDERS...

I'VE EVEN MADE A CLARK KENT ROOM! CLARK IS KNOWN TO BE A FRIEND OF **SUPERMAN**, AND IF SOME UNEXPECTED EARTHQUAKE EVER OPENED MY SECRET CAVE TO A STRANGER THAT WAX CLARK WOULD HELP PRESERVE THE SECRET OF MY IDENTITY!

AND, EVEN A **SUPERMAN** MUST HAVE HOBBIES... OR SUPER-HOBBIES!

NOW TO ENJOY SOME PAINTING! THIS ISN'T THE RESULT OF MY IMAGINATION -- IT'S A REALISTIC PICTURE OF A MARTIAN LANDSCAPE, AS OBSERVED BY MY TELESCOPIC VISION!

YES, IT'S A BUSY, PLEASANT VISIT FOR **SUPERMAN** AS HE WINDS UP THE DAY WITH AN IMPORTANT EXPERIMENT!

IN THIS LEAD ARMOR, I'M IMMUNE TO **KRYPTONITE** RAYS... AND CAN STUDY IT TO SEE IF I CAN OVERCOME ITS DANGEROUS EFFECT ON ME. WHEN I'VE FINISHED EXPERIMENTING, I'LL PUT IT BACK IN A LEAD CONTAINER.

FINALLY, THE **MAN OF STEEL** PAYS A RELUCTANT FAREWELL TO HIS MOUNTAIN FORTRESS OF SILENCE AND SOLITUDE...

WHAT A WONDERFUL NIGHT! IT'S NOT OFTEN I GET TIME TO MYSELF...TIME WHICH I CAN USE FOR MY HOBBIES AND SELF-IMPROVEMENT!

NEXT DAY, AS **SUPERMAN** RESPONDS TO AN URGENT CALL FROM A FAMOUS SCIENTIST...

I'VE CREATED A METAL WHICH I THINK EVEN **YOU** CAN'T BREAK! PLEASE TRY IT OUT IN SOME ISOLATED PLACE. I'M AFRAID REVERBERATIONS MAY SHATTER BUILDINGS IF YOU HIT IT WITH ALL YOUR STRENGTH!

GOOD! IT GIVES ME AN EXCUSE TO PAY ANOTHER VISIT TO MY HIDEOUT!

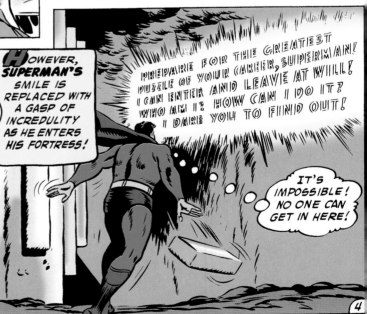

HOWEVER, **SUPERMAN'S** SMILE IS REPLACED WITH A GASP OF INCREDULITY AS HE ENTERS HIS FORTRESS!

PREPARE FOR THE GREATEST PUZZLE OF YOUR CAREER, SUPERMAN! I CAN ENTER AND LEAVE AT WILL! WHO AM I? HOW CAN I DO IT? I DARE YOU TO FIND OUT!

IT'S IMPOSSIBLE! NO ONE CAN GET IN HERE!

4

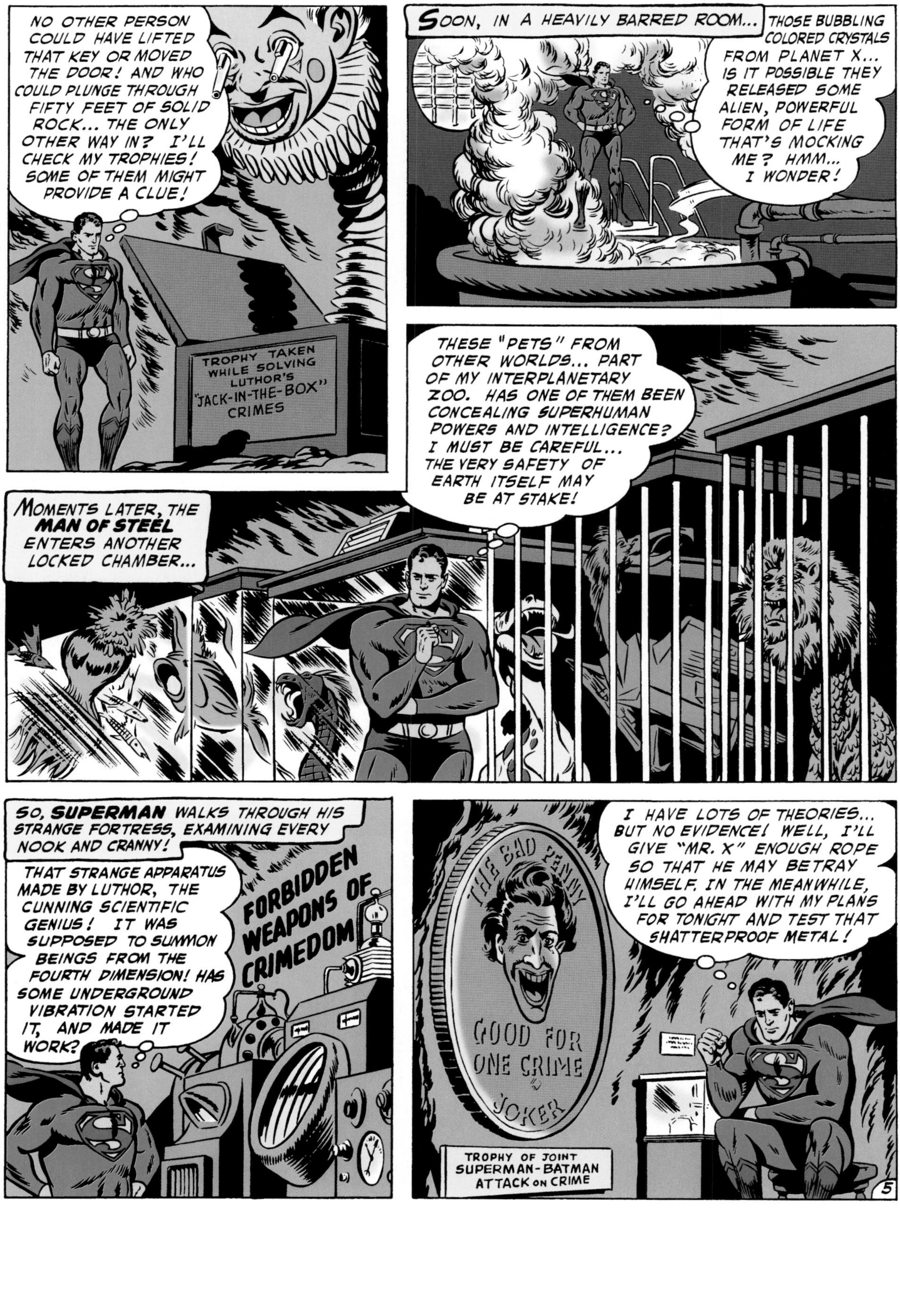
NO OTHER PERSON COULD HAVE LIFTED THAT KEY OR MOVED THE DOOR! AND WHO COULD PLUNGE THROUGH FIFTY FEET OF SOLID ROCK... THE ONLY OTHER WAY IN? I'LL CHECK MY TROPHIES! SOME OF THEM MIGHT PROVIDE A CLUE!
TROPHY TAKEN WHILE SOLVING LUTHOR'S "JACK-IN-THE-BOX" CRIMES
SOON, IN A HEAVILY BARRED ROOM...
THOSE BUBBLING COLORED CRYSTALS FROM PLANET X... IS IT POSSIBLE THEY RELEASED SOME ALIEN, POWERFUL FORM OF LIFE THAT'S MOCKING ME? HMM... I WONDER!
MOMENTS LATER, THE MAN OF STEEL ENTERS ANOTHER LOCKED CHAMBER...
THESE "PETS" FROM OTHER WORLDS... PART OF MY INTERPLANETARY ZOO. HAS ONE OF THEM BEEN CONCEALING SUPERHUMAN POWERS AND INTELLIGENCE? I MUST BE CAREFUL... THE VERY SAFETY OF EARTH ITSELF MAY BE AT STAKE!
SO, SUPERMAN WALKS THROUGH HIS STRANGE FORTRESS, EXAMINING EVERY NOOK AND CRANNY!
THAT STRANGE APPARATUS MADE BY LUTHOR, THE CUNNING SCIENTIFIC GENIUS! IT WAS SUPPOSED TO SUMMON BEINGS FROM THE FOURTH DIMENSION! HAS SOME UNDERGROUND VIBRATION STARTED IT, AND MADE IT WORK?
FORBIDDEN WEAPONS OF CRIMEDOM
I HAVE LOTS OF THEORIES... BUT NO EVIDENCE! WELL, I'LL GIVE "MR. X" ENOUGH ROPE SO THAT HE MAY BETRAY HIMSELF. IN THE MEANWHILE, I'LL GO AHEAD WITH MY PLANS FOR TONIGHT AND TEST THAT SHATTERPROOF METAL!
THE BAD PENNY
GOOD FOR ONE CRIME
JOKER
TROPHY OF JOINT SUPERMAN-BATMAN ATTACK ON CRIME
5

Presently, **SUPERMAN** drives his mighty fist at the metal, and...

I'M AFRAID THE PROFESSOR'S METAL IS NOT SO SHATTERPROOF AS HE THINKS! I'LL HAVE TO PATCH THAT WALL, AND THEN MAKE A FEW ENTRIES IN MY DIARY!

WHAMMMP!

THERE'S NO CHANCE MY DIARY WILL EVER BE DESTROYED! THE PAGES ARE MADE OF METAL AND I ENGRAVE ALL MY ENTRIES WITH MY FINGERNAILS!

AND THERE'S NO DANGER THAT ANYONE WILL EVER READ THESE PAGES. I WRITE EVERYTHING IN **KRYPTONESE**, THE LANGUAGE OF THE PLANET ON WHICH I WAS BORN!

Later, after **SUPERMAN** leaves, and locks the ponderous door that leads to his fortress...

IT'S JUST POSSIBLE SOMEONE FOUND MY KEY AND WAS ABLE TO LIFT IT SOMEHOW! I'LL USE THE HEAT OF MY X-RAY VISION TO MELT THE DOOR AND FUSE IT INTO THE ROCK OF THE MOUNTAIN! THEN THERE WILL BE **NO ENTRANCE!**

Next day, back in Metropolis, **SUPERMAN** answers a fire alarm...

USING THESE WATER MAINS AS HOSES IS THE BEST WAY TO EXTINGUISH THIS FIRE! I'LL REPAIR THEM LATER! I'D LIKE TO SPEND ALL DAY WATCHING AT MY CAVE...BUT THE WORLD NEEDS **SUPERMAN'S** POWERS!

And, that evening, when his super-work is done, **SUPERMAN** speeds to his arctic retreat, where...

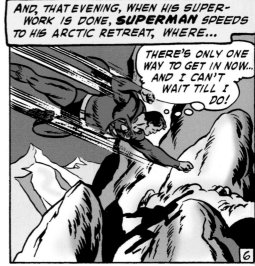

THERE'S ONLY ONE WAY TO GET IN NOW... AND I CAN'T WAIT TILL I DO!

6

AS A HOT KNIFE SLICES THROUGH BUTTER, **SUPERMAN** CLEAVES THROUGH FIFTY FEET OF SOLID ROCK, AND...

I'LL USE THAT ROCK DEBRIS I'VE DISLODGED TO SEAL UP THIS ENTRANCE I'VE MADE, AND THEN LOOK TO SEE IF THERE ARE ANY OTHER SIGNS OF THE INTRUDER!

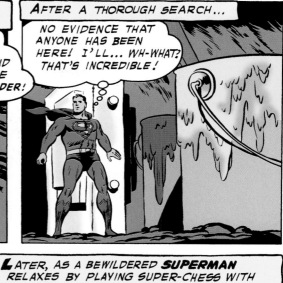

AFTER A THOROUGH SEARCH...

NO EVIDENCE THAT ANYONE HAS BEEN HERE! I'LL... WH-WHAT? THAT'S INCREDIBLE!

SOMEONE COMPLETED THAT PAINTING I'D STARTED! BUT IT'S **NOT** A MARTIAN LANDSCAPE! I'VE NEVER SEEN ANYTHING LIKE THAT... IN ALL MY TRAVELS THROUGH THE SOLAR SYSTEM! IT'S WEIRD-- UTTERLY WEIRD!

*L*ATER, AS A BEWILDERED **SUPERMAN** RELAXES BY PLAYING SUPER-CHESS WITH A GREAT ROBOT HE HAS BUILT AS A PLAYMATE FOR HIMSELF...

THIS ROBOT POSSESSES A SUPER-ELECTRONIC BRAIN! HE CAN THINK AND PLAY WITH THE SPEED OF LIGHTNING, AND PLANS A MILLION MOVES AT ONCE! IT'S TOUGH BEATING HIM!

MOMENTS AFTERWARD, IN A GAME THAT'S PLAYED SO FAST THE PIECES MOVE IN A BLUR OF SPEED...

BUT I DID... BY THINKING **FASTER!** CHECKMATE! IT SURE SHARPENED MY WITS HAVING **YOU** AS AN OPPONENT OLD MAN!

AND LATER, IN ANOTHER CHAMBER OF THE FORTRESS...

I'VE BEEN EXPERIMENTING WITH THESE GLASSES TO DISCOVER IF THEY WILL ENABLE MY X-RAY VISION TO PENETRATE **LEAD**... THE ONE SUBSTANCE I CAN'T SEE THROUGH.

7

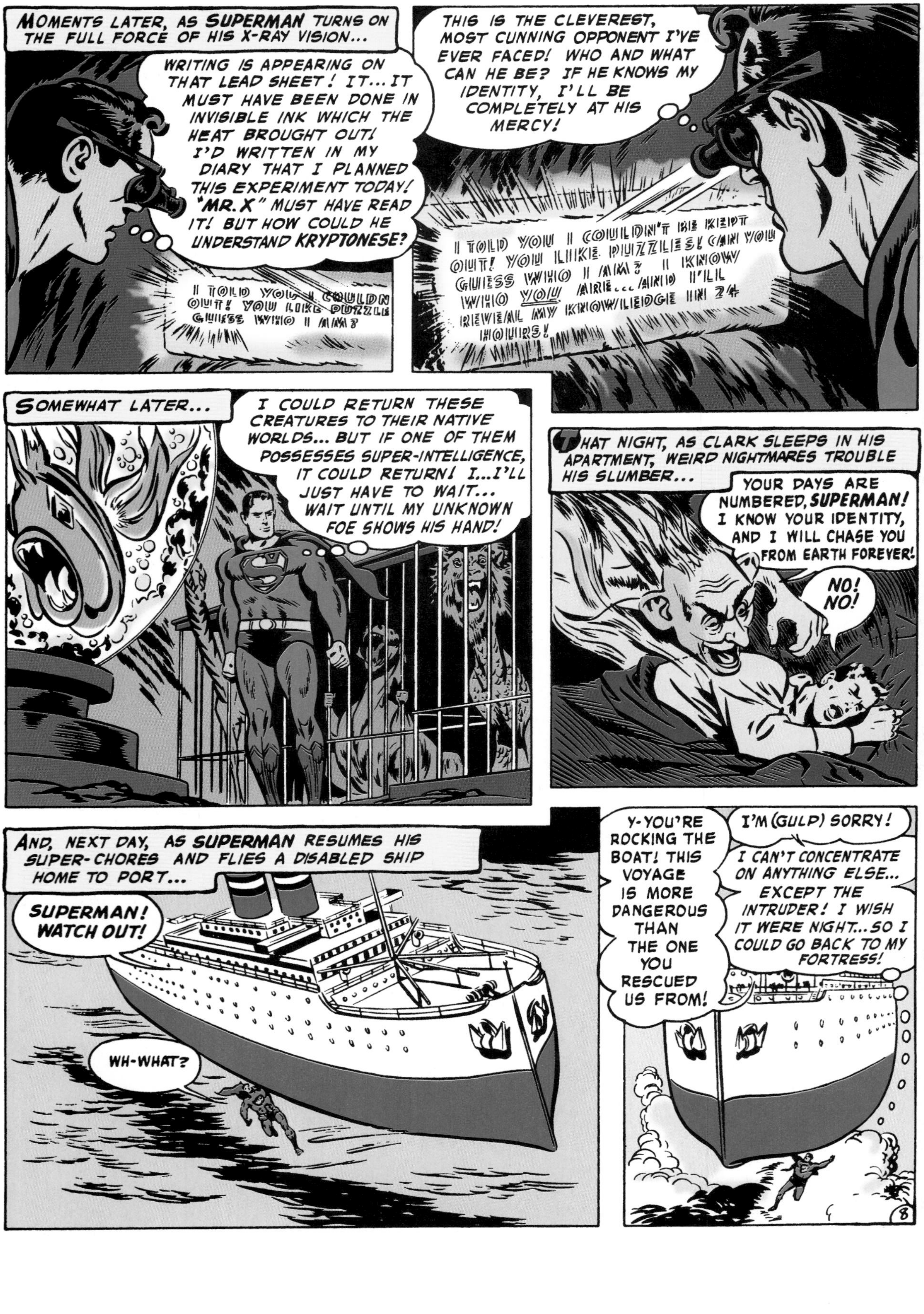
MOMENTS LATER, AS SUPERMAN TURNS ON THE FULL FORCE OF HIS X-RAY VISION...
WRITING IS APPEARING ON THAT LEAD SHEET! IT... IT MUST HAVE BEEN DONE IN INVISIBLE INK WHICH THE HEAT BROUGHT OUT! I'D WRITTEN IN MY DIARY THAT I PLANNED THIS EXPERIMENT TODAY! "MR. X" MUST HAVE READ IT! BUT HOW COULD HE UNDERSTAND KRYPTONESE?
I TOLD YOU I COULDN OUT! YOU LIKE PUZZLE GUESS WHO I AM?
THIS IS THE CLEVEREST, MOST CUNNING OPPONENT I'VE EVER FACED! WHO AND WHAT CAN HE BE? IF HE KNOWS MY IDENTITY, I'LL BE COMPLETELY AT HIS MERCY!
I TOLD YOU I COULDN'T BE KEPT OUT! YOU LIKE PUZZLES! CAN YOU GUESS WHO I AM? I KNOW WHO YOU ARE... AND I'LL REVEAL MY KNOWLEDGE IN 24 HOURS!
SOMEWHAT LATER...
I COULD RETURN THESE CREATURES TO THEIR NATIVE WORLDS... BUT IF ONE OF THEM POSSESSES SUPER-INTELLIGENCE, IT COULD RETURN! I... I'LL JUST HAVE TO WAIT... WAIT UNTIL MY UNKNOWN FOE SHOWS HIS HAND!
THAT NIGHT, AS CLARK SLEEPS IN HIS APARTMENT, WEIRD NIGHTMARES TROUBLE HIS SLUMBER...
YOUR DAYS ARE NUMBERED, SUPERMAN! I KNOW YOUR IDENTITY, AND I WILL CHASE YOU FROM EARTH FOREVER!
NO! NO!
AND, NEXT DAY, AS SUPERMAN RESUMES HIS SUPER-CHORES AND FLIES A DISABLED SHIP HOME TO PORT...
SUPERMAN! WATCH OUT!
WH-WHAT?
Y-YOU'RE ROCKING THE BOAT! THIS VOYAGE IS MORE DANGEROUS THAN THE ONE YOU RESCUED US FROM!
I'M (GULP) SORRY!
I CAN'T CONCENTRATE ON ANYTHING ELSE... EXCEPT THE INTRUDER! I WISH IT WERE NIGHT... SO I COULD GO BACK TO MY FORTRESS!
8

THAT EVENING, *SUPERMAN* SPEEDS NORTHWARD AND PLUNGES INTO THE ROCK ROOF OF HIS FORTRESS...

IF THE INTRUDER KNOWS THE SECRET OF MY IDENTITY, IT MAY MEAN THE END OF MY CAREER! I HAVE A FEELING THAT TONIGHT WE WILL COME FACE TO FACE!

WHAMMP!

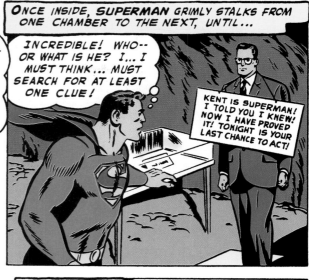

ONCE INSIDE, *SUPERMAN* GRIMLY STALKS FROM ONE CHAMBER TO THE NEXT, UNTIL...

INCREDIBLE! WHO-- OR WHAT IS HE? I... I MUST THINK... MUST SEARCH FOR AT LEAST ONE CLUE!

KENT IS SUPERMAN! I TOLD YOU I KNEW! NOW I HAVE PROVED IT! TONIGHT IS YOUR LAST CHANCE TO ACT!

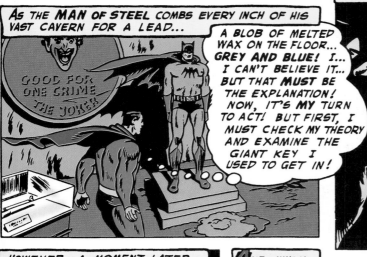

AS THE *MAN OF STEEL* COMBS EVERY INCH OF HIS VAST CAVERN FOR A LEAD...

GOOD FOR ONE CRIME — THE JOKER

A BLOB OF MELTED WAX ON THE FLOOR... GREY AND BLUE! I... I CAN'T BELIEVE IT... BUT THAT *MUST* BE THE EXPLANATION! NOW, IT'S *MY* TURN TO ACT! BUT FIRST, I MUST CHECK MY THEORY AND EXAMINE THE GIANT KEY I USED TO GET IN!

MEANWHILE...

HA, HA! *SUPERMAN* HAS NOT GUESSED WHO I AM... OR HOW I GOT IN! WHEN HE RETURNS, I WILL REVEAL MYSELF, AND HE'LL GET THE SHOCK OF HIS LIFE!

HOWEVER, A MOMENT LATER...

THE WALLS OF THIS FORTRESS ARE SHAKING! IT'S AN EARTHQUAKE!

AND, WHEN *SUPERMAN* RETURNS...

GREAT SCOTT! I'LL NEVER BE ABLE TO GET OUT OF HERE ALIVE! I'M SEALED IN BY TONS OF ROCKS! AND *SUPERMAN* CAN'T HELP ME, EITHER-- THE QUAKE DISLODGED THAT CHUNK OF *KRYPTONITE* HE WAS WORKING ON!

(9)

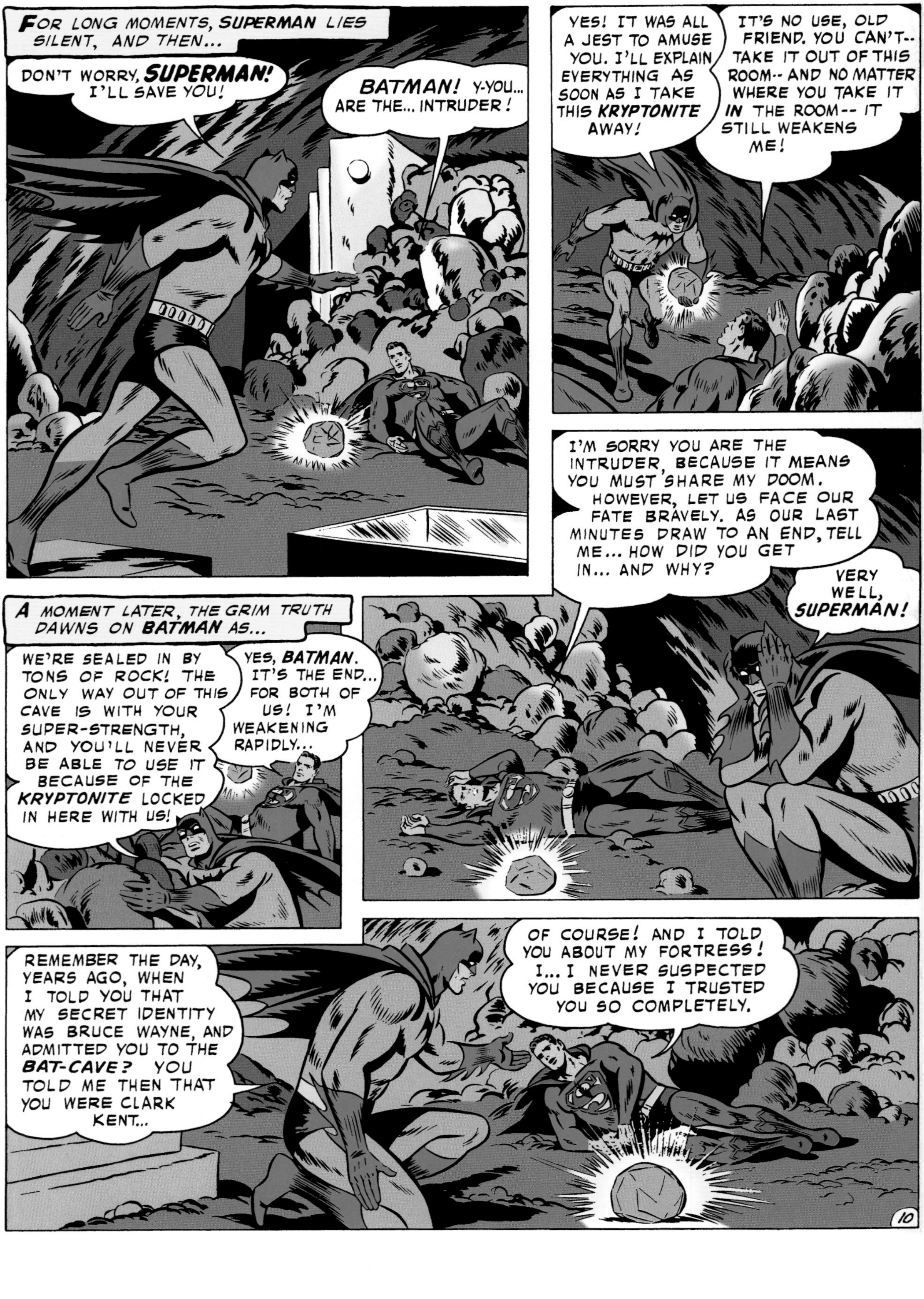
FOR LONG MOMENTS, SUPERMAN LIES SILENT, AND THEN...
DON'T WORRY, SUPERMAN! I'LL SAVE YOU!
BATMAN! Y-YOU... ARE THE... INTRUDER!
YES! IT WAS ALL A JEST TO AMUSE YOU. I'LL EXPLAIN EVERYTHING AS SOON AS I TAKE THIS KRYPTONITE AWAY!
IT'S NO USE, OLD FRIEND. YOU CAN'T-- TAKE IT OUT OF THIS ROOM-- AND NO MATTER WHERE YOU TAKE IT IN THE ROOM-- IT STILL WEAKENS ME!
A MOMENT LATER, THE GRIM TRUTH DAWNS ON BATMAN AS...
WE'RE SEALED IN BY TONS OF ROCK! THE ONLY WAY OUT OF THIS CAVE IS WITH YOUR SUPER-STRENGTH, AND YOU'LL NEVER BE ABLE TO USE IT BECAUSE OF THE KRYPTONITE LOCKED IN HERE WITH US!
YES, BATMAN. IT'S THE END... FOR BOTH OF US! I'M WEAKENING RAPIDLY...
I'M SORRY YOU ARE THE INTRUDER, BECAUSE IT MEANS YOU MUST SHARE MY DOOM. HOWEVER, LET US FACE OUR FATE BRAVELY. AS OUR LAST MINUTES DRAW TO AN END, TELL ME... HOW DID YOU GET IN... AND WHY?
VERY WELL, SUPERMAN!
REMEMBER THE DAY, YEARS AGO, WHEN I TOLD YOU THAT MY SECRET IDENTITY WAS BRUCE WAYNE, AND ADMITTED YOU TO THE BAT-CAVE? YOU TOLD ME THEN THAT YOU WERE CLARK KENT...
OF COURSE! AND I TOLD YOU ABOUT MY FORTRESS! I... I NEVER SUSPECTED YOU BECAUSE I TRUSTED YOU SO COMPLETELY.
10

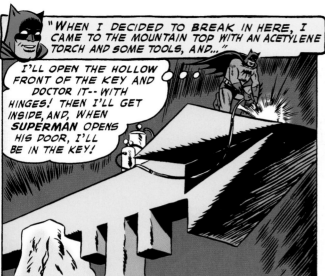

"WHEN I DECIDED TO BREAK IN HERE, I CAME TO THE MOUNTAIN TOP WITH AN ACETYLENE TORCH AND SOME TOOLS, AND..."

I'LL OPEN THE HOLLOW FRONT OF THE KEY AND DOCTOR IT-- WITH HINGES! THEN I'LL GET INSIDE, AND, WHEN SUPERMAN OPENS HIS DOOR, I'LL BE IN THE KEY!

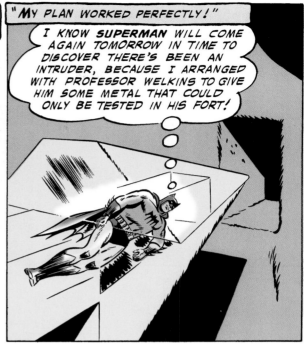

"MY PLAN WORKED PERFECTLY!"

I KNOW SUPERMAN WILL COME AGAIN TOMORROW IN TIME TO DISCOVER THERE'S BEEN AN INTRUDER, BECAUSE I ARRANGED WITH PROFESSOR WELKINS TO GIVE HIM SOME METAL THAT COULD ONLY BE TESTED IN HIS FORT!

"WHILE YOU WERE BUSY, I SLIPPED OUT OF THE KEY AND HID. THEN, WHEN YOU LEFT..."

I KNEW THIS "BAD PENNY" WAS ONE OF SUPERMAN'S TROPHIES... SINCE WE WORKED ON THE CASE TOGETHER! AND, AS IT'S MADE OF LEAD WHICH HIS X-RAY VISION CAN'T PIERCE, ITS INTERIOR WILL BE A PERFECT HIDING PLACE! WHAT A PUZZLE I'LL GIVE HIM!

"EARLIER TONIGHT I MELTED DOWN THE WAX FIGURE OF YOU IN THE "BATMAN" ROOM WITH A FLARE FROM MY UTILITY BELT..."

IF HE DOESN'T GUESS THE SOLUTION TONIGHT, I'LL LEAP DOWN, SURPRISE HIM, AND TELL HIM!

I NEVER GUESSED WE'D SHARE OUR DOOM INSTEAD OF... WH-WHAT? Y-YOU'RE LAUGHING!

S-SORRY (HA-HA) BATMAN! I CAN'T CONTROL MYSELF ANY LONGER. YOU SEE, SINCE YOU TRICKED ME, I DECIDED IT WAS ONLY FAIR FOR ME TO TRICK YOU!

SUDDENLY, THE MAN OF STEEL LEAPS UP, AND...

THAT KRYPTONITE IS PHONY AND THE 'QUAKE WAS CAUSED BY VIBRATIONS FROM A SUPER-CLAP OF MY HANDS. THE REST OF THE FORT IS STILL UNHARMED!

WHEW! YOU CERTAINLY FOOLED ME--AS MUCH AS I FOOLED YOU! BUT HOW DID YOU GUESS I WAS THE INTRUDER?

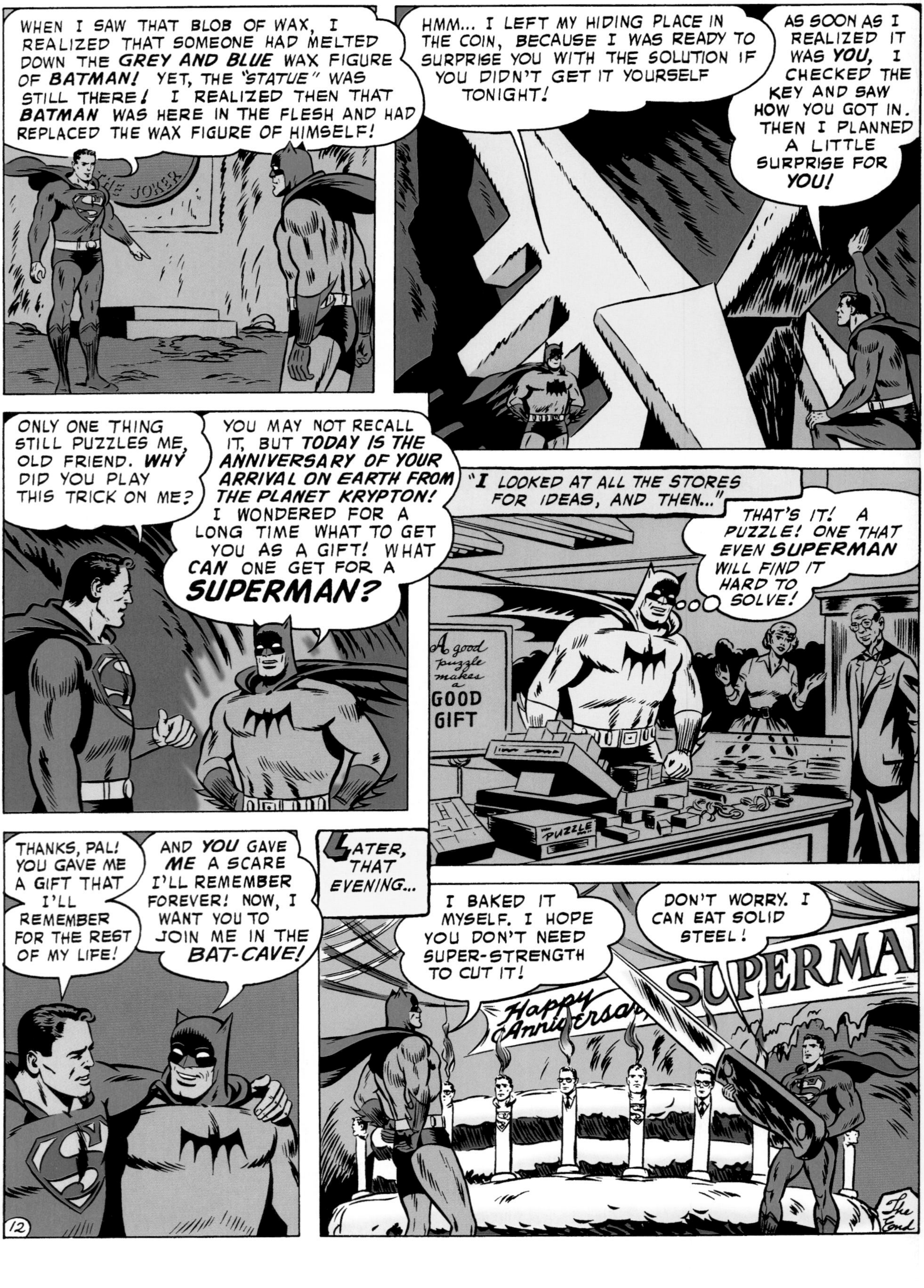
WHEN I SAW THAT BLOB OF WAX, I REALIZED THAT SOMEONE HAD MELTED DOWN THE GREY AND BLUE WAX FIGURE OF BATMAN! YET, THE "STATUE" WAS STILL THERE! I REALIZED THEN THAT BATMAN WAS HERE IN THE FLESH AND HAD REPLACED THE WAX FIGURE OF HIMSELF!
THE JOKER
HMM... I LEFT MY HIDING PLACE IN THE COIN, BECAUSE I WAS READY TO SURPRISE YOU WITH THE SOLUTION IF YOU DIDN'T GET IT YOURSELF TONIGHT!
AS SOON AS I REALIZED IT WAS YOU, I CHECKED THE KEY AND SAW HOW YOU GOT IN. THEN I PLANNED A LITTLE SURPRISE FOR YOU!
ONLY ONE THING STILL PUZZLES ME, OLD FRIEND. WHY DID YOU PLAY THIS TRICK ON ME?
YOU MAY NOT RECALL IT, BUT TODAY IS THE ANNIVERSARY OF YOUR ARRIVAL ON EARTH FROM THE PLANET KRYPTON! I WONDERED FOR A LONG TIME WHAT TO GET YOU AS A GIFT! WHAT CAN ONE GET FOR A SUPERMAN?
"I LOOKED AT ALL THE STORES FOR IDEAS, AND THEN..."
THAT'S IT! A PUZZLE! ONE THAT EVEN SUPERMAN WILL FIND IT HARD TO SOLVE!
A good puzzle makes a GOOD GIFT
PUZZLE
THANKS, PAL! YOU GAVE ME A GIFT THAT I'LL REMEMBER FOR THE REST OF MY LIFE!
AND YOU GAVE ME A SCARE I'LL REMEMBER FOREVER! NOW, I WANT YOU TO JOIN ME IN THE BAT-CAVE!
12
LATER, THAT EVENING...
I BAKED IT MYSELF. I HOPE YOU DON'T NEED SUPER-STRENGTH TO CUT IT!
DON'T WORRY. I CAN EAT SOLID STEEL!
Happy Anniversary
SUPERMA
The End

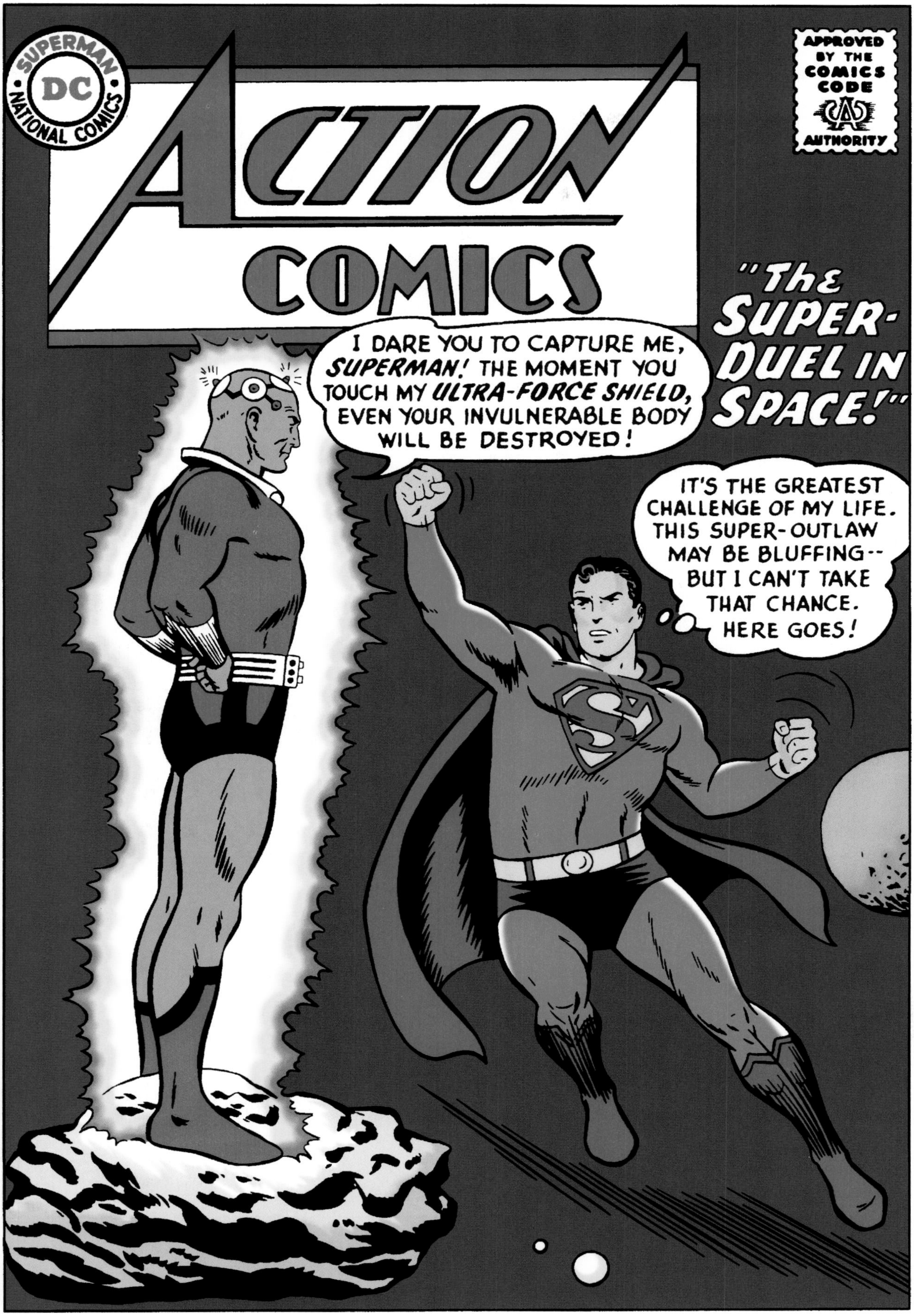
SUPERMAN
DC
NATIONAL COMICS
APPROVED BY THE COMICS CODE AUTHORITY
ACTION COMICS
"The SUPER-DUEL IN SPACE!"
I DARE YOU TO CAPTURE ME, SUPERMAN! THE MOMENT YOU TOUCH MY ULTRA-FORCE SHIELD, EVEN YOUR INVULNERABLE BODY WILL BE DESTROYED!
IT'S THE GREATEST CHALLENGE OF MY LIFE. THIS SUPER-OUTLAW MAY BE BLUFFING-- BUT I CAN'T TAKE THAT CHANCE. HERE GOES!

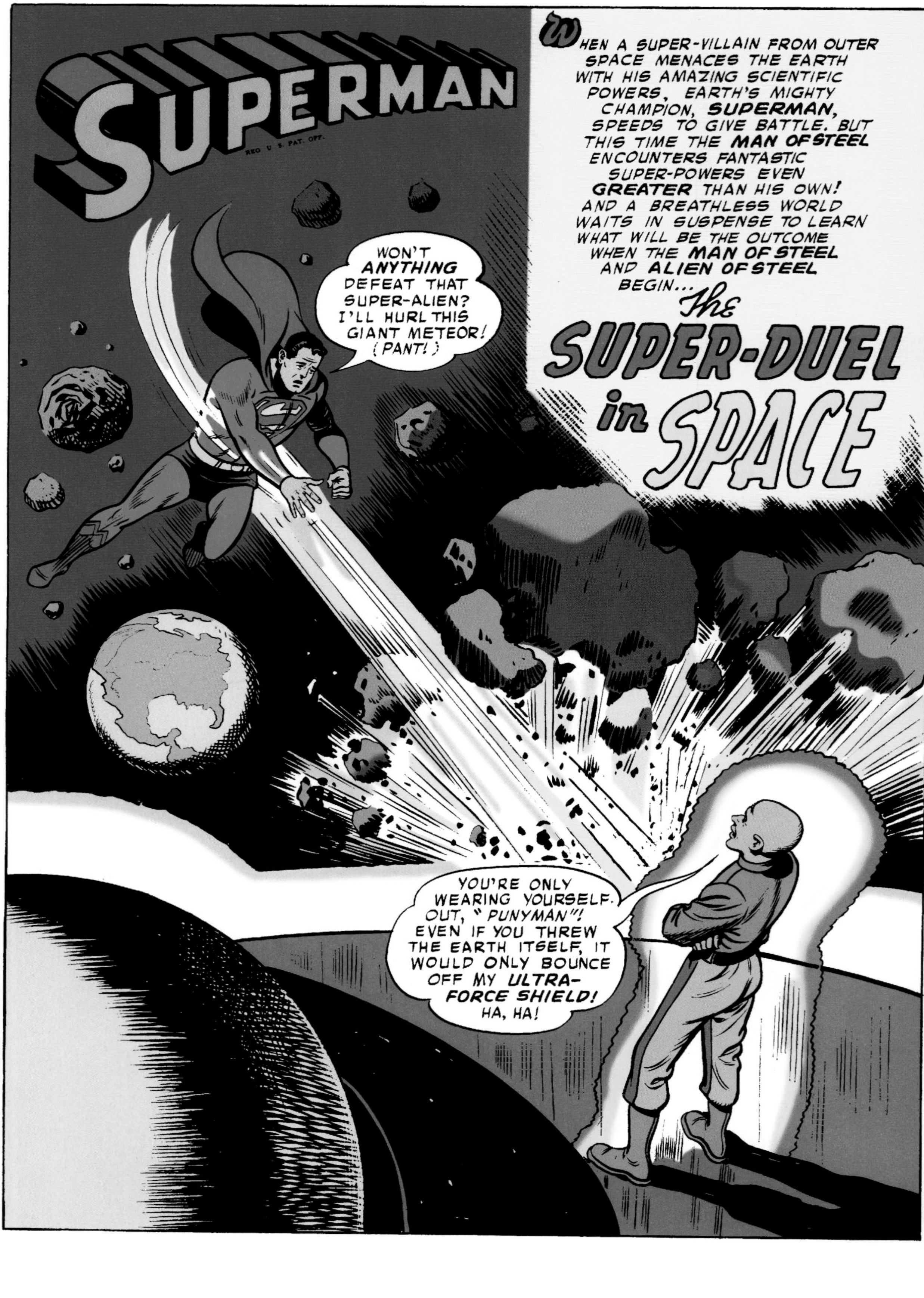
SUPERMAN
REG. U.S. PAT. OFF.
WHEN A SUPER-VILLAIN FROM OUTER SPACE MENACES THE EARTH WITH HIS AMAZING SCIENTIFIC POWERS, EARTH'S MIGHTY CHAMPION, SUPERMAN, SPEEDS TO GIVE BATTLE. BUT THIS TIME THE MAN OF STEEL ENCOUNTERS FANTASTIC SUPER-POWERS EVEN GREATER THAN HIS OWN! AND A BREATHLESS WORLD WAITS IN SUSPENSE TO LEARN WHAT WILL BE THE OUTCOME WHEN THE MAN OF STEEL AND ALIEN OF STEEL BEGIN...
The SUPER-DUEL in SPACE
WON'T ANYTHING DEFEAT THAT SUPER-ALIEN? I'LL HURL THIS GIANT METEOR! (PANT!)
YOU'RE ONLY WEARING YOURSELF OUT, "PUNYMAN"! EVEN IF YOU THREW THE EARTH ITSELF, IT WOULD ONLY BOUNCE OFF MY ULTRA-FORCE SHIELD! HA, HA!

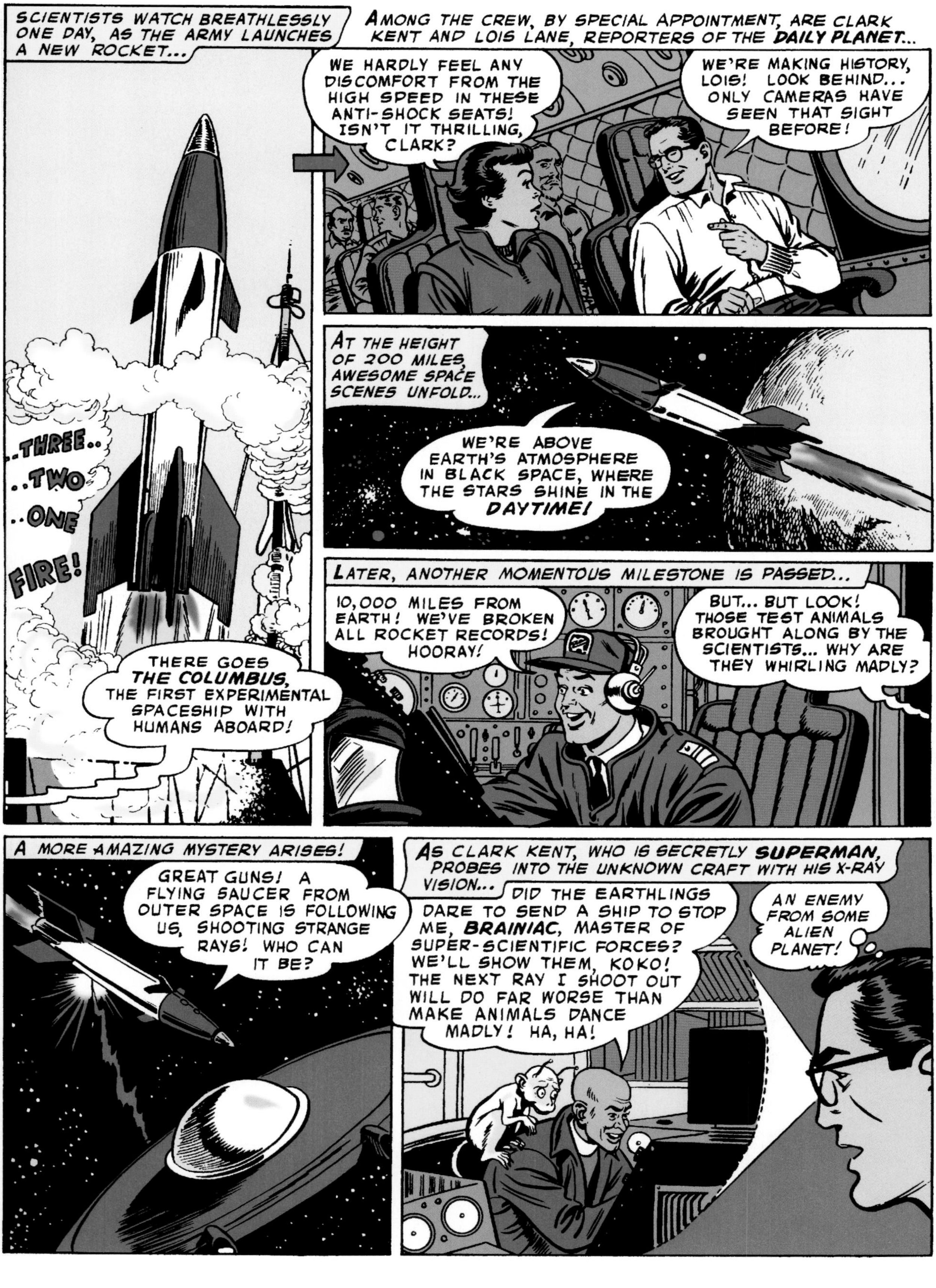
SCIENTISTS WATCH BREATHLESSLY ONE DAY, AS THE ARMY LAUNCHES A NEW ROCKET...
..THREE.. ..TWO.. ..ONE FIRE!
THERE GOES THE COLUMBUS, THE FIRST EXPERIMENTAL SPACESHIP WITH HUMANS ABOARD!
AMONG THE CREW, BY SPECIAL APPOINTMENT, ARE CLARK KENT AND LOIS LANE, REPORTERS OF THE DAILY PLANET...
WE HARDLY FEEL ANY DISCOMFORT FROM THE HIGH SPEED IN THESE ANTI-SHOCK SEATS! ISN'T IT THRILLING, CLARK?
WE'RE MAKING HISTORY, LOIS! LOOK BEHIND... ONLY CAMERAS HAVE SEEN THAT SIGHT BEFORE!
AT THE HEIGHT OF 200 MILES, AWESOME SPACE SCENES UNFOLD...
WE'RE ABOVE EARTH'S ATMOSPHERE IN BLACK SPACE, WHERE THE STARS SHINE IN THE DAYTIME!
LATER, ANOTHER MOMENTOUS MILESTONE IS PASSED...
10,000 MILES FROM EARTH! WE'VE BROKEN ALL ROCKET RECORDS! HOORAY!
BUT... BUT LOOK! THOSE TEST ANIMALS BROUGHT ALONG BY THE SCIENTISTS... WHY ARE THEY WHIRLING MADLY?
A MORE AMAZING MYSTERY ARISES!
GREAT GUNS! A FLYING SAUCER FROM OUTER SPACE IS FOLLOWING US, SHOOTING STRANGE RAYS! WHO CAN IT BE?
AS CLARK KENT, WHO IS SECRETLY SUPERMAN, PROBES INTO THE UNKNOWN CRAFT WITH HIS X-RAY VISION...
DID THE EARTHLINGS DARE TO SEND A SHIP TO STOP ME, BRAINIAC, MASTER OF SUPER-SCIENTIFIC FORCES? WE'LL SHOW THEM, KOKO! THE NEXT RAY I SHOOT OUT WILL DO FAR WORSE THAN MAKE ANIMALS DANCE MADLY! HA, HA!
AN ENEMY FROM SOME ALIEN PLANET!

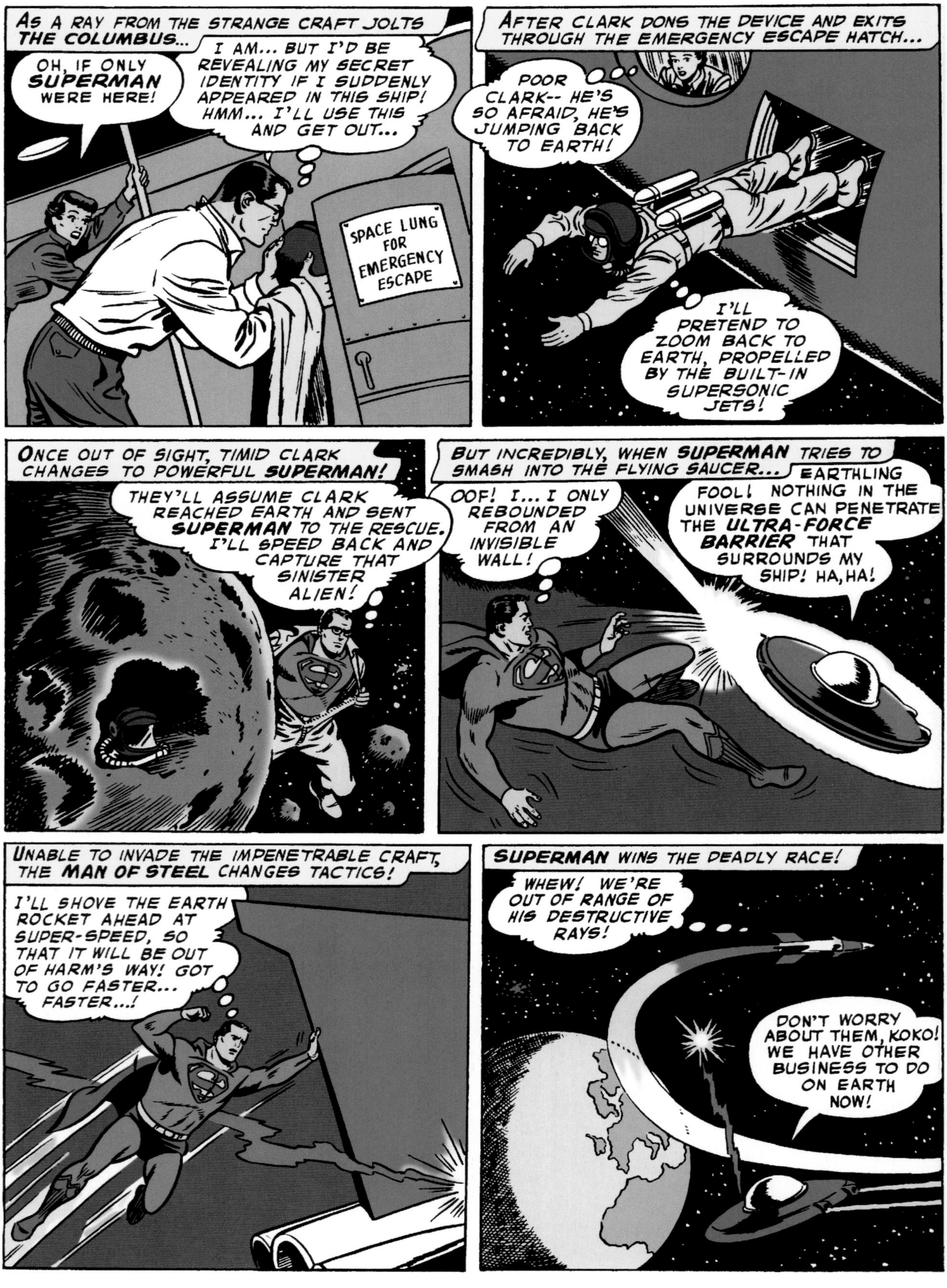

AS A RAY FROM THE STRANGE CRAFT JOLTS THE COLUMBUS...
OH, IF ONLY SUPERMAN WERE HERE!
I AM... BUT I'D BE REVEALING MY SECRET IDENTITY IF I SUDDENLY APPEARED IN THIS SHIP! HMM... I'LL USE THIS AND GET OUT...
SPACE LUNG FOR EMERGENCY ESCAPE
AFTER CLARK DONS THE DEVICE AND EXITS THROUGH THE EMERGENCY ESCAPE HATCH...
POOR CLARK-- HE'S SO AFRAID, HE'S JUMPING BACK TO EARTH!
I'LL PRETEND TO ZOOM BACK TO EARTH, PROPELLED BY THE BUILT-IN SUPERSONIC JETS!
ONCE OUT OF SIGHT, TIMID CLARK CHANGES TO POWERFUL SUPERMAN!
THEY'LL ASSUME CLARK REACHED EARTH AND SENT SUPERMAN TO THE RESCUE. I'LL SPEED BACK AND CAPTURE THAT SINISTER ALIEN!
BUT INCREDIBLY, WHEN SUPERMAN TRIES TO SMASH INTO THE FLYING SAUCER...
OOF! I... I ONLY REBOUNDED FROM AN INVISIBLE WALL!
EARTHLING FOOL! NOTHING IN THE UNIVERSE CAN PENETRATE THE ULTRA-FORCE BARRIER THAT SURROUNDS MY SHIP! HA, HA!
UNABLE TO INVADE THE IMPENETRABLE CRAFT, THE MAN OF STEEL CHANGES TACTICS!
I'LL SHOVE THE EARTH ROCKET AHEAD AT SUPER-SPEED, SO THAT IT WILL BE OUT OF HARM'S WAY! GOT TO GO FASTER... FASTER...!
SUPERMAN WINS THE DEADLY RACE!
WHEW! WE'RE OUT OF RANGE OF HIS DESTRUCTIVE RAYS!
DON'T WORRY ABOUT THEM, KOKO! WE HAVE OTHER BUSINESS TO DO ON EARTH NOW!

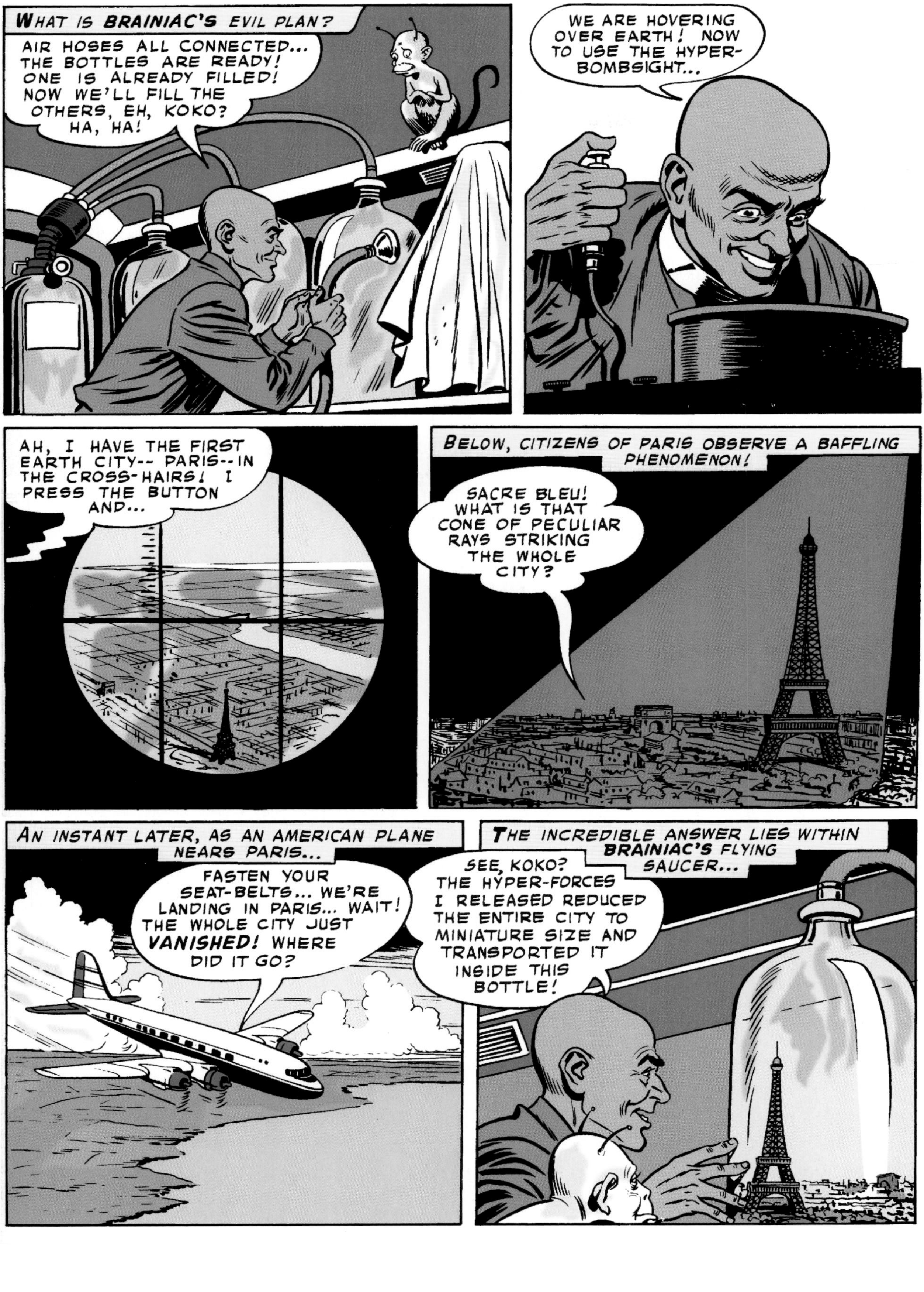
WHAT IS BRAINIAC'S EVIL PLAN?
AIR HOSES ALL CONNECTED... THE BOTTLES ARE READY! ONE IS ALREADY FILLED! NOW WE'LL FILL THE OTHERS, EH, KOKO? HA, HA!
WE ARE HOVERING OVER EARTH! NOW TO USE THE HYPER-BOMBSIGHT...
AH, I HAVE THE FIRST EARTH CITY-- PARIS--IN THE CROSS-HAIRS! I PRESS THE BUTTON AND...
BELOW, CITIZENS OF PARIS OBSERVE A BAFFLING PHENOMENON!
SACRE BLEU! WHAT IS THAT CONE OF PECULIAR RAYS STRIKING THE WHOLE CITY?
AN INSTANT LATER, AS AN AMERICAN PLANE NEARS PARIS...
FASTEN YOUR SEAT-BELTS... WE'RE LANDING IN PARIS... WAIT! THE WHOLE CITY JUST VANISHED! WHERE DID IT GO?
THE INCREDIBLE ANSWER LIES WITHIN BRAINIAC'S FLYING SAUCER...
SEE, KOKO? THE HYPER-FORCES I RELEASED REDUCED THE ENTIRE CITY TO MINIATURE SIZE AND TRANSPORTED IT INSIDE THIS BOTTLE!

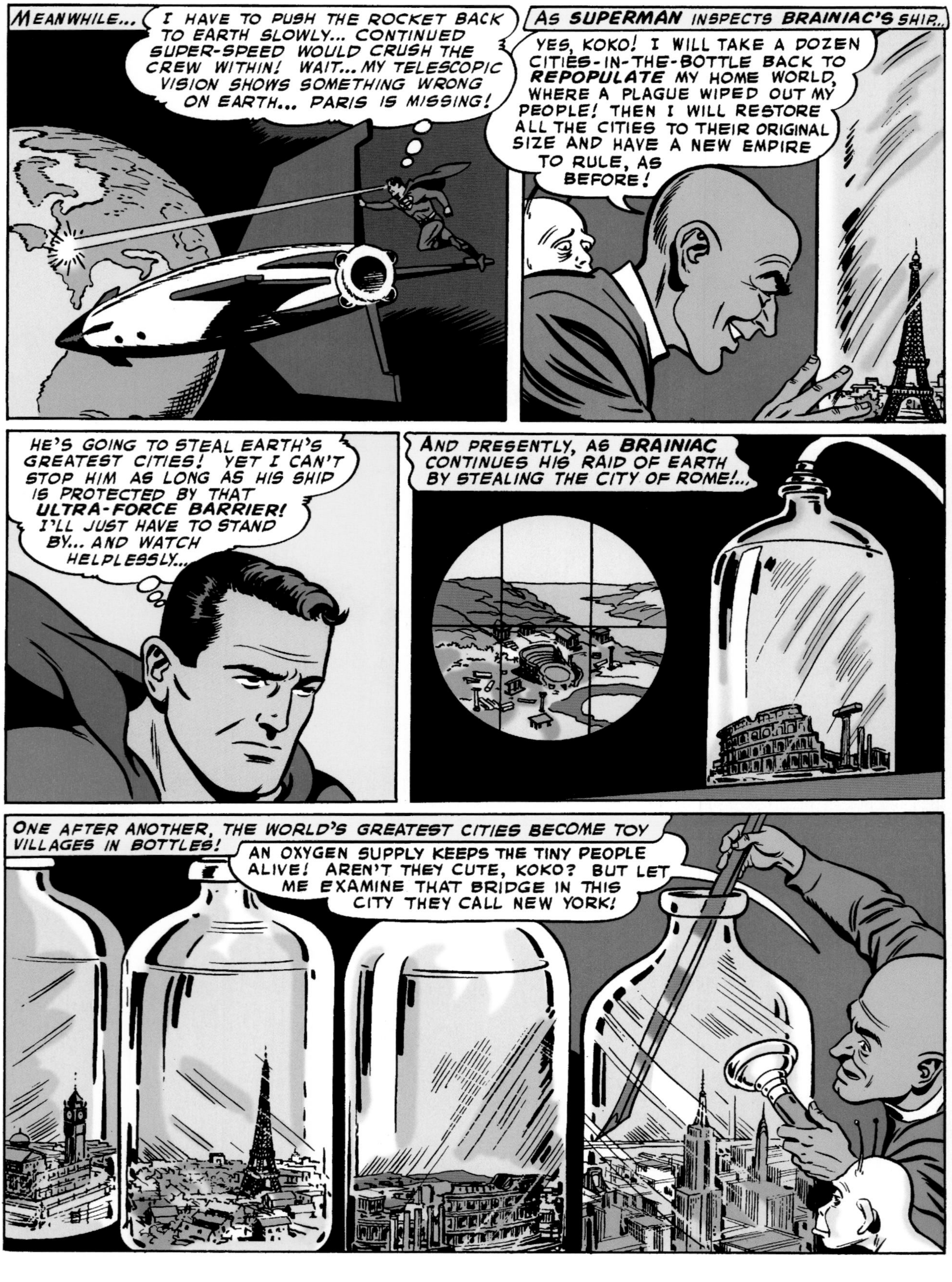
MEANWHILE...
I HAVE TO PUSH THE ROCKET BACK TO EARTH SLOWLY... CONTINUED SUPER-SPEED WOULD CRUSH THE CREW WITHIN! WAIT... MY TELESCOPIC VISION SHOWS SOMETHING WRONG ON EARTH... PARIS IS MISSING!
AS SUPERMAN INSPECTS BRAINIAC'S SHIP...
YES, KOKO! I WILL TAKE A DOZEN CITIES-IN-THE-BOTTLE BACK TO REPOPULATE MY HOME WORLD, WHERE A PLAGUE WIPED OUT MY PEOPLE! THEN I WILL RESTORE ALL THE CITIES TO THEIR ORIGINAL SIZE AND HAVE A NEW EMPIRE TO RULE, AS BEFORE!
HE'S GOING TO STEAL EARTH'S GREATEST CITIES! YET I CAN'T STOP HIM AS LONG AS HIS SHIP IS PROTECTED BY THAT ULTRA-FORCE BARRIER! I'LL JUST HAVE TO STAND BY... AND WATCH HELPLESSLY...
AND PRESENTLY, AS BRAINIAC CONTINUES HIS RAID OF EARTH BY STEALING THE CITY OF ROME!...
ONE AFTER ANOTHER, THE WORLD'S GREATEST CITIES BECOME TOY VILLAGES IN BOTTLES!
AN OXYGEN SUPPLY KEEPS THE TINY PEOPLE ALIVE! AREN'T THEY CUTE, KOKO? BUT LET ME EXAMINE THAT BRIDGE IN THIS CITY THEY CALL NEW YORK!

HELP! GIANT TWEEZERS RIPPED THE GEORGE WASHINGTON BRIDGE LOOSE!

ALL THE WHILE, SUPERMAN OBSERVES HELPLESSLY VIA TELESCOPIC VISION AND SUPER-HEARING...

BAH! SUCH PRIMITIVE STRUCTURES!

HE'S EXAMINING THE MINIATURE CITIES AS THOUGH THEY WERE "ANT NESTS!" YET I... I CAN'T GET INTO HIS SHIP AND STOP HIM!

BUT HOPE RISES IN SUPERMAN AS THEIR SPACE PATHS CROSS AGAIN...

TIME TO RECHARGE MY HYPER-BATTERIES WITH COSMIC RAY POWER! MEANWHILE, WE'LL LAND ON THAT PLANETOID AND STRETCH OUR MUSCLES, KOKO!

HMM... MAYBE I CAN DEFEAT HIM OUTSIDE OF HIS SHIP! I'LL LET THE EARTH-ROCKET FLOAT IN SPACE NEARBY!

SHORTLY...

SO THE FLYING FOOL IS GOING TO TRY TO DEFEAT ME AGAIN, EH? WELL, I'M WAITING!

THE HEAT OF MY X-RAY EYES OUGHT TO MAKE YOU YELL "UNCLE"!

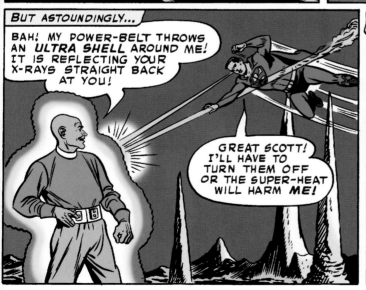

BUT ASTOUNDINGLY...

BAH! MY POWER-BELT THROWS AN ULTRA SHELL AROUND ME! IT IS REFLECTING YOUR X-RAYS STRAIGHT BACK AT YOU!

GREAT SCOTT! I'LL HAVE TO TURN THEM OFF OR THE SUPER-HEAT WILL HARM ME!

DESPERATELY, SUPERMAN USES THE NEAREST WEAPON AT HAND...

I BROKE OFF ONE OF THESE STALAGMITES AND HURLED IT LIKE A SUPER-LANCE!

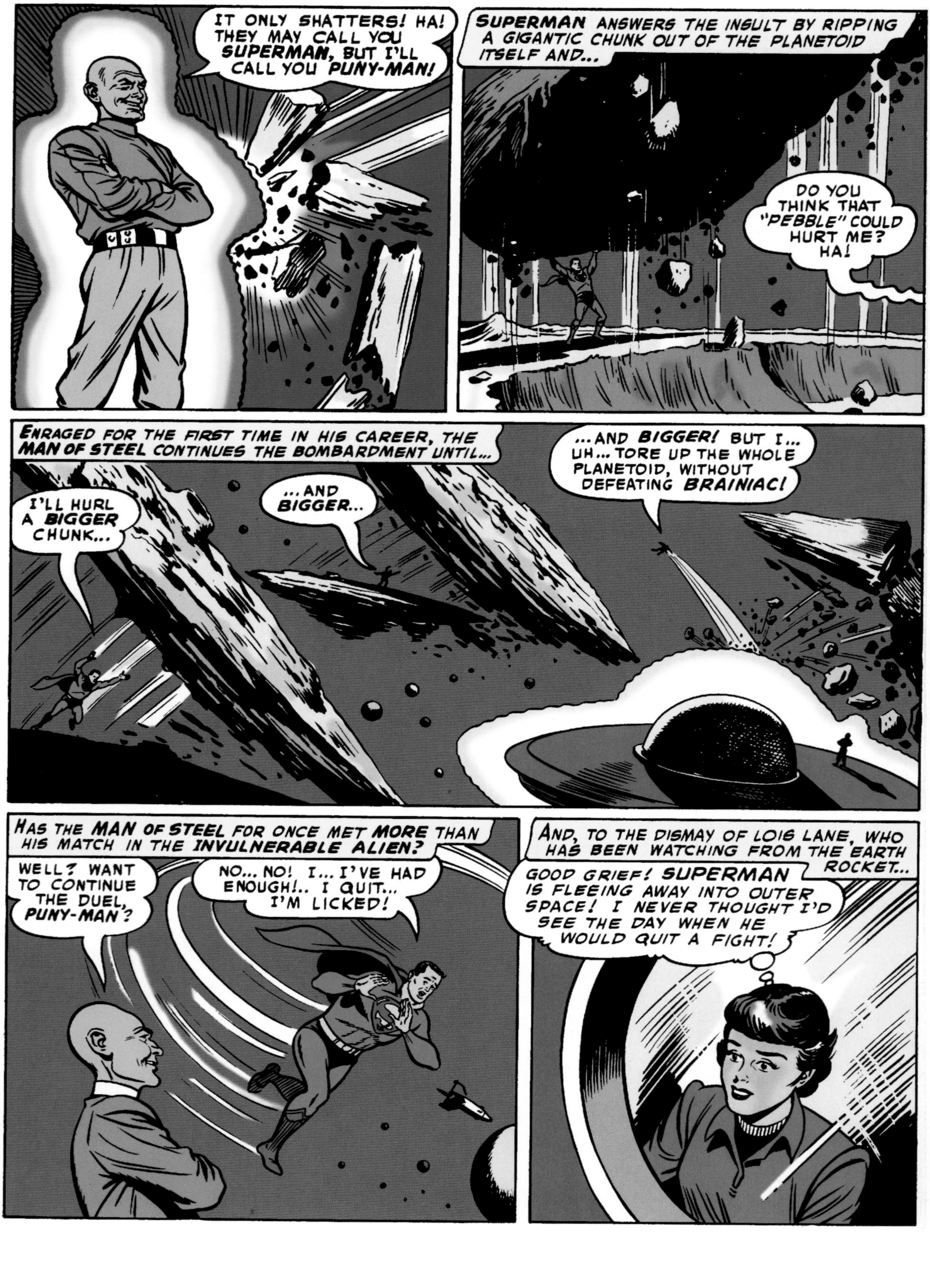
IT ONLY SHATTERS! HA! THEY MAY CALL YOU SUPERMAN, BUT I'LL CALL YOU PUNY-MAN!
SUPERMAN ANSWERS THE INSULT BY RIPPING A GIGANTIC CHUNK OUT OF THE PLANETOID ITSELF AND...
DO YOU THINK THAT "PEBBLE" COULD HURT ME? HA!
ENRAGED FOR THE FIRST TIME IN HIS CAREER, THE MAN OF STEEL CONTINUES THE BOMBARDMENT UNTIL...
I'LL HURL A BIGGER CHUNK...
...AND BIGGER...
...AND BIGGER! BUT I... UH... TORE UP THE WHOLE PLANETOID, WITHOUT DEFEATING BRAINIAC!
HAS THE MAN OF STEEL FOR ONCE MET MORE THAN HIS MATCH IN THE INVULNERABLE ALIEN?
WELL? WANT TO CONTINUE THE DUEL, PUNY-MAN?
NO... NO! I... I'VE HAD ENOUGH!.. I QUIT... I'M LICKED!
AND, TO THE DISMAY OF LOIS LANE, WHO HAS BEEN WATCHING FROM THE EARTH ROCKET...
GOOD GRIEF! SUPERMAN IS FLEEING AWAY INTO OUTER SPACE! I NEVER THOUGHT I'D SEE THE DAY WHEN HE WOULD QUIT A FIGHT!

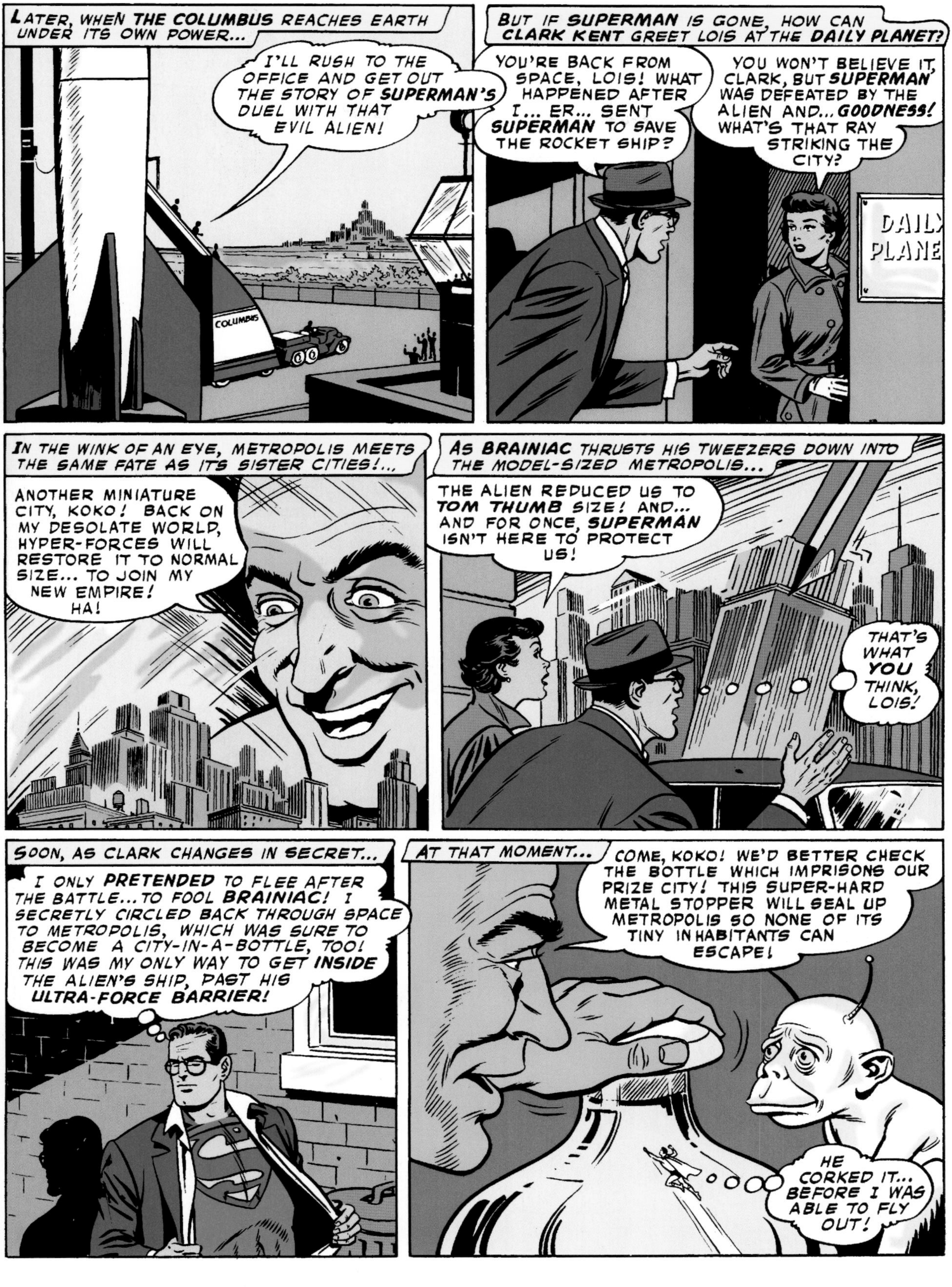

LATER, WHEN THE COLUMBUS REACHES EARTH UNDER ITS OWN POWER...
I'LL RUSH TO THE OFFICE AND GET OUT THE STORY OF SUPERMAN'S DUEL WITH THAT EVIL ALIEN!
COLUMBUS
BUT IF SUPERMAN IS GONE, HOW CAN CLARK KENT GREET LOIS AT THE DAILY PLANET?
YOU'RE BACK FROM SPACE, LOIS! WHAT HAPPENED AFTER I... ER... SENT SUPERMAN TO SAVE THE ROCKET SHIP?
YOU WON'T BELIEVE IT, CLARK, BUT SUPERMAN WAS DEFEATED BY THE ALIEN AND... GOODNESS! WHAT'S THAT RAY STRIKING THE CITY?
DAILY PLANE
IN THE WINK OF AN EYE, METROPOLIS MEETS THE SAME FATE AS ITS SISTER CITIES!...
ANOTHER MINIATURE CITY, KOKO! BACK ON MY DESOLATE WORLD, HYPER-FORCES WILL RESTORE IT TO NORMAL SIZE... TO JOIN MY NEW EMPIRE! HA!
AS BRAINIAC THRUSTS HIS TWEEZERS DOWN INTO THE MODEL-SIZED METROPOLIS...
THE ALIEN REDUCED US TO TOM THUMB SIZE! AND... AND FOR ONCE, SUPERMAN ISN'T HERE TO PROTECT US!
THAT'S WHAT YOU THINK, LOIS!
SOON, AS CLARK CHANGES IN SECRET...
I ONLY PRETENDED TO FLEE AFTER THE BATTLE...TO FOOL BRAINIAC! I SECRETLY CIRCLED BACK THROUGH SPACE TO METROPOLIS, WHICH WAS SURE TO BECOME A CITY-IN-A-BOTTLE, TOO! THIS WAS MY ONLY WAY TO GET INSIDE THE ALIEN'S SHIP, PAST HIS ULTRA-FORCE BARRIER!
AT THAT MOMENT...
COME, KOKO! WE'D BETTER CHECK THE BOTTLE WHICH IMPRISONS OUR PRIZE CITY! THIS SUPER-HARD METAL STOPPER WILL SEAL UP METROPOLIS SO NONE OF ITS TINY INHABITANTS CAN ESCAPE!
HE CORKED IT... BEFORE I WAS ABLE TO FLY OUT!

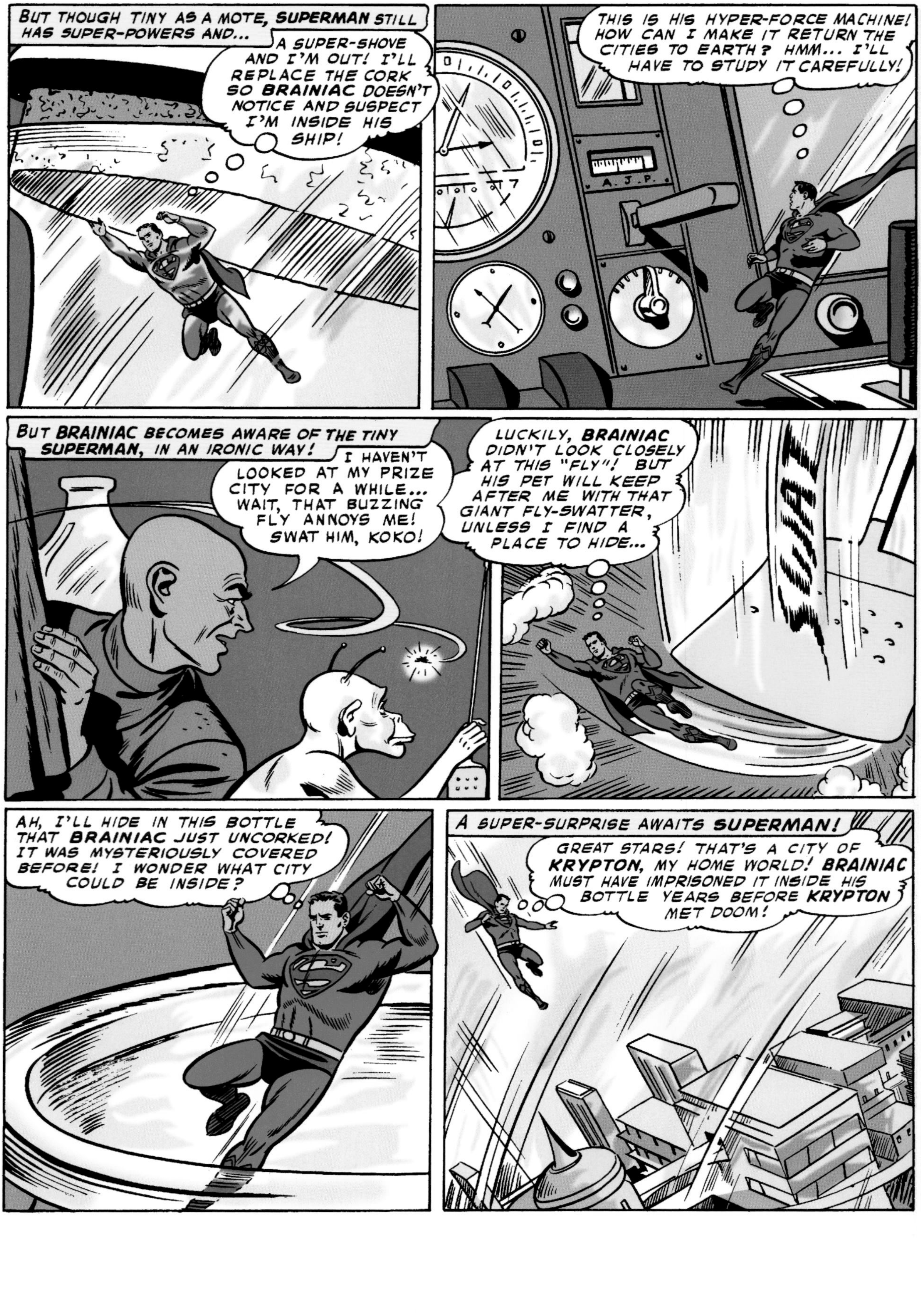

BUT THOUGH TINY AS A MOTE, SUPERMAN STILL HAS SUPER-POWERS AND...
A SUPER-SHOVE AND I'M OUT! I'LL REPLACE THE CORK SO BRAINIAC DOESN'T NOTICE AND SUSPECT I'M INSIDE HIS SHIP!
THIS IS HIS HYPER-FORCE MACHINE! HOW CAN I MAKE IT RETURN THE CITIES TO EARTH? HMM... I'LL HAVE TO STUDY IT CAREFULLY!
A. J. P.
BUT BRAINIAC BECOMES AWARE OF THE TINY SUPERMAN, IN AN IRONIC WAY!
I HAVEN'T LOOKED AT MY PRIZE CITY FOR A WHILE... WAIT, THAT BUZZING FLY ANNOYS ME! SWAT HIM, KOKO!
LUCKILY, BRAINIAC DIDN'T LOOK CLOSELY AT THIS "FLY"! BUT HIS PET WILL KEEP AFTER ME WITH THAT GIANT FLY-SWATTER, UNLESS I FIND A PLACE TO HIDE...
AH, I'LL HIDE IN THIS BOTTLE THAT BRAINIAC JUST UNCORKED! IT WAS MYSTERIOUSLY COVERED BEFORE! I WONDER WHAT CITY COULD BE INSIDE?
A SUPER-SURPRISE AWAITS SUPERMAN!
GREAT STARS! THAT'S A CITY OF KRYPTON, MY HOME WORLD! BRAINIAC MUST HAVE IMPRISONED IT INSIDE HIS BOTTLE YEARS BEFORE KRYPTON MET DOOM!

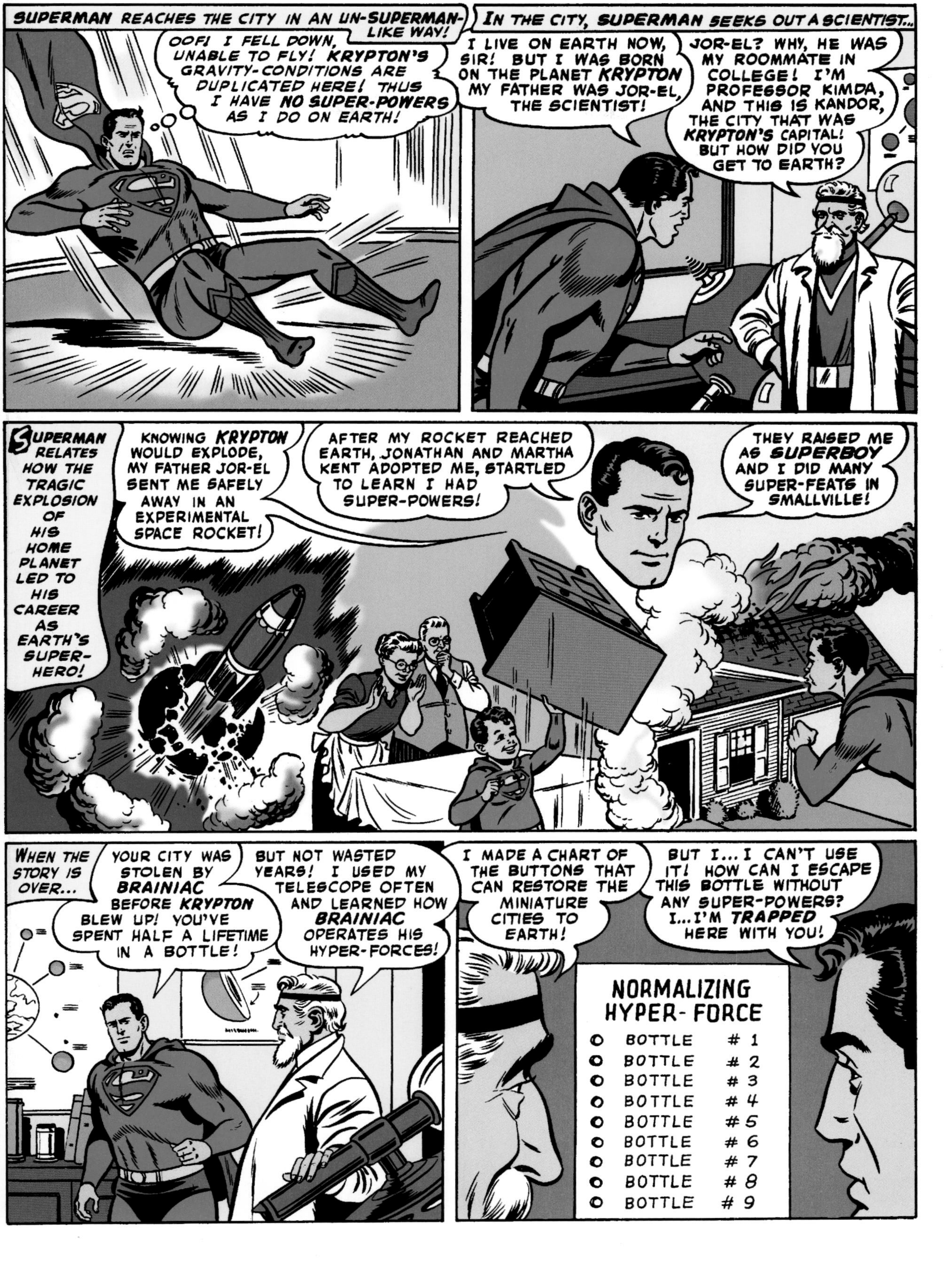
SUPERMAN REACHES THE CITY IN AN UN-SUPERMAN-LIKE WAY!
OOF! I FELL DOWN, UNABLE TO FLY! KRYPTON'S GRAVITY-CONDITIONS ARE DUPLICATED HERE! THUS I HAVE NO SUPER-POWERS AS I DO ON EARTH!
IN THE CITY, SUPERMAN SEEKS OUT A SCIENTIST...
I LIVE ON EARTH NOW, SIR! BUT I WAS BORN ON THE PLANET KRYPTON MY FATHER WAS JOR-EL, THE SCIENTIST!
JOR-EL? WHY, HE WAS MY ROOMMATE IN COLLEGE! I'M PROFESSOR KIMDA, AND THIS IS KANDOR, THE CITY THAT WAS KRYPTON'S CAPITAL! BUT HOW DID YOU GET TO EARTH?
SUPERMAN RELATES HOW THE TRAGIC EXPLOSION OF HIS HOME PLANET LED TO HIS CAREER AS EARTH'S SUPER-HERO!
KNOWING KRYPTON WOULD EXPLODE, MY FATHER JOR-EL SENT ME SAFELY AWAY IN AN EXPERIMENTAL SPACE ROCKET!
AFTER MY ROCKET REACHED EARTH, JONATHAN AND MARTHA KENT ADOPTED ME, STARTLED TO LEARN I HAD SUPER-POWERS!
THEY RAISED ME AS SUPERBOY AND I DID MANY SUPER-FEATS IN SMALLVILLE!
WHEN THE STORY IS OVER...
YOUR CITY WAS STOLEN BY BRAINIAC BEFORE KRYPTON BLEW UP! YOU'VE SPENT HALF A LIFETIME IN A BOTTLE!
BUT NOT WASTED YEARS! I USED MY TELESCOPE OFTEN AND LEARNED HOW BRAINIAC OPERATES HIS HYPER-FORCES!
I MADE A CHART OF THE BUTTONS THAT CAN RESTORE THE MINIATURE CITIES TO EARTH!
BUT I... I CAN'T USE IT! HOW CAN I ESCAPE THIS BOTTLE WITHOUT ANY SUPER-POWERS? I...I'M TRAPPED HERE WITH YOU!
NORMALIZING HYPER-FORCE
BOTTLE # 1
BOTTLE # 2
BOTTLE # 3
BOTTLE # 4
BOTTLE # 5
BOTTLE # 6
BOTTLE # 7
BOTTLE # 8
BOTTLE # 9

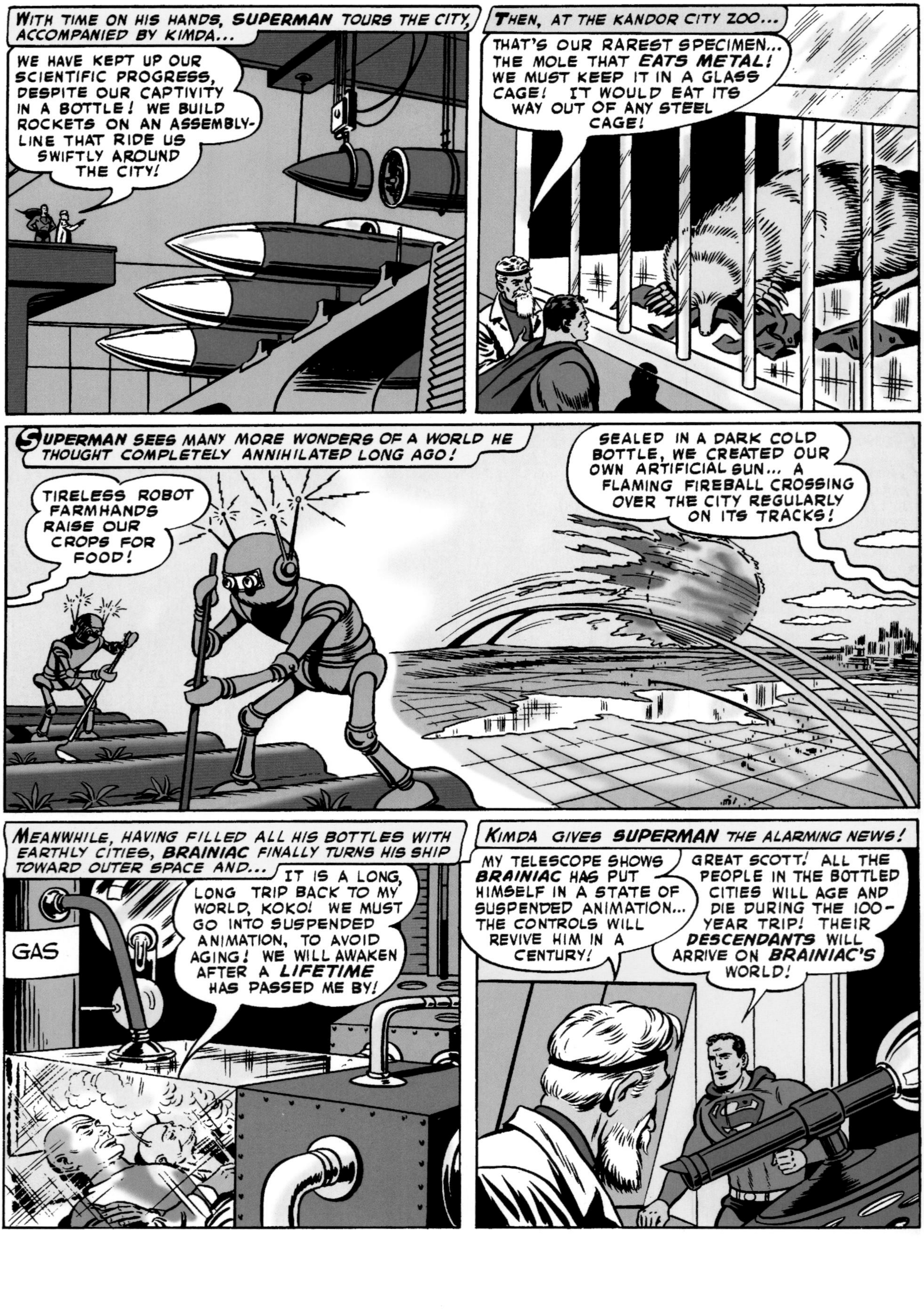
WITH TIME ON HIS HANDS, SUPERMAN TOURS THE CITY, ACCOMPANIED BY KIMDA...
WE HAVE KEPT UP OUR SCIENTIFIC PROGRESS, DESPITE OUR CAPTIVITY IN A BOTTLE! WE BUILD ROCKETS ON AN ASSEMBLY-LINE THAT RIDE US SWIFTLY AROUND THE CITY!
THEN, AT THE KANDOR CITY ZOO...
THAT'S OUR RAREST SPECIMEN... THE MOLE THAT EATS METAL! WE MUST KEEP IT IN A GLASS CAGE! IT WOULD EAT ITS WAY OUT OF ANY STEEL CAGE!
SUPERMAN SEES MANY MORE WONDERS OF A WORLD HE THOUGHT COMPLETELY ANNIHILATED LONG AGO!
TIRELESS ROBOT FARMHANDS RAISE OUR CROPS FOR FOOD!
SEALED IN A DARK COLD BOTTLE, WE CREATED OUR OWN ARTIFICIAL SUN... A FLAMING FIREBALL CROSSING OVER THE CITY REGULARLY ON ITS TRACKS!
MEANWHILE, HAVING FILLED ALL HIS BOTTLES WITH EARTHLY CITIES, BRAINIAC FINALLY TURNS HIS SHIP TOWARD OUTER SPACE AND...
IT IS A LONG, LONG TRIP BACK TO MY WORLD, KOKO! WE MUST GO INTO SUSPENDED ANIMATION, TO AVOID AGING! WE WILL AWAKEN AFTER A LIFETIME HAS PASSED ME BY!
GAS
KIMDA GIVES SUPERMAN THE ALARMING NEWS!
MY TELESCOPE SHOWS BRAINIAC HAS PUT HIMSELF IN A STATE OF SUSPENDED ANIMATION... THE CONTROLS WILL REVIVE HIM IN A CENTURY!
GREAT SCOTT! ALL THE PEOPLE IN THE BOTTLED CITIES WILL AGE AND DIE DURING THE 100-YEAR TRIP! THEIR DESCENDANTS WILL ARRIVE ON BRAINIAC'S WORLD!

Suddenly, SUPERMAN thinks of a SUPER-STRATEGY...

HMM... THIS CHART, AND TWO OTHER THINGS IN YOUR CITY, MAY SAVE US! I WANT YOUR MOST POWERFUL ROCKET! AND A CERTAIN ANIMAL FROM THE ZOO!

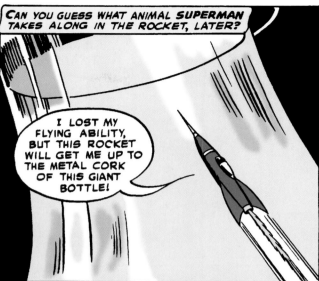

CAN YOU GUESS WHAT ANIMAL SUPERMAN TAKES ALONG IN THE ROCKET, LATER?

I LOST MY FLYING ABILITY, BUT THIS ROCKET WILL GET ME UP TO THE METAL CORK OF THIS GIANT BOTTLE!

SUPERMAN PURPOSELY RAMS THE ROCKET'S NOSE INTO THE UNDERSIDE OF THE CORK, AND THEN...

NOW TO LET THE METAL-EATING MOLE FEAST HIS WAY UP THROUGH THE CORK! HE'LL BURROW A TUNNEL BIG ENOUGH FOR ME TO CLIMB THROUGH!

THE INGENIOUS PLAN WORKS!..

NOW THAT I'M OUTSIDE THE BOTTLE, I'M FREE OF THE KRYPTON-GRAVITY WITHIN THE BOTTLE! MY SUPER-POWERS RETURNED! I CAN FLY TO THE CONTROL PANEL AND USE KIMDA'S OPERATIONAL CHART!

WITH NO INTERFERENCE FROM THE SLEEPING ALIEN, THE MOTE OF STEEL PUNCHES THE CORRECT BUTTONS... IN A SPECIAL WAY!

MY FINGER'S TOO SMALL...BUT THIS IS USING MY HEAD! EACH BUTTON I PRESS MAKES A CITY REAPPEAR BACK ON EARTH IN NORMAL SIZE, UNHARMED!

LOOK! METROPOLIS SUDDENLY RETURNED, AS MYSTERIOUSLY AS IT VANISHED YESTERDAY!

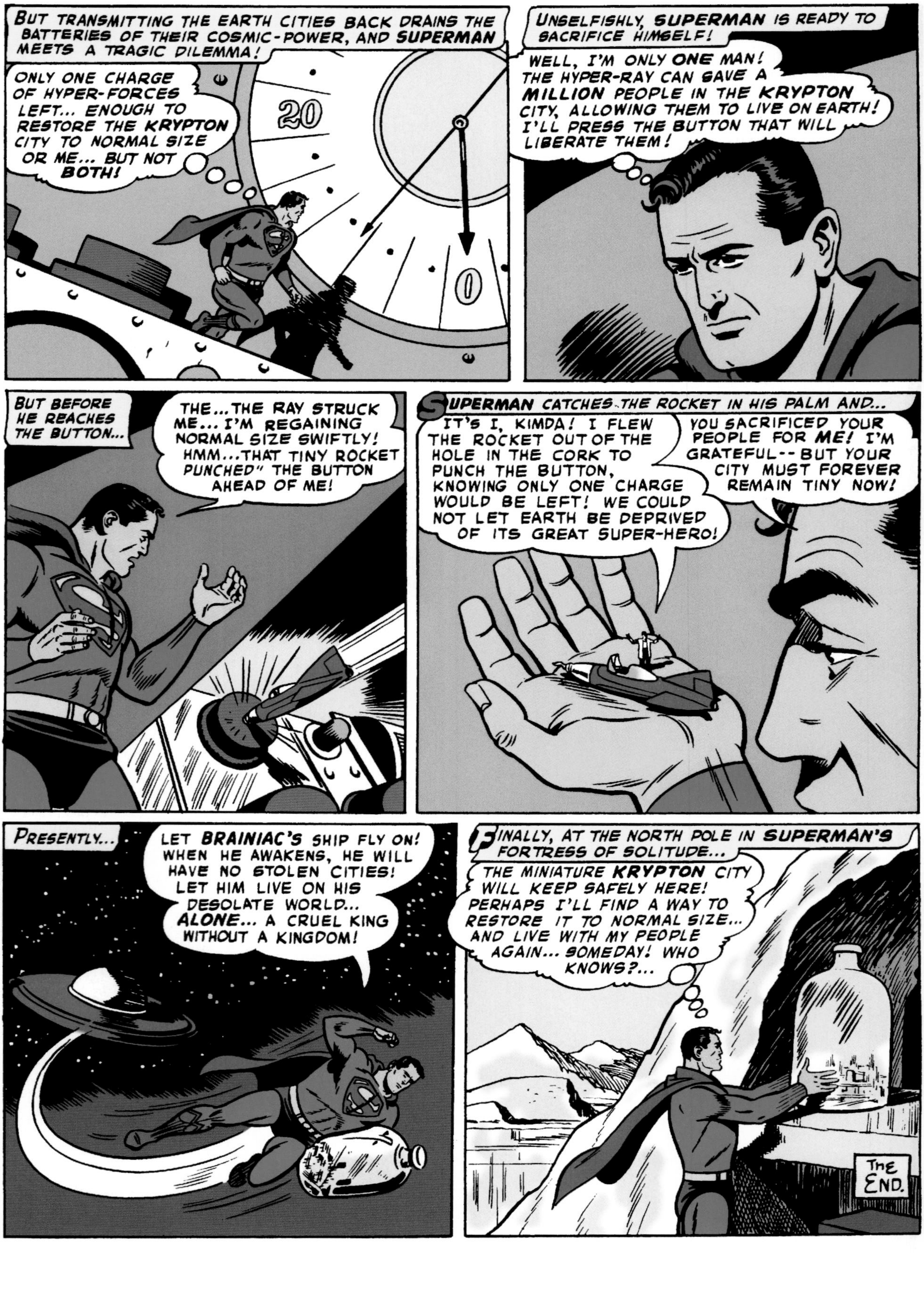
BUT TRANSMITTING THE EARTH CITIES BACK DRAINS THE BATTERIES OF THEIR COSMIC-POWER, AND SUPERMAN MEETS A TRAGIC DILEMMA!
ONLY ONE CHARGE OF HYPER-FORCES LEFT... ENOUGH TO RESTORE THE KRYPTON CITY TO NORMAL SIZE OR ME... BUT NOT BOTH!
20
0
UNSELFISHLY, SUPERMAN IS READY TO SACRIFICE HIMSELF!
WELL, I'M ONLY ONE MAN! THE HYPER-RAY CAN SAVE A MILLION PEOPLE IN THE KRYPTON CITY, ALLOWING THEM TO LIVE ON EARTH! I'LL PRESS THE BUTTON THAT WILL LIBERATE THEM!
BUT BEFORE HE REACHES THE BUTTON...
THE...THE RAY STRUCK ME... I'M REGAINING NORMAL SIZE SWIFTLY! HMM...THAT TINY ROCKET PUNCHED" THE BUTTON AHEAD OF ME!
SUPERMAN CATCHES THE ROCKET IN HIS PALM AND...
IT'S I, KIMDA! I FLEW THE ROCKET OUT OF THE HOLE IN THE CORK TO PUNCH THE BUTTON, KNOWING ONLY ONE CHARGE WOULD BE LEFT! WE COULD NOT LET EARTH BE DEPRIVED OF ITS GREAT SUPER-HERO!
YOU SACRIFICED YOUR PEOPLE FOR ME! I'M GRATEFUL--BUT YOUR CITY MUST FOREVER REMAIN TINY NOW!
PRESENTLY...
LET BRAINIAC'S SHIP FLY ON! WHEN HE AWAKENS, HE WILL HAVE NO STOLEN CITIES! LET HIM LIVE ON HIS DESOLATE WORLD... ALONE... A CRUEL KING WITHOUT A KINGDOM!
FINALLY, AT THE NORTH POLE IN SUPERMAN'S FORTRESS OF SOLITUDE...
THE MINIATURE KRYPTON CITY WILL KEEP SAFELY HERE! PERHAPS I'LL FIND A WAY TO RESTORE IT TO NORMAL SIZE... AND LIVE WITH MY PEOPLE AGAIN... SOMEDAY! WHO KNOWS?...
THE END.

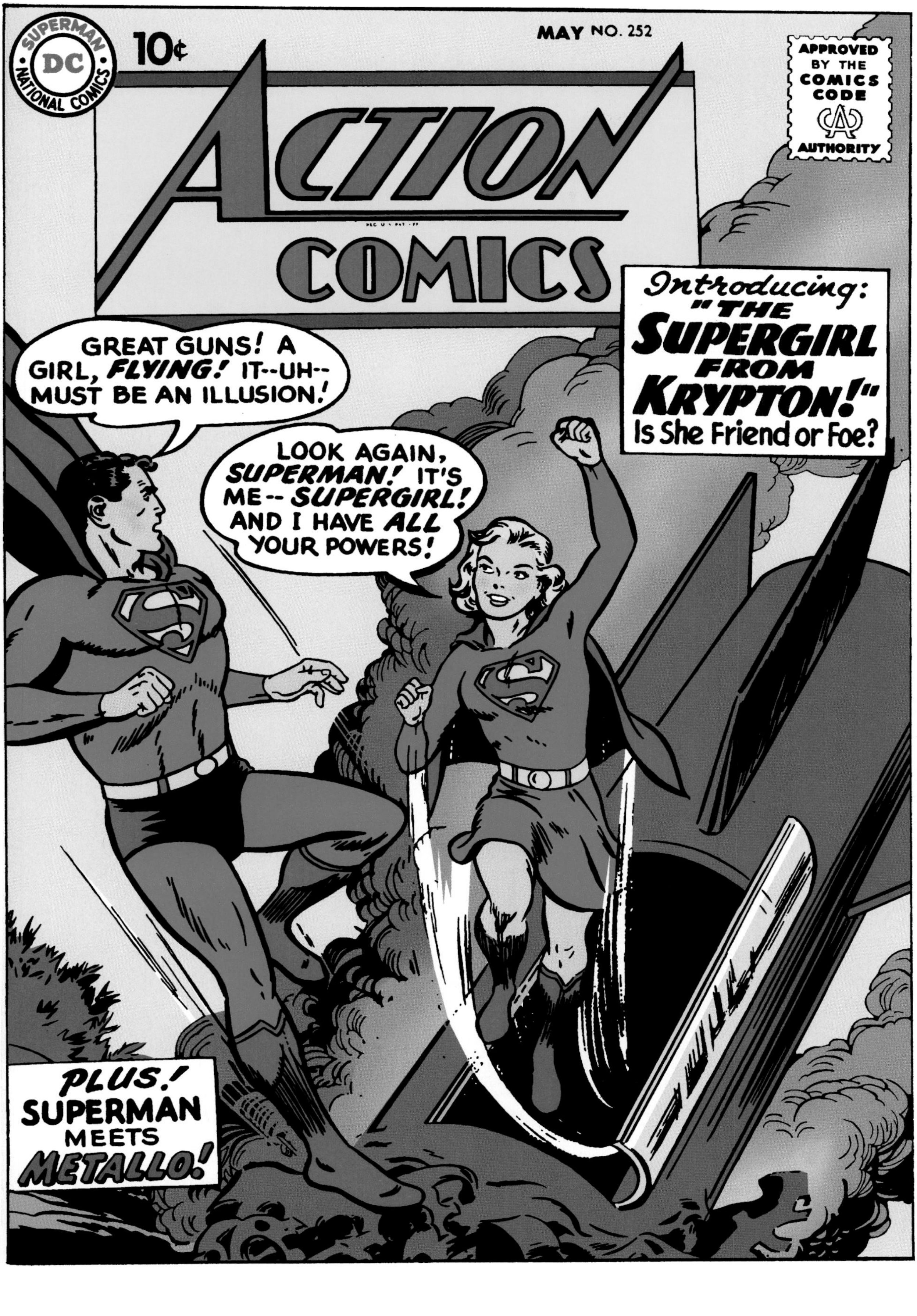
10¢
MAY NO. 252
APPROVED BY THE COMICS CODE AUTHORITY
ACTION COMICS
Introducing: "THE SUPERGIRL FROM KRYPTON!" Is She Friend or Foe?
GREAT GUNS! A GIRL, FLYING! IT--UH-- MUST BE AN ILLUSION!
LOOK AGAIN, SUPERMAN! IT'S ME-- SUPERGIRL! AND I HAVE ALL YOUR POWERS!
PLUS! SUPERMAN MEETS METALLO!

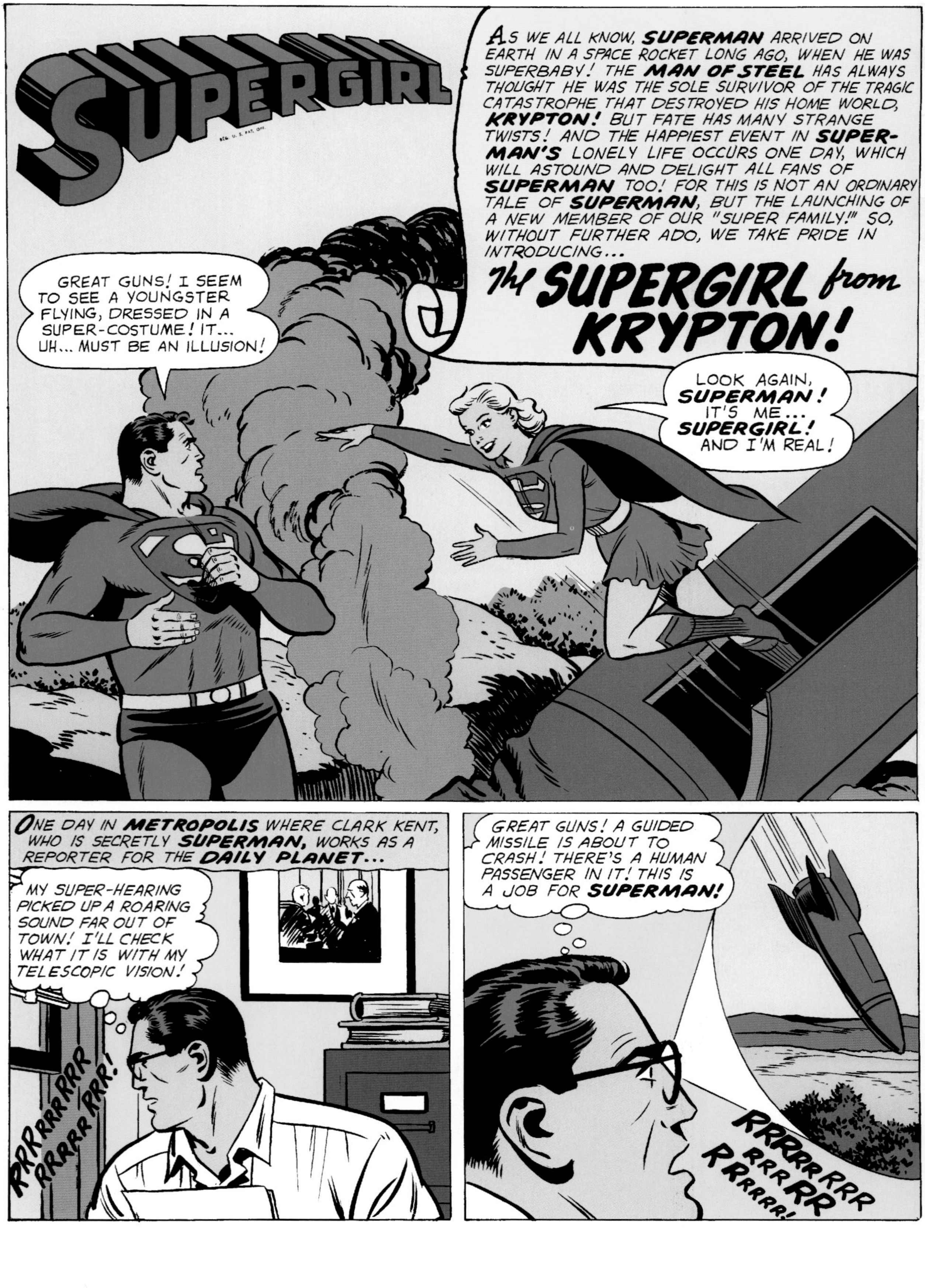
SUPERGIRL
REG. U.S. PAT. OFF.
AS WE ALL KNOW, SUPERMAN ARRIVED ON EARTH IN A SPACE ROCKET LONG AGO, WHEN HE WAS SUPERBABY! THE MAN OF STEEL HAS ALWAYS THOUGHT HE WAS THE SOLE SURVIVOR OF THE TRAGIC CATASTROPHE THAT DESTROYED HIS HOME WORLD, KRYPTON! BUT FATE HAS MANY STRANGE TWISTS! AND THE HAPPIEST EVENT IN SUPERMAN'S LONELY LIFE OCCURS ONE DAY, WHICH WILL ASTOUND AND DELIGHT ALL FANS OF SUPERMAN TOO! FOR THIS IS NOT AN ORDINARY TALE OF SUPERMAN, BUT THE LAUNCHING OF A NEW MEMBER OF OUR "SUPER FAMILY!" SO, WITHOUT FURTHER ADO, WE TAKE PRIDE IN INTRODUCING...
The SUPERGIRL from KRYPTON!
GREAT GUNS! I SEEM TO SEE A YOUNGSTER FLYING, DRESSED IN A SUPER-COSTUME! IT... UH... MUST BE AN ILLUSION!
LOOK AGAIN, SUPERMAN! IT'S ME... SUPERGIRL! AND I'M REAL!
ONE DAY IN METROPOLIS WHERE CLARK KENT, WHO IS SECRETLY SUPERMAN, WORKS AS A REPORTER FOR THE DAILY PLANET...
MY SUPER-HEARING PICKED UP A ROARING SOUND FAR OUT OF TOWN! I'LL CHECK WHAT IT IS WITH MY TELESCOPIC VISION!
RRRRRRRRR RRRRR RRR!
GREAT GUNS! A GUIDED MISSILE IS ABOUT TO CRASH! THERE'S A HUMAN PASSENGER IN IT! THIS IS A JOB FOR SUPERMAN!
RRRRRRRR RRRRR RRRRRR!

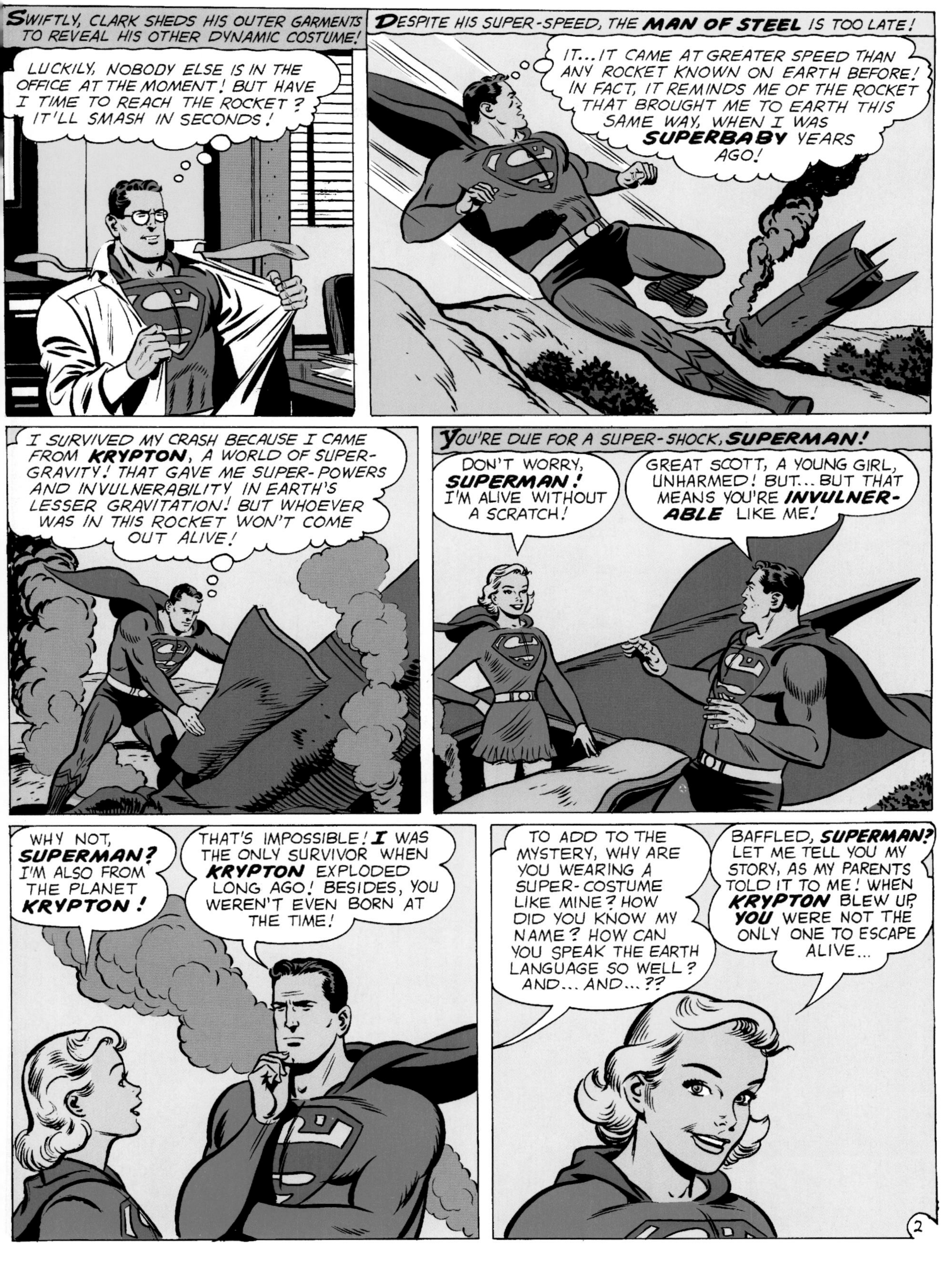
SWIFTLY, CLARK SHEDS HIS OUTER GARMENTS TO REVEAL HIS OTHER DYNAMIC COSTUME!
LUCKILY, NOBODY ELSE IS IN THE OFFICE AT THE MOMENT! BUT HAVE I TIME TO REACH THE ROCKET? IT'LL SMASH IN SECONDS!
DESPITE HIS SUPER-SPEED, THE MAN OF STEEL IS TOO LATE!
IT... IT CAME AT GREATER SPEED THAN ANY ROCKET KNOWN ON EARTH BEFORE! IN FACT, IT REMINDS ME OF THE ROCKET THAT BROUGHT ME TO EARTH THIS SAME WAY, WHEN I WAS SUPERBABY YEARS AGO!
I SURVIVED MY CRASH BECAUSE I CAME FROM KRYPTON, A WORLD OF SUPER-GRAVITY! THAT GAVE ME SUPER-POWERS AND INVULNERABILITY IN EARTH'S LESSER GRAVITATION! BUT WHOEVER WAS IN THIS ROCKET WON'T COME OUT ALIVE!
YOU'RE DUE FOR A SUPER-SHOCK, SUPERMAN!
DON'T WORRY, SUPERMAN! I'M ALIVE WITHOUT A SCRATCH!
GREAT SCOTT, A YOUNG GIRL, UNHARMED! BUT... BUT THAT MEANS YOU'RE INVULNERABLE LIKE ME!
WHY NOT, SUPERMAN? I'M ALSO FROM THE PLANET KRYPTON!
THAT'S IMPOSSIBLE! I WAS THE ONLY SURVIVOR WHEN KRYPTON EXPLODED LONG AGO! BESIDES, YOU WEREN'T EVEN BORN AT THE TIME!
TO ADD TO THE MYSTERY, WHY ARE YOU WEARING A SUPER-COSTUME LIKE MINE? HOW DID YOU KNOW MY NAME? HOW CAN YOU SPEAK THE EARTH LANGUAGE SO WELL? AND... AND...??
BAFFLED, SUPERMAN? LET ME TELL YOU MY STORY, AS MY PARENTS TOLD IT TO ME! WHEN KRYPTON BLEW UP, YOU WERE NOT THE ONLY ONE TO ESCAPE ALIVE...
2

"BY SHEER LUCK, A LARGE CHUNK OF THE PLANET WAS HURLED AWAY INTACT, WITH PEOPLE ON IT..."

OUR STREET OF HOMES IS BEING FLUNG FREE INTO *SPACE*, SAVING US FROM THE CONCUSSION THAT WIPED OUT ALL OTHERS!

"AMONG THE PITIFUL FEW SURVIVORS WAS A SCIENTIST, ZOR-EL..."

FORTUNATELY, A LARGE BUBBLE OF AIR CAME ALONG WITH THIS CHUNK! ALSO, THIS **FOOD MACHINE** IS STILL WORKING! WE CAN STAY ALIVE INDEFINITELY!

"BUT THEIR JOY WAS SHORT-LIVED, FOR, WHEN NIGHT FELL..."

OHH... I FEEL WEAK!

GREAT STARS! THE GROUND IS GLOWING GREEN! THE NUCLEAR EXPLOSION CONVERTED OUR SHATTERED PLANET INTO **KRYPTONITE**, AN ELEMENT WHOSE RADIATIONS CAN POISON AND DESTROY US IN TIME!

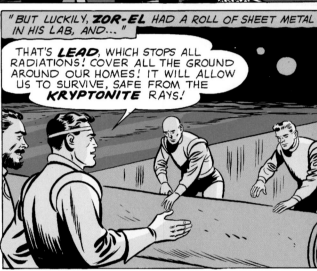

"BUT LUCKILY, **ZOR-EL** HAD A ROLL OF SHEET METAL IN HIS LAB, AND..."

THAT'S **LEAD**, WHICH STOPS ALL RADIATIONS! COVER ALL THE GROUND AROUND OUR HOMES! IT WILL ALLOW US TO SURVIVE, SAFE FROM THE **KRYPTONITE** RAYS!

"LIFE SETTLED DOWN FOR THE **KRYPTON** REFUGEES AND, SOME YEARS LATER, **ZOR-EL** TOOK A WIFE AND A DAUGHTER WAS BORN TO THEM....**ME!**"

IT'S TIME FOR **KARA'S** BOTTLE, DEAR!

OUR CHILD CAN GROW UP SAFELY AS LONG AS THE LEADEN SHIELD UNDER OUR COMMUNITY WARDS OFF THOSE **KRYPTONITE** RADIATIONS!

"BUT FATE PLAYED A CRUEL TRICK, WHEN I HAD GROWN INTO GIRLHOOD..."

INTO THE HOUSE, **KARA!** A METEOR FLOCK IS SMASHING HOLES IN THE LEADEN SHIELD, RELEASING **KRYPTONITE** RADIATIONS! WE ARE ALL DOOMED... ≡CHOKE!≡

3

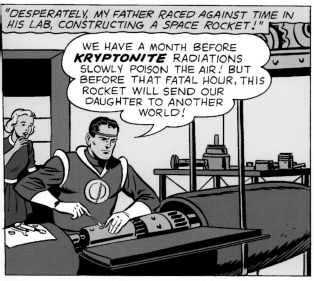

"DESPERATELY, MY FATHER RACED AGAINST TIME IN HIS LAB, CONSTRUCTING A SPACE ROCKET!"

WE HAVE A MONTH BEFORE **KRYPTONITE** RADIATIONS SLOWLY POISON THE AIR! BUT BEFORE THAT FATAL HOUR, THIS ROCKET WILL SEND OUR DAUGHTER TO ANOTHER WORLD!

BUT WHICH WORLD? I'LL USE THE **SUPER-SPACE TELESCOPE** TO FIND SOME CIVILIZED WORLD WHERE **KARA** CAN GROW UP SAFELY!

"EXAMINING MANY PLANETS, MY MOTHER SPIED A STARTLING PHENOMENON ON ONE PARTICULAR WORLD..."

LOOK, MOTHER! WHO IS THAT FLYING MAN?

I...I DON'T KNOW, DEAR! BUT THAT IS A CIVILIZED WORLD! I'LL PICK UP THEIR BROADCASTS WITH OUR SPACE RADIO, AND DECIPHER THEIR LANGUAGE!

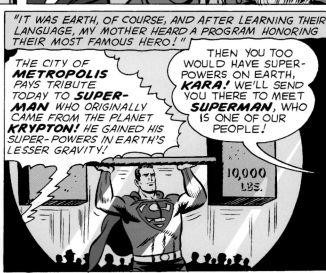

"IT WAS EARTH, OF COURSE, AND AFTER LEARNING THEIR LANGUAGE, MY MOTHER HEARD A PROGRAM HONORING THEIR MOST FAMOUS HERO!"

THE CITY OF **METROPOLIS** PAYS TRIBUTE TODAY TO **SUPER-MAN** WHO ORIGINALLY CAME FROM THE PLANET **KRYPTON!** HE GAINED HIS SUPER-POWERS IN EARTH'S LESSER GRAVITY!

THEN YOU TOO WOULD HAVE SUPER-POWERS ON EARTH, **KARA!** WE'LL SEND YOU THERE TO MEET **SUPERMAN**, WHO IS ONE OF OUR PEOPLE!

10,000 LBS.

"MY MOTHER ALSO MADE ME A SPECIAL COSTUME..."

I'LL MAKE IT LIKE **SUPERMAN'S** SUIT SO HE'LL KNOW YOU FOR A **KRYPTON** GIRL! I CAN CUT AND SEW IT HERE, BUT ON EARTH IT WILL BECOME INDESTRUCTIBLE **SUPER-CLOTH!**

THE SPACE ROCKET IS FINISHED, TOO! HURRY! THE **KRYPTONITE** RADIATIONS ARE FILLING THE AIR LIKE POISON!

"BARELY IN TIME, I WAS SHOT FREE OF MY DOOMED PEOPLE!"

WE HAVE AIMED THE ROCKET FOR EARTH! FAREWELL, **KARA** ...≷GASP!≶

MY FATHER... MOTHER... ALL THE PEOPLE ARE DYING! I'M AN **ORPHAN** OF SPACE NOW... ≷SOB!≶

4

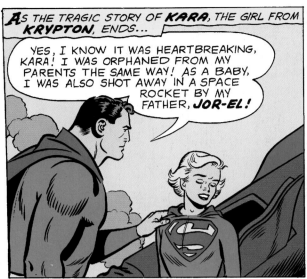

As the tragic story of **KARA**, the girl from **KRYPTON**, ends...

YES, I KNOW IT WAS HEARTBREAKING, KARA! I WAS ORPHANED FROM MY PARENTS THE SAME WAY! AS A BABY, I WAS ALSO SHOT AWAY IN A SPACE ROCKET BY MY FATHER, **JOR-EL!**

JOR-EL? WHY, MY FATHER'S NAME WAS **ZOR-EL**, YOUR FATHER'S **BROTHER!**

GREAT SCOTT! THEN YOU'RE MY-- **COUSIN!**

THIS IS PERHAPS THE HAPPIEST MOMENT IN **SUPERMAN'S** LIFE, TO FIND HE HAS A LONG-LOST LIVING RELATIVE FROM HIS NATIVE WORLD!

WE MAY BE ORPHANS, BUT WE HAVE EACH OTHER NOW! I'LL TAKE CARE OF YOU LIKE A BIG BROTHER, COUSIN **KARA!**

THANKS, COUSIN **SUPERMAN!** ... ≡CHOKE!≡ YOU MEAN I'LL COME AND LIVE WITH YOU?

HMM... NO! THAT WOULDN'T WORK! YOU SEE, I'VE ADOPTED A SECRET IDENTITY ON EARTH WHICH MIGHT BE JEOPARDIZED! BUT I HAVE A GREAT IDEA FOR YOUR FUTURE LIFE! FIRST, LET'S SEE IF YOU CAN FLY!

I...I CAN! I HAVE SUPER-POWERS JUST LIKE YOU DO, COUSIN!

I JUST WANTED TO MAKE SURE! IN MY YOUTH IN SMALLVILLE, I WAS HONORED AS **SUPER-BOY!** YOU TOO CAN GAIN FAME AS **SUPER-GIRL**, THE **GIRL OF STEEL!**

OH, HOW THRILLING, **SUPERMAN!** CAN I BEGIN MY SUPER-CAREER RIGHT AWAY?

NO, KARA! YOU'LL NEED LONG PRACTICE BEFORE YOU CAN USE YOUR SUPER-POWERS PROPERLY. MEANWHILE, THIS ORPHANAGE WILL BE YOUR HOME!

MIDVALE ORPHANGE

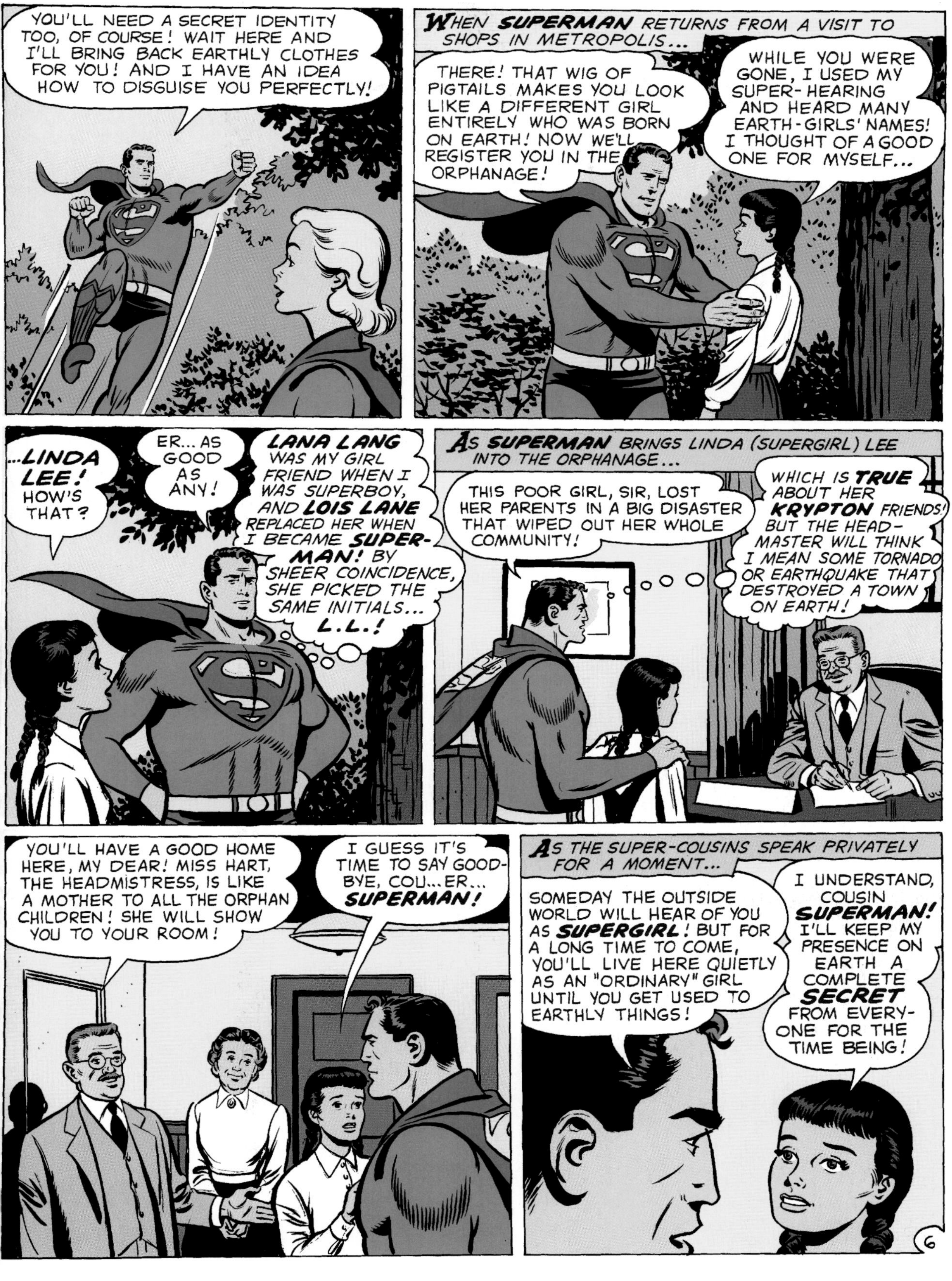
YOU'LL NEED A SECRET IDENTITY TOO, OF COURSE! WAIT HERE AND I'LL BRING BACK EARTHLY CLOTHES FOR YOU! AND I HAVE AN IDEA HOW TO DISGUISE YOU PERFECTLY!
WHEN SUPERMAN RETURNS FROM A VISIT TO SHOPS IN METROPOLIS...
THERE! THAT WIG OF PIGTAILS MAKES YOU LOOK LIKE A DIFFERENT GIRL ENTIRELY WHO WAS BORN ON EARTH! NOW WE'LL REGISTER YOU IN THE ORPHANAGE!
WHILE YOU WERE GONE, I USED MY SUPER-HEARING AND HEARD MANY EARTH-GIRLS' NAMES! I THOUGHT OF A GOOD ONE FOR MYSELF...
...LINDA LEE! HOW'S THAT?
ER... AS GOOD AS ANY!
LANA LANG WAS MY GIRL FRIEND WHEN I WAS SUPERBOY, AND LOIS LANE REPLACED HER WHEN I BECAME SUPER-MAN! BY SHEER COINCIDENCE, SHE PICKED THE SAME INITIALS... L.L.!
AS SUPERMAN BRINGS LINDA (SUPERGIRL) LEE INTO THE ORPHANAGE...
THIS POOR GIRL, SIR, LOST HER PARENTS IN A BIG DISASTER THAT WIPED OUT HER WHOLE COMMUNITY!
WHICH IS TRUE ABOUT HER KRYPTON FRIENDS! BUT THE HEAD-MASTER WILL THINK I MEAN SOME TORNADO OR EARTHQUAKE THAT DESTROYED A TOWN ON EARTH!
YOU'LL HAVE A GOOD HOME HERE, MY DEAR! MISS HART, THE HEADMISTRESS, IS LIKE A MOTHER TO ALL THE ORPHAN CHILDREN! SHE WILL SHOW YOU TO YOUR ROOM!
I GUESS IT'S TIME TO SAY GOOD-BYE, COU...ER... SUPERMAN!
AS THE SUPER-COUSINS SPEAK PRIVATELY FOR A MOMENT...
SOMEDAY THE OUTSIDE WORLD WILL HEAR OF YOU AS SUPERGIRL! BUT FOR A LONG TIME TO COME, YOU'LL LIVE HERE QUIETLY AS AN "ORDINARY" GIRL UNTIL YOU GET USED TO EARTHLY THINGS!
I UNDERSTAND, COUSIN SUPERMAN! I'LL KEEP MY PRESENCE ON EARTH A COMPLETE SECRET FROM EVERY-ONE FOR THE TIME BEING!
6

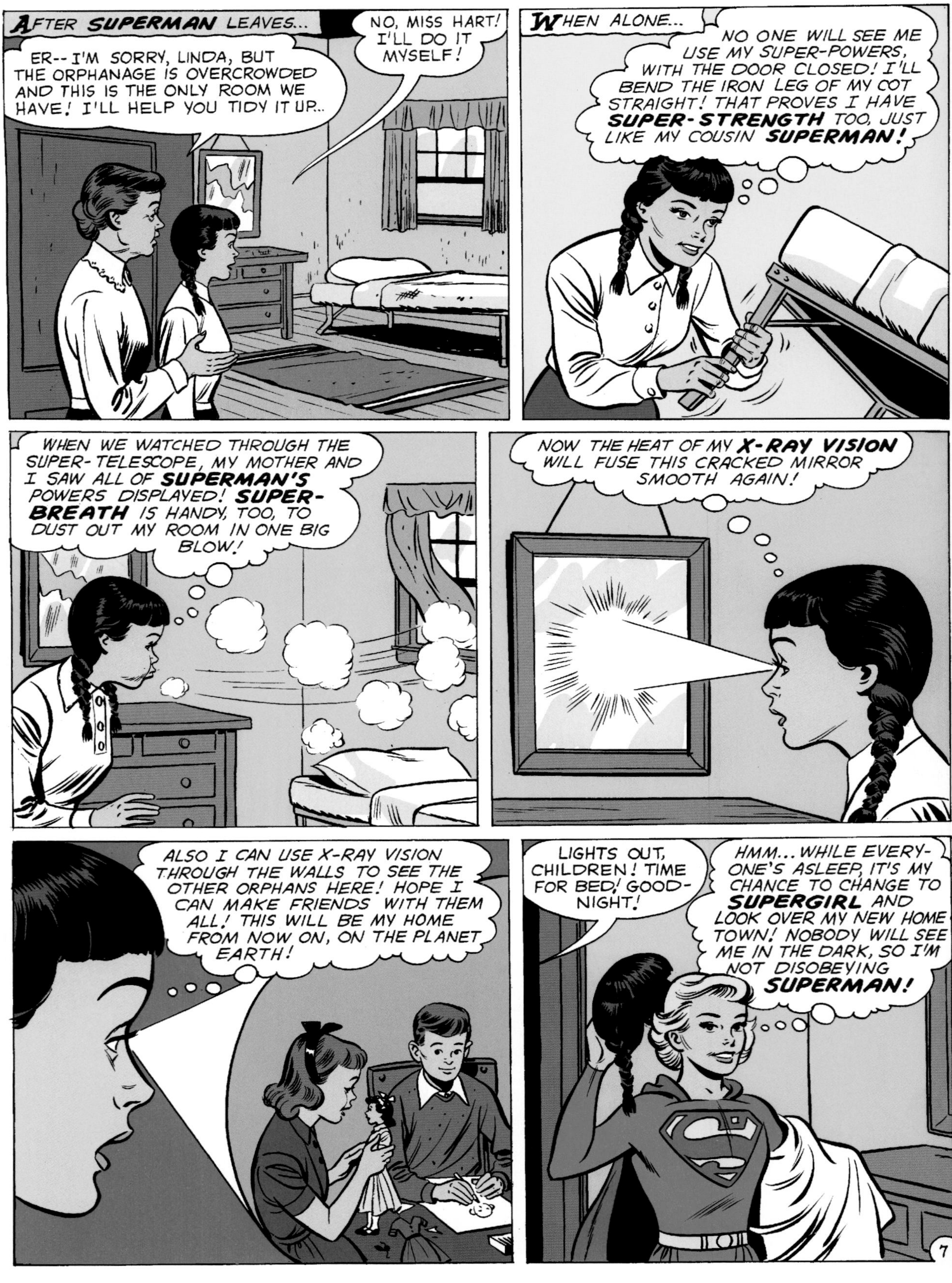
AFTER SUPERMAN LEAVES...
ER-- I'M SORRY, LINDA, BUT THE ORPHANAGE IS OVERCROWDED AND THIS IS THE ONLY ROOM WE HAVE! I'LL HELP YOU TIDY IT UP...
NO, MISS HART! I'LL DO IT MYSELF!
WHEN ALONE...
NO ONE WILL SEE ME USE MY SUPER-POWERS, WITH THE DOOR CLOSED! I'LL BEND THE IRON LEG OF MY COT STRAIGHT! THAT PROVES I HAVE SUPER-STRENGTH TOO, JUST LIKE MY COUSIN SUPERMAN!
WHEN WE WATCHED THROUGH THE SUPER-TELESCOPE, MY MOTHER AND I SAW ALL OF SUPERMAN'S POWERS DISPLAYED! SUPER-BREATH IS HANDY, TOO, TO DUST OUT MY ROOM IN ONE BIG BLOW!
NOW THE HEAT OF MY X-RAY VISION WILL FUSE THIS CRACKED MIRROR SMOOTH AGAIN!
ALSO I CAN USE X-RAY VISION THROUGH THE WALLS TO SEE THE OTHER ORPHANS HERE! HOPE I CAN MAKE FRIENDS WITH THEM ALL! THIS WILL BE MY HOME FROM NOW ON, ON THE PLANET EARTH!
LIGHTS OUT, CHILDREN! TIME FOR BED! GOOD-NIGHT!
HMM... WHILE EVERY-ONE'S ASLEEP, IT'S MY CHANCE TO CHANGE TO SUPERGIRL AND LOOK OVER MY NEW HOME TOWN! NOBODY WILL SEE ME IN THE DARK, SO I'M NOT DISOBEYING SUPERMAN!
7

SOON, *SUPERGIRL* IS ON A SECRET "PATROL" OF MIDVALE!

MIDVALE IS A PRETTY LITTLE TOWN! I LIKE IT ALREADY! MAYBE I CAN STILL DO SUPER-DEEDS FOR WORTHY PEOPLE WITHOUT BEING SEEN, LIKE A SORT OF "GUARDIAN ANGEL!"

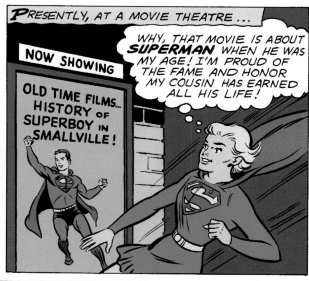

PRESENTLY, AT A MOVIE THEATRE...

NOW SHOWING

OLD TIME FILMS... HISTORY OF SUPERBOY IN SMALLVILLE!

WHY, THAT MOVIE IS ABOUT *SUPERMAN* WHEN HE WAS MY AGE! I'M PROUD OF THE FAME AND HONOR MY COUSIN HAS EARNED ALL HIS LIFE!

WILL I SOMEDAY DO AS GOOD A JOB IN MIDVALE, AS *SUPERGIRL?* WHAT WILL THE FUTURE BRING FOR ME?

8

MIDVALE ORPHANAGE

IF YOU WANT TO FIND OUT, READERS, YOU CAN! *SUPER-GIRL'S* ADVENTURES WILL CONTINUE *REGULARLY* HEREAFTER IN *ACTION COMICS,* ALONG WITH THE DOINGS OF HER FAMOUS COUSIN, *SUPER-MAN!* SEE THE NEXT ISSUE FOR ANOTHER THRILLING STORY ABOUT THIS *GIRL OF STEEL,* A BRAND-NEW MEMBER OF OUR *SUPER-FAMILY* ALONG WITH *SUPERBOY* AND *SUPERMAN!*

The End

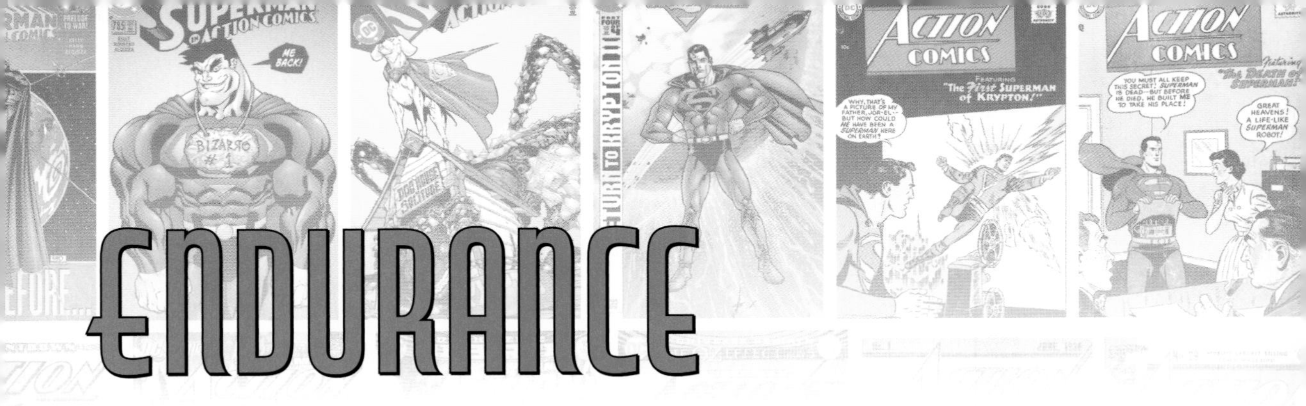
ACTION COMICS
The First SUPERMAN of KRYPTON!
ACTION COMICS
BIZARRO #1

ENDURANCE

by **LARRY TYE**

The most enduring American hero of the last century is someone who lived half his life in disguise and the other half as the world's most recognizable man. He is not Jack Kennedy or Joltin' Joe DiMaggio, Batman or Jerry Seinfeld, although all of them were inspired by him. It was on his muscle-bound back that the iconic comic book took flight and that the very idea of the superhero was born. He appeared on more radio broadcasts than Ellery Queen and in more movies than Marlon Brando, who once pretended to be his father. He helped give America the confidence to wage war against Adolf Hitler, the Great Depression and the Ku Klux Klan. He is an intimate to kids from Boston to Belgrade and has adult devotees who, like Talmudic scholars, anatomize his every utterance. And he did it all with an innocence and confidence that let him appear in public in full-body tights and underpants and assume an alter ego who forever pursued the prettiest girl, even if he seldom got her.

The most enduring American hero was an alien from outer space who, once he reached Earth, swiftly traded in his foreign-sounding name Kal-El for the singularly American handle of Superman.

Ah, you say, the Man of Steel. I know him! But do you really? Do you know the wrenching story of his birth and nurturing at the hands of a parade of young creators yearning for their own absent fathers? The first was the youngest child of Lithuanian immigrants, who was devastated when his dad died during a robbery of his store. While there was no bringing back his father and role model, Jerry Siegel did bring to life a hero able not just to run fast and jump high but, as we see early on, to fend off a robber. Who would buy this fanciful tale? How about Jack Liebowitz, a hard-headed comic book entrepreneur whose own dad died just after he was born and who could use a champion? While many baby boomers discovered that costumed hero in the comics, even more got to know him when he hurtled onto their television screens in the 1950s. Whitney Ellsworth, the man who wrote, edited and produced nearly all of those shows, was just 14 when he lost his 45 year-old father to a heart attack. George Reeves, TV's original Clark Kent and Superman, didn't even know who his real father was until he was in his twenties. Who better to create the ultimate childhood fantasy figure than men whose childhoods were stolen from them?

Superman's rivals also were more than they seemed and more than just fantasy. Many were real-world menaces, which made the stories timely and authentic. Superman stood up to Hitler and Stalin before America did. The Metropolis Marvel used his radio broadcast to expose the savagery of the Ku Klux Klan, and in his comic books he upended slumlords and wife beaters. Lex Luthor, Superman's most persistent foe, likely came from Jerry Siegel's boyhood. The day after Jerry's father died, his hometown newspaper published a letter denouncing the vigilante justice that would become Superman's early signature. The letter writer: A.L. Luther.

The superhero never revealed how he voted, but during the Great Depression he was a New Dealer hell-bent on truth and justice, and during the Reagan Revolution he was a patriot trumpeting the American way. His sex life underwent an even more drastic about-face—from celibate to satisfied husband. There is one more thing that even his most fervent fans may not know about the Man of Steel: he is Jewish.

I knew when I decided to write a book about him that I cared about Superman but was not sure anyone else still did. Sure, he was a big deal when I was coming of age in the 1960s, but I suspected he was passé in the virtual realities of the new millennium. Then I started paying attention. My four-year-old nephew showed up one night wearing a Superman shirt. My 16-year-old stepdaughter told me how, when she was four, she trick-or-treated dressed as Superman. When a neighbor said she made an adorable Supergirl, she set him straight: "I'm Superman!" My oldest friend's 14-year-old daughter showed me her DVD collection of *Smallville*, a show I had never heard of that for nine seasons chronicled the adventures of a young Clark Kent. The final test was on Halloween. Merchants in my hometown of Lexington, Massachusetts hand out candy all afternoon, packing sidewalks with costumed

ACTION COMICS
Sensational! SUPERMAN GOES WILD!
Introducing The SON of the MAN of STEEL— "Superman, Junior!"
SON OF THE ANNIHILATOR
THE KID WITH THE SUPER-FISTS!
SUPERMAN
ACTION COMICS
TRUTH, JUSTICE & THE AMERICAN WAY?

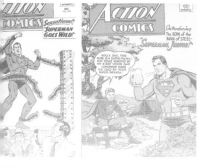

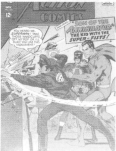

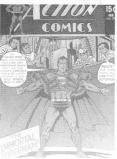

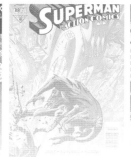

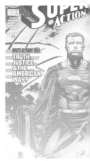

kids and providing the perfect sampling of who's hot in the world of heroes. Spider-Man did well, with half a dozen children dressed in webbed costumes, but the hands-down winner was the blue tights, red cape and bright yellow *S* of Superman.

I still had doubts, but they had changed from *whether* anyone cared to *why*. Why did Barack Obama pose in front of a Superman statue and later, just before his election as president, joke that he, too, came from Krypton? Surely he understood better than anyone the value of bonding to such a symbol of strength and honor. Why is the Man of Steel as popular today as he was in my era and every era back to his begetting in the 1930s? That is more than we can say for Jim Thorpe or Dwight Eisenhower, the Phantom, the Lone Ranger or Tarzan the Ape Man. Heroes, understandably, are woven into their times and seldom wear well.

So how has Superman managed to thrive for 80 years and counting?

It starts with the intrinsic simplicity of his story. *Little Orphan Annie* and *Oliver Twist* reminded us how compelling a foundling's tale can be, and Superman, the sole survivor of a doomed planet, is a super-foundling. The love triangle connecting Clark Kent, Lois Lane and Superman has a side for everyone, whether you are the boy who can't get the girl, the girl pursued by the wrong boy, or the conflicted hero. His secret identity might have been annoying if we hadn't been let in on the joke, and if we didn't each have a hero hidden within ourselves. He was not just any hero, but one with the very powers we would have: the strength to lift boulders and planets, the speed to outrun a locomotive or a bullet and, coolest on anyone's fantasy list, the gift of flight.

Superpowers are just half the equation. More essential is knowing what to do with them, and nobody has a more instinctive sense than Superman of right and wrong. He is an archetype of mankind at its pinnacle. Like John Wayne, he sweeps in to solve our problems. No thank-you needed. Like Jesus Christ, he descended from the heavens to help us discover our humanity. He is neither cynical like Batman nor fraught like Spider-Man. For the religious, he can reinforce whatever faith they profess; for nonbelievers, he is a secular messiah. The more jaded the era, the more we have been lured back to his clunky familiarity. No matter that the upshot of his adventures is as predictable as those of Sherlock Holmes, with the good guy never losing. That, too, is reassuring.

That does not mean he hasn't changed with the times. Superman has evolved more than the fruit fly. In the 1930s he was just the crime-fighter we needed to take on Al Capone and the robber barons. In the '40s he defended the home front while brave GIs battled overseas. In the early years of the Cold War he took on communist spies, while in its waning days he tried to single-handedly eliminate nuclear stockpiles. For each era, he zeroed in on the threats that scared us most, using powers that grew or diminished depending on the need. So did his spectacles, hairstyle and job title. Each generation got the Superman it needed and deserved. Each change offered a Rorschach test of the pulse of that time and its dreams. Superman, always a beacon of life, was a work in progress.

Over the years comics, too, have transformed—from childhood entertainment to art form to mythology, and Superman helped drive that progress. The comic book and its leading man could only have taken root in America. What could be more USA than an orphaned outsider who arrives in this land of immigrants, reinvents himself and reminds us that we can reach for the sky? Yet today this flying Uncle Sam is global in his reach, having written himself into the national folklore everywhere from Beirut to Buenos Aires. It is that constancy and purity—knowing that he was not merely the oldest of our superheroes but the most transcendent—that has reeled back aging devotees like me and drawn in new ones like my stepdaughter and nephew. It is what makes the Man of Tomorrow timeless as well as ageless.

LARRY TYE is a Boston-based journalist and author, having published biographies of Bobby Kennedy, Edward L. Bernays, Satchel Paige and Superman. He is currently writing a bio of Senator Joseph McCarthy for Houghton-Mifflin-Harcourt.

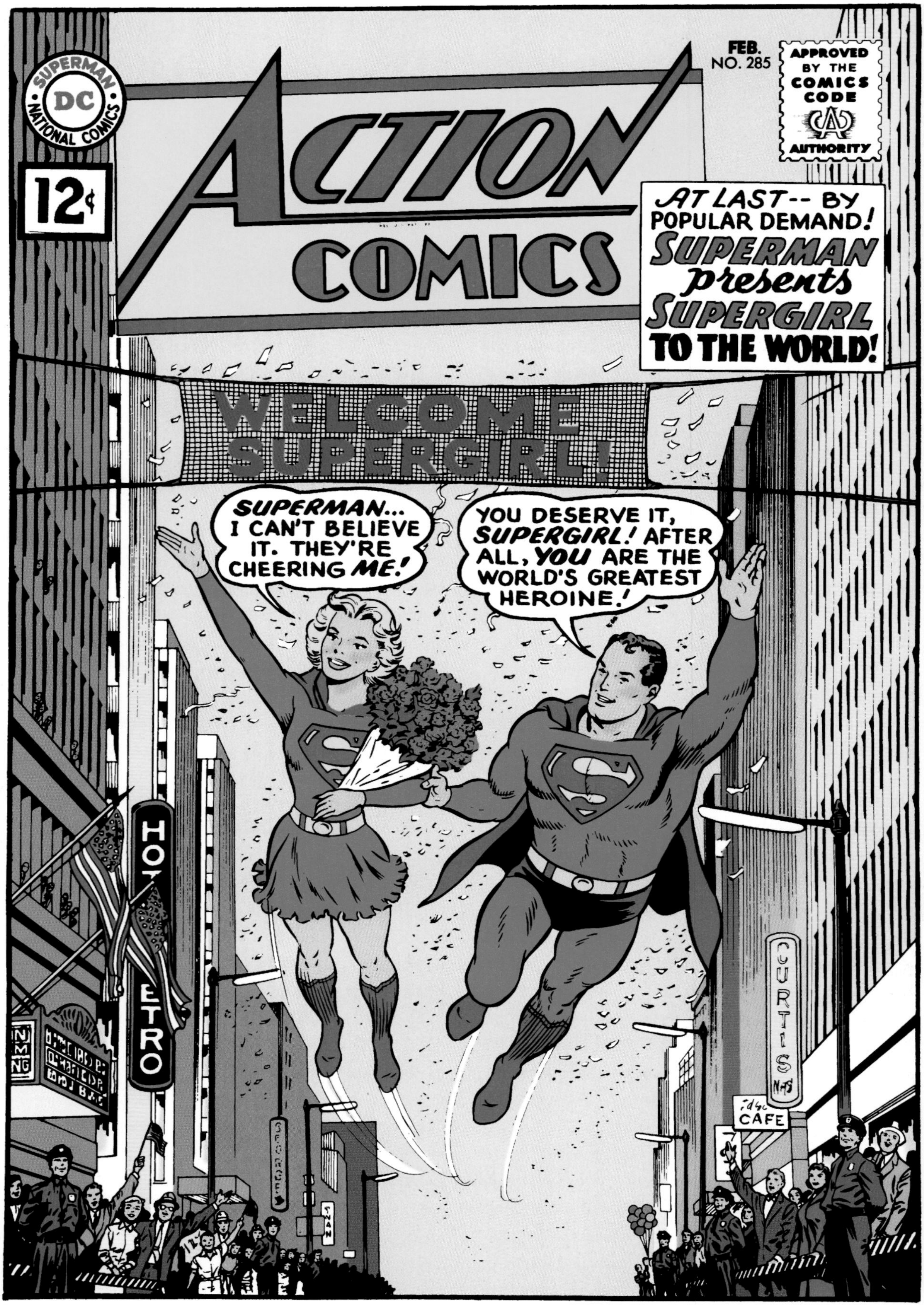
SUPERMAN DC NATIONAL COMICS
12¢
ACTION COMICS
FEB. NO. 285
APPROVED BY THE COMICS CODE AUTHORITY
AT LAST-- BY POPULAR DEMAND! SUPERMAN presents SUPERGIRL TO THE WORLD!
WELCOME SUPERGIRL!
SUPERMAN... I CAN'T BELIEVE IT. THEY'RE CHEERING ME!
YOU DESERVE IT, SUPERGIRL! AFTER ALL, YOU ARE THE WORLD'S GREATEST HEROINE!
HOT
METRO
CURTIS
CAFE

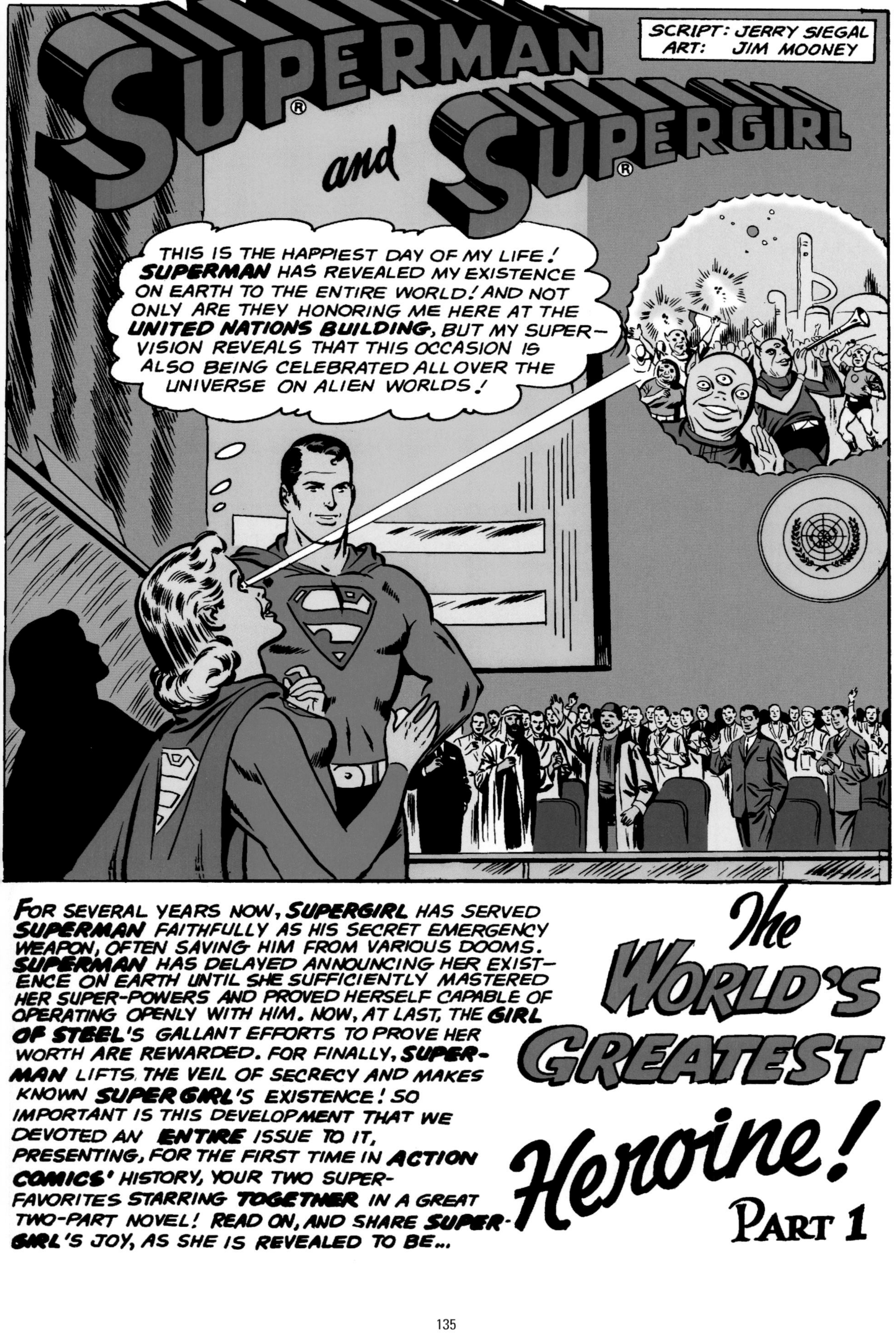

SCRIPT: JERRY SIEGAL
ART: JIM MOONEY
SUPERMAN and SUPERGIRL
THIS IS THE HAPPIEST DAY OF MY LIFE! SUPERMAN HAS REVEALED MY EXISTENCE ON EARTH TO THE ENTIRE WORLD! AND NOT ONLY ARE THEY HONORING ME HERE AT THE UNITED NATIONS BUILDING, BUT MY SUPER-VISION REVEALS THAT THIS OCCASION IS ALSO BEING CELEBRATED ALL OVER THE UNIVERSE ON ALIEN WORLDS!

FOR SEVERAL YEARS NOW, **SUPERGIRL** HAS SERVED **SUPERMAN** FAITHFULLY AS HIS SECRET EMERGENCY WEAPON, OFTEN SAVING HIM FROM VARIOUS DOOMS. **SUPERMAN** HAS DELAYED ANNOUNCING HER EXISTENCE ON EARTH UNTIL SHE SUFFICIENTLY MASTERED HER SUPER-POWERS AND PROVED HERSELF CAPABLE OF OPERATING OPENLY WITH HIM. NOW, AT LAST, THE **GIRL OF STEEL**'S GALLANT EFFORTS TO PROVE HER WORTH ARE REWARDED. FOR FINALLY, **SUPERMAN** LIFTS THE VEIL OF SECRECY AND MAKES KNOWN **SUPERGIRL**'S EXISTENCE! SO IMPORTANT IS THIS DEVELOPMENT THAT WE DEVOTED AN **ENTIRE** ISSUE TO IT, PRESENTING, FOR THE FIRST TIME IN **ACTION COMICS'** HISTORY, YOUR TWO SUPER-FAVORITES STARRING **TOGETHER** IN A GREAT TWO-PART NOVEL! **READ ON, AND SHARE SUPERGIRL**'S JOY, AS SHE IS **REVEALED TO BE**...

The World's Greatest Heroine!

Part 1

ONE AFTERNOON, ON THE OUTSKIRTS OF MIDVALE...

YOU'VE BEEN A SPLENDID "SECRET EMERGENCY WEAPON", SUPER-GIRL! BUT NOW THAT YOU'VE LEARNED HOW TO HANDLE YOUR SUPER-POWERS WISELY, IT WOULD BE UNFAIR FOR ME TO KEEP YOUR EXISTENCE A SECRET ANY LONGER!

OH, HOW WONDERFUL, SUPERMAN! I JUST CAN'T BELIEVE IT!

AND SO I'LL PUBLICLY REVEAL YOUR EXISTENCE! FIRST, HOWEVER, WE'LL DISCLOSE IT TO YOUR FOSTER PARENTS, TOGETHER WITH THE FACT THAT YOU, THEIR ADOPTED DAUGHTER, LINDA, ARE SUPERGIRL'S SECRET IDENTITY!

I'M SO HAPPY!

I'LL MEET YOU AT 9 O'CLOCK TONIGHT! WE'LL TELL THEM TOGETHER! BUT NOW I MUST RESUME MY PATROL OF METROPOLIS!

SUPERMAN'S SUCH A DEAR! I REALIZE NOW HOW WISE HE WAS TO DELAY ANNOUNCING MY EXISTENCE UNTIL I WAS REALLY READY!

SHORTLY, AS SUPERGIRL CHANGES TO HER LINDA LEE DANVERS IDENTITY, AND RETURNS HOME...

I CAN HARDLY KEEP FROM BLURTING OUT MY BIG SECRET TO MY FOLKS!... IT SEEMS LIKE 9 O'CLOCK WILL NEVER COME!

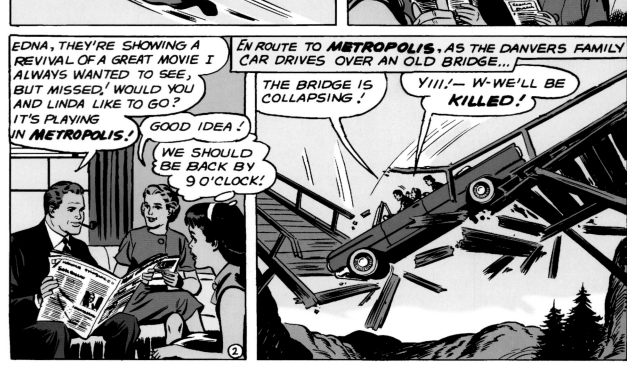

EDNA, THEY'RE SHOWING A REVIVAL OF A GREAT MOVIE I ALWAYS WANTED TO SEE, BUT MISSED! WOULD YOU AND LINDA LIKE TO GO? IT'S PLAYING IN METROPOLIS!

GOOD IDEA!

WE SHOULD BE BACK BY 9 O'CLOCK!

EN ROUTE TO METROPOLIS, AS THE DANVERS FAMILY CAR DRIVES OVER AN OLD BRIDGE...

THE BRIDGE IS COLLAPSING!

YIII!— W-WE'LL BE KILLED!

2

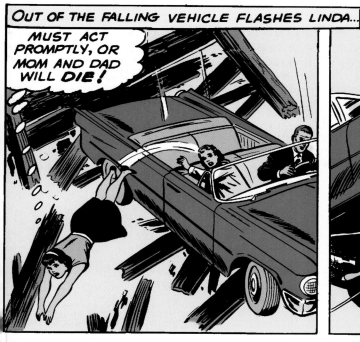

OUT OF THE FALLING VEHICLE FLASHES LINDA...

MUST ACT PROMPTLY, OR MOM AND DAD WILL *DIE!*

CAUGHT THE FALLING CAR! NOW TO FLY IT BACK TO SAFETY!

MOMENTS AFTERWARD...

THEY'RE ALL RIGHT NOW!

JUMPING JEHOSHAPHAT! THIS IS IMPOSSIBLE!

LINDA *CAUGHT THE CAR* AND FLEW US HERE!

I SAVED THEM... BUT IN SO DOING, I DISOBEYED *SUPERMAN'S* INSTRUCTIONS NOT TO REVEAL MY EXISTENCE AS *SUPERGIRL* UNTIL THE AGREED TIME! ≷CHOKE≷

LINDA! YOU'RE *SUPER-STRONG!* YOU CAN *FLY!*

NO ORDINARY HUMAN COULD DO THOSE THINGS! WE'RE GRATEFUL YOU SAVED OUR LIVES... BUT WE'RE YOUR PARENTS, DEAR, AND WE'RE ENTITLED TO AN EXPLANATION!

I *CAN'T* EXPLAIN! PLEASE DON'T ASK ME TO... YET! PLEASE!

EVASION IS SO USELESS! IT'S OBVIOUS I'M A *SUPERGIRL!* ≷CHOKE≷ – WILL *SUPERMAN* NOW DECIDE *NOT* TO ANNOUNCE MY EXISTENCE TO THE WORLD?

3

SUDDENLY... IT'S ALL RIGHT, LINDA! TELL YOUR PARENTS *EVERYTHING!*

SUPERMAN! WHAT...?!

SUPERMAN DOESN'T LOOK ANGRY!

I FINISHED MY PATROL EARLIER THAN EXPECTED, LINDA, AND WAS FLYING TOWARD YOUR HOME WHEN I SIGHTED THE RESCUE WITH MY TELESCOPIC VISION!... NATURALLY YOU HAD TO SAVE YOUR PARENTS, THOUGH IT MEANT DISCLOSING YOUR SUPER-POWERS!

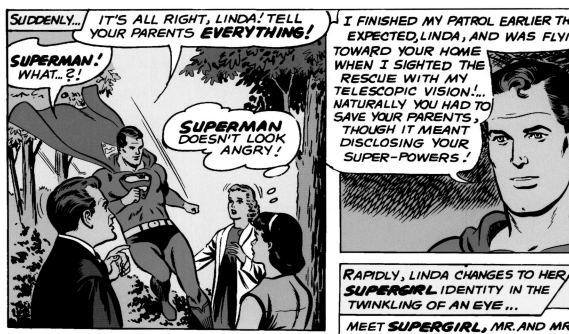

YOU MEAN ... YOU HAVEN'T CHANGED YOUR MIND ABOUT...?

REVEALING YOUR SECRET IDENTITY? OF COURSE NOT! LET'S DO IT *RIGHT NOW!*

"SECRET IDENTITY"? WHAT ARE THE TWO OF YOU TALKING ABOUT?!

RAPIDLY, LINDA CHANGES TO HER *SUPERGIRL* IDENTITY IN THE TWINKLING OF AN EYE ...

MEET *SUPERGIRL,* MR. AND MRS. DANVERS! YOUR DAUGHTER LINDA IS ACTUALLY MY COUSIN FROM THE DESTROYED PLANET *KRYPTON!*

OH MY!

GASP!

SEE? SHE HAS SUPER-POWERS AS GREAT AS MINE!

BUT *KRYPTON* EXPLODED WHEN YOU LEFT IT IN A ROCKET SHIP AS A BABY! SINCE *SUPERGIRL'S* MUCH YOUNGER THAN YOU, *HOW* COULD SHE HAVE ESCAPED *KRYPTON'S* DESTRUCTION?

"I'LL EXPLAIN!—MOMENTS AFTER *SUPERMAN'S* PARENTS SENT THEIR CHILD KAL-EL TOWARD EARTH IN A MODEL SPACESHIP... *KRYPTON* WAS BLASTED APART BY AN ATOMIC CHAIN-REACTION, AND A CHUNK OF THE PLANET WAS HURLED AWAY UNDER A PLASTIC DOME..."

4

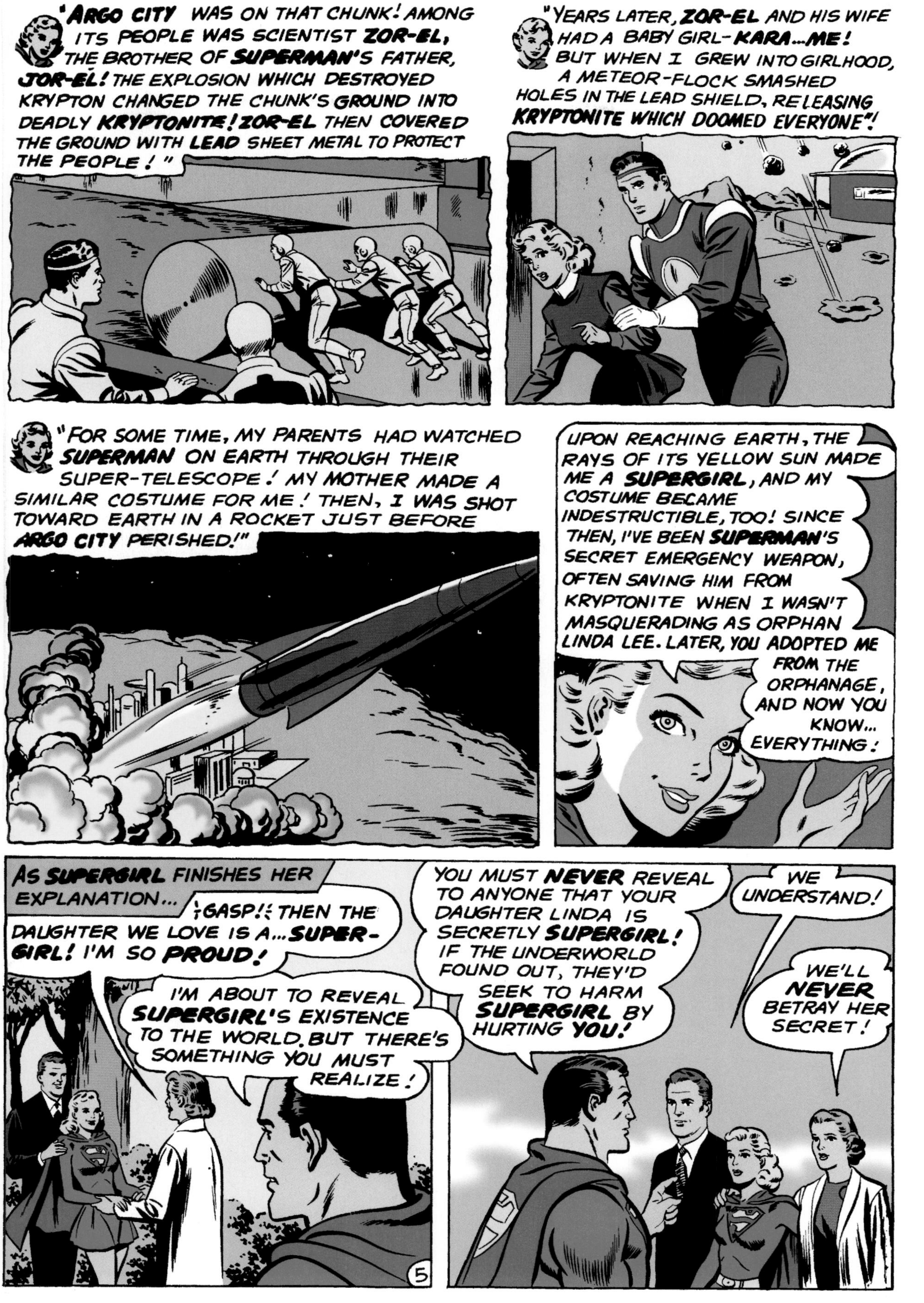

"ARGO CITY WAS ON THAT CHUNK! AMONG ITS PEOPLE WAS SCIENTIST ZOR-EL, THE BROTHER OF SUPERMAN'S FATHER, JOR-EL! THE EXPLOSION WHICH DESTROYED KRYPTON CHANGED THE CHUNK'S GROUND INTO DEADLY KRYPTONITE! ZOR-EL THEN COVERED THE GROUND WITH LEAD SHEET METAL TO PROTECT THE PEOPLE!"
"YEARS LATER, ZOR-EL AND HIS WIFE HAD A BABY GIRL-KARA...ME! BUT WHEN I GREW INTO GIRLHOOD, A METEOR-FLOCK SMASHED HOLES IN THE LEAD SHIELD, RELEASING KRYPTONITE WHICH DOOMED EVERYONE"!
"FOR SOME TIME, MY PARENTS HAD WATCHED SUPERMAN ON EARTH THROUGH THEIR SUPER-TELESCOPE! MY MOTHER MADE A SIMILAR COSTUME FOR ME! THEN, I WAS SHOT TOWARD EARTH IN A ROCKET JUST BEFORE ARGO CITY PERISHED!"
UPON REACHING EARTH, THE RAYS OF ITS YELLOW SUN MADE ME A SUPERGIRL, AND MY COSTUME BECAME INDESTRUCTIBLE, TOO! SINCE THEN, I'VE BEEN SUPERMAN'S SECRET EMERGENCY WEAPON, OFTEN SAVING HIM FROM KRYPTONITE WHEN I WASN'T MASQUERADING AS ORPHAN LINDA LEE. LATER, YOU ADOPTED ME FROM THE ORPHANAGE, AND NOW YOU KNOW... EVERYTHING!
AS SUPERGIRL FINISHES HER EXPLANATION...
GASP! THEN THE DAUGHTER WE LOVE IS A...SUPER-GIRL! I'M SO PROUD!
I'M ABOUT TO REVEAL SUPERGIRL'S EXISTENCE TO THE WORLD. BUT THERE'S SOMETHING YOU MUST REALIZE!
5
YOU MUST NEVER REVEAL TO ANYONE THAT YOUR DAUGHTER LINDA IS SECRETLY SUPERGIRL! IF THE UNDERWORLD FOUND OUT, THEY'D SEEK TO HARM SUPERGIRL BY HURTING YOU!
WE UNDERSTAND!
WE'LL NEVER BETRAY HER SECRET!

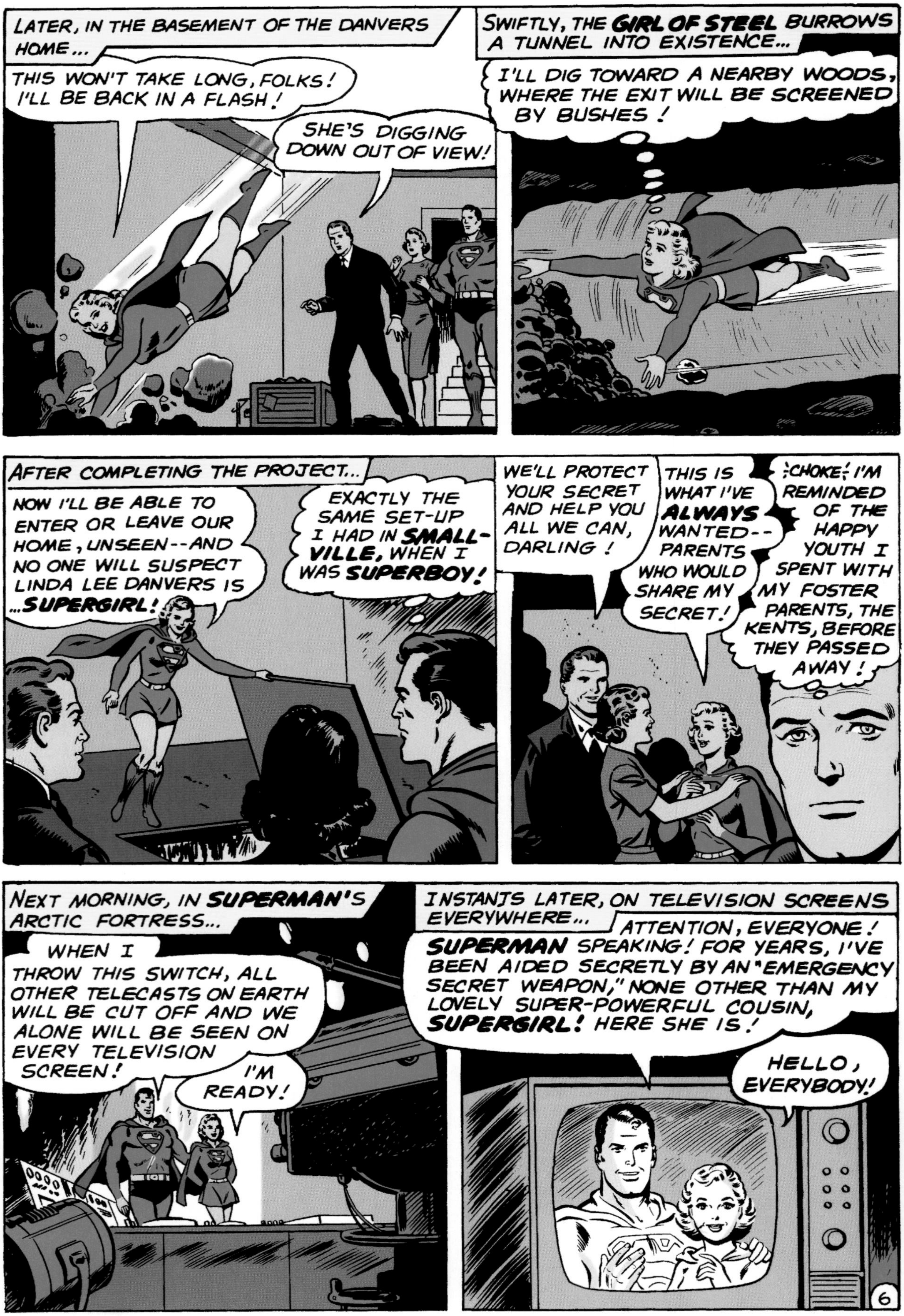
LATER, IN THE BASEMENT OF THE DANVERS HOME...
THIS WON'T TAKE LONG, FOLKS! I'LL BE BACK IN A FLASH!
SHE'S DIGGING DOWN OUT OF VIEW!
SWIFTLY, THE GIRL OF STEEL BURROWS A TUNNEL INTO EXISTENCE...
I'LL DIG TOWARD A NEARBY WOODS, WHERE THE EXIT WILL BE SCREENED BY BUSHES!
AFTER COMPLETING THE PROJECT...
NOW I'LL BE ABLE TO ENTER OR LEAVE OUR HOME, UNSEEN--AND NO ONE WILL SUSPECT LINDA LEE DANVERS IS ...SUPERGIRL!
EXACTLY THE SAME SET-UP I HAD IN SMALLVILLE, WHEN I WAS SUPERBOY!
WE'LL PROTECT YOUR SECRET AND HELP YOU ALL WE CAN, DARLING!
THIS IS WHAT I'VE ALWAYS WANTED--PARENTS WHO WOULD SHARE MY SECRET!
CHOKE! I'M REMINDED OF THE HAPPY YOUTH I SPENT WITH MY FOSTER PARENTS, THE KENTS, BEFORE THEY PASSED AWAY!
NEXT MORNING, IN SUPERMAN'S ARCTIC FORTRESS...
WHEN I THROW THIS SWITCH, ALL OTHER TELECASTS ON EARTH WILL BE CUT OFF AND WE ALONE WILL BE SEEN ON EVERY TELEVISION SCREEN!
I'M READY!
INSTANTS LATER, ON TELEVISION SCREENS EVERYWHERE...
ATTENTION, EVERYONE! SUPERMAN SPEAKING! FOR YEARS, I'VE BEEN AIDED SECRETLY BY AN "EMERGENCY SECRET WEAPON," NONE OTHER THAN MY LOVELY SUPER-POWERFUL COUSIN, SUPERGIRL! HERE SHE IS!
HELLO, EVERYBODY!
6

THE AMAZING NEWS BURSTS LIKE A BOMBSHELL, ASTOUNDING VIEWERS ALL OVER THE GLOBE...

SHE'S ADORABLE! I *LOVE* HER HAIR!

I'M HOLLYWOOD'S MOST BEAUTIFUL ACTRESS! BUT SHE'LL ATTRACT MORE ATTENTION THAN ME!...*BAH!*

IT'S UNFAIR! PEOPLE WILL LAUGH AT MY ACT, KNOWING A YOUNG GIRL IS STRONGER THAN ME!

;GROAN; HOW CAN THIS SNIP OF A CHILD BE MIGHTIER THAN ALL THE SOVIET ATOMIC BOMBS PUT TOGETHER? IT MUST BE A CAPITALISTIC *HOAX!*

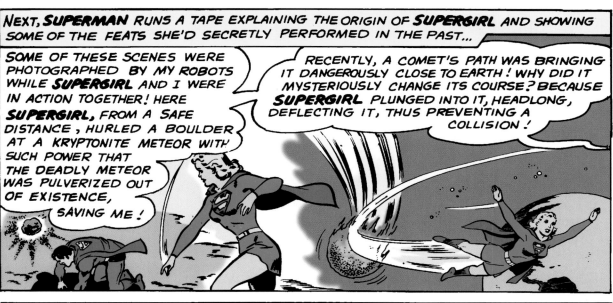

NEXT, *SUPERMAN* RUNS A TAPE EXPLAINING THE ORIGIN OF *SUPERGIRL* AND SHOWING SOME OF THE FEATS SHE'D SECRETLY PERFORMED IN THE PAST...

SOME OF THESE SCENES WERE PHOTOGRAPHED BY MY ROBOTS WHILE *SUPERGIRL* AND I WERE IN ACTION TOGETHER! HERE *SUPERGIRL*, FROM A SAFE DISTANCE, HURLED A BOULDER AT A KRYPTONITE METEOR WITH SUCH POWER THAT THE DEADLY METEOR WAS PULVERIZED OUT OF EXISTENCE, SAVING ME!

RECENTLY, A COMET'S PATH WAS BRINGING IT DANGEROUSLY CLOSE TO EARTH! WHY DID IT MYSTERIOUSLY CHANGE ITS COURSE? BECAUSE *SUPERGIRL* PLUNGED INTO IT, HEADLONG, DEFLECTING IT, THUS PREVENTING A COLLISION!

BUT THOUGH HONEST, LAW-ABIDING CITIZENS *REJOICE* EVERYWHERE, GANGLAND MOURNS...

IT WAS BAD ENOUGH HAVING *SUPERMAN* AFTER US, BUT NOW--

--WE GOTTA WORRY ABOUT A *SUPER-DAME*, TOO! DISGUSTING, AIN'T IT?

PRISON CELLS BECOME EVEN GLOOMIER...

THE GRAPEVINE SAYS A *SUPERGIRL* HAS BEEN ANNOUNCED ON EARTH! FORGET OUR PERFECT ESCAPE PLAN!

RIGHT!! IF THAT YOUNG GIRL CAPTURED US, THE OTHER CONS WOULD NEVER STOP RAZZING US!

7

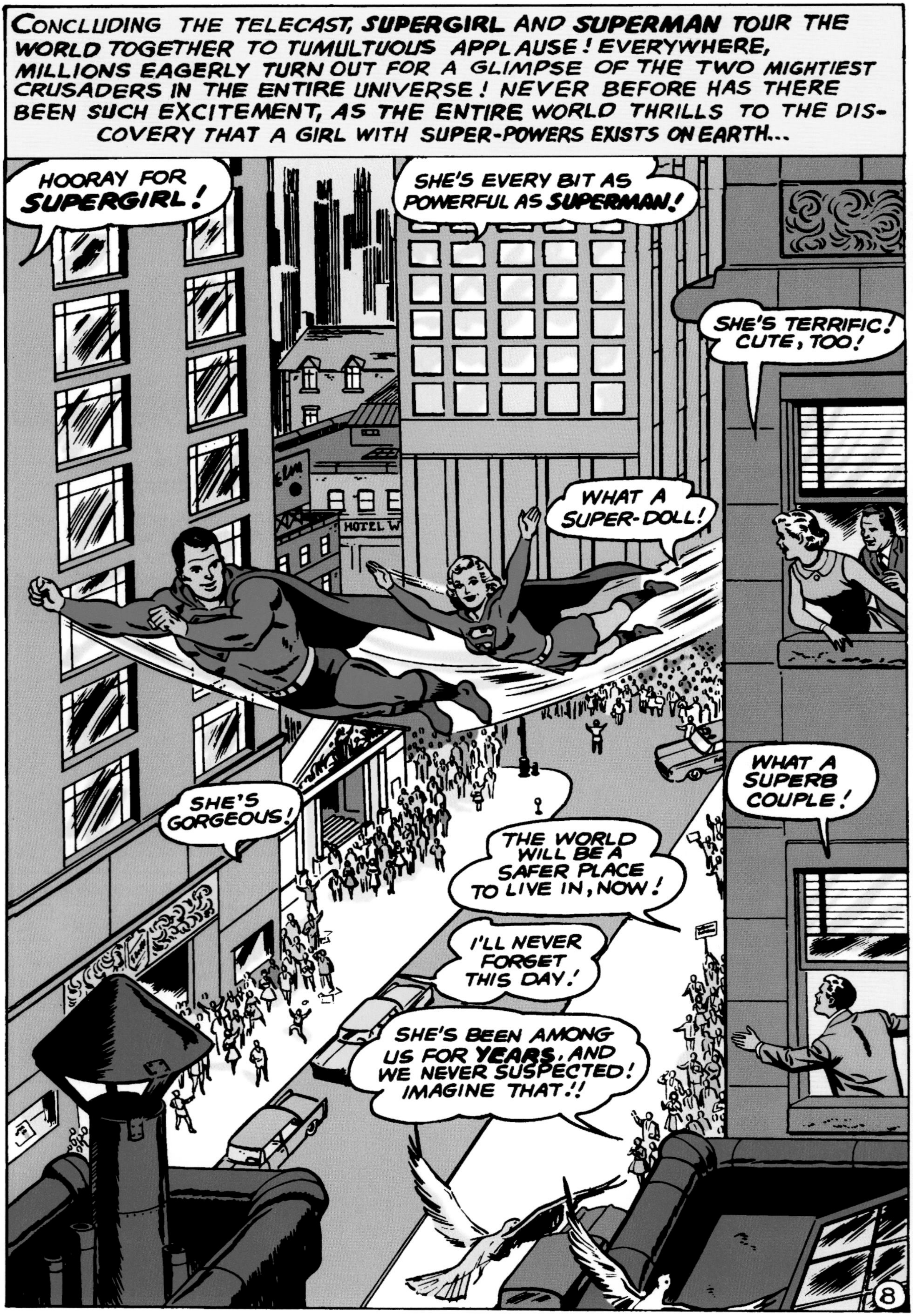
CONCLUDING THE TELECAST, SUPERGIRL AND SUPERMAN TOUR THE WORLD TOGETHER TO TUMULTUOUS APPLAUSE! EVERYWHERE, MILLIONS EAGERLY TURN OUT FOR A GLIMPSE OF THE TWO MIGHTIEST CRUSADERS IN THE ENTIRE UNIVERSE! NEVER BEFORE HAS THERE BEEN SUCH EXCITEMENT, AS THE ENTIRE WORLD THRILLS TO THE DISCOVERY THAT A GIRL WITH SUPER-POWERS EXISTS ON EARTH...
HOORAY FOR SUPERGIRL!
SHE'S EVERY BIT AS POWERFUL AS SUPERMAN!
SHE'S TERRIFIC! CUTE, TOO!
HOTEL W
WHAT A SUPER-DOLL!
WHAT A SUPERB COUPLE!
SHE'S GORGEOUS!
THE WORLD WILL BE A SAFER PLACE TO LIVE IN, NOW!
I'LL NEVER FORGET THIS DAY!
SHE'S BEEN AMONG US FOR YEARS, AND WE NEVER SUSPECTED! IMAGINE THAT!!
8

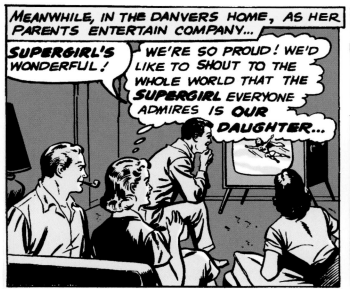

MEANWHILE, IN THE DANVERS HOME, AS HER PARENTS ENTERTAIN COMPANY...

SUPERGIRL'S WONDERFUL!

WE'RE SO PROUD! WE'D LIKE TO SHOUT TO THE WHOLE WORLD THAT THE SUPERGIRL EVERYONE ADMIRES IS OUR DAUGHTER...

...BUT WE MUSTN'T! WE'VE PROMISED TO TELL NO ONE, AND WE'LL KEEP OUR WORD... THOUGH IT ISN'T EASY!

I COULD BURST WITH PRIDE! IF OUR FRIENDS KNEW THAT SUPERGIRL IS OUR LINDA, THEY'D FAINT!

PRESENTLY, AT THE WHITE HOUSE IN WASHINGTON, D.C. ...

SUPERGIRL, I KNOW YOU'LL USE YOUR SUPER-POWERS NOT ONLY TO FIGHT CRIME, BUT TO PRESERVE PEACE IN OUR TROUBLED WORLD!

THANK YOU, MR. PRESIDENT! ... I WILL!

AFTERWARD...

SUPERMAN, I'M COMPLETELY OVERWHELMED BY ALL THESE HONORS! GOODNESS! I...

YOU DESERVE THEM! BUT THE GREATEST ACCLAIM OF ALL AWAITS YOU IN THE UNITED NATIONS BUILDING BELOW!

MOMENTS LATER, INSIDE THE U.N. BUILDING, SUPERGIRL RECEIVES A STANDING OVATION FROM THE DISTINGUISHED REPRESENTATIVES OF MEMBER NATIONS...

¡CHOKE! ... I'M SO... OVERWHELMED! I-I'M AFRAID I'M GOING TO CRY...

PHYSICALLY, SHE'S THE MIGHTIEST FEMALE OF ALL TIME! BUT AT HEART, SHE'S AS GENTLE AND SWEET AND AS QUICK TO TEARS--AS ANY ORDINARY GIRL! I GUESS THAT'S WHY EVERYONE WHO MEETS HER LOVES HER!

9

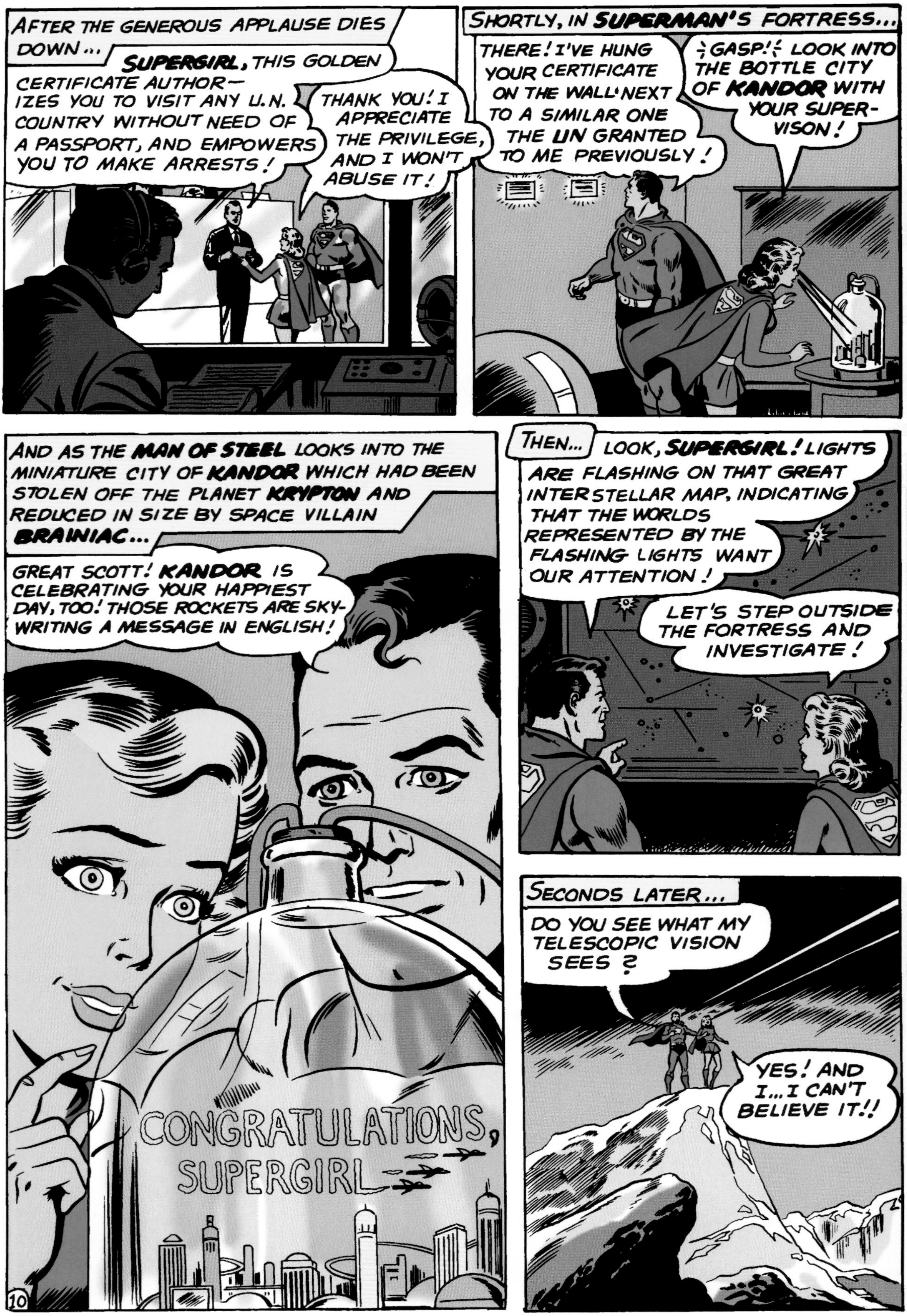
AFTER THE GENEROUS APPLAUSE DIES DOWN...
SUPERGIRL, THIS GOLDEN CERTIFICATE AUTHOR-IZES YOU TO VISIT ANY U.N. COUNTRY WITHOUT NEED OF A PASSPORT, AND EMPOWERS YOU TO MAKE ARRESTS!
THANK YOU! I APPRECIATE THE PRIVILEGE, AND I WON'T ABUSE IT!
SHORTLY, IN SUPERMAN'S FORTRESS...
THERE! I'VE HUNG YOUR CERTIFICATE ON THE WALL NEXT TO A SIMILAR ONE THE UN GRANTED TO ME PREVIOUSLY!
-GASP!- LOOK INTO THE BOTTLE CITY OF KANDOR WITH YOUR SUPER-VISON!
AND AS THE MAN OF STEEL LOOKS INTO THE MINIATURE CITY OF KANDOR WHICH HAD BEEN STOLEN OFF THE PLANET KRYPTON AND REDUCED IN SIZE BY SPACE VILLAIN BRAINIAC...
GREAT SCOTT! KANDOR IS CELEBRATING YOUR HAPPIEST DAY, TOO! THOSE ROCKETS ARE SKY-WRITING A MESSAGE IN ENGLISH!
CONGRATULATIONS, SUPERGIRL
10
THEN...
LOOK, SUPERGIRL! LIGHTS ARE FLASHING ON THAT GREAT INTERSTELLAR MAP, INDICATING THAT THE WORLDS REPRESENTED BY THE FLASHING LIGHTS WANT OUR ATTENTION!
LET'S STEP OUTSIDE THE FORTRESS AND INVESTIGATE!
SECONDS LATER...
DO YOU SEE WHAT MY TELESCOPIC VISION SEES?
YES! AND I...I CAN'T BELIEVE IT!!

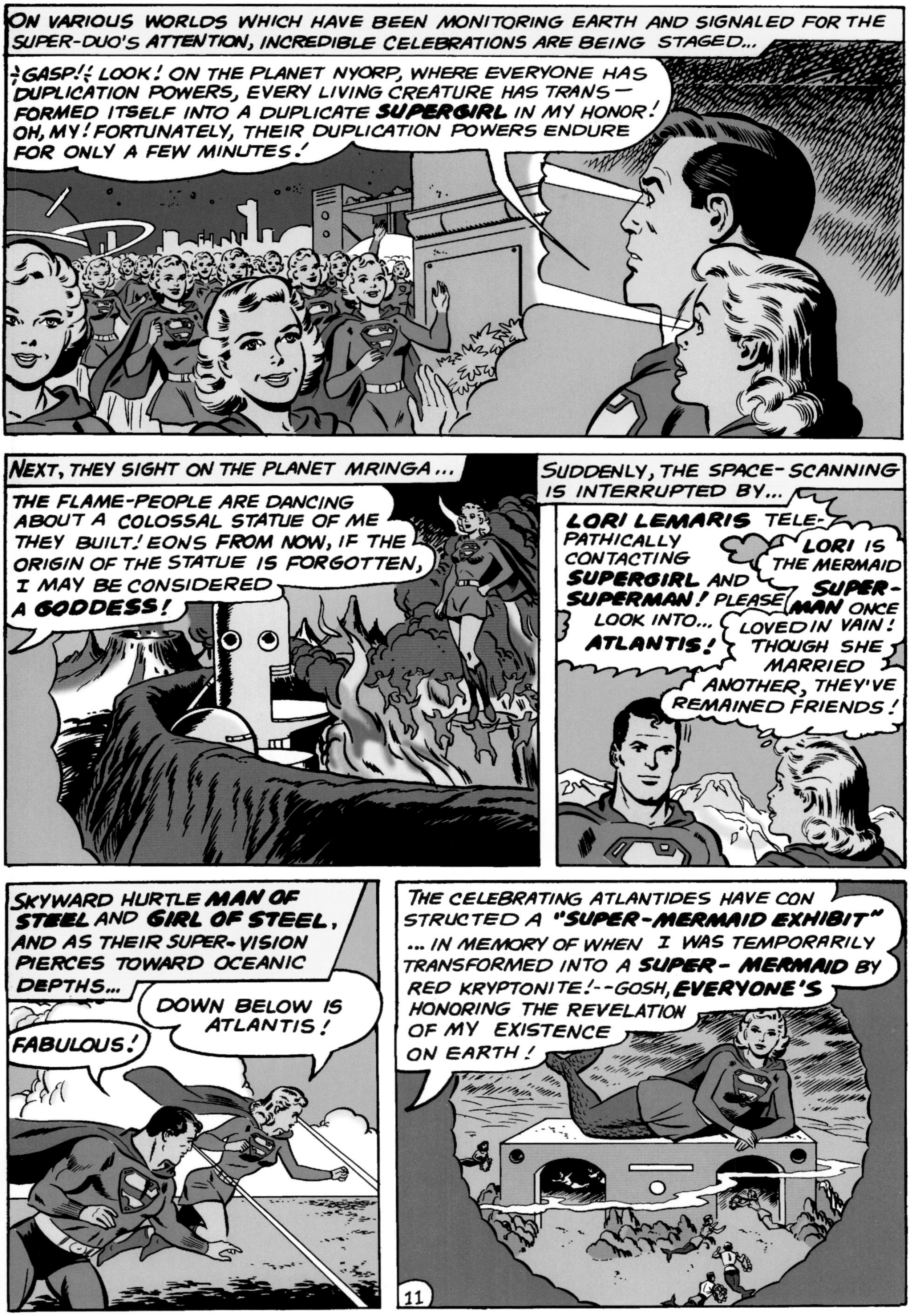

ON VARIOUS WORLDS WHICH HAVE BEEN MONITORING EARTH AND SIGNALED FOR THE SUPER-DUO'S ATTENTION, INCREDIBLE CELEBRATIONS ARE BEING STAGED...
GASP! LOOK! ON THE PLANET NYORP, WHERE EVERYONE HAS DUPLICATION POWERS, EVERY LIVING CREATURE HAS TRANS-FORMED ITSELF INTO A DUPLICATE SUPERGIRL IN MY HONOR! OH, MY! FORTUNATELY, THEIR DUPLICATION POWERS ENDURE FOR ONLY A FEW MINUTES!
NEXT, THEY SIGHT ON THE PLANET MRINGA...
THE FLAME-PEOPLE ARE DANCING ABOUT A COLOSSAL STATUE OF ME THEY BUILT! EONS FROM NOW, IF THE ORIGIN OF THE STATUE IS FORGOTTEN, I MAY BE CONSIDERED A GODDESS!
SUDDENLY, THE SPACE-SCANNING IS INTERRUPTED BY...
LORI LEMARIS TELE-PATHICALLY CONTACTING SUPERGIRL AND SUPERMAN! PLEASE LOOK INTO... ATLANTIS!
LORI IS THE MERMAID SUPER-MAN ONCE LOVED IN VAIN! THOUGH SHE MARRIED ANOTHER, THEY'VE REMAINED FRIENDS!
SKYWARD HURTLE MAN OF STEEL AND GIRL OF STEEL, AND AS THEIR SUPER-VISION PIERCES TOWARD OCEANIC DEPTHS...
DOWN BELOW IS ATLANTIS!
FABULOUS!
THE CELEBRATING ATLANTIDES HAVE CON STRUCTED A "SUPER-MERMAID EXHIBIT" ... IN MEMORY OF WHEN I WAS TEMPORARILY TRANSFORMED INTO A SUPER-MERMAID BY RED KRYPTONITE!--GOSH, EVERYONE'S HONORING THE REVELATION OF MY EXISTENCE ON EARTH!
11

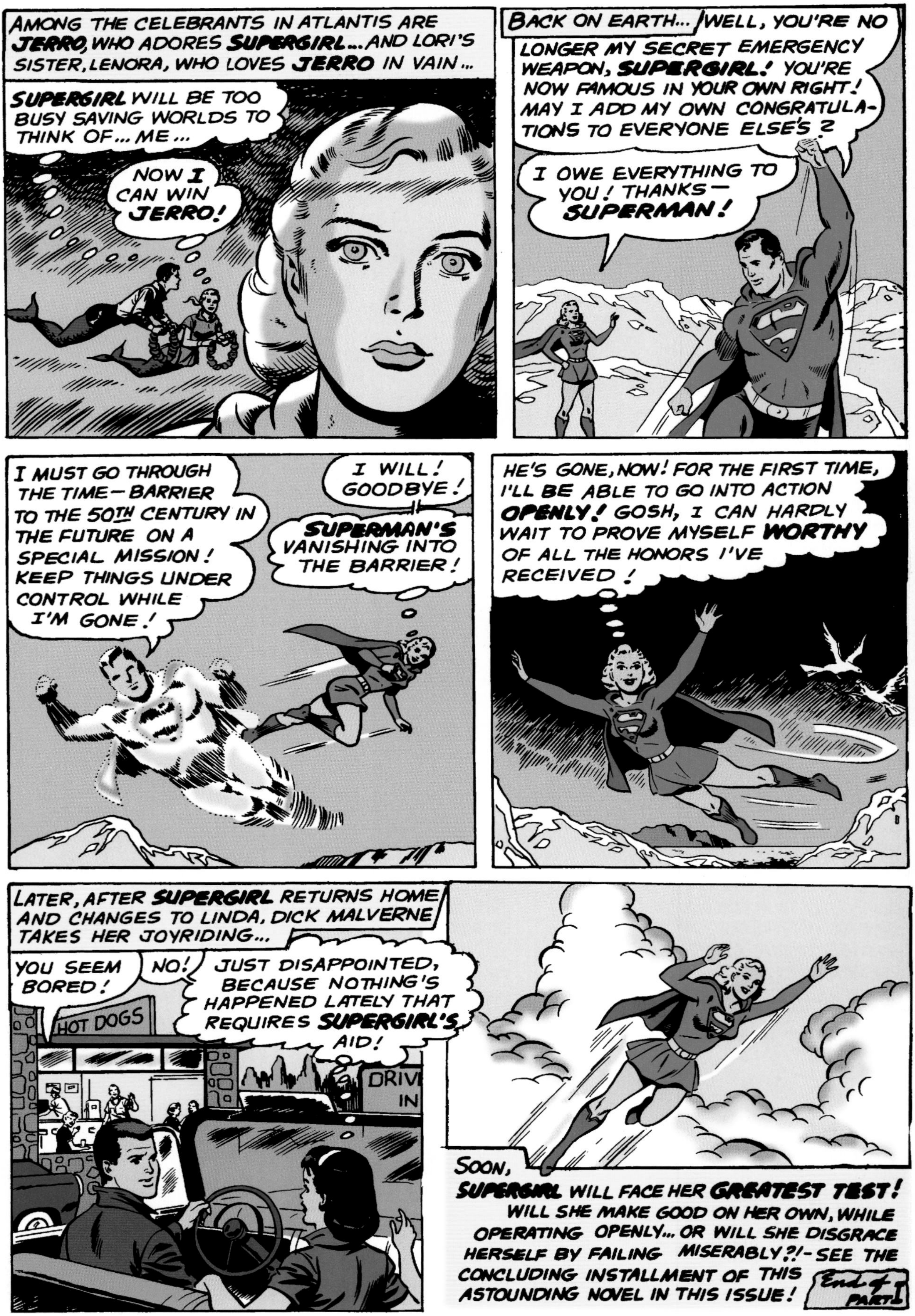

AMONG THE CELEBRANTS IN ATLANTIS ARE JERRO, WHO ADORES SUPERGIRL... AND LORI'S SISTER, LENORA, WHO LOVES JERRO IN VAIN...
SUPERGIRL WILL BE TOO BUSY SAVING WORLDS TO THINK OF... ME...
NOW I CAN WIN JERRO!
BACK ON EARTH...
WELL, YOU'RE NO LONGER MY SECRET EMERGENCY WEAPON, SUPERGIRL! YOU'RE NOW FAMOUS IN YOUR OWN RIGHT! MAY I ADD MY OWN CONGRATULATIONS TO EVERYONE ELSE'S?
I OWE EVERYTHING TO YOU! THANKS— SUPERMAN!
I MUST GO THROUGH THE TIME-BARRIER TO THE 50TH CENTURY IN THE FUTURE ON A SPECIAL MISSION! KEEP THINGS UNDER CONTROL WHILE I'M GONE!
I WILL! GOODBYE!
SUPERMAN'S VANISHING INTO THE BARRIER!
HE'S GONE, NOW! FOR THE FIRST TIME, I'LL BE ABLE TO GO INTO ACTION OPENLY! GOSH, I CAN HARDLY WAIT TO PROVE MYSELF WORTHY OF ALL THE HONORS I'VE RECEIVED!
LATER, AFTER SUPERGIRL RETURNS HOME AND CHANGES TO LINDA, DICK MALVERNE TAKES HER JOYRIDING...
YOU SEEM BORED!
NO!
JUST DISAPPOINTED, BECAUSE NOTHING'S HAPPENED LATELY THAT REQUIRES SUPERGIRL'S AID!
HOT DOGS
DRIVE IN
SOON, SUPERGIRL WILL FACE HER GREATEST TEST! WILL SHE MAKE GOOD ON HER OWN, WHILE OPERATING OPENLY... OR WILL SHE DISGRACE HERSELF BY FAILING MISERABLY?!- SEE THE CONCLUDING INSTALLMENT OF THIS ASTOUNDING NOVEL IN THIS ISSUE!
End of PART I

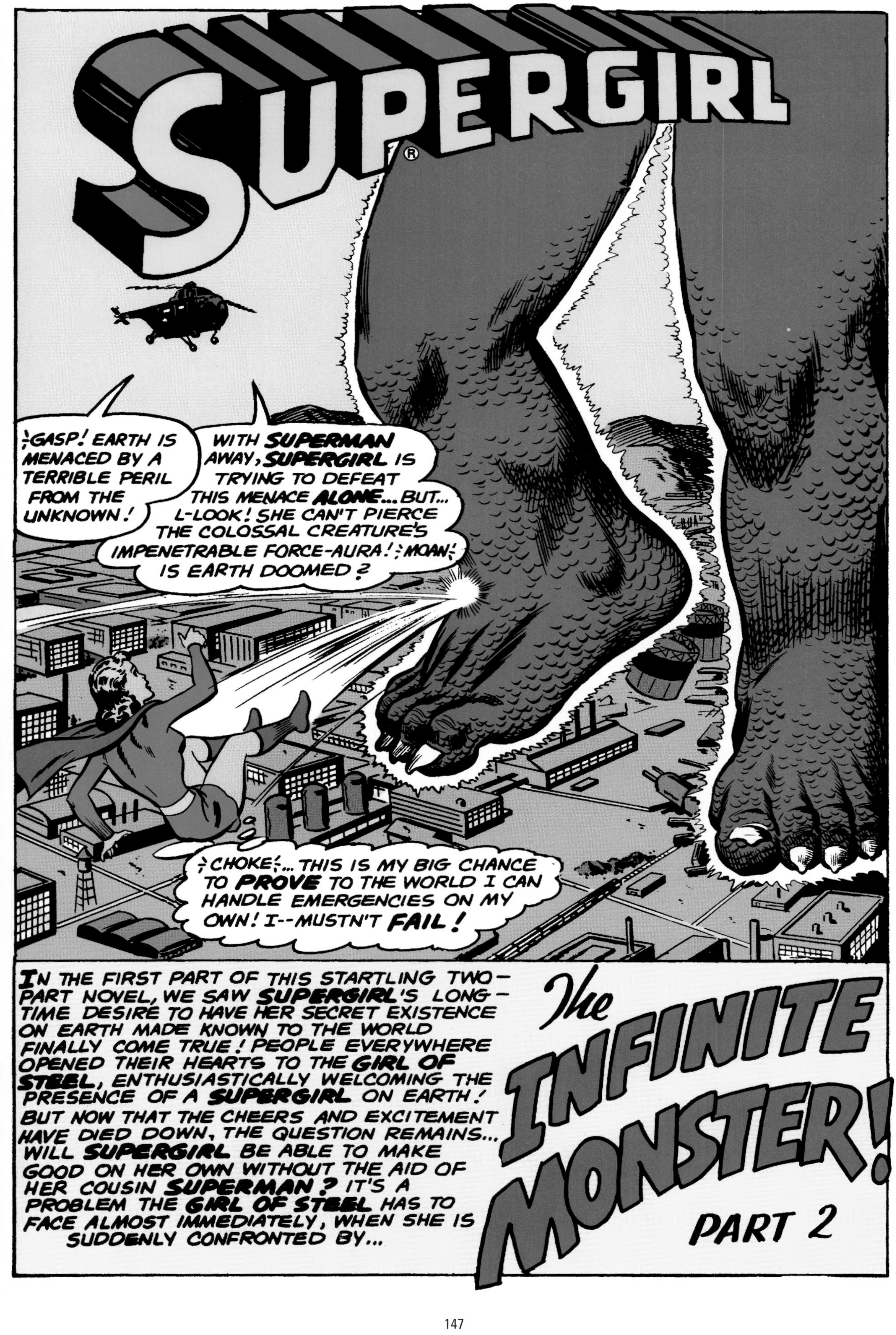
SUPERGIRL®
¡GASP! EARTH IS MENACED BY A TERRIBLE PERIL FROM THE UNKNOWN!
WITH SUPERMAN AWAY, SUPERGIRL IS TRYING TO DEFEAT THIS MENACE ALONE... BUT... L-LOOK! SHE CAN'T PIERCE THE COLOSSAL CREATURE'S IMPENETRABLE FORCE-AURA! ¡MOAN! IS EARTH DOOMED?
¡CHOKE!... THIS IS MY BIG CHANCE TO PROVE TO THE WORLD I CAN HANDLE EMERGENCIES ON MY OWN! I--MUSTN'T FAIL!
IN THE FIRST PART OF THIS STARTLING TWO-PART NOVEL, WE SAW SUPERGIRL'S LONG-TIME DESIRE TO HAVE HER SECRET EXISTENCE ON EARTH MADE KNOWN TO THE WORLD FINALLY COME TRUE! PEOPLE EVERYWHERE OPENED THEIR HEARTS TO THE GIRL OF STEEL, ENTHUSIASTICALLY WELCOMING THE PRESENCE OF A SUPERGIRL ON EARTH! BUT NOW THAT THE CHEERS AND EXCITEMENT HAVE DIED DOWN, THE QUESTION REMAINS... WILL SUPERGIRL BE ABLE TO MAKE GOOD ON HER OWN WITHOUT THE AID OF HER COUSIN SUPERMAN? IT'S A PROBLEM THE GIRL OF STEEL HAS TO FACE ALMOST IMMEDIATELY, WHEN SHE IS SUDDENLY CONFRONTED BY...
The INFINITE MONSTER!
PART 2

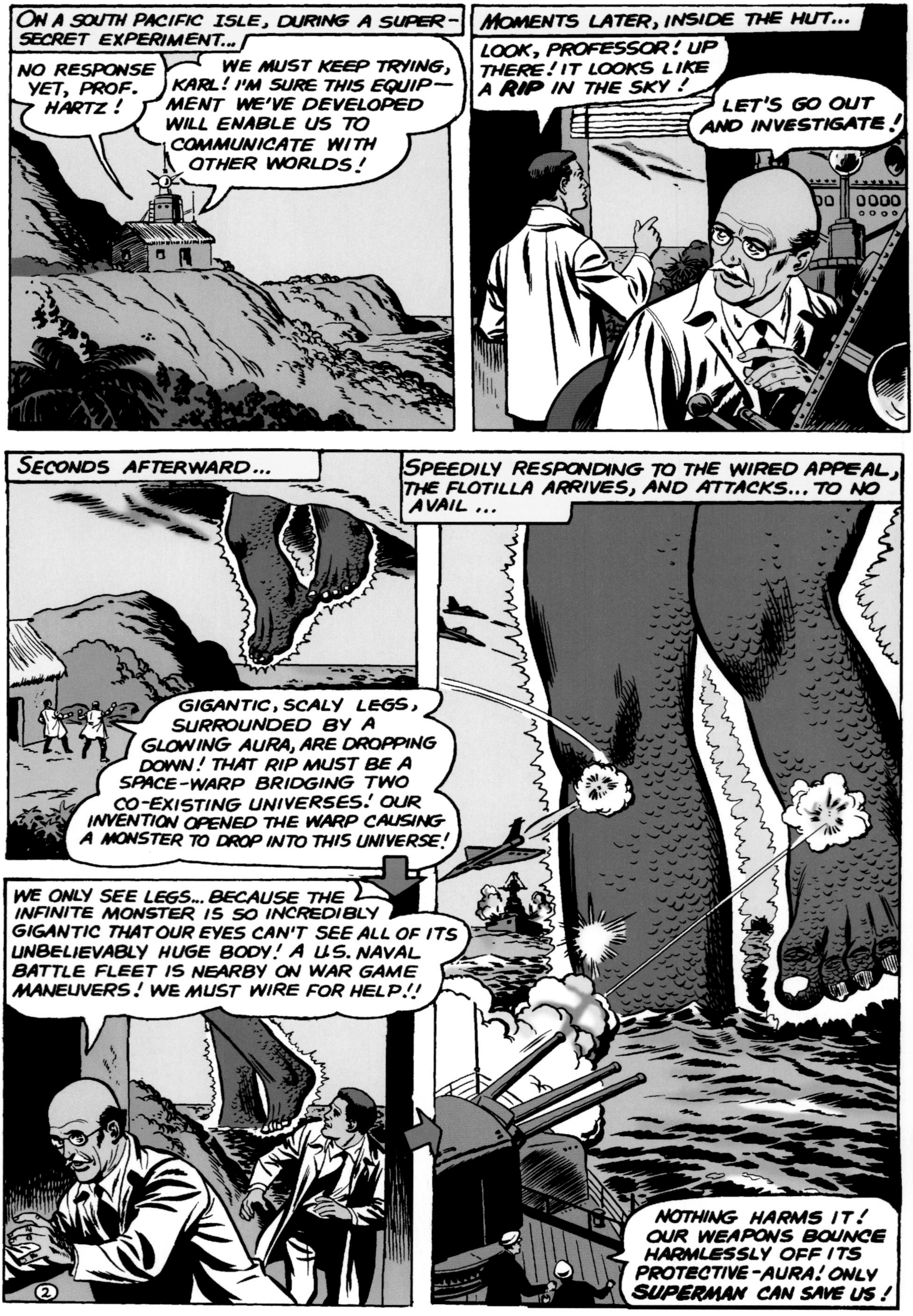

ON A SOUTH PACIFIC ISLE, DURING A SUPER-SECRET EXPERIMENT...
NO RESPONSE YET, PROF. HARTZ!
WE MUST KEEP TRYING, KARL! I'M SURE THIS EQUIPMENT WE'VE DEVELOPED WILL ENABLE US TO COMMUNICATE WITH OTHER WORLDS!
MOMENTS LATER, INSIDE THE HUT...
LOOK, PROFESSOR! UP THERE! IT LOOKS LIKE A RIP IN THE SKY!
LET'S GO OUT AND INVESTIGATE!
SECONDS AFTERWARD...
GIGANTIC, SCALY LEGS, SURROUNDED BY A GLOWING AURA, ARE DROPPING DOWN! THAT RIP MUST BE A SPACE-WARP BRIDGING TWO CO-EXISTING UNIVERSES! OUR INVENTION OPENED THE WARP CAUSING A MONSTER TO DROP INTO THIS UNIVERSE!
WE ONLY SEE LEGS... BECAUSE THE INFINITE MONSTER IS SO INCREDIBLY GIGANTIC THAT OUR EYES CAN'T SEE ALL OF ITS UNBELIEVABLY HUGE BODY! A U.S. NAVAL BATTLE FLEET IS NEARBY ON WAR GAME MANEUVERS! WE MUST WIRE FOR HELP!!
2
SPEEDILY RESPONDING TO THE WIRED APPEAL, THE FLOTILLA ARRIVES, AND ATTACKS... TO NO AVAIL...
NOTHING HARMS IT! OUR WEAPONS BOUNCE HARMLESSLY OFF ITS PROTECTIVE-AURA! ONLY SUPERMAN CAN SAVE US!

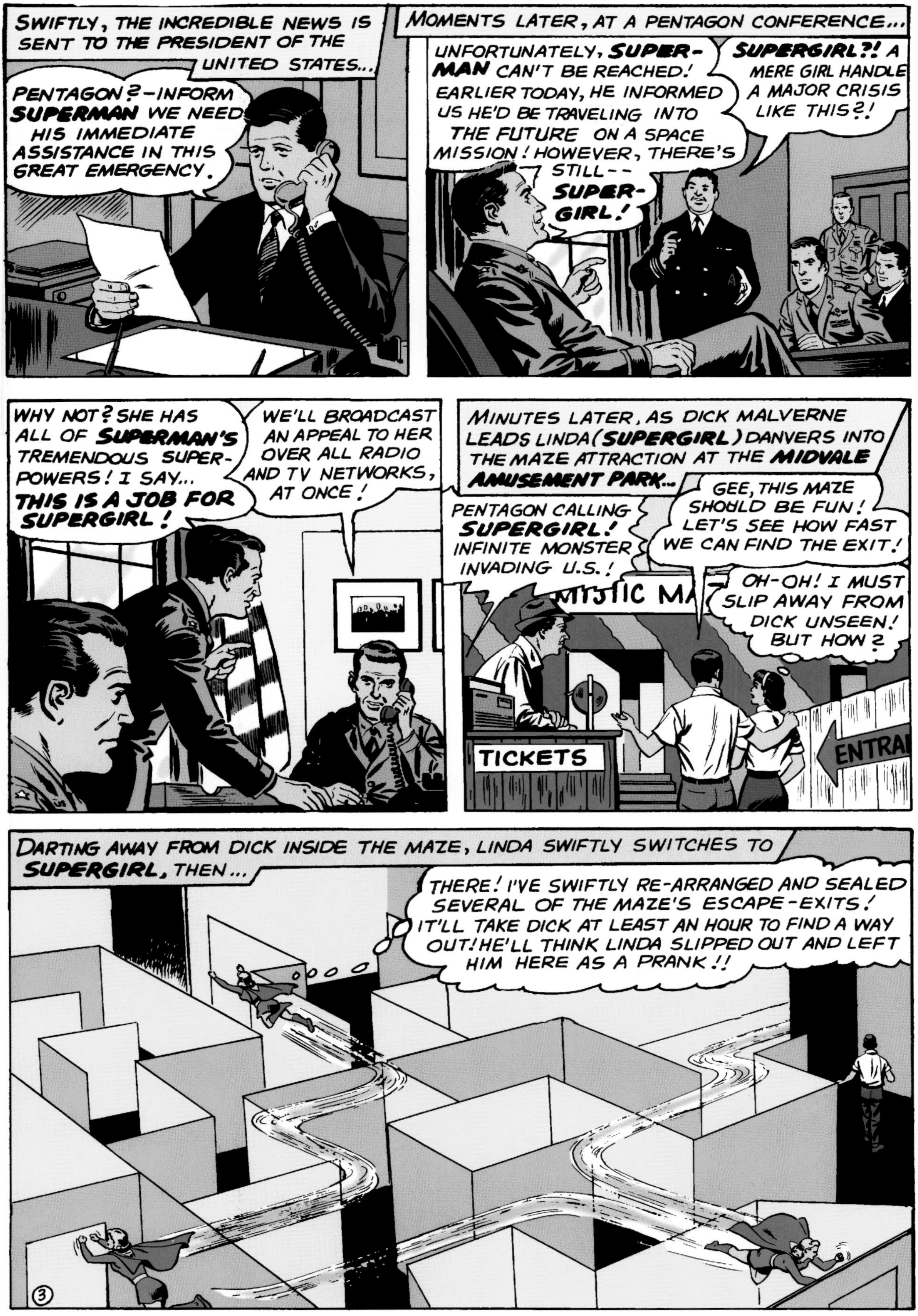
SWIFTLY, THE INCREDIBLE NEWS IS SENT TO THE PRESIDENT OF THE UNITED STATES...
PENTAGON?–INFORM SUPERMAN WE NEED HIS IMMEDIATE ASSISTANCE IN THIS GREAT EMERGENCY.
MOMENTS LATER, AT A PENTAGON CONFERENCE...
UNFORTUNATELY, SUPERMAN CAN'T BE REACHED! EARLIER TODAY, HE INFORMED US HE'D BE TRAVELING INTO THE FUTURE ON A SPACE MISSION! HOWEVER, THERE'S STILL-- SUPERGIRL!
SUPERGIRL?! A MERE GIRL HANDLE A MAJOR CRISIS LIKE THIS?!
WHY NOT? SHE HAS ALL OF SUPERMAN'S TREMENDOUS SUPER-POWERS! I SAY... THIS IS A JOB FOR SUPERGIRL!
WE'LL BROADCAST AN APPEAL TO HER OVER ALL RADIO AND TV NETWORKS, AT ONCE!
MINUTES LATER, AS DICK MALVERNE LEADS LINDA (SUPERGIRL) DANVERS INTO THE MAZE ATTRACTION AT THE MIDVALE AMUSEMENT PARK...
PENTAGON CALLING SUPERGIRL! INFINITE MONSTER INVADING U.S.!
GEE, THIS MAZE SHOULD BE FUN! LET'S SEE HOW FAST WE CAN FIND THE EXIT!
OH-OH! I MUST SLIP AWAY FROM DICK UNSEEN! BUT HOW?
MYSTIC MA
TICKETS
ENTRA
DARTING AWAY FROM DICK INSIDE THE MAZE, LINDA SWIFTLY SWITCHES TO SUPERGIRL, THEN...
THERE! I'VE SWIFTLY RE-ARRANGED AND SEALED SEVERAL OF THE MAZE'S ESCAPE-EXITS! IT'LL TAKE DICK AT LEAST AN HOUR TO FIND A WAY OUT! HE'LL THINK LINDA SLIPPED OUT AND LEFT HIM HERE AS A PRANK!!
3

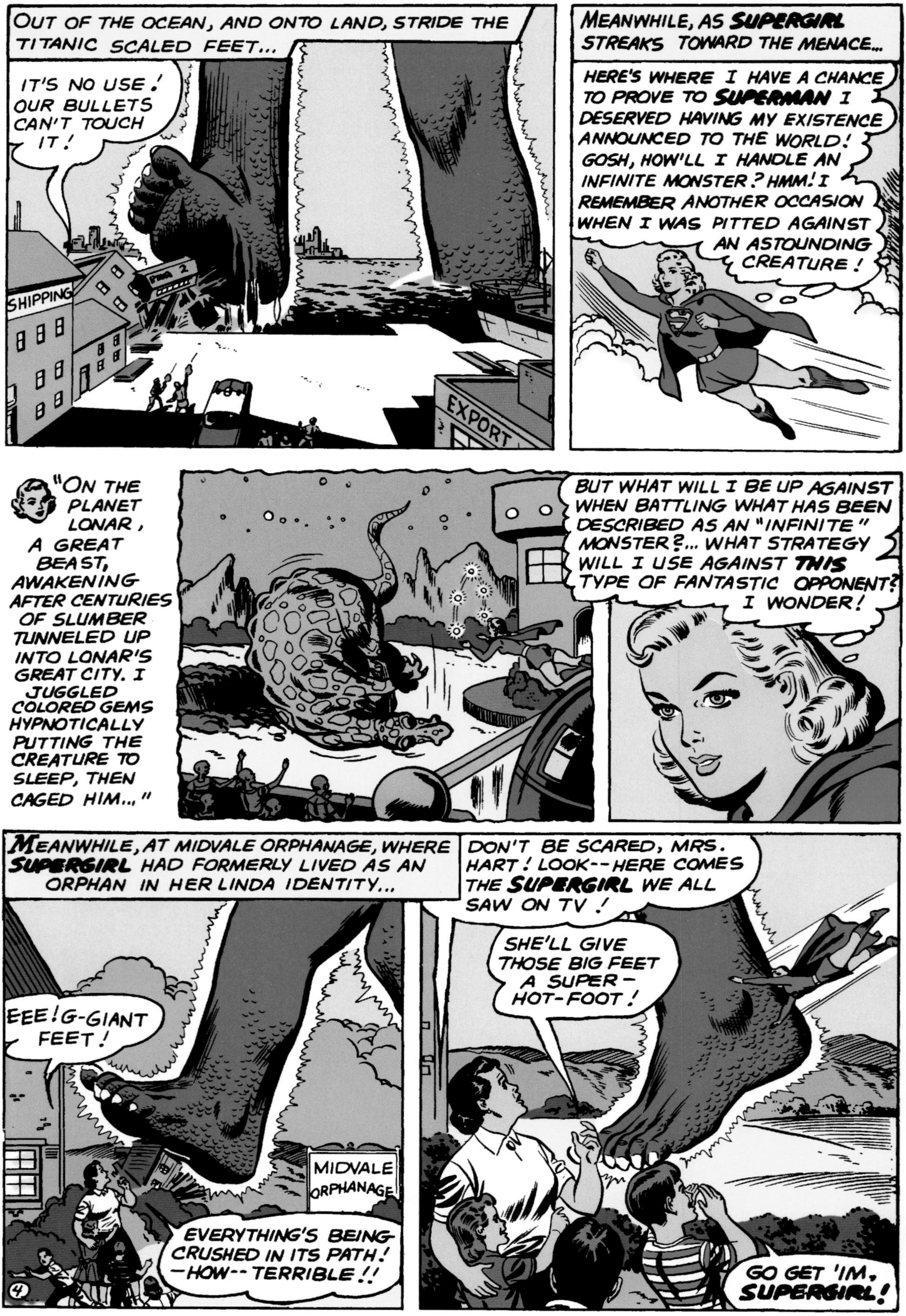

OUT OF THE OCEAN, AND ONTO LAND, STRIDE THE TITANIC SCALED FEET...
IT'S NO USE! OUR BULLETS CAN'T TOUCH IT!
SHIPPING
EXPORT
MEANWHILE, AS SUPERGIRL STREAKS TOWARD THE MENACE...
HERE'S WHERE I HAVE A CHANCE TO PROVE TO SUPERMAN I DESERVED HAVING MY EXISTENCE ANNOUNCED TO THE WORLD! GOSH, HOW'LL I HANDLE AN INFINITE MONSTER? HMM! I REMEMBER ANOTHER OCCASION WHEN I WAS PITTED AGAINST AN ASTOUNDING CREATURE!
"ON THE PLANET LONAR, A GREAT BEAST, AWAKENING AFTER CENTURIES OF SLUMBER TUNNELED UP INTO LONAR'S GREAT CITY. I JUGGLED COLORED GEMS HYPNOTICALLY PUTTING THE CREATURE TO SLEEP, THEN CAGED HIM..."
BUT WHAT WILL I BE UP AGAINST WHEN BATTLING WHAT HAS BEEN DESCRIBED AS AN "INFINITE" MONSTER?... WHAT STRATEGY WILL I USE AGAINST THIS TYPE OF FANTASTIC OPPONENT? I WONDER!
MEANWHILE, AT MIDVALE ORPHANAGE, WHERE SUPERGIRL HAD FORMERLY LIVED AS AN ORPHAN IN HER LINDA IDENTITY...
EEE! G-GIANT FEET!
MIDVALE ORPHANAGE
EVERYTHING'S BEING CRUSHED IN ITS PATH! --HOW-- TERRIBLE!!
4
DON'T BE SCARED, MRS. HART! LOOK--HERE COMES THE SUPERGIRL WE ALL SAW ON TV!
SHE'LL GIVE THOSE BIG FEET A SUPER-HOT-FOOT!
GO GET 'IM, SUPERGIRL!

INCREDIBLY GIGANTIC LEGS! I'LL BRING IT DOWN IN A *FLYING TACKLE...!*

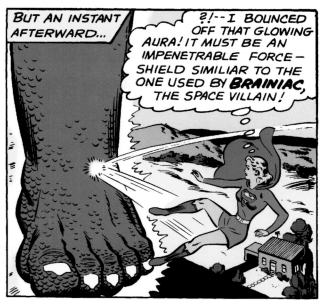

BUT AN INSTANT AFTERWARD...

?!-- I BOUNCED OFF THAT GLOWING AURA! IT MUST BE AN IMPENETRABLE FORCE-SHIELD SIMILIAR TO THE ONE USED BY *BRAINIAC,* THE SPACE VILLAIN!

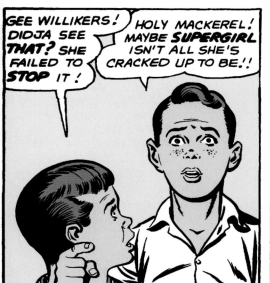

GEE WILLIKERS! DIDJA SEE *THAT?* SHE FAILED TO *STOP* IT!

HOLY MACKEREL! MAYBE *SUPERGIRL* ISN'T ALL SHE'S CRACKED UP TO BE.!!

AS SEVERAL GIGANTIC STRIDES OF THE COLOSSAL FEET TAKE THE HUGE INVADER INTO THE *METROPOLIS* STEEL YARDS, *SUPERGIRL* HURLS HERSELF ONCE MORE AT IT DESPERATELY, BUT TO NO AVAIL...

SUPERGIRL CAN'T STOP THAT CREATURE! HOW I WISH WE HAD *SUPERMAN* HERE INSTEAD OF THAT GIRL!

DESPERATELY, *SUPERGIRL* TRIES ANOTHER METHOD AS THE HUGE FEET ADVANCE...

MUST STOP THE DESTRUCTIVE MARCH OF THOSE TITANIC FEET! PERHAPS IF I GRAB HOLD, THEN FLIP IT UPWARD...!

⑤

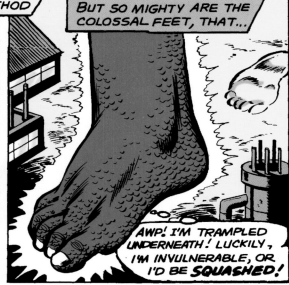

BUT SO MIGHTY ARE THE COLOSSAL FEET, THAT...

AWP! I'M TRAMPLED UNDERNEATH! LUCKILY, I'M INVULNERABLE, OR I'D BE *SQUASHED!*

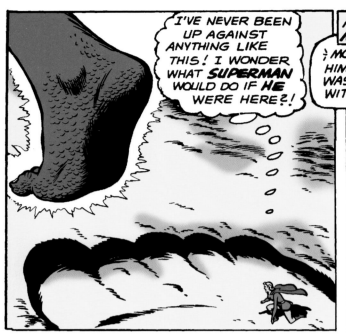

I'VE NEVER BEEN UP AGAINST ANYTHING LIKE THIS! I WONDER WHAT **SUPERMAN** WOULD DO IF **HE** WERE HERE?!

AS **SUPERGIRL** PURSUES THE FOE TO **METROPOLIS'** OUTSKIRTS...

¡MOAN¡ HOW TRAGIC THAT **SUPERMAN** HIMSELF ISN'T HERE AT A TIME LIKE THIS! WAS HE UNWISE TO ENTRUST **SUPERGIRL** WITH THE FATE OF THE WORLD?

EARTH IS DOOMED!

MY SUPER-HEARING OVERHEARD THOSE DOUBTING REMARKS ABOUT MY ABILITY! I-I'VE GOT TO MAKE GOOD! HMM... I THINK I KNOW WHAT TO DO NOW!

SCRAP METAL

BUILDING A CAPSULE FROM SCRAP METAL, **SUPERGIRL** WRITES A NOTE WITH MATERIALS TAKEN FROM HER CAPE'S POUCH, THEN...

I NEED ASSISTANCE, BUT THE ONE PERSON WHO CAN HELP ME LIVES IN THE DISTANT FUTURE! THERE'S ONLY ONE WAY TO CON-TACT HIM!

I'M HURLING THE CAPSULE SO SWIFTLY, IT'S VANISHING INTO THE TIME-BARRIER! IT'S STREAKING AT SUCH SUPER-SPEED THAT IT CAN'T BE DESTROYED BY FRICTION WITH THE AIR!

6

THROUGH THE TIME-BARRIER WHIZZES THE MESSAGE CAPSULE...

1962

2060

2161

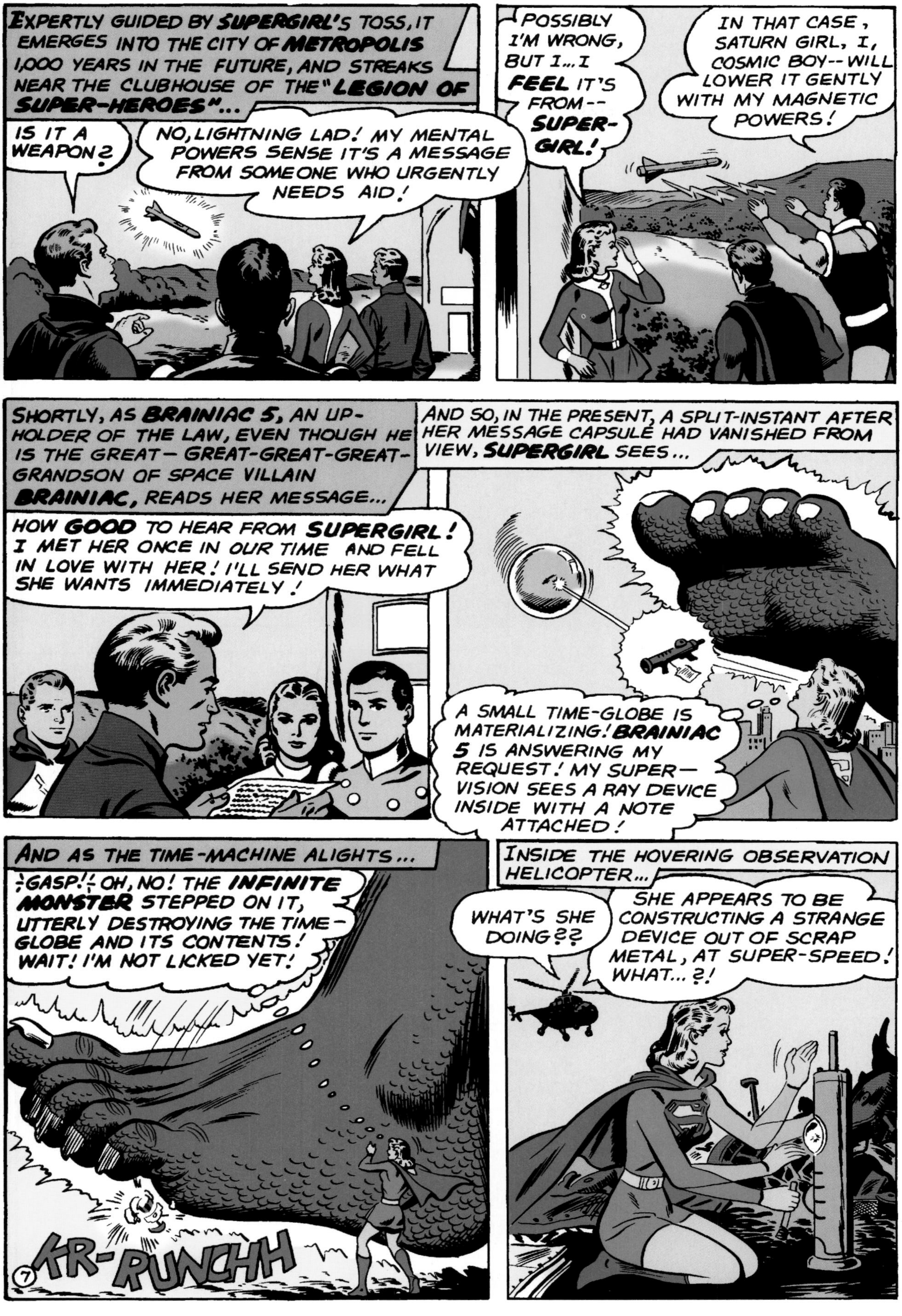
EXPERTLY GUIDED BY SUPERGIRL'S TOSS, IT EMERGES INTO THE CITY OF METROPOLIS 1,000 YEARS IN THE FUTURE, AND STREAKS NEAR THE CLUBHOUSE OF THE "LEGION OF SUPER-HEROES"...
IS IT A WEAPON?
NO, LIGHTNING LAD! MY MENTAL POWERS SENSE IT'S A MESSAGE FROM SOMEONE WHO URGENTLY NEEDS AID!
POSSIBLY I'M WRONG, BUT I...I FEEL IT'S FROM--SUPER-GIRL!
IN THAT CASE, SATURN GIRL, I, COSMIC BOY--WILL LOWER IT GENTLY WITH MY MAGNETIC POWERS!
SHORTLY, AS BRAINIAC 5, AN UPHOLDER OF THE LAW, EVEN THOUGH HE IS THE GREAT-GREAT-GREAT-GREAT-GRANDSON OF SPACE VILLAIN BRAINIAC, READS HER MESSAGE...
HOW GOOD TO HEAR FROM SUPERGIRL! I MET HER ONCE IN OUR TIME AND FELL IN LOVE WITH HER! I'LL SEND HER WHAT SHE WANTS IMMEDIATELY!
AND SO, IN THE PRESENT, A SPLIT-INSTANT AFTER HER MESSAGE CAPSULE HAD VANISHED FROM VIEW, SUPERGIRL SEES...
A SMALL TIME-GLOBE IS MATERIALIZING! BRAINIAC 5 IS ANSWERING MY REQUEST! MY SUPER—VISION SEES A RAY DEVICE INSIDE WITH A NOTE ATTACHED!
AND AS THE TIME-MACHINE ALIGHTS...
-GASP!- OH, NO! THE INFINITE MONSTER STEPPED ON IT, UTTERLY DESTROYING THE TIME-GLOBE AND ITS CONTENTS! WAIT! I'M NOT LICKED YET!
KR-RUNCHH
7
INSIDE THE HOVERING OBSERVATION HELICOPTER...
WHAT'S SHE DOING??
SHE APPEARS TO BE CONSTRUCTING A STRANGE DEVICE OUT OF SCRAP METAL, AT SUPER-SPEED! WHAT...?!

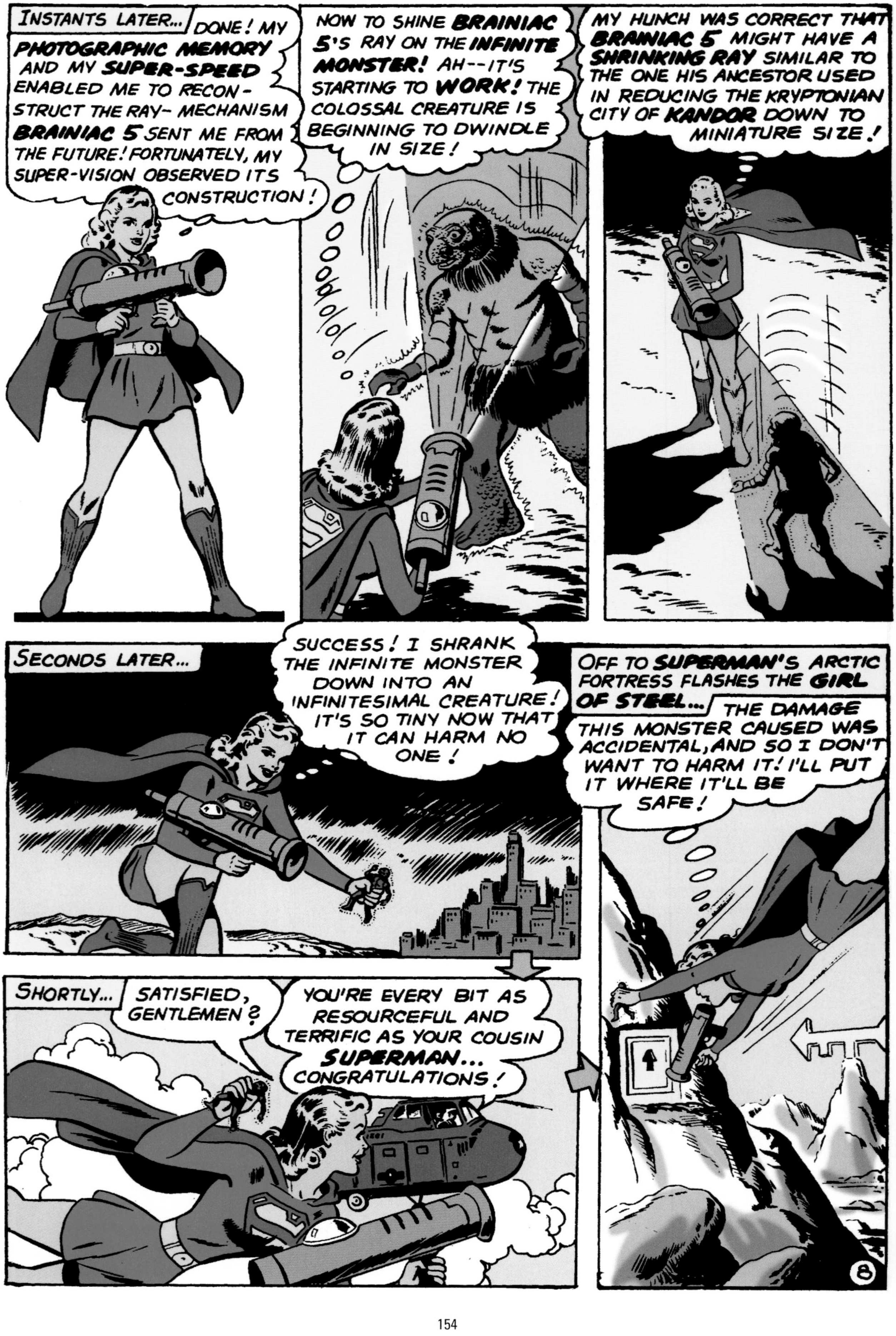
INSTANTS LATER...
DONE! MY PHOTOGRAPHIC MEMORY AND MY SUPER-SPEED ENABLED ME TO RECON-STRUCT THE RAY-MECHANISM BRAINIAC 5 SENT ME FROM THE FUTURE! FORTUNATELY, MY SUPER-VISION OBSERVED ITS CONSTRUCTION!
NOW TO SHINE BRAINIAC 5'S RAY ON THE INFINITE MONSTER! AH--IT'S STARTING TO WORK! THE COLOSSAL CREATURE IS BEGINNING TO DWINDLE IN SIZE!
MY HUNCH WAS CORRECT THAT BRAINIAC 5 MIGHT HAVE A SHRINKING RAY SIMILAR TO THE ONE HIS ANCESTOR USED IN REDUCING THE KRYPTONIAN CITY OF KANDOR DOWN TO MINIATURE SIZE!
SECONDS LATER...
SUCCESS! I SHRANK THE INFINITE MONSTER DOWN INTO AN INFINITESIMAL CREATURE! IT'S SO TINY NOW THAT IT CAN HARM NO ONE!
SHORTLY...
SATISFIED, GENTLEMEN?
YOU'RE EVERY BIT AS RESOURCEFUL AND TERRIFIC AS YOUR COUSIN SUPERMAN... CONGRATULATIONS!
OFF TO SUPERMAN'S ARCTIC FORTRESS FLASHES THE GIRL OF STEEL...
THE DAMAGE THIS MONSTER CAUSED WAS ACCIDENTAL, AND SO I DON'T WANT TO HARM IT! I'LL PUT IT WHERE IT'LL BE SAFE!
8

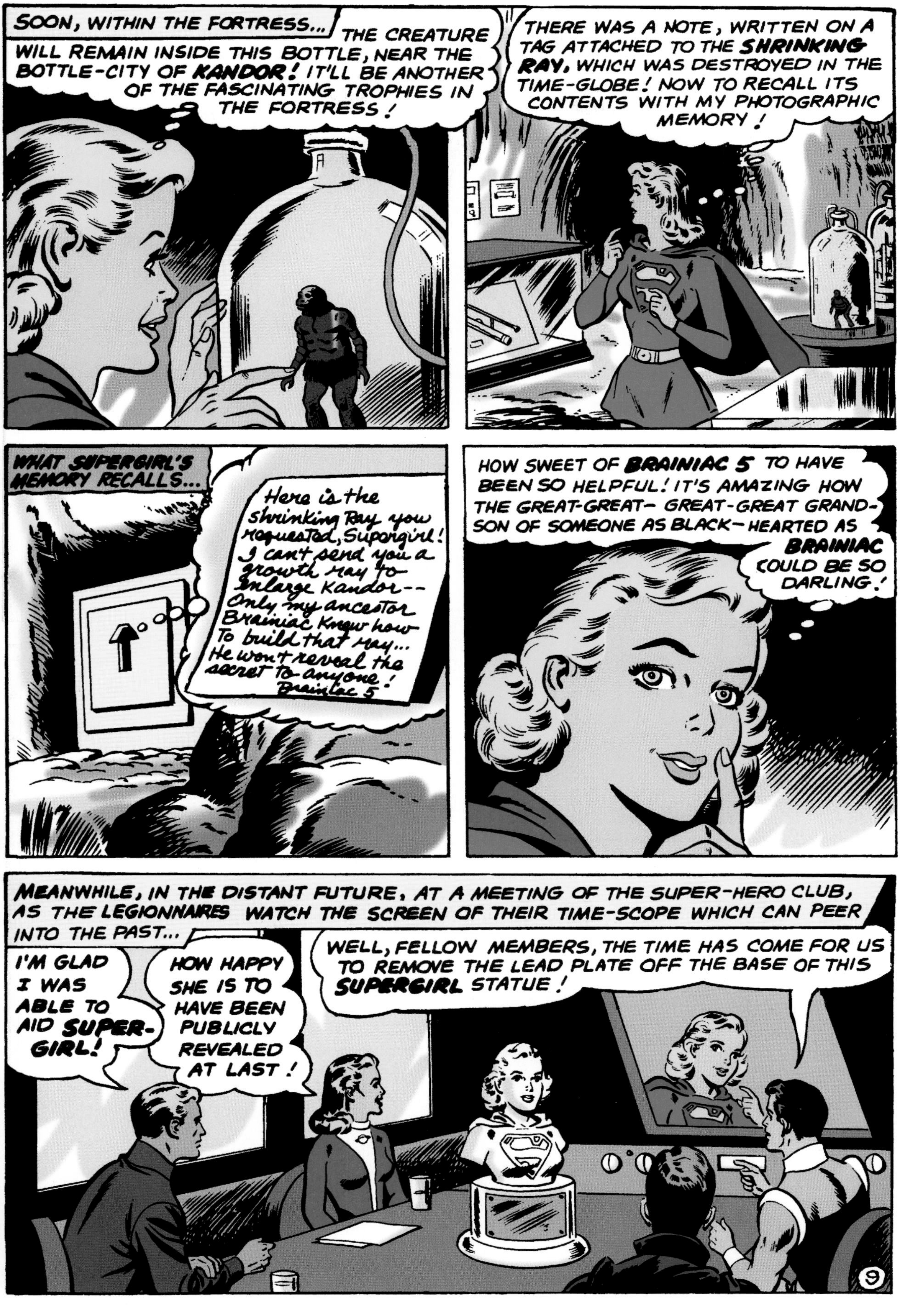
SOON, WITHIN THE FORTRESS...
THE CREATURE WILL REMAIN INSIDE THIS BOTTLE, NEAR THE BOTTLE-CITY OF KANDOR! IT'LL BE ANOTHER OF THE FASCINATING TROPHIES IN THE FORTRESS!
THERE WAS A NOTE, WRITTEN ON A TAG ATTACHED TO THE SHRINKING RAY, WHICH WAS DESTROYED IN THE TIME-GLOBE! NOW TO RECALL ITS CONTENTS WITH MY PHOTOGRAPHIC MEMORY!
WHAT SUPERGIRL'S MEMORY RECALLS...
Here is the shrinking Ray you requested, Supergirl! I can't send you a growth ray to Enlarge Kandor-- Only my ancestor Brainiac Knew how To build that ray... He won't reveal the secret to anyone! Brainiac 5
HOW SWEET OF BRAINIAC 5 TO HAVE BEEN SO HELPFUL! IT'S AMAZING HOW THE GREAT-GREAT- GREAT-GREAT GRAND-SON OF SOMEONE AS BLACK-HEARTED AS BRAINIAC COULD BE SO DARLING!
MEANWHILE, IN THE DISTANT FUTURE, AT A MEETING OF THE SUPER-HERO CLUB, AS THE LEGIONNAIRES WATCH THE SCREEN OF THEIR TIME-SCOPE WHICH CAN PEER INTO THE PAST...
I'M GLAD I WAS ABLE TO AID SUPER-GIRL!
HOW HAPPY SHE IS TO HAVE BEEN PUBLICLY REVEALED AT LAST!
WELL, FELLOW MEMBERS, THE TIME HAS COME FOR US TO REMOVE THE LEAD PLATE OFF THE BASE OF THIS SUPERGIRL STATUE!
9

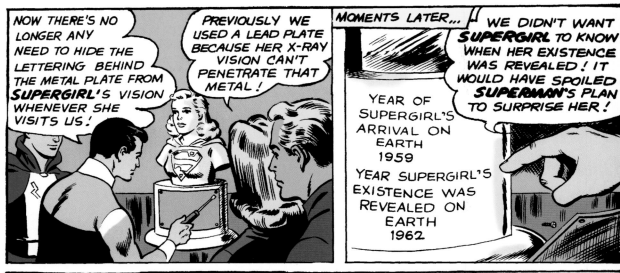

NOW THERE'S NO LONGER ANY NEED TO HIDE THE LETTERING BEHIND THE METAL PLATE FROM *SUPERGIRL'S* VISION WHENEVER SHE VISITS US!

PREVIOUSLY WE USED A LEAD PLATE BECAUSE HER X-RAY VISION CAN'T PENETRATE THAT METAL!

MOMENTS LATER...

WE DIDN'T WANT *SUPERGIRL* TO KNOW WHEN HER EXISTENCE WAS REVEALED! IT WOULD HAVE SPOILED *SUPERMAN'S* PLAN TO SURPRISE HER!

YEAR OF SUPERGIRL'S ARRIVAL ON EARTH 1959

YEAR SUPERGIRL'S EXISTENCE WAS REVEALED ON EARTH 1962

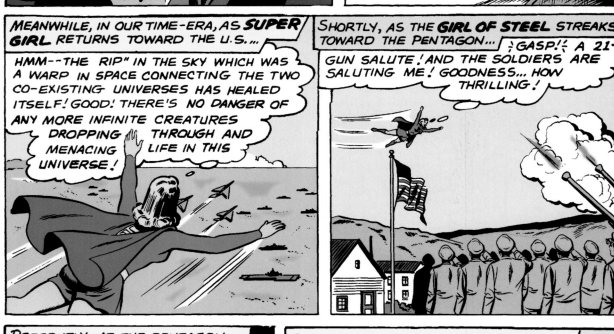

MEANWHILE, IN OUR TIME-ERA, AS *SUPERGIRL* RETURNS TOWARD THE U.S....

HMM--THE "RIP" IN THE SKY WHICH WAS A WARP IN SPACE CONNECTING THE TWO CO-EXISTING UNIVERSES HAS HEALED ITSELF! GOOD! THERE'S NO DANGER OF ANY MORE INFINITE CREATURES DROPPING THROUGH AND MENACING LIFE IN THIS UNIVERSE!

SHORTLY, AS THE *GIRL OF STEEL* STREAKS TOWARD THE PENTAGON...

GASP! A 21-GUN SALUTE! AND THE SOLDIERS ARE SALUTING ME! GOODNESS... HOW THRILLING!

PRESENTLY, AT THE PENTAGON...

SUPERGIRL, YOU HANDLED THE *INFINITE MONSTER* EMERGENCY MAGNIFICENTLY! WE'RE EXTREMELY GRATEFUL TO YOU! THE PRESIDENT WANTS TO THANK YOU PERSONALLY AT A PARTY IN YOUR HONOR!

SHORTLY, ON THE WHITE HOUSE LAWN...

YOU'RE AS RESOURCEFUL AS YOU ARE LOVELY, *SUPERGIRL*! THANKS A MILLION!

THE PRESIDENT'S WIFE LOOKS-- GORGEOUS!

10

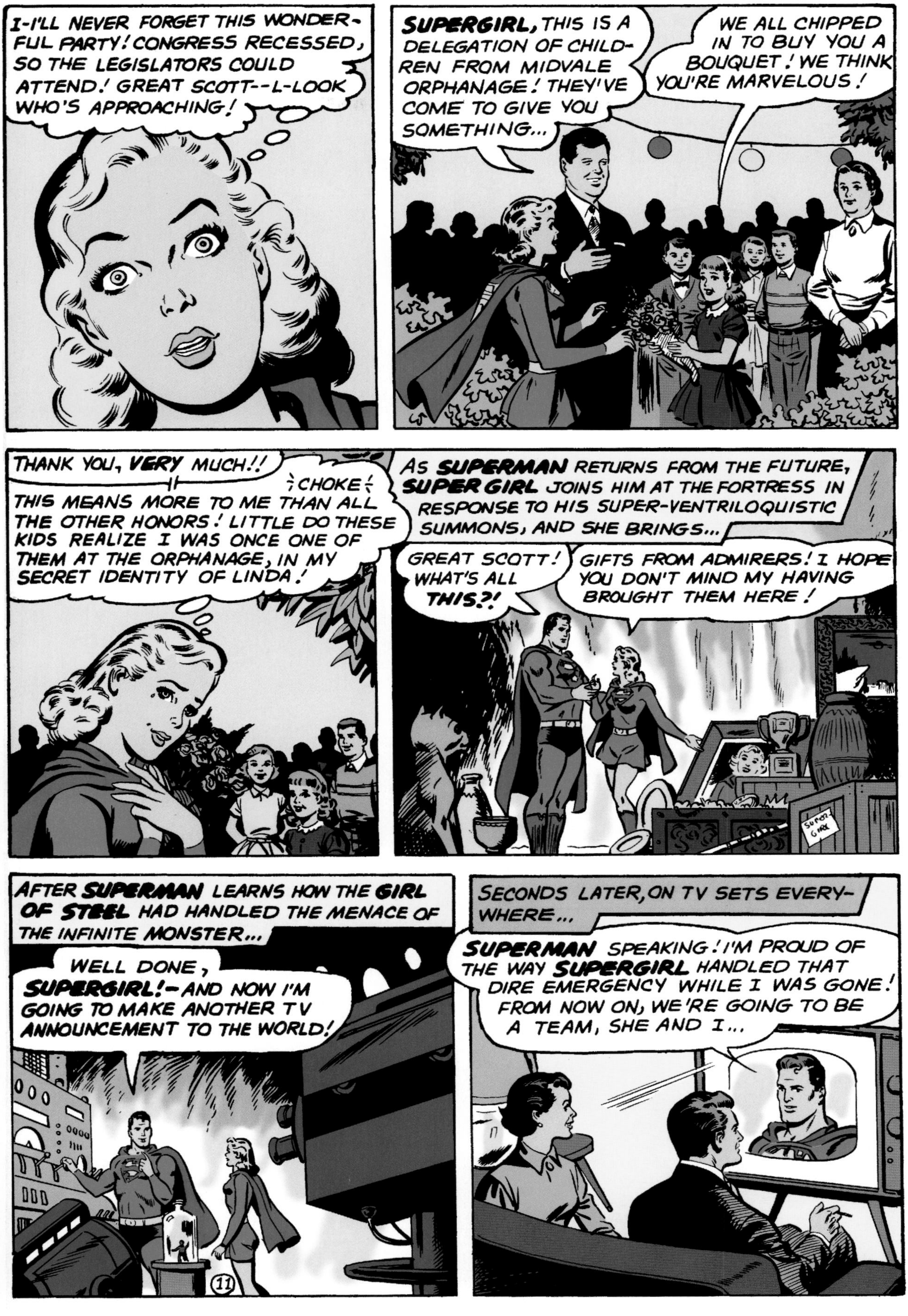
I-I'LL NEVER FORGET THIS WONDERFUL PARTY! CONGRESS RECESSED, SO THE LEGISLATORS COULD ATTEND! GREAT SCOTT--L-LOOK WHO'S APPROACHING!
SUPERGIRL, THIS IS A DELEGATION OF CHILDREN FROM MIDVALE ORPHANAGE! THEY'VE COME TO GIVE YOU SOMETHING...
WE ALL CHIPPED IN TO BUY YOU A BOUQUET! WE THINK YOU'RE MARVELOUS!
THANK YOU, VERY MUCH!!
CHOKE
THIS MEANS MORE TO ME THAN ALL THE OTHER HONORS! LITTLE DO THESE KIDS REALIZE I WAS ONCE ONE OF THEM AT THE ORPHANAGE, IN MY SECRET IDENTITY OF LINDA!
AS SUPERMAN RETURNS FROM THE FUTURE, SUPERGIRL JOINS HIM AT THE FORTRESS IN RESPONSE TO HIS SUPER-VENTRILOQUISTIC SUMMONS, AND SHE BRINGS...
GREAT SCOTT! WHAT'S ALL THIS?!
GIFTS FROM ADMIRERS! I HOPE YOU DON'T MIND MY HAVING BROUGHT THEM HERE!
AFTER SUPERMAN LEARNS HOW THE GIRL OF STEEL HAD HANDLED THE MENACE OF THE INFINITE MONSTER...
WELL DONE, SUPERGIRL!-- AND NOW I'M GOING TO MAKE ANOTHER TV ANNOUNCEMENT TO THE WORLD!
SECONDS LATER, ON TV SETS EVERYWHERE...
SUPERMAN SPEAKING! I'M PROUD OF THE WAY SUPERGIRL HANDLED THAT DIRE EMERGENCY WHILE I WAS GONE! FROM NOW ON, WE'RE GOING TO BE A TEAM, SHE AND I...

WHENEVER ONE OF US JOURNEYS INTO THE FUTURE OR THE PAST... OFF INTO OUTER SPACE... OR INTO ANOTHER DIMENSIONAL WORLD... THE OTHER WILL CONTINUE TO PATROL EARTH!

EARTH'S SECURITY WILL BE STRENGTHENED! HAVE YOU ANYTHING TO ADD, *SUPERGIRL*?

ONLY THAT YOU'RE THE MOST WONDERFUL PARTNER ANYONE EVER HAD! I'LL *ALWAYS* BE GRATEFUL TO YOU!

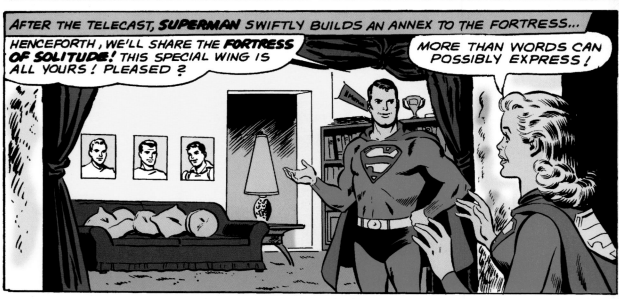

AFTER THE TELECAST, *SUPERMAN* SWIFTLY BUILDS AN ANNEX TO THE FORTRESS...

HENCEFORTH, WE'LL SHARE THE **FORTRESS OF SOLITUDE!** THIS SPECIAL WING IS ALL YOURS! PLEASED?

MORE THAN WORDS CAN POSSIBLY EXPRESS!

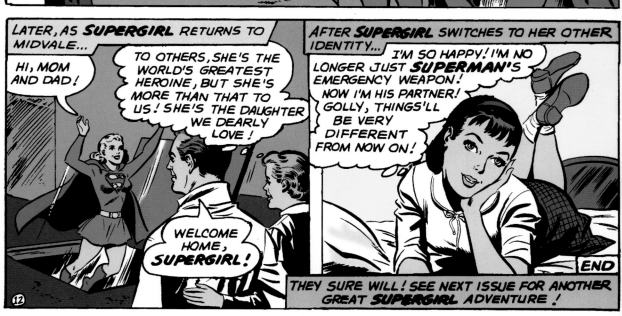

LATER, AS *SUPERGIRL* RETURNS TO MIDVALE...

HI, MOM AND DAD!

TO OTHERS, SHE'S THE WORLD'S GREATEST HEROINE, BUT SHE'S MORE THAN THAT TO US! SHE'S THE DAUGHTER WE DEARLY LOVE!

WELCOME HOME, SUPERGIRL!

AFTER *SUPERGIRL* SWITCHES TO HER OTHER IDENTITY...

I'M SO HAPPY! I'M NO LONGER JUST *SUPERMAN'S* EMERGENCY WEAPON! NOW I'M HIS PARTNER! GOLLY, THINGS'LL BE VERY DIFFERENT FROM NOW ON!

END

THEY SURE WILL! SEE NEXT ISSUE FOR ANOTHER GREAT *SUPERGIRL* ADVENTURE!

12

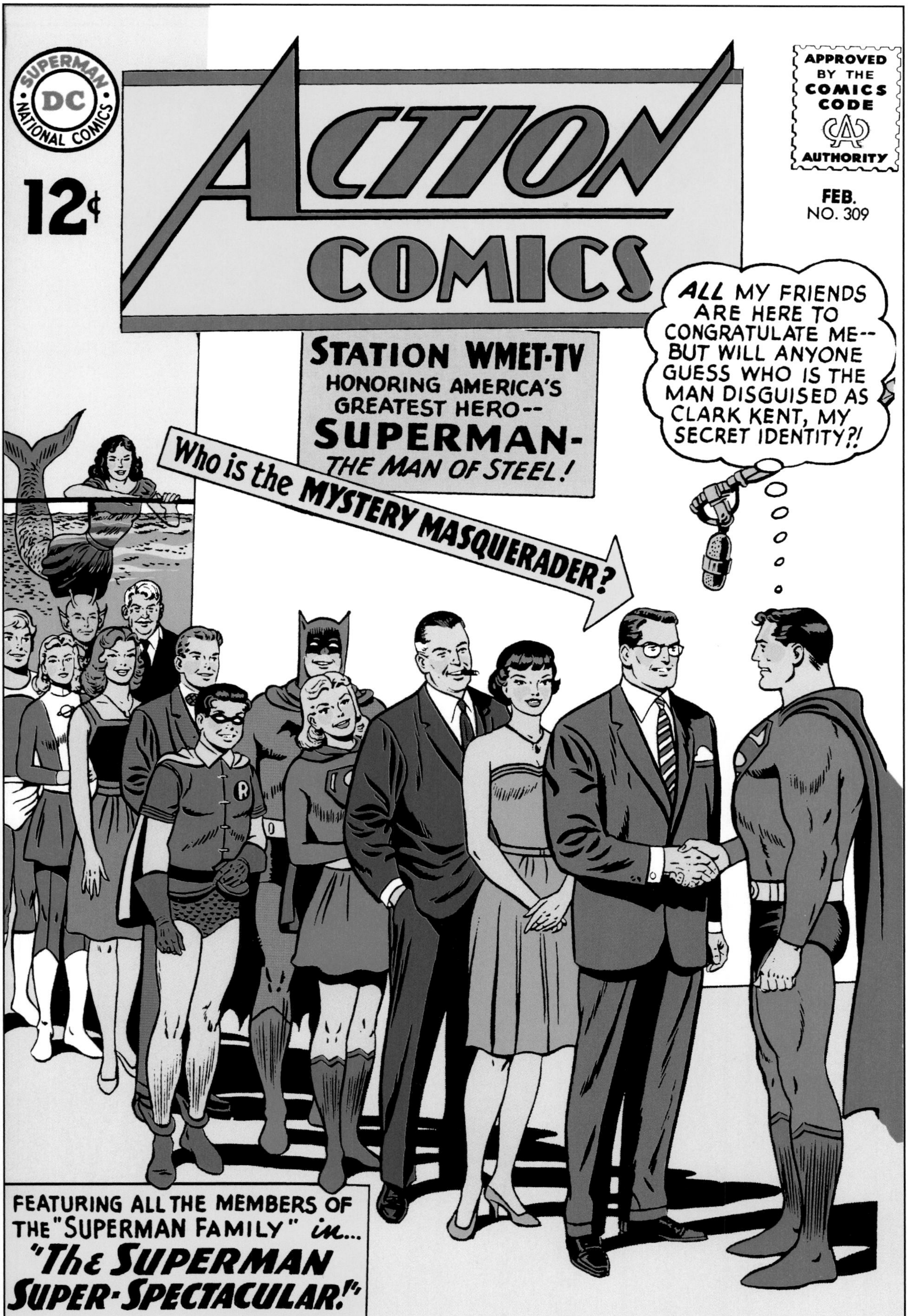
SUPERMAN DC NATIONAL COMICS
12¢
ACTION COMICS
APPROVED BY THE COMICS CODE AUTHORITY
FEB. NO. 309
STATION WMET-TV HONORING AMERICA'S GREATEST HERO-- SUPERMAN- THE MAN OF STEEL!
Who is the MYSTERY MASQUERADER?
ALL MY FRIENDS ARE HERE TO CONGRATULATE ME-- BUT WILL ANYONE GUESS WHO IS THE MAN DISGUISED AS CLARK KENT, MY SECRET IDENTITY?!
FEATURING ALL THE MEMBERS OF THE "SUPERMAN FAMILY" in...
"The SUPERMAN SUPER-SPECTACULAR!"

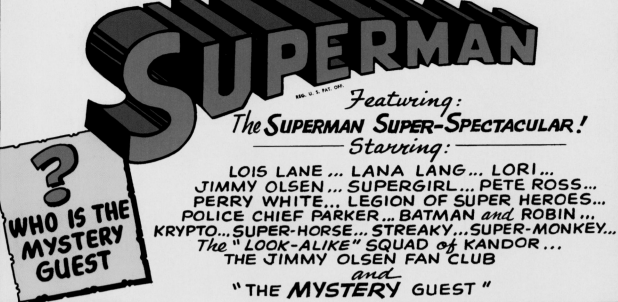

SUPERMAN

REG. U. S. PAT. OFF.

Featuring:
The SUPERMAN SUPER-SPECTACULAR!
—— Starring: ——

LOIS LANE... LANA LANG... LORI...
JIMMY OLSEN... SUPERGIRL... PETE ROSS...
PERRY WHITE... LEGION OF SUPER HEROES...
POLICE CHIEF PARKER... BATMAN and ROBIN...
KRYPTO...SUPER-HORSE...STREAKY...SUPER-MONKEY...
The "LOOK-ALIKE" SQUAD of KANDOR...
THE JIMMY OLSEN FAN CLUB
and
"THE MYSTERY GUEST"

?
WHO IS THE MYSTERY GUEST

LANA, IF EITHER CLARK KENT OR **SUPERMAN** WERE A ROBOT, THIS DETECTOR–GADGET WOULD CLICK! BUT NOTHING IS HAPPENING! THAT MEANS THEY'RE **TWO** DIFFERENT PEOPLE! OUR THEORY ABOUT **SUPERMAN** IS–– **WRONG!**

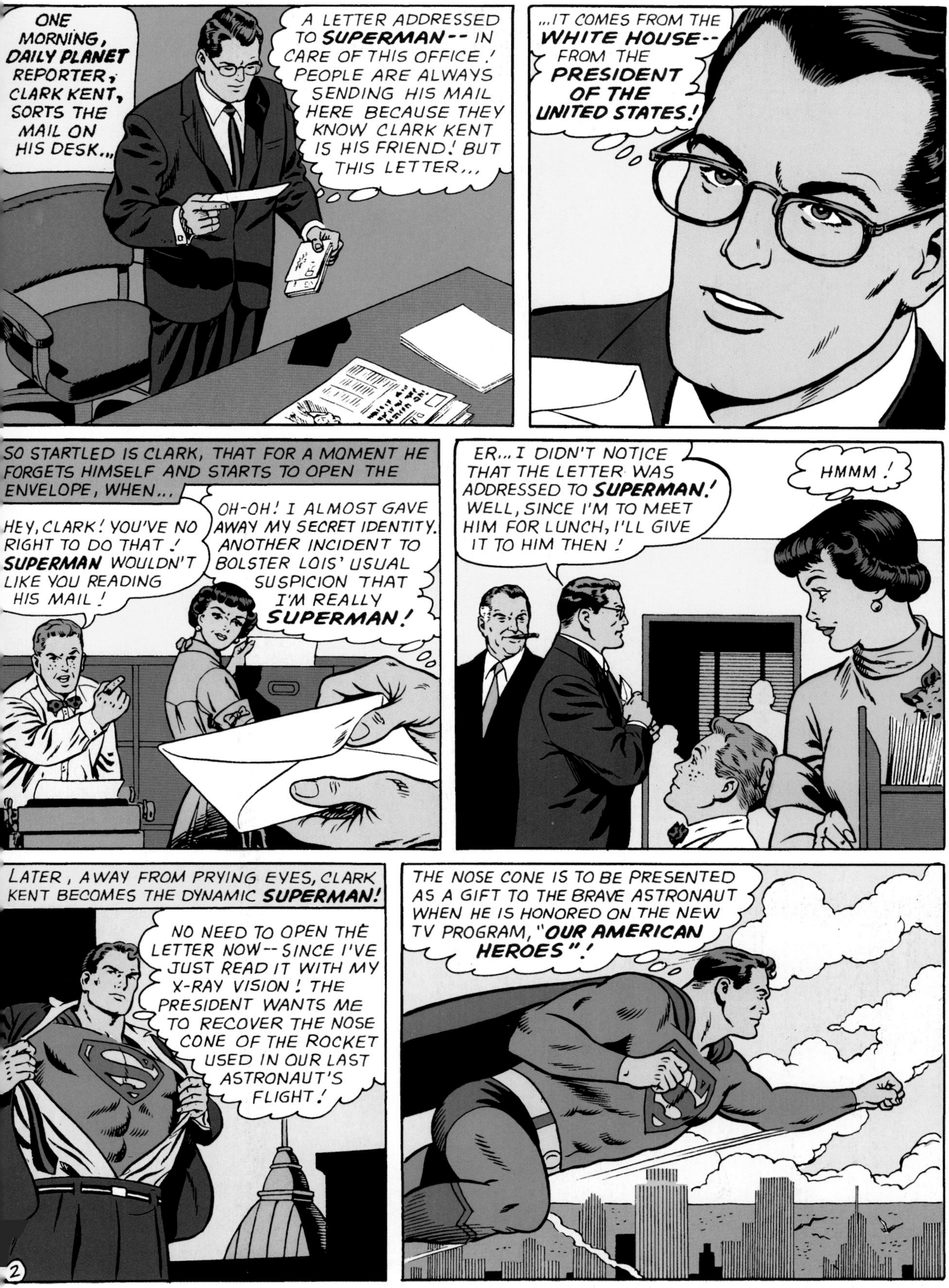
ONE MORNING, DAILY PLANET REPORTER, CLARK KENT, SORTS THE MAIL ON HIS DESK...
A LETTER ADDRESSED TO SUPERMAN-- IN CARE OF THIS OFFICE! PEOPLE ARE ALWAYS SENDING HIS MAIL HERE BECAUSE THEY KNOW CLARK KENT IS HIS FRIEND! BUT THIS LETTER...
...IT COMES FROM THE WHITE HOUSE-- FROM THE PRESIDENT OF THE UNITED STATES!
SO STARTLED IS CLARK, THAT FOR A MOMENT HE FORGETS HIMSELF AND STARTS TO OPEN THE ENVELOPE, WHEN...
HEY, CLARK! YOU'VE NO RIGHT TO DO THAT! SUPERMAN WOULDN'T LIKE YOU READING HIS MAIL!
OH-OH! I ALMOST GAVE AWAY MY SECRET IDENTITY. ANOTHER INCIDENT TO BOLSTER LOIS' USUAL SUSPICION THAT I'M REALLY SUPERMAN!
ER... I DIDN'T NOTICE THAT THE LETTER WAS ADDRESSED TO SUPERMAN! WELL, SINCE I'M TO MEET HIM FOR LUNCH, I'LL GIVE IT TO HIM THEN!
HMMM!
LATER, AWAY FROM PRYING EYES, CLARK KENT BECOMES THE DYNAMIC SUPERMAN!
NO NEED TO OPEN THE LETTER NOW-- SINCE I'VE JUST READ IT WITH MY X-RAY VISION! THE PRESIDENT WANTS ME TO RECOVER THE NOSE CONE OF THE ROCKET USED IN OUR LAST ASTRONAUT'S FLIGHT!
2
THE NOSE CONE IS TO BE PRESENTED AS A GIFT TO THE BRAVE ASTRONAUT WHEN HE IS HONORED ON THE NEW TV PROGRAM, "OUR AMERICAN HEROES"!

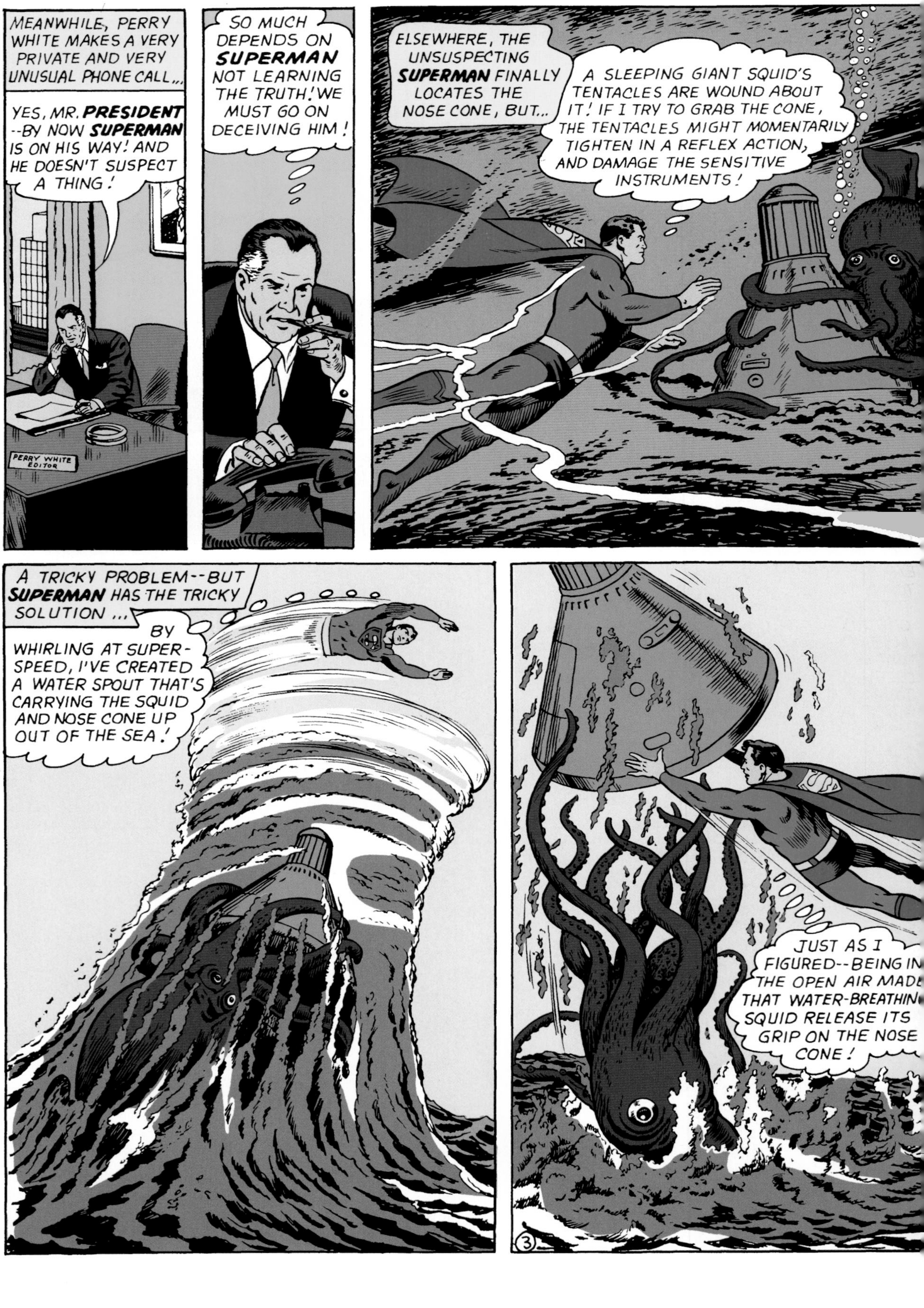
MEANWHILE, PERRY WHITE MAKES A VERY PRIVATE AND VERY UNUSUAL PHONE CALL...
YES, MR. PRESIDENT --BY NOW SUPERMAN IS ON HIS WAY! AND HE DOESN'T SUSPECT A THING!
PERRY WHITE EDITOR
SO MUCH DEPENDS ON SUPERMAN NOT LEARNING THE TRUTH! WE MUST GO ON DECEIVING HIM!
ELSEWHERE, THE UNSUSPECTING SUPERMAN FINALLY LOCATES THE NOSE CONE, BUT...
A SLEEPING GIANT SQUID'S TENTACLES ARE WOUND ABOUT IT! IF I TRY TO GRAB THE CONE, THE TENTACLES MIGHT MOMENTARILY TIGHTEN IN A REFLEX ACTION, AND DAMAGE THE SENSITIVE INSTRUMENTS!
A TRICKY PROBLEM--BUT SUPERMAN HAS THE TRICKY SOLUTION...
BY WHIRLING AT SUPER-SPEED, I'VE CREATED A WATER SPOUT THAT'S CARRYING THE SQUID AND NOSE CONE UP OUT OF THE SEA!
JUST AS I FIGURED--BEING IN THE OPEN AIR MADE THAT WATER-BREATHING SQUID RELEASE ITS GRIP ON THE NOSE CONE!
3

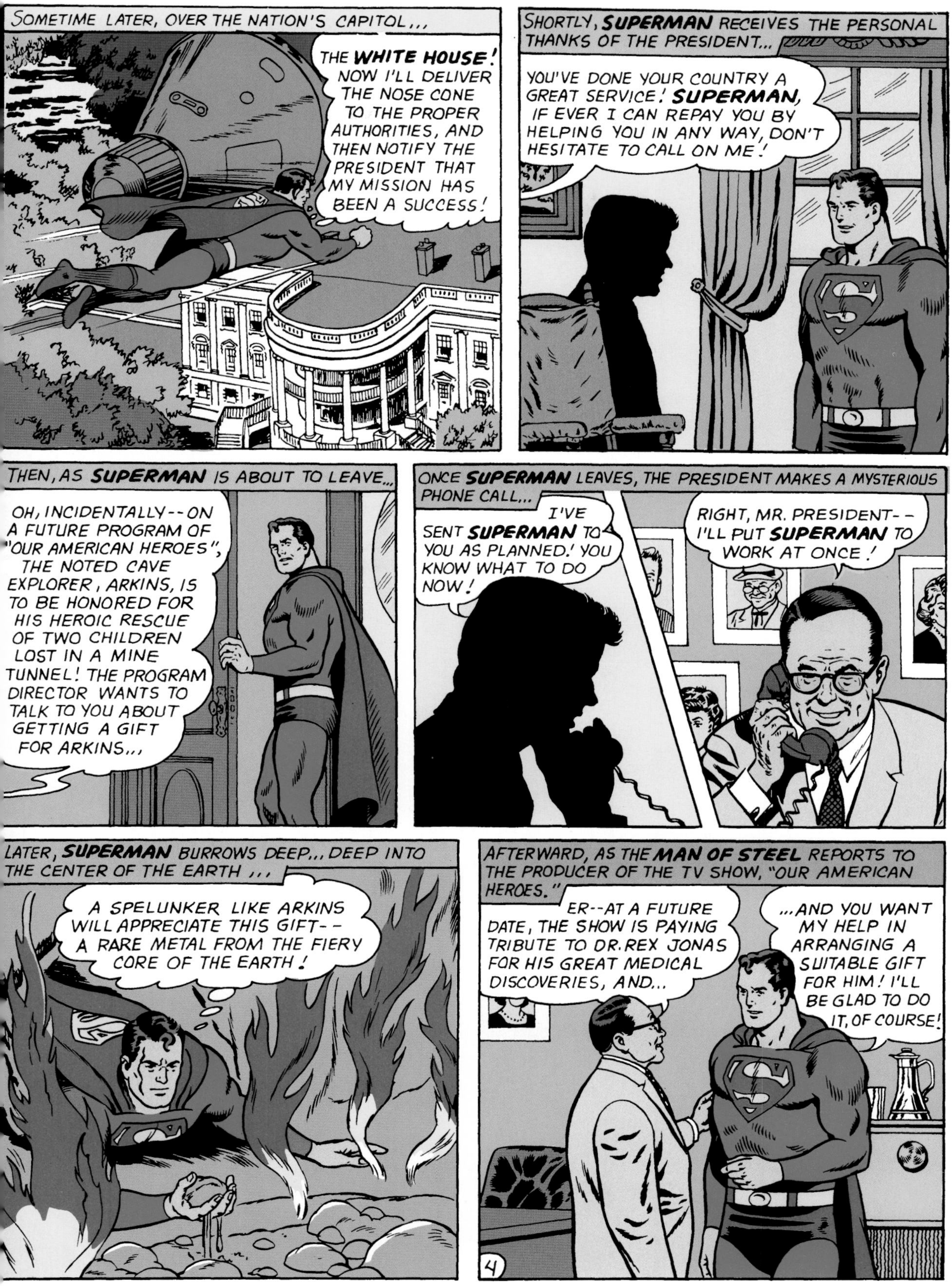
SOMETIME LATER, OVER THE NATION'S CAPITOL,,,
THE WHITE HOUSE! NOW I'LL DELIVER THE NOSE CONE TO THE PROPER AUTHORITIES, AND THEN NOTIFY THE PRESIDENT THAT MY MISSION HAS BEEN A SUCCESS!
SHORTLY, SUPERMAN RECEIVES THE PERSONAL THANKS OF THE PRESIDENT...
YOU'VE DONE YOUR COUNTRY A GREAT SERVICE! SUPERMAN, IF EVER I CAN REPAY YOU BY HELPING YOU IN ANY WAY, DON'T HESITATE TO CALL ON ME!
THEN, AS SUPERMAN IS ABOUT TO LEAVE...
OH, INCIDENTALLY--ON A FUTURE PROGRAM OF "OUR AMERICAN HEROES", THE NOTED CAVE EXPLORER, ARKINS, IS TO BE HONORED FOR HIS HEROIC RESCUE OF TWO CHILDREN LOST IN A MINE TUNNEL! THE PROGRAM DIRECTOR WANTS TO TALK TO YOU ABOUT GETTING A GIFT FOR ARKINS...
ONCE SUPERMAN LEAVES, THE PRESIDENT MAKES A MYSTERIOUS PHONE CALL...
I'VE SENT SUPERMAN TO YOU AS PLANNED! YOU KNOW WHAT TO DO NOW!
RIGHT, MR. PRESIDENT--I'LL PUT SUPERMAN TO WORK AT ONCE!
LATER, SUPERMAN BURROWS DEEP... DEEP INTO THE CENTER OF THE EARTH ...
A SPELUNKER LIKE ARKINS WILL APPRECIATE THIS GIFT--A RARE METAL FROM THE FIERY CORE OF THE EARTH!
AFTERWARD, AS THE MAN OF STEEL REPORTS TO THE PRODUCER OF THE TV SHOW, "OUR AMERICAN HEROES."
ER--AT A FUTURE DATE, THE SHOW IS PAYING TRIBUTE TO DR. REX JONAS FOR HIS GREAT MEDICAL DISCOVERIES, AND...
...AND YOU WANT MY HELP IN ARRANGING A SUITABLE GIFT FOR HIM! I'LL BE GLAD TO DO IT, OF COURSE!
4

LATER, SOMEWHERE IN THE AMAZON JUNGLE... THE JUICES OF THIS UNIQUE PLANT HAVE BEEN USED FOR HEALING BY AMAZON INDIANS FOR CENTURIES! DR. JONAS WILL APPRECIATE HAVING THE PLANT FOR RESEARCH!

THAT JOB DONE, **SUPERMAN** IS GIVEN STILL ANOTHER TASK--THEN ANOTHER--AND ANOTHER!

I'VE HAD QUITE A BUSY DAY--RUSHING FROM ONE CHORE TO ANOTHER! NOW THE PROGRAM DIRECTOR WANTS ME IN THE STOREROOM FOR ANOTHER JOB!

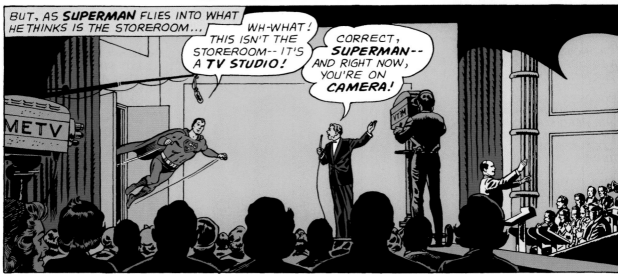

BUT, AS **SUPERMAN** FLIES INTO WHAT HE THINKS IS THE STOREROOM...

WH-WHAT! THIS ISN'T THE STOREROOM-- IT'S A **TV STUDIO!**

CORRECT, **SUPERMAN**-- AND RIGHT NOW, YOU'RE ON **CAMERA!**

METV

KNOWING YOU ARE TOO MODEST TO ACCEPT PRAISE, WE KEPT YOU DISTRACTED WITH VARIOUS MISSIONS SO YOU WOULDN'T GUESS THE TRUTH! EVERYONE'S COOPERATED --PERRY WHITE--AND EVEN THE PRESIDENT!

BUT-- WHY...?

5

THIS IS THE FIRST TELECAST OF THE TV SHOW **"OUR AMERICAN HEROES".** IT'S ONLY FITTING THAT YOU BE OUR FIRST HONORED GUEST, FOR YOU, **SUPERMAN,** ARE-- OUR **GREATEST AMERICAN HERO!**

TIME OUT FOR THE COMMERCIAL--AND SUPERMAN'S SUPER-HEARING PICKS UP WHISPERED WORDS...

THIS SHOW SHOULD BE A BLOCK-BUSTER! ALL OF SUPERMAN'S GOOD FRIENDS PROMISED TO BE HERE! DID YOU NOTIFY CLARK KENT?

HE WAS STILL OUT WHEN I LEFT THE OFFICE--BUT I LEFT A NOTE ON HIS DESK TELLING HIM ABOUT THE SHOW!

HMM! AT THE PROPER TIME, I'LL USE SUPER-VENTRILOQUISM TO SUMMON ONE OF MY ROBOTS--AND COMMAND IT TO MASQUERADE HERE AS CLARK KENT!

NOW, SUPERMAN-- A SUPER-TRIBUTE TO YOU IS ABOUT TO BEGIN!

THAT IS A LEAD-LINED CURTAIN SO THAT YOUR X-RAY VISION CAN'T SEE THE SURPRISE GUEST BEHIND IT! BUT, PERHAPS THAT IDENTIFYING INITIAL CAN HELP YOU GUESS WHO IT IS...

THE LETTER "P" --COULD BE FOR PERRY WHITE...

IT'S POLICE CHIEF PARKER OF SMALLVILLE--THE TOWN WHERE I GREW UP AS SUPERBOY!

I'M NO LONGER POLICE CHIEF, BUT THOUGH I'M RETIRED, I STILL KEEP MY MEMORIES ALIVE--

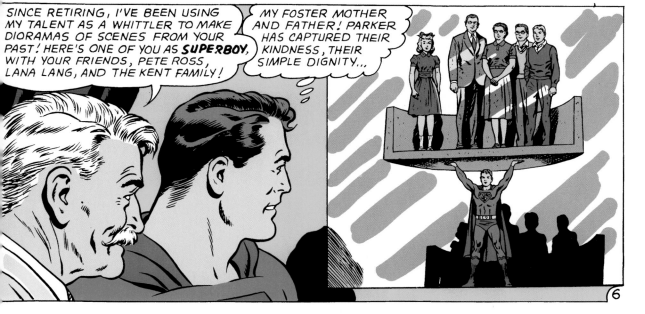

SINCE RETIRING, I'VE BEEN USING MY TALENT AS A WHITTLER TO MAKE DIORAMAS OF SCENES FROM YOUR PAST! HERE'S ONE OF YOU AS SUPERBOY, WITH YOUR FRIENDS, PETE ROSS, LANA LANG, AND THE KENT FAMILY!

MY FOSTER MOTHER AND FATHER! PARKER HAS CAPTURED THEIR KINDNESS, THEIR SIMPLE DIGNITY...

6

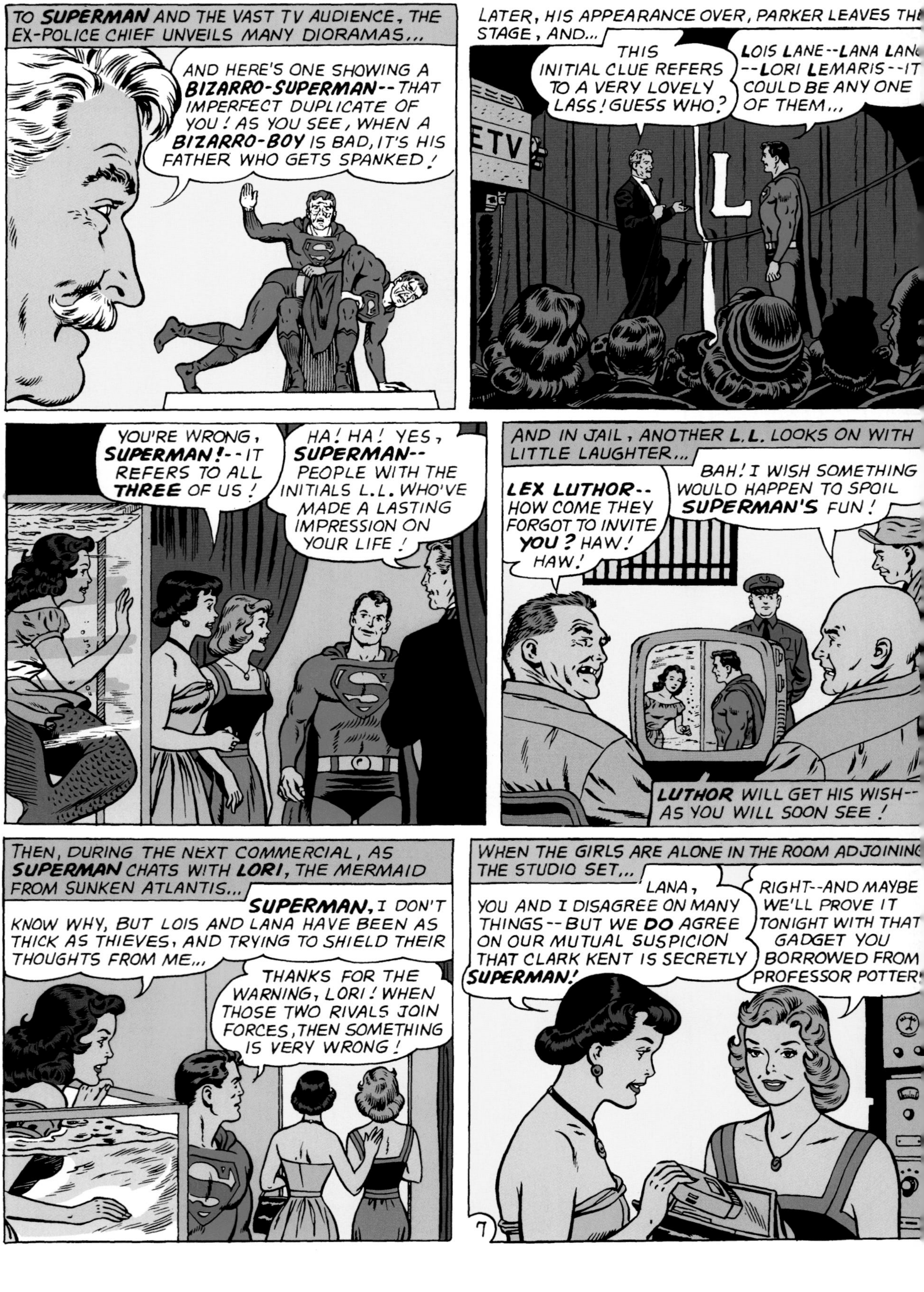

TO SUPERMAN AND THE VAST TV AUDIENCE, THE EX-POLICE CHIEF UNVEILS MANY DIORAMAS...
AND HERE'S ONE SHOWING A BIZARRO-SUPERMAN-- THAT IMPERFECT DUPLICATE OF YOU! AS YOU SEE, WHEN A BIZARRO-BOY IS BAD, IT'S HIS FATHER WHO GETS SPANKED!
LATER, HIS APPEARANCE OVER, PARKER LEAVES THE STAGE, AND...
THIS INITIAL CLUE REFERS TO A VERY LOVELY LASS! GUESS WHO?
LOIS LANE--LANA LANG --LORI LEMARIS--IT COULD BE ANY ONE OF THEM...
ETV
L
YOU'RE WRONG, SUPERMAN!--IT REFERS TO ALL THREE OF US!
HA! HA! YES, SUPERMAN-- PEOPLE WITH THE INITIALS L.L. WHO'VE MADE A LASTING IMPRESSION ON YOUR LIFE!
AND IN JAIL, ANOTHER L.L. LOOKS ON WITH LITTLE LAUGHTER...
LEX LUTHOR-- HOW COME THEY FORGOT TO INVITE YOU? HAW! HAW!
BAH! I WISH SOMETHING WOULD HAPPEN TO SPOIL SUPERMAN'S FUN!
LUTHOR WILL GET HIS WISH-- AS YOU WILL SOON SEE!
THEN, DURING THE NEXT COMMERCIAL, AS SUPERMAN CHATS WITH LORI, THE MERMAID FROM SUNKEN ATLANTIS...
SUPERMAN, I DON'T KNOW WHY, BUT LOIS AND LANA HAVE BEEN AS THICK AS THIEVES, AND TRYING TO SHIELD THEIR THOUGHTS FROM ME...
THANKS FOR THE WARNING, LORI! WHEN THOSE TWO RIVALS JOIN FORCES, THEN SOMETHING IS VERY WRONG!
WHEN THE GIRLS ARE ALONE IN THE ROOM ADJOINING THE STUDIO SET...
LANA, YOU AND I DISAGREE ON MANY THINGS--BUT WE DO AGREE ON OUR MUTUAL SUSPICION THAT CLARK KENT IS SECRETLY SUPERMAN!
RIGHT--AND MAYBE WE'LL PROVE IT TONIGHT WITH THAT GADGET YOU BORROWED FROM PROFESSOR POTTER!
7

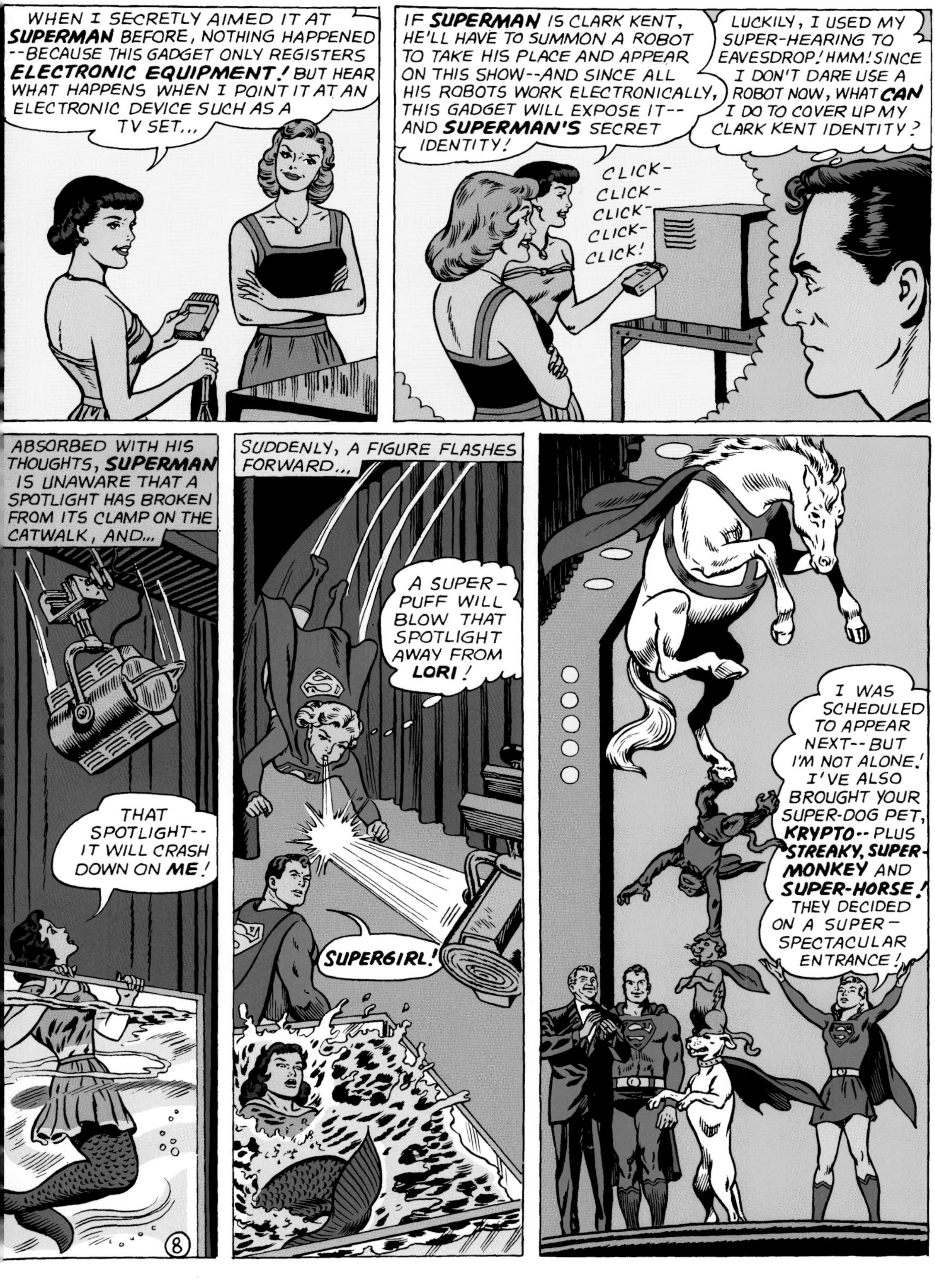

WHEN I SECRETLY AIMED IT AT SUPERMAN BEFORE, NOTHING HAPPENED --BECAUSE THIS GADGET ONLY REGISTERS ELECTRONIC EQUIPMENT! BUT HEAR WHAT HAPPENS WHEN I POINT IT AT AN ELECTRONIC DEVICE SUCH AS A TV SET...
IF SUPERMAN IS CLARK KENT, HE'LL HAVE TO SUMMON A ROBOT TO TAKE HIS PLACE AND APPEAR ON THIS SHOW--AND SINCE ALL HIS ROBOTS WORK ELECTRONICALLY, THIS GADGET WILL EXPOSE IT--AND SUPERMAN'S SECRET IDENTITY!
CLICK-CLICK-CLICK-CLICK-CLICK!
LUCKILY, I USED MY SUPER-HEARING TO EAVESDROP! HMM! SINCE I DON'T DARE USE A ROBOT NOW, WHAT CAN I DO TO COVER UP MY CLARK KENT IDENTITY?
ABSORBED WITH HIS THOUGHTS, SUPERMAN IS UNAWARE THAT A SPOTLIGHT HAS BROKEN FROM ITS CLAMP ON THE CATWALK, AND...
THAT SPOTLIGHT--IT WILL CRASH DOWN ON ME!
8
SUDDENLY, A FIGURE FLASHES FORWARD...
A SUPER-PUFF WILL BLOW THAT SPOTLIGHT AWAY FROM LORI!
SUPERGIRL!
I WAS SCHEDULED TO APPEAR NEXT--BUT I'M NOT ALONE! I'VE ALSO BROUGHT YOUR SUPER-DOG PET, KRYPTO--PLUS STREAKY, SUPER-MONKEY AND SUPER-HORSE! THEY DECIDED ON A SUPER-SPECTACULAR ENTRANCE!

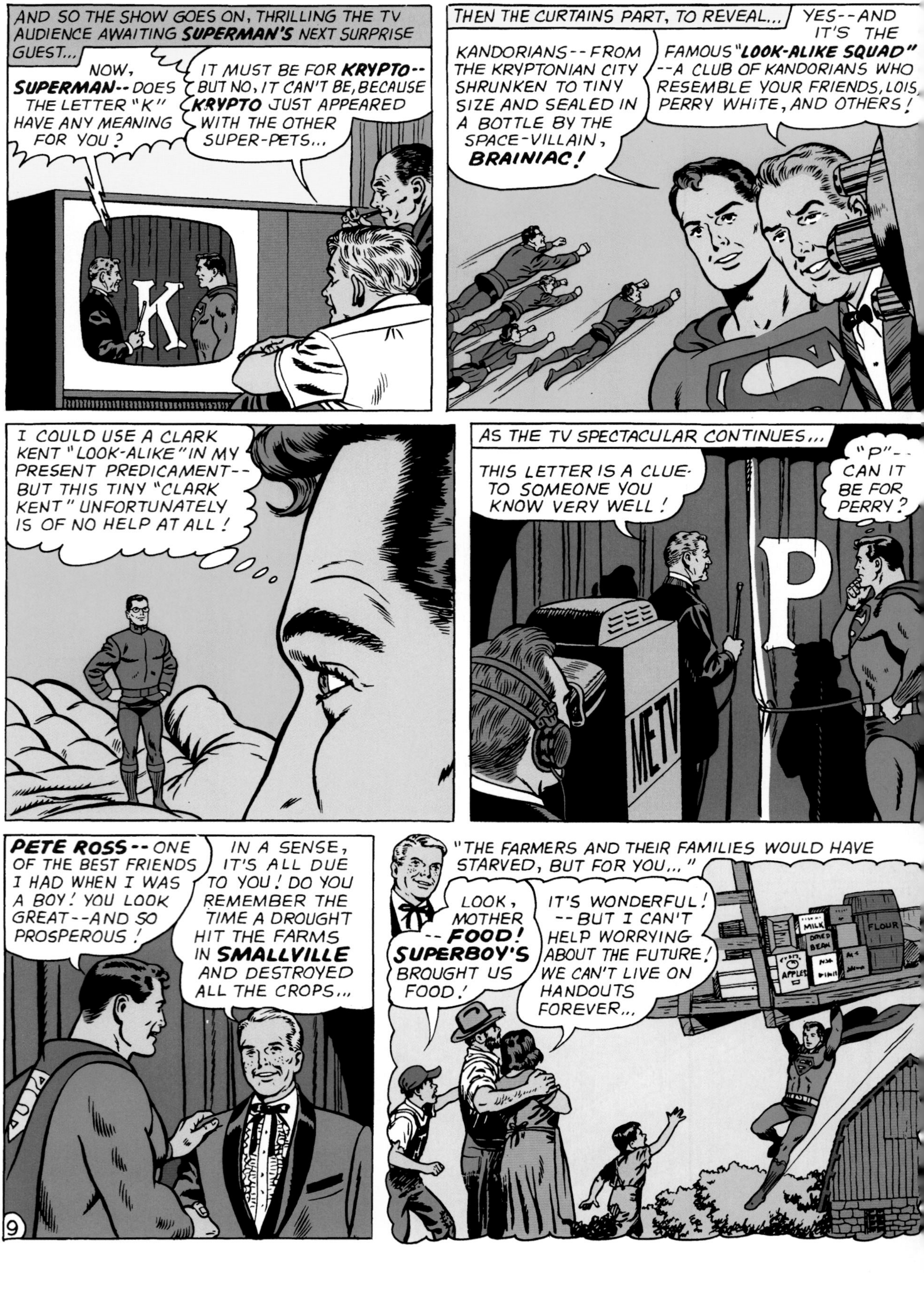
AND SO THE SHOW GOES ON, THRILLING THE TV AUDIENCE AWAITING SUPERMAN'S NEXT SURPRISE GUEST...
NOW, SUPERMAN-- DOES THE LETTER "K" HAVE ANY MEANING FOR YOU?
IT MUST BE FOR KRYPTO-- BUT NO, IT CAN'T BE, BECAUSE KRYPTO JUST APPEARED WITH THE OTHER SUPER-PETS...
K
THEN THE CURTAINS PART, TO REVEAL...
KANDORIANS-- FROM THE KRYPTONIAN CITY SHRUNKEN TO TINY SIZE AND SEALED IN A BOTTLE BY THE SPACE-VILLAIN, BRAINIAC!
YES--AND IT'S THE FAMOUS "LOOK-ALIKE SQUAD" --A CLUB OF KANDORIANS WHO RESEMBLE YOUR FRIENDS, LOIS, PERRY WHITE, AND OTHERS!
I COULD USE A CLARK KENT "LOOK-ALIKE" IN MY PRESENT PREDICAMENT-- BUT THIS TINY "CLARK KENT" UNFORTUNATELY IS OF NO HELP AT ALL!
AS THE TV SPECTACULAR CONTINUES...
THIS LETTER IS A CLUE TO SOMEONE YOU KNOW VERY WELL!
"P"-- CAN IT BE FOR PERRY?
P
METV
PETE ROSS-- ONE OF THE BEST FRIENDS I HAD WHEN I WAS A BOY! YOU LOOK GREAT--AND SO PROSPEROUS!
IN A SENSE, IT'S ALL DUE TO YOU! DO YOU REMEMBER THE TIME A DROUGHT HIT THE FARMS IN SMALLVILLE AND DESTROYED ALL THE CROPS...
9
"THE FARMERS AND THEIR FAMILIES WOULD HAVE STARVED, BUT FOR YOU..."
LOOK, MOTHER --FOOD! SUPERBOY'S BROUGHT US FOOD!
IT'S WONDERFUL! --BUT I CAN'T HELP WORRYING ABOUT THE FUTURE! WE CAN'T LIVE ON HANDOUTS FOREVER...
MILK
FLOUR
APPLES

"YOU KNEW THE PROUD FARMERS WOULDN'T GO ON ACCEPTING CHARITY--SO YOU SEARCHED FOR AN ANSWER--AND FOUND IT!"

SUPERBOY--BURROWING INTO THE GROUND? BUT WHY?

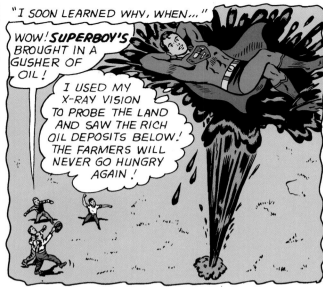

"I SOON LEARNED WHY, WHEN..."

WOW! SUPERBOY'S BROUGHT IN A GUSHER OF OIL!

I USED MY X-RAY VISION TO PROBE THE LAND AND SAW THE RICH OIL DEPOSITS BELOW! THE FARMERS WILL NEVER GO HUNGRY AGAIN!

THAT FEAT INSPIRED ME TO BECOME A GEOLOGIST! I'VE BECOME RICH--BUT I'VE HAD THE SATISFACTION OF KNOWING I'VE MADE OTHERS RICH, TOO--BY FINDING OIL IN FIELDS ONCE CONSIDERED WORTHLESS!

THUS, PETE ROSS PAYS TRIBUTE TO SUPERMAN, BUT MORE WELL-WISHERS MAKE THEIR APPEARANCE...

JIMMY OLSEN!

YUP--AND WITH ME ARE SOME MEMBERS OF THE JIMMY OLSEN FAN CLUB! ONE OF THEM HAS A GIFT FOR YOU!

A LEAD BOX?

YES--TO MAKE SURE YOUR X-RAY VISION COULDN'T SEE THE SURPRISE GIFT INSIDE THE BOX UNTIL THE PROPER MOMENT!

MY DAD AND OTHER MEMBERS OF HIS SKIN-DIVING CLUB FOUND A CHUNK OF GOLD IN THE SEA--AND DECIDED TO GIVE IT TO YOU TO CONTRIBUTE TO YOUR FAVORITE CHARITY!

10

ABRUPTLY... SATURN GIRL-- ELEMENT LAD-- CHAMELEON BOY-- AND OTHER MEMBERS OF THE **LEGION OF SUPER-HEROES!**

GREAT SCOTT! IT'S ONLY BECAUSE OF MY ABILITY TO INSTANTLY ANALYZE ALL ELEMENTS THAT I CAN SEE THAT THE LEAD BOX DOES **NOT** CONTAIN GOLD BUT **GOLD KRYPTONITE!**

GOLD KRYPTONITE-- IT CAN **PERMANENTLY** TAKE AWAY **SUPERMAN'S** POWERS!

I'LL SIMPLY USE MY **ELEMENT-CHANGING POWER** TO TURN IT INTO **PLATINUM**-- SO **SUPERMAN** WILL STILL HAVE HIS SUPER-POWERS, AND HIS CHARITY WILL STILL HAVE ITS DONATION!

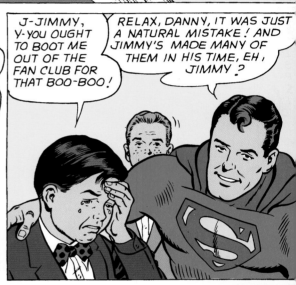

J-JIMMY, Y-YOU OUGHT TO BOOT ME OUT OF THE FAN CLUB FOR THAT BOO-BOO!

RELAX, DANNY, IT WAS JUST A NATURAL MISTAKE! AND JIMMY'S MADE MANY OF THEM IN HIS TIME, EH, JIMMY?

WE TRAVELED FROM THE 30TH CENTURY AS REPRESENTATIVES OF THE **LEGION** IN ORDER TO HONOR YOU ON THIS OCCASION!

I'M GLAD YOU DID! GLADDER THAN YOU REALIZE-- BECAUSE NOW I CAN GET **CHAMELEON BOY** TO SECRETLY CHANGE HIS APPEARANCE AND RETURN LATER AS **CLARK KENT!**

BUT SUDDENLY... BUZZ-ZZ-ZZ-ZZZ-

OH-OH! THE ALERT SIGNAL SUMMONING US BACK! THE LEGION MUST NEED US TO HELP FIGHT SOME EMERGENCY! SORRY, **SUPERMAN**-- BUT WE MUST RETURN TO OUR OWN TIME AT ONCE!

11

AS THE **LEGION OF SUPER-HEROES** LEAVES, PETE ROSS OVERHEARS...

PSST! PERRY-- KENT'S LATE! AND HE'S DUE TO APPEAR ON STAGE AFTER THE NEXT COMMERCIAL!

HMM! **SUPERMAN** LOOKS WORRIED! IS IT POSSIBLE HE'S ON A SPOT? **SUPERMAN** DOESN'T KNOW I'VE ALWAYS BEEN AWARE THAT HE'S CLARK KENT...

"IT HAPPENED DURING A CAMPING TRIP-- WHEN **SUPERBOY** WAS NEEDED..."

GREAT SCOTT! CLARK THINKS I'M ASLEEP-- AND DOESN'T REALIZE HE'S EXPOSING HIS SECRET IDENTITY TO ME! BUT I'LL NEVER BETRAY HIM -- NOR LET HIM HIM KNOW THAT I KNOW!

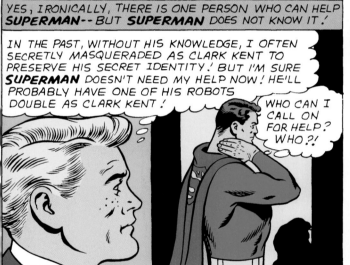

YES, IRONICALLY, THERE IS ONE PERSON WHO CAN HELP **SUPERMAN**-- BUT **SUPERMAN** DOES NOT KNOW IT!

IN THE PAST, WITHOUT HIS KNOWLEDGE, I OFTEN SECRETLY MASQUERADED AS CLARK KENT TO PRESERVE HIS SECRET IDENTITY! BUT I'M SURE **SUPERMAN** DOESN'T NEED MY HELP NOW! HE'LL PROBABLY HAVE ONE OF HIS ROBOTS DOUBLE AS CLARK KENT!

WHO CAN I CALL ON FOR HELP? WHO?!

AH! I HAVE IT! **BATMAN!** HE'S DOUBLED FOR ME BEFORE! I'LL SUMMON HIM VIA SUPER- VENTRILOQUISM!

SUPER-VISION PROBES THE SUBTERRANEAN SANCTUM OF **BATMAN** AND **ROBIN**, BUT...

THEY'RE NOT IN THE **BAT-CAVE!** WHERE CAN THEY BE?

THEN, AS THE PROGRAM CONTINUES...

AND NOW, **SUPERMAN** -- HERE'S ANOTHER INITIAL CLUE FOR YOU TO DECIPHER...

A "B"! OH, NO -- I HOPE IT ISN'T...

B

12

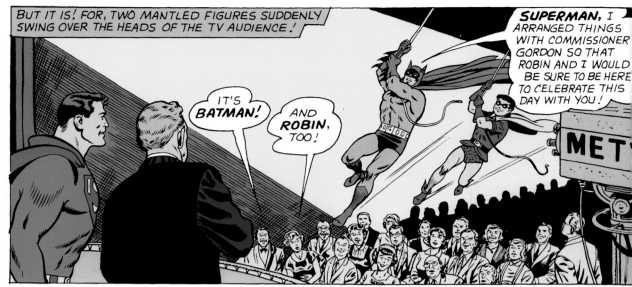

BUT IT IS! FOR, TWO MANTLED FIGURES SUDDENLY SWING OVER THE HEADS OF THE TV AUDIENCE!

IT'S BATMAN!

AND ROBIN, TOO!

SUPERMAN, I ARRANGED THINGS WITH COMMISSIONER GORDON SO THAT ROBIN AND I WOULD BE SURE TO BE HERE TO CELEBRATE THIS DAY WITH YOU!

MET

NOW THAT BATMAN IS HERE, I CAN'T POSSIBLY ASK HIM TO LEAVE THE STUDIO AND RETURN AS CLARK KENT! THAT WOULD ONLY HEIGHTEN LOIS' SUSPICIONS!

HMM! SUPERMAN LOOKS REAL WORRIED! I WONDER IF HE'LL SECRETLY ASK BATMAN TO DISGUISE HIMSELF AS CLARK KENT LATER?

LATER, DURING THE COMMERCIAL, AS BATMAN WANDERS IN THE WINGS, HE SPEAKS STARTLING WORDS...

LOIS, YOU'RE ALWAYS TRYING TO LEARN SUPERMAN'S IDENTITY-- AND MINE, TOO -- SO, I'M GOING TO SATISFY YOUR CURIOSITY ABOUT ME -- AND UNMASK!

HUH?

THE DARK COWL IS WHIPPED AWAY, TO REVEAL...

EEK! YOU'RE A BIZARRO!

HA! HA! IT'S JUST MAKE-UP LOIS! I WANTED TO TEASE YOU A BIT BY SHOWING YOU WHAT A BIZARRO-BATMAN WOULD LOOK LIKE! HA! HA!

WELL--ALL THAT HEAVY MAKE-UP WOULD TAKE AN HOUR TO REMOVE! BATMAN COULD NEVER DOUBLE FOR CLARK KENT IN TIME NOW!

13

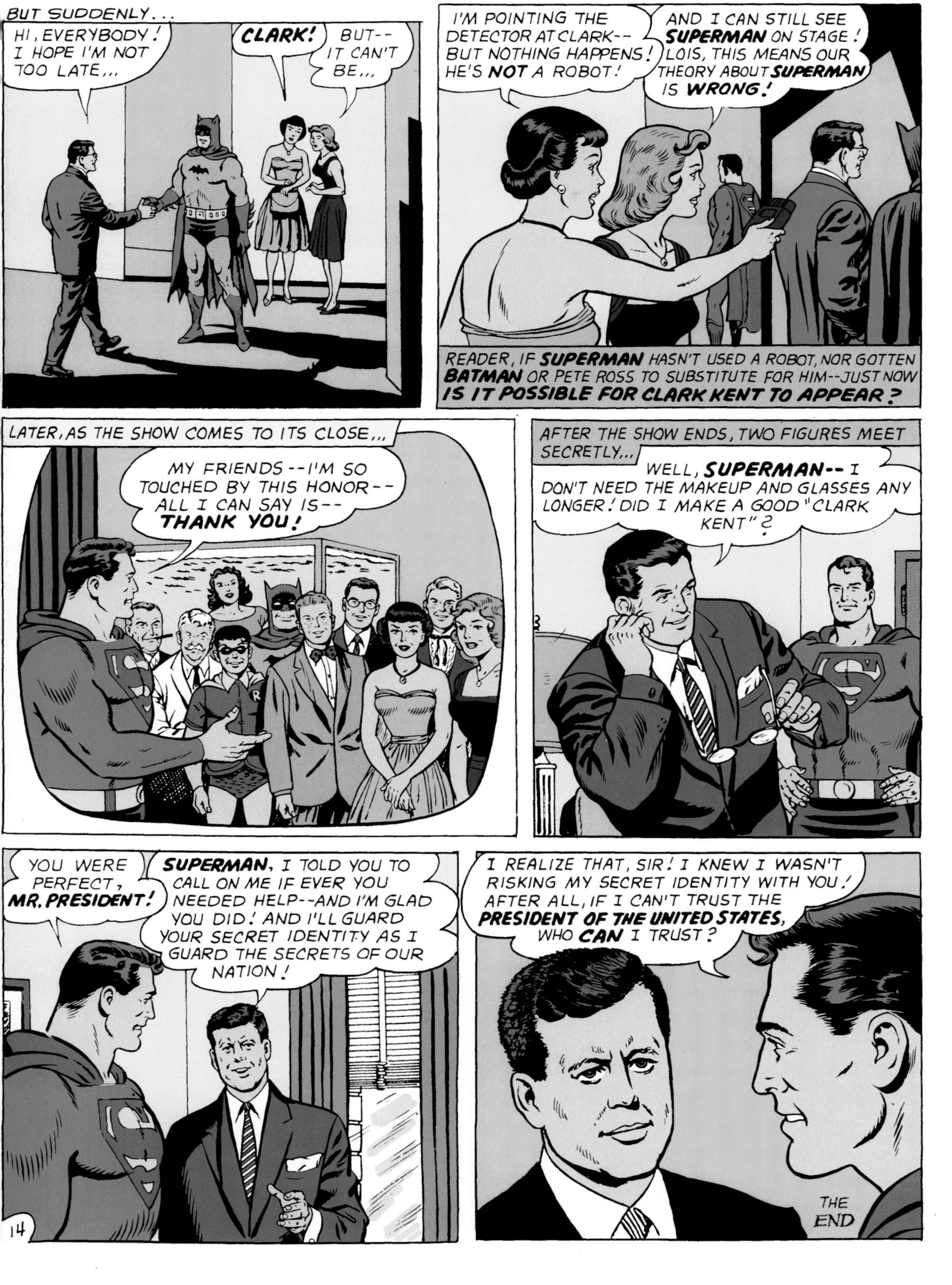

BUT SUDDENLY...
HI, EVERYBODY! I HOPE I'M NOT TOO LATE...
CLARK!
BUT-- IT CAN'T BE...
I'M POINTING THE DETECTOR AT CLARK-- BUT NOTHING HAPPENS! HE'S NOT A ROBOT!
AND I CAN STILL SEE SUPERMAN ON STAGE! LOIS, THIS MEANS OUR THEORY ABOUT SUPERMAN IS WRONG!
READER, IF SUPERMAN HASN'T USED A ROBOT, NOR GOTTEN BATMAN OR PETE ROSS TO SUBSTITUTE FOR HIM--JUST NOW IS IT POSSIBLE FOR CLARK KENT TO APPEAR?
LATER, AS THE SHOW COMES TO ITS CLOSE...
MY FRIENDS--I'M SO TOUCHED BY THIS HONOR-- ALL I CAN SAY IS-- THANK YOU!
AFTER THE SHOW ENDS, TWO FIGURES MEET SECRETLY...
WELL, SUPERMAN-- I DON'T NEED THE MAKEUP AND GLASSES ANY LONGER! DID I MAKE A GOOD "CLARK KENT"?
YOU WERE PERFECT, MR. PRESIDENT!
SUPERMAN, I TOLD YOU TO CALL ON ME IF EVER YOU NEEDED HELP--AND I'M GLAD YOU DID! AND I'LL GUARD YOUR SECRET IDENTITY AS I GUARD THE SECRETS OF OUR NATION!
14
I REALIZE THAT, SIR! I KNEW I WASN'T RISKING MY SECRET IDENTITY WITH YOU! AFTER ALL, IF I CAN'T TRUST THE PRESIDENT OF THE UNITED STATES, WHO CAN I TRUST?
THE END

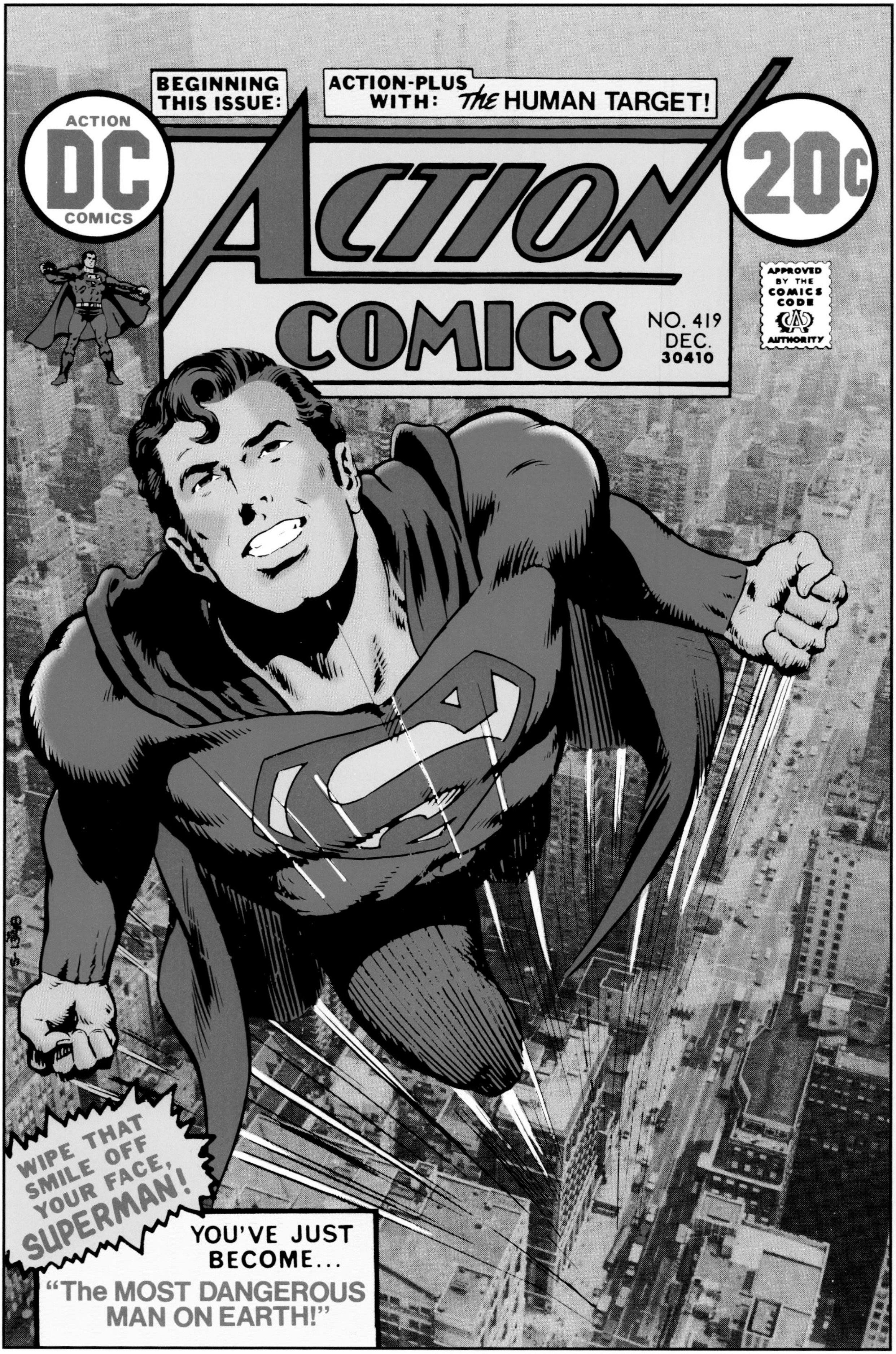
BEGINNING THIS ISSUE:
ACTION-PLUS WITH: THE HUMAN TARGET!
ACTION DC COMICS
ACTION COMICS
20c
APPROVED BY THE COMICS CODE AUTHORITY
NO. 419 DEC. 30410
WIPE THAT SMILE OFF YOUR FACE, SUPERMAN!
YOU'VE JUST BECOME...
"The MOST DANGEROUS MAN ON EARTH!"

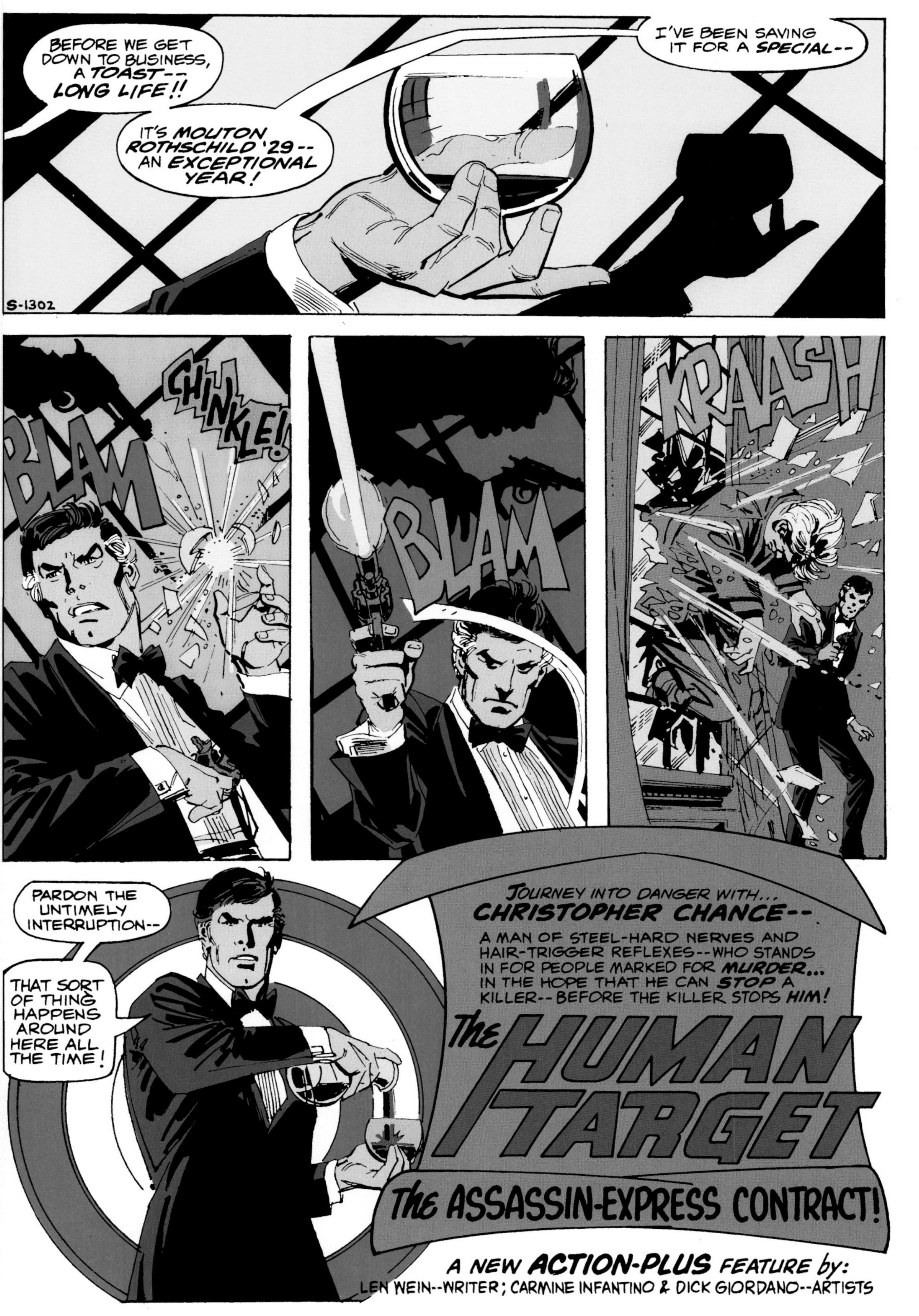

BEFORE WE GET DOWN TO BUSINESS, A TOAST-- LONG LIFE!!
I'VE BEEN SAVING IT FOR A SPECIAL--
IT'S MOUTON ROTHSCHILD '29-- AN EXCEPTIONAL YEAR!
S-1302
CHINKLE!
BLAM
BLAM
KRAASH
PARDON THE UNTIMELY INTERRUPTION--
THAT SORT OF THING HAPPENS AROUND HERE ALL THE TIME!
JOURNEY INTO DANGER WITH... CHRISTOPHER CHANCE--
A MAN OF STEEL-HARD NERVES AND HAIR-TRIGGER REFLEXES--WHO STANDS IN FOR PEOPLE MARKED FOR MURDER... IN THE HOPE THAT HE CAN STOP A KILLER--BEFORE THE KILLER STOPS HIM!
The HUMAN TARGET
The ASSASSIN-EXPRESS CONTRACT!
A NEW ACTION-PLUS FEATURE by:
LEN WEIN--WRITER; CARMINE INFANTINO & DICK GIORDANO--ARTISTS

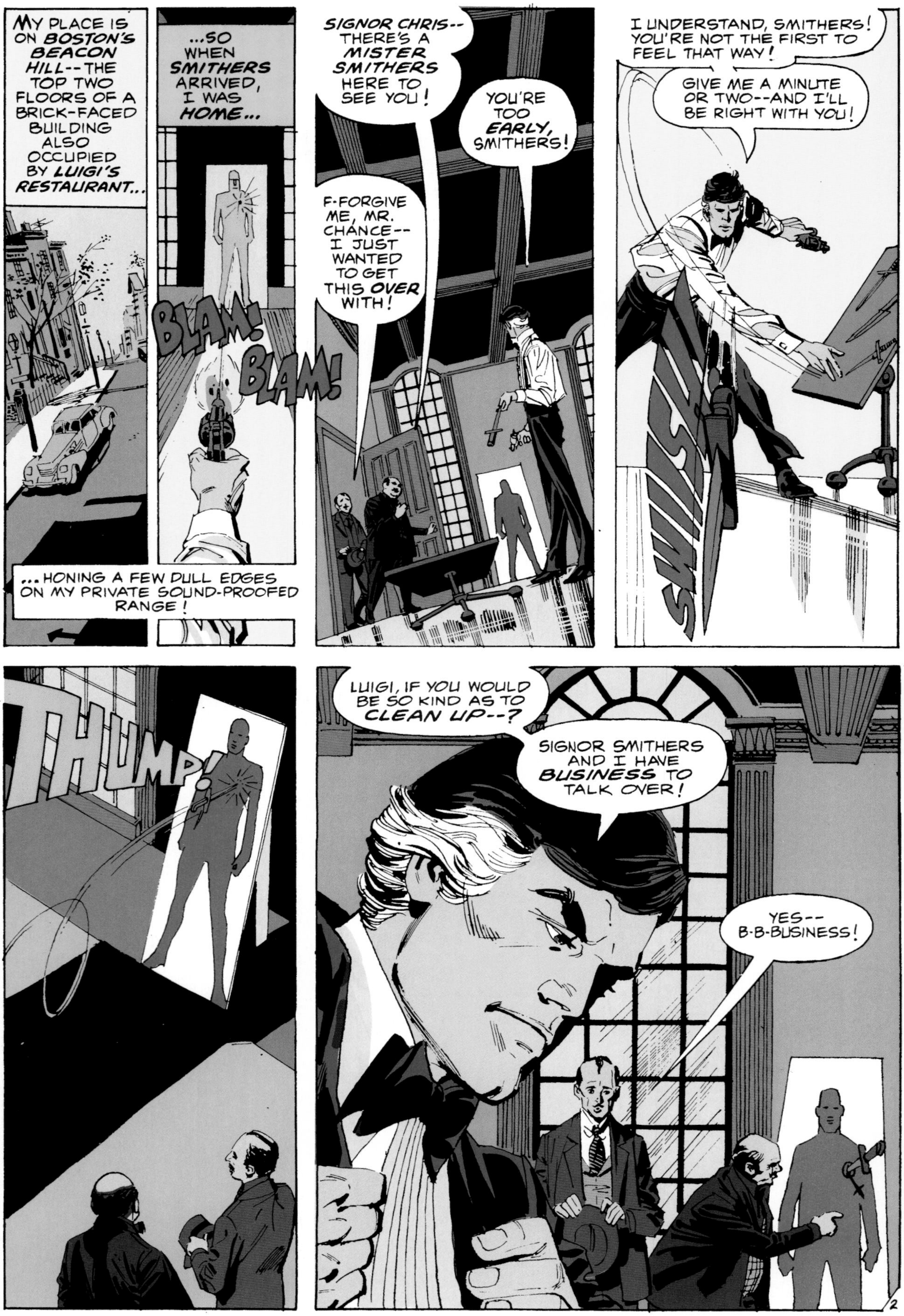
MY PLACE IS ON BOSTON'S BEACON HILL--THE TOP TWO FLOORS OF A BRICK-FACED BUILDING ALSO OCCUPIED BY LUIGI'S RESTAURANT...
...SO WHEN SMITHERS ARRIVED, I WAS HOME...
BLAM! BLAM!
...HONING A FEW DULL EDGES ON MY PRIVATE SOUND-PROOFED RANGE!
SIGNOR CHRIS--THERE'S A MISTER SMITHERS HERE TO SEE YOU!
YOU'RE TOO EARLY, SMITHERS!
F-FORGIVE ME, MR. CHANCE--I JUST WANTED TO GET THIS OVER WITH!
I UNDERSTAND, SMITHERS! YOU'RE NOT THE FIRST TO FEEL THAT WAY!
GIVE ME A MINUTE OR TWO--AND I'LL BE RIGHT WITH YOU!
SWISH
THUMP!
LUIGI, IF YOU WOULD BE SO KIND AS TO CLEAN UP--?
SIGNOR SMITHERS AND I HAVE BUSINESS TO TALK OVER!
YES--B-B-BUSINESS!
2

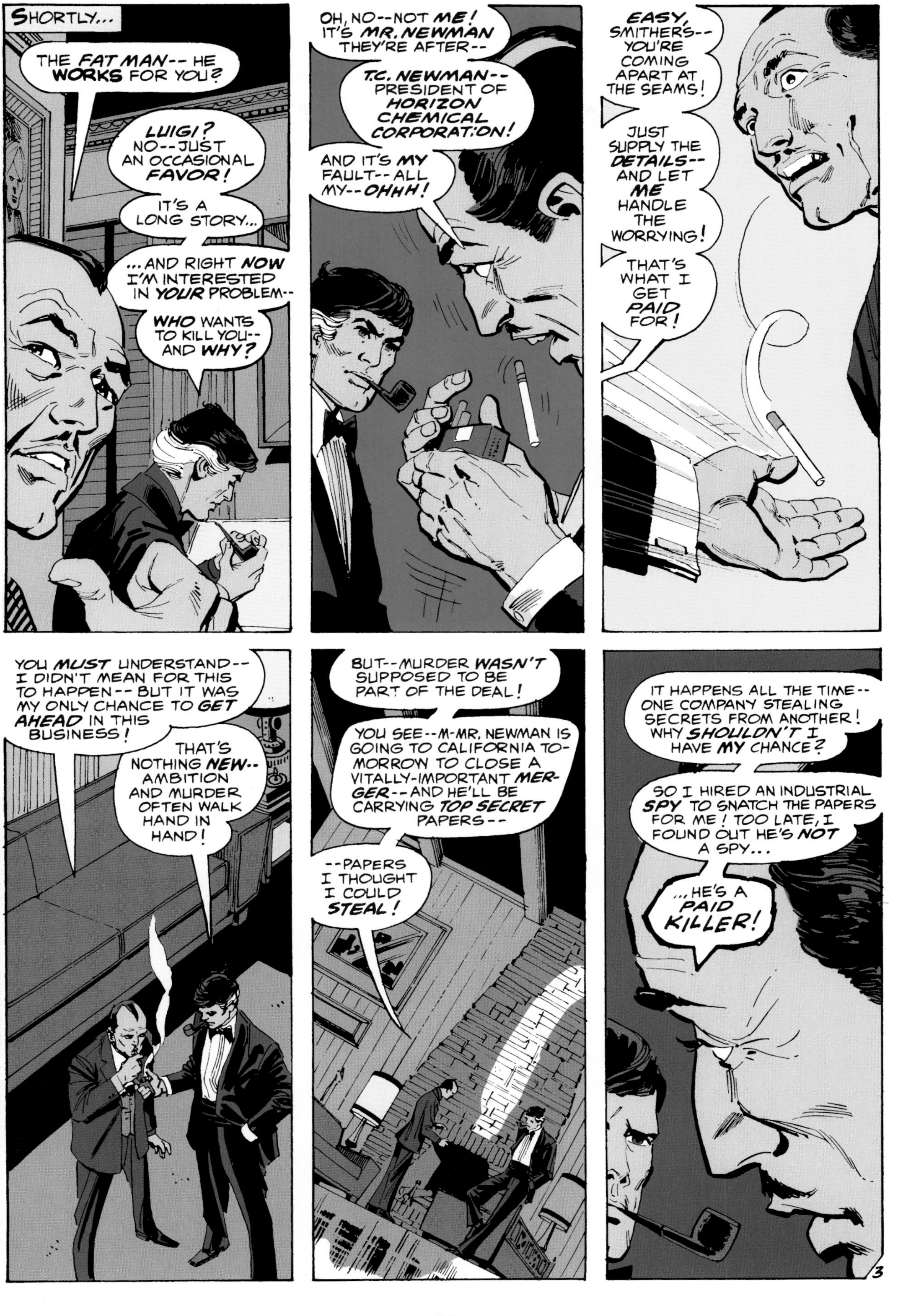
SHORTLY...
THE FAT MAN-- HE WORKS FOR YOU?
LUIGI? NO--JUST AN OCCASIONAL FAVOR!
IT'S A LONG STORY...
...AND RIGHT NOW I'M INTERESTED IN YOUR PROBLEM--
WHO WANTS TO KILL YOU-- AND WHY?
OH, NO--NOT ME! IT'S MR. NEWMAN THEY'RE AFTER--
T.C. NEWMAN-- PRESIDENT OF HORIZON CHEMICAL CORPORATION!
AND IT'S MY FAULT--ALL MY--OHHH!
EASY, SMITHERS-- YOU'RE COMING APART AT THE SEAMS!
JUST SUPPLY THE DETAILS-- AND LET ME HANDLE THE WORRYING!
THAT'S WHAT I GET PAID FOR!
YOU MUST UNDERSTAND-- I DIDN'T MEAN FOR THIS TO HAPPEN-- BUT IT WAS MY ONLY CHANCE TO GET AHEAD IN THIS BUSINESS!
THAT'S NOTHING NEW-- AMBITION AND MURDER OFTEN WALK HAND IN HAND!
BUT--MURDER WASN'T SUPPOSED TO BE PART OF THE DEAL!
YOU SEE--M-MR. NEWMAN IS GOING TO CALIFORNIA TO-MORROW TO CLOSE A VITALLY-IMPORTANT MER-GER--AND HE'LL BE CARRYING TOP SECRET PAPERS--
--PAPERS I THOUGHT I COULD STEAL!
IT HAPPENS ALL THE TIME-- ONE COMPANY STEALING SECRETS FROM ANOTHER! WHY SHOULDN'T I HAVE MY CHANCE?
SO I HIRED AN INDUSTRIAL SPY TO SNATCH THE PAPERS FOR ME! TOO LATE, I FOUND OUT HE'S NOT A SPY...
...HE'S A PAID KILLER!
3

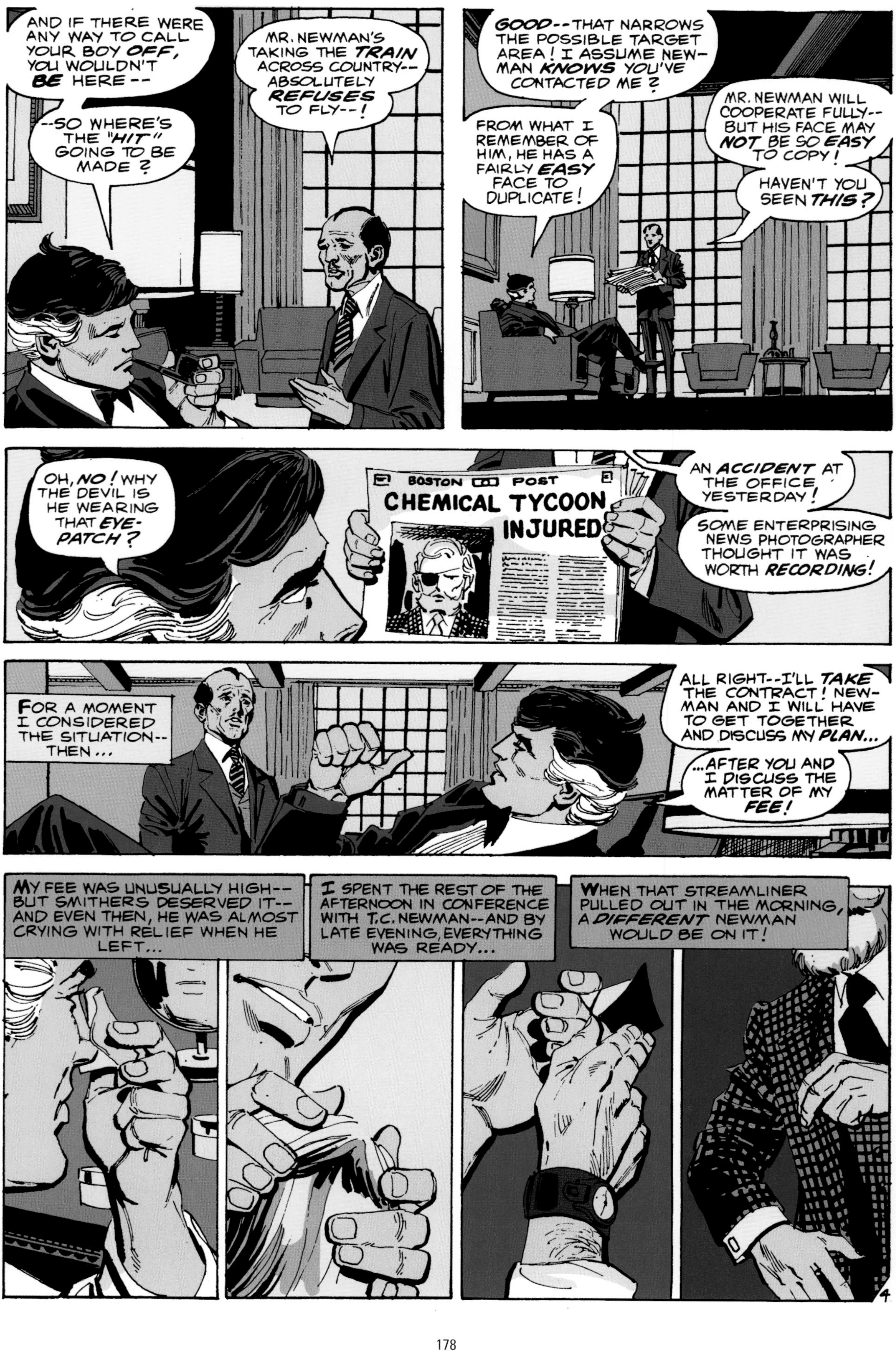
AND IF THERE WERE ANY WAY TO CALL YOUR BOY OFF, YOU WOULDN'T BE HERE--
--SO WHERE'S THE "HIT" GOING TO BE MADE?
MR. NEWMAN'S TAKING THE TRAIN ACROSS COUNTRY-- ABSOLUTELY REFUSES TO FLY--!
GOOD--THAT NARROWS THE POSSIBLE TARGET AREA! I ASSUME NEW-MAN KNOWS YOU'VE CONTACTED ME?
FROM WHAT I REMEMBER OF HIM, HE HAS A FAIRLY EASY FACE TO DUPLICATE!
MR. NEWMAN WILL COOPERATE FULLY-- BUT HIS FACE MAY NOT BE SO EASY TO COPY!
HAVEN'T YOU SEEN THIS?
OH, NO! WHY THE DEVIL IS HE WEARING THAT EYE-PATCH?
BOSTON POST
CHEMICAL TYCOON INJURED
AN ACCIDENT AT THE OFFICE YESTERDAY!
SOME ENTERPRISING NEWS PHOTOGRAPHER THOUGHT IT WAS WORTH RECORDING!
FOR A MOMENT I CONSIDERED THE SITUATION-- THEN...
ALL RIGHT--I'LL TAKE THE CONTRACT! NEW-MAN AND I WILL HAVE TO GET TOGETHER AND DISCUSS MY PLAN...
...AFTER YOU AND I DISCUSS THE MATTER OF MY FEE!
MY FEE WAS UNUSUALLY HIGH-- BUT SMITHERS DESERVED IT-- AND EVEN THEN, HE WAS ALMOST CRYING WITH RELIEF WHEN HE LEFT...
I SPENT THE REST OF THE AFTERNOON IN CONFERENCE WITH T.C. NEWMAN--AND BY LATE EVENING, EVERYTHING WAS READY...
WHEN THAT STREAMLINER PULLED OUT IN THE MORNING, A DIFFERENT NEWMAN WOULD BE ON IT!
4

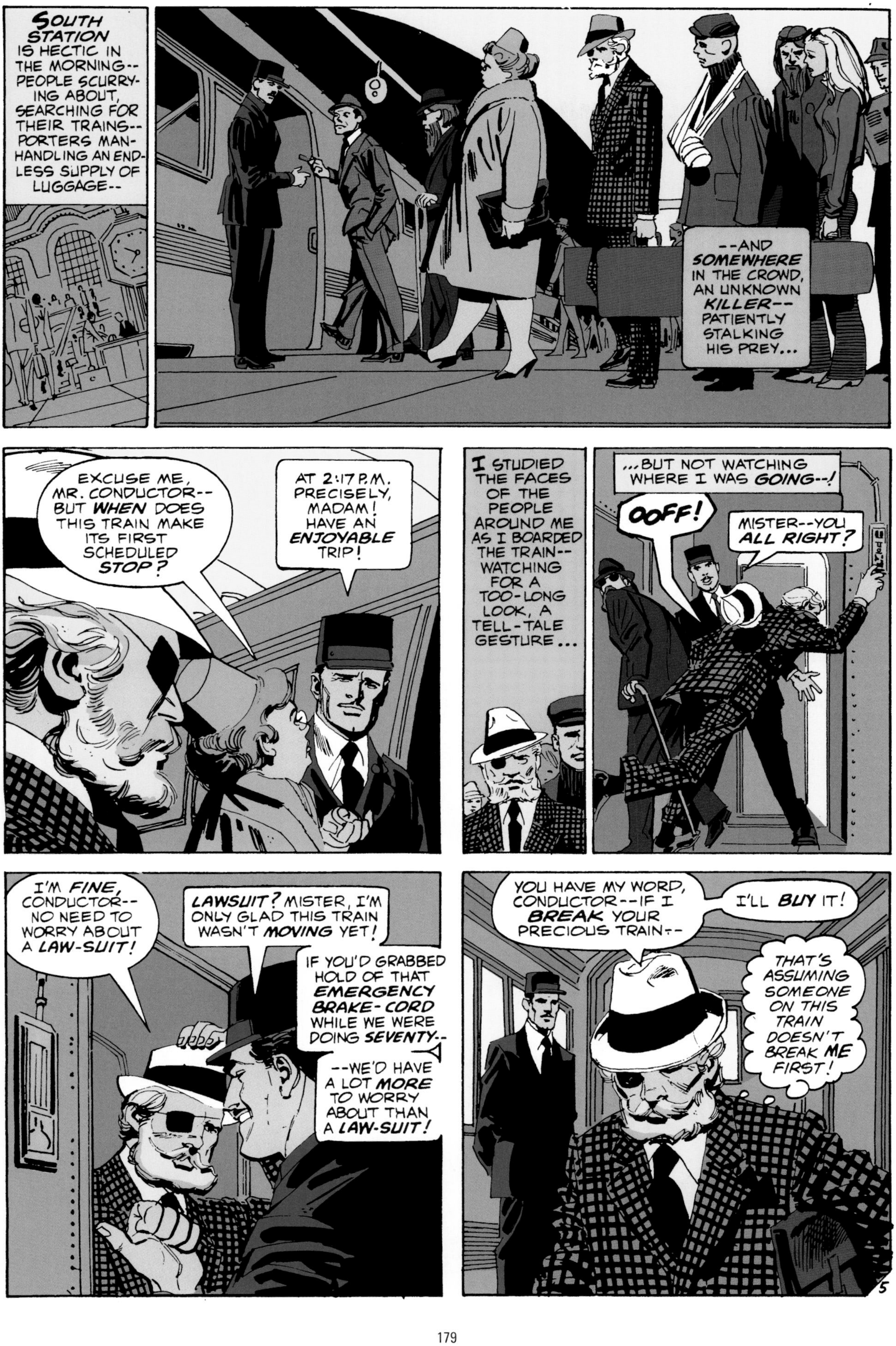
SOUTH STATION IS HECTIC IN THE MORNING-- PEOPLE SCURRYING ABOUT, SEARCHING FOR THEIR TRAINS-- PORTERS MANHANDLING AN ENDLESS SUPPLY OF LUGGAGE--
--AND SOMEWHERE IN THE CROWD, AN UNKNOWN KILLER-- PATIENTLY STALKING HIS PREY...
EXCUSE ME, MR. CONDUCTOR-- BUT WHEN DOES THIS TRAIN MAKE ITS FIRST SCHEDULED STOP?
AT 2:17 P.M. PRECISELY, MADAM! HAVE AN ENJOYABLE TRIP!
I STUDIED THE FACES OF THE PEOPLE AROUND ME AS I BOARDED THE TRAIN-- WATCHING FOR A TOO-LONG LOOK, A TELL-TALE GESTURE...
...BUT NOT WATCHING WHERE I WAS GOING--!
OOFF!
MISTER--YOU ALL RIGHT?
I'M FINE, CONDUCTOR-- NO NEED TO WORRY ABOUT A LAW-SUIT!
LAWSUIT? MISTER, I'M ONLY GLAD THIS TRAIN WASN'T MOVING YET!
IF YOU'D GRABBED HOLD OF THAT EMERGENCY BRAKE-CORD WHILE WE WERE DOING SEVENTY--
--WE'D HAVE A LOT MORE TO WORRY ABOUT THAN A LAW-SUIT!
YOU HAVE MY WORD, CONDUCTOR--IF I BREAK YOUR PRECIOUS TRAIN--
I'LL BUY IT!
THAT'S ASSUMING SOMEONE ON THIS TRAIN DOESN'T BREAK ME FIRST!
5

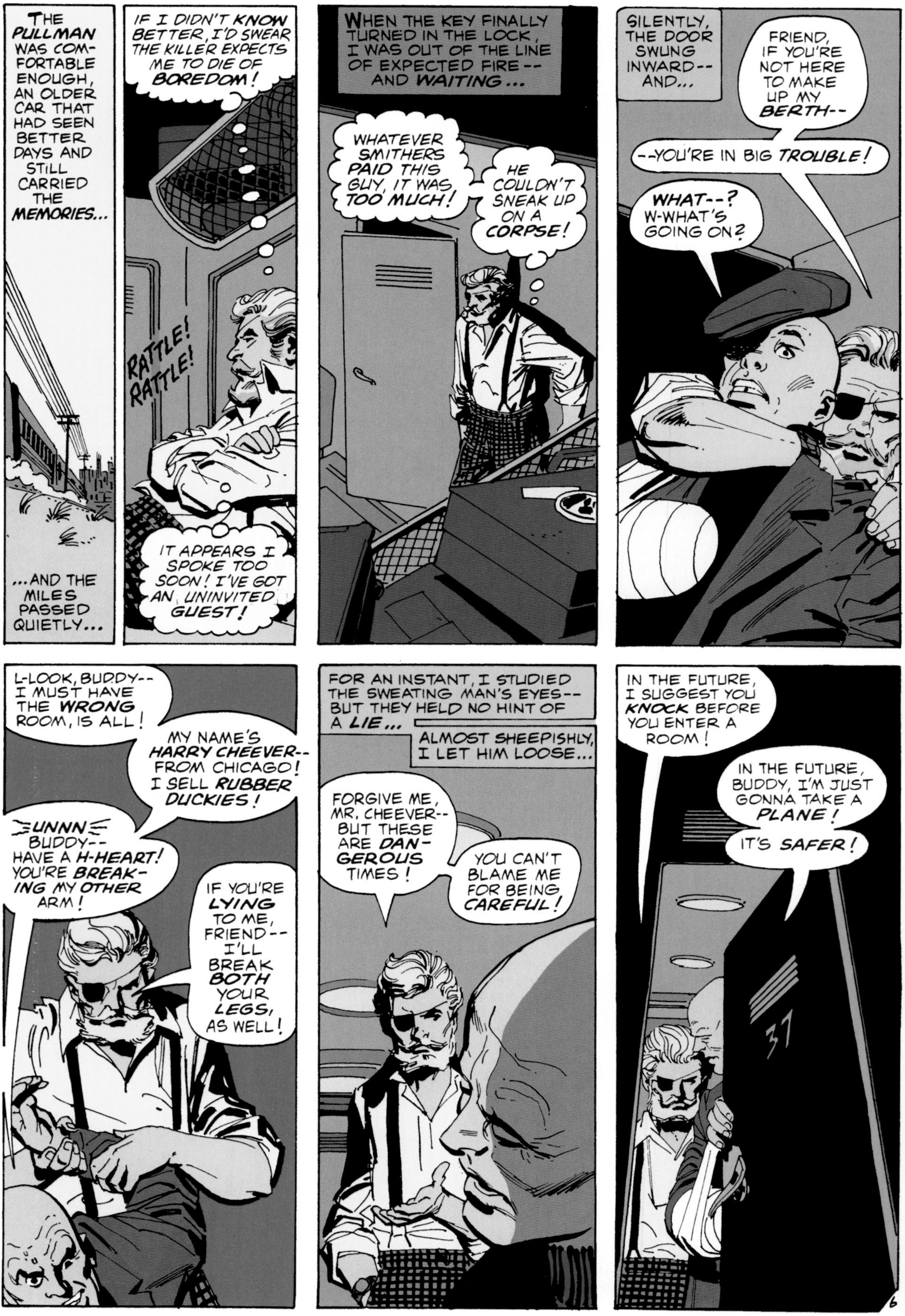

THE PULLMAN WAS COMFORTABLE ENOUGH, AN OLDER CAR THAT HAD SEEN BETTER DAYS AND STILL CARRIED THE MEMORIES...
...AND THE MILES PASSED QUIETLY...
IF I DIDN'T KNOW BETTER, I'D SWEAR THE KILLER EXPECTS ME TO DIE OF BOREDOM!
RATTLE! RATTLE!
IT APPEARS I SPOKE TOO SOON! I'VE GOT AN UNINVITED GUEST!
WHEN THE KEY FINALLY TURNED IN THE LOCK, I WAS OUT OF THE LINE OF EXPECTED FIRE -- AND WAITING...
WHATEVER SMITHERS PAID THIS GUY, IT WAS TOO MUCH!
HE COULDN'T SNEAK UP ON A CORPSE!
SILENTLY, THE DOOR SWUNG INWARD -- AND...
FRIEND, IF YOU'RE NOT HERE TO MAKE UP MY BERTH--
--YOU'RE IN BIG TROUBLE!
WHAT--? W-WHAT'S GOING ON?
L-LOOK, BUDDY-- I MUST HAVE THE WRONG ROOM, IS ALL!
MY NAME'S HARRY CHEEVER-- FROM CHICAGO! I SELL RUBBER DUCKIES!
UNNN BUDDY-- HAVE A H-HEART! YOU'RE BREAKING MY OTHER ARM!
IF YOU'RE LYING TO ME, FRIEND-- I'LL BREAK BOTH YOUR LEGS, AS WELL!
FOR AN INSTANT, I STUDIED THE SWEATING MAN'S EYES-- BUT THEY HELD NO HINT OF A LIE...
ALMOST SHEEPISHLY, I LET HIM LOOSE...
FORGIVE ME, MR. CHEEVER-- BUT THESE ARE DANGEROUS TIMES!
YOU CAN'T BLAME ME FOR BEING CAREFUL!
IN THE FUTURE, I SUGGEST YOU KNOCK BEFORE YOU ENTER A ROOM!
IN THE FUTURE, BUDDY, I'M JUST GONNA TAKE A PLANE!
IT'S SAFER!
37
6

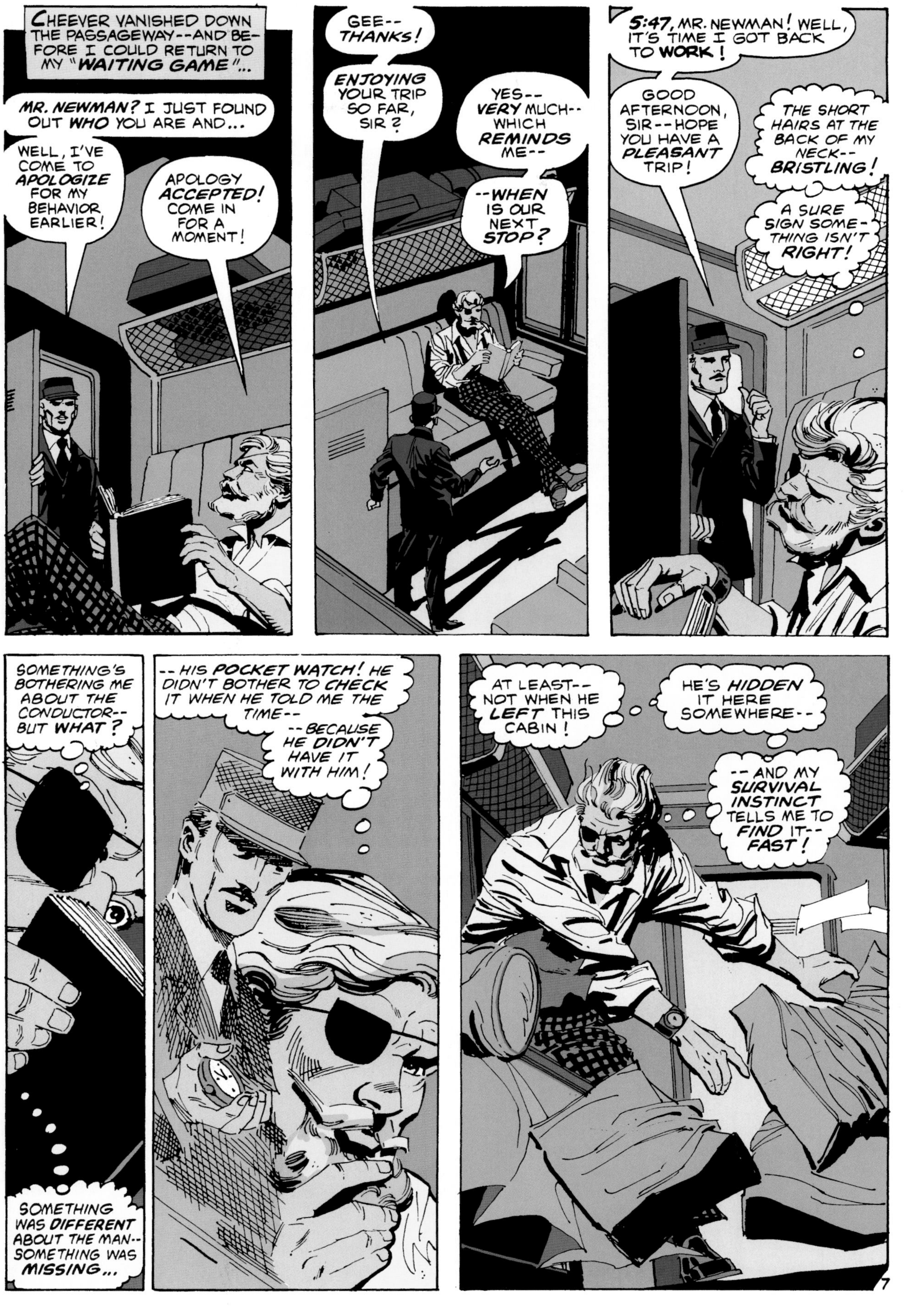

CHEEVER VANISHED DOWN THE PASSAGEWAY--AND BEFORE I COULD RETURN TO MY "WAITING GAME"...
MR. NEWMAN? I JUST FOUND OUT WHO YOU ARE AND...
WELL, I'VE COME TO APOLOGIZE FOR MY BEHAVIOR EARLIER!
APOLOGY ACCEPTED! COME IN FOR A MOMENT!
GEE--THANKS!
ENJOYING YOUR TRIP SO FAR, SIR?
YES--VERY MUCH--WHICH REMINDS ME--
--WHEN IS OUR NEXT STOP?
5:47, MR. NEWMAN! WELL, IT'S TIME I GOT BACK TO WORK!
GOOD AFTERNOON, SIR--HOPE YOU HAVE A PLEASANT TRIP!
THE SHORT HAIRS AT THE BACK OF MY NECK--BRISTLING!
A SURE SIGN SOMETHING ISN'T RIGHT!
SOMETHING'S BOTHERING ME ABOUT THE CONDUCTOR--BUT WHAT?
SOMETHING WAS DIFFERENT ABOUT THE MAN--SOMETHING WAS MISSING...
--HIS POCKET WATCH! HE DIDN'T BOTHER TO CHECK IT WHEN HE TOLD ME THE TIME--
--BECAUSE HE DIDN'T HAVE IT WITH HIM!
AT LEAST--NOT WHEN HE LEFT THIS CABIN!
HE'S HIDDEN IT HERE SOMEWHERE--
--AND MY SURVIVAL INSTINCT TELLS ME TO FIND IT--FAST!
7

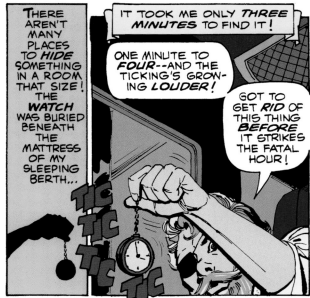

THERE AREN'T MANY PLACES TO HIDE SOMETHING IN A ROOM THAT SIZE! THE WATCH WAS BURIED BENEATH THE MATTRESS OF MY SLEEPING BERTH...

IT TOOK ME ONLY THREE MINUTES TO FIND IT!

ONE MINUTE TO FOUR--AND THE TICKING'S GROWING LOUDER!

GOT TO GET RID OF THIS THING BEFORE IT STRIKES THE FATAL HOUR!

TIC TIC TIC TIC

NO TIME FOR ANYTHING BUT THE WINDOW-- AND THAT WAS STUCK TIGHT WITH AGE...

SO I OPENED IT-- THE HARD WAY!...

ONLY SECONDS TO GO!

CRASH!

GOT TO TRACK DOWN THAT CONDUCTOR-- BEFORE HE CAN GET ANOTHER CRACK AT ME!

BLAM!

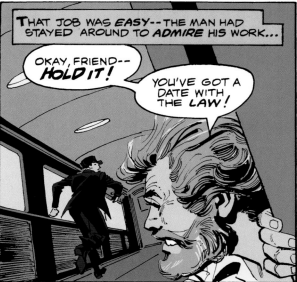

THAT JOB WAS EASY--THE MAN HAD STAYED AROUND TO ADMIRE HIS WORK...

OKAY, FRIEND-- HOLD IT!

YOU'VE GOT A DATE WITH THE LAW!

MISTER, YOU'VE GOT TO BE KIDDING!

MAGNESIUM FLARE! HE'S BLINDED ME--!

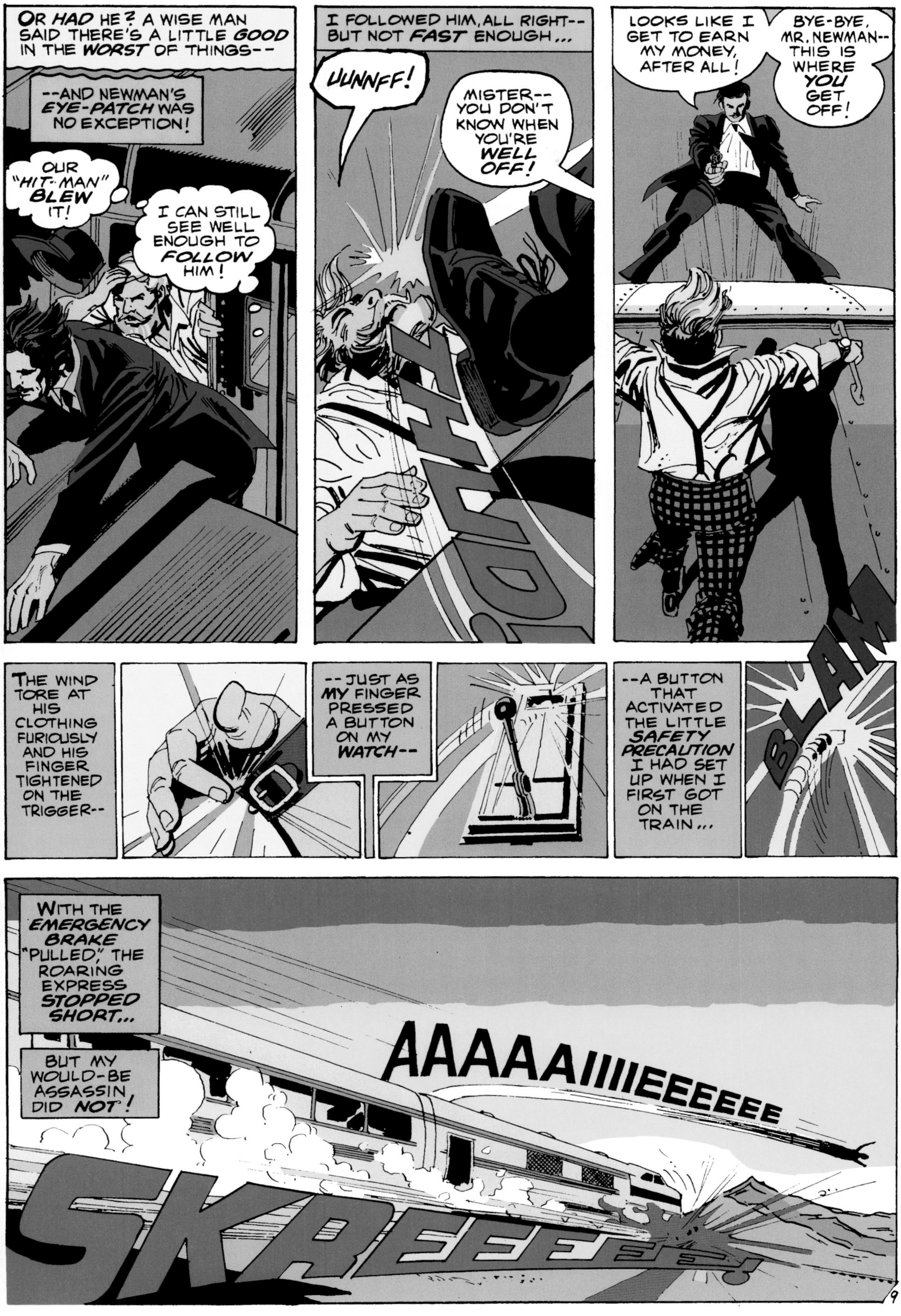
OR HAD HE? A WISE MAN SAID THERE'S A LITTLE GOOD IN THE WORST OF THINGS--
--AND NEWMAN'S EYE-PATCH WAS NO EXCEPTION!
OUR "HIT-MAN" BLEW IT!
I CAN STILL SEE WELL ENOUGH TO FOLLOW HIM!
I FOLLOWED HIM, ALL RIGHT-- BUT NOT FAST ENOUGH...
UUNNFF!
MISTER-- YOU DON'T KNOW WHEN YOU'RE WELL OFF!
THUD!
LOOKS LIKE I GET TO EARN MY MONEY, AFTER ALL!
BYE-BYE, MR. NEWMAN-- THIS IS WHERE YOU GET OFF!
THE WIND TORE AT HIS CLOTHING FURIOUSLY AND HIS FINGER TIGHTENED ON THE TRIGGER--
--JUST AS MY FINGER PRESSED A BUTTON ON MY WATCH--
--A BUTTON THAT ACTIVATED THE LITTLE SAFETY PRECAUTION I HAD SET UP WHEN I FIRST GOT ON THE TRAIN...
BLAM
WITH THE EMERGENCY BRAKE "PULLED," THE ROARING EXPRESS STOPPED SHORT...
BUT MY WOULD-BE ASSASSIN DID NOT!
AAAAAIIIIIEEEEEE
SKREEEEE!
9

10
THEY SCRAPED UP WHAT WAS LEFT OF THE "CON-DUCTOR"-- AND THE REST OF THE TRIP PASSED QUIETLY...
SO, SEVERAL DAYS LATER, IN SAN FRANCISCO...
MR. CHANCE-- YOU MADE IT! THANK HEAVENS!
THAT'S WHAT YOU HIRED ME FOR, ISN'T IT?
BUT MR. NEWMAN--? WHERE IS HE?
YOU SAID HE WAS COMING WITH YOU!
AND HE DID, SMITHERS!
CAN'T YOU EVEN RECOGNIZE YOUR OWN BOSS?
YOU MEAN HIS EX-BOSS, DON'T YOU, MR. CHANCE?
REALLY? WELL-- CONGRATULATIONS, SMITHERS--
--IT COULDN'T HAVE HAPPENED TO A MORE DESERVING FELLOW!
THE END

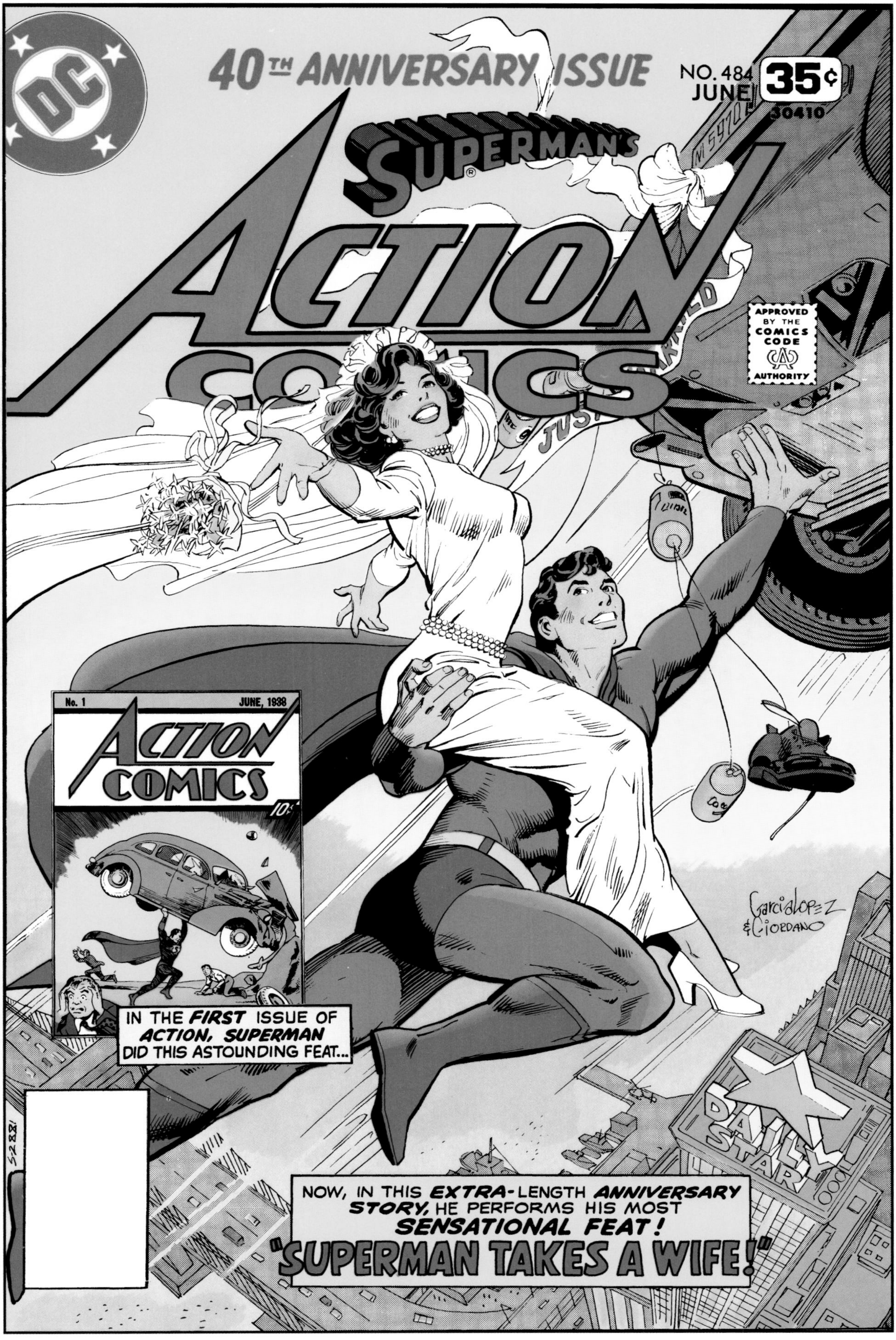
40TH ANNIVERSARY ISSUE
NO. 484
JUNE
35¢
30410
SUPERMAN'S
ACTION COMICS
APPROVED BY THE COMICS CODE AUTHORITY
No. 1
JUNE, 1938
ACTION COMICS
10¢
IN THE FIRST ISSUE OF ACTION, SUPERMAN DID THIS ASTOUNDING FEAT...
GarciaLopez & Giordano
DAILY STAR
NOW, IN THIS EXTRA-LENGTH ANNIVERSARY STORY, HE PERFORMS HIS MOST SENSATIONAL FEAT!
"SUPERMAN TAKES A WIFE!"

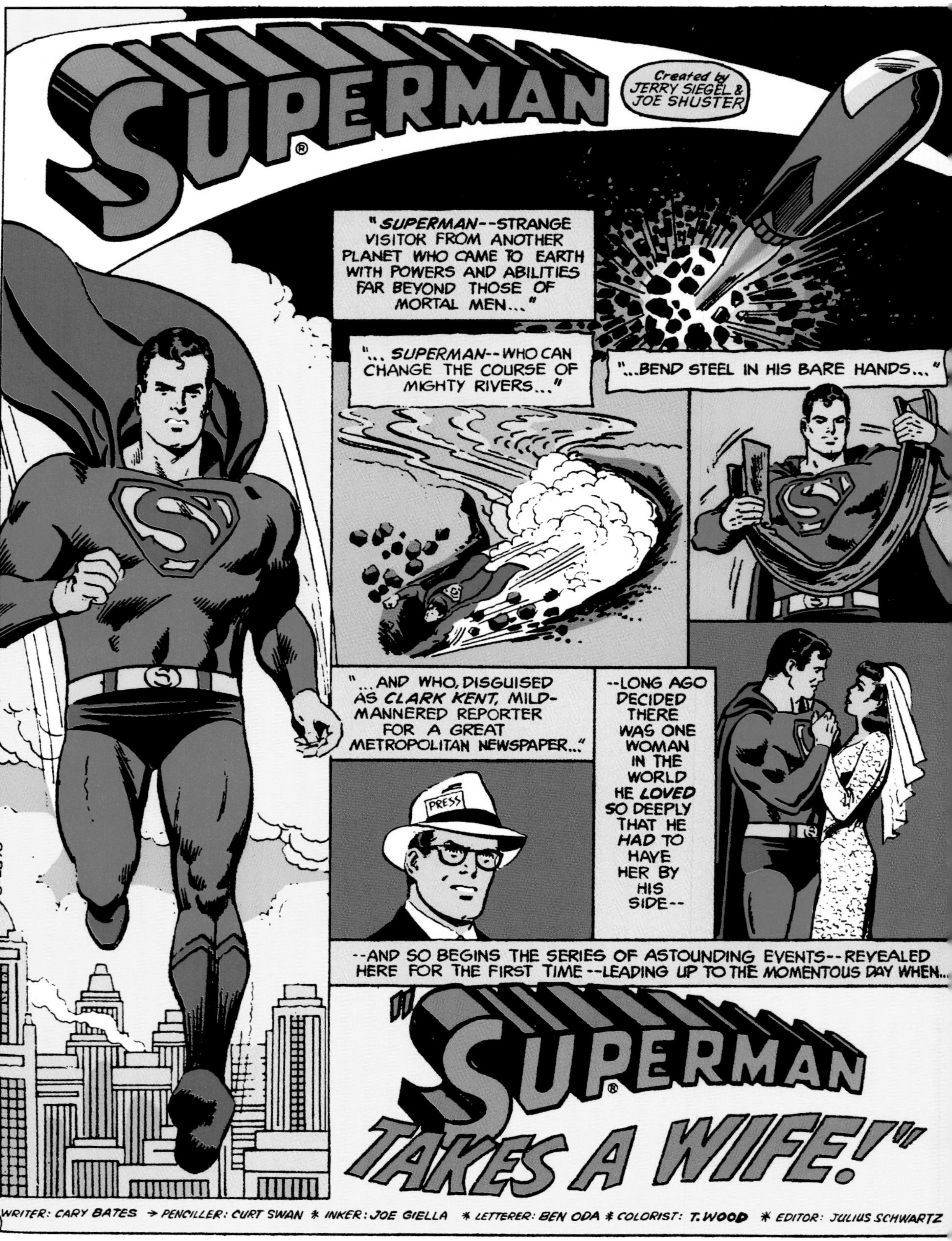
SUPERMAN
Created by JERRY SIEGEL & JOE SHUSTER
"SUPERMAN--STRANGE VISITOR FROM ANOTHER PLANET WHO CAME TO EARTH WITH POWERS AND ABILITIES FAR BEYOND THOSE OF MORTAL MEN..."
"...SUPERMAN--WHO CAN CHANGE THE COURSE OF MIGHTY RIVERS..."
"...BEND STEEL IN HIS BARE HANDS..."
"...AND WHO, DISGUISED AS CLARK KENT, MILD-MANNERED REPORTER FOR A GREAT METROPOLITAN NEWSPAPER..."
PRESS
--LONG AGO DECIDED THERE WAS ONE WOMAN IN THE WORLD HE LOVED SO DEEPLY THAT HE HAD TO HAVE HER BY HIS SIDE--
--AND SO BEGINS THE SERIES OF ASTOUNDING EVENTS--REVEALED HERE FOR THE FIRST TIME--LEADING UP TO THE MOMENTOUS DAY WHEN...
"SUPERMAN TAKES A WIFE!"
WRITER: CARY BATES → PENCILLER: CURT SWAN ✱ INKER: JOE GIELLA ✱ LETTERER: BEN ODA ✱ COLORIST: T. WOOD ✱ EDITOR: JULIUS SCHWARTZ

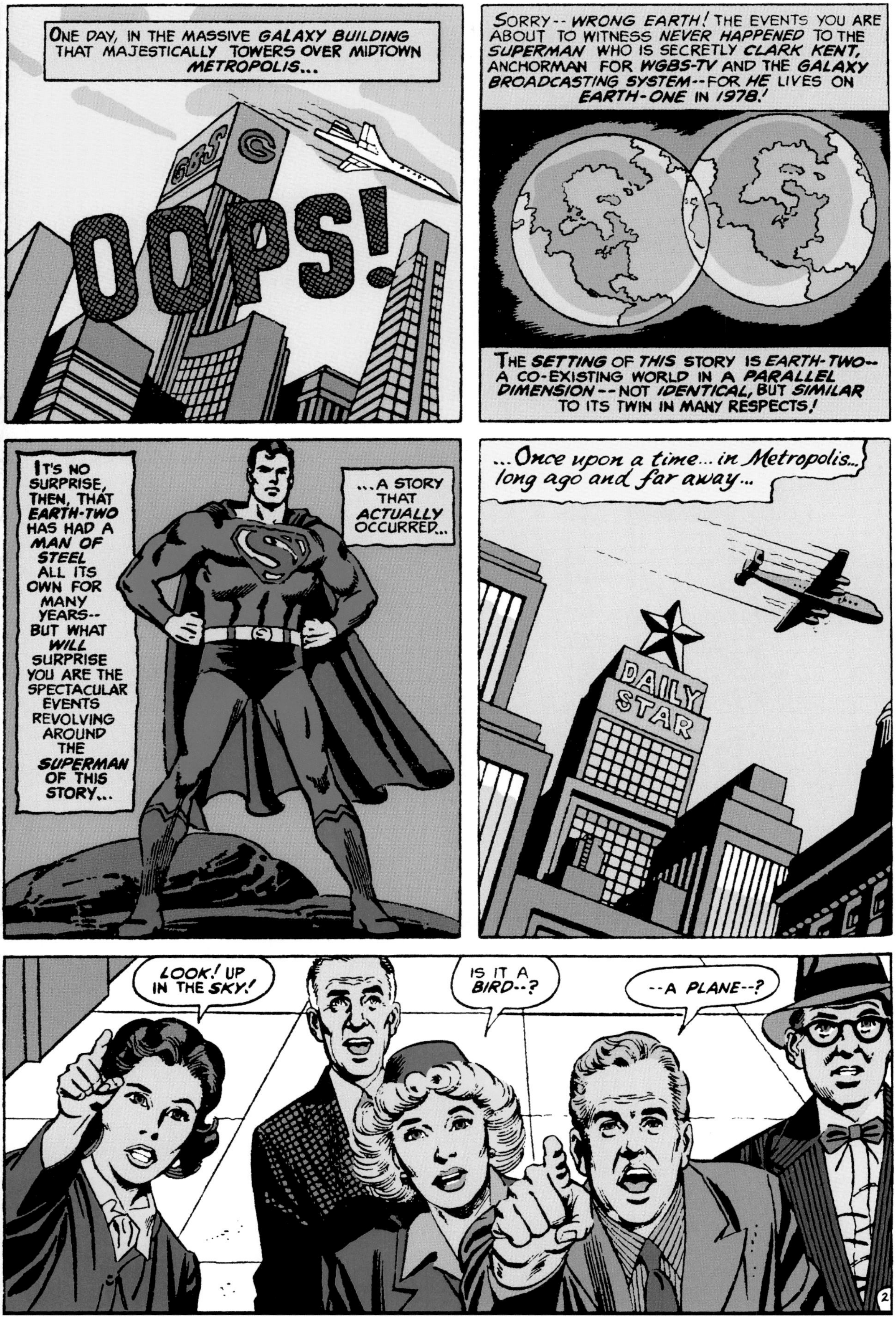
ONE DAY, IN THE MASSIVE GALAXY BUILDING THAT MAJESTICALLY TOWERS OVER MIDTOWN METROPOLIS...
GBS
OOPS!
SORRY--WRONG EARTH! THE EVENTS YOU ARE ABOUT TO WITNESS NEVER HAPPENED TO THE SUPERMAN WHO IS SECRETLY CLARK KENT, ANCHORMAN FOR WGBS-TV AND THE GALAXY BROADCASTING SYSTEM--FOR HE LIVES ON EARTH-ONE IN 1978!
THE SETTING OF THIS STORY IS EARTH-TWO--A CO-EXISTING WORLD IN A PARALLEL DIMENSION--NOT IDENTICAL, BUT SIMILAR TO ITS TWIN IN MANY RESPECTS!
IT'S NO SURPRISE, THEN, THAT EARTH-TWO HAS HAD A MAN OF STEEL ALL ITS OWN FOR MANY YEARS--BUT WHAT WILL SURPRISE YOU ARE THE SPECTACULAR EVENTS REVOLVING AROUND THE SUPERMAN OF THIS STORY...
...A STORY THAT ACTUALLY OCCURRED...
...Once upon a time... in Metropolis... long ago and far away...
DAILY STAR
LOOK! UP IN THE SKY!
IS IT A BIRD--?
--A PLANE--?
2

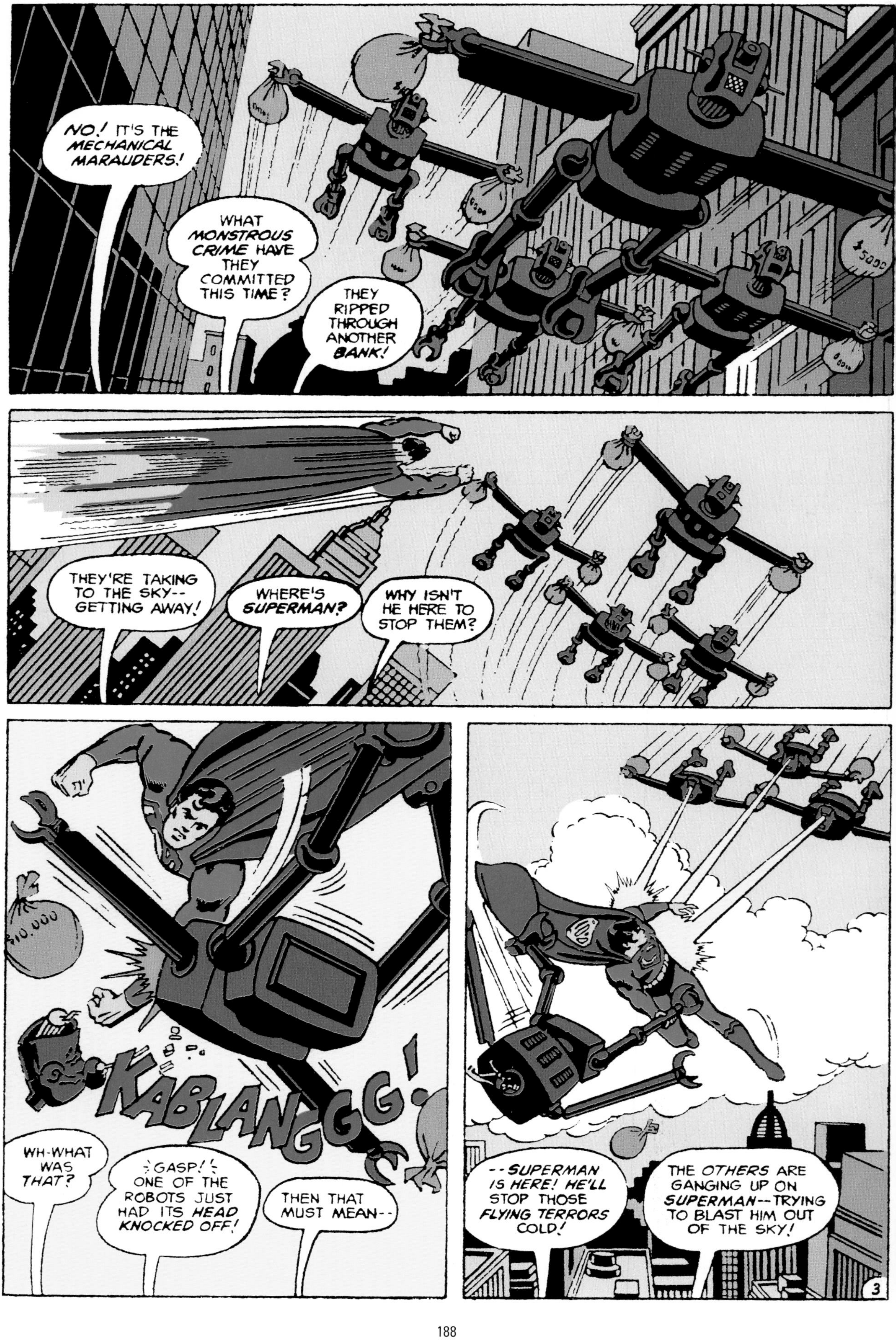
NO! IT'S THE MECHANICAL MARAUDERS!
WHAT MONSTROUS CRIME HAVE THEY COMMITTED THIS TIME?
THEY RIPPED THROUGH ANOTHER BANK!
THEY'RE TAKING TO THE SKY-- GETTING AWAY!
WHERE'S SUPERMAN?
WHY ISN'T HE HERE TO STOP THEM?
KABLANGGG!
WH-WHAT WAS THAT?
GASP! ONE OF THE ROBOTS JUST HAD ITS HEAD KNOCKED OFF!
THEN THAT MUST MEAN--
--SUPERMAN IS HERE! HE'LL STOP THOSE FLYING TERRORS COLD!
THE OTHERS ARE GANGING UP ON SUPERMAN--TRYING TO BLAST HIM OUT OF THE SKY!
3

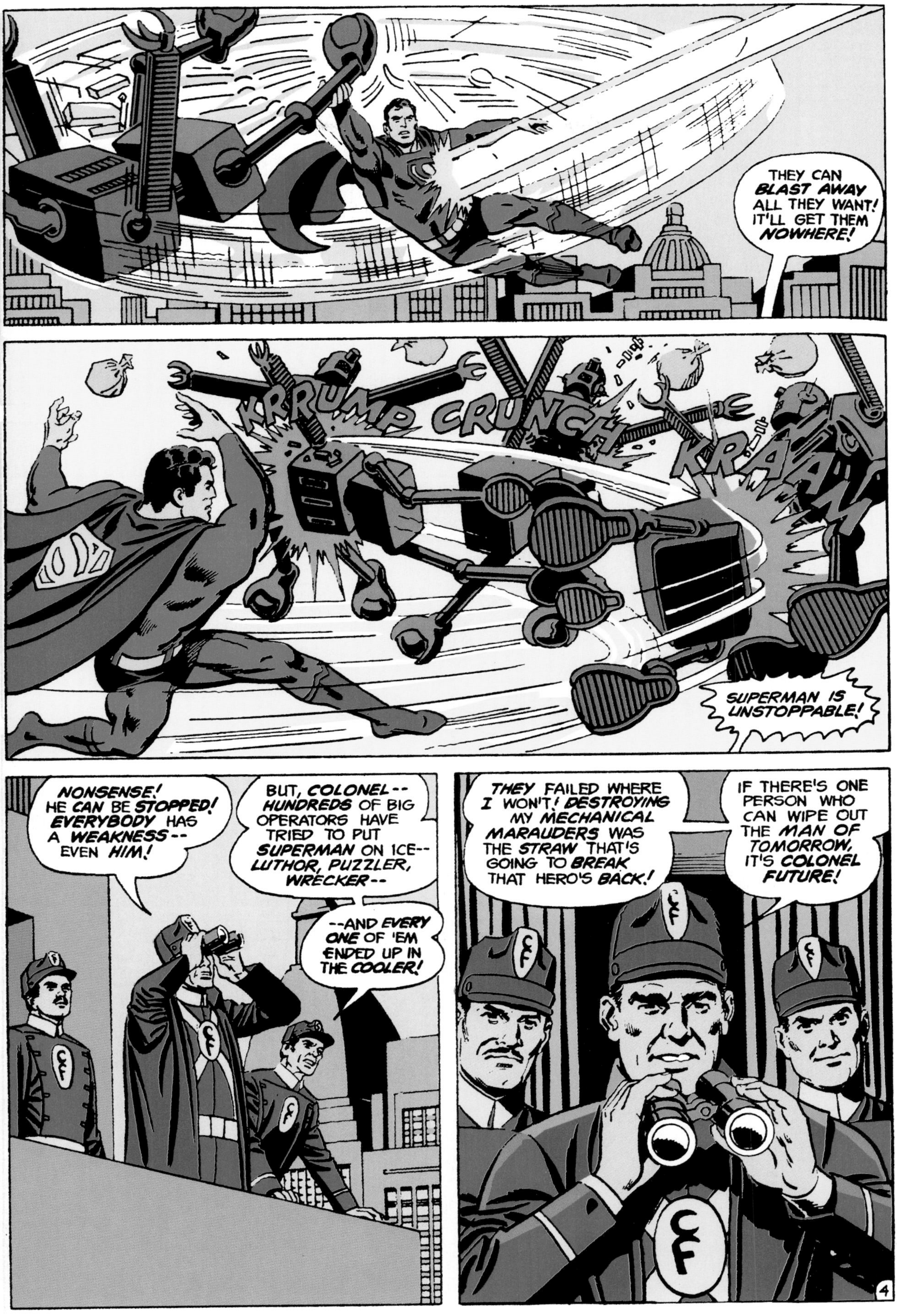
THEY CAN BLAST AWAY ALL THEY WANT! IT'LL GET THEM NOWHERE!
KRRUMP CRUNCH KRAAM
SUPERMAN IS UNSTOPPABLE!
NONSENSE! HE CAN BE STOPPED! EVERYBODY HAS A WEAKNESS -- EVEN HIM!
BUT, COLONEL -- HUNDREDS OF BIG OPERATORS HAVE TRIED TO PUT SUPERMAN ON ICE -- LUTHOR, PUZZLER, WRECKER --
--AND EVERY ONE OF 'EM ENDED UP IN THE COOLER!
THEY FAILED WHERE I WON'T! DESTROYING MY MECHANICAL MARAUDERS WAS THE STRAW THAT'S GOING TO BREAK THAT HERO'S BACK!
IF THERE'S ONE PERSON WHO CAN WIPE OUT THE MAN OF TOMORROW, IT'S COLONEL FUTURE!
4

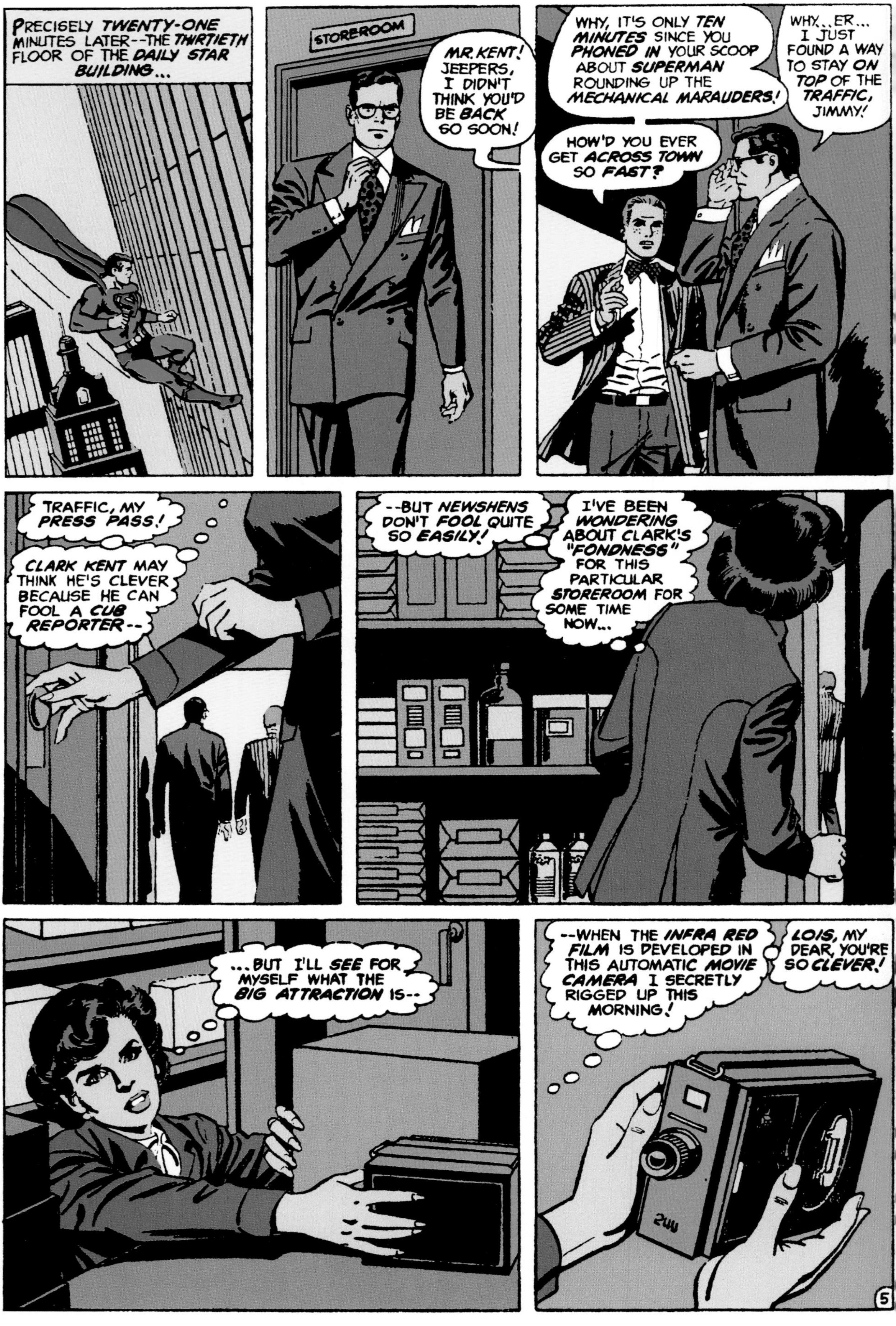

PRECISELY TWENTY-ONE MINUTES LATER--THE THIRTIETH FLOOR OF THE DAILY STAR BUILDING...
STOREROOM
MR. KENT! JEEPERS, I DIDN'T THINK YOU'D BE BACK SO SOON!
WHY, IT'S ONLY TEN MINUTES SINCE YOU PHONED IN YOUR SCOOP ABOUT SUPERMAN ROUNDING UP THE MECHANICAL MARAUDERS!
HOW'D YOU EVER GET ACROSS TOWN SO FAST?
WHY...ER... I JUST FOUND A WAY TO STAY ON TOP OF THE TRAFFIC, JIMMY!
TRAFFIC, MY PRESS PASS!
CLARK KENT MAY THINK HE'S CLEVER BECAUSE HE CAN FOOL A CUB REPORTER--
--BUT NEWSHENS DON'T FOOL QUITE SO EASILY!
I'VE BEEN WONDERING ABOUT CLARK'S "FONDNESS" FOR THIS PARTICULAR STOREROOM FOR SOME TIME NOW...
...BUT I'LL SEE FOR MYSELF WHAT THE BIG ATTRACTION IS--
--WHEN THE INFRA RED FILM IS DEVELOPED IN THIS AUTOMATIC MOVIE CAMERA I SECRETLY RIGGED UP THIS MORNING!
LOIS, MY DEAR, YOU'RE SO CLEVER!
5

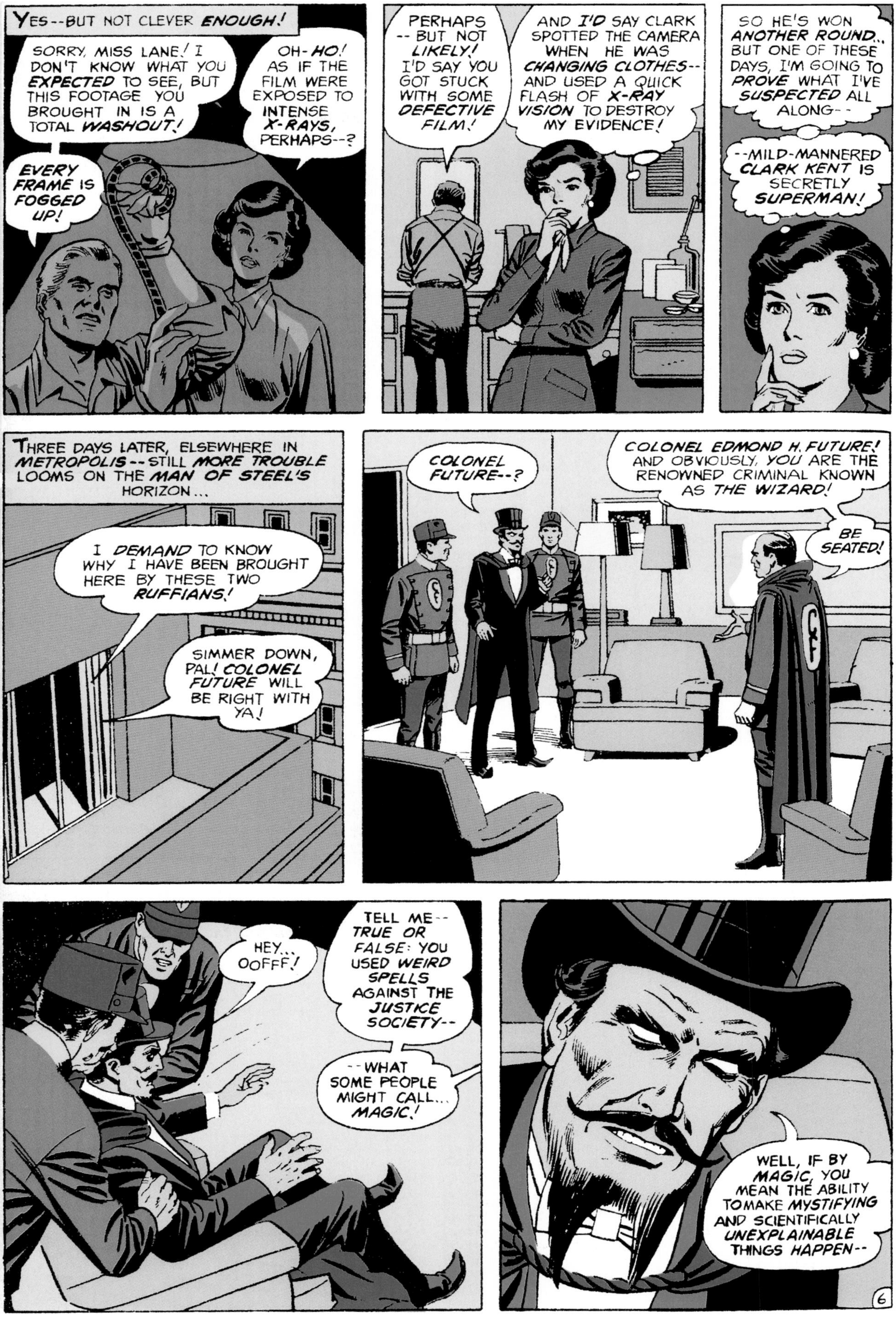
YES--BUT NOT CLEVER ENOUGH!
SORRY, MISS LANE! I DON'T KNOW WHAT YOU EXPECTED TO SEE, BUT THIS FOOTAGE YOU BROUGHT IN IS A TOTAL WASHOUT!
OH-HO! AS IF THE FILM WERE EXPOSED TO INTENSE X-RAYS, PERHAPS--?
EVERY FRAME IS FOGGED UP!
PERHAPS -- BUT NOT LIKELY! I'D SAY YOU GOT STUCK WITH SOME DEFECTIVE FILM!
AND I'D SAY CLARK SPOTTED THE CAMERA WHEN HE WAS CHANGING CLOTHES--AND USED A QUICK FLASH OF X-RAY VISION TO DESTROY MY EVIDENCE!
SO HE'S WON ANOTHER ROUND... BUT ONE OF THESE DAYS, I'M GOING TO PROVE WHAT I'VE SUSPECTED ALL ALONG--
--MILD-MANNERED CLARK KENT IS SECRETLY SUPERMAN!
THREE DAYS LATER, ELSEWHERE IN METROPOLIS--STILL MORE TROUBLE LOOMS ON THE MAN OF STEEL'S HORIZON...
I DEMAND TO KNOW WHY I HAVE BEEN BROUGHT HERE BY THESE TWO RUFFIANS!
SIMMER DOWN, PAL! COLONEL FUTURE WILL BE RIGHT WITH YA!
COLONEL FUTURE--?
COLONEL EDMOND H. FUTURE! AND OBVIOUSLY, YOU ARE THE RENOWNED CRIMINAL KNOWN AS THE WIZARD!
BE SEATED!
HEY... OOFFF!
TELL ME--TRUE OR FALSE: YOU USED WEIRD SPELLS AGAINST THE JUSTICE SOCIETY--
--WHAT SOME PEOPLE MIGHT CALL... MAGIC!
WELL, IF BY MAGIC, YOU MEAN THE ABILITY TO MAKE MYSTIFYING AND SCIENTIFICALLY UNEXPLAINABLE THINGS HAPPEN--
6

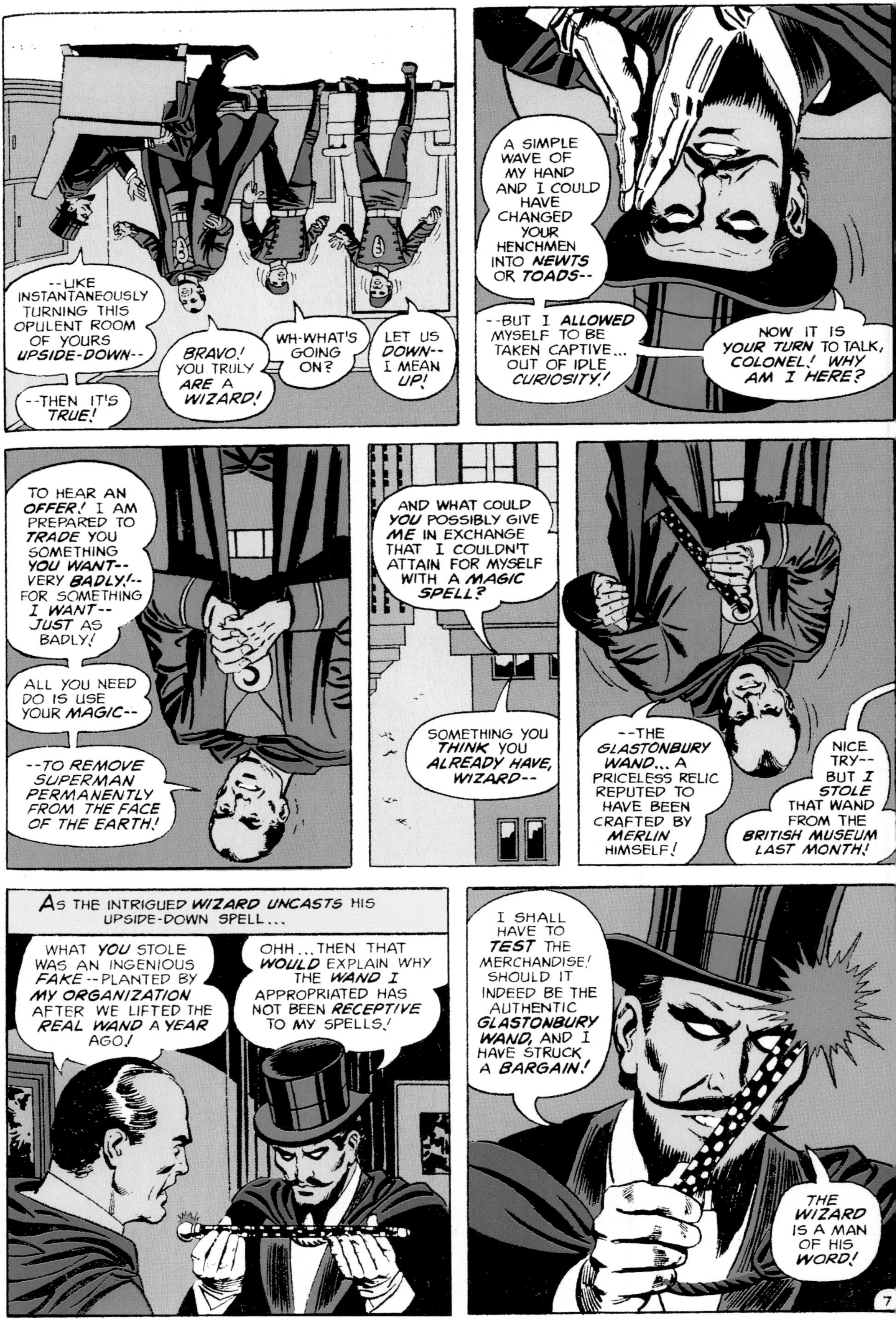
--LIKE INSTANTANEOUSLY TURNING THIS OPULENT ROOM OF YOURS UPSIDE-DOWN--
--THEN IT'S TRUE!
BRAVO! YOU TRULY ARE A WIZARD!
WH-WHAT'S GOING ON?
LET US DOWN-- I MEAN UP!
A SIMPLE WAVE OF MY HAND AND I COULD HAVE CHANGED YOUR HENCHMEN INTO NEWTS OR TOADS--
--BUT I ALLOWED MYSELF TO BE TAKEN CAPTIVE... OUT OF IDLE CURIOSITY!
NOW IT IS YOUR TURN TO TALK, COLONEL! WHY AM I HERE?
TO HEAR AN OFFER! I AM PREPARED TO TRADE YOU SOMETHING YOU WANT-- VERY BADLY!-- FOR SOMETHING I WANT-- JUST AS BADLY!
ALL YOU NEED DO IS USE YOUR MAGIC--
--TO REMOVE SUPERMAN PERMANENTLY FROM THE FACE OF THE EARTH!
AND WHAT COULD YOU POSSIBLY GIVE ME IN EXCHANGE THAT I COULDN'T ATTAIN FOR MYSELF WITH A MAGIC SPELL?
SOMETHING YOU THINK YOU ALREADY HAVE, WIZARD--
--THE GLASTONBURY WAND... A PRICELESS RELIC REPUTED TO HAVE BEEN CRAFTED BY MERLIN HIMSELF!
NICE TRY-- BUT I STOLE THAT WAND FROM THE BRITISH MUSEUM LAST MONTH!
AS THE INTRIGUED WIZARD UNCASTS HIS UPSIDE-DOWN SPELL...
WHAT YOU STOLE WAS AN INGENIOUS FAKE--PLANTED BY MY ORGANIZATION AFTER WE LIFTED THE REAL WAND A YEAR AGO!
OHH... THEN THAT WOULD EXPLAIN WHY THE WAND I APPROPRIATED HAS NOT BEEN RECEPTIVE TO MY SPELLS!
I SHALL HAVE TO TEST THE MERCHANDISE! SHOULD IT INDEED BE THE AUTHENTIC GLASTONBURY WAND, AND I HAVE STRUCK A BARGAIN!
THE WIZARD IS A MAN OF HIS WORD!
7

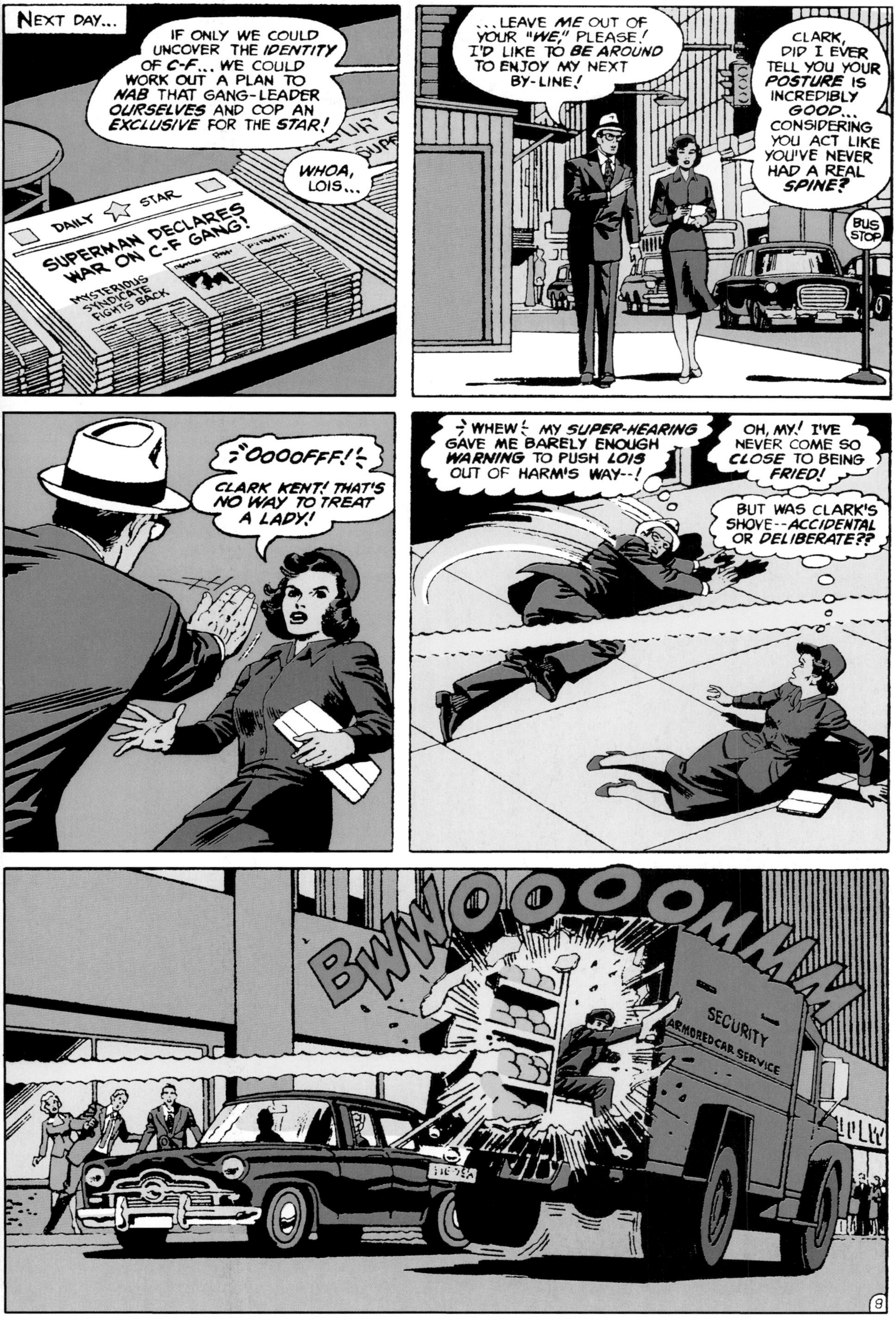
NEXT DAY...
IF ONLY WE COULD UNCOVER THE IDENTITY OF C-F... WE COULD WORK OUT A PLAN TO NAB THAT GANG-LEADER OURSELVES AND COP AN EXCLUSIVE FOR THE STAR!
WHOA, LOIS...
DAILY STAR
SUPERMAN DECLARES WAR ON C-F GANG!
MYSTERIOUS SYNDICATE FIGHTS BACK
...LEAVE ME OUT OF YOUR "WE," PLEASE! I'D LIKE TO BE AROUND TO ENJOY MY NEXT BY-LINE!
CLARK, DID I EVER TELL YOU YOUR POSTURE IS INCREDIBLY GOOD... CONSIDERING YOU ACT LIKE YOU'VE NEVER HAD A REAL SPINE?
BUS STOP
OOOOFFF!
CLARK KENT! THAT'S NO WAY TO TREAT A LADY!
WHEW! MY SUPER-HEARING GAVE ME BARELY ENOUGH WARNING TO PUSH LOIS OUT OF HARM'S WAY--!
OH, MY! I'VE NEVER COME SO CLOSE TO BEING FRIED!
BUT WAS CLARK'S SHOVE--ACCIDENTAL OR DELIBERATE??
BWWOOOOMMMM
SECURITY
ARMORED CAR SERVICE
9

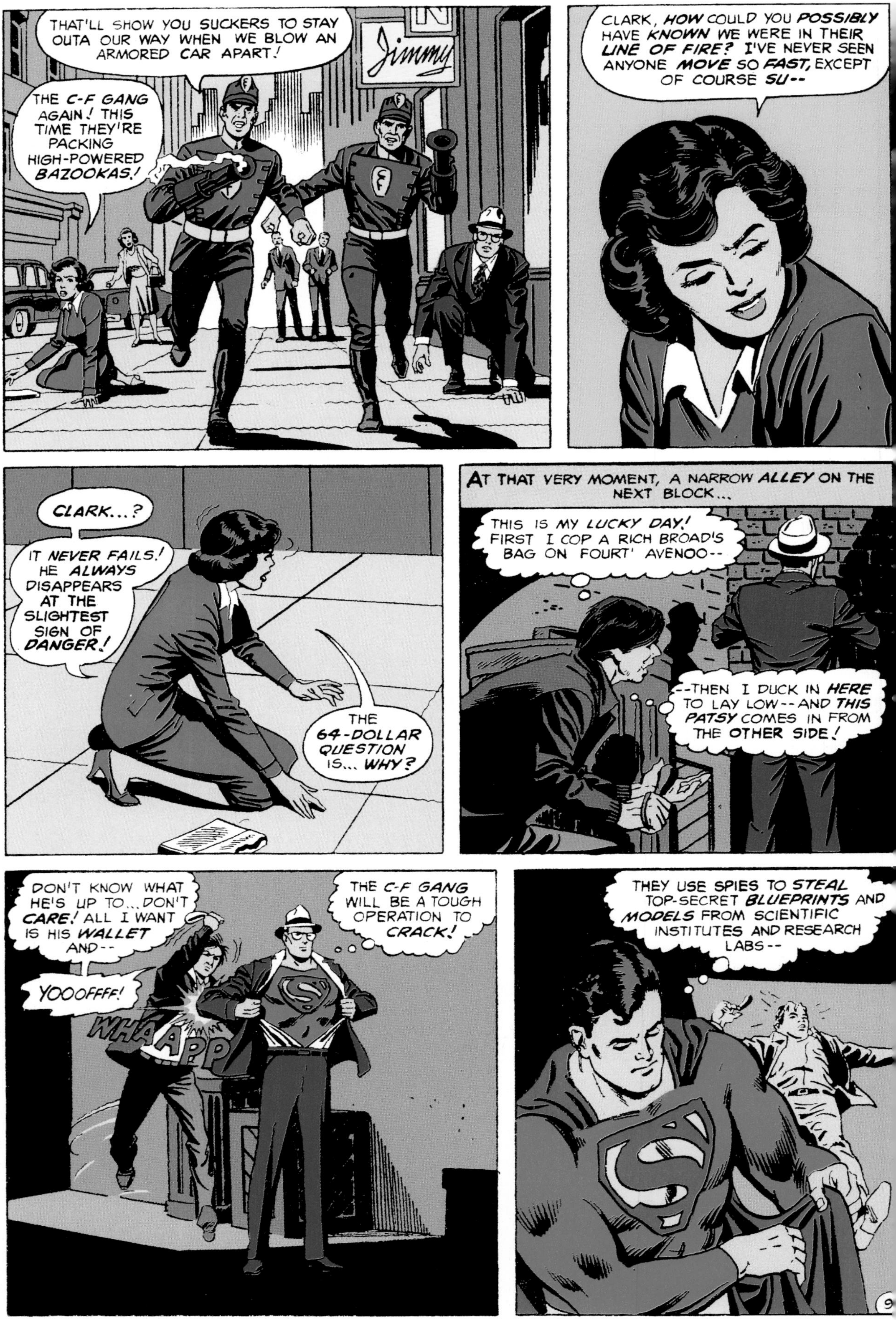
THAT'LL SHOW YOU SUCKERS TO STAY OUTA OUR WAY WHEN WE BLOW AN ARMORED CAR APART!
THE C-F GANG AGAIN! THIS TIME THEY'RE PACKING HIGH-POWERED BAZOOKAS!
Jimmy
CLARK, HOW COULD YOU POSSIBLY HAVE KNOWN WE WERE IN THEIR LINE OF FIRE? I'VE NEVER SEEN ANYONE MOVE SO FAST, EXCEPT OF COURSE SU--
CLARK...?
IT NEVER FAILS! HE ALWAYS DISAPPEARS AT THE SLIGHTEST SIGN OF DANGER!
THE 64-DOLLAR QUESTION IS... WHY?
AT THAT VERY MOMENT, A NARROW ALLEY ON THE NEXT BLOCK...
THIS IS MY LUCKY DAY! FIRST I COP A RICH BROAD'S BAG ON FOURT' AVENOO--
--THEN I DUCK IN HERE TO LAY LOW--AND THIS PATSY COMES IN FROM THE OTHER SIDE!
DON'T KNOW WHAT HE'S UP TO...DON'T CARE! ALL I WANT IS HIS WALLET AND--
THE C-F GANG WILL BE A TOUGH OPERATION TO CRACK!
YOOOFFFF!
WHAAPP
THEY USE SPIES TO STEAL TOP-SECRET BLUEPRINTS AND MODELS FROM SCIENTIFIC INSTITUTES AND RESEARCH LABS--
9

--WHICH THEIR HIGHLY SKILLED ENGINEERS TURN INTO ELABORATE DEVICES FOR COMMITTING CRIMES!

THIS HAUL WAS A *BREEZE!* NOW TO USE OUR *BAZOOKAS* TO *JET AWAY* ON OUR *GETAWAY!*

SECURITY ARMORED CAR SERVICE

TELL ME--DO YOU GUYS HAVE A *LICENSE* TO FLY?

SUPERMAN--!?

--OR A *PERMIT* TO CARRY THOSE *WEAPONS?*

;GAAA! HE'S *FUSING* THE BARRELS *TOGETHER* WITH *HEAT VISION!*

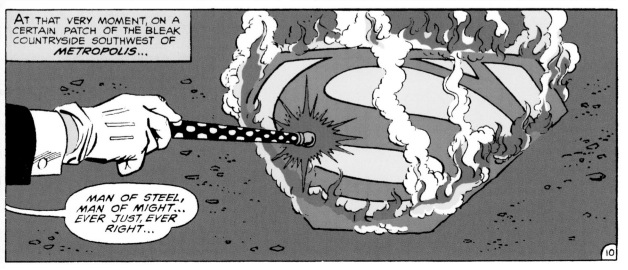

AT THAT VERY MOMENT, ON A CERTAIN PATCH OF THE BLEAK COUNTRYSIDE SOUTHWEST OF *METROPOLIS...*

MAN OF STEEL, MAN OF MIGHT... EVER JUST, EVER RIGHT...

10

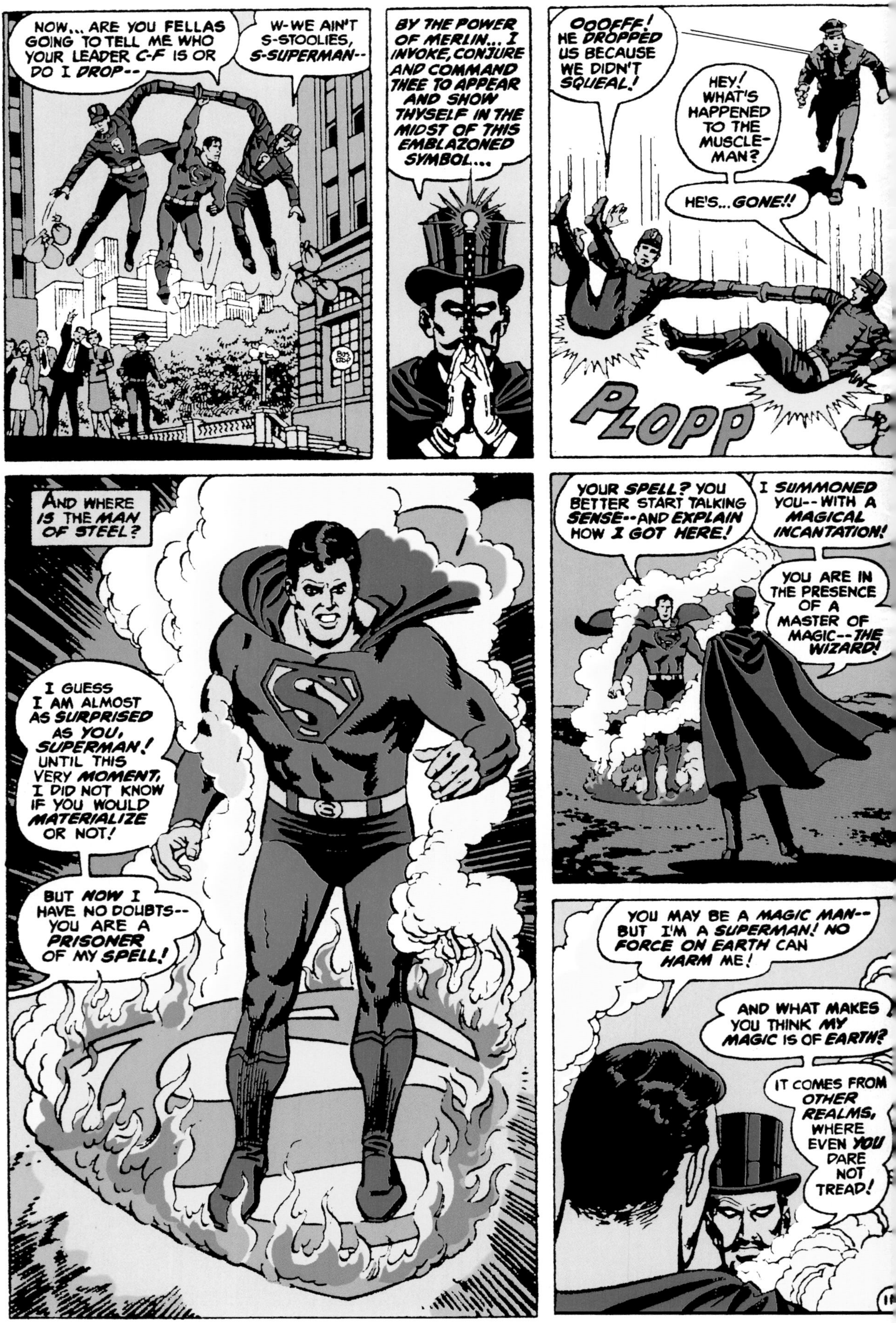
NOW... ARE YOU FELLAS GOING TO TELL ME WHO YOUR LEADER C-F IS OR DO I DROP--
W-WE AIN'T S-STOOLIES, S-SUPERMAN--
BUS STOP
BY THE POWER OF MERLIN... I INVOKE, CONJURE AND COMMAND THEE TO APPEAR AND SHOW THYSELF IN THE MIDST OF THIS EMBLAZONED SYMBOL...
OOOFFF! HE DROPPED US BECAUSE WE DIDN'T SQUEAL!
HEY! WHAT'S HAPPENED TO THE MUSCLE-MAN?
HE'S...GONE!!
PLOPP
AND WHERE IS THE MAN OF STEEL?
I GUESS I AM ALMOST AS SURPRISED AS YOU, SUPERMAN! UNTIL THIS VERY MOMENT, I DID NOT KNOW IF YOU WOULD MATERIALIZE OR NOT!
BUT NOW I HAVE NO DOUBTS-- YOU ARE A PRISONER OF MY SPELL!
YOUR SPELL? YOU BETTER START TALKING SENSE--AND EXPLAIN HOW I GOT HERE!
I SUMMONED YOU-- WITH A MAGICAL INCANTATION!
YOU ARE IN THE PRESENCE OF A MASTER OF MAGIC--THE WIZARD!
YOU MAY BE A MAGIC MAN-- BUT I'M A SUPERMAN! NO FORCE ON EARTH CAN HARM ME!
AND WHAT MAKES YOU THINK MY MAGIC IS OF EARTH?
IT COMES FROM OTHER REALMS, WHERE EVEN YOU DARE NOT TREAD!

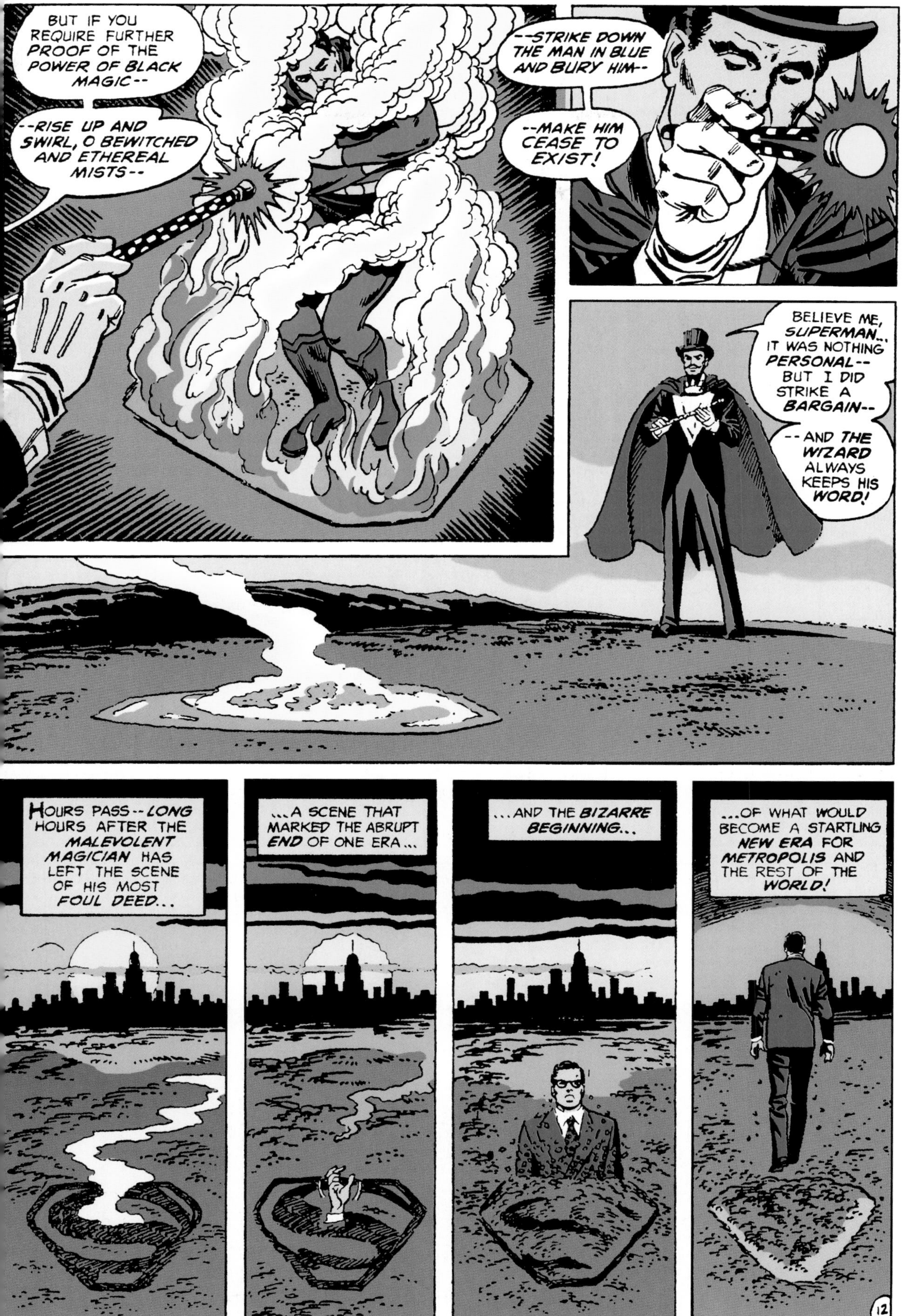
BUT IF YOU REQUIRE FURTHER PROOF OF THE POWER OF BLACK MAGIC--
--RISE UP AND SWIRL, O BEWITCHED AND ETHEREAL MISTS--
--STRIKE DOWN THE MAN IN BLUE AND BURY HIM--
--MAKE HIM CEASE TO EXIST!
BELIEVE ME, SUPERMAN... IT WAS NOTHING PERSONAL-- BUT I DID STRIKE A BARGAIN--
--AND THE WIZARD ALWAYS KEEPS HIS WORD!
HOURS PASS--LONG HOURS AFTER THE MALEVOLENT MAGICIAN HAS LEFT THE SCENE OF HIS MOST FOUL DEED...
...A SCENE THAT MARKED THE ABRUPT END OF ONE ERA...
...AND THE BIZARRE BEGINNING...
...OF WHAT WOULD BECOME A STARTLING NEW ERA FOR METROPOLIS AND THE REST OF THE WORLD!
12

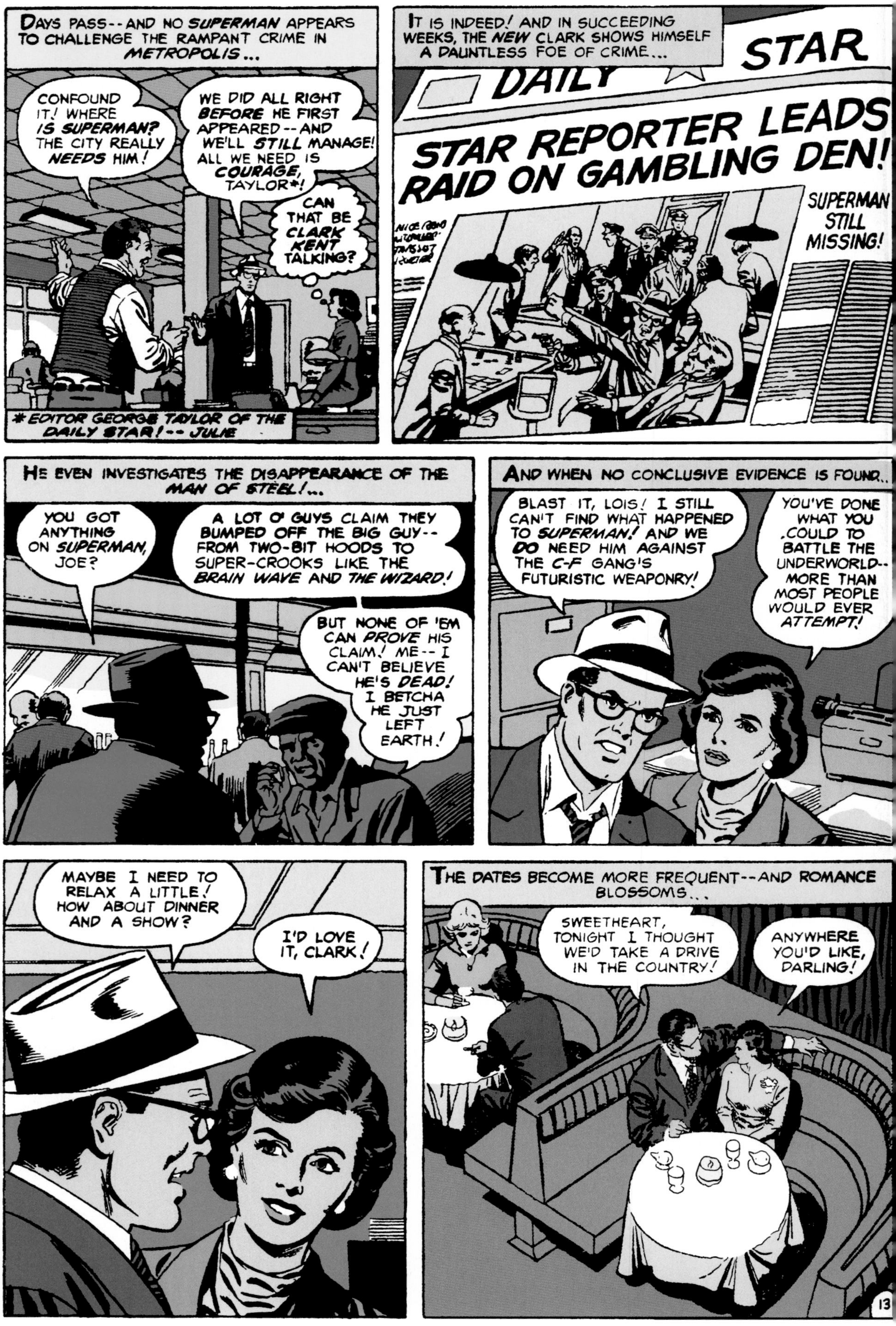
DAYS PASS--AND NO SUPERMAN APPEARS TO CHALLENGE THE RAMPANT CRIME IN METROPOLIS...
CONFOUND IT! WHERE IS SUPERMAN? THE CITY REALLY NEEDS HIM!
WE DID ALL RIGHT BEFORE HE FIRST APPEARED--AND WE'LL STILL MANAGE! ALL WE NEED IS COURAGE, TAYLOR*!
CAN THAT BE CLARK KENT TALKING?
*EDITOR GEORGE TAYLOR OF THE DAILY STAR!--JULIE
IT IS INDEED! AND IN SUCCEEDING WEEKS, THE NEW CLARK SHOWS HIMSELF A DAUNTLESS FOE OF CRIME...
DAILY STAR
STAR REPORTER LEADS RAID ON GAMBLING DEN!
SUPERMAN STILL MISSING!
HE EVEN INVESTIGATES THE DISAPPEARANCE OF THE MAN OF STEEL!...
YOU GOT ANYTHING ON SUPERMAN, JOE?
A LOT O' GUYS CLAIM THEY BUMPED OFF THE BIG GUY--FROM TWO-BIT HOODS TO SUPER-CROOKS LIKE THE BRAIN WAVE AND THE WIZARD!
BUT NONE OF 'EM CAN PROVE HIS CLAIM! ME--I CAN'T BELIEVE HE'S DEAD! I BETCHA HE JUST LEFT EARTH!
AND WHEN NO CONCLUSIVE EVIDENCE IS FOUND...
BLAST IT, LOIS! I STILL CAN'T FIND WHAT HAPPENED TO SUPERMAN! AND WE DO NEED HIM AGAINST THE C-F GANG'S FUTURISTIC WEAPONRY!
YOU'VE DONE WHAT YOU COULD TO BATTLE THE UNDERWORLD--MORE THAN MOST PEOPLE WOULD EVER ATTEMPT!
MAYBE I NEED TO RELAX A LITTLE! HOW ABOUT DINNER AND A SHOW?
I'D LOVE IT, CLARK!
THE DATES BECOME MORE FREQUENT--AND ROMANCE BLOSSOMS...
SWEETHEART, TONIGHT I THOUGHT WE'D TAKE A DRIVE IN THE COUNTRY!
ANYWHERE YOU'D LIKE, DARLING!
13

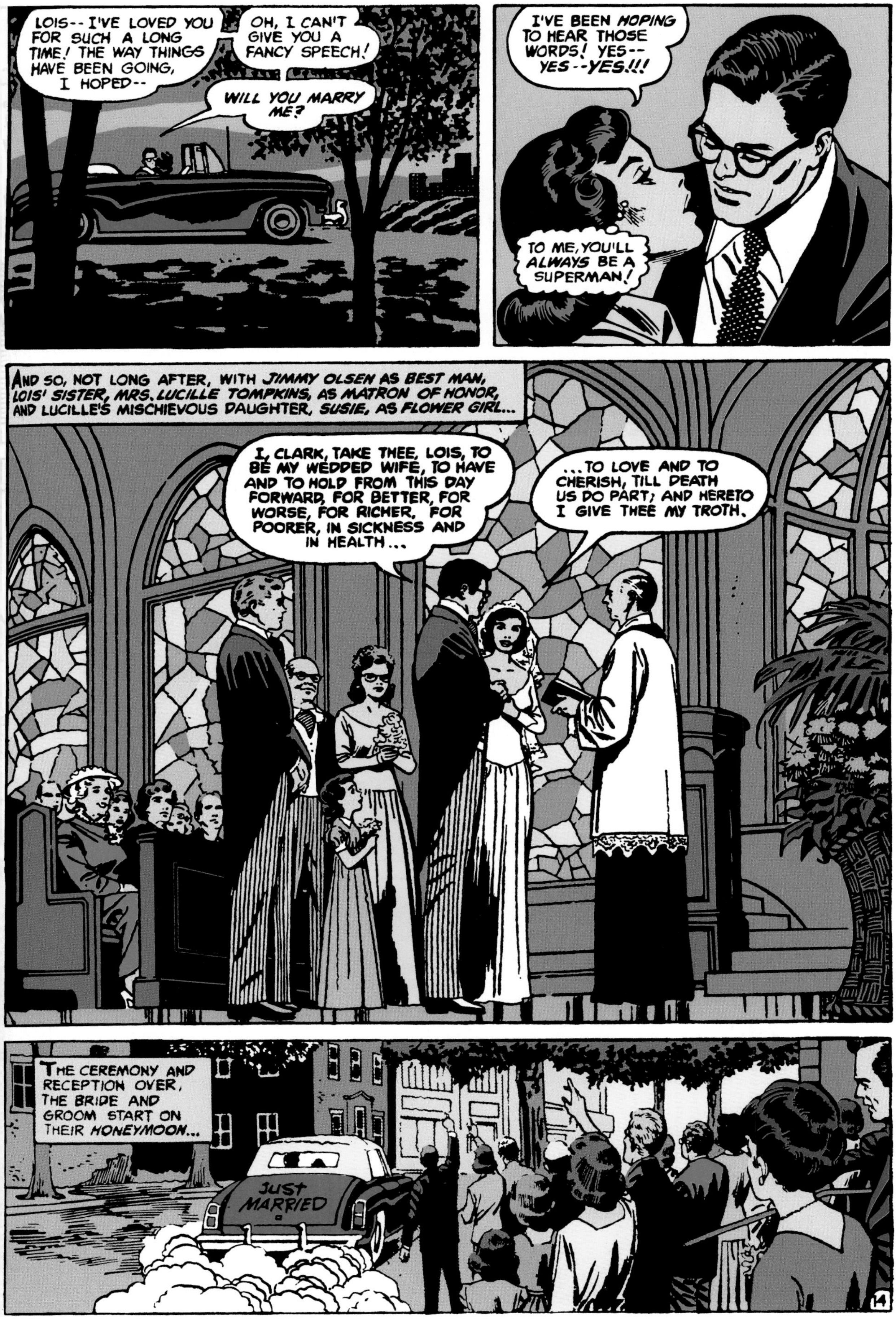
LOIS-- I'VE LOVED YOU FOR SUCH A LONG TIME! THE WAY THINGS HAVE BEEN GOING, I HOPED--
OH, I CAN'T GIVE YOU A FANCY SPEECH!
WILL YOU MARRY ME?
I'VE BEEN HOPING TO HEAR THOSE WORDS! YES-- YES--YES!!!
TO ME, YOU'LL ALWAYS BE A SUPERMAN!
AND SO, NOT LONG AFTER, WITH JIMMY OLSEN AS BEST MAN, LOIS' SISTER, MRS. LUCILLE TOMPKINS, AS MATRON OF HONOR, AND LUCILLE'S MISCHIEVOUS DAUGHTER, SUSIE, AS FLOWER GIRL...
I, CLARK, TAKE THEE, LOIS, TO BE MY WEDDED WIFE, TO HAVE AND TO HOLD FROM THIS DAY FORWARD, FOR BETTER, FOR WORSE, FOR RICHER, FOR POORER, IN SICKNESS AND IN HEALTH...
...TO LOVE AND TO CHERISH, TILL DEATH US DO PART; AND HERETO I GIVE THEE MY TROTH.
THE CEREMONY AND RECEPTION OVER, THE BRIDE AND GROOM START ON THEIR HONEYMOON...
JUST MARRIED
14

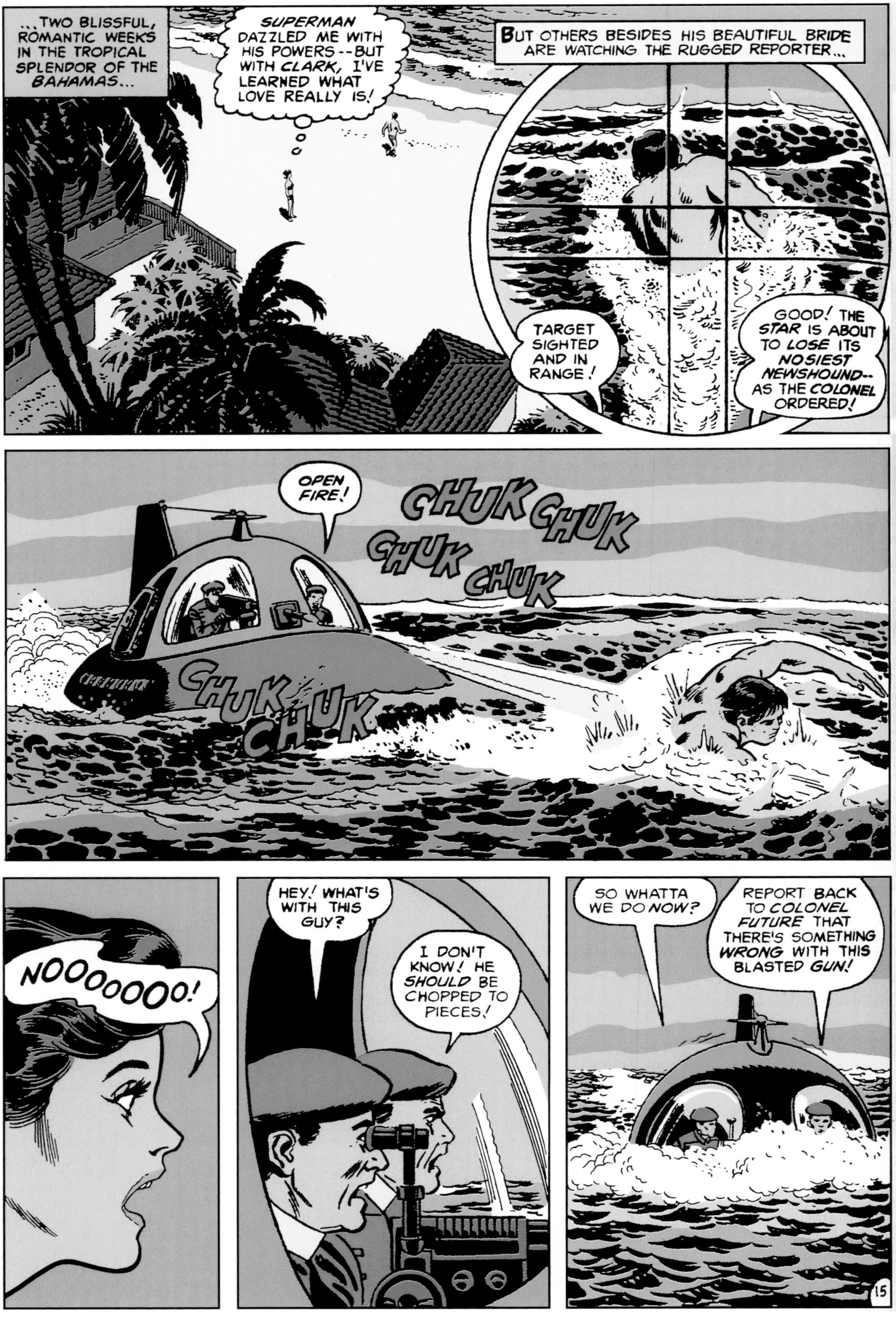

...TWO BLISSFUL, ROMANTIC WEEKS IN THE TROPICAL SPLENDOR OF THE BAHAMAS...
SUPERMAN DAZZLED ME WITH HIS POWERS--BUT WITH CLARK, I'VE LEARNED WHAT LOVE REALLY IS!
BUT OTHERS BESIDES HIS BEAUTIFUL BRIDE ARE WATCHING THE RUGGED REPORTER...
TARGET SIGHTED AND IN RANGE!
GOOD! THE STAR IS ABOUT TO LOSE ITS NOSIEST NEWSHOUND--AS THE COLONEL ORDERED!
OPEN FIRE!
CHUK CHUK
CHUK CHUK
CHUK CHUK
NOOOOOOO!
HEY! WHAT'S WITH THIS GUY?
I DON'T KNOW! HE SHOULD BE CHOPPED TO PIECES!
SO WHATTA WE DO NOW?
REPORT BACK TO COLONEL FUTURE THAT THERE'S SOMETHING WRONG WITH THIS BLASTED GUN!
15

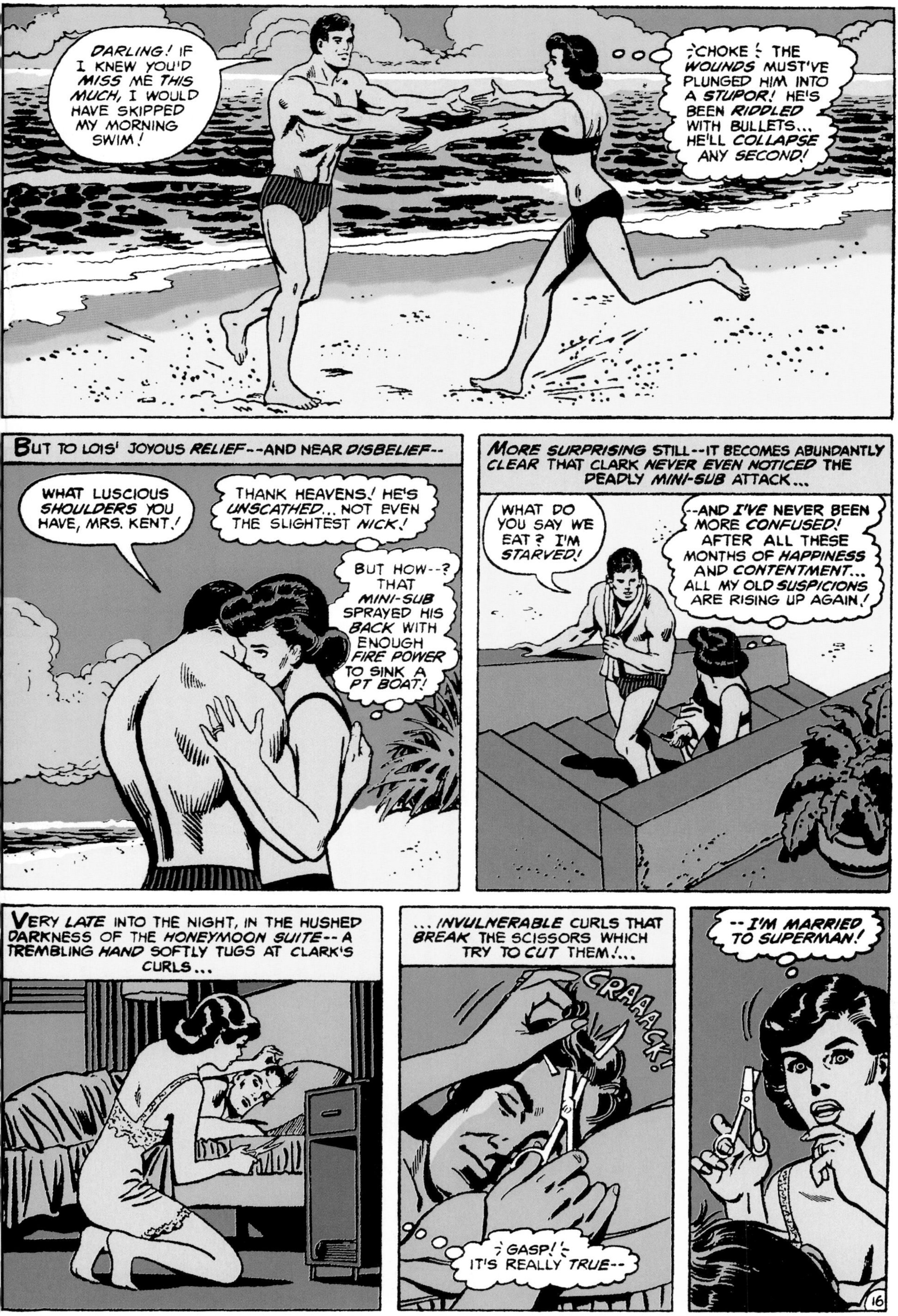
DARLING! IF I KNEW YOU'D MISS ME THIS MUCH, I WOULD HAVE SKIPPED MY MORNING SWIM!
CHOKE THE WOUNDS MUST'VE PLUNGED HIM INTO A STUPOR! HE'S BEEN RIDDLED WITH BULLETS... HE'LL COLLAPSE ANY SECOND!
BUT TO LOIS' JOYOUS RELIEF--AND NEAR DISBELIEF--
WHAT LUSCIOUS SHOULDERS YOU HAVE, MRS. KENT!
THANK HEAVENS! HE'S UNSCATHED... NOT EVEN THE SLIGHTEST NICK!
BUT HOW--? THAT MINI-SUB SPRAYED HIS BACK WITH ENOUGH FIRE POWER TO SINK A PT BOAT!
MORE SURPRISING STILL--IT BECOMES ABUNDANTLY CLEAR THAT CLARK NEVER EVEN NOTICED THE DEADLY MINI-SUB ATTACK...
WHAT DO YOU SAY WE EAT? I'M STARVED!
--AND I'VE NEVER BEEN MORE CONFUSED! AFTER ALL THESE MONTHS OF HAPPINESS AND CONTENTMENT... ALL MY OLD SUSPICIONS ARE RISING UP AGAIN!
VERY LATE INTO THE NIGHT, IN THE HUSHED DARKNESS OF THE HONEYMOON SUITE--A TREMBLING HAND SOFTLY TUGS AT CLARK'S CURLS...
...INVULNERABLE CURLS THAT BREAK THE SCISSORS WHICH TRY TO CUT THEM!...
CRAAACK!
GASP! IT'S REALLY TRUE--
--I'M MARRIED TO SUPERMAN!
16

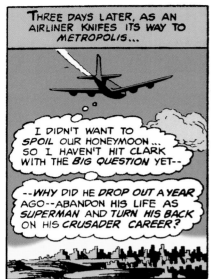

THREE DAYS LATER, AS AN AIRLINER KNIFES ITS WAY TO METROPOLIS...

I DIDN'T WANT TO *SPOIL* OUR HONEYMOON... SO I HAVEN'T HIT CLARK WITH THE *BIG QUESTION* YET--

--WHY DID HE *DROP OUT* A YEAR AGO--ABANDON HIS LIFE AS *SUPERMAN* AND TURN HIS BACK ON HIS *CRUSADER CAREER?*

AND *WORST* OF ALL-- WHY COULDN'T HE TRUST *ME* WITH HIS *SECRET?*

WHY-- UNLESS ... UNLESS... GOOD GRIEF! AN INCREDIBLE THOUGHT JUST STRUCK ME:

WHAT IF CLARK REALLY *DOESN'T KNOW* HE'S SUPERMAN?

WHAT IF SOME *FORCE* PREVENTS HIM FROM *REALIZING* HE HAS SUPER-POWERS?

NEXT DAY, AS *MRS. LOIS KENT* RESUMES HER REPORTING CAREER...

A *NICE IDEA* FOR A SUNDAY PIECE, *LOIS*... BUT YOU'VE TAKEN ON A *BIG JOB!* OUR FILES SHOW NO LESS THAN *FIFTY-THREE CROOKS* HAVE TRIED TO *TAKE CREDIT* FOR IT OVER THE PAST YEAR--

DAILY STAR

--EACH ONE SWEARING *HE* WAS THE ONE WHO GOT RID OF *SUPERMAN!*

I NEVER SAID IT WOULD BE *EASY,* TAYLOR-- BUT JUST THINK WHAT A *SCOOP* WE'D HAVE IF *ONE* OF THEM WAS TELLING THE *TRUTH!*

MANY HOURS OF PAINSTAKING RESEARCH LATER...

SOME OF THESE CLAIMS *SEEM* PLAUSIBLE... BUT I'M LOOKING FOR SOMETHING TOTALLY *UNORTHODOX...* SOMETHING *SUPERMAN* WOULD NEVER *EXPECT...*

HMMM... SOMETHING LIKE *THIS*--!

LATER THAT DAY, IN *METROPOLIS PARK...*

PARDON ME, SIR-- ARE YOU *FREDERICK P. GARTH*--

-- THE CRIMINAL *MASTER MAGICIAN* KNOWN AS *THE WIZARD?*

17

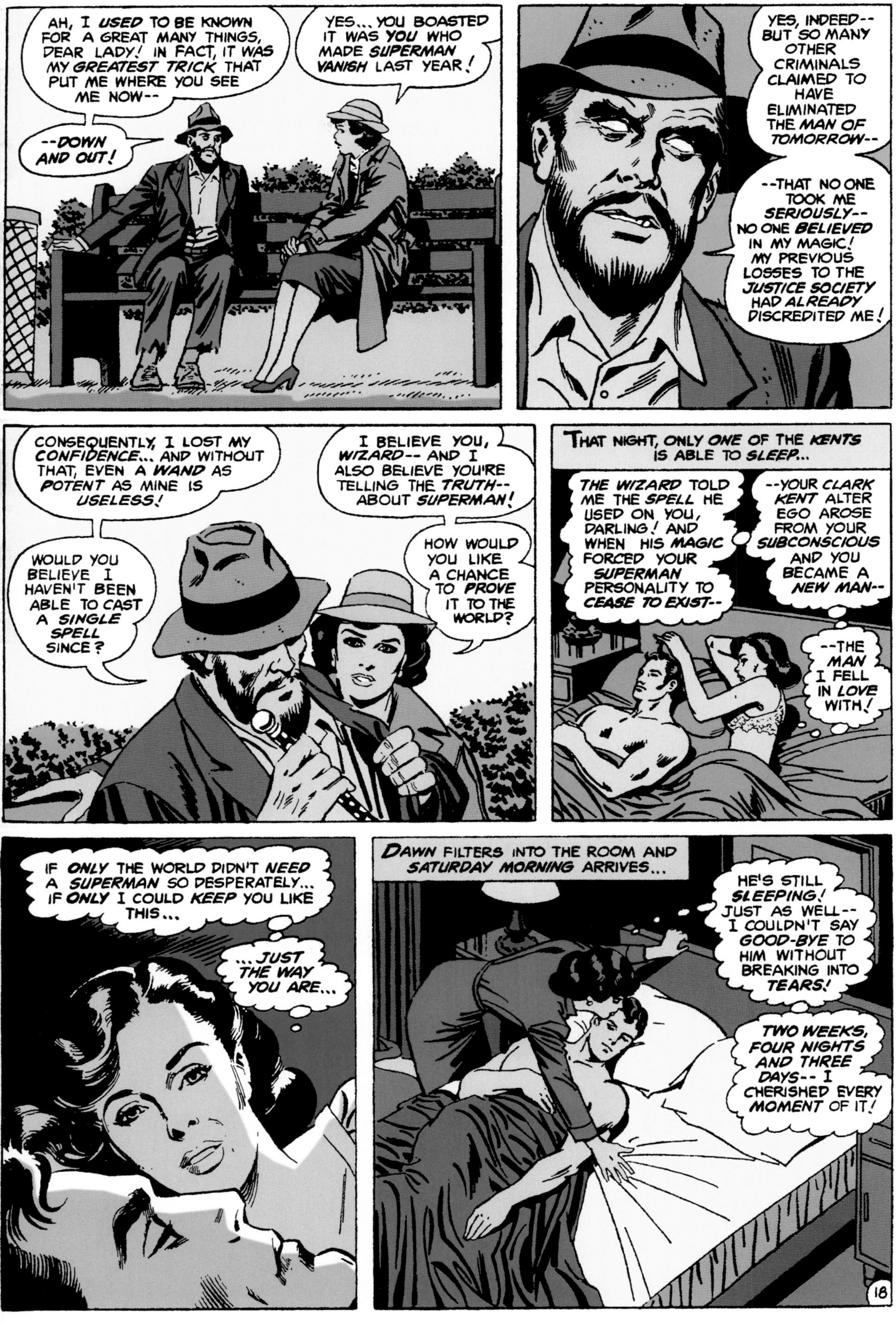

AH, I USED TO BE KNOWN FOR A GREAT MANY THINGS, DEAR LADY! IN FACT, IT WAS MY GREATEST TRICK THAT PUT ME WHERE YOU SEE ME NOW--
--DOWN AND OUT!
YES... YOU BOASTED IT WAS YOU WHO MADE SUPERMAN VANISH LAST YEAR!
YES, INDEED-- BUT SO MANY OTHER CRIMINALS CLAIMED TO HAVE ELIMINATED THE MAN OF TOMORROW--
--THAT NO ONE TOOK ME SERIOUSLY-- NO ONE BELIEVED IN MY MAGIC! MY PREVIOUS LOSSES TO THE JUSTICE SOCIETY HAD ALREADY DISCREDITED ME!
CONSEQUENTLY, I LOST MY CONFIDENCE... AND WITHOUT THAT, EVEN A WAND AS POTENT AS MINE IS USELESS!
WOULD YOU BELIEVE I HAVEN'T BEEN ABLE TO CAST A SINGLE SPELL SINCE?
I BELIEVE YOU, WIZARD-- AND I ALSO BELIEVE YOU'RE TELLING THE TRUTH-- ABOUT SUPERMAN!
HOW WOULD YOU LIKE A CHANCE TO PROVE IT TO THE WORLD?
THAT NIGHT, ONLY ONE OF THE KENTS IS ABLE TO SLEEP...
THE WIZARD TOLD ME THE SPELL HE USED ON YOU, DARLING! AND WHEN HIS MAGIC FORCED YOUR SUPERMAN PERSONALITY TO CEASE TO EXIST--
--YOUR CLARK KENT ALTER EGO AROSE FROM YOUR SUBCONSCIOUS AND YOU BECAME A NEW MAN--
--THE MAN I FELL IN LOVE WITH!
IF ONLY THE WORLD DIDN'T NEED A SUPERMAN SO DESPERATELY... IF ONLY I COULD KEEP YOU LIKE THIS...
...JUST THE WAY YOU ARE...
DAWN FILTERS INTO THE ROOM AND SATURDAY MORNING ARRIVES...
HE'S STILL SLEEPING! JUST AS WELL-- I COULDN'T SAY GOOD-BYE TO HIM WITHOUT BREAKING INTO TEARS!
TWO WEEKS, FOUR NIGHTS AND THREE DAYS-- I CHERISHED EVERY MOMENT OF IT!
18

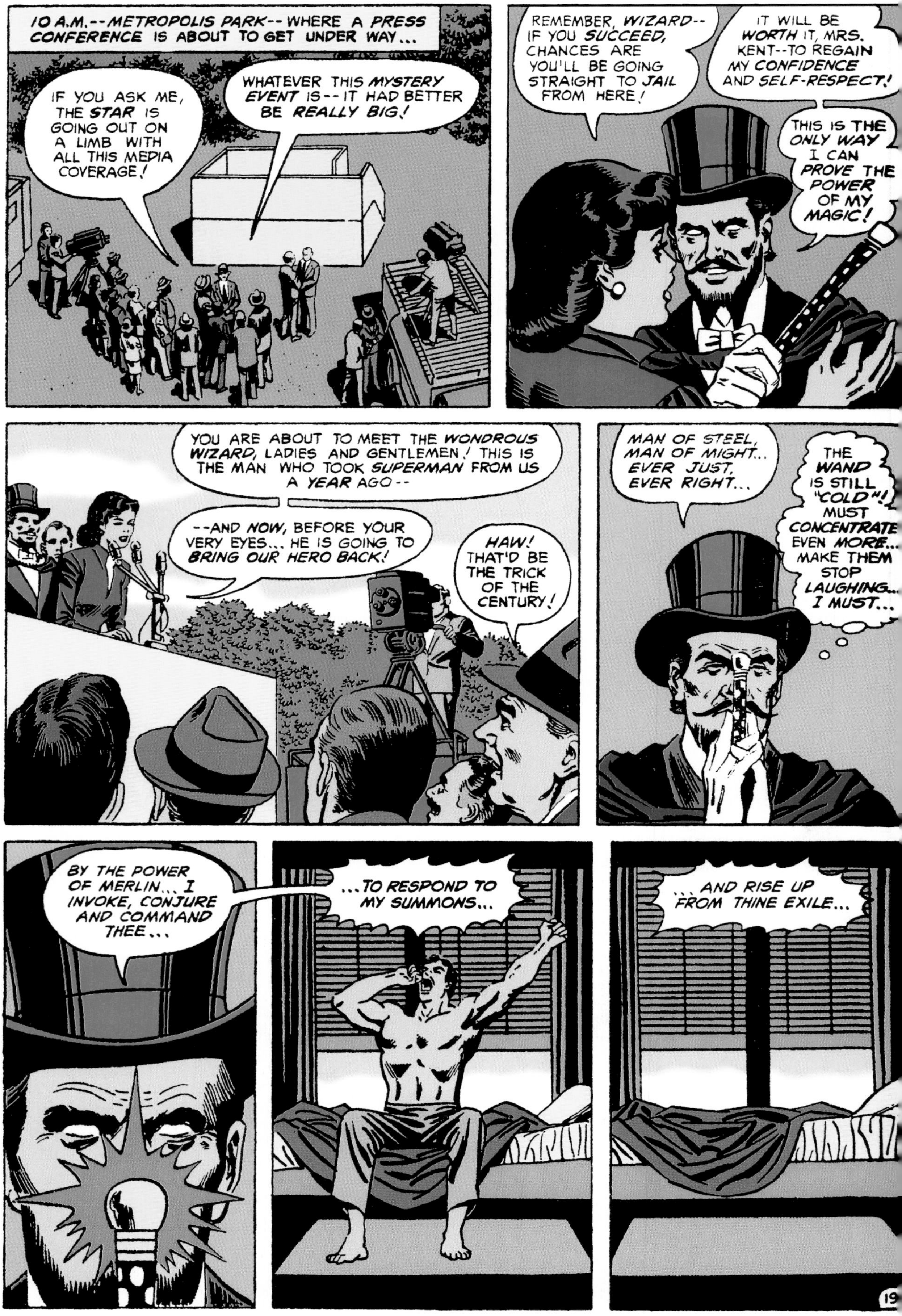
10 A.M.--METROPOLIS PARK--WHERE A PRESS CONFERENCE IS ABOUT TO GET UNDER WAY...
IF YOU ASK ME, THE STAR IS GOING OUT ON A LIMB WITH ALL THIS MEDIA COVERAGE!
WHATEVER THIS MYSTERY EVENT IS--IT HAD BETTER BE REALLY BIG!
REMEMBER, WIZARD--IF YOU SUCCEED, CHANCES ARE YOU'LL BE GOING STRAIGHT TO JAIL FROM HERE!
IT WILL BE WORTH IT, MRS. KENT--TO REGAIN MY CONFIDENCE AND SELF-RESPECT!
THIS IS THE ONLY WAY I CAN PROVE THE POWER OF MY MAGIC!
YOU ARE ABOUT TO MEET THE WONDROUS WIZARD, LADIES AND GENTLEMEN! THIS IS THE MAN WHO TOOK SUPERMAN FROM US A YEAR AGO--
--AND NOW, BEFORE YOUR VERY EYES... HE IS GOING TO BRING OUR HERO BACK!
HAW! THAT'D BE THE TRICK OF THE CENTURY!
MAN OF STEEL, MAN OF MIGHT... EVER JUST, EVER RIGHT...
THE WAND IS STILL "COLD"! MUST CONCENTRATE EVEN MORE... MAKE THEM STOP LAUGHING... I MUST...
BY THE POWER OF MERLIN... I INVOKE, CONJURE AND COMMAND THEE...
...TO RESPOND TO MY SUMMONS...
...AND RISE UP FROM THINE EXILE...
19

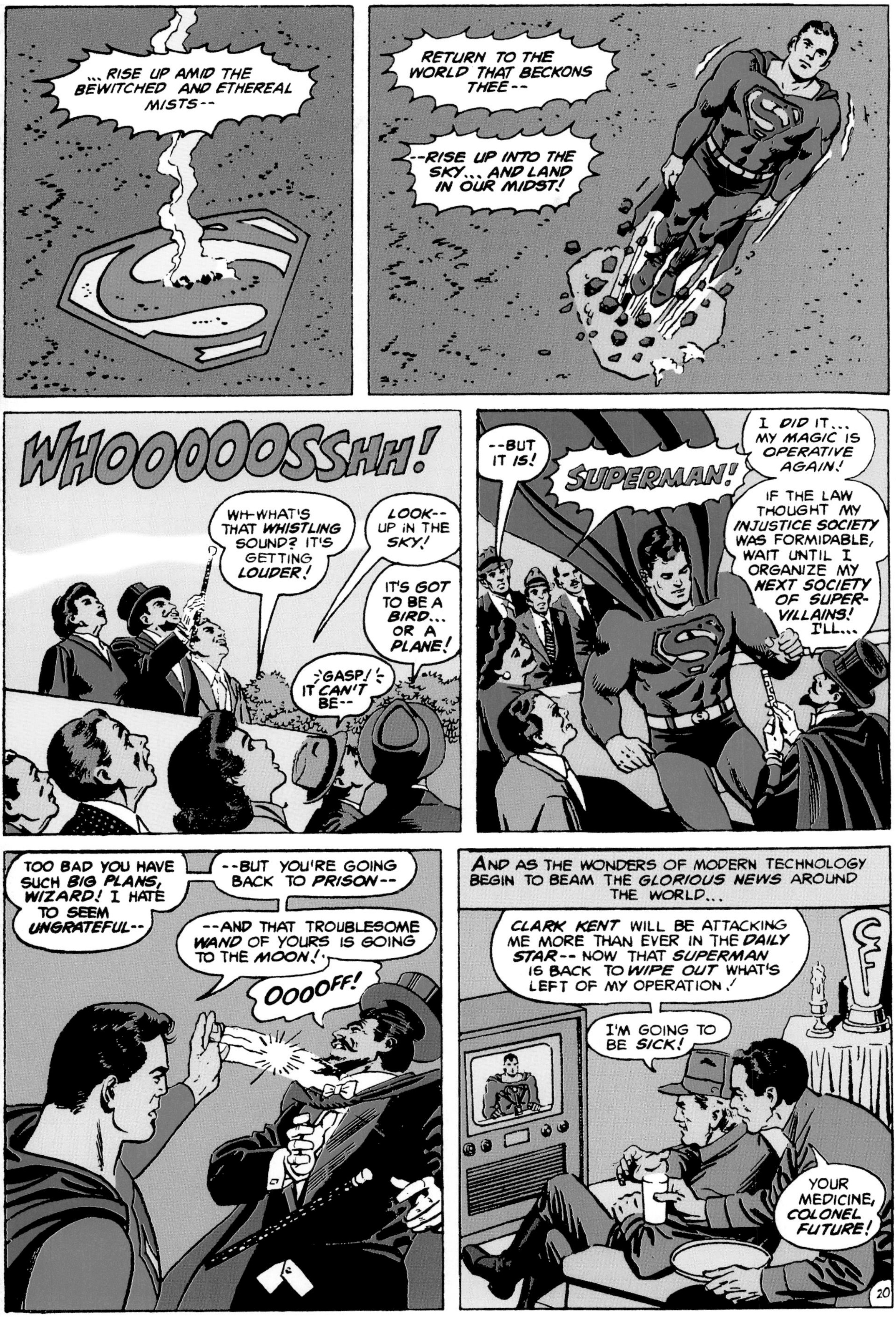
...RISE UP AMID THE BEWITCHED AND ETHEREAL MISTS--
RETURN TO THE WORLD THAT BECKONS THEE--
--RISE UP INTO THE SKY... AND LAND IN OUR MIDST!
WHOOOOOOSSHH!
WH-WHAT'S THAT WHISTLING SOUND? IT'S GETTING LOUDER!
LOOK-- UP IN THE SKY!
IT'S GOT TO BE A BIRD... OR A PLANE!
GASP! IT CAN'T BE--
--BUT IT IS!
SUPERMAN!
I DID IT... MY MAGIC IS OPERATIVE AGAIN!
IF THE LAW THOUGHT MY INJUSTICE SOCIETY WAS FORMIDABLE, WAIT UNTIL I ORGANIZE MY NEXT SOCIETY OF SUPER-VILLAINS! I'LL...
TOO BAD YOU HAVE SUCH BIG PLANS, WIZARD! I HATE TO SEEM UNGRATEFUL--
--BUT YOU'RE GOING BACK TO PRISON--
--AND THAT TROUBLESOME WAND OF YOURS IS GOING TO THE MOON!
OOOOFF!
AND AS THE WONDERS OF MODERN TECHNOLOGY BEGIN TO BEAM THE GLORIOUS NEWS AROUND THE WORLD...
CLARK KENT WILL BE ATTACKING ME MORE THAN EVER IN THE DAILY STAR-- NOW THAT SUPERMAN IS BACK TO WIPE OUT WHAT'S LEFT OF MY OPERATION!
I'M GOING TO BE SICK!
YOUR MEDICINE, COLONEL FUTURE!
20

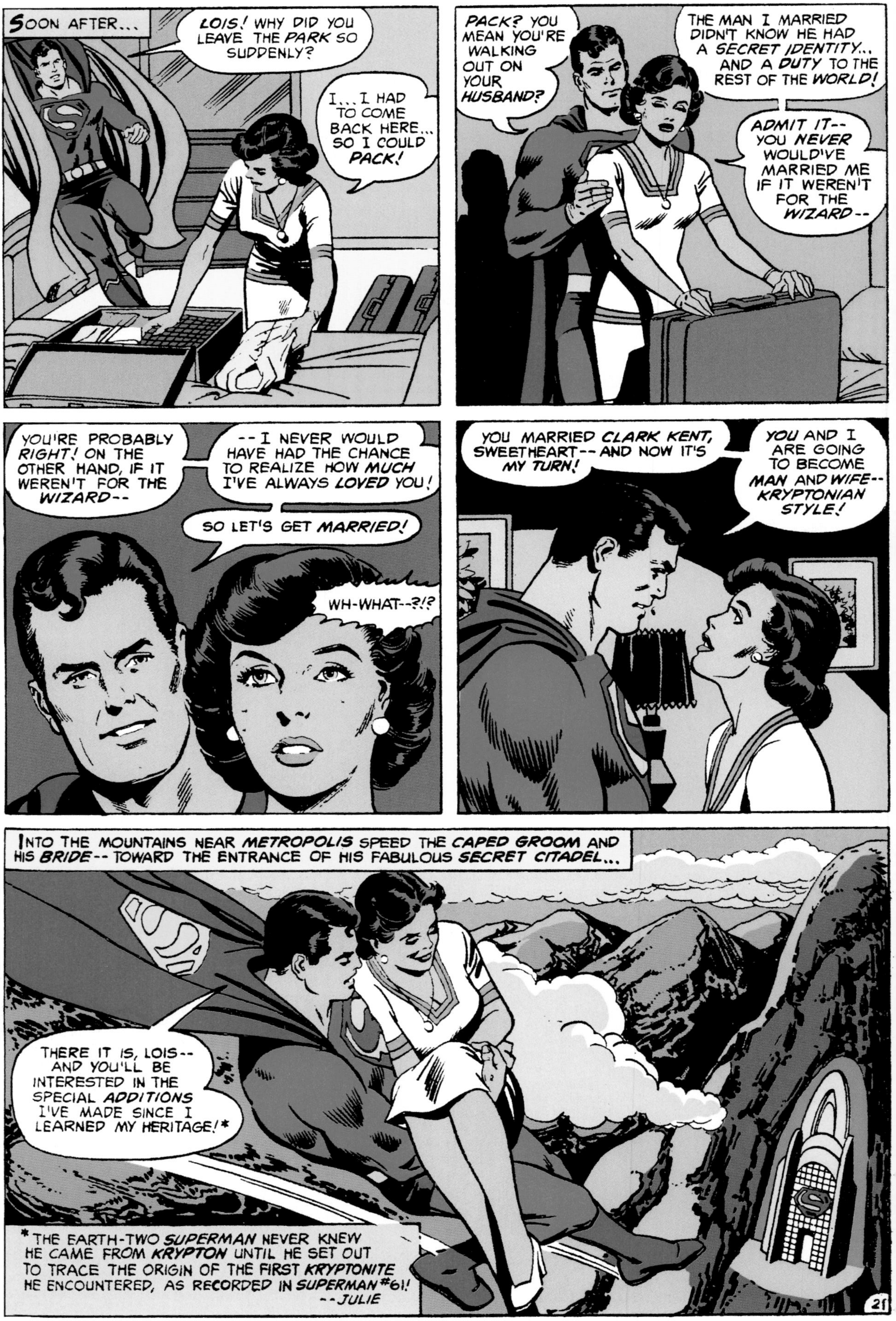
SOON AFTER...
LOIS! WHY DID YOU LEAVE THE PARK SO SUDDENLY?
I... I HAD TO COME BACK HERE... SO I COULD PACK!
PACK? YOU MEAN YOU'RE WALKING OUT ON YOUR HUSBAND?
THE MAN I MARRIED DIDN'T KNOW HE HAD A SECRET IDENTITY... AND A DUTY TO THE REST OF THE WORLD!
ADMIT IT-- YOU NEVER WOULD'VE MARRIED ME IF IT WEREN'T FOR THE WIZARD--
YOU'RE PROBABLY RIGHT! ON THE OTHER HAND, IF IT WEREN'T FOR THE WIZARD--
--I NEVER WOULD HAVE HAD THE CHANCE TO REALIZE HOW MUCH I'VE ALWAYS LOVED YOU!
SO LET'S GET MARRIED!
WH-WHAT--?!?
YOU MARRIED CLARK KENT, SWEETHEART-- AND NOW IT'S MY TURN!
YOU AND I ARE GOING TO BECOME MAN AND WIFE-- KRYPTONIAN STYLE!
INTO THE MOUNTAINS NEAR METROPOLIS SPEED THE CAPED GROOM AND HIS BRIDE-- TOWARD THE ENTRANCE OF HIS FABULOUS SECRET CITADEL...
THERE IT IS, LOIS-- AND YOU'LL BE INTERESTED IN THE SPECIAL ADDITIONS I'VE MADE SINCE I LEARNED MY HERITAGE!*
*THE EARTH-TWO SUPERMAN NEVER KNEW HE CAME FROM KRYPTON UNTIL HE SET OUT TO TRACE THE ORIGIN OF THE FIRST KRYPTONITE HE ENCOUNTERED, AS RECORDED IN SUPERMAN #61! --JULIE
21

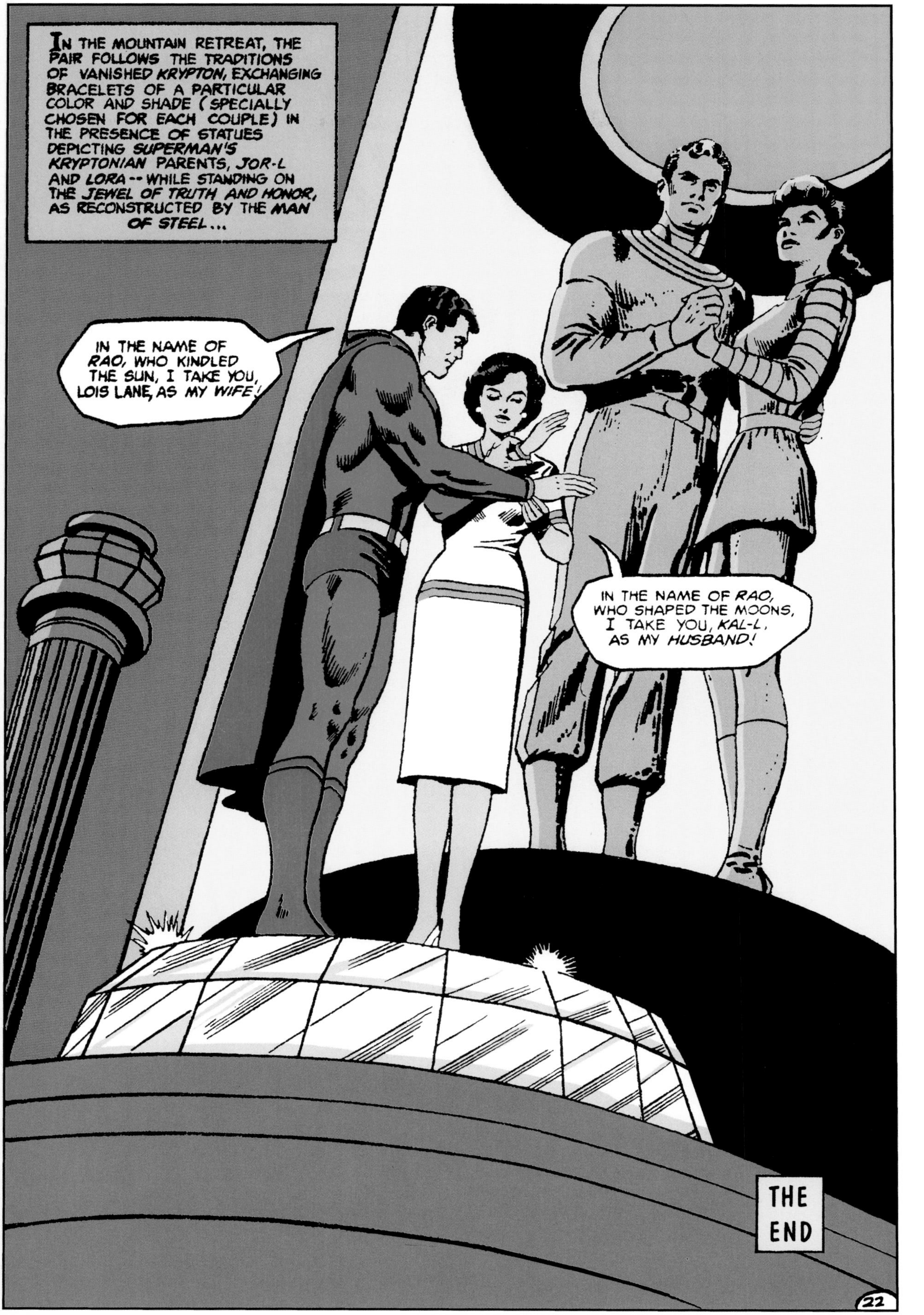
IN THE MOUNTAIN RETREAT, THE PAIR FOLLOWS THE TRADITIONS OF VANISHED KRYPTON, EXCHANGING BRACELETS OF A PARTICULAR COLOR AND SHADE (SPECIALLY CHOSEN FOR EACH COUPLE) IN THE PRESENCE OF STATUES DEPICTING SUPERMAN'S KRYPTONIAN PARENTS, JOR-L AND LORA -- WHILE STANDING ON THE JEWEL OF TRUTH AND HONOR, AS RECONSTRUCTED BY THE MAN OF STEEL...
IN THE NAME OF RAO, WHO KINDLED THE SUN, I TAKE YOU, LOIS LANE, AS MY WIFE!
IN THE NAME OF RAO, WHO SHAPED THE MOONS, I TAKE YOU, KAL-L, AS MY HUSBAND!
THE END
22

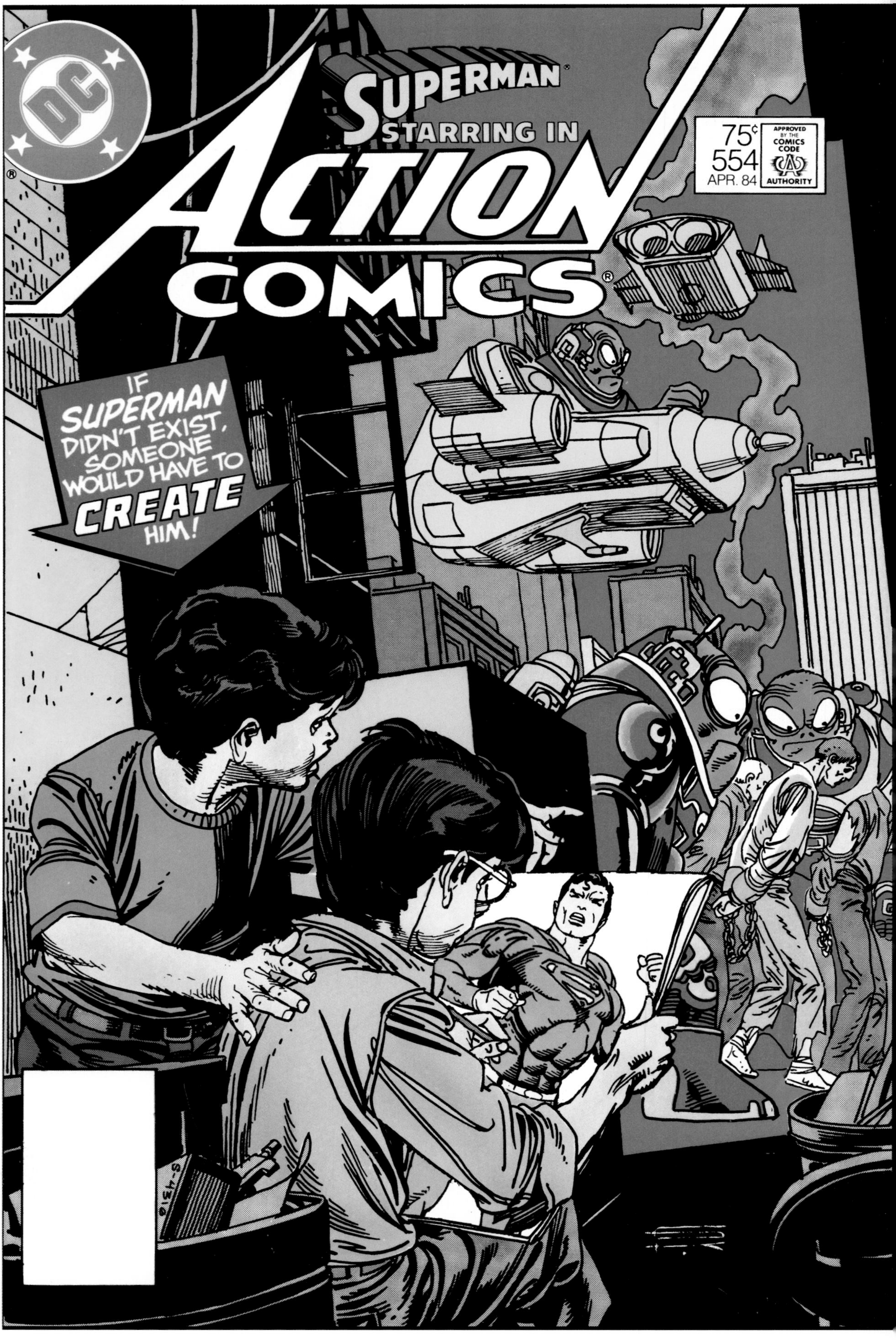
SUPERMAN
STARRING IN
ACTION COMICS
75¢
554
APR. 84
APPROVED BY THE COMICS CODE AUTHORITY
IF SUPERMAN DIDN'T EXIST, SOMEONE WOULD HAVE TO CREATE HIM!

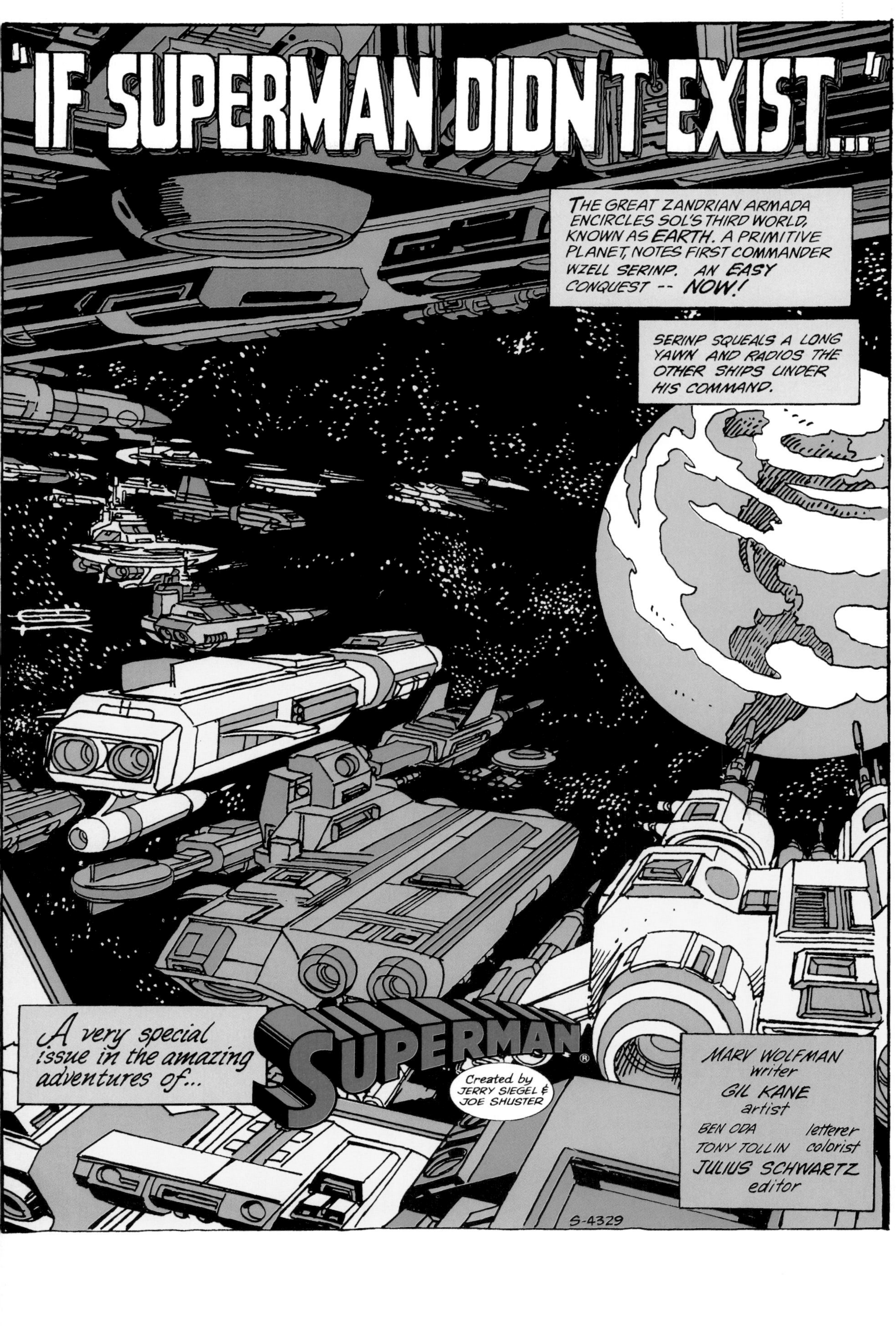
"IF SUPERMAN DIDN'T EXIST..."
THE GREAT ZANDRIAN ARMADA ENCIRCLES SOL'S THIRD WORLD, KNOWN AS EARTH. A PRIMITIVE PLANET, NOTES FIRST COMMANDER WZELL SERINP. AN EASY CONQUEST -- NOW!
SERINP SQUEALS A LONG YAWN AND RADIOS THE OTHER SHIPS UNDER HIS COMMAND.
A very special issue in the amazing adventures of...
SUPERMAN®
Created by JERRY SIEGEL & JOE SHUSTER
MARV WOLFMAN writer
GIL KANE artist
BEN ODA letterer
TONY TOLLIN colorist
JULIUS SCHWARTZ editor
S-4329

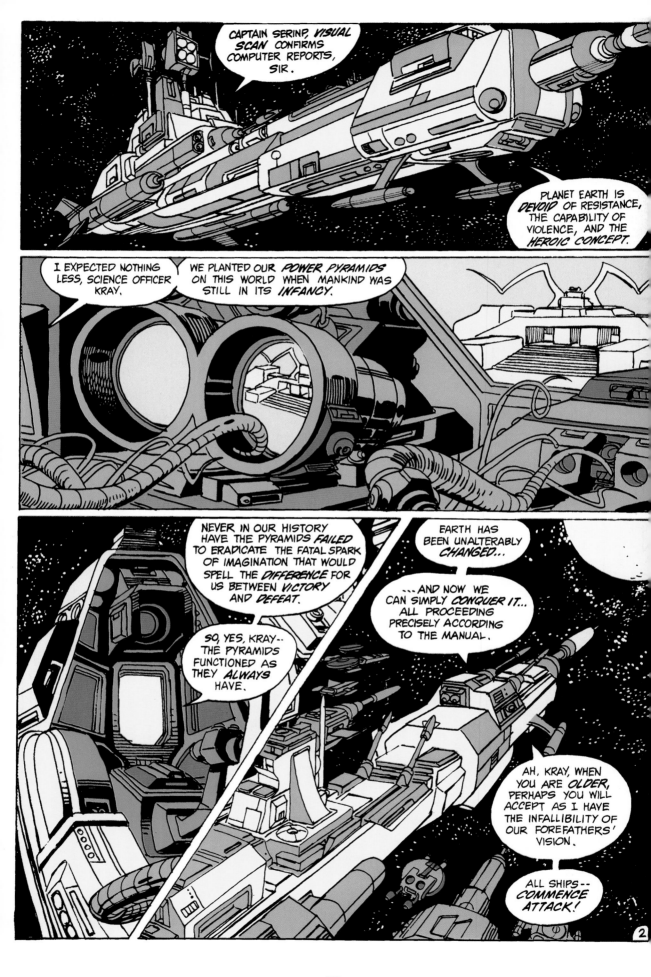

CAPTAIN SERINP, *VISUAL SCAN* CONFIRMS COMPUTER REPORTS, SIR.

PLANET EARTH IS *DEVOID* OF RESISTANCE, THE CAPABILITY OF VIOLENCE, AND THE *HEROIC CONCEPT.*

I EXPECTED NOTHING LESS, SCIENCE OFFICER KRAY.

WE PLANTED OUR *POWER PYRAMIDS* ON THIS WORLD WHEN MANKIND WAS STILL IN ITS *INFANCY.*

NEVER IN OUR HISTORY HAVE THE PYRAMIDS *FAILED* TO ERADICATE THE FATAL SPARK OF IMAGINATION THAT WOULD SPELL THE *DIFFERENCE* FOR US BETWEEN *VICTORY* AND *DEFEAT.*

SO, YES, KRAY-- THE PYRAMIDS FUNCTIONED AS THEY *ALWAYS* HAVE.

EARTH HAS BEEN UNALTERABLY *CHANGED...*

...AND NOW WE CAN SIMPLY *CONQUER IT...* ALL PROCEEDING PRECISELY ACCORDING TO THE MANUAL.

AH, KRAY, WHEN YOU ARE *OLDER,* PERHAPS YOU WILL ACCEPT AS I HAVE THE INFALLIBILITY OF OUR FOREFATHERS' VISION.

ALL SHIPS-- *COMMENCE ATTACK!*

2

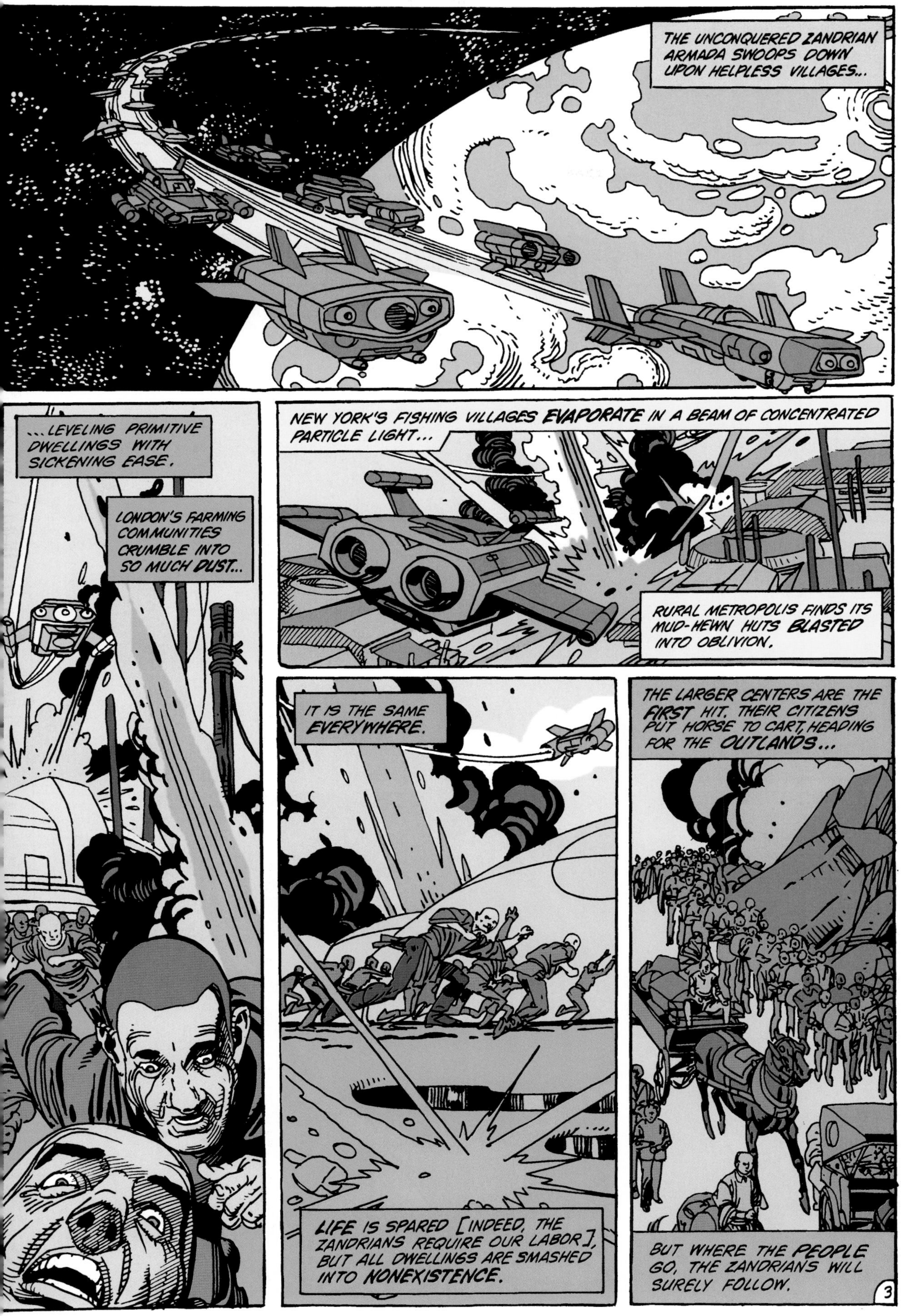
THE UNCONQUERED ZANDRIAN ARMADA SWOOPS DOWN UPON HELPLESS VILLAGES...
...LEVELING PRIMITIVE DWELLINGS WITH SICKENING EASE.
LONDON'S FARMING COMMUNITIES CRUMBLE INTO SO MUCH DUST...
NEW YORK'S FISHING VILLAGES EVAPORATE IN A BEAM OF CONCENTRATED PARTICLE LIGHT...
RURAL METROPOLIS FINDS ITS MUD-HEWN HUTS BLASTED INTO OBLIVION.
IT IS THE SAME EVERYWHERE.
LIFE IS SPARED [INDEED, THE ZANDRIANS REQUIRE OUR LABOR], BUT ALL DWELLINGS ARE SMASHED INTO NONEXISTENCE.
THE LARGER CENTERS ARE THE FIRST HIT. THEIR CITIZENS PUT HORSE TO CART, HEADING FOR THE OUTLANDS...
BUT WHERE THE PEOPLE GO, THE ZANDRIANS WILL SURELY FOLLOW.
3

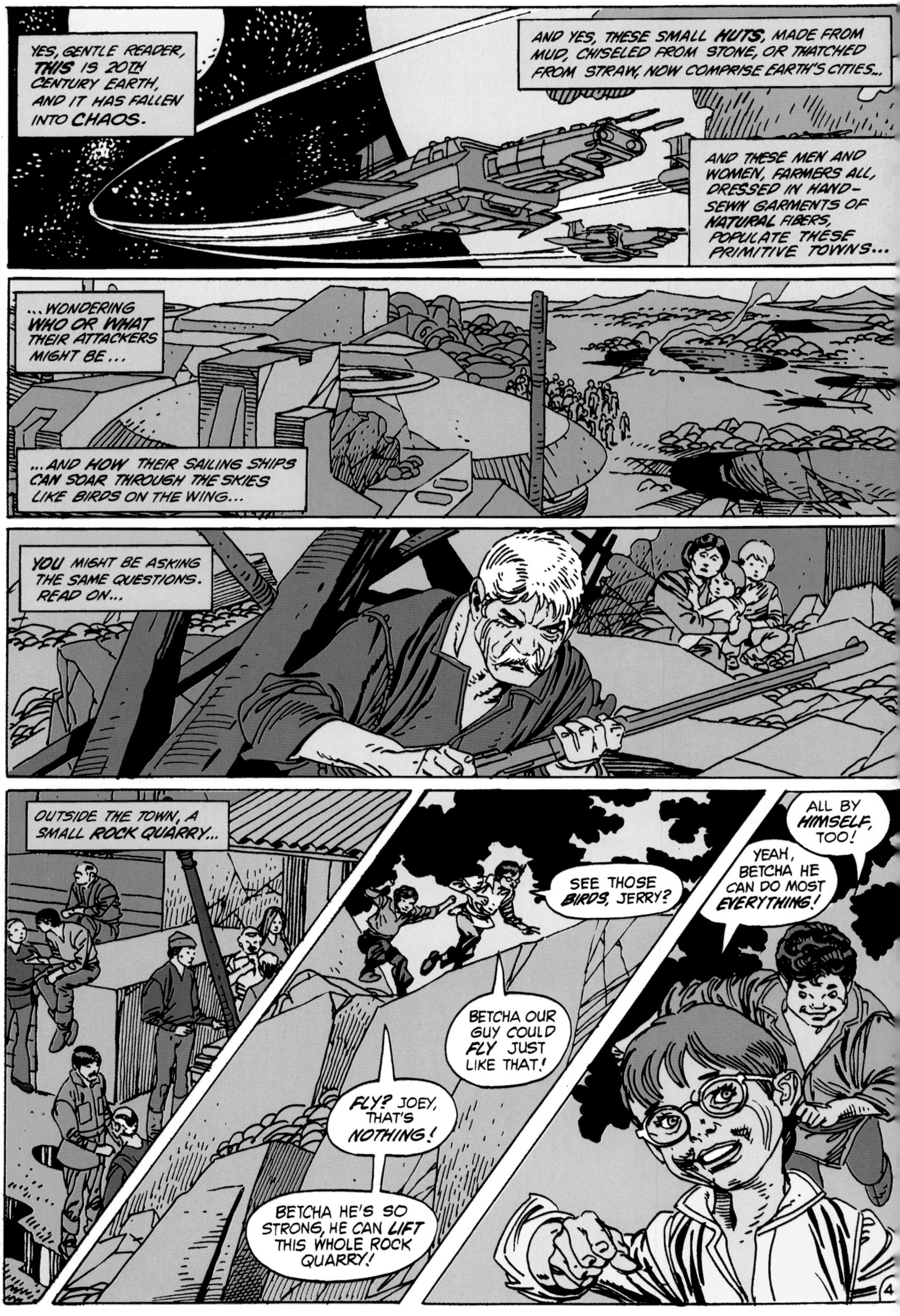
YES, GENTLE READER, THIS IS 20TH CENTURY EARTH, AND IT HAS FALLEN INTO CHAOS.
AND YES, THESE SMALL HUTS, MADE FROM MUD, CHISELED FROM STONE, OR THATCHED FROM STRAW, NOW COMPRISE EARTH'S CITIES...
AND THESE MEN AND WOMEN, FARMERS ALL, DRESSED IN HAND-SEWN GARMENTS OF NATURAL FIBERS, POPULATE THESE PRIMITIVE TOWNS...
...WONDERING WHO OR WHAT THEIR ATTACKERS MIGHT BE...
...AND HOW THEIR SAILING SHIPS CAN SOAR THROUGH THE SKIES LIKE BIRDS ON THE WING...
YOU MIGHT BE ASKING THE SAME QUESTIONS. READ ON...
OUTSIDE THE TOWN, A SMALL ROCK QUARRY...
SEE THOSE BIRDS, JERRY?
BETCHA OUR GUY COULD FLY JUST LIKE THAT!
FLY? JOEY, THAT'S NOTHING!
BETCHA HE'S SO STRONG, HE CAN LIFT THIS WHOLE ROCK QUARRY!
ALL BY HIMSELF, TOO!
YEAH, BETCHA HE CAN DO MOST EVERYTHING!
4

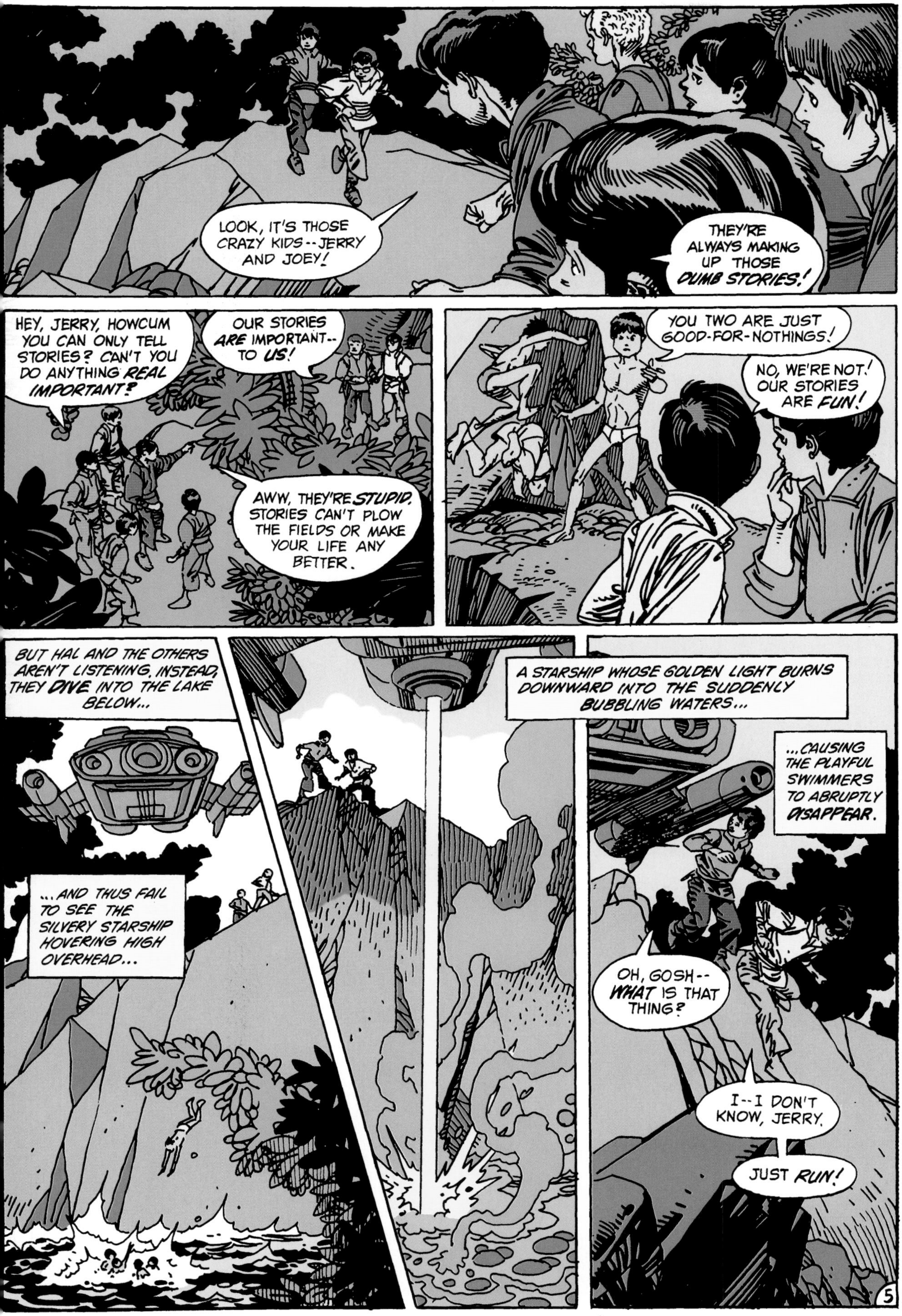
LOOK, IT'S THOSE CRAZY KIDS--JERRY AND JOEY!
THEY'RE ALWAYS MAKING UP THOSE DUMB STORIES!
HEY, JERRY, HOWCUM YOU CAN ONLY TELL STORIES? CAN'T YOU DO ANYTHING REAL IMPORTANT?
OUR STORIES ARE IMPORTANT-- TO US!
AWW, THEY'RE STUPID. STORIES CAN'T PLOW THE FIELDS OR MAKE YOUR LIFE ANY BETTER.
YOU TWO ARE JUST GOOD-FOR-NOTHINGS!
NO, WE'RE NOT! OUR STORIES ARE FUN!
BUT HAL AND THE OTHERS AREN'T LISTENING. INSTEAD, THEY DIVE INTO THE LAKE BELOW...
...AND THUS FAIL TO SEE THE SILVERY STARSHIP HOVERING HIGH OVERHEAD...
A STARSHIP WHOSE GOLDEN LIGHT BURNS DOWNWARD INTO THE SUDDENLY BUBBLING WATERS...
...CAUSING THE PLAYFUL SWIMMERS TO ABRUPTLY DISAPPEAR.
OH, GOSH-- WHAT IS THAT THING?
I--I DON'T KNOW, JERRY.
JUST RUN!
5

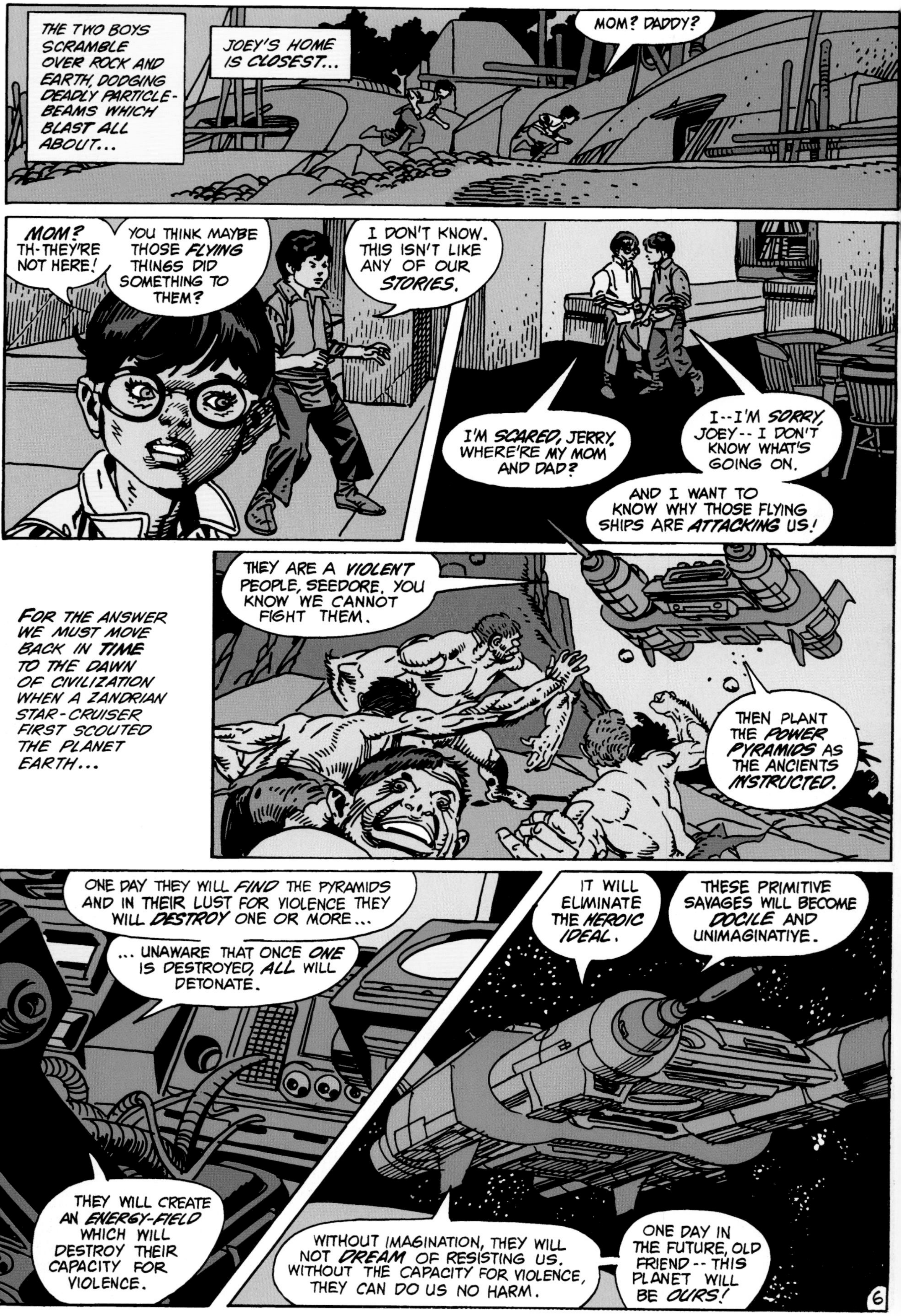
THE TWO BOYS SCRAMBLE OVER ROCK AND EARTH, DODGING DEADLY PARTICLE-BEAMS WHICH BLAST ALL ABOUT...
JOEY'S HOME IS CLOSEST...
MOM? DADDY?
MOM? TH-THEY'RE NOT HERE!
YOU THINK MAYBE THOSE FLYING THINGS DID SOMETHING TO THEM?
I DON'T KNOW. THIS ISN'T LIKE ANY OF OUR STORIES.
I'M SCARED, JERRY. WHERE'RE MY MOM AND DAD?
I--I'M SORRY, JOEY-- I DON'T KNOW WHAT'S GOING ON.
AND I WANT TO KNOW WHY THOSE FLYING SHIPS ARE ATTACKING US!
FOR THE ANSWER WE MUST MOVE BACK IN TIME TO THE DAWN OF CIVILIZATION WHEN A ZANDRIAN STAR-CRUISER FIRST SCOUTED THE PLANET EARTH...
THEY ARE A VIOLENT PEOPLE, SEEDORE. YOU KNOW WE CANNOT FIGHT THEM.
THEN PLANT THE POWER PYRAMIDS AS THE ANCIENTS INSTRUCTED.
ONE DAY THEY WILL FIND THE PYRAMIDS AND IN THEIR LUST FOR VIOLENCE THEY WILL DESTROY ONE OR MORE...
... UNAWARE THAT ONCE ONE IS DESTROYED, ALL WILL DETONATE.
THEY WILL CREATE AN ENERGY-FIELD WHICH WILL DESTROY THEIR CAPACITY FOR VIOLENCE.
IT WILL ELIMINATE THE HEROIC IDEAL.
THESE PRIMITIVE SAVAGES WILL BECOME DOCILE AND UNIMAGINATIVE.
WITHOUT IMAGINATION, THEY WILL NOT DREAM OF RESISTING US. WITHOUT THE CAPACITY FOR VIOLENCE, THEY CAN DO US NO HARM.
ONE DAY IN THE FUTURE, OLD FRIEND-- THIS PLANET WILL BE OURS!
6

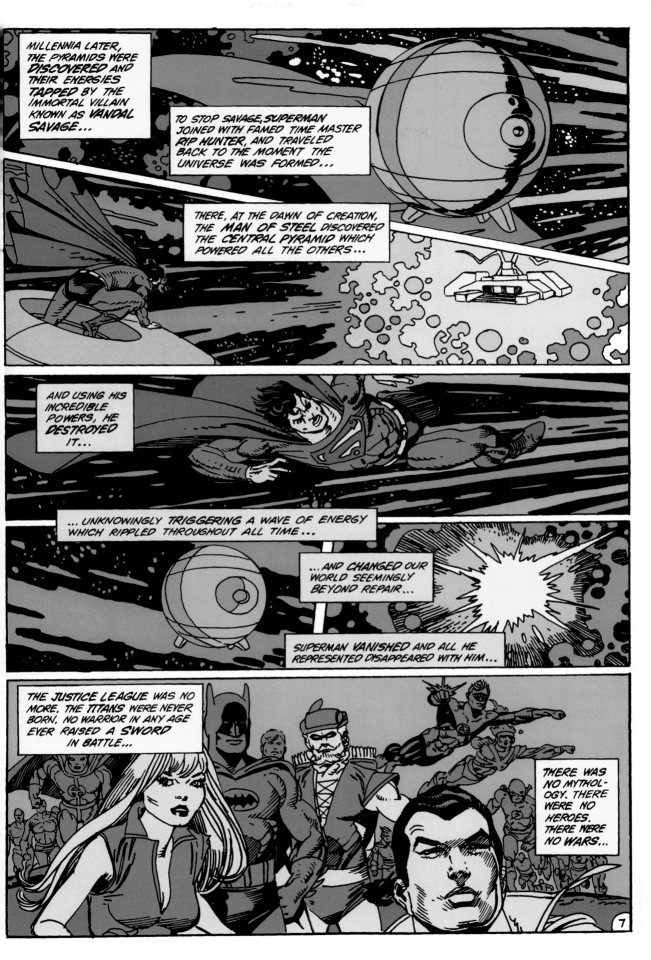

MILLENNIA LATER, THE PYRAMIDS WERE *DISCOVERED* AND THEIR ENERGIES TAPPED BY THE IMMORTAL VILLAIN KNOWN AS *VANDAL SAVAGE*...

TO STOP SAVAGE, SUPERMAN JOINED WITH FAMED TIME MASTER *RIP HUNTER*, AND TRAVELED BACK TO THE MOMENT THE UNIVERSE WAS FORMED...

THERE, AT THE DAWN OF CREATION, THE *MAN OF STEEL* DISCOVERED THE *CENTRAL PYRAMID* WHICH POWERED ALL THE OTHERS...

AND USING HIS INCREDIBLE POWERS, HE *DESTROYED* IT...

...UNKNOWINGLY TRIGGERING A WAVE OF ENERGY WHICH RIPPLED THROUGHOUT ALL TIME...

...AND *CHANGED* OUR WORLD SEEMINGLY BEYOND REPAIR...

SUPERMAN VANISHED AND ALL HE REPRESENTED DISAPPEARED WITH HIM...

THE JUSTICE LEAGUE WAS NO MORE. THE TITANS WERE NEVER BORN. NO WARRIOR IN ANY AGE EVER RAISED A SWORD IN BATTLE...

THERE WAS NO MYTHOLOGY. THERE WERE NO HEROES. THERE WERE NO WARS...

7

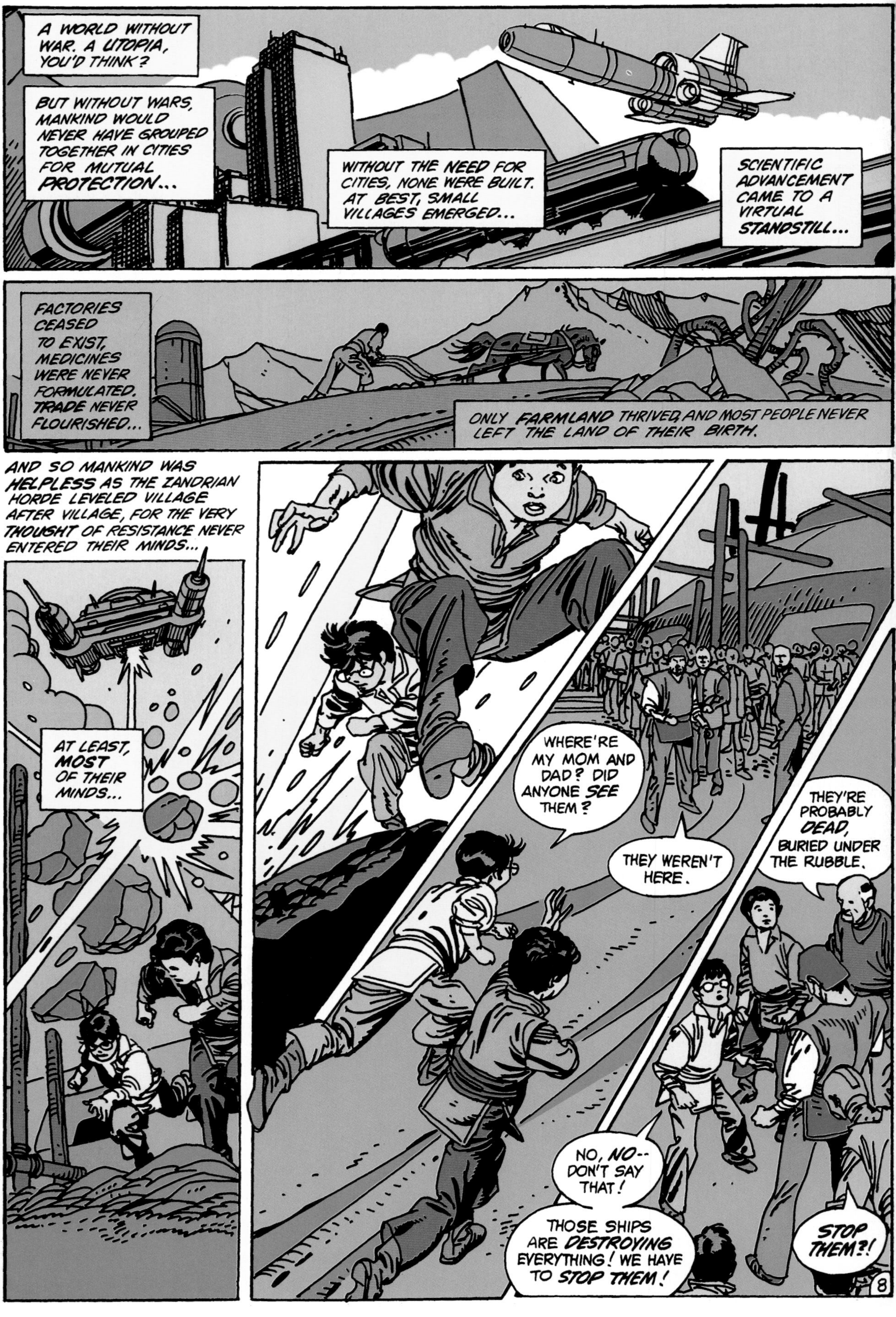
A WORLD WITHOUT WAR. A UTOPIA, YOU'D THINK?
BUT WITHOUT WARS, MANKIND WOULD NEVER HAVE GROUPED TOGETHER IN CITIES FOR MUTUAL PROTECTION...
WITHOUT THE NEED FOR CITIES, NONE WERE BUILT. AT BEST, SMALL VILLAGES EMERGED...
SCIENTIFIC ADVANCEMENT CAME TO A VIRTUAL STANDSTILL...
FACTORIES CEASED TO EXIST, MEDICINES WERE NEVER FORMULATED, TRADE NEVER FLOURISHED...
ONLY FARMLAND THRIVED, AND MOST PEOPLE NEVER LEFT THE LAND OF THEIR BIRTH.
AND SO MANKIND WAS HELPLESS AS THE ZANDRIAN HORDE LEVELED VILLAGE AFTER VILLAGE, FOR THE VERY THOUGHT OF RESISTANCE NEVER ENTERED THEIR MINDS...
AT LEAST, MOST OF THEIR MINDS...
WHERE'RE MY MOM AND DAD? DID ANYONE SEE THEM?
THEY WEREN'T HERE.
THEY'RE PROBABLY DEAD, BURIED UNDER THE RUBBLE.
NO, NO-- DON'T SAY THAT!
THOSE SHIPS ARE DESTROYING EVERYTHING! WE HAVE TO STOP THEM!
STOP THEM?!
8

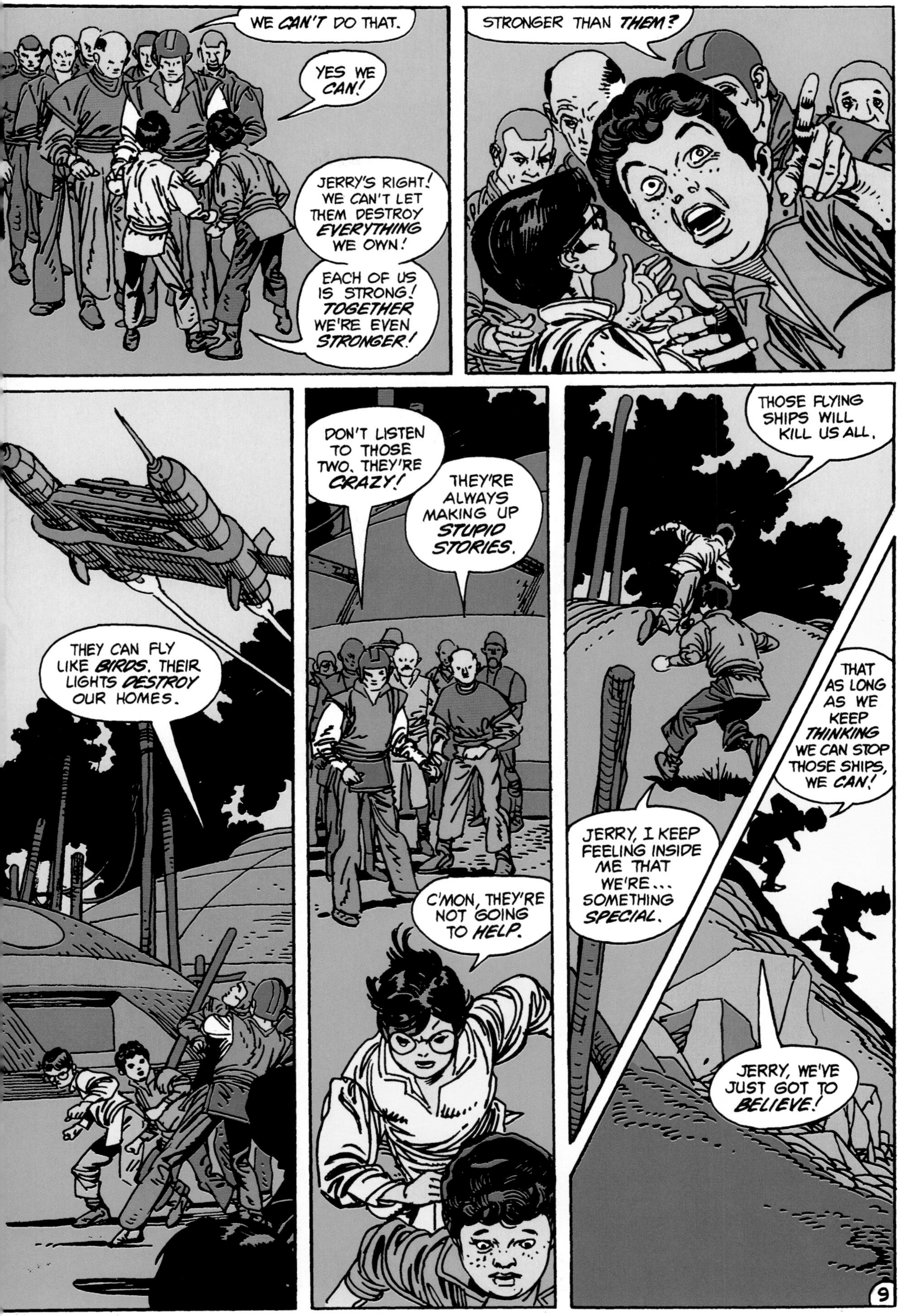
WE CAN'T DO THAT.
YES WE CAN!
JERRY'S RIGHT! WE CAN'T LET THEM DESTROY EVERYTHING WE OWN!
EACH OF US IS STRONG! TOGETHER WE'RE EVEN STRONGER!
STRONGER THAN THEM?
THEY CAN FLY LIKE BIRDS. THEIR LIGHTS DESTROY OUR HOMES.
DON'T LISTEN TO THOSE TWO. THEY'RE CRAZY!
THEY'RE ALWAYS MAKING UP STUPID STORIES.
C'MON, THEY'RE NOT GOING TO HELP.
THOSE FLYING SHIPS WILL KILL US ALL.
JERRY, I KEEP FEELING INSIDE ME THAT WE'RE... SOMETHING SPECIAL.
THAT AS LONG AS WE KEEP THINKING WE CAN STOP THOSE SHIPS, WE CAN!
JERRY, WE'VE JUST GOT TO BELIEVE!
9

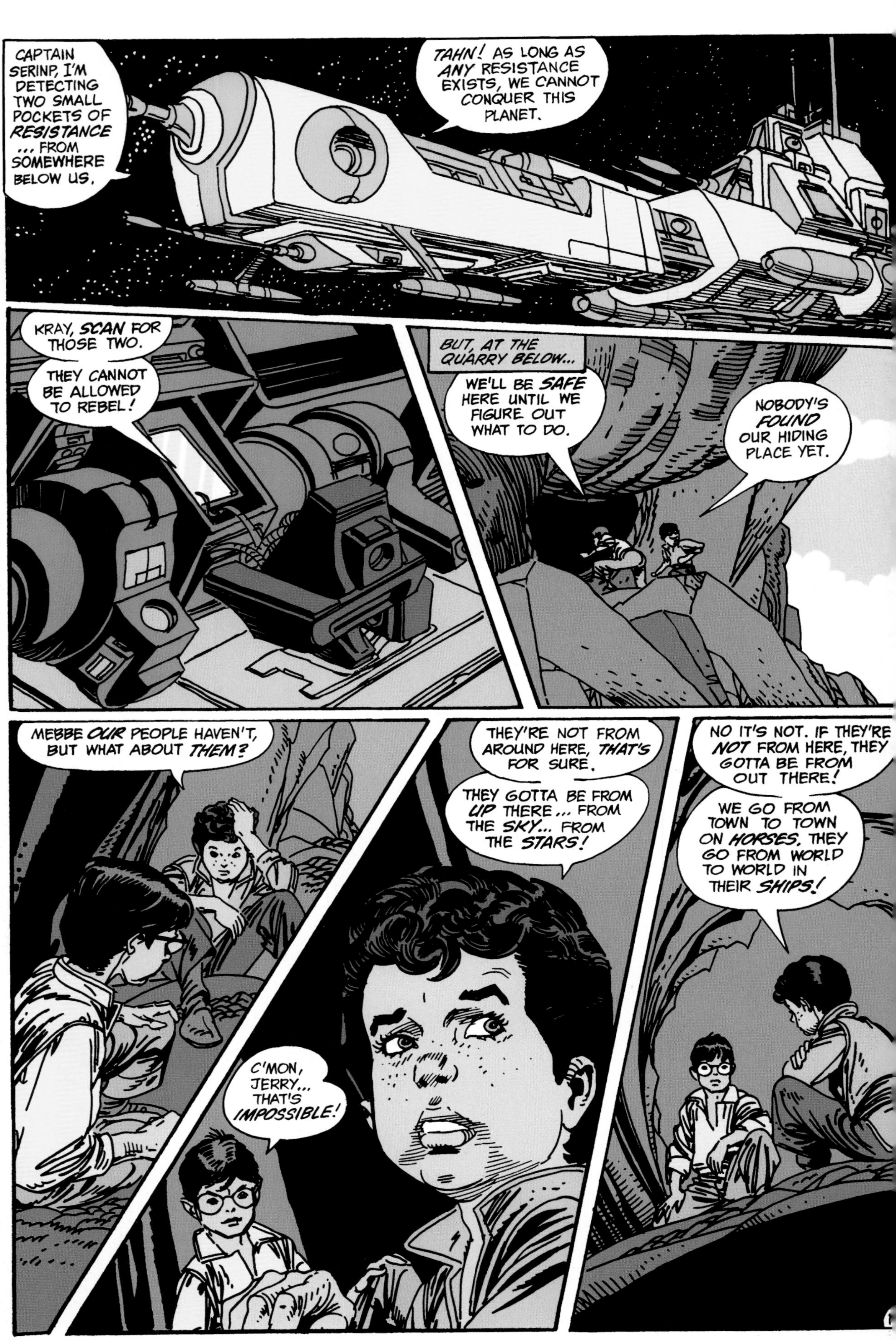
CAPTAIN SERINP, I'M DETECTING TWO SMALL POCKETS OF RESISTANCE ... FROM SOMEWHERE BELOW US.
TAHN! AS LONG AS ANY RESISTANCE EXISTS, WE CANNOT CONQUER THIS PLANET.
KRAY, SCAN FOR THOSE TWO.
THEY CANNOT BE ALLOWED TO REBEL!
BUT, AT THE QUARRY BELOW...
WE'LL BE SAFE HERE UNTIL WE FIGURE OUT WHAT TO DO.
NOBODY'S FOUND OUR HIDING PLACE YET.
MEBBE OUR PEOPLE HAVEN'T, BUT WHAT ABOUT THEM?
THEY'RE NOT FROM AROUND HERE, THAT'S FOR SURE.
THEY GOTTA BE FROM UP THERE... FROM THE SKY... FROM THE STARS!
C'MON, JERRY... THAT'S IMPOSSIBLE!
NO IT'S NOT. IF THEY'RE NOT FROM HERE, THEY GOTTA BE FROM OUT THERE!
WE GO FROM TOWN TO TOWN ON HORSES. THEY GO FROM WORLD TO WORLD IN THEIR SHIPS!

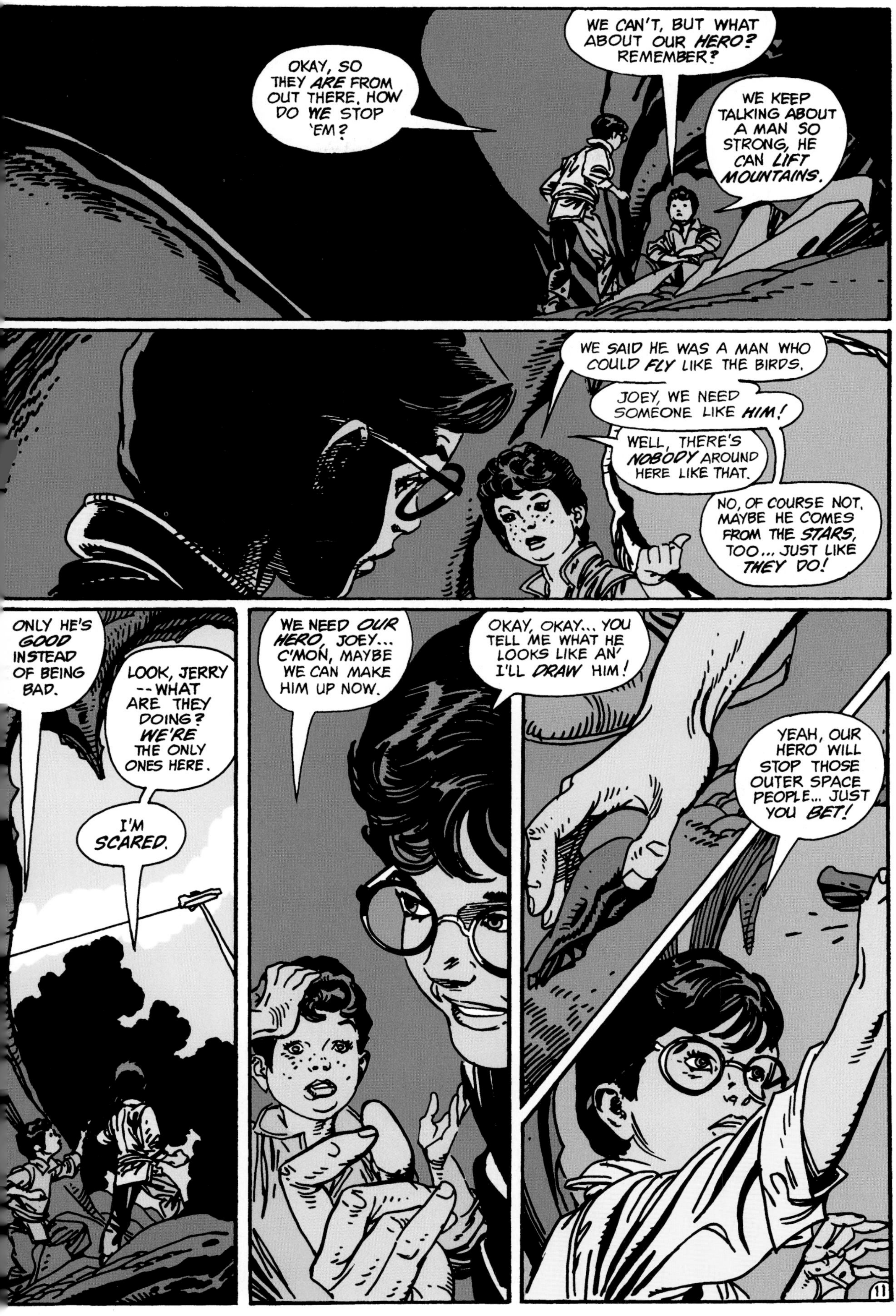
OKAY, SO THEY ARE FROM OUT THERE. HOW DO WE STOP 'EM?
WE CAN'T, BUT WHAT ABOUT OUR HERO? REMEMBER?
WE KEEP TALKING ABOUT A MAN SO STRONG, HE CAN LIFT MOUNTAINS.
WE SAID HE WAS A MAN WHO COULD FLY LIKE THE BIRDS.
JOEY, WE NEED SOMEONE LIKE HIM!
WELL, THERE'S NOBODY AROUND HERE LIKE THAT.
NO, OF COURSE NOT. MAYBE HE COMES FROM THE STARS, TOO... JUST LIKE THEY DO!
ONLY HE'S GOOD INSTEAD OF BEING BAD.
LOOK, JERRY --WHAT ARE THEY DOING? WE'RE THE ONLY ONES HERE.
I'M SCARED.
WE NEED OUR HERO, JOEY... C'MON, MAYBE WE CAN MAKE HIM UP NOW.
OKAY, OKAY... YOU TELL ME WHAT HE LOOKS LIKE AN' I'LL DRAW HIM!
YEAH, OUR HERO WILL STOP THOSE OUTER SPACE PEOPLE... JUST YOU BET!
11

SIR, RESISTANCE ENERGY IS *INCREASING*. THE HEROIC CONCEPT IS RE-FORMING.

WE'VE CONQUERED *HUNDREDS* OF WORLDS THIS WAY BEFORE. WHY DOES *THIS* PLANET REBEL?

THIS HAS ALWAYS BEEN A WORLD OF IDEAS. *TAHN!*-- THERE MUST BE SOME WAY TO SNUFF THAT SPARK OF IMAGINATION!

FIND THOSE TWO QUICKLY...

...BEFORE THEY *DESTROY* US!

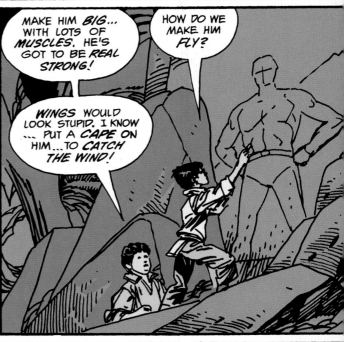

MAKE HIM *BIG*... WITH LOTS OF *MUSCLES*. HE'S GOT TO BE *REAL STRONG!*

HOW DO WE MAKE HIM *FLY?*

WINGS WOULD LOOK STUPID. I KNOW ... PUT A *CAPE* ON HIM...TO *CATCH THE WIND!*

AND GIVE HIM *SPECIAL BOOTS*... SO HE CAN *RUN* FASTER THAN ANYONE!

WE SHOULD PUT A *SYMBOL* ON HIM ... SOMETHING THAT WOULD MAKE PEOPLE KNOW HE'S *MORE* THAN JUST A MAN.

THEY SHOULD KNOW HE'S A...*SUPER MAN!*

I KNOW JUST THE SYMBOL, JERRY...

WELL, WHAT DO YOU THINK?

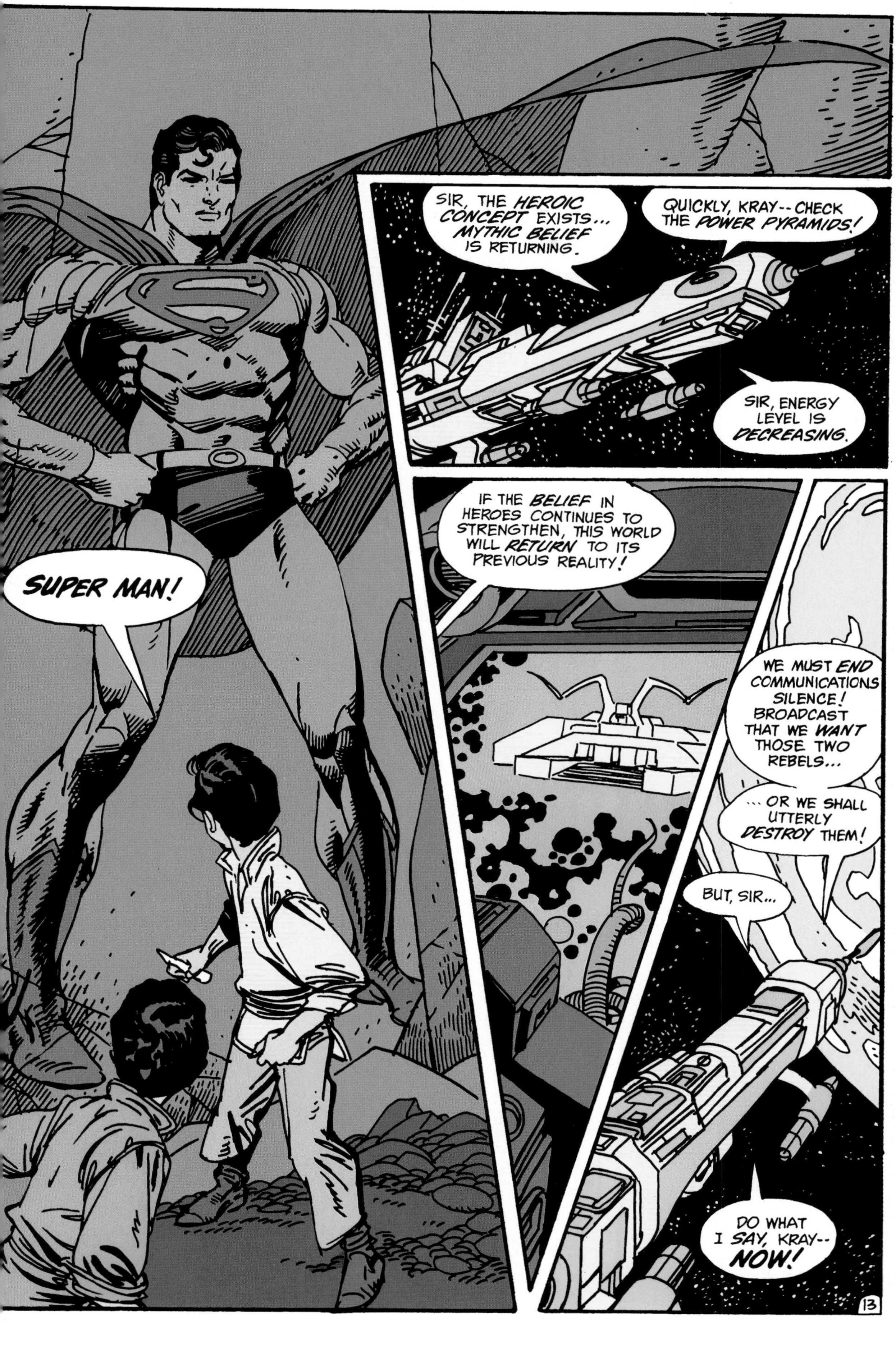
SUPER MAN!
SIR, THE HEROIC CONCEPT EXISTS... MYTHIC BELIEF IS RETURNING.
QUICKLY, KRAY--CHECK THE POWER PYRAMIDS!
SIR, ENERGY LEVEL IS DECREASING.
IF THE BELIEF IN HEROES CONTINUES TO STRENGTHEN, THIS WORLD WILL RETURN TO ITS PREVIOUS REALITY!
WE MUST END COMMUNICATIONS SILENCE! BROADCAST THAT WE WANT THOSE TWO REBELS...
...OR WE SHALL UTTERLY DESTROY THEM!
BUT, SIR...
DO WHAT I SAY, KRAY-- NOW!
13

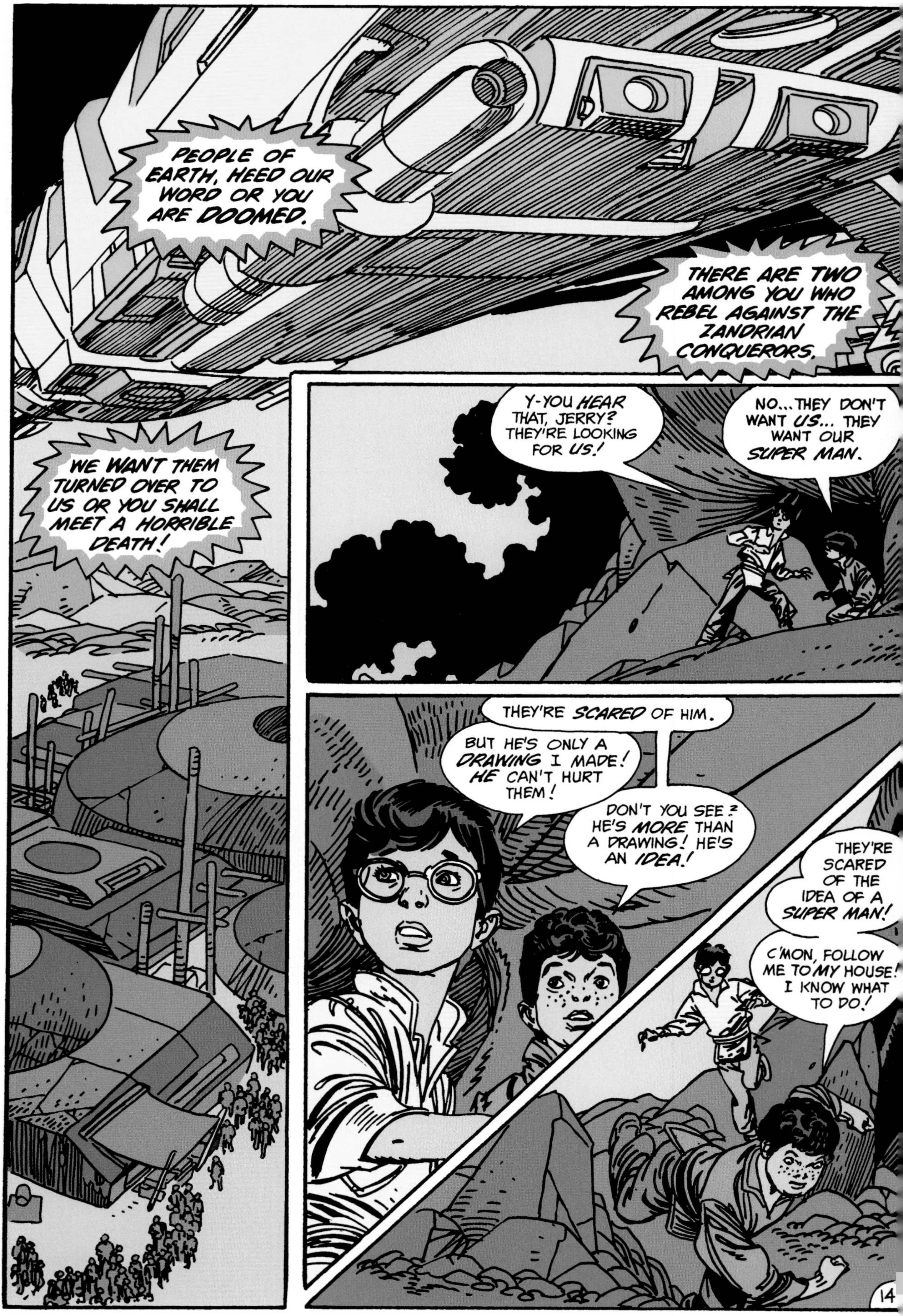
PEOPLE OF EARTH, HEED OUR WORD OR YOU ARE DOOMED.
THERE ARE TWO AMONG YOU WHO REBEL AGAINST THE ZANDRIAN CONQUERORS.
WE WANT THEM TURNED OVER TO US OR YOU SHALL MEET A HORRIBLE DEATH!
Y-YOU HEAR THAT, JERRY? THEY'RE LOOKING FOR US!
NO...THEY DON'T WANT US... THEY WANT OUR SUPER MAN.
THEY'RE SCARED OF HIM.
BUT HE'S ONLY A DRAWING I MADE! HE CAN'T HURT THEM!
DON'T YOU SEE? HE'S MORE THAN A DRAWING! HE'S AN IDEA!
THEY'RE SCARED OF THE IDEA OF A SUPER MAN!
C'MON, FOLLOW ME TO MY HOUSE! I KNOW WHAT TO DO!
14

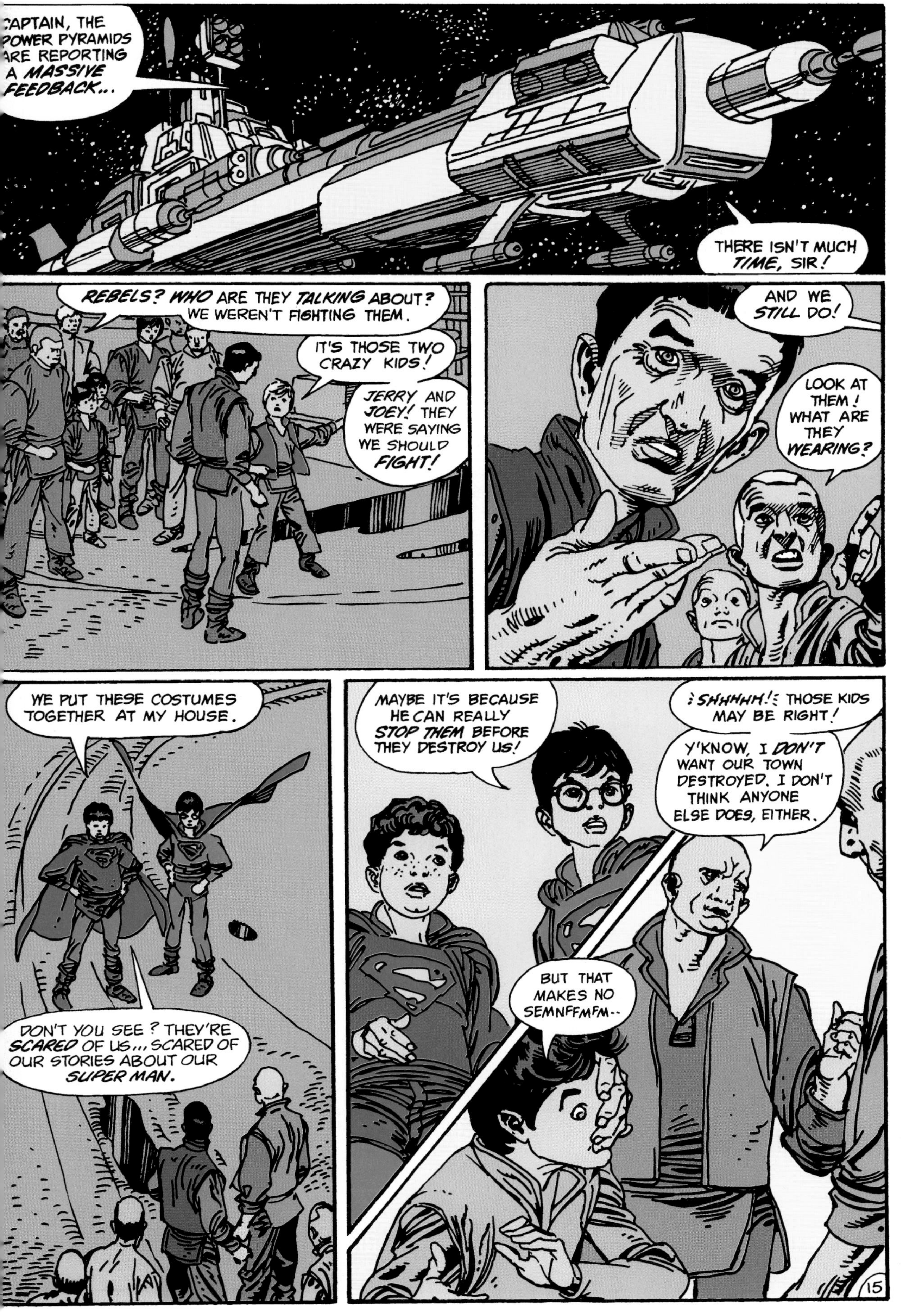
CAPTAIN, THE POWER PYRAMIDS ARE REPORTING A MASSIVE FEEDBACK...
THERE ISN'T MUCH TIME, SIR!
REBELS? WHO ARE THEY TALKING ABOUT? WE WEREN'T FIGHTING THEM.
IT'S THOSE TWO CRAZY KIDS!
JERRY AND JOEY! THEY WERE SAYING WE SHOULD FIGHT!
AND WE STILL DO!
LOOK AT THEM! WHAT ARE THEY WEARING?
WE PUT THESE COSTUMES TOGETHER AT MY HOUSE.
DON'T YOU SEE? THEY'RE SCARED OF US... SCARED OF OUR STORIES ABOUT OUR SUPER MAN.
MAYBE IT'S BECAUSE HE CAN REALLY STOP THEM BEFORE THEY DESTROY US!
SHHHHH! THOSE KIDS MAY BE RIGHT!
Y'KNOW, I DON'T WANT OUR TOWN DESTROYED. I DON'T THINK ANYONE ELSE DOES, EITHER.
BUT THAT MAKES NO SEMNFFMFM--
15

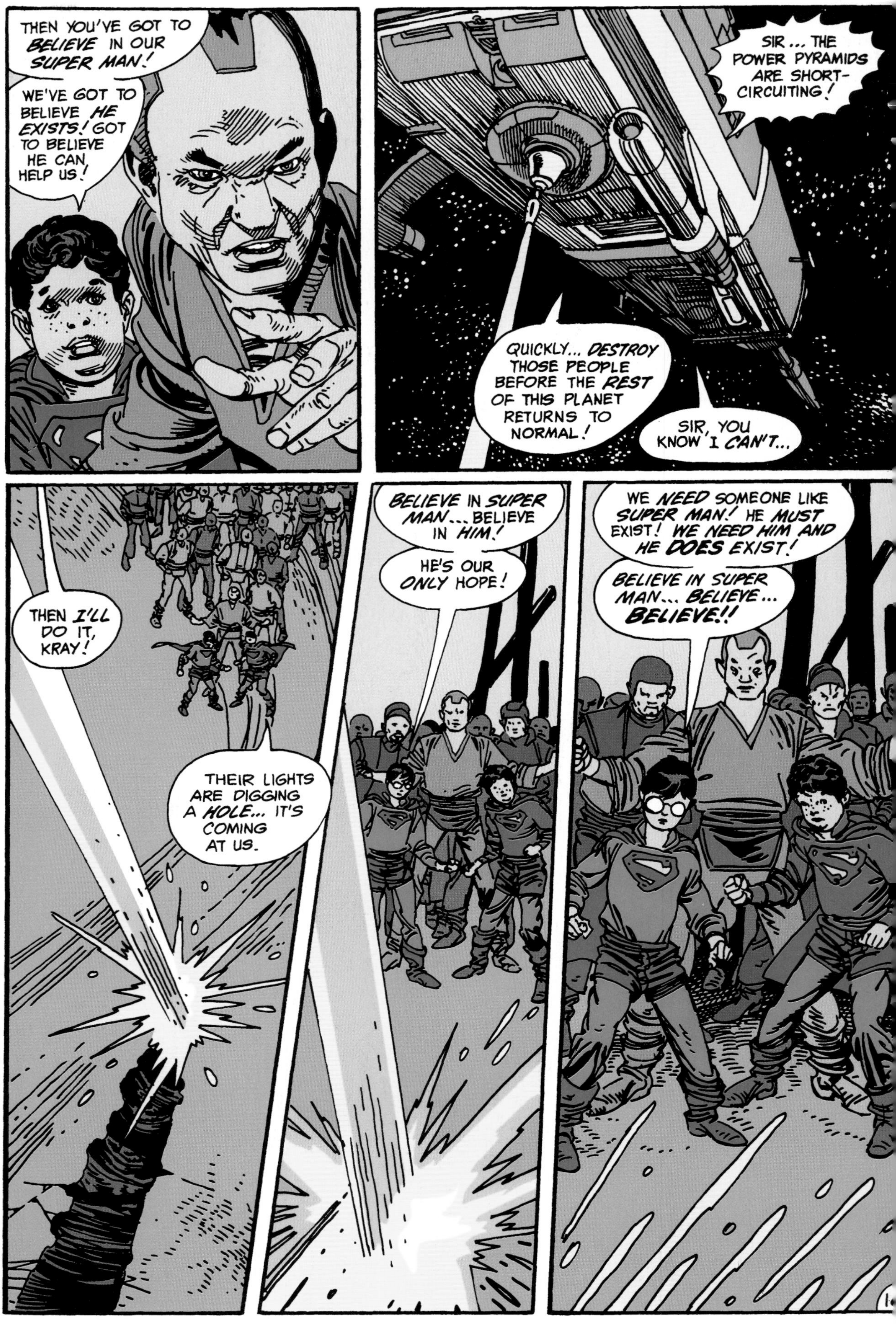
THEN YOU'VE GOT TO BELIEVE IN OUR SUPER MAN!
WE'VE GOT TO BELIEVE HE EXISTS! GOT TO BELIEVE HE CAN HELP US!
SIR... THE POWER PYRAMIDS ARE SHORT-CIRCUITING!
QUICKLY... DESTROY THOSE PEOPLE BEFORE THE REST OF THIS PLANET RETURNS TO NORMAL!
SIR, YOU KNOW I CAN'T...
THEN I'LL DO IT, KRAY!
THEIR LIGHTS ARE DIGGING A HOLE... IT'S COMING AT US.
BELIEVE IN SUPER MAN... BELIEVE IN HIM!
HE'S OUR ONLY HOPE!
WE NEED SOMEONE LIKE SUPER MAN! HE MUST EXIST! WE NEED HIM AND HE DOES EXIST!
BELIEVE IN SUPER MAN... BELIEVE... BELIEVE!!

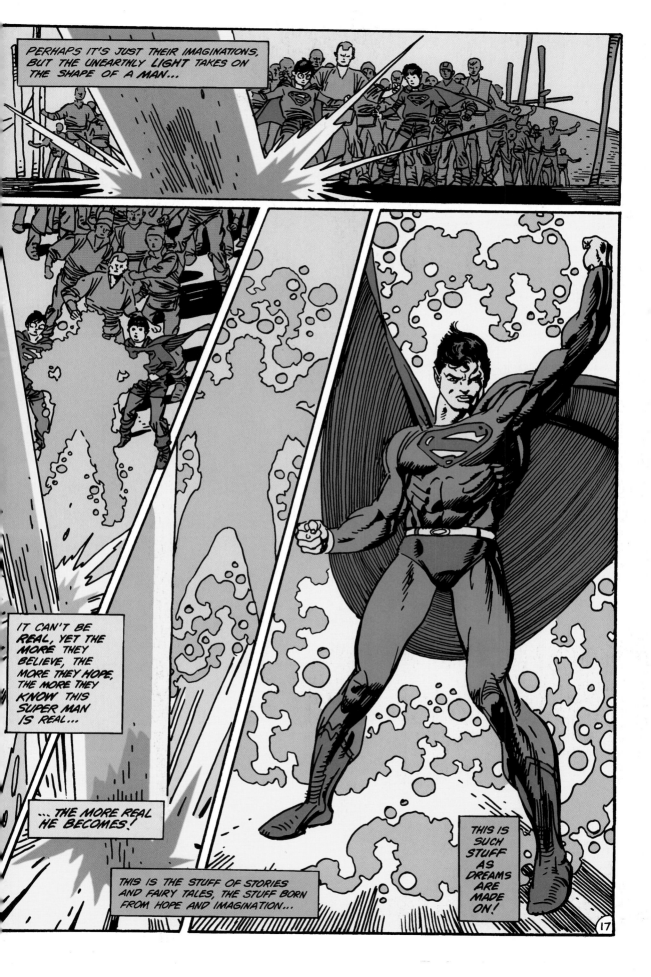

PERHAPS IT'S JUST THEIR IMAGINATIONS, BUT THE UNEARTHLY *LIGHT* TAKES ON THE SHAPE OF A *MAN*...

IT CAN'T BE *REAL*, YET THE MORE THEY *BELIEVE*, THE MORE THEY *HOPE*, THE MORE THEY *KNOW* THIS *SUPER MAN* IS REAL...

...THE MORE REAL HE *BECOMES!*

THIS IS THE STUFF OF STORIES AND FAIRY TALES, THE STUFF BORN FROM HOPE AND IMAGINATION...

THIS IS SUCH STUFF AS DREAMS ARE MADE ON!

17

HE IS EVERY SILENT KNIGHT MARCHING OFF TO BATTLE THE DASTARDLY FOE. HE IS EVERY HERO BORN TO SAVE THE DISTRESSED MAIDEN.

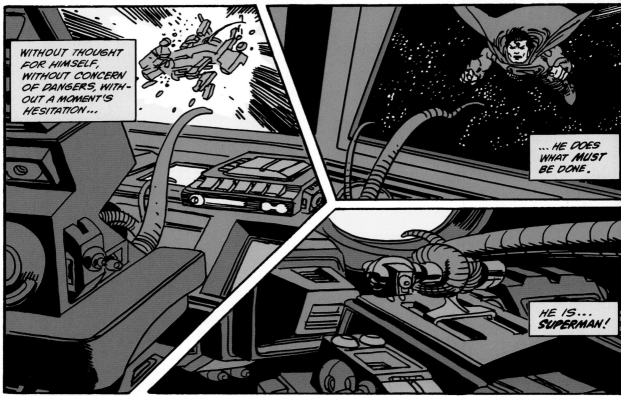

WITHOUT THOUGHT FOR HIMSELF, WITHOUT CONCERN OF DANGERS, WITHOUT A MOMENT'S HESITATION...

...HE DOES WHAT MUST BE DONE.

HE IS... SUPERMAN!

STOP HIM, KRAY! STOP HIM!

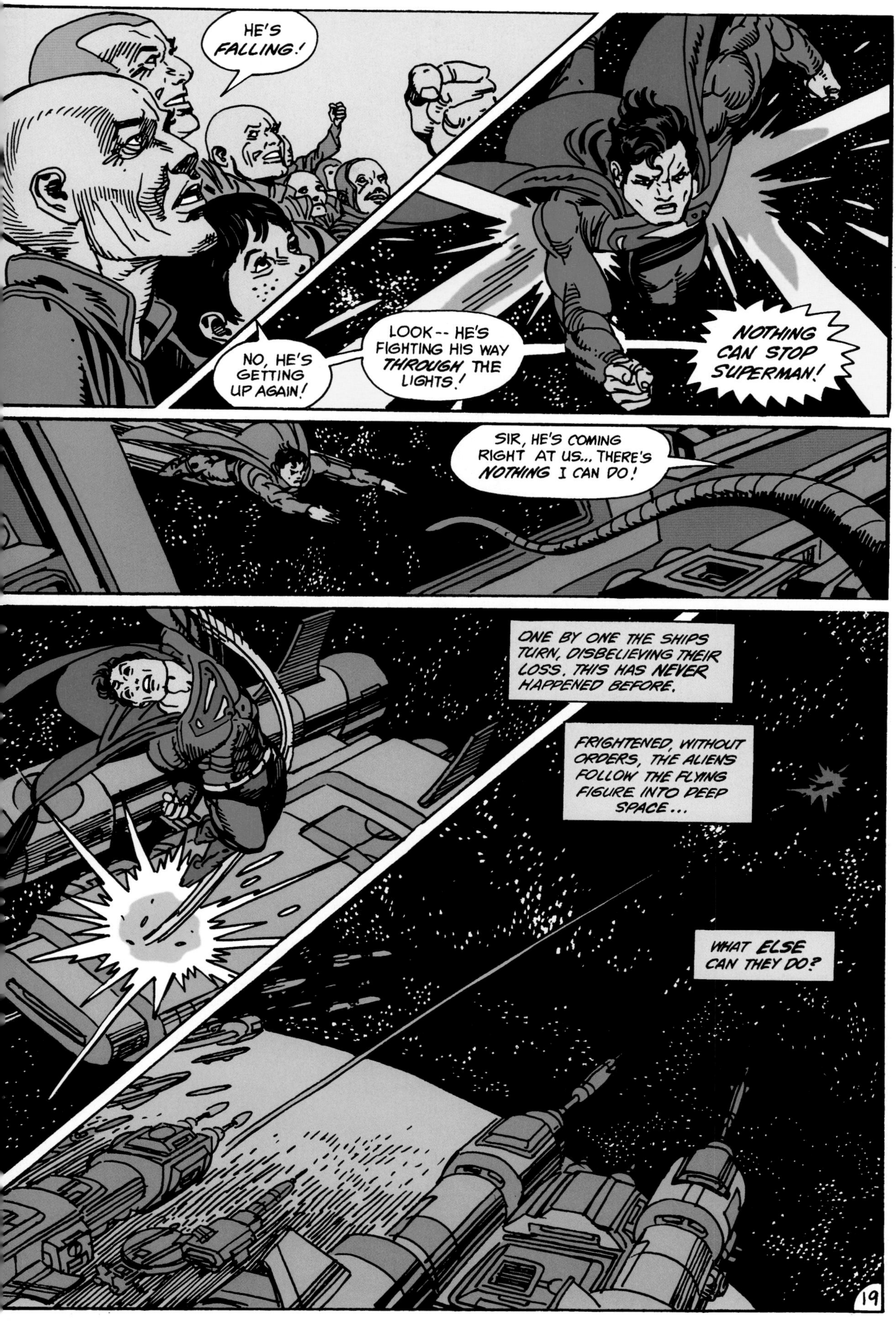
HE'S FALLING!
NO, HE'S GETTING UP AGAIN!
LOOK -- HE'S FIGHTING HIS WAY THROUGH THE LIGHTS!
NOTHING CAN STOP SUPERMAN!
SIR, HE'S COMING RIGHT AT US... THERE'S NOTHING I CAN DO!
ONE BY ONE THE SHIPS TURN, DISBELIEVING THEIR LOSS. THIS HAS NEVER HAPPENED BEFORE.
FRIGHTENED, WITHOUT ORDERS, THE ALIENS FOLLOW THE FLYING FIGURE INTO DEEP SPACE...
WHAT ELSE CAN THEY DO?
19

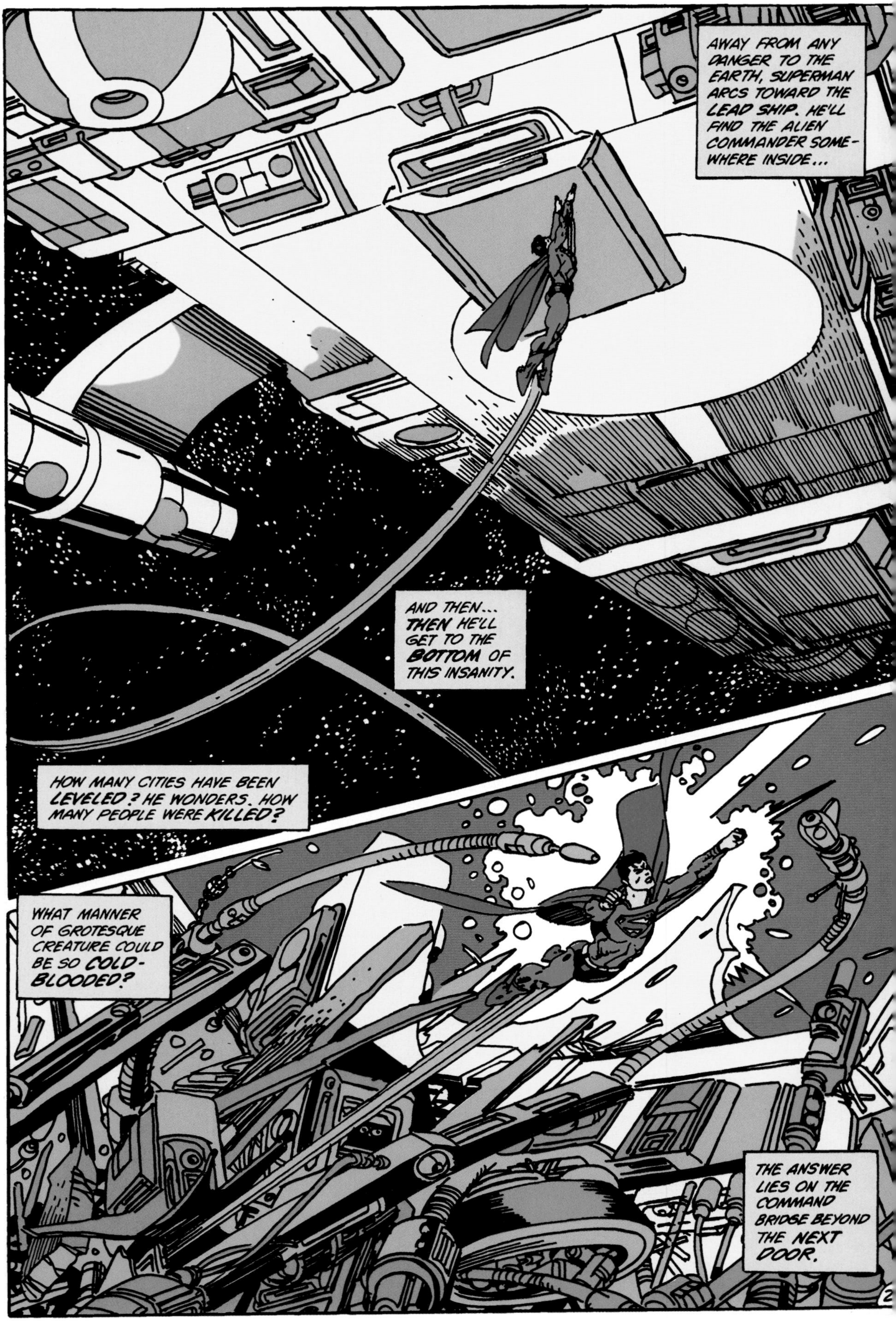
AWAY FROM ANY DANGER TO THE EARTH, SUPERMAN ARCS TOWARD THE LEAD SHIP. HE'LL FIND THE ALIEN COMMANDER SOME-WHERE INSIDE...
AND THEN... THEN HE'LL GET TO THE BOTTOM OF THIS INSANITY.
HOW MANY CITIES HAVE BEEN LEVELED? HE WONDERS. HOW MANY PEOPLE WERE KILLED?
WHAT MANNER OF GROTESQUE CREATURE COULD BE SO COLD-BLOODED?
THE ANSWER LIES ON THE COMMAND BRIDGE BEYOND THE NEXT DOOR.

SUPERMAN? PLEASE DON'T *ATTACK* US.

W-WE'RE *SORRY* FOR WHAT WE HAVE DONE.

DON'T *LOOK* AT US LIKE THAT. WE'RE NOT MURDERERS. WE'VE *NEVER* KILLED... NO MATTER WHAT WE SAID.

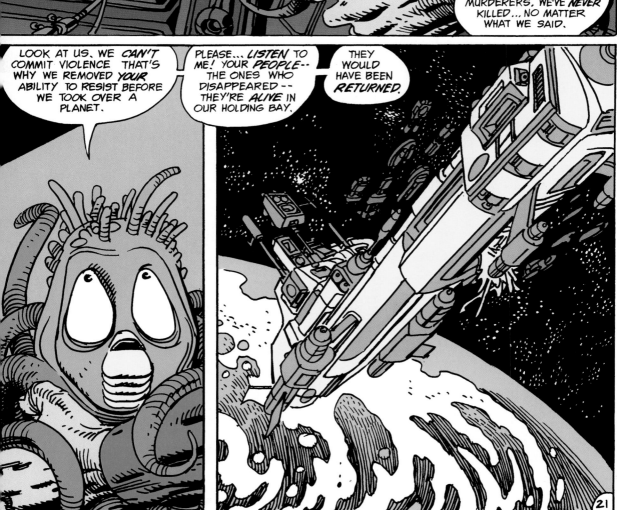

LOOK AT US. WE *CAN'T* COMMIT VIOLENCE. THAT'S WHY WE REMOVED *YOUR* ABILITY TO RESIST BEFORE WE TOOK OVER A PLANET.

PLEASE... *LISTEN* TO ME! YOUR *PEOPLE*-- THE ONES WHO DISAPPEARED -- THEY'RE *ALIVE* IN OUR HOLDING BAY.

THEY WOULD HAVE BEEN *RETURNED.*

21

229

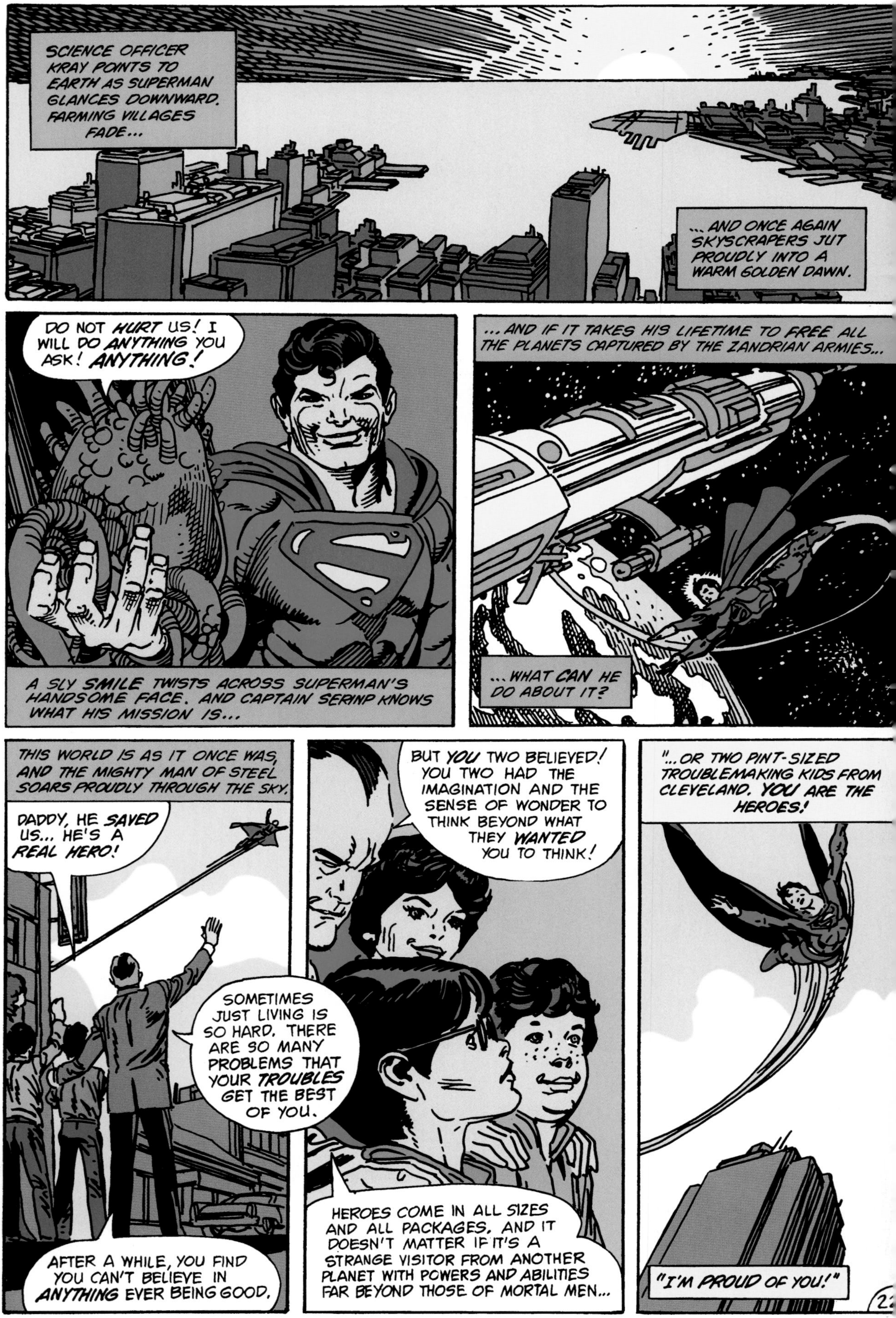
SCIENCE OFFICER KRAY POINTS TO EARTH AS SUPERMAN GLANCES DOWNWARD. FARMING VILLAGES FADE...
...AND ONCE AGAIN SKYSCRAPERS JUT PROUDLY INTO A WARM GOLDEN DAWN.
DO NOT HURT US! I WILL DO ANYTHING YOU ASK! ANYTHING!
A SLY SMILE TWISTS ACROSS SUPERMAN'S HANDSOME FACE. AND CAPTAIN SERINP KNOWS WHAT HIS MISSION IS...
...AND IF IT TAKES HIS LIFETIME TO FREE ALL THE PLANETS CAPTURED BY THE ZANDRIAN ARMIES...
...WHAT CAN HE DO ABOUT IT?
THIS WORLD IS AS IT ONCE WAS, AND THE MIGHTY MAN OF STEEL SOARS PROUDLY THROUGH THE SKY.
DADDY, HE SAVED US... HE'S A REAL HERO!
SOMETIMES JUST LIVING IS SO HARD. THERE ARE SO MANY PROBLEMS THAT YOUR TROUBLES GET THE BEST OF YOU.
AFTER A WHILE, YOU FIND YOU CAN'T BELIEVE IN ANYTHING EVER BEING GOOD.
BUT YOU TWO BELIEVED! YOU TWO HAD THE IMAGINATION AND THE SENSE OF WONDER TO THINK BEYOND WHAT THEY WANTED YOU TO THINK!
HEROES COME IN ALL SIZES AND ALL PACKAGES, AND IT DOESN'T MATTER IF IT'S A STRANGE VISITOR FROM ANOTHER PLANET WITH POWERS AND ABILITIES FAR BEYOND THOSE OF MORTAL MEN...
"...OR TWO PINT-SIZED TROUBLEMAKING KIDS FROM CLEVELAND. YOU ARE THE HEROES!
"I'M PROUD OF YOU!"

HIS MISSION IS DONE AND SUPERMAN IS PLEASED, NOT WITH HIMSELF... BUT WITH HIS SUCCESS.

NOW IT'S TIME TO RETURN HOME.

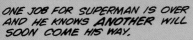

ONE JOB FOR SUPERMAN IS OVER AND HE KNOWS *ANOTHER* WILL SOON COME HIS WAY.

MEANWHILE, IN A SMALL HOUSE IN SUBURBAN METROPOLIS...

FORGET IT, JACK-- I CAN'T THINK OF ANYTHING.

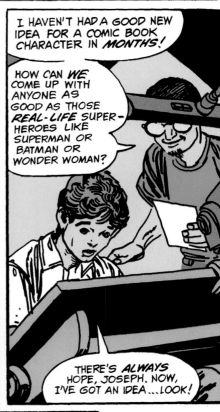

I HAVEN'T HAD A GOOD NEW IDEA FOR A COMIC BOOK CHARACTER IN *MONTHS!*

HOW CAN *WE* COME UP WITH ANYONE AS GOOD AS THOSE *REAL-LIFE* SUPER-HEROES LIKE SUPERMAN OR BATMAN OR WONDER WOMAN?

THERE'S *ALWAYS* HOPE, JOSEPH. NOW, I'VE GOT AN IDEA...LOOK!

WHAT DO YOU *THINK?*

WOW! SUDDENLY I'M GETTING AN IDEA, TOO!

HE'S GONNA BE *GREAT!* LISTEN, HERE'S WHAT WE DO...

THIS IS GOING TO BE OUR *GREATEST* IDEA EVER!

Dedicated to JERRY SIEGEL and JOE SHUSTER, whose imagination led generations to even more imaginings. With deep respect from JULIE, MARV, and GIL.

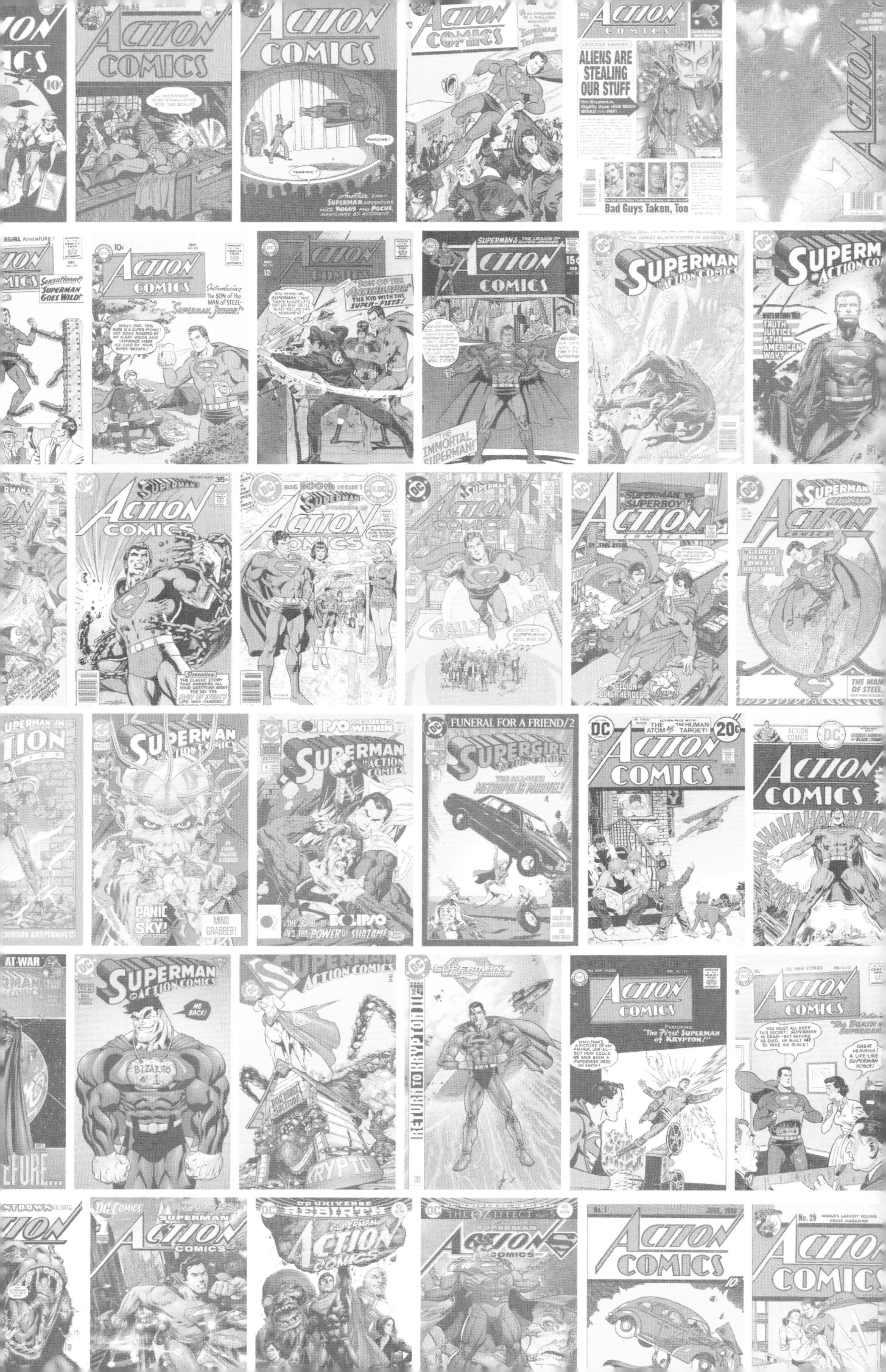

ACTION COMICS
10¢
No. 85
ACTION COMICS
...MASSAGE IS SO STIMULATING FOR THE SCALP!
ACTION COMICS
AMAZING!
TERRIFIC!
Another ZANY SUPERMAN ADVENTURE with HOCUS and POCUS, MAGICIANS BY ACCIDENT!
ACTION COMICS
BE AN EYEWITNESS TO A THRILLING MANHUNT
SUPERMAN ON TELEVISION
ACTION COMICS
SHOCKER REPORT:
ALIENS ARE STEALING OUR STUFF
EXCLUSIVE!
Bad Guys Taken, Too
ACTION
Sensational!
"SUPERMAN GOES WILD!"
10¢
ACTION COMICS
Introducing The SON of the MAN of STEEL--
"SUPERMAN, JUNIOR"
GOLLY, DAD, THIS SURE IS A SUPER-PICNIC! HOT DOGS ROASTED BY MY X-RAY VISION AND LEMONADE MADE ICE-COLD BY YOUR SUPER-BREATH!
ACTION COMICS
12¢
SON OF THE ANNIHILATOR! THE KID WITH THE SUPER-FISTS!
SUPERMAN & THE LEGION OF SUPER-HEROES
ACTION COMICS
15¢
THE IMMORTAL SUPERMAN!
THE GREAT SLIMP WORKS OF KANDOR
SUPERMAN IN ACTION COMICS
SUPERMAN IN ACTION COMICS
TRUTH, JUSTICE & THE AMERICAN WAY?
SUPERMAN
ACTION COMICS
35¢
Presenting: THE CLASSIC STORY THAT ANSWERS ALL YOUR QUESTIONS ABOUT THE DAY THE MAN OF STEEL'S LIFE WAS CHANGED!
BIG 500th ISSUE!
$1.00
SUPERMAN STARRING IN ACTION COMICS
SUPERMAN
ACTION COMICS
DAILY PLANET
GOOD-BYE, SUPERMAN! WE'LL MISS YOU!
SUPERMAN VS. SUPERBOY
ACTION COMICS
BY JOHN BYRNE
LEGION OF SUPER-HEROES
SUPERMAN
ACTION COMICS
GEORGE PEREZ BRETT BREEDING
THE MAN OF STEEL
SUPERMAN IN ACTION COMICS
SUPERMAN IN ACTION COMICS
PANIC IN THE SKY!
MIND GRABBER!
ECLIPSO THE DARKNESS WITHIN
SUPERMAN IN ACTION COMICS
THE EVIL OF ECLIPSO VS. THE POWER OF SHAZAM!
FUNERAL FOR A FRIEND/2
SUPERGIRL IN ACTION COMICS
THE ALL-NEW METROPOLIS MARVEL!
ACTION COMICS
IN THIS ISSUE THE ATOM AND THE HUMAN TARGET!
20¢
ACTION COMICS
HAHAHAHAHAHA
AT WAR
SUPERMAN IN ACTION COMICS
ME BACK!
BIZARRO #1
SUPERMAN IN ACTION COMICS
KRYPTO
SUPERMAN IN ACTION COMICS
RETURN TO KRYPTON II
ALL NEW STORIES
ACTION COMICS
FEATURING "The First SUPERMAN of KRYPTON!"
WHY, THAT'S A PICTURE OF MY FATHER, JOR-EL-- BUT HOW COULD HE HAVE BEEN A SUPERMAN HERE ON EARTH?
ALL NEW STORIES
ACTION COMICS
"The Death of Superman!"
YOU MUST ALL KEEP THIS SECRET! SUPERMAN IS DEAD--BUT BEFORE HE DIED, HE BUILT ME TO TAKE HIS PLACE!
GREAT HEAVENS! A LIFE-LIKE SUPERMAN ROBOT!
ACTION
DC COMICS
THE NEW 52!
SUPERMAN
ACTION COMICS
DC UNIVERSE REBIRTH
SUPERMAN ACTION COMICS
THE OZ EFFECT
SUPERMAN ACTION COMICS
No. 1
JUNE, 1938
ACTION COMICS
10¢
No. 29
WORLD'S LARGEST SELLING COMIC MAGAZINE!
ACTION COMICS

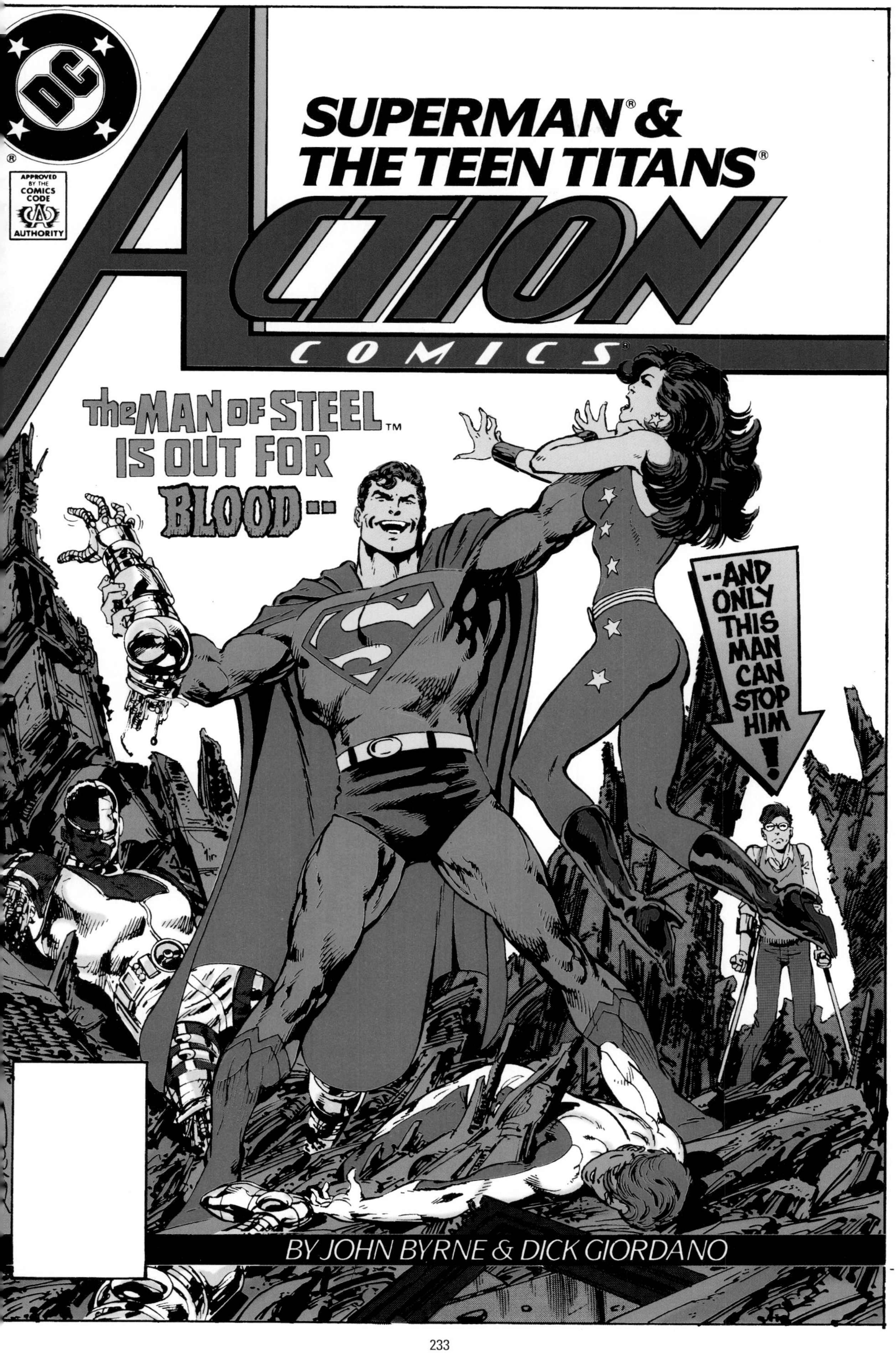

APPROVED BY THE COMICS CODE AUTHORITY
SUPERMAN® & THE TEEN TITANS®
ACTION COMICS®
The MAN of STEEL™ IS OUT FOR BLOOD--
--AND ONLY THIS MAN CAN STOP HIM!
BY JOHN BYRNE & DICK GIORDANO

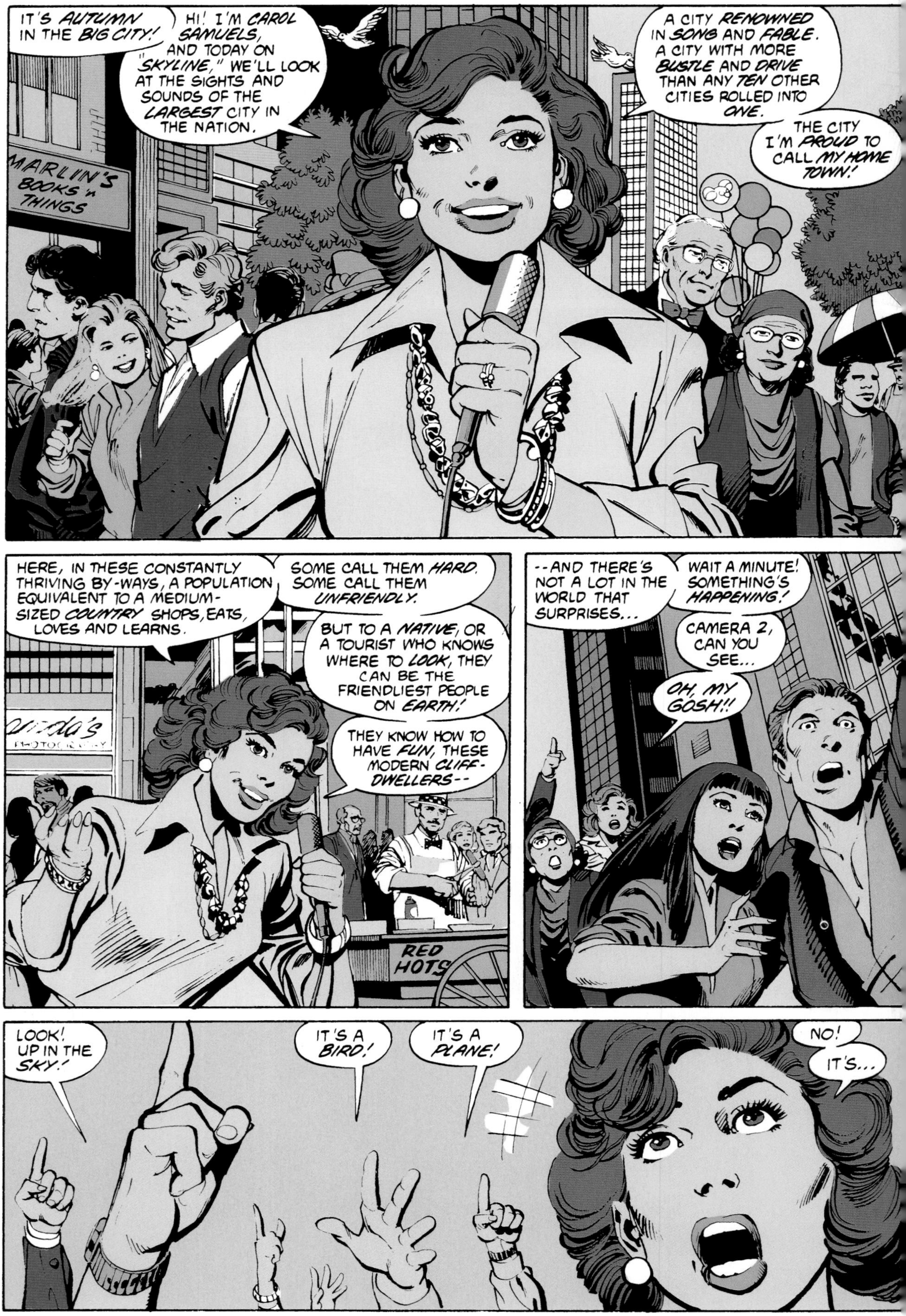
IT'S AUTUMN IN THE BIG CITY!
HI! I'M CAROL SAMUELS, AND TODAY ON "SKYLINE," WE'LL LOOK AT THE SIGHTS AND SOUNDS OF THE LARGEST CITY IN THE NATION.
MARLIN'S BOOKS 'n THINGS
A CITY RENOWNED IN SONG AND FABLE. A CITY WITH MORE BUSTLE AND DRIVE THAN ANY TEN OTHER CITIES ROLLED INTO ONE.
THE CITY I'M PROUD TO CALL MY HOME TOWN!
HERE, IN THESE CONSTANTLY THRIVING BY-WAYS, A POPULATION EQUIVALENT TO A MEDIUM-SIZED COUNTRY SHOPS, EATS, LOVES AND LEARNS.
SOME CALL THEM HARD. SOME CALL THEM UNFRIENDLY.
BUT TO A NATIVE, OR A TOURIST WHO KNOWS WHERE TO LOOK, THEY CAN BE THE FRIENDLIEST PEOPLE ON EARTH!
THEY KNOW HOW TO HAVE FUN, THESE MODERN CLIFF-DWELLERS--
RED HOTS
--AND THERE'S NOT A LOT IN THE WORLD THAT SURPRISES...
WAIT A MINUTE! SOMETHING'S HAPPENING!
CAMERA 2, CAN YOU SEE...
OH, MY GOSH!!
LOOK! UP IN THE SKY!
IT'S A BIRD!
IT'S A PLANE!
NO!
IT'S...

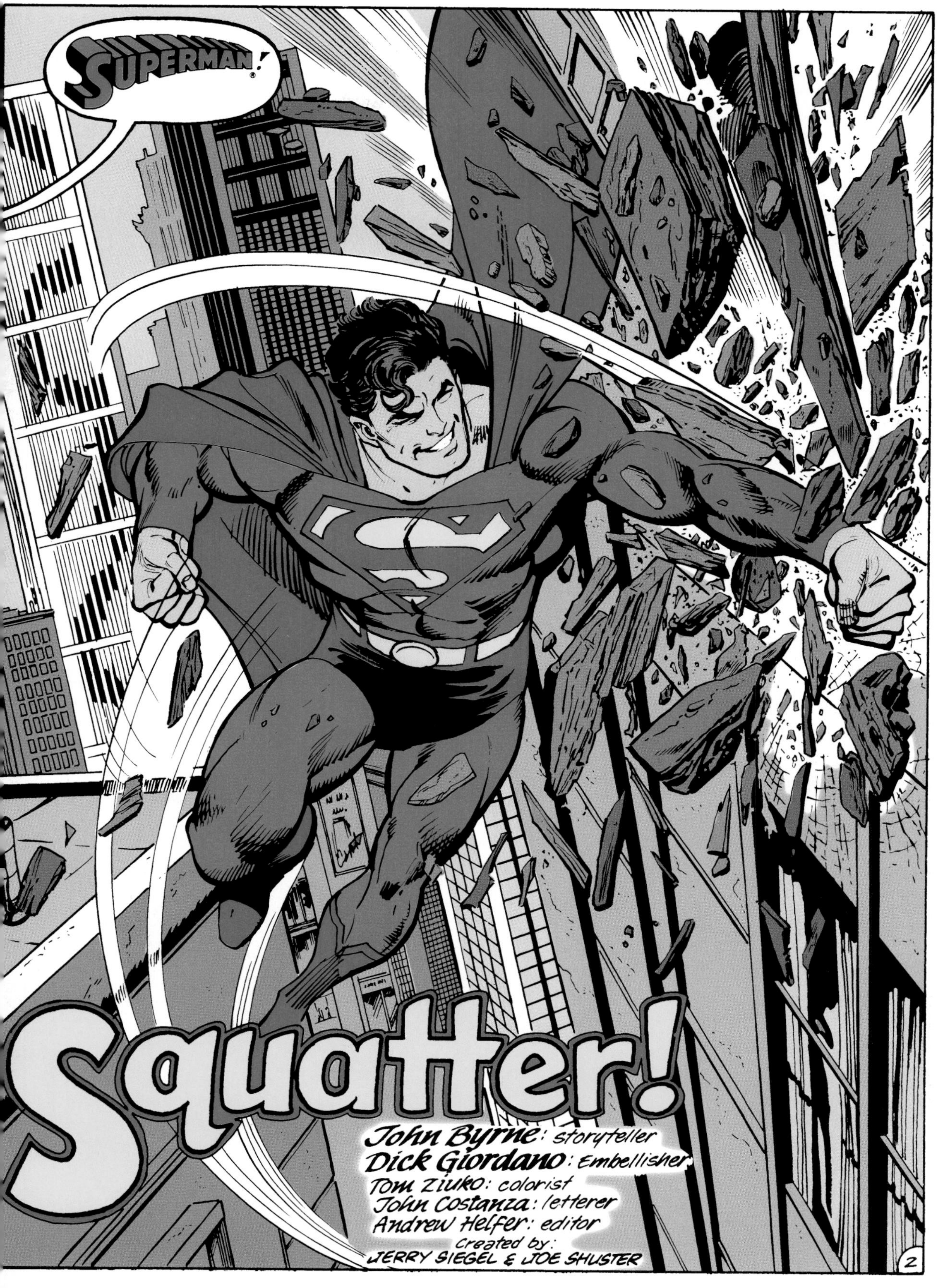
SUPERMAN!
Squatter!
John Byrne: storyteller
Dick Giordano: Embellisher
Tom Ziuko: colorist
John Costanza: letterer
Andrew Helfer: editor
Created by:
JERRY SIEGEL & JOE SHUSTER
2

WHAT... WHAT'S HE *DOING*?

HE'S *SMASHING* THROUGH ALL THE SKY-SCRAPERS!!

HE'S GONE *CRAZY*!!

SUPERMAN HAS GONE *MAD*!!

SH-OOM!

KRAM!

KRAK!

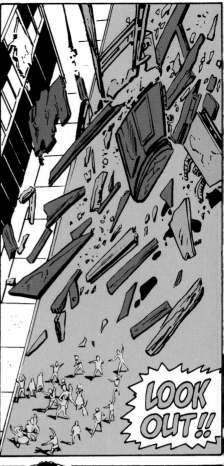

LOOK OUT!!

HOLY...!!

TH' WHOLE *TOP* OF THAT TOWER'S COMIN' DOWN ON TH' *STREET*!!

THERE'S *NO WAY* ALL THOSE PEDESTRIANS CAN GET *CLEAR* IN TIME!

CAN'T SOMEBODY *DO* SOMETHING?!?

SOMEBODY CAN SURE *TRY*, MA'AM.

--AND HIS *NAME* IS *CYBORG*!!

3

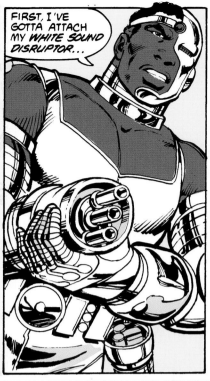

FIRST, I'VE GOTTA ATTACH MY *WHITE SOUND DISRUPTOR*...

...THEN FIRE MY *GRAPPLING LINE* UP TO THE TOP OF THE *UNDAMAGED* TOWERS...

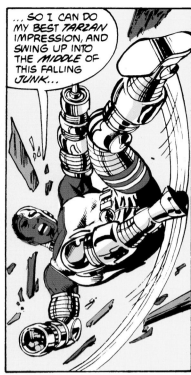

...SO I CAN DO MY BEST *TARZAN* IMPRESSION, AND SWING UP INTO THE *MIDDLE* OF THIS FALLING *JUNK*...

...AND BLAST IT ALL TO *DUST* BEFORE IT HITS THE STREET!

IT *WORKED!*

SOME OF THOSE FOLKS DOWN BELOW MAY FIND THEMSELVES *ITCHING* AND *SNEEZING* FOR A WHILE...

...BUT THAT'S A WHOLE LOT BETTER'N BEING *DEAD.*

NOW...

...LET'S SEE IF WE CAN'T FIND OUT WHAT'S GOT *INTO* THE *MAN OF STEEL!*

4

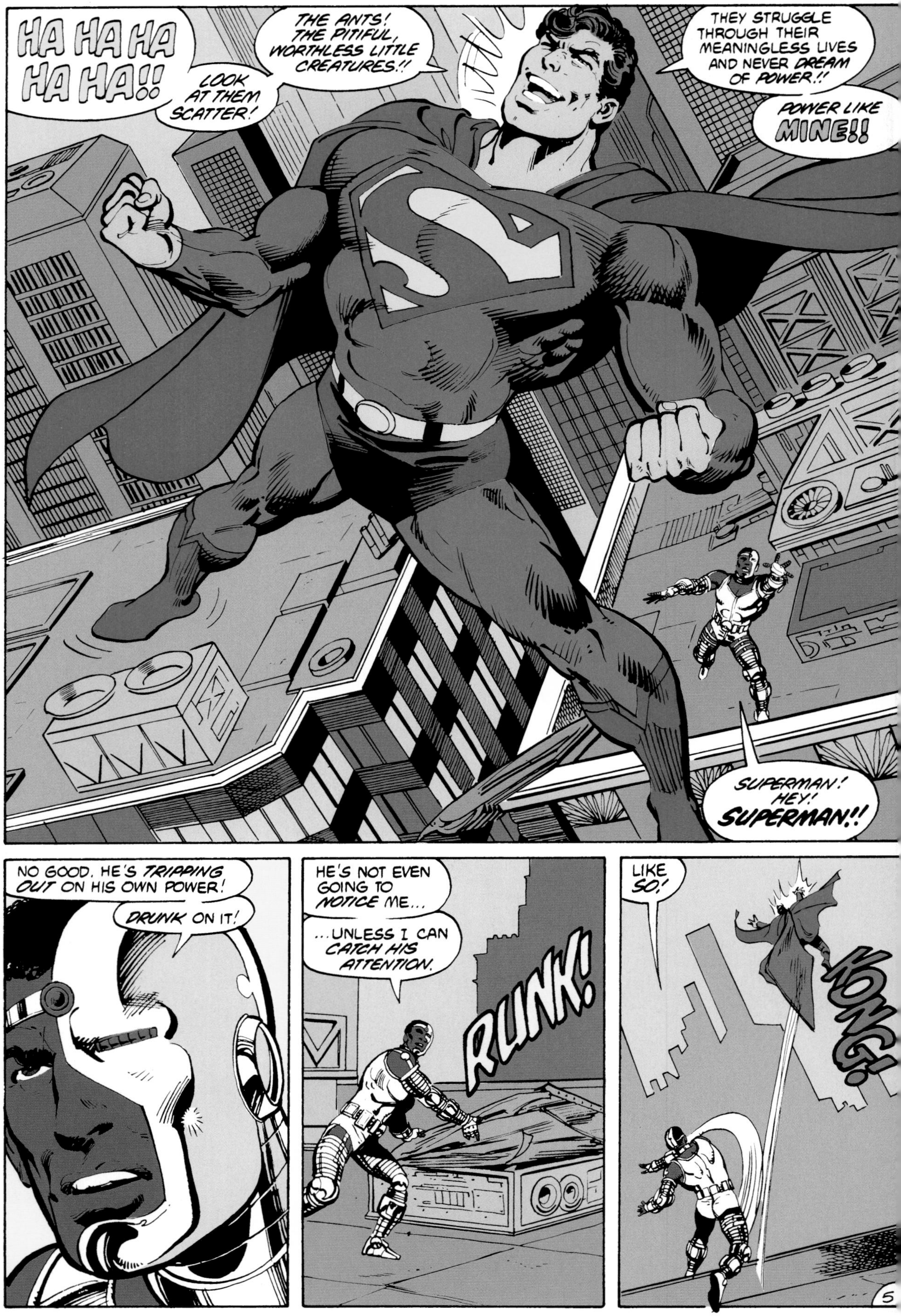
HA HA HA
HA HA!!
LOOK AT THEM SCATTER!
THE ANTS! THE PITIFUL, WORTHLESS LITTLE CREATURES!!
THEY STRUGGLE THROUGH THEIR MEANINGLESS LIVES AND NEVER DREAM OF POWER!!
POWER LIKE MINE!!
SUPERMAN! HEY! SUPERMAN!!
NO GOOD. HE'S TRIPPING OUT ON HIS OWN POWER!
DRUNK ON IT!
HE'S NOT EVEN GOING TO NOTICE ME...
...UNLESS I CAN CATCH HIS ATTENTION.
RUNK!
LIKE SO!
KONG!
5

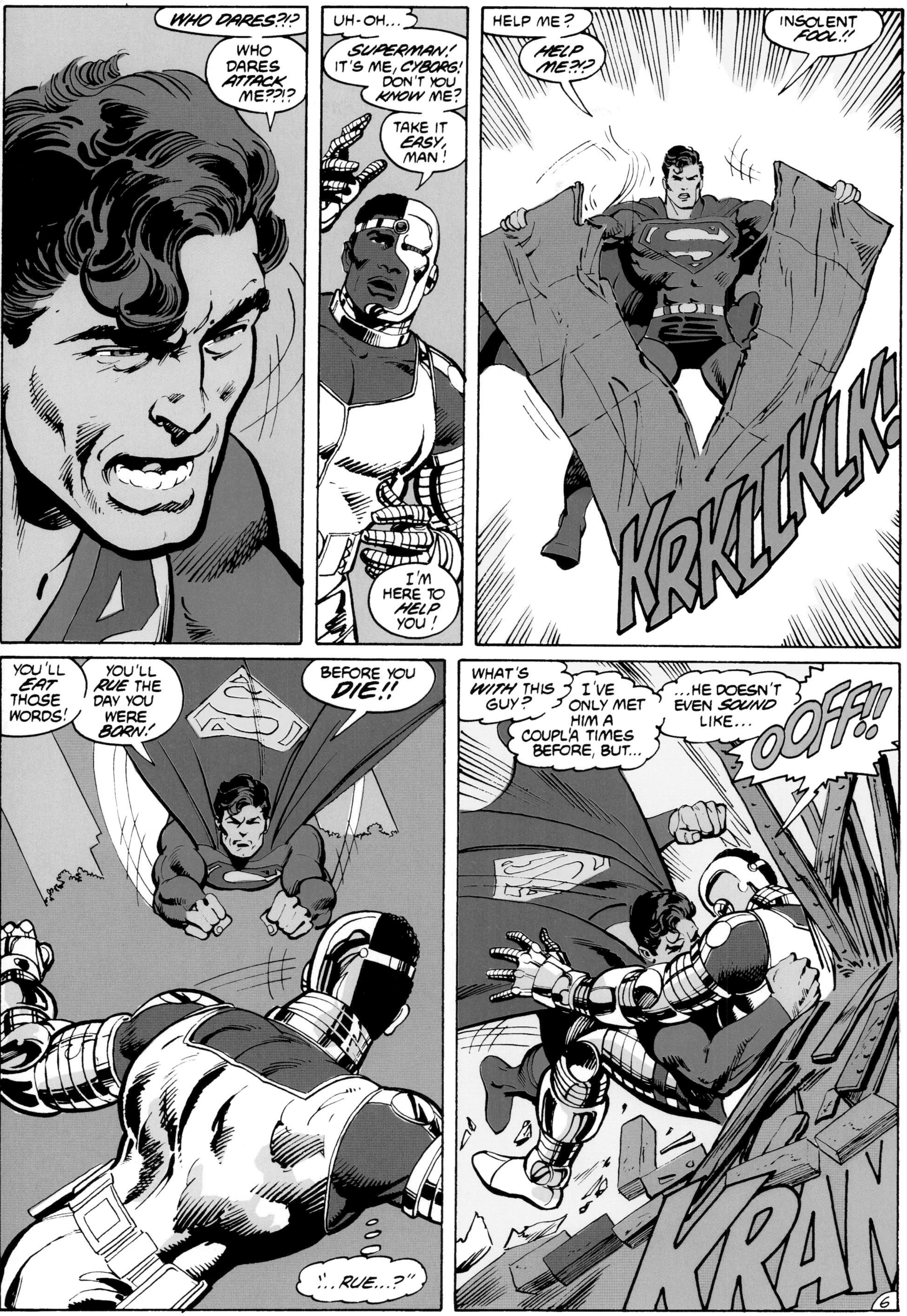
WHO DARES?!?
WHO DARES ATTACK ME??!?
UH-OH...
SUPERMAN! IT'S ME, CYBORG! DON'T YOU KNOW ME?
TAKE IT EASY, MAN!
I'M HERE TO HELP YOU!
HELP ME?
HELP ME?!?
INSOLENT FOOL!!
KRKLLKLK!
YOU'LL EAT THOSE WORDS!
YOU'LL RUE THE DAY YOU WERE BORN!
BEFORE YOU DIE!!
"...RUE...?"
WHAT'S WITH THIS GUY?
I'VE ONLY MET HIM A COUPL'A TIMES BEFORE, BUT...
...HE DOESN'T EVEN SOUND LIKE...
OOFF!!
KRAN
6

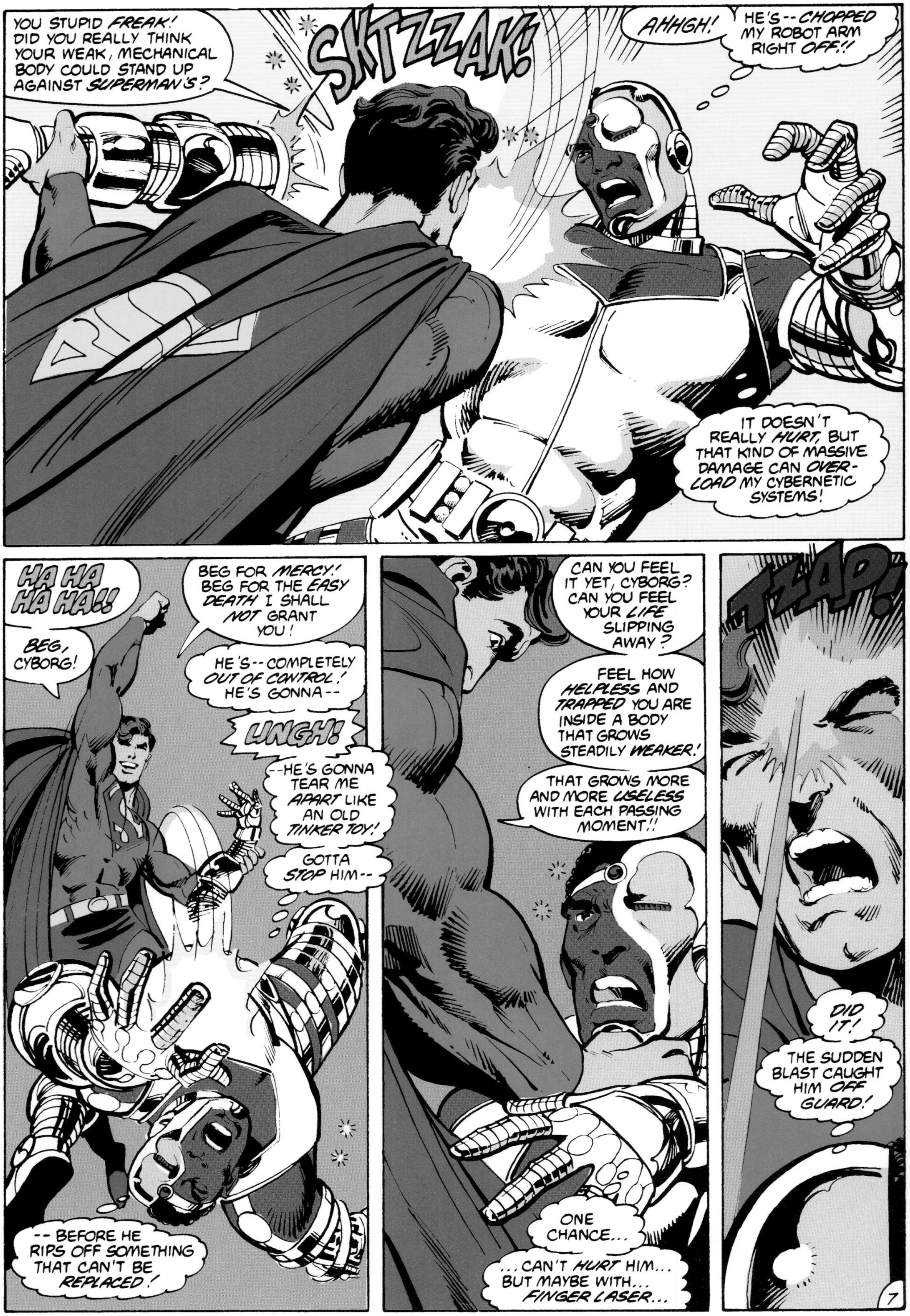
YOU STUPID FREAK! DID YOU REALLY THINK YOUR WEAK, MECHANICAL BODY COULD STAND UP AGAINST SUPERMAN'S?
SKTZZZAK!
AHHGH!
HE'S--CHOPPED MY ROBOT ARM RIGHT OFF!!
IT DOESN'T REALLY HURT, BUT THAT KIND OF MASSIVE DAMAGE CAN OVER-LOAD MY CYBERNETIC SYSTEMS!
HA HA HA HA!!
BEG, CYBORG!
BEG FOR MERCY! BEG FOR THE EASY DEATH I SHALL NOT GRANT YOU!
HE'S--COMPLETELY OUT OF CONTROL! HE'S GONNA--
UNGH!
--HE'S GONNA TEAR ME APART LIKE AN OLD TINKER TOY!
GOTTA STOP HIM--
--BEFORE HE RIPS OFF SOMETHING THAT CAN'T BE REPLACED!
CAN YOU FEEL IT YET, CYBORG? CAN YOU FEEL YOUR LIFE SLIPPING AWAY?
FEEL HOW HELPLESS AND TRAPPED YOU ARE INSIDE A BODY THAT GROWS STEADILY WEAKER!
THAT GROWS MORE AND MORE USELESS WITH EACH PASSING MOMENT!!
ONE CHANCE...
...CAN'T HURT HIM... BUT MAYBE WITH... FINGER LASER...
TZAP!
DID IT!
THE SUDDEN BLAST CAUGHT HIM OFF GUARD!
7

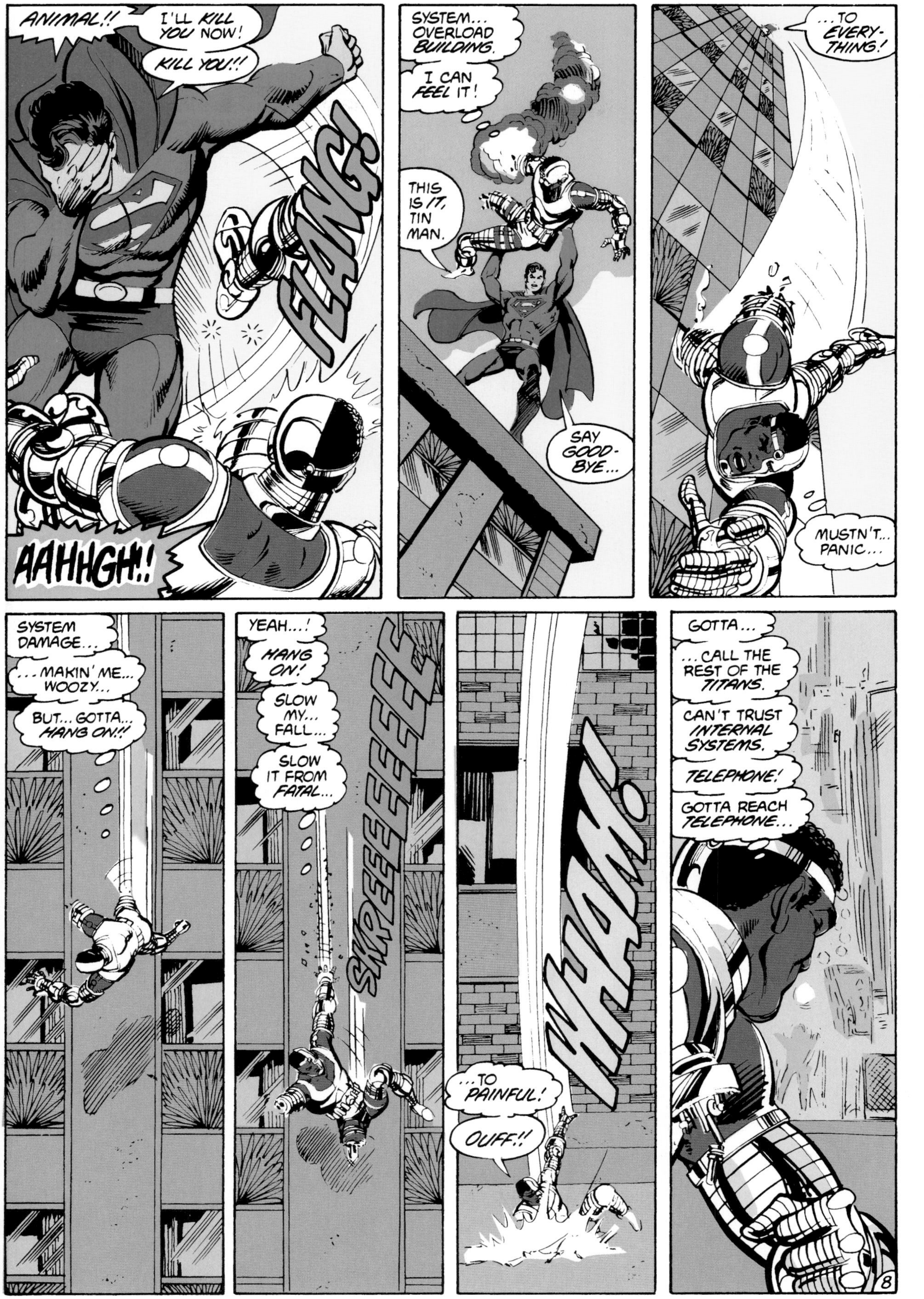
ANIMAL!!
I'LL KILL YOU NOW!
KILL YOU!!
FLANG!
AAHHGH!!
SYSTEM... OVERLOAD BUILDING.
I CAN FEEL IT!
THIS IS IT, TIN MAN.
SAY GOOD-BYE...
...TO EVERY-THING!
MUSTN'T... PANIC...
SYSTEM DAMAGE...
...MAKIN' ME... WOOZY...
BUT... GOTTA... HANG ON!!
YEAH...!
HANG ON!
SLOW MY... FALL...
SLOW IT FROM FATAL...
SKREEEEEEEE
WHAM!
...TO PAINFUL!
OUFF!!
GOTTA...
...CALL THE REST OF THE TITANS.
CAN'T TRUST INTERNAL SYSTEMS.
TELEPHONE!
GOTTA REACH TELEPHONE...
8

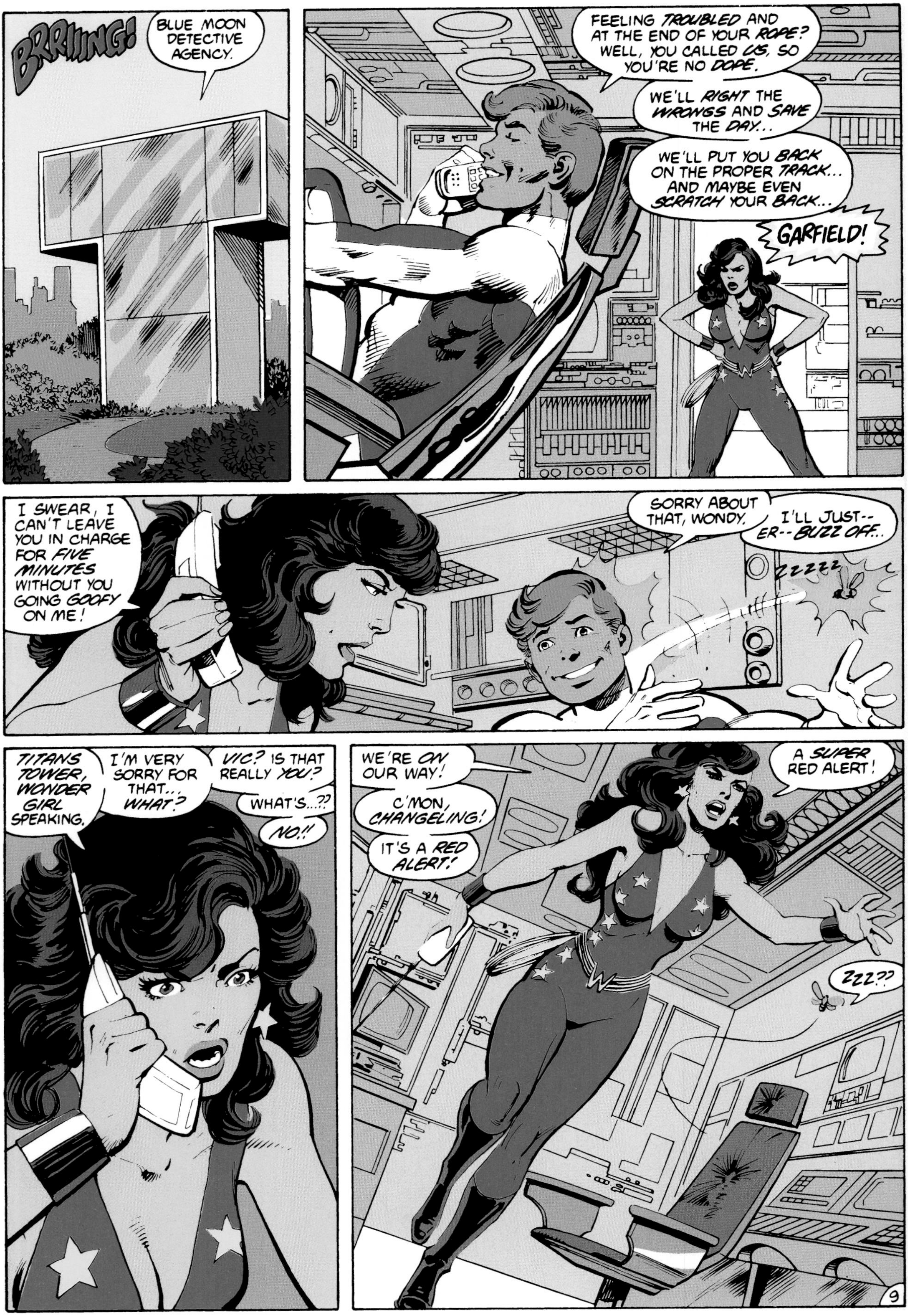
BRRIIING!
BLUE MOON DETECTIVE AGENCY.
FEELING TROUBLED AND AT THE END OF YOUR ROPE? WELL, YOU CALLED US, SO YOU'RE NO DOPE.
WE'LL RIGHT THE WRONGS AND SAVE THE DAY...
WE'LL PUT YOU BACK ON THE PROPER TRACK... AND MAYBE EVEN SCRATCH YOUR BACK...
GARFIELD!
I SWEAR, I CAN'T LEAVE YOU IN CHARGE FOR FIVE MINUTES WITHOUT YOU GOING GOOFY ON ME!
SORRY ABOUT THAT, WONDY.
I'LL JUST-- ER--BUZZ OFF...
ZZZZZ
TITANS TOWER, WONDER GIRL SPEAKING.
I'M VERY SORRY FOR THAT... WHAT?
VIC? IS THAT REALLY YOU?
WHAT'S...??
NO!!
WE'RE ON OUR WAY!
C'MON, CHANGELING!
IT'S A RED ALERT!
A SUPER RED ALERT!
ZZZ??
9

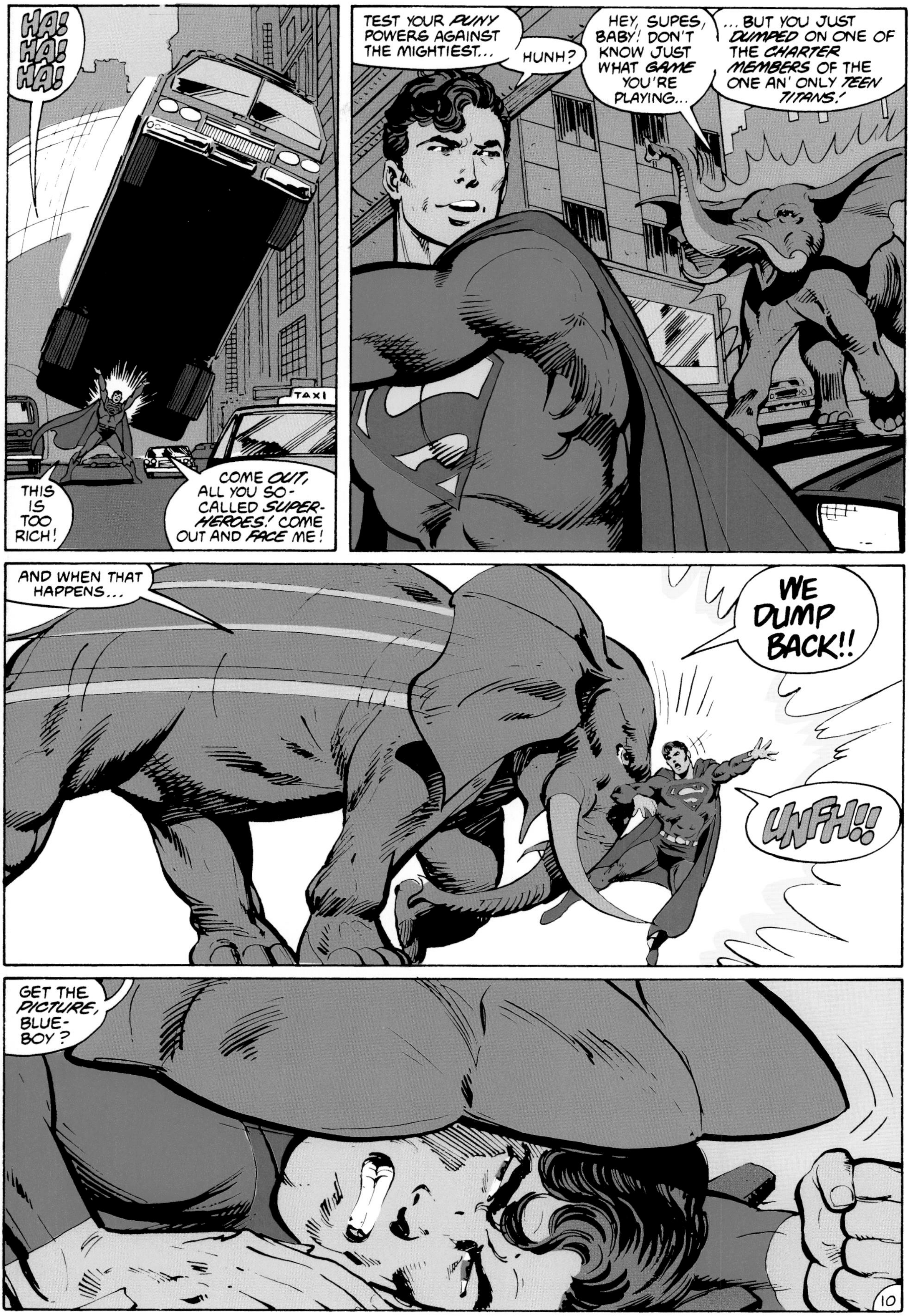
HA! HA! HA!
THIS IS TOO RICH!
COME OUT, ALL YOU SO-CALLED SUPER-HEROES! COME OUT AND FACE ME!
TAXI
TEST YOUR PUNY POWERS AGAINST THE MIGHTIEST...
HUNH?
HEY, SUPES, BABY! DON'T KNOW JUST WHAT GAME YOU'RE PLAYING...
...BUT YOU JUST DUMPED ON ONE OF THE CHARTER MEMBERS OF THE ONE AN' ONLY TEEN TITANS!
AND WHEN THAT HAPPENS...
WE DUMP BACK!!
UNFH!!
GET THE PICTURE, BLUE-BOY?
10

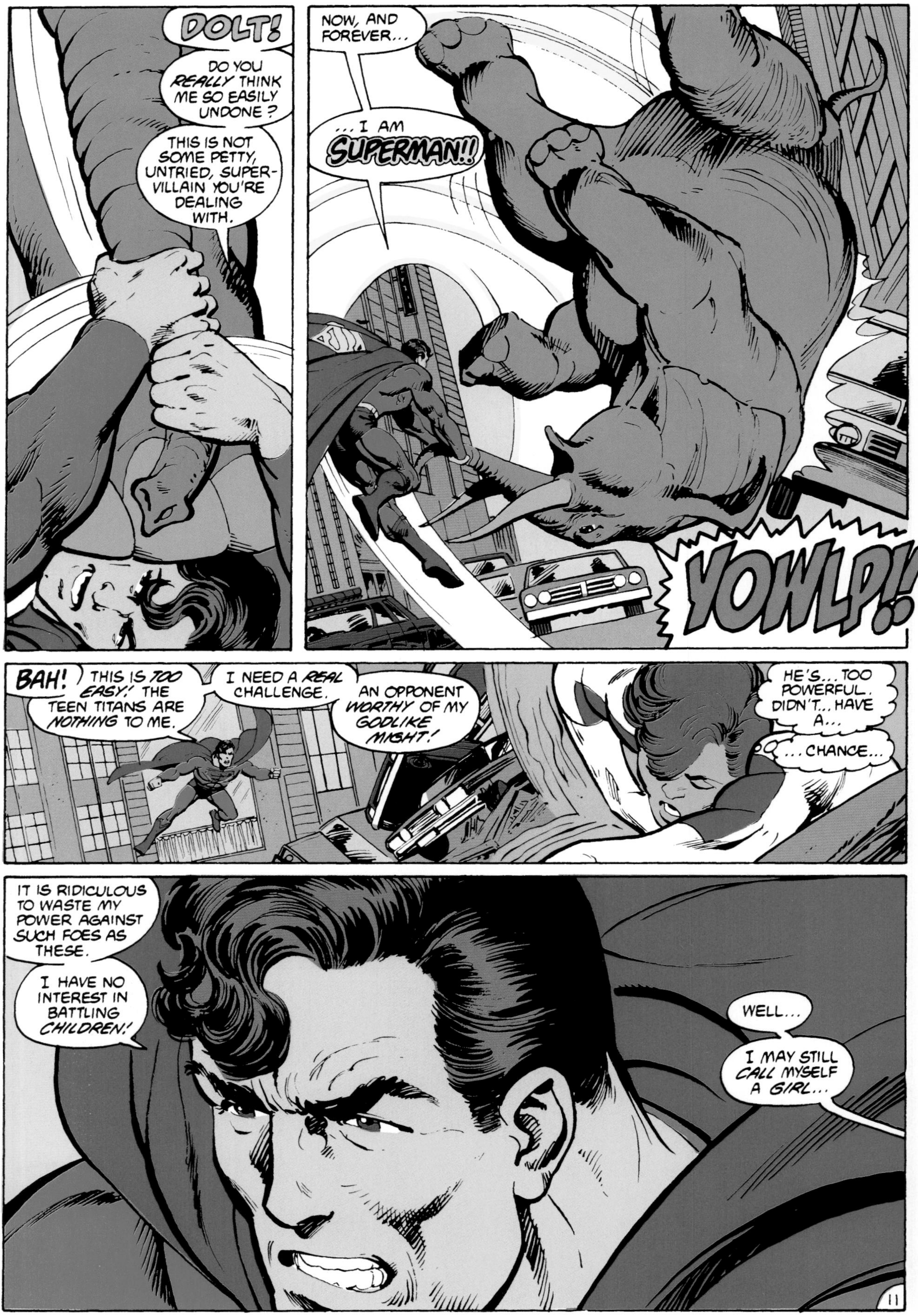
DOLT!
DO YOU REALLY THINK ME SO EASILY UNDONE?
THIS IS NOT SOME PETTY, UNTRIED, SUPER-VILLAIN YOU'RE DEALING WITH.
NOW, AND FOREVER...
...I AM SUPERMAN!!
YOWLP!!
BAH! THIS IS TOO EASY! THE TEEN TITANS ARE NOTHING TO ME.
I NEED A REAL CHALLENGE.
AN OPPONENT WORTHY OF MY GODLIKE MIGHT!
HE'S...TOO POWERFUL. DIDN'T...HAVE A...
...CHANCE...
IT IS RIDICULOUS TO WASTE MY POWER AGAINST SUCH FOES AS THESE.
I HAVE NO INTEREST IN BATTLING CHILDREN!
WELL...
I MAY STILL CALL MYSELF A GIRL...
11

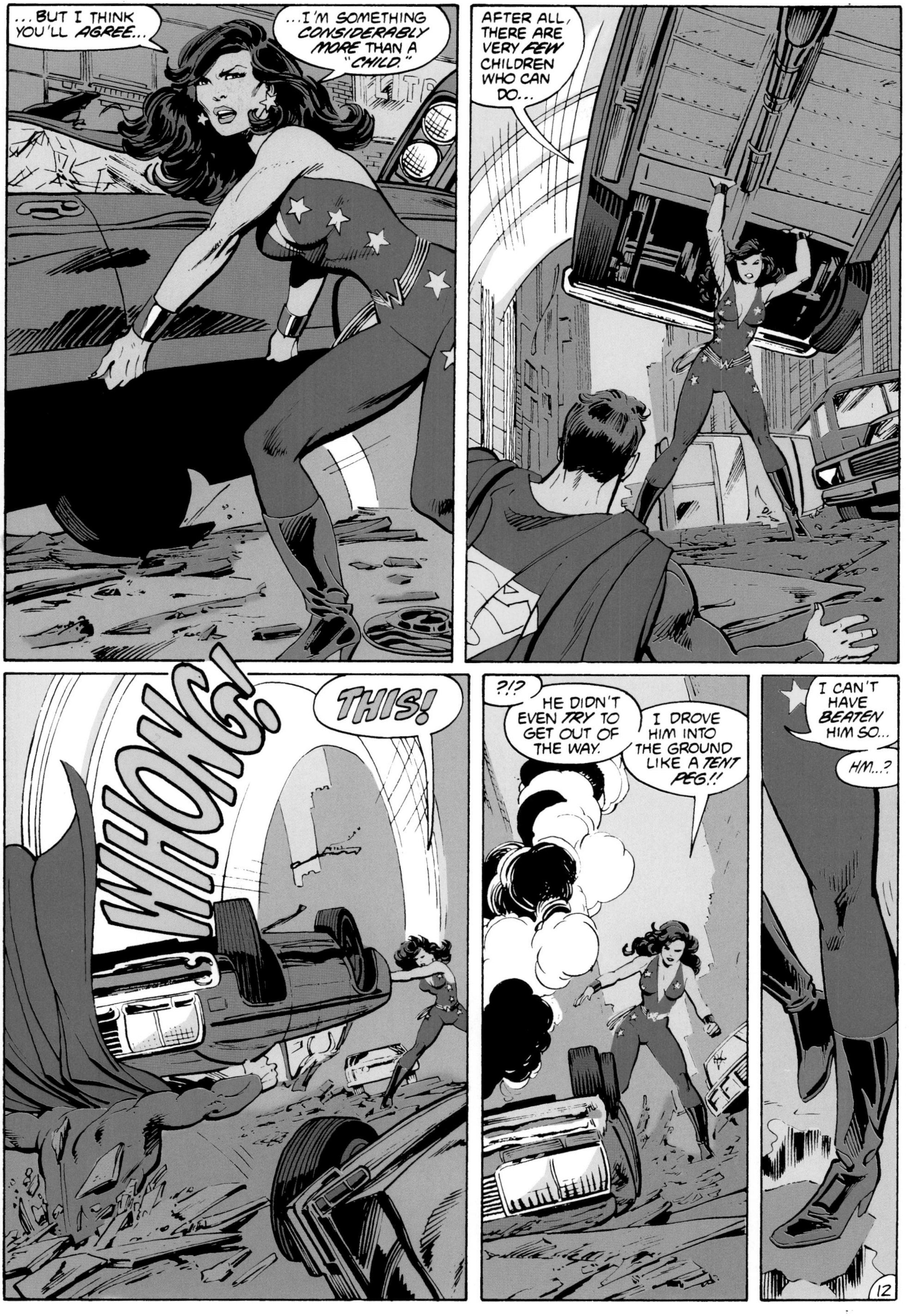
...BUT I THINK YOU'LL AGREE...
...I'M SOMETHING CONSIDERABLY MORE THAN A "CHILD."
AFTER ALL, THERE ARE VERY FEW CHILDREN WHO CAN DO...
WHONG!
THIS!
?!?
HE DIDN'T EVEN TRY TO GET OUT OF THE WAY.
I DROVE HIM INTO THE GROUND LIKE A TENT PEG!!
I CAN'T HAVE BEATEN HIM SO...
HM...?
12

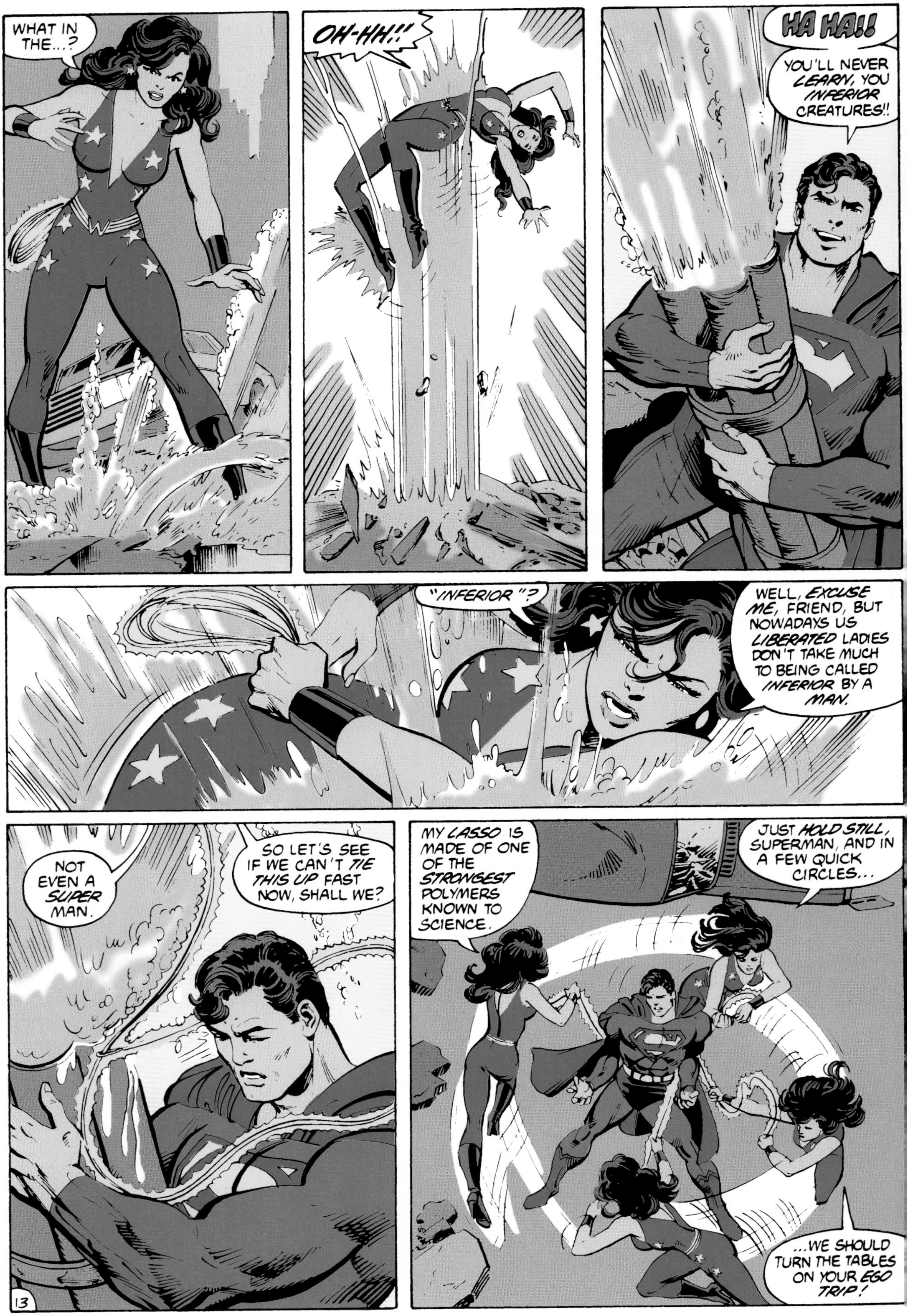
WHAT IN THE...?
OH-HH!!
HA HA!!
YOU'LL NEVER LEARN, YOU INFERIOR CREATURES!!
"INFERIOR"?
WELL, EXCUSE ME, FRIEND, BUT NOWADAYS US LIBERATED LADIES DON'T TAKE MUCH TO BEING CALLED INFERIOR BY A MAN.
NOT EVEN A SUPER MAN.
SO LET'S SEE IF WE CAN'T TIE THIS UP FAST NOW, SHALL WE?
13
MY LASSO IS MADE OF ONE OF THE STRONGEST POLYMERS KNOWN TO SCIENCE.
JUST HOLD STILL, SUPERMAN, AND IN A FEW QUICK CIRCLES...
...WE SHOULD TURN THE TABLES ON YOUR EGO TRIP!

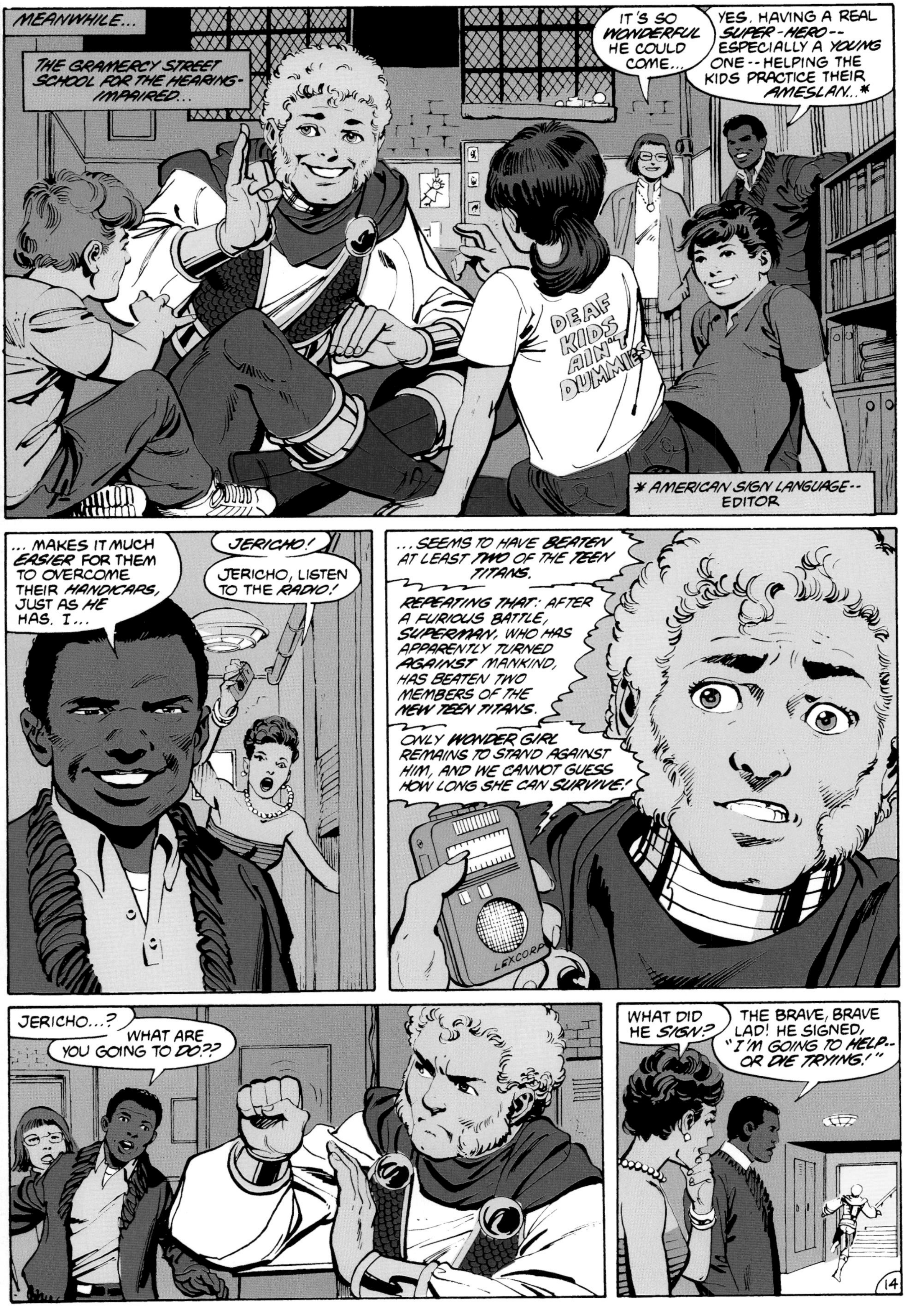
MEANWHILE...
THE GRAMERCY STREET SCHOOL FOR THE HEARING-IMPAIRED...
IT'S SO WONDERFUL HE COULD COME...
YES. HAVING A REAL SUPER-HERO--ESPECIALLY A YOUNG ONE--HELPING THE KIDS PRACTICE THEIR AMESLAN..*
DEAF KIDS AIN'T DUMMIES
* AMERICAN SIGN LANGUAGE--EDITOR
...MAKES IT MUCH EASIER FOR THEM TO OVERCOME THEIR HANDICAPS, JUST AS HE HAS. I...
JERICHO!
JERICHO, LISTEN TO THE RADIO!
...SEEMS TO HAVE BEATEN AT LEAST TWO OF THE TEEN TITANS.
REPEATING THAT: AFTER A FURIOUS BATTLE, SUPERMAN, WHO HAS APPARENTLY TURNED AGAINST MANKIND, HAS BEATEN TWO MEMBERS OF THE NEW TEEN TITANS.
ONLY WONDER GIRL REMAINS TO STAND AGAINST HIM, AND WE CANNOT GUESS HOW LONG SHE CAN SURVIVE!
LEXCORP
JERICHO...?
WHAT ARE YOU GOING TO DO??
WHAT DID HE SIGN?
THE BRAVE, BRAVE LAD! HE SIGNED, "I'M GOING TO HELP--OR DIE TRYING!"
14

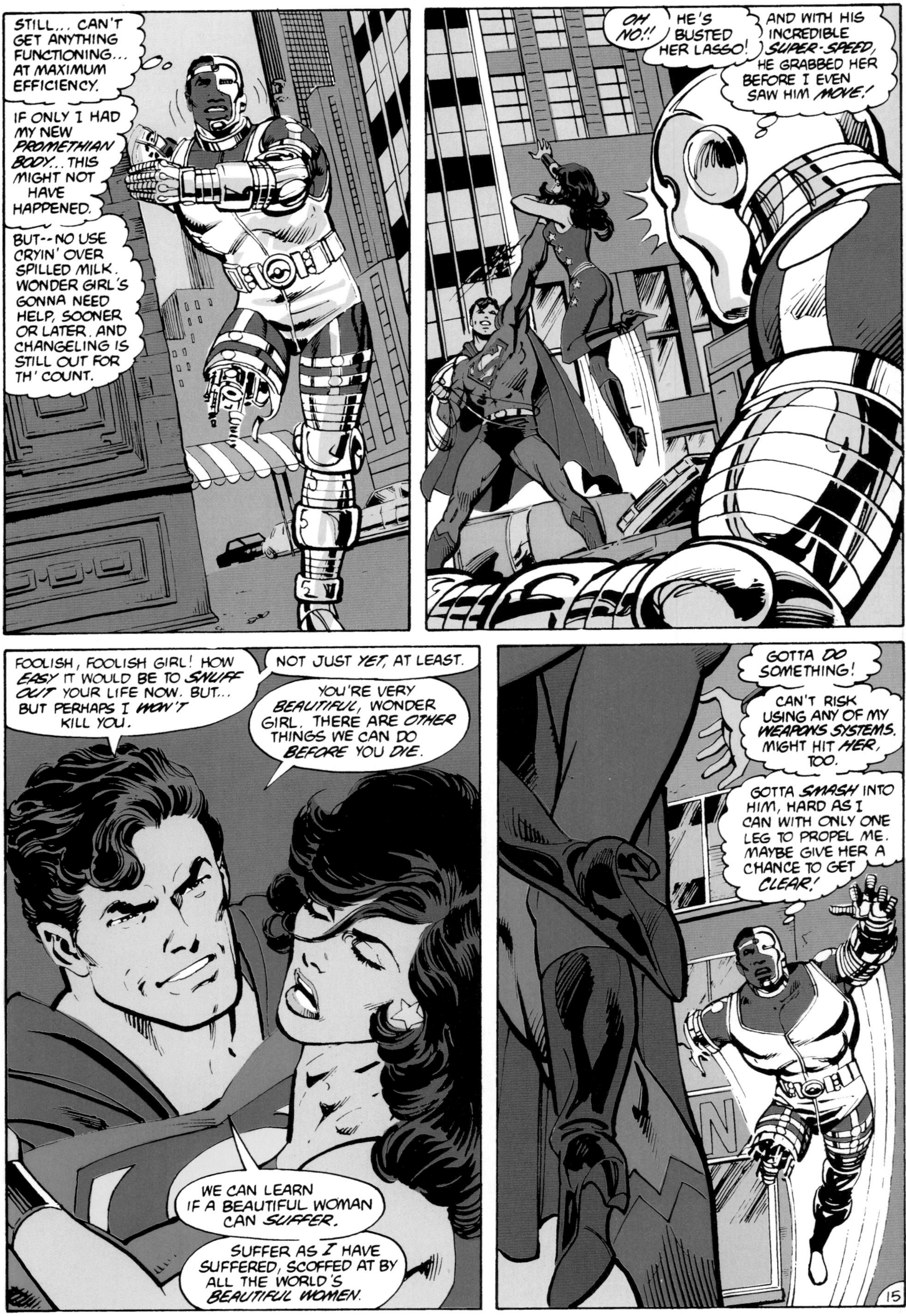
STILL... CAN'T GET ANYTHING FUNCTIONING... AT MAXIMUM EFFICIENCY.
IF ONLY I HAD MY NEW PROMETHIAN BODY... THIS MIGHT NOT HAVE HAPPENED.
BUT--NO USE CRYIN' OVER SPILLED MILK. WONDER GIRL'S GONNA NEED HELP, SOONER OR LATER. AND CHANGELING IS STILL OUT FOR TH' COUNT.
OH NO!!
HE'S BUSTED HER LASSO!
AND WITH HIS INCREDIBLE SUPER-SPEED, HE GRABBED HER BEFORE I EVEN SAW HIM MOVE!
FOOLISH, FOOLISH GIRL! HOW EASY IT WOULD BE TO SNUFF OUT YOUR LIFE NOW. BUT... BUT PERHAPS I WON'T KILL YOU.
NOT JUST YET, AT LEAST.
YOU'RE VERY BEAUTIFUL, WONDER GIRL. THERE ARE OTHER THINGS WE CAN DO BEFORE YOU DIE.
WE CAN LEARN IF A BEAUTIFUL WOMAN CAN SUFFER.
SUFFER AS I HAVE SUFFERED, SCOFFED AT BY ALL THE WORLD'S BEAUTIFUL WOMEN.
GOTTA DO SOMETHING!
CAN'T RISK USING ANY OF MY WEAPONS SYSTEMS. MIGHT HIT HER, TOO.
GOTTA SMASH INTO HIM, HARD AS I CAN WITH ONLY ONE LEG TO PROPEL ME. MAYBE GIVE HER A CHANCE TO GET CLEAR!
N
15

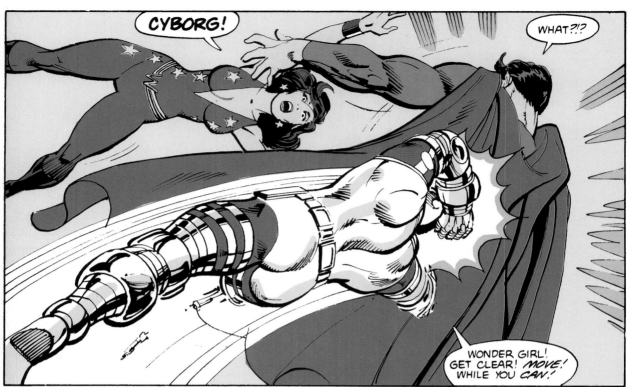

CYBORG!

WHAT?!?

WONDER GIRL! GET CLEAR! *MOVE!* WHILE YOU *CAN!*

MISERABLE, INTERFERING *SWINE!* DON'T YOU HAVE EVEN ENOUGH *SENSE* TO STAY OUT OF THE WAY??

YOU ESCAPED *ONCE* WITH YOUR LIFE, *HALF-MAN.*

YOU SHALL NOT DO SO A *SECOND TIME!*

NOW YOU *DIE!!*

UNGH!

MANAGED TO *ROLL* OUT OF THE WAY.

BUT CAN'T KEEP DOIN' THAT *FOREVER!*

I'M *DONE FOR!!*

KROM!

WHAT TH'....?!?

SPLOT!

16

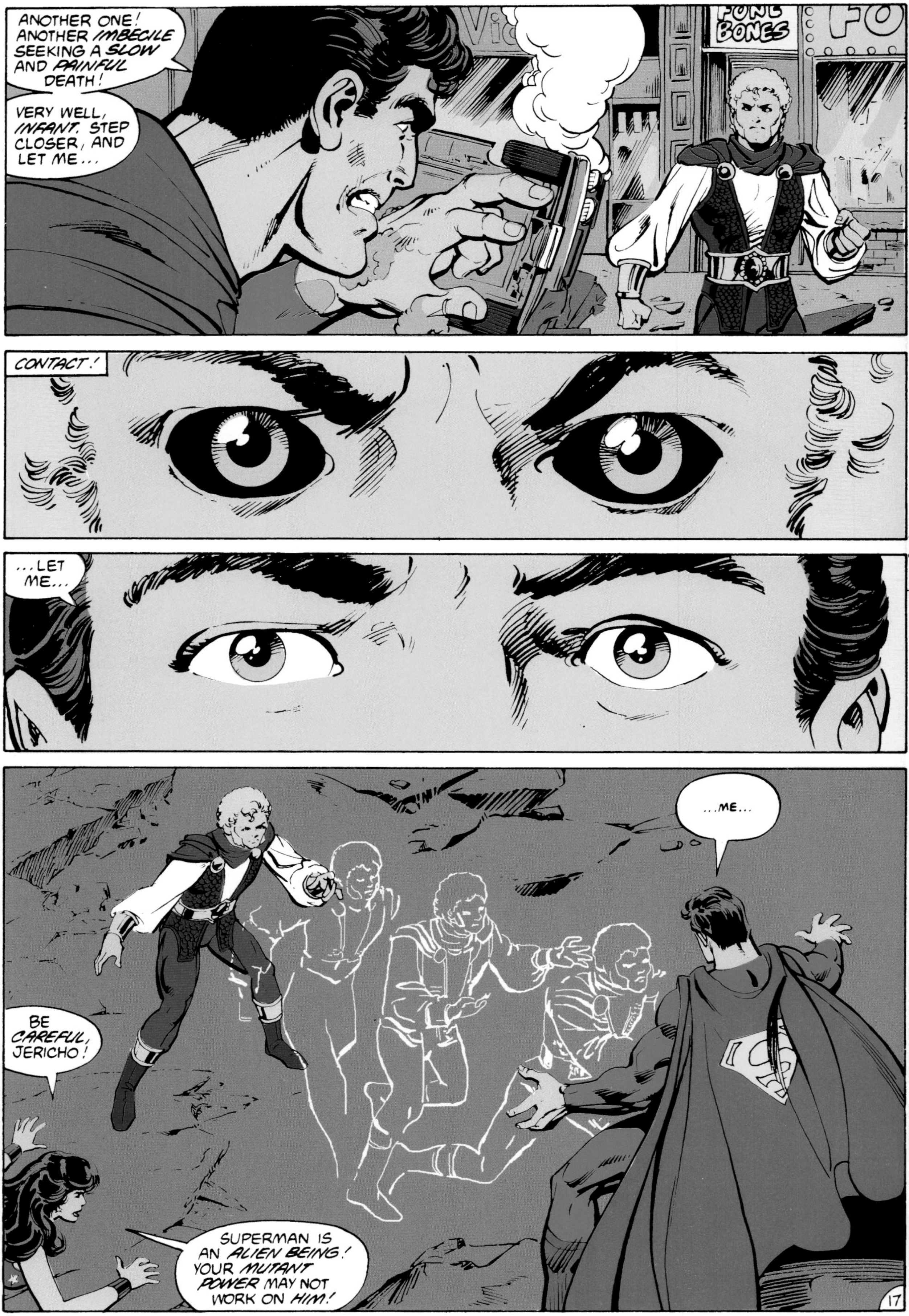
ANOTHER ONE! ANOTHER IMBECILE SEEKING A SLOW AND PAINFUL DEATH!
VERY WELL, INFANT. STEP CLOSER, AND LET ME...
FONE BONES
CONTACT!
...LET ME...
...ME...
BE CAREFUL, JERICHO!
SUPERMAN IS AN ALIEN BEING! YOUR MUTANT POWER MAY NOT WORK ON HIM!
17

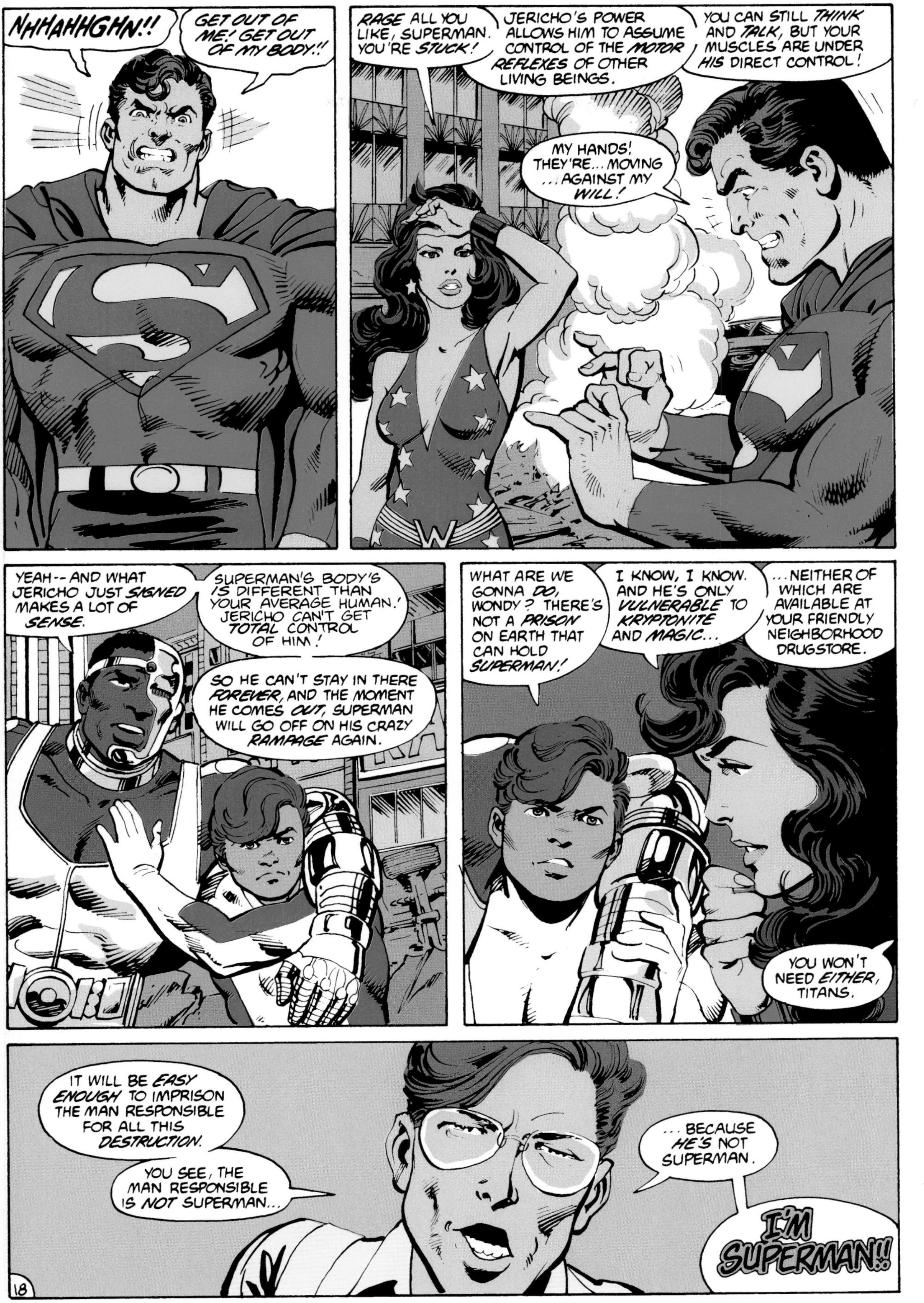
NHHAHHGHN!!
GET OUT OF ME! GET OUT OF MY BODY!!
RAGE ALL YOU LIKE, SUPERMAN. YOU'RE STUCK!
JERICHO'S POWER ALLOWS HIM TO ASSUME CONTROL OF THE MOTOR REFLEXES OF OTHER LIVING BEINGS.
YOU CAN STILL THINK AND TALK, BUT YOUR MUSCLES ARE UNDER HIS DIRECT CONTROL!
MY HANDS! THEY'RE... MOVING ...AGAINST MY WILL!
YEAH--AND WHAT JERICHO JUST SIGNED MAKES A LOT OF SENSE.
SUPERMAN'S BODY'S IS DIFFERENT THAN YOUR AVERAGE HUMAN! JERICHO CAN'T GET TOTAL CONTROL OF HIM!
SO HE CAN'T STAY IN THERE FOREVER, AND THE MOMENT HE COMES OUT, SUPERMAN WILL GO OFF ON HIS CRAZY RAMPAGE AGAIN.
WHAT ARE WE GONNA DO, WONDY? THERE'S NOT A PRISON ON EARTH THAT CAN HOLD SUPERMAN!
I KNOW, I KNOW. AND HE'S ONLY VULNERABLE TO KRYPTONITE AND MAGIC...
...NEITHER OF WHICH ARE AVAILABLE AT YOUR FRIENDLY NEIGHBORHOOD DRUGSTORE.
YOU WON'T NEED EITHER, TITANS.
IT WILL BE EASY ENOUGH TO IMPRISON THE MAN RESPONSIBLE FOR ALL THIS DESTRUCTION.
YOU SEE, THE MAN RESPONSIBLE IS NOT SUPERMAN...
...BECAUSE HE'S NOT SUPERMAN.
I'M SUPERMAN!!
18

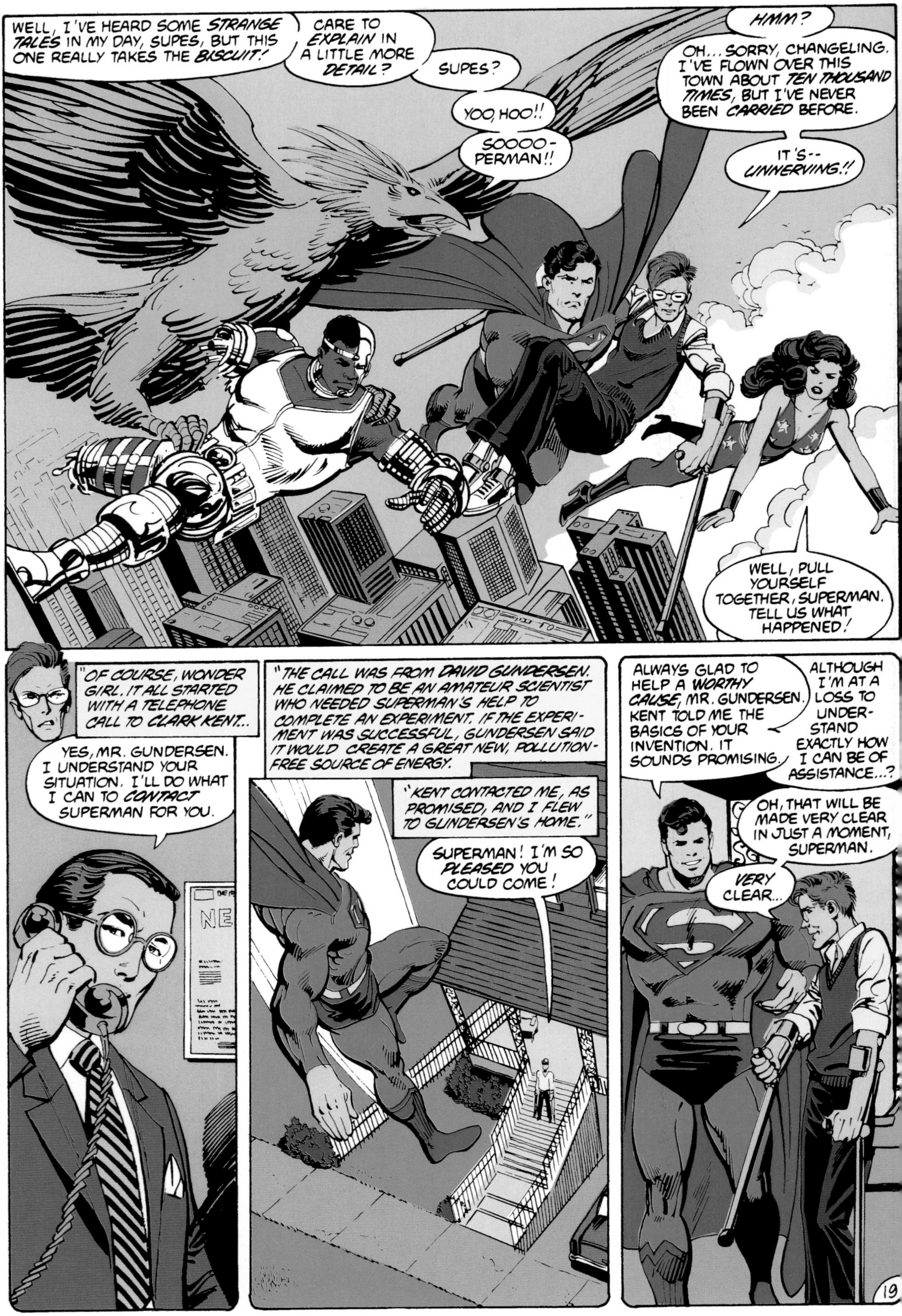

WELL, I'VE HEARD SOME STRANGE TALES IN MY DAY, SUPES, BUT THIS ONE REALLY TAKES THE BISCUIT!
CARE TO EXPLAIN IN A LITTLE MORE DETAIL?
SUPES?
YOO, HOO!!
SOOOO-PERMAN!!
HMM?
OH... SORRY, CHANGELING. I'VE FLOWN OVER THIS TOWN ABOUT TEN THOUSAND TIMES, BUT I'VE NEVER BEEN CARRIED BEFORE.
IT'S-- UNNERVING!!
WELL, PULL YOURSELF TOGETHER, SUPERMAN. TELL US WHAT HAPPENED!
"OF COURSE, WONDER GIRL. IT ALL STARTED WITH A TELEPHONE CALL TO CLARK KENT...
YES, MR. GUNDERSEN. I UNDERSTAND YOUR SITUATION. I'LL DO WHAT I CAN TO CONTACT SUPERMAN FOR YOU.
NE
"THE CALL WAS FROM DAVID GUNDERSEN. HE CLAIMED TO BE AN AMATEUR SCIENTIST WHO NEEDED SUPERMAN'S HELP TO COMPLETE AN EXPERIMENT. IF THE EXPERIMENT WAS SUCCESSFUL, GUNDERSEN SAID IT WOULD CREATE A GREAT NEW, POLLUTION-FREE SOURCE OF ENERGY.
"KENT CONTACTED ME, AS PROMISED, AND I FLEW TO GUNDERSEN'S HOME."
SUPERMAN! I'M SO PLEASED YOU COULD COME!
ALWAYS GLAD TO HELP A WORTHY CAUSE, MR. GUNDERSEN. KENT TOLD ME THE BASICS OF YOUR INVENTION. IT SOUNDS PROMISING.
ALTHOUGH I'M AT A LOSS TO UNDERSTAND EXACTLY HOW I CAN BE OF ASSISTANCE...?
OH, THAT WILL BE MADE VERY CLEAR IN JUST A MOMENT, SUPERMAN.
VERY CLEAR...
19

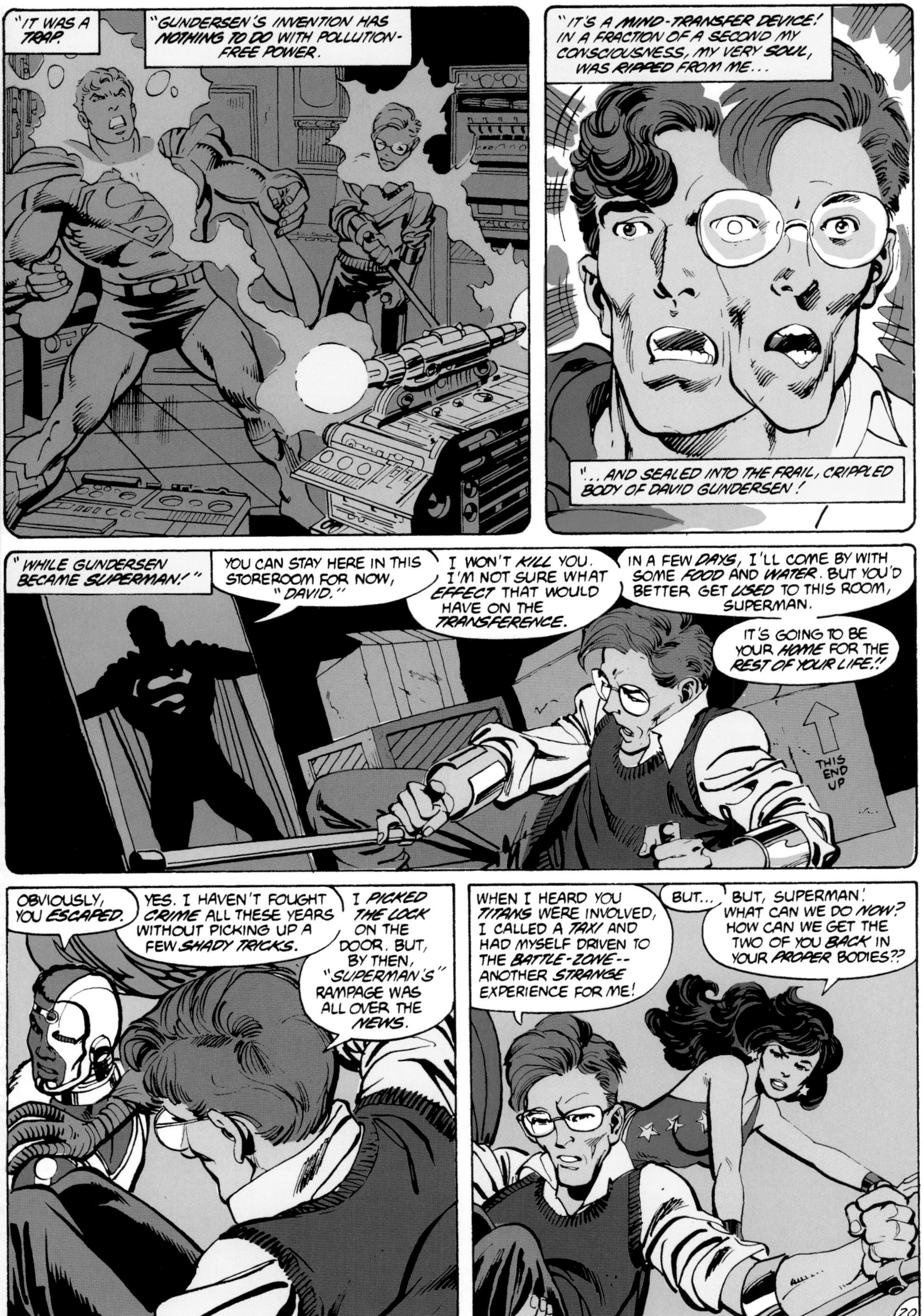
"IT WAS A TRAP.
"GUNDERSEN'S INVENTION HAS NOTHING TO DO WITH POLLUTION-FREE POWER.
"IT'S A MIND-TRANSFER DEVICE! IN A FRACTION OF A SECOND MY CONSCIOUSNESS, MY VERY SOUL, WAS RIPPED FROM ME...
"...AND SEALED INTO THE FRAIL, CRIPPLED BODY OF DAVID GUNDERSEN!
"WHILE GUNDERSEN BECAME SUPERMAN!"
YOU CAN STAY HERE IN THIS STOREROOM FOR NOW, "DAVID."
I WON'T KILL YOU. I'M NOT SURE WHAT EFFECT THAT WOULD HAVE ON THE TRANSFERENCE.
IN A FEW DAYS, I'LL COME BY WITH SOME FOOD AND WATER. BUT YOU'D BETTER GET USED TO THIS ROOM, SUPERMAN.
IT'S GOING TO BE YOUR HOME FOR THE REST OF YOUR LIFE!!
THIS END UP
OBVIOUSLY, YOU ESCAPED.
YES. I HAVEN'T FOUGHT CRIME ALL THESE YEARS WITHOUT PICKING UP A FEW SHADY TRICKS.
I PICKED THE LOCK ON THE DOOR. BUT, BY THEN, "SUPERMAN'S" RAMPAGE WAS ALL OVER THE NEWS.
WHEN I HEARD YOU TITANS WERE INVOLVED, I CALLED A TAXI AND HAD MYSELF DRIVEN TO THE BATTLE-ZONE-- ANOTHER STRANGE EXPERIENCE FOR ME!
BUT...
BUT, SUPERMAN! WHAT CAN WE DO NOW? HOW CAN WE GET THE TWO OF YOU BACK IN YOUR PROPER BODIES??
20

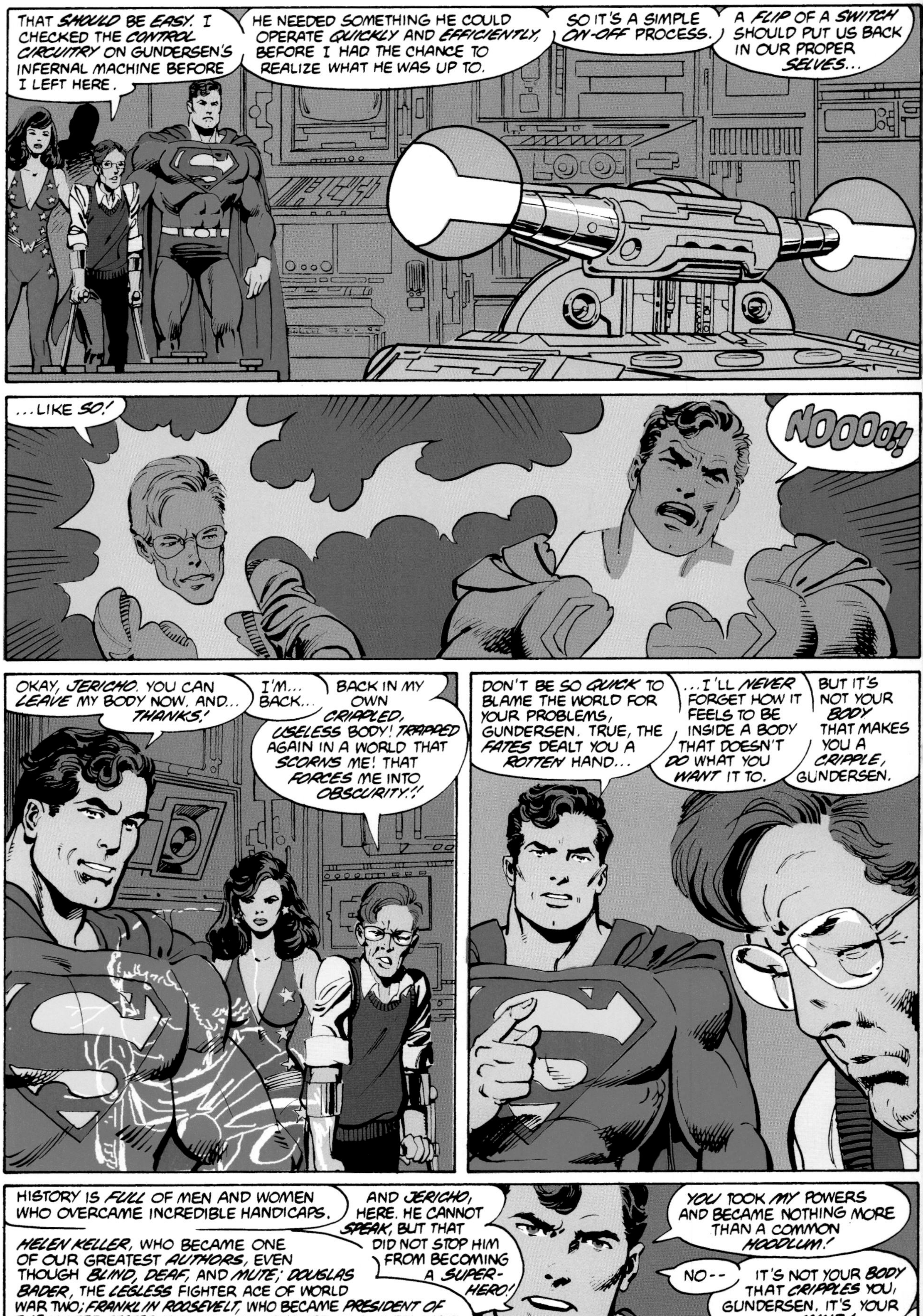
THAT SHOULD BE EASY. I CHECKED THE CONTROL CIRCUITRY ON GUNDERSEN'S INFERNAL MACHINE BEFORE I LEFT HERE.
HE NEEDED SOMETHING HE COULD OPERATE QUICKLY AND EFFICIENTLY, BEFORE I HAD THE CHANCE TO REALIZE WHAT HE WAS UP TO.
SO IT'S A SIMPLE ON-OFF PROCESS.
A FLIP OF A SWITCH SHOULD PUT US BACK IN OUR PROPER SELVES...
...LIKE SO!
NOOOo!!
OKAY, JERICHO. YOU CAN LEAVE MY BODY NOW. AND... THANKS!
I'M... BACK...
BACK IN MY OWN CRIPPLED, USELESS BODY! TRAPPED AGAIN IN A WORLD THAT SCORNS ME! THAT FORCES ME INTO OBSCURITY!!
DON'T BE SO QUICK TO BLAME THE WORLD FOR YOUR PROBLEMS, GUNDERSEN. TRUE, THE FATES DEALT YOU A ROTTEN HAND...
...I'LL NEVER FORGET HOW IT FEELS TO BE INSIDE A BODY THAT DOESN'T DO WHAT YOU WANT IT TO.
BUT IT'S NOT YOUR BODY THAT MAKES YOU A CRIPPLE, GUNDERSEN.
HISTORY IS FULL OF MEN AND WOMEN WHO OVERCAME INCREDIBLE HANDICAPS.
HELEN KELLER, WHO BECAME ONE OF OUR GREATEST AUTHORS, EVEN THOUGH BLIND, DEAF, AND MUTE; DOUGLAS BADER, THE LEGLESS FIGHTER ACE OF WORLD WAR TWO; FRANKLIN ROOSEVELT, WHO BECAME PRESIDENT OF THE UNITED STATES, EVEN THOUGH CONFINED TO A WHEELCHAIR.
AND JERICHO, HERE. HE CANNOT SPEAK, BUT THAT DID NOT STOP HIM FROM BECOMING A SUPER-HERO!
YOU TOOK MY POWERS AND BECAME NOTHING MORE THAN A COMMON HOODLUM!
NO--
IT'S NOT YOUR BODY THAT CRIPPLES YOU, GUNDERSEN. IT'S YOUR MIND!
21

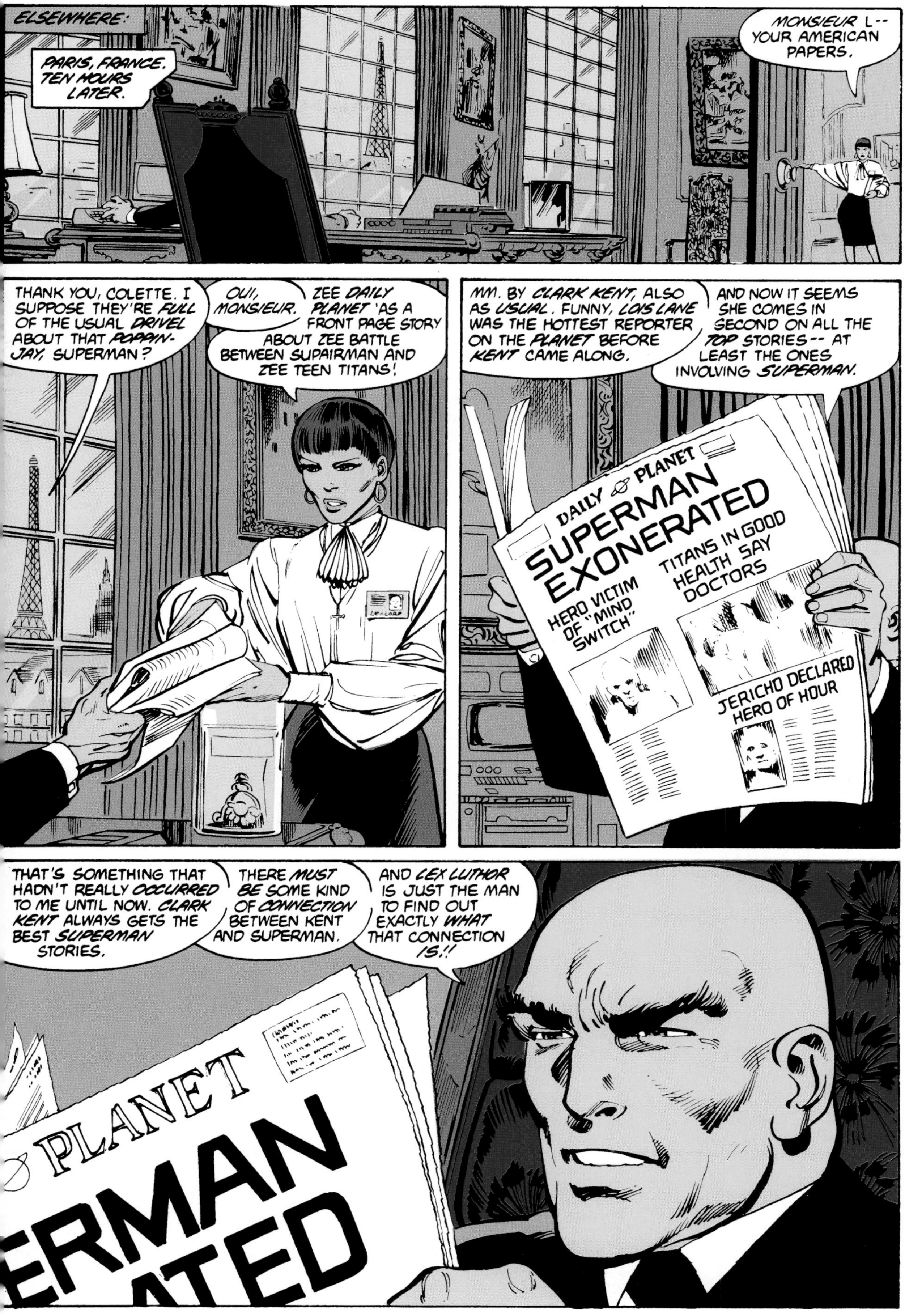
ELSEWHERE:
PARIS, FRANCE. TEN HOURS LATER.
MONSIEUR L-- YOUR AMERICAN PAPERS.
THANK YOU, COLETTE. I SUPPOSE THEY'RE FULL OF THE USUAL DRIVEL ABOUT THAT POPPIN-JAY, SUPERMAN?
OUI, MONSIEUR.
ZEE DAILY PLANET 'AS A FRONT PAGE STORY ABOUT ZEE BATTLE BETWEEN SUPAIRMAN AND ZEE TEEN TITANS!
MM. BY CLARK KENT, ALSO AS USUAL. FUNNY, LOIS LANE WAS THE HOTTEST REPORTER ON THE PLANET BEFORE KENT CAME ALONG.
AND NOW IT SEEMS SHE COMES IN SECOND ON ALL THE TOP STORIES-- AT LEAST THE ONES INVOLVING SUPERMAN.
DAILY PLANET
SUPERMAN EXONERATED
HERO VICTIM OF "MIND SWITCH"
TITANS IN GOOD HEALTH SAY DOCTORS
JERICHO DECLARED HERO OF HOUR
THAT'S SOMETHING THAT HADN'T REALLY OCCURRED TO ME UNTIL NOW. CLARK KENT ALWAYS GETS THE BEST SUPERMAN STORIES.
THERE MUST BE SOME KIND OF CONNECTION BETWEEN KENT AND SUPERMAN.
AND LEX LUTHOR IS JUST THE MAN TO FIND OUT EXACTLY WHAT THAT CONNECTION IS!!
PLANET
ERMAN
ATED

SUPERSQUARE

A Comics Essay About Superman by Gene Luen Yang

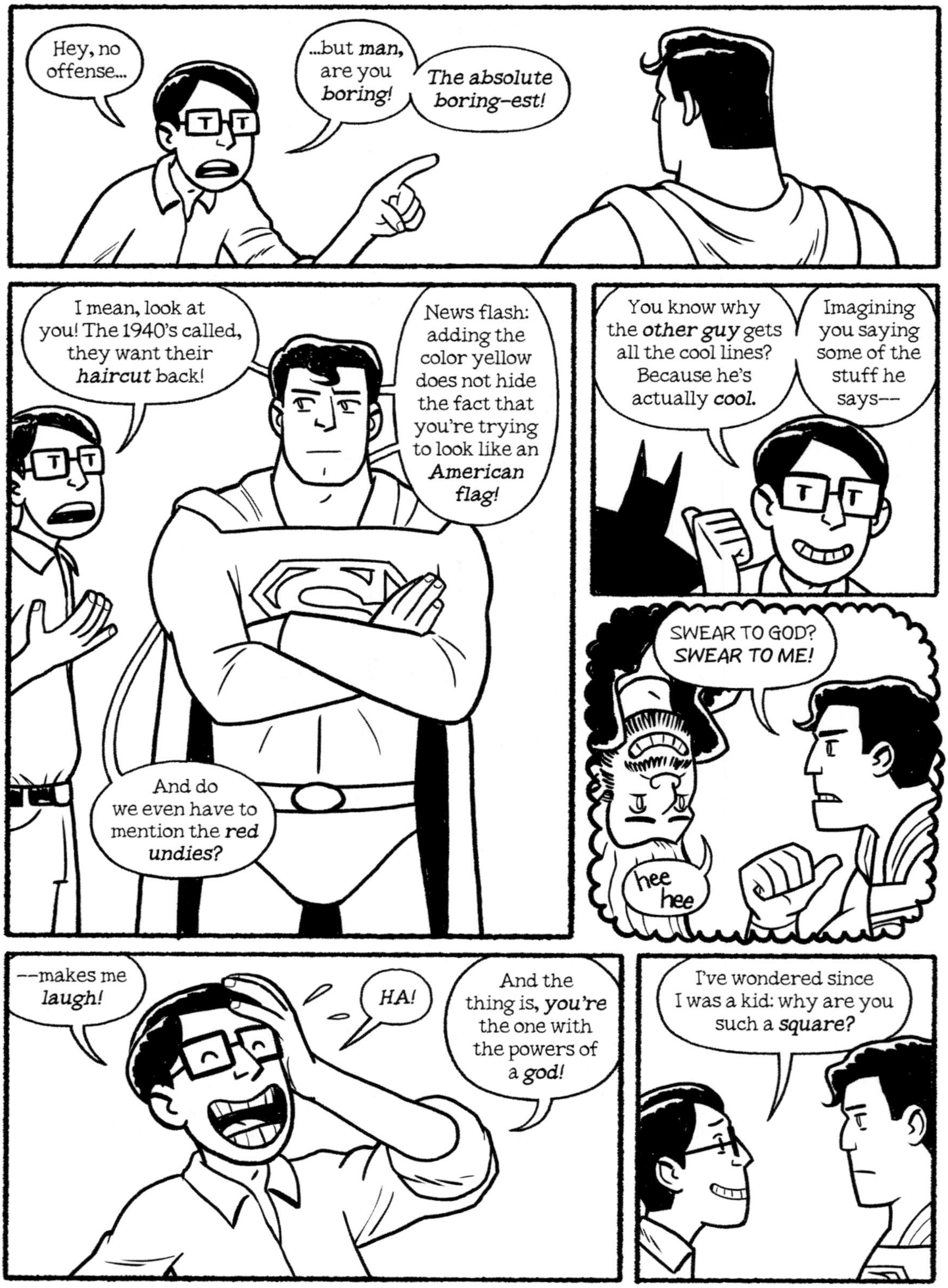
Hey, no offense...
...but *man*, are you *boring!*
The absolute boring-est!
I mean, look at you! The 1940's called, they want their *haircut* back!
News flash: adding the color yellow does not hide the fact that you're trying to look like an *American flag!*
And do we even have to mention the *red undies?*
You know why the *other guy* gets all the cool lines? Because he's actually *cool.*
Imagining you saying some of the stuff he says--
SWEAR TO GOD? *SWEAR TO ME!*
hee hee
--makes me *laugh!*
HA!
And the thing is, *you're* the one with the powers of a *god!*
I've wondered since I was a kid: why are you such a *square?*

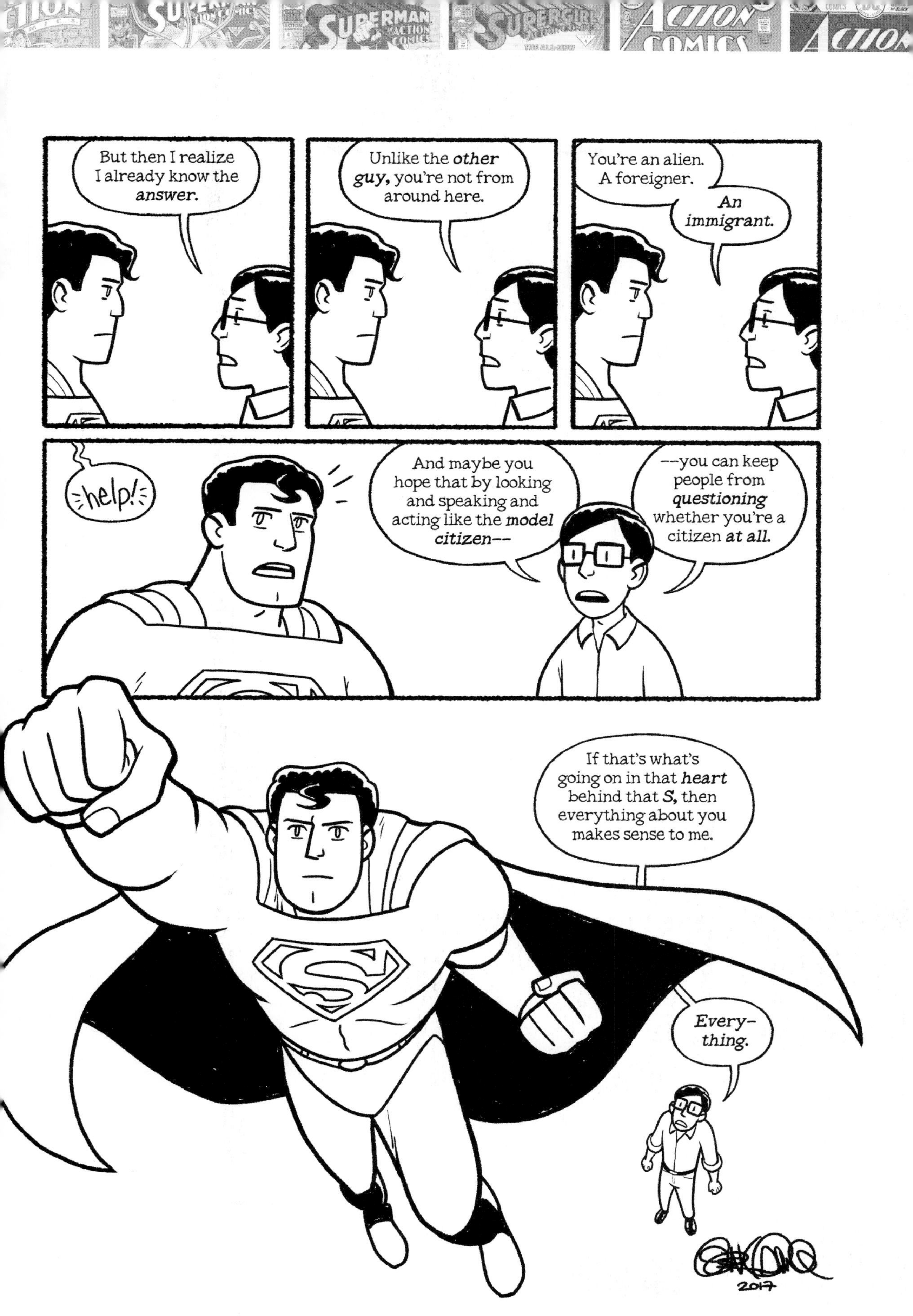

But then I realize I already know the *answer.*
Unlike the *other guy,* you're not from around here.
You're an alien. A foreigner.
An immigrant.
help!
And maybe you hope that by looking and speaking and acting like the *model citizen--*
--you can keep people from *questioning* whether you're a citizen *at all.*
If that's what's going on in that *heart* behind that *S,* then everything about you makes sense to me.
Every-thing.
2017

GENE LUEN YANG is an accomplished cartoonist and graphic novelist, including authoring* American Born Chinese*, and has served as the Library of Congress' ambassador for young people's literature. He currently writes the NEW SUPER-MAN series for DC.

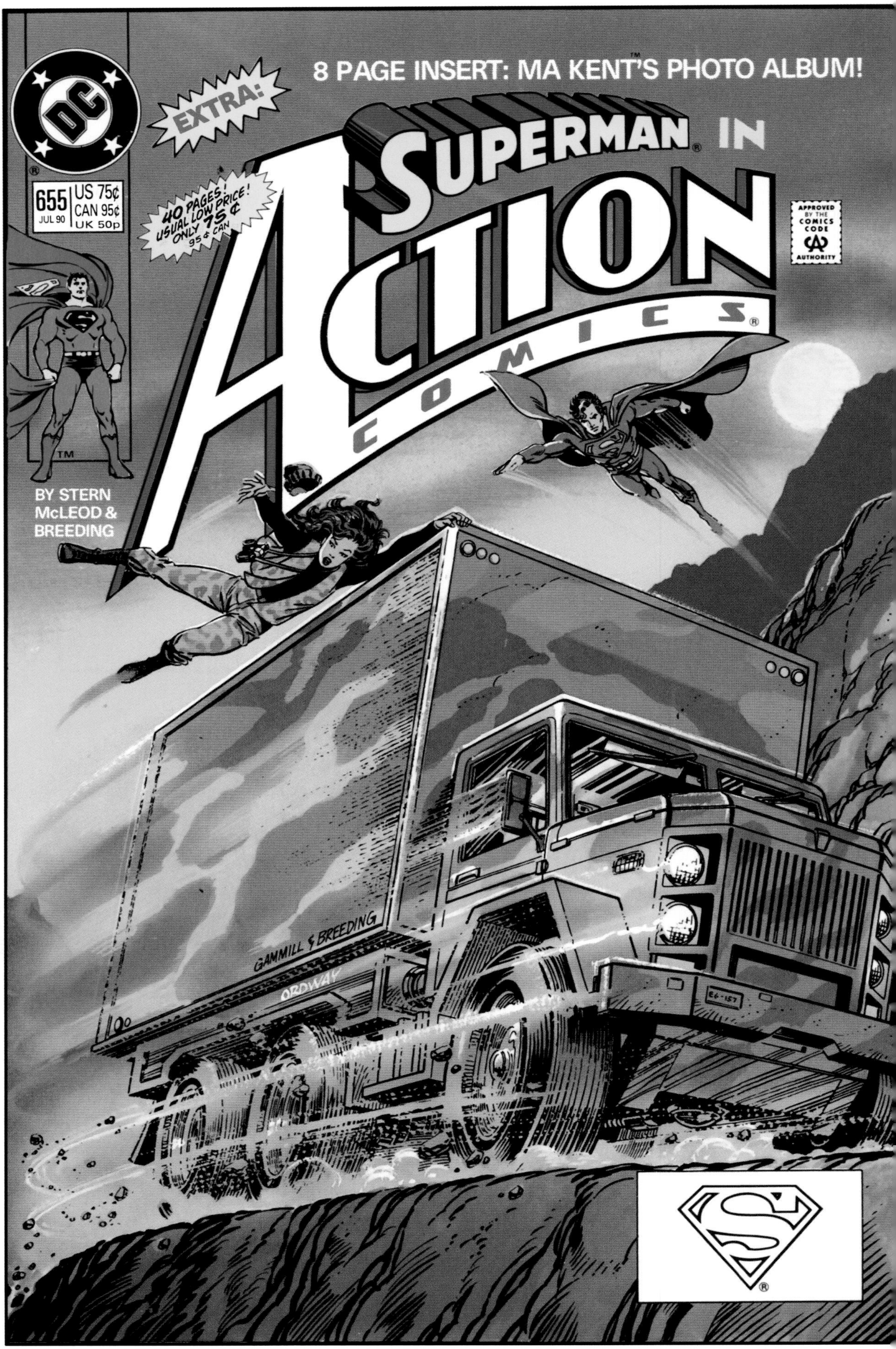
8 PAGE INSERT: MA KENT'S PHOTO ALBUM!
EXTRA:
SUPERMAN IN
ACTION COMICS
655 JUL 90
US 75¢
CAN 95¢
UK 50p
40 PAGES! USUAL LOW PRICE! ONLY 75¢ 95¢ CAN
APPROVED BY THE COMICS CODE AUTHORITY
BY STERN
McLEOD &
BREEDING
GAMMILL & BREEDING
ORDWAY

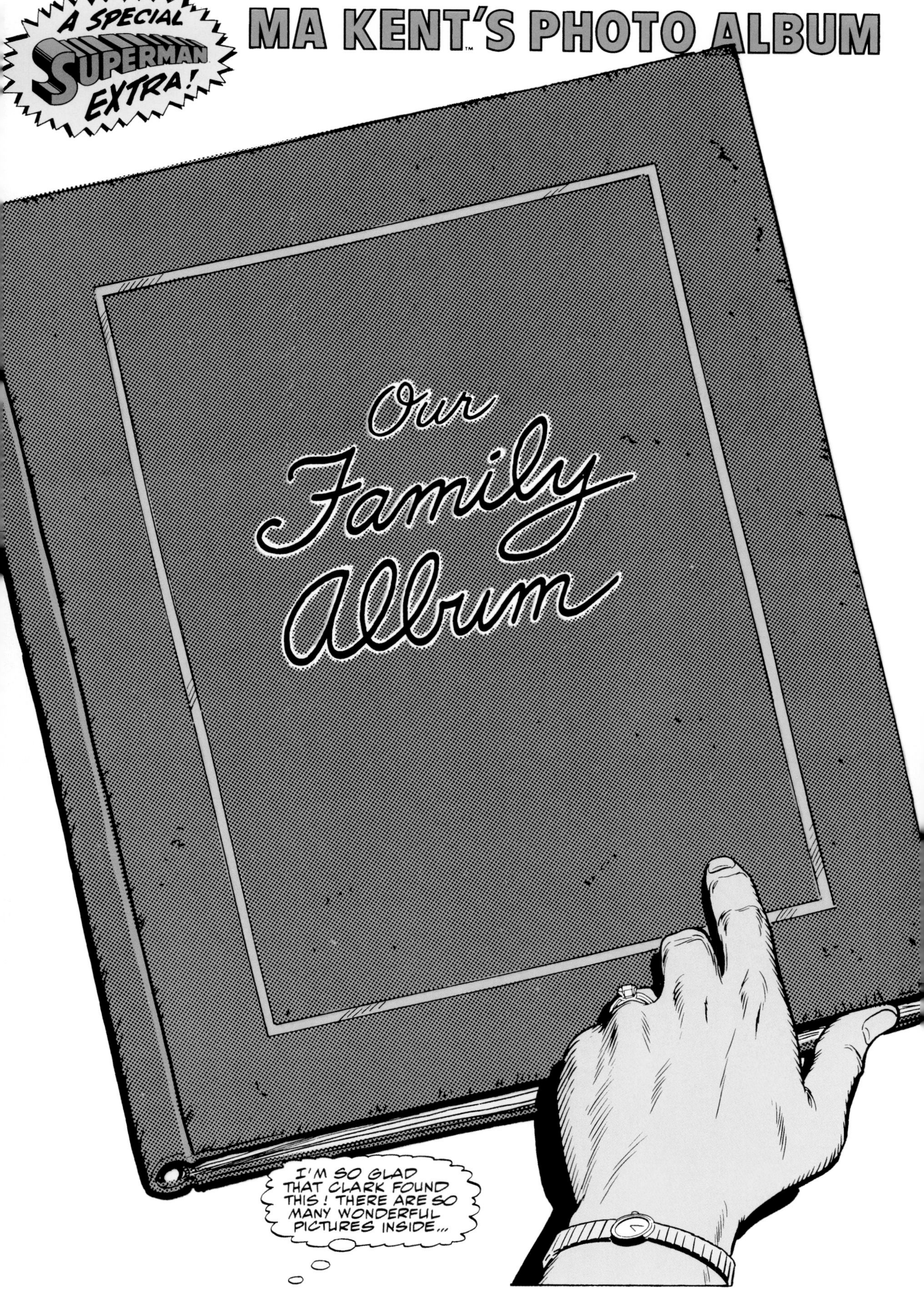
A SPECIAL SUPERMAN EXTRA!
MA KENT'S PHOTO ALBUM
Our Family Album
I'M SO GLAD THAT CLARK FOUND THIS! THERE ARE SO MANY WONDERFUL PICTURES INSIDE...

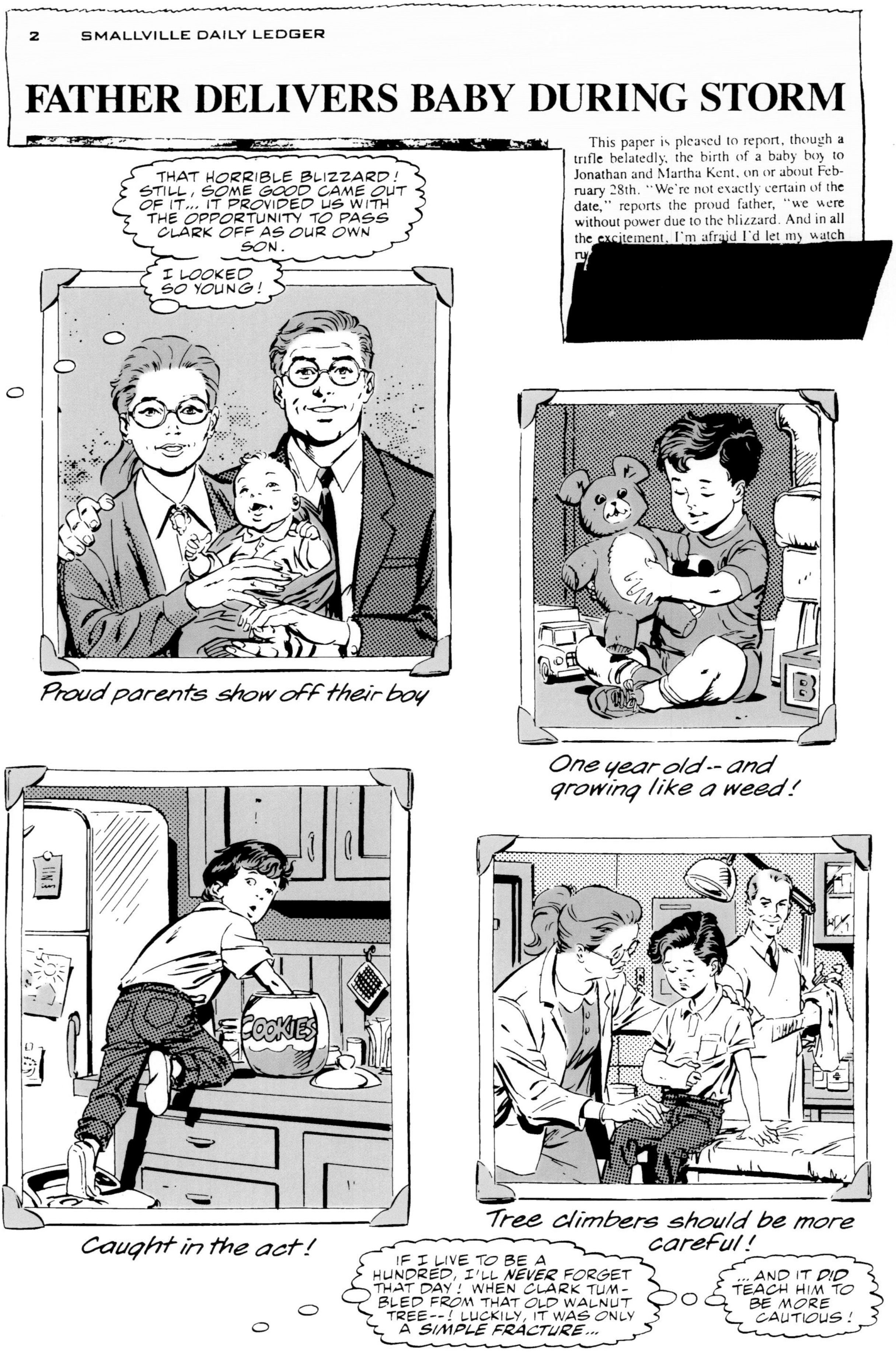
2 SMALLVILLE DAILY LEDGER
FATHER DELIVERS BABY DURING STORM
This paper is pleased to report, though a trifle belatedly, the birth of a baby boy to Jonathan and Martha Kent, on or about February 28th. "We're not exactly certain of the date," reports the proud father, "we were without power due to the blizzard. And in all the excitement, I'm afraid I'd let my watch [redacted]
THAT HORRIBLE BLIZZARD! STILL, SOME GOOD CAME OUT OF IT... IT PROVIDED US WITH THE OPPORTUNITY TO PASS CLARK OFF AS OUR OWN SON.
I LOOKED SO YOUNG!
Proud parents show off their boy
One year old -- and growing like a weed!
COOKIES
Caught in the act!
Tree climbers should be more careful!
IF I LIVE TO BE A HUNDRED, I'LL NEVER FORGET THAT DAY! WHEN CLARK TUMBLED FROM THAT OLD WALNUT TREE--! LUCKILY, IT WAS ONLY A SIMPLE FRACTURE...
...AND IT DID TEACH HIM TO BE MORE CAUTIOUS!

Best of pals!

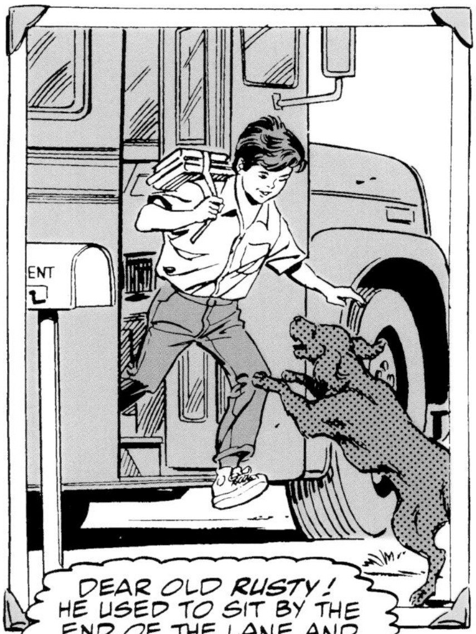
ENT
DEAR OLD RUSTY! HE USED TO SIT BY THE END OF THE LANE AND WAIT FOR CLARK TO GET HOME FROM SCHOOL! I STILL MISS THAT DOG!

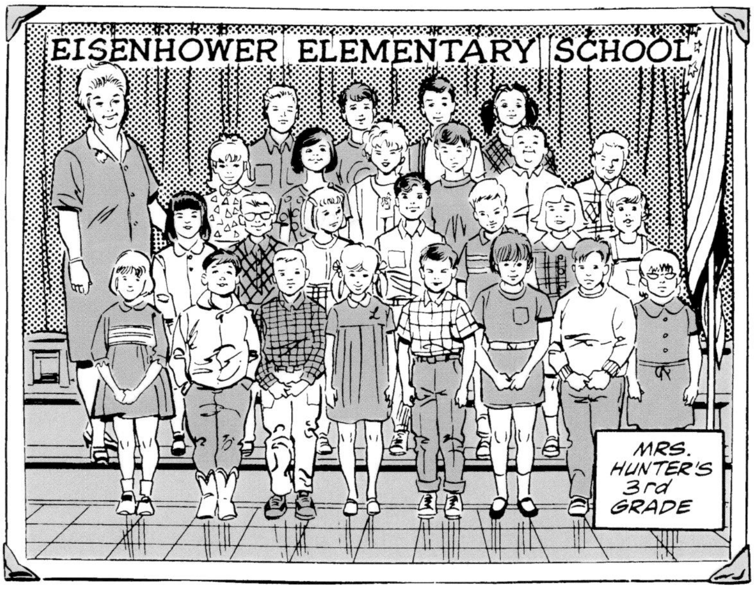
EISENHOWER ELEMENTARY SCHOOL
MRS. HUNTER'S 3rd GRADE

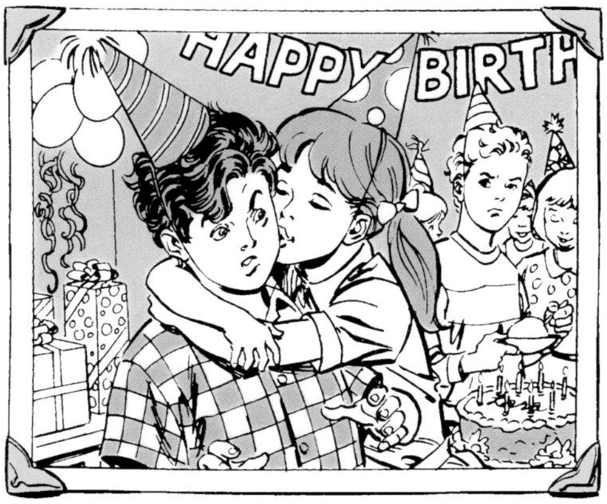
HAPPY BIRTH

Clark at Lana Lang's 8th birthday party

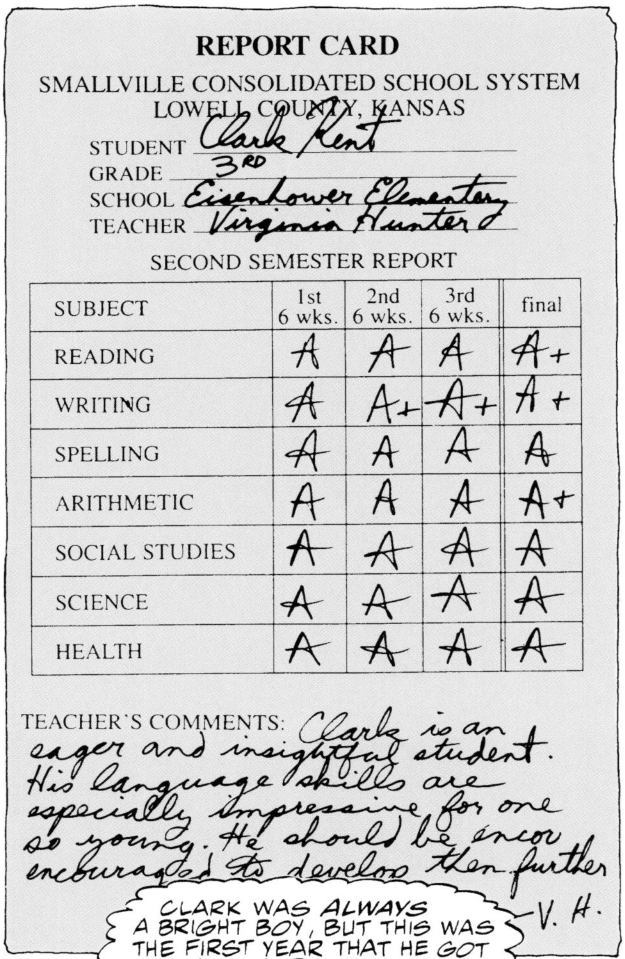

REPORT CARD

SMALLVILLE CONSOLIDATED SCHOOL SYSTEM
LOWELL COUNTY, KANSAS

STUDENT Clark Kent
GRADE 3RD
SCHOOL Eisenhower Elementary
TEACHER Virginia Hunter

SECOND SEMESTER REPORT

SUBJECT	1st 6 wks.	2nd 6 wks.	3rd 6 wks.	final
READING	A	A	A	A+
WRITING	A	A+	A+	A+
SPELLING	A	A	A	A
ARITHMETIC	A	A	A	A+
SOCIAL STUDIES	A	A	A	A
SCIENCE	A	A	A	A
HEALTH	A	A	A	A

TEACHER'S COMMENTS: Clark is an eager and insightful student. His language skills are especially impressive for one so young. He should be encor encouraged to develop them further
-V. H.

CLARK WAS ALWAYS A BRIGHT BOY, BUT THIS WAS THE FIRST YEAR THAT HE GOT ALL A'S. AND I STILL SAY THAT VIRGIE HUNTER WAS THE REASON!
SHE GOT ALL THE CHILDREN TO ENJOY LEARNING! WE WERE SO LUCKY TO HAVE TEACHERS LIKE HER IN THIS COUNTY!

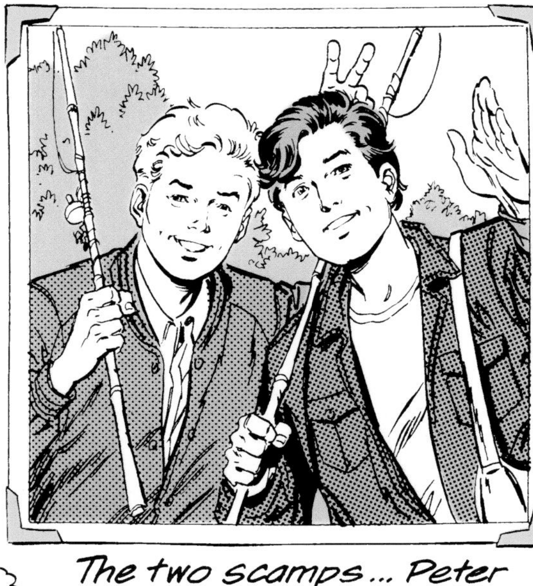

The two scamps... Peter Ross and Clark off for a day of fishing!

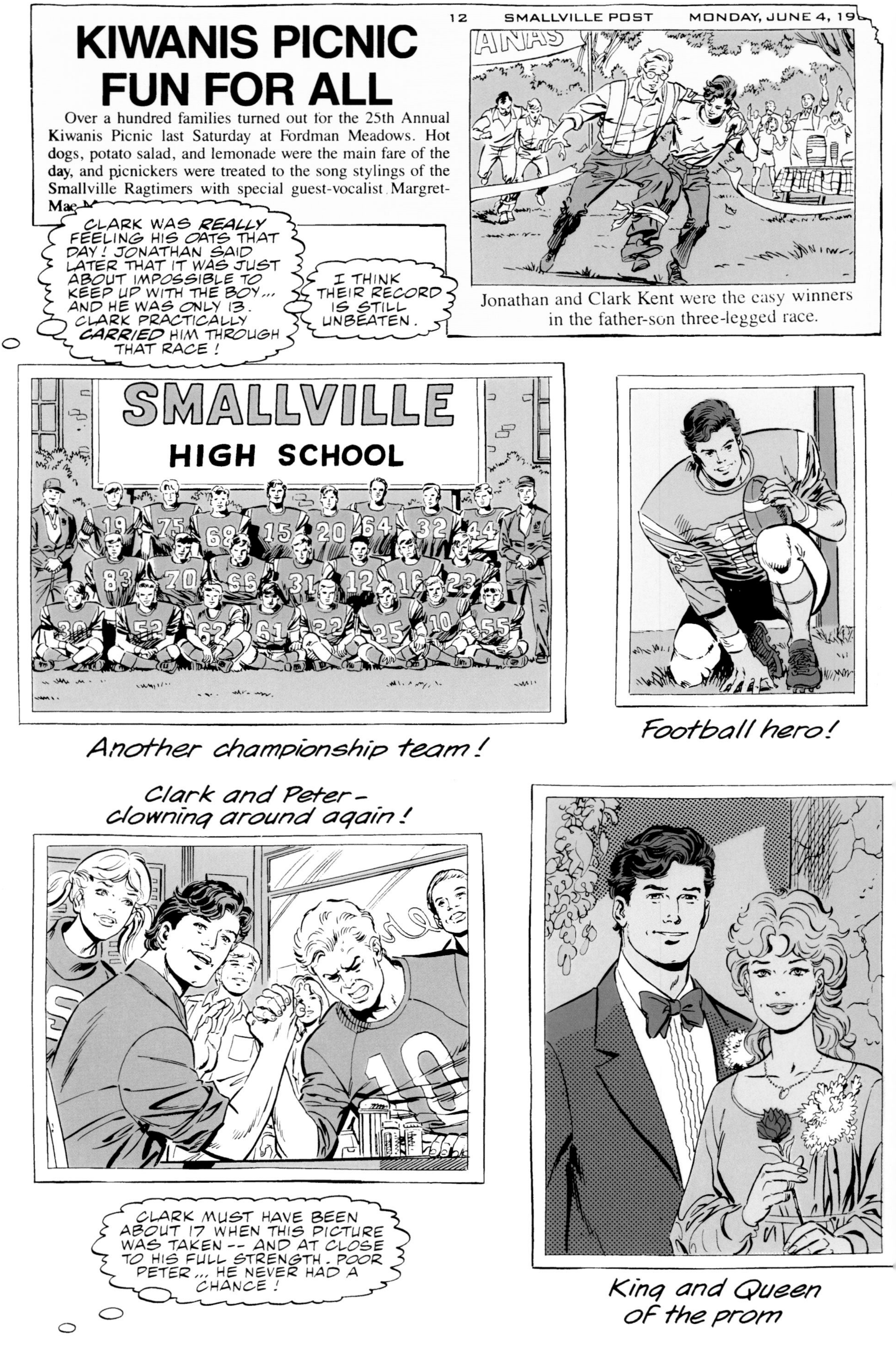
12 SMALLVILLE POST MONDAY, JUNE 4, 19
KIWANIS PICNIC FUN FOR ALL
Over a hundred families turned out for the 25th Annual Kiwanis Picnic last Saturday at Fordman Meadows. Hot dogs, potato salad, and lemonade were the main fare of the day, and picnickers were treated to the song stylings of the Smallville Ragtimers with special guest-vocalist Margret-Mae
Jonathan and Clark Kent were the easy winners in the father-son three-legged race.
CLARK WAS REALLY FEELING HIS OATS THAT DAY! JONATHAN SAID LATER THAT IT WAS JUST ABOUT IMPOSSIBLE TO KEEP UP WITH THE BOY... AND HE WAS ONLY 13. CLARK PRACTICALLY CARRIED HIM THROUGH THAT RACE!
I THINK THEIR RECORD IS STILL UNBEATEN.
SMALLVILLE HIGH SCHOOL
Another championship team!
Football hero!
Clark and Peter - clowning around again!
CLARK MUST HAVE BEEN ABOUT 17 WHEN THIS PICTURE WAS TAKEN -- AND AT CLOSE TO HIS FULL STRENGTH. POOR PETER... HE NEVER HAD A CHANCE!
King and Queen of the prom

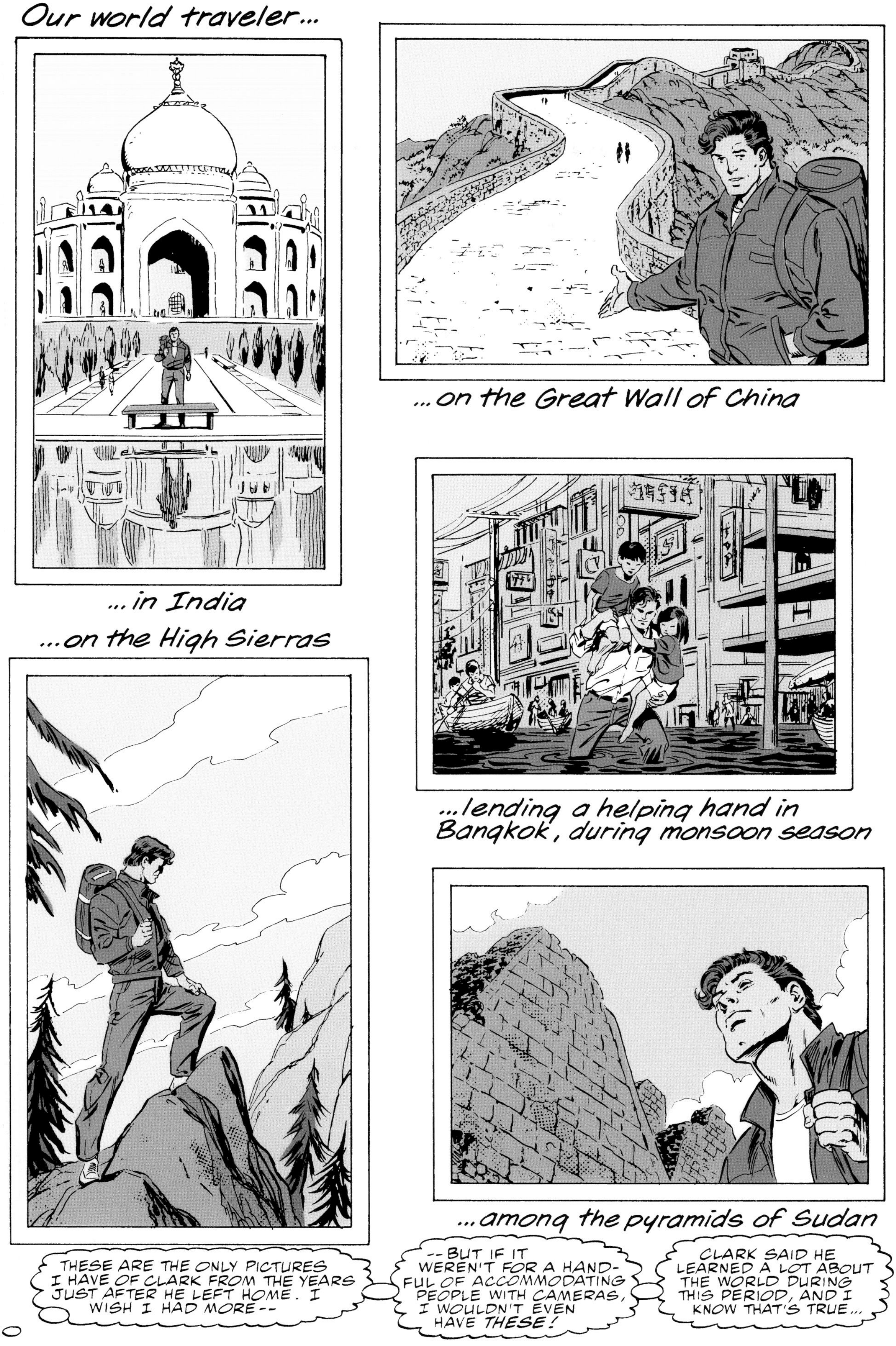
Our world traveler...
...in India
...on the Great Wall of China
...on the High Sierras
...lending a helping hand in Bangkok, during monsoon season
...among the pyramids of Sudan
THESE ARE THE ONLY PICTURES I HAVE OF CLARK FROM THE YEARS JUST AFTER HE LEFT HOME. I WISH I HAD MORE--
--BUT IF IT WEREN'T FOR A HANDFUL OF ACCOMMODATING PEOPLE WITH CAMERAS, I WOULDN'T EVEN HAVE THESE!
CLARK SAID HE LEARNED A LOT ABOUT THE WORLD DURING THIS PERIOD, AND I KNOW THAT'S TRUE...

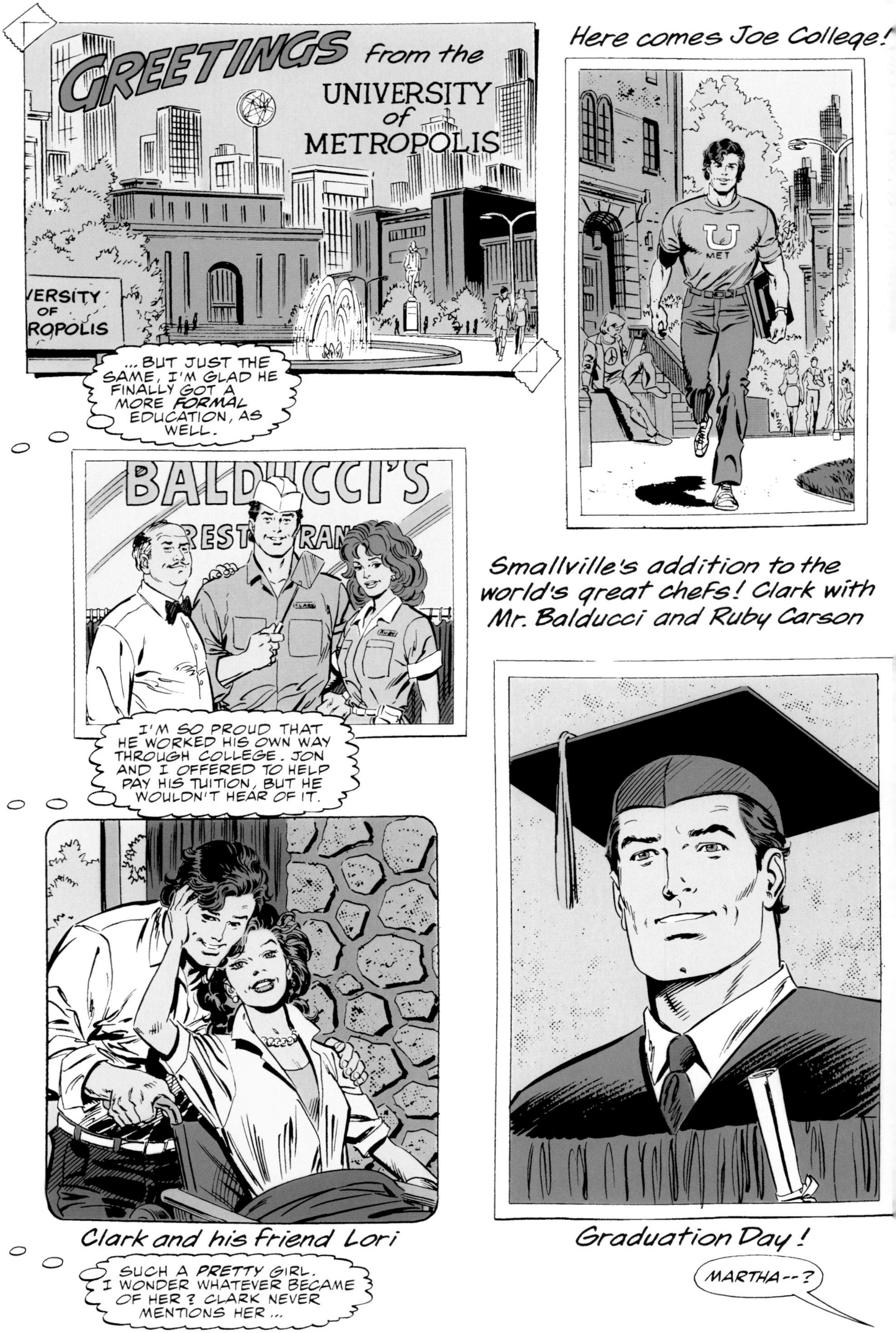
GREETINGS from the UNIVERSITY of METROPOLIS
VERSITY OF ROPOLIS
Here comes Joe College!
U MET
...BUT JUST THE SAME, I'M GLAD HE FINALLY GOT A MORE FORMAL EDUCATION, AS WELL.
BALDUCCI'S RESTAURANT
CLARK
RUBY
Smallville's addition to the world's great chefs! Clark with Mr. Balducci and Ruby Carson
I'M SO PROUD THAT HE WORKED HIS OWN WAY THROUGH COLLEGE. JON AND I OFFERED TO HELP PAY HIS TUITION, BUT HE WOULDN'T HEAR OF IT.
Clark and his friend Lori
SUCH A PRETTY GIRL. I WONDER WHATEVER BECAME OF HER? CLARK NEVER MENTIONS HER...
Graduation Day!
MARTHA--?

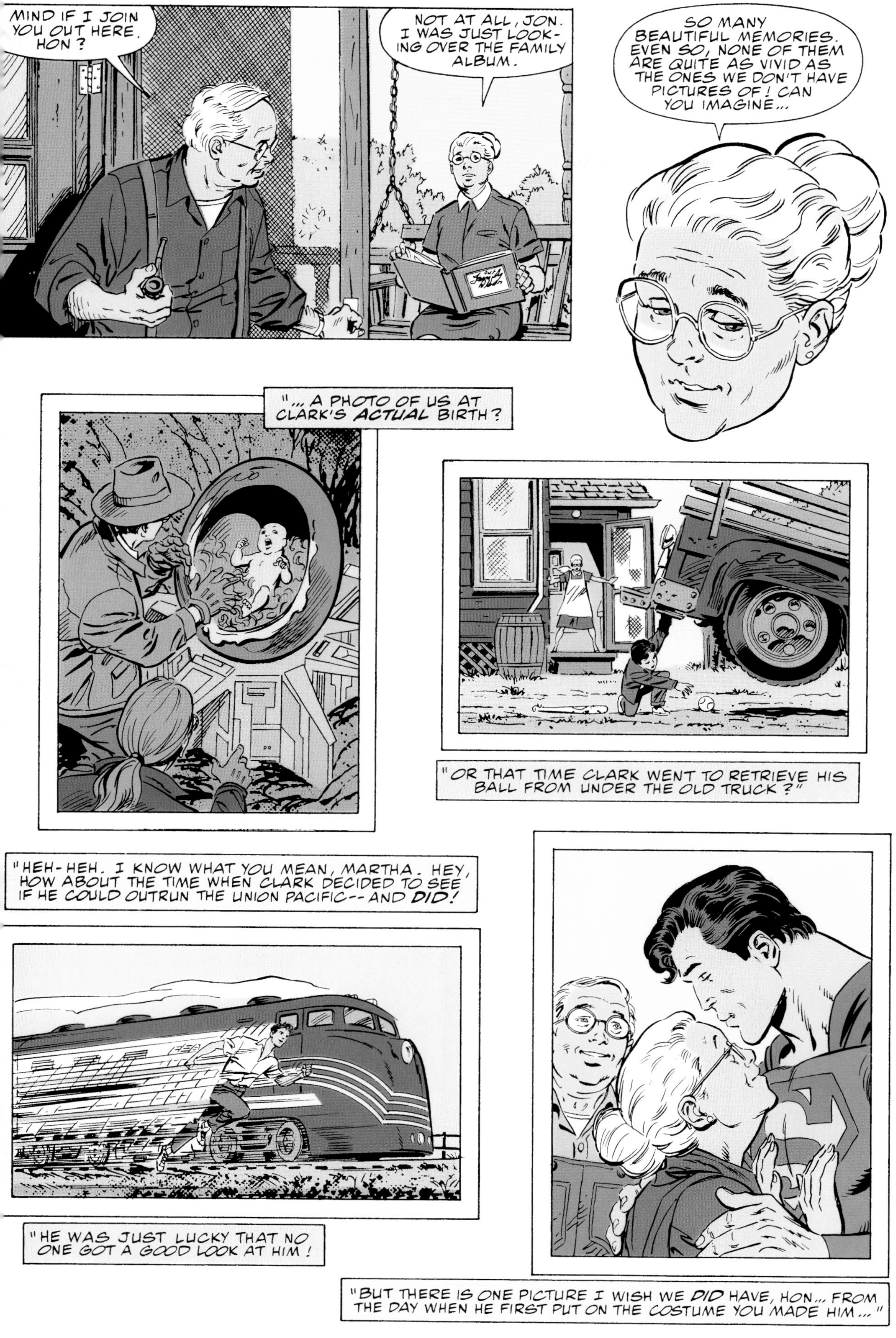

MIND IF I JOIN YOU OUT HERE, HON?
NOT AT ALL, JON. I WAS JUST LOOKING OVER THE FAMILY ALBUM.
SO MANY BEAUTIFUL MEMORIES. EVEN SO, NONE OF THEM ARE QUITE AS VIVID AS THE ONES WE DON'T HAVE PICTURES OF! CAN YOU IMAGINE...
"...A PHOTO OF US AT CLARK'S ACTUAL BIRTH?
"OR THAT TIME CLARK WENT TO RETRIEVE HIS BALL FROM UNDER THE OLD TRUCK?"
"HEH-HEH. I KNOW WHAT YOU MEAN, MARTHA. HEY, HOW ABOUT THE TIME WHEN CLARK DECIDED TO SEE IF HE COULD OUTRUN THE UNION PACIFIC--AND DID!
"HE WAS JUST LUCKY THAT NO ONE GOT A GOOD LOOK AT HIM!
"BUT THERE IS ONE PICTURE I WISH WE DID HAVE, HON... FROM THE DAY WHEN HE FIRST PUT ON THE COSTUME YOU MADE HIM..."

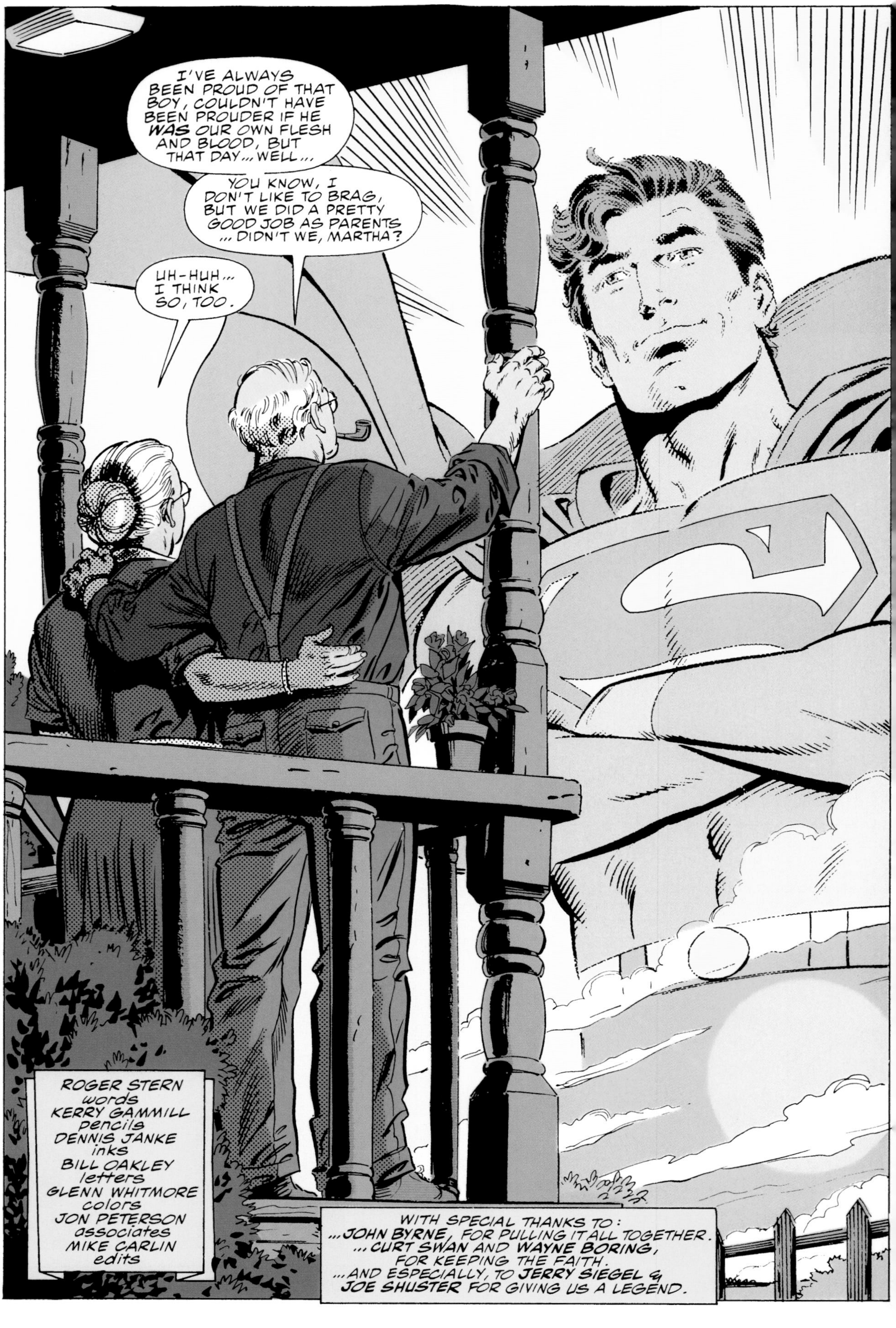
I'VE ALWAYS BEEN PROUD OF THAT BOY, COULDN'T HAVE BEEN PROUDER IF HE WAS OUR OWN FLESH AND BLOOD, BUT THAT DAY... WELL...
YOU KNOW, I DON'T LIKE TO BRAG, BUT WE DID A PRETTY GOOD JOB AS PARENTS ... DIDN'T WE, MARTHA?
UH-HUH... I THINK SO, TOO.
ROGER STERN words KERRY GAMMILL pencils DENNIS JANKE inks BILL OAKLEY letters GLENN WHITMORE colors JON PETERSON associates MIKE CARLIN edits
WITH SPECIAL THANKS TO: ...JOHN BYRNE, FOR PULLING IT ALL TOGETHER. ...CURT SWAN AND WAYNE BORING, FOR KEEPING THE FAITH. ...AND ESPECIALLY, TO JERRY SIEGEL & JOE SHUSTER FOR GIVING US A LEGEND.

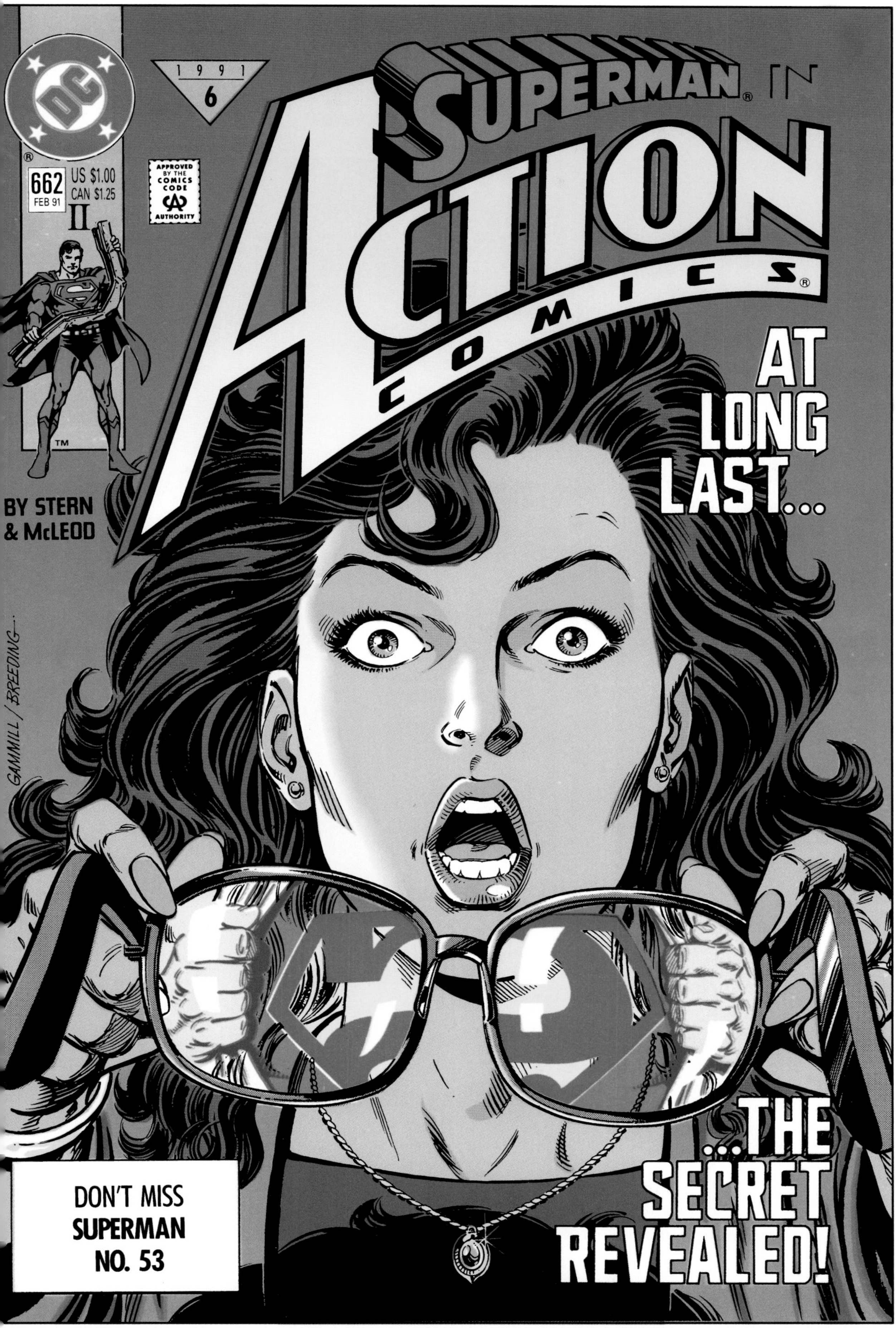
1991
6
SUPERMAN IN
ACTION COMICS
662
FEB 91
US $1.00
CAN $1.25
II
APPROVED BY THE COMICS CODE AUTHORITY
BY STERN & McLEOD
GAMMILL / BREEDING
AT LONG LAST...
...THE SECRET REVEALED!
DON'T MISS SUPERMAN NO. 53

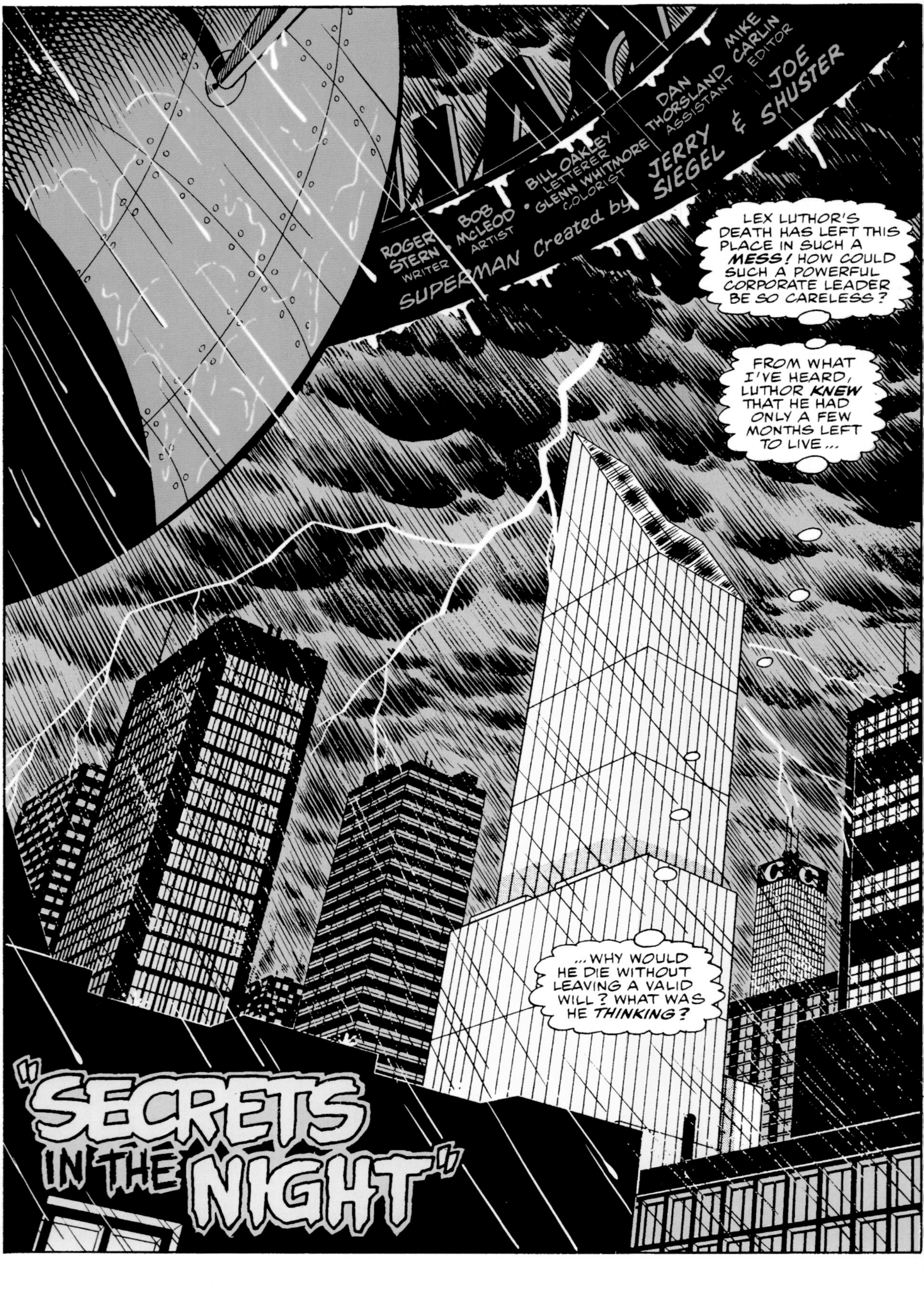
ROGER STERN WRITER
BOB McLEOD ARTIST
BILL OAKLEY LETTERER
GLENN WHITMORE COLORIST
DAN THORSLAND ASSISTANT
MIKE CARLIN EDITOR
SUPERMAN Created by JERRY SIEGEL & JOE SHUSTER
LEX LUTHOR'S DEATH HAS LEFT THIS PLACE IN SUCH A MESS! HOW COULD SUCH A POWERFUL CORPORATE LEADER BE SO CARELESS?
FROM WHAT I'VE HEARD, LUTHOR KNEW THAT HE HAD ONLY A FEW MONTHS LEFT TO LIVE...
...WHY WOULD HE DIE WITHOUT LEAVING A VALID WILL? WHAT WAS HE THINKING?
"SECRETS IN THE NIGHT"

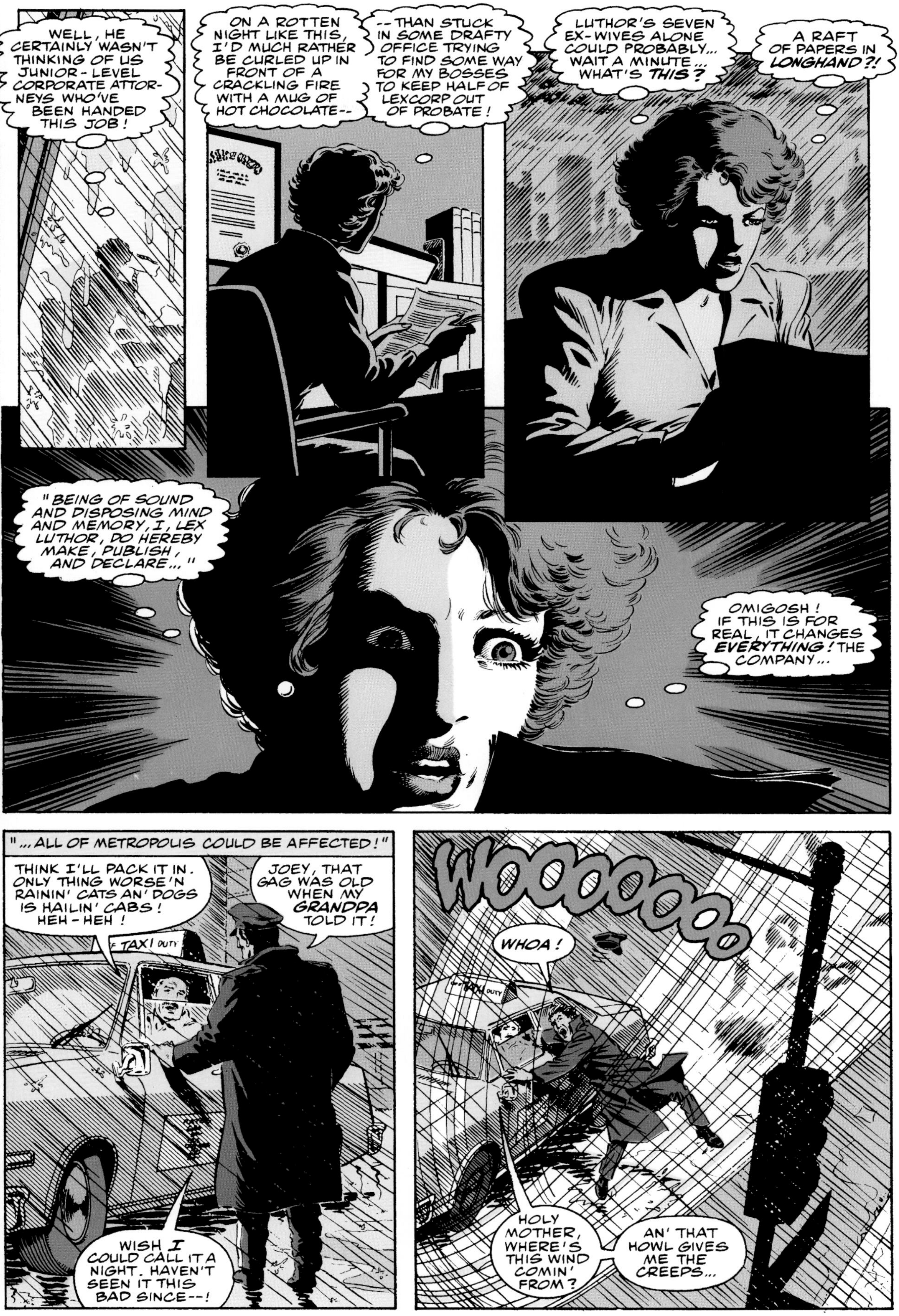

WELL, HE CERTAINLY WASN'T THINKING OF US JUNIOR-LEVEL CORPORATE ATTORNEYS WHO'VE BEEN HANDED THIS JOB!
ON A ROTTEN NIGHT LIKE THIS, I'D MUCH RATHER BE CURLED UP IN FRONT OF A CRACKLING FIRE WITH A MUG OF HOT CHOCOLATE--
--THAN STUCK IN SOME DRAFTY OFFICE TRYING TO FIND SOME WAY FOR MY BOSSES TO KEEP HALF OF LEXCORP OUT OF PROBATE!
LUTHOR'S SEVEN EX-WIVES ALONE COULD PROBABLY... WAIT A MINUTE... WHAT'S THIS?
A RAFT OF PAPERS IN LONGHAND?!
"BEING OF SOUND AND DISPOSING MIND AND MEMORY, I, LEX LUTHOR, DO HEREBY MAKE, PUBLISH, AND DECLARE..."
OMIGOSH! IF THIS IS FOR REAL, IT CHANGES EVERYTHING! THE COMPANY...
"...ALL OF METROPOLIS COULD BE AFFECTED!"
THINK I'LL PACK IT IN. ONLY THING WORSE'N RAININ' CATS AN' DOGS IS HAILIN' CABS! HEH-HEH!
JOEY, THAT GAG WAS OLD WHEN MY GRANDPA TOLD IT!
WISH I COULD CALL IT A NIGHT. HAVEN'T SEEN IT THIS BAD SINCE--!
WOOOOOOO
WHOA!
HOLY MOTHER, WHERE'S THIS WIND COMIN' FROM?
AN' THAT HOWL GIVES ME THE CREEPS...

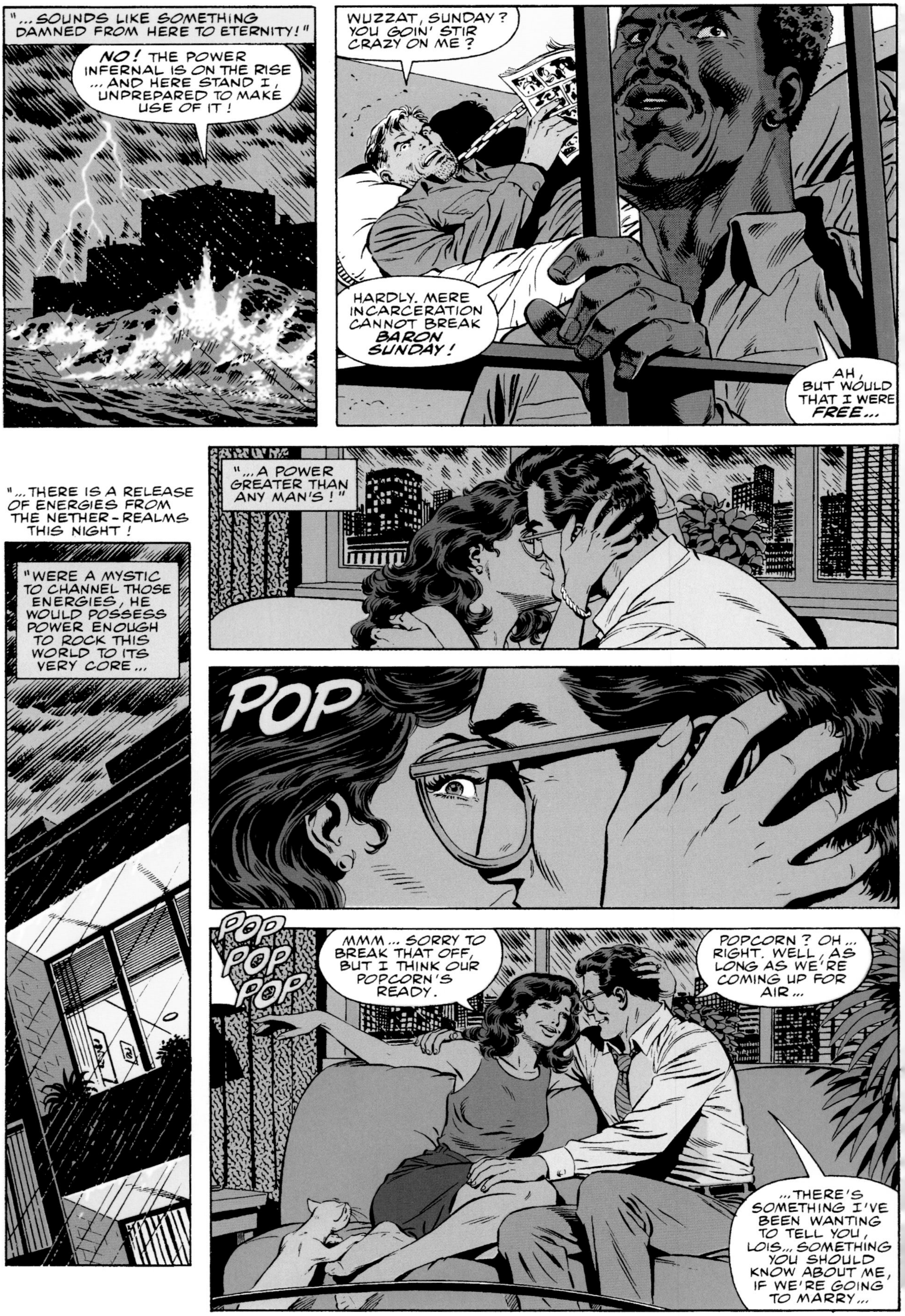
"...SOUNDS LIKE SOMETHING DAMNED FROM HERE TO ETERNITY!"
NO! THE POWER INFERNAL IS ON THE RISE ...AND HERE STAND I, UNPREPARED TO MAKE USE OF IT!
WUZZAT, SUNDAY? YOU GOIN' STIR CRAZY ON ME?
HARDLY. MERE INCARCERATION CANNOT BREAK BARON SUNDAY!
AH, BUT WOULD THAT I WERE FREE...
"...THERE IS A RELEASE OF ENERGIES FROM THE NETHER-REALMS THIS NIGHT!
"WERE A MYSTIC TO CHANNEL THOSE ENERGIES, HE WOULD POSSESS POWER ENOUGH TO ROCK THIS WORLD TO ITS VERY CORE...
"...A POWER GREATER THAN ANY MAN'S!"
POP
POP POP POP
MMM... SORRY TO BREAK THAT OFF, BUT I THINK OUR POPCORN'S READY.
POPCORN? OH... RIGHT. WELL, AS LONG AS WE'RE COMING UP FOR AIR...
...THERE'S SOMETHING I'VE BEEN WANTING TO TELL YOU, LOIS... SOMETHING YOU SHOULD KNOW ABOUT ME, IF WE'RE GOING TO MARRY...

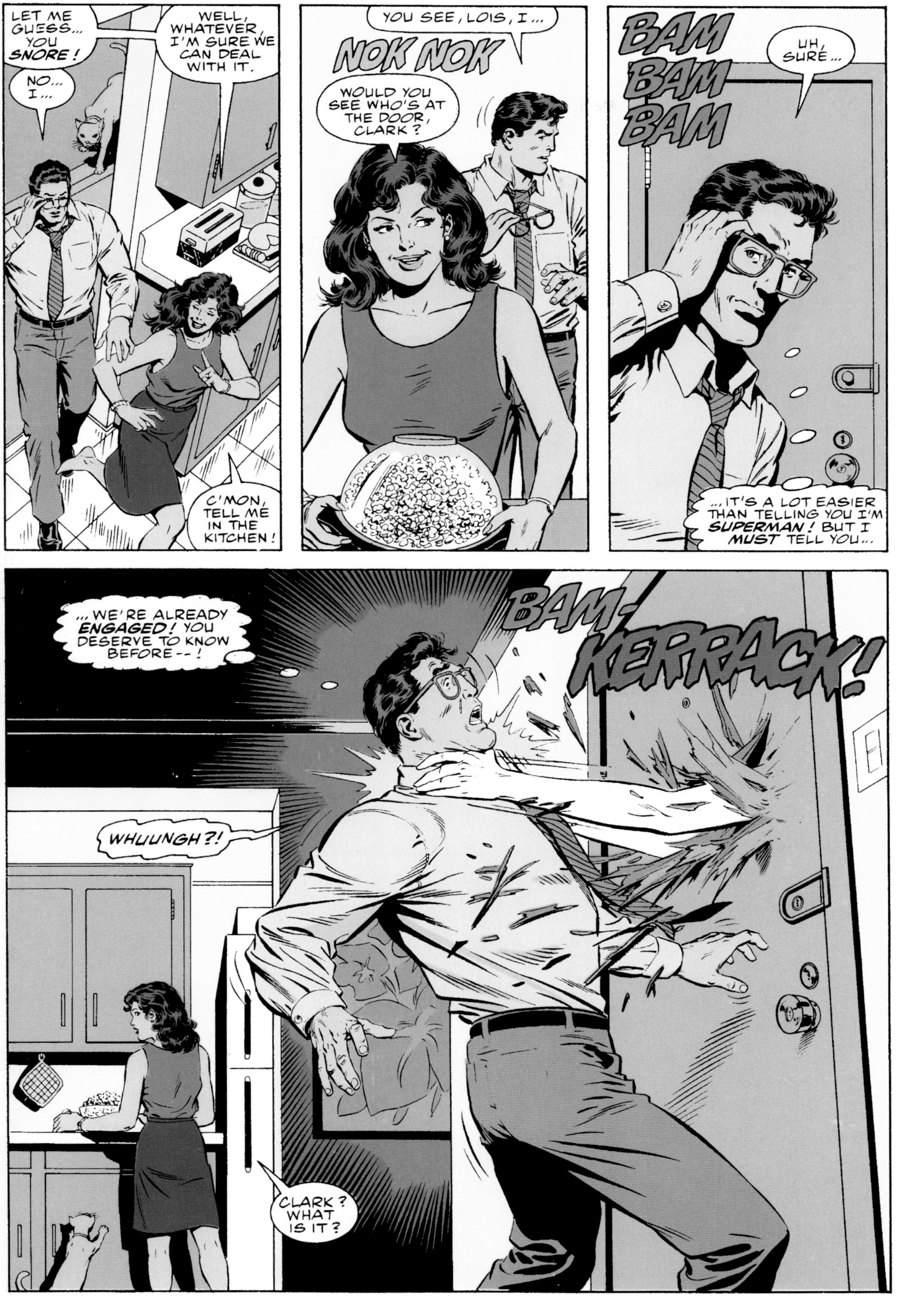

LET ME GUESS... YOU SNORE!
NO... I...
WELL, WHATEVER, I'M SURE WE CAN DEAL WITH IT.
C'MON, TELL ME IN THE KITCHEN!
YOU SEE, LOIS, I...
NOK NOK
WOULD YOU SEE WHO'S AT THE DOOR, CLARK?
BAM BAM BAM
UH, SURE...
...IT'S A LOT EASIER THAN TELLING YOU I'M SUPERMAN! BUT I MUST TELL YOU...
...WE'RE ALREADY ENGAGED! YOU DESERVE TO KNOW BEFORE--!
BAM-KERRACK!
WHUUNGH?!
CLARK? WHAT IS IT?

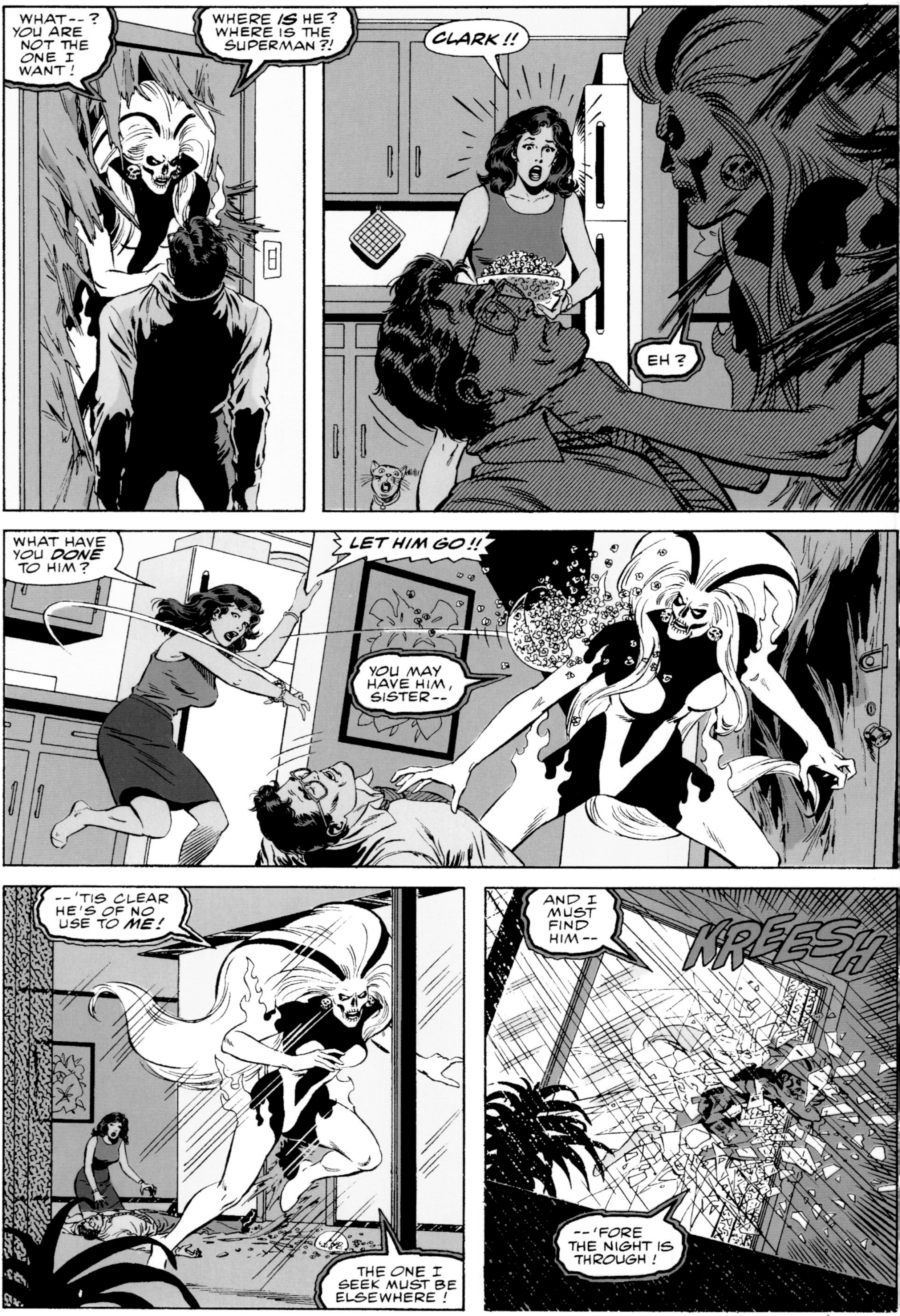
WHAT--? YOU ARE NOT THE ONE I WANT!
WHERE IS HE? WHERE IS THE SUPERMAN?!
CLARK!!
EH?
WHAT HAVE YOU DONE TO HIM?
LET HIM GO!!
YOU MAY HAVE HIM, SISTER--
--'TIS CLEAR HE'S OF NO USE TO ME!
THE ONE I SEEK MUST BE ELSEWHERE!
AND I MUST FIND HIM--
KREESH
--'FORE THE NIGHT IS THROUGH!

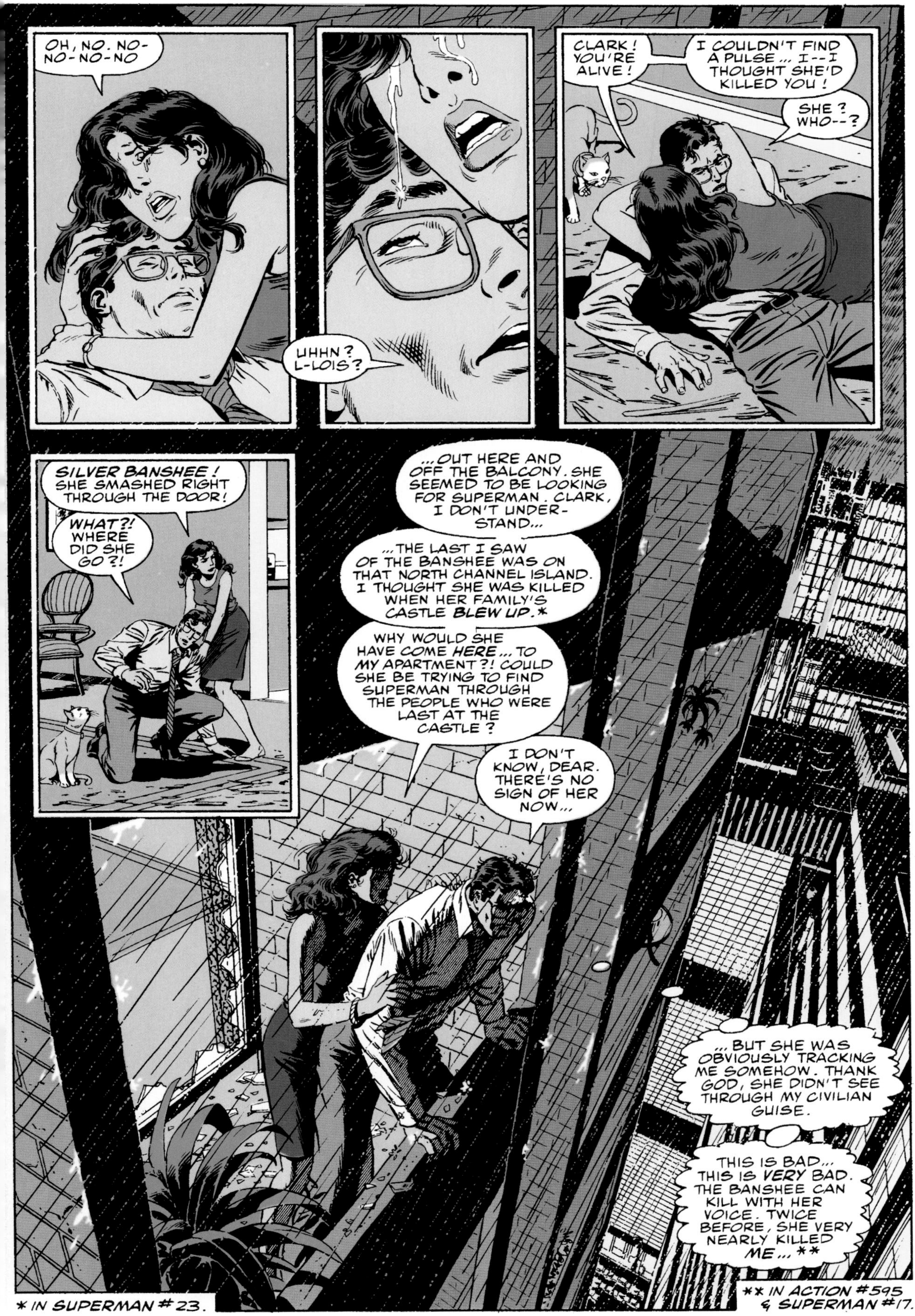
OH, NO. NO-NO-NO-NO
UHHN? L-LOIS?
CLARK! YOU'RE ALIVE!
I COULDN'T FIND A PULSE... I--I THOUGHT SHE'D KILLED YOU!
SHE? WHO--?
SILVER BANSHEE! SHE SMASHED RIGHT THROUGH THE DOOR!
WHAT?! WHERE DID SHE GO?!
...OUT HERE AND OFF THE BALCONY. SHE SEEMED TO BE LOOKING FOR SUPERMAN. CLARK, I DON'T UNDERSTAND...
...THE LAST I SAW OF THE BANSHEE WAS ON THAT NORTH CHANNEL ISLAND. I THOUGHT SHE WAS KILLED WHEN HER FAMILY'S CASTLE BLEW UP.*
WHY WOULD SHE HAVE COME HERE... TO MY APARTMENT?! COULD SHE BE TRYING TO FIND SUPERMAN THROUGH THE PEOPLE WHO WERE LAST AT THE CASTLE?
I DON'T KNOW, DEAR. THERE'S NO SIGN OF HER NOW...
...BUT SHE WAS OBVIOUSLY TRACKING ME SOMEHOW. THANK GOD, SHE DIDN'T SEE THROUGH MY CIVILIAN GUISE.
THIS IS BAD... THIS IS VERY BAD. THE BANSHEE CAN KILL WITH HER VOICE. TWICE BEFORE, SHE VERY NEARLY KILLED ME...**

* IN SUPERMAN #23.

** IN ACTION #595 & SUPERMAN #17.

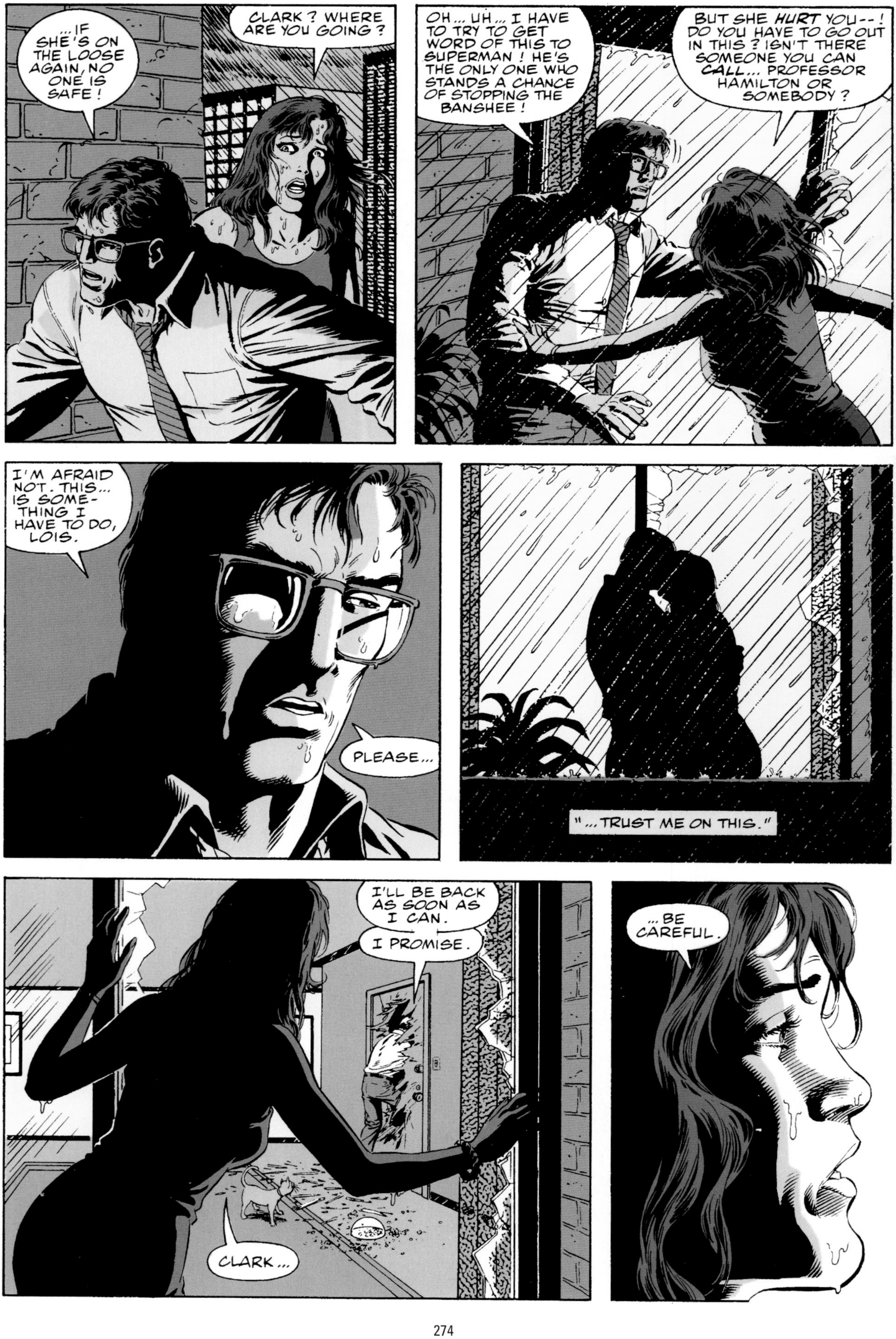

...IF SHE'S ON THE LOOSE AGAIN, NO ONE IS SAFE!
CLARK? WHERE ARE YOU GOING?
OH... UH... I HAVE TO TRY TO GET WORD OF THIS TO SUPERMAN! HE'S THE ONLY ONE WHO STANDS A CHANCE OF STOPPING THE BANSHEE!
BUT SHE HURT YOU--! DO YOU HAVE TO GO OUT IN THIS? ISN'T THERE SOMEONE YOU CAN CALL... PROFESSOR HAMILTON OR SOMEBODY?
I'M AFRAID NOT. THIS... IS SOMETHING I HAVE TO DO, LOIS.
PLEASE...
"...TRUST ME ON THIS."
I'LL BE BACK AS SOON AS I CAN.
I PROMISE.
CLARK...
...BE CAREFUL.

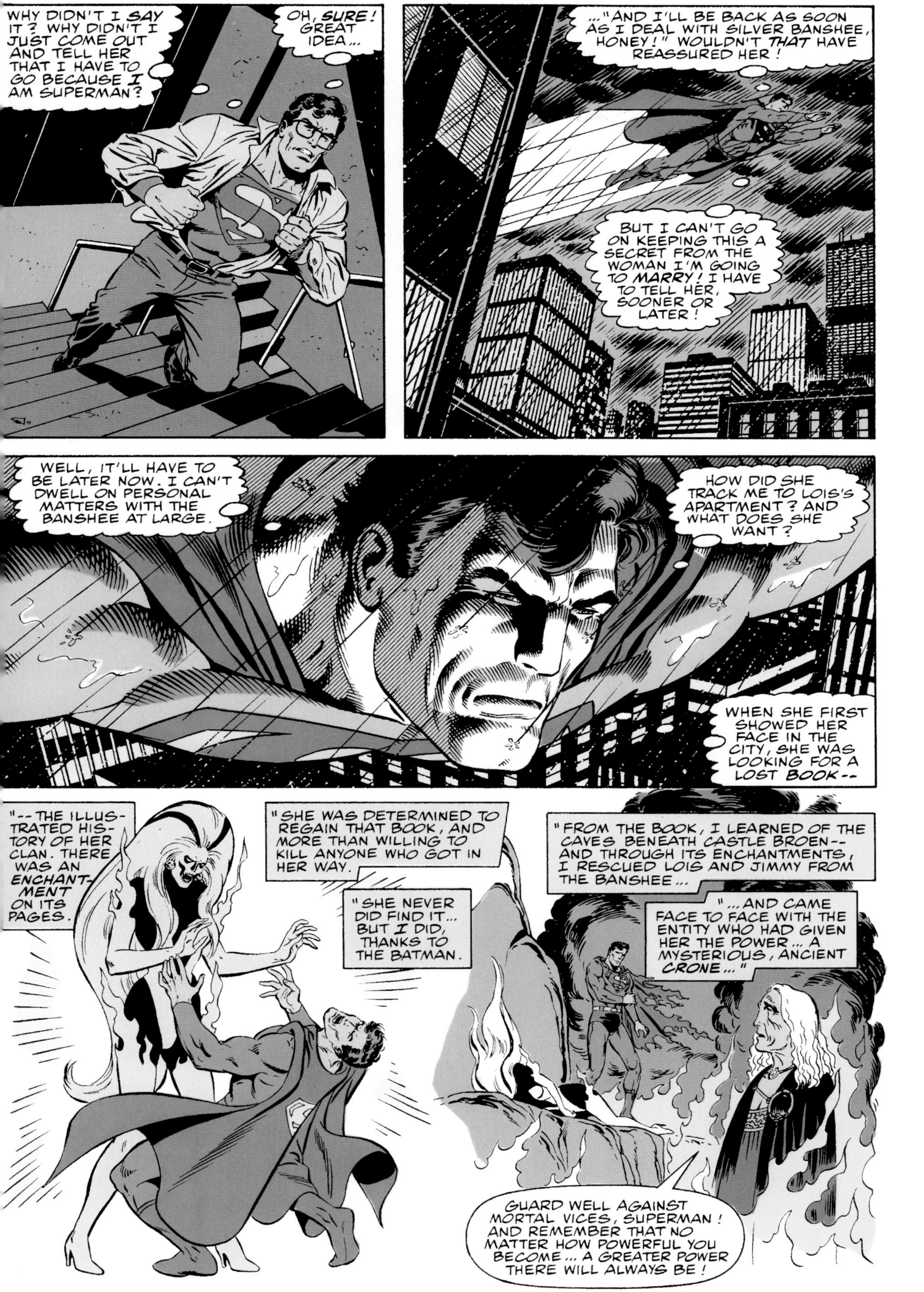
WHY DIDN'T I SAY IT? WHY DIDN'T I JUST COME OUT AND TELL HER THAT I HAVE TO GO BECAUSE I AM SUPERMAN?
OH, SURE! GREAT IDEA...
..."AND I'LL BE BACK AS SOON AS I DEAL WITH SILVER BANSHEE, HONEY!" WOULDN'T THAT HAVE REASSURED HER!
BUT I CAN'T GO ON KEEPING THIS A SECRET FROM THE WOMAN I'M GOING TO MARRY! I HAVE TO TELL HER, SOONER OR LATER!
WELL, IT'LL HAVE TO BE LATER NOW. I CAN'T DWELL ON PERSONAL MATTERS WITH THE BANSHEE AT LARGE.
HOW DID SHE TRACK ME TO LOIS'S APARTMENT? AND WHAT DOES SHE WANT?
WHEN SHE FIRST SHOWED HER FACE IN THE CITY, SHE WAS LOOKING FOR A LOST BOOK--
"--THE ILLUSTRATED HISTORY OF HER CLAN. THERE WAS AN ENCHANTMENT ON ITS PAGES.
"SHE WAS DETERMINED TO REGAIN THAT BOOK, AND MORE THAN WILLING TO KILL ANYONE WHO GOT IN HER WAY.
"SHE NEVER DID FIND IT... BUT I DID, THANKS TO THE BATMAN.
"FROM THE BOOK, I LEARNED OF THE CAVES BENEATH CASTLE BROEN--AND THROUGH ITS ENCHANTMENTS, I RESCUED LOIS AND JIMMY FROM THE BANSHEE...
"...AND CAME FACE TO FACE WITH THE ENTITY WHO HAD GIVEN HER THE POWER... A MYSTERIOUS, ANCIENT CRONE..."
GUARD WELL AGAINST MORTAL VICES, SUPERMAN! AND REMEMBER THAT NO MATTER HOW POWERFUL YOU BECOME... A GREATER POWER THERE WILL ALWAYS BE!

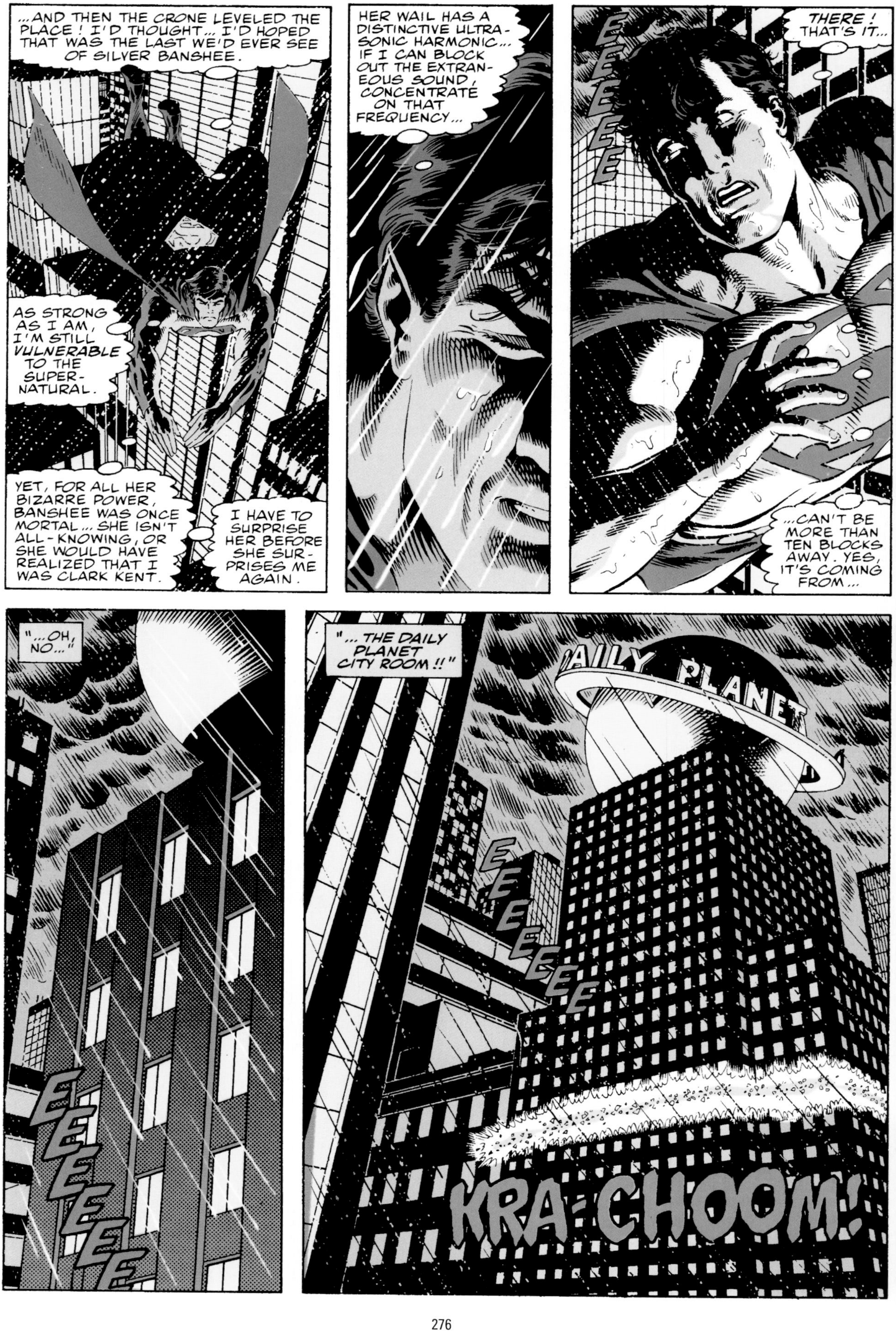
...AND THEN THE CRONE LEVELED THE PLACE! I'D THOUGHT... I'D HOPED THAT WAS THE LAST WE'D EVER SEE OF SILVER BANSHEE.
AS STRONG AS I AM, I'M STILL VULNERABLE TO THE SUPER-NATURAL.
YET, FOR ALL HER BIZARRE POWER, BANSHEE WAS ONCE MORTAL... SHE ISN'T ALL-KNOWING, OR SHE WOULD HAVE REALIZED THAT I WAS CLARK KENT.
I HAVE TO SURPRISE HER BEFORE SHE SUR-PRISES ME AGAIN.
HER WAIL HAS A DISTINCTIVE ULTRA-SONIC HARMONIC... IF I CAN BLOCK OUT THE EXTRAN-EOUS SOUND, CONCENTRATE ON THAT FREQUENCY...
EEEEEE
THERE! THAT'S IT...
...CAN'T BE MORE THAN TEN BLOCKS AWAY. YES, IT'S COMING FROM...
"...OH, NO..."
EEEEEEE
"...THE DAILY PLANET CITY ROOM!!"
AILY PLANET
EEEEEEE
KRA-CHOOM!

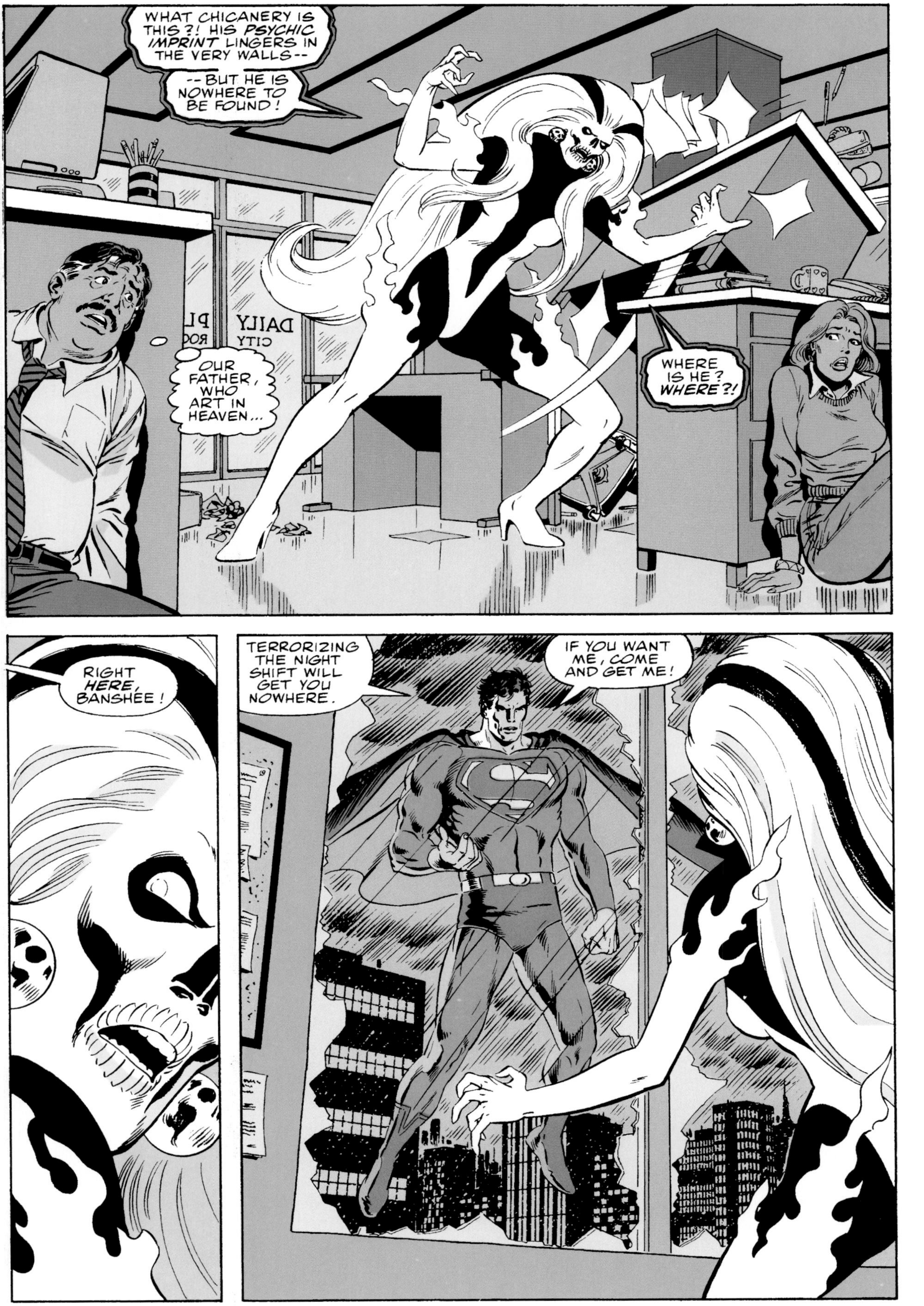
WHAT CHICANERY IS THIS?! HIS PSYCHIC IMPRINT LINGERS IN THE VERY WALLS--
--BUT HE IS NOWHERE TO BE FOUND!
OUR FATHER, WHO ART IN HEAVEN...
WHERE IS HE? WHERE?!
RIGHT HERE, BANSHEE!
TERRORIZING THE NIGHT SHIFT WILL GET YOU NOWHERE.
IF YOU WANT ME, COME AND GET ME!

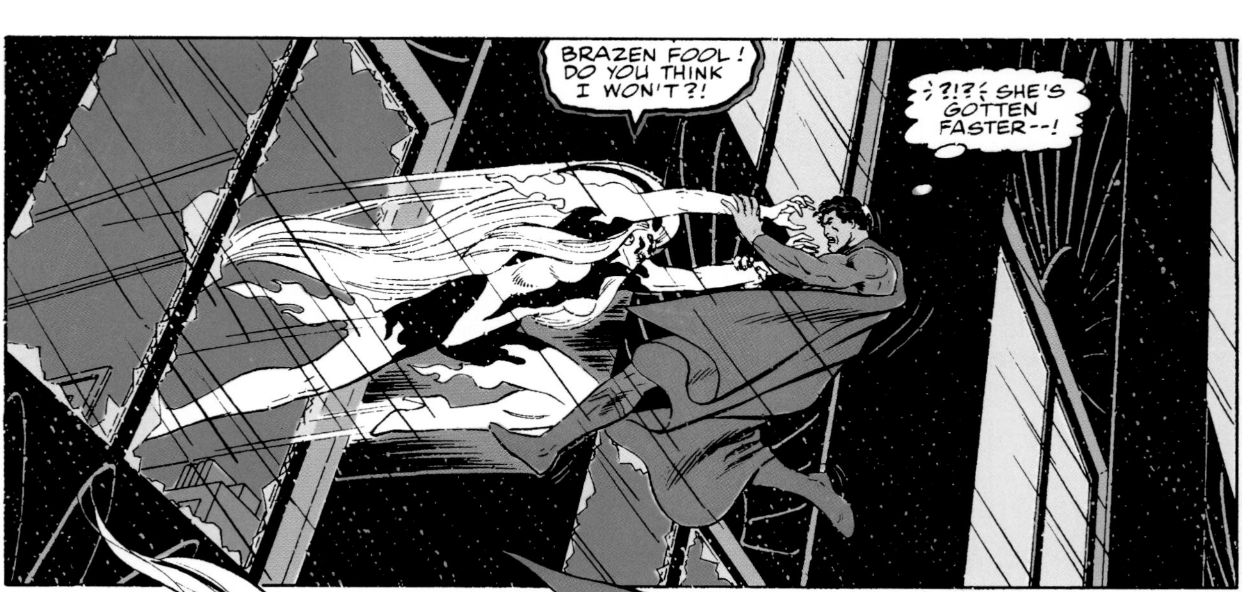
BRAZEN FOOL! DO YOU THINK I WON'T?!
¿?!?¿ SHE'S GOTTEN FASTER--!

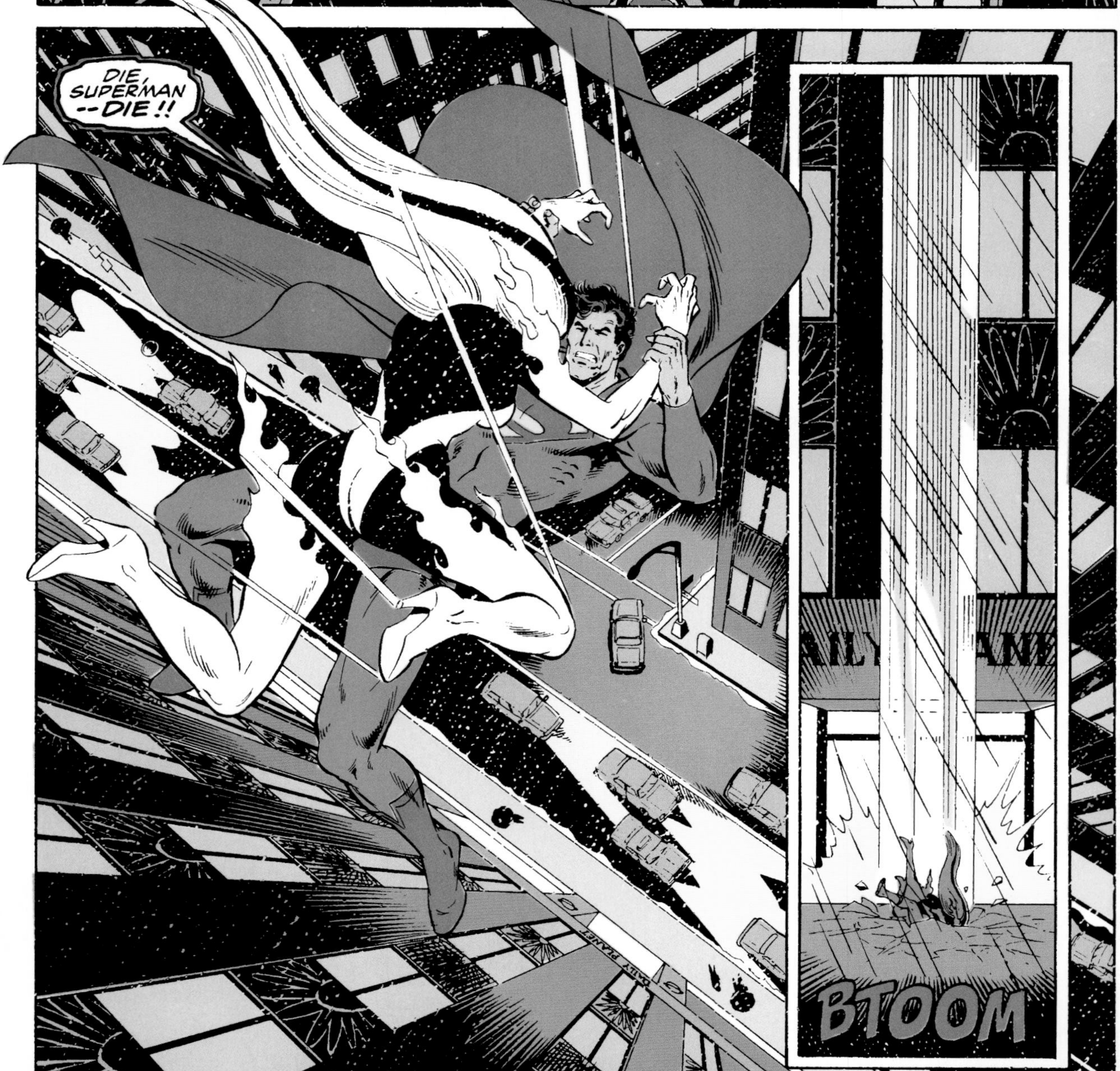
DIE, SUPERMAN --DIE!!
DAILY PLANET
BTOOM

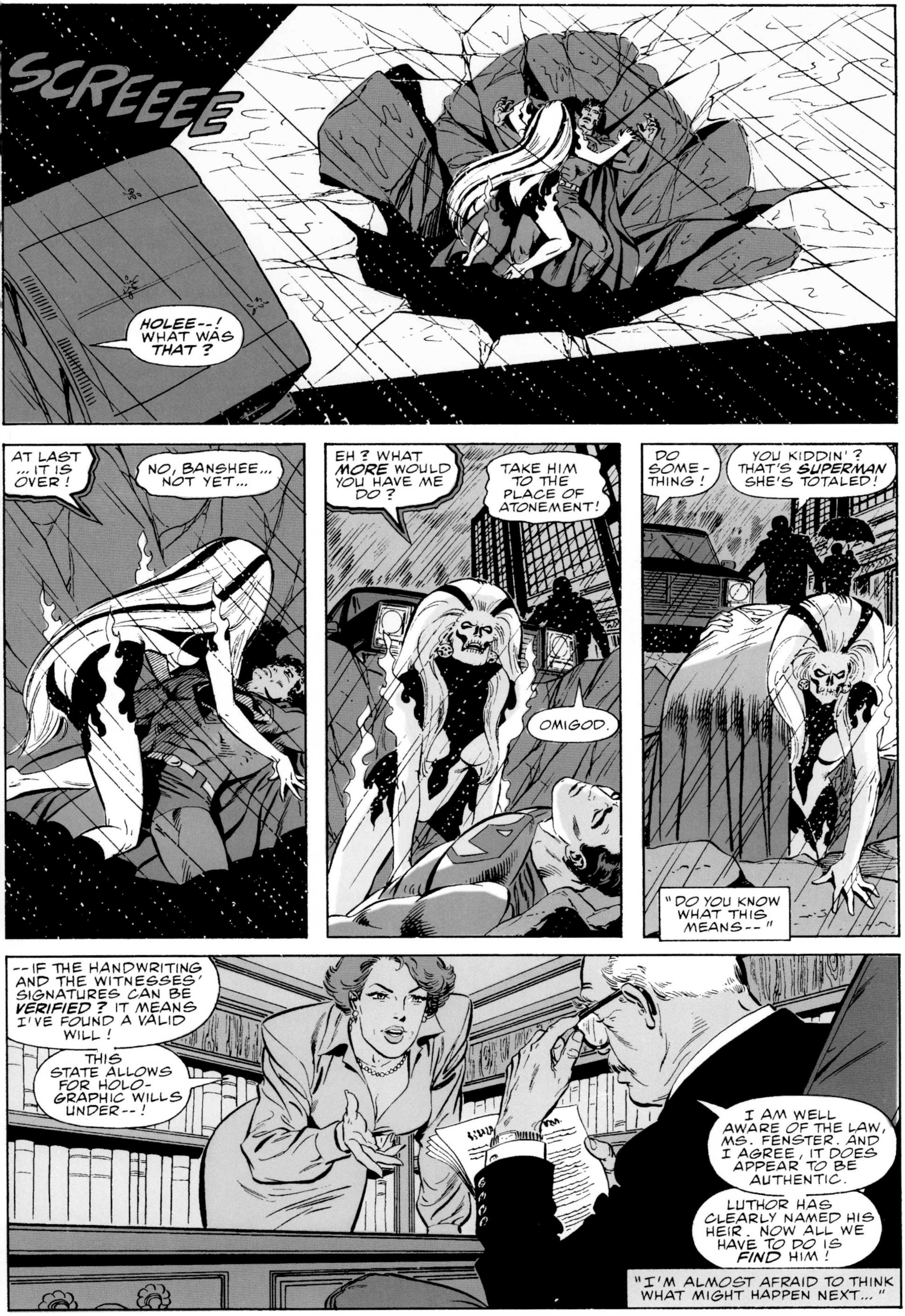
SCREEEEE
HOLEE--! WHAT WAS THAT?
AT LAST ...IT IS OVER!
NO, BANSHEE... NOT YET...
EH? WHAT MORE WOULD YOU HAVE ME DO?
TAKE HIM TO THE PLACE OF ATONEMENT!
OMIGOD.
DO SOME-THING!
YOU KIDDIN'? THAT'S SUPERMAN SHE'S TOTALED!
"DO YOU KNOW WHAT THIS MEANS--"
--IF THE HANDWRITING AND THE WITNESSES' SIGNATURES CAN BE VERIFIED? IT MEANS I'VE FOUND A VALID WILL!
THIS STATE ALLOWS FOR HOLO-GRAPHIC WILLS UNDER--!
I AM WELL AWARE OF THE LAW, MS. FENSTER. AND I AGREE, IT DOES APPEAR TO BE AUTHENTIC.
LUTHOR HAS CLEARLY NAMED HIS HEIR. NOW ALL WE HAVE TO DO IS FIND HIM!
"I'M ALMOST AFRAID TO THINK WHAT MIGHT HAPPEN NEXT..."

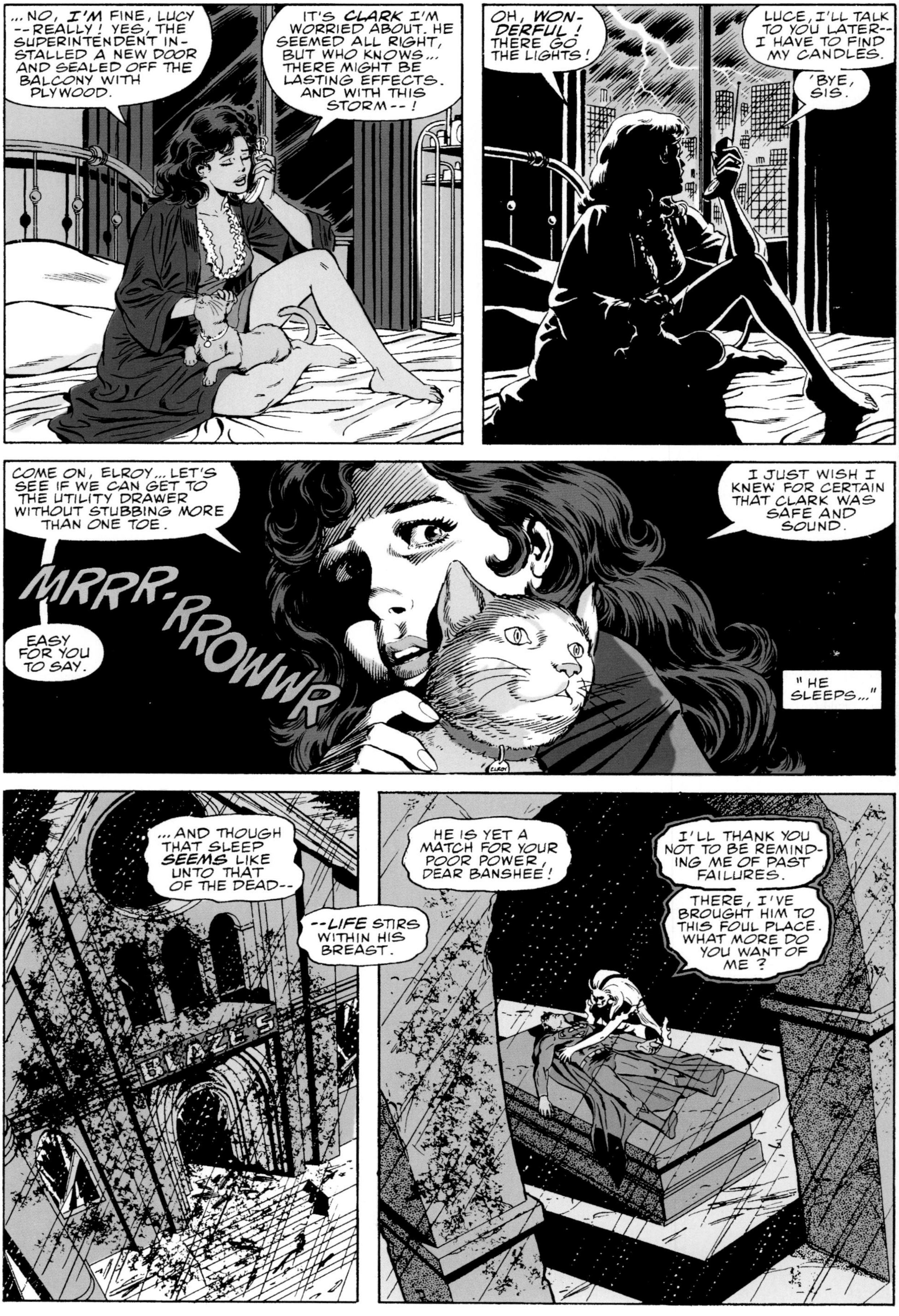

...NO, I'M FINE, LUCY --REALLY! YES, THE SUPERINTENDENT INSTALLED A NEW DOOR AND SEALED OFF THE BALCONY WITH PLYWOOD.
IT'S CLARK I'M WORRIED ABOUT. HE SEEMED ALL RIGHT, BUT WHO KNOWS... THERE MIGHT BE LASTING EFFECTS. AND WITH THIS STORM--!
OH, WONDERFUL! THERE GO THE LIGHTS!
LUCE, I'LL TALK TO YOU LATER-- I HAVE TO FIND MY CANDLES.
'BYE, SIS.
COME ON, ELROY... LET'S SEE IF WE CAN GET TO THE UTILITY DRAWER WITHOUT STUBBING MORE THAN ONE TOE.
MRRR-RROWWR
EASY FOR YOU TO SAY.
I JUST WISH I KNEW FOR CERTAIN THAT CLARK WAS SAFE AND SOUND.
"HE SLEEPS..."
...AND THOUGH THAT SLEEP SEEMS LIKE UNTO THAT OF THE DEAD--
--LIFE STIRS WITHIN HIS BREAST.
BLAZE'S
HE IS YET A MATCH FOR YOUR POOR POWER, DEAR BANSHEE!
I'LL THANK YOU NOT TO BE REMINDING ME OF PAST FAILURES.
THERE, I'VE BROUGHT HIM TO THIS FOUL PLACE. WHAT MORE DO YOU WANT OF ME?

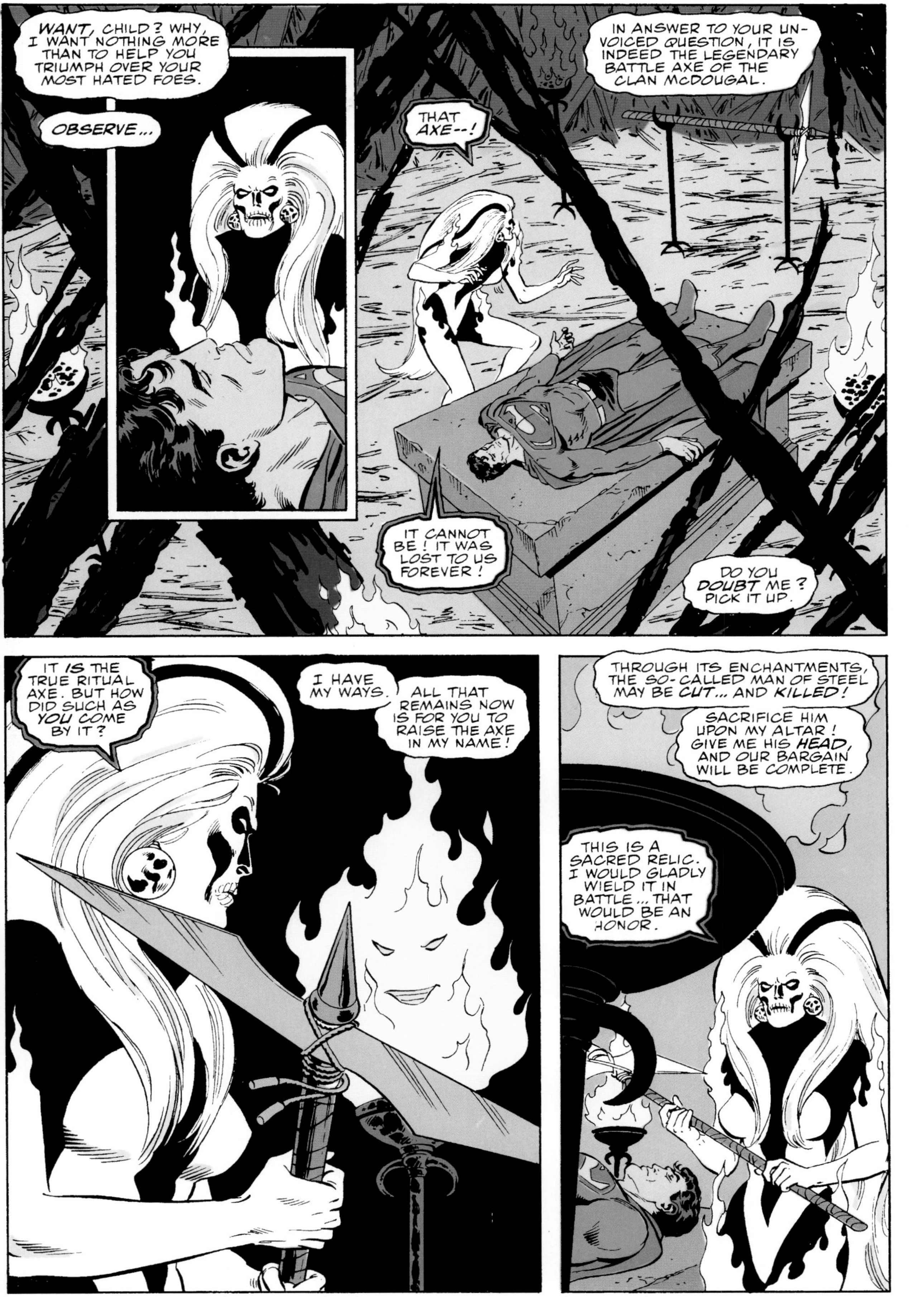
WANT, CHILD? WHY, I WANT NOTHING MORE THAN TO HELP YOU TRIUMPH OVER YOUR MOST HATED FOES.
OBSERVE...
THAT AXE--!
IN ANSWER TO YOUR UNVOICED QUESTION, IT IS INDEED THE LEGENDARY BATTLE AXE OF THE CLAN McDOUGAL.
IT CANNOT BE! IT WAS LOST TO US FOREVER!
DO YOU DOUBT ME? PICK IT UP.
IT IS THE TRUE RITUAL AXE. BUT HOW DID SUCH AS YOU COME BY IT?
I HAVE MY WAYS.
ALL THAT REMAINS NOW IS FOR YOU TO RAISE THE AXE IN MY NAME!
THROUGH ITS ENCHANTMENTS, THE SO-CALLED MAN OF STEEL MAY BE CUT... AND KILLED!
SACRIFICE HIM UPON MY ALTAR! GIVE ME HIS HEAD, AND OUR BARGAIN WILL BE COMPLETE.
THIS IS A SACRED RELIC. I WOULD GLADLY WIELD IT IN BATTLE... THAT WOULD BE AN HONOR.

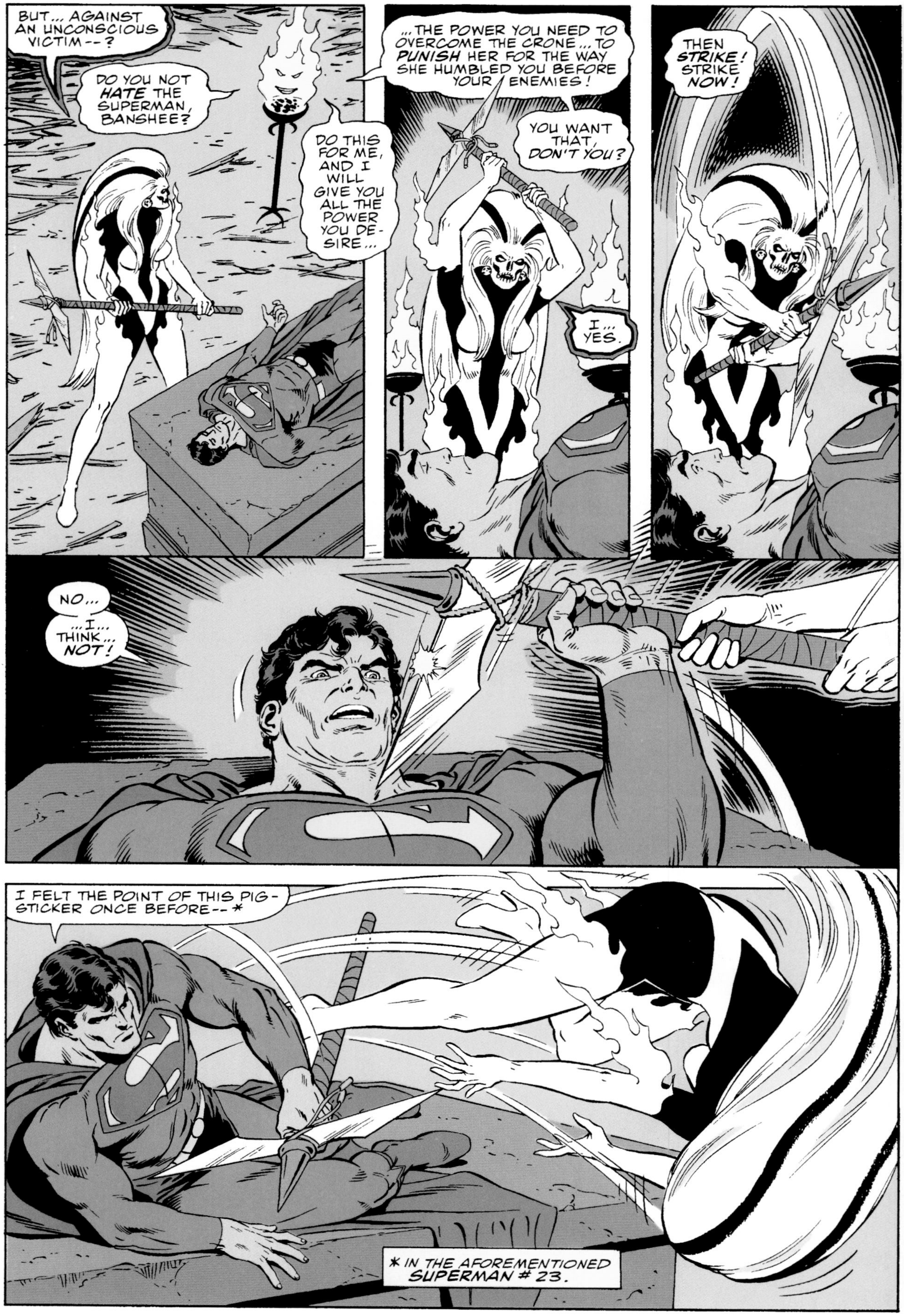
BUT... AGAINST AN UNCONSCIOUS VICTIM--?
DO YOU NOT HATE THE SUPERMAN, BANSHEE?
DO THIS FOR ME, AND I WILL GIVE YOU ALL THE POWER YOU DESIRE...
...THE POWER YOU NEED TO OVERCOME THE CRONE... TO PUNISH HER FOR THE WAY SHE HUMBLED YOU BEFORE YOUR ENEMIES!
YOU WANT THAT, DON'T YOU?
I... YES.
THEN STRIKE! STRIKE NOW!
NO...
...I... THINK... NOT!
I FELT THE POINT OF THIS PIG-STICKER ONCE BEFORE--*
*IN THE AFOREMENTIONED SUPERMAN #23.

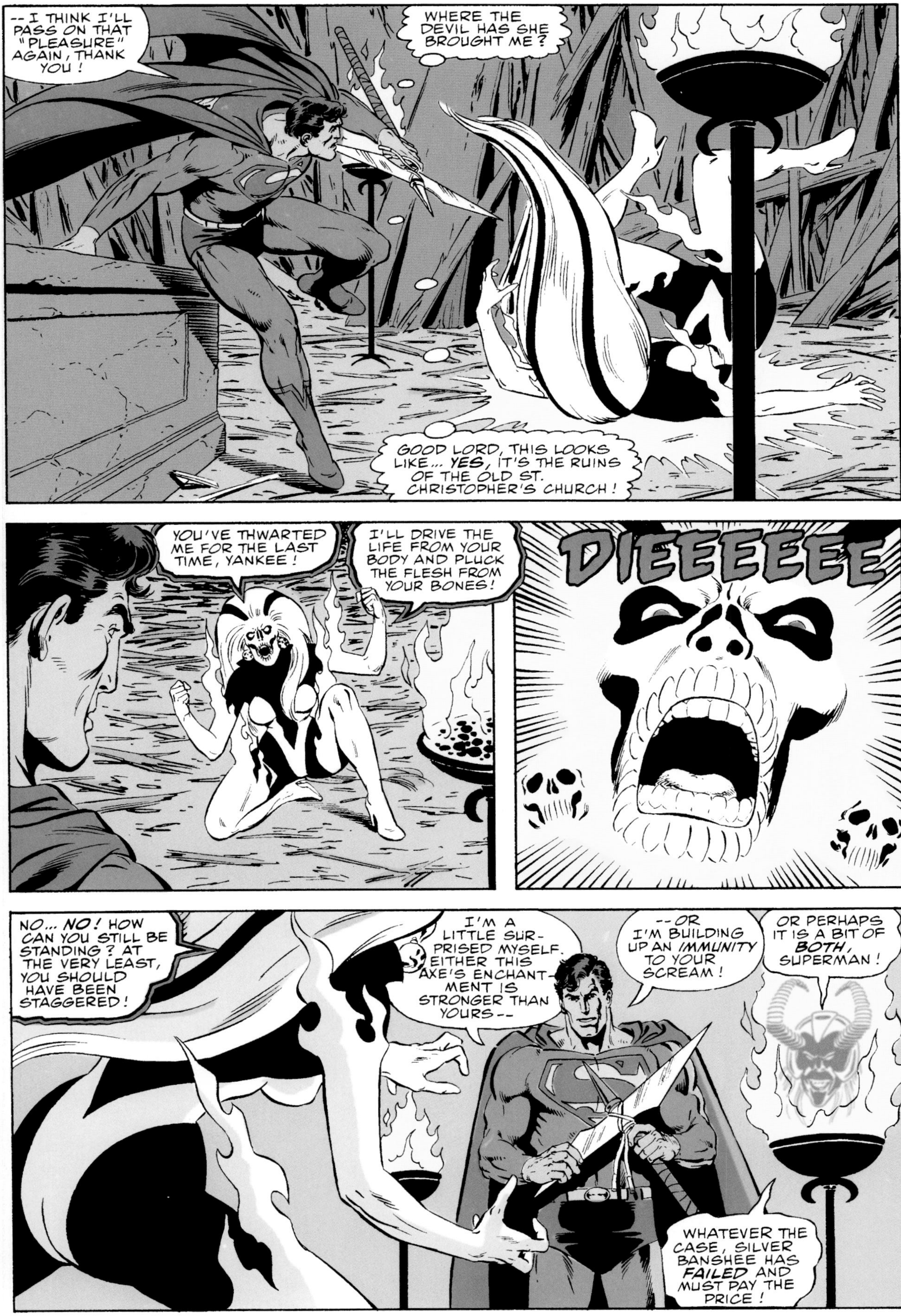
--I THINK I'LL PASS ON THAT "PLEASURE" AGAIN, THANK YOU!
WHERE THE DEVIL HAS SHE BROUGHT ME?
GOOD LORD, THIS LOOKS LIKE... YES, IT'S THE RUINS OF THE OLD ST. CHRISTOPHER'S CHURCH!
YOU'VE THWARTED ME FOR THE LAST TIME, YANKEE!
I'LL DRIVE THE LIFE FROM YOUR BODY AND PLUCK THE FLESH FROM YOUR BONES!
DIEEEEEE
NO... NO! HOW CAN YOU STILL BE STANDING? AT THE VERY LEAST, YOU SHOULD HAVE BEEN STAGGERED!
I'M A LITTLE SUR-PRISED MYSELF. EITHER THIS AXE'S ENCHANT-MENT IS STRONGER THAN YOURS--
--OR I'M BUILDING UP AN IMMUNITY TO YOUR SCREAM!
OR PERHAPS IT IS A BIT OF BOTH, SUPERMAN!
WHATEVER THE CASE, SILVER BANSHEE HAS FAILED AND MUST PAY THE PRICE!

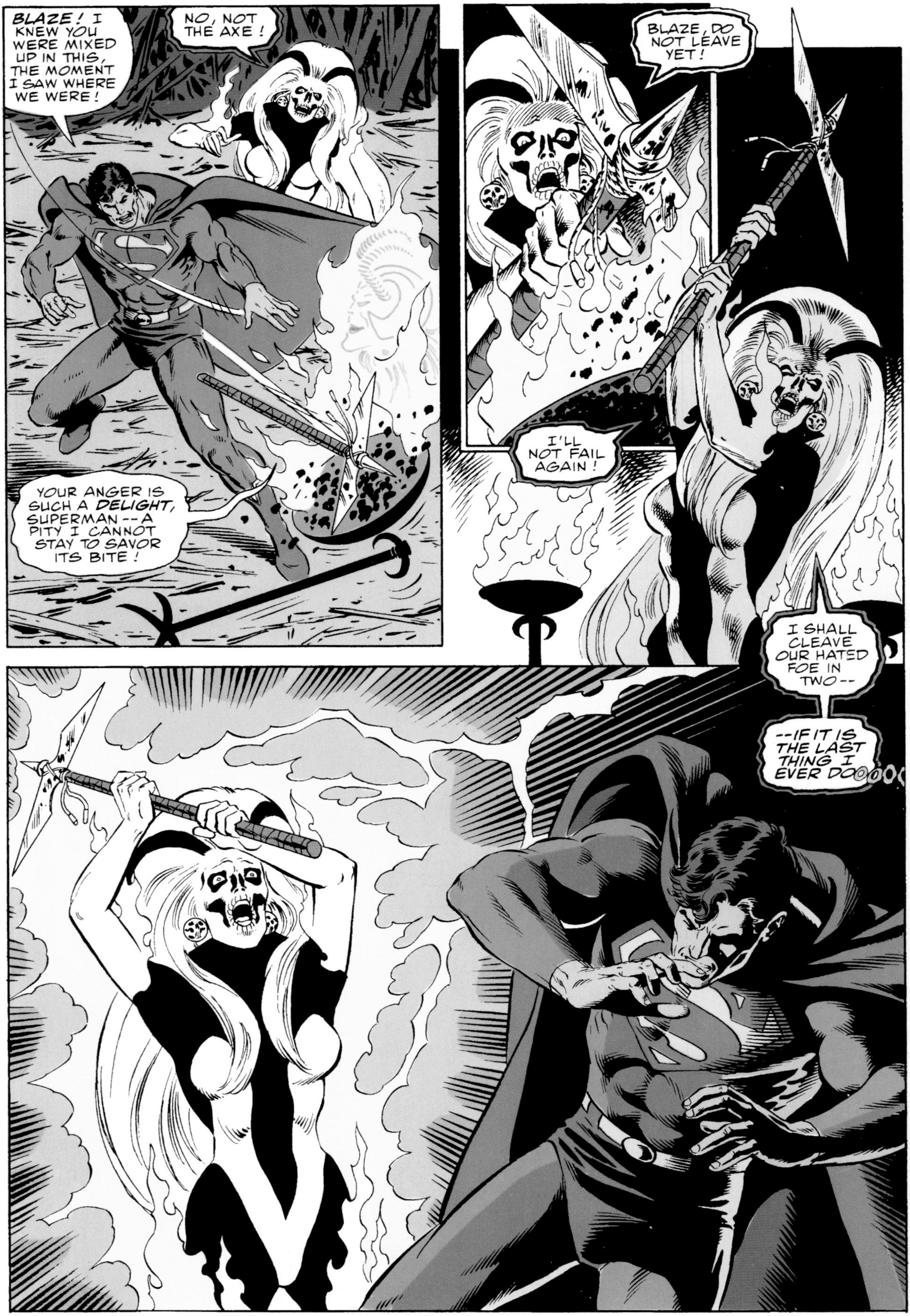
BLAZE! I KNEW YOU WERE MIXED UP IN THIS, THE MOMENT I SAW WHERE WE WERE!
NO, NOT THE AXE!
YOUR ANGER IS SUCH A DELIGHT, SUPERMAN -- A PITY I CANNOT STAY TO SAVOR ITS BITE!
BLAZE, DO NOT LEAVE YET!
I'LL NOT FAIL AGAIN!
I SHALL CLEAVE OUR HATED FOE IN TWO --
-- IF IT IS THE LAST THING I EVER DOOOOO

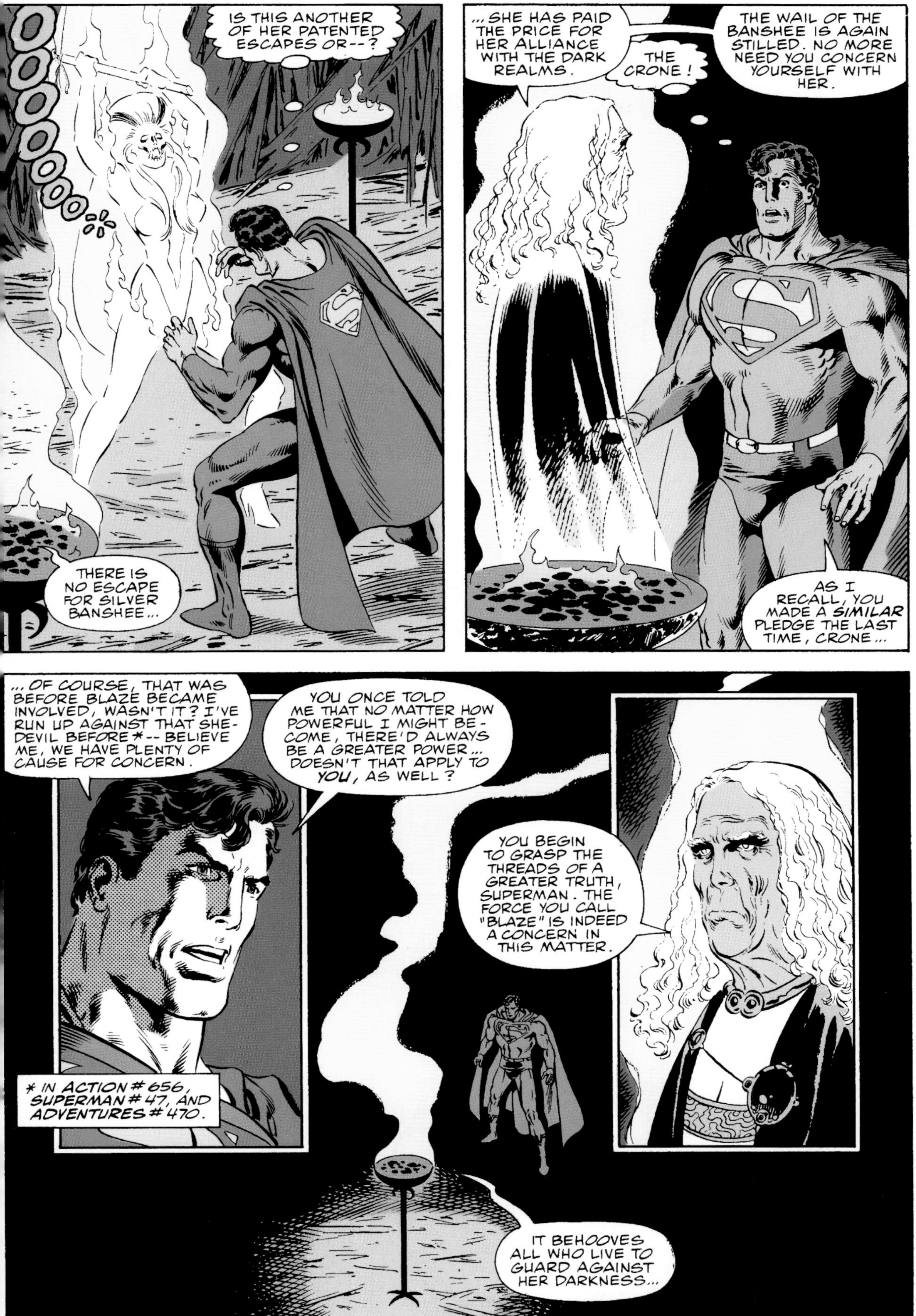
OOOOOOOOO...
IS THIS ANOTHER OF HER PATENTED ESCAPES OR--?
THERE IS NO ESCAPE FOR SILVER BANSHEE...
...SHE HAS PAID THE PRICE FOR HER ALLIANCE WITH THE DARK REALMS.
THE CRONE!
THE WAIL OF THE BANSHEE IS AGAIN STILLED. NO MORE NEED YOU CONCERN YOURSELF WITH HER.
AS I RECALL, YOU MADE A SIMILAR PLEDGE THE LAST TIME, CRONE...
...OF COURSE, THAT WAS BEFORE BLAZE BECAME INVOLVED, WASN'T IT? I'VE RUN UP AGAINST THAT SHE-DEVIL BEFORE*-- BELIEVE ME, WE HAVE PLENTY OF CAUSE FOR CONCERN.
YOU ONCE TOLD ME THAT NO MATTER HOW POWERFUL I MIGHT BE-COME, THERE'D ALWAYS BE A GREATER POWER... DOESN'T THAT APPLY TO YOU, AS WELL?
*IN ACTION #656, SUPERMAN #47, AND ADVENTURES #470.
YOU BEGIN TO GRASP THE THREADS OF A GREATER TRUTH, SUPERMAN. THE FORCE YOU CALL "BLAZE" IS INDEED A CONCERN IN THIS MATTER.
IT BEHOOVES ALL WHO LIVE TO GUARD AGAINST HER DARKNESS...

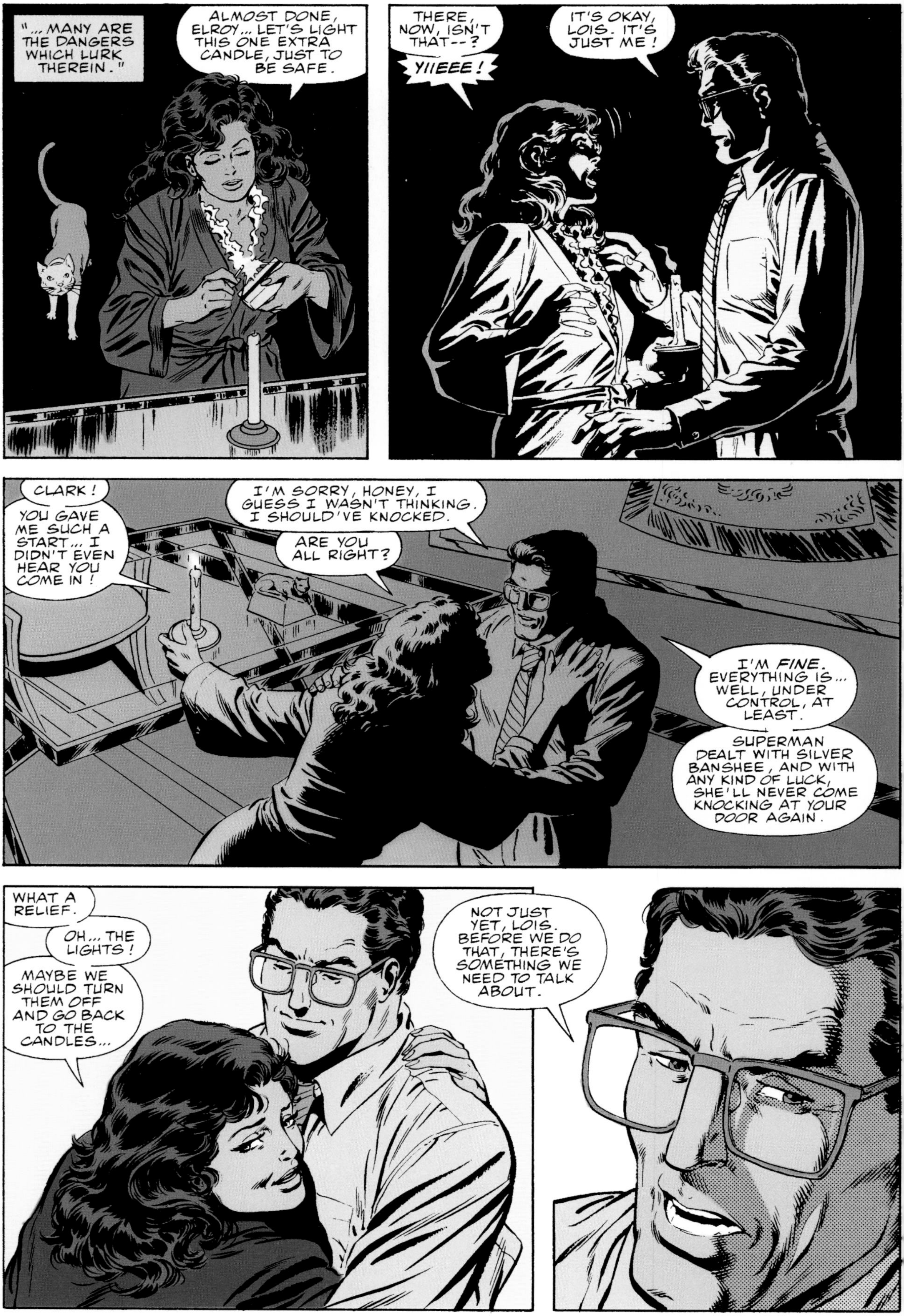
"... MANY ARE THE DANGERS WHICH LURK THEREIN."
ALMOST DONE, ELROY... LET'S LIGHT THIS ONE EXTRA CANDLE, JUST TO BE SAFE.
THERE, NOW, ISN'T THAT--?
YIIEEE!
IT'S OKAY, LOIS. IT'S JUST ME!
CLARK!
YOU GAVE ME SUCH A START... I DIDN'T EVEN HEAR YOU COME IN!
I'M SORRY, HONEY, I GUESS I WASN'T THINKING. I SHOULD'VE KNOCKED.
ARE YOU ALL RIGHT?
I'M FINE. EVERYTHING IS... WELL, UNDER CONTROL, AT LEAST.
SUPERMAN DEALT WITH SILVER BANSHEE, AND WITH ANY KIND OF LUCK, SHE'LL NEVER COME KNOCKING AT YOUR DOOR AGAIN.
WHAT A RELIEF.
OH... THE LIGHTS!
MAYBE WE SHOULD TURN THEM OFF AND GO BACK TO THE CANDLES...
NOT JUST YET, LOIS. BEFORE WE DO THAT, THERE'S SOMETHING WE NEED TO TALK ABOUT.

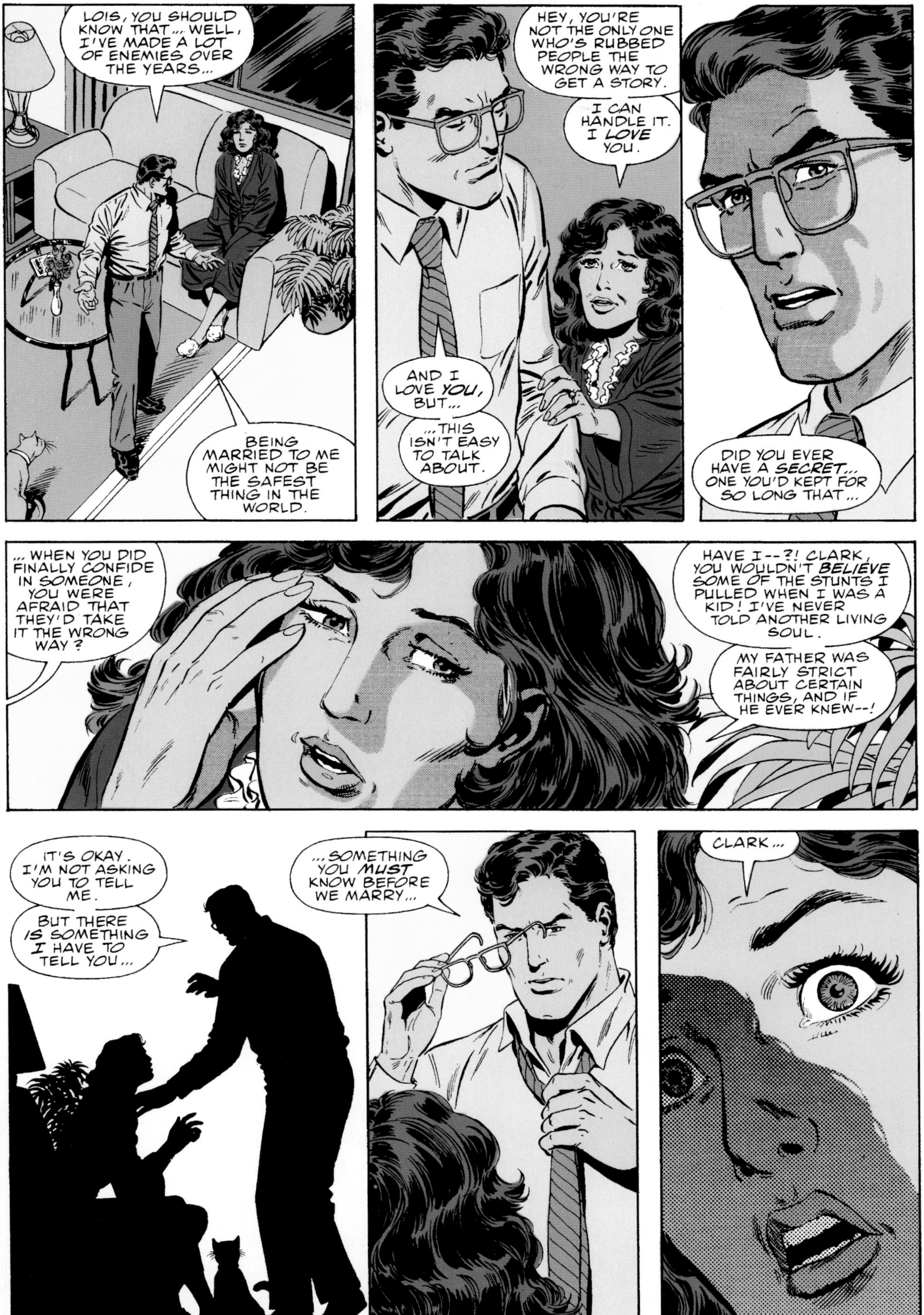
LOIS, YOU SHOULD KNOW THAT... WELL, I'VE MADE A LOT OF ENEMIES OVER THE YEARS...
BEING MARRIED TO ME MIGHT NOT BE THE SAFEST THING IN THE WORLD.
HEY, YOU'RE NOT THE ONLY ONE WHO'S RUBBED PEOPLE THE WRONG WAY TO GET A STORY.
I CAN HANDLE IT. I LOVE YOU.
AND I LOVE YOU, BUT...
...THIS ISN'T EASY TO TALK ABOUT.
DID YOU EVER HAVE A SECRET... ONE YOU'D KEPT FOR SO LONG THAT...
...WHEN YOU DID FINALLY CONFIDE IN SOMEONE, YOU WERE AFRAID THAT THEY'D TAKE IT THE WRONG WAY?
HAVE I--?! CLARK, YOU WOULDN'T BELIEVE SOME OF THE STUNTS I PULLED WHEN I WAS A KID! I'VE NEVER TOLD ANOTHER LIVING SOUL.
MY FATHER WAS FAIRLY STRICT ABOUT CERTAIN THINGS, AND IF HE EVER KNEW--!
IT'S OKAY. I'M NOT ASKING YOU TO TELL ME.
BUT THERE IS SOMETHING I HAVE TO TELL YOU...
...SOMETHING YOU MUST KNOW BEFORE WE MARRY...
CLARK...

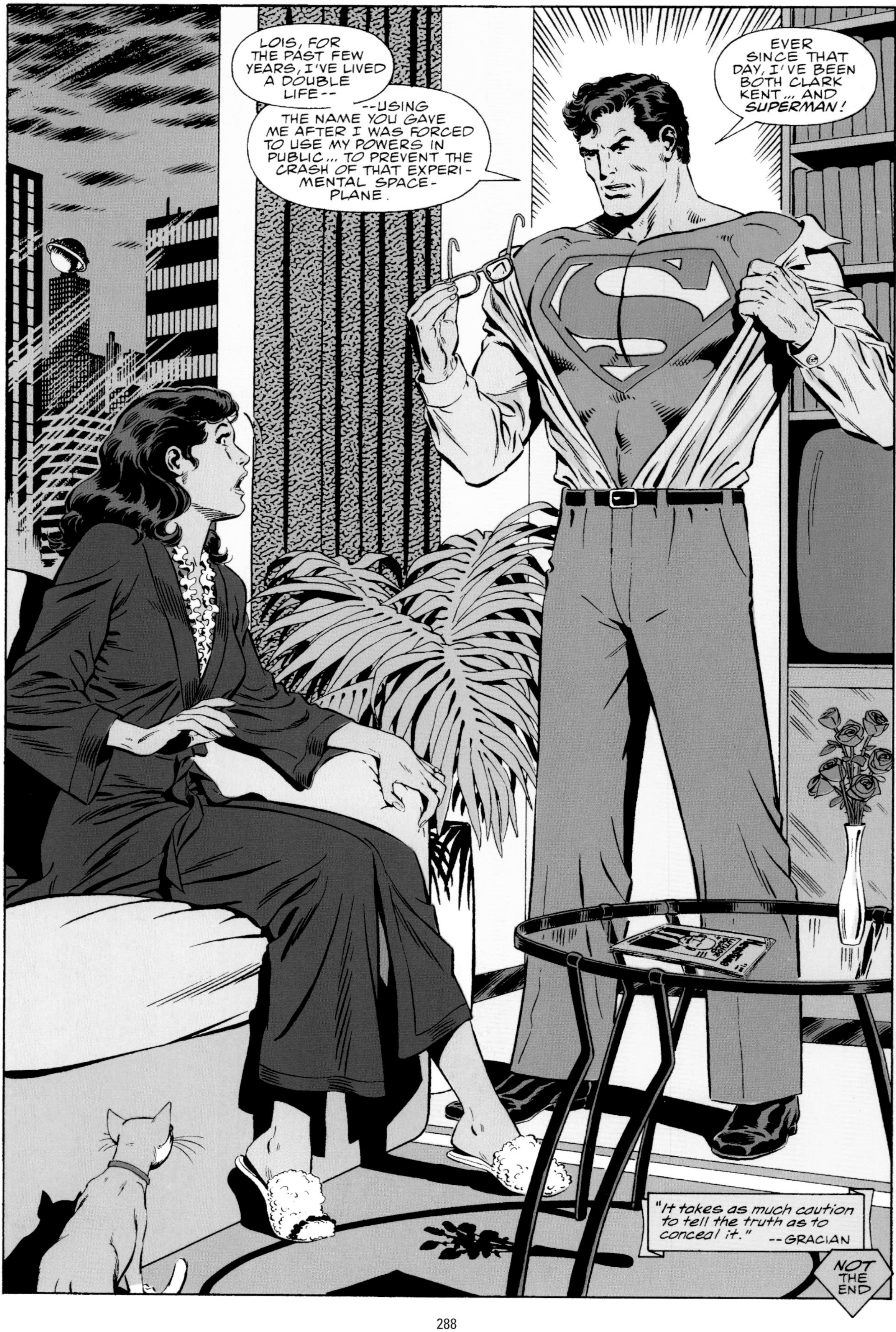
LOIS, FOR THE PAST FEW YEARS, I'VE LIVED A DOUBLE LIFE--
--USING THE NAME YOU GAVE ME AFTER I WAS FORCED TO USE MY POWERS IN PUBLIC... TO PREVENT THE CRASH OF THAT EXPERIMENTAL SPACE-PLANE.
EVER SINCE THAT DAY, I'VE BEEN BOTH CLARK KENT... AND SUPERMAN!
"It takes as much caution to tell the truth as to conceal it." --GRACIAN
NOT THE END

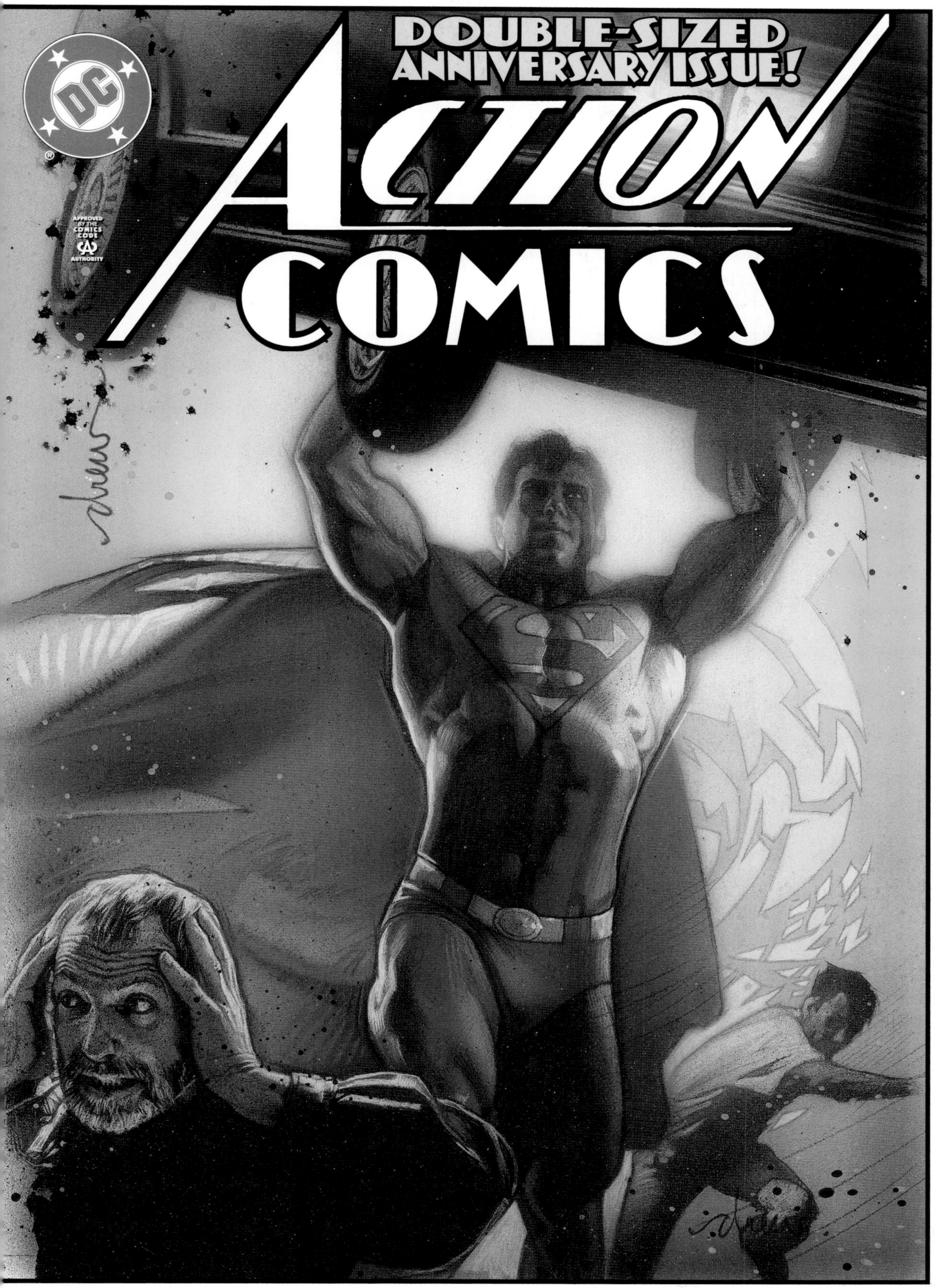
DOUBLE-SIZED
ANNIVERSARY ISSUE!
DC
APPROVED BY THE COMICS CODE AUTHORITY
ACTION
COMICS

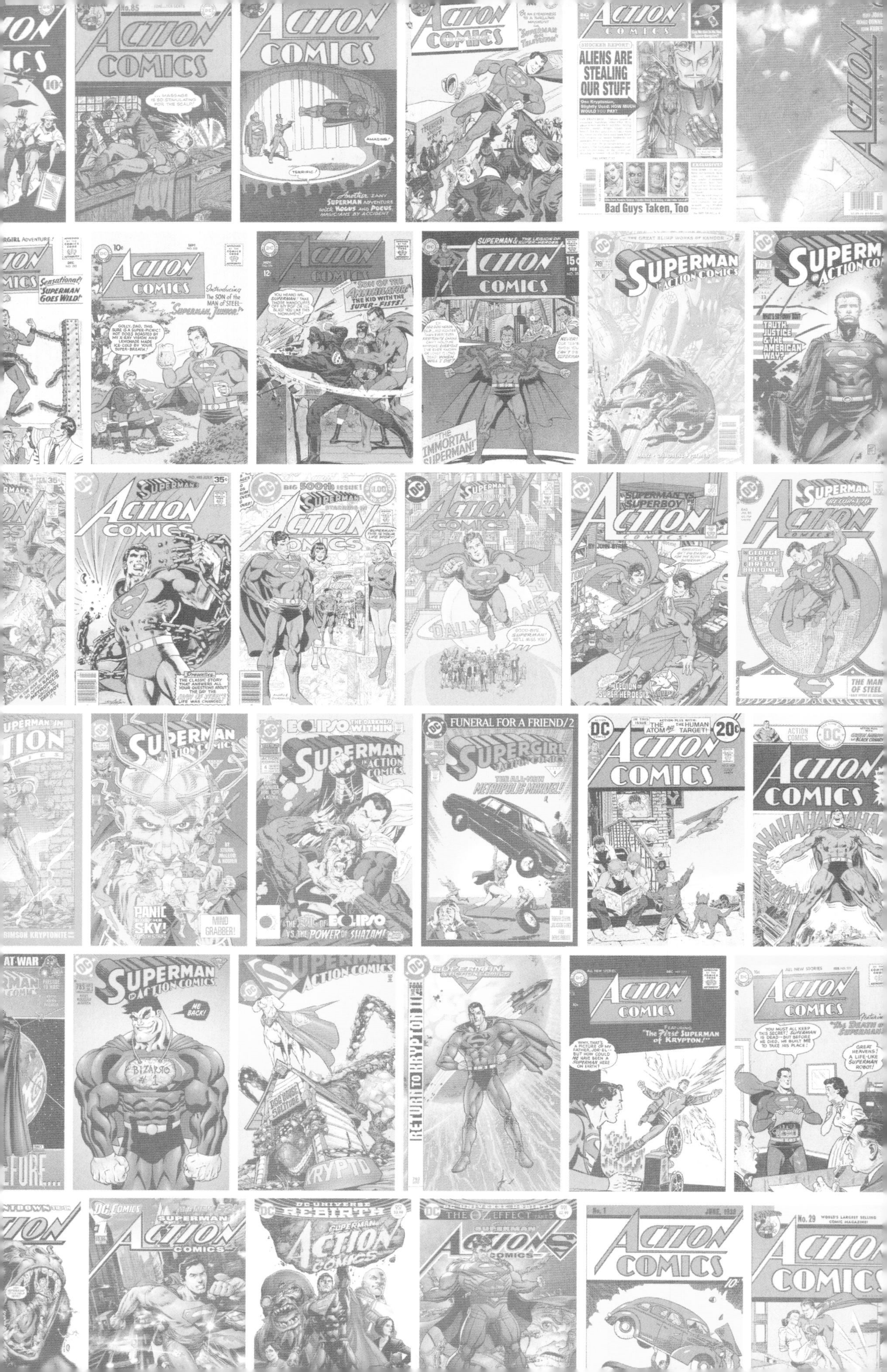

No.85
ACTION COMICS
... MASSAGE IS SO STIMULATING FOR THE SCALP!
ACTION COMICS
AMAZING!
TERRIFIC!
Another ZANY SUPERMAN ADVENTURE WITH HOCUS AND POCUS, MAGICIANS BY ACCIDENT
ACTION COMICS
BE AN EYEWITNESS TO A THRILLING MANHUNT IN "SUPERMAN ON TELEVISION"
ACTION COMICS
SHOCKER REPORT
ALIENS ARE STEALING OUR STUFF
One Kryptonian, Slightly Used: HOW MUCH WOULD YOU PAY?
EXCLUSIVE!
Bad Guys Taken, Too
Sensational! "SUPERMAN GOES WILD!"
ACTION COMICS
Introducing The SON of the MAN of STEEL— "SUPERMAN, JUNIOR!"
GOLLY, DAD, THIS SURE IS A SUPER-PICNIC! HOT DOGS ROASTED BY MY X-RAY VISION AND LEMONADE MADE ICE-COLD BY YOUR SUPER-BREATH!
ACTION COMICS
SON OF THE ANNIHILATOR! THE KID WITH THE SUPER-FISTS!
SUPERMAN & THE LEGION OF SUPER-HEROES
ACTION COMICS
15¢
NEVER!
THE IMMORTAL SUPERMAN!
SUPERMAN IN ACTION COMICS
SUPERMAN IN ACTION COMICS
TRUTH, JUSTICE & THE AMERICAN WAY?
35¢
SUPERMAN
ACTION COMICS
BIG 500th ISSUE!
$1.00
SUPERMAN STARRING IN ACTION COMICS
SUPERMAN
ACTION COMICS
DAILY PLANET
GOOD-BYE, SUPERMAN! WE'LL MISS YOU!
SUPERMAN VS. SUPERBOY
ACTION COMICS
BY JOHN BYRNE
LEGION OF SUPER-HEROES
SUPERMAN
ACTION COMICS
GEORGE PEREZ
BRETT BREEDING
THE MAN OF STEEL
SUPERMAN IN ACTION COMICS
CRIMSON KRYPTONITE
SUPERMAN IN ACTION COMICS
PANIC IN THE SKY!
MIND GRABBER!
ECLIPSO THE DARKNESS WITHIN
SUPERMAN IN ACTION COMICS
THE EVIL OF ECLIPSO VS. THE POWER OF SHAZAM!
FUNERAL FOR A FRIEND/2
SUPERGIRL
THE ALL-NEW METROPOLIS MARVEL!
IN THIS ISSUE THE ATOM
ACTION-PLUS WITH THE HUMAN TARGET!
20¢
ACTION COMICS
ACTION COMICS
HAHAHAHAHAHAHA
AT WAR
SUPERMAN IN ACTION COMICS
ME BACK!
BIZARRO #1
SUPERMAN ACTION COMICS
KRYPTO
RETURN TO KRYPTON II
SUPERMAN IN ACTION COMICS
ALL NEW STORIES
ACTION COMICS
FEATURING "The First SUPERMAN of KRYPTON!"
WHY, THAT'S A PICTURE OF MY FATHER, JOR-EL— BUT HOW COULD HE HAVE BEEN A SUPERMAN HERE ON EARTH?
ALL NEW STORIES
ACTION COMICS
Featuring "The DEATH of SUPERMAN"
YOU MUST ALL KEEP THIS SECRET! SUPERMAN IS DEAD—BUT BEFORE HE DIED, HE BUILT ME TO TAKE HIS PLACE!
GREAT HEAVENS! A LIFE-LIKE SUPERMAN ROBOT!
DC COMICS
SUPERMAN
ACTION COMICS
DC UNIVERSE REBIRTH
SUPERMAN
ACTION COMICS
THE OZ EFFECT
SUPERMAN
ACTION COMICS
No. 1
JUNE, 1938
ACTION COMICS
No. 29
WORLD'S LARGEST SELLING COMIC MAGAZINE!
ACTION COMICS

He turns all of his injuries into strengths, that which does not kill him makes him stronger, he is superman."

-- Friedrich Wilhelm Nietzsche,
Thus Spake Zarathustra

"The future belongs to those who believe in the beauty of their dreams."

-- Eleanor Roosevelt

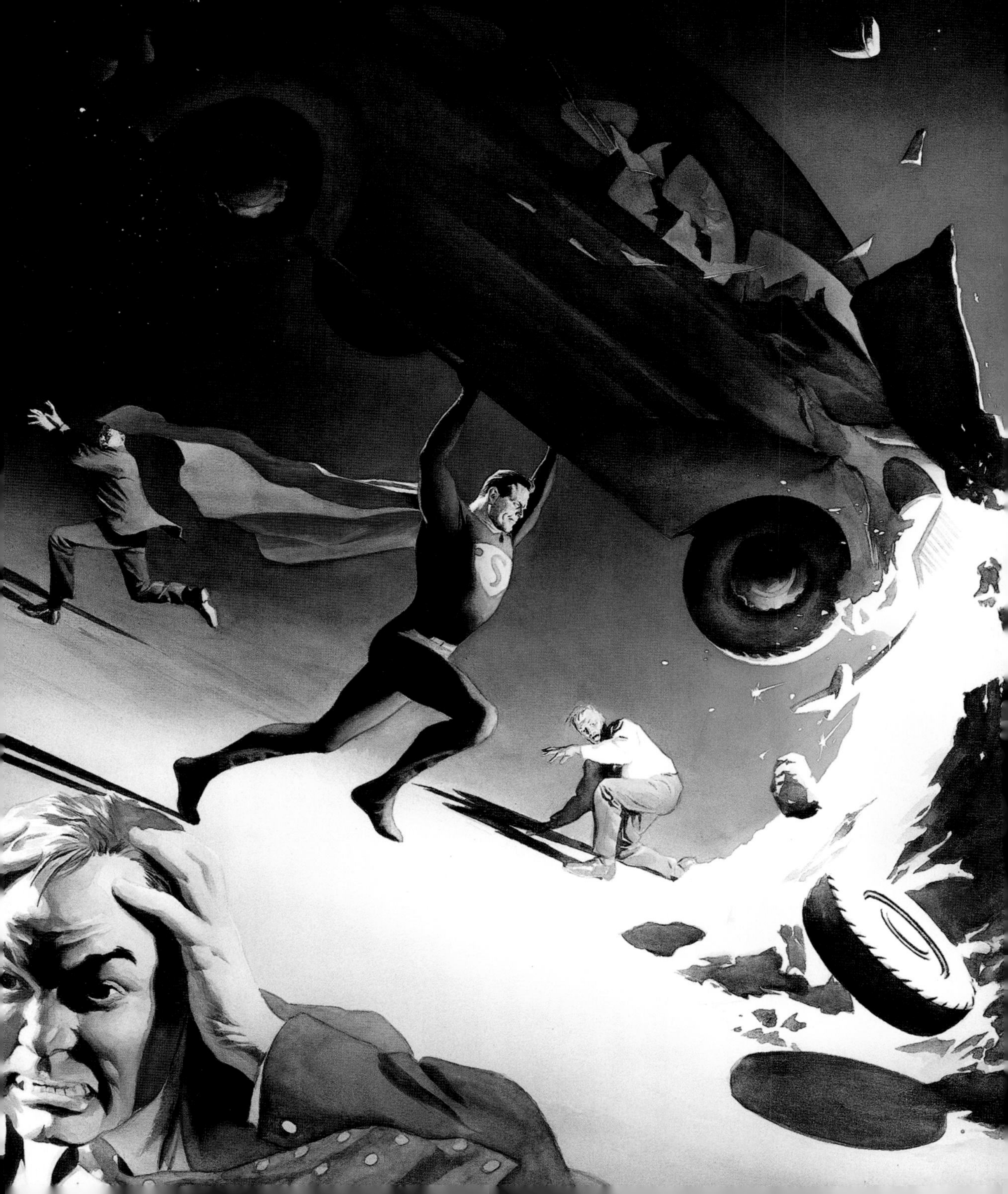

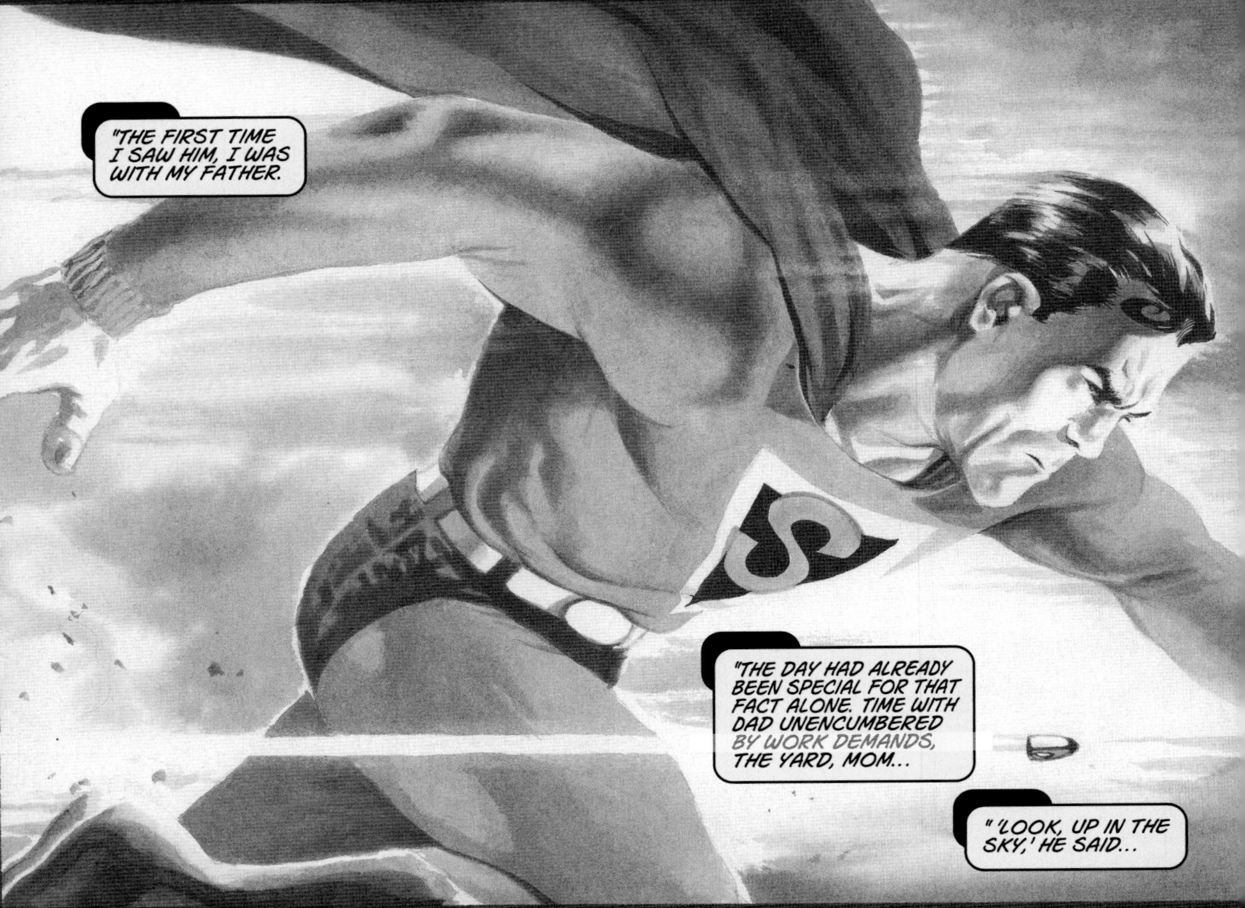
"THE FIRST TIME I SAW HIM, I WAS WITH MY FATHER.
"THE DAY HAD ALREADY BEEN SPECIAL FOR THAT FACT ALONE. TIME WITH DAD UNENCUMBERED BY WORK DEMANDS, THE YARD, MOM...
"'LOOK, UP IN THE SKY,' HE SAID...

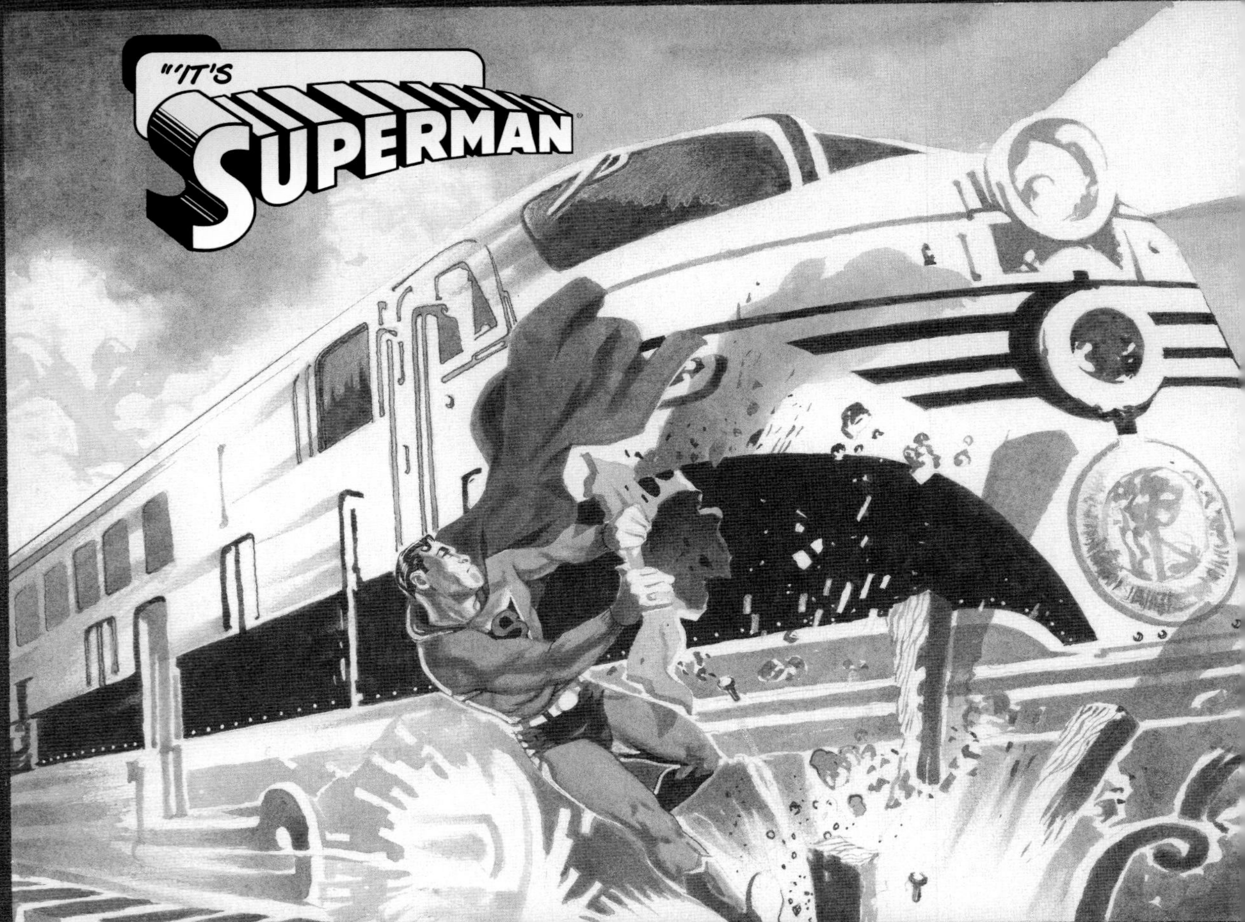
"'IT'S SUPERMAN

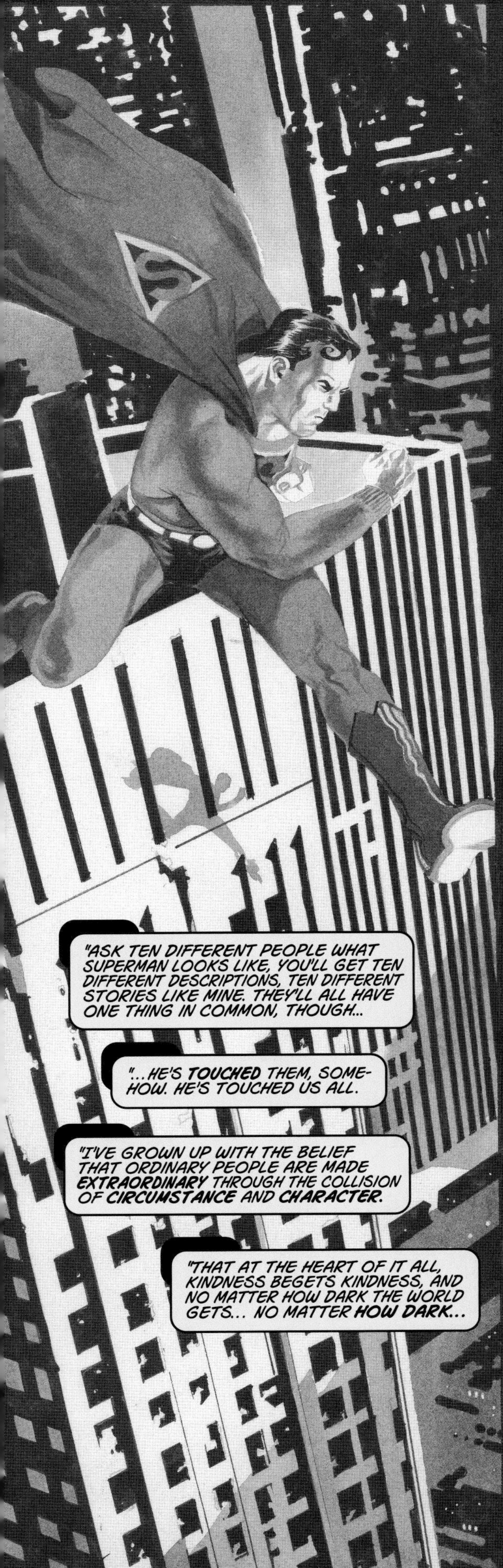
"ASK TEN DIFFERENT PEOPLE WHAT SUPERMAN LOOKS LIKE, YOU'LL GET TEN DIFFERENT DESCRIPTIONS, TEN DIFFERENT STORIES LIKE MINE. THEY'LL ALL HAVE ONE THING IN COMMON, THOUGH...
"...HE'S **TOUCHED** THEM, SOMEHOW. HE'S TOUCHED US ALL.
"I'VE GROWN UP WITH THE BELIEF THAT ORDINARY PEOPLE ARE MADE **EXTRAORDINARY** THROUGH THE COLLISION OF **CIRCUMSTANCE** AND **CHARACTER**.
"THAT AT THE HEART OF IT ALL, KINDNESS BEGETS KINDNESS, AND NO MATTER HOW DARK THE WORLD GETS... NO MATTER **HOW DARK**...

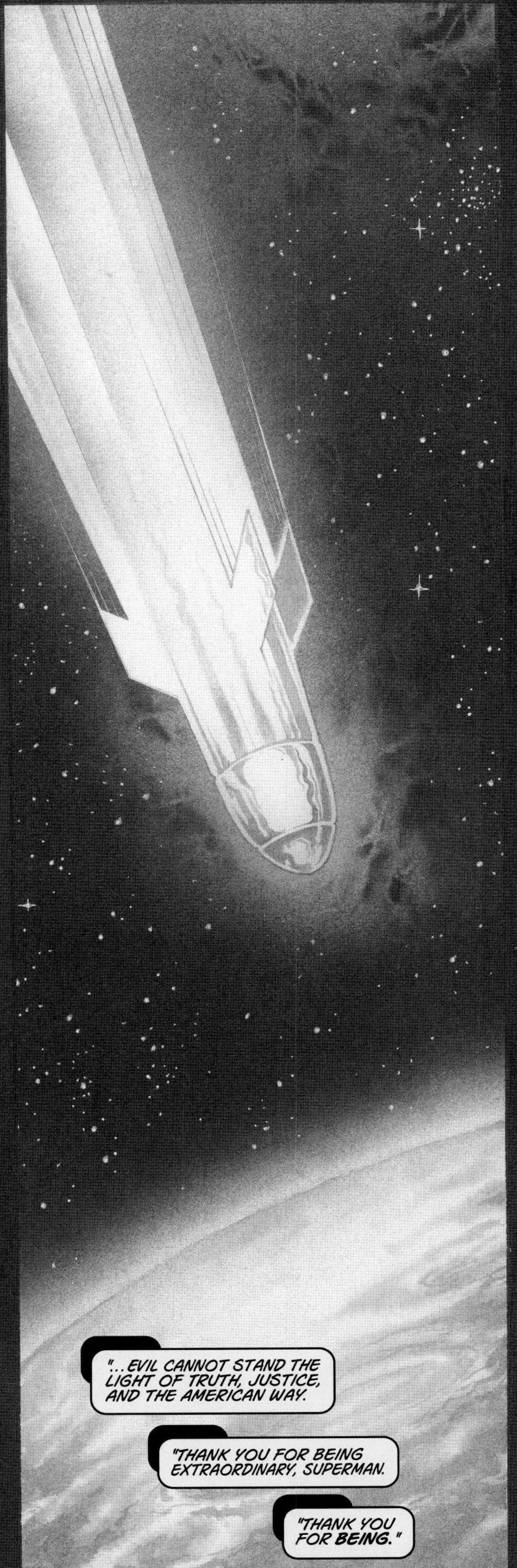
"...EVIL CANNOT STAND THE LIGHT OF TRUTH, JUSTICE, AND THE AMERICAN WAY.
"THANK YOU FOR BEING EXTRAORDINARY, SUPERMAN.
"THANK YOU FOR **BEING**."

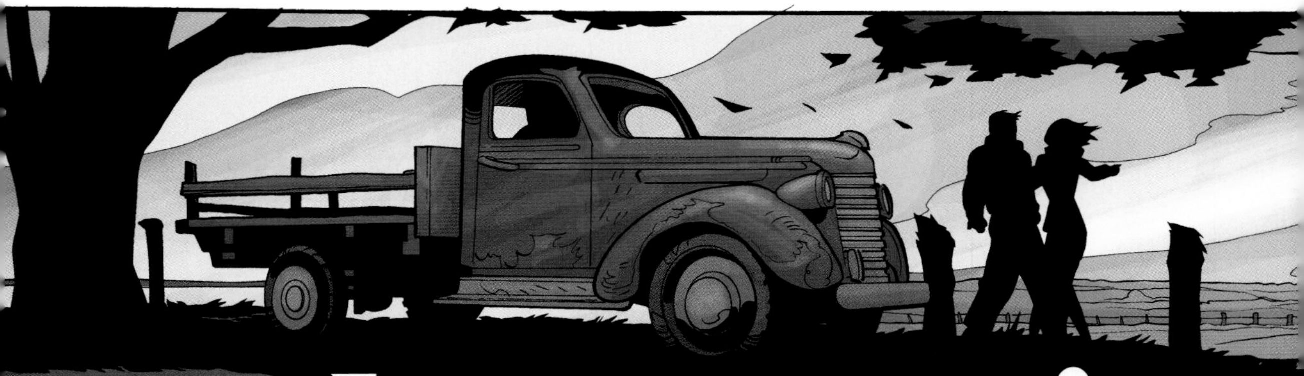

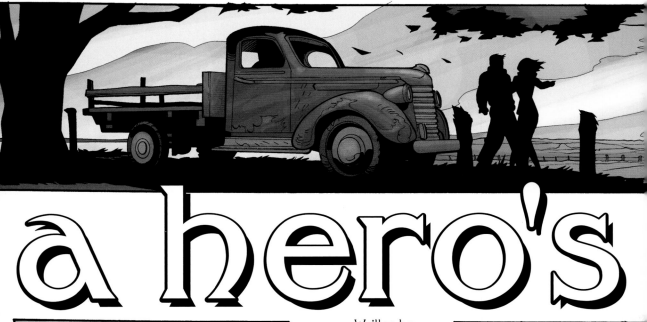

a hero's

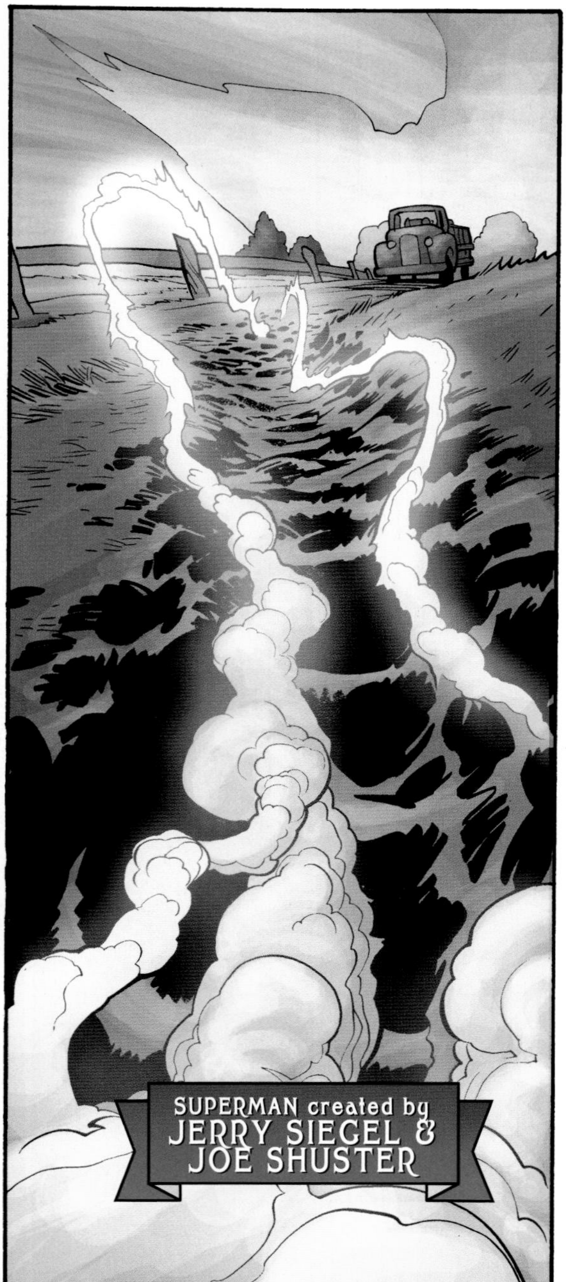

SUPERMAN created by
JERRY SIEGEL &
JOE SHUSTER

Written by
JOE KELLY

Pencilled by
PASCUAL FERRY &
DUNCAN ROULEAU

with Special Guests:
ALEX ROSS
TONY HARRIS
BILL SIENKIEWICZ
DAVE BULLOCK
ED McGUINNESS
J.H. WILLIAMS
DAN JURGENS &
KLAUS JANSON
KILIAN PLUNKETT
JIM LEE
TIM SALE
LEE BERMEJO

Inked by
CAM SMITH
MARLO ALQUIZA
SCOTT HANNA
DUNCAN ROULEAU

Colored by
MOOSE BAUMANN
JEROMY COX
GUY MAJOR

Lettered by
COMICRAFT

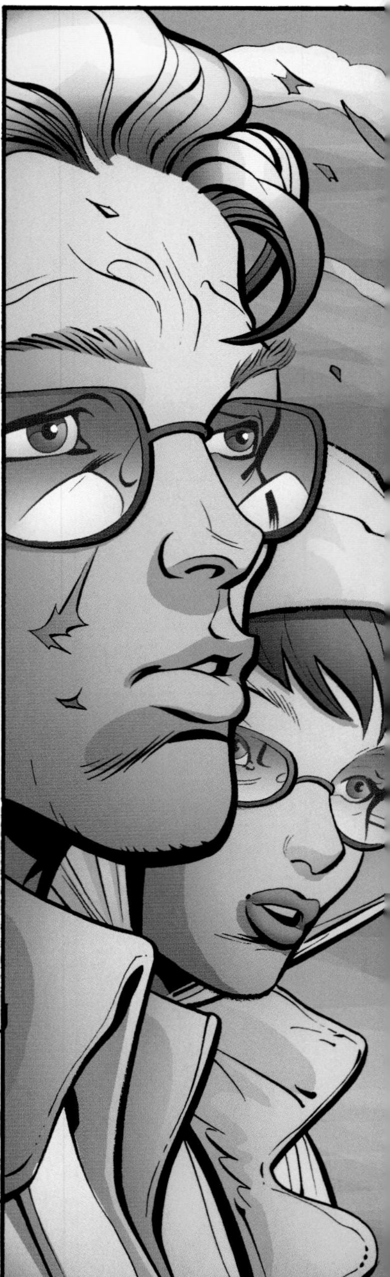

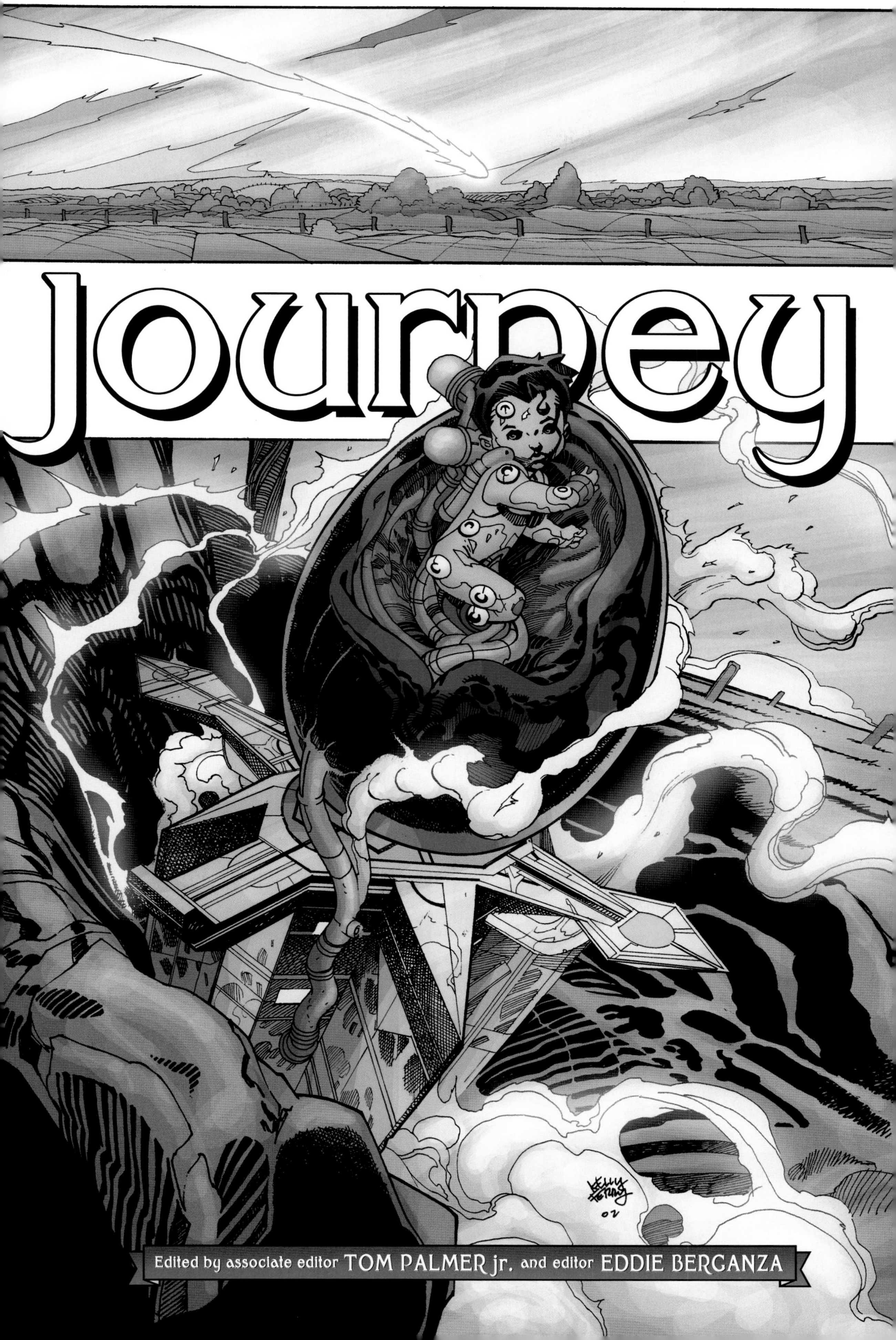
Journey
Edited by associate editor TOM PALMER jr. and editor EDDIE BERGANZA

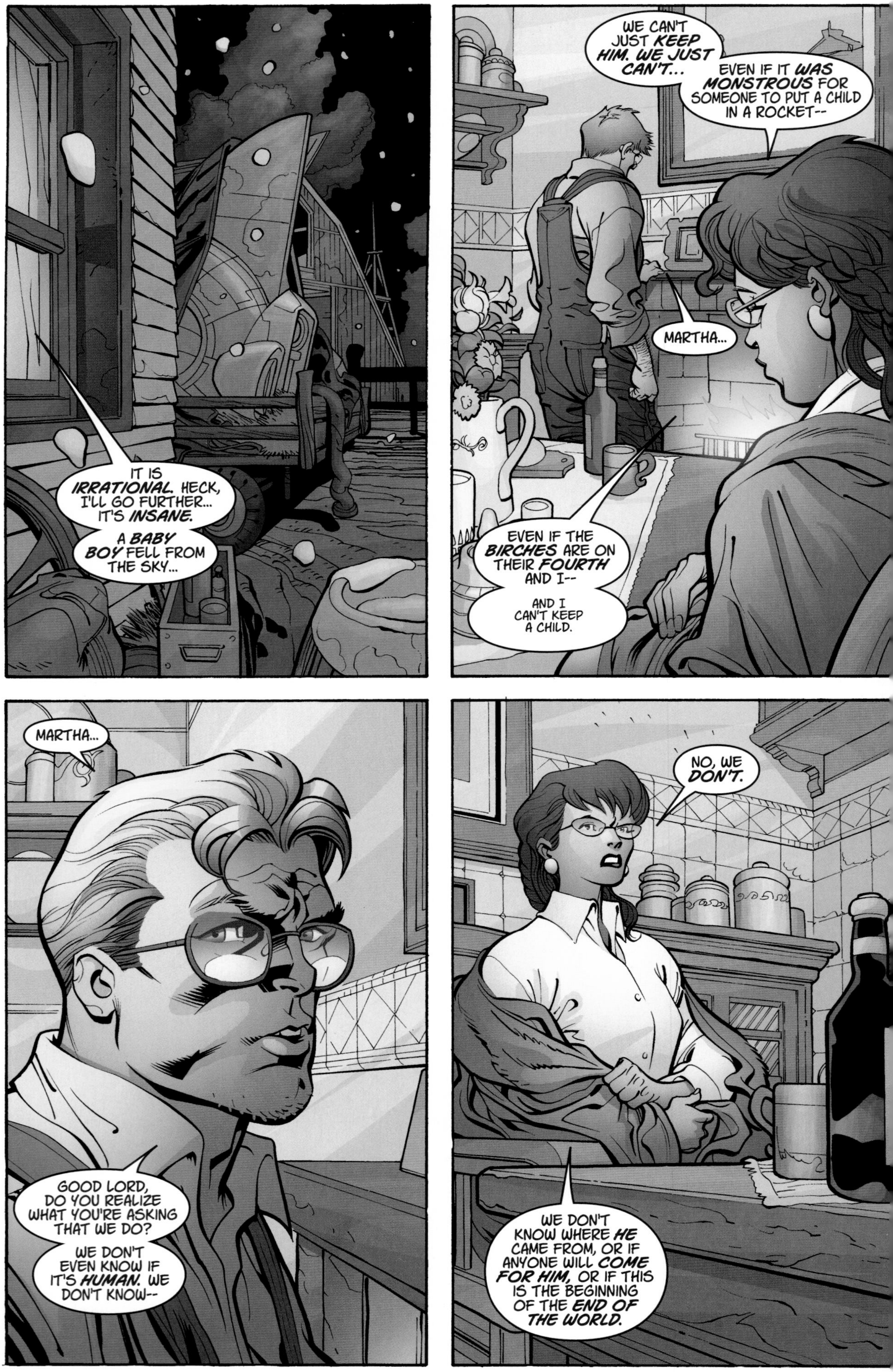
IT IS IRRATIONAL. HECK, I'LL GO FURTHER... IT'S INSANE.
A BABY BOY FELL FROM THE SKY...
WE CAN'T JUST KEEP HIM. WE JUST CAN'T...
EVEN IF IT WAS MONSTROUS FOR SOMEONE TO PUT A CHILD IN A ROCKET--
MARTHA...
EVEN IF THE BIRCHES ARE ON THEIR FOURTH AND I--
AND I CAN'T KEEP A CHILD.
MARTHA...
GOOD LORD, DO YOU REALIZE WHAT YOU'RE ASKING THAT WE DO?
WE DON'T EVEN KNOW IF IT'S HUMAN. WE DON'T KNOW--
NO, WE DON'T.
WE DON'T KNOW WHERE HE CAME FROM, OR IF ANYONE WILL COME FOR HIM, OR IF THIS IS THE BEGINNING OF THE END OF THE WORLD.

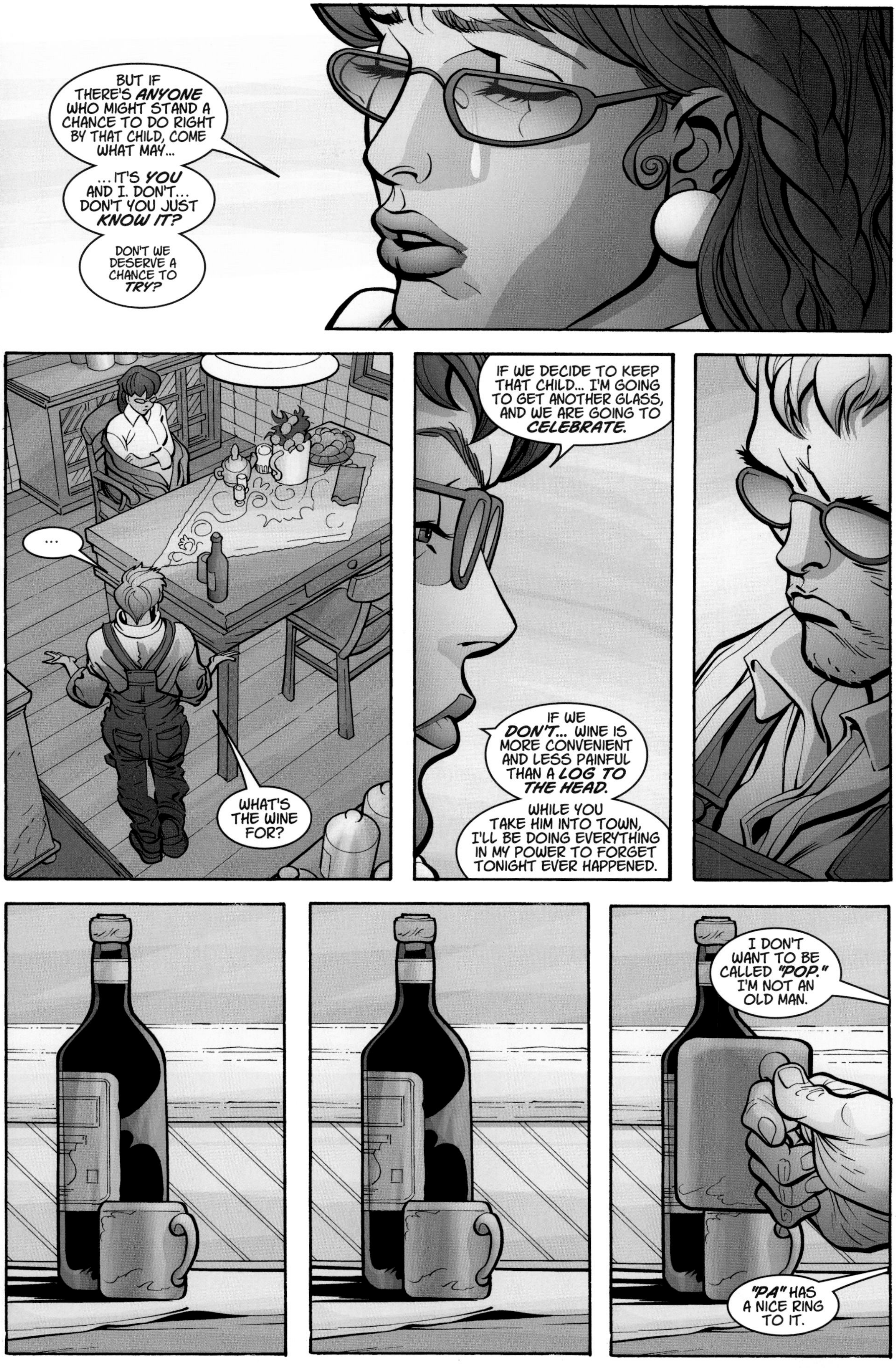
BUT IF THERE'S *ANYONE* WHO MIGHT STAND A CHANCE TO DO RIGHT BY THAT CHILD, COME WHAT MAY...
...IT'S *YOU* AND I. DON'T... DON'T YOU JUST *KNOW IT?*
DON'T WE DESERVE A CHANCE TO *TRY?*
...
WHAT'S THE WINE FOR?
IF WE DECIDE TO KEEP THAT CHILD... I'M GOING TO GET ANOTHER GLASS, AND WE ARE GOING TO *CELEBRATE.*
IF WE *DON'T...* WINE IS MORE CONVENIENT AND LESS PAINFUL THAN A *LOG TO THE HEAD.*
WHILE YOU TAKE HIM INTO TOWN, I'LL BE DOING EVERYTHING IN MY POWER TO FORGET TONIGHT EVER HAPPENED.
I DON'T WANT TO BE CALLED *"POP."* I'M NOT AN OLD MAN.
"PA" HAS A NICE RING TO IT.

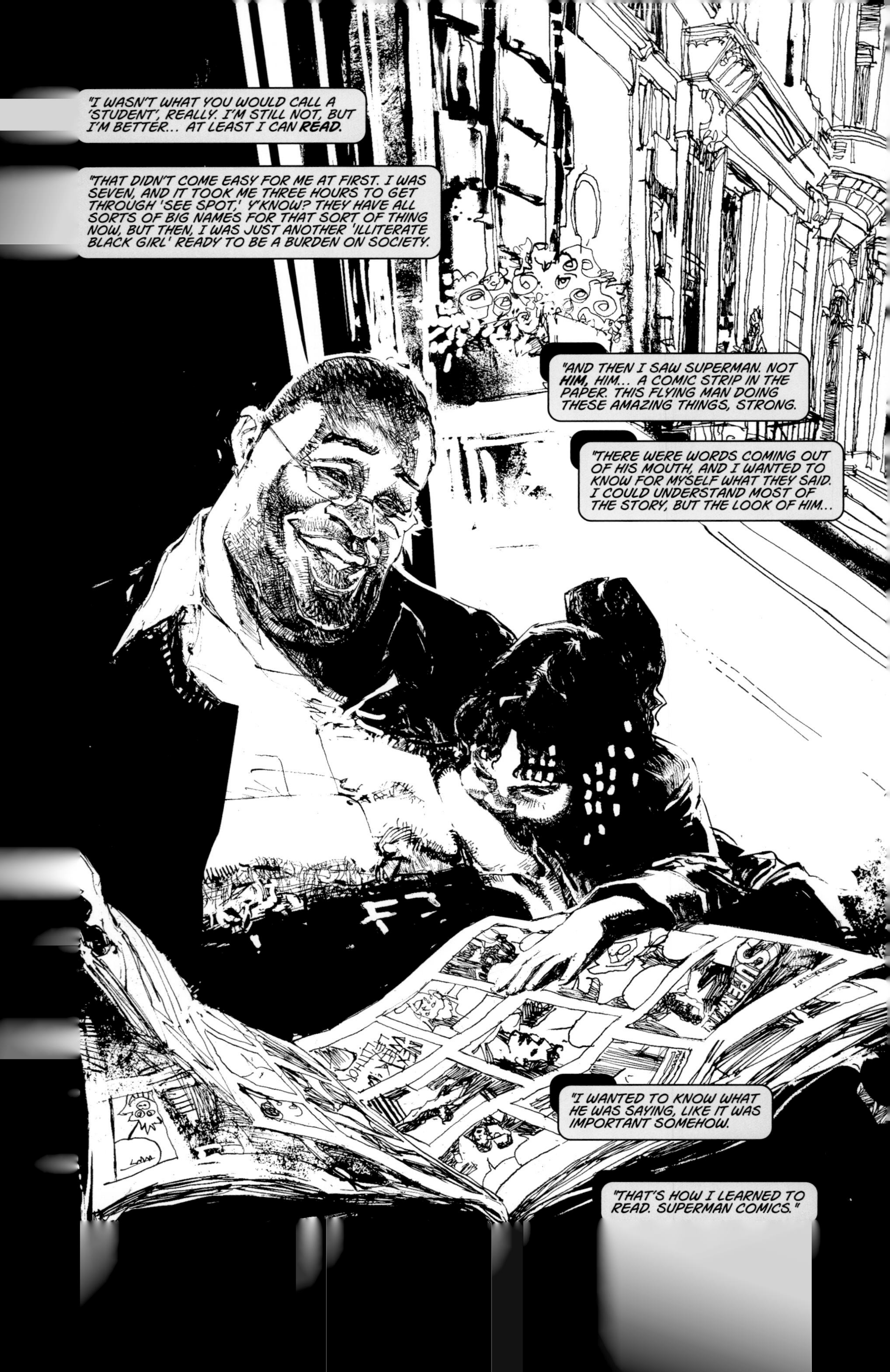
"I WASN'T WHAT YOU WOULD CALL A 'STUDENT', REALLY. I'M STILL NOT, BUT I'M BETTER... AT LEAST I CAN **READ**.
"THAT DIDN'T COME EASY FOR ME AT FIRST. I WAS SEVEN, AND IT TOOK ME THREE HOURS TO GET THROUGH 'SEE SPOT,' Y'KNOW? THEY HAVE ALL SORTS OF BIG NAMES FOR THAT SORT OF THING NOW, BUT THEN, I WAS JUST ANOTHER 'ILLITERATE BLACK GIRL' READY TO BE A BURDEN ON SOCIETY.
"AND THEN I SAW SUPERMAN. NOT **HIM,** HIM... A COMIC STRIP IN THE PAPER. THIS FLYING MAN DOING THESE AMAZING THINGS, STRONG.
"THERE WERE WORDS COMING OUT OF HIS MOUTH, AND I WANTED TO KNOW FOR MYSELF WHAT THEY SAID. I COULD UNDERSTAND MOST OF THE STORY, BUT THE LOOK OF HIM...
"I WANTED TO KNOW WHAT HE WAS SAYING, LIKE IT WAS IMPORTANT SOMEHOW.
"THAT'S HOW I LEARNED TO READ. SUPERMAN COMICS."

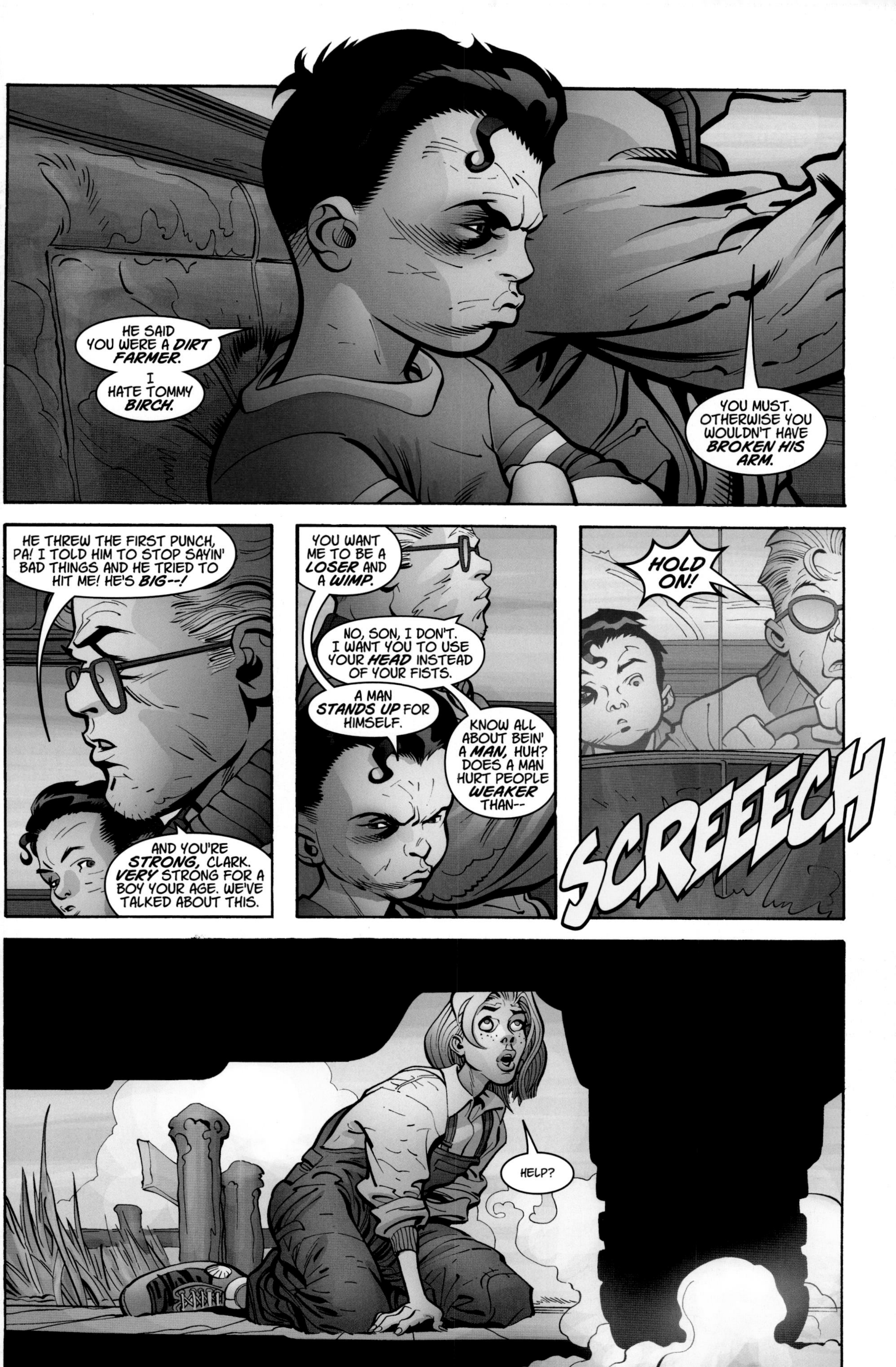
HE SAID YOU WERE A DIRT FARMER.
I HATE TOMMY BIRCH.
YOU MUST. OTHERWISE YOU WOULDN'T HAVE BROKEN HIS ARM.
HE THREW THE FIRST PUNCH, PA! I TOLD HIM TO STOP SAYIN' BAD THINGS AND HE TRIED TO HIT ME! HE'S BIG--!
AND YOU'RE STRONG, CLARK. VERY STRONG FOR A BOY YOUR AGE. WE'VE TALKED ABOUT THIS.
YOU WANT ME TO BE A LOSER AND A WIMP.
NO, SON, I DON'T. I WANT YOU TO USE YOUR HEAD INSTEAD OF YOUR FISTS.
A MAN STANDS UP FOR HIMSELF.
KNOW ALL ABOUT BEIN' A MAN, HUH? DOES A MAN HURT PEOPLE WEAKER THAN--
HOLD ON!
SCREEECH
HELP?

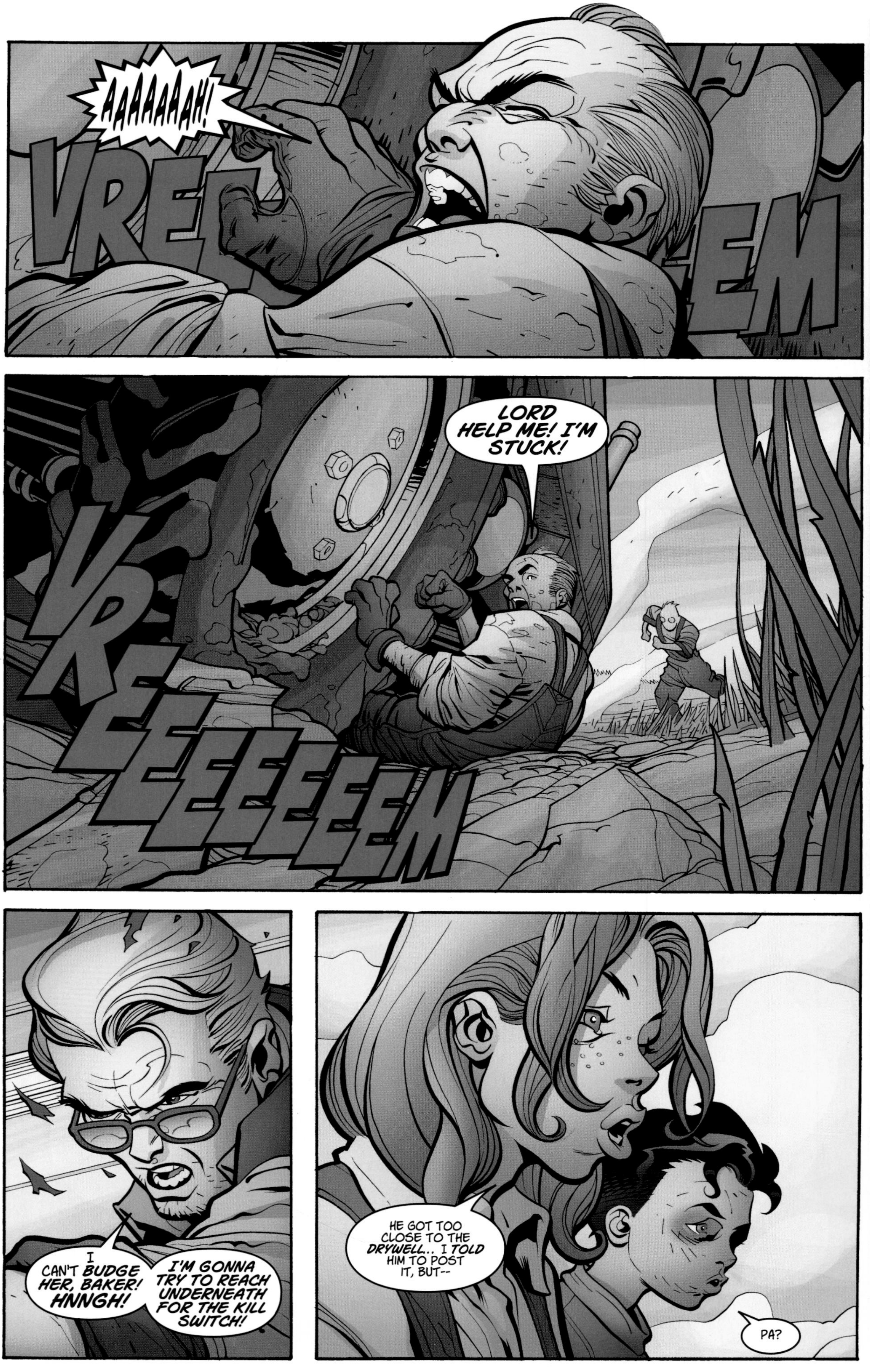
AAAAAAAH!
VREEEM
LORD HELP ME! I'M STUCK!
VREEEEEEEEM
I CAN'T BUDGE HER, BAKER! HNNGH!
I'M GONNA TRY TO REACH UNDERNEATH FOR THE KILL SWITCH!
HE GOT TOO CLOSE TO THE DRYWELL... I TOLD HIM TO POST IT, BUT--
PA?

VREE

OH JESUS! HURRY, KENT! THE THRESHER BLADES! PLEASE--!

ALL RIGHT, BAKER. YOU GOTTA LET GO...

EEE

...AND DO NOT MOVE!

EEE

THE BLADES ARE GETTING CLOSER!

EEE

SHUT UP, BAKER!

VREE

SHRPPT

AAAAGH!

EEEE

ECLK

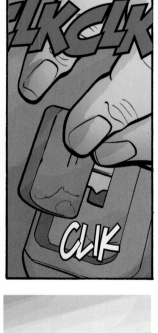

LKCLK

CLIK

P-PA?

I'M OKAY, SON...

WE'RE OKAY.

WOW.

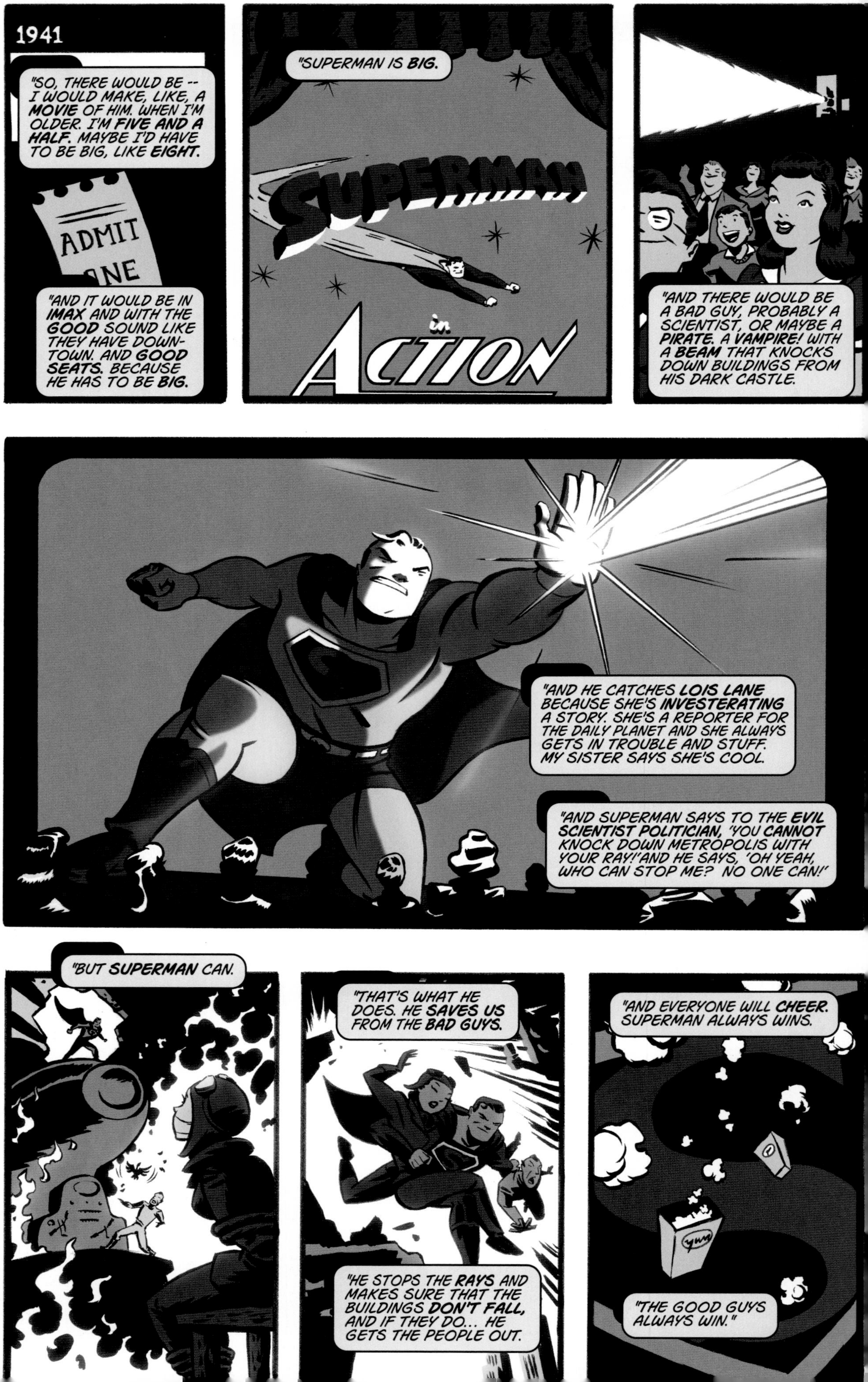
1941
"SO, THERE WOULD BE -- I WOULD MAKE, LIKE, A MOVIE OF HIM. WHEN I'M OLDER. I'M FIVE AND A HALF. MAYBE I'D HAVE TO BE BIG, LIKE EIGHT.
ADMIT
"AND IT WOULD BE IN IMAX AND WITH THE GOOD SOUND LIKE THEY HAVE DOWN-TOWN. AND GOOD SEATS. BECAUSE HE HAS TO BE BIG.
"SUPERMAN IS BIG.
SUPERMAN
in
ACTION
"AND THERE WOULD BE A BAD GUY, PROBABLY A SCIENTIST, OR MAYBE A PIRATE. A VAMPIRE! WITH A BEAM THAT KNOCKS DOWN BUILDINGS FROM HIS DARK CASTLE.
"AND HE CATCHES LOIS LANE BECAUSE SHE'S INVESTERATING A STORY. SHE'S A REPORTER FOR THE DAILY PLANET AND SHE ALWAYS GETS IN TROUBLE AND STUFF. MY SISTER SAYS SHE'S COOL.
"AND SUPERMAN SAYS TO THE EVIL SCIENTIST POLITICIAN, 'YOU CANNOT KNOCK DOWN METROPOLIS WITH YOUR RAY!' AND HE SAYS, 'OH YEAH, WHO CAN STOP ME? NO ONE CAN!'
"BUT SUPERMAN CAN.
"THAT'S WHAT HE DOES. HE SAVES US FROM THE BAD GUYS.
"HE STOPS THE RAYS AND MAKES SURE THAT THE BUILDINGS DON'T FALL, AND IF THEY DO... HE GETS THE PEOPLE OUT.
"AND EVERYONE WILL CHEER. SUPERMAN ALWAYS WINS.
"THE GOOD GUYS ALWAYS WIN."

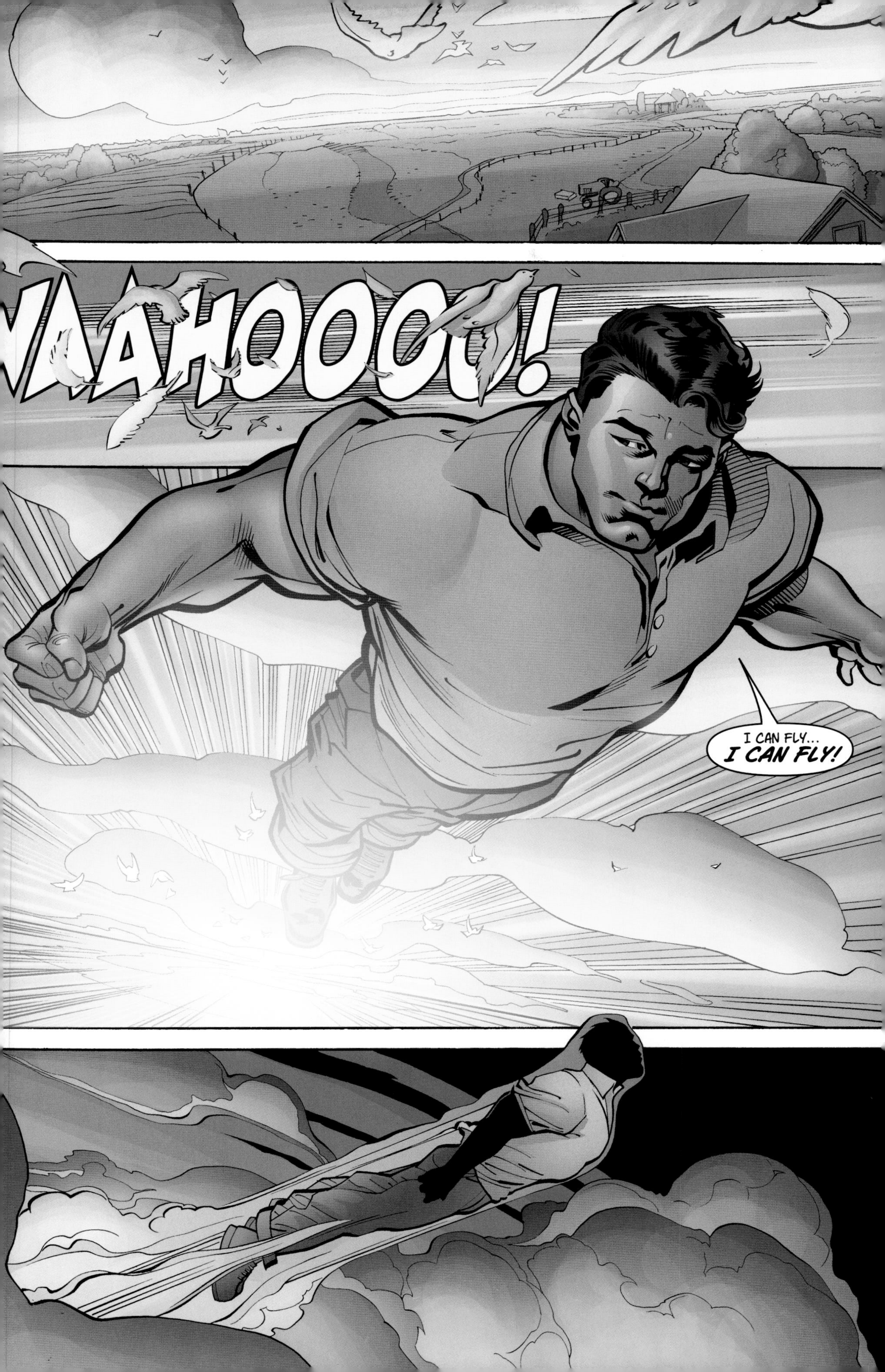
WAAHOOOOO!
I CAN FLY...
I CAN FLY!

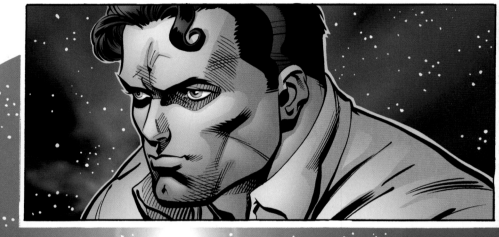

"I HAD THE CAPE. I HAD THE LOOK. I KNEW EXACTLY HOW MY ARMS WOULD GO...

"I WAS READY TO FLY.

"BUT METROPOLIS'S A MILLION MILES FROM BROOKLYN, AND MAMMA WOULDN'T EVEN LET ME CROSS THE STREET.

"I'M TEN THOUGH, RIGHT? INVINCIBLE AND FLYING MAKES COMPLETE SENSE. I PROMISE I'M NEVER GIVING UP UNTIL I CAN FLY LIKE SUPERMAN.

"I DON'T KNOW HOW MANY TIMES THE WRIGHT BROTHERS WERE GROUNDED, BUT I FIGURE IT HAD TO BE A LOT.

"TELL MAMMA WE WOULDN'T EVEN HAVE THE TERM 'GROUNDED' IF THEY HADN'T LEARNED TO FLY.

"SHE LAUGHS AND CALLS ME 'FLYBOY'. I LIKE IT.

"SUPERMAN'S SIDEKICK, 'FLYBOY'. I'M TEN, DON'T FORGET.

"SO FLYBOY HITS THE BOOKS. CAPE TUCKED UNDER MY COAT AT THE LIBRARY... MY FORTRESS OF SOLITUDE.

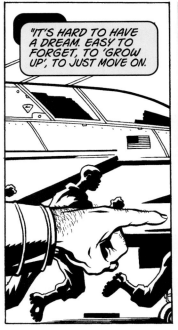

"IT'S HARD TO HAVE A DREAM. EASY TO FORGET, TO 'GROW UP', TO JUST MOVE ON.

"BUT ANYTIME I CHECKED, SUPERMAN WAS STILL TEARING THROUGH THE CLOUDS AT MACH TEN...

"SO WHY SHOULDN'T 'FLYBOY'?

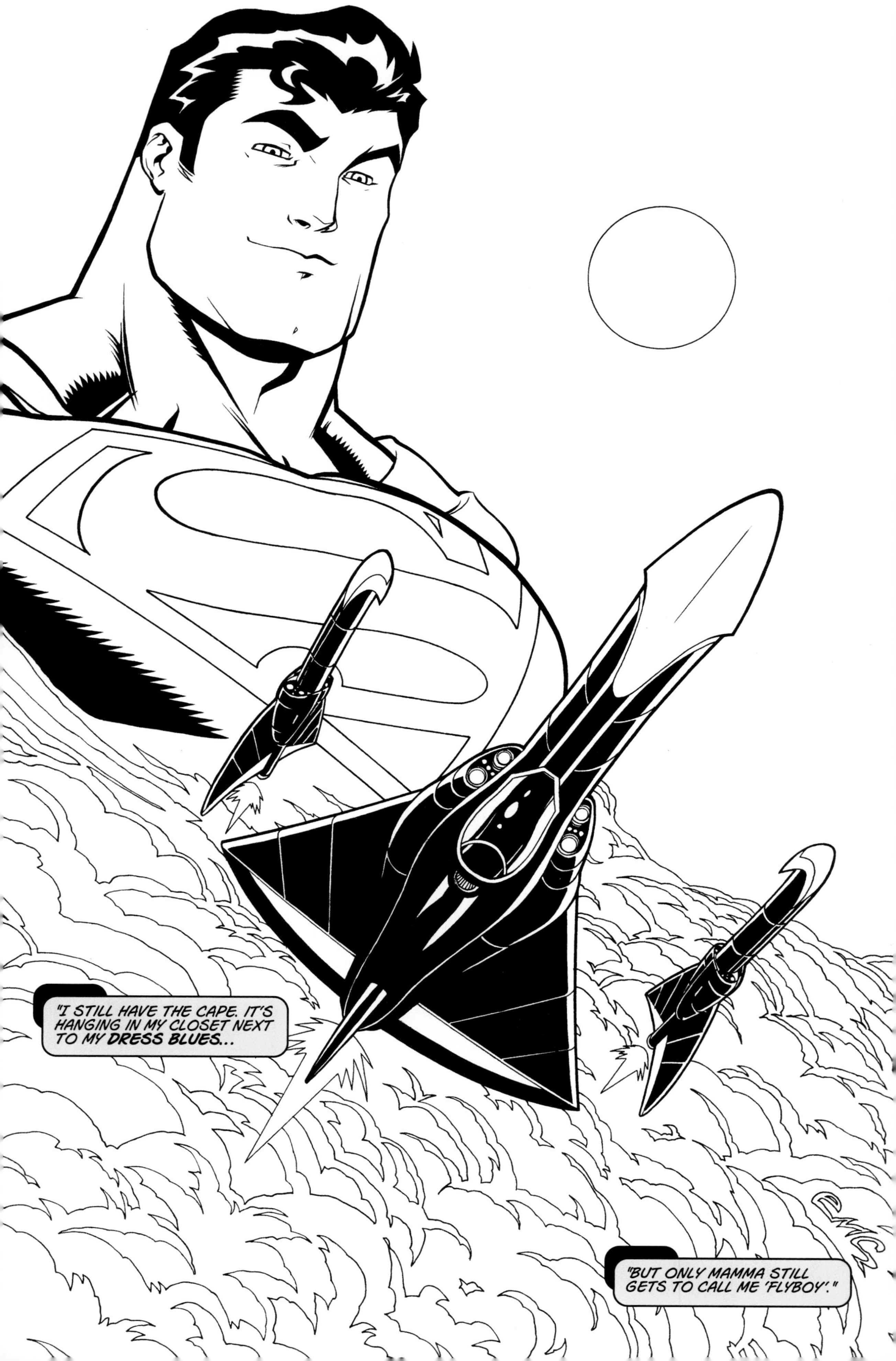
"I STILL HAVE THE CAPE. IT'S HANGING IN MY CLOSET NEXT TO MY DRESS BLUES...
"BUT ONLY MAMMA STILL GETS TO CALL ME 'FLYBOY'."

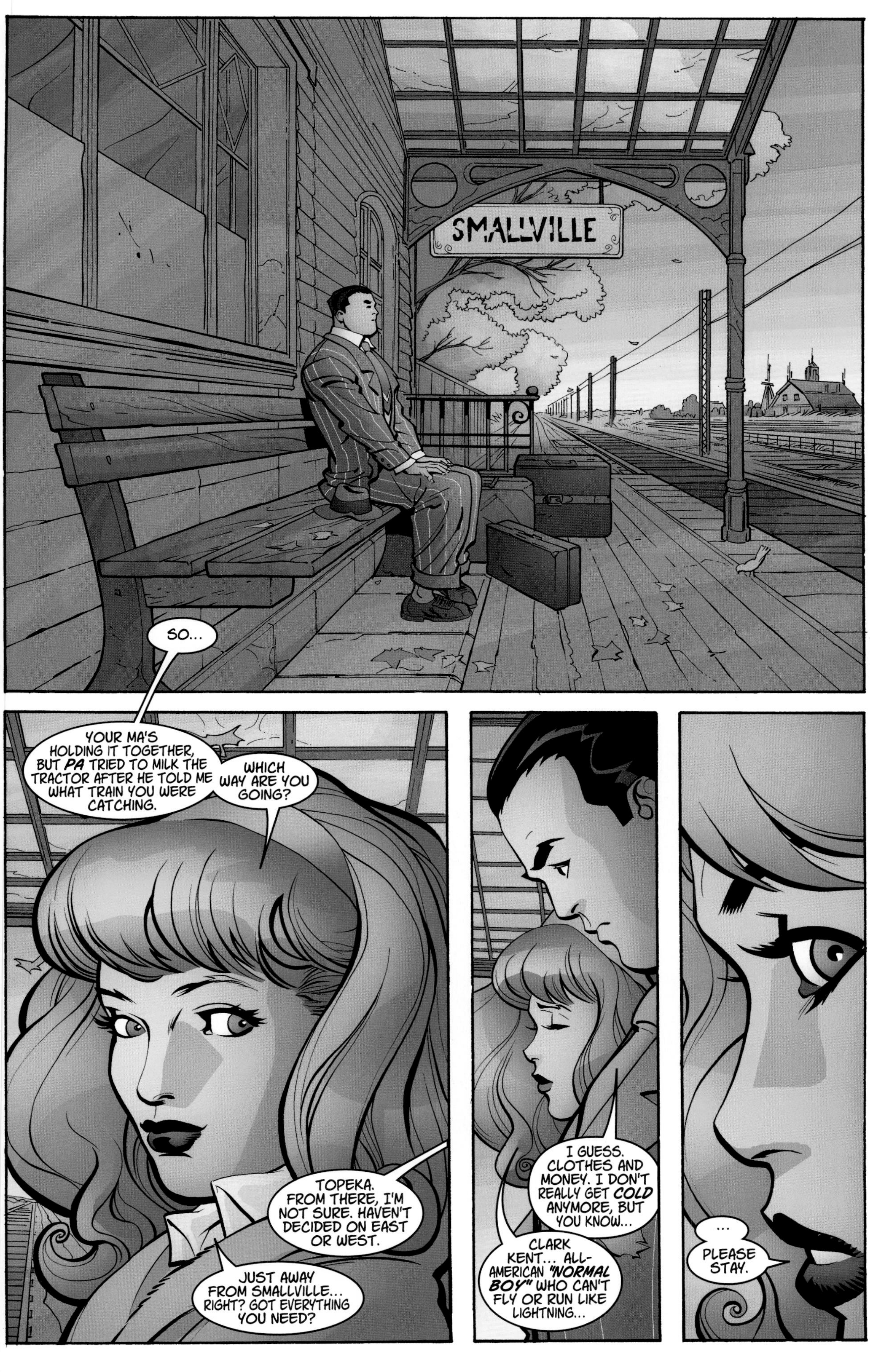
SMALLVILLE
SO...
YOUR MA'S HOLDING IT TOGETHER, BUT PA TRIED TO MILK THE TRACTOR AFTER HE TOLD ME WHAT TRAIN YOU WERE CATCHING.
WHICH WAY ARE YOU GOING?
TOPEKA. FROM THERE, I'M NOT SURE. HAVEN'T DECIDED ON EAST OR WEST.
JUST AWAY FROM SMALLVILLE... RIGHT? GOT EVERYTHING YOU NEED?
I GUESS. CLOTHES AND MONEY. I DON'T REALLY GET COLD ANYMORE, BUT YOU KNOW...
CLARK KENT... ALL-AMERICAN "NORMAL BOY" WHO CAN'T FLY OR RUN LIKE LIGHTNING...
...
PLEASE STAY.

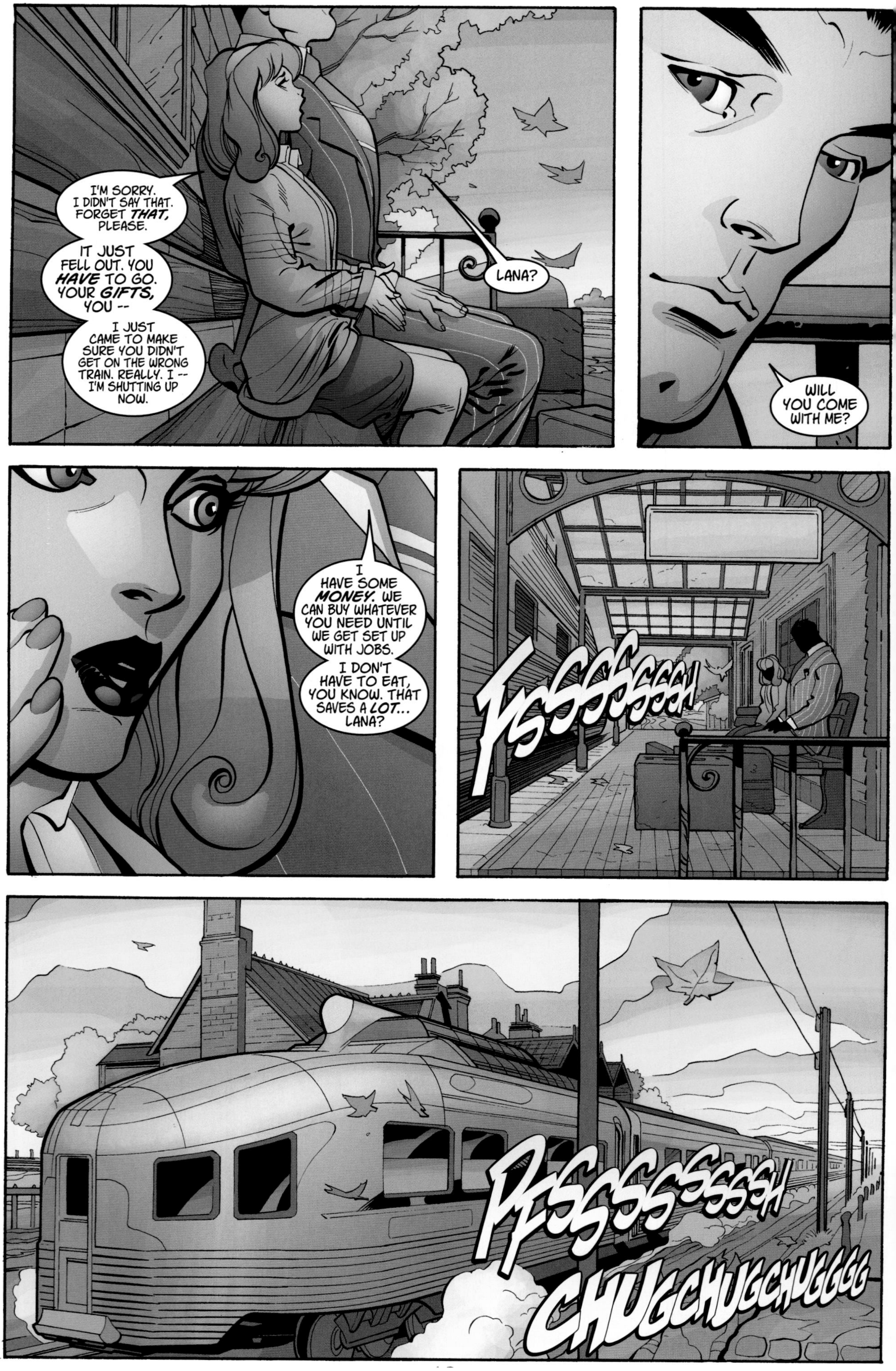

I'M SORRY. I DIDN'T SAY THAT. FORGET THAT, PLEASE.
IT JUST FELL OUT. YOU HAVE TO GO. YOUR GIFTS, YOU --
I JUST CAME TO MAKE SURE YOU DIDN'T GET ON THE WRONG TRAIN. REALLY. I -- I'M SHUTTING UP NOW.
LANA?
WILL YOU COME WITH ME?
I HAVE SOME MONEY. WE CAN BUY WHATEVER YOU NEED UNTIL WE GET SET UP WITH JOBS.
I DON'T HAVE TO EAT, YOU KNOW. THAT SAVES A LOT... LANA?
FSSSSSSSH
PFSSSSSSSSH
CHUGCHUGCHUGGGG

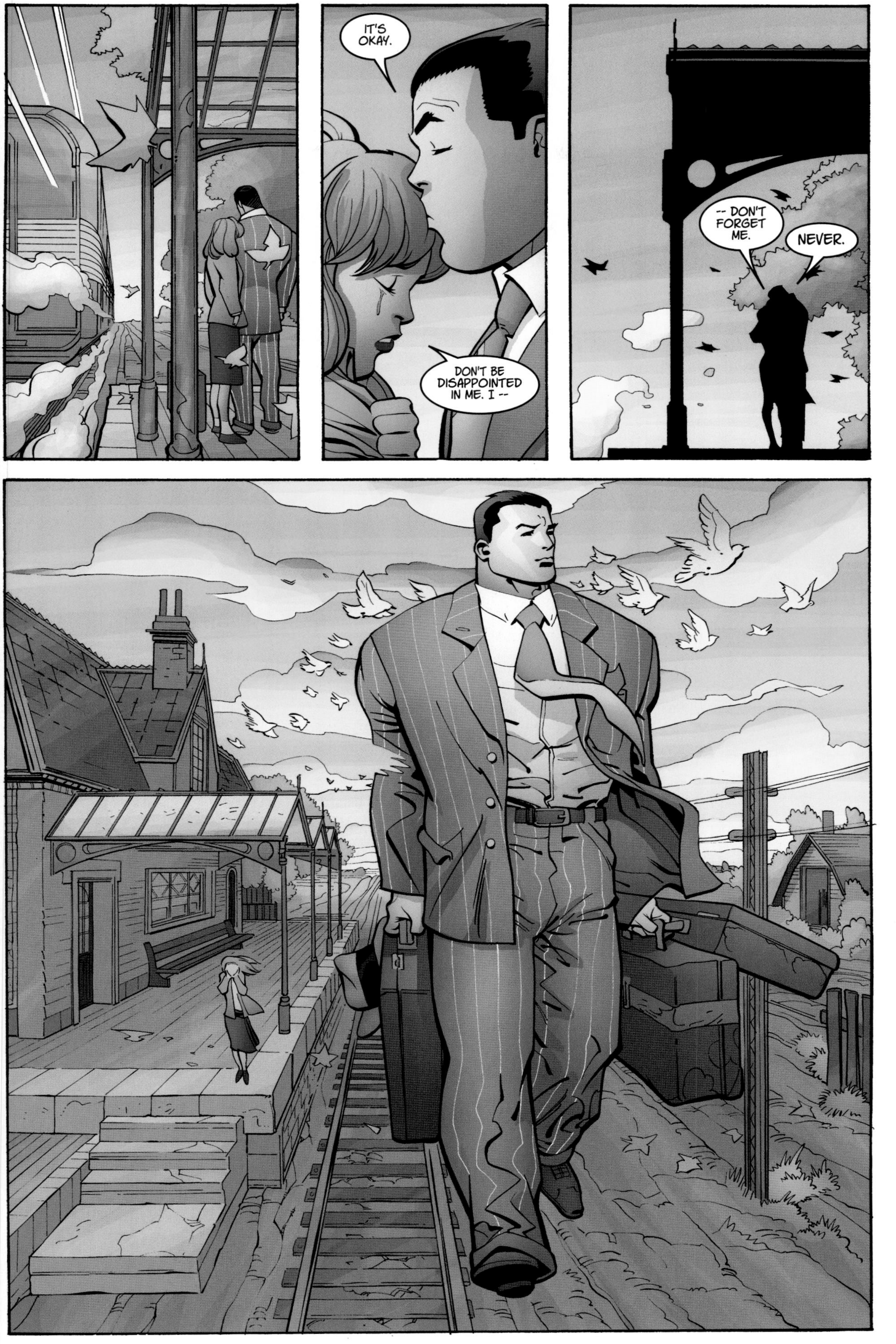
IT'S OKAY.
DON'T BE DISAPPOINTED IN ME. I --
-- DON'T FORGET ME.
NEVER.

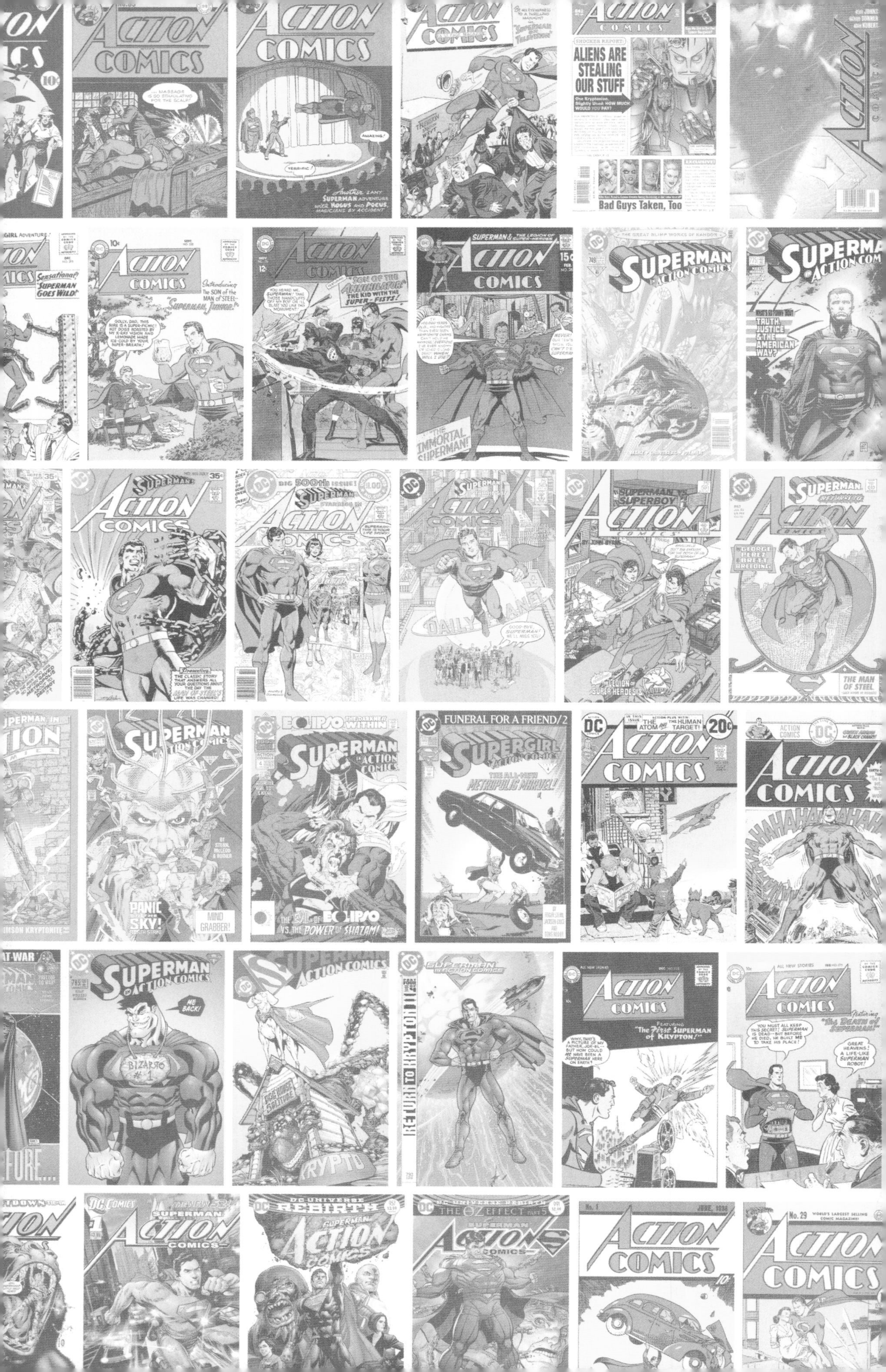
ACTION COMICS
...MASSAGE IS SO STIMULATING FOR THE SCALP!
AMAZING!
TERRIFIC!
Another ZANY SUPERMAN ADVENTURE with HOCUS AND POCUS, MAGICIANS BY ACCIDENT
SHOCKER REPORT:
ALIENS ARE STEALING OUR STUFF
One Kryptonian, Slightly Used: HOW MUCH WOULD YOU PAY?
EXCLUSIVE!
Bad Guys Taken, Too
Sensational! SUPERMAN GOES WILD!
Introducing The SON of the MAN of STEEL— "Superman, Junior!"
SON OF THE ANNIHILATOR! THE KID WITH THE SUPER-FISTS
SUPERMAN & THE LEGION OF SUPER-HEROES
THE IMMORTAL SUPERMAN!
SUPERMAN IN ACTION COMICS
WHAT'S SO FUNNY ABOUT TRUTH JUSTICE & THE AMERICAN WAY?
SUPERMAN'S ACTION COMICS
BIG 500th ISSUE!
SUPERMAN STARRING IN ACTION COMICS
DAILY PLANET
GOOD-BYE, SUPERMAN! WE'LL MISS YOU!
SUPERMAN VS. SUPERBOY
BY JOHN BYRNE
SUPERMAN RETURNS TO ACTION COMICS
GEORGE PEREZ BRETT BREEDING
THE MAN OF STEEL
PANIC IN THE SKY!
MIND GRABBER!
ECLIPSO THE DARKNESS WITHIN
THE EVIL OF ECLIPSO VS. THE POWER OF SHAZAM!
FUNERAL FOR A FRIEND/2
SUPERGIRL IN ACTION COMICS
THE ALL-NEW METROPOLIS MARVEL!
IN THIS ISSUE THE ATOM AND THE HUMAN TARGET!
20¢
ME BACK!
BIZARRO #1
KRYPTO
RETURN TO KRYPTON II
The First Superman of Krypton!
WHY, THAT'S A PICTURE OF MY FATHER, JOR-EL! BUT HOW COULD HE HAVE BEEN A SUPERMAN HERE ON EARTH?
YOU MUST ALL KEEP THIS SECRET! SUPERMAN IS DEAD—BUT BEFORE HE DIED, HE BUILT ME TO TAKE HIS PLACE!
GREAT HEAVENS! A LIFE-LIKE SUPERMAN ROBOT!
The Death of Superman!
DC COMICS #1
THE NEW 52!
SUPERMAN ACTION COMICS
DC UNIVERSE REBIRTH
THE OZ EFFECT PART 5
No. 1
JUNE, 1938
10¢
No. 29
WORLD'S LARGEST SELLING COMIC MAGAZINE!

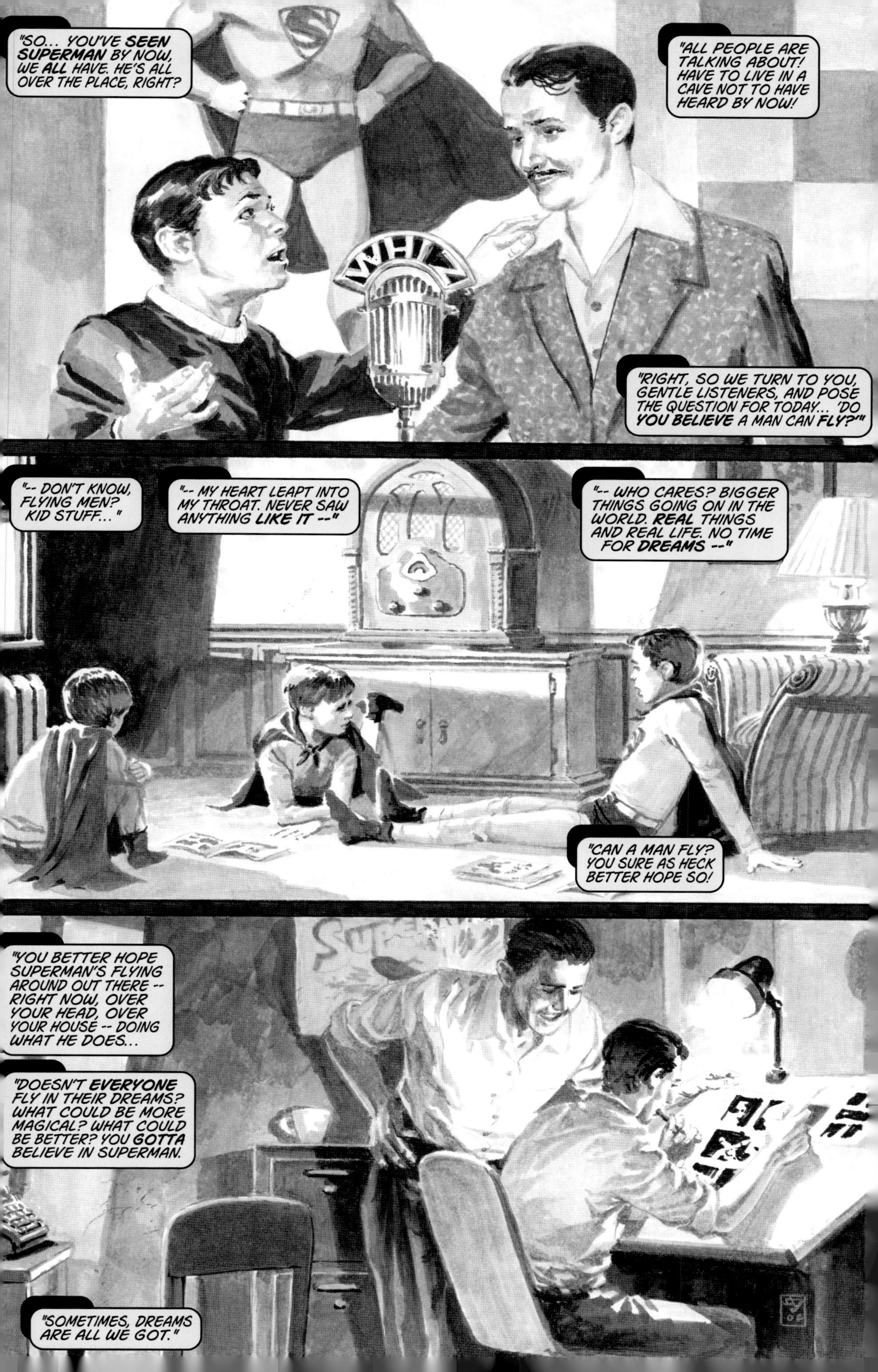
"SO... YOU'VE SEEN SUPERMAN BY NOW, WE ALL HAVE. HE'S ALL OVER THE PLACE, RIGHT?
"ALL PEOPLE ARE TALKING ABOUT! HAVE TO LIVE IN A CAVE NOT TO HAVE HEARD BY NOW!
"RIGHT, SO WE TURN TO YOU, GENTLE LISTENERS, AND POSE THE QUESTION FOR TODAY... 'DO YOU BELIEVE A MAN CAN FLY?'"
"-- DON'T KNOW, FLYING MEN? KID STUFF..."
"-- MY HEART LEAPT INTO MY THROAT. NEVER SAW ANYTHING LIKE IT --"
"-- WHO CARES? BIGGER THINGS GOING ON IN THE WORLD. REAL THINGS AND REAL LIFE. NO TIME FOR DREAMS --"
"CAN A MAN FLY? YOU SURE AS HECK BETTER HOPE SO!
"YOU BETTER HOPE SUPERMAN'S FLYING AROUND OUT THERE -- RIGHT NOW, OVER YOUR HEAD, OVER YOUR HOUSE -- DOING WHAT HE DOES...
"DOESN'T EVERYONE FLY IN THEIR DREAMS? WHAT COULD BE MORE MAGICAL? WHAT COULD BE BETTER? YOU GOTTA BELIEVE IN SUPERMAN.
"SOMETIMES, DREAMS ARE ALL WE GOT."

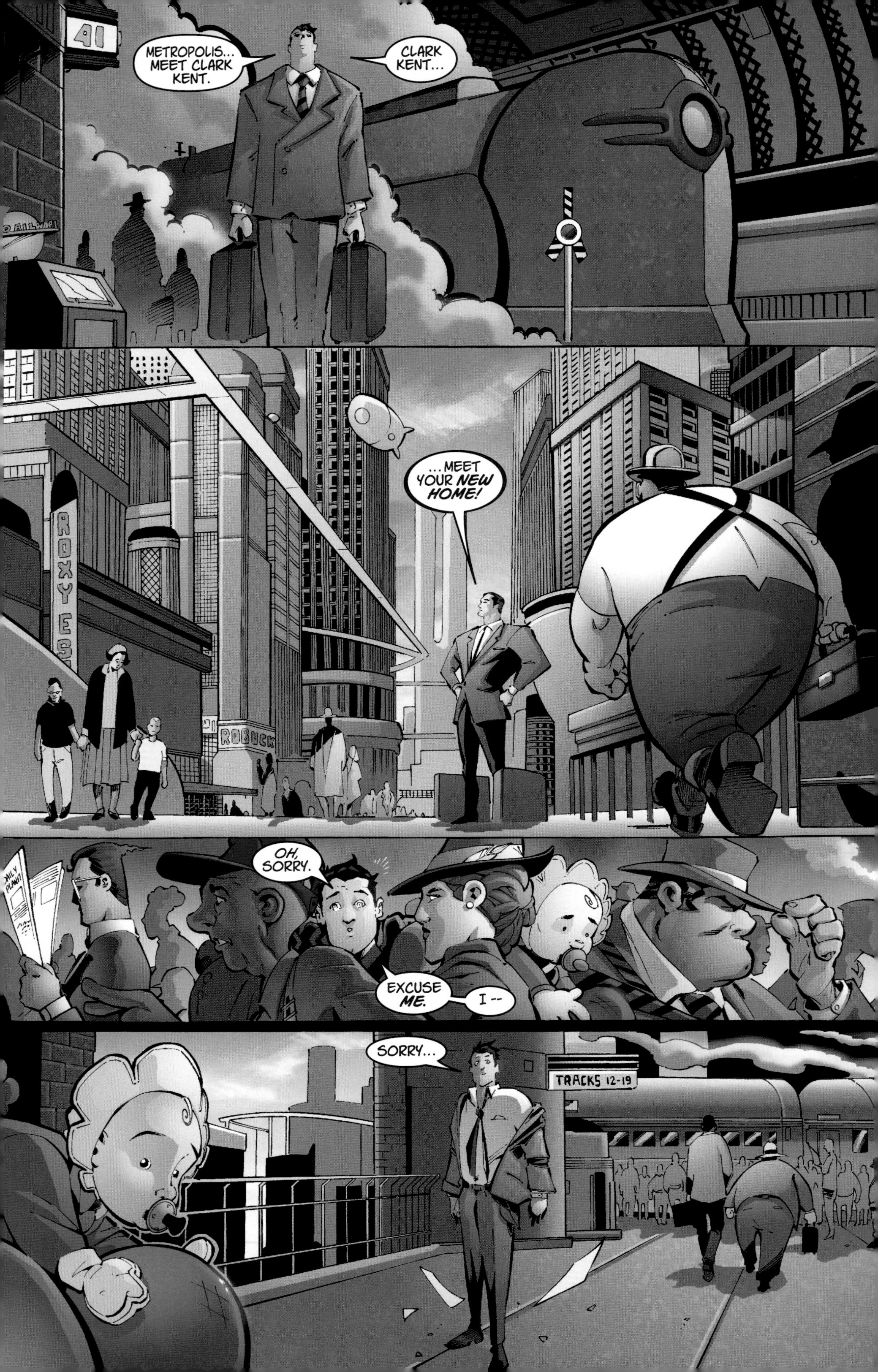

41
METROPOLIS... MEET CLARK KENT.
CLARK KENT...
...MEET YOUR NEW HOME!
ROXY
ES
ROBUCK
OH, SORRY.
EXCUSE ME.
I --
SORRY...
TRACKS 12-19

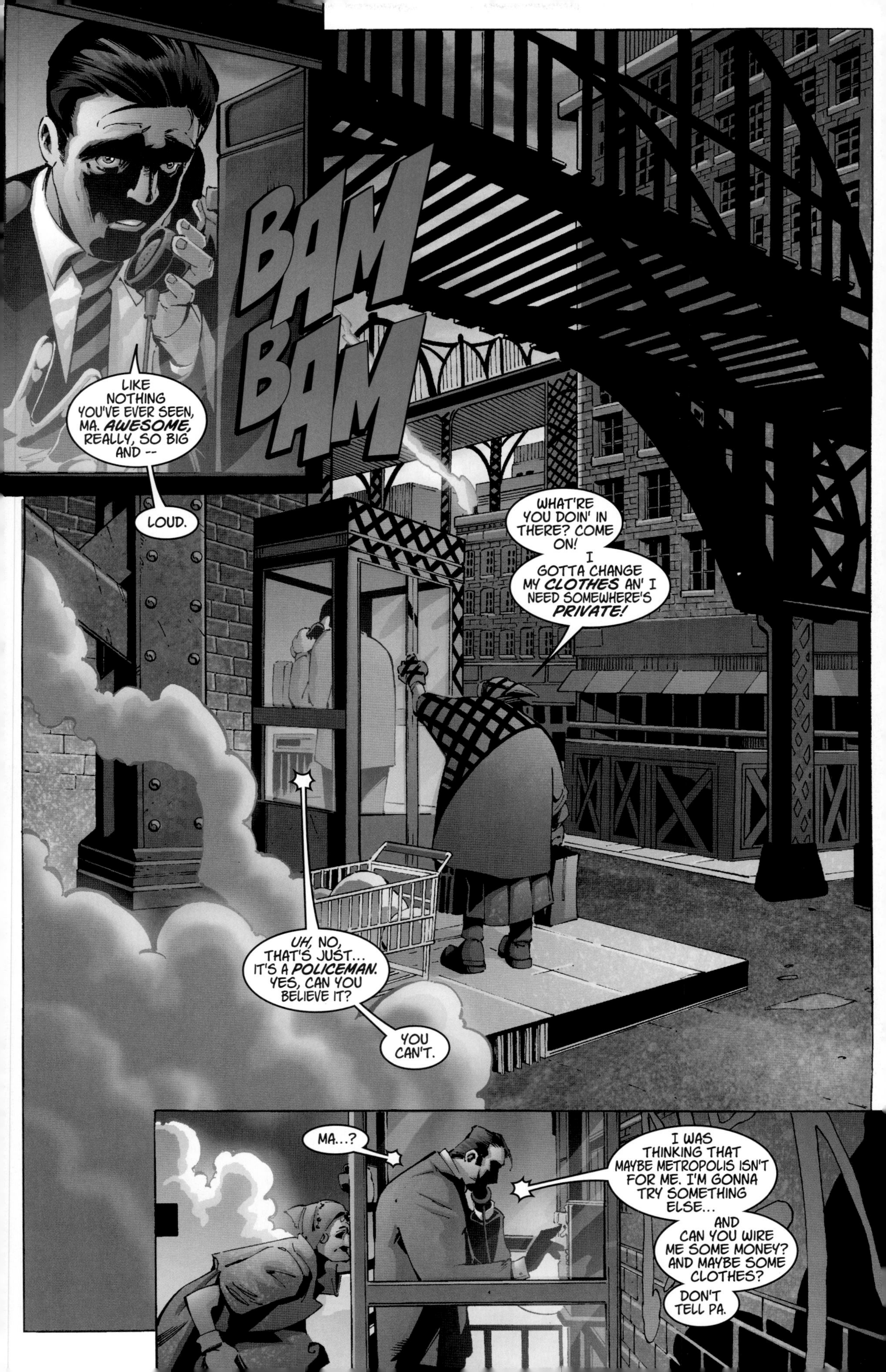
BAM
BAM
LIKE NOTHING YOU'VE EVER SEEN, MA. AWESOME, REALLY, SO BIG AND --
LOUD.
WHAT'RE YOU DOIN' IN THERE? COME ON!
I GOTTA CHANGE MY CLOTHES AN' I NEED SOMEWHERE'S PRIVATE!
UH, NO, THAT'S JUST... IT'S A POLICEMAN. YES, CAN YOU BELIEVE IT?
YOU CAN'T.
MA...?
I WAS THINKING THAT MAYBE METROPOLIS ISN'T FOR ME. I'M GONNA TRY SOMETHING ELSE...
AND CAN YOU WIRE ME SOME MONEY? AND MAYBE SOME CLOTHES?
DON'T TELL PA.

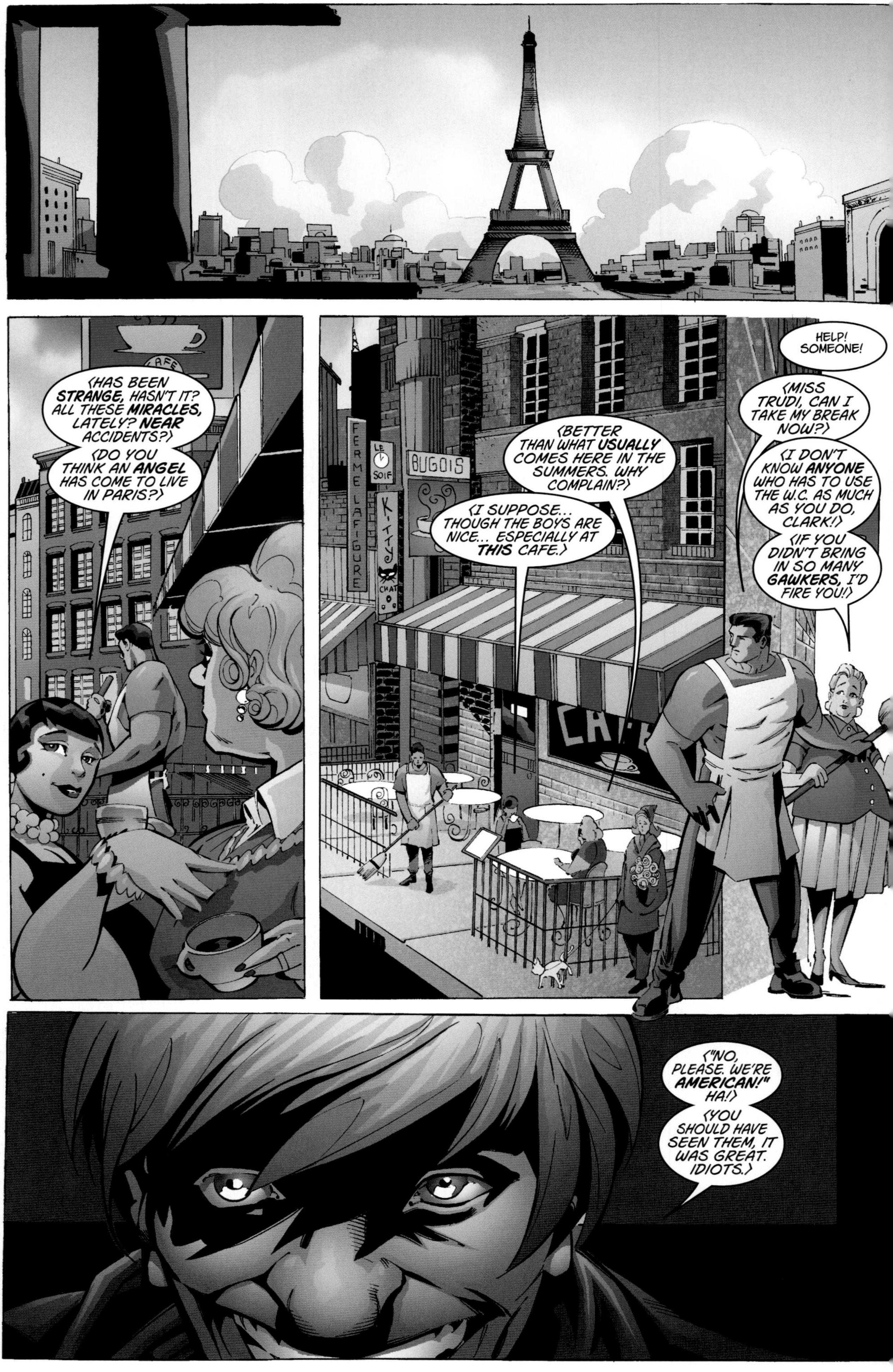
⟨HAS BEEN STRANGE, HASN'T IT? ALL THESE MIRACLES, LATELY? NEAR ACCIDENTS?⟩
⟨DO YOU THINK AN ANGEL HAS COME TO LIVE IN PARIS?⟩
CAFE
FERME LAFIGURE
LE SOIF
BUGOIS
KITTY
CHAT
⟨BETTER THAN WHAT USUALLY COMES HERE IN THE SUMMERS. WHY COMPLAIN?⟩
⟨I SUPPOSE... THOUGH THE BOYS ARE NICE... ESPECIALLY AT THIS CAFE.⟩
HELP! SOMEONE!
⟨MISS TRUDI, CAN I TAKE MY BREAK NOW?⟩
⟨I DON'T KNOW ANYONE WHO HAS TO USE THE W.C. AS MUCH AS YOU DO, CLARK!⟩
⟨IF YOU DIDN'T BRING IN SO MANY GAWKERS, I'D FIRE YOU!⟩
⟨"NO, PLEASE. WE'RE AMERICAN!" HA!⟩
⟨YOU SHOULD HAVE SEEN THEM, IT WAS GREAT. IDIOTS.⟩

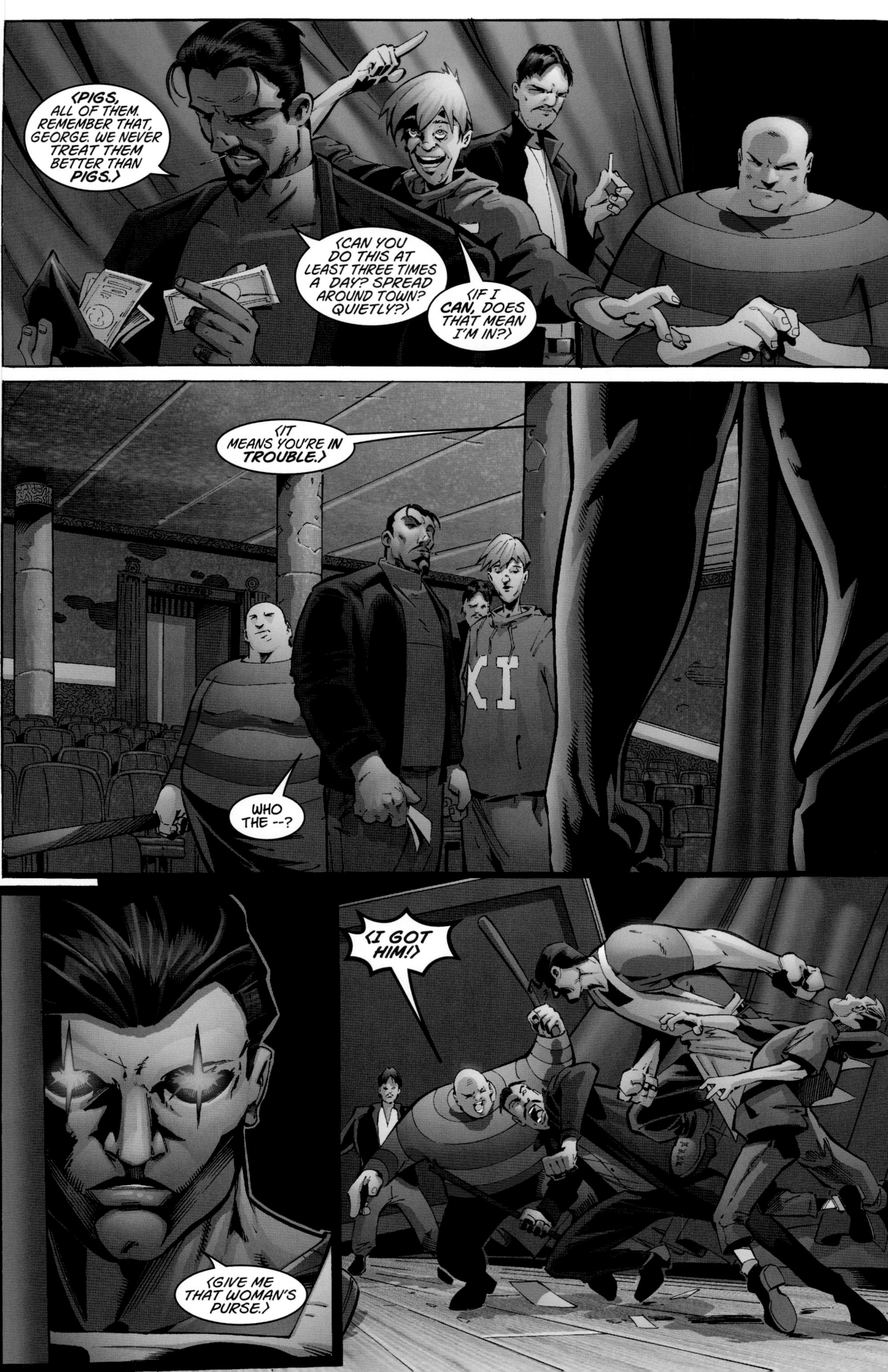

<PIGS, ALL OF THEM. REMEMBER THAT, GEORGE. WE NEVER TREAT THEM BETTER THAN PIGS.>
<CAN YOU DO THIS AT LEAST THREE TIMES A DAY? SPREAD AROUND TOWN? QUIETLY?>
<IF I CAN, DOES THAT MEAN I'M IN?>
<IT MEANS YOU'RE IN TROUBLE.>
WHO THE --?
<GIVE ME THAT WOMAN'S PURSE.>
<I GOT HIM!>

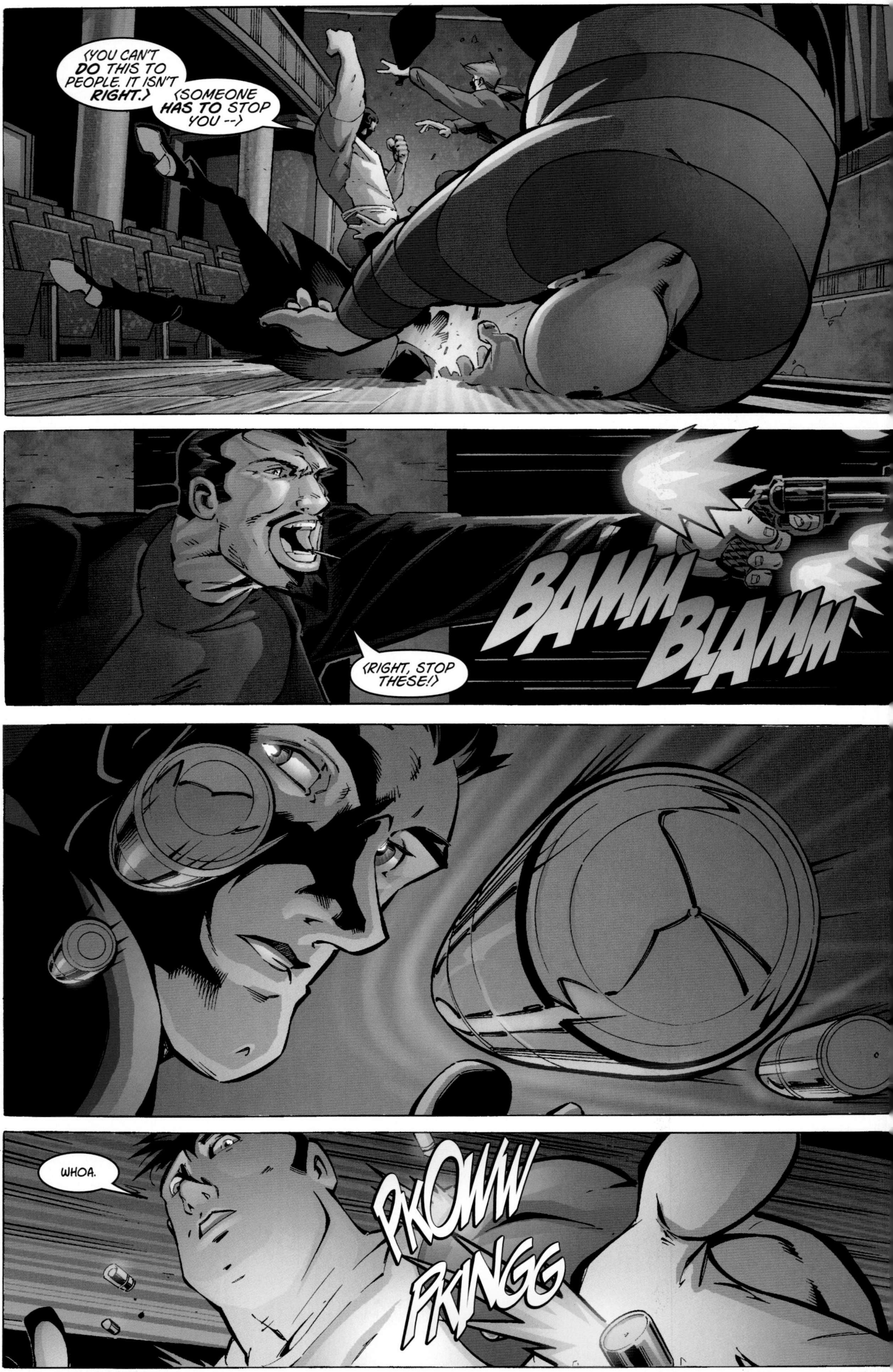
‹YOU CAN'T DO THIS TO PEOPLE. IT ISN'T RIGHT.›
‹SOMEONE HAS TO STOP YOU --›
BAMM BLAMM
‹RIGHT, STOP THESE!›
WHOA.
PKOWW
PKINGG

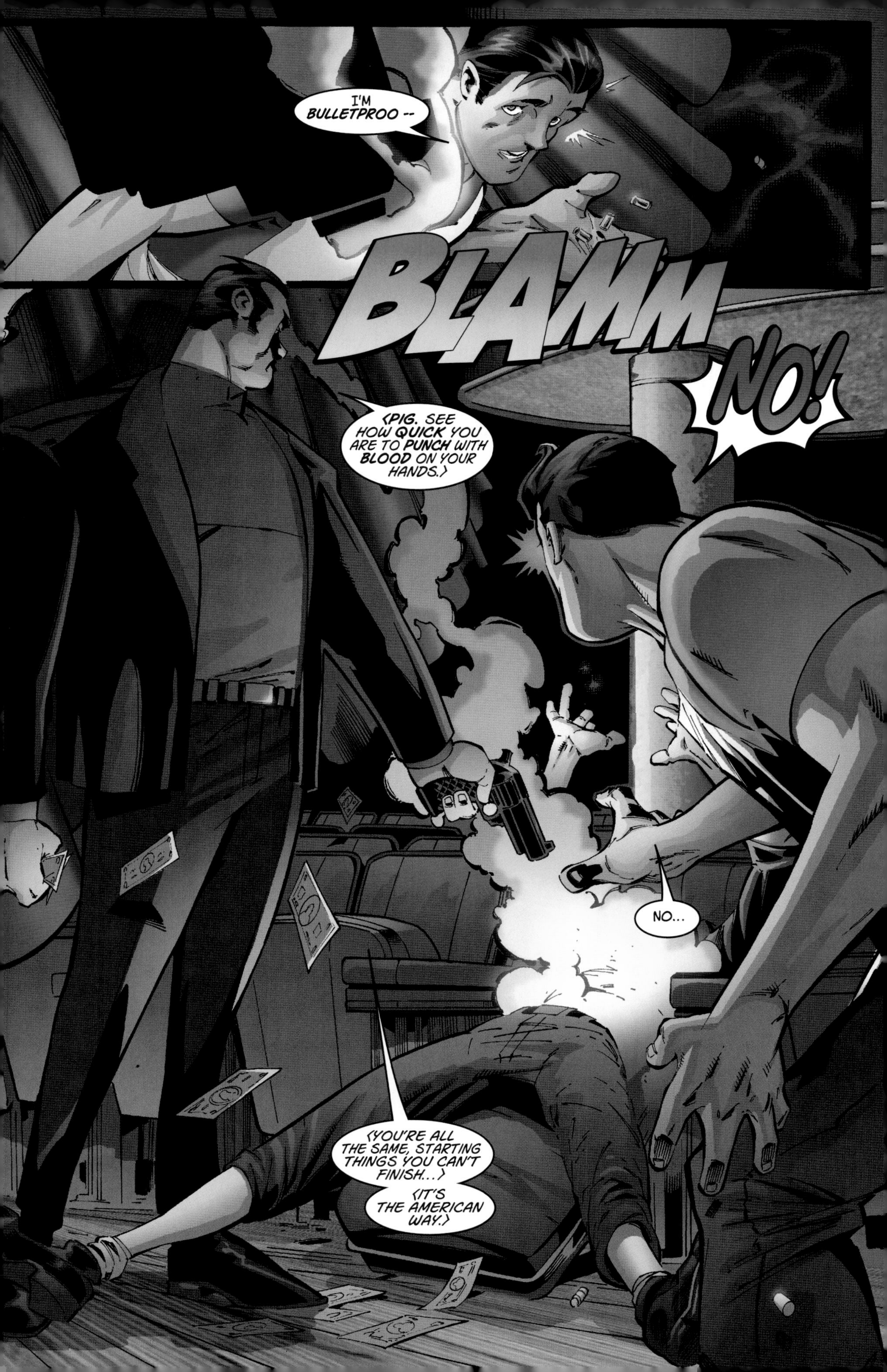
I'M BULLETPROO --
BLAMM
NO!
⟨PIG. SEE HOW QUICK YOU ARE TO PUNCH WITH BLOOD ON YOUR HANDS.⟩
NO...
⟨YOU'RE ALL THE SAME, STARTING THINGS YOU CAN'T FINISH...⟩
⟨IT'S THE AMERICAN WAY.⟩

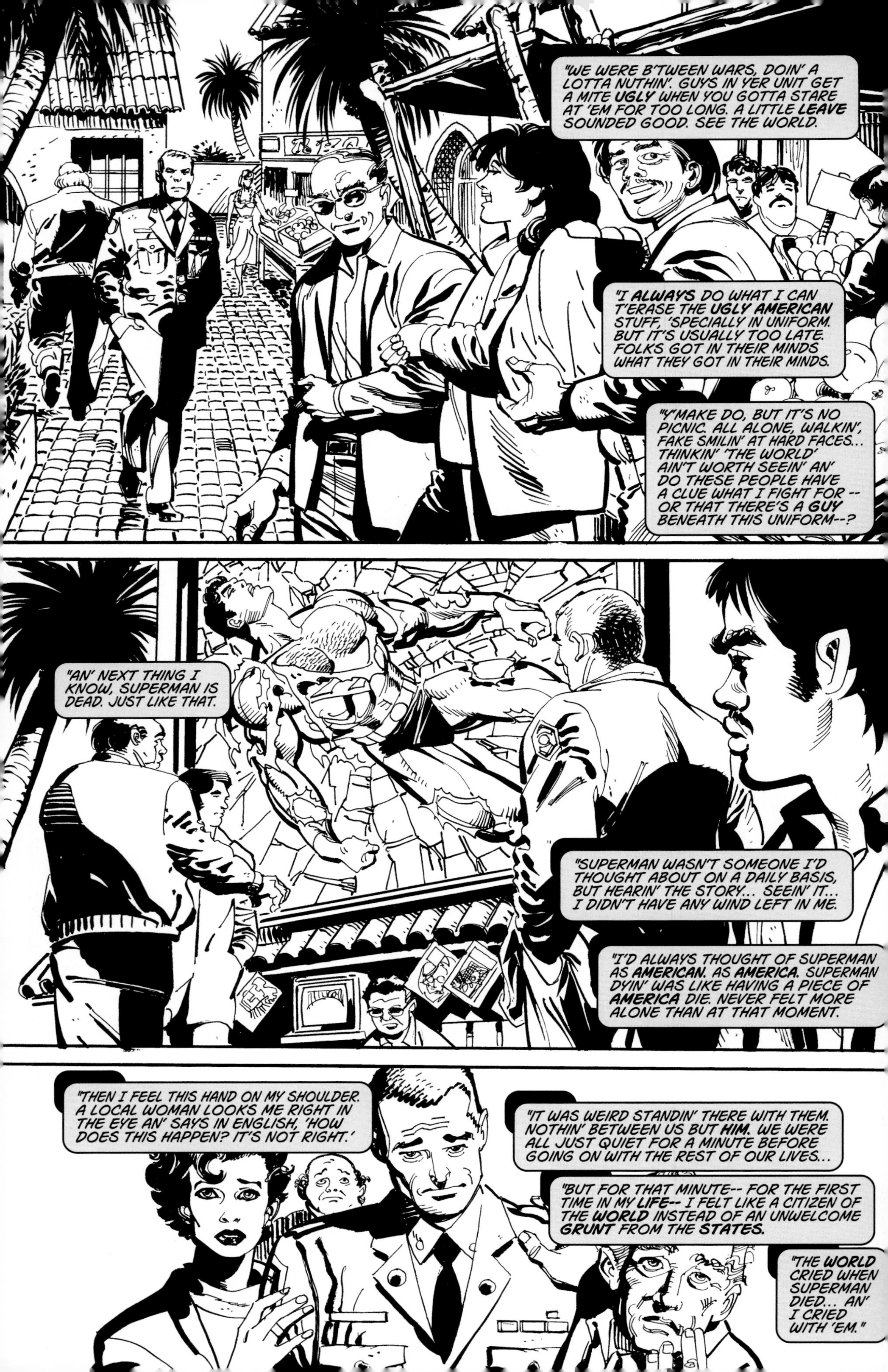
"WE WERE B'TWEEN WARS, DOIN' A LOTTA NUTHIN'. GUYS IN YER UNIT GET A MITE UGLY WHEN YOU GOTTA STARE AT 'EM FOR TOO LONG. A LITTLE LEAVE SOUNDED GOOD. SEE THE WORLD.
"I ALWAYS DO WHAT I CAN T'ERASE THE UGLY AMERICAN STUFF, 'SPECIALLY IN UNIFORM. BUT IT'S USUALLY TOO LATE. FOLKS GOT IN THEIR MINDS WHAT THEY GOT IN THEIR MINDS.
"Y'MAKE DO, BUT IT'S NO PICNIC. ALL ALONE, WALKIN', FAKE SMILIN' AT HARD FACES... THINKIN' 'THE WORLD' AIN'T WORTH SEEIN' AN' DO THESE PEOPLE HAVE A CLUE WHAT I FIGHT FOR -- OR THAT THERE'S A GUY BENEATH THIS UNIFORM--?
"AN' NEXT THING I KNOW, SUPERMAN IS DEAD. JUST LIKE THAT.
"SUPERMAN WASN'T SOMEONE I'D THOUGHT ABOUT ON A DAILY BASIS, BUT HEARIN' THE STORY... SEEIN' IT... I DIDN'T HAVE ANY WIND LEFT IN ME.
"I'D ALWAYS THOUGHT OF SUPERMAN AS AMERICAN. AS AMERICA. SUPERMAN DYIN' WAS LIKE HAVING A PIECE OF AMERICA DIE. NEVER FELT MORE ALONE THAN AT THAT MOMENT.
"THEN I FEEL THIS HAND ON MY SHOULDER. A LOCAL WOMAN LOOKS ME RIGHT IN THE EYE AN' SAYS IN ENGLISH, 'HOW DOES THIS HAPPEN? IT'S NOT RIGHT.'
"IT WAS WEIRD STANDIN' THERE WITH THEM. NOTHIN' BETWEEN US BUT HIM. WE WERE ALL JUST QUIET FOR A MINUTE BEFORE GOING ON WITH THE REST OF OUR LIVES...
"BUT FOR THAT MINUTE-- FOR THE FIRST TIME IN MY LIFE-- I FELT LIKE A CITIZEN OF THE WORLD INSTEAD OF AN UNWELCOME GRUNT FROM THE STATES.
"THE WORLD CRIED WHEN SUPERMAN DIED... AN' I CRIED WITH 'EM."

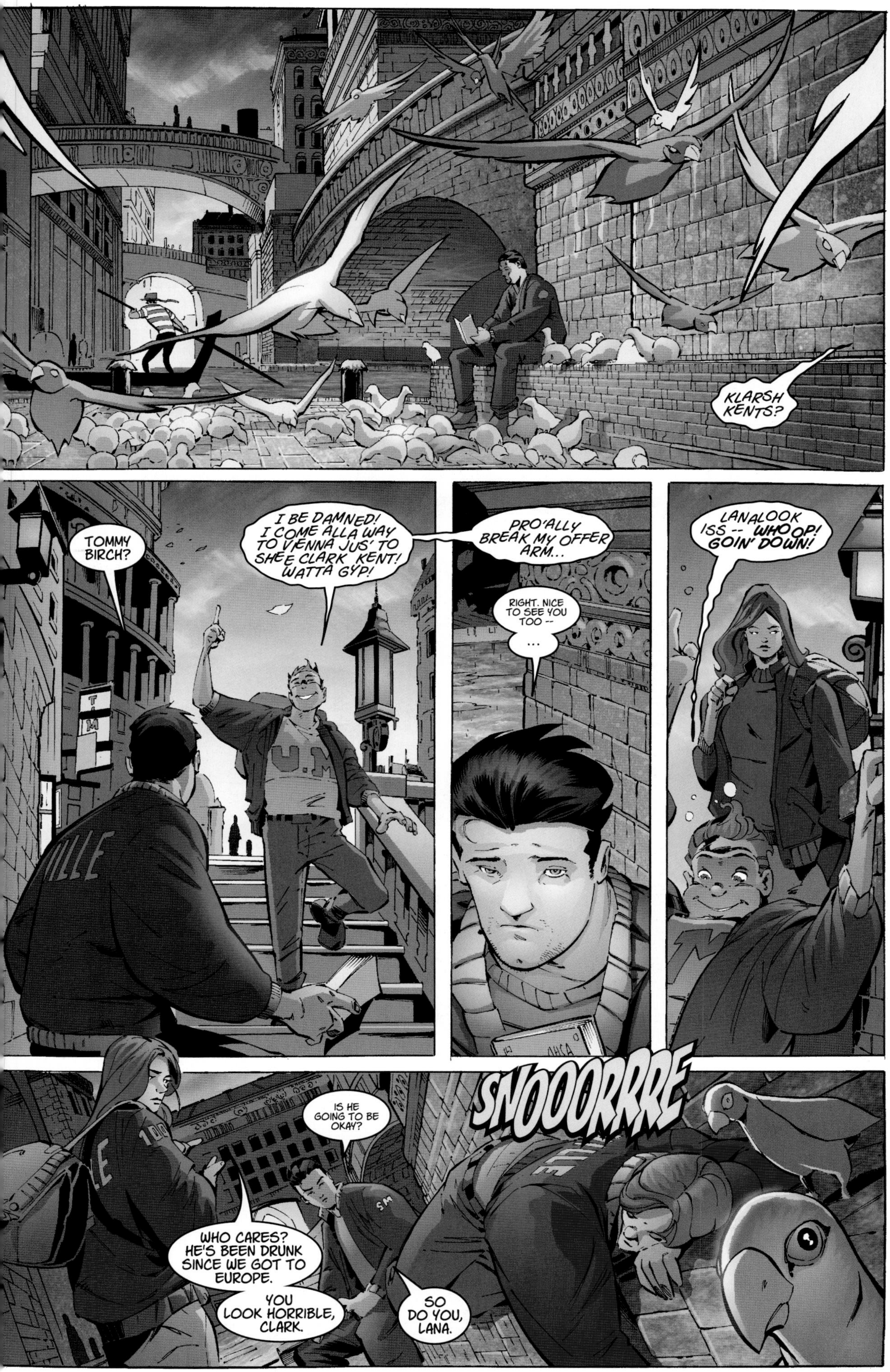
KLARSH KENTS?
TOMMY BIRCH?
I BE DAMNED! I COME ALLA WAY TO VIENNA JUS' TO SHEE CLARK KENT! WATTA GYP!
PRO'ALLY BREAK MY OFFER ARM...
RIGHT. NICE TO SEE YOU TOO --
...
LANALOOK ISS -- WHOOP! GOIN' DOWN!
SNOOORRRE
IS HE GOING TO BE OKAY?
WHO CARES? HE'S BEEN DRUNK SINCE WE GOT TO EUROPE.
YOU LOOK HORRIBLE, CLARK.
SO DO YOU, LANA.

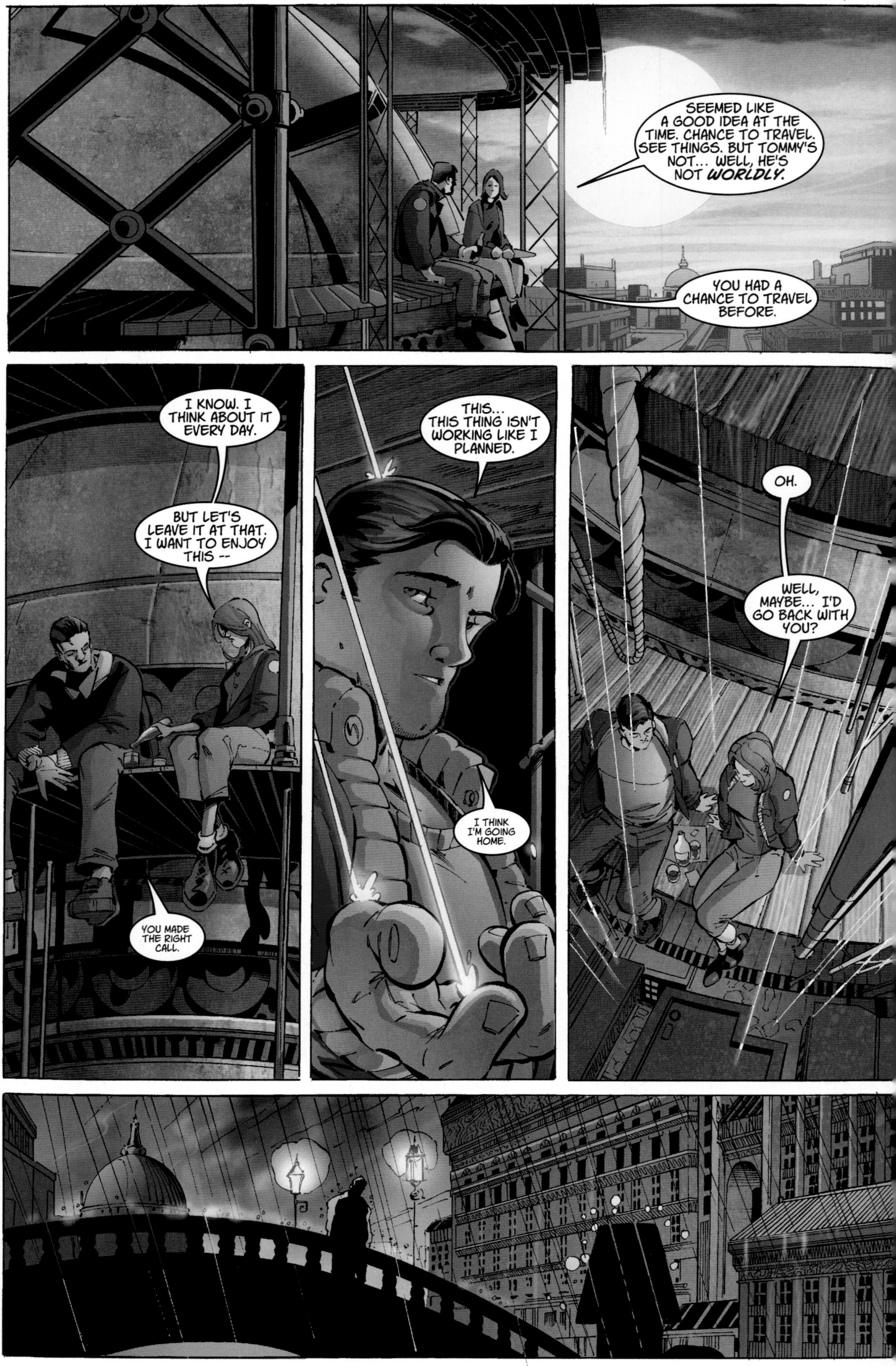
SEEMED LIKE A GOOD IDEA AT THE TIME. CHANCE TO TRAVEL. SEE THINGS. BUT TOMMY'S NOT... WELL, HE'S NOT *WORLDLY*.
YOU HAD A CHANCE TO TRAVEL BEFORE.
I KNOW. I THINK ABOUT IT EVERY DAY.
BUT LET'S LEAVE IT AT THAT. I WANT TO ENJOY THIS --
YOU MADE THE RIGHT CALL.
THIS... THIS THING ISN'T WORKING LIKE I PLANNED.
I THINK I'M GOING HOME.
OH.
WELL, MAYBE... I'D GO BACK WITH YOU?

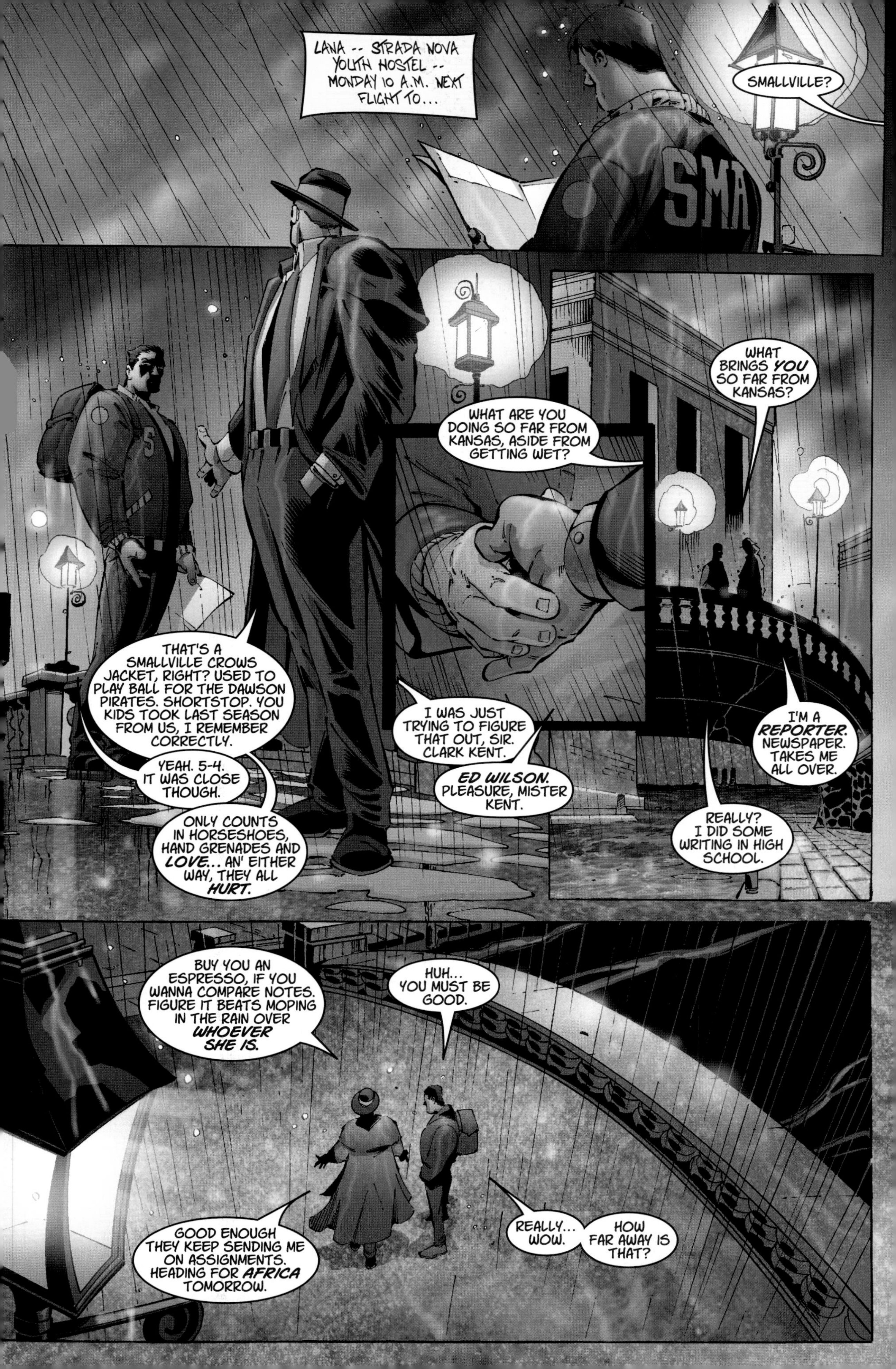
LANA -- STRADA NOVA YOUTH HOSTEL -- MONDAY 10 A.M. NEXT FLIGHT TO...
SMALLVILLE?
WHAT BRINGS YOU SO FAR FROM KANSAS?
WHAT ARE YOU DOING SO FAR FROM KANSAS, ASIDE FROM GETTING WET?
THAT'S A SMALLVILLE CROWS JACKET, RIGHT? USED TO PLAY BALL FOR THE DAWSON PIRATES. SHORTSTOP. YOU KIDS TOOK LAST SEASON FROM US, I REMEMBER CORRECTLY.
YEAH. 5-4. IT WAS CLOSE THOUGH.
ONLY COUNTS IN HORSESHOES, HAND GRENADES AND LOVE... AN' EITHER WAY, THEY ALL HURT.
I WAS JUST TRYING TO FIGURE THAT OUT, SIR. CLARK KENT.
ED WILSON. PLEASURE, MISTER KENT.
I'M A REPORTER. NEWSPAPER. TAKES ME ALL OVER.
REALLY? I DID SOME WRITING IN HIGH SCHOOL.
BUY YOU AN ESPRESSO, IF YOU WANNA COMPARE NOTES. FIGURE IT BEATS MOPING IN THE RAIN OVER WHOEVER SHE IS.
HUH... YOU MUST BE GOOD.
GOOD ENOUGH THEY KEEP SENDING ME ON ASSIGNMENTS. HEADING FOR AFRICA TOMORROW.
REALLY... WOW.
HOW FAR AWAY IS THAT?

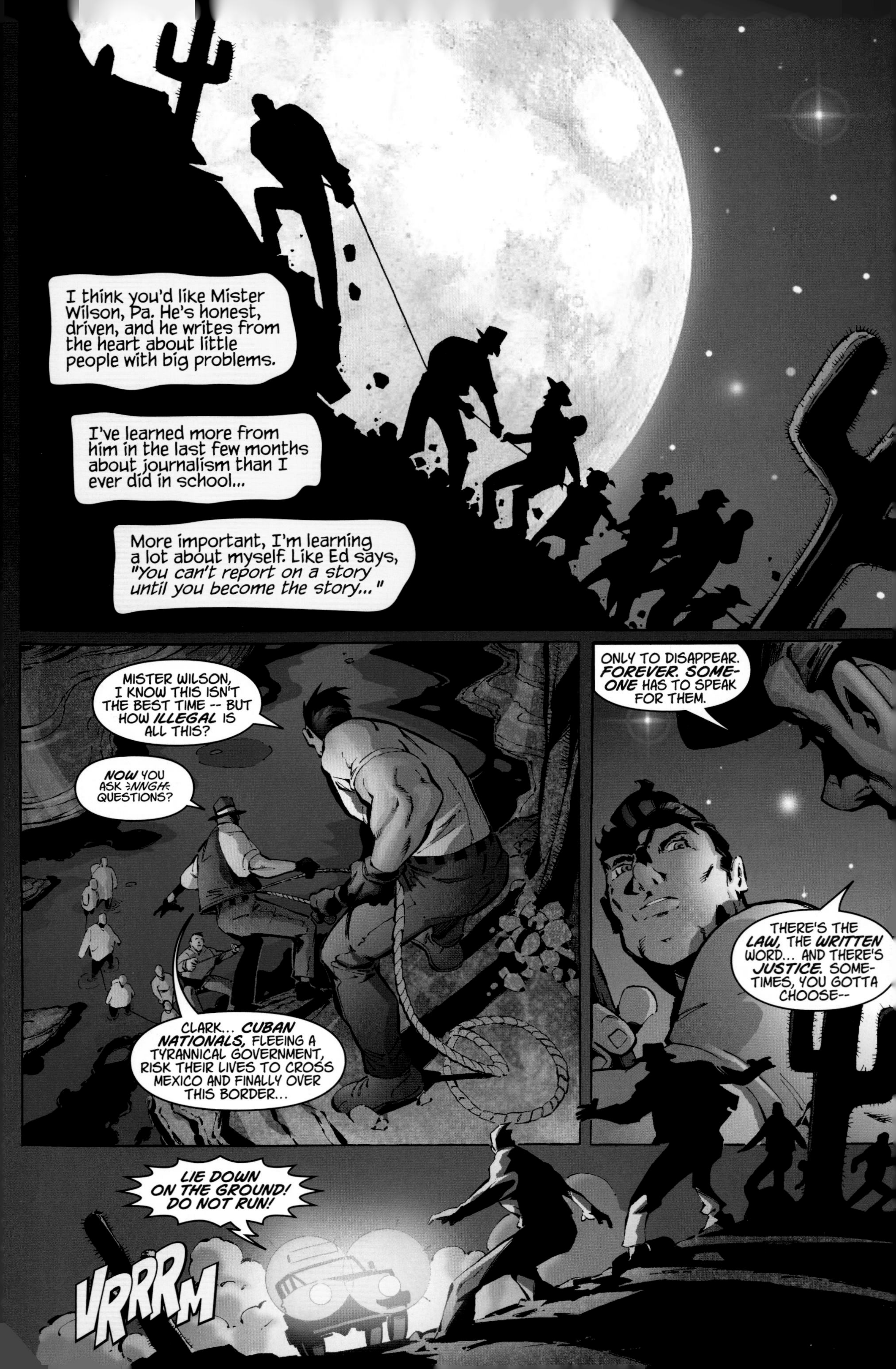

I think you'd like Mister Wilson, Pa. He's honest, driven, and he writes from the heart about little people with big problems.
I've learned more from him in the last few months about journalism than I ever did in school...
More important, I'm learning a lot about myself. Like Ed says, *"You can't report on a story until you become the story..."*
MISTER WILSON, I KNOW THIS ISN'T THE BEST TIME -- BUT HOW *ILLEGAL* IS ALL THIS?
NOW YOU ASK ≶NNGH≶ QUESTIONS?
CLARK... *CUBAN NATIONALS,* FLEEING A TYRANNICAL GOVERNMENT, RISK THEIR LIVES TO CROSS MEXICO AND FINALLY OVER THIS BORDER...
ONLY TO DISAPPEAR. *FOREVER. SOMEONE* HAS TO SPEAK FOR THEM.
THERE'S THE *LAW,* THE *WRITTEN* WORD... AND THERE'S *JUSTICE.* SOMETIMES, YOU GOTTA CHOOSE--
LIE DOWN ON THE GROUND! DO NOT RUN!
VRRRM

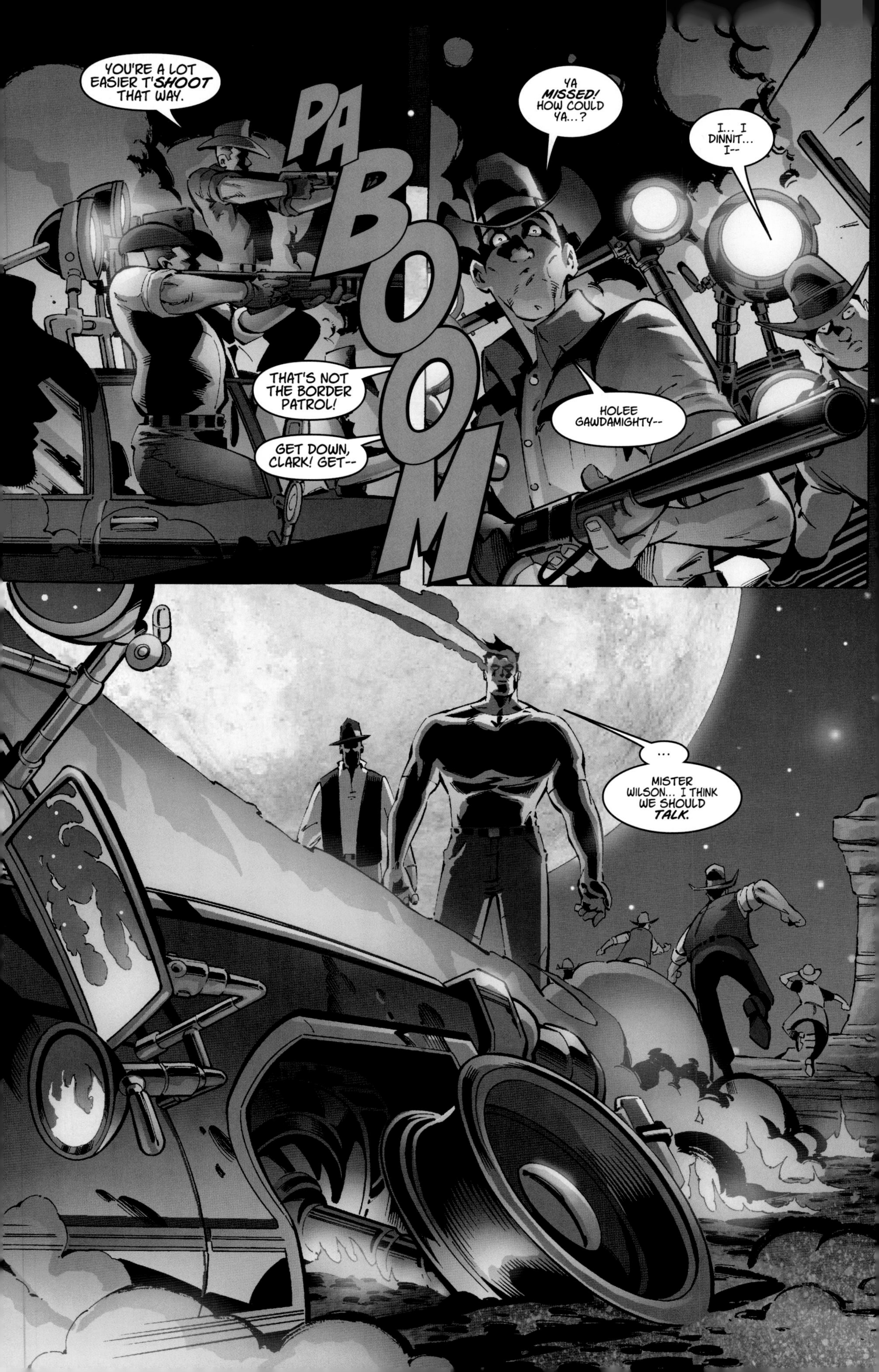
YOU'RE A LOT EASIER T'SHOOT THAT WAY.
PABOOM
THAT'S NOT THE BORDER PATROL!
GET DOWN, CLARK! GET--
YA MISSED! HOW COULD YA...?
HOLEE GAWDAMIGHTY--
I... I DINNIT... I--
...
MISTER WILSON... I THINK WE SHOULD TALK.

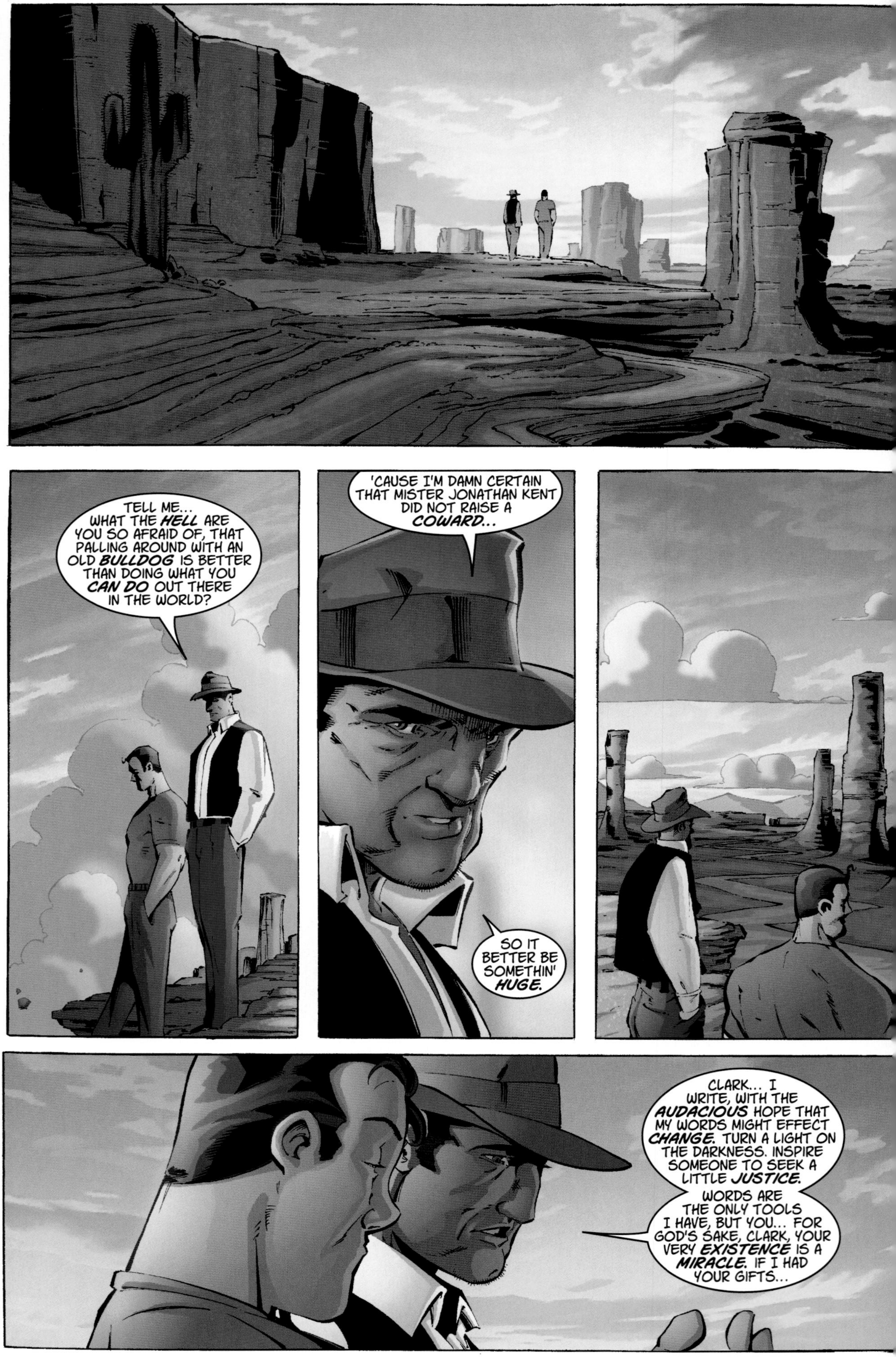
TELL ME... WHAT THE *HELL* ARE YOU SO AFRAID OF, THAT PALLING AROUND WITH AN OLD *BULLDOG* IS BETTER THAN DOING WHAT YOU *CAN DO* OUT THERE IN THE WORLD?
'CAUSE I'M DAMN CERTAIN THAT MISTER JONATHAN KENT DID NOT RAISE A *COWARD*...
SO IT BETTER BE SOMETHIN' *HUGE*.
CLARK... I WRITE, WITH THE *AUDACIOUS* HOPE THAT MY WORDS MIGHT EFFECT *CHANGE*. TURN A LIGHT ON THE DARKNESS. INSPIRE SOMEONE TO SEEK A LITTLE *JUSTICE*.
WORDS ARE THE ONLY TOOLS I HAVE, BUT YOU... FOR GOD'S SAKE, CLARK, YOUR VERY *EXISTENCE* IS A *MIRACLE*. IF I HAD YOUR GIFTS...

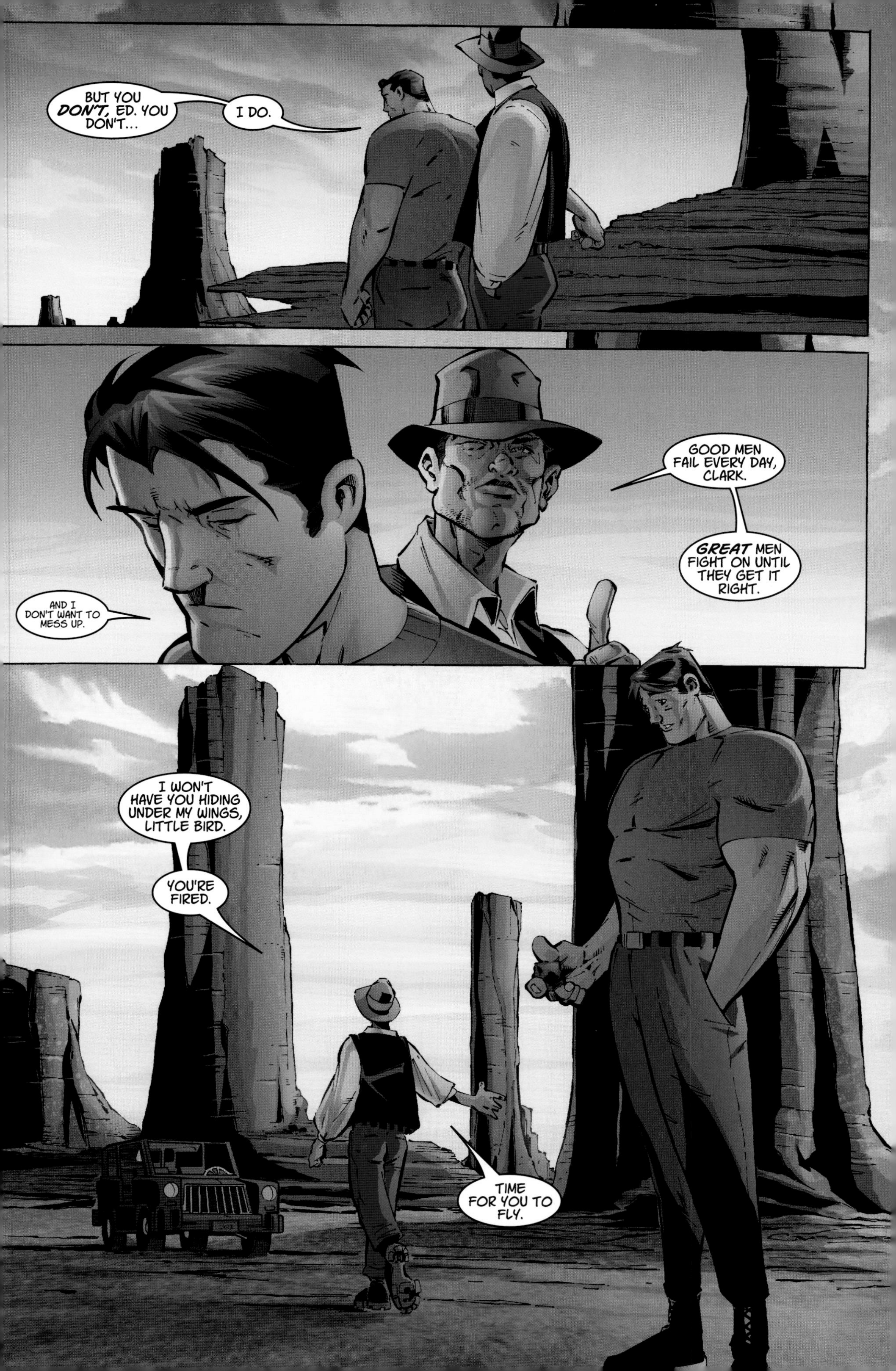
BUT YOU DON'T, ED. YOU DON'T...
I DO.
AND I DON'T WANT TO MESS UP.
GOOD MEN FAIL EVERY DAY, CLARK.
GREAT MEN FIGHT ON UNTIL THEY GET IT RIGHT.
I WON'T HAVE YOU HIDING UNDER MY WINGS, LITTLE BIRD.
YOU'RE FIRED.
TIME FOR YOU TO FLY.

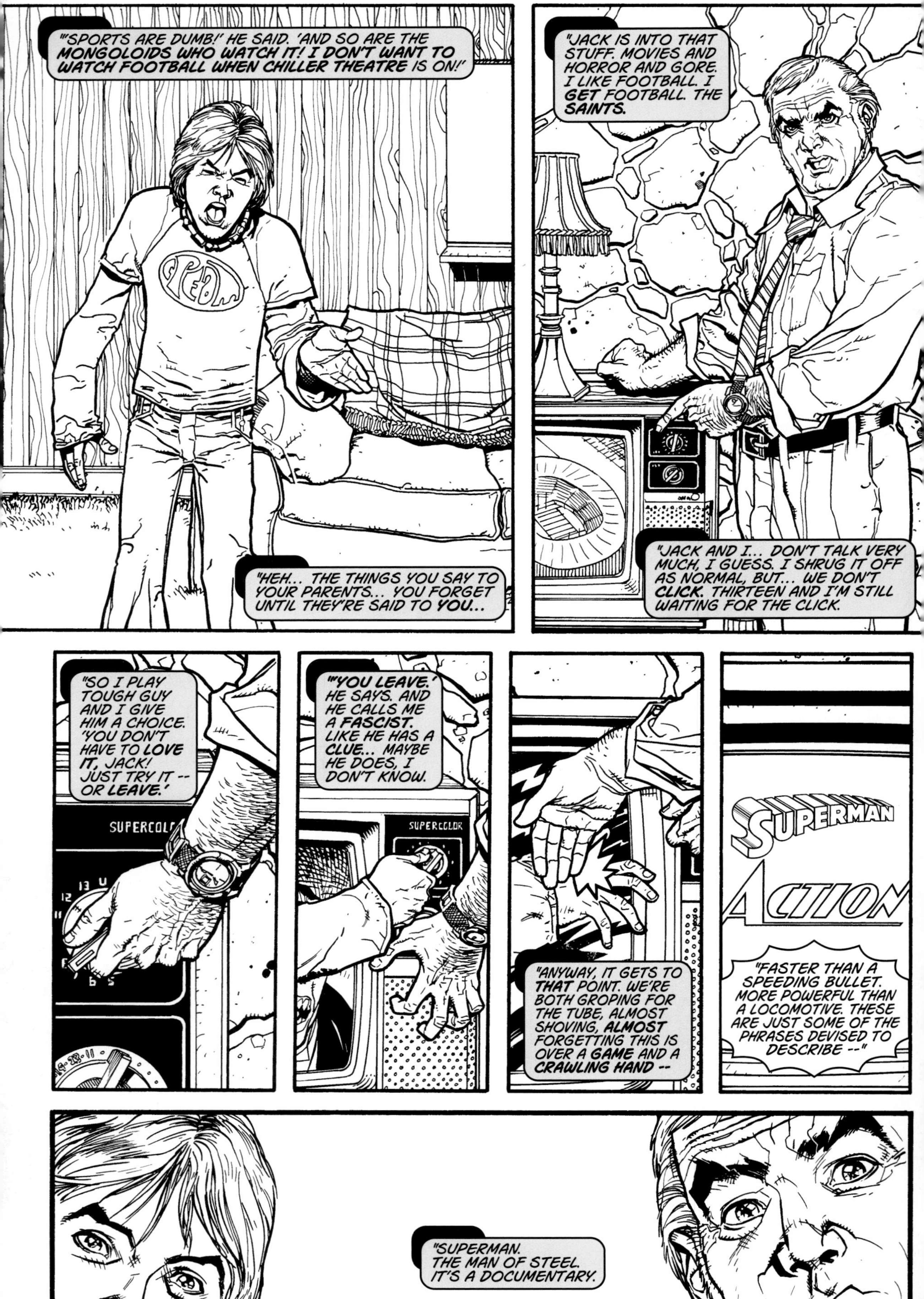

"'SPORTS ARE DUMB!' HE SAID. 'AND SO ARE THE MONGOLOIDS WHO WATCH IT! I DON'T WANT TO WATCH FOOTBALL WHEN CHILLER THEATRE IS ON!'
"HEH... THE THINGS YOU SAY TO YOUR PARENTS... YOU FORGET UNTIL THEY'RE SAID TO YOU...
"JACK IS INTO THAT STUFF. MOVIES AND HORROR AND GORE. I LIKE FOOTBALL. I GET FOOTBALL. THE SAINTS.
"JACK AND I... DON'T TALK VERY MUCH, I GUESS. I SHRUG IT OFF AS NORMAL, BUT... WE DON'T CLICK. THIRTEEN AND I'M STILL WAITING FOR THE CLICK.
"SO I PLAY TOUGH GUY AND I GIVE HIM A CHOICE. 'YOU DON'T HAVE TO LOVE IT, JACK! JUST TRY IT -- OR LEAVE.'
SUPERCOLOR
"'YOU LEAVE.' HE SAYS. AND HE CALLS ME A FASCIST. LIKE HE HAS A CLUE... MAYBE HE DOES, I DON'T KNOW.
SUPERCOLOR
"ANYWAY, IT GETS TO THAT POINT. WE'RE BOTH GROPING FOR THE TUBE, ALMOST SHOVING, ALMOST FORGETTING THIS IS OVER A GAME AND A CRAWLING HAND --
SUPERMAN
ACTION
"FASTER THAN A SPEEDING BULLET. MORE POWERFUL THAN A LOCOMOTIVE. THESE ARE JUST SOME OF THE PHRASES DEVISED TO DESCRIBE --"
"SUPERMAN. THE MAN OF STEEL. IT'S A DOCUMENTARY.

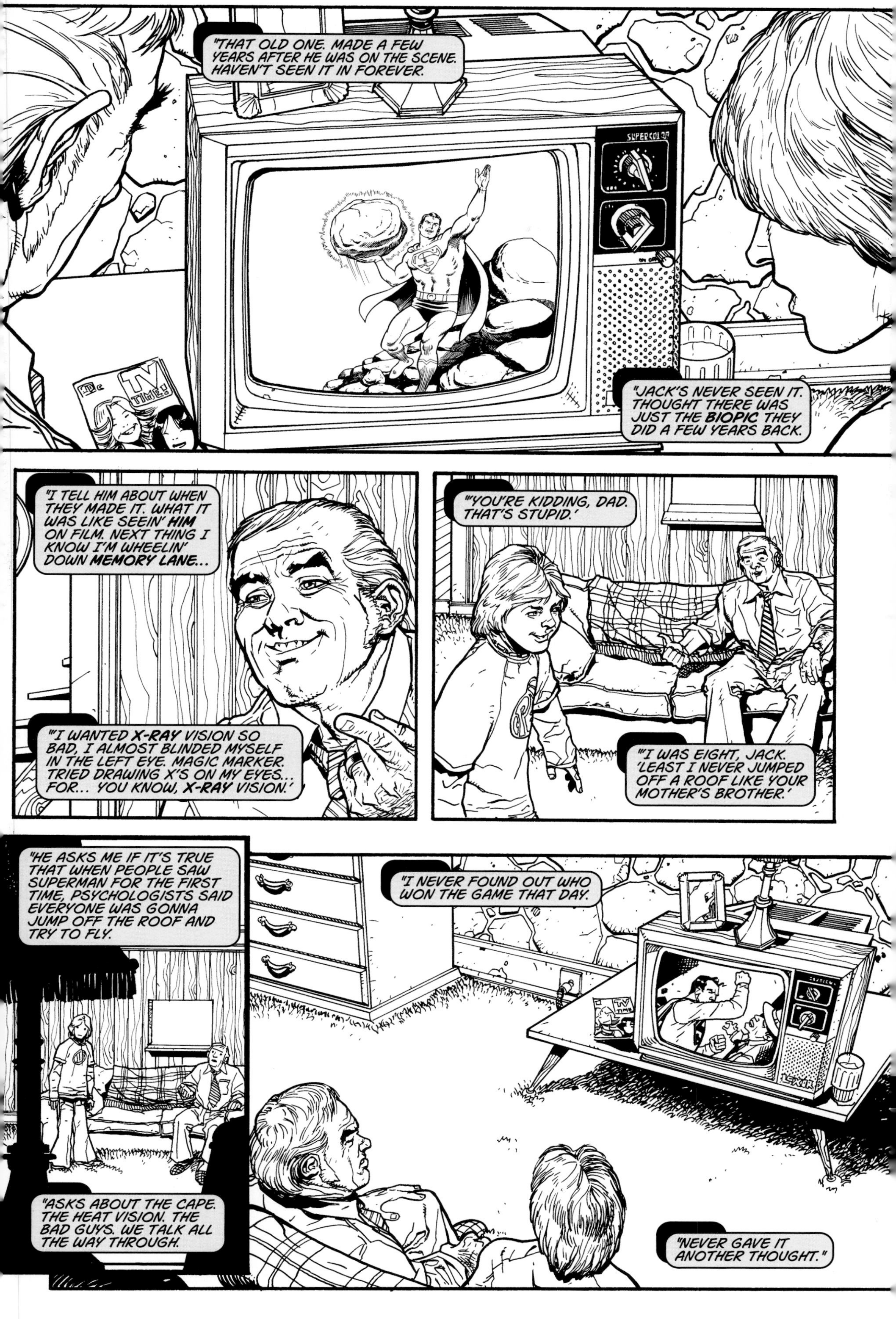
"THAT OLD ONE. MADE A FEW YEARS AFTER HE WAS ON THE SCENE. HAVEN'T SEEN IT IN FOREVER.
SUPERCOLOR
TV TIME!
"JACK'S NEVER SEEN IT. THOUGHT THERE WAS JUST THE BIOPIC THEY DID A FEW YEARS BACK.
"I TELL HIM ABOUT WHEN THEY MADE IT. WHAT IT WAS LIKE SEEIN' HIM ON FILM. NEXT THING I KNOW I'M WHEELIN' DOWN MEMORY LANE...
"'I WANTED X-RAY VISION SO BAD, I ALMOST BLINDED MYSELF IN THE LEFT EYE. MAGIC MARKER. TRIED DRAWING X'S ON MY EYES... FOR... YOU KNOW, X-RAY VISION.'
"'YOU'RE KIDDING, DAD. THAT'S STUPID.'
"'I WAS EIGHT, JACK. 'LEAST I NEVER JUMPED OFF A ROOF LIKE YOUR MOTHER'S BROTHER.'
"HE ASKS ME IF IT'S TRUE THAT WHEN PEOPLE SAW SUPERMAN FOR THE FIRST TIME, PSYCHOLOGISTS SAID EVERYONE WAS GONNA JUMP OFF THE ROOF AND TRY TO FLY.
"ASKS ABOUT THE CAPE. THE HEAT VISION. THE BAD GUYS. WE TALK ALL THE WAY THROUGH.
"I NEVER FOUND OUT WHO WON THE GAME THAT DAY.
"NEVER GAVE IT ANOTHER THOUGHT."

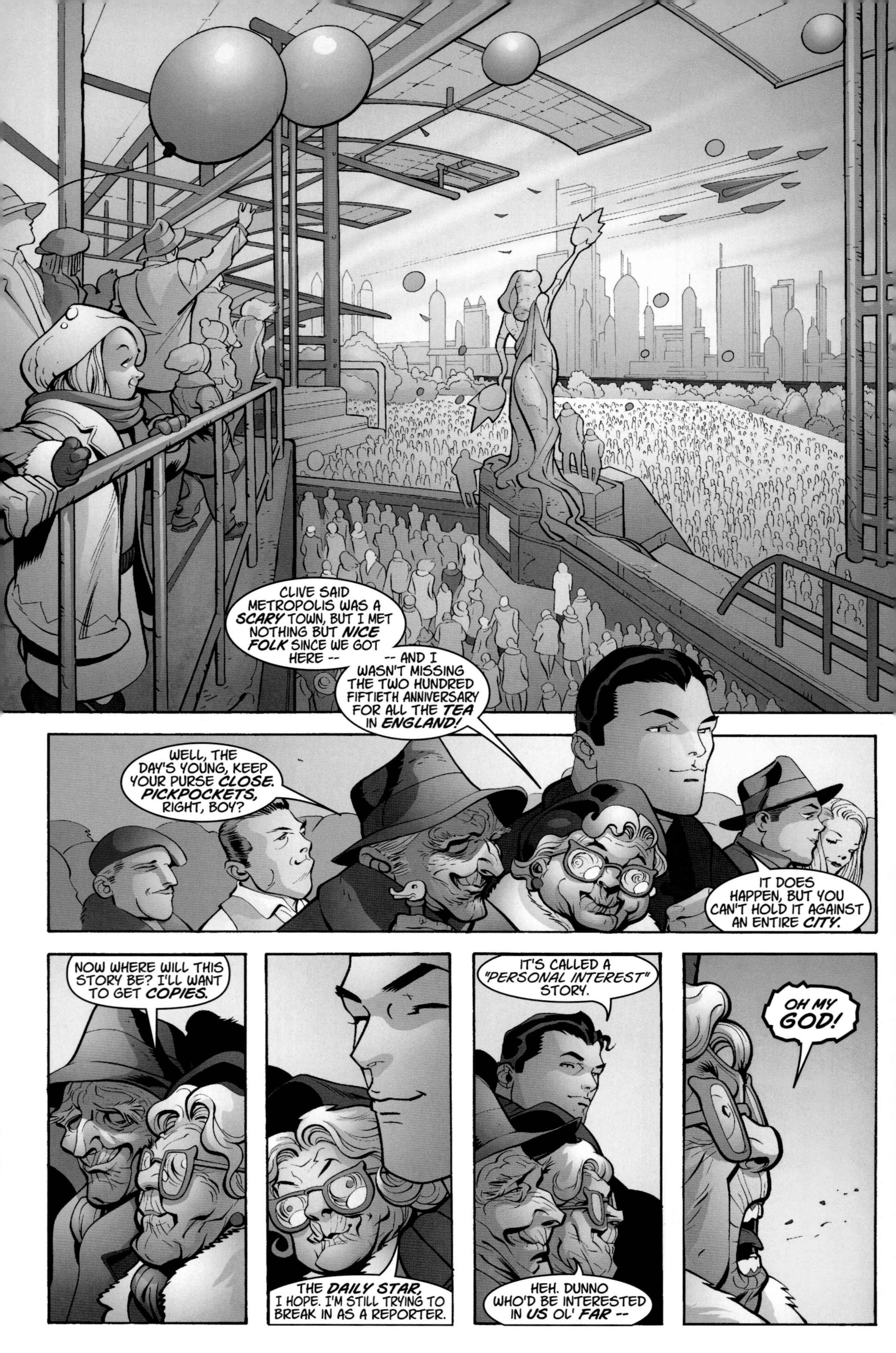
CLIVE SAID METROPOLIS WAS A SCARY TOWN, BUT I MET NOTHING BUT NICE FOLK SINCE WE GOT HERE --
-- AND I WASN'T MISSING THE TWO HUNDRED FIFTIETH ANNIVERSARY FOR ALL THE TEA IN ENGLAND!
WELL, THE DAY'S YOUNG, KEEP YOUR PURSE CLOSE. PICKPOCKETS, RIGHT, BOY?
IT DOES HAPPEN, BUT YOU CAN'T HOLD IT AGAINST AN ENTIRE CITY.
NOW WHERE WILL THIS STORY BE? I'LL WANT TO GET COPIES.
THE DAILY STAR, I HOPE. I'M STILL TRYING TO BREAK IN AS A REPORTER.
IT'S CALLED A "PERSONAL INTEREST" STORY.
HEH. DUNNO WHO'D BE INTERESTED IN US OL' FAR --
OH MY GOD!

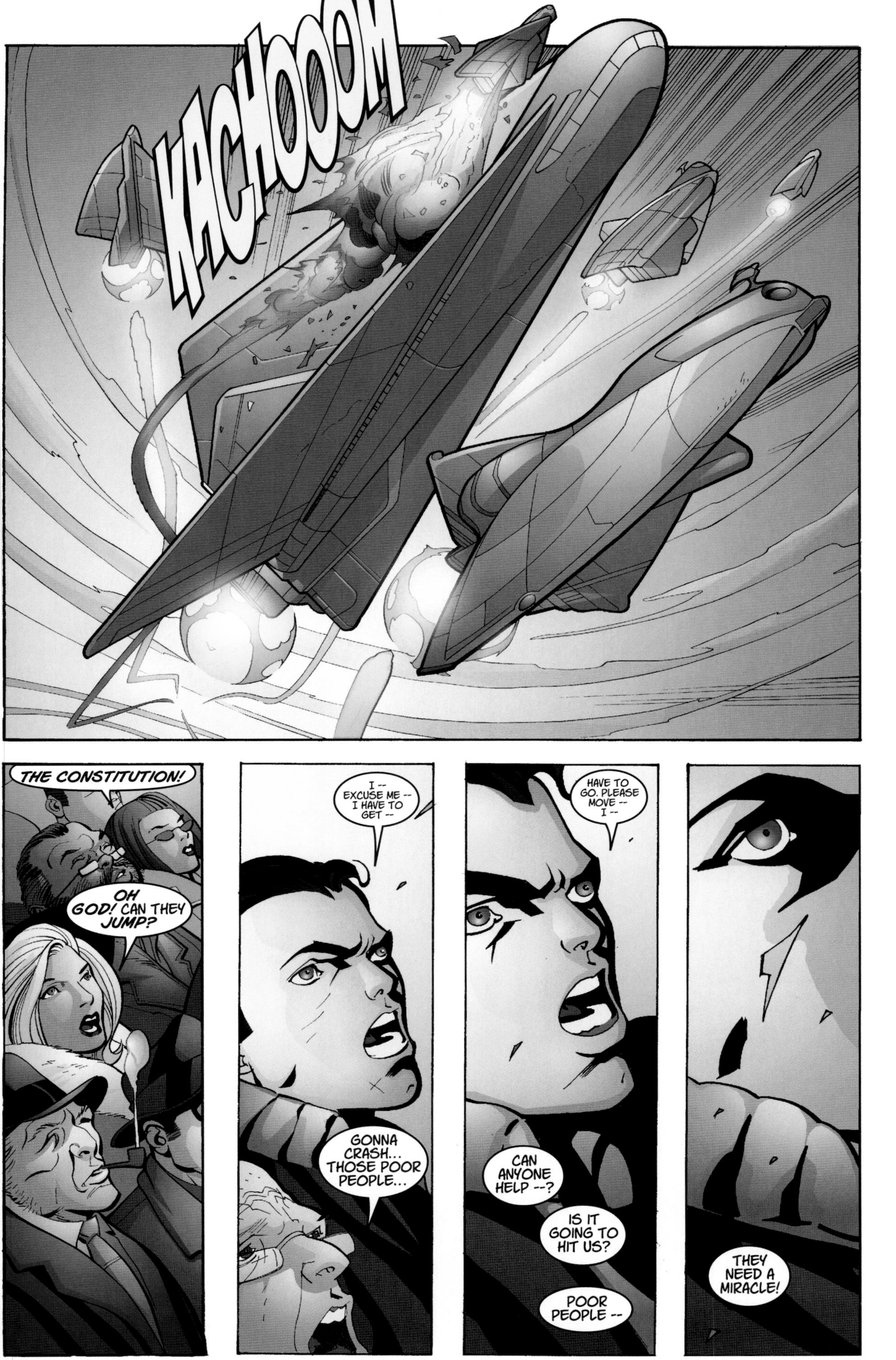
KACHOOOM
THE CONSTITUTION!
OH GOD! CAN THEY JUMP?
I -- EXCUSE ME -- I HAVE TO GET --
GONNA CRASH... THOSE POOR PEOPLE...
HAVE TO GO. PLEASE MOVE -- I --
CAN ANYONE HELP --?
IS IT GOING TO HIT US?
POOR PEOPLE --
THEY NEED A MIRACLE!

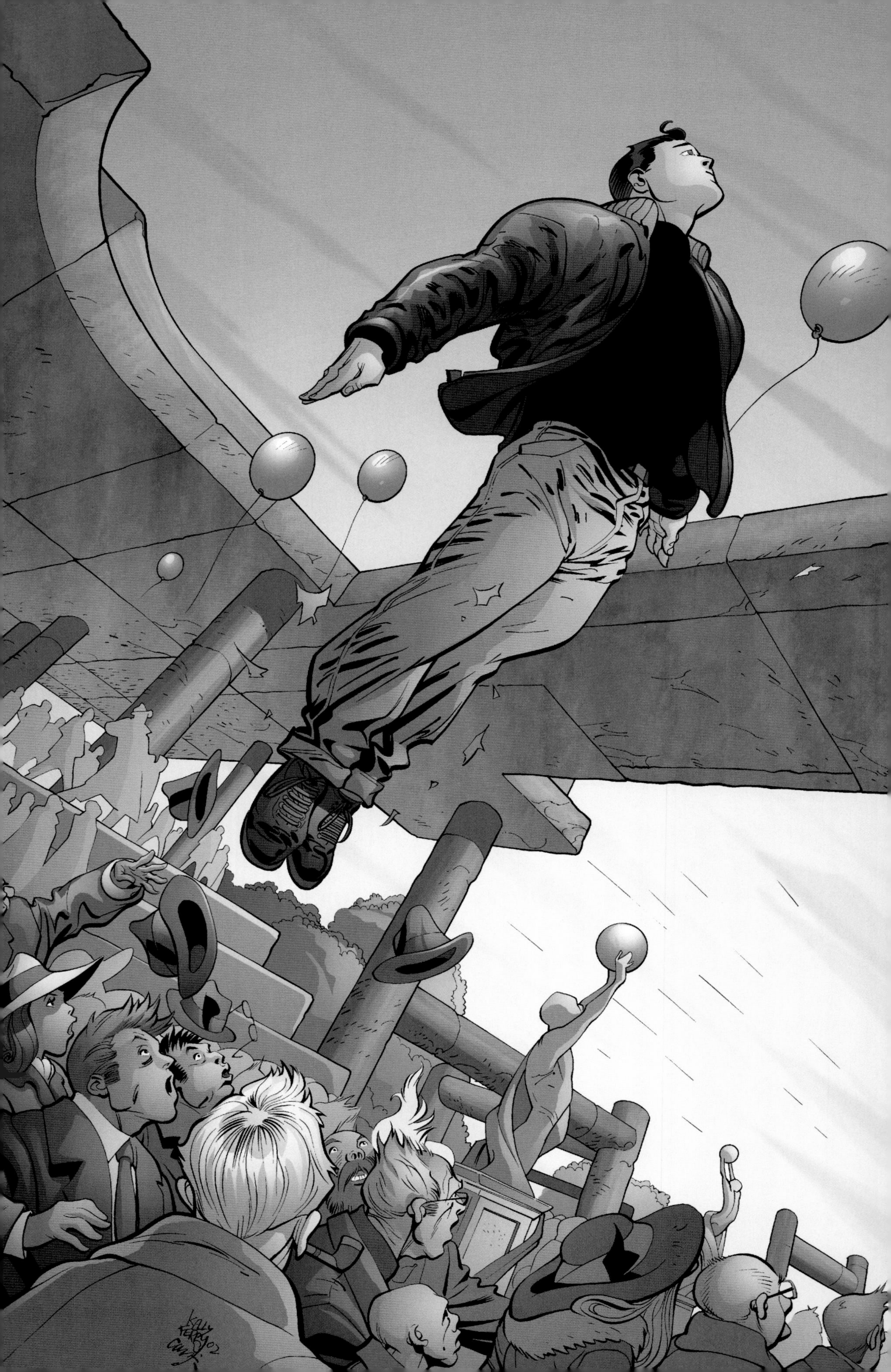

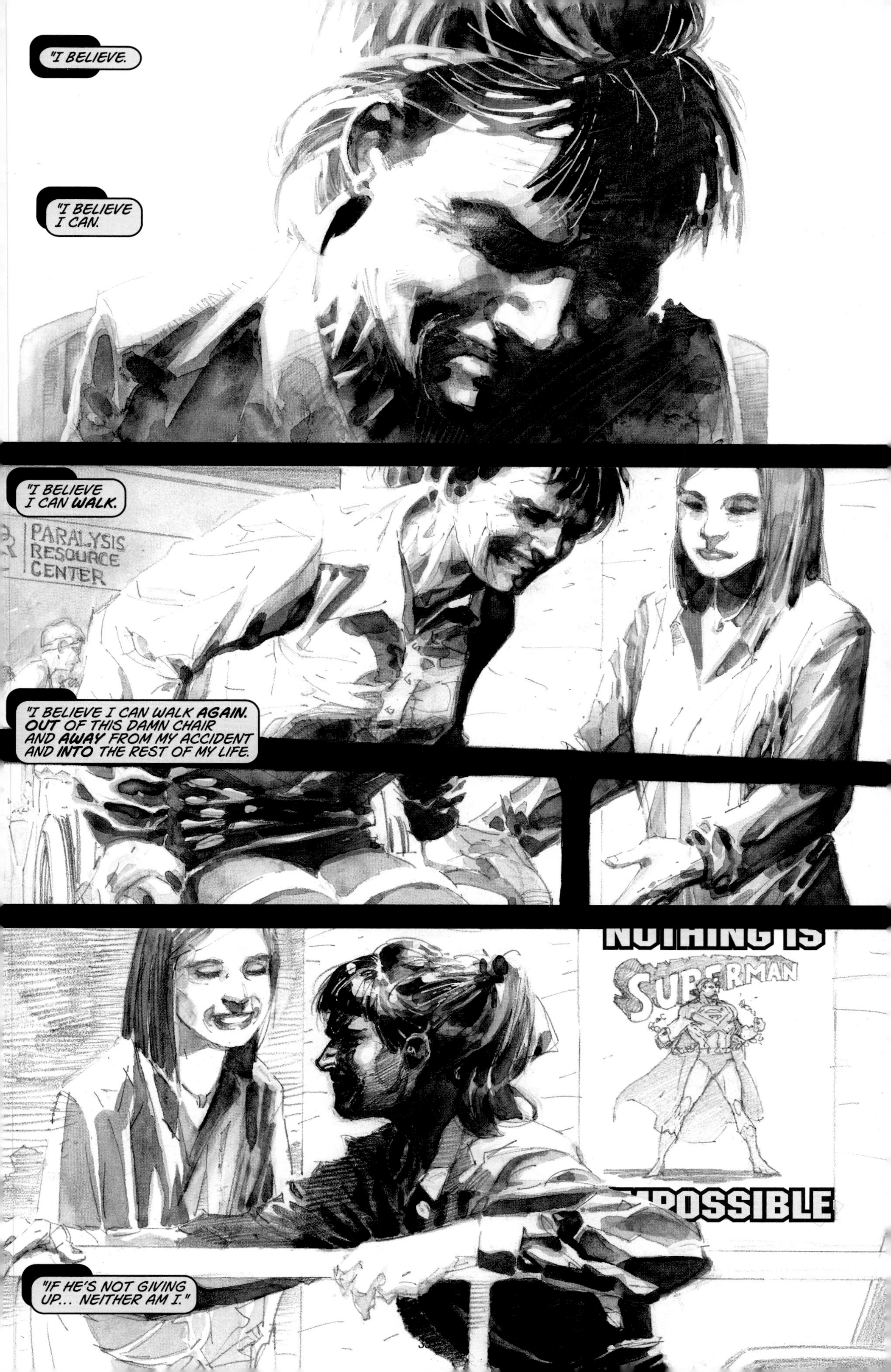
"I BELIEVE.
"I BELIEVE I CAN.
"I BELIEVE I CAN WALK.
PARALYSIS RESOURCE CENTER
"I BELIEVE I CAN WALK AGAIN. OUT OF THIS DAMN CHAIR AND AWAY FROM MY ACCIDENT AND INTO THE REST OF MY LIFE.
NOTHING IS
SUPERMAN
POSSIBLE
"IF HE'S NOT GIVING UP... NEITHER AM I."

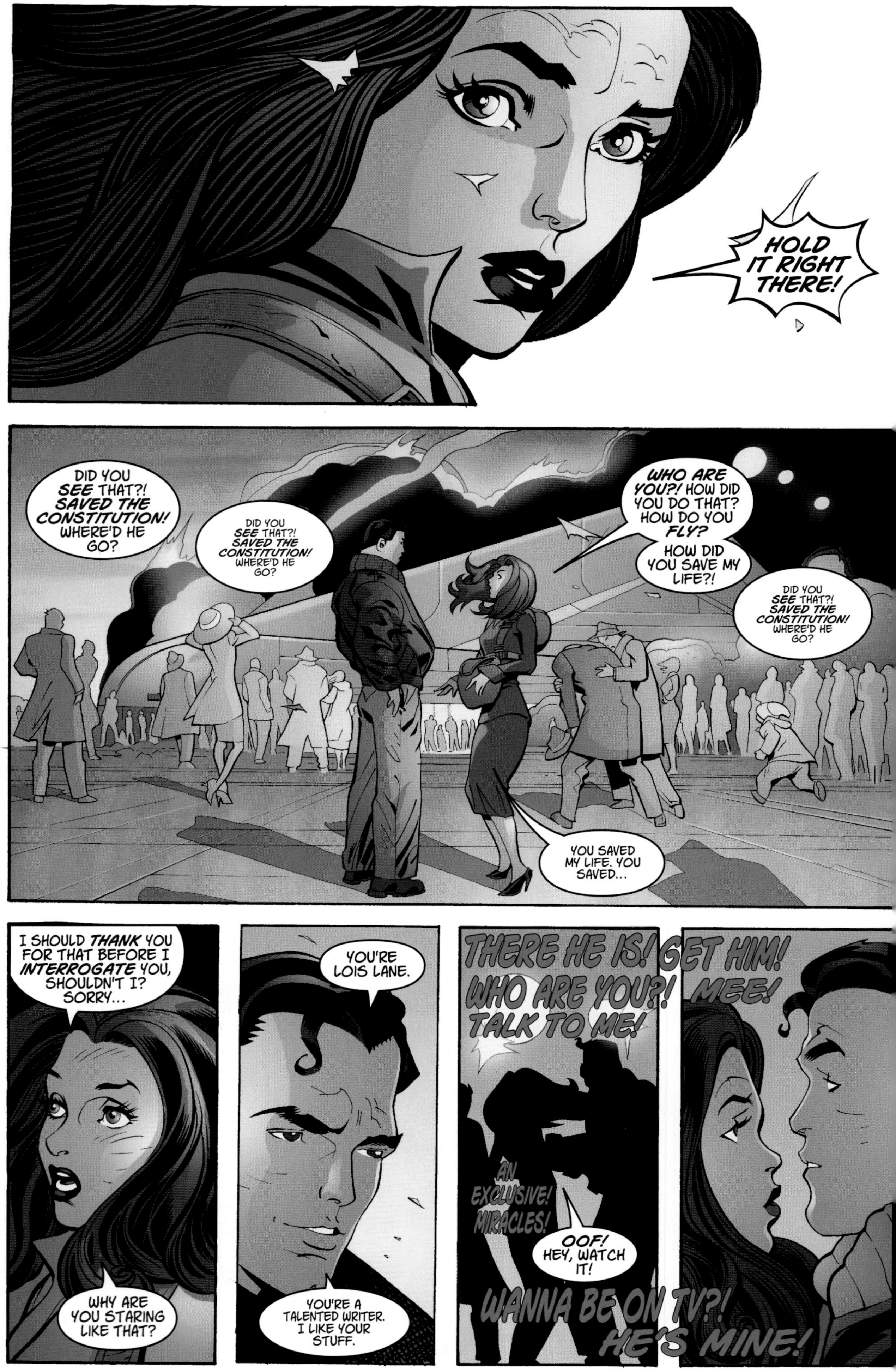
HOLD IT RIGHT THERE!
DID YOU SEE THAT?! SAVED THE CONSTITUTION! WHERE'D HE GO?
DID YOU SEE THAT?! SAVED THE CONSTITUTION! WHERE'D HE GO?
WHO ARE YOU?! HOW DID YOU DO THAT? HOW DO YOU FLY?
HOW DID YOU SAVE MY LIFE?!
DID YOU SEE THAT?! SAVED THE CONSTITUTION! WHERE'D HE GO?
YOU SAVED MY LIFE. YOU SAVED...
I SHOULD THANK YOU FOR THAT BEFORE I INTERROGATE YOU, SHOULDN'T I? SORRY...
WHY ARE YOU STARING LIKE THAT?
YOU'RE LOIS LANE.
YOU'RE A TALENTED WRITER. I LIKE YOUR STUFF.
THERE HE IS! GET HIM!
WHO ARE YOU?! MEE!
TALK TO ME!
AN EXCLUSIVE! MIRACLES!
OOF! HEY, WATCH IT!
WANNA BE ON TV?!
HE'S MINE!

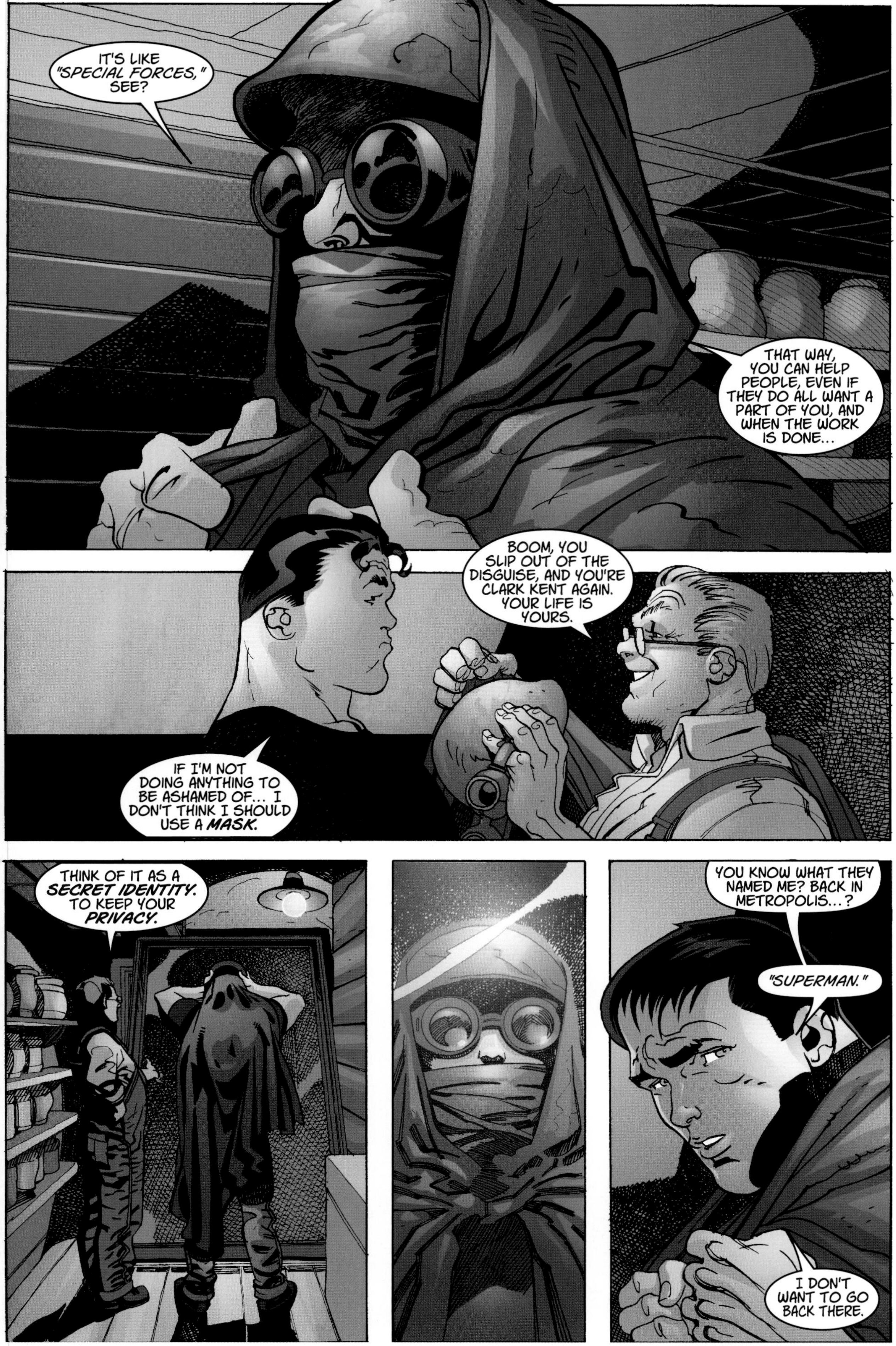
IT'S LIKE "SPECIAL FORCES," SEE?
THAT WAY, YOU CAN HELP PEOPLE, EVEN IF THEY DO ALL WANT A PART OF YOU, AND WHEN THE WORK IS DONE...
BOOM, YOU SLIP OUT OF THE DISGUISE, AND YOU'RE CLARK KENT AGAIN. YOUR LIFE IS YOURS.
IF I'M NOT DOING ANYTHING TO BE ASHAMED OF... I DON'T THINK I SHOULD USE A MASK.
THINK OF IT AS A SECRET IDENTITY. TO KEEP YOUR PRIVACY.
YOU KNOW WHAT THEY NAMED ME? BACK IN METROPOLIS...?
"SUPERMAN."
I DON'T WANT TO GO BACK THERE.

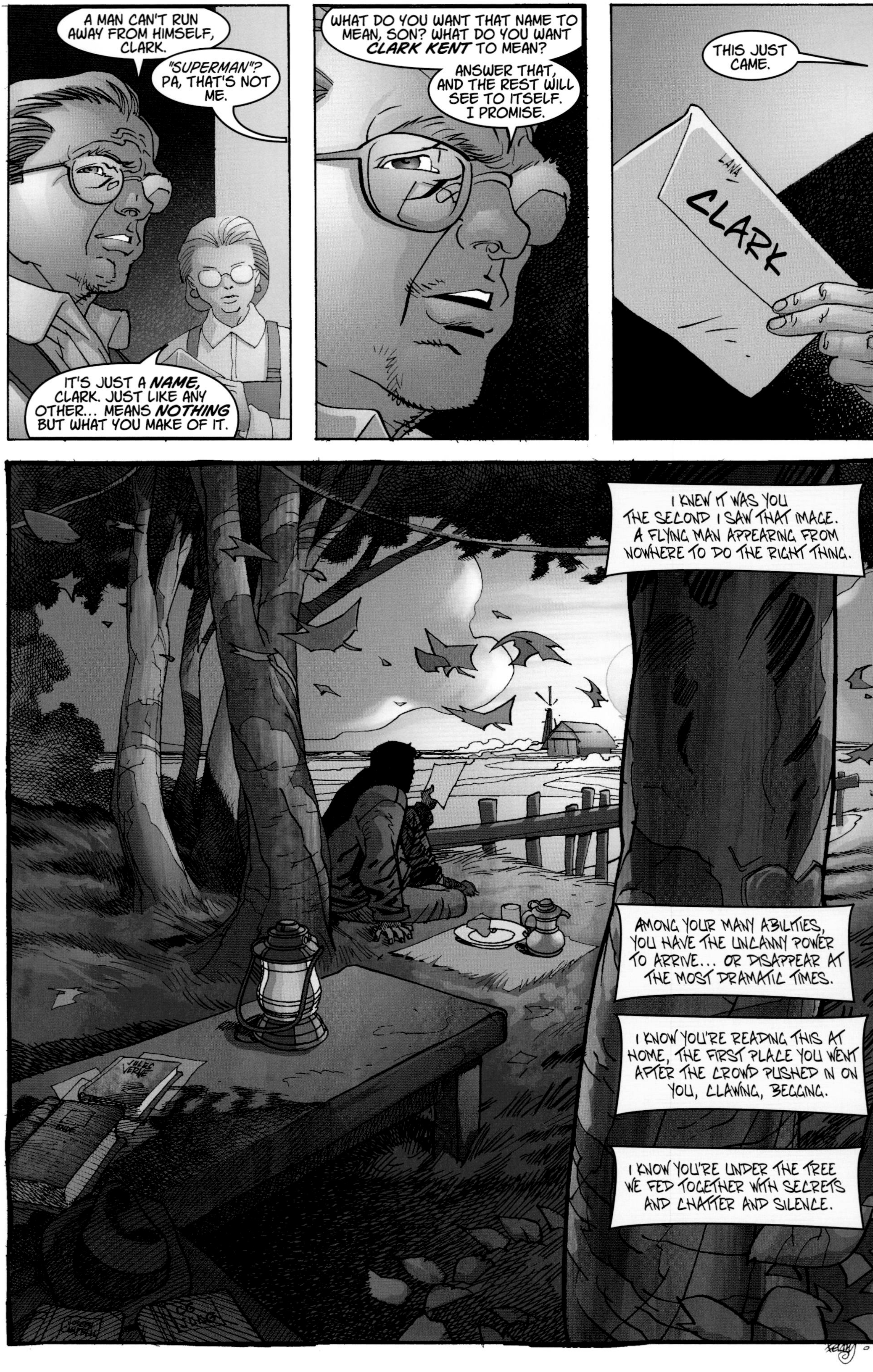
A MAN CAN'T RUN AWAY FROM HIMSELF, CLARK.
"SUPERMAN"? PA, THAT'S NOT ME.
IT'S JUST A NAME, CLARK. JUST LIKE ANY OTHER... MEANS NOTHING BUT WHAT YOU MAKE OF IT.
WHAT DO YOU WANT THAT NAME TO MEAN, SON? WHAT DO YOU WANT CLARK KENT TO MEAN?
ANSWER THAT, AND THE REST WILL SEE TO ITSELF. I PROMISE.
THIS JUST CAME.
LANA
CLARK
I KNEW IT WAS YOU THE SECOND I SAW THAT IMAGE. A FLYING MAN APPEARING FROM NOWHERE TO DO THE RIGHT THING.
AMONG YOUR MANY ABILITIES, YOU HAVE THE UNCANNY POWER TO ARRIVE... OR DISAPPEAR AT THE MOST DRAMATIC TIMES.
I KNOW YOU'RE READING THIS AT HOME, THE FIRST PLACE YOU WENT AFTER THE CROWD PUSHED IN ON YOU, CLAWING, BEGGING.
I KNOW YOU'RE UNDER THE TREE WE FED TOGETHER WITH SECRETS AND CHATTER AND SILENCE.
JULES VERNE

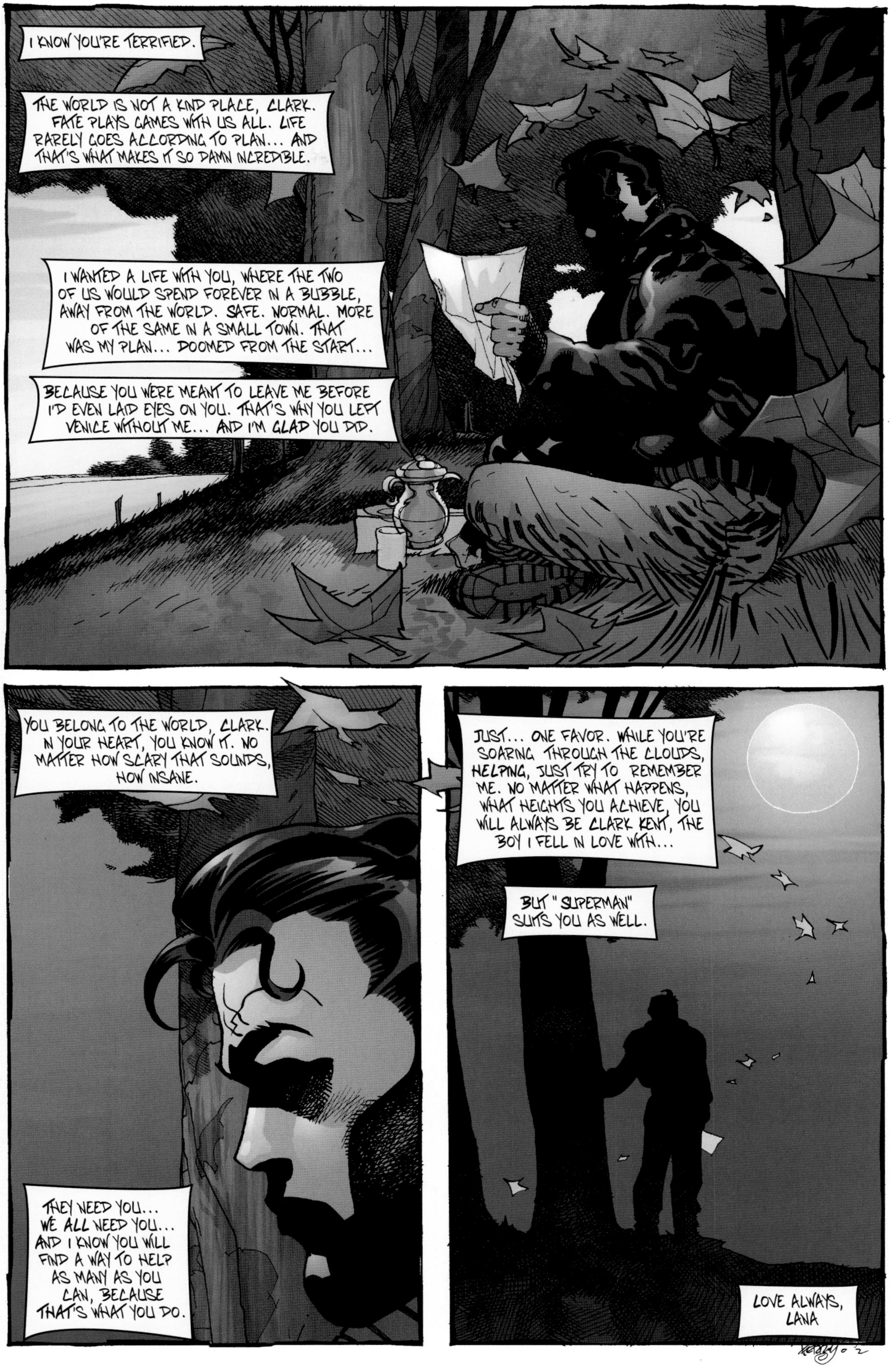
I KNOW YOU'RE TERRIFIED.
THE WORLD IS NOT A KIND PLACE, CLARK. FATE PLAYS GAMES WITH US ALL. LIFE RARELY GOES ACCORDING TO PLAN... AND THAT'S WHAT MAKES IT SO DAMN INCREDIBLE.
I WANTED A LIFE WITH YOU, WHERE THE TWO OF US WOULD SPEND FOREVER IN A BUBBLE, AWAY FROM THE WORLD. SAFE. NORMAL. MORE OF THE SAME IN A SMALL TOWN. THAT WAS MY PLAN... DOOMED FROM THE START...
BECAUSE YOU WERE MEANT TO LEAVE ME BEFORE I'D EVEN LAID EYES ON YOU. THAT'S WHY YOU LEFT VENICE WITHOUT ME... AND I'M GLAD YOU DID.
YOU BELONG TO THE WORLD, CLARK. IN YOUR HEART, YOU KNOW IT. NO MATTER HOW SCARY THAT SOUNDS, HOW INSANE.
THEY NEED YOU... WE ALL NEED YOU... AND I KNOW YOU WILL FIND A WAY TO HELP AS MANY AS YOU CAN, BECAUSE THAT'S WHAT YOU DO.
JUST... ONE FAVOR. WHILE YOU'RE SOARING THROUGH THE CLOUDS, HELPING, JUST TRY TO REMEMBER ME. NO MATTER WHAT HAPPENS, WHAT HEIGHTS YOU ACHIEVE, YOU WILL ALWAYS BE CLARK KENT, THE BOY I FELL IN LOVE WITH...
BUT "SUPERMAN" SUITS YOU AS WELL.
LOVE ALWAYS, LANA

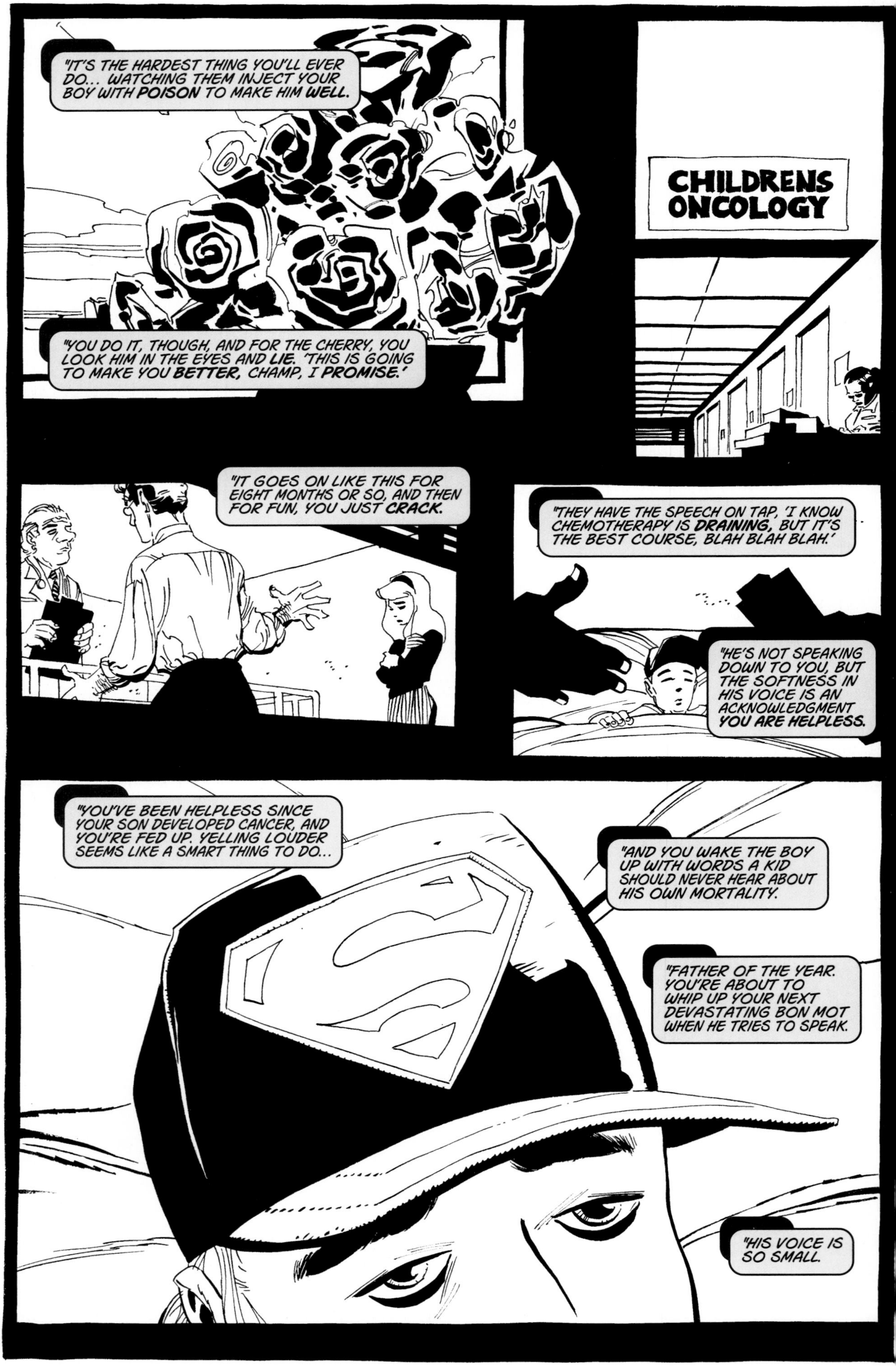
"IT'S THE HARDEST THING YOU'LL EVER DO... WATCHING THEM INJECT YOUR BOY WITH POISON TO MAKE HIM WELL.
"YOU DO IT, THOUGH, AND FOR THE CHERRY, YOU LOOK HIM IN THE EYES AND LIE. 'THIS IS GOING TO MAKE YOU BETTER, CHAMP, I PROMISE.'
CHILDRENS ONCOLOGY
"IT GOES ON LIKE THIS FOR EIGHT MONTHS OR SO, AND THEN FOR FUN, YOU JUST CRACK.
"THEY HAVE THE SPEECH ON TAP, 'I KNOW CHEMOTHERAPY IS DRAINING, BUT IT'S THE BEST COURSE, BLAH BLAH BLAH.'
"HE'S NOT SPEAKING DOWN TO YOU, BUT THE SOFTNESS IN HIS VOICE IS AN ACKNOWLEDGMENT YOU ARE HELPLESS.
"YOU'VE BEEN HELPLESS SINCE YOUR SON DEVELOPED CANCER, AND YOU'RE FED UP. YELLING LOUDER SEEMS LIKE A SMART THING TO DO...
"AND YOU WAKE THE BOY UP WITH WORDS A KID SHOULD NEVER HEAR ABOUT HIS OWN MORTALITY.
"FATHER OF THE YEAR. YOU'RE ABOUT TO WHIP UP YOUR NEXT DEVASTATING BON MOT WHEN HE TRIES TO SPEAK.
"HIS VOICE IS SO SMALL.

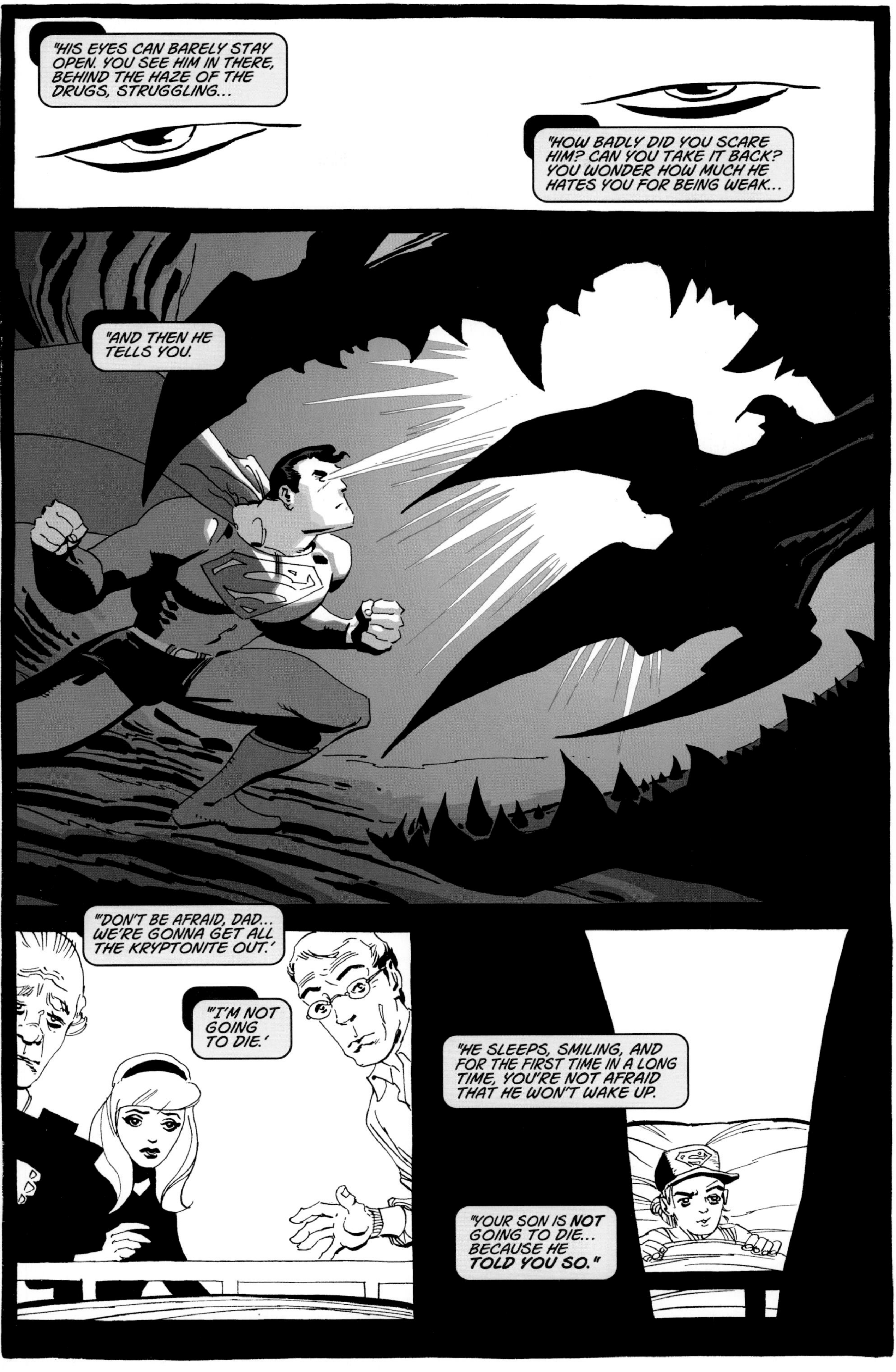
"HIS EYES CAN BARELY STAY OPEN. YOU SEE HIM IN THERE, BEHIND THE HAZE OF THE DRUGS, STRUGGLING...
"HOW BADLY DID YOU SCARE HIM? CAN YOU TAKE IT BACK? YOU WONDER HOW MUCH HE HATES YOU FOR BEING WEAK...
"AND THEN HE TELLS YOU.
"'DON'T BE AFRAID, DAD... WE'RE GONNA GET ALL THE KRYPTONITE OUT.'
"'I'M NOT GOING TO DIE.'
"HE SLEEPS, SMILING, AND FOR THE FIRST TIME IN A LONG TIME, YOU'RE NOT AFRAID THAT HE WON'T WAKE UP.
"YOUR SON IS NOT GOING TO DIE... BECAUSE HE TOLD YOU SO."

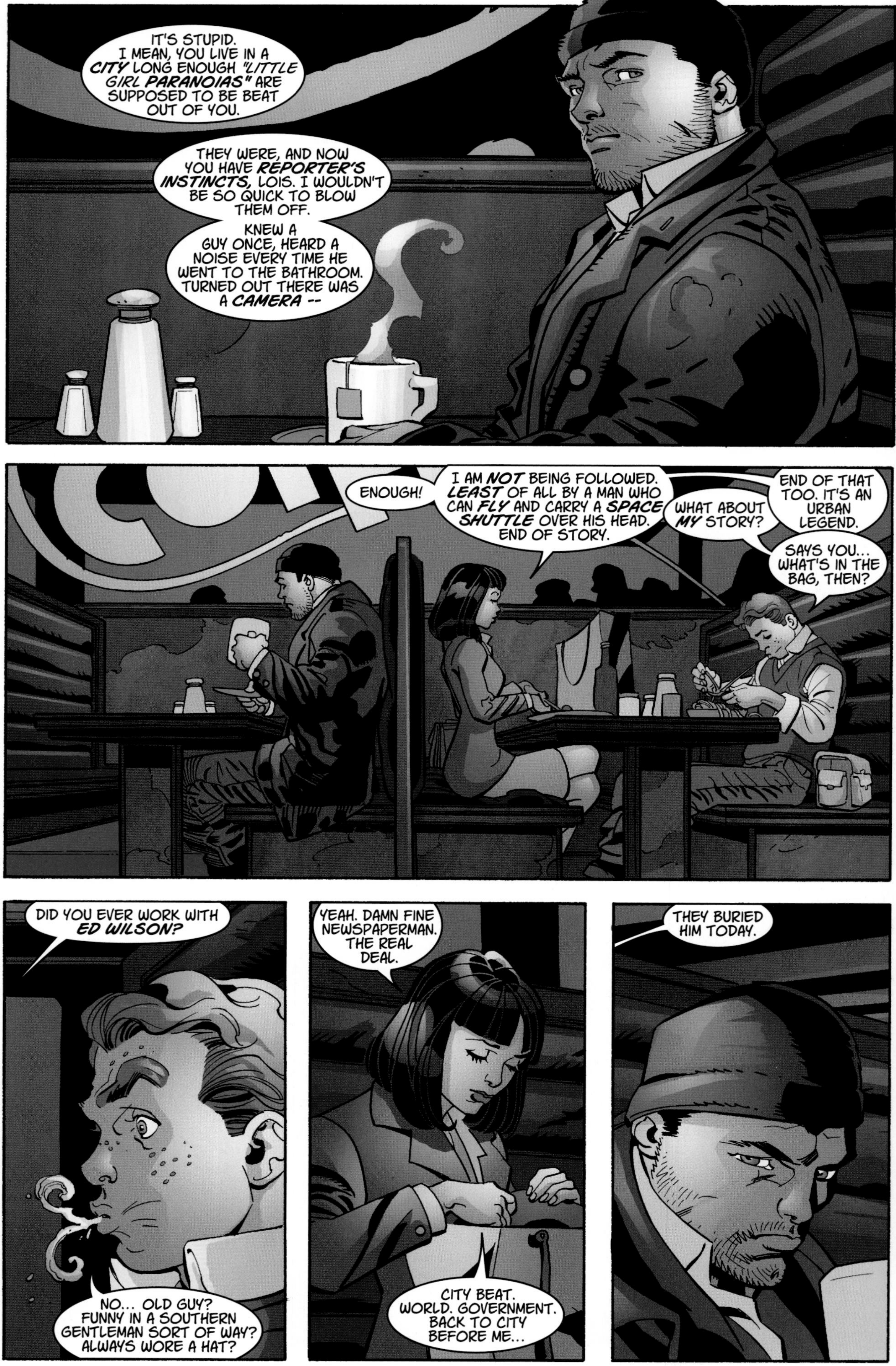
IT'S STUPID. I MEAN, YOU LIVE IN A CITY LONG ENOUGH "LITTLE GIRL PARANOIAS" ARE SUPPOSED TO BE BEAT OUT OF YOU.
THEY WERE, AND NOW YOU HAVE REPORTER'S INSTINCTS, LOIS. I WOULDN'T BE SO QUICK TO BLOW THEM OFF.
KNEW A GUY ONCE, HEARD A NOISE EVERY TIME HE WENT TO THE BATHROOM. TURNED OUT THERE WAS A CAMERA --
ENOUGH!
I AM NOT BEING FOLLOWED. LEAST OF ALL BY A MAN WHO CAN FLY AND CARRY A SPACE SHUTTLE OVER HIS HEAD. END OF STORY.
WHAT ABOUT MY STORY?
END OF THAT TOO. IT'S AN URBAN LEGEND.
SAYS YOU... WHAT'S IN THE BAG, THEN?
DID YOU EVER WORK WITH ED WILSON?
NO... OLD GUY? FUNNY IN A SOUTHERN GENTLEMAN SORT OF WAY? ALWAYS WORE A HAT?
YEAH. DAMN FINE NEWSPAPERMAN. THE REAL DEAL.
CITY BEAT. WORLD. GOVERNMENT. BACK TO CITY BEFORE ME...
THEY BURIED HIM TODAY.

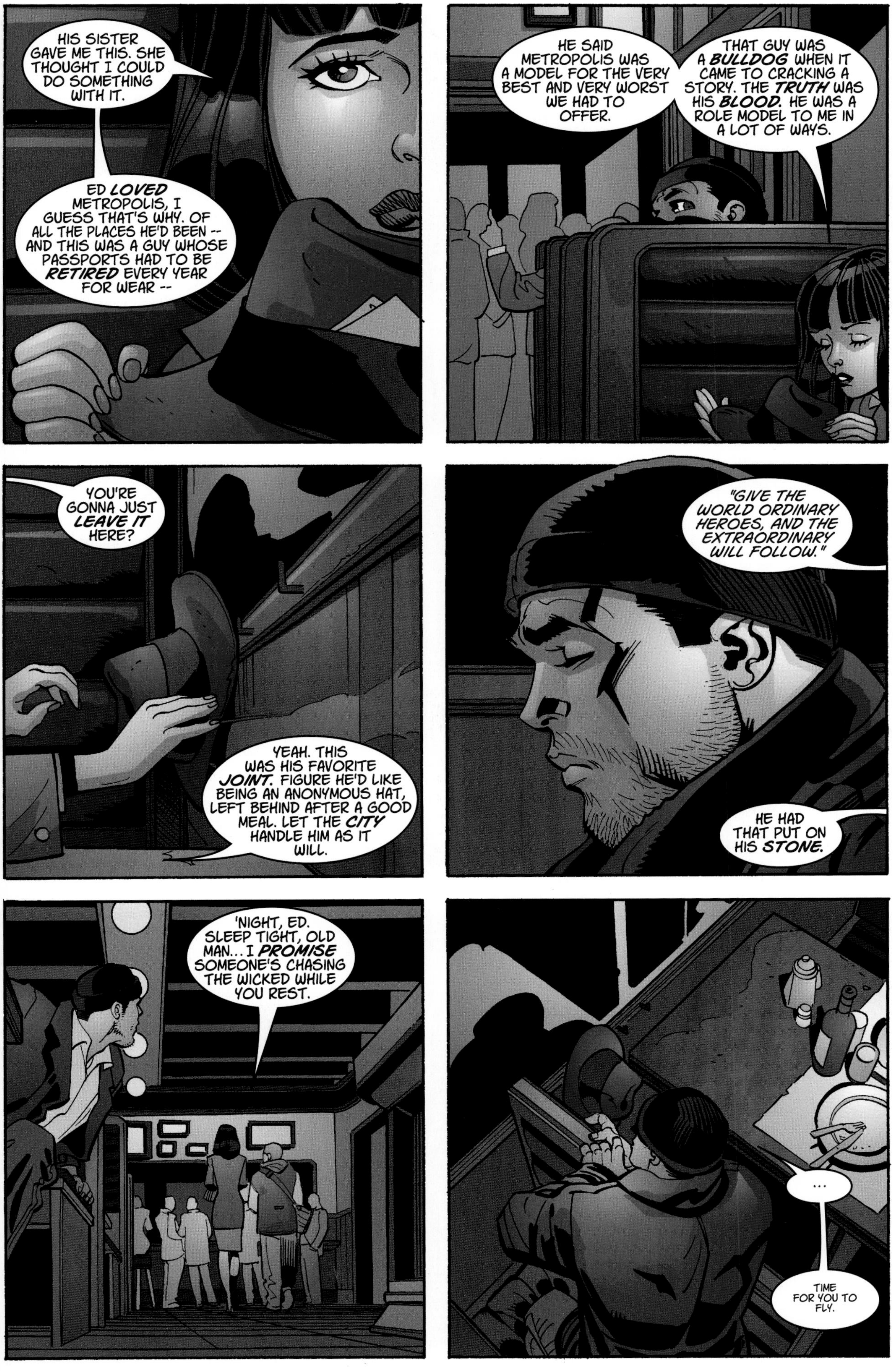
HIS SISTER GAVE ME THIS. SHE THOUGHT I COULD DO SOMETHING WITH IT.
ED LOVED METROPOLIS, I GUESS THAT'S WHY. OF ALL THE PLACES HE'D BEEN -- AND THIS WAS A GUY WHOSE PASSPORTS HAD TO BE RETIRED EVERY YEAR FOR WEAR --
HE SAID METROPOLIS WAS A MODEL FOR THE VERY BEST AND VERY WORST WE HAD TO OFFER.
THAT GUY WAS A BULLDOG WHEN IT CAME TO CRACKING A STORY. THE TRUTH WAS HIS BLOOD. HE WAS A ROLE MODEL TO ME IN A LOT OF WAYS.
YOU'RE GONNA JUST LEAVE IT HERE?
YEAH. THIS WAS HIS FAVORITE JOINT. FIGURE HE'D LIKE BEING AN ANONYMOUS HAT, LEFT BEHIND AFTER A GOOD MEAL. LET THE CITY HANDLE HIM AS IT WILL.
"GIVE THE WORLD ORDINARY HEROES, AND THE EXTRAORDINARY WILL FOLLOW."
HE HAD THAT PUT ON HIS STONE.
'NIGHT, ED. SLEEP TIGHT, OLD MAN... I PROMISE SOMEONE'S CHASING THE WICKED WHILE YOU REST.
...
TIME FOR YOU TO FLY.

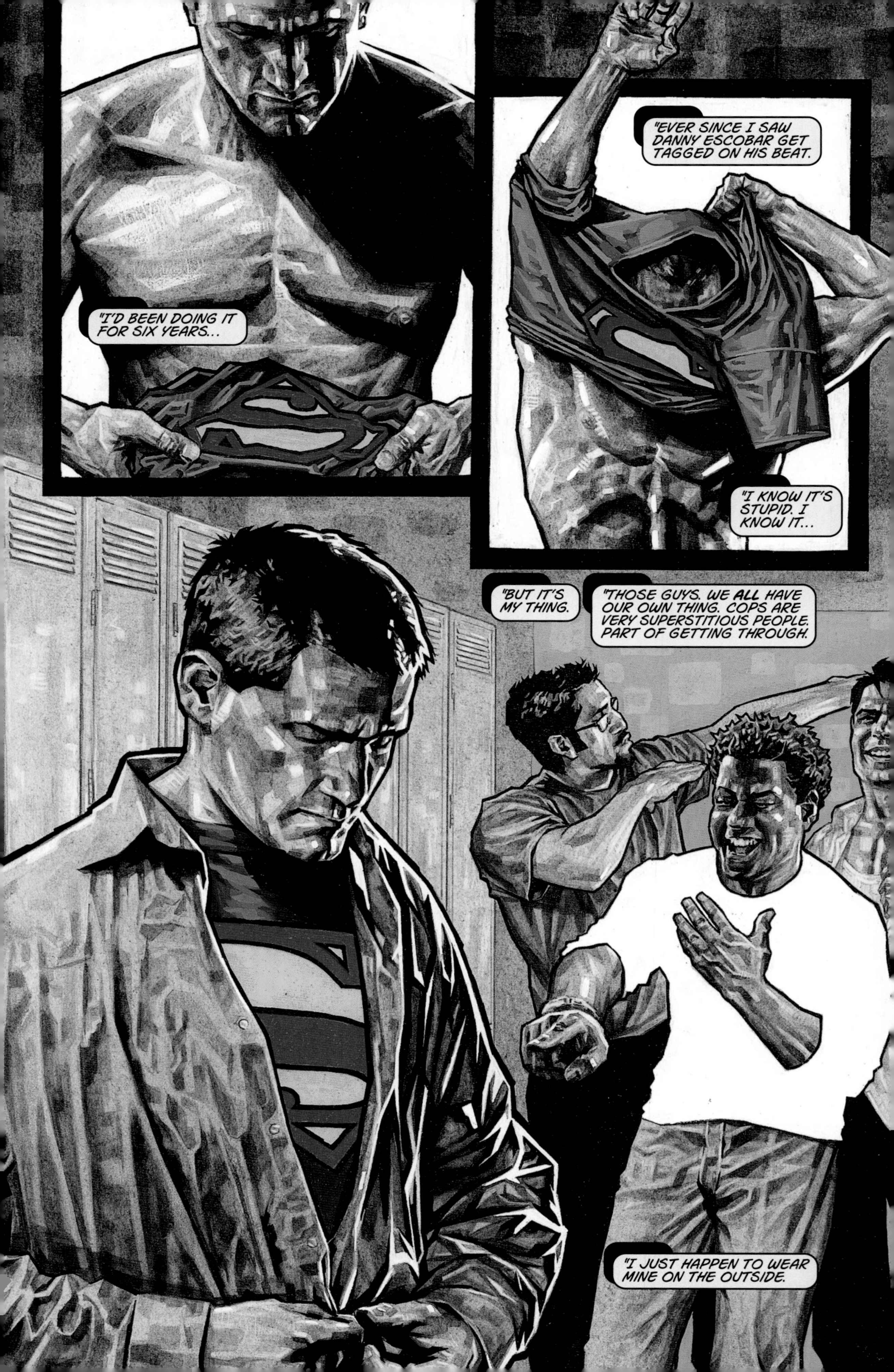
"I'D BEEN DOING IT FOR SIX YEARS...
"EVER SINCE I SAW DANNY ESCOBAR GET TAGGED ON HIS BEAT.
"I KNOW IT'S STUPID. I KNOW IT...
"BUT IT'S MY THING.
"THOSE GUYS. WE ALL HAVE OUR OWN THING. COPS ARE VERY SUPERSTITIOUS PEOPLE. PART OF GETTING THROUGH.
"I JUST HAPPEN TO WEAR MINE ON THE OUTSIDE.

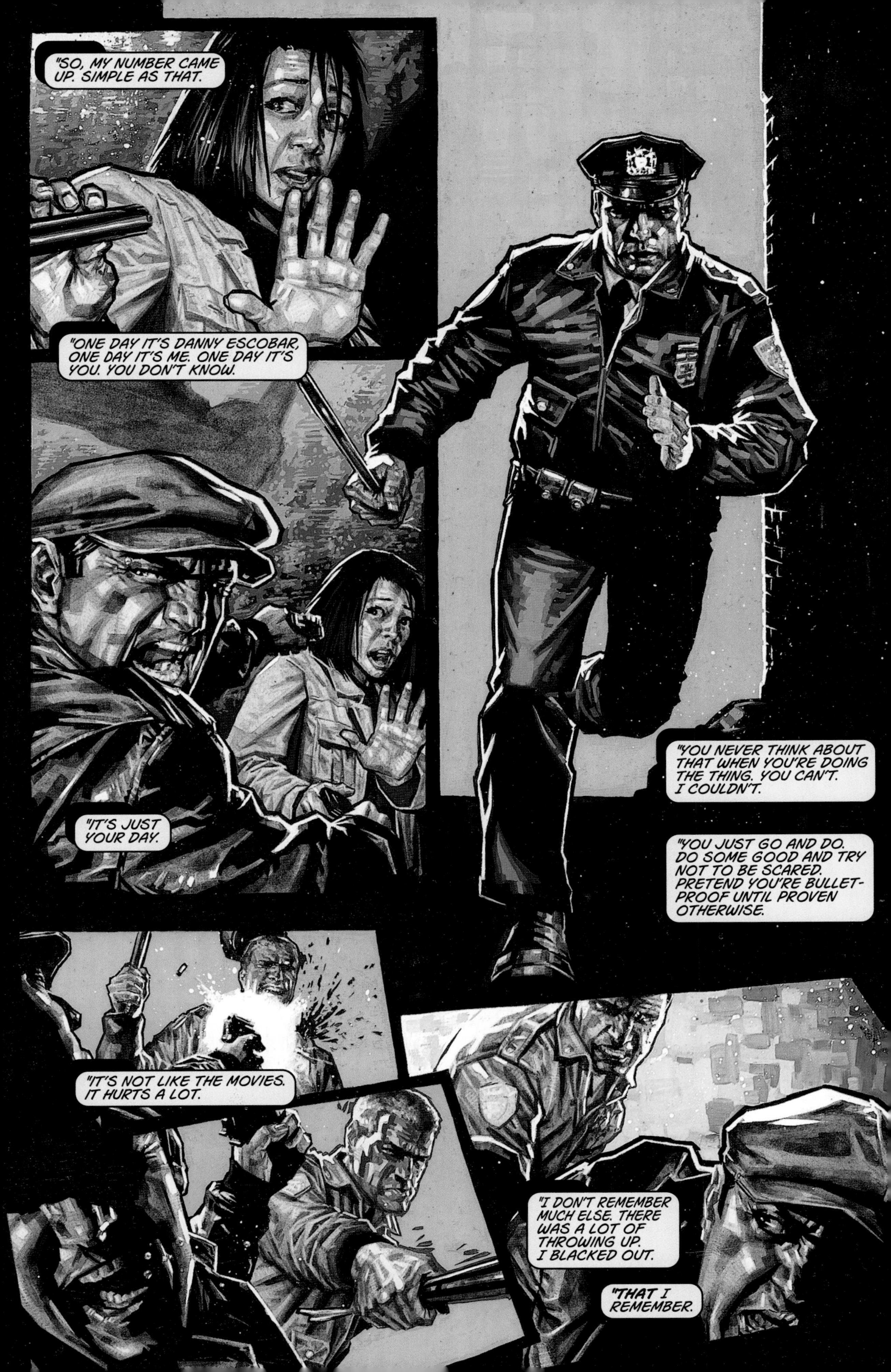
"SO, MY NUMBER CAME UP. SIMPLE AS THAT.
"ONE DAY IT'S DANNY ESCOBAR, ONE DAY IT'S ME. ONE DAY IT'S YOU. YOU DON'T KNOW.
"IT'S JUST YOUR DAY.
"YOU NEVER THINK ABOUT THAT WHEN YOU'RE DOING THE THING. YOU CAN'T. I COULDN'T.
"YOU JUST GO AND DO. DO SOME GOOD AND TRY NOT TO BE SCARED. PRETEND YOU'RE BULLET-PROOF UNTIL PROVEN OTHERWISE.
"IT'S NOT LIKE THE MOVIES. IT HURTS A LOT.
"I DON'T REMEMBER MUCH ELSE. THERE WAS A LOT OF THROWING UP. I BLACKED OUT.
"THAT I REMEMBER.

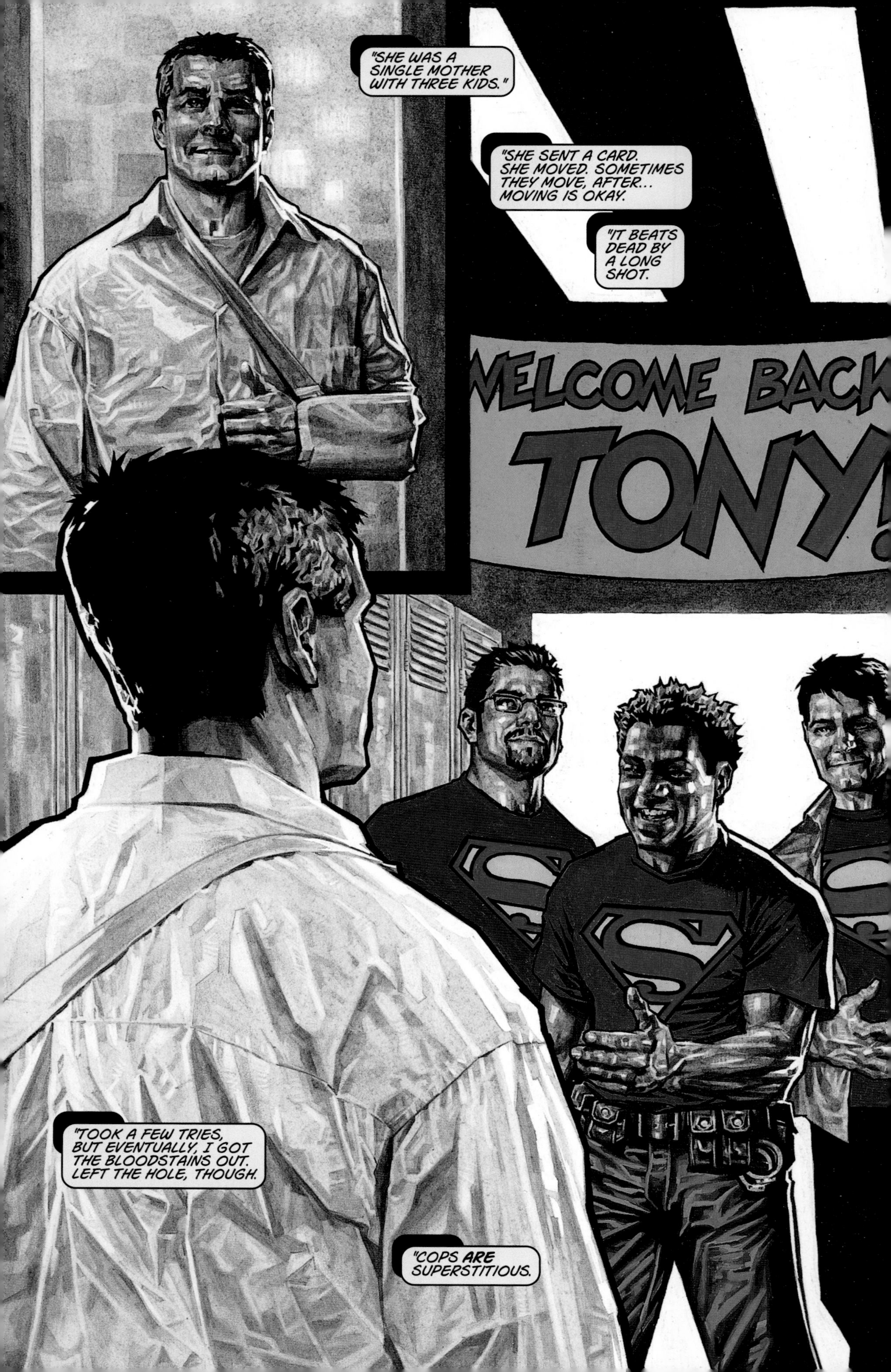
"SHE WAS A SINGLE MOTHER WITH THREE KIDS."
"SHE SENT A CARD. SHE MOVED. SOMETIMES THEY MOVE, AFTER... MOVING IS OKAY.
"IT BEATS DEAD BY A LONG SHOT.
WELCOME BACK TONY!
"TOOK A FEW TRIES, BUT EVENTUALLY, I GOT THE BLOODSTAINS OUT. LEFT THE HOLE, THOUGH.
"COPS **ARE** SUPERSTITIOUS.

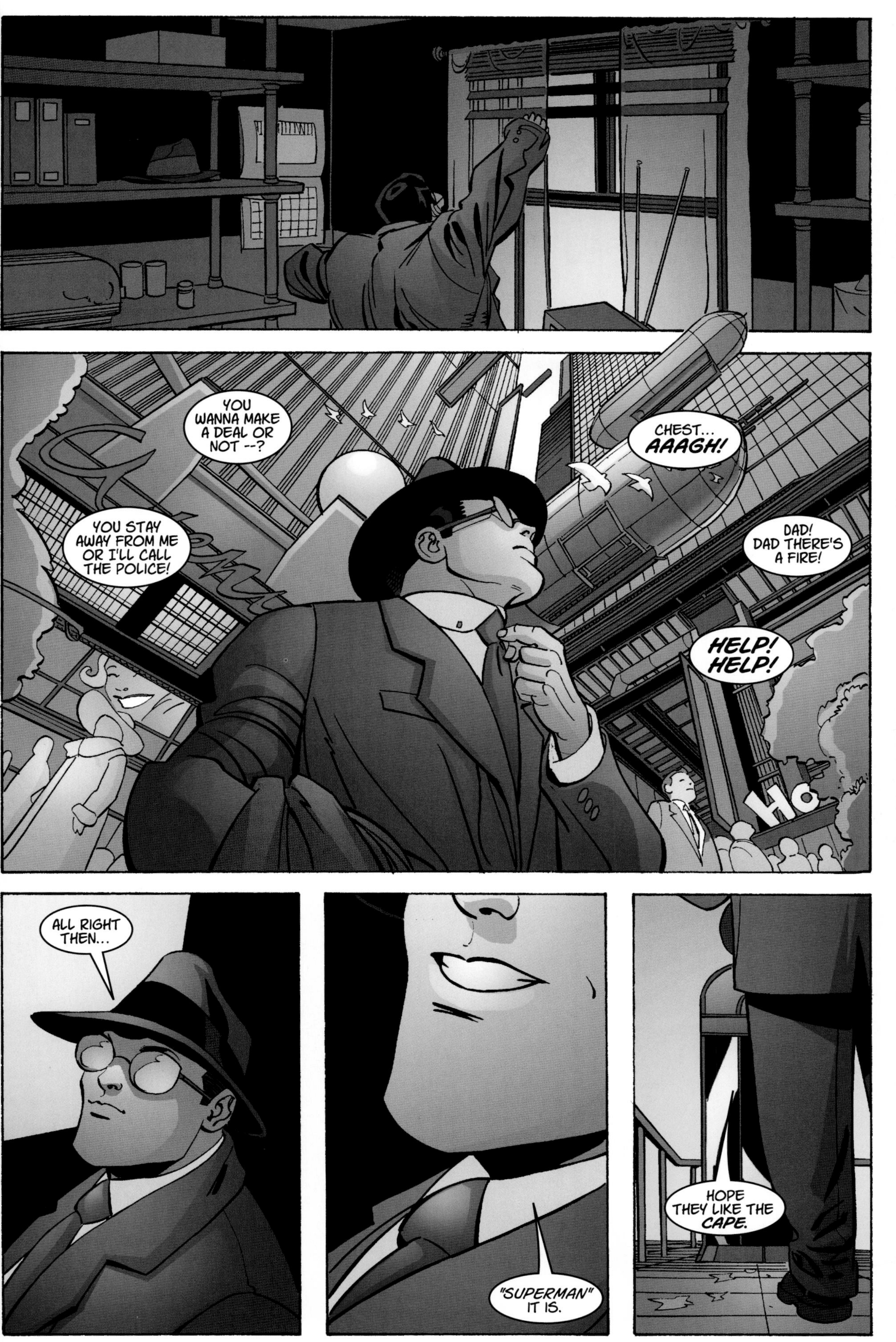

YOU WANNA MAKE A DEAL OR NOT --?
YOU STAY AWAY FROM ME OR I'LL CALL THE POLICE!
CHEST... AAAGH!
DAD! DAD THERE'S A FIRE!
HELP! HELP!
ALL RIGHT THEN...
"SUPERMAN" IT IS.
HOPE THEY LIKE THE CAPE.

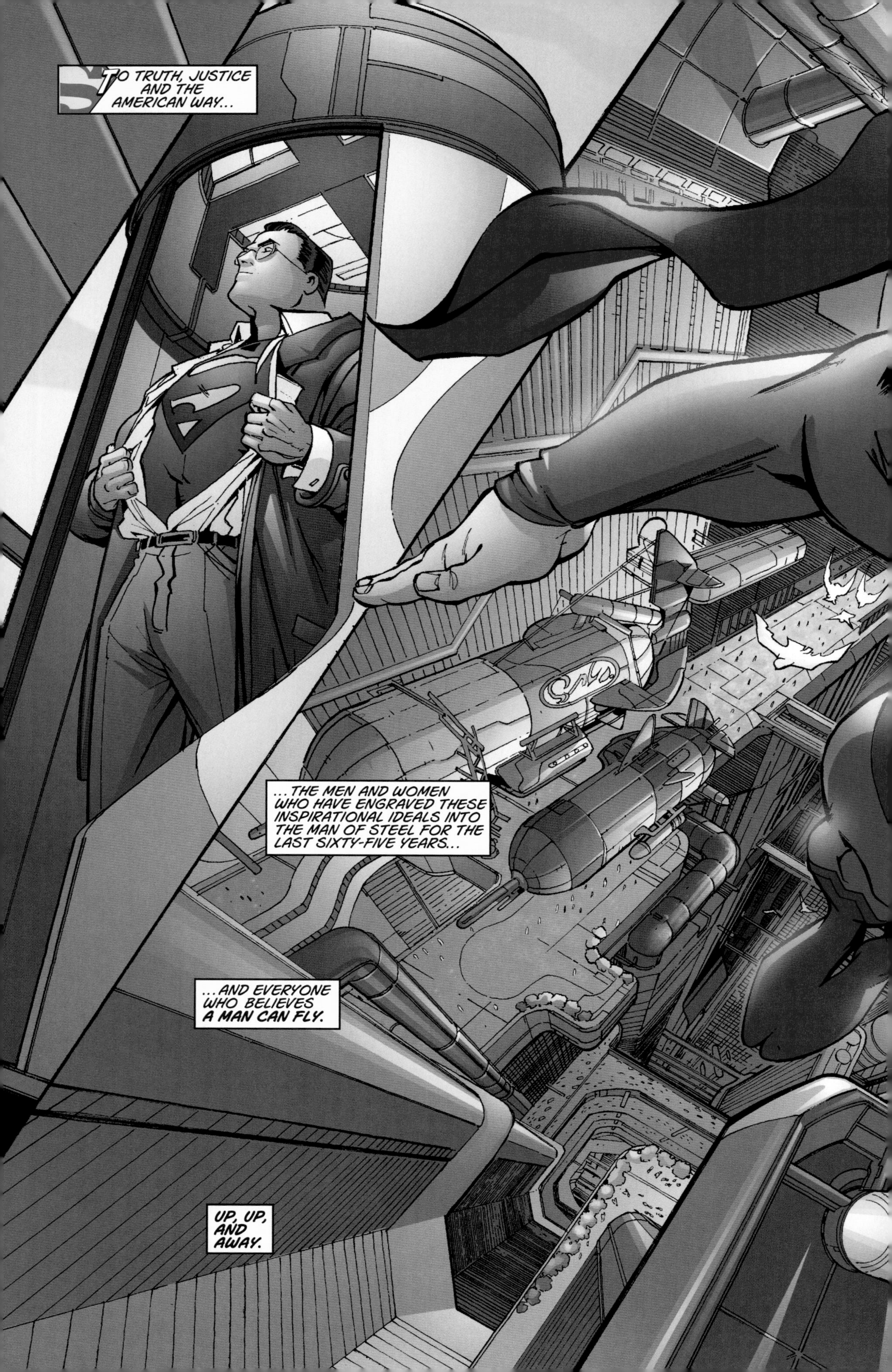
TO TRUTH, JUSTICE AND THE AMERICAN WAY...
...THE MEN AND WOMEN WHO HAVE ENGRAVED THESE INSPIRATIONAL IDEALS INTO THE MAN OF STEEL FOR THE LAST SIXTY-FIVE YEARS...
...AND EVERYONE WHO BELIEVES A MAN CAN FLY.
UP, UP, AND AWAY.

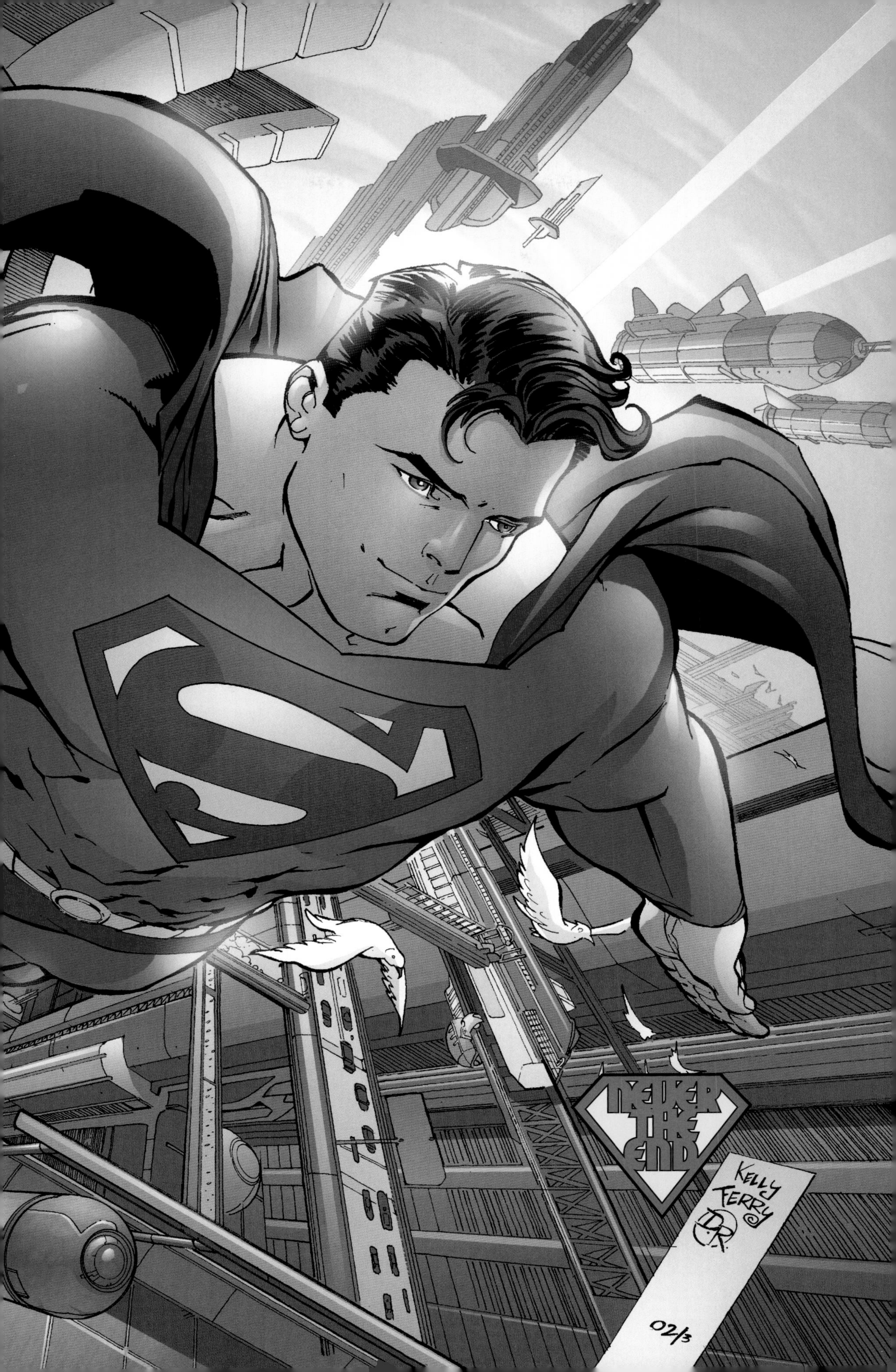
NEVER THE END
KELLY
FERRY
D.R.
02/3

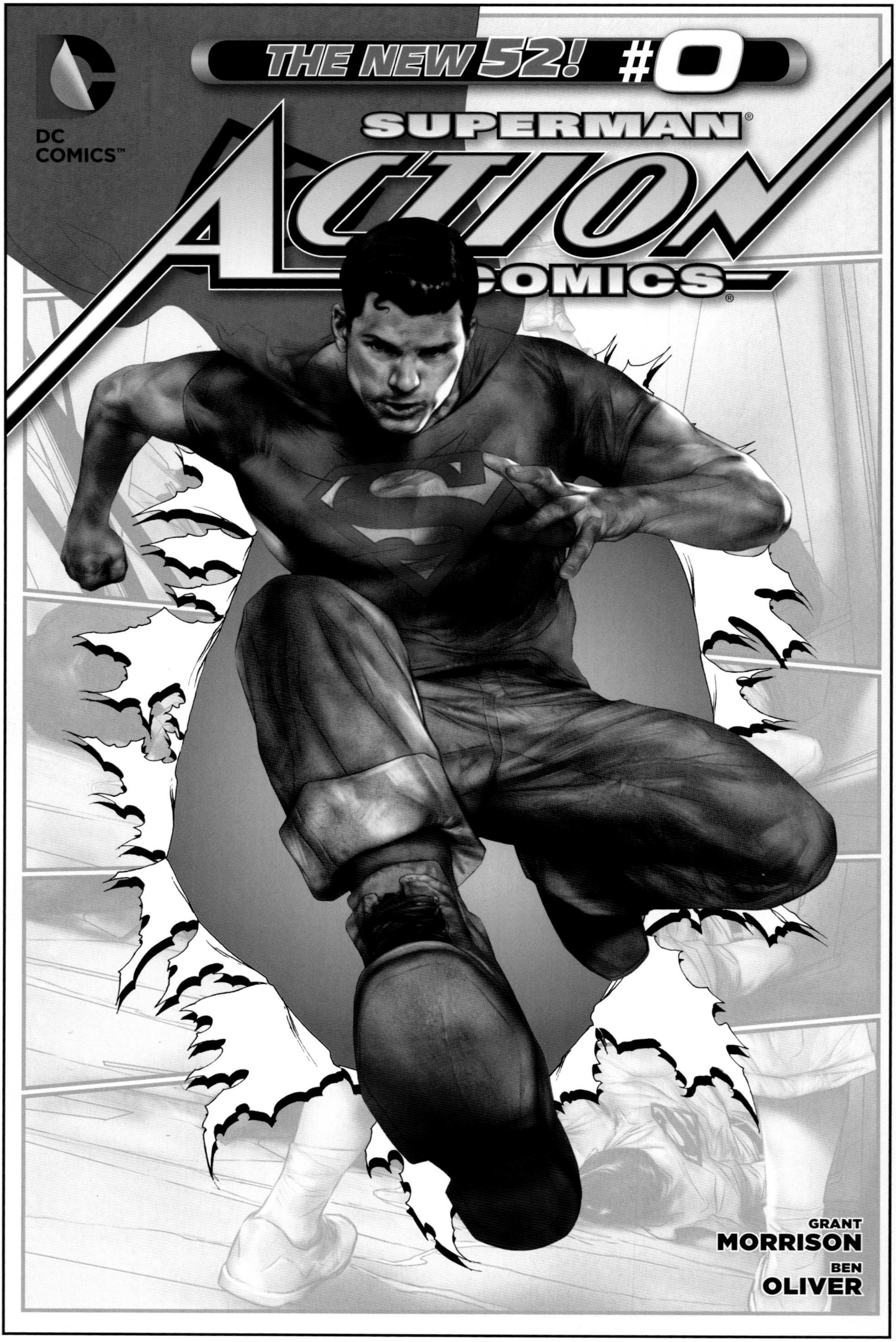
DC COMICS™
THE NEW 52! #0
SUPERMAN®
ACTION COMICS®
GRANT MORRISON
BEN OLIVER

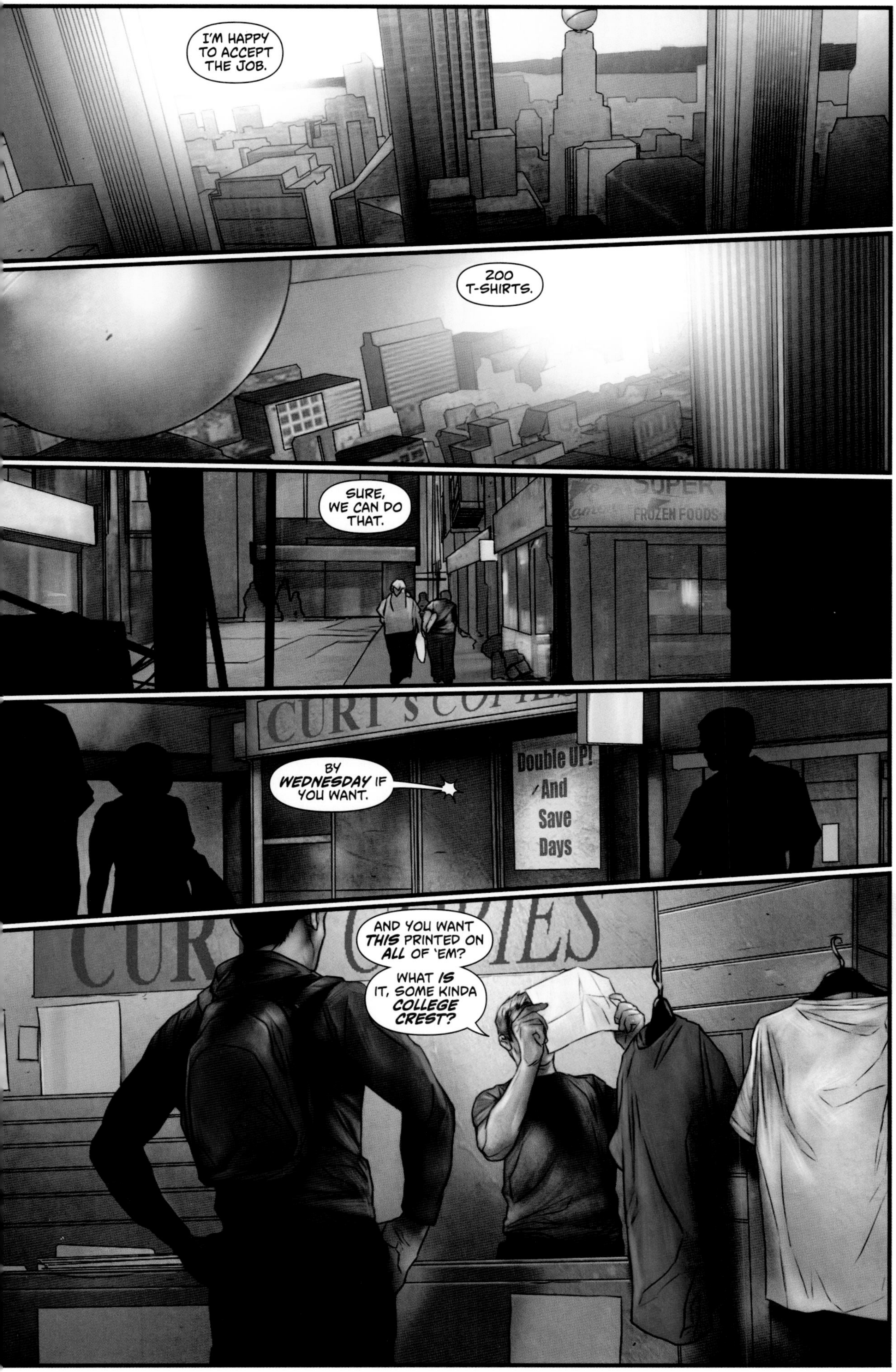
I'M HAPPY TO ACCEPT THE JOB.
200 T-SHIRTS.
SURE, WE CAN DO THAT.
SUPER FROZEN FOODS
CURT'S COPIES
BY *WEDNESDAY* IF YOU WANT.
Double UP! And Save Days
AND YOU WANT *THIS* PRINTED ON *ALL* OF 'EM?
WHAT *IS* IT, SOME KINDA *COLLEGE CREST?*

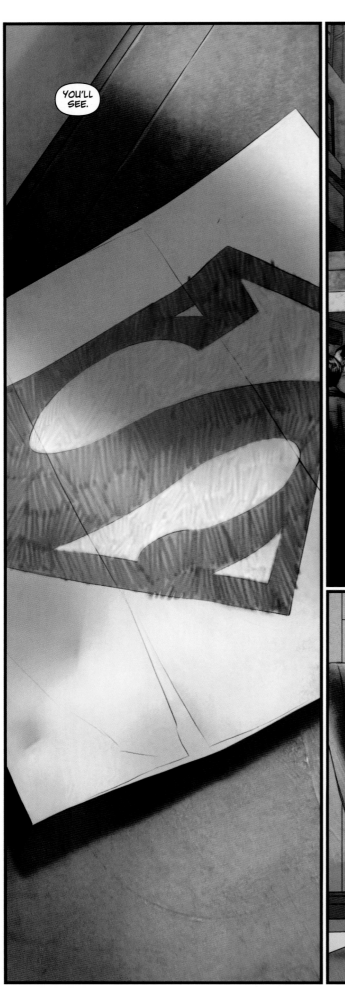

YOU'LL SEE.

I'LL TELL YOU WHAT *MY* FIRST EDITOR TOLD ME, CLARK.

THE STORY NEVER COMES BEFORE THE *PEOPLE* IN THE STORY.

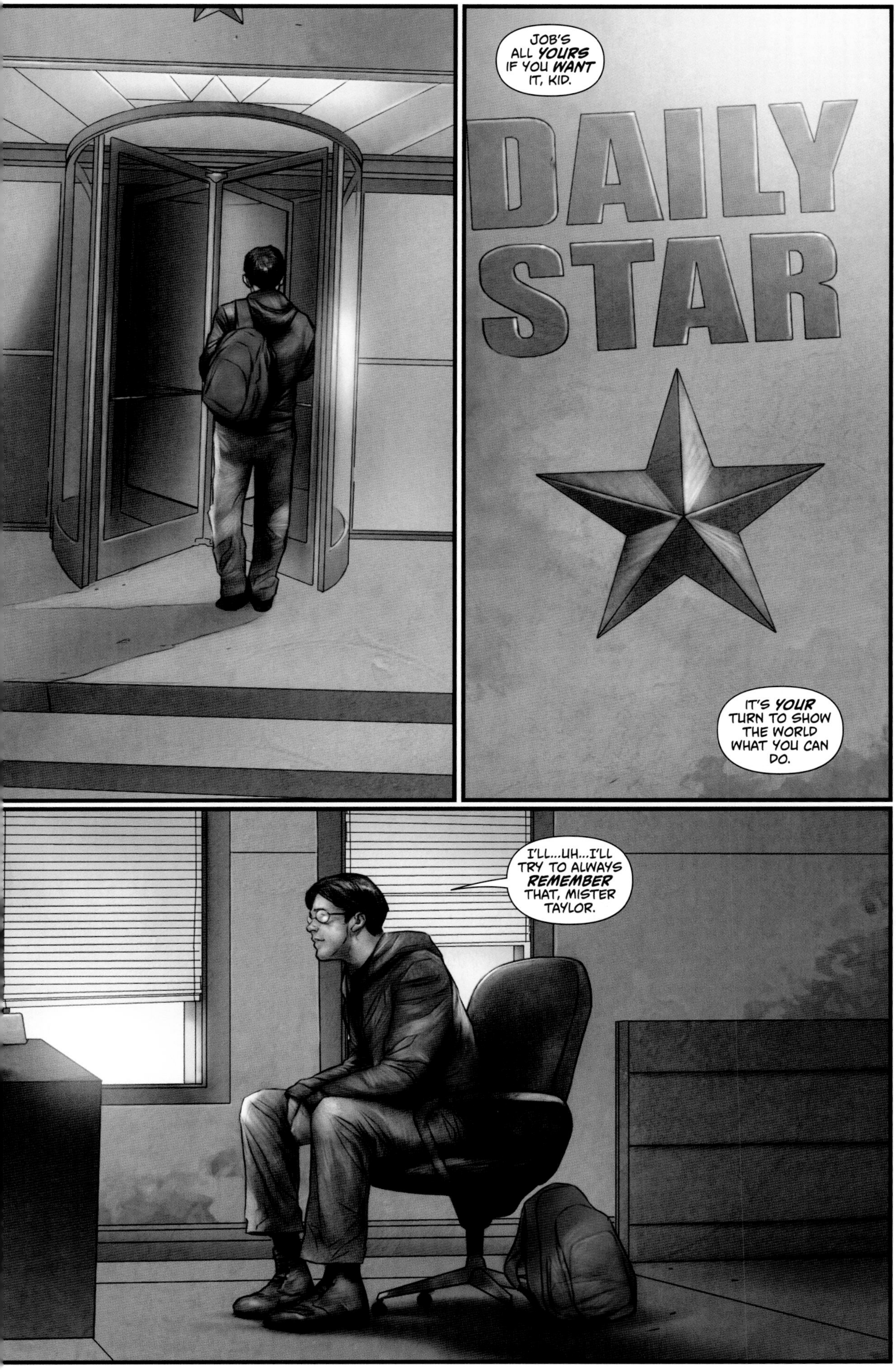
JOB'S ALL YOURS IF YOU WANT IT, KID.
DAILY STAR
IT'S YOUR TURN TO SHOW THE WORLD WHAT YOU CAN DO.
I'LL...UH...I'LL TRY TO ALWAYS REMEMBER THAT, MISTER TAYLOR.

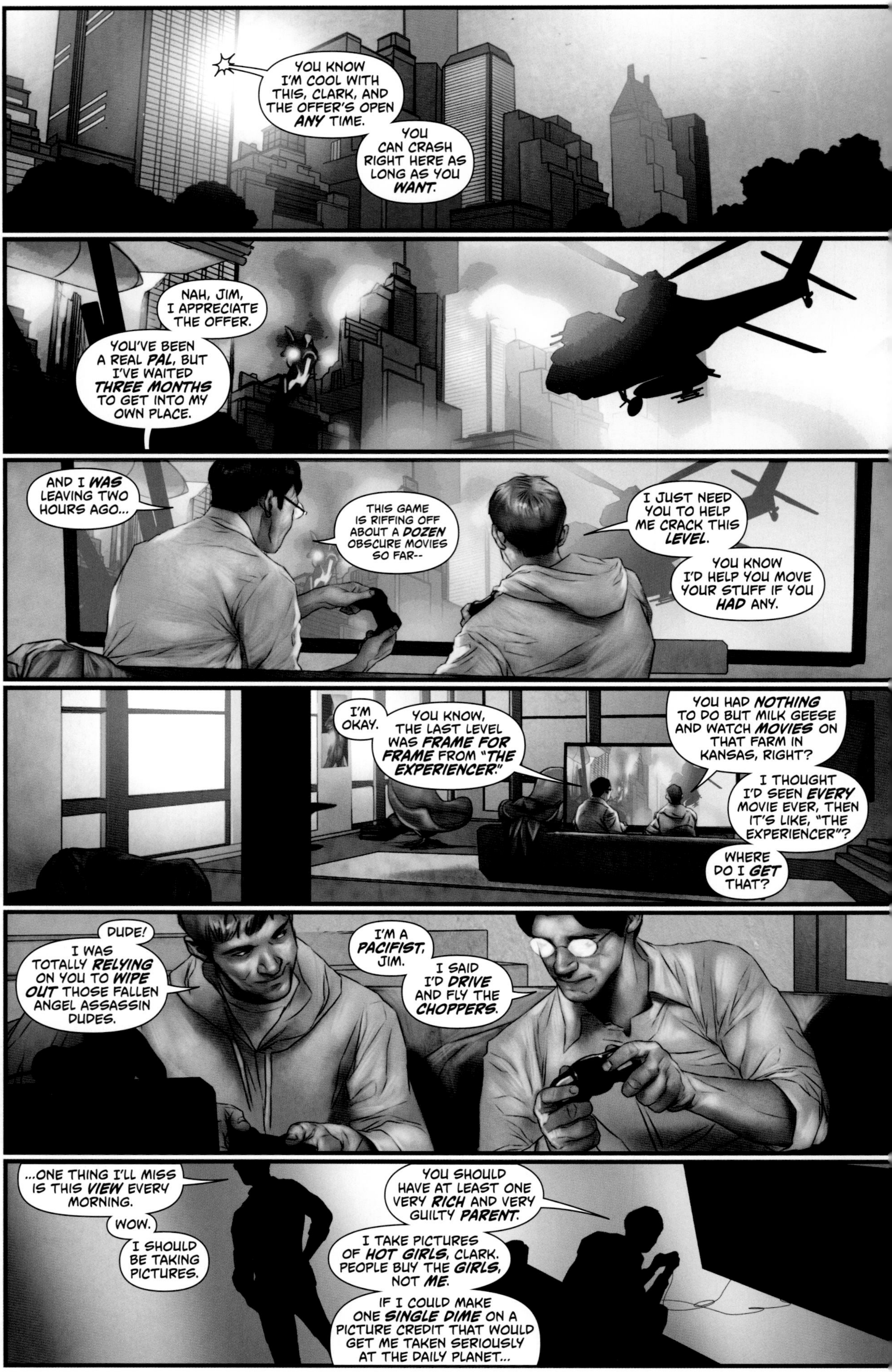
YOU KNOW I'M COOL WITH THIS, CLARK, AND THE OFFER'S OPEN ANY TIME.
YOU CAN CRASH RIGHT HERE AS LONG AS YOU WANT.
NAH, JIM, I APPRECIATE THE OFFER.
YOU'VE BEEN A REAL PAL, BUT I'VE WAITED THREE MONTHS TO GET INTO MY OWN PLACE.
AND I WAS LEAVING TWO HOURS AGO...
THIS GAME IS RIFFING OFF ABOUT A DOZEN OBSCURE MOVIES SO FAR--
I JUST NEED YOU TO HELP ME CRACK THIS LEVEL.
YOU KNOW I'D HELP YOU MOVE YOUR STUFF IF YOU HAD ANY.
I'M OKAY.
YOU KNOW, THE LAST LEVEL WAS FRAME FOR FRAME FROM "THE EXPERIENCER."
YOU HAD NOTHING TO DO BUT MILK GEESE AND WATCH MOVIES ON THAT FARM IN KANSAS, RIGHT?
I THOUGHT I'D SEEN EVERY MOVIE EVER, THEN IT'S LIKE, "THE EXPERIENCER"?
WHERE DO I GET THAT?
DUDE!
I WAS TOTALLY RELYING ON YOU TO WIPE OUT THOSE FALLEN ANGEL ASSASSIN DUDES.
I'M A PACIFIST, JIM.
I SAID I'D DRIVE AND FLY THE CHOPPERS.
...ONE THING I'LL MISS IS THIS VIEW EVERY MORNING.
WOW.
I SHOULD BE TAKING PICTURES.
YOU SHOULD HAVE AT LEAST ONE VERY RICH AND VERY GUILTY PARENT.
I TAKE PICTURES OF HOT GIRLS, CLARK. PEOPLE BUY THE GIRLS, NOT ME.
IF I COULD MAKE ONE SINGLE DIME ON A PICTURE CREDIT THAT WOULD GET ME TAKEN SERIOUSLY AT THE DAILY PLANET...

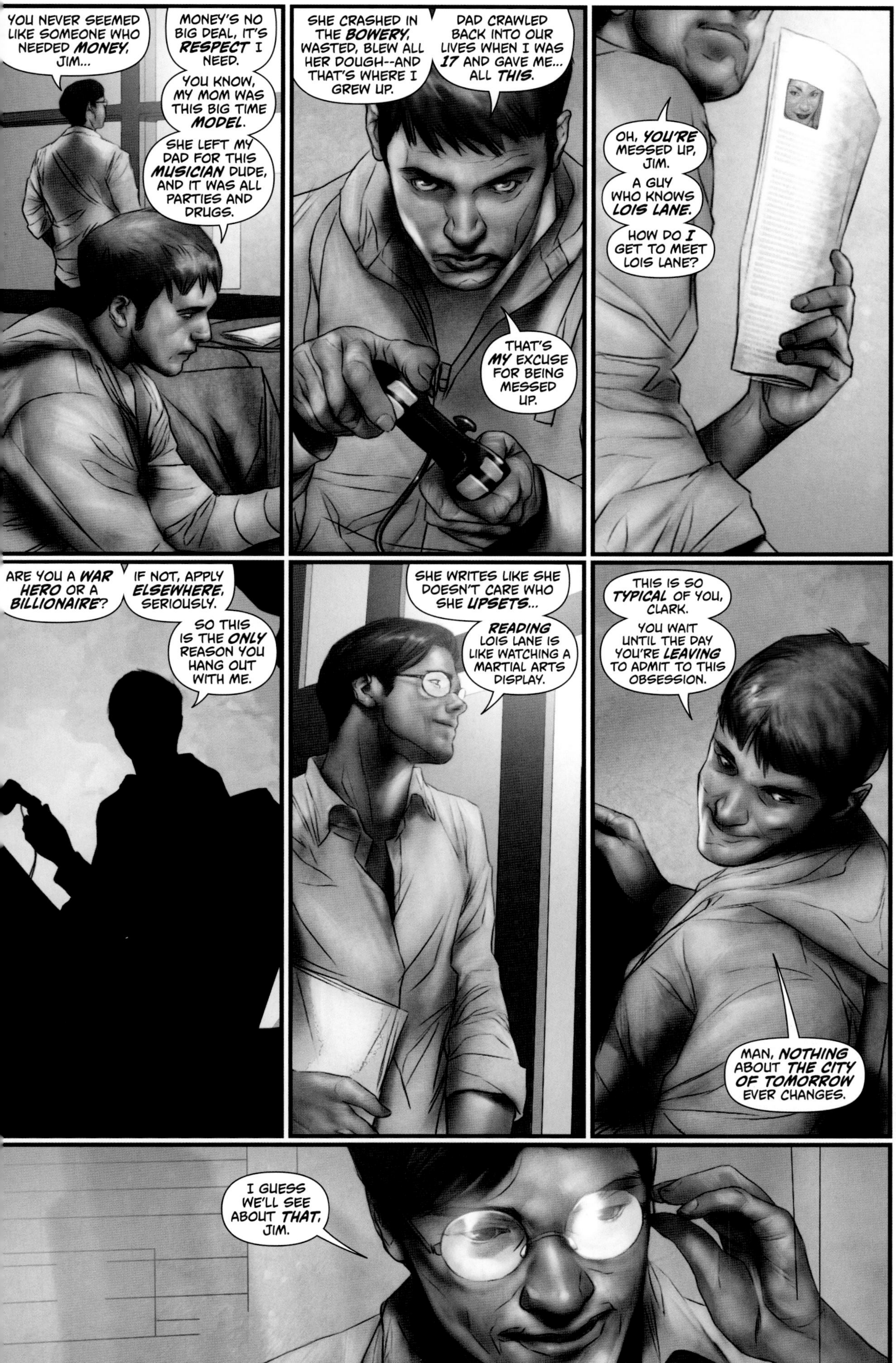

YOU NEVER SEEMED LIKE SOMEONE WHO NEEDED MONEY, JIM...
MONEY'S NO BIG DEAL, IT'S RESPECT I NEED.
YOU KNOW, MY MOM WAS THIS BIG TIME MODEL.
SHE LEFT MY DAD FOR THIS MUSICIAN DUDE, AND IT WAS ALL PARTIES AND DRUGS.
SHE CRASHED IN THE BOWERY, WASTED, BLEW ALL HER DOUGH--AND THAT'S WHERE I GREW UP.
DAD CRAWLED BACK INTO OUR LIVES WHEN I WAS 17 AND GAVE ME... ALL THIS.
THAT'S MY EXCUSE FOR BEING MESSED UP.
OH, YOU'RE MESSED UP, JIM.
A GUY WHO KNOWS LOIS LANE.
HOW DO I GET TO MEET LOIS LANE?
ARE YOU A WAR HERO OR A BILLIONAIRE?
IF NOT, APPLY ELSEWHERE, SERIOUSLY.
SO THIS IS THE ONLY REASON YOU HANG OUT WITH ME.
SHE WRITES LIKE SHE DOESN'T CARE WHO SHE UPSETS...
READING LOIS LANE IS LIKE WATCHING A MARTIAL ARTS DISPLAY.
THIS IS SO TYPICAL OF YOU, CLARK.
YOU WAIT UNTIL THE DAY YOU'RE LEAVING TO ADMIT TO THIS OBSESSION.
MAN, NOTHING ABOUT THE CITY OF TOMORROW EVER CHANGES.
I GUESS WE'LL SEE ABOUT THAT, JIM.

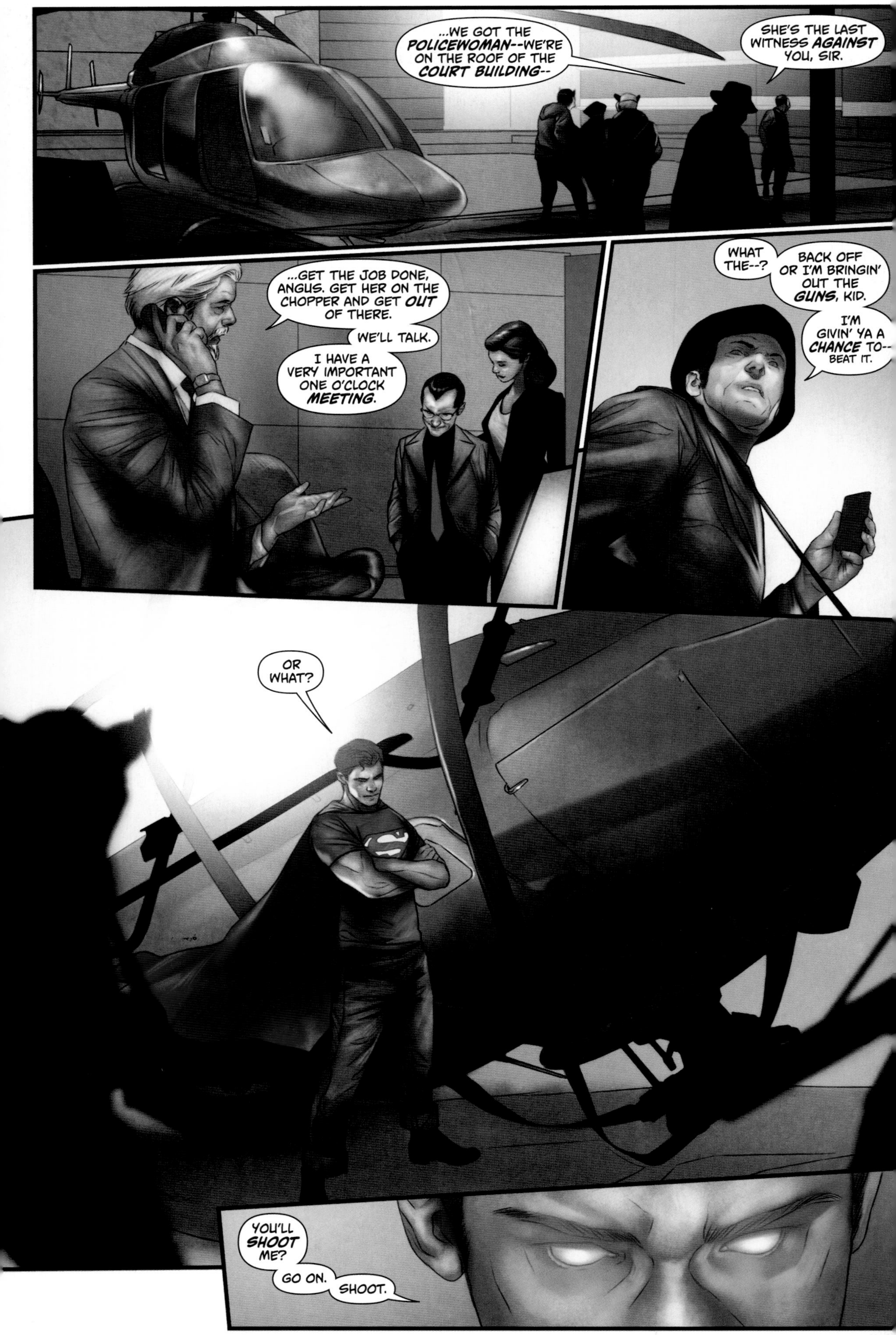
...WE GOT THE POLICEWOMAN--WE'RE ON THE ROOF OF THE COURT BUILDING--
SHE'S THE LAST WITNESS AGAINST YOU, SIR.
...GET THE JOB DONE, ANGUS. GET HER ON THE CHOPPER AND GET OUT OF THERE.
WE'LL TALK.
I HAVE A VERY IMPORTANT ONE O'CLOCK MEETING.
WHAT THE--?
BACK OFF OR I'M BRINGIN' OUT THE GUNS, KID.
I'M GIVIN' YA A CHANCE TO-- BEAT IT.
OR WHAT?
YOU'LL SHOOT ME?
GO ON.
SHOOT.

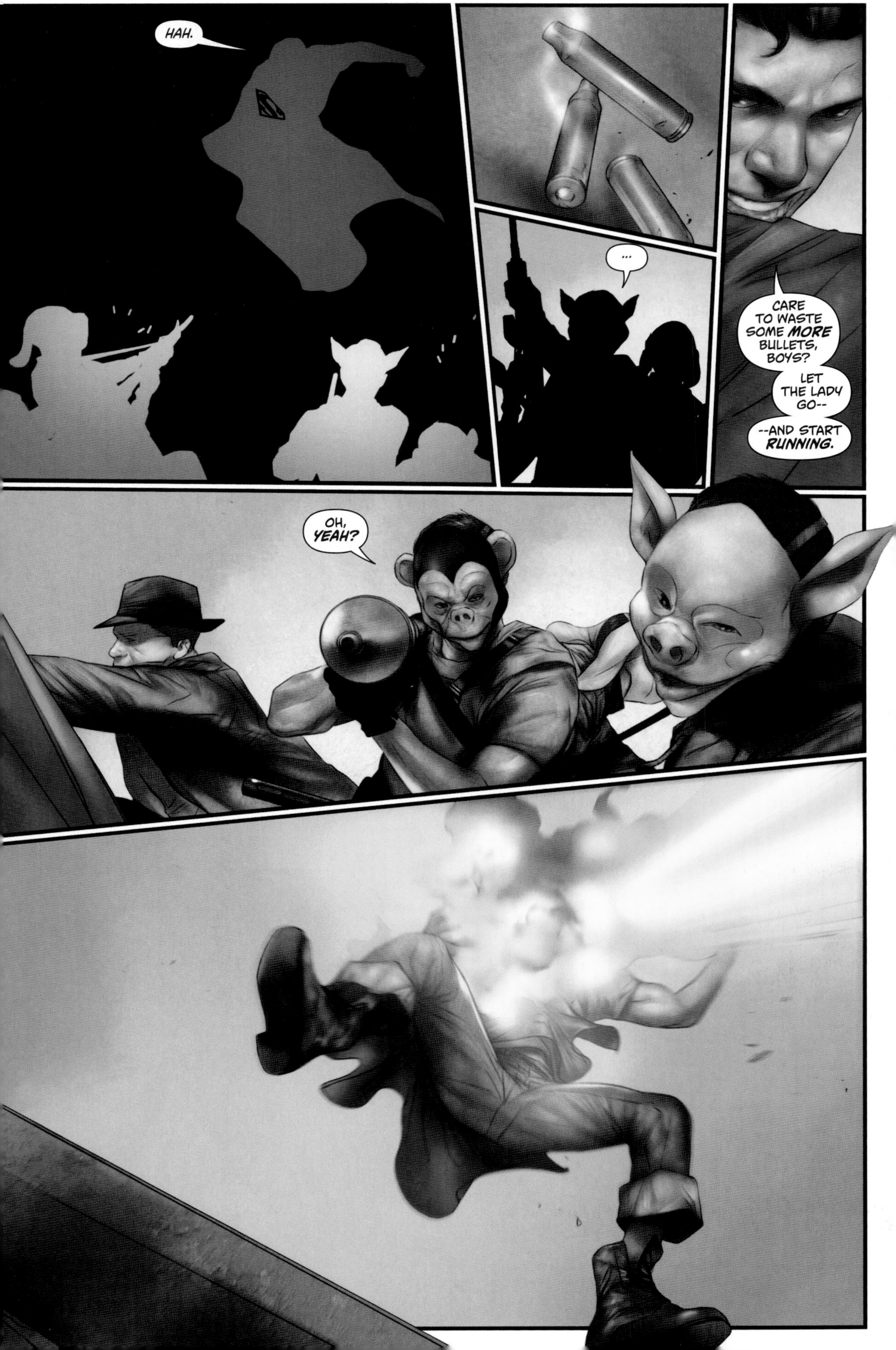

HAH.
...
CARE TO WASTE SOME MORE BULLETS, BOYS?
LET THE LADY GO--
--AND START RUNNING.
OH, YEAH?

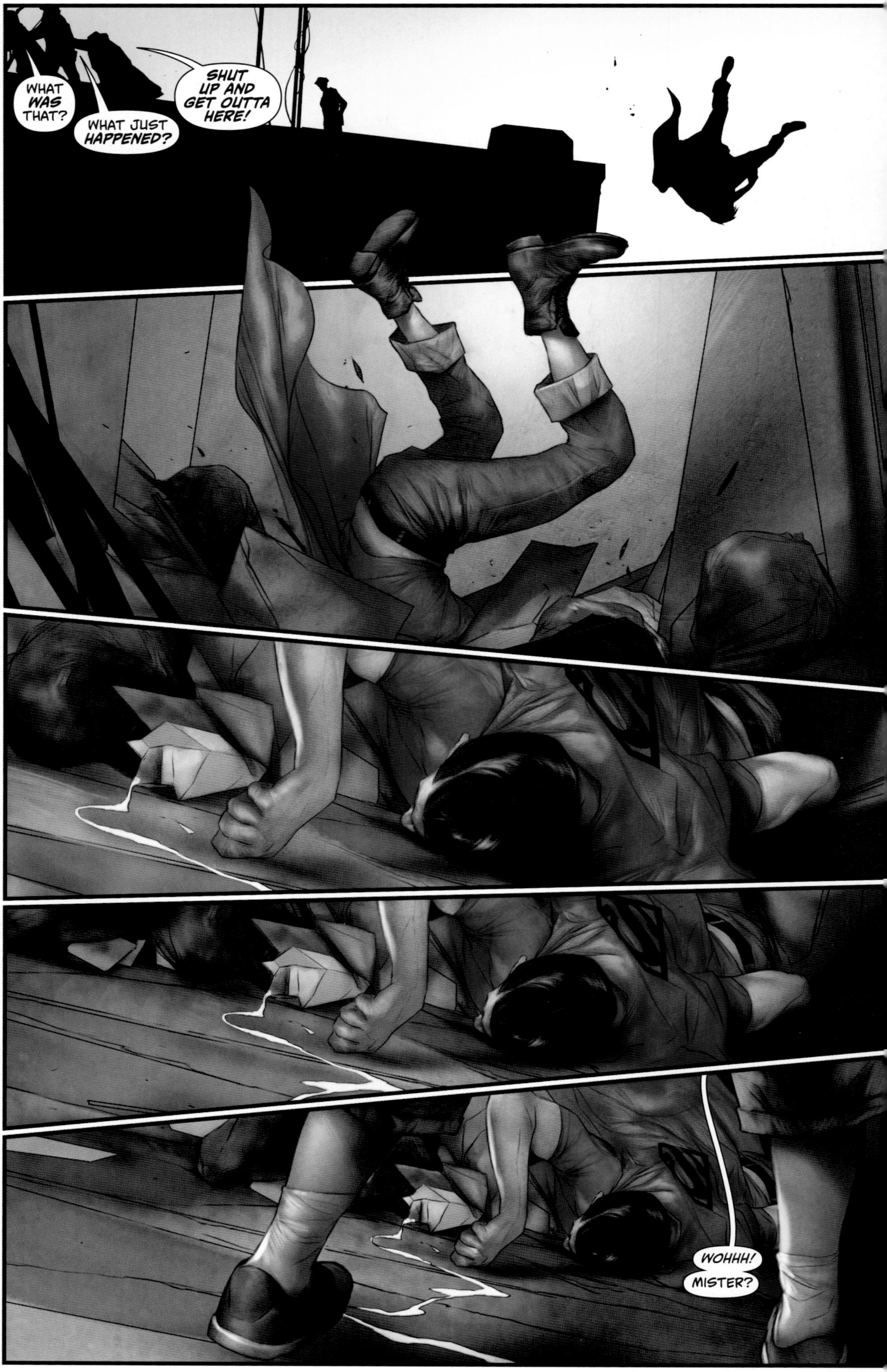
WHAT WAS THAT?
WHAT JUST HAPPENED?
SHUT UP AND GET OUTTA HERE!
WOHHH!
MISTER?

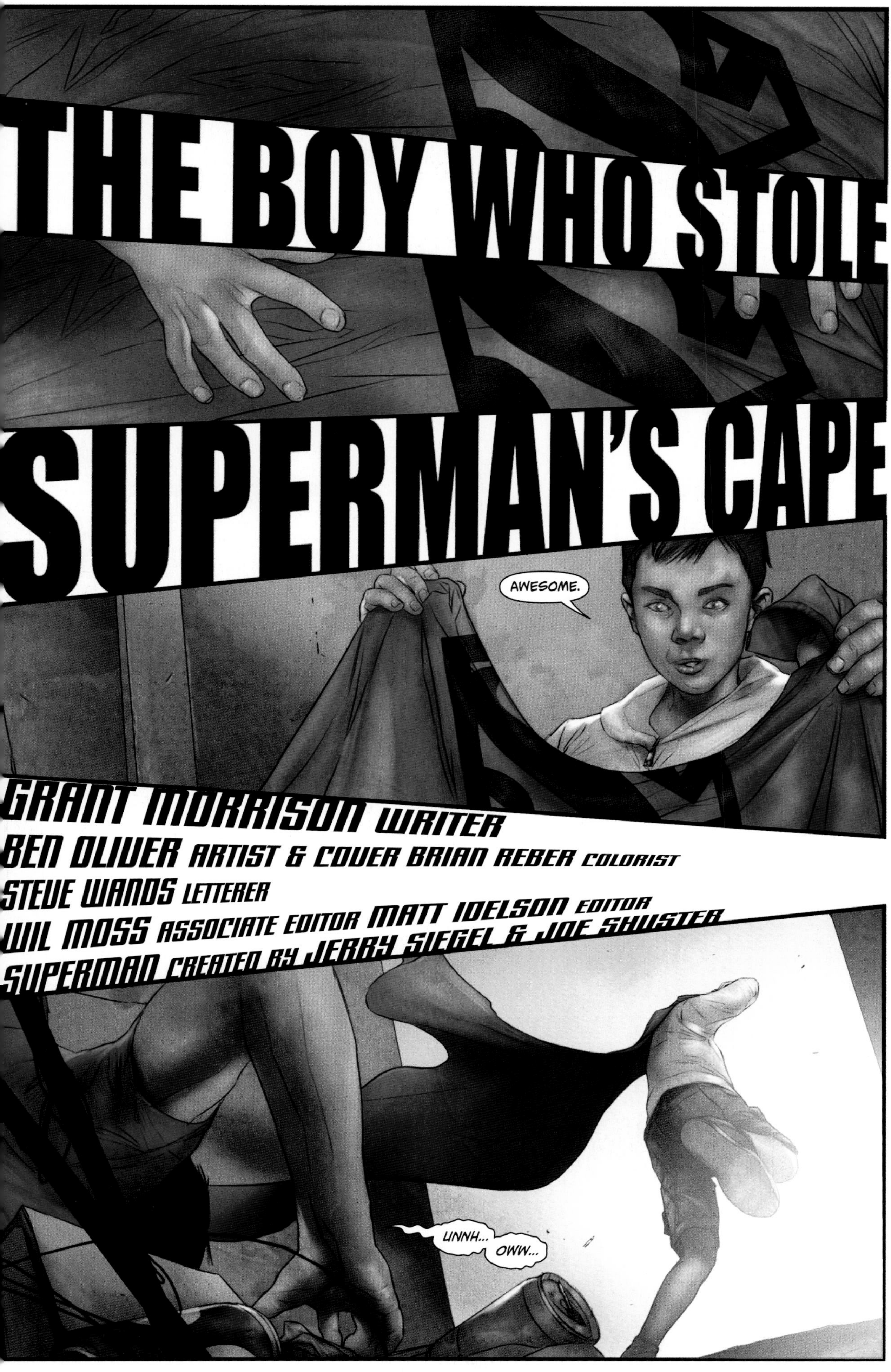
THE BOY WHO STOLE
SUPERMAN'S CAPE
AWESOME.
GRANT MORRISON WRITER
BEN OLIVER ARTIST & COVER BRIAN REBER COLORIST
STEVE WANDS LETTERER
WIL MOSS ASSOCIATE EDITOR MATT IDELSON EDITOR
SUPERMAN CREATED BY JERRY SIEGEL & JOE SHUSTER
UNNH...
OWW...

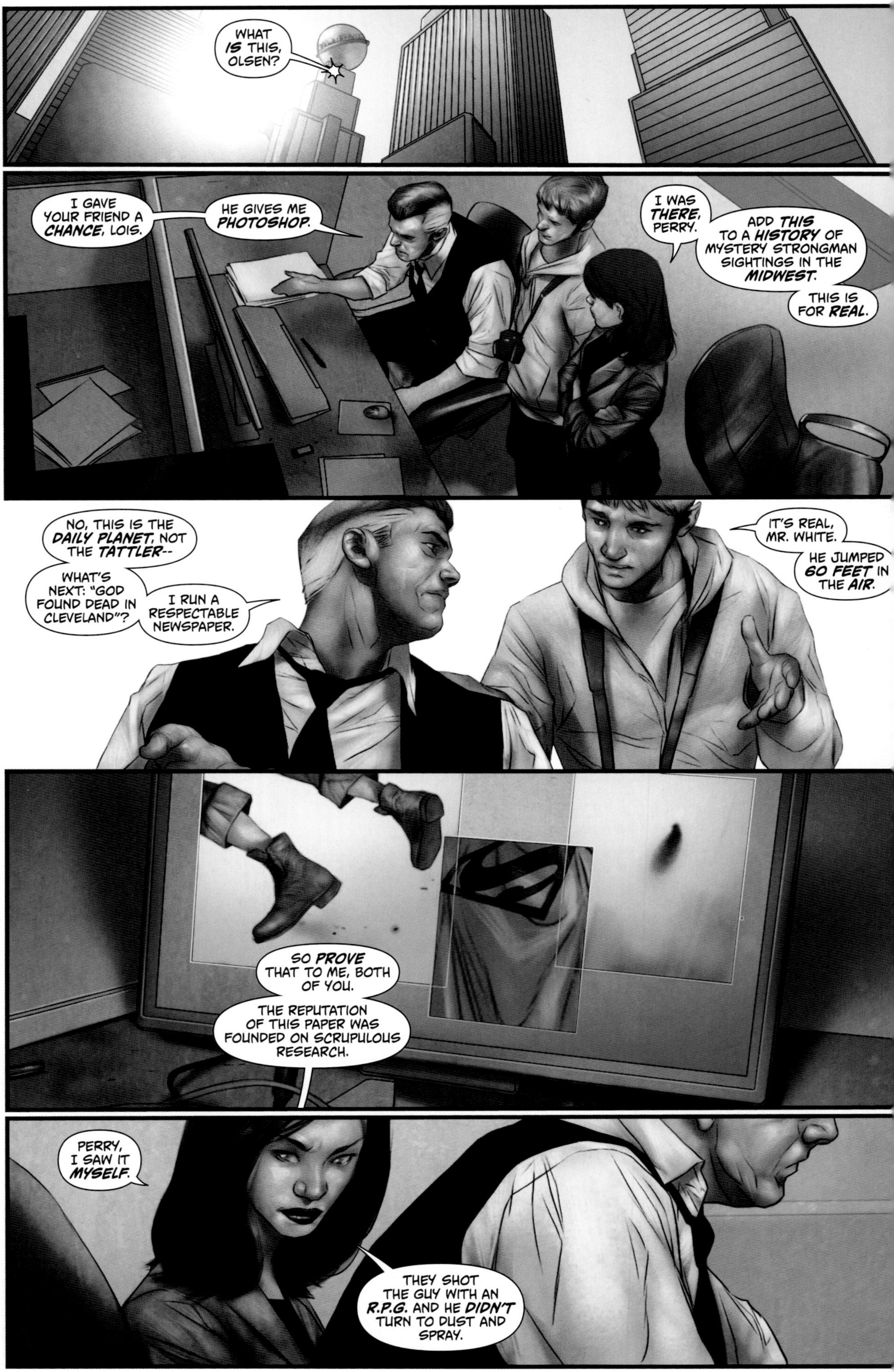

WHAT *IS* THIS, OLSEN?
I GAVE YOUR FRIEND A *CHANCE*, LOIS.
HE GIVES ME *PHOTOSHOP*.
I WAS *THERE*, PERRY.
ADD *THIS* TO A *HISTORY* OF MYSTERY STRONGMAN SIGHTINGS IN THE *MIDWEST*.
THIS IS FOR *REAL*.
NO, THIS IS THE *DAILY PLANET*, NOT THE *TATTLER*--
WHAT'S NEXT: "GOD FOUND DEAD IN CLEVELAND"?
I RUN A RESPECTABLE NEWSPAPER.
IT'S REAL, MR. WHITE.
HE JUMPED *60 FEET* IN THE *AIR*.
SO *PROVE* THAT TO ME, BOTH OF YOU.
THE REPUTATION OF THIS PAPER WAS FOUNDED ON SCRUPULOUS RESEARCH.
PERRY, I SAW IT *MYSELF*.
THEY SHOT THE GUY WITH AN *R.P.G.* AND HE *DIDN'T* TURN TO DUST AND SPRAY.

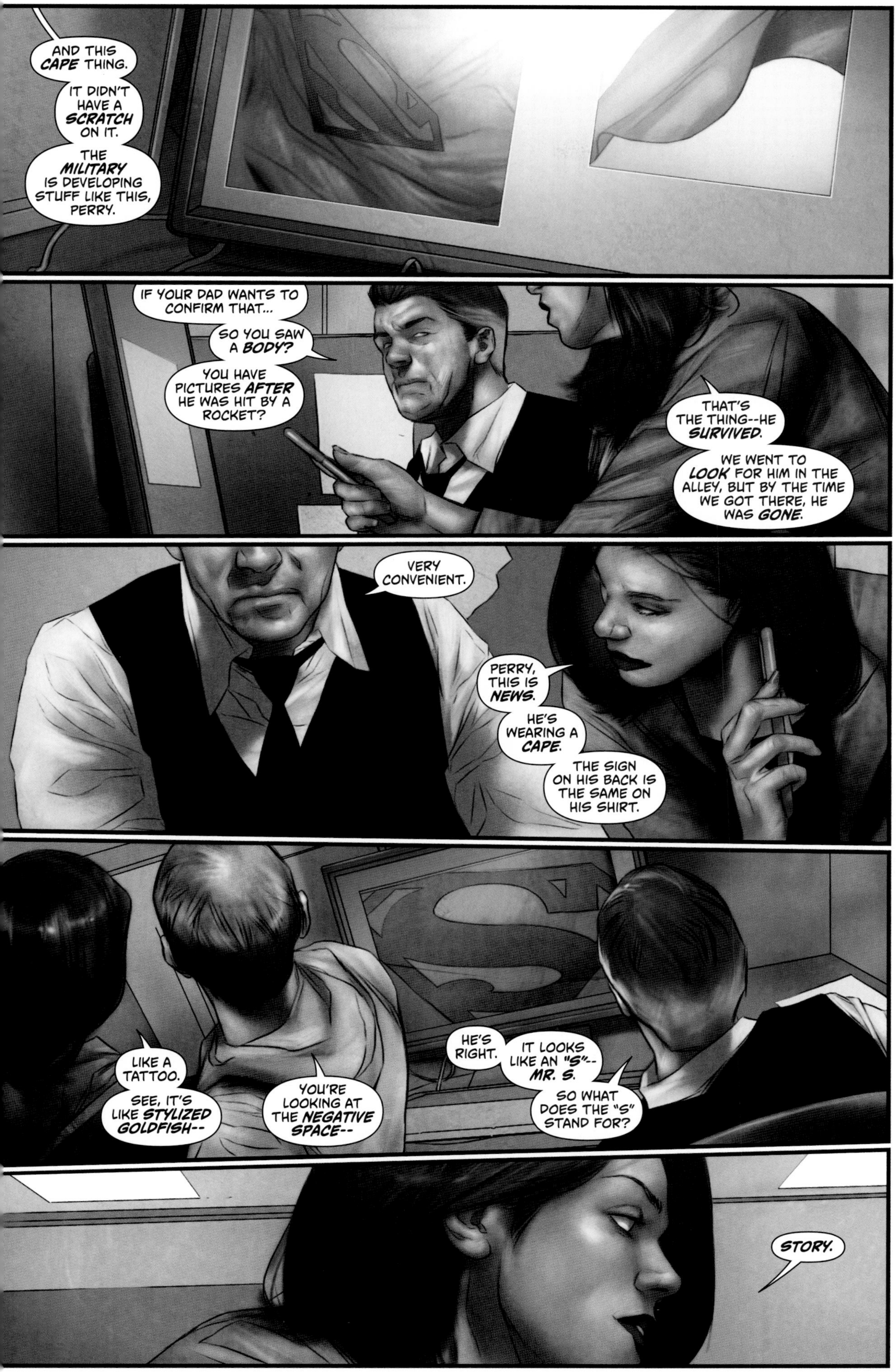
AND THIS CAPE THING.
IT DIDN'T HAVE A SCRATCH ON IT.
THE MILITARY IS DEVELOPING STUFF LIKE THIS, PERRY.
IF YOUR DAD WANTS TO CONFIRM THAT...
SO YOU SAW A BODY?
YOU HAVE PICTURES AFTER HE WAS HIT BY A ROCKET?
THAT'S THE THING--HE SURVIVED.
WE WENT TO LOOK FOR HIM IN THE ALLEY, BUT BY THE TIME WE GOT THERE, HE WAS GONE.
VERY CONVENIENT.
PERRY, THIS IS NEWS.
HE'S WEARING A CAPE.
THE SIGN ON HIS BACK IS THE SAME ON HIS SHIRT.
LIKE A TATTOO.
SEE, IT'S LIKE STYLIZED GOLDFISH--
YOU'RE LOOKING AT THE NEGATIVE SPACE--
HE'S RIGHT.
IT LOOKS LIKE AN "S"-- MR. S.
SO WHAT DOES THE "S" STAND FOR?
STORY.

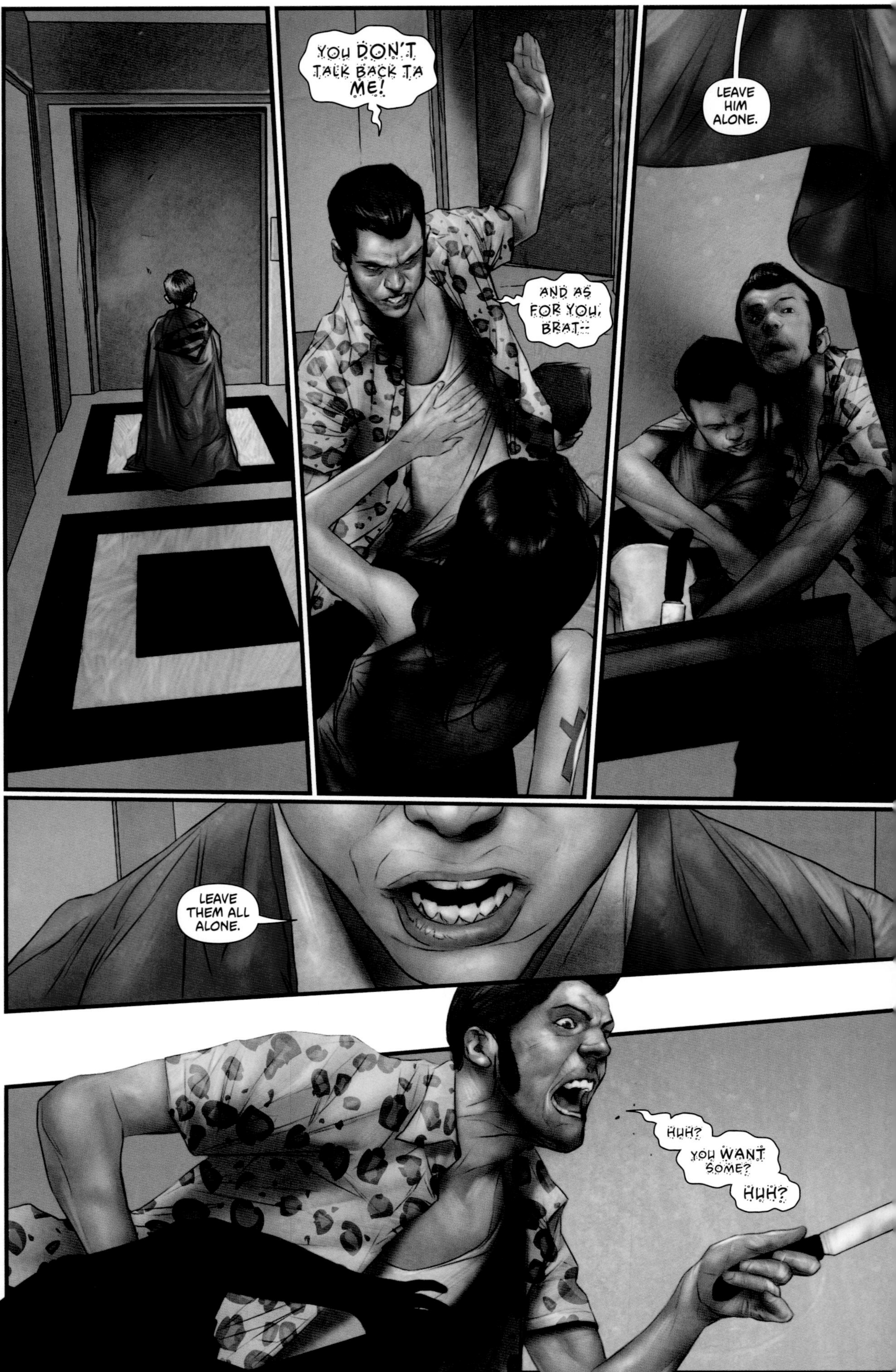
YOU DON'T TALK BACK TA ME!
AND AS FOR YOU, BRAT--
LEAVE HIM ALONE.
LEAVE THEM ALL ALONE.
HUH?
YOU WANT SOME?
HUH?

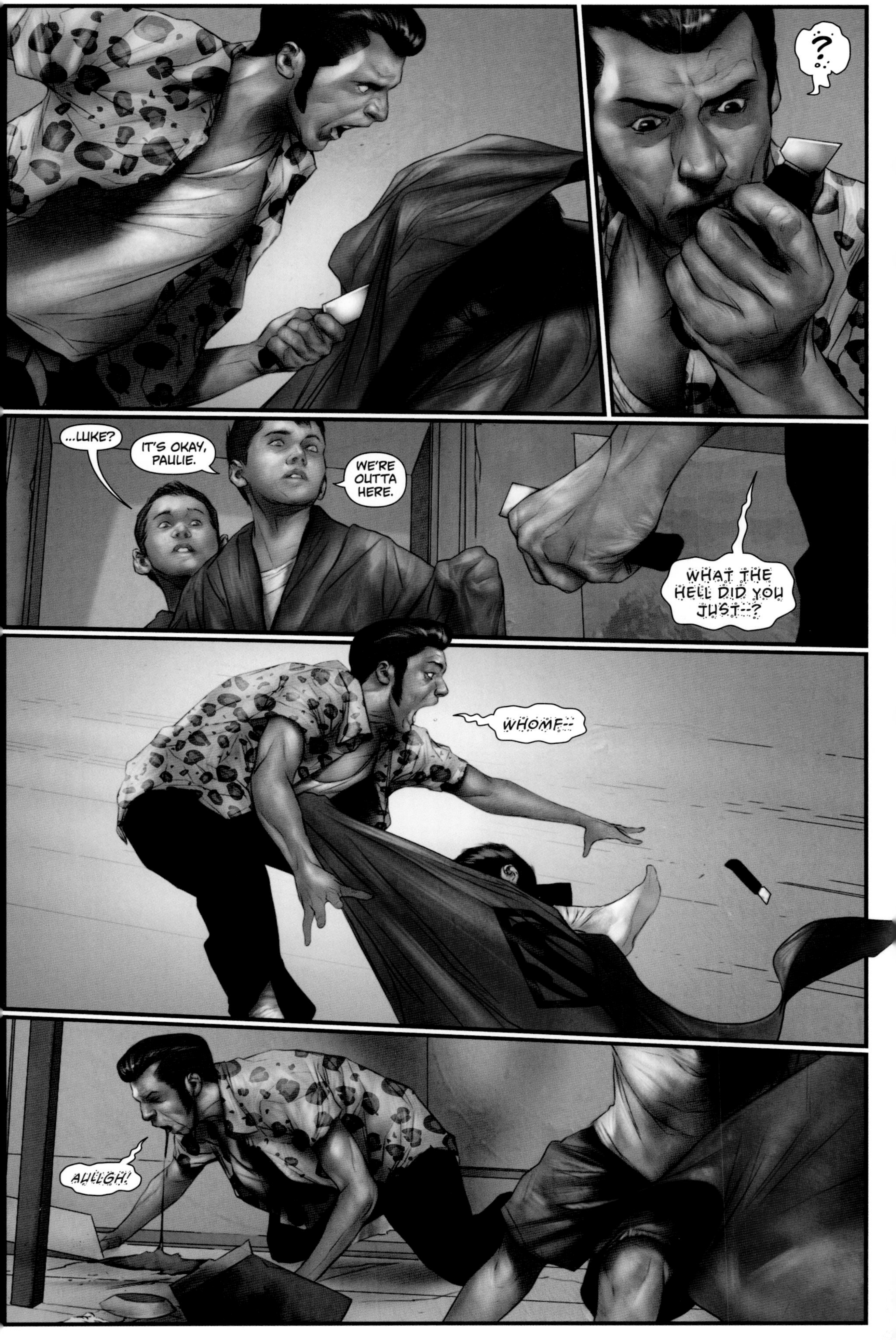
?
...LUKE?
IT'S OKAY, PAULIE.
WE'RE OUTTA HERE.
WHAT THE HELL DID YOU JUST--?
WHOMF--
AULLGH!

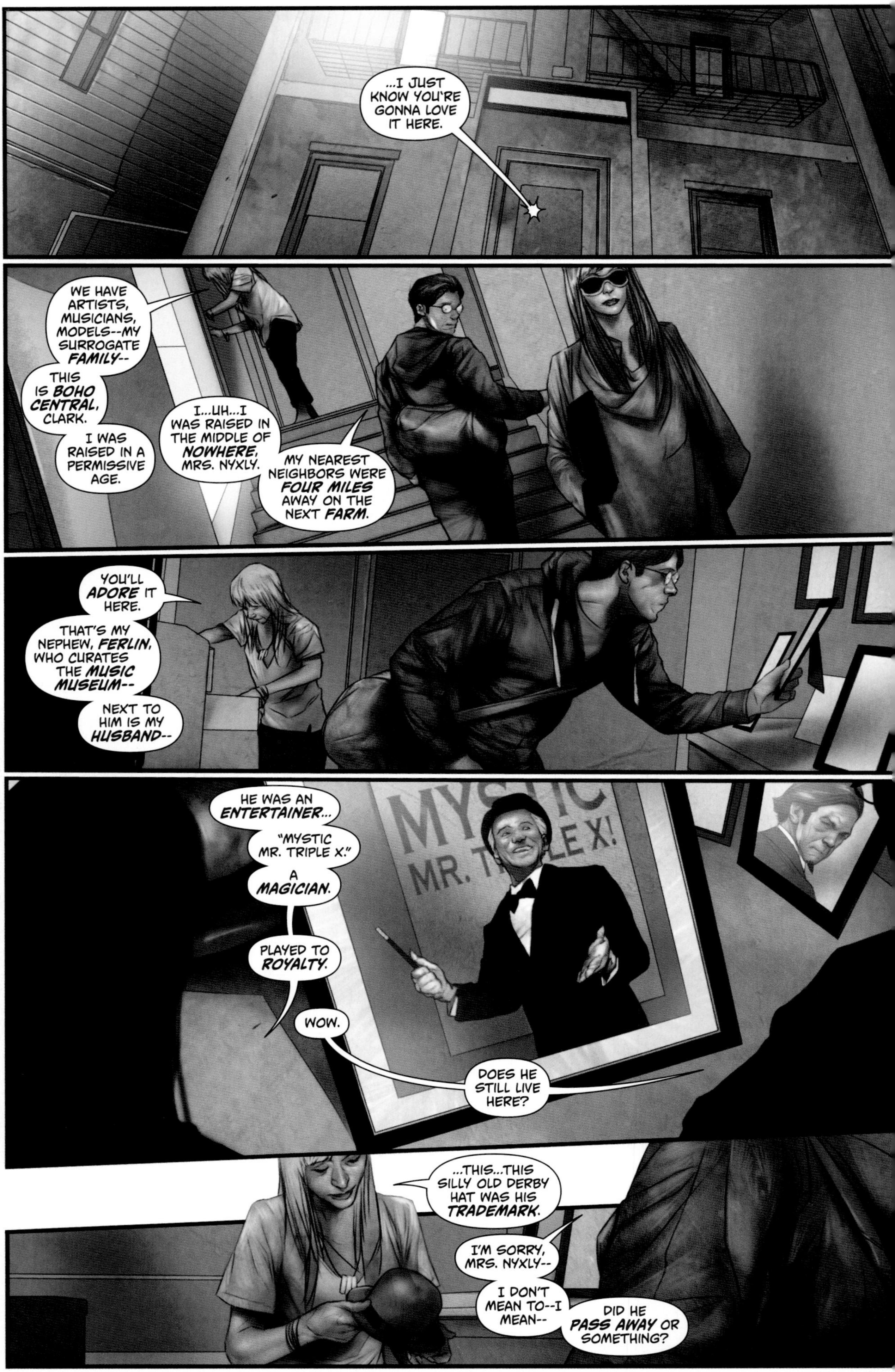
...I JUST KNOW YOU'RE GONNA LOVE IT HERE.
WE HAVE ARTISTS, MUSICIANS, MODELS--MY SURROGATE FAMILY--
THIS IS BOHO CENTRAL, CLARK.
I WAS RAISED IN A PERMISSIVE AGE.
I...UH...I WAS RAISED IN THE MIDDLE OF NOWHERE, MRS. NYXLY.
MY NEAREST NEIGHBORS WERE FOUR MILES AWAY ON THE NEXT FARM.
YOU'LL ADORE IT HERE.
THAT'S MY NEPHEW, FERLIN, WHO CURATES THE MUSIC MUSEUM--
NEXT TO HIM IS MY HUSBAND--
HE WAS AN ENTERTAINER...
"MYSTIC MR. TRIPLE X."
A MAGICIAN.
PLAYED TO ROYALTY.
WOW.
DOES HE STILL LIVE HERE?
...THIS...THIS SILLY OLD DERBY HAT WAS HIS TRADEMARK.
I'M SORRY, MRS. NYXLY--
I DON'T MEAN TO--I MEAN--
DID HE PASS AWAY OR SOMETHING?

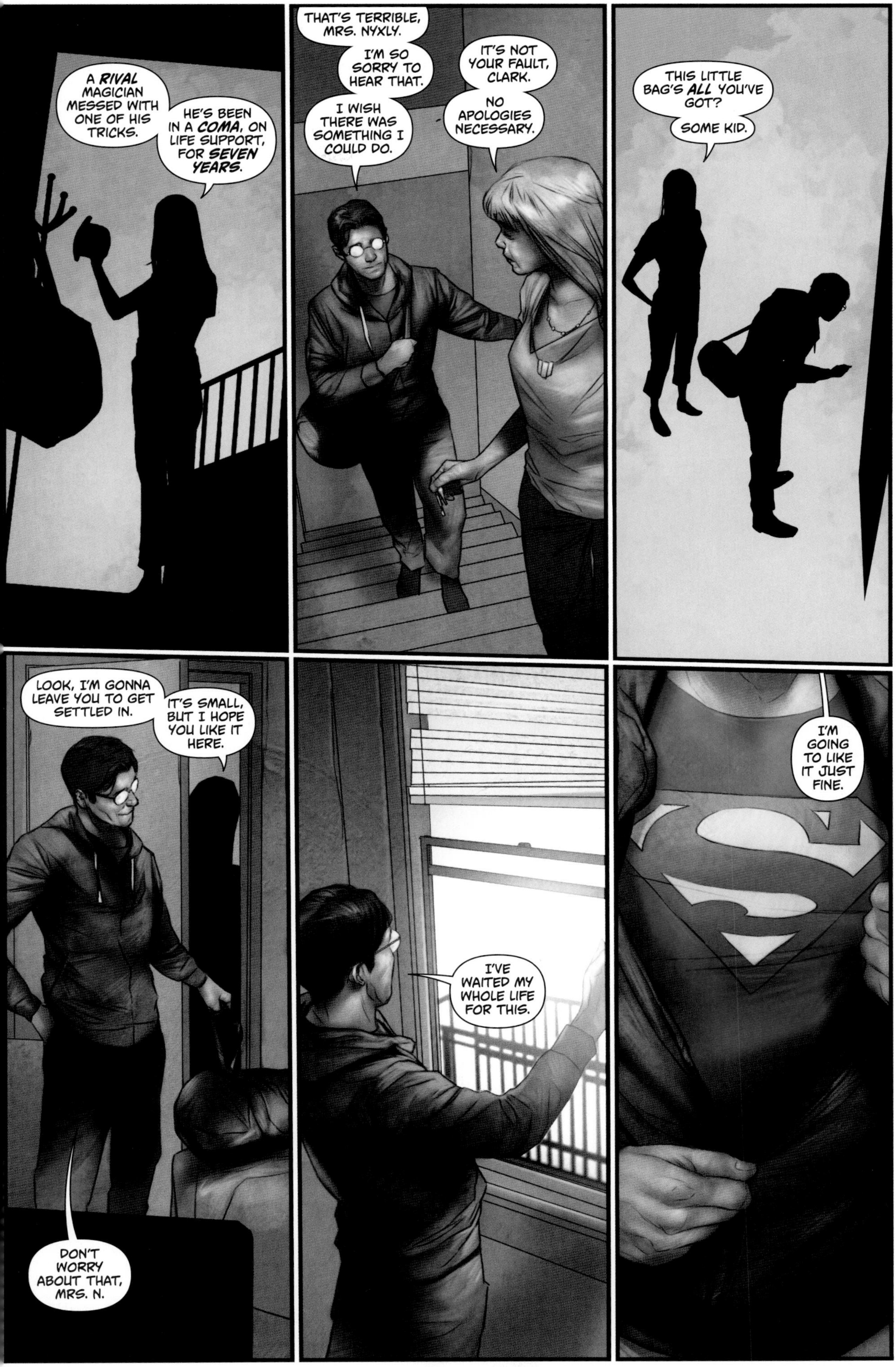
A RIVAL MAGICIAN MESSED WITH ONE OF HIS TRICKS.
HE'S BEEN IN A COMA, ON LIFE SUPPORT, FOR SEVEN YEARS.
THAT'S TERRIBLE, MRS. NYXLY.
I'M SO SORRY TO HEAR THAT.
I WISH THERE WAS SOMETHING I COULD DO.
IT'S NOT YOUR FAULT, CLARK.
NO APOLOGIES NECESSARY.
THIS LITTLE BAG'S ALL YOU'VE GOT?
SOME KID.
LOOK, I'M GONNA LEAVE YOU TO GET SETTLED IN.
IT'S SMALL, BUT I HOPE YOU LIKE IT HERE.
DON'T WORRY ABOUT THAT, MRS. N.
I'VE WAITED MY WHOLE LIFE FOR THIS.
I'M GOING TO LIKE IT JUST FINE.

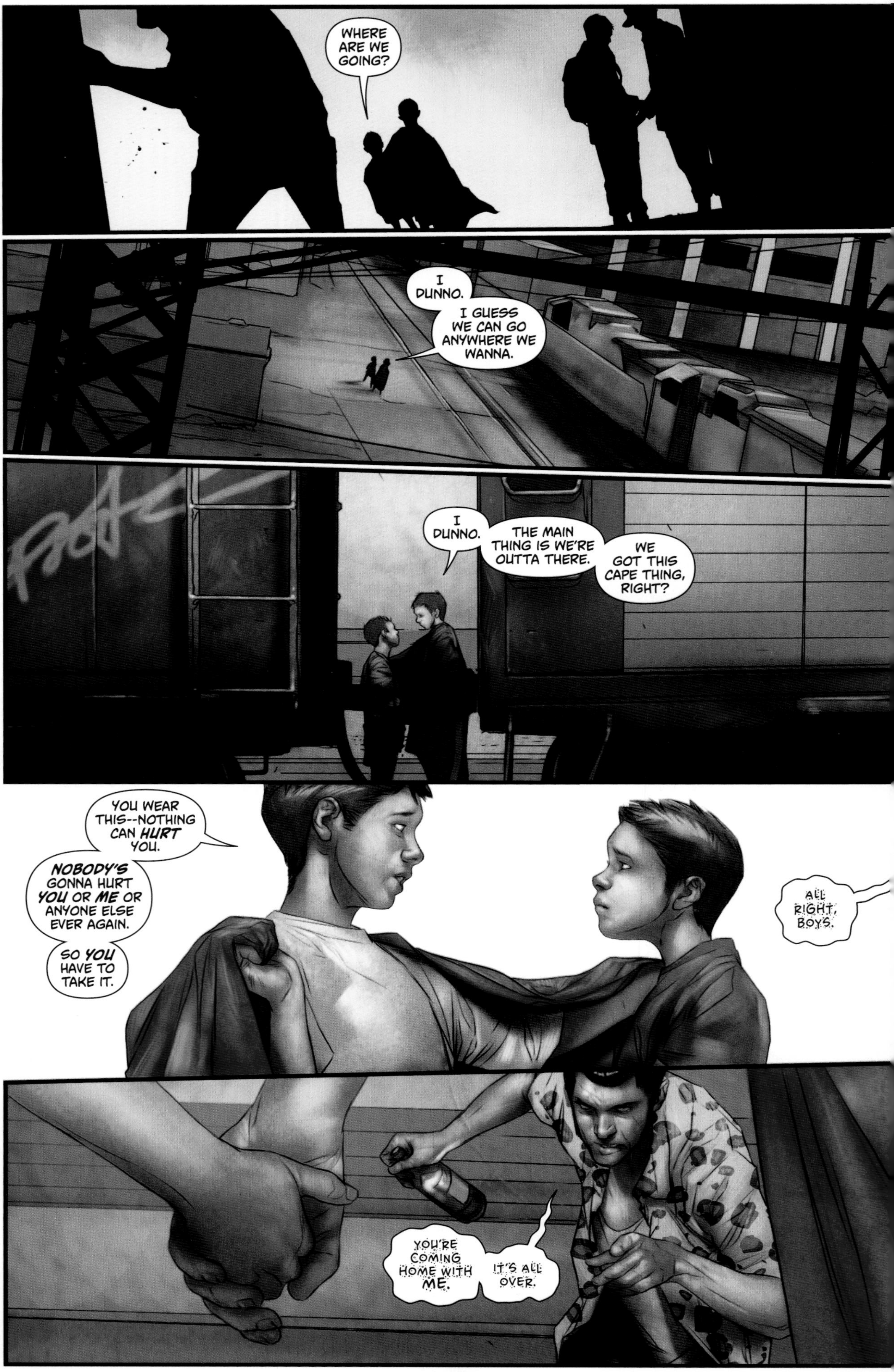
WHERE ARE WE GOING?
I DUNNO.
I GUESS WE CAN GO ANYWHERE WE WANNA.
I DUNNO.
THE MAIN THING IS WE'RE OUTTA THERE.
WE GOT THIS CAPE THING, RIGHT?
YOU WEAR THIS--NOTHING CAN HURT YOU.
NOBODY'S GONNA HURT YOU OR ME OR ANYONE ELSE EVER AGAIN.
SO YOU HAVE TO TAKE IT.
ALL RIGHT, BOYS.
YOU'RE COMING HOME WITH ME.
IT'S ALL OVER.

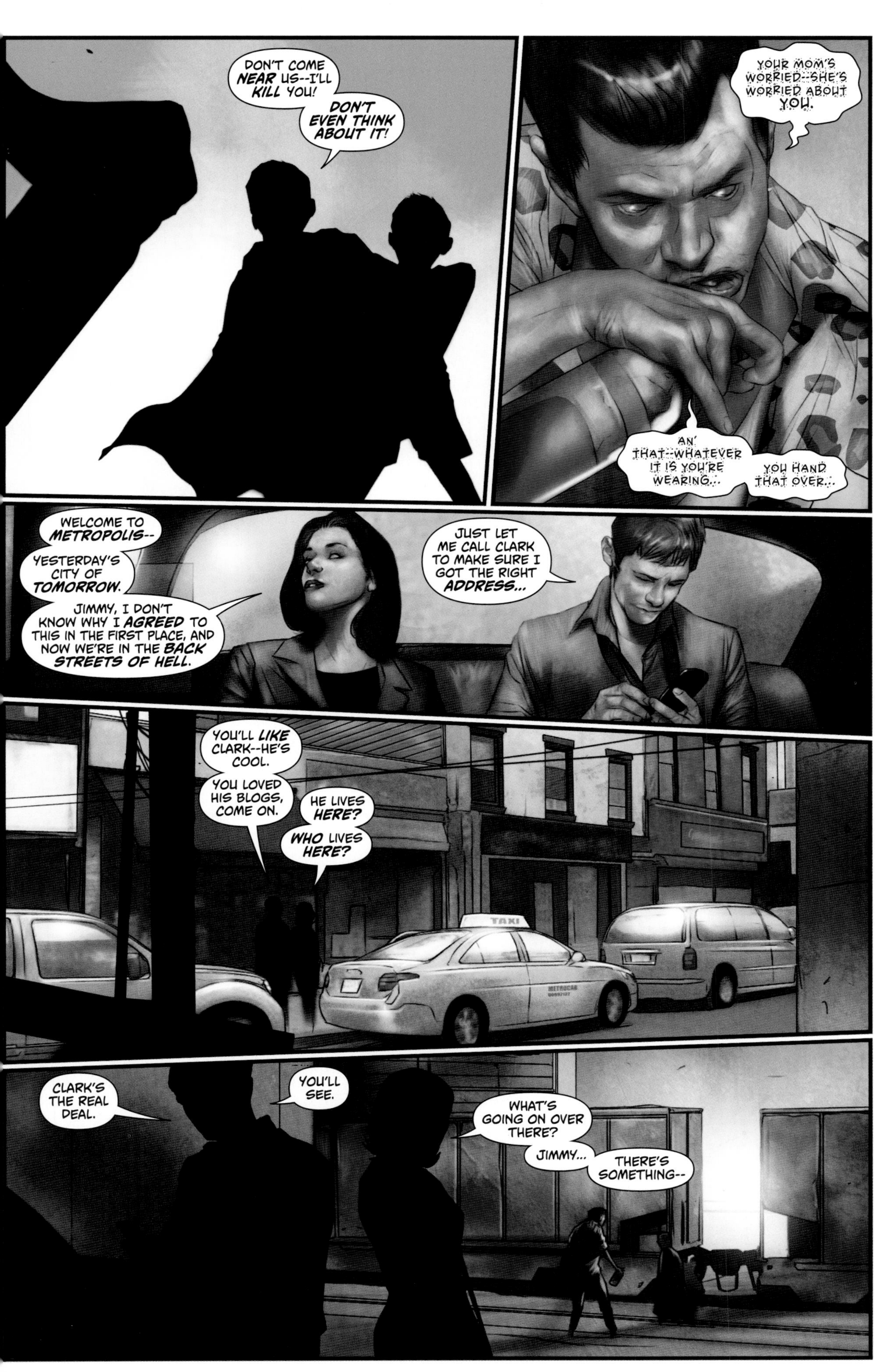
DON'T COME NEAR US--I'LL KILL YOU!
DON'T EVEN THINK ABOUT IT!
YOUR MOM'S WORRIED--SHE'S WORRIED ABOUT YOU.
AN' THAT--WHATEVER IT IS YOU'RE WEARING...
YOU HAND THAT OVER...
WELCOME TO METROPOLIS--
YESTERDAY'S CITY OF TOMORROW.
JIMMY, I DON'T KNOW WHY I AGREED TO THIS IN THE FIRST PLACE, AND NOW WE'RE IN THE BACK STREETS OF HELL.
JUST LET ME CALL CLARK TO MAKE SURE I GOT THE RIGHT ADDRESS...
YOU'LL LIKE CLARK--HE'S COOL.
YOU LOVED HIS BLOGS, COME ON.
HE LIVES HERE?
WHO LIVES HERE?
TAXI
CLARK'S THE REAL DEAL.
YOU'LL SEE.
WHAT'S GOING ON OVER THERE?
JIMMY...
THERE'S SOMETHING--

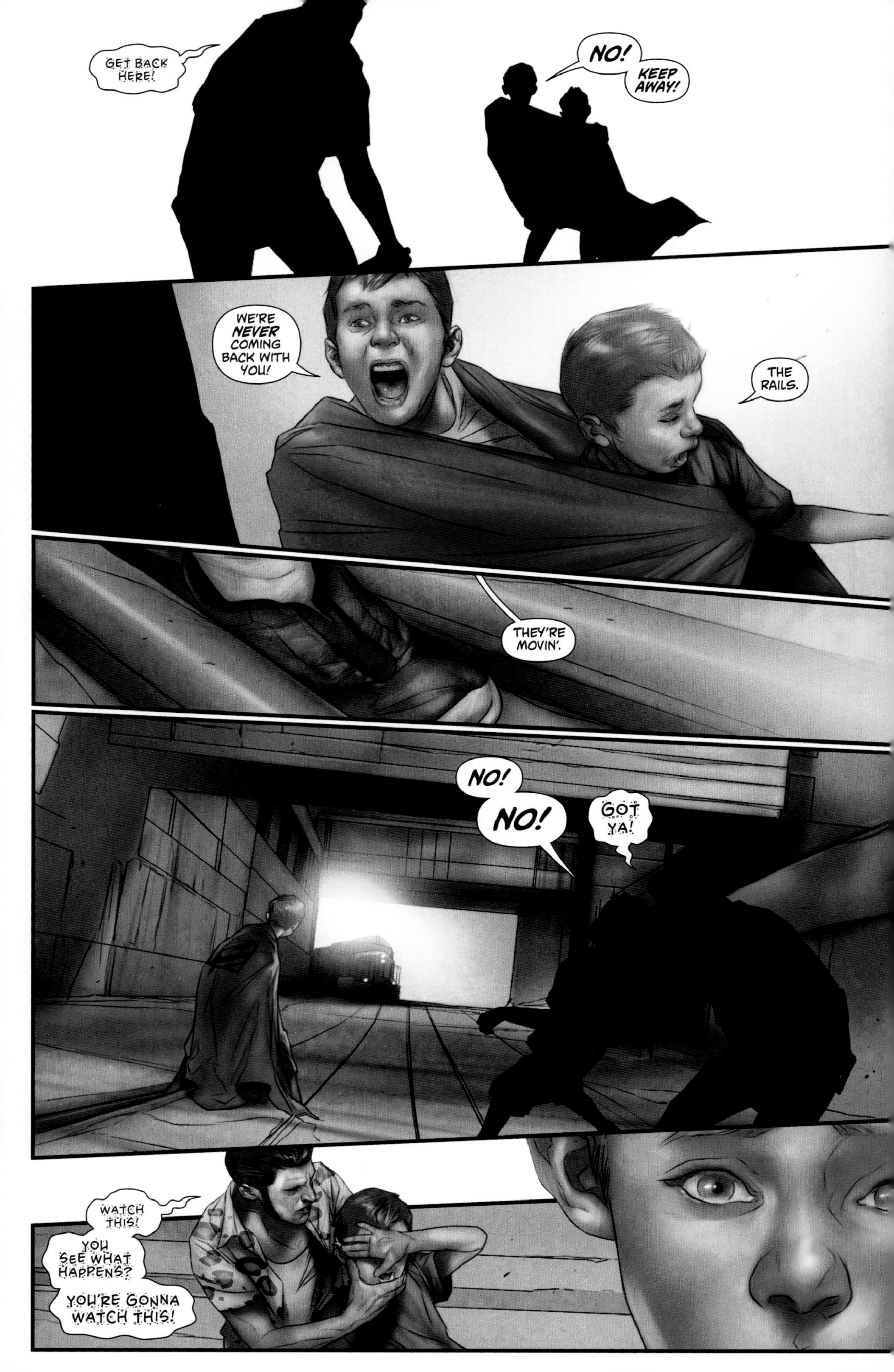
GET BACK HERE!
NO!
KEEP AWAY!
WE'RE NEVER COMING BACK WITH YOU!
THE RAILS.
THEY'RE MOVIN'.
NO!
NO!
GOT YA!
WATCH THIS!
YOU SEE WHAT HAPPENS?
YOU'RE GONNA WATCH THIS!

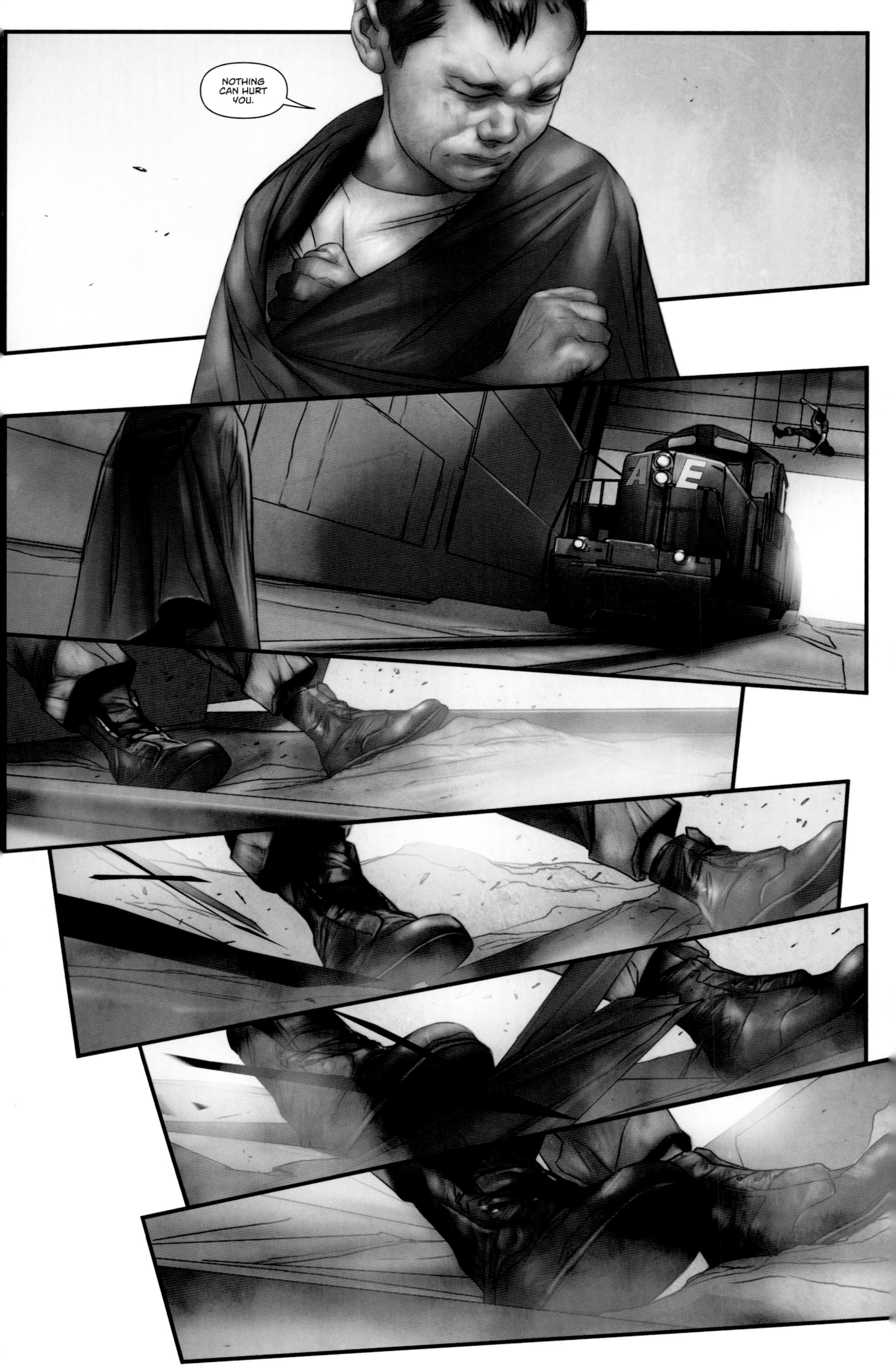
NOTHING CAN HURT YOU.

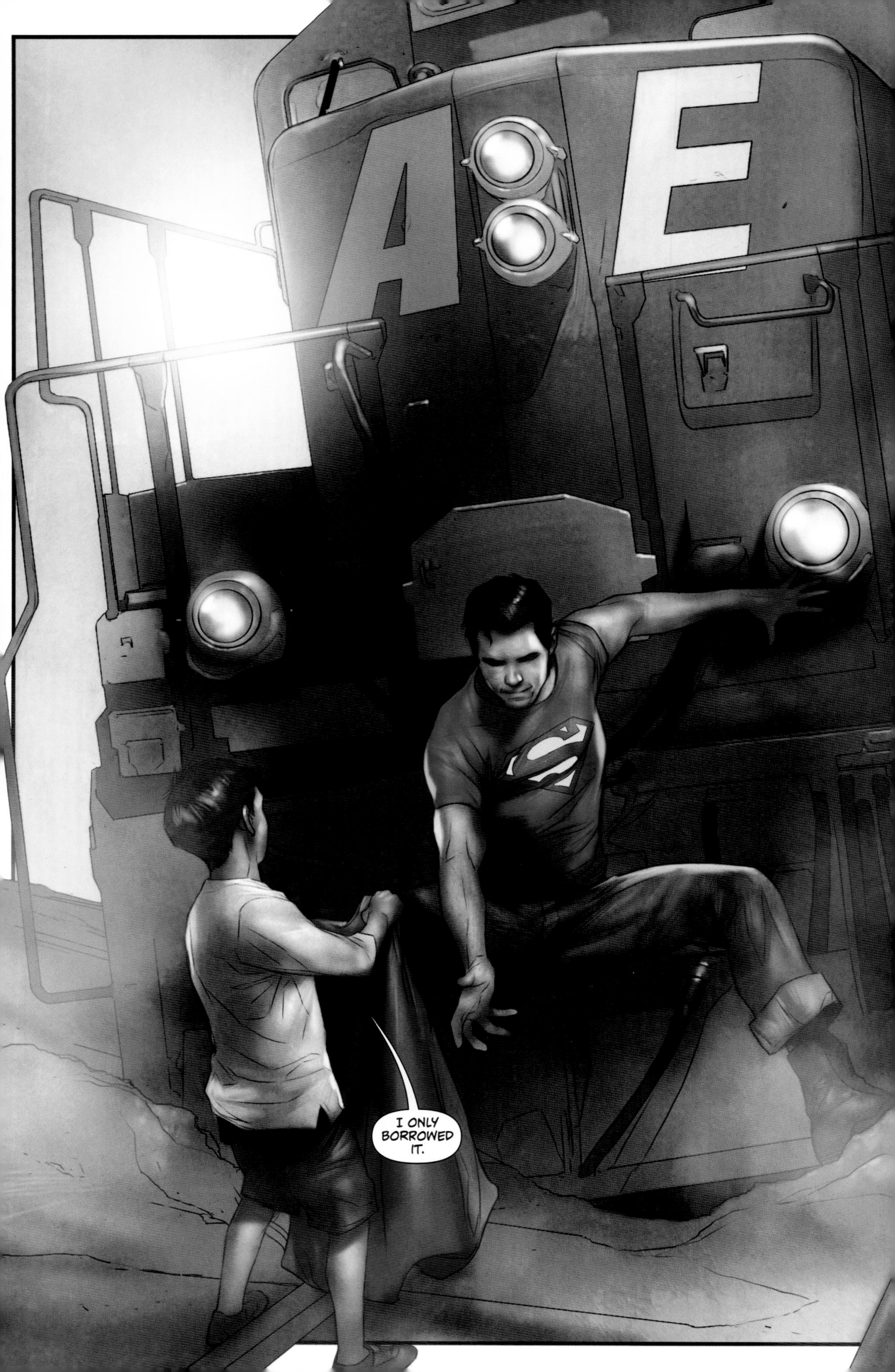
I ONLY BORROWED IT.

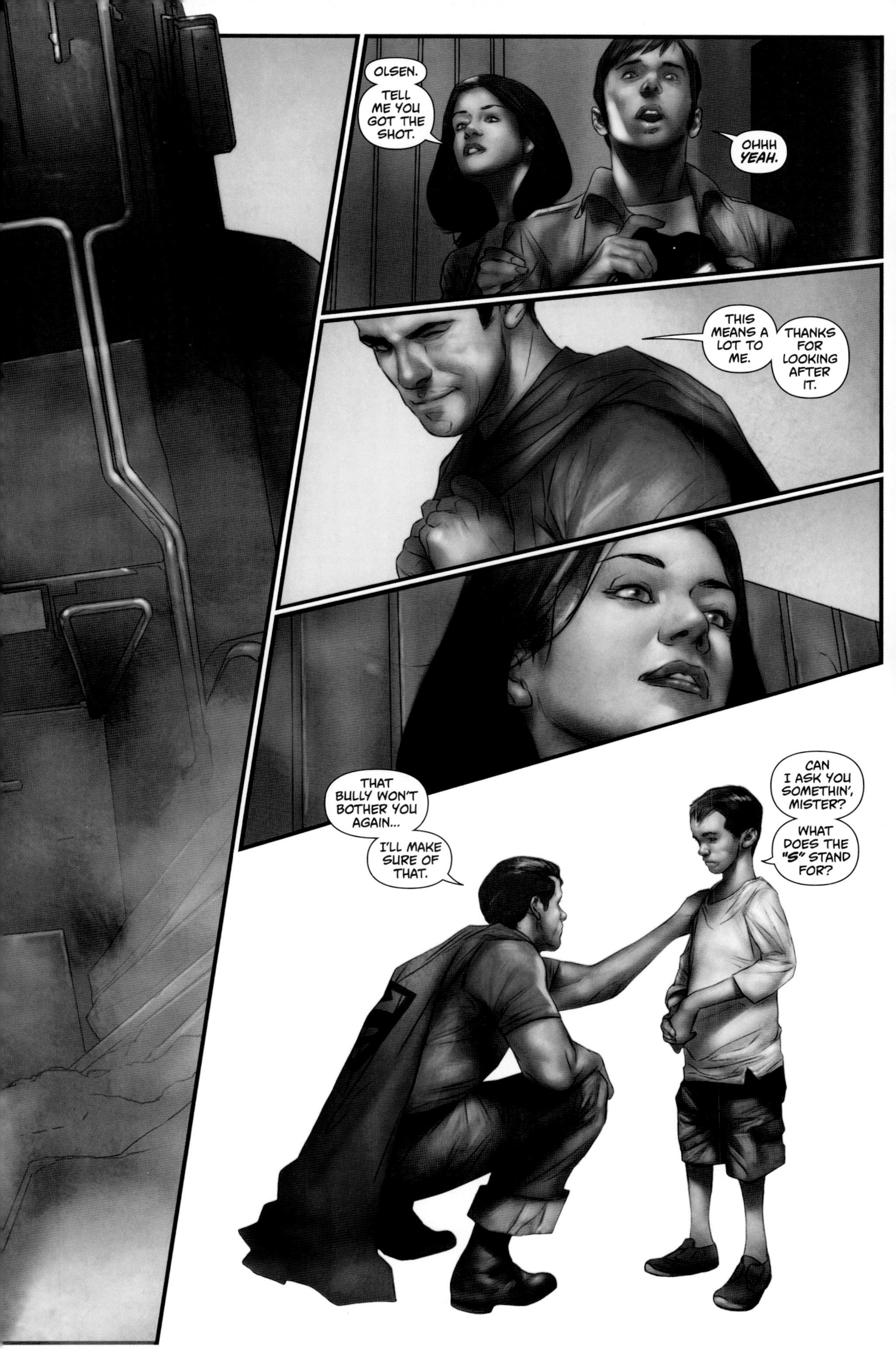
OLSEN.
TELL ME YOU GOT THE SHOT.
OHHH YEAH.
THIS MEANS A LOT TO ME.
THANKS FOR LOOKING AFTER IT.
THAT BULLY WON'T BOTHER YOU AGAIN...
I'LL MAKE SURE OF THAT.
CAN I ASK YOU SOMETHIN', MISTER?
WHAT DOES THE "S" STAND FOR?

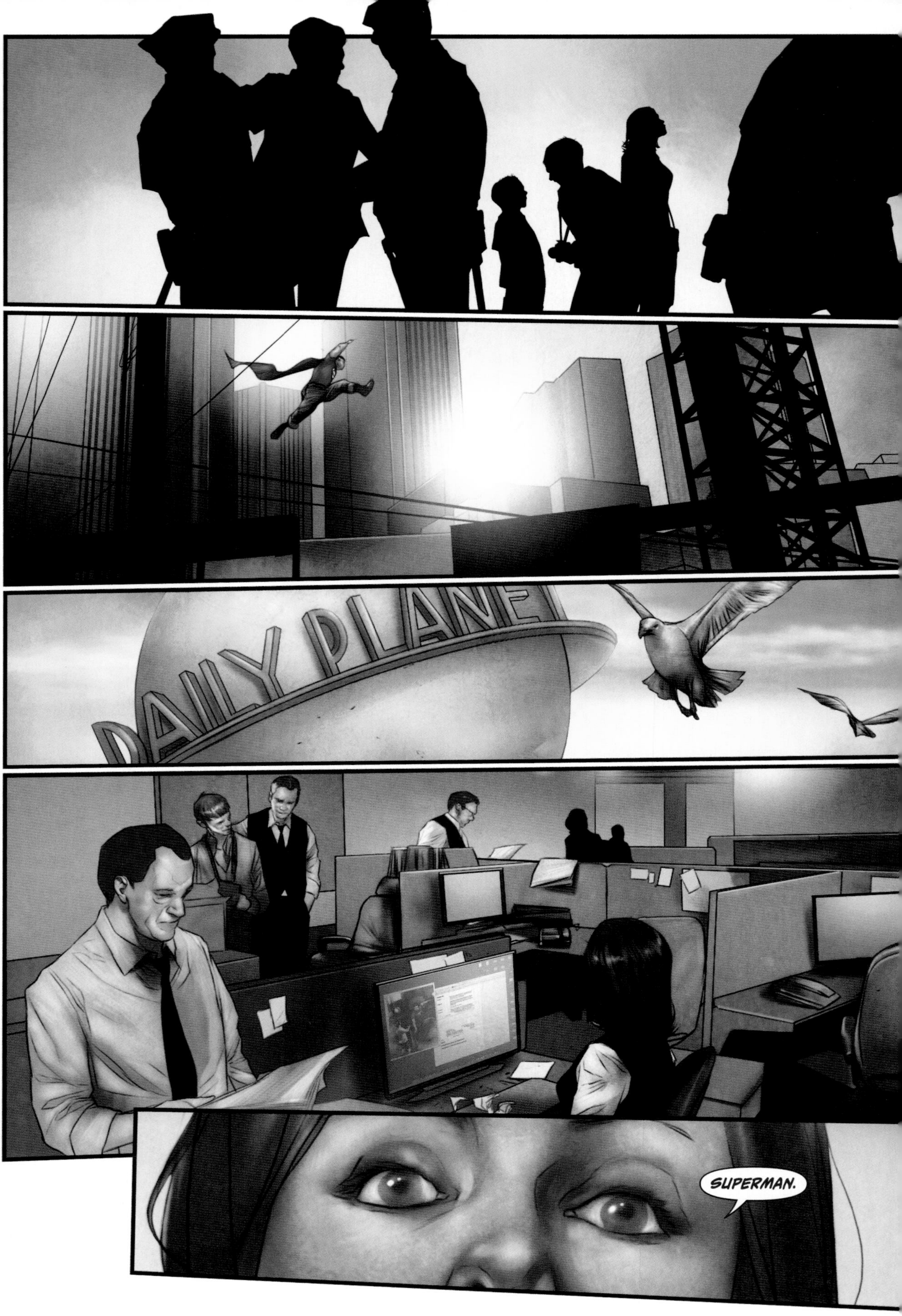
DAILY PLANET
SUPERMAN.

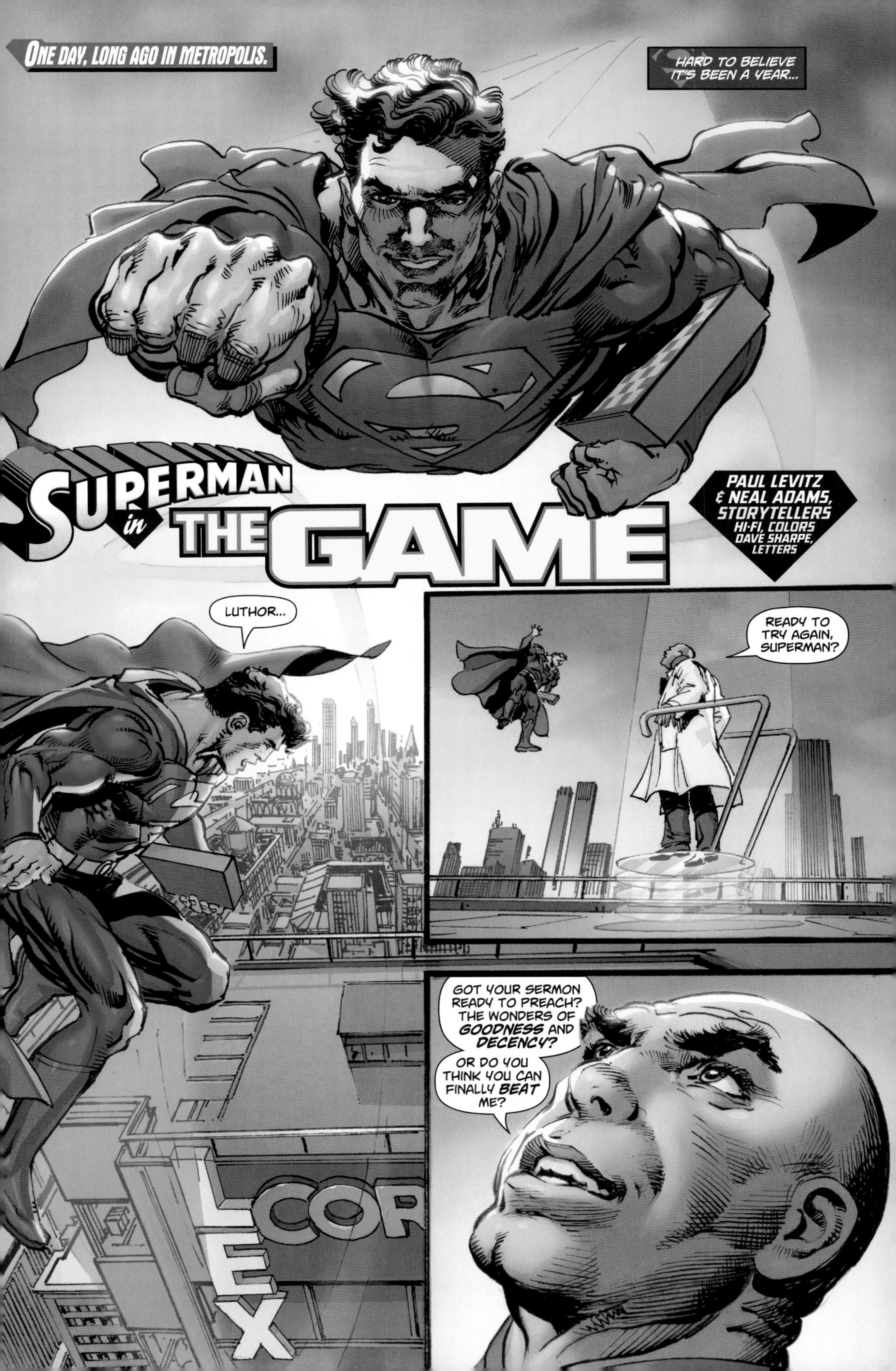
ONE DAY, LONG AGO IN METROPOLIS.
HARD TO BELIEVE IT'S BEEN A YEAR...
SUPERMAN in THE GAME
PAUL LEVITZ & NEAL ADAMS, STORYTELLERS
HI-FI, COLORS
DAVE SHARPE, LETTERS
LUTHOR...
READY TO TRY AGAIN, SUPERMAN?
GOT YOUR SERMON READY TO PREACH? THE WONDERS OF GOODNESS AND DECENCY?
OR DO YOU THINK YOU CAN FINALLY BEAT ME?
LEX COR

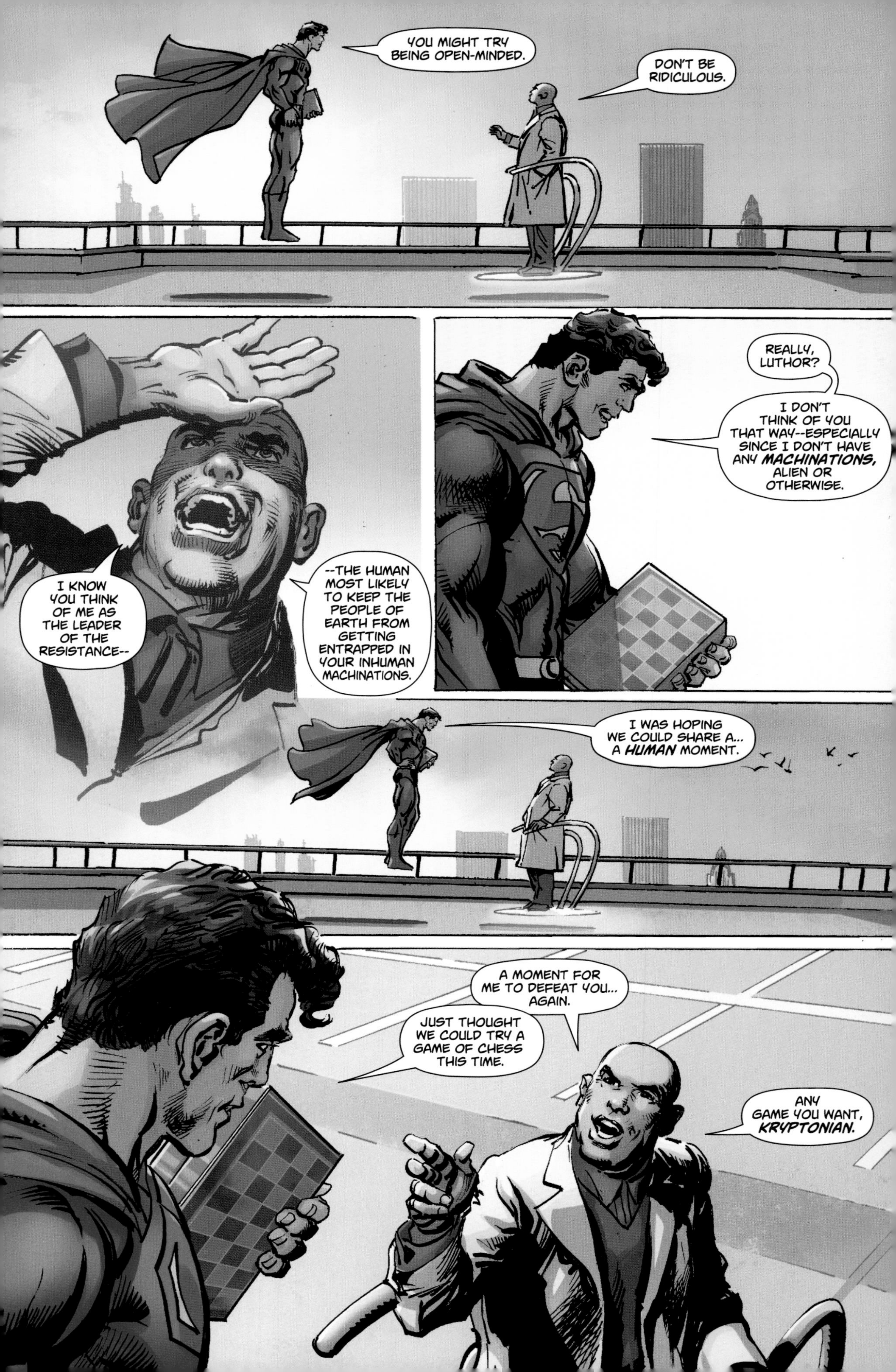

YOU MIGHT TRY BEING OPEN-MINDED.
DON'T BE RIDICULOUS.
I KNOW YOU THINK OF ME AS THE LEADER OF THE RESISTANCE--
--THE HUMAN MOST LIKELY TO KEEP THE PEOPLE OF EARTH FROM GETTING ENTRAPPED IN YOUR INHUMAN MACHINATIONS.
REALLY, LUTHOR?
I DON'T THINK OF YOU THAT WAY--ESPECIALLY SINCE I DON'T HAVE ANY MACHINATIONS, ALIEN OR OTHERWISE.
I WAS HOPING WE COULD SHARE A... A HUMAN MOMENT.
A MOMENT FOR ME TO DEFEAT YOU... AGAIN.
JUST THOUGHT WE COULD TRY A GAME OF CHESS THIS TIME.
ANY GAME YOU WANT, KRYPTONIAN.

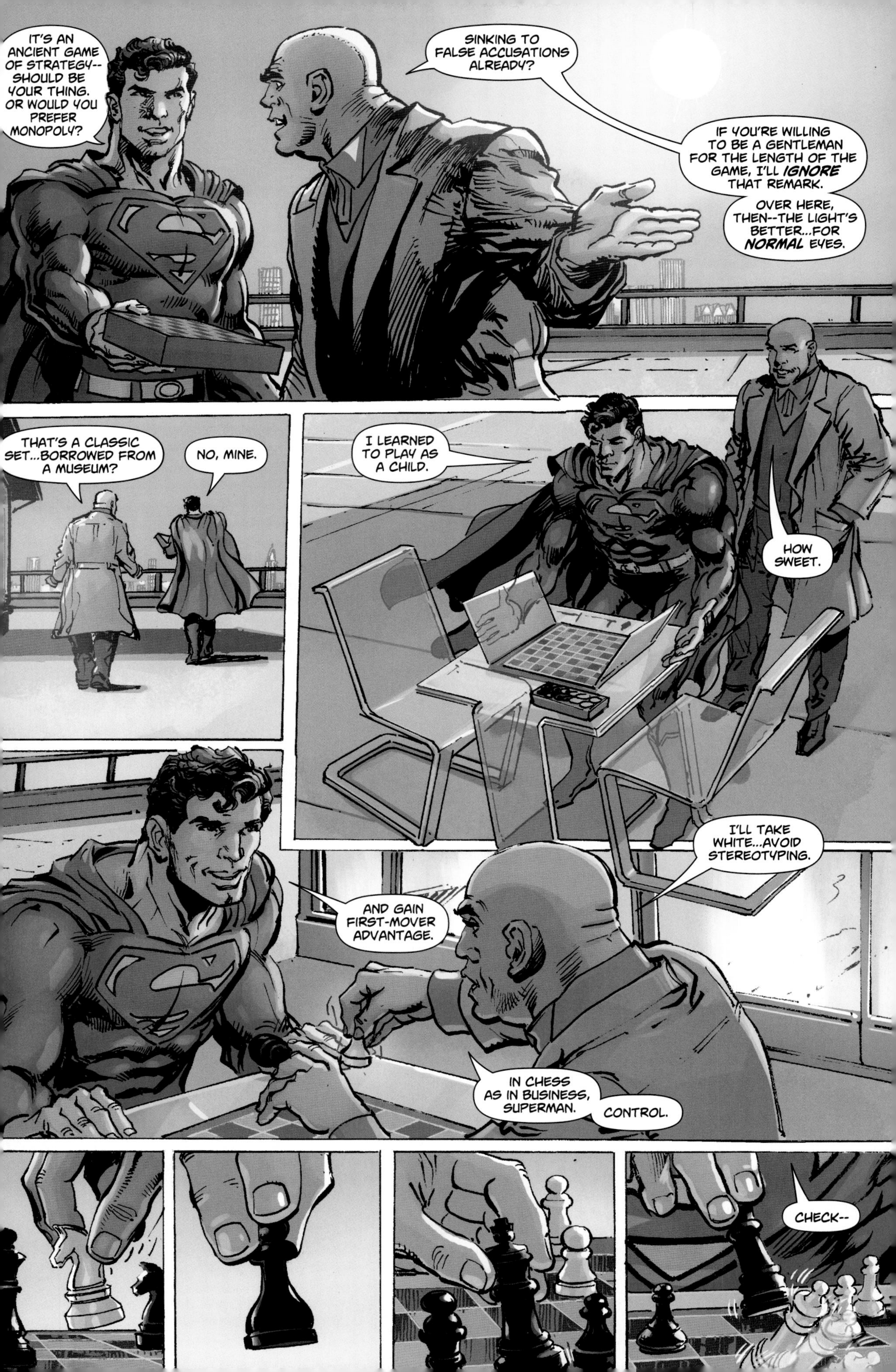
IT'S AN ANCIENT GAME OF STRATEGY-- SHOULD BE YOUR THING. OR WOULD YOU PREFER MONOPOLY?
SINKING TO FALSE ACCUSATIONS ALREADY?
IF YOU'RE WILLING TO BE A GENTLEMAN FOR THE LENGTH OF THE GAME, I'LL IGNORE THAT REMARK.
OVER HERE, THEN--THE LIGHT'S BETTER...FOR NORMAL EYES.
THAT'S A CLASSIC SET...BORROWED FROM A MUSEUM?
NO, MINE.
I LEARNED TO PLAY AS A CHILD.
HOW SWEET.
I'LL TAKE WHITE...AVOID STEREOTYPING.
AND GAIN FIRST-MOVER ADVANTAGE.
IN CHESS AS IN BUSINESS, SUPERMAN.
CONTROL.
CHECK--

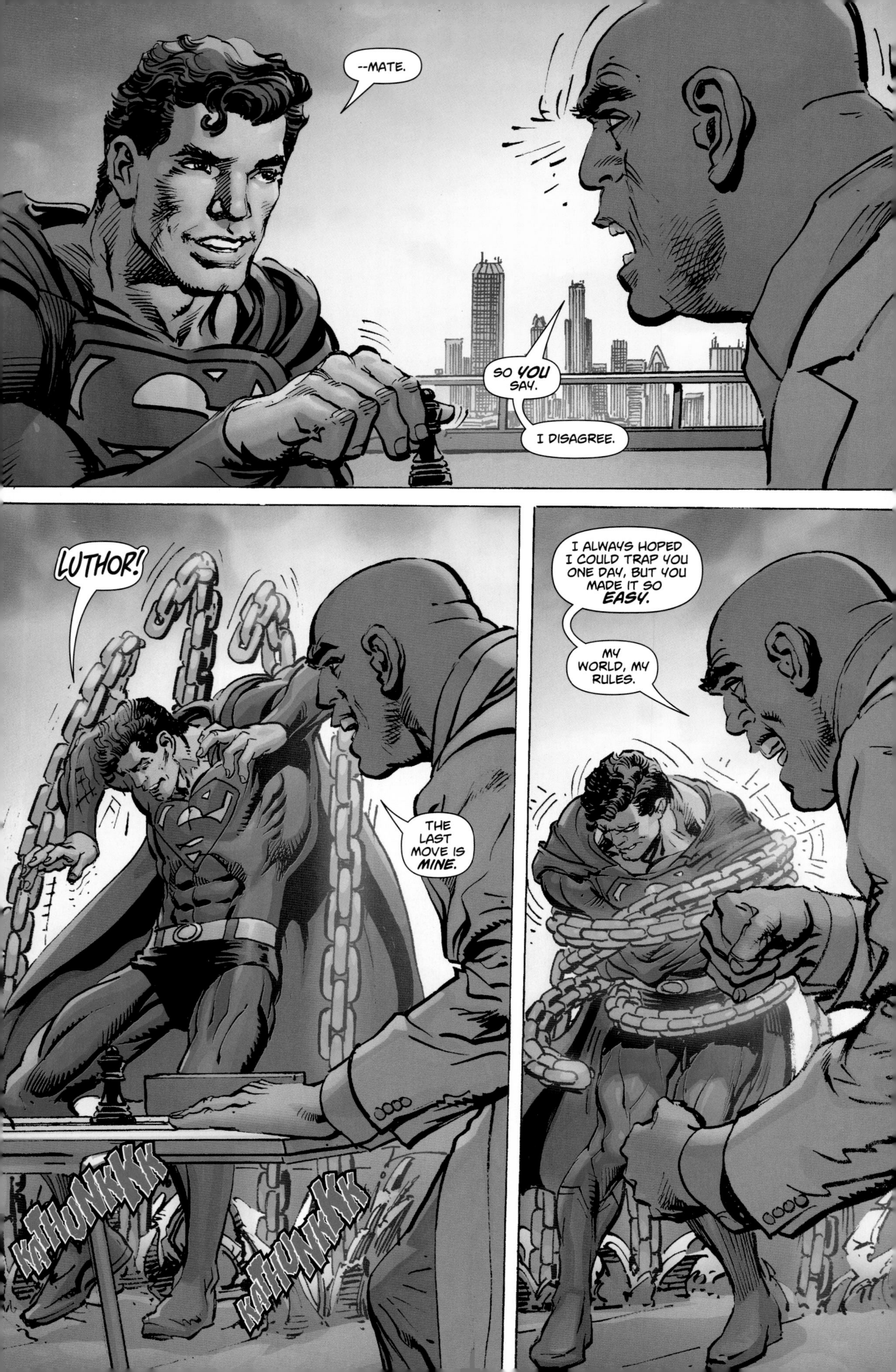
--MATE.
SO YOU SAY.
I DISAGREE.
LUTHOR!
THE LAST MOVE IS MINE.
KATHUNKKK
KATHUNKKK
I ALWAYS HOPED I COULD TRAP YOU ONE DAY, BUT YOU MADE IT SO EASY.
MY WORLD, MY RULES.

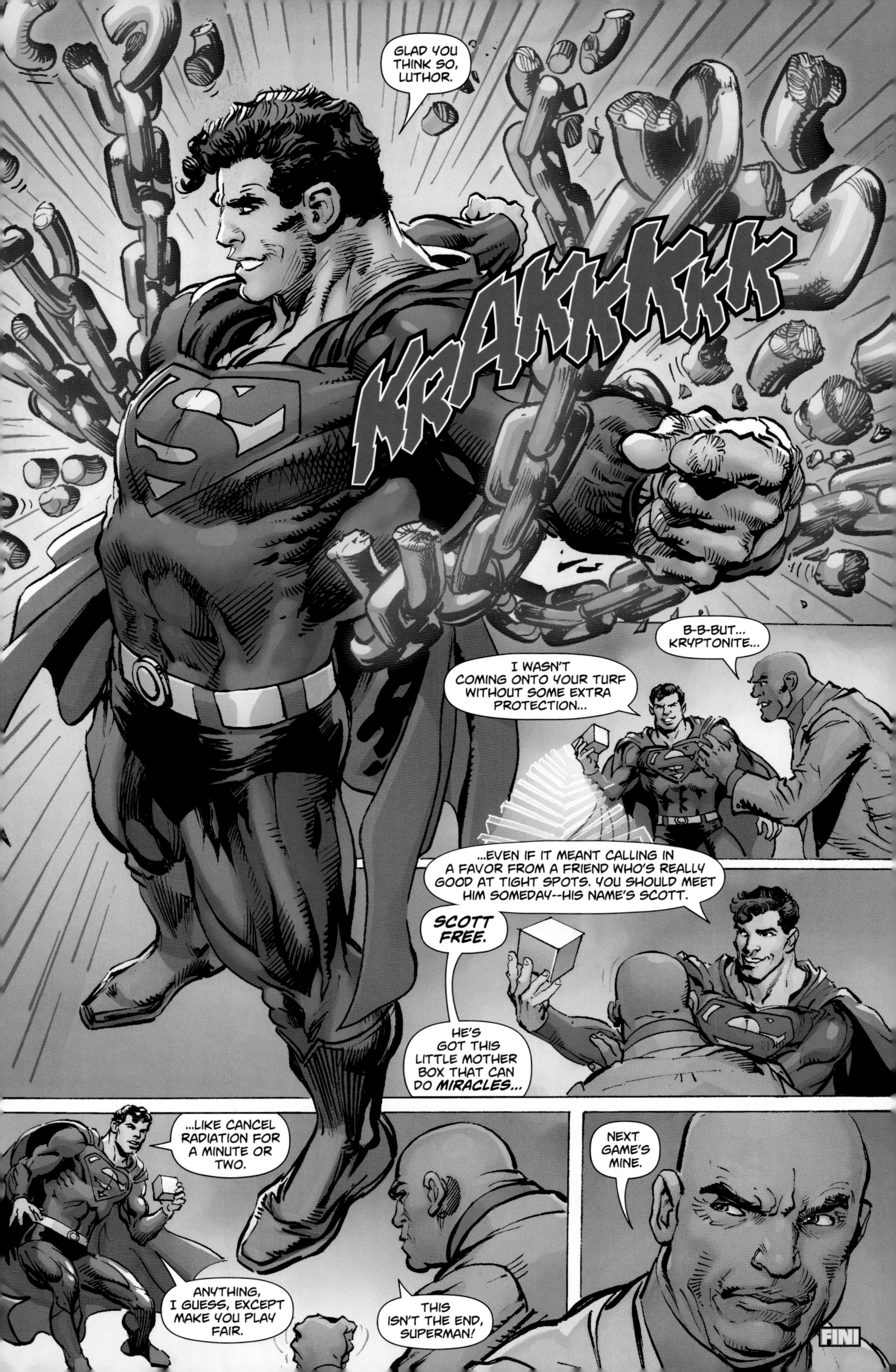
GLAD YOU THINK SO, LUTHOR.
KRAKKKKKK
B-B-BUT... KRYPTONITE...
I WASN'T COMING ONTO YOUR TURF WITHOUT SOME EXTRA PROTECTION...
...EVEN IF IT MEANT CALLING IN A FAVOR FROM A FRIEND WHO'S REALLY GOOD AT TIGHT SPOTS. YOU SHOULD MEET HIM SOMEDAY--HIS NAME'S SCOTT.
SCOTT FREE.
HE'S GOT THIS LITTLE MOTHER BOX THAT CAN DO MIRACLES...
...LIKE CANCEL RADIATION FOR A MINUTE OR TWO.
ANYTHING, I GUESS, EXCEPT MAKE YOU PLAY FAIR.
THIS ISN'T THE END, SUPERMAN!
NEXT GAME'S MINE.
FINI

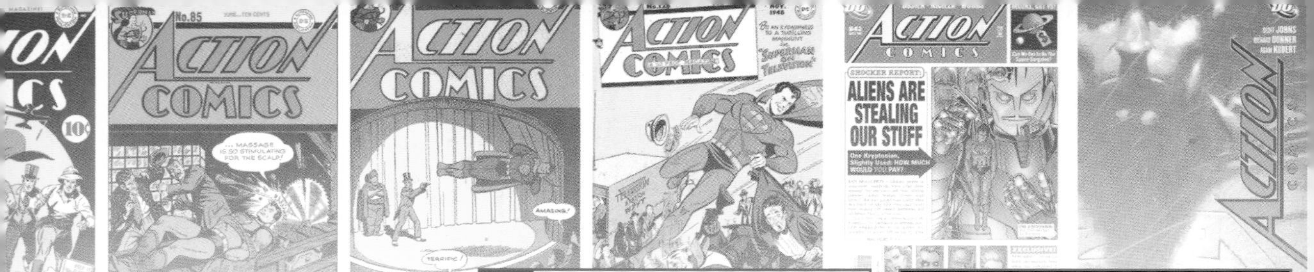
ACTION COMICS
ALIENS ARE STEALING OUR STUFF

the GOLDEN AGE

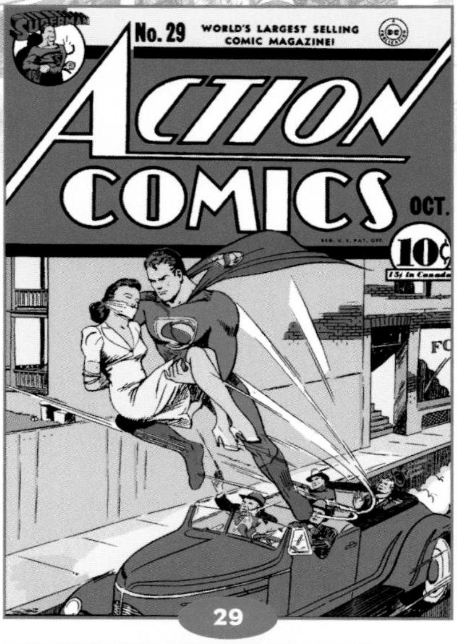
No. 29
WORLD'S LARGEST SELLING COMIC MAGAZINE!
ACTION COMICS
OCT.
10¢
15¢ in Canada

29

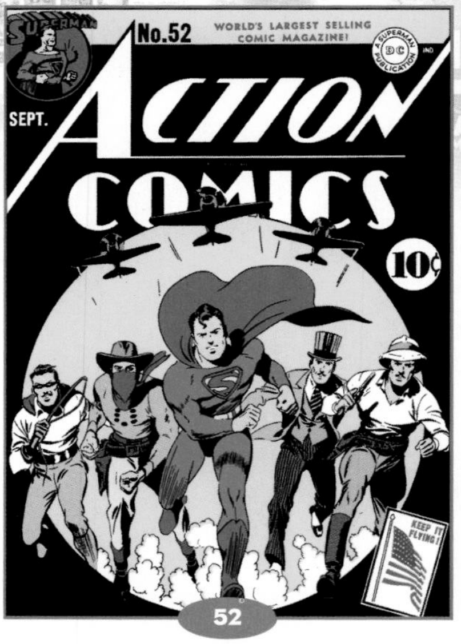
No.52
WORLD'S LARGEST SELLING COMIC MAGAZINE!
SEPT.
ACTION COMICS
10¢
KEEP IT FLYING!

52

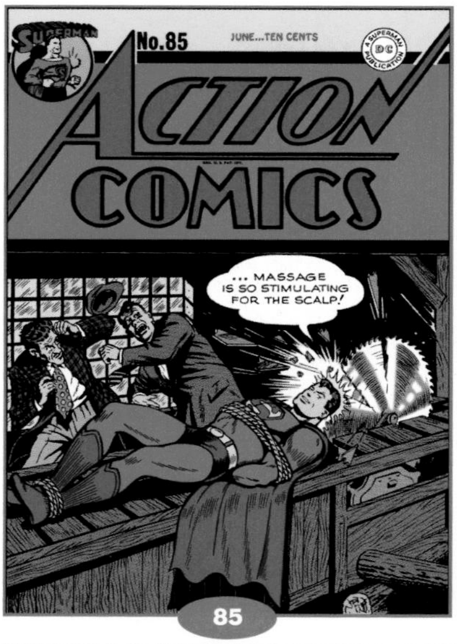
No.85
JUNE...TEN CENTS
ACTION COMICS
... MASSAGE IS SO STIMULATING FOR THE SCALP!

85

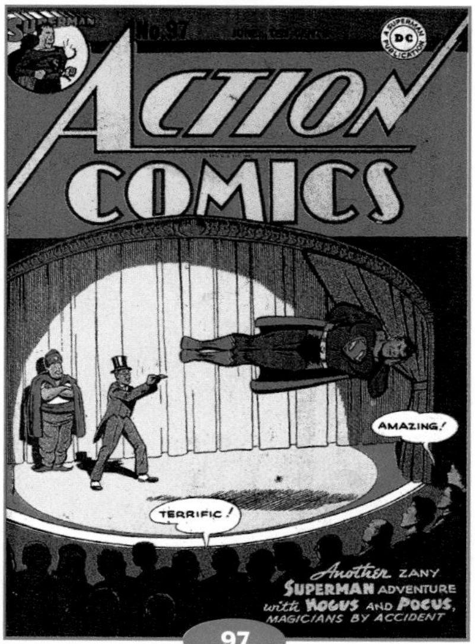
ACTION COMICS
AMAZING!
TERRIFIC!
Another ZANY SUPERMAN ADVENTURE with HOGUS AND POCUS, MAGICIANS BY ACCIDENT

97

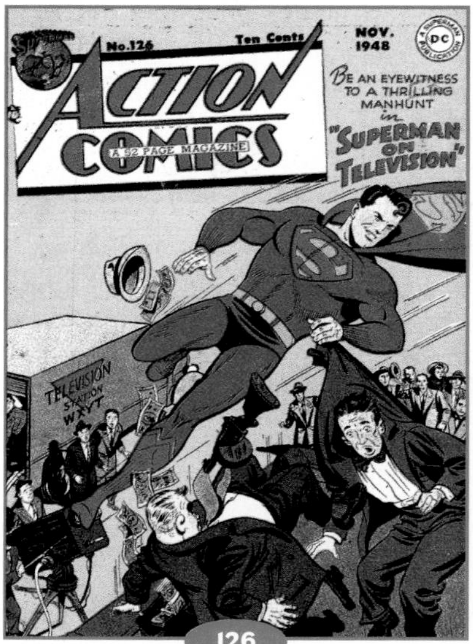
No.126
Ten Cents
NOV. 1948
ACTION COMICS
A 52 PAGE MAGAZINE
BE AN EYEWITNESS TO A THRILLING MANHUNT in "SUPERMAN ON TELEVISION"
TELEVISION STATION WXYT

126

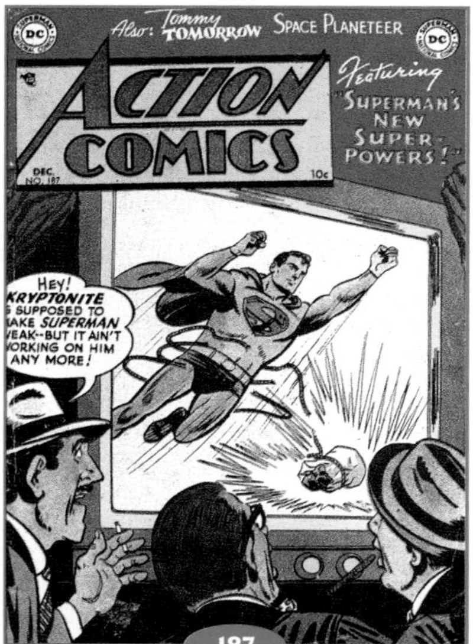
Also: Tommy TOMORROW SPACE PLANETEER
ACTION COMICS
Featuring "SUPERMAN'S NEW SUPER-POWERS!"
DEC. NO. 187
10¢

187

Moments from the Golden Age: Superman's first cover rescue of Lois (by **Wayne Boring**); the stars of the ACTION anthology rushing at us (**Fred Ray**); the covers getting more humorous (**Jack Burnley**); the last cover by **Joe Shuster**; a prophetic view of Superman conquering a new medium (**Al Plastino**); and an early moment of increasing super-mythology (**Win Mortimer**). Boring and Plastino would vie to be the definitive Superman artist after Shuster.

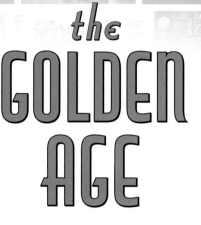

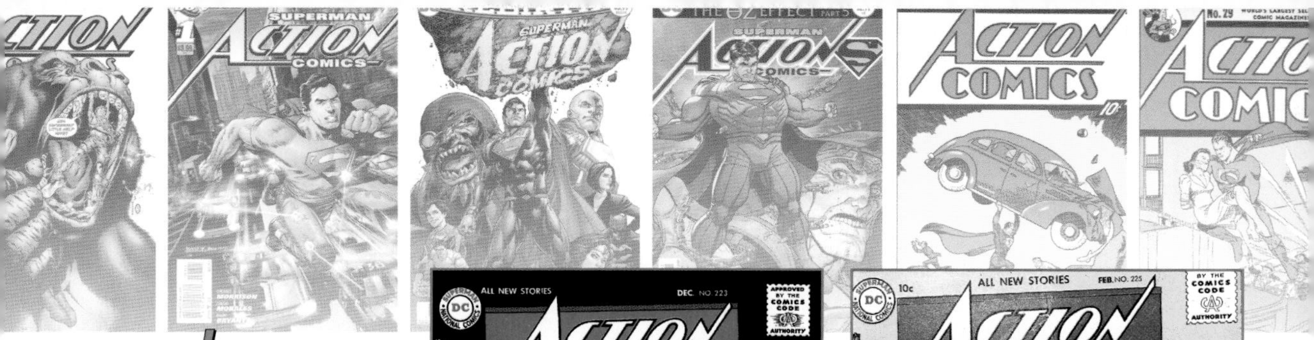

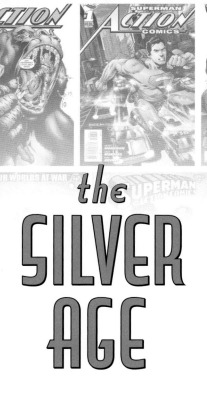

the SILVER AGE

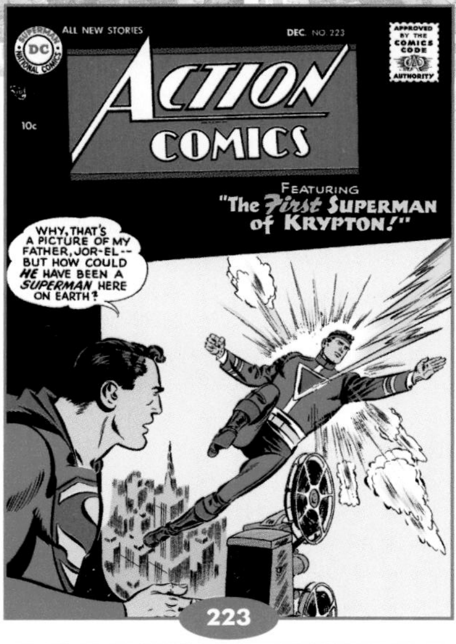
ALL NEW STORIES
DEC. NO. 223
APPROVED BY THE COMICS CODE AUTHORITY
10¢
ACTION COMICS
FEATURING "The First SUPERMAN of KRYPTON!"
WHY, THAT'S A PICTURE OF MY FATHER, JOR-EL-- BUT HOW COULD HE HAVE BEEN A SUPERMAN HERE ON EARTH?

223

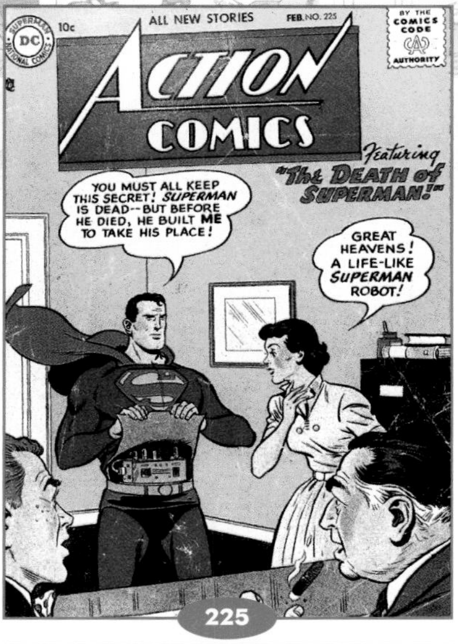
10¢
ALL NEW STORIES
FEB. NO. 225
BY THE COMICS CODE AUTHORITY
ACTION COMICS
Featuring "The DEATH of SUPERMAN!"
YOU MUST ALL KEEP THIS SECRET! SUPERMAN IS DEAD--BUT BEFORE HE DIED, HE BUILT ME TO TAKE HIS PLACE!
GREAT HEAVENS! A LIFE-LIKE SUPERMAN ROBOT!

225

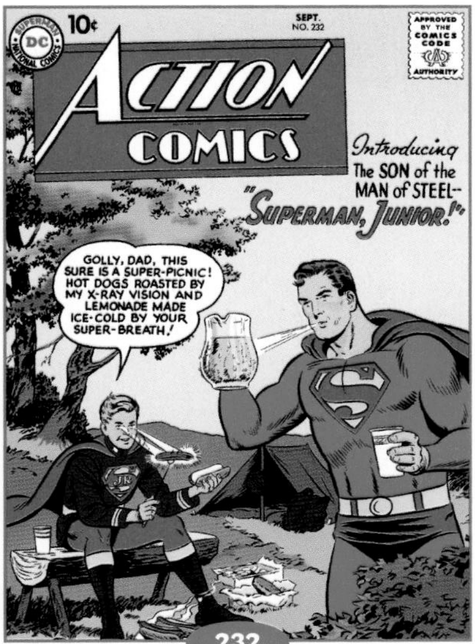
10¢
SEPT. NO. 232
APPROVED BY THE COMICS CODE AUTHORITY
ACTION COMICS
Introducing The SON of the MAN of STEEL-- "SUPERMAN, JUNIOR!"
GOLLY, DAD, THIS SURE IS A SUPER-PICNIC! HOT DOGS ROASTED BY MY X-RAY VISION AND LEMONADE MADE ICE-COLD BY YOUR SUPER-BREATH!

232

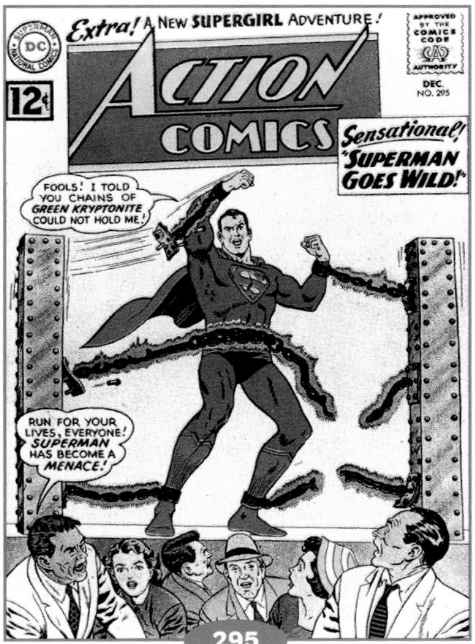
Extra! A NEW SUPERGIRL ADVENTURE!
APPROVED BY THE COMICS CODE AUTHORITY
12¢
DEC. NO. 295
ACTION COMICS
Sensational! "SUPERMAN GOES WILD!"
FOOLS! I TOLD YOU CHAINS OF GREEN KRYPTONITE COULD NOT HOLD ME!
RUN FOR YOUR LIVES, EVERYONE! SUPERMAN HAS BECOME A MENACE!

295

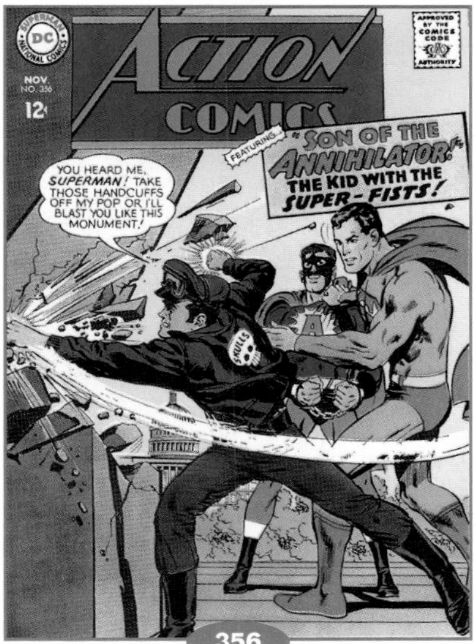
APPROVED BY THE COMICS CODE AUTHORITY
NOV. NO. 356
12¢
ACTION COMICS
FEATURING "SON OF THE ANNIHILATOR!" THE KID WITH THE SUPER-FISTS!
YOU HEARD ME, SUPERMAN! TAKE THOSE HANDCUFFS OFF MY POP OR I'LL BLAST YOU LIKE THIS MONUMENT!

356

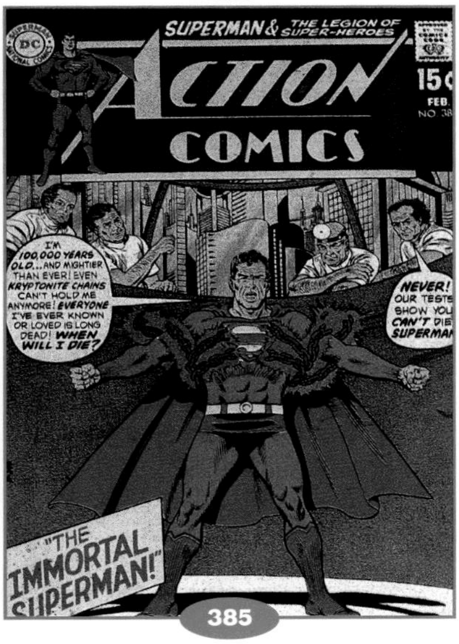
SUPERMAN & THE LEGION OF SUPER-HEROES
ACTION COMICS
15¢
FEB.
I'M 100,000 YEARS OLD...AND MIGHTIER THAN EVER! EVEN KRYPTONITE CHAINS CAN'T HOLD ME ANYMORE! EVERYONE I'VE EVER KNOWN OR LOVED IS LONG DEAD! WHEN WILL I DIE?
NEVER! OUR TESTS SHOW YOU CAN'T DIE SUPERMAN
"THE IMMORTAL SUPERMAN!"

385

Moments from the Silver Age: a prescient look at Krypton's past (Boring/**Stan Kaye**); a death that didn't become a media event (Plastino); the cover debut of **Curt Swan**, the dominant Superman artist for a generation (Swan/Kaye); an early Kryptonite-chains cover (Swan/Klein); the cover debut of the inimitable **Neal Adams** as art director **Carmine Infantino** begins a decade of designing DC covers; and chains once more (Swan/**Murphy Anderson**).

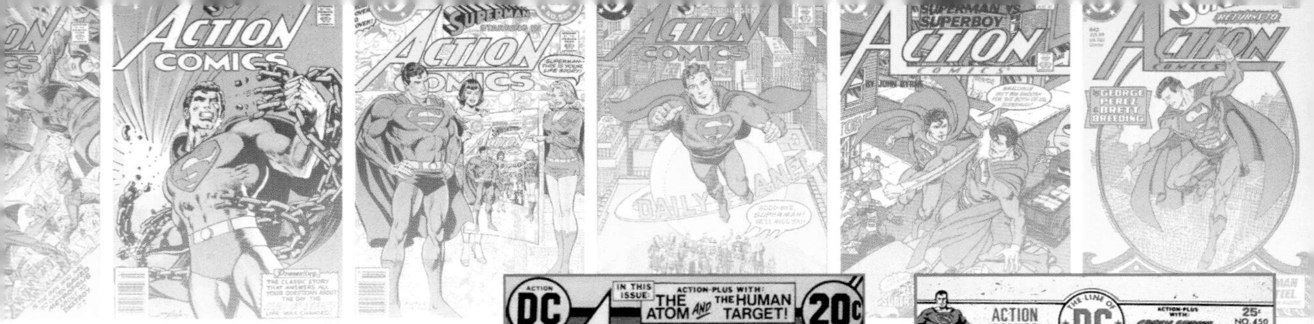

the BRONZE AGE

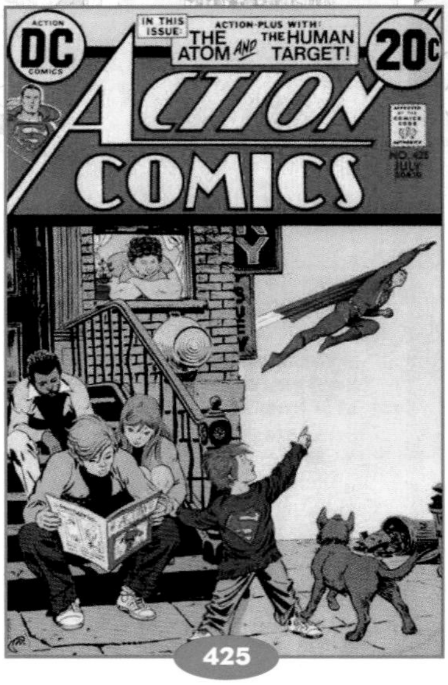
DC COMICS
IN THIS ISSUE:
ACTION-PLUS WITH: THE ATOM AND THE HUMAN TARGET!
20¢
ACTION COMICS
425

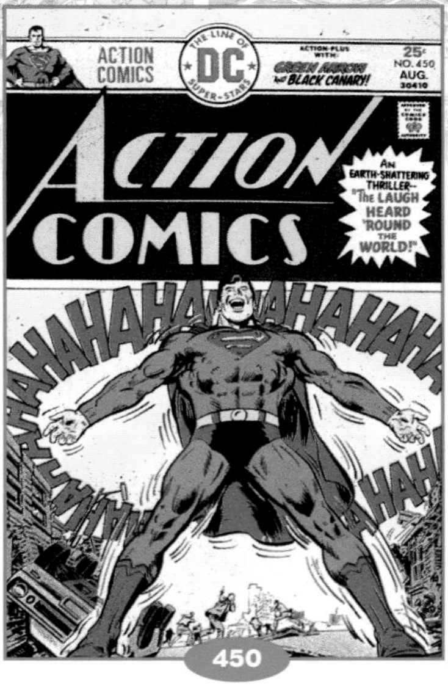
ACTION COMICS
THE LINE OF DC SUPER-STARS
ACTION-PLUS WITH: GREEN ARROW and BLACK CANARY!
25¢ NO. 450 AUG.
AN EARTH-SHATTERING THRILLER— "The LAUGH HEARD 'ROUND THE WORLD!"
HAHAHAHA
450

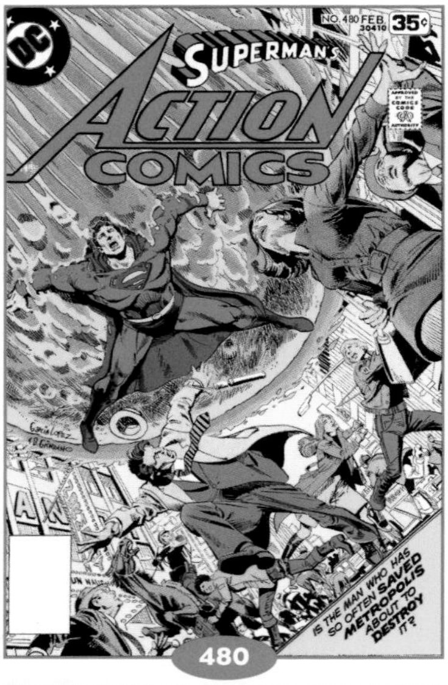
NO. 480 FEB. 35¢
SUPERMAN'S ACTION COMICS
IS THE MAN WHO HAS SO OFTEN SAVED METROPOLIS ABOUT TO DESTROY IT?
480

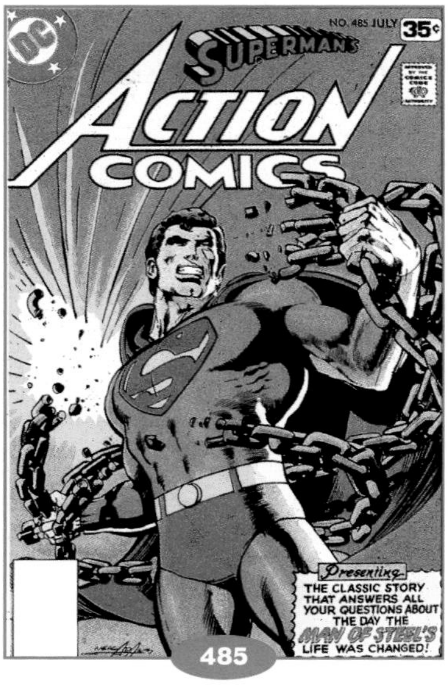
NO. 485 JULY 35¢
SUPERMAN'S ACTION COMICS
Presenting: THE CLASSIC STORY THAT ANSWERS ALL YOUR QUESTIONS ABOUT THE DAY THE MAN OF STEEL'S LIFE WAS CHANGED!
485

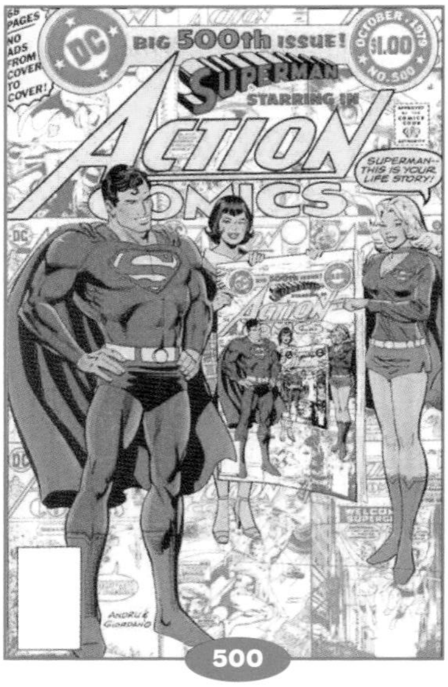
BIG 500th ISSUE!
$1.00 NO. 500
SUPERMAN STARRING IN ACTION COMICS
SUPERMAN— THIS IS YOUR LIFE STORY!
NO ADS FROM COVER TO COVER!
500

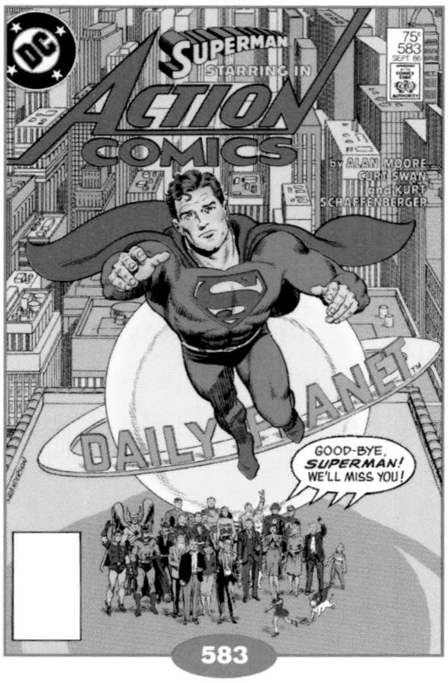
SUPERMAN STARRING IN ACTION COMICS
75¢ 583
by ALAN MOORE, CURT SWAN and KURT SCHAFFENBERGER
DAILY PLANET
GOOD-BYE, SUPERMAN! WE'LL MISS YOU!
583

Moments from the Bronze Age: **Nick Cardy** often depicted charming kids on his covers; a moment of laughter (**Bob Oksner**); a dramatic moment by the artists who would do a generation's Superman merchandise (**José Luis García-López/Dick Giordano**); Neal Adams does chains, though not his most famous cover of Superman with them; the first ACTION cover to celebrate a commemorative issue (**Ross Andru/** Giordano); and the issue that ended an era of mythology (Swan/Anderson)

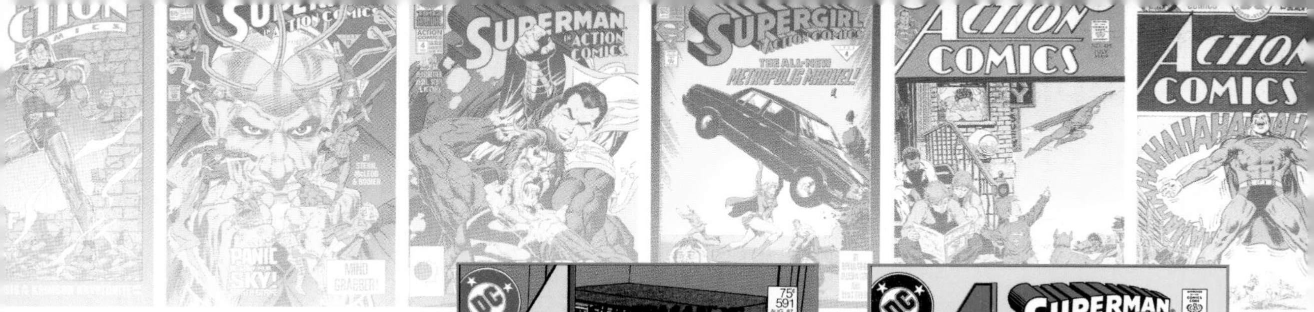

the DARK AGE

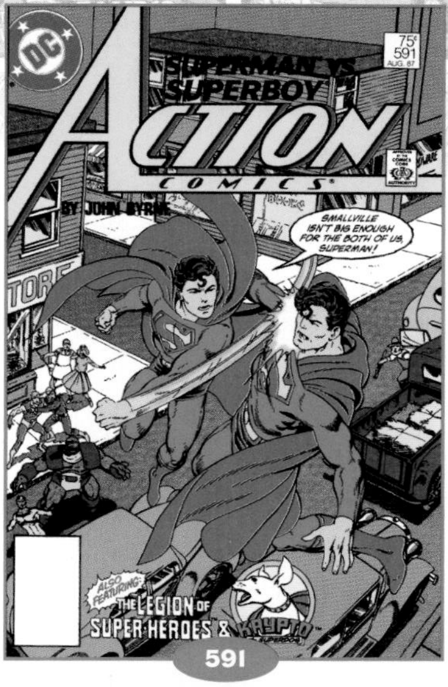

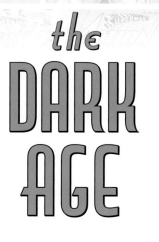

SUPERMAN VS. SUPERBOY
ACTION COMICS
75¢ 591 AUG. 87
BY JOHN BYRNE
SMALLVILLE ISN'T BIG ENOUGH FOR THE BOTH OF US, SUPERMAN!
ALSO FEATURING: THE LEGION OF SUPER-HEROES & KRYPTO

591

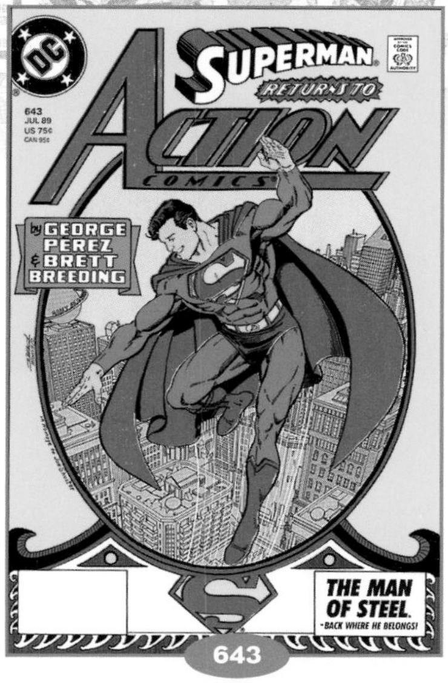

SUPERMAN RETURNS TO ACTION COMICS
643 JUL 89 US 75¢
by GEORGE PEREZ & BRETT BREEDING
THE MAN OF STEEL. BACK WHERE HE BELONGS!

643

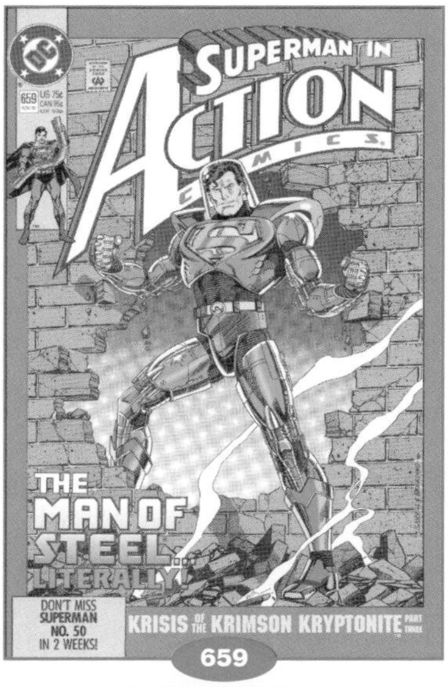

SUPERMAN IN ACTION COMICS
659 US 75¢
THE MAN OF STEEL... LITERALLY!
DON'T MISS SUPERMAN NO. 50 IN 2 WEEKS!
KRISIS OF THE KRIMSON KRYPTONITE PART THREE

659

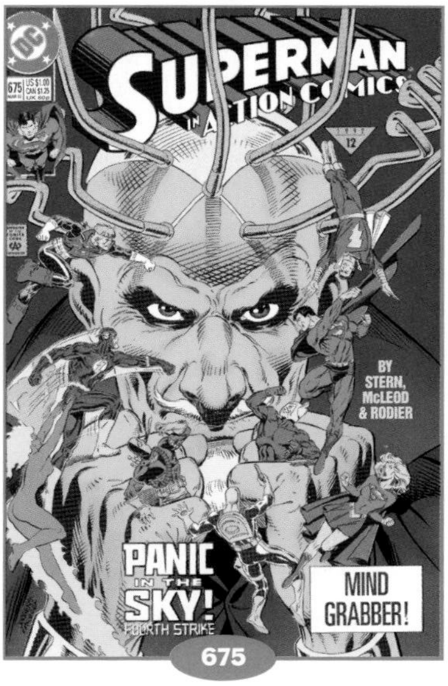

SUPERMAN IN ACTION COMICS
675 US $1.00
BY STERN, McLEOD & RODIER
PANIC IN THE SKY! FOURTH STRIKE
MIND GRABBER!

675

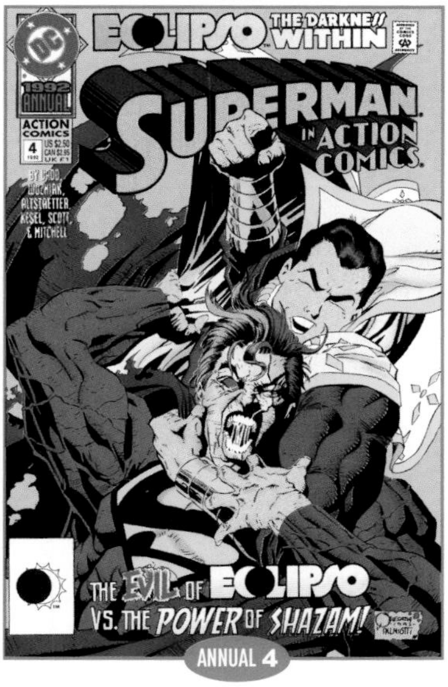

ECLIPSO THE DARKNESS WITHIN
1992 ANNUAL
SUPERMAN IN ACTION COMICS
ACTION COMICS 4
THE EVIL OF ECLIPSO VS. THE POWER OF SHAZAM!

ANNUAL 4

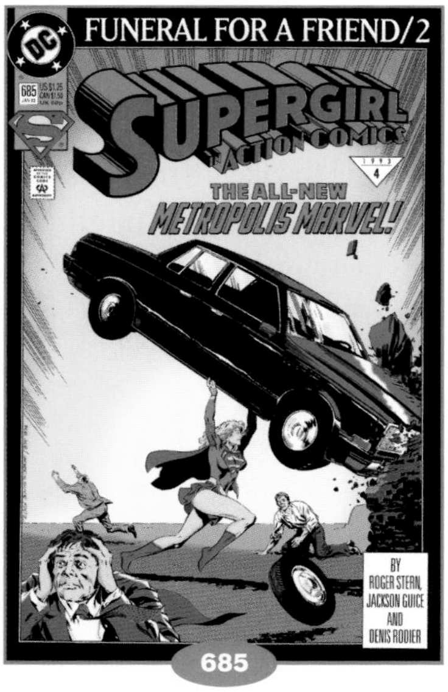

FUNERAL FOR A FRIEND/2
SUPERGIRL IN ACTION COMICS
685
THE ALL-NEW METROPOLIS MARVEL!
BY ROGER STERN, JACKSON GUICE AND DENIS RODIER

685

Moments from the Dark Age: **John Byrne** remakes Superman; **George Pérez** pays homage to SUPERMAN #1; a very metallic Man of Steel (**Kerry Gammill/Brett Breeding**); Brainiac for a new era (**Dan Jurgens**); the only ACTION cover by Marvel chief creative officer **Joe Quesada** (and **Jimmy Palmiotti**); and the death tale everyone read (**Jackson Guice**).

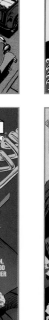

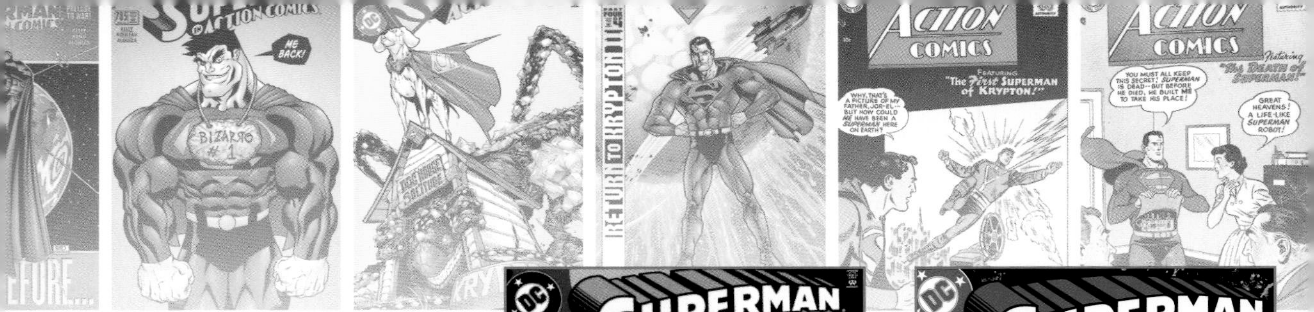

the MODERN AGE

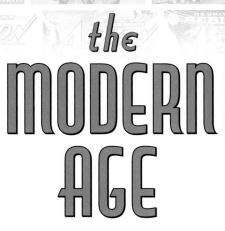

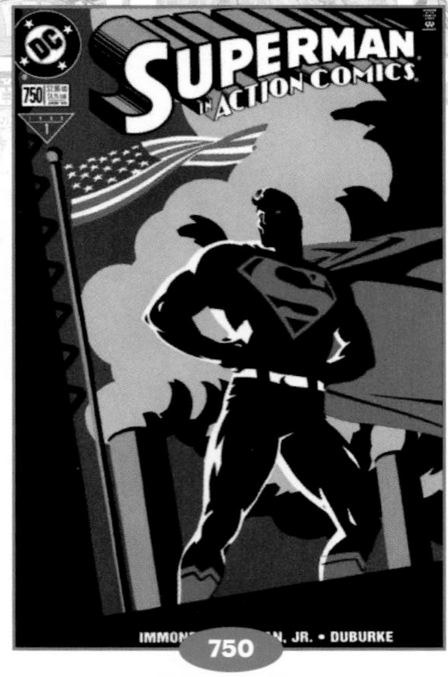
SUPERMAN
IN ACTION COMICS
750
750

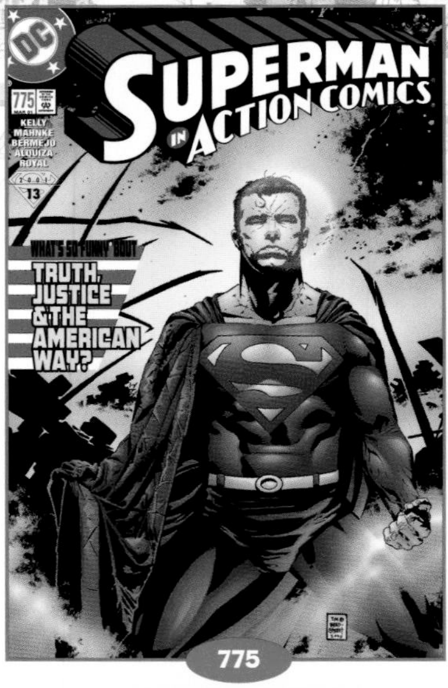
SUPERMAN
IN ACTION COMICS
775
KELLY
MAHNKE
BERMEJO
ALQUIZA
ROYAL
WHAT'S SO FUNNY 'BOUT
TRUTH, JUSTICE & THE AMERICAN WAY?
775

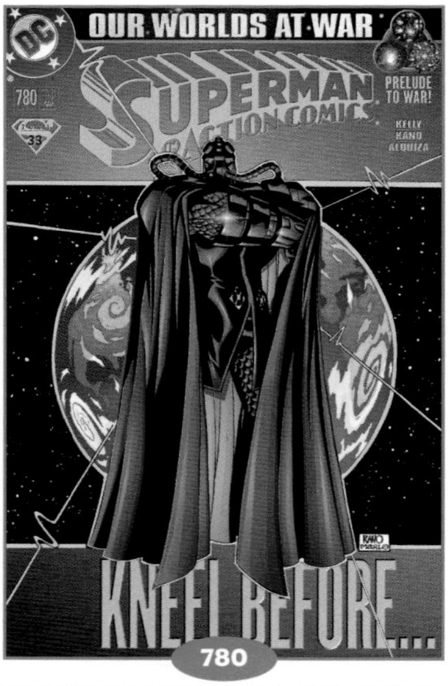
OUR WORLDS AT WAR
SUPERMAN
IN ACTION COMICS
780
PRELUDE TO WAR!
KELLY
KANO
ALQUIZA
KNEEL BEFORE...
780

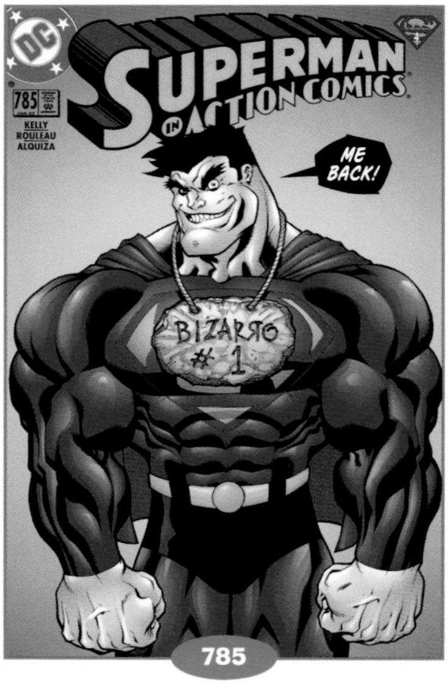
SUPERMAN
IN ACTION COMICS
785
KELLY
ROULEAU
ALQUIZA
ME BACK!
BIZARRO #1
785

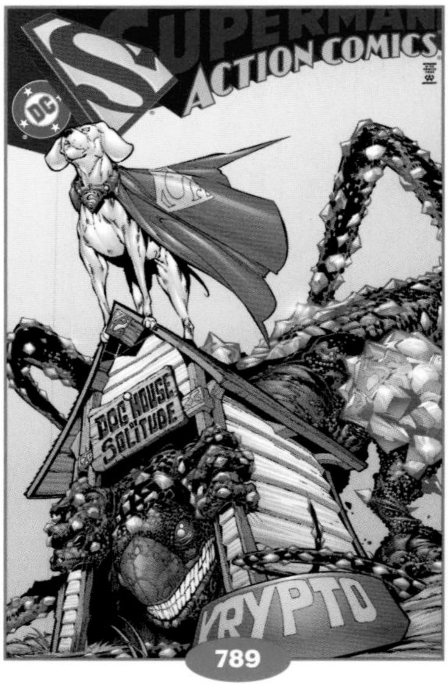
SUPERMAN
ACTION COMICS
DOG HOUSE OF SOLITUDE
KRYPTO
789

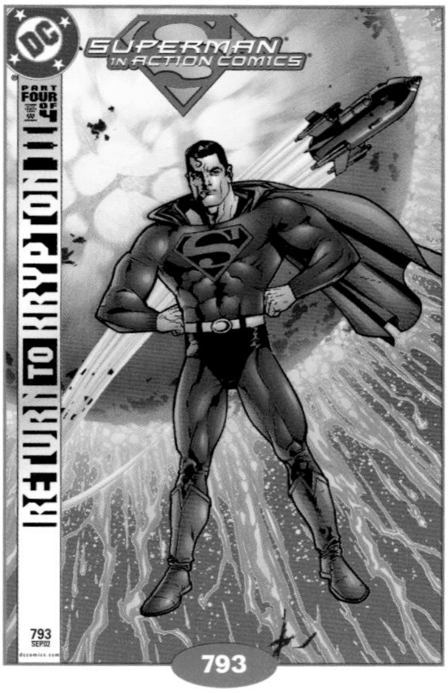
SUPERMAN
IN ACTION COMICS
PART FOUR OF 4
RETURN TO KRYPTON II
793
793

Moments from the Modern Age: Superman and the flag (**Stuart Immonen/Jose Marzan Jr.**); as well as his classic motto (**Timothy Bradstreet**); an example of the story arc emerging as a subtitle (**Jose Angel Cano Lopez/Marlo Alquiza**); Bizarro never dies (**Ed McGuinness/Cam Smith**); Krypto finally gets a solo cover (**Duncan Rouleau**/Alquiza); and another journey to Krypton (**Kilian Plunkett**).

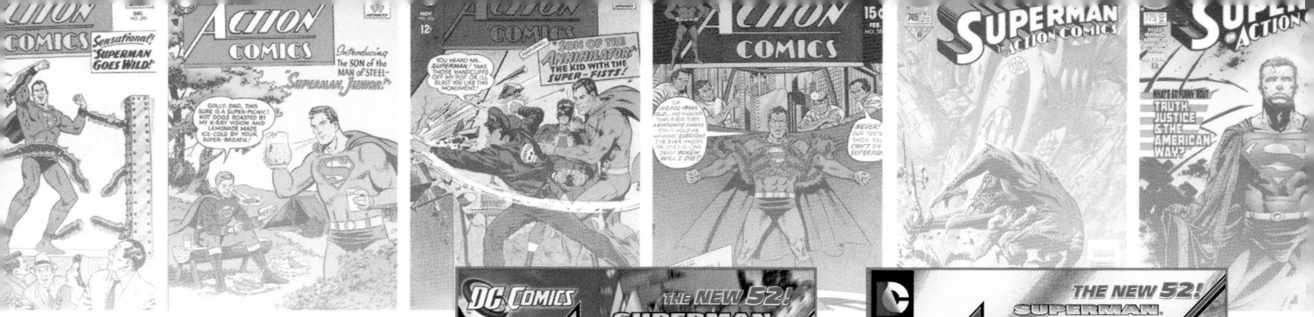
ACTION COMICS
Sensational! "Superman Goes Wild!"
Introducing The SON of the MAN of STEEL— "Superman, Junior!"
GOLLY, DAD, THIS SURE IS A SUPER-PICNIC! HOT DOGS ROASTED BY MY X-RAY VISION AND LEMONADE MADE ICE-COLD BY YOUR SUPER-BREATH!
SON OF THE ANNIHILATOR! THE KID WITH THE SUPER-FISTS!
SUPERMAN ACTION COMICS
WHAT'S SO FUNNY 'BOUT TRUTH, JUSTICE & THE AMERICAN WAY?

now

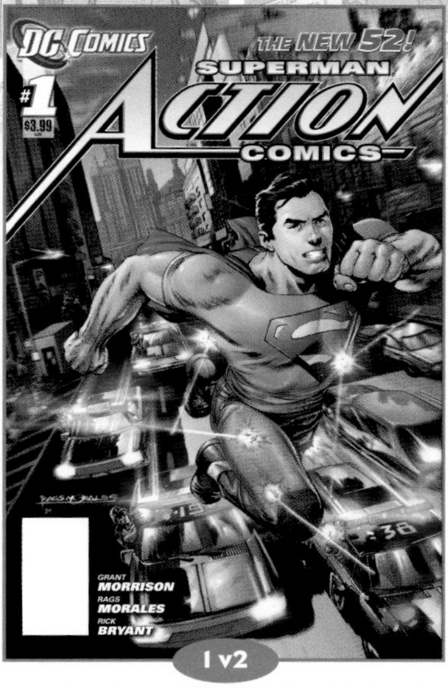
DC COMICS
THE NEW 52!
SUPERMAN
ACTION COMICS
#1
$3.99
GRANT MORRISON
RAGS MORALES
RICK BRYANT

1 v2

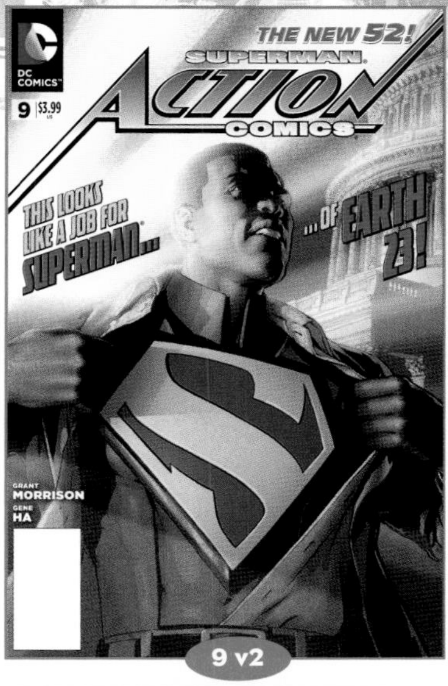
THE NEW 52!
SUPERMAN
ACTION COMICS
DC COMICS
9 $3.99
THIS LOOKS LIKE A JOB FOR SUPERMAN...
...OF EARTH 23!
GRANT MORRISON
GENE HA

9 v2

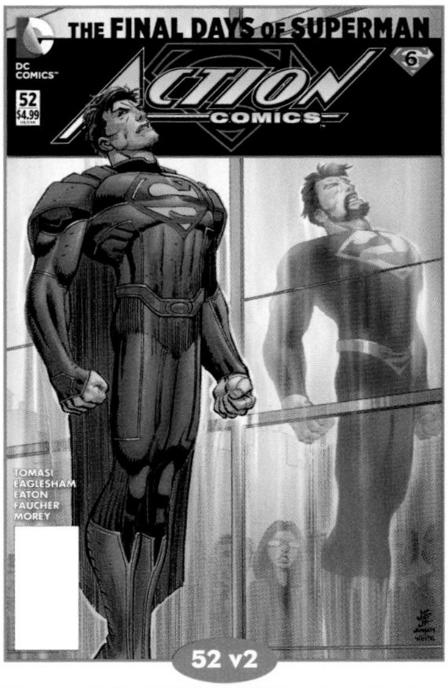
THE FINAL DAYS OF SUPERMAN
DC COMICS
ACTION COMICS
52
$4.99
6
TOMASI
EAGLESHAM
EATON
FAUCHER
MOREY

52 v2

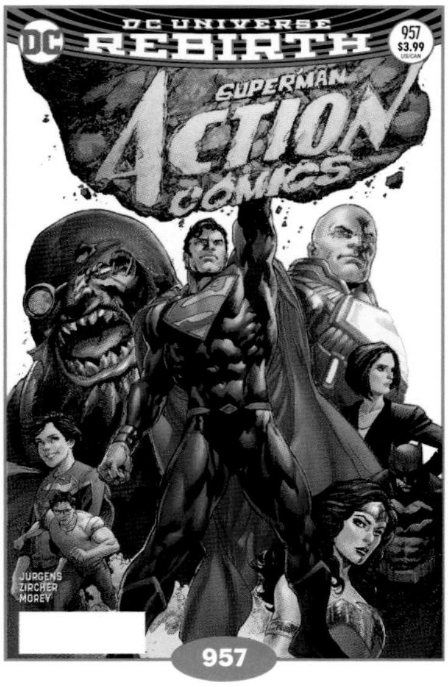
DC UNIVERSE REBIRTH
957
$3.99
SUPERMAN
ACTION COMICS
JURGENS
ZIRCHER
MOREY

957

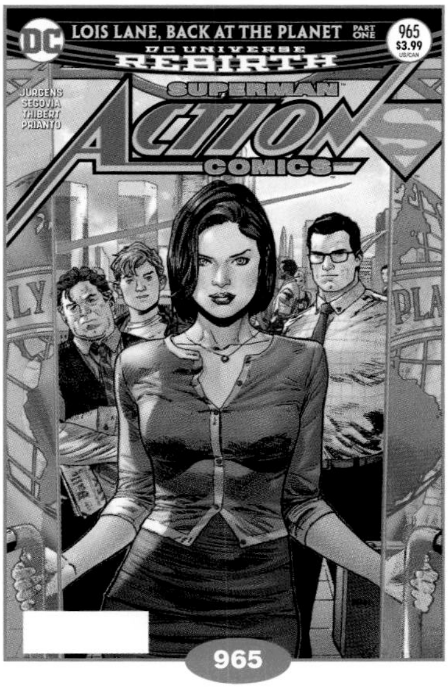
LOIS LANE, BACK AT THE PLANET PART ONE
965
$3.99
DC UNIVERSE REBIRTH
SUPERMAN
ACTION COMICS
JURGENS
SEGOVIA
THIBERT
PRIANTO

965

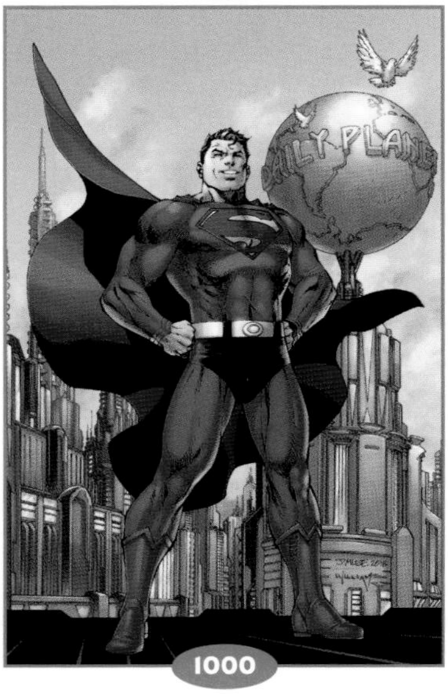

1000

Recent ACTION COMICS moments: a new Man of Steel for a new DC Universe (**Rags Morales**); hail to the Chief: it's President Superman of Earth 23(**Gene Ha**); **John Romita Jr.** introduces Supermen past and present (with **Klaus Janson**); the return of pre-Flashpoint Superman—and ACTION's original numbering (**Ivan Reis/Joe Prado**); Lois Lane, back at the Planet (**Clay Mann**); and the first superhero comic to reach #1000 (**Jim Lee/Scott Williams**).

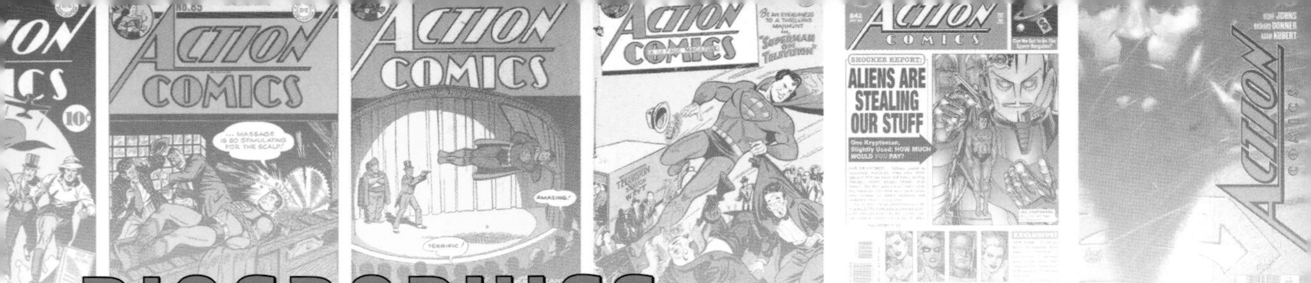
ACTION COMICS
ACTION COMICS
ACTION COMICS
ACTION COMICS
ALIENS ARE STEALING OUR STUFF

BIOGRAPHIES

Born on June 15, 1941, in New York City, **Neal Adams** began his career in comics and illustration immediately after high school and has worked in the field ever since. He first began freelancing for DC Comics in 1965, and he quickly became one of their top cover artists, contributing radical and dynamic illustrations to nearly every series the company published. His first interior work was done for editor Robert Kanigher's war titles, but it was his celebrated run on a new book called DEADMAN that began to build his reputation as a revolutionary creative force.

That reputation was cemented in the early 1970s with DC's publication of a series of collaborations between Adams, writer Dennis O'Neil and inker Dick Giordano starring Batman, Green Lantern and Green Arrow. These stories revolutionized a struggling industry and flew in the face of—and finally removed the teeth from—the repressive "Comics Code," while breaking new ground for mainstream comics and attracting major (and overwhelmingly positive) national media attention to the art form. Years later, Adams opened Continuity Associates (which would become Continuity Studios) and invited Giordano to join. Capitalizing on their comics experience, they produced advertising artwork for clients around the world.

In addition to his pivotal artistic and business roles, Adams is also one of the founders of the movement for creators' rights in the comics industry, which has worked to establish as standard practices the return of original art, the payment of royalties and the use of better-quality color separation and printing methodologies, as well as helping individual creators and their families in protecting and asserting their rights.

Marlo Alquiza was born in 1970, raised on comics, *Star Wars* and toys. After graduating with a degree in art from UC Berkeley in 1993, he entered the comics industry, first working for Image Comics (*Prophet, Darkchylde,* etc.). He subsequently went freelance and worked with Top Cow (*The Darkness, Rising Stars, Tomb Raider*) and Marvel (*X-Men*). After joining DC, Marlo inked stories found in CATWOMAN, ACTION COMICS and TEEN TITANS.

Born in 1925, **Ross Andru** first began drawing comic books in 1951 for Ziff-Davis. While there he met Mike Esposito, the man who would become his artistic partner for more than a quarter of a century. The two set up their own short-lived company called Mikeross Publications in the early 1950s, but by the end of the decade the team was firmly ensconced at DC Comics, where they contributed to editor Robert Kanigher's war books before moving on to such titles as WONDER WOMAN, METAL MEN, THE FLASH and SUPERMAN. In 1970 they shifted their efforts to Marvel Comics, becoming the regular art team on *The Amazing Spider-Man* as well as contributing to numerous other titles. Andru returned to DC as an editor in 1978, working mostly with licensed properties and drawing the occasional cover or story. He passed away in 1993.

Eduardo Barreto was a Uruguayan artist who rose to prominence in the U.S. in the 1980s working on a variety of series, mainly for DC Comics. In addition to covers and fill-in issues for titles including ACTION COMICS, SUPERMAN, WONDER WOMAN, SUPERGIRL and many, many more, Barreto drew notable runs on THE SHADOW STRIKES and THE NEW TEEN TITANS. He passed away in 2011.

Born in 1948 in Ohio, **Cary Bates** was, along with 13-year-old Jim Shooter, one of Mort Weisinger's teen *wunderkinds*, contributing story ideas and cover sketches to Weisinger when he was barely 17. In time, Weisinger encouraged Bates to submit scripts to DC, and as a Superman author Bates found himself with a steady job that lasted for nearly two decades. In the late 1980s, Bates—by then a story editor for the *Superboy* television series—left the comics field altogether to pursue a television and movie career, having left behind a vast body of work that forever defined him as one of the preeminent Superman writers.

Award-winning artist **Lee Bermejo** is the illustrator of the graphic novels BATMAN/DEATHBLOW, LUTHOR, BEFORE WATCHMEN: RORSCHACH and the *New York Times* best-selling JOKER, all of which were done in collaboration with writer Brian Azzarello.

Bermejo's other work for DC includes the titles GLOBAL FREQUENCY (with Warren Ellis), SUPERMAN/GEN 13 (with Adam Hughes), HELLBLAZER (with Mike Carey) and his creator-owned Vertigo series SUICIDERS, as well as several dozen painted covers and the best-selling graphic novel BATMAN: NOËL, which he wrote and illustrated. He currently lives with his wife, Sara, in Italy.

Otto Oscar Binder's résumé reads like a who's who of American folk heroes. During his 30-year comics career, the veteran science fiction writer penned the comic book adventures of Superman, Doc Savage, the Shadow, Captain America, Blackhawk and most notably Captain Marvel and his supporting cast, the majority of whose Golden Age exploits sprang from Binder's fertile imagination.

The secret of Binder's productivity was his versatility. Though a science fiction writer by nature, he scripted horror tales, Westerns and humor with the same professionalism he lent to his superhero work, while simultaneously producing dozens of science fiction novels and short stories. Binder retired from comics in 1969; he passed away in 1974.

Born on June 5, 1905 in Minnesota, **Wayne Boring** studied for three years at the Minneapolis Institute of Art, and then briefly at the Chicago Art Institute under J. Allen St. John. In 1938 Boring responded to Jerry Siegel's magazine advertisement searching for a cartoonist. He worked by mail on features such as *Spy* and *Federal Men,* eventually moving to Cleveland in 1940. Almost from the beginning of the syndicated *Superman* newspaper strip in 1939, Boring's chief job was to draw the daily and Sunday strips (Joe Shuster would ink the faces of the main characters). Within a few years, he was illustrating covers and stories for DC. Boring was best known for his work on the newspaper strip (which he continued to illustrate until its demise in 1966) and the SUPERMAN comic books. He died in 1987.

Since his first work was published in 1967's *Flash Gordon* #10, **Rich Buckler** went on to draw virtually every major character at DC and Marvel. In addition to his interior work on series including *Fantastic Four,* JUSTICE LEAGUE and WORLD'S FINEST COMICS, Buckler is perhaps best known for the legendary covers he created for SUPERMAN, WONDER WOMAN and ACTION COMICS, among many others. He died in 2017.

David Bullock has served as a director and/or story artist on many animated movies and TV shows, including *Batman Beyond, Kim Possible, Teen Titans* and *Star Wars: The Clone Wars.* His comics work can be seen in SUPERMAN, BLOODSHOT, the "Deadman" feature in WEDNESDAY COMICS and his own creation, *King Ronok.*

Born in England and raised in Canada, **John Byrne** discovered superheroes through *The Adventures of Superman* on television. After studying at the Alberta College of Art and Design, he broke into comics first with Skywald and then at Charlton, where he created the character Rog-2000. Following his tenure at Charlton, Byrne moved to Marvel, where his acclaimed runs on *The Uncanny X-Men* and *The Fantastic Four* soon made him one of the most popular artists in the industry. In 1986 he came to DC to revamp Superman from the ground up, and since then he has gone on to draw and/or write every major character at both DC and Marvel.

Donald Clough Cameron was born on December 21, 1905 in Detroit. He grew up in Michigan and later attended St. John's Military Academy in Delafield, Wisconsin. His first newspaper job was at the *Detroit Free Press* as a crime reporter during the Prohibition era. After working for area newspapers, he moved to New York in 1934 and began writing pulp fiction in 1935, including a Phantom Detective novel in 1939. Additional pulp work lasted into the mid-1940s, but in September 1941 Cameron began scripting for DC, which became his chief source of income for more than six years.

He handled a wide range of characters for DC, including Batman, Superman, the Boy Commandos, Johnny Quick, Liberty Belle and some funny-animal stories, as well as six of Superboy's initial seven appearances in MORE FUN COMICS. Cameron scripted at least one episode ("The Ghost of Garrett the Great") of an apparently unproduced Batman radio series, *The Batman Mystery Club.* He also wrote for Fawcett, and his first mystery novel, written in 1937, appeared in 1939 (*Murder's Coming,* Henry Holt). His other novels include *And So He Had to Die* (1941, Henry Holt) and *Dig Another Grave* (1946, Mystery House).

Cameron evidently left comics permanently in November of 1947, although his inventoried scripts continued to appear after that date. He went back to Michigan and, during 1948, was working as a staff reporter for the *Windsor*

ACTION COMICS
ACTION COMICS
ACTION COMICS

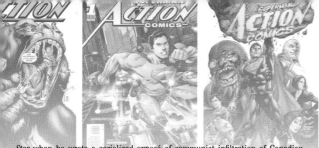

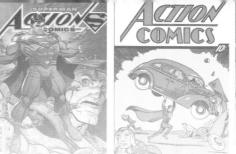

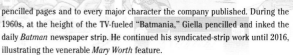

Star when he wrote a serialized exposé of communist infiltration of Canadian trade unions, which was syndicated in American and Canadian papers. Cameron eventually returned to New York City and its newspapers, and was working on a book about occultism when he passed away in 1954.

Nicholas Peter Viscardi was born in 1920. He was an early recruit in the shop of the legendary Will Eisner, where, among other features, he worked on Lady Luck, one of the backups of the Spirit comics sections. Under the name of **Nick Cardy**, he went on to work directly for Fiction House and Quality, where he was an early artist on Wonder Boy and the original Quicksilver.

Cardy became one of DC's top talents of the 1950s and 1960s, becoming the main artist on AQUAMAN and TEEN TITANS while also inking other pencillers including Irv Novick, Gil Kane, Neal Adams, George Tuska and Art Saaf. Cardy also drew the entire run of DC's short-lived but fondly remembered Western hero of the 1960s, Bat Lash.

In 1971 Nick Cardy became the main cover artist for most of the DC line, and remained so for several years. He dropped out of comics shortly afterward to concentrate on advertising art, until DC editor Mark Waid tracked him down and talked him into drawing occasional covers and other work. He passed away in 2013.

Ernie Chan was born in 1940 and had been working as a professional artist for many years in his native Philippine Islands. Recruited in 1970 by DC publisher Carmine Infantino, Chan ended up coming to America to live. An immigration official misspelled Chan's last name, rendering it "Chua." Rather than try to explain it, Chan signed that name to his art for the next few years, before resuming his original name upon becoming an American citizen.

Ernie Chan went on to work for other employers, including Warren and Marvel, and distinguished himself as an inker on Marvel's *Conan the Barbarian,* as well as on other titles including *Dr. Strange, Red Sonja* and many more. Carmine Infantino lured him back by offering him the chance to become the main cover artist for the entire DC line, where he went on to draw characters as diverse as Batman, the Bronze Age Sandman created by Joe Simon and Jack Kirby and Claw the Unconquered. He passed away in 2012.

Little is know about writer **Jerry Coleman**, who worked for DC Comics from 1951 through 1962 scripting stories for such titles as STRANGE ADVENTURES, SUPERMAN, BATMAN, LOIS LANE, SUPERBOY and MYSTERY IN SPACE.

Edward Dobrotka was born on August 15, 1917. Intent from childhood on becoming an artist, he earned a degree in mural painting and illustration in 1939 from the Cleveland Institute of Art. That same year he had four paintings accepted in the May Show at the Cleveland Museum of Art and produced 14 paintings for the Western Reserve Historical Society.

In 1941 Dobrotka married an art school classmate and began ghosting for Joe Shuster. Dobrotka joined the Shuster studio around August 1941, just before Leo Nowak's departure, and worked on comic book stories. He served in the U.S. Army Air Corps from 1943-45 and was stationed in Texas and England. Following World War II, Dobrotka lived in the New York area for a while, earning a Bachelor of Science degree at Columbia University Teachers College and working on SUPERBOY, often inking John Sikela's stories. His comics art at that point was done directly for DC, not through Shuster.

While Dobrotka made a living from comics for many years, he apparently disliked the medium, perhaps because he was a very good painter and would have preferred to pay the bills exclusively by painting. He jokingly yet disparagingly referred to his comic book art in a 1950 application for a Guggenheim Foundation fellowship, which he failed to win. Dobrotka died in 1977.

Pasqual Ferry is a Spanish artist best known for his work on series including *Heroes for Hire, Ultimate Fantastic Four* and *Thor* for Marvel, and SUPERBOY, ADAM STRANGE and ACTION COMICS for DC.

Kerry Gammill got his start drawing titles including *Marvel Team-Up* and *Power Man and Iron Fist,* co-creating many characters including Frog-Man, White Rabbit and more. At DC, he drew several Superman titles, including ACTION COMICS and SUPERMAN.

Joe Giella began his long career as a comic book artist in the 1940s, working for Hillman Publications and for Timely, the company that was later to become Marvel Comics. Giella came to DC in 1951 and over the next three decades worked predominantly as an inker, lending his clean, tight line to thousands of pencilled pages and to every major character the company published. During the 1960s, at the height of the TV-fueled "Batmania," Giella pencilled and inked the daily *Batman* newspaper strip. He continued his syndicated-strip work until 2016, illustrating the venerable *Mary Worth* feature.

A veteran of more than five decades in the comic book field, **Dick Giordano** began his career as an artist for Charlton Comics in 1952 and became the company's editor-in-chief in 1965, launching the short-lived but well-remembered Action Heroes line. In 1967 he moved to DC for a three-year stint as an editor and became part of a creative team that helped to change the face of comic books in the late 1960s and early 1970s. Together with writer Dennis O'Neil and penciller Neal Adams, he helped to bring Batman back to his roots as a dark, brooding "creature of the night," and to raise awareness of contemporary social issues through the adventures of Green Lantern and Green Arrow. The winner of numerous industry awards, Giordano later returned to DC and rose to the position of Vice President – Executive Editor before "retiring" in 1993 to once again pursue a full-time freelance career as a penciller and inker. He passed away in 2010.

Based in Saskatoon, Saskatchewan, **Tom Grummett** is best known for his work as a penciller on such DC series as THE NEW TITANS, THE ADVENTURES OF SUPERMAN, SUPERBOY, POWER COMPANY and ROBIN. His work on these titles afforded him the opportunity to draw for some of the biggest publishing events in DC's history, including A LONELY PLACE OF DYING, THE DEATH AND RETURN OF SUPERMAN and the BATMAN story arcs KNIGHTFALL, KNIGHTQUEST and KNIGHTSEND.

Born in Albany, New York, **Fred Guardineer** was a prolific artist in the comics industry during the Golden Age. He was best known for creating the characters of Pep Morgan and Zatara for DC in ACTION COMICS #1. He went on to draw Gardner Fox's Old West crime-fighter series, THE DURANGO KID, as well as titles including *Black Diamond Western* and *Crime Does Not Pay* until his retirement from comics in 1955. Guardineer passed away in 2002.

Jackson Guice is an artist who was given his first comics work by Marvel editor Al Milgrom on *Micronauts*. He went on to illustrate a plethora of notable work spanning over 30 years, including all 27 issues of RESURRECTION MAN, *Captain America* with Ed Brubaker and the famous "Death of Superman" storyline in ACTION COMICS.

Edmond Hamilton came to comics from science fiction pulp magazines, for which he was the creator of grand space operas such as "The Star Kings" and classic short stories like the intense, introspective "What's It Like Out There?" He created Captain Future for pulp editor Mort Weisinger in 1939, and upon moving to DC Comics in 1941, Weisinger offered Hamilton work on comics scripts. Hamilton quickly became a major Superman writer. In addition, he wrote Tommy Tomorrow features for ACTION COMICS and classic stories for DC editor Julius Schwartz's science fiction comics.

In 1952, Hamilton teamed Superman and Batman in "The Mightiest Team in the World" (SUPERMAN #76), a story he conceived as a minor one-shot adventure. Editor Jack Schiff soon made the Superman-Batman team a regular feature in WORLD'S FINEST, where Hamilton wrote the majority of stories until 1966. In other Batman, Superman and Legion of Super-Heroes stories, Hamilton introduced such memorable characters as Batwoman, the Composite Superman, Element Lad, Dream Girl, Timber Wolf and Brainiac 5.

Hamilton retired from comics in 1966 and lived with his wife, Leigh Brackett (a science fiction novelist and screenwriter whose credits include *The Big Sleep* and *The Empire Strikes Back*), until his death in 1977.

A third-generation artist, **Scott Hanna** has been drawing and inking comics for over 25 years. He has produced nearly 14,000 pages of graphic art in the course of his career, including lengthy runs on DC's Batman series and Marvel's Spider-Man titles, and he has drawn nearly every major character at both companies. His most recent work is on display in the pages of DC's GREEN LANTERN CORPS and SUICIDE SQUAD and Marvel's *Avengers vs. X-Men.* A winner of the Eisner, Inkwell and Wizard Fan awards, he has also taught inking and sequential art and has lectured on the subject at a wide variety of media and educational venues. He lives in Bucks County, Pennsylvania with his wife and two cats.

Tony Harris began his career as a professional illustrator in the early nineties working for small gaming companies, then moved up through the ranks

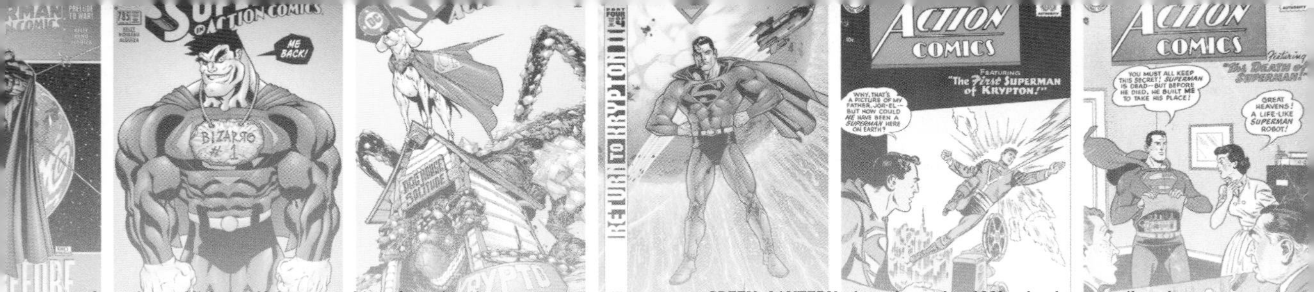
ACTION COMICS
ME BACK!
BIZARRO #1
RETURN TO KRYPTON
ACTION COMICS
"The First Superman of Krypton!"
WHY, THAT'S A PICTURE OF MY FATHER, JOR-EL-- BUT HOW COULD HE HAVE BEEN A SUPERMAN HERE ON EARTH?
ACTION COMICS
Featuring "The DEATH of SUPERMAN!"
YOU MUST ALL KEEP THIS SECRET! SUPERMAN IS DEAD--BUT BEFORE HE DIED, HE BUILT ME TO TAKE HIS PLACE!
GREAT HEAVENS! A LIFE-LIKE SUPERMAN ROBOT!

of comics publishers (doing everything from interior story pages to cover illustrations) before breaking into the industry's big leagues. This led to memorable runs on STARMAN for DC, *Nightbreed* for Marvel, *The Mummy* for Dark Horse and EX MACHINA for WildStorm, as well as lots of illustration work for television commercials and film studios. To date, he has received 19 nominations for Eisner Awards and won two — one for his work on STARMAN and one for his work on EX MACHINA.

Stuart Immonen has pursued a career in the entertainment arts since 1986. After attending Toronto's York University, he and his partner, Kathryn Kuder, self-published his first comics series, *Playground*, which was subsequently collected by Caliber Press in 1990. In 1993, following several jobs at Rip Off Press, Innovation and Revolutionary Comics, Immonen found work at DC and Marvel and kicked off a series of successful runs on a variety of high-profile and critically acclaimed titles, including SUPERMAN, LEGION OF SUPER-HEROES, *X-Men, The Fantastic Four, The Incredible Hulk, Ultimate Fantastic Four, The New Avengers* and *Ultimate Spider-Man.* In addition to providing art for these books, he also wrote and drew the INFERNO miniseries as well as DC's first original Superman hardcover graphic novel, SUPERMAN: END OF THE CENTURY.

The man most closely associated with the Silver Age Flash, **Carmine Infantino** began working in comics in the mid-1940s as the artist on such characters as Green Lantern, Black Canary, Ghost Patrol...and the original Golden Age Flash. Infantino lent his unique style to a variety of superhero, supernatural and Western features throughout the 1950s, until he was tapped to pencil the 1956 revival of the Flash. While continuing to pencil THE FLASH series, he also provided art for other strips, including Batman, the Elongated Man and Adam Strange. Infantino became DC's editorial director in 1967 and, later, its publisher before he returned to freelancing in 1976. After that he pencilled and inked numerous features, including the *Batman* newspaper strip, GREEN LANTERN CORPS and DANGER TRAIL. Infantino passed away in 2013.

Dennis Janke first broke into the comics industry with an illustration in HOUSE OF SECRETS in 1976, but rose to prominence as an inker. He is best known for his work on ADVENTURES OF SUPERMAN and SUPERMAN, and most especially his nine-year run on SUPERMAN: THE MAN OF STEEL.

Klaus Janson was born in 1952 in Coburg, Germany, and came to America in 1957. As a child growing up in Connecticut, he learned how to read and write the English language almost exclusively from Lois Lane and Superman comics. An apprenticeship with mentor Dick Giordano encouraged Janson to continue with his passion, and after many summers of portfolio reviews and rejections, in 1973 Marvel Comics offered him a part-time office job applying gray tones to the black-and-white horror-comic reprints that were then glutting the market.

In the 1980s Janson got his big break as an artist working with Frank Miller on the groundbreaking comic book series *Daredevil* and BATMAN: THE DARK KNIGHT RETURNS. Their success kicked off a long and celebrated career spent working on such titles as *The Amazing Spider-Man, The Mighty Thor, World War Hulk* and *Wolverine.* Janson lives in New York City, where he writes, draws, inks and colors comics, and teaches at the School of Visual Arts.

Dan Jurgens is a writer and artist most famous for creating Booster Gold, as well as for being one of the main forces behind THE DEATH OF SUPERMAN. He has written and illustrated such titles as JUSTICE LEAGUE AMERICA, *Captain America, The Sensational Spider-Man, Thor,* TEEN TITANS, AQUAMAN and the DC Universe-spanning crossover known as ZERO HOUR.

Born in 1926, **Gil Kane** and his family moved from their native Latvia to New York City when Kane was three. By his late teens, Kane, an artistic prodigy, had left his mark on every major comics publisher of the day, including MLJ, Prize, Quality, Marvel and DC, for whom he drew Wildcat, Johnny Thunder and a plethora of Western, science fiction and true-crime tales. In 1959 he joined with John Broome to revive the Golden Age hero Green Lantern, and in the process totally revamped the look of the feature, giving the Emerald Gladiator the trademark sleek, streamlined costume he wears to this day.

Over the years, Kane's work has come to stand as the textbook definition of dynamic drawing. A master of style, he imbued each of his drawings with an unequaled sense of power and motion. Though Kane continued to illustrate GREEN LANTERN throughout the 1960s, he lent pencil and pen to many other series as well, including Marvel's *The Amazing Spider-Man* and *Captain America* and Tower's *T.H.U.N.D.E.R. Agents*. Kane passed away in 2000.

Stan Kaye got his start in comics during World War II, drawing and often writing humor strips such as *Drafty*, starring a bumbling soldier whose antics made things tough for the Axis powers. He also worked on Hayfoot Henry, an ACTION COMICS backup about a poetic cop, scripted entirely in verse by Alvin Schwartz.

In 1944, when Wayne Boring accepted the Sunday *Superman* newspaper strip in addition to his pencilling and inking responsibilities on the dailies, he chose to pass the inking job on to Kaye. Together, Boring and Kaye brought a smooth, clean look that appealed to a wider audience than those who read the comic book. In 1948 the Boring-Kaye team added their talents to the Superman books.

Kaye inked Curt Swan on the WORLD'S FINEST team-ups to keep Superman consistent with the way he was drawn in his own titles. When Batman artist Dick Sprang began pencilling WORLD'S FINEST, his and Kaye's experience with the characters made them a perfect pair to work on the Superman-Batman team.

Kaye left comics in 1962 to enter his family's business. He passed away in 1967.

Joe Kelly began writing for Marvel after graduating from college, on titles including *Deadpool, Daredevil* and *X-Men.* He went on to write several series for DC as well, with runs on SUPERBOY and JLA, among many others, and most notably ACTION COMICS for nearly five years. As part of the Man of Action collective of creators, Kelly co-created the animated series *Ben 10*.

Little is known of **George Klein**'s early comics career, save that it began in 1942 at Marvel (then Timely), where Klein pencilled and inked funny-animal strips for *Krazy Komics.* During the 1950s he went on to provide pencils and inks for ACG's *Forbidden Worlds* and *Adventures into the Unknown*.

In 1962 Klein came to DC and quickly became one of the most revered and respected comic book inkers in the business. He set new standards for his craft with his razor-crisp brushline, which brought a new dimension to the art of Curt Swan, the penciller with whom Klein was most frequently paired. Together, Swan and Klein defined for years to come the look of Superman and his cast of characters; to this day, most Legion of Super-Heroes aficionados consider Swan and Klein to be the all-time finest Legion art team.

In 1968 Klein left DC for Marvel, where he inked several issues of *The Avengers, Daredevil* and *The Mighty Thor.* He died in 1969.

Jim Lee is a renowned comic book artist and the co-publisher of DC Entertainment. Prior to his current position, Lee served as DC's editorial director, overseeing WildStorm Studios and providing art for many of DC Comics' best-selling comic books and graphic novels, including SUPERMAN: FOR TOMORROW, BATMAN: HUSH and JUSTICE LEAGUE: ORIGIN. Lee also served as the executive creative director for the massively multiplayer action game *DC Universe Online* from Sony Online Entertainment.

Paul Levitz has worked for DC Comics in various capacities for over 45 years, with tenures as an editor (ADVENTURE COMICS, BATMAN), a writer (ALL STAR COMICS, LEGION OF SUPER-HEROES) and ultimately president and publisher. As a writer, he is best known for his long association with the Legion, which began in 1974 and has continued off and on ever since—with a particularly fan-favored run published between 1982 and 1989. In 2009 Levitz stepped down from his executive role at DC to pursue writing again full-time.

Born in New York City, **Jose Marzan Jr.** has worked in the comics industry for the past 20 years, contributing to such titles as THE ADVENTURES OF SUPERMAN, THE FLASH, JUSTICE LEAGUE OF AMERICA, Y: THE LAST MAN and many others. He lives in Florida with his wife, two sons and their dog, Krypto. He collects soundtrack CDs and runs marathons.

Ed McGuinness first gained the notice of comic book fans with his work on *Deadpool* and *Vampirella*. His short run on WildStorm's MR. MAJESTIC landed him a gig on the monthly SUPERMAN title with Jeph Loeb, which led to his groundbreaking work with Loeb on the best-selling SUPERMAN/BATMAN monthly series. He lives in Maine with his wife and four kids.

A graduate of the Art Institute of Fort Lauderdale, **Bob McLeod** honed his skills first at Marvel Comics' *Crazy* magazine and then as a member of Neal Adams' Continuity Studios. Soon after that, his indelible inks began gracing countless comics titles, including THE NEW TITANS, DETECTIVE

ACTION COMICS
Sensational! SUPERMAN GOES WILD!
ACTION COMICS
Introducing The SON of the MAN of STEEL— Superman, Junior!
ACTION COMICS
SON OF THE ANNIHILATOR! THE KID WITH THE SUPER-FISTS!
ACTION COMICS
SUPERMAN IN ACTION COMICS
SUPERMAN IN ACTION COMICS
TRUTH, JUSTICE & THE AMERICAN WAY?

COMICS and *The Incredible Hulk,* while his pencils on *The New Mutants* (which he co-created with writer Chris Claremont), *Star Wars* and ACTION COMICS earned him even greater fan acclaim. The author and illustrator of the children's book *Superhero ABC,* McLeod currently teaches at the Pennsylvania College of Art and Design in Lancaster, Pennsylvania.

With his stylized, cinematic technique and lush use of black, **Mort Meskin** has long been considered one of the finest illustrators of comics' Golden Age. Born on May 30, 1916, Meskin was educated at New York City's Pratt Institute and Art Students League and began his career doing illustrations for newspapers and pulp magazines in the 1930s. His first comic book work appeared in Fiction House's *Sheena* in 1938 when he was working in the Eisner & Iger shop. Over the next several years Meskin worked primarily for Archie, and in 1941 he began a long association with DC Comics, working first on the Vigilante, Wildcat and Johnny Quick features before branching out into long runs on several of DC's war, suspense and romance titles. From the late 1940s through the mid-1960s he worked on a wide variety of genres for a host of publishers (including DC, Marvel, Better, Feature, Harvey, Hillman and Mainline) before eventually leaving the industry in 1966 to work in the advertising field. Meskin passed away in 1995.

Born in 1919, **James Noel Mooney** began his long career in comics at age 21 as an artist for Ace Publishing, where he illustrated such features as Lash Lightning and Magna. By the late 1940s Mooney was firmly in place as one of DC Comics' most productive penciller/inkers, contributing Batman stories to BATMAN and DETECTIVE COMICS, Robin tales to STAR SPANGLED COMICS and monthly Tommy Tomorrow installments to ACTION COMICS through most of the 1950s.

In the 1960s, Mooney concentrated his efforts on ACTION COMICS' Supergirl, the feature for which he is best known to this day. His prolific talent and ability to make deadlines also ensured that he always had a script in hand for one of Superman editor Mort Weisinger's other titles (such as SUPERMAN, WORLD'S FINEST COMICS or ADVENTURE COMICS).

By the 1970s Mooney had left DC for Marvel Comics, where he both pencilled *The Amazing Spider-Man, Ghost Rider, Son of Satan* and *Marvel Team-Up* and, at one time or another, inked virtually every title Marvel published. In 1991 he returned to DC briefly as the artist of THE ADVENTURES OF SUPERBOY. Mooney passed away in 2008.

Grant Morrison has been working with DC Comics for more than 20 years, beginning with his legendary runs on the revolutionary titles ANIMAL MAN and DOOM PATROL. Since then he has written numerous bestsellers—including JLA, BATMAN and *New X-Men*—as well as the critically acclaimed creator-owned series THE INVISIBLES, SEAGUY, THE FILTH, WE3 and JOE THE BARBARIAN. Morrison has also expanded the borders of the DC Universe in the award-winning pages of ALL-STAR SUPERMAN, FINAL CRISIS, BATMAN INCORPORATED, ACTION COMICS and the Grand DC Unification Theory that is THE MULTIVERSITY.

In his secret identity, Morrison is a "counterculture" spokesperson, a musician, an award-winning playwright and a chaos magician. He is also the author of the *New York Times* bestseller *Supergods*, a groundbreaking psycho-historic mapping of the superhero as a cultural organism. He divides his time between his homes in Los Angeles and Scotland.

James Winslow "Win" Mortimer was born on May 1, 1919, and studied at the Art Students League of New York City before being hired by DC Comics in 1945. In addition to pencilling and inking many stories for such titles as WORLD'S FINEST COMICS and BATMAN, Mortimer was also DC's most frequent cover artist for their main titles from 1949 through 1956. He maintained an unbroken string of 46 covers for DETECTIVE COMICS (issues #169-214), and ultimately pencilled and inked 87 of the 121 covers for issues #110-230 as well as numerous covers for ADVENTURE COMICS, BATMAN, WORLD'S FINEST COMICS, ACTION COMICS, SUPERBOY, SUPERMAN, MR. DISTRICT ATTORNEY and STAR SPANGLED COMICS. He also worked on the *Superman* daily syndicated newspaper strip from 1949 through 1956. Mortimer's art was unsigned, but he was fond of sneaking his name—Win or Winslow—into his early DC material on trucks, storefronts and billboards.

Mortimer left DC in early 1956 to illustrate *David Crane,* a daily newspaper strip about a minister. He departed *Crane* in 1960, and from 1961 through 1968 he worked on another strip, *Larry Brannon.* After the mid-1960s he moved in and out of comic books, doing occasional work for DC as well as Gold Key and Marvel. Mortimer died in 1998.

George Pérez started drawing at the age of five and hasn't stopped since. Born on June 9, 1954, Pérez began his professional comics career as an assistant to Rich Buckler in 1973. After establishing himself as a penciller at Marvel Comics, Pérez came to DC in 1980, bringing his highly detailed art style to such titles as JUSTICE LEAGUE OF AMERICA and FIRESTORM. After co-creating THE NEW TEEN TITANS in 1980, Pérez and writer Marv Wolfman reunited for the landmark miniseries CRISIS ON INFINITE EARTHS in 1985. In the aftermath of that universe-smashing event, Pérez revitalized WONDER WOMAN as the series' writer and artist, reestablishing the Amazon Princess as one of DC's preeminent characters and bringing in some of the best sales the title has ever experienced. He has since gone on to illustrate celebrated runs on Marvel's *The Avengers,* CrossGen's *Solus* and DC's THE BRAVE AND THE BOLD.

Al Plastino's work on Superman and Batman was probably seen by more people internationally than any of his artistic contemporaries, due to the fact that he drew both characters' syndicated comic strips in the 1960s and 1970s, appearing daily in newspapers around the world. Plastino's work was a constant fixture in DC titles of the 1940s, 1950s and 1960s. Originally just another Superman artist in the Joe Shuster shop, Plastino broke away from the pack to become, along with Shuster and Wayne Boring, one of the three definitive Superman artists during comics' Golden Age. Plastino passed away in 2013.

Born and raised outside Dublin, Ireland, **Kilian Plunkett** had no sooner arrived in the U.S. than he was hired as the illustrator for Dark Horse Comics' *Aliens: Labyrinth.* From there, Plunkett plied his midichlorian-charged artistry on numerous *Star Wars* tie-ins for Dark Horse, then on DC and Vertigo titles such as UNKNOWN SOLDIER, LEGION WORLDS and the BATMAN BEGINS movie adaptation. Since claimed by the Force as Lucasfilm Animation's lead designer on *Star Wars: The Clone Wars,* Plunkett has yet to disclose his "Master Plan."

Frederic Ray Jr. was born in Pennsylvania in 1922. Hired by Whitney Ellsworth, he went to work in the DC Comics bullpen in 1940 handling a variety of projects, including pencilling and inking covers for SUPERMAN, ACTION COMICS and LEADING COMICS. He also wrote, illustrated and sometimes colored Congo Bill for ACTION COMICS and pencilled covers for BATMAN, WORLD'S FINEST COMICS and DETECTIVE COMICS.

Although he was drafted in May 1942, Ray continued to occasionally draw for DC while in the Air Force as a staff sergeant. He was discharged in December 1945 and attended the Pennsylvania Academy of Fine Arts in 1946.

His primary job after 1945 was to draw Tomahawk for STAR SPANGLED COMICS, WORLD'S FINEST COMICS and TOMAHAWK. He worked on several of DC's war titles during the 1960s, including OUR FIGHTING FORCES, G.I. COMBAT and OUR ARMY AT WAR. His last DC work appeared in 1971.

Beginning in the 1950s, Ray wrote, illustrated and self-published a number of history booklets. Around 1960 he became the art director and cover artist for *American History Illustrated* and *Civil War Times.* He was associated with those publishers for about 20 years. Ray did illustrations for various Western magazines during the 1960s and 1970s and compiled a book of famous historical paintings entitled *Oh, Say, Can You See?,* which was published in 1970. He died in 2001.

Alex Ross studied illustration at the American Academy of Art in Chicago, then honed his craft as a storyboard artist before entering the comics field. His miniseries *Marvels* opened a wider acceptance for painted comics. He moved on to produce the equally successful KINGDOM COME for DC. Receiving critical acclaim and multiple awards for these best-selling works, Ross made a name as both an artist and storyteller, dedicating himself to bold experiments within the comics medium. In addition to the six graphic novels collected in this volume, his extensive work for DC/Vertigo includes UNCLE SAM, ASTRO CITY, JUSTICE and JUSTICE SOCIETY OF AMERICA. Ross has continued producing work for Marvel Comics, including the *Earth X* trilogy, *Spider-Man* and *Avengers.* His work outside of comics includes magazine and album covers as well as the poster for the 2002 Academy Awards. Ross is currently creating a variety of art prints, including works of the Beatles, Universal Monsters and Disney characters, among others.

Duncan Rouleau has worked in a variety of capacities in the comics industry. He's pencilled and inked series including X-Factor, Alpha Flight and

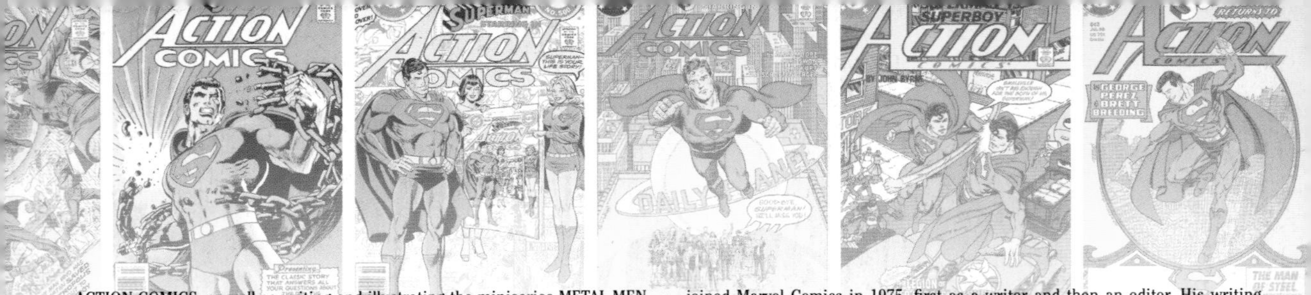
ACTION COMICS
ACTION COMICS
ACTION COMICS
SUPERBOY
ACTION COMICS
ACTION COMICS

ACTION COMICS, as well as writing and illustrating the miniseries METAL MEN. He's also the co-creator of the super-team Big Hero 6.

Born in August of 1920, **George Roussos** was 19 years old when he was hired by Jerry Robinson to assist on Batman. Roussos started on May 30, 1940, inking backgrounds and handling lettering. His first work appeared in BATMAN #2 (Summer 1940), and he became a mainstay on the character until 1944, when he left the DC bullpen to freelance.

Roussos pencilled, inked and colored Airwave, as well as inking Superman, Johnny Quick, Vigilante, the Star-Spangled Kid and many other DC heroes.

From the late 1940s into the 1950s, Roussos worked freelance for a number of comic book publishers, including Harvey, Hillman, Avon, Ziff-Davis, Fiction House, EC, Timely, Prize and Pines. In 1963 he began inking stories for Marvel (sometimes using the name George Bell), ultimately leaving DC around 1970 to work full time as their cover colorist. Other efforts included work on syndicated newspaper strips and in advertising. Roussos remained in the comics industry well into the 1990s. He died in 2000.

Tim Sale was born in Ithaca, New York and grew up in Seattle, Washington. After studying at the University of Washington and the School of Visual Arts in New York City, he began his career inking *Myth Adventures* for WaRP Graphics and illustrating the *Thieves' World* series of graphic novels for Donning/Starblaze. His extended collaboration with writer Jeph Loeb has yielded a string of popular and critically acclaimed projects, including BATMAN: THE LONG HALLOWEEN, BATMAN: DARK VICTORY, SUPERMAN FOR ALL SEASONS and the "color" series from Marvel featuring Daredevil, Spider-Man, Captain America and the Hulk. Sale has also illustrated the titles *Bili 99, Grendel,* DEATHBLOW and SUPERMAN CONFIDENTIAL, and his contributions to the comics medium have been chronicled in the retrospective volume *Tim Sale: Black and White.* He lives in Seattle with his loves, Susan, Jackie and Sammy.

Joseph Shuster was born in 1914 in Toronto, Canada. When he was nine, his family moved to Cleveland, Ohio, where he met Jerry Siegel. The two became fast friends and collaborators; together, they published the earliest science fiction fan magazines, where Shuster honed his fledgling art skills. In 1936 he and Siegel began providing DC Comics with such new features as Dr. Occult, Slam Bradley and Radio Squad before selling Superman to DC in 1938. Influenced by such comic-strip greats as *Wash Tubbs*' Roy Crane, Joe Shuster drew Superman through 1947, after which he left comic books to create the comic strip *Funnyman*, again with Siegel. Failing eyesight cut short his career, but not before his place in the history of American culture was assured. Joe Shuster died of heart failure in 1992.

Born in 1914 in Cleveland, Ohio, **Jerome Siegel** was a fan of the emerging literary genre that came to be known as science fiction. Together with schoolmate Joe Shuster, Siegel published several science fiction fan magazines, and in 1933 they came up with their own science fiction hero—Superman. Siegel scripted and Shuster drew several weeks' worth of newspaper strips featuring their new creation, but garnered no interest from publishers or newspaper syndicates. It wasn't until the two established themselves as reliable adventure-strip creators at DC Comics that the editors at DC offered to take a chance on the Superman material—provided it was re-pasted into comic book format for DC's new magazine, ACTION COMICS. Siegel wrote the adventures of Superman (as well as other DC heroes) through 1948 and then again from 1959-1966, in the interim scripting several newspaper strips, including *Funnyman* and *Ken Winston*. Jerry Siegel died in 1996.

Bill Sienkiewicz has had a major impact on the comic book field with his innovative use of multimedia, collage, illustration techniques and storytelling. He has won nearly every major comics award in the U.S. and abroad, and has exhibited his art worldwide. Among his best-known works are the series *Elektra: Assassin,* for which he received the prestigious Yellow Kid Award, and the critically acclaimed *Stray Toasters*, which he both wrote and illustrated. He was nominated for two Emmy awards for his work on the animated series *Where in the World Is Carmen Sandiego?,* and he also worked on the Academy Award-winning film *Unforgiven* as well as contributing cover and interior illustrations for the DVD and Blu-ray releases of *The Venture Bros.* seasons one and three.

Born in 1950, **Roger Stern** began his love affair with comics by helping produce the popular fanzine *CPL (Contemporary Pictorial Literature)*. He then joined Marvel Comics in 1975, first as a writer and then an editor. His writing credits at Marvel include celebrated runs on *The Amazing Spider-Man* and *Captain America.* In 1987, Stern began writing for DC, where he quickly became an integral part of the Superman team. His other DC credits include POWER OF THE ATOM and STARMAN, and he has also written the prose novels *The Death and Life of Superman, Smallville: Strange Visitors* and *Superman: The Never-Ending Battle.*

Curt Swan entered the art field intending to become not a cartoonist but a "slick" magazine illustrator like Norman Rockwell or Joseph Leyendecker. While serving during World War II illustrating the Army newspaper *Stars and Stripes,* Swan worked with DC writer France E. Herron. On Herron's suggestion, Swan found work at DC after the war. Swan's versatile pencils, which he remembers applying first to BOY COMMANDOS, soon appeared on various DC features, including Superman, Batman, the Newsboy Legion, Big Town, Mr. District Attorney, Tommy Tomorrow and Swan's longest assignment up to that time, Superboy. His familiarity with both Superman and Batman specially suited him to draw the original Superman-Batman team-up in 1952. Swan served various stints, regular and semi-regular, on almost all the Superman titles of the 1950s and 1960s, and remained the near-exclusive Superman penciller throughout the 1970s and much of the 1980s. Although he "retired" in 1986, Swan continued to work for DC until his death in 1996. To generations of professionals and fans, Curt Swan's Superman will always be the definitive version.

Veteran comics writer and editor **Len Wein** created such memorable characters as Wolverine, the New X-Men and the Human Target, as well as co-creating (with Bernie Wrightson) the Swamp Thing. In his long and prolific career he wrote for hundreds of titles, encompassing nearly every significant character in the medium. He also served as senior editor at DC Comics and as editor-in-chief at both Marvel and Disney Comics, and built a successful career in TV animation, scripting such hit series as *X-Men, Spider-Man* and *Batman: The Animated Series.* He passed away in 2017.

Born on April 25, 1915 in New York City, editor **Mort Weisinger** was a fan of science fiction from its earliest days and is credited with co-publishing the first science fiction fanzine. He came to work for DC Comics in 1940, where he coordinated many characters and titles. Beginning in the mid-1950s he became the sole editor of the Superman brand. Under his legendarily stern guidance, writers such as Jerry Siegel, Otto Binder and Jim Shooter carefully wove a sprawling, imaginative mythos around the Man of Steel that is still celebrated to this day. Weisinger died in 1978.

J.H. Williams III is a multiple-award-winning creator known for his fine work on a wide array of titles, including THE SANDMAN: OVERTURE, BATMAN, STARMAN, CHASE, SON OF SUPERMAN, SEVEN SOLDIERS OF VICTORY, JONAH HEX, DESOLATION JONES (co-created with Warren Ellis), the revered PROMETHEA (co-created with Alan Moore), DETECTIVE COMICS (with writer Greg Rucka) and a celebrated run on BATWOMAN (as writer and artist). He has also provided art and designs for music releases, including the albums *Apocryphon* by The Sword and *Ghosts of Download* by the legendary Blondie, and he occasionally dabbles in fashion. J.H. and his wife, Wendy, live in the ethereal.

One of the most prolific and influential writers in modern comics, **Marv Wolfman** began his career as an artist. Realizing that his talents lay more in writing the stories than in drawing them, Wolfman soon became known for his carefully crafted, character-driven tales.

In a career that has spanned 50 years, Wolfman has helped shape the heroic journeys of DC Comics' Green Lantern, Blackhawk and the original Teen Titans, as well as Marvel Comics' Fantastic Four, Spider-Man and Nova. In addition to co-creating THE NEW TEEN TITANS and the universe-shattering CRISIS ON INFINITE EARTHS with George Pérez, Wolfman was instrumental in the revamp of Superman after CRISIS, the development of THE NEW TEEN TITANS spin-off series VIGILANTE, DEATHSTROKE THE TERMINATOR and TEAM TITANS and created such characters as Blade for Marvel, along with NIGHT FORCE and the retooled DIAL "H" FOR HERO for DC.

In addition to his numerous comic book credits, Wolfman has also written several novels and worked in series television and animation, including the *Superman* cartoon of the late 1980s and the hit *Teen Titans* show on Cartoon Network.

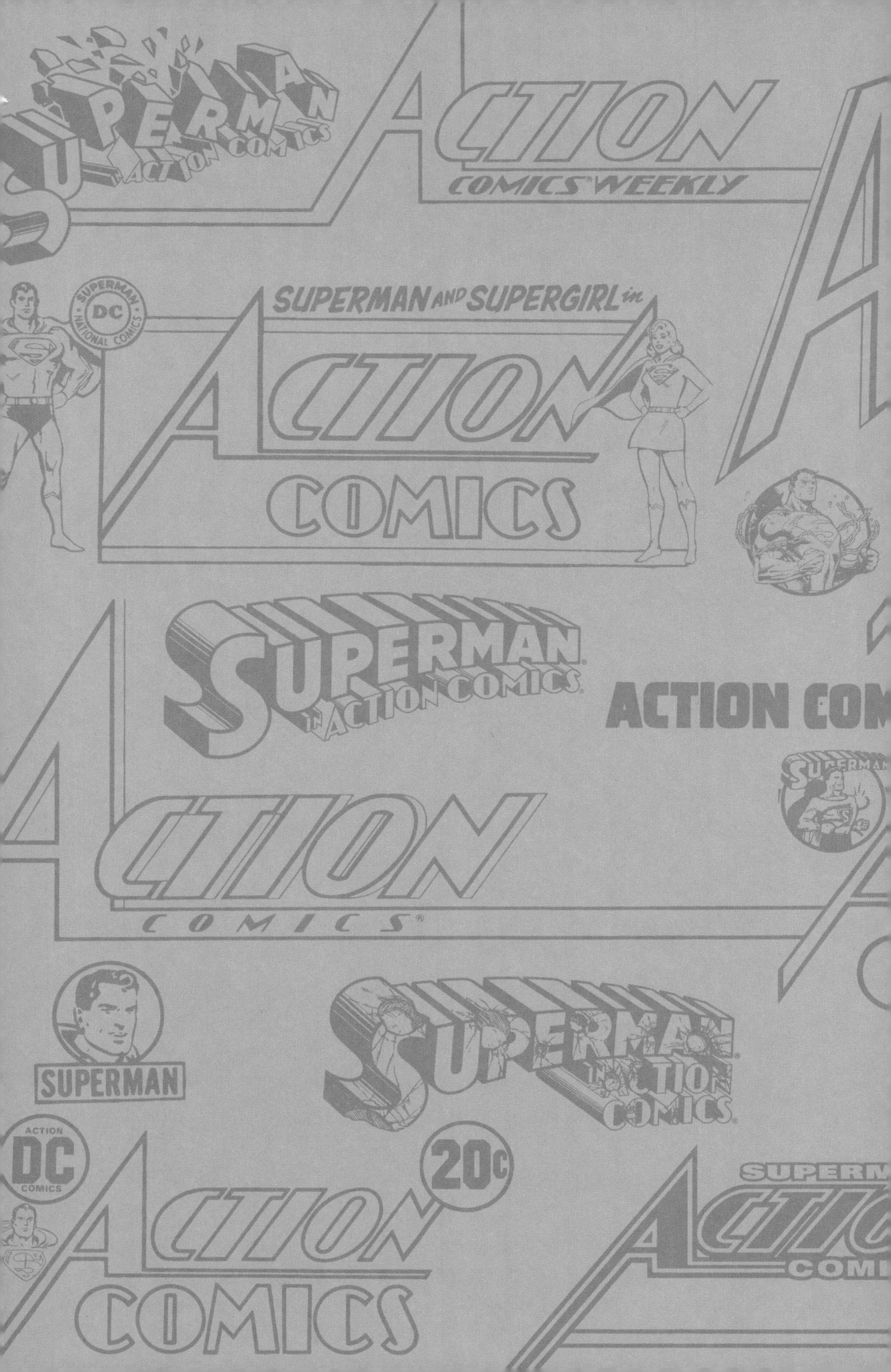
SUPERMAN
ACTION COMICS
ACTION
COMICS WEEKLY
SUPERMAN AND SUPERGIRL in
SUPERMAN
DC
NATIONAL COMICS
ACTION
COMICS
SUPERMAN
IN ACTION COMICS
ACTION COM
SUPERMAN
ACTION
COMICS
SUPERMAN
SUPERMAN
IN ACTION
COMICS
ACTION
DC
COMICS
20¢
ACTION
COMICS
SUPERM
ACTIO
COM

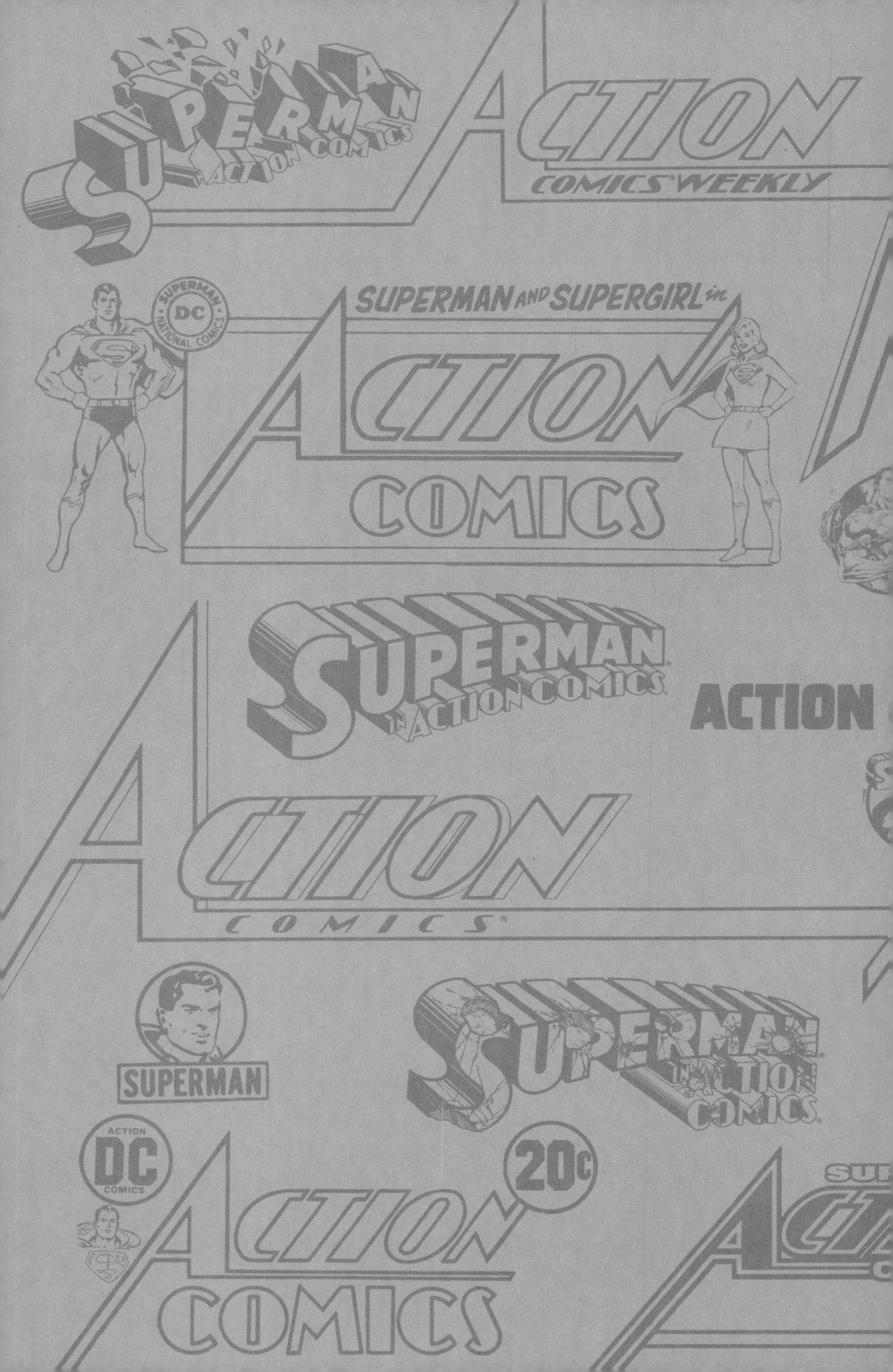
SUPERMAN
ACTION COMICS
ACTION
COMICS WEEKLY
SUPERMAN
DC
NATIONAL COMICS
SUPERMAN AND SUPERGIRL in
ACTION
COMICS
SUPERMAN
in ACTION COMICS
ACTION
ACTION
COMICS
SUPERMAN
SUPERMAN
in ACTION
COMICS
ACTION
DC
COMICS
20¢
ACTION
COMICS